Sports Illustrated 2013 Almanac

By the Editors of Sports Illustrated

BASEBALL

PRO
FOOTBALL

COLLEGE
FOOTBALL

PRO
BASKETBALL

COLLEGE
BASKETBALL

HOCKEY

OLYMPICS

TENNIS

GOLF

SOCCER

MOTOR
SPORTS

Published by Sports Illustrated Books, an imprint of Time Home Entertainment Inc.
135 West 50th Street
New York, New York 10020

ISBN 10: 1-60320-934-4
ISBN 13: 978-1-60320-934-2

SPORTS ILLUSTRATED is a registered trademark of Time Inc.

SPORTS ILLUSTRATED 2013 Almanac was prepared by:
Kensington Media Group, Inc.

Editorial Director: Morin Bishop	Art Director: Barbara Chilenskas
Proofreader: Wade Martin	Photo Editor: John Blackmar

Cover photography credits:
ELI MANNING: Heinz Kluetmeier
MIKE TROUT: Robert Beck
SERENA WILLIAMS: Simon Bruty/Sports Illustrated/Getty Images
LEBRON JAMES: Greg Nelson

Back cover photography credits:
ANTHONY DAVIS: Greg Nelson
JONATHAN QUICK: David E. Klutho
GABBY DOUGLAS: Al Tielemans

Spine photography credit: RORY MCILROY: Fred Vuich

TIME HOME ENTERTAINMENT

Publisher .... Jim Childs
Vice President, Business Development & Strategy .... Steven Sandonato
Executive Director, Marketing Services .... Carol Pittard
Executive Director, Retail & Special Sales .... Tom Mifsud
Executive Publishing Director .... Joy Butts
Director, Bookazine Development & Marketing .... Laura Adam
Finance Director .... Glenn Buonocore
Associate Publishing Director .... Megan Pearlman
Assistant General Counsel .... Helen Wan
Assistant Director, Special Sales .... Ilene Schreider
Senior Book Production Manager .... Susan Chodakiewicz
Design & Prepress Manager .... Anne-Michelle Gallero
Brand Manager .... Michele Bové
Associate Prepress Manager .... Alex Voznesenskiy
Assistant Brand Manager .... Stephanie Braga

Editorial Director .... Stephen Koepp
Editorial Operations Director .... Michael Q. Bullerdick

Special thanks: Amy Migliaccio, Nina Mistry, Dave Rozzelle, Ricardo Santiago, Adriana Tierno,
Vanessa Wu.

We welcome your comments and suggestions about Sports Illustrated Books. Please write to us
at: Sports Illustrated, Attention: Book Editors, P.O. Box 11016, Des Moines, IA 50336-1016.
If you would like to order any of our hardcover Collector's Edition books, please call us at
1-800-327-6388 (Monday through Friday, 7:00 a.m.–8:00 p.m. or Saturday, 7:00 a.m.–6:00 p.m.
Central Time).

CONTENTS

BASEBALL   by Merrell Noden 5

PRO FOOTBALL   by Hank Hersch 83

COLLEGE FOOTBALL   by B.J. Schecter 171

PRO BASKETBALL   by Chris Mannix 237

COLLEGE BASKETBALL   by B.J. Schecter 273

HOCKEY   by Mark Beech 315

OLYMPICS   by Merrell Noden 357

TENNIS 393

GOLF 415

SOCCER 443

MOTOR SPORTS 453

HORSE RACING 471

BOXING 483

NCAA SPORTS 497

TRACK AND FIELD 509

MISCELLANEOUS SPORTS 521

2013 MAJOR EVENTS 543

SOURCES

In compiling the *Sports Illustrated 2013 Almanac*, the editors would like to extend their gratitude to the following organizations for their help in providing information and materials relating to their sports: Major League Baseball; the National Football League; the National Collegiate Athletic Association; the National Basketball Association; the National Hockey League; the Association of Tennis Professionals; the Women's Tennis Association; the U.S. Tennis Association; the U.S. Golf Association; the Ladies Professional Golf Association; the Professional Golfers Association; National Thoroughbred Racing Association; the Breeders' Cup; Churchill Downs; the National Association for Stock Car Auto Racing; Major League Soccer; the Fédération Internationale de Futbol Association; the U.S. Olympic Committee; USA Track & Field; USA Gymnastics.

The following sources were consulted in gathering information:

Baseball mlb.com, worldseries.com, baseballhalloffame.org, baseball-reference.com, *Associated Press* (LCS, WS game recaps)

Pro Football nfl.com, superbowl.com, profootballhof.com, cfl.ca, greycup.cfl.ca

College Football ncaasports.com, heisman.com, *Official 2012 NCAA Division I-A and I-AA Football Records Book, Official 2012 Division II and III Football Records Book*

Pro Basketball nba.com, hoophall.com

College Basketball ncaasports.com, *Official 20012–13 NCAA Division I Men's Basketball Records Book, Official 2012–13 NCAA Division I Women's Basketball Records Book, Official 2012–13 NCAA Division II and III Men's Basketball Records Book*

Hockey nhl.com, hhof.com, ushockeyhall.com

Tennis atptennis.com, sonyericssonwtatour.com, usopen.org, australianopen.com, wimbledon.org, rolandgarros.com, masters-cup.com, daviscup.com, fedcup.com, tennisfame.com

Golf pgatour.com, masters.org, usopen.org, usga.org, opengolf.com, pga.com, lpga.com, knc.com, ussenioropen.com, usamateur.org, rydercup.com, walkercup.org, curtiscup.org, pinggolf.com

Boxing boxrec.com, wbaonline.com, wbcboxing.com, ibf-usba-boxing.com, ibhof.com, thering-online.com, usaboxing.org, olympic.org

Horse Racing ntra.com, equibase.com, bloodhorse.com, kentuckyderby.com, preakness.com, belmontstakes.nyra.com

Motor Sports nascar.com, formula1.com, indycar.com, americanlemans.com, lemans.org, champcarworldseries.com, indy500.com, daytona24hr.com

Soccer fifa.com, mlsnet.com, ussoccer.com, soccernet.com, uslsoccer.com,

NCAA Sports ncaasports.com

Olympics olympic.org, usoc.org

Track and Field iaaf.org, usatf.org, usoc.org

Miscellaneous Sports letour.fr, usarchery.org, pba.com, fide.com, worldcurling.org, usacurl.org, usacycling.org, iditarod.com, usfigureskating.org, isu.org, fig-gymnastics.com, usa-gymnastics.org, ushandball.org, uscla.com, nll.com, littleleague.org, us-polo.org, prorodeo.org, usrowing.org, usarugby.org, rugbyworldcup.com, amnrl.com, fis-ski.com, asasoftball.com, us-squash.org, ironmanlive.com, usatriathlon.org, fivb.org, usavolleyball.org, themat.com

Baseball

As Miguel Cabrera trudged off, Buster Posey and Sergio Romo celebrated the final out of the Giants sweep over the Tigers in the World Series

Giants On Top Again

After a season full of surprises, the colorful San Francisco Giants rode a run of brilliant pitching to their second World Series title in three seasons

BY MERRELL NODEN

THEIR MOTTO WAS "PLAY FOR the guy next to you," and in seven amazing games at the end of the season, the San Francisco Giants showed what such loyalty—backed by outrageously effective pitching—can do for a team. In their four-game World Series sweep of Detroit, the Giants strangled any hope the poor Tigers might have had of winning, shutting them out in Games Two and Three, while holding them to a Series batting average of .159.

These Giants were fun to watch. They played hard, held pre-game dugout rallies that resembled mosh pits, and even contributed a new concept to the world of horseplay, Romobombing, in which bearded, wide-eyed relief pitcher Sergio Romo pops up out of nowhere, eyes wide with excitement. With Romo and several of his teammates sporting thick beards, the Giants sometimes resembled a village of Amish men finally busting loose. At the center of this giddy storm was manager Bruce Bochy, scruffy and unflappable. His Giants became the first National League team to win two championships in three years since Cincinnati's Big Red Machine won in 1975 and '76.

In many ways, the regular season felt like "opposite day." Everything was turned on its head. At the All Star break, the Washington Nationals, who had never finished higher than third in their division, had the best record in the National League, while the Pittsburgh Pirates, whose last winning season came in 1992, were leading the NL Central.

In the American League, the Bronx was still up, in the form of the home run-slugging Yankees. But the Yankees, who led the AL East by 10 games on July 17, were caught in early September by the no-name Baltimore Orioles. The Red Sox were a seething pit of dysfunction all season.

The Texas Rangers started strong but collapsed late, losing seven of their last nine games and the AL West to the young Oakland A's. A major highlight for the Rangers came on May 8, when Josh Hamilton became the 16th major leaguer to hit four homers in a game. In the final weeks of the season, Hamilton's home run total was all that stood between Detroit's Miguel Cabrera and the majors' first Triple Crown since Carl Yastrzemski achieved the feat in 1967. Cabrera hit his 44th homer on Oct. 1 to slip past Hamilton, 44 to 43. He finished with a batting average of .330, 44 homers and 139 RBIs, league leaders all.

Milwaukee's Ryan Braun led the National League with 41 homers and would have been a strong contender to repeat as MVP,

but for the feeling in many quarters that he'd beaten a positive drug test. No such doubt surrounded Melky Cabrera, whose positive test for testosterone was announced on August 15, along with a 50-game suspension. With his batting average frozen at a league leading .346, Cabrera ultimately removed himself from the race for the batting title, which wound up going to teammate Buster Posey (.336).

Still, the most intriguing man in the majors may have been R.A. Dickey of the Mets. At age 37, following a peripatetic and mostly lackluster career, Dickey led the NL in strikeouts (230) and was second in wins (20), behind only Geo Gonzalez of Washington (21). Dickey is a rarity in baseball: a deep reader, author of an acclaimed autobiography (*Wherever I Wind Up*), and the last of a dying breed, the knuckleballer.

This was a season of exciting new stars.

The year's most exciting rookie was Trout, who was oustanding on defense, electrified on the bases with 49 steals and led the majors in runs scored with 129.

Mike Trout, who turned 21 on August 7, led the American League in batting for almost the entire season before slipping in September to .326. Trout did, however, lead the majors in runs scored (129) and stolen bases (49) despite playing most of April in the minors.

Trout's National League counterparts both happened to play in Washington, D.C., whose Nationals won 98 games, more than any other team in the majors. Fearless outfielder Bryce Harper made the NL All Star team at age 19, while flame-throwing pitcher Stephen Strasburg, coming back from Tommy John surgery, bolstered the Nationals' strong pitching staff.

AL TIELEMANS

The Tigers also showed late-season toughness, chasing down the White Sox in September, then beating the A's in five games. They next demolished the punchless Yankees in four straight to reach the Series. Perhaps it was the loss of captain Derek Jeter, who broke his ankle in Game One, but against Detroit, New York looked old and powerless, hitting just .157 and getting outscored 19–6.

The Giants, World Series champs in 2010, demonstrated a knack for playoff brinksmanship. After losing the first two games of the first round at home, they won three straight in Cincinnati. Then, down 3–1 against St. Louis, they used superb starting pitching to win three straight at home, outscoring the Cardinals 20–1 in those three games to move on to the Series against Detroit. Series MVP Marco Scutaro went 14 for 28 to lead the feisty Giants.

But it was pitching that carried the Giants when it counted most. Over those seven final games, San Francisco pitchers surrendered just seven runs and combined for four shutouts. In the Series, Prince Fielder, the Tigers' mammoth clean-up hitter, went just 1 for 14, while Cabrera hit .231 with a single home run. By contrast, Pablo Sandoval, the Giants' rotund third baseman known as Panda to the San Francisco faithful, had an outstanding Series, batting .500, with three Game One homers, to claim MVP honors. Everyone chipped in when they were needed. Said Matt Cain, the starting pitcher in Game Four, "It seemed all the pieces fit together."

For seven amazing games, what pieces they were!

One of the season's ongoing mysteries was whether the Nationals would stick to their promise to limit Strasburg to between 160 and 180 innings, no matter where they stood. They did. After 159⅓ innings pitched, his final start came on Sept. 7. Washington fans may still be wondering what might have been after watching the Cardinals come back from 6–0 down to beat the Nationals in the fifth and final game of their playoff series.

This was the first season in which two teams in each league earned wildcard spots, then competed in a one-game playoff for the right to continue in the divisional playoffs. The added team made for an exciting September, as three or four more teams in each league had a realistic shot at playing in October than otherwise would have been the case. In the National League the Cardinals, with both experience and destiny on their sides, looked capable of repeating their stunning heroics of last year. Having lost two future Hall of Famers in slugger Albert Pujols and manager Tony LaRussa, St. Louis beat Atlanta in the one-game playoff before eliminating Washington.

2012 Final Regular Season Standings

National League

EASTERN DIVISION

Team	Won	Lost	Pct	GB	Home	Away
Washington	98	64	.605	—	50-31	48-33
Atlanta	94	68	.580	4.0	48-33	46-35
Philadelphia	81	81	.500	17.0	40-41	41-40
NY Mets	74	88	.457	24.0	36-45	38-43
Miami	69	93	.426	29.0	38-43	31-50

CENTRAL DIVISION

Team	Won	Lost	Pct	GB	Home	Away
Cincinnati	97	65	.599	—	50-31	47-34
St. Louis	88	74	.543	9.0	50-31	38-43
Milwaukee	83	79	.512	14.0	49-32	34-47
Pittsburgh	79	83	.488	18.0	45-36	34-47
Chi. Cubs	61	101	.377	36.0	38-43	23-58
Houston	55	107	.340	42.0	35-46	20-61

WESTERN DIVISION

Team	Won	Lost	Pct	GB	Home	Away
San Francisco	94	68	.580	—	48-33	46-35
LA Dodgers	86	76	.531	8.0	45-36	41-40
Arizona	81	81	.500	13.0	41-40	40-41
San Diego	76	86	.469	18.0	42-39	34-47
Colorado	64	98	.395	30.0	35-46	29-52

Wild-card teams.

American League

EASTERN DIVISION

Team	Won	Lost	Pct	GB	Home	Away
NY Yankees	95	67	.586	—	51-30	44-37
†Baltimore	93	69	.574	2.0	47-34	46-35
Tampa Bay	90	72	.556	5.0	46-35	44-37
Toronto	73	89	.451	22.0	41-40	32-49
Boston	69	93	.426	26.0	34-47	35-46

CENTRAL DIVISION

Team	Won	Lost	Pct	GB	Home	Away
Detroit	88	74	.543	—	50-31	38-43
Chi. White Sox	85	77	.525	3.0	45-36	40-41
Kansas City	72	90	.444	16.0	37-44	35-46
Cleveland	68	94	.420	20.0	37-44	31-50
Minnesota	66	96	.407	22.0	31-50	35-46

WESTERN DIVISION

Team	Won	Lost	Pct	GB	Home	Away
Oakland	94	68	.580	—	50-31	44-37
†Texas	93	69	.574	1.0	50-31	43-38
LA Angels	89	73	.549	5.0	46-35	43-38
Seattle	75	87	.463	19.0	40-41	35-46

2012 Playoffs

National League wild-card play-in game

St. Louis 6 at Atlanta 3

National League Division Playoffs

Game 1 ....Cincinnati 5 at San Francisco 2
Game 2 ....Cincinnati 9 at San Francisco 0
Game 3 ....San Francisco 2 at Cincinnati 1 (10)
Game 4 ....San Francisco 8 at Cincinnati 3
Game 5 ....San Francisco 6 at Cincinnati 4

(San Francisco won series 3–2)

Game 1 ....Washington 3 at St. Louis 2
Game 2 ....Washington 4 at St. Louis 12
Game 3 ....St. Louis 8 at Washington 0
Game 4 ....St. Louis 1 at Washington 2
Game 5 ....St. Louis 9 at Washington 7

(St. Louis won series 3–2)

National League Championship Series

Game 1 ....St. Louis 6 at San Francisco 4
Game 2 ....St. Louis 1 at San Francisco 7
Game 3 ....San Francisco 1 at St. Louis 3
Game 4 ....San Francisco 3 at St. Louis 8
Game 5 ....San Francisco 5 at St. Louis 0
Game 6 ....St. Louis 1 at San Francisco 6
Game 7 ....St. Louis 0 at San Francisco 9

(San Francisco won series 4–3)

GAME 1

											R	H	E
St. Louis	0	2	0	4	0	0	0	0	0	6	8	0
San Francisco	0	0	0	4	0	0	0	0	0	4	7	1

W—StL: Mujica. **L**—SF: Bumgarner. **SV**—StL: Motte. **LOB**—StL: 4; SF: 7. **2B**—StL: Descalso, Kozma; SF: Crawford. **3B**—SF: Blanco. **HR**—StL: Freese, Beltran. **RBI**—StL: Freese (2), Kozma, Jay, Beltran (2); SF: Belt, Blanco (2), Crawford. **SB**—StL: Holliday, Kozma. **GIDP**—StL: Freese. **E**—SF: Sandoval,

T—3:21. **A**—42,534.

Recap: (AP) Ahead by a lot or behind by a bunch, these St. Louis Cardinals are winning every which way. Boosted by two-run homers from proven postseason stars Carlos Beltran and David Freese, and 5⅓ innings from a steady bullpen, these wild, wild-card Cardinals beat the San Francisco Giants 6–4 in Game 1 of the NL championship series. The defending World Series champions built an early 6–0 cushion and held on. Only two nights earlier, the Cardinals came back from the same deficit, using a four-run rally in the ninth inning at Washington in the deciding Game 5 of the division series.

National League Championship Series (Cont.)

GAME 2

St. Louis	0	1 0	0 0 0	0 0 0	**1**	**5**	**2**
San Francisco	1	0 0	4 0 0	0 2 x	**7**	**12**	**0**

W—SF: Vogelsong. **L**—StL: Carpenter. **LOB**—StL: 7; SF: 9. **2B**—StL: Carpenter, Beltran; SF: Belt, Vogelsong. **HR**—SF: Pagan. **RBI**—StL: Carpenter; SF: Pagan, Crawford (2), Scutaro (2) Theriot (2). **SAC**—SF: Vogelsong. **E**—StL: Carpenter, Holliday.

T—3:10. **A**—42,679.

Recap: (AP) Marco Scutaro singled in two runs during a four-run fourth inning before leaving with a hip injury, sparking San Francisco's first home win this postseason, 7-1 over the St. Louis Cardinals to tie the NL championship series at one game apiece. Ryan Vogelsong pitched seven strong innings, Angel Pagan hit a leadoff homer and Scutaro stayed in until breaking the game open with his single off Chris Carpenter.

GAME 3

San Francisco	0 0 1	0 0 0	0 0 0	**1**	**9**	**1**
St. Louis	0 0 2	0 0 0	1 0 x	**3**	**6**	**0**

W—StL: Lohse. **L**—SF: Cain. **SV**—StL: Motte. **LOB**—SF: 11; StL: 5. **2B**—SF: Scutaro; StL: Freese. **HR**—StL: M. Carpenter. **RBI**—SF: Sandoval; StL: M. Carpenter (2), Robinson. **SAC**—SF: Cain. **GIDP**—SF: Pence, Sandoval; StL: Beltran.

T—3:02. **A**—45,850.

Recap: (AP) Super sub Matt Carpenter hit a two-run homer after replacing an injured Carlos Beltran and the Cardinals chased Matt Cain before a 3½-hour rain delay in the seventh inning of a 3-1 victory over the San Francisco Giants for a 2-1 series lead. Kyle Lohse worked around a season-worst five walks in 5⅔ innings. Mitchell Boggs struck out Hunter Pence and Brandon Belt with two out to end the seventh. Jason Motte earned the first two-inning save of his career.

GAME 4

San Francisco	0 0 1	0 0 0	0 0 2	**3**	**6**	**1**
St. Louis	2 0 0	0 2 2	2 0 x	**8**	**12**	**0**

W—StL: Wainwright. **L**—SF: Lincecum. **LOB**—SF: 3; StL: 7. **2B**—SF: Scutaro; StL: M. Carpenter, Jay, Molina. **3B**—SF: Pagan. **HR**—SF: Pence, Sandoval. **RBI**—SF: Pence, Sandoval (2); StL: Holliday (2), Craig, Molina (2), Jay (2), Kozma. **SAC**—StL: Wainwright. **SF**—StL: Craig. **CS**—StL: Kozma. **E**—SF: Sandoval. **WP**—SF: Affeldt.

T—3:17. **A**—47,062.

Recap: (AP) "We're not taking the last game to get into the World Series for granted," Matt Holliday said after an 8-3 win put St. Louis up 3-1 in the best-of-seven NL championship series with a chance to wrap it up at home. "The Giants have proven they're a great team and they had their backs to the wall against the Reds." The Giants are in a hole after Adam Wainwright threw seven innings of four-hit ball and St. Louis' offense roughed up Tim Lincecum and the San Francisco bullpen. Holliday, Jon Jay and Yadier Molina had two RBIs apiece to lead a 12-hit outburst by a team that batted just .198 through the first three games of the series.

GAME 5

San Francisco	0 0 0	4 0 0	0 1 0	**5**	**6**	**0**
St. Louis	0 0 0	0 0 0	0 0 0	**0**	**7**	**0**

W—SF: Zito. **L**—StL: Lynn. **LOB**—SF: 5; StL: 7. **2B**—StL: Craig. **HR**—SF: Sandoval. **RBI**—SF: Sandoval,

GAME 5 (CONT.)

Crawford (2), Zito. **SB**—SF: Belt; StL: Beltran. **GIDP**—StL: Lynn. **IBB**—StL: Kozma. **E**—StL: Lynn.

T—3:03. **A**—47,075.

Recap: (AP) Barry Zito was at his best Friday night, pitching San Francisco back into the NL championship series with a 5-0 win over the St. Louis Cardinals that narrowed its deficit to 3-2. Pablo Sandoval homered for the second straight night and once again this postseason, the Giants benefited from a big error. The Giants had runners on first and second with one out in the fourth inning when St. Louis pitcher Lance Lynn threw a low dart off the second-base bag with the ball bounding into shallow right field and Marco Scutaro scoring without a play from second. Eighth-place hitter Brandon Crawford singled up the middle with the bases loaded on a full-count with two outs for two more runs. Zito, who has just 30 career hits in 310 at-bats in the regular season with nine RBIs, laid down a perfect bunt for a fourth run.

GAME 6

St. Louis	0 0 0	0 0 1	0 0 0	**1**	**5**	
San Francisco	1 4 0	0 0 0	0 1 x	**6**	**9**	

W—SF: Vogelsong. **L**—StL: Carpenter. **LOB**—StL: 6; SF: 7. **2B**—StL: Beltran; SF: Sandoval, Scutaro, Blanco. **3B**—SF: Belt. **RBI**—SF: Craig; SF: Posey, Vogelsong, Scutaro (2), Sandoval, Theriot. **E**—StL: Kozma; SF: Blanco. **IBB**—SF: Crawford.

T—2:55. **A**—43,070.

Recap: (AP) Ryan Vogelsong struck out a career-best nine in another postseason gem and on his biggest stage yet, and San Francisco staved off elimination for the second straight game, pushing St Louis to a winner-take-all Game 7 with a 6-1 victory. Marco Scutaro delivered a two-run double and Buster Posey drove in his first run of the series with a groundout in the first inning as San Francisco struck early to support Vogelsong. The Giants again got to St. Louis ace Chris Carpenter, who was done in by one big inning this time, too. He allowed six hits and five runs, two earned, in four innings.

GAME 7

St. Louis	0 0 0	0 0 0	0 0 0	**0**	**7**	**2**
San Francisco	1 1 5	0 0 0	1 1 x	**9**	**14**	**0**

W—SF: Cain. **L**—StL: Lohse. **LOB**—SF: 12; SF: 10. **2B**—Sandoval, Pence. **HR**—SF: Belt. **RBI**—SF: Sandoval, Cain, Pence (2), Crawford, Pagan, Belt. **SB**—StL: Beltran, Descalso. **GIDP**—SF: Huff. **E**—StL: Jay, Kozma. **HBP**—StL: Holliday (by Cain). **WP**—SF: Casilla, Romo.

T—3:35. **A**—43,056.

Recap: (AP) Hunter Pence got the Giants going with a weird double, Matt Cain pitched his second clincher of October and San Francisco closed out Game 7 of the NL championship series in a rainstorm, routing the St. Louis Cardinals 9-0. San Francisco won its record-tying sixth elimination game of the postseason, completing a lopsided rally from a 3-1 deficit. Marco Scutaro produced his sixth multi-hit game of the series and matched an LCS record with 14 hits and Pablo Sandoval drove in a run for his fifth straight game. "These guys never quit," manager Bruce Bochy said. "They just kept believing and they got it done."

American League wild-card play-in game

Baltimore 5 at Texas 1

American League Division Playoffs

Game 1 ....Oakland 1 at Detroit 3	Game 4 ....Detroit 3 at Oakland 4
Game 2 ....Oakland 4 at Detroit 5	Game 5 ....Detroit 6 at Oakland 0
Game 3 ....Detroit 0 at Oakland 2	

(Detroit won series 3–2)

Game 1 ....New York 7 at Baltimore 2	Game 4 ....Baltimore 2 at New York 1 (13)
Game 2 ....New York 2 at Baltimore 3	Game 5 ....Baltimore 1 at New York 3
Game 3 ....Baltimore 2 at New York 3 (12)	

(New York won series 3–2)

American League Championship Series

Game 1 ....Detroit 6 at New York 4 (12)	Game 3 ....New York 1 at Detroit 3
Game 2 ....Detroit 3 at New York 0	Game 4 ....New York 1 at Detroit 8

(Detroit won series 4–0)

GAME 1

														R	H	E
Detroit	0	0	0	0	0	2	0	2	0	0	0	2	**6**	**15**	**1**
New York	0	0	0	0	0	0	0	4	0	0	0	0	**4**	**11**	**0**

W—Det: Smyly. **L**—NY: Phelps. **LOB**—Det: 12; NY: 13. **2B**—Det: Peralta, Jackson, Young; NY: Ibanez, Swisher. **3B**—Det: Jackson. **HR**—Det: Young; NY: Suzuki, Ibanez. **RBI**—Det: Fielder, Young (3), Garcia, Dirks; NY: Suzuki (2), Ibanez (2). **SB**—NY: Gardner (2). **GIDP**—Det: Jackson. **E**—Det: Infante. **IBB**—Det: Cabrera.

T—4:54. A—47,122.

Recap: (AP) The Detroit Tigers took the lead on Delmon Young's ringing double in the 12th inning. Then came the blow that really staggered the New York Yankees. A little grounder up the middle left Derek Jeter sprawled in the dirt, screaming in pain and out for the rest of the postseason with a broken left ankle. Detroit's 6-4 win and Jeter's injury capped a game of wild swings and wild swings of emotion. Detroit was coasting toward a 4–0 win behind outstanding pitching by Doug Fister before the Yankees rocked Tigers closer Jose Valverde in the ninth. Ichiro Suzuki started the Yankees' comeback with a two-run homer with one out in the ninth, and the 40-year-old Raul Ibanez hit another two-run drive with two outs. But in the twelfth inning, Young's one-out double off David Phelps, which followed a leadoff walk by Triple Crown winner Miguel Cabrera, sliced in right and eluded Nick Swisher, allowing Cabrera to score the winning run.

GAME 2

										R	H	E
Detroit	0	0	0	0	0	0	1	2	0	**3**	**8**	**1**
New York	0	0	0	0	0	0	0	0	0	**0**	**4**	**0**

W—Det: Sanchez. **L**—NY: Kuroda. **SV**—Det: Coke. **LOB**—Det: 6; NY: 7. **2B**—Det: Berry; NY: Teixeira. **RBI**—Det: Young, Garcia, Cabrera. **SB**—NY: Granderson. **CS**—NY: Ibanez. **E**—Det: Sanchez. **IBB**—NY: Ibanez.

T—3:18. A—47,082.

Recap: (AP) The Detroit Tigers got a big boost from Anibal Sanchez's arm. They got a helping hand from an umpire, too. The reward: a commanding 2–0 lead in the AL championship series, and a trip home with their ace ready to start. Delmon Young gave Sanchez his first run of support in these playoffs with a fielder's choice in the seventh. The Tigers then scored twice in the eighth after second base umpire Jeff Nelson missed a call on a two-out tag at second base.

GAME 3

										R	H	E
New York	0	0	0	0	0	0	0	0	1	**1**	**5**	**1**
Detroit	0	0	1	1	0	0	0	0	x	**2**	**7**	**0**

W—Det: Verlander. **L**—NY: Hughes. **SV**—Det: Coke. **LOB**—NY: 4; Det: 10. **2B**—Det: Cabrera. **HR**—NY: Nunez. Det: Young. **RBI**—NY: Nunez; Det: Young, Cabrera. **SB**—Det: Berry, Infante. **GIDP**—Det: Cabrera. **E**—NY: Chavez. **IBB**—Det: Young.

T—3:28. A—42,490.

Recap: (AP) Justin Verlander and Detroit's stellar starters are on quite a roll—no matter who is in the opposing lineup. Verlander took a shutout into the ninth inning and the Tigers held on to beat New York 2–1 for a 3–0 lead in the AL championship series. Yankees manager Joe Girardi changed his batting order again, benching Alex Rodriguez and Nick Swisher in a futile effort to snap his team out of an untimely hitting funk. Phil Coke gave up consecutive singles with two outs in the ninth before striking out postseason star Raul Ibanez for his second save in two games. Verlander allowed only a pair of singles by Ichiro Suzuki and a leadoff homer by Eduardo Nunez in the ninth. Delmon Young hit a solo home run for the Tigers, and Miguel Cabrera had an RBI double.

GAME 4

										R	H	E
New York	0	0	0	0	0	1	0	0	0	**1**	**2**	**2**
Detroit	1	0	1	4	0	0	1	1	x	**8**	**16**	**1**

W—Det: Scherzer. **L**—NY: Sabathia. **LOB**—NY: 5; Det: 12. **2B**—NY: Swisher; Det: Dirks, Garcia. **3B**—NY: Nunez. **HR**—Det: Cabrera, Peralta (2), Jackson. **RBI**—NY: Nunez; Det: Young, Garcia, Cabrera (2), Peralta (3), Jackson. **SB**—NY: Nunez; Det: Garcia. **CS**—Tex: Cruz; Det; Jackson. **E**—NY: Teixeira, Nunez; Det: Fielder.

T—3:27. A—42,477.

Recap: (AP) Max Scherzer capped a stupendous stretch for Detroit's rotation, and the Tigers won their second pennant in seven years by beating the Yankees 8-1 for a four-game sweep of the ALCS. Miguel Cabrera and Jhonny Peralta hit two-run homers in a four-run fourth inning against CC Sabathia, who was unable to prevent the Yankees from getting swept in a seven-game postseason series for the first time in 36 years. Scherzer took a no-hit bid into the sixth against a starting lineup that was again without Alex Rodriguez, who flied out with two on in the sixth as a pinch hitter. Austin Jackson added a solo shot in the seventh for Detroit, and Peralta hit another homer an inning later.

Game 1 ....Detroit 3 at San Francisco 8
Game 2 ....Detroit 0 at San Francisco 2

Game 3 ....San Francisco 2 at Detroit 0
Game 4 ....San Francisco 4 at Detroit 3 (10)

(San Francisco won series 4–0)

GAME I

Detroit	0	0	0	0	0	1	0	0	2	**3**	**8**	**0**
San Francisco	1	0	3	1	1	0	2	0	x	**8**	**11**	**0**

W—SF: Zito. **L**—Det: Verlander. **LOB**—Det: 6; SF: 4. **2B**—Det: Jackson; SF: Pagan (2). **HR**—Det: Peralta; SF: Sandoval (3). **RBI**—Det: Cabrera, Peralta (2); SF: Sandoval (4), Scutaro (2), Zito, Posey. **GIDP**—Det: Young. **WP**—Det: Benoit.

T—3:26. **A**—42,855.

Recap: (AP) The Babe. Mr. October. El Hombre. And now Kung Fu Panda. Pablo Sandoval joined Babe Ruth, Reggie Jackson and Albert Pujols as the only sluggers to hit three home runs in a World Series game, and the San Francisco Giants rolled over Justin Verlander and the Detroit Tigers 8–3 in Game 1. Barry Zito—remember him?—won in his World Series debut, two years after poor performances caused the Giants to drop him from their postseason roster. Sandoval hit a solo home run to right-center on a 95 mph 0–2 fastball at the letters in the first. He reached outside and hit a two-run, opposite-field drive to left in the third on another 95 mph pitch from Verlander, the reigning AL MVP and Cy Young winner. Then he added another bases-empty shot into the center-field batter's eye in the fifth, this time on an 84 mph offspeed offering from Al Alburquerque. Verlander was chased after allowing five runs and six hits in four innings, his shortest start this year, and he dropped to 0–3 with a 7.20 ERA in World Series play.

GAME 2

Detroit	0	0	0	0	0	0	0	0	0	**0**	**2**	**0**
San Francisco	0	0	0	0	0	0	1	1	x	**2**	**5**	**0**

W—SF: Bumgarner. **L**—Det: Fister. **SV**—SF: Romo. **LOB**—Det: 2; SF: 7. **2B**—Det: Young. **RBI**—SF: Pence. **SF**—SF: Pence. **GIDP**—Det: Fielder; SF: Crawford. **SB**—SF: Pagan. **CS**—Det:Infante. **PO**—Det: Infante. **IBB**—SF: Sandoval. **HBP**—Det: Fielder (by Bumgarner)

T—3:05. **A**—42,982.

Recap: (AP) Long ball one night, a Giant dose of small ball the next. Madison Bumgarner shut down the Detroit Tigers for seven innings, then the Giants took advantage of a bunt that stayed fair to eke out the go-ahead run in a 2–0 win for a 2–0 edge in the World Series. Gregor Blanco's single trickled to a stop inches fair on the infield dirt, setting up Brandon Crawford's run-scoring double-play grounder in the seventh. Hunter Pence added a sacrifice fly in the eighth, and that was plenty for these masters of the October comeback.

GAME 3

San Francisco	0	2	0	0	0	0	0	0	0	**2**	**7**	**1**
Detroit	0	0	0	0	0	0	0	0	0	**0**	**5**	**1**

W—SF: Vogelsong. **L**—Det: Sanchez. **SV**—SF: Romo. **LOB**—SF: 6; Det: 9. **2B**—SF: Sandoval. **3B**—SF: Blanco. **RBI**—SF: Blanco, Crawford. **GIDP**—Det: Fielder, Berry. **SB**—SF: Pence, Crawford. **E**—SF: Crawford; Det: Jackson. **WP**—Det: Sanchez.

T—3:25. **A**—42,262.

GAME 3 *(CONT.)*

Recap: (AP) Nothing is stopping them—not even the Triple Crown winner at the plate with the bases loaded. Armed and accelerating, the San Francisco Giants became the first team to throw consecutive World Series shutouts in nearly a half-century, blanking Miguel Cabrera and the Detroit Tigers 2–0 on a chilly night for a commanding 3–0 lead. Gregor Blanco hit an RBI triple and trotted home on Brandon Crawford's single in the second inning, and that was ample for the Giants. Timely hits, combined with another dominant effort on the mound and sharp defense, put them close to their second title in three years. Ryan Vogelsong, a career journeyman whose path to the World Series took a detour to Japan, improved to 3-0 with a 1.09 ERA in four starts this postseason. Tim Lincecum took over with two outs in the sixth, and the two-time Cy Young Award winner looked as if he had been coming out of the bullpen his whole life and shut down the Tigers. Closer Sergio Romo finished off the combined five-hitter with his second save of the Series.

GAME 4

San Francisco	0	1	0	0	0	2	0	0	0	1	**4**	**9**	**0**
Detroit	0	0	2	0	0	1	0	0	0	0	**3**	**5**	**0**

W—SF: Casilla. **L**—Det: Coke. **SV**—SF: Romo. **LOB**—SF: 5; Det: 6. **2B**—SF: Pence. **3B**—SF: Belt. **HR**—SF: Posey; Det: Cabrera, Young. **RBI**—SF: Belt, Posey, Scutaro; Det: Cabrera (2), Young. **GIDP**—SF: Sandoval. **CS**—SF: Belt. **HBP**—Det: Infante, by Casilla.

T—3:34. **A**—42,152.

Recap: (AP) Marco Scutaro delivered one more key hit, a go-ahead single with two outs in the 10th inning against Phil Coke to help the Giants sweep the Detroit Tigers with a 4–3, 10-inning win. On a night of biting cold, stiff breezes and some rain, the Giants sealed the title when Sergio Romo got Triple Crown winner Miguel Cabrera to look at strike three for the final out. Ryan Theriot led off the 10th with a single against Phil Coke, moved up on Brandon Crawford's sacrifice and scored on a shallow single by Scutaro, the MVP of the NL championship series.

Once again, San Francisco took an early lead. Pence hit a one-hop drive over the center-field fence for a double and Brandon Belt tripled off the right-field wall on the next pitch for a 1–0 lead in the second. The next inning, with two outs and a runner on first, Cabrera lofted an opposite-field fly to right—off the bat, it looked like a routine out shy of the warning track. But with winds gusting over 25 mph, the ball kept carrying, Pence kept drifting toward the wall and the crowd kept getting louder. Just like that, it was gone. But Scutaro led off the sixth with a single and clapped all the way around the bases when Buster Posey sent a shot that sailed just inside the left-field foul pole for a 3–2 San Francisco lead. Delmon Young, the ALCS MVP against the Yankees, made it 3–all with another opposite-field homer to right, this one a no-doubt drive. Pablo Sandoval, benched for most of the 2010 Series, went 8 for 16 this year, including a three-homer performance in Game 1, to win World Series MVP honors.

DETROIT

BATTING	AB	R	H	HR	RBI	Avg
Omar Infante ...15	0	5	0	0	.333
Jhonny Peralta..15	1	1	1	2	.067
Prince Fielder..14	0	1	0	0	.071
D. Young 14	2	5	1	0	.357
M. Cabrera 13	1	3	1	3	.231
A. Jackson 13	2	3	0	0	.231
Andy Dirks.........9	0	1	0	0	.111
Quintin Berry 8	0	0	0	0	.000
Alex Avila 7	0	1	0	0	.143
Gerald Laird 7	0	0	0	0	.000
Avisail Garcia 5	0	0	0	0	.000
Doug Fister........2	0	0	0	0	.000
Don Kelly...........1	0	0	0	0	.000
R. Santiago........1	0	0	0	0	.000
J. Verlander.......1	0	0	0	0	.000
Danny Worth 1	0	0	0	0	.000
Totals 126	**6**	**20**	**3**	**6**	**.159**

PITCHING	G	IP	W	L	SV	H	BB	SO	ERA
Anibal Sanchez..1	7.0	0	1	0	6	1	8	2.57
Max Scherzer.....1	6.1	0	0	0	7	1	8	4.26
Doug Fister 1	6.0	0	1	0	4	1	3	1.50
J. Verlander 1	4.0	0	1	0	6	1	4	11.25
Phil Coke...........3	3.1	0	1	0	2	0	8	2.70
A. Alburquerque ..1	2.0	0	0	0	1	0	2	4.50
Joaquin Benoit ..2	1.2	0	0	0	1	0	3	0.00
Octavio Dotel 2	1.2	0	0	0	0	2	1	0.00
Drew Smyly........2	1.2	0	0	0	1	3	2	5.40
Rick Porcello......1	1.0	0	0	0	0	0	1	0.00
Jose Valverde 1	0.1	0	0	0	4	0	0	154.00
Totals 35.0	**0**	**4**	**0**	**32**	**9**	**41**	**4.11**

SAN FRANCISCO

BATTING	AB	R	H	HR	RBI	Avg
Angel Pagan ...16	3	2	0	0	.125
P. Sandoval.....16	3	8	3	4	.500
M. Scutaro.......16	3	4	0	3	.250
Gregor Blanco.15	1	4	0	1	.267
Buster Posey ...15	1	4	1	3	.267
Hunter Pence ..14	3	4	0	1	.286
Brandon Belt ..13	1	1	0	1	.077
B. Crawford.....12	0	3	0	1	.250
Ryan Theriot......5	1	1	0	0	.200
H. Sanchez 4	0	0	0	0	.000
M. Bumgarner ..2	0	0	0	0	.000
Barry Zito..........2	0	1	0	1	.500
Aubrey Huff.......1	0	0	0	0	.000
Tim Lincecum....1	0	0	0	0	.000
Totals 132	**16**	**32**	**4**	**15**	**.242**

PITCHING	G	IP	W	L	SV	H	BB	SO	ERA
M. Bumgarner....1	7.0	1	0	0	2	2	8	0.00
Matt Cain 1	7.0	0	0	0	5	2	5	3.86
Ryan Vogelsong 1	5.2	1	0	0	5	4	3	0.00
Barry Zito 1	5.2	1	0	0	6	1	3	1.59
Tim Lincecum 2	4.2	0	0	0	1	8	0.00
Sergio Romo 3	3.0	0	0	3	0	0	5	0.00
Jeremy Affeldt...2	2.0	0	0	0	0	1	4	0.00
Santiago Casilla .2	1.1	0	0	0	0	0	0	0.00
George Kontos ..1	0.1	0	0	0	2	1	0	54.00
Jose Mijares.......1	0.1	0	0	0	0	0	0	0.00
Totals.................................37.0	**4**	**0**	**3**	**20**	**12**	**36**	**1.46**

National League Batting

BATTING AVERAGE

Buster Posey, SF	.336
Andrew McCutchen, Pit	.327
Ryan Braun, Mil	.319
Yadier Molina, StL	.315
Jordan Pacheco, Col	.309
Allen Craig, StL	.307
Marco Scutaro, SF/Col	.306
David Wright, NYM	.306
Carlos Gonzalez, Col	.303
Aaron Hill, Ari	.302

HITS

Andrew McCutchen, Pit	194
Ryan Braun, Mil	191
Marco Scutaro, SF/Col	190
Martin Prado, Atl	186
Jose Reyes, Mia	184
Aaron Hill, Ari	184
Starlin Castro, Chi	183
David Wright, NYM	178
Buster Posey, SF	178
Matt Holliday, StL	177

DOUBLES

Aramis Ramirez, Mil	50
Aaron Hill, Ari	44
Joey Votto, Cin	44
Paul Goldschmidt, Ari	43
Martin Prado, Atl	42
David Wright, NYM	41
Daniel Murphy, NYM	40

TRIPLES

Angel Pagan, SF	15
Jose Reyes, Mia	12
Starlin Castro, Chi	12
Dexter Fowler, Col	11
Melky Cabrera, SF	10
Michael Bourn, Atl	10
Tyler Colvin, Col	10

STOLEN BASES

Everth Cabrera, SD	44
Michael Bourn, Atl	42
Jose Reyes, Mia	40
Shane Victorino, LA/Phi	39
Juan Pierre, Phi	37
Carlos Gomez, Mil	37
Jose Altuve, Hou	33
Dee Gordon, LA	32

Six tied with 30

HOME RUNS

Ryan Braun, Mil	41
Giancarlo Stanton, Mia	37
Jay Bruce, Cin	34
Adam LaRoche, Wash	33
Carlos Beltran, StL	32
Alfonso Soriano, Chi	32
Ike Davis, NYM	32
Andrew McCutchen, Pit	31
Chase Headley, SD	31
Corey Hart, Mil	30
Jason Kubel, Ari	30
Pedro Alvarez, Pit	30

RUNS SCORED

Ryan Braun, Mil	108
Andrew McCutchen, Pit	107
Justin Upton, Ari	107
Jimmy Rollins, Phi	102
Bryce Harper, Wash	98
Michael Bourn, Atl	96
Matt Holliday, StL	95
Angel Pagan, SF	95
Chase Headley, SD	95
Aaron Hill, Ari	93
Ryan Zimmerman, Wash	93
Jason Heyward, Atl	93

RUNS BATTED IN

Chase Headley, SD	115
Ryan Braun, Mil	112
Alfonso Soriano, Chi	108
Aramis Ramirez, Mil	105
Hunter Pence, Phi/SF	104
Buster Posey, SF	103
Matt Holliday, StL	102
Adam LaRoche, Wash	100
Jay Bruce, Cin	99
Carlos Beltran, StL	97

ON-BASE PERCENTAGE

Joey Votto, Cin	.474
Buster Posey, SF	.408
Andrew McCutchen, Pit	.400
Ryan Braun, Mil	.391
David Wright, NYM	.391
Miguel Montero, Ari	.391
Dexter Fowler, Col	.389
Matt Holliday, StL	.379
Chase Headley, SD	.376

SLUGGING PERCENTAGE

Giancarlo Stanton, Mia	.608
Ryan Braun, Mil	.595
Andrew McCutchen, Pit	.553
Buster Posey, SF	.549
Aramis Ramirez, Mil	.540
Allen Craig, StL	.522
Aaron Hill, Ari	.522
Garrett Jones, Pit	.516
Jay Bruce, Cin	.514
Ian Desmond, Wash	.511

BASES ON BALLS

Dan Uggla, Atl	94
Joey Votto, Cin	94
Chase Headley, SD	86
David Wright, NYM	81
Matt Holliday, StL	75

National League Pitching

EARNED RUN AVERAGE

Clayton Kershaw, LA	2.53
R.A. Dickey, NYM	2.73
Johnny Cueto, Cin	2.78
Matt Cain, SF	2.79
Kyle Lohse, StL	2.86
Gio Gonzalez, Wash	2.89
Jordan Zimmermann, Wash	2.94
Cole Hamels, Phi	3.05
Cliff Lee, Phi	3.16
Wade Miley, Ari	3.33

SAVES

Jason Motte, StL	42
Craig Kimbrel, Atl	42
Jonathan Papelbon, Phi	38
Aroldis Chapman, Cin	38
Joel Hanrahan, Pit	36
John Axford, Mil	35
J.J. Putz, Ari	32
Tyler Clippard, Wash	32
Rafael Betancourt, Col	31

WINS

Gio Gonzalez, Wash	21
R.A. Dickey, NYM	20
Johnny Cueto, Cin	19
Lance Lynn, StL	18
Cole Hamels, Phi	17
Tim Hudson, Atl	16
A.J. Burnett, Pit	16
Kyle Lohse, StL	16
Matt Cain, SF	16
Yovani Gallardo, Mil	16
Madison Bumgarner, SF	16
Wade Miley, Ari	16

GAMES PITCHED

Randy Choate, LA/Mia	80
Matt Belisle, Col	80
Shawn Camp, Chi	80
Francisco Rodriguez, Mil	78
Mitchell Boggs, StL	78

SHUTOUTS

R.A. Dickey, NYM	3

Six tied with 2.

INNINGS PITCHED

R.A. Dickey, NYM	233.2
Clayton Kershaw, LA	227.2
Matt Cain, SF	219.1
Clayton Richard, SD	218.2
Johnny Cueto, Cin	217.0

STRIKEOUTS

R.A. Dickey, NYM	230
Clayton Kershaw, LA	229
Cole Hamels, Phi	216
Cliff Lee, Phi	207
Gio Gonzalez, Wash	207

COMPLETE GAMES

R.A. Dickey, NYM	5
Adam Wainwright, StL	3
Ricky Nolasco, Mia	3
Chris Carpenter, StL	4

13 tied with 3.

American League Batting

BATTING AVERAGE

Miguel Cabrera, Det .... .330
Mike Trout, LA .... .326
Adrian Beltre, Tex .... .321
Joe Mauer, Minn .... .319
Derek Jeter, NY .... .316
Prince Fielder, Det .... .313
Torii Hunter, LA .... .313
Billy Butler, KC .... .313
Robinson Cano, NY .... .313
David Murphy, Tex .... .304

HITS

Derek Jeter, NY 216
Miguel Cabrera, Det 205
Robinson Cano, NY 196
Adrian Beltre, Tex 194
Billy Butler, KC 192
Alex Gordon, KC 189
Adam Jones, Bal 186
Alex Rios, Chi 184
Prince Fielder, Det 182
Mike Trout, LA 182

DOUBLES

Alex Gordon, KC 51
Albert Pujols, LA 50
Robinson Cano, NY 48
Nelson Cruz, Tex 45
Shin-Soo Choo, Cle 43
Ian Kinsler, Tex 42
Miguel Cabrera, Det 40
Three tied with 39.

TRIPLES

Peter Bourjos, LA 11
Austin Jackson, Det 10
Elvis Andrus, Tex 9
Alex Rios, Chi 8
Jemile Weeks, Oak 8
Mike Trout, LA 8

EARNED RUN AVERAGE

David Price, TB 2.56
Justin Verlander, Det 2.64
Jered Weaver, LA 2.81
Chris Sale, Chi 3.05
Felix Hernandez, Sea 3.06
Jeremy Hellickson, TB 3.10
Matt Harrison, Tex 3.29
Hiroki Kuroda, NY 3.32
Jake Peavy, Chi 3.37
CC Sabathia, NY 3.38

SAVES

Jim Johnson, Bal 51
Fernando Rodney, TB 48
Rafael Soriano, NY 42
Chris Perez, Cle 39
Joe Nathan, Tex 37
Jose Valverde, Det 35
Addison Reed, Chi 29
Tom Wilhelmsen, Sea 29
Alfredo Aceves, Bos 25
Grant Balfour, Oak 24

STOLEN BASES

Mike Trout, LA 49
Rajai Davis, Tor 46
Ben Revere, Min 40
Coco Crisp, Oak 39
Alcides Escobar, KC 35
B.J. Upton, TB 31
Desmond Jennings, TB 31
Jason Kipnis, Cle 31
Jarrod Dyson, KC 30
Ichiro Suzuki, NY/Sea 29

HOME RUNS

Miguel Cabrera, Det 44
Josh Hamilton, Tex 43
Curtis Granderson, NY 43
Edwin Encarnacion, Tor 42
Adam Dunn, Chi 41
Adrian Beltre, Tex 36
Josh Willingham, Min 35
Robinson Cano, NY 33
Chris Davis, Bal 33
Adam Jones, Bal 32

RUNS SCORED

Mike Trout, LA 129
Miguel Cabrera, Det 109
Ian Kinsler, Tex 105
Robinson Cano, NY 105
Josh Hamilton, Tex 103
Adam Jones, Bal 103
Austin Jackson, Det 103
Curtis Granderson, NY 102
Derek Jeter, NY 99
Adrian Beltre, Tex 95

RUNS BATTED IN

Miguel Cabrera, Det 139
Josh Hamilton, Tex 128
Edwin Encarnacion, Tor 110
Josh Willingham, Min 110
Prince Fielder, Det 108

American League Pitching

WINS

David Price, TB 20
Jered Weaver, LA 20
Matt Harrison, Tex 18
Justin Verlander, Det 17
Chris Sale, Chi 17
Phil Hughes, NY 16
Hiroki Kuroda, NY 16
Max Scherzer, Det 16
Yu Darvish, Tex 16
CC Sabathia, NY 15
James Shields, TB 15

GAMES PITCHED

Boone Logan, NY 80
Fernando Rodney, TB 76
Joel Peralta, TB 76
Kelvin Herrera, KC 76
Grant Balfour, Oak 75

SHUTOUTS

Felix Hernandez, Sea 5
Brandon Morrow, Tor 3
Four tied with 2.

RUNS BATTED IN (CONT.)

Billy Butler, KC 107
Curtis Granderson, NY 106
Albert Pujols, LA 105
Adrian Beltre, Tex 102
Adam Dunn, Chi 96

ON-BASE PERCENTAGE

Miguel Cabrera, Det .... .448
Joe Mauer, Min .... .446
Prince Fielder, Det .... .412
Mike Trout, LA .... .399
Miguel Cabrera, Det .... .393
Edwin Encarnacion, Tor .... .384
David Murphy, Tex .... .380
Robinson Cano, NY .... .379
Austin Jackson, Det .... .377
Ben Zobrist, TB .... .377
Shin-Soo Choo, Cle .... .373
Billy Butler, KC .... .373

SLUGGING PERCENTAGE

Miguel Cabrera, Det .... .606
Josh Hamilton, Tex .... .577
Mike Trout, LA .... .564
Adrian Beltre, Tex .... .561
Edwin Encarnacion, Tor .... .557
Robinson Cano, NY .... .550
Prince Fielder, Det .... .528
Josh Willingham, Min .... .524
Alex Rios, Chi .... .516
Albert Pujols, LA .... .516

BASES ON BALLS

Adam Dunn, Chi 105
Ben Zobrist, TB 97
Carlos Santana, Cle 91
Joe Mauer, Min 90
Carlos Pena, TB 87
Prince Fielder, Det 84
Edwin Encarnacion, Tor 84
Nick Swisher, NY 77
Josh Willingham, Min 76
Curtis Granderson, NY 75

INNINGS PITCHED

Justin Verlander, Det 238.1
Felix Hernandez, Sea 232.0
James Shields, TB 227.2
Hiroki Kuroda, NY 219.2
Jake Peavy, Chi 219.0

STRIKEOUTS

Justin Verlander, Det 239
Max Scherzer, Det 231
Felix Hernandez, Sea 223
James Shields, TB 223
Yu Darvish, Tex 221

COMPLETE GAMES

Justin Verlander, Det 6
Felix Hernandez, Sea 5
Jake Peavy, Chi 4
Matt Harrison, Tex 4
Five tied with 3.

National League

TEAM BATTING

TEAM BATTING	G	AB	R	H	2B	3B	HR	TB	RBI	OBP	SLG	OPS	BAVG
Colorado Rockies	162	5577	758	1526	306	52	166	2434	716	.330	.436	.766	.274
St. Louis Cardinals	162	5622	765	1526	290	37	159	2367	732	.338	.421	.759	.271
San Francisco Giants	162	5558	718	1495	287	57	103	2205	675	.327	.397	.724	.269
Washington Nationals	162	5615	731	1468	301	25	194	2401	688	.322	.428	.750	.261
Milwaukee Brewers	162	5557	776	1442	300	39	202	2426	741	.325	.437	.762	.259
Arizona Diamondbacks	162	5462	734	1416	307	33	165	2284	710	.328	.418	.746	.259
Philadelphia Phillies	162	5544	684	1414	271	28	158	2215	659	.317	.400	.716	.255
Los Angeles Dodgers	162	5438	637	1369	269	23	116	2032	607	.317	.374	.690	.252
Cincinnati Reds	162	5477	669	1377	296	30	172	2249	636	.315	.411	.726	.251
New York Mets	162	5450	650	1357	286	21	139	2102	625	.316	.386	.701	.249
Atlanta Braves	162	5425	700	1341	263	30	149	2111	660	.320	.389	.709	.247
San Diego Padres	162	5422	651	1339	272	43	121	2060	610	.319	.380	.699	.247
Miami Marlins	162	5437	609	1327	261	39	137	2077	576	.308	.382	.690	.244
Pittsburgh Pirates	162	5412	651	1313	241	37	170	2138	620	.304	.395	.699	.243
Chicago Cubs	162	5411	613	1297	265	36	137	2045	570	.302	.378	.680	.240
Houston Astros	162	5407	583	1276	238	28	146	2008	545	.302	.371	.673	.236

TEAM PITCHING

TEAM PITCHING	GP	W	L	SV	SVO	CG	SHO	R	IP	Ks	BB	ERA
Washington Nationals	162	98	64	51	68	3	9	594	1468.1	1325	497	3.33
Los Angeles Dodgers	162	86	76	40	59	2	10	597	1449.2	1276	539	3.34
Cincinnati Reds	162	97	65	56	74	9	12	588	1453.0	1248	427	3.34
Atlanta Braves	162	94	68	47	60	5	16	600	1445.1	1232	464	3.42
San Francisco Giants	162	94	68	53	67	5	14	649	1451.0	1237	489	3.68
St. Louis Cardinals	162	88	74	42	64	4	10	648	1462.2	1218	436	3.71
Philadelphia Phillies	162	81	81	42	61	5	11	680	1451.1	1385	409	3.83
Pittsburgh Pirates	162	79	83	45	59	2	10	674	1433.1	1192	490	3.86
Arizona Diamondbacks	162	81	81	39	59	4	9	688	1433.2	1200	417	3.93
San Diego Padres	162	76	86	43	60	4	11	710	1434.2	1205	539	4.01
New York Mets	162	74	88	36	55	7	13	709	1434.0	1240	488	4.09
Miami Marlins	162	69	93	38	60	5	7	724	1440.2	1113	495	4.09
Milwaukee Brewers	162	83	79	44	73	0	9	733	1453.2	1402	525	4.22
Chicago Cubs	162	61	101	28	49	1	9	759	1413.2	1128	573	4.51
Houston Astros	162	55	107	31	50	3	11	794	1423.1	1170	540	4.56
Colorado Rockies	162	64	98	36	63	0	7	890	1422.0	1144	566	5.22

American League

TEAM BATTING	G	AB	R	H	2B	3B	HR	TB	RBI	OBP	SLG	OPS	BAVG
Los Angeles Angels	162	5536	767	1518	273	22	187	2396	732	.332	.433	.764	.274
Texas Rangers	162	5590	808	1526	303	32	200	2493	780	.334	.446	.780	.273
Detroit Tigers	162	5476	726	1467	279	39	163	2313	698	.335	.422	.757	.268
Kansas City Royals	162	5636	676	1492	295	37	131	2254	643	.317	.400	.716	.265
New York Yankees	162	5524	804	1462	280	13	245	2503	774	.337	.453	.790	.265
Boston Red Sox	162	5604	734	1459	339	16	165	2325	695	.315	.415	.730	.260
Minnesota Twins	162	5562	701	1448	270	30	131	2171	667	.325	.390	.715	.260
Chicago White Sox	162	5518	748	1409	228	29	211	2328	726	.318	.422	.740	.255
Cleveland Indians	162	5525	667	1385	266	24	136	2107	635	.324	.381	.705	.251
Baltimore Orioles	162	5560	712	1375	270	16	214	2319	677	.311	.417	.728	.247
Toronto Blue Jays	162	5487	716	1346	247	22	198	2231	677	.309	.407	.716	.245
Tampa Bay Rays	162	5398	697	1293	250	30	175	2128	665	.317	.394	.711	.240
Oakland Athletics	162	5527	713	1315	267	32	195	2231	676	.310	.404	.714	.238
Seattle Mariners	162	5494	619	1285	241	27	149	2027	584	.296	.369	.665	.234

TEAM PITCHING	GP	W	L	SV	SVO	CG	SHO	R	IP	Ks	BB	ERA
Tampa Bay Rays	162	90	72	50	58	7	15	577	1459.2	1383	469	3.19
Oakland Athletics	162	94	68	47	64	1	13	614	1470.0	1136	462	3.48
Detroit Tigers	162	88	74	40	56	9	8	670	1430.2	1318	438	3.75
Seattle Mariners	162	75	87	43	63	8	11	651	1456.2	1166	449	3.76
New York Yankees	162	95	67	51	64	6	9	668	1445.1	1318	431	3.85
Baltimore Orioles	162	93	69	55	73	1	10	705	1483.0	1177	481	3.90
Texas Rangers	162	93	69	43	52	7	10	707	1442.0	1286	446	3.99
Los Angeles Angels	162	89	73	38	60	6	16	699	1433.1	1157	483	4.02
Chicago White Sox	162	85	77	37	57	6	11	676	1445.2	1246	503	4.02
Kansas City Royals	162	72	90	44	64	2	12	746	1451.1	1177	542	4.30
Toronto Blue Jays	162	73	89	29	44	5	11	784	1443.2	1142	574	4.64
Boston Red Sox	162	69	93	35	57	6	4	806	1443.0	1176	529	4.70
Minnesota Twins	162	66	96	35	49	3	6	832	1438.2	943	465	4.77
Cleveland Indians	162	68	94	43	56	2	6	845	1442.0	1086	543	4.78

Arizona Diamondbacks

BATTING	G	AB	R	H	2B	3B	HR	RBI	TB	BB	SO	SB	OBP	SLG	BAVG
Aaron Hill	156	609	93	184	44	6	26	85	318	52	86	14	.360	.522	.302
Justin Upton	150	554	107	155	24	4	17	67	238	63	121	18	.355	.430	.280
Paul Goldschmidt	145	514	82	147	43	1	20	82	252	60	130	18	.359	.490	.286
Jason Kubel	141	506	75	128	30	4	30	90	256	57	151	1	.327	.506	.253
Miguel Montero	141	486	65	139	25	2	15	88	213	73	130	0	.391	.438	.286
Gerardo Parra	133	385	58	105	21	2	7	36	151	33	77	15	.335	.392	.273
Chris Young	101	325	36	75	24	0	14	41	141	36	79	8	.311	.434	.231
Willie Bloomquist	80	324	47	98	21	5	0	23	129	12	55	7	.325	.398	.302
*Ryan Roberts	83	252	28	63	9	0	6	34	90	22	45	6	.306	.357	.250
John McDonald	70	197	16	49	9	0	6	22	76	12	33	0	.295	.386	.249
*Chris Johnson	44	147	12	42	7	2	7	35	74	8	40	1	.321	.503	.286
*Stephen Drew	40	135	17	26	8	1	2	12	42	19	35	0	.290	.311	.193
Ryan Wheeler	50	109	11	26	6	1	1	10	37	9	22	1	.294	.339	.239
*Lyle Overbay	45	96	11	28	9	0	2	10	43	12	26	0	.367	.448	.292
Adam Eaton	22	85	19	22	3	2	2	5	35	14	15	2	.382	.412	.259

PITCHING	GP	GS	IP	W–L	SV	HLD	H	ER	HR	BB	SO	ERA
Ian Kennedy	33	33	208.1	15-12	0	0	216	93	28	55	187	4.02
Trevor Cahill	32	32	200.0	13-12	0	0	184	84	16	74	156	3.78
Wade Miley	32	29	194.2	16-11	0	0	193	72	14	37	144	3.33
*Joe Saunders	21	21	130.0	6-10	0	0	146	61	17	31	89	4.22
Patrick Corbin	22	17	107.0	6-8	1	0	117	54	14	25	86	4.54
Josh Collmenter	28	11	90.1	5-3	0	0	92	37	13	22	80	3.69
Brad Ziegler	77	0	68.2	6-1	0	17	54	19	2	21	42	2.49
David Hernandez	72	0	68.1	2-3	4	25	48	19	4	22	98	2.50
Bryan Shaw	64	0	59.1	1-6	2	10	60	23	4	24	41	3.49
J.J. Putz	57	0	54.1	1-5	32	0	45	17	4	11	65	2.82
Daniel Hudson	9	9	45.1	3-2	0	0	62	37	9	12	37	7.35
*Craig Breslow	40	0	43.1	2-0	0	4	38	13	5	13	42	2.70
Mike Zagurski	45	0	37.1	0-0	0	4	37	23	5	19	34	5.54
Brad Bergesen	19	0	29.2	2-1	0	0	29	12	2	7	18	3.64
Tyler Skaggs	6	6	29.1	1-3	0	0	30	19	6	13	21	5.83

Atlanta Braves

BATTING	G	AB	R	H	2B	3B	HR	RBI	TB	BB	SO	SB	OBP	SLG	BAVG
Michael Bourn	155	624	96	171	26	10	9	57	244	70	155	42	.348	.391	.274
Martin Prado	156	617	81	186	42	6	10	70	270	58	69	17	.359	.438	.301
Jason Heyward	158	587	93	158	30	6	27	82	281	58	152	21	.335	.479	.269
Freddie Freeman	147	540	91	140	33	2	23	94	246	64	129	2	.340	.456	.259
Dan Uggla	154	523	86	115	29	0	19	78	201	94	168	4	.348	.384	.220
Brian McCann	121	439	44	101	14	0	20	67	175	44	76	3	.300	.399	.230
Chipper Jones	112	387	58	111	23	0	14	62	176	57	51	1	.377	.455	.287
Juan Francisco	93	192	17	45	11	0	9	32	83	11	70	1	.278	.432	.234
David Ross	62	176	18	45	7	0	9	23	79	18	60	1	.321	.449	.256
Tyler Pastornicky	76	169	21	41	6	1	2	13	55	10	32	2	.287	.325	.243
Paul Janish	55	167	18	31	6	1	0	9	39	17	30	1	.269	.234	.186
Andrelton Simmons	49	166	17	48	8	2	3	19	69	12	21	1	.335	.416	.289
Eric Hinske	91	132	9	26	7	1	2	13	41	14	41	0	.272	.311	.197
Matt Diaz	51	108	10	24	6	0	2	13	36	9	21	0	.280	.333	.222
*Reed Johnson	43	100	7	27	5	0	0	4	32	3	18	0	.305	.320	.270

PITCHING	GP	GS	IP	W–L	SV	HLD	H	ER	HR	BB	SO	ERA
Mike Minor	30	30	179.1	11-10	0	0	151	82	26	56	145	4.12
Tim Hudson	28	28	179.0	16-7	0	0	168	72	12	48	102	3.62
Tommy Hanson	31	31	174.2	13-10	0	0	183	87	27	71	161	4.48
Kris Medlen	50	12	138.0	10-1	1	7	103	24	6	23	120	1.57
Randall Delgado	18	17	92.2	4-9	0	0	89	45	8	42	76	4.37
Brandon Beachy	13	13	81.0	5-5	0	0	49	18	6	29	68	2.00
Cristhian Martinez	54	0	73.2	5-4	1	1	80	32	6	19	65	3.91
*Paul Maholm	11	11	68.2	4-5	0	0	63	27	8	19	59	3.54
Craig Kimbrel	63	0	62.2	3-1	42	0	27	7	3	14	116	1.01
Chad Durbin	76	0	61.0	4-1	1	15	52	21	9	28	49	3.10
Jonny Venters	66	0	58.2	5-4	0	20	61	21	6	28	69	3.22
Eric O'Flaherty	64	0	57.1	3-0	0	28	47	11	3	19	46	1.73
Ben Sheets	9	9	49.1	4-2	0	0	52	19	6	16	35	3.47
Jair Jurrjens	11	10	48.1	3-4	0	0	72	37	8	18	19	6.89
Luis Avilan	31	0	36.0	1-0	0	5	27	8	1	10	33	2.00

*Mid-season trade.

Chicago Cubs

BATTING	G	AB	R	H	2B	3B	HR	RBI	TB	BB	SO	SB	OBP	SLG	BAVG
Starlin Castro	162	646	78	183	29	12	14	78	278	36	100	25	.323	.430	.283
Alfonso Soriano	151	561	68	147	33	2	32	108	280	44	153	6	.322	.499	.262
Darwin Barney	156	548	73	139	26	4	7	44	194	33	58	6	.299	.354	.254
David DeJesus	148	506	76	133	28	8	9	50	204	61	89	7	.350	.403	.263
Bryan LaHair	130	340	42	88	17	0	16	40	153	39	124	4	.334	.450	.259
Anthony Rizzo	87	337	44	96	15	0	15	48	156	27	62	3	.342	.463	.285
Luis Valbuena	90	265	26	58	20	0	4	28	90	36	55	0	.310	.340	.219
Joe Mather	103	225	18	47	11	0	5	19	73	14	46	5	.256	.324	.209
Steve Clevenger	69	199	16	40	12	0	1	16	55	16	39	0	.260	.276	.201
Ian Stewart	55	179	16	36	5	2	5	17	60	21	46	0	.292	.335	.201
*Geovany Soto	52	176	26	35	6	1	6	14	61	19	35	0	.284	.347	.199
Tony Campana	89	174	26	46	6	0	0	5	52	11	43	30	.308	.299	.264
Welington Castillo	52	170	16	45	11	0	5	22	71	17	51	0	.337	.418	.265
*Reed Johnson	76	169	23	51	9	3	3	16	75	10	43	2	.355	.444	.302
*Jeff Baker	54	134	16	36	10	1	4	20	60	8	28	4	.306	.448	.269

PITCHING	GP	GS	IP	W-L	SV	HLD	H	ER	HR	BB	SO	ERA
Jeff Samardzija	28	28	174.2	9-13	0	0	157	74	20	56	180	3.81
Travis Wood	26	26	156.0	6-13	0	0	133	74	25	54	119	4.27
*Paul Maholm	21	20	120.1	9-6	0	0	115	50	12	34	81	3.74
Chris Volstad	21	21	111.1	3-12	0	0	137	78	16	43	61	6.31
*Ryan Dempster	16	16	104.0	5-5	0	0	81	26	9	27	83	2.25
Matt Garza	18	18	103.2	5-7	0	0	90	45	15	32	96	3.91
Shawn Camp	80	0	77.2	3-6	2	18	79	31	7	21	54	3.59
James Russell	77	0	69.1	7-1	2	13	67	25	5	23	55	3.25
*Justin Germano	13	12	64.0	2-10	0	0	81	48	7	19	45	6.75
Carlos Marmol	61	0	55.1	3-3	20	2	40	21	4	45	72	3.42
Manny Corpas	48	0	46.2	0-2	0	6	50	26	7	16	28	5.01
Rafael Dolis	34	0	38.0	2-4	4	3	40	27	5	23	24	6.39
*Michael Bowden	30	0	36.2	0-0	0	2	30	12	4	16	29	2.95
Chris Rusin	7	7	29.2	2-3	0	0	38	21	4	11	21	6.37

Cincinnati Reds

BATTING	G	AB	R	H	2B	3B	HR	RBI	TB	BB	SO	SB	OBP	SLG	BAVG
Brandon Phillips	147	580	86	163	30	1	18	77	249	28	79	15	.321	.429	.281
Zack Cozart	138	561	72	138	33	4	15	35	224	31	113	4	.288	.399	.246
Jay Bruce	155	560	89	141	35	5	34	99	288	62	155	9	.327	.514	.252
Drew Stubbs	136	493	75	105	13	2	14	40	164	42	166	30	.277	.333	.213
Ryan Ludwick	125	422	53	116	28	1	26	80	224	42	97	0	.346	.531	.275
Todd Frazier	128	422	55	115	26	6	19	67	210	36	103	3	.331	.498	.273
Joey Votto	111	374	59	126	44	0	14	56	212	94	85	5	.474	.567	.337
Chris Heisey	120	347	44	92	16	5	7	31	139	18	81	6	.315	.401	.265
Ryan Hanigan	112	317	25	87	14	0	2	24	107	44	37	0	.365	.338	.274
Scott Rolen	92	294	26	72	17	2	8	39	117	30	62	2	.318	.398	.245
Wilson Valdez	77	194	15	40	4	0	0	15	44	8	36	3	.236	.227	.206
Devin Mesoraco	54	165	17	35	8	0	5	14	58	17	33	1	.288	.352	.212
Miguel Cairo	70	150	9	28	7	2	1	13	42	4	20	4	.212	.280	.187
Xavier Paul	55	86	8	27	5	1	2	7	40	9	18	4	.379	.465	.314
Homer Bailey	34	70	1	8	1	0	0	5	9	1	29	0	.127	.129	.114

PITCHING	GP	GS	IP	W-L	SV	HLD	H	ER	HR	BB	SO	ERA
Johnny Cueto	33	33	217.0	19-9	0	0	205	67	15	49	170	2.78
Mat Latos	33	33	209.1	14-4	0	0	179	81	25	64	185	3.48
Homer Bailey	33	33	208.0	13-10	0	0	206	85	26	52	168	3.68
Bronson Arroyo	32	32	202.0	12-10	0	0	209	84	26	35	129	3.74
Mike Leake	30	30	179.0	8-9	0	0	201	91	26	41	116	4.58
Aroldis Chapman	68	0	71.2	5-5	38	6	35	12	4	23	122	1.51
Sean Marshall	73	0	61.0	5-5	9	22	55	17	3	16	74	2.51
Jose Arredondo	66	0	61.0	6-2	1	12	50	20	7	34	62	2.95
Alfredo Simon	36	0	61.0	3-2	1	1	65	18	2	22	52	2.66
Sam LeCure	48	0	57.1	3-3	0	7	46	20	3	23	61	3.14
Logan Ondrusek	63	0	54.2	5-2	2	13	51	21	8	31	39	3.46
J.J. Hoover	28	0	30.2	1-0	1	1	17	7	2	13	31	2.05
*Jonathan Broxton	25	0	22.1	3-3	4	10	20	7	1	3	20	2.82

*Mid-season trade.

Colorado Rockies

BATTING	G	AB	R	H	2B	3B	HR	RBI	TB	BB	SO	SB	OBP	SLG	BAVG
Carlos Gonzalez	135	518	89	157	31	5	22	85	264	56	115	20	.371	.510	.303
Jordan Pacheco	132	475	51	147	32	3	5	54	200	22	61	7	.341	.421	.309
Dexter Fowler	143	454	72	136	18	11	13	53	215	68	128	12	.389	.474	.300
Tyler Colvin	136	420	62	122	27	10	18	72	223	21	117	7	.327	.531	.290
Wilin Rosario	117	396	67	107	19	0	28	71	210	25	99	4	.312	.530	.270
*Marco Scutaro	95	377	47	102	16	3	4	30	136	27	35	7	.324	.361	.271
Michael Cuddyer	101	358	53	93	30	2	16	58	175	32	78	8	.317	.489	.260
Chris Nelson	111	345	45	104	21	3	9	53	158	27	84	2	.352	.458	.301
Josh Rutledge	73	277	37	76	20	5	8	37	130	9	54	7	.306	.469	.274
Todd Helton	69	240	31	57	16	1	7	37	96	39	44	1	.343	.400	.238
DJ LeMahieu	81	229	26	68	12	4	2	22	94	13	42	1	.332	.410	.297
Jonathan Herrera	86	225	29	59	9	1	3	12	79	16	39	4	.317	.351	.262
Ramon Hernandez	52	184	16	40	10	0	5	28	65	6	32	0	.247	.353	.217
Troy Tulowitzki	47	181	33	52	8	2	8	27	88	19	19	2	.360	.486	.287
Eric Young Jr.	98	174	36	55	7	2	4	15	78	13	31	14	.377	.448	.316
Charlie Blackmon	42	113	15	32	8	0	2	9	46	4	17	1	.325	.407	.283
Andrew Brown	46	112	14	26	7	0	5	11	48	12	34	2	.302	.429	.232

PITCHING	GP	GS	IP	W–L	SV	HLD	H	ER	HR	BB	SO	ERA
Jeff Francis	24	24	113.0	6-7	0	0	145	70	15	22	76	5.58
Alex White	23	20	98.0	2-9	0	0	114	60	13	51	64	5.51
Drew Pomeranz	22	22	96.2	2-9	0	0	97	53	14	46	83	4.93
*Jeremy Guthrie	19	15	90.2	3-9	0	0	122	64	21	31	45	6.35
Josh Roenicke	63	0	88.2	4-2	1	8	85	32	9	43	54	3.25
Christian Friedrich	16	16	84.2	5-8	0	0	102	58	14	30	74	6.17
Matt Belisle	80	0	80.0	3-8	3	26	91	33	5	18	69	3.71
Adam Ottavino	53	0	79.0	5-1	0	7	76	40	9	34	81	4.56
Jhoulys Chacin	14	14	69.0	3-5	0	0	80	34	10	32	45	4.43
Rex Brothers	75	0	67.2	8-2	0	18	63	29	5	37	83	3.86
Tyler Chatwood	19	12	64.2	5-6	1	0	74	39	9	33	41	5.43
Juan Nicasio	11	11	58.0	2-3	0	0	72	34	7	22	54	5.28
Rafael Betancourt	60	0	57.2	1-4	31	1	53	18	6	12	57	2.81
Matt Reynolds	71	0	57.1	3-1	0	2	65	28	11	17	51	4.40
Jamie Moyer	10	10	53.2	2-5	0	0	75	34	11	18	36	5.70

Houston Astros

BATTING	G	AB	R	H	2B	3B	HR	RBI	TB	BB	SO	SB	OBP	SLG	BAVG
Jose Altuve	147	576	80	167	34	4	7	37	230	40	74	33	.340	.399	.290
J.D. Martinez	113	395	34	95	14	3	11	55	148	40	96	0	.311	.375	.241
Brian Bogusevic	146	355	39	72	9	2	7	28	106	41	96	15	.297	.299	.203
*Chris Johnson	92	341	36	95	21	3	8	41	146	23	92	4	.329	.428	.279
Jed Lowrie	97	340	43	83	18	0	16	42	149	43	65	2	.331	.438	.244
Justin Maxwell	124	315	46	72	13	3	18	53	145	32	114	9	.304	.460	.229
Jordan Schafer	106	313	40	66	10	2	4	23	92	36	106	27	.297	.294	.211
*Carlos Lee	66	258	24	74	15	1	5	29	106	19	17	0	.336	.411	.287
Jason Castro	87	257	29	66	15	2	6	29	103	31	61	0	.334	.401	.257
Brett Wallace	66	229	24	58	10	1	9	24	97	18	73	0	.323	.424	.253
Chris Snyder	76	221	23	39	8	0	7	24	68	33	70	0	.295	.308	.176
Marwin Gonzalez	80	205	21	48	13	0	2	12	67	13	29	3	.280	.327	.234
Scott Moore	72	201	23	52	11	0	9	26	90	16	56	0	.330	.448	.259
Matt Downs	91	178	15	36	4	1	8	16	66	8	38	2	.253	.371	.202
*Tyler Greene	39	126	18	31	6	0	7	11	58	6	39	3	.278	.460	.246

PITCHING	GP	GS	IP	W–L	SV	HLD	H	ER	HR	BB	SO	ERA
Lucas Harrell	32	32	193.2	11-11	0	0	185	81	13	78	140	3.76
Bud Norris	29	29	168.1	7-13	0	0	165	87	23	66	165	4.65
Jordan Lyles	25	25	141.1	5-12	0	0	159	80	20	42	99	5.09
*Wandy Rodriguez	21	21	130.2	7-9	0	0	134	55	13	32	89	3.79
*J.A. Happ	18	18	104.1	7-9	0	0	112	56	17	39	98	4.83
Dallas Keuchel	16	16	85.1	3-8	0	0	93	50	14	39	38	5.27
Fernando Rodriguez	71	0	70.1	2-10	0	13	68	42	10	34	78	5.37
Wilton Lopez	64	0	66.1	6-3	10	9	61	16	4	8	54	2.17
Rhiner Cruz	52	0	55.0	1-1	0	0	65	37	8	29	46	6.05
Wesley Wright	77	0	52.1	2-2	1	20	45	19	4	17	54	3.27
Fernando Abad	37	6	46.0	0-6	0	3	57	26	6	19	38	5.09
*Brandon Lyon	37	0	36.0	0-2	0	5	37	13	3	11	35	3.25
Xavier Cedeno	44	0	31.0	0-1	1	6	30	13	3	14	36	3.77
*Brett Myers	35	0	30.2	0-4	19	0	35	12	4	6	20	3.52
Mickey Storey	26	0	30.1	0-1	0	3	27	13	2	10	34	3.86

*Mid-season trade.

Los Angeles Dodgers

BATTING	G	AB	R	H	2B	3B	HR	RBI	TB	BB	SO	SB	OBP	SLG	BAVG
Andre Ethier	149	556	79	158	36	1	20	89	256	50	124	2	.351	.460	.284
A.J. Ellis	133	423	44	114	20	1	13	52	175	65	107	0	.373	.414	.270
Mark Ellis	110	415	62	107	21	1	7	31	151	40	70	5	.333	.364	.258
Matt Kemp	106	403	74	122	22	2	23	69	217	40	103	9	.367	.538	.303
*James Loney	114	334	32	85	18	0	4	33	115	23	39	0	.302	.344	.254
Juan Rivera	109	312	30	76	14	0	9	47	117	18	35	1	.286	.375	.244
Dee Gordon	87	303	38	69	9	2	1	17	85	20	62	32	.280	.281	.228
Luis Cruz	78	283	26	84	20	0	6	40	122	9	34	2	.322	.431	.297
Tony Gwynn	103	259	29	60	8	4	0	17	76	16	52	13	.276	.293	.232
*Hanley Ramirez	64	251	30	68	11	2	10	44	113	17	60	7	.324	.450	.271
Jerry Hairston Jr.	78	238	19	65	13	1	4	26	92	23	27	1	.342	.387	.273
*Shane Victorino	53	208	26	51	12	2	2	15	73	18	31	15	.316	.351	.245
*Bobby Abreu	92	195	28	48	8	1	3	19	67	35	51	6	.361	.344	.246
Elian Herrera	67	187	26	47	10	1	1	17	62	23	50	4	.340	.332	.251
Adam Kennedy	86	168	22	44	8	1	2	16	60	23	33	1	.345	.357	.262
Juan Uribe	66	162	15	31	9	0	2	17	46	13	37	0	.258	.284	.191
*Adrian Gonzalez	36	145	12	43	10	1	3	22	64	11	29	2	.344	.441	.297

PITCHING	GP	GS	IP	W-L	SV	HLD	H	ER	HR	BB	SO	ERA
Clayton Kershaw	33	33	227.2	14-9	0	0	170	64	16	63	229	2.53
Chris Capuano	33	33	198.1	12-12	0	0	188	82	25	54	162	3.72
Aaron Harang	31	31	179.2	10-10	0	0	167	72	14	85	131	3.61
Chad Billingsley	25	25	149.2	10-9	0	0	148	59	11	45	128	3.55
Ronald Belisario	68	0	71.0	8-1	1	23	47	20	3	29	69	2.54
Jamey Wright	66	0	67.2	5-3	0	6	72	28	2	30	54	3.72
Kenley Jansen	65	0	65.0	5-3	25	8	33	17	6	22	99	2.35
*Joe Blanton	10	10	57.2	2-4	0	0	66	32	7	16	51	4.99
*Nate Eovaldi	10	10	56.1	1-6	0	0	63	26	5	20	34	4.15
Ted Lilly	8	8	48.2	5-1	0	0	36	17	3	19	31	3.14
*Josh Lindblom	48	0	47.2	2-2	0	15	42	16	9	18	43	3.02
Javy Guerra	45	0	45.0	2-3	8	4	44	13	1	23	37	2.60
*Josh Beckett	7	7	43.0	2-3	0	0	43	14	5	14	38	2.93
Shawn Tolleson	40	0	37.2	3-1	0	2	30	18	4	20	39	4.30
Scott Elbert	43	0	32.2	1-1	0	9	27	8	3	13	29	2.20

Miami Marlins

BATTING	G	AB	R	H	2B	3B	HR	RBI	TB	BB	SO	SB	OBP	SLG	BAVG
Jose Reyes	160	642	86	184	37	12	11	57	278	63	56	40	.347	.433	.287
Giancarlo Stanton	123	449	75	130	30	1	37	86	273	46	143	6	.361	.608	.290
*Hanley Ramirez	93	353	49	87	18	2	14	48	151	37	72	14	.322	.428	.246
John Buck	106	343	29	66	15	1	12	41	119	49	103	0	.297	.347	.192
*Omar Infante	85	328	42	94	23	2	8	33	145	12	42	10	.312	.442	.287
Greg Dobbs	120	319	26	91	13	2	5	39	123	14	53	4	.313	.386	.285
Logan Morrison	93	296	30	68	15	1	11	36	118	31	58	1	.308	.399	.230
*Carlos Lee	81	292	29	71	12	0	4	48	95	39	32	3	.328	.325	.243
Justin Ruggiano	91	288	38	90	23	1	13	36	154	29	84	14	.374	.535	.313
Donovan Solano	93	285	29	84	11	3	2	28	107	21	58	7	.342	.375	.295
Emilio Bonifacio	64	244	30	63	3	4	1	11	77	25	52	30	.330	.316	.258
Bryan Petersen	84	241	29	47	9	3	0	17	62	25	58	8	.272	.257	.195
*Gaby Sanchez	55	183	12	37	10	0	3	17	56	12	36	1	.250	.306	.202
Austin Kearns	87	147	21	36	6	0	4	16	54	22	44	2	.366	.367	.245
*Gorkys Hernandez	45	132	16	28	2	3	3	11	45	12	37	5	.288	.341	.212
Donnie Murphy	52	116	13	25	6	2	3	12	44	9	35	1	.281	.379	.216

PITCHING	GP	GS	IP	W-L	SV	HLD	H	ER	HR	BB	SO	ERA
Mark Buehrle	31	31	202.1	13-13	0	0	197	84	26	40	125	3.74
Josh Johnson	31	31	191.1	8-14	0	0	180	81	14	65	165	3.81
Ricky Nolasco	31	31	191.0	12-13	0	0	214	95	18	47	125	4.48
Carlos Zambrano	35	20	132.1	7-10	0	0	123	66	9	75	95	4.49
*Anibal Sanchez	19	19	121.0	5-7	0	0	119	53	12	33	110	3.94
Chad Gaudin	46	0	69.1	4-2	0	1	72	35	6	26	57	4.54
Wade LeBlanc	25	9	68.2	2-5	0	1	71	28	7	19	43	3.67
Heath Bell	73	0	63.2	4-5	19	13	70	36	5	29	59	5.09
Steve Cishek	68	0	63.2	5-2	15	13	54	19	3	29	68	2.69
*Nate Eovaldi	12	12	63.0	3-7	0	0	70	31	5	27	44	4.43
Ryan Webb	65	0	60.1	4-3	0	10	72	27	2	20	44	4.03
Mike Dunn	60	0	44.0	0-3	1	18	49	24	3	29	47	4.91
*Jacob Turner	7	7	42.2	1-4	0	0	33	16	1	9	29	3.38
*Edward Mujica	41	0	39.0	0-3	2	12	36	19	6	9	26	4.38

*Mid-season trade.

Milwaukee Brewers

BATTING	G	AB	R	H	2B	3B	HR	RBI	TB	BB	SO	SB	OBP	SLG	BAVG
Ryan Braun	154	598	108	191	36	3	41	112	356	63	128	30	.391	.595	.319
Rickie Weeks	157	588	85	135	29	4	21	63	235	74	169	16	.328	.400	.230
Aramis Ramirez	149	570	92	171	50	3	27	105	308	44	82	9	.360	.540	.300
Corey Hart	149	562	91	152	35	4	30	83	285	44	151	5	.334	.507	.270
Norichika Aoki	151	520	81	150	37	4	10	50	225	43	55	30	.355	.433	.288
Carlos Gomez	137	415	72	108	19	4	19	51	192	20	98	37	.305	.463	.260
Jonathan Lucroy	96	316	46	101	17	4	12	58	162	22	44	4	.368	.513	.320
Nyjer Morgan	122	289	44	69	5	3	3	16	89	20	63	12	.302	.308	.239
Martin Maldonado	78	233	22	62	9	0	8	30	95	17	56	1	.321	.408	.266
*Cody Ransom	64	168	18	33	7	0	6	26	58	23	79	0	.293	.345	.196
*Cesar Izturis	57	162	9	38	6	2	2	11	54	3	13	1	.248	.333	.235
Travis Ishikawa	94	152	19	39	12	1	4	30	65	13	42	0	.329	.428	.257
*Jean Segura	44	148	19	39	4	3	0	14	49	13	21	7	.321	.331	.264
Taylor Green	58	103	8	19	7	0	3	14	35	10	24	0	.265	.340	.184

PITCHING	GP	GS	IP	W-L	SV	HLD	H	ER	HR	BB	SO	ERA
Yovani Gallardo	33	33	204.0	16-9	0	0	185	83	26	81	204	3.66
*Randy Wolf	25	24	142.1	3-10	0	0	179	90	21	45	96	5.69
Marco Estrada	29	23	138.1	5-7	0	1	129	56	18	29	143	3.64
Mike Fiers	23	22	127.2	9-10	0	0	125	53	12	36	135	3.74
Shaun Marcum	21	21	124.0	7-4	0	0	116	51	16	41	109	3.70
*Zack Greinke	21	21	123.0	9-3	0	0	120	47	7	28	122	3.44
Francisco Rodriguez	78	0	72.0	2-7	3	32	65	35	8	31	72	4.38
John Axford	75	0	69.1	5-8	35	3	61	36	10	39	93	4.67
Kameron Loe	70	0	68.1	6-5	2	7	78	35	9	20	55	4.61
Jose Veras	72	0	67.0	5-4	1	11	61	27	5	40	79	3.63
Manny Parra	62	0	58.2	2-3	0	9	62	33	3	35	61	5.06
Mark Rogers	7	7	39.0	3-1	0	0	36	17	5	14	41	3.92
Tim Dillard	34	0	37.0	0-2	0	1	45	18	3	14	29	4.38
*Livan Hernandez	26	0	36.1	3-0	0	2	44	31	10	8	29	7.68
Jim Henderson	36	0	30.2	1-3	3	15	26	12	1	13	45	3.52

New York Mets

BATTING	G	AB	R	H	2B	3B	HR	RBI	TB	BB	SO	SB	OBP	SLG	BAVG
David Wright	156	581	91	178	41	2	21	93	286	81	112	15	.391	.492	.306
Daniel Murphy	156	571	62	166	40	3	6	65	230	36	82	10	.332	.403	.291
Ike Davis	156	519	66	118	26	0	32	90	240	61	141	0	.308	.462	.227
Ruben Tejada	114	464	53	134	26	0	1	25	163	27	73	4	.333	.351	.289
Lucas Duda	121	401	43	96	15	0	15	57	156	51	120	1	.329	.389	.239
Scott Hairston	134	377	52	99	25	3	20	57	190	19	83	8	.299	.504	.263
Andres Torres	132	374	47	86	17	7	3	35	126	52	90	13	.327	.337	.230
Josh Thole	104	321	24	75	15	0	1	21	93	27	50	0	.294	.290	.234
Kirk Nieuwenhuis	91	282	40	71	12	1	7	28	106	25	98	4	.315	.376	.252
Jason Bay	70	194	21	32	2	0	8	20	58	19	58	5	.237	.299	.165
Jordany Valdespin	94	191	28	46	9	1	8	26	81	10	44	10	.286	.424	.241
Mike Baxter	89	179	26	47	14	2	3	17	74	25	45	5	.365	.413	.263
Justin Turner	94	171	20	46	13	1	2	19	67	9	24	1	.319	.392	.269
Ronny Cedeno	78	166	18	43	11	1	4	22	68	17	35	0	.332	.410	.259
Mike Nickeas	47	109	8	19	3	0	1	13	25	8	27	0	.242	.229	.174

PITCHING	GP	GS	IP	W-L	SV	HLD	H	ER	HR	BB	SO	ERA
R.A. Dickey	34	33	233.2	20-6	0	0	192	71	24	54	230	2.73
Jonathon Niese	30	30	190.1	13-9	0	0	174	72	22	49	155	3.40
Johan Santana	21	21	117.0	6-9	0	0	117	63	17	39	111	4.85
Chris Young	20	20	115.0	4-9	0	0	119	53	16	36	80	4.15
Dillon Gee	17	17	109.2	6-7	0	0	108	50	12	29	97	4.10
Jeremy Hefner	26	13	93.2	4-7	0	0	110	53	18	62	82	5.09
Bobby Parnell	74	0	68.2	5-4	7	18	65	19	4	20	61	2.49
Ramon Ramirez	58	0	63.2	3-4	1	1	58	30	4	35	52	4.24
Matt Harvey	10	10	59.1	3-5	0	0	42	18	5	26	70	2.73
Jon Rauch	73	0	57.2	3-7	4	16	45	23	7	12	42	3.59
Manny Acosta	45	0	47.1	1-3	1	4	48	34	7	25	46	6.46
*Miguel Batista	30	5	46.2	1-3	0	0	53	25	5	31	34	4.82
Frank Francisco	48	0	42.1	1-3	23	1	47	26	5	21	47	5.53
Tim Byrdak	56	0	30.2	2-2	0	17	18	15	2	18	34	4.40
Josh Edgin	34	0	25.2	1-2	0	5	19	13	5	10	30	4.56

*Mid-season trade.

Philadelphia Phillies

BATTING	G	AB	R	H	2B	3B	HR	RBI	TB	BB	SO	SB	OBP	SLG	BAVG
Jimmy Rollins	156	632	102	158	33	5	23	68	270	62	96	30	.316	.427	.250
John Mayberry Jr.	149	441	53	108	24	0	14	46	174	34	111	1	.301	.395	.245
*Hunter Pence	101	398	59	108	15	2	17	59	178	37	85	4	.336	.447	.271
Juan Pierre	130	394	59	121	10	6	1	25	146	23	27	37	.351	.371	.307
*Shane Victorino	101	387	46	101	17	5	9	40	155	35	49	24	.324	.401	.261
Carlos Ruiz	114	372	56	121	32	0	16	68	201	29	50	4	.394	.540	.325
Ty Wigginton	125	315	40	74	11	0	11	43	118	37	81	1	.314	.375	.235
Placido Polanco	90	303	28	78	15	0	2	19	99	18	25	0	.302	.327	.257
Chase Utley	83	301	48	77	15	2	11	45	129	43	43	11	.365	.429	.256
Ryan Howard	71	260	28	57	11	0	14	56	110	25	99	0	.295	.423	.219
Kevin Frandsen	55	195	24	66	10	3	2	14	88	9	18	0	.383	.451	.338
Freddy Galvis	58	190	14	43	15	1	3	24	69	7	29	0	.254	.363	.226
Domonic Brown	56	187	21	44	11	2	5	26	74	21	34	0	.316	.396	.235
Erik Kratz	50	141	14	35	9	0	9	26	71	11	34	0	.306	.504	.248
Michael Martinez	45	115	10	20	3	0	2	7	29	5	21	0	.208	.252	.174
Laynce Nix	70	114	13	28	10	0	3	16	47	12	42	0	.315	.412	.246

PITCHING	GP	GS	IP	W-L	SV	HLD	H	ER	HR	BB	SO	ERA
Cole Hamels	31	31	215.1	17-6	0	0	190	73	24	52	216	3.05
Cliff Lee	30	30	211.0	6-9	0	0	207	74	26	28	207	3.16
Kyle Kendrick	37	25	159.1	11-12	0	2	154	69	20	49	116	3.90
Roy Halladay	25	25	156.1	11-8	0	0	155	78	18	36	132	4.49
*Joe Blanton	21	20	133.1	8-9	0	0	141	68	22	18	115	4.59
Vance Worley	23	23	133.0	6-9	0	0	154	62	12	47	107	4.20
Jonathan Papelbon	70	0	70.0	5-6	38	0	56	19	8	18	92	2.44
Antonio Bastardo	65	0	52.0	2-5	1	26	40	25	7	26	81	4.33
Michael Schwimer	35	0	34.1	2-1	0	1	30	17	3	16	36	4.46
Tyler Cloyd	6	6	33.0	2-2	0	0	33	18	8	7	30	4.91
*Chad Qualls	35	0	31.1	1-1	0	12	39	16	7	9	19	4.60
Jeremy Horst	32	0	31.1	2-0	0	6	21	4	1	14	40	1.15
Raul Valdes	27	1	31.0	3-2	0	2	18	10	3	5	35	2.90
Jacob Diekman	32	0	27.1	1-1	0	4	25	12	1	20	35	3.95

Pittsburgh Pirates

BATTING	G	AB	R	H	2B	3B	HR	RBI	TB	BB	SO	SB	OBP	SLG	BAVG
Andrew McCutchen	157	593	107	194	29	6	31	96	328	70	132	20	.400	.553	.327
Pedro Alvarez	149	525	64	128	25	1	30	85	245	57	180	1	.317	.467	.244
Garrett Jones	145	475	68	130	28	3	27	86	245	33	103	2	.317	.516	.274
Neil Walker	129	472	62	132	27	0	14	69	201	47	104	7	.342	.426	.280
Clint Barmes	144	455	34	104	16	1	8	45	146	20	106	0	.272	.321	.229
Alex Presley	104	346	46	82	14	7	10	25	140	18	72	9	.279	.405	.237
Jose Tabata	103	333	43	81	20	3	3	16	116	29	58	8	.315	.348	.243
Rod Barajas	104	321	29	66	11	0	11	31	110	29	69	0	.283	.343	.206
*Casey McGehee	92	265	27	61	13	1	8	35	100	24	60	1	.297	.377	.230
Josh Harrison	104	249	34	58	9	5	3	16	86	10	37	7	.279	.345	.233
Michael McKenry	88	240	25	56	14	0	12	39	106	29	73	0	.320	.442	.233
Starling Marte	47	167	18	43	3	6	5	17	73	8	50	12	.300	.437	.257
*Travis Snider	50	128	17	32	5	1	1	9	42	14	34	2	.324	.328	.250
*Gaby Sanchez	50	116	18	28	6	0	4	13	46	13	20	0	.323	.397	.241

PITCHING	GP	GS	IP	W-L	SV	HLD	H	ER	HR	BB	SO	ERA
A.J. Burnett	31	31	202.1	16-10	0	0	189	79	18	62	180	3.51
James McDonald	30	29	171.0	12-8	0	0	147	80	21	69	151	4.21
Kevin Correia	32	28	171.0	12-11	0	0	176	80	20	46	89	4.21
Erik Bedard	24	24	125.2	7-14	0	0	129	70	14	56	118	5.01
Jeff Karstens	19	15	90.2	5-4	0	1	89	40	8	15	66	3.97
Jared Hughes	66	0	75.2	2-2	2	12	65	24	7	22	50	2.85
*Wandy Rodriguez	13	12	75.0	5-4	0	0	71	31	8	24	50	3.72
Chris Resop	61	0	73.2	1-4	1	8	81	32	6	24	46	3.91
Joel Hanrahan	63	0	59.2	5-2	36	0	40	18	8	36	67	2.72
*Brad Lincoln	28	5	59.1	4-2	1	5	51	18	8	14	60	2.73
Jason Grilli	64	0	58.2	1-6	2	32	45	19	7	22	90	2.91
Tony Watson	68	0	53.1	5-2	0	16	37	20	5	23	53	3.38
Charlie Morton	9	9	50.1	2-6	0	0	62	26	5	11	25	4.65
Juan Cruz	43	0	35.2	1-1	3	14	39	11	3	19	33	2.78
Jeff Locke	8	6	34.1	1-3	0	0	36	21	6	11	34	5.50

*Mid-season trade.

St. Louis Cardinals

BATTING

	G	AB	R	H	2B	3B	HR	RBI	TB	BB	SO	SB	OBP	SLG	BAVG
Matt Holliday	157	599	95	177	36	2	27	102	298	75	132	4	.379	.497	.295
Carlos Beltran	151	547	83	147	26	1	32	97	271	65	124	13	.346	.495	.269
Yadier Molina	138	505	65	159	28	0	22	76	253	45	55	12	.373	.501	.315
David Freese	144	501	70	147	25	1	20	79	234	57	122	3	.372	.467	.293
Rafael Furcal	121	477	69	126	18	3	5	49	165	44	57	12	.325	.346	.264
Allen Craig	119	469	76	144	35	0	22	92	245	37	89	2	.354	.522	.307
Jon Jay	117	443	70	135	22	4	4	40	177	34	71	19	.373	.400	.305
Daniel Descalso	143	374	41	85	10	7	4	26	121	37	83	6	.303	.324	.227
Matt Carpenter	114	296	44	87	22	5	6	46	137	34	63	1	.365	.463	.294
Skip Schumaker	107	272	37	75	14	4	1	28	100	27	50	1	.339	.368	.276
*Tyler Greene	77	179	16	39	9	2	4	19	64	13	56	9	.272	.358	.218
Shane Robinson	102	166	20	42	8	0	3	16	59	14	32	1	.309	.355	.253
Tony Cruz	51	126	11	32	9	1	1	11	46	3	19	0	.267	.365	.254
Matt Adams	27	86	8	21	6	0	2	13	33	5	24	0	.286	.384	.244
Lance Berkman	32	81	12	21	7	1	2	7	36	14	19	2	.381	.444	.259

PITCHING

	GP	GS	IP	W-L	SV	HLD	H	ER	HR	BB	SO	ERA
Kyle Lohse	33	33	211.0	16-3	0	0	192	67	19	38	143	2.86
Adam Wainwright	32	32	198.2	14-13	0	0	196	87	15	52	184	3.94
Lance Lynn	35	29	176.0	18-7	0	1	168	74	16	64	180	3.78
Jake Westbrook	28	28	174.2	13-11	0	0	191	77	12	52	106	3.97
Jaime Garcia	20	20	121.2	7-7	0	0	136	53	7	30	98	3.92
Joe Kelly	24	16	107.0	5-7	0	0	112	42	10	36	75	3.53
Mitchell Boggs	78	0	73.1	4-1	0	34	56	18	5	21	58	2.21
Jason Motte	67	0	72.0	4-5	42	0	49	22	9	17	86	2.75
Fernando Salas	65	0	58.2	1-4	0	7	56	28	5	27	60	4.30
Marc Rzepczynski	70	0	46.2	1-3	0	18	46	22	7	17	33	4.24
Victor Marte	48	0	40.1	3-2	0	9	51	22	6	14	36	4.91
*Edward Mujica	29	0	26.1	0-0	0	18	20	3	1	3	21	1.03

San Diego Padres

BATTING

	G	AB	R	H	2B	3B	HR	RBI	TB	BB	SO	SB	OBP	SLG	BAVG
Chase Headley	161	604	95	173	31	2	31	115	301	86	157	17	.376	.498	.286
Yonder Alonso	155	549	47	150	39	0	9	62	216	62	101	3	.348	.393	.273
Cameron Maybin	147	507	67	123	20	5	8	45	177	44	110	26	.306	.349	.243
Will Venable	148	417	62	110	26	8	9	45	179	41	94	24	.335	.429	.264
Everth Cabrera	115	398	49	98	19	3	2	24	129	43	110	44	.324	.324	.246
Chris Denorfia	130	348	56	102	19	6	8	36	157	27	52	13	.345	.451	.293
Logan Forsythe	91	315	46	86	13	3	6	26	123	28	57	8	.343	.390	.273
Jesus Guzman	120	287	32	71	18	2	9	48	120	29	71	3	.319	.418	.247
Carlos Quentin	86	284	44	74	21	0	16	46	143	36	41	0	.374	.504	.261
*Alexi Amarista	105	275	35	66	15	5	5	32	106	17	42	8	.282	.385	.240
Nick Hundley	58	204	14	32	7	1	3	22	50	15	56	0	.219	.245	.157
John Baker	63	193	17	46	8	0	0	14	54	20	41	2	.310	.280	.238
Yasmani Grandal	60	192	28	57	7	1	8	36	90	31	39	0	.394	.469	.297
Mark Kotsay	82	143	9	37	8	0	2	14	51	11	14	0	.314	.357	.259
*Orlando Hudson	35	123	11	26	0	5	1	11	39	8	27	3	.260	.317	.211
Andy Parrino	55	116	9	24	5	0	1	6	32	17	35	1	.316	.276	.207

PITCHING

	GP	GS	IP	W-L	SV	HLD	H	ER	HR	BB	SO	ERA
Clayton Richard	33	33	218.2	14-14	0	0	228	97	31	42	107	3.99
Edinson Volquez	32	32	182.2	11-11	0	0	160	84	14	105	174	4.14
Anthony Bass	24	15	97.0	2-8	1	1	89	51	10	39	80	4.73
*Jason Marquis	15	15	93.2	6-7	0	0	94	42	14	28	79	4.04
*Eric Stults	18	14	92.1	8-3	0	0	86	30	7	23	51	2.92
Luke Gregerson	77	0	71.2	2-0	9	24	57	19	7	21	72	2.39
Brad Brach	67	0	66.2	2-4	0	15	50	28	11	33	75	3.78
Dale Thayer	64	0	57.2	2-2	7	22	53	22	4	12	47	3.43
Ross Ohlendorf	13	9	48.2	4-4	0	0	62	42	7	24	39	7.77
Andrew Cashner	33	5	46.1	3-4	0	6	42	22	5	19	52	4.27
Andrew Werner	8	8	40.1	2-3	0	0	45	25	5	14	35	5.58
Huston Street	40	0	39.0	2-1	23	0	17	8	2	11	47	1.85
Kip Wells	7	7	37.1	2-4	0	0	41	19	6	20	19	4.58
Miles Mikolas	25	0	32.1	2-1	0	1	32	13	4	15	23	3.62
Joe Thatcher	55	0	31.2	1-4	1	14	30	12	2	14	39	3.41

*Mid-season trade.

San Francisco Giants

BATTING	G	AB	R	H	2B	3B	HR	RBI	TB	BB	SO	SB	OBP	SLG	BAVG
Angel Pagan	154	605	95	174	38	15	8	56	266	48	97	29	.338	.440	.288
Buster Posey	148	530	78	178	39	1	24	103	291	69	96	1	.408	.549	.336
Melky Cabrera	113	459	84	159	25	10	11	60	237	36	63	13	.390	.516	.346
Brandon Crawford	143	435	44	108	26	3	4	45	152	33	95	1	.304	.349	.248
Brandon Belt	145	411	47	113	27	6	7	56	173	54	106	12	.360	.421	.275
Pablo Sandoval	108	396	59	112	25	2	12	63	177	38	59	1	.342	.447	.283
Gregor Blanco	141	393	56	96	14	5	5	34	135	51	104	26	.333	.344	.244
Ryan Theriot	104	352	45	95	16	1	0	28	113	24	47	13	.316	.321	.270
Joaquin Arias	112	319	30	86	13	5	5	34	124	13	44	5	.304	.389	.270
*Marco Scutaro	61	243	40	88	16	1	3	44	115	13	14	2	.385	.473	.362
*Hunter Pence	59	219	28	48	11	2	7	45	84	19	60	1	.287	.384	.219
Hector Sanchez	74	218	22	61	15	0	3	34	85	5	52	0	.295	.390	.280
*Nate Schierholtz	77	175	15	44	4	5	5	16	73	18	36	3	.321	.417	.251
Emmanuel Burriss	60	136	15	29	1	0	0	7	30	10	25	5	.270	.221	.213
Brett Pill	48	105	10	22	3	0	4	11	37	6	19	1	.265	.352	.210

PITCHING	GP	GS	IP	W-L	SV	HLD	H	ER	HR	BB	SO	ERA
Matt Cain	32	32	219.1	16-5	0	0	177	68	21	51	193	2.79
Madison Bumgarner	32	32	208.1	16-11	0	0	183	78	23	49	191	3.37
Ryan Vogelsong	31	31	189.2	14-9	0	0	171	71	17	62	158	3.37
Tim Lincecum	33	33	186.0	10-15	0	0	183	107	23	90	190	5.18
Barry Zito	32	32	184.1	15-8	0	0	186	85	20	70	114	4.15
Jeremy Affeldt	67	0	63.1	1-2	3	16	57	19	1	23	57	2.70
Santiago Casilla	73	0	63.1	7-6	25	12	55	20	8	22	55	2.84
Sergio Romo	69	0	55.1	4-2	14	23	37	11	5	10	63	1.79
Clay Hensley	60	0	50.2	4-5	3	8	50	26	5	30	42	4.62
George Kontos	44	0	43.2	2-1	0	5	34	12	3	12	44	2.47
Javier Lopez	70	0	36.0	3-0	7	18	37	10	1	14	28	2.50
Brad Penny	22	0	28.0	0-1	0	2	42	19	4	9	10	6.11

Washington Nationals

BATTING	G	AB	R	H	2B	3B	HR	RBI	TB	BB	SO	SB	OBP	SLG	BAVG
Danny Espinosa	160	594	82	147	37	2	17	56	239	46	189	20	.315	.402	.247
Ryan Zimmerman	145	578	93	163	36	1	25	95	276	57	116	5	.346	.478	.282
Adam LaRoche	154	571	76	155	35	1	33	100	291	67	138	1	.343	.510	.271
Bryce Harper	139	533	98	144	26	9	22	59	254	56	120	18	.340	.477	.270
Ian Desmond	130	513	72	150	33	2	25	73	262	30	113	21	.335	.511	.292
Michael Morse	102	406	53	118	17	1	18	62	191	16	97	0	.321	.470	.291
Stephen Lombardozzi	126	384	40	105	16	3	3	27	136	19	46	5	.317	.354	.273
Jayson Werth	81	300	42	90	21	3	5	31	132	42	57	8	.387	.440	.300
Jesus Flores	83	277	22	59	12	1	6	26	91	13	59	1	.248	.329	.213
Roger Bernadina	129	227	25	66	11	0	5	25	92	28	53	15	.372	.405	.291
Rick Ankiel	68	158	15	36	10	2	5	15	65	12	59	1	.282	.411	.228
Tyler Moore	75	156	20	41	9	0	10	29	80	14	46	3	.327	.513	.263
*Kurt Suzuki	43	146	17	39	5	0	5	25	59	11	20	1	.321	.404	.267
*Xavier Nady	40	102	6	16	3	0	3	6	28	7	24	1	.211	.275	.157

PITCHING	GP	GS	IP	W-L	SV	HLD	H	ER	HR	BB	SO	ERA
Gio Gonzalez	32	32	199.1	21-8	0	0	149	64	9	76	207	2.89
Jordan Zimmermann	32	32	195.2	12-8	0	0	186	64	18	43	153	2.94
Edwin Jackson	31	31	189.2	10-11	0	0	173	85	23	58	168	4.03
Ross Detwiler	33	27	164.1	10-8	0	1	149	62	15	52	105	3.40
Stephen Strasburg	28	28	159.1	15-6	0	0	136	56	15	48	197	3.16
Craig Stammen	59	0	88.1	6-1	1	10	70	23	7	36	87	2.34
Tyler Clippard	74	0	72.2	2-6	32	13	55	30	7	29	84	3.72
Tom Gorzelanny	45	1	72.0	4-2	1	9	65	23	7	30	62	2.88
Ryan Mattheus	66	0	66.1	5-3	0	18	57	21	8	19	41	2.85
Sean Burnett	70	0	56.2	1-2	2	31	58	15	4	12	57	2.38
Mike Gonzalez	47	0	35.2	0-0	0	7	31	12	2	16	39	3.03
John Lannan	6	6	32.2	4-1	0	0	33	15	0	14	17	4.13
Chien-Ming Wang	10	5	32.1	2-3	0	0	50	24	5	15	15	6.68
Drew Storen	37	0	30.1	3-1	4	10	22	8	0	8	24	2.37

*Mid-season trade.

Baltimore Orioles

BATTING	G	AB	R	H	2B	3B	HR	RBI	TB	BB	SO	SB	OBP	SLG	BAVG
J.J. Hardy	158	663	85	158	30	2	22	68	258	38	106	0	.282	.389	.238
Adam Jones	162	648	103	186	39	3	32	82	327	34	126	16	.334	.505	.287
Matt Wieters	144	526	67	131	27	1	23	83	229	60	112	3	.329	.435	.249
Chris Davis	139	515	75	139	20	0	33	85	258	37	169	2	.326	.501	.270
Mark Reynolds	135	457	65	101	26	0	23	69	196	73	159	1	.335	.429	.221
Nick Markakis	104	420	59	125	28	3	13	54	198	42	51	1	.363	.471	.298
Robert Andino	127	384	41	81	13	1	7	28	117	37	100	5	.283	.305	.211
Wilson Betemit	102	341	41	89	19	0	12	40	144	31	103	0	.322	.422	.261
*Nate McLouth	55	209	35	56	12	1	7	18	91	22	43	12	.342	.435	.268
Manny Machado	51	191	24	50	8	3	7	26	85	9	38	2	.294	.445	.262
Endy Chavez	64	158	15	32	6	0	2	12	44	6	24	3	.236	.278	.203
Ryan Flaherty	77	153	15	33	2	1	6	19	55	6	43	1	.258	.359	.216
*Jim Thome	28	101	8	26	5	0	3	10	40	14	40	0	.348	.396	.257

PITCHING	GP	GS	IP	W–L	SV	HLD	H	ER	HR	BB	SO	ERA
Wei-Yin Chen	32	32	192.2	12-11	0	0	186	86	29	57	154	4.02
Tommy Hunter	33	20	133.2	7-8	0	0	161	81	32	27	77	5.45
Jason Hammel	20	20	118.0	8-6	0	0	104	45	9	42	113	3.43
Jake Arrieta	24	18	114.2	3-9	0	1	122	79	16	35	109	6.20
Miguel Gonzalez	18	15	105.1	9-4	0	0	92	38	13	35	77	3.25
Brian Matusz	34	16	98.0	6-10	0	5	112	53	15	41	81	4.87
Chris Tillman	15	15	86.0	9-3	0	0	66	28	12	24	66	2.93
Luis Ayala	66	0	75.0	5-5	1	11	81	22	7	14	51	2.64
Jim Johnson	71	0	68.2	2-1	51	0	55	19	3	15	41	2.49
Darren O'Day	69	0	67.0	7-1	0	15	49	17	6	14	69	2.28
Pedro Strop	70	0	66.1	5-2	3	24	52	18	2	37	58	2.44
Zach Britton	12	11	60.1	5-3	0	0	61	34	6	32	53	5.07
Troy Patton	54	0	55.2	1-0	0	9	45	15	5	12	49	2.43
*Joe Saunders	7	7	44.2	3-3	0	0	49	18	4	8	23	3.63
Kevin Gregg	40	0	43.2	3-2	0	1	50	24	6	24	37	4.95
Steve Johnson	12	4	38.1	4-0	0	0	23	9	4	18	46	2.11

Boston Red Sox

BATTING	G	AB	R	H	2B	3B	HR	RBI	TB	BB	SO	SB	OBP	SLG	BAVG
Dustin Pedroia	141	563	81	163	39	3	15	65	253	48	60	20	.347	.449	.290
Mike Aviles	136	512	57	128	28	0	13	60	195	23	77	14	.282	.381	.250
*Adrian Gonzalez	123	484	63	145	37	0	15	86	227	31	81	0	.343	.469	.300
Cody Ross	130	476	70	127	34	1	22	81	229	42	129	2	.326	.481	.267
Jarrod Saltalamacchia	121	405	55	90	17	1	25	59	184	38	139	0	.288	.454	.222
David Ortiz	90	324	65	103	26	0	23	60	198	56	51	0	.415	.611	.318
Jacoby Ellsbury	74	303	43	82	18	0	4	26	112	19	43	14	.313	.370	.271
Will Middlebrooks	75	267	34	77	14	0	15	54	136	13	70	4	.325	.509	.288
Daniel Nava	88	267	38	65	21	0	6	33	104	37	63	3	.352	.390	.243
Pedro Ciriaco	76	259	33	76	15	2	2	19	101	8	47	16	.315	.390	.293
Ryan Sweeney	63	204	22	53	19	2	0	16	76	12	43	0	.303	.373	.260
Scott Podsednik	63	199	19	60	7	0	1	12	70	6	35	8	.322	.352	.302
Ryan Lavarnway	46	153	11	24	8	0	2	12	38	11	41	0	.211	.248	.157
*Kevin Youkilis	42	146	25	34	7	1	4	14	55	14	39	1	.315	.377	.233
*Kelly Shoppach	48	140	16	35	12	2	5	17	66	11	62	1	.327	.471	.250
*Nick Punto	65	125	14	25	6	0	1	10	34	19	33	5	.301	.272	.200
Carl Crawford	31	117	23	33	10	2	3	19	56	3	22	5	.306	.479	.282
Mauro Gomez	37	102	14	28	5	2	2	17	43	8	26	0	.324	.422	.275

PITCHING	GP	GS	IP	W–L	SV	HLD	H	ER	HR	BB	SO	ERA
Jon Lester	33	33	205.1	9-14	0	0	216	110	25	68	166	4.82
Clay Buchholz	29	29	189.1	11-8	0	0	187	96	25	64	129	4.56
Felix Doubront	29	29	161.0	11-10	0	0	162	87	24	71	167	4.86
*Josh Beckett	21	21	127.1	5-11	0	0	131	74	16	38	94	5.23
Aaron Cook	18	18	94.0	4-11	0	0	117	59	15	21	20	5.65
Alfredo Aceves	69	0	84.0	2-10	25	0	80	50	11	31	75	5.36
Franklin Morales	37	9	76.1	3-4	1	8	64	32	11	30	76	3.77
Daniel Bard	17	10	59.1	5-6	0	0	60	41	9	43	38	6.22
Scott Atchison	42	0	51.1	2-1	0	5	42	9	2	9	36	1.58
Vicente Padilla	56	0	50.0	4-1	1	23	59	25	7	15	51	4.50
Daisuke Matsuzaka	11	11	45.2	1-7	0	0	58	42	11	20	41	8.28
Mark Melancon	41	0	45.0	0-2	1	2	45	31	8	12	41	6.20
Junichi Tazawa	37	0	44.0	1-1	1	5	37	7	1	5	45	1.43
Clayton Mortensen	26	0	42.0	1-1	0	1	32	15	7	19	41	3.21
Andrew Miller	53	0	40.1	3-2	0	13	28	15	3	20	51	3.35

*Mid-season trade.

Chicago White Sox

BATTING	G	AB	R	H	2B	3B	HR	RBI	TB	BB	SO	SB	OBP	SLG	BAVG
Alex Rios	157	605	93	184	37	8	25	91	312	26	92	23	.334	.516	.304
Alexei Ramirez	158	593	59	157	24	4	9	73	216	16	77	20	.287	.364	.265
Adam Dunn	151	539	87	110	19	0	41	96	252	105	222	2	.333	.468	.204
Paul Konerko	144	533	66	159	22	0	26	75	259	56	83	0	.371	.486	.298
Gordon Beckham	151	525	62	123	24	0	16	60	195	40	89	5	.296	.371	.234
Alejandro De Aza	131	524	81	147	29	6	9	50	215	47	109	26	.349	.410	.281
Dayan Viciedo	147	505	64	129	18	1	25	78	224	28	120	0	.300	.444	.255
A.J. Pierzynski	135	479	68	133	18	4	27	77	240	28	78	0	.326	.501	.278
*Kevin Youkilis	80	292	47	69	8	1	15	46	124	37	69	0	.346	.425	.236
*Dewayne Wise	45	163	20	42	7	1	5	22	66	9	40	12	.295	.405	.258
*Orlando Hudson	51	137	10	27	3	3	2	17	42	12	24	3	.262	.307	.197
Tyler Flowers	52	136	19	29	6	0	7	13	56	12	56	2	.296	.412	.213
Brent Morel	35	113	14	20	2	0	0	5	22	7	39	4	.225	.195	.177
*Eduardo Escobar	36	87	14	18	4	1	0	3	24	9	23	2	.281	.276	.207

PITCHING	GP	GS	IP	W-L	SV	HLD	H	ER	HR	BB	SO	ERA
Jake Peavy	32	32	219.0	11-12	0	0	191	82	27	49	194	3.37
Chris Sale	30	29	192.0	17-8	0	0	167	65	19	51	192	3.05
Gavin Floyd	29	29	168.0	12-11	0	0	166	80	22	63	144	4.29
Jose Quintana	25	22	136.1	6-6	0	0	142	57	14	42	81	3.76
Philip Humber	26	16	102.0	5-5	0	0	113	73	23	44	85	6.44
Nate Jones	65	0	71.2	8-0	0	7	67	19	4	32	65	2.39
Hector Santiago	42	4	70.1	4-1	4	4	54	26	10	40	79	3.33
Matt Thornton	74	0	65.0	4-10	3	26	63	25	4	17	53	3.46
*Francisco Liriano	12	11	56.2	3-2	0	0	54	34	7	32	58	5.40
Addison Reed	62	0	55.0	3-2	29	4	57	29	6	18	54	4.75
John Danks	9	9	53.2	3-4	0	0	57	34	7	23	30	5.70
Dylan Axelrod	14	7	51.0	2-2	0	0	56	31	8	21	40	5.47
Jesse Crain	51	0	48.0	2-3	0	10	29	13	5	23	60	2.44
*Brett Myers	35	0	34.2	3-4	0	8	30	12	4	9	21	3.12
*Zach Stewart	18	1	30.0	1-2	0	0	41	20	10	4	16	6.00

Cleveland Indians

BATTING	G	AB	R	H	2B	3B	HR	RBI	TB	BB	SO	SB	OBP	SLG	BAVG
Shin-Soo Choo	155	598	88	169	43	2	16	67	264	73	150	21	.373	.441	.283
Jason Kipnis	152	591	86	152	22	4	14	76	224	67	109	31	.335	.379	.257
Asdrubal Cabrera	143	555	70	150	35	1	16	68	235	52	99	9	.338	.423	.270
Michael Brantley	149	552	63	159	37	4	6	60	222	53	56	12	.348	.402	.288
Carlos Santana	143	507	72	128	27	2	18	76	213	91	101	3	.365	.420	.252
Casey Kotchman	142	463	46	106	12	0	12	55	154	26	49	3	.280	.333	.229
Jack Hannahan	105	287	23	70	16	0	4	29	98	27	63	0	.312	.341	.244
Shelley Duncan	81	232	29	47	10	0	11	31	90	28	59	1	.288	.388	.203
Travis Hafner	66	219	23	50	6	2	12	34	96	32	47	0	.346	.438	.228
*Jose Lopez	66	213	16	53	13	0	4	28	78	8	35	0	.272	.366	.249
Johnny Damon	64	207	25	46	6	2	4	19	68	17	27	4	.281	.329	.222
Lou Marson	70	195	27	44	8	2	0	13	56	36	44	4	.348	.287	.226
Ezequiel Carrera	48	147	20	40	6	3	2	11	58	8	35	8	.312	.395	.272
Lonnie Chisenhall	43	142	16	38	6	1	5	16	61	8	27	2	.311	.430	.268
Jason Donald	43	124	18	25	2	1	2	11	35	5	40	4	.246	.282	.202
*Brent Lillibridge	43	111	15	24	5	0	3	8	38	7	40	6	.276	.342	.216

PITCHING	GP	GS	IP	W-L	SV	HLD	H	ER	HR	BB	SO	ERA
Justin Masterson	34	34	206.1	11-15	0	0	212	113	18	88	159	4.93
Ubaldo Jimenez	31	31	176.2	9-17	0	0	190	106	25	95	143	5.40
Zach McAllister	22	22	125.1	6-8	0	0	133	59	19	38	110	4.24
*Derek Lowe	21	21	119.0	8-10	0	0	156	73	8	45	41	5.52
Josh Tomlin	21	16	103.1	5-8	0	0	126	73	18	25	56	6.36
Jeanmar Gomez	20	17	90.2	5-8	0	0	95	60	15	34	47	5.96
Vinnie Pestano	70	0	70.0	3-3	2	36	53	20	7	24	76	2.57
Joe Smith	72	0	67.0	7-4	0	21	53	22	4	25	53	2.96
Corey Kluber	12	12	63.0	2-5	0	0	76	36	9	18	54	5.14
Chris Perez	61	0	57.2	0-4	39	0	49	23	6	16	59	3.59
Tony Sipp	63	0	55.0	1-2	1	12	47	27	9	23	51	4.42
*Esmil Rogers	44	0	53.0	3-1	0	6	47	18	5	12	54	3.06
*Jeremy Accardo	26	0	35.1	0-0	0	0	38	18	3	16	28	4.58
Chris Seddon	17	2	34.1	1-1	0	1	35	14	2	13	18	3.67

*Mid-season trade.

Detroit Tigers

BATTING	G	AB	R	H	2B	3B	HR	RBI	TB	BB	SO	SB	OBP	SLG	BAVG
Miguel Cabrera 161	622	109	205	40	0	44	139	377	66	98	4	.393	.606	.330
Prince Fielder 162	581	83	182	33	1	30	108	307	85	84	1	.412	.528	.313
Delmon Young 151	574	54	153	27	1	18	74	236	20	112	0	.296	.411	.267
Austin Jackson 137	543	103	163	29	10	16	66	260	67	134	12	.377	.479	.300
Jhonny Peralta 150	531	58	127	32	3	13	63	204	49	105	1	.305	.384	.239
Brennan Boesch 132	470	52	113	22	2	12	54	175	26	104	6	.286	.372	.240
Alex Avila 116	367	42	89	21	2	9	48	141	61	104	2	.352	.384	.243
Andy Dirks................88	314	56	101	18	5	8	35	153	23	53	1	.370	.487	.322
Quintin Berry 94	291	44	75	10	6	2	29	103	25	80	21	.330	.354	.258
Ramon Santiago.........93	228	19	47	7	1	2	17	62	20	39	1	.283	.272	.206
*Omar Infante............64	226	27	58	7	5	4	20	87	9	23	7	.283	.385	.257
Ryan Raburn 66	205	14	35	14	0	1	12	52	13	53	1	.226	.254	.171
Gerald Laird 63	174	24	49	8	1	2	11	65	14	21	0	.337	.374	.282
Don Kelly.................75	113	14	21	2	1	1	7	28	14	22	2	.276	.248	.186

PITCHING	GP	GS	IP	W-L	SV	HLD	H	ER	HR	BB	SO	EF
Justin Verlander 33	33	238.1	17-8	0	0	192	70	19	60	239	2.6
Max Scherzer 32	32	187.2	16-7	0	0	179	78	23	60	231	3.7
Rick Porcello 31	31	176.1	10-12	0	0	226	90	16	44	107	4.5
Doug Fister 26	26	161.2	10-10	0	0	156	62	15	37	137	3.4
Drew Smyly.................23	18	99.1	4-3	0	1	93	44	12	33	94	3.9
*Anibal Sanchez.............12	12	74.2	4-6	0	0	81	31	8	15	57	3.7
Joaquin Benoit 73	0	71.0	5-3	2	30	59	29	14	22	84	3.6
Jose Valverde 71	0	69.0	3-4	35	0	59	29	3	27	48	3.7
Octavio Dotel................57	0	58.0	5-3	1	11	50	23	3	12	62	3.5
Brayan Villarreal.............50	0	54.2	3-5	0	9	38	16	3	28	66	2.6
Phil Coke 66	0	54.0	2-3	1	20	71	24	5	18	51	4.0
Duane Below 27	1	46.1	2-1	0	0	49	20	6	8	29	3.8
Luis Marte....................13	0	22.1	1-0	0	0	19	7	4	9	19	2.8

Kansas City Royals

BATTING	G	AB	R	H	2B	3B	HR	RBI	TB	BB	SO	SB	OBP	SLG	BAVG
Alex Gordon 161	642	93	189	51	5	14	72	292	73	140	10	.368	.455	.294
Billy Butler 161	614	72	192	32	1	29	107	313	54	111	2	.373	.510	.313
Alcides Escobar.........155	605	68	177	30	7	5	52	236	27	100	35	.331	.390	.293
Mike Moustakas 149	563	69	136	34	1	20	73	232	39	124	5	.296	.412	.242
Jeff Francoeur 148	561	58	132	26	3	16	49	212	34	119	4	.287	.378	.235
Eric Hosmer 152	535	65	124	22	2	14	60	192	56	95	16	.304	.359	.232
Jarrod Dyson............102	292	52	76	8	5	0	9	94	30	56	30	.328	.322	.260
Salvador Perez...........76	289	38	87	16	0	11	39	136	12	27	0	.328	.471	.301
Lorenzo Cain............61	222	27	59	9	2	7	31	93	15	56	10	.316	.419	.266
Yuniesky Betancourt .57	215	21	49	14	1	7	36	86	9	25	0	.256	.400	.228
Brayan Pena...............68	212	16	50	10	1	2	25	68	9	24	0	.262	.321	.236
Chris Getz 64	189	22	52	10	3	0	17	68	11	17	9	.312	.360	.275
Johnny Giavotella.......53	181	21	43	7	1	1	15	55	8	35	3	.270	.304	.238
Humberto Quintero 43	138	7	32	12	0	1	19	47	4	28	0	.257	.341	.232
Irving Falu 24	85	14	29	6	1	0	7	37	4	9	0	.371	.435	.341

PITCHING	GP	GS	IP	W-L	SV	HLD	H	ER	HR	BB	SO	EF
Bruce Chen 34	34	191.2	11-14	0	0	215	108	33	47	140	5.0
Luke Hochevar 32	32	185.1	8-16	0	0	202	118	27	61	144	5.7
Luis Mendoza................30	25	166.0	8-10	0	0	176	78	15	59	104	4.2
*Jeremy Guthrie 14	14	91.0	5-3	0	0	84	32	9	19	56	3.1
Will Smith....................16	16	89.2	6-9	0	0	111	53	12	33	59	5.3
Kelvin Herrera 76	0	84.1	4-3	3	19	79	22	4	21	77	2.3
Tim Collins...................72	0	69.2	5-4	0	11	55	26	8	34	93	3.3
Greg Holland.................67	0	67.0	7-4	16	9	58	22	2	34	91	2.9
Aaron Crow 73	0	64.2	3-1	2	19	54	25	4	22	65	3.4
Everett Teaford.............18	5	61.1	1-4	0	0	68	34	11	21	35	4.9
*Jonathan Sanchez 12	12	53.1	1-6	0	0	65	46	8	44	36	7.7
Louis Coleman 42	0	51.0	0-0	0	2	41	21	10	26	65	3.7
Vin Mazzaro.................18	6	44.0	4-3	0	0	55	28	3	19	26	5.7
*Jose Mijares...............51	0	38.2	2-2	0	11	36	11	3	13	37	2.5
Felipe Paulino...............7	7	37.2	3-1	0	0	31	7	3	15	39	1.6
*Jonathan Broxton..........35	0	35.2	1-2	23	0	36	9	1	14	25	2.2
Nate Adcock 12	2	34.2	0-3	0	1	37	9	4	13	22	2.3

*Mid-season trade.

Los Angeles Angels

BATTING

	G	AB	R	H	2B	3B	HR	RBI	TB	BB	SO	SB	OBP	SLG	BAVG
Albert Pujols	154	607	85	173	50	0	30	105	313	52	76	8	.343	.516	.285
Mike Trout	139	559	129	182	27	8	30	83	315	67	139	49	.399	.564	.326
Howard Kendrick	147	550	57	158	32	3	8	67	220	29	115	14	.325	.400	.287
Mark Trumbo	144	544	66	146	19	3	32	95	267	36	153	4	.317	.491	.268
Torii Hunter	140	534	81	167	24	1	16	92	241	38	133	9	.365	.451	.313
Erick Aybar	141	517	67	150	31	5	8	45	215	22	61	20	.324	.416	.290
Kendrys Morales	134	484	61	132	26	1	22	73	226	31	116	0	.320	.467	.273
Alberto Callaspo	138	457	55	115	20	0	10	53	165	56	59	4	.331	.361	.252
Maicer Izturis	100	289	35	74	11	0	2	20	91	25	38	17	.320	.315	.256
Vernon Wells	77	243	36	56	9	0	11	29	98	16	35	3	.279	.403	.230
Chris Iannetta	79	221	27	53	6	1	9	26	88	29	60	1	.332	.398	.240
Bobby Wilson	75	171	19	36	5	0	3	13	50	15	33	0	.277	.292	.211
Peter Bourjos	101	168	27	37	7	0	3	19	53	15	44	3	.291	.315	.220
John Hester	39	85	14	18	1	0	3	4	28	8	25	0	.287	.329	.212

PITCHING

	GP	GS	IP	W-L	SV	HLD	H	ER	HR	BB	SO	ERA
C.J. Wilson	34	34	202.1	13-10	0	0	181	86	19	91	173	3.83
Jered Weaver	30	30	188.2	20-5	0	0	147	59	20	45	142	2.81
Ervin Santana	30	30	178.0	9-13	0	0	165	102	39	61	133	5.16
Dan Haren	30	30	176.2	12-13	0	0	190	85	28	38	142	4.33
Jerome Williams	32	15	137.2	6-8	1	0	139	70	17	35	98	4.58
*Zack Greinke	13	13	89.1	6-2	0	0	80	35	11	26	78	3.53
Garrett Richards	30	9	71.0	4-3	1	5	77	37	7	34	47	4.69
*Ernesto Frieri	56	0	54.1	4-2	23	6	26	14	7	26	80	2.32
Scott Downs	57	0	45.2	1-1	9	24	43	16	3	17	32	3.15
Jason Isringhausen	50	0	45.2	3-2	0	4	44	21	7	19	31	4.14
Kevin Jepsen	49	0	44.2	3-2	2	18	39	15	3	12	38	3.02
LaTroy Hawkins	48	0	42.0	2-3	1	6	45	17	5	13	23	3.64
*Hisanori Takahashi	42	0	42.0	0-3	0	5	39	23	6	10	41	4.93
David Carpenter	28	0	39.2	1-2	0	2	42	21	6	17	28	4.76
Jordan Walden	45	0	39.0	3-2	1	8	35	15	3	18	48	3.46

Minnesota Twins

BATTING

	G	AB	R	H	2B	3B	HR	RBI	TB	BB	SO	SB	OBP	SLG	BAVG
Joe Mauer	147	545	81	174	31	4	10	85	243	90	88	8	.416	.446	.319
Josh Willingham	145	519	85	135	30	1	35	110	272	76	141	3	.366	.524	.260
Denard Span	128	516	71	146	38	4	4	41	204	47	62	17	.342	.395	.283
Ben Revere	124	511	70	150	13	6	0	32	175	29	54	40	.333	.342	.294
Justin Morneau	134	505	63	135	26	2	19	77	222	49	102	1	.333	.440	.267
Ryan Doumit	134	484	56	133	34	1	18	75	223	29	98	0	.320	.461	.275
Jamey Carroll	138	470	65	126	18	1	1	40	149	52	65	9	.343	.317	.268
Trevor Plouffe	119	422	56	99	19	1	24	55	192	37	92	1	.301	.455	.235
Brian Dozier	84	316	33	74	11	1	6	33	105	16	58	9	.271	.332	.234
Alexi Casilla	106	299	33	72	17	2	1	30	96	16	52	21	.282	.321	.241
Chris Parmelee	64	192	18	44	10	2	5	20	73	13	52	0	.290	.380	.229
Darin Mastroianni	77	163	22	41	3	2	3	17	57	18	45	21	.328	.350	.252
Pedro Florimon	43	137	16	30	5	2	1	10	42	10	30	3	.272	.307	.219
*Danny Valencia	34	126	13	25	6	1	2	17	39	3	32	0	.212	.310	.198
Drew Butera	42	111	7	22	6	0	1	5	31	9	26	0	.270	.279	.198

PITCHING

	GP	GS	IP	W-L	SV	HLD	H	ER	HR	BB	SO	ERA
Scott Diamond	27	27	173.0	12-9	0	0	184	68	17	31	90	3.54
Brian Duensing	55	11	109.0	4-12	0	7	126	62	10	27	69	5.12
*Francisco Liriano	22	17	100.0	3-10	0	1	89	59	12	55	109	5.31
Nick Blackburn	19	19	98.2	4-9	0	0	143	81	23	26	42	7.39
Anthony Swarzak	44	5	96.2	3-6	0	1	106	54	15	31	62	5.03
Cole De Vries	17	16	87.2	5-5	0	0	88	40	16	18	58	4.11
Liam Hendriks	16	16	85.1	1-8	0	0	106	53	17	26	50	5.59
Samuel Deduno	15	15	79.0	6-5	0	0	69	39	10	53	57	4.44
Alex Burnett	67	0	71.2	4-4	0	10	71	28	4	26	36	3.52
Glen Perkins	70	0	70.1	3-1	16	11	57	20	8	16	78	2.56
Carl Pavano	11	11	63.0	2-5	0	0	80	42	9	8	33	6.00
Jared Burton	64	0	62.0	3-2	5	18	41	15	5	16	55	2.18
P.J. Walters	12	12	61.2	2-5	0	0	71	39	12	22	42	5.69
Jeff Gray	49	0	52.0	6-1	0	1	58	33	9	22	26	5.71

*Mid-season trade.

New York Yankees

BATTING	G	AB	R	H	2B	3B	HR	RBI	TB	BB	SO	SB	OBP	SLG	BAVG
Derek Jeter	159	683	99	216	32	0	15	58	293	45	90	9	.362	.429	.316
Robinson Cano	161	627	105	196	48	1	33	94	345	61	96	3	.379	.550	.313
Curtis Granderson	160	596	102	138	18	4	43	106	293	75	195	10	.319	.492	.232
Nick Swisher	148	537	75	146	36	0	24	93	254	77	141	2	.364	.473	.272
Alex Rodriguez	122	463	74	126	17	1	18	57	199	51	116	13	.353	.430	.272
Mark Teixeira	123	451	66	113	27	1	24	84	214	54	83	2	.332	.475	.251
Russell Martin	133	422	50	89	18	0	21	53	170	53	95	6	.311	.403	.211
Raul Ibanez	130	384	50	92	19	3	19	62	174	35	67	3	.308	.453	.240
Eric Chavez	113	278	36	78	12	0	16	37	138	30	59	0	.348	.496	.281
Andruw Jones	94	233	27	46	7	0	14	34	95	28	71	0	.294	.408	.197
*Ichiro Suzuki	67	227	28	73	13	1	5	27	103	5	21	14	.340	.454	.322
Jayson Nix	74	177	24	43	13	0	4	18	68	14	53	6	.306	.384	.243
Chris Stewart	55	141	15	34	8	0	1	13	45	10	21	2	.292	.319	.241
Eduardo Nunez	38	89	14	26	4	1	1	11	35	6	12	11	.330	.393	.292

PITCHING	GP	GS	IP	W–L	SV	HLD	H	ER	HR	BB	SO	ERA
Hiroki Kuroda	33	33	219.2	16-11	0	0	205	81	25	51	167	3.32
CC Sabathia	28	28	200.0	15-6	0	0	184	75	22	44	197	3.38
Phil Hughes	32	32	191.1	16-13	0	0	196	90	35	46	165	4.23
Ivan Nova	28	28	170.1	12-8	0	0	194	95	28	56	153	5.02
Freddy Garcia	30	17	107.1	7-6	0	0	112	62	18	35	89	5.20
David Phelps	33	11	99.2	4-4	0	2	81	37	14	38	96	3.34
Andy Pettitte	12	12	75.1	5-4	0	0	65	24	8	21	69	2.87
Rafael Soriano	69	0	67.2	2-1	42	4	55	17	6	24	69	2.26
David Robertson	65	0	60.2	2-7	2	30	52	18	5	19	81	2.67
Boone Logan	80	0	55.1	7-2	1	23	48	23	6	28	68	3.74
Cody Eppley	59	0	46.0	1-2	0	9	46	17	3	17	32	3.33
Cory Wade	39	0	39.0	1-1	0	8	46	28	8	8	38	6.46
Clay Rapada	70	0	38.1	3-0	0	6	29	12	2	17	38	2.82
*Derek Lowe	17	0	23.2	1-1	1	1	24	8	2	6	14	3.04
Joba Chamberlain	22	0	20.2	1-0	0	4	26	10	3	6	22	4.35

Oakland Athletics

BATTING	G	AB	R	H	2B	3B	HR	RBI	TB	BB	SO	SB	OBP	SLG	BAVG
Josh Reddick	156	611	85	148	29	5	32	85	283	55	151	11	.305	.463	.242
Yoenis Cespedes	129	487	70	142	25	5	23	82	246	43	102	16	.356	.505	.292
Coco Crisp	120	455	68	118	25	7	11	46	190	45	64	39	.325	.418	.259
Jemile Weeks	118	444	54	98	15	8	2	20	135	50	70	16	.305	.304	.221
Cliff Pennington	125	418	50	90	18	2	6	28	130	35	90	15	.278	.311	.215
Seth Smith	125	383	55	92	23	2	14	52	161	50	98	2	.333	.420	.240
*Brandon Inge	74	283	31	64	13	0	11	52	110	24	85	0	.286	.389	.226
Jonny Gomes	99	279	46	73	10	0	18	47	137	44	104	3	.377	.491	.262
Josh Donaldson	75	274	34	66	16	0	9	33	109	14	61	4	.289	.398	.241
Brandon Moss	84	265	48	77	18	0	21	52	158	26	90	1	.358	.596	.291
*Kurt Suzuki	75	262	19	57	15	0	1	18	75	9	53	1	.250	.286	.218
Chris Carter	67	218	38	52	12	0	16	39	112	39	83	0	.350	.514	.239
Derek Norris	60	209	19	42	8	1	7	34	73	21	66	5	.276	.349	.201
*Stephen Drew	39	152	21	38	5	0	5	16	58	18	41	1	.326	.382	.250
Kila Ka'aihue	39	128	13	30	9	0	4	14	51	10	28	1	.295	.398	.234
Daric Barton	46	113	8	23	7	0	1	6	33	22	32	1	.338	.292	.204

PITCHING	GP	GS	IP	W–L	SV	HLD	H	ER	HR	BB	SO	ERA
Tommy Milone	31	31	190.0	13-10	0	0	207	79	24	36	137	3.74
Jarrod Parker	29	29	181.1	13-8	0	0	166	70	11	63	140	3.47
Bartolo Colon	24	24	152.1	10-9	0	0	161	58	17	23	91	3.43
Brandon McCarthy	18	18	111.0	8-6	0	0	115	40	10	24	73	3.24
*Travis Blackley	24	15	102.2	6-4	0	0	91	44	10	30	69	3.86
A.J. Griffin	15	15	82.1	7-1	0	0	74	28	10	19	64	3.06
Grant Balfour	75	0	74.2	3-2	24	15	41	21	4	28	72	2.53
Ryan Cook	71	0	73.1	6-2	14	21	42	17	4	27	80	2.09
Tyson Ross	18	13	73.1	2-11	0	0	96	53	7	37	46	6.50
Jerry Blevins	63	0	65.1	5-1	1	14	45	18	7	25	54	2.48
Jordan Norberto	39	0	52.0	4-1	1	4	37	16	5	22	46	2.77
Jim Miller	33	0	48.2	2-1	0	0	39	14	6	27	44	2.59
Sean Doolittle	44	0	47.1	2-1	1	18	40	16	3	11	60	3.04
Dan Straily	7	7	39.1	2-1	0	0	36	17	11	16	32	3.89
Evan Scribner	30	0	35.1	2-0	1	0	30	10	2	12	30	2.55
Brett Anderson	6	6	35.0	4-2	0	0	29	10	1	7	25	2.57

*Mid-season trade.

Seattle Mariners

BATTING	G	AB	R	H	2B	3B	HR	RBI	TB	BB	SO	SB	OBP	SLG	BAVG
Dustin Ackley	153	607	84	137	22	2	12	50	199	59	124	13	.294	.328	.226
Kyle Seager	155	594	62	154	35	1	20	86	251	46	110	13	.316	.423	.259
Jesus Montero	135	515	46	134	20	0	15	62	199	29	99	0	.298	.386	.260
Michael Saunders	139	507	71	125	31	3	19	57	219	43	132	21	.306	.432	.247
Justin Smoak	132	483	49	105	14	0	19	51	176	49	111	1	.290	.364	.217
Brendan Ryan	141	407	42	79	19	3	3	31	113	44	98	11	.277	.278	.194
*Ichiro Suzuki	95	402	49	105	15	5	4	28	142	17	40	15	.288	.353	.261
Miguel Olivo	87	315	27	70	14	0	12	29	120	7	85	3	.239	.381	.222
John Jaso	108	294	41	81	19	2	10	50	134	56	51	5	.394	.456	.276
Casper Wells	93	285	42	65	12	3	10	36	113	26	80	3	.302	.396	.228
Chone Figgins	66	166	18	30	5	2	2	11	45	19	48	4	.262	.271	.181
Mike Carp	59	164	17	35	6	0	5	20	56	21	46	1	.312	.341	.213
Franklin Gutierrez	40	150	18	39	10	1	4	17	63	9	31	3	.309	.420	.260
Trayvon Robinson	46	145	16	32	4	1	3	12	47	14	43	6	.294	.324	.221
*Eric Thames	40	123	10	27	5	2	6	14	54	6	47	1	.256	.439	.220
Alex Liddi	38	116	8	26	4	1	3	10	41	9	49	2	.278	.353	.224
Munenori Kawasaki	61	104	13	20	1	0	0	7	21	8	18	2	.257	.202	.192

PITCHING	GP	GS	IP	W–L	SV	HLD	H	ER	HR	BB	SO	ERA
Felix Hernandez	33	33	232.0	13-9	0	0	209	79	14	56	223	3.06
Jason Vargas	33	33	217.1	14-11	0	0	201	93	35	55	141	3.85
Kevin Millwood	28	28	161.0	6-12	0	0	168	76	13	56	107	4.25
Blake Beavan	26	26	152.1	11-11	0	0	168	75	23	24	67	4.43
Hisashi Iwakuma	30	16	125.1	9-5	2	0	117	44	17	43	101	3.16
Hector Noesi	22	18	106.2	2-12	0	0	107	69	21	39	68	5.82
Tom Wilhelmsen	73	0	79.1	4-3	29	7	59	22	5	29	87	2.50
Erasmo Ramirez	16	8	59.0	1-3	0	0	47	22	6	12	48	3.36
Charlie Furbush	48	0	46.1	5-2	0	6	28	14	3	16	53	2.72
*Brandon League	46	0	44.2	0-5	9	6	48	18	1	19	27	3.63
Shawn Kelley	47	0	44.1	2-4	0	6	43	16	5	15	45	3.25
Lucas Luetge	63	0	40.2	2-2	2	12	37	18	3	24	38	3.98
*Steve Delabar	34	0	36.2	2-1	0	3	23	17	9	11	46	4.17
Josh Kinney	35	0	32.0	0-3	1	9	24	14	3	15	36	3.94

Tampa Bay Rays

BATTING	G	AB	R	H	2B	3B	HR	RBI	TB	BB	SO	SB	OBP	SLG	BAVG
B.J. Upton	146	573	79	141	29	3	28	78	260	45	169	31	.298	.454	.246
Ben Zobrist	157	560	88	151	39	7	20	74	264	97	103	14	.377	.471	.270
Desmond Jennings	132	505	85	124	19	7	13	47	196	46	120	31	.314	.388	.246
Carlos Pena	160	497	72	98	17	2	19	61	176	87	182	2	.330	.354	.197
Matt Joyce	124	399	55	96	18	3	17	59	171	55	102	4	.341	.429	.241
Jeff Keppinger	115	385	46	125	15	1	9	40	169	24	31	1	.367	.439	.325
Luke Scott	96	314	35	72	22	1	14	55	138	21	80	5	.285	.439	.229
Sean Rodriguez	112	301	36	64	14	1	6	32	98	27	75	5	.281	.326	.213
Elliot Johnson	123	297	32	72	10	2	6	33	104	24	84	18	.304	.350	.242
Evan Longoria	74	273	39	79	14	0	17	55	144	33	61	2	.369	.527	.289
Jose Molina	102	251	27	56	9	0	8	32	89	20	60	3	.286	.355	.223
*Ryan Roberts	60	187	23	40	10	0	6	18	68	18	47	4	.284	.364	.214
Jose Lobaton	69	167	16	37	10	0	2	20	53	24	46	0	.323	.317	.222
Will Rhymes	47	123	11	28	2	1	1	8	35	10	17	1	.299	.285	.228
Chris Gimenez	42	100	10	26	4	0	1	9	33	8	24	0	.315	.330	.260

PITCHING	GP	GS	IP	W–L	SV	HLD	H	ER	HR	BB	SO	ERA
James Shields	33	33	227.2	15-10	0	0	208	89	25	58	223	3.52
David Price	31	31	211.0	20-5	0	0	173	60	16	59	205	2.56
Matt Moore	31	31	177.1	11-11	0	0	158	75	18	81	175	3.81
Jeremy Hellickson	31	31	177.0	10-11	0	0	163	61	25	59	124	3.10
Alex Cobb	23	23	136.1	11-9	0	0	130	61	11	40	106	4.03
Fernando Rodney	76	0	74.2	2-2	48	0	43	5	2	15	76	0.60
Wade Davis	54	0	70.1	3-0	0	7	48	19	5	29	87	2.43
Joel Peralta	76	0	67.0	2-6	2	37	49	27	9	17	84	3.63
Burke Badenhop	66	0	62.1	3-2	0	5	63	21	6	12	42	3.03
Jake McGee	69	0	55.1	5-2	0	20	33	12	3	11	73	1.95
J.P. Howell	55	0	50.1	1-0	0	3	39	17	7	22	42	3.04
Jeff Niemann	8	8	38.0	2-3	0	0	30	13	2	12	34	3.08
Cesar Ramos	17	1	30.0	1-0	0	0	19	7	2	10	29	2.10

*Mid-season trade.

Texas Rangers

BATTING	G	AB	R	H	2B	3B	HR	RBI	TB	BB	SO	SB	OBP	SLG	BAVG
Ian Kinsler	157	655	105	168	42	5	19	72	277	60	90	21	.326	.423	.256
Elvis Andrus	158	629	85	180	31	9	3	62	238	57	96	21	.349	.378	.286
Michael Young	156	611	79	169	27	3	8	67	226	33	70	2	.312	.370	.277
Adrian Beltre	156	604	95	194	33	2	36	102	339	36	82	1	.359	.561	.321
Nelson Cruz	159	585	86	152	45	0	24	90	269	48	140	8	.319	.460	.260
Josh Hamilton	148	562	103	160	31	2	43	128	324	60	162	7	.354	.577	.285
David Murphy	147	457	65	139	29	3	15	61	219	54	74	10	.380	.479	.304
Mike Napoli	108	352	53	80	9	2	24	56	165	56	125	1	.343	.469	.227
Mitch Moreland	114	327	41	90	18	0	15	50	153	23	71	1	.321	.468	.275
Craig Gentry	122	240	31	73	12	3	1	26	94	14	41	13	.367	.392	.304
*Yorvit Torrealba	49	161	16	38	8	0	3	12	55	14	31	1	.302	.342	.236
*Geovany Soto	47	148	19	29	6	0	5	25	50	11	41	1	.253	.338	.196
Brandon Snyder	40	65	11	18	2	0	3	9	29	3	26	0	.309	.446	.277

PITCHING	GP	GS	IP	W–L	SV	HLD	H	ER	HR	BB	SO	ERA
Matt Harrison	32	32	213.1	18-11	0	0	210	78	22	59	133	3.29
Yu Darvish	29	29	191.1	16-9	0	0	156	83	14	89	221	3.90
Derek Holland	29	27	175.1	12-7	0	0	162	91	32	52	145	4.67
Scott Feldman	29	21	123.2	6-11	0	0	139	70	14	32	96	5.09
Colby Lewis	16	16	105.0	6-6	0	0	99	40	16	14	93	3.43
*Ryan Dempster	12	12	69.0	7-3	0	0	74	39	10	25	70	5.09
Alexi Ogando	58	1	66.0	2-0	3	12	49	24	9	17	66	3.27
Robbie Ross	58	0	65.0	6-0	0	9	55	16	3	23	47	2.22
Joe Nathan	66	0	64.1	3-5	37	0	55	20	7	13	78	2.80
Roy Oswalt	17	9	59.0	4-3	0	0	79	38	11	11	59	5.80
Mike Adams	61	0	52.1	5-3	1	27	56	19	4	17	45	3.27
Neftali Feliz	8	7	42.2	3-1	0	0	28	15	5	23	37	3.16
Mark Lowe	36	0	39.1	0-2	0	1	35	15	5	13	28	3.43
Martin Perez	12	6	38.0	1-4	0	0	47	23	3	15	25	5.45
Koji Uehara	37	0	36.0	0-0	1	7	20	7	4	3	43	1.75
Michael Kirkman	28	0	35.1	1-2	0	2	24	15	5	17	38	3.82
Tanner Scheppers	39	0	32.1	1-1	1	4	47	16	6	9	30	4.45

Toronto Blue Jays

BATTING	G	AB	R	H	2B	3B	HR	RBI	TB	BB	SO	SB	OBP	SLG	BAVG
Colby Rasmus	151	565	75	126	21	5	23	75	226	47	149	4	.289	.400	.223
Yunel Escobar	145	558	58	141	22	1	9	51	192	35	70	5	.300	.344	.253
Edwin Encarnacion	151	542	93	152	24	0	42	110	302	84	94	13	.384	.557	.280
Kelly Johnson	142	507	61	114	19	2	16	55	185	62	159	14	.313	.365	.225
Brett Lawrie	125	494	73	135	26	3	11	48	200	33	86	13	.324	.405	.273
Rajai Davis	142	447	64	115	24	3	8	43	169	29	102	46	.309	.378	.257
J.P. Arencibia	102	347	45	81	16	0	18	56	151	18	108	1	.275	.435	.233
Jose Bautista	92	332	64	80	14	0	27	65	175	59	63	5	.358	.527	.241
Adam Lind	93	321	28	82	14	2	11	45	133	29	61	0	.314	.414	.255
Jeff Mathis	71	211	25	46	13	0	8	27	83	9	68	1	.249	.393	.218
Anthony Gose	56	166	25	37	7	3	1	11	53	17	59	15	.303	.319	.223
Omar Vizquel	60	153	13	36	5	1	0	7	43	7	17	3	.265	.281	.235
*Eric Thames	46	148	17	36	7	1	3	11	54	9	40	0	.288	.365	.243
Moises Sierra	49	147	14	33	4	0	6	15	55	8	44	1	.274	.374	.224
David Cooper	45	140	16	42	11	0	4	11	65	4	22	0	.324	.464	.300
Adeiny Hechavarria	41	126	10	32	8	0	2	15	46	4	32	1	.280	.365	.254

PITCHING	GP	GS	IP	W–L	SV	HLD	H	ER	HR	BB	SO	ERA
Henderson Alvarez	31	31	187.1	9-14	0	0	216	101	29	54	79	4.85
Ricky Romero	32	32	181.0	9-14	0	0	198	116	21	105	124	5.77
Carlos Villanueva	38	16	125.1	7-7	0	2	113	58	23	46	122	4.16
Brandon Morrow	21	21	124.2	10-7	0	0	98	41	12	41	108	2.96
Aaron Laffey	22	16	100.2	4-6	0	0	100	51	17	37	48	4.56
Kyle Drabek	13	13	71.1	4-7	0	0	67	37	10	47	47	4.67
Casey Janssen	62	0	63.2	1-1	22	1	44	18	7	11	67	2.54
Brett Cecil	21	9	61.1	2-4	0	0	70	39	11	23	51	5.72
Drew Hutchison	11	11	58.2	5-3	0	0	59	30	8	20	49	4.60
Darren Oliver	62	0	56.2	3-4	2	16	43	13	3	15	52	2.06
Jason Frasor	50	0	43.2	1-1	0	13	42	20	6	22	53	4.12
Luis Perez	35	0	42.0	2-2	0	4	38	16	3	16	39	3.43
*J.A. Happ	10	6	40.1	3-2	0	1	35	21	2	17	46	4.69
*Francisco Cordero	41	0	34.1	3-5	2	6	48	22	7	14	26	5.77

*Mid-season trade.

The World Series

Results

1903	Boston (A) 5, Pittsburgh (N) 3
1904	No series
1905	New York (N) 4, Philadelphia (A) 1
1906	Chicago (A) 4, Chicago (N) 2
1907	Chicago (N) 4, Detroit (A) 0; 1 tie
1908	Chicago (N) 4, Detroit (A) 1
1909	Pittsburgh (N) 4, Detroit (A) 3
1910	Philadelphia (A) 4, Chicago (N) 1
1911	Philadelphia (A) 4, New York (N) 2
1912	Boston (A) 4, New York (N) 3; 1 tie
1913	Philadelphia (A) 4, New York (N) 1
1914	Boston (N) 4, Philadelphia (A) 0
1915	Boston (A) 4, Philadelphia (N) 1
1916	Boston (A) 4, Brooklyn (N) 1
1917	Chicago (A) 4, New York (N) 2
1918	Boston (A) 4, Chicago (N) 2
1919	Cincinnati (N) 5, Chicago (A) 3
1920	Cleveland (A) 5, Brooklyn (N) 2
1921	New York (N) 5, New York (A) 3
1922	New York (N) 4, New York (A) 0; 1 tie
1923	New York (A) 4, New York (N) 2
1924	Washington (A) 4, New York (N) 3
1925	Pittsburgh (N) 4, Washington (A) 3
1926	St. Louis (N) 4, New York (A) 3
1927	New York (A) 4, Pittsburgh (N) 0
1928	New York (A) 4, St. Louis (N) 0
1929	Philadelphia (A) 4, Chicago (N) 1
1930	Philadelphia (A) 4, St. Louis (N) 2
1931	St. Louis (N) 4, Philadelphia (A) 3
1932	New York (A) 4, Chicago (N) 0
1933	New York (N) 4, Washington (A) 1
1934	St. Louis (N) 4, Detroit (A) 3
1935	Detroit (A) 4, Chicago (N) 2
1936	New York (A) 4, New York (N) 2
1937	New York (A) 4, New York (N) 1
1938	New York (A) 4, Chicago (N) 0
1939	New York (A) 4, Cincinnati (N) 0
1940	Cincinnati (N) 4, Detroit (A) 3
1941	New York (A) 4, Brooklyn (N) 1
1942	St. Louis (N) 4, New York (A) 1
1943	New York (A) 4, St. Louis (N) 1
1944	St. Louis (N) 4, St. Louis (A) 2
1945	Detroit (A) 4, Chicago (N) 3
1946	St. Louis (N) 4, Boston (A) 3
1947	New York (A) 4, Brooklyn (N) 3
1948	Cleveland (A) 4, Boston (N) 2
1949	New York (A) 4, Brooklyn (N) 1
1950	New York (A) 4, Philadelphia (N) 0
1951	New York (A) 4, New York (N) 2
1952	New York (A) 4, Brooklyn (N) 3
1953	New York (A) 4, Brooklyn (N) 2
1954	New York (N) 4, Cleveland (A) 0
1955	Brooklyn (N) 4, New York (A) 3
1956	New York (A) 4, Brooklyn (N) 3
1957	Milwaukee (N) 4, New York (A) 3
1958	New York (A) 4, Milwaukee (N) 3
1959	Los Angeles (N) 4, Chicago (A) 2
1960	Pittsburgh (N) 4, New York (A) 3
1961	New York (A) 4, Cincinnati (N) 1
1962	New York (A) 4, San Francisco (N) 3
1963	Los Angeles (N) 4, New York (A) 0
1964	St. Louis (N) 4, New York (A) 3
1965	Los Angeles (N) 4, Minnesota (A) 3
1966	Baltimore (A) 4, Los Angeles (N) 0
1967	St. Louis (N) 4, Boston (A) 3
1968	Detroit (A) 4, St. Louis (N) 3
1969	New York (N) 4, Baltimore (A) 1
1970	Baltimore (A) 4, Cincinnati (N) 1
1971	Pittsburgh (N) 4, Baltimore (A) 3
1972	Oakland (A) 4, Cincinnati (N) 3
1973	Oakland (A) 4, New York (N) 3
1974	Oakland (A) 4, Los Angeles (N) 1
1975	Cincinnati (N) 4, Boston (A) 3
1976	Cincinnati (N) 4, New York (A) 0
1977	New York (A) 4, Los Angeles (N) 2
1978	New York (A) 4, Los Angeles (N) 2
1979	Pittsburgh (N) 4, Baltimore (A) 3
1980	Philadelphia (N) 4, Kansas City (A) 2
1981	Los Angeles (N) 4, New York (A) 2
1982	St. Louis (N) 4, Milwaukee (A) 3
1983	Baltimore (A) 4, Philadelphia (N) 1
1984	Detroit (A) 4, San Diego (N) 1
1985	Kansas City (A) 4, St. Louis (N) 3
1986	New York (N) 4, Boston (A) 3
1987	Minnesota (A) 4, St. Louis (N) 3
1988	Los Angeles (N) 4, Oakland (A) 1
1989	Oakland (A) 4, San Francisco (N) 0
1990	Cincinnati (N) 4, Oakland (A) 0
1991	Minnesota (A) 4, Atlanta (N) 3
1992	Toronto (A) 4, Atlanta (N) 2
1993	Toronto (A) 4, Philadelphia (N) 2
1994	Series canceled due to players' strike.
1995	Atlanta (N) 4, Cleveland (A) 2
1996	New York (A) 4, Atlanta (N) 2
1997	Florida (N) 4, Cleveland (A) 3
1998	New York (A) 4, San Diego (N) 0
1999	New York (A) 4, Atlanta (N) 0
2000	New York (A) 4 , New York (N) 1
2001	Arizona (N) 4, New York (A) 3
2002	Anaheim (A) 4, San Francisco (N) 3
2003	Florida (N) 4, New York (A) 2
2004	Boston (A) 4, St. Louis (N) 0
2005	Chicago (A) 4, Houston (N) 0
2006	St. Louis (N) 4, Detroit (A) 1
2007	Boston (A) 4, Colorado (N) 0
2008	Philadelphia (N) 4, Tampa Bay (A) 1
2009	New York (A) 4, Philadelphia (N) 2
2010	San Francisco (N) 4, Texas (A) 1
2011	St. Louis (N) 4, Texas (A) 3
2012	San Francisco (N) 4, Detroit (A) 0

Most Valuable Players

1955	Johnny Podres, Bklyn
1956	Don Larsen, NY (A)
1957	Lew Burdette, Mil
1958	Bob Turley, NY (A)
1959	Larry Sherry, LA
1960	Bobby Richardson, NY (A)
1961	Whitey Ford, NY (A)
1962	Ralph Terry, NY (A)
1963	Sandy Koufax, LA
1964	Bob Gibson, StL
1965	Sandy Koufax, LA
1966	Frank Robinson, Balt
1967	Bob Gibson, StL
1968	Mickey Lolich, Det
1969	Donn Clendenon, NY (N)
1970	Brooks Robinson, Balt
1971	Roberto Clemente, Pitt
1972	Gene Tenace, Oak
1973	Reggie Jackson, Oak
1974	Rollie Fingers, Oak
1975	Pete Rose, Cin
1976	Johnny Bench, Cin
1977	Reggie Jackson, NY (A)
1978	Bucky Dent, NY (A)
1979	Willie Stargell, Pitt
1980	Mike Schmidt, Phil
1981	Ron Cey, LA; Steve Yeager, LA; Pedro Guerrero, LA
1982	Darrell Porter, StL
1983	Rick Dempsey, Balt
1984	Alan Trammell, Det
1985	Bret Saberhagen, KC
1986	Ray Knight, NY (N)
1987	Frank Viola, Minn
1988	Orel Hershiser, LA
1989	Dave Stewart, Oak
1990	Jose Rijo, Cin
1991	Jack Morris, Minn
1992	Pat Borders, Tor
1993	Paul Molitor, Tor
1994	Series canceled due to strike.
1995	Tom Glavine, Atl
1996	John Wetteland, NY (A)
1997	Livan Hernandez, Fla
1998	Scott Brosius, NY (A)
1999	Mariano Rivera, NY (A)
2000	Derek Jeter, NY (A)
2001	Randy Johnson, Ariz; Curt Schilling, Ariz
2002	Troy Glaus, Ana
2003	Josh Beckett, Fla
2004	Manny Ramirez, Bos
2005	Jermaine Dye, Chi (A)
2006	David Eckstein, StL
2007	Mike Lowell, Bos
2008	Cole Hamels, Phi
2009	Hideki Matsui, NY (A)
2010	Edgar Renteria, SF
2011	David Freese, StL
2012	Pablo Sandoval, SF

Career Batting Leaders (Minimum 40 at bats)

GAMES

Yogi Berra	75
Mickey Mantle	65
Elston Howard	54
Hank Bauer	53
Gil McDougald	53
Phil Rizzuto	52
Joe DiMaggio	51
Frankie Frisch	50
Pee Wee Reese	44
Roger Maris	41
Babe Ruth	41

AT BATS

Yogi Berra	259
Mickey Mantle	230
Joe DiMaggio	199
Frankie Frisch	197
Gil McDougald	190
Hank Bauer	188
Phil Rizzuto	183
Elston Howard	171
Pee Wee Reese	169
Derek Jeter	156
Roger Maris	152

BATTING AVERAGE

Bobby Brown	.439
Paul Molitor	.418
Pepper Martin	.418
Hal McRae	.400
Lou Brock	.391
Marquis Grissom	.390
Thurman Munson	.373
George Brett	.373
Pat Borders	.372
Hank Aaron	.364

TOTAL BASES

Mickey Mantle	123
Yogi Berra	117
Babe Ruth	96
Lou Gehrig	87
Joe DiMaggio	84
Duke Snider	79
Hank Bauer	75
Reggie Jackson	74
Frankie Frisch	74
Gil McDougald	72

HOME RUNS

Mickey Mantle	18
Babe Ruth	15
Yogi Berra	12
Duke Snider	11
Reggie Jackson	10
Lou Gehrig	10
Frank Robinson	8
Bill Skowron	8
Joe DiMaggio	8
Goose Goslin	7
Hank Bauer	7
Gil McDougald	7
Chase Utley	7

RUNS

Mickey Mantle	42
Yogi Berra	41
Babe Ruth	37
Derek Jeter	32
Lou Gehrig	30
Joe DiMaggio	27
Derek Jeter	27
Roger Maris	26
Elston Howard	25
Gil McDougald	23
Jackie Robinson	22

RUNS BATTED IN

Mickey Mantle	40
Yogi Berra	39
Lou Gehrig	35
Babe Ruth	33
Joe DiMaggio	30
Bill Skowron	29
Duke Snider	26
Reggie Jackson	24
Bill Dickey	24
Hank Bauer	24
Gil McDougald	24

HITS

Yogi Berra	71
Mickey Mantle	59
Frankie Frisch	58
Joe DiMaggio	54
Derek Jeter	50
Pee Wee Reese	46
Hank Bauer	46
Phil Rizzuto	45
Gil McDougald	45
Lou Gehrig	43
Eddie Collins	42
Babe Ruth	42
Elston Howard	42

STOLEN BASES

Lou Brock	14
Eddie Collins	14
Frank Chance	10
Davey Lopes	10
Phil Rizzuto	10
Honus Wagner	9
Frankie Frisch	9
Kenny Lofton	9

Career Batting Leaders *(Cont.)*

STOLEN BASES (CONT.)

Johnny Evers 8
Roberto Alomar 7
Joe Tinker 7
Pepper Martin..........................7
Joe Morgan 7
Rickey Henderson 7

SLUGGING AVERAGE

Reggie Jackson................ .755
Babe Ruth ,....................... .744
Lou Gehrig .... .731
Bobby Brown..................... .707
Lenny Dykstra.................... .700
Al Simmons....................... .658
Lou Brock .... .655
Pepper Martin.................... .636
Paul Molitor....................... .636
Joe Harris .... .625

STRIKEOUTS

Mickey Mantle 54
Derek Jeter............................39
Elston Howard......................37
Duke Snider..........................33
Jorge Posada 31
Babe Ruth............................30
David Justice 30
Gil McDougald 29
Bill Skowron 26
Bernie Williams 26
Hank Bauer..........................25

Career Pitching Leaders

GAMES

Mariano Rivera 24
Whitey Ford 22
Mike Stanton..........................19
Jeff Nelson............................16
Rollie Fingers........................16
Allie Reynolds........................15
Bob Turley 15
Clay Carroll 14
Clem Labine 13
Mark Wohlers........................13
Andy Pettitte 13

LOSSES

Whitey Ford 8
Eddie Plank............................5
Schoolboy Rowe....................5
Joe Bush................................5
Rube Marquard 5
Christy Mathewson 5

COMPLETE GAMES

Christy Mathewson 10
Chief Bender 9
Bob Gibson 8
Red Ruffing............................7
Whitey Ford 7
George Mullin 6
Eddie Plank 6
Art Nehf 6
Waite Hoyt 6

INNINGS PITCHED

Whitey Ford 146
Christy Mathewson 101.2
Red Ruffing..........................85.2
Chief Bender 85
Waite Hoyt 83.2
Bob Gibson 81
Art Nehf 79
Andy Pettitte 77.2
Allie Reynolds........................77

SAVES

Mariano Rivera 11
Rollie Fingers 6
Allie Reynolds........................4
Johnny Murphy......................4
John Wetteland......................4
Robb Nen..............................4

STRIKEOUTS

Whitey Ford 94
Bob Gibson 92
Allie Reynolds........................62
Sandy Koufax 61
Red Ruffing............................61
Chief Bender 59
Andy Pettitte 56
George Earnshaw..................56
John Smoltz..........................52
Waite Hoyt 49
Roger Clemens......................49
Christy Mathewson 48

*EARNED RUN AVERAGE

Jack Billingham 0.36
Harry Brecheen 0.83
Babe Ruth 0.87
Sherry Smith 0.89
Sandy Koufax 0.95
Mariano Rivera 0.99
Hippo Vaughn 1.00
Monte Pearson 1.01
Christy Mathewson 1.06
Babe Adams........................1.29

WINS

Whitey Ford 10
Bob Gibson 7
Red Ruffing............................7
Allie Reynolds........................7
Lefty Gomez 6
Chief Bender 6
Waite Hoyt 6
Jack Coombs 5
Three Finger Brown................5
Herb Pennock 5
Christy Mathewson 5
Vic Raschi 5
Catfish Hunter 5
Andy Pettitte 5

SHUTOUTS

Christy Mathewson 4
Three Finger Brown................3
Whitey Ford 3
Bill Hallahan..........................2
Lew Burdette 2
Bill Dinneen 2
Sandy Koufax 2
Allie Reynolds........................2
Art Nehf 2
Bob Gibson 2

BASES ON BALLS

Whitey Ford 34
Allie Reynolds........................32
Art Nehf 32
Jim Palmer............................31
Bob Turley 29
Paul Derringer 27
Red Ruffing............................27
Don Gullett............................26
Burleigh Grimes....................26
Andy Pettitte 26
Vic Raschi............................25

*Minimum 25 innings pitched.

Alltime Team Rankings, by Championships

Team	W	L	Appearances	Pct.	Most Recent App.	Last Championship
New York Yankees.....................27	13	40	.675	2009	2009
St. Louis Cardinals.......................11	7	18	.611	2011	2011
Phila./K.C./Oakland Athletics..........9	5	14	.643	1990	1989
Boston Red Sox...............7	5	12	.583	2007	2007
New York/San Francisco Giants.....7	12	19	.368	2012	2012
Brooklyn/Los Angeles Dodgers......6	12	18	.333	1988	1988
Pittsburgh Pirates 5	2	7	.714	1979	1979
Cincinnati Reds 5	4	9	.556	1990	1990
Detroit Tigers 4	7	11	.364	2012	1984
Chicago White Sox 3	2	5	.600	2005	2005
Wash. Senators/Minnesota Twins......3	3	6	.500	1991	1991
St. Louis Browns/Baltimore Orioles...3	4	7	.429	1983	1983
Boston/Milwaukee/Atlanta Braves...3	6	9	.333	1999	1995
Florida Marlins 2	0	2	1.000	2003	2003

Alltime Team Rankings, by Championships (Cont.)

Team	W	L	Appearances	Pct.	Most Recent App.	Last Championship
Toronto Blue Jays	2	0	2	1.000	1993	1993
New York Mets	2	2	4	.500	2000	1986
Cleveland Indians	2	3	5	.400	1997	1948
Philadelphia Phillies	2	5	7	.286	2009	2008
Chicago Cubs	2	8	10	.200	1945	1908
California/Anaheim/L.A. Angels	1	0	1	1.000	2002	2002
Arizona Diamondbacks	1	0	1	1.000	2001	2001
Kansas City Royals	1	1	2	.500	1985	1985
Tampa Bay Rays	0	1	1	.000	2008	—
Colorado Rockies	0	1	1	.000	2007	—
Houston Astros	0	1	1	.000	2005	—
Seattle Pilots/Milwaukee Brewers	0	1	1	.000	1982	—
Texas Rangers	0	2	2	.000	2011	—
San Diego Padres	0	2	2	.000	1998	—

League Pennant Winners

National League

Year	Team	Manager	W	L	Pct	GA
1900	Brooklyn	Ned Hanlon	82	54	.603	4½
1901	Pittsburgh	Fred Clarke	90	49	.647	7½
1902	Pittsburgh	Fred Clarke	103	36	.741	27½
1903	Pittsburgh	Fred Clarke	91	49	.650	6½
1904	New York	John McGraw	106	47	.693	13
1905	New York	John McGraw	105	48	.686	9
1906	Chicago	Frank Chance	116	36	.763	20
1907	Chicago	Frank Chance	107	45	.704	17
1908	Chicago	Frank Chance	99	55	.643	1
1909	Pittsburgh	Fred Clarke	110	42	.724	6½
1910	Chicago	Frank Chance	104	50	.675	13
1911	New York	John McGraw	99	54	.647	7½
1912	New York	John McGraw	103	48	.682	10
1913	New York	John McGraw	101	51	.664	12½
1914	Boston	George Stallings	94	59	.614	10½
1915	Philadelphia	Pat Moran	90	62	.592	7
1916	Brooklyn	Wilbert Robinson	94	60	.610	2½
1917	New York	John McGraw	98	56	.636	10
1918	Chicago	Fred Mitchell	84	45	.651	10½
1919	Cincinnati	Pat Moran	96	44	.686	9
1920	Brooklyn	Wilbert Robinson	93	61	.604	7
1921	New York	John McGraw	94	59	.614	4
1922	New York	John McGraw	93	61	.604	7
1923	New York	John McGraw	95	58	.621	4½
1924	New York	John McGraw	93	60	.608	1½
1925	Pittsburgh	Bill McKechnie	95	58	.621	8½
1926	St. Louis	Rogers Hornsby	89	65	.578	2
1927	Pittsburgh	Donie Bush	94	60	.610	1½
1928	St. Louis	Bill McKechnie	95	59	.617	2
1929	Chicago	Joe McCarthy	98	54	.645	10½
1930	St. Louis	Gabby Street	92	62	.597	2
1931	St. Louis	Gabby Street	101	53	.656	13
1932	Chicago	Charlie Grimm	90	64	.584	4
1933	New York	Bill Terry	91	61	.599	5
1934	St. Louis	Frankie Frisch	95	58	.621	2
1935	Chicago	Charlie Grimm	100	54	.649	4
1936	New York	Bill Terry	92	62	.597	5
1937	New York	Bill Terry	95	57	.625	3
1938	Chicago	Gabby Hartnett	89	63	.586	2
1939	Cincinnati	Bill McKechnie	97	57	.630	4½
1940	Cincinnati	Bill McKechnie	100	53	.654	12
1941	Brooklyn	Leo Durocher	100	54	.649	2½
1942	St. Louis	Billy Southworth	106	48	.688	2
1943	St. Louis	Billy Southworth	105	49	.682	18
1944	St. Louis	Billy Southworth	105	49	.682	14½
1945	Chicago	Charlie Grimm	98	56	.636	3
1946	St. Louis*	Eddie Dyer	98	58	.628	2
1947	Brooklyn	Burt Shotton	94	60	.610	5

National League *(Cont.)*

Year	Team	Manager	W	L	Pct	GA
1948	Boston	Billy Southworth	91	62	.595	6½
1949	Brooklyn	Burt Shotton	97	57	.630	1
1950	Philadelphia	Eddie Sawyer	91	63	.591	2
1951	New York†	Leo Durocher	98	59	.624	1
1952	Brooklyn	Chuck Dressen	96	57	.627	4½
1953	Brooklyn	Chuck Dressen	105	49	.682	13
1954	New York	Leo Durocher	97	57	.630	5
1955	Brooklyn	Walter Alston	98	55	.641	13½
1956	Brooklyn	Walter Alston	93	61	.604	1
1957	Milwaukee	Fred Haney	95	59	.617	8
1958	Milwaukee	Fred Haney	92	62	.597	8
1959	Los Angeles‡	Walter Alston	88	68	.564	2
1960	Pittsburgh	Danny Murtaugh	95	59	.617	7
1961	Cincinnati	Fred Hutchinson	93	61	.604	4
1962	San Francisco#	Al Dark	103	62	.624	1
1963	Los Angeles	Walter Alston	99	63	.611	6
1964	St. Louis	Johnny Keane	93	69	.574	1
1965	Los Angeles	Walter Alston	97	65	.599	2
1966	Los Angeles	Walter Alston	95	67	.586	1½
1967	St. Louis	Red Schoendienst	101	60	.627	10½
1968	St. Louis	Red Schoendienst	97	65	.599	9
1969	New York (E)††	Gil Hodges	100	62	.617	8
1970	Cincinnati (W)††	Sparky Anderson	102	60	.630	14½
1971	Pittsburgh (E)††	Danny Murtaugh	97	65	.599	7
1972	Cincinnati (W)††	Sparky Anderson	95	59	.617	10½
1973	New York (E)††	Yogi Berra	82	79	.509	1½
1974	Los Angeles (W)††	Walter Alston	102	60	.630	4
1975	Cincinnati (W)††	Sparky Anderson	108	54	.667	20
1976	Cincinnati (W)††	Sparky Anderson	102	60	.630	10
1977	Los Angeles (W)††	Tommy Lasorda	98	64	.605	10
1978	Los Angeles (W)††	Tommy Lasorda	95	67	.586	2½
1979	Pittsburgh (E)††	Chuck Tanner	98	64	.605	2
1980	Philadelphia (E)††	Dallas Green	91	71	.562	1
1981	Los Angeles (W)††	Tommy Lasorda	63	47	.573	**
1982	St. Louis (E)††	Whitey Herzog	92	70	.568	3
1983	Philadelphia (E)††	Pat Corrales/Paul Owens	90	72	.556	6
1984	San Diego (W)††	Dick Williams	92	70	.568	12
1985	St. Louis (E)††	Whitey Herzog	101	61	.623	3
1986	New York (E)††	Davey Johnson	108	54	.667	21½
1987	St. Louis (E)††	Whitey Herzog	95	67	.586	3
1988	Los Angeles (W)††	Tommy Lasorda	94	67	.584	7
1989	San Francisco (W)††	Roger Craig	92	70	.568	3
1990	Cincinnati (W)††	Lou Piniella	91	71	.562	5
1991	Atlanta (W)††	Bobby Cox	94	68	.580	1
1992	Atlanta (W)††	Bobby Cox	98	64	.605	8
1993	Philadelphia (E)††	Jim Fregosi	97	65	.599	3
1994	Season ended Aug. 11 due to players' strike.					
1995	Atlanta (E)††	Bobby Cox	90	54	.625	21
1996	Atlanta (E)††	Bobby Cox	96	66	.593	8
1997	Florida (wc)††	Jim Leyland	92	70	.568	-9
1998	San Diego (W)††	Bruce Bochy	98	64	.605	9½
1999	Atlanta (E)††	Bobby Cox	103	59	.636	6½
2000	New York (wc)††	Bobby Valentine	94	68	.580	-6½
2001	Arizona (W)††	Bob Brenly	92	70	.568	2
2002	San Francisco (wc)††	Dusty Baker	95	66	.590	-2½
2003	Florida (wc)††	Jack McKeon	91	71	.562	-10
2004	St. Louis (C)††	Tony LaRussa	105	57	.648	13
2005	Houston (wc)††	Phil Garner	89	73	.549	-11
2006	St. Louis (C)††	Tony LaRussa	83	78	.516	1½
2007	Colorado (wc)††§	Clint Hurdle	89	73	.549	-1
2008	Philadelphia (E)††	Charlie Manuel	92	70	.568	3
2009	Philadelphia (E)††	Charlie Manuel	93	69	.574	6
2010	San Francisco (W)††	Bruce Bochy	92	70	.568	2
2011	St. Louis (wc)††	Tony LaRussa	90	72	.556	-6
2012	San Francisco (W)††	Bruce Bochy	94	68	.580	8

*Defeated Brooklyn, two games to none, in playoff for pennant. †Defeated Brooklyn, two games to one, in playoff for pennant. ‡Defeated Milwaukee, two games to none, in playoff for pennant. #Defeated Los Angeles, two games to one, in playoff for pennant. § Defeated San Diego in one-game playoff for wild card. ††Won Championship Series. **First half 36–21; second half 27–26, in season split by strike; defeated Houston in playoff for Western Division title.

American League

Year	Team	Manager	W	L	Pct	GA
1901	Chicago	Clark Griffith	83	53	.610	4
1902	Philadelphia	Connie Mack	83	53	.610	5
1903	Boston	Jimmy Collins	91	47	.659	14½
1904	Boston	Jimmy Collins	95	59	.617	1½
1905	Philadelphia	Connie Mack	92	56	.622	2
1906	Chicago	Fielder Jones	93	58	.616	3
1907	Detroit	Hughie Jennings	92	58	.613	1½
1908	Detroit	Hughie Jennings	90	63	.588	½
1909	Detroit	Hughie Jennings	98	54	.645	3½
1910	Philadelphia	Connie Mack	102	48	.680	14½
1911	Philadelphia	Connie Mack	101	50	.669	13½
1912	Boston	Jake Stahl	105	47	.691	14
1913	Philadelphia	Connie Mack	96	57	.627	6½
1914	Philadelphia	Connie Mack	99	53	.651	8½
1915	Boston	Bill Carrigan	101	50	.669	2½
1916	Boston	Bill Carrigan	91	63	.591	2
1917	Chicago	Pants Rowland	100	54	.649	9
1918	Boston	Ed Barrow	75	51	.595	2½
1919	Chicago	Kid Gleason	88	52	.629	3½
1920	Cleveland	Tris Speaker	98	56	.636	2
1921	New York	Miller Huggins	98	55	.641	4½
1922	New York	Miller Huggins	94	60	.610	1
1923	New York	Miller Huggins	98	54	.645	16
1924	Washington	Bucky Harris	92	62	.597	2
1925	Washington	Bucky Harris	96	55	.636	8½
1926	New York	Miller Huggins	91	63	.591	3
1927	New York	Miller Huggins	110	44	.714	19
1928	New York	Miller Huggins	101	53	.656	2½
1929	Philadelphia	Connie Mack	104	46	.693	18
1930	Philadelphia	Connie Mack	102	52	.662	8
1931	Philadelphia	Connie Mack	107	45	.704	13½
1932	New York	Joe McCarthy	107	47	.695	13
1933	Washington	Joe Cronin	99	53	.651	7
1934	Detroit	Mickey Cochrane	101	53	.656	7
1935	Detroit	Mickey Cochrane	93	58	.616	3
1936	New York	Joe McCarthy	102	51	.667	19½
1937	New York	Joe McCarthy	102	52	.662	13
1938	New York	Joe McCarthy	99	53	.651	9½
1939	New York	Joe McCarthy	106	45	.702	17
1940	Detroit	Del Baker	90	64	.584	1
1941	New York	Joe McCarthy	101	53	.656	17
1942	New York	Joe McCarthy	103	51	.669	9
1943	New York	Joe McCarthy	98	56	.636	13½
1944	St. Louis	Luke Sewell	89	65	.578	1
1945	Detroit	Steve O'Neill	88	65	.575	1½
1946	Boston	Joe Cronin	104	50	.675	12
1947	New York	Bucky Harris	97	57	.630	12
1948	Cleveland†	Lou Boudreau	97	58	.626	1
1949	New York	Casey Stengel	97	57	.630	1
1950	New York	Casey Stengel	98	56	.636	3
1951	New York	Casey Stengel	98	56	.636	5
1952	New York	Casey Stengel	95	59	.617	2
1953	New York	Casey Stengel	99	52	.656	8½
1954	Cleveland	Al Lopez	111	43	.721	8
1955	New York	Casey Stengel	96	58	.623	3
1956	New York	Casey Stengel	97	57	.630	9
1957	New York	Casey Stengel	98	56	.636	8
1958	New York	Casey Stengel	92	62	.597	10
1959	Chicago	Al Lopez	94	60	.610	5
1960	New York	Casey Stengel	97	57	.630	8
1961	New York	Ralph Houk	109	53	.673	8
1962	New York	Ralph Houk	96	66	.593	5
1963	New York	Ralph Houk	104	57	.646	10½
1964	New York	Yogi Berra	99	63	.611	1
1965	Minnesota	Sam Mele	102	60	.630	7
1966	Baltimore	Hank Bauer	97	63	.606	9
1967	Boston	Dick Williams	92	70	.568	1

†Defeated Boston in one-game playoff.

American League *(Cont.)*

Year	Team	Manager	W	L	Pct	GA
1968	Detroit	Mayo Smith	103	59	.636	12
1969	Baltimore (E)‡	Earl Weaver	109	53	.673	19
1970	Baltimore (E)‡	Earl Weaver	108	54	.667	15
1971	Baltimore (E)‡	Earl Weaver	101	57	.639	12
1972	Oakland (W)‡	Dick Williams	93	62	.600	5½
1973	Oakland (W)‡	Dick Williams	94	68	.580	6
1974	Oakland (W)‡	Al Dark	90	72	.556	5
1975	Boston (E)‡	Darrell Johnson	95	65	.594	4½
1976	New York (E)‡	Billy Martin	97	62	.610	10½
1977	New York (E)‡	Billy Martin	100	62	.617	2½
1978	New York (E)†‡	Billy Martin/Bob Lemon	100	63	.613	1
1979	Baltimore (E)‡	Earl Weaver	102	57	.642	8
1980	Kansas City (W)‡	Jim Frey	97	65	.599	14
1981	New York (E)‡	Gene Michael/Bob Lemon	59	48	.551	#
1982	Milwaukee (E)‡	Buck Rodgers/ Harvey Kuenn	95	67	.586	1
1983	Baltimore (E)‡	Joe Altobelli	98	64	.605	6
1984	Detroit (E)‡	Sparky Anderson	104	58	.642	15
1985	Kansas City (W)‡	Dick Howser	91	71	.562	1
1986	Boston (E)‡	John McNamara	95	66	.590	5½
1987	Minnesota (W)‡	Tom Kelly	85	77	.525	2
1988	Oakland (W)‡	Tony LaRussa	104	58	.642	13
1989	Oakland (W)‡	Tony LaRussa	99	63	.611	7
1990	Oakland (W)‡	Tony LaRussa	103	59	.636	9
1991	Minnesota (W)‡	Tom Kelly	95	67	.586	8
1992	Toronto (E)‡	Cito Gaston	96	66	.593	4
1993	Toronto (E)‡	Cito Gaston	95	67	.586	7
1994	Season ended Aug. 11 due to players' strike.					
1995	Cleveland (C)‡	Mike Hargrove	100	44	.694	30
1996	New York (E)‡	Joe Torre	92	70	.568	4
1997	Cleveland (C)‡	Mike Hargrove	86	75	.534	6
1998	New York (E)‡	Joe Torre	114	48	.704	22
1999	New York (E)‡	Joe Torre	98	64	.605	4
2000	New York (E)‡	Joe Torre	87	74	.540	2½
2001	New York (E)‡	Joe Torre	95	65	.594	13½
2002	Anaheim (wc)‡	Mike Scioscia	99	63	.611	-4
2003	New York (E)‡	Joe Torre	101	61	.623	6
2004	Boston (wc)‡	Terry Francona	98	64	.605	-3
2005	Chicago (C)‡	Ozzie Guillen	99	63	.611	6
2006	Detroit (wc)‡	Jim Leyland	95	67	.586	-1
2007	Boston (E)‡	Terry Francona	96	66	.593	2
2008	Tampa Bay (E)‡	Joe Maddon	97	65	.599	2
2009	New York (E)‡	Joe Girardi	103	59	.636	8
2010	Texas (W)‡	Ron Washington	90	72	.556	9
2011	Texas (W)‡	Ron Washington	96	66	.593	5
2012	Detroit (C)‡	Jim Leyland	88	74	.543	3

‡Won championship series. †Defeated Boston in one-game playoff.

League Championship Series

National League

1969	New York (E) 3, Atlanta (W) 0
1970	Cincinnati (W) 3, Pittsburgh (E) 0
1971	Pittsburgh (E) 3, San Francisco (W) 1
1972	Cincinnati (W) 3, Pittsburgh (E) 2
1973	New York (E) 3, Cincinnati (W) 2
1974	Los Angeles (W) 3, Pittsburgh (E) 1
1975	Cincinnati (W) 3, Pittsburgh (E) 0
1976	Cincinnati (W) 3, Philadelphia (E) 0
1977	Los Angeles (W) 3, Philadelphia (E) 1
1978	Los Angeles (W) 3, Philadelphia (E) 1
1979	Pittsburgh (E) 3, Cincinnati (W) 0
1980	Philadelphia (E) 3, Houston (W) 2
1981	Los Angeles (W) 3, Montreal (E) 2
1982	St. Louis (E) 3, Atlanta (W) 0
1983	Philadelphia (E) 3, Los Angeles (W) 1

American League

1969	Baltimore (E) 3, Minnesota (W) 0
1970	Baltimore (E) 3, Minnesota (W) 0
1971	Baltimore (E) 3, Oakland (W) 0
1972	Oakland (W) 3, Detroit (E) 2
1973	Oakland (W) 3, Baltimore (E) 2
1974	Oakland (W) 3, Baltimore (E) 1
1975	Boston (E) 3, Oakland (W) 0
1976	New York (E) 3, Kansas City (W) 2
1977	New York (E) 3, Kansas City (W) 2
1978	New York (E) 3, Kansas City (W) 1
1979	Baltimore (E) 3, California (W) 1
1980	Kansas City (W) 3, New York (E) 0
1981	New York (E) 3, Oakland (W) 0
1982	Milwaukee (E) 3, California (W) 2
1983	Baltimore (E) 3, Chicago (W) 1

National League *(Cont.)*

1984	San Diego (W) 3, Chicago (E) 2
1985	St. Louis (E) 4, Los Angeles (W) 2
1986	New York (E) 4, Houston (W) 2
1987	St. Louis (E) 4, San Francisco (W) 3
1988	Los Angeles (W) 4, New York (E) 3
1989	San Francisco (W) 4, Chicago (E) 1
1990	Cincinnati (W) 4, Pittsburgh (E) 2
1991	Atlanta (W) 4, Pittsburgh (E) 3
1992	Atlanta (W) 4, Pittsburgh (E) 3
1993	Philadelphia (E) 4, Atlanta (W) 2
1994	Playoffs canceled due to players' strike.
1995	Atlanta (E) 4, Cincinnati (C) 0
1996	Atlanta (E) 4, St. Louis (C) 3
1997	Florida (wc) 4, Atlanta (E) 2
1998	San Diego (W) 4, Atlanta (E) 2
1999	Atlanta (E) 4, New York (wc) 2
2000	New York (wc) 4, St. Louis (C) 1
2001	Arizona (W) 4, Atlanta (E) 1
2002	San Francisco (wc) 4, St. Louis (C) 1
2003	Florida (wc) 4, Chicago (C) 3
2004	St. Louis (C) 4, Houston (wc) 3
2005	Houston (wc) 4, St. Louis (C) 2
2006	St. Louis (C) 4, New York (E) 3
2007	Colorado (wc) 4, Arizona (W) 0
2008	Philadelphia (E) 4, Los Angeles (W) 1
2009	Philadelphia (E) 4, Los Angeles (W) 1
2010	San Francisco (W) 4, Philadelphia (E) 2
2011	St. Louis (wc) 4, Milwaukee (C) 2
2012	San Francisco (W) 4, St. Louis (wc) 3

American League *(Cont.)*

1984	Detroit (E) 3, Kansas City (W) 0
1985	Kansas City (W) 4, Toronto (E) 3
1986	Boston (E) 4, California (W) 3
1987	Minnesota (W) 4, Detroit (E) 1
1988	Oakland (W) 4, Boston (E) 0
1989	Oakland (W) 4, Toronto (E) 1
1990	Oakland (W) 4, Boston (E) 0
1991	Minnesota (W) 4, Toronto (E) 1
1992	Toronto (E) 4, Oakland (W) 2
1993	Toronto (E) 4, Chicago (W) 2
1994	Playoffs canceled due to players' strike.
1995	Cleveland (C) 4, Seattle (W) 2
1996	New York (E) 4, Baltimore (wc) 1
1997	Cleveland (C) 4, Baltimore (E) 2
1998	New York (E) 4, Cleveland (C) 2
1999	New York (E) 4, Boston (wc) 1
2000	New York (E) 4, Seattle (wc) 2
2001	New York (E) 4, Seattle (W) 1
2002	Anaheim (wc) 4, Minnesota (C) 1
2003	New York (E) 4, Boston (wc) 3
2004	Boston (wc) 4, New York (E) 3
2005	Chicago (C) 4, Los Angeles (W) 1
2006	Detroit (wc) 4, Oakland (W) 0
2007	Boston (E) 4, Cleveland (C) 3
2008	Tampa Bay (E) 4, Boston (wc) 3
2009	New York (E) 4, Los Angeles (W) 2
2010	Texas (W) 4, New York (E) 2
2011	Texas (W) 4, Detroit (C) 2
2012	Detroit (C) 4, New York (E) 0

NLCS Most Valuable Player

1977	Dusty Baker, LA	1989	Will Clark, SF	2001	Craig Counsell, Ariz
1978	Steve Garvey, LA	1990	R. Myers/R. Dibble, Cin	2002	Benito Santiago, SF
1979	Willie Stargell, Pitt	1991	Steve Avery, Atl	2003	Ivan Rodriguez, Fla
1980	Manny Trillo, Phi	1992	John Smoltz, Atl	2004	Albert Pujols, StL
1981	Burt Hooton, LA	1993	Curt Schilling, Phi	2005	Roy Oswalt, Hou
1982	Darrell Porter, StL	1994	Playoffs canceled	2006	Jeff Suppan, StL
1983	Gary Matthews, Phi	1995	Mike Devereaux, Atl	2007	Matt Holliday, Col
1984	Steve Garvey, SD	1996	Javier Lopez, Atl	2008	Cole Hamels, Phi
1985	Ozzie Smith, StL	1997	Livan Hernandez, Fla	2009	Ryan Howard, Phi
1986	Mike Scott, Hou	1998	Sterling Hitchcock, SD	2010	Cody Ross, SF
1987	Jeffrey Leonard, SF	1999	Eddie Perez, Atl	2011	David Freese, StL
1988	Orel Hershiser, LA	2000	Mike Hampton, NY	2012	Marco Scutaro, SF

ALCS Most Valuable Player

1980	Frank White, KC	1991	Kirby Puckett, Minn	2002	Adam Kennedy, Ana
1981	Graig Nettles, NY	1992	Roberto Alomar, Tor	2003	Mariano Rivera, NY
1982	Fred Lynn, Calif	1993	Dave Stewart, Tor	2004	David Ortiz, Bos
1983	Mike Boddicker, Balt	1994	Playoffs canceled	2005	Paul Konerko, Chi
1984	Kirk Gibson, Det	1995	Orel Hershiser, Clev	2006	Placido Polanco, Det
1985	George Brett, KC	1996	Bernie Williams, NY	2007	Josh Beckett, Bos
1986	Marty Barrett, Bos	1997	Marquis Grissom, Clev	2008	Matt Garza, TB
1987	Gary Gaetti, Minn	1998	David Wells, NY	2009	CC Sabathia, NY
1988	Dennis Eckersley, Oak	1999	Orlando Hernandez, NY	2010	Josh Hamilton, Tex
1989	Rickey Henderson, Oak	2000	David Justice, NY	2011	Nelson Cruz, Tex
1990	Dave Stewart, Oak	2001	Andy Pettitte, NY	2012	Delmon Young, Det

Divisional Playoffs

National League

1995	Atlanta (E) 3, Colorado (wc) 1
	Cincinnati (C) 3, Los Angeles (W) 0
1996	St. Louis (C) 3, San Diego (W) 0
	Atlanta (E) 3, Los Angeles (wc) 0
1997	Atlanta (E) 3, Houston (C) 0
	Florida (wc) 3, San Francisco (W) 0
1998	San Diego (W) 3, Houston (C) 1
	Atlanta (E) 3, Chicago (wc) 0

American League

1995	Cleveland (C) 3, Boston (E) 0
	Seattle (W) 3, New York (wc) 2
1996	Baltimore (wc) 3, Cleveland (C) 1
	New York (E) 3, Texas (W) 1
1997	Baltimore (E) 3, Seattle (W) 1
	Cleveland (C) 3, New York (wc) 2
1998	New York (E) 3, Texas (W) 0
	Cleveland (C) 3, Boston (wc) 1

National League *(Cont.)*

1999	Atlanta (E) 3, Houston (C) 1
	New York (wc) 3, Arizona (W) 1
2000	St. Louis (C) 3, Atlanta (E) 0
	New York (wc) 3, San Francisco (W) 1
2001	Atlanta (E) 3, Houston (C) 0
	Arizona (W) 3, St. Louis (wc) 2
2002	St. Louis (C) 3, Arizona (W) 0
	San Francisco (wc) 3, Atlanta (E) 2
2003	Chicago (C) 3, Atlanta (E) 2
	Florida (wc) 3, San Francisco (W) 1
2004	St. Louis (C) 3, Los Angeles (W) 1
	Houston (wc) 3, Atlanta (E) 2
2005	Houston (wc) 3, Atlanta (E) 1
	St. Louis (C) 3, San Diego (W) 1
2006	St. Louis (C) 3, San Diego (W) 1
	New York (E) 3, Los Angeles (wc) 0
2007	Colorado (wc) 3, Philadelphia (E) 0
	Arizona (W) 3, Chicago (C) 0
2008	Los Angeles (W) 3, Chicago (C) 0
	Philadelphia (E) 3, Milwaukee (wc) 1
2009	Los Angeles (W) 3, St. Louis, (C) 0
	Philadelphia (E) 3, Colorado (wc) 1
2010	San Francisco (W) 3, Atlanta (wc) 1
	Philadelphia (E) 3, Cincinnati (C) 0
2011	Milwaukee (C) 3, Arizona (W) 2
	St. Louis (wc) 3, Philadelphia (E) 2
2012	San Francisco (W) 3, Cincinnati (C) 2
	St. Louis (wc) 3, Washington (E) 2

American League *(Cont.)*

1999	New York (E) 3, Texas (W) 1
	Boston (wc) 3, Cleveland (C) 2
2000	New York (E) 3, Oakland (W) 2
	Seattle (wc) 3, Chicago (C) 0
2001	Seattle (W) 3, Cleveland (wc) 2
	New York (E) 3, Oakland (wc) 2
2002	Minnesota (C) 3, Oakland (W) 2
	Anaheim (wc) 3, New York (E) 1
2003	New York (E) 3, Minnesota (C) 1
	Boston (wc) 3, Oakland (W) 2
2004	New York (E) 3, Minnesota (C) 1
	Boston (wc) 3 Anaheim (W) 0
2005	Los Angeles (W) 3, New York (E) 2
	Chicago (C) 3, Boston (wc) 0
2006	Oakland (W) 3, Minnesota (C) 0
	Detroit (wc) 3, New York (E) 1
2007	Boston (E) 3, Los Angeles (W) 0
	Cleveland (C) 3, New York (wc) 1
2008	Boston (wc) 3, Los Angeles (W) 1
	Tampa Bay (E) 3, Chicago (C) 1
2009	Los Angeles (W) 3, Boston (wc) 0
	New York (E) 3, Minnesota (C) 0
2010	Texas (W) 3, Tampa Bay (E) 2
	New York (wc) 3, Minnesota (C) 0
2011	Detroit (C) 3, New York (E) 2
	Texas (W) 3, Tampa Bay (wc) 1
2012	New York (E) 3, Baltimore (wc) 2
	Detroit (C) 3, Oakland (W) 2

The All-Star Game

Date	Winner	Score	Site	Date	Winner	Score	Site
7-6-33	American	4–2	Comiskey Park, Chi	7-12-66	National	2–1	Busch Stadium, StL
7-10-34	American	9–7	Polo Grounds, NY	7-11-67	National	2–1	Anaheim Stadium, Cal
7-8-35	American	4–1	Municipal Stadium, Clev	7-9-68	National	1–0	Astrodome, Hou
7-7-36	National	4–3	Braves Field, Bos	7-23-69	National	9–3	R.F.K. Stadium, Wash.
7-7-37	American	8–3	Griffith Stadium, Wash	7-14-70	National	5–4	Riverfront Stadium, Cin
7-6-38	National	4–1	Crosley Field, Cin	7-13-71	American	6–4	Tiger Stadium, Det
7-11-39	American	3–1	Yankee Stadium, NY	7-25-72	National	4–3	Atlanta Stadium, Atl
7-10-40	National	4–0	Sportsman's Park, StL	7-24-73	National	7–1	Royals Stadium, KC
7-8-41	American	7–5	Briggs Stadium, Det	7-23-74	National	7–2	Three Rivers Stadium, Pitt
7-6-42	American	3–1	Polo Grounds, NY	7-15-75	National	6–3	County Stadium, Mil
7-13-43	American	5–3	Shibe Park, Phi	7-13-76	National	7–1	Veterans Stadium, Phi
7-11-44	National	7–1	Forbes Field, Pitt	7-19-77	National	7–5	Yankee Stadium, NY
1945	No game due to wartime travel restrictions.			7-11-78	National	7–3	Jack Murphy Stadium, SD
7-9-46	American	12–0	Fenway Park, Bos	7-17-79	National	7–6	Kingdome, Sea
7-8-47	American	2–1	Wrigley Field, Chi	7-8-80	National	4–2	Dodger Stadium, LA
7-13-48	American	5–2	Sportsman's Park, StL	8-9-81	National	5–4	Municipal Stadium, Clev
7-12-49	American	11–7	Ebbets Field, Bklyn	7-13-82	National	4–1	Olympic Stadium, Mtl
7-11-50	National	4–3	Comiskey Park, Chi	7-6-83	American	13–3	Comiskey Park, Chi
7-10-51	National	8–3	Briggs Stadium, Det	7-10-84	National	3–1	Candlestick Park, SF
7-8-52	National	3–2	Shibe Park, Phi	7-16-85	National	6–1	Metrodome, Minn
7-14-53	National	5–1	Crosley Field, Cin	7-15-86	American	3–2	Astrodome, Hou
7-13-54	American	11–9	Municipal Stadium, Clev	7-14-87	National	2–0	Oakland Coliseum, Oak
7-12-55	National	6–5	County Stadium, Mil	7-12-88	American	2–1	Riverfront Stadium, Cin
7-10-56	National	7–3	Griffith Stadium, Wash	7-11-89	American	5–3	Anaheim Stadium, Cal
7-9-57	American	6–5	Busch Stadium, StL	7-10-90	American	2–0	Wrigley Field, Chi
7-8-58	American	4–3	Memorial Stadium, Balt	7-9-91	American	4–2	SkyDome, Tor
7-7-59	National	5–4	Forbes Field, Pitt	7-14-92	American	13–6	Jack Murphy Stadium, SD
8-3-59	American	5–3	Memorial Coliseum, LA	7-13-93	American	9–3	Camden Yards, Balt
7-11-60	National	5–3	Municipal Stadium, KC	7-12-94	National	8–7	Three Rivers Stadium, Pitt
7-13-60	National	6–0	Yankee Stadium, NY	7-11-95	National	3–2	Ballpark in Arlington, Tex
7-11-61	National	5–4	Candlestick Park, SF	7-9-96	National	6–0	Veterans Stadium, Phi
7-31-61	Tie*	1–1	Fenway Park, Bos	7-8-97	American	3–1	Jacobs Field, Cle
7-10-62	National	3–1	D.C. Stadium, Wash	7-7-98	American	13–8	Coors Field, Col
7-30-62	American	9–4	Wrigley Field, Chi	7-13-99	American	4–1	Fenway Park, Bos
7-9-63	National	5–3	Municipal Stadium, Clev	7-11-00	American	6–3	Turner Field, Atl
7-7-64	National	7–4	Shea Stadium, NY	7-10-01	American	4–1	Safeco Field, Sea
7-13-65	National	6–5	Metro. Stadium, Minn	7-9-02	Tie (11 inn)	7–7	Miller Park, Mil

*Game called because of rain after nine innings.

Results (Cont.)

Date	Winner	Score	Site	Date	Winner	Score	Site
7-15-03	American	7–6	Comiskey Park, Chi	7-15-08	American	4–3	Yankee Stadium, NY
7-13-04	American	9–4	Minute Maid Park, Hou	7-14-09	American	4–3	Busch Stadium, StL
7-12-05	American	7–5	Comerica Park, Det	7-13-10	National	3–1	Angel Stadium, LA
7-11-06	American	3–2	PNC Park, Pitt	7-12-11	National	5–1	Chase Field, Ari
7-10-07	American	5–4	AT&T Park, SF	7-12-12	National	8–0	Kauffman Stadium, KC

Most Valuable Players

1962	Maury Wills, LA	NL	1978	Steve Garvey, LA	NL	1996	Mike Piazza, LA	NL
	Leon Wagner, LA	AL	1979	Dave Parker, Pitt	NL	1997	Sandy Alomar, Clev	AL
1963	Willie Mays, SF	NL	1980	Ken Griffey, Cin	NL	1998	Roberto Alomar, Balt	AL
1964	Johnny Callison, Phi	NL	1981	Gary Carter, Mtl	NL	1999	Pedro Martinez, Bos	AL
1965	Juan Marichal, SF	NL	1982	Dave Concepcion, Cin	NL	2000	Derek Jeter, NY	AL
1966	Brooks Robinson, Balt	AL	1983	Fred Lynn, Calif	AL	2001	Cal Ripken Jr., Balt	AL
1967	Tony Perez, Cin	NL	1984	Gary Carter, Mtl	NL	2002	None selected	
1968	Willie Mays, SF	NL	1985	LaMarr Hoyt, SD	NL	2003	Garret Anderson, Ana	AL
1969	Willie McCovey, SF	NL	1986	Roger Clemens, Bos	AL	2004	Alfonso Soriano, Tex	AL
1970	Carl Yastrzemski, Bos	AL	1987	Tim Raines, Mtl	NL	2005	Miguel Tejada, Balt	AL
1971	Frank Robinson, Balt	AL	1988	Terry Steinbach, Oak	AL	2006	Michael Young, Tex	AL
1972	Joe Morgan, Cin	NL	1989	Bo Jackson, KC	AL	2007	Ichiro Suzuki, Sea	AL
1973	Bobby Bonds, SF	NL	1990	Julio Franco, Tex	AL	2008	J.D. Drew, Bos	AL
1974	Steve Garvey, LA	NL	1991	Cal Ripken Jr., Balt	AL	2009	Carl Crawford, TB	AL
1975	Bill Madlock, Chi	NL	1992	Ken Griffey Jr., Sea	AL	2010	Brian McCann, Atl	NL
	Jon Matlack, NY	NL	1993	Kirby Puckett, Minn	AL	2011	Prince Fielder, Mil	NL
1976	George Foster, Cin	NL	1994	Fred McGriff, Atl	NL	2012	Melky Cabrera, SF	NL
1977	Don Sutton, LA	NL	1995	Jeff Conine, Fla	NL			

The Regular Season

Most Valuable Players
NATIONAL LEAGUE

Year	Name and Team	Position	Noteworthy
1911	Wildfire Schulte, Chi	Outfield	21 HR†, 121 RBI†, .300
1912	*Larry Doyle, NY	Second base	10 HR, 90 RBI, .330
1913	Jake Daubert, Bklyn	First base	52 RBI, .350†
1914	*Johnny Evers, Bos	Second base	FA .976†, .279
1915–23	No selection		
1924	Dazzy Vance, Bklyn	Pitcher	28†–6, 2.16 ERA†, 262 K†
1925	Rogers Hornsby, StL	Second base, Manager	39 HR†, 143 RBI†, .403†
1926	*Bob O'Farrell, StL	Catcher	7 HR, 68 RBI, .293
1927	*Paul Waner, Pitt	Outfield	237 hits†, 131 RBI†, .380†
1928	*Jim Bottomley, StL	First base	31 HR†, 136 RBI†, .325
1929	*Rogers Hornsby, Chi	Second base	39 HR, 149 RBI, 156 runs†, .380
1930	No selection		
1931	*Frankie Frisch, StL	Second base	4 HR, 82 RBI, 28 SB†, .311
1932	Chuck Klein, Phi	Outfield	38 HR†, 137 RBI, 226 hits†, .348
1933	*Carl Hubbell, NY	Pitcher	23†–12, 1.66 ERA†, 10 SO†
1934	*Dizzy Dean, StL	Pitcher	30†–7, 2.66 ERA, 195 K†
1935	*Gabby Hartnett, Chi	Catcher	13 HR, 91 RBI, .344
1936	*Carl Hubbell, NY	Pitcher	26†–6, 2.31 ERA†
1937	Joe Medwick, StL	Outfield	31 HR‡, 154 RBI†, 111 runs†, .374†
1938	Ernie Lombardi, Cin	Catcher	19 HR, 95 RBI, .342†
1939	*Bucky Walters, Cin	Pitcher	27†–11, 2.29 ERA†, 137 K‡
1940	*Frank McCormick, Cin	First base	19 HR, 127 RBI, 191 hits†, .309
1941	*Dolph Camilli, Bklyn	First base	34 HR†, 120 RBI†, .285
1942	*Mort Cooper, StL	Pitcher	22†–7, 1.78 ERA†, 10 SO†
1943	*Stan Musial, StL	Outfield	13 HR, 81 RBI, 220 hits†, .357†
1944	*Marty Marion, StL	Shortstop	FA .972†, 63 RBI
1945	*Phil Cavarretta, Chi	First base	6 HR, 97 RBI, .355†
1946	*Stan Musial, StL	First base, Outfield	103 RBI, 124 runs†, 228 hits†, .365†
1947	Bob Elliott, Bos	Third base	22 HR, 113 RBI, .317
1948	Stan Musial, StL	Outfield	39 HR, 131 RBI†, .376†
1949	*Jackie Robinson, Bklyn	Second base	16 HR, 124 RBI, 37 SB†, .342†
1950	*Jim Konstanty, Phi	Pitcher	16–7, 22 saves†, 2.66 ERA
1951	Roy Campanella, Bklyn	Catcher	33 HR, 108 RBI, .325
1952	Hank Sauer, Chi	Outfield	37 HR‡, 121 RBI†, .270
1953	*Roy Campanella, Bklyn	Catcher	41 HR, 142 RBI†, .312

*Played for pennant or, after 1968, division winner. †Led league. ‡Tied for league lead.

Most Valuable Players *(Cont.)*
NATIONAL LEAGUE *(Cont.)*

Year	Name and Team	Position	Noteworthy
1954	*Willie Mays, NY	Outfield	41 HR, 110 RBI, 13 3B†, .345†
1955	*Roy Campanella, Bklyn	Catcher	32 HR, 107 RBI, .318
1956	*Don Newcombe, Bklyn	Pitcher	27†–7, 3.06 ERA
1957	*Hank Aaron, Mil	Outfield	44 HR†, 132 RBI†, .322
1958	Ernie Banks, Chi	Shortstop	47 HR†, 129 RBI†, .313
1959	Ernie Banks, Chi	Shortstop	45 HR, 143 RBI†, .304
1960	*Dick Groat, Pitt	Shortstop	2 HR, 50 RBI, .325†
1961	*Frank Robinson, Cin	Outfield	37 HR, 124 RBI, .323
1962	Maury Wills, LA	Shortstop	104 SB†, 208 hits, .299, GG
1963	*Sandy Koufax, LA	Pitcher	25†–5, 1.88 ERA†, 306 K†
1964	*Ken Boyer, StL	Third Base	24 HR, 119 RBI†, .295
1965	Willie Mays, SF	Outfield	52 HR†, 112 RBI, .317, GG
1966	Roberto Clemente, Pitt	Outfield	29 HR, 119 RBI, 202 hits, .317, GG
1967	*Orlando Cepeda, StL	First base	25 HR, 111 RBI†, .325
1968	*Bob Gibson, StL	Pitcher	22–9, 1.12 ERA†, 268 K†, 13 SO†, GG
1969	Willie McCovey, SF	First base	45 HR†, 126 RBI†, .320
1970	*Johnny Bench, Cin	Catcher	45 HR†, 148 RBI†, .293, GG
1971	Joe Torre, StL	Third base	24 HR, 137 RBI†, .363†
1972	*Johnny Bench, Cin	Catcher	40 HR†, 125 RBI†, .270, GG
1973	*Pete Rose, Cin	Outfield	5 HR, 64 RBI, .338†, 230 hits†
1974	*Steve Garvey, LA	First base	21 HR, 111 RBI, 200 hits, .312, GG
1975	*Joe Morgan, Cin	Second base	17 HR, 94 RBI, 67 SB, .327, GG
1976	*Joe Morgan, Cin	Second base	27 HR, 111 RBI, 60 SB, .320, GG
1977	George Foster, Cin	Outfield	52 HR†, 149 RBI†, .320
1978	Dave Parker, Pitt	Outfield	30 HR, 117 RBI, .334†, GG
1979	Keith Hernandez, StL	First base	11 HR, 105 RBI, 210 hits, .344†, GG
	*Willie Stargell, Pitt	First base	32 HR, 82 RBI, .281
1980	*Mike Schmidt, Phi	Third base	48 HR†, 121 RBI†, .286, GG
1981	Mike Schmidt, Phi	Third base	31 HR†, 91 RBI†, 78 runs†, .316, GG
1982	*Dale Murphy, Atl	Outfield	36 HR, 109 RBI‡, .281, GG
1983	Dale Murphy, Atl	Outfield	36 HR, 121 RBI†, .302, GG
1984	*Ryne Sandberg, Chi	Second base	19 HR, 84 RBI, 114 runs†, .314, GG
1985	*Willie McGee, StL	Outfield	10 HR, 82 RBI, 18 3B†, .353†, GG
1986	Mike Schmidt, Phi	Third base	37 HR†, 119 RBI†, .290, GG
1987	Andre Dawson, Chi	Outfield	49 HR†, 137 RBI†, .287, GG
1988	*Kirk Gibson, LA	Outfield	25 HR, 76 RBI, 106 runs, .290
1989	*Kevin Mitchell, SF	Outfield	47 HR†, 125 RBI†, .291
1990	*Barry Bonds, Pitt	Outfield	33 HR, 114 RBI, .301
1991	*Terry Pendleton, Atl	Third base	23 HR, 86 RBI, .319†
1992	Barry Bonds, Pitt	Outfield	34 HR, 103 RBI, .311
1993	Barry Bonds, SF	Outfield	46 HR†, 123 RBI†, .336
1994	Jeff Bagwell, Hou	First base	39 HR, 116 RBI†, .368
1995	*Barry Larkin, Cin	Shortstop	15 HR, 66 RBI, 51 SB, .319
1996	*Ken Caminiti, SD	Third base	40 HR, 130 RBI, .326
1997	Larry Walker, Col	Outfield	49 HR†, 130 RBI, .452 OBA†, .366, GG
1998	Sammy Sosa, Chi	Outfield	66 HR, 158 RBI†, 134 runs†, 416 TB†, .308
1999	*Chipper Jones, Atl	Third Base	45 HR, 110 RBI, 116 runs, .319
2000	*Jeff Kent, SF	Second Base	33 HR, 125 RBI, 114 runs, .334
2001	Barry Bonds, SF	Outfield	73 HR†, 137 RBI, 177 BB†, .328, .863 SLG†
2002	*Barry Bonds, SF	Outfield	46 HR, 110 RBI, .582 OBP, 198 BB† .370
2003	*Barry Bonds, SF	Outfield	45 HR, .341, .529 OBP†, .749 SLG†
2004	Barry Bonds, SF	Outfield	45 HR, 101 RBI, .609 OBP, .812 SLG
2005	*Albert Pujols, StL	First Base	41 HR, 117 RBI, .330, .430 OBP†, .609 SLG†
2006	Ryan Howard, Phi	First Base	58 HR†, 149 RBI†, .313, .425 OBP, .659 SLG
2007	*Jimmy Rollins, Phi	Shortstop	30 HR, 94 RBI, .296, 139 runs†, 41 SB, GG
2008	Albert Pujols, StL	First Base	37 HR, 116 RBI, 100 runs, .357, .653 SLG†
2009	*Albert Pujols, StL	First Base	47 HR†, 135 RBI, 124 runs†, .327, .658 SLG†
2010	*Joey Votto, Cin	First Base	37 HR, 113 RBI, 106 runs, .324, .600 SLG†
2011	*Ryan Braun, Mil	Outfield	33 HR, 111 RBI, 109 runs, .332, .597 SLG†

*Played for pennant or, after 1968, division winner. †Led league. ‡Tied for league lead. Notes: 2B=doubles; 3B=triples; FA=fielding average; GG=won Gold Glove, award begun in 1957; K=strikeouts; O=shutouts; SB=stolen bases; TB=total bases.

Most Valuable Players (Cont.)

AMERICAN LEAGUE

Year	Name and Team	Position	Noteworthy
1911	Ty Cobb, Det	Outfield	8 HR, 144 RBI†, 24 3B†, .420†
1912	*Tris Speaker, Bos	Outfield	10 HR‡, 98 RBI, 53 2B†, .383
1913	Walter Johnson, Wash	Pitcher	36†–7, 1.09 ERA†, 11 SO†, 243 K†
1914	*Eddie Collins, Phi	Second base	2 HR, 85 RBI, 122 runs†, .344
1915–21	No selection		
1922	George Sisler, StL	First base	8 HR, 105 RBI, 246 hits†, .420†
1923	*Babe Ruth, NY	Outfield	41 HR†, 131 RBI†, .393
1924	*Walter Johnson, Wash	Pitcher	23†–7, 2.72 ERA†, 158 K†
1925	*Roger Peckinpaugh, Wash	Shortstop	4 HR, 64 RBI, .294
1926	George Burns, Clev	First base	114 RBI, 216 hits‡, 64 2B†, .358
1927	*Lou Gehrig, NY	First base	47 HR, 175 RBI†, 52 2B†, .373
1928	Mickey Cochrane, Phi	Catcher	10 HR, 57 RBI, .293
1929	No selection		
1930	No selection		
1931	*Lefty Grove, Phi	Pitcher	31†–4, 2.06 ERA†, 175 K†
1932	Jimmie Foxx, Phi	First base	58 HR†, 169 RBI†, 151 runs†, .364
1933	Jimmie Foxx, Phi	First base	48 HR†, 163 RBI†, .356†
1934	*Mickey Cochrane, Det	Catcher	2 HR, 76 RBI, .320
1935	*Hank Greenberg, Det	First base	36 HR†, 170 RBI†, 203 hits, .328
1936	*Lou Gehrig, NY	First base	49 HR‡, 152 RBI, 167 runs†, .354
1937	Charlie Gehringer, Det	Second base	14 HR, 96 RBI, 133 runs, .371†
1938	Jimmie Foxx, Phi	First base	50 HR, 175 RBI†, .349†
1939	*Joe DiMaggio, NY	Outfield	30 HR, 126 RBI, .381†
1940	*Hank Greenberg, Det	Outfield	41 HR†, 150 RBI†, 50 2B†, .340
1941	*Joe DiMaggio, NY	Outfield	30 HR, 125 RBI†, .357
1942	*Joe Gordon, NY	Second base	18 HR, 103 RBI, .322
1943	*Spud Chandler, NY	Pitcher	20†–4, 1.64 ERA†, 5 SO‡
1944	Hal Newhouser, Det	Pitcher	29†–9, 2.22 ERA†, 187 K†
1945	Hal Newhouser, Det	Pitcher	25†–9, 1.81 ERA†, 8 SO†, 212 K†
1946	*Ted Williams, Bos	Outfield	38 HR, 123 RBI, 142 runs†, .342
1947	*Joe DiMaggio, NY	Outfield	20 HR, 97 RBI, .315
1948	*Lou Boudreau, Clev	Shortstop	18 HR, 106 RBI, .355
1949	Ted Williams, Bos	Outfield	43 HR‡, 159 RBI‡, 150 runs†, .343
1950	*Phil Rizzuto, NY	Shortstop	125 runs, 200 hits, .324
1951	*Yogi Berra, NY	Catcher	27 HR, 88 RBI, .294
1952	Bobby Shantz, Phi	Pitcher	24†–7, 2.48 ERA
1953	Al Rosen, Clev	Third base	43 HR†, 145 RBI†, 115 runs†, .336
1954	Yogi Berra, NY	Catcher	22 HR, 125 RBI, .307
1955	*Yogi Berra, NY	Catcher	27 HR, 108 RBI, .272
1956	*Mickey Mantle, NY	Outfield	52 HR†, 130 RBI†, 132 runs†, .353†
1957	*Mickey Mantle, NY	Outfield	34 HR, 94 RBI, 121 runs†, .365
1958	Jackie Jensen, Bos	Outfield	35 HR, 122 RBI†, .286
1959	*Nellie Fox, Chi	Second base	2 HR, 70 RBI, .306, GG
1960	*Roger Maris, NY	Outfield	39 HR, 112 RBI†, .283, GG
1961	*Roger Maris, NY	Outfield	61 HR†, 142 RBI†, .269
1962	*Mickey Mantle, NY	Outfield	30 HR, 89 RBI, .321, GG
1963	*Elston Howard, NY	Catcher	28 HR, 85 RBI, .287, GG
1964	Brooks Robinson, Balt	Third base	28 HR, 118 RBI†, .317, GG
1965	*Zoilo Versalles, Minn	Shortstop	126 runs†, 45 2B†, 12 3B‡, GG
1966	*Frank Robinson, Balt	Outfield	49 HR†, 122 RBI†, 122 runs†, .316†
1967	*Carl Yastrzemski, Bos	Outfield	44 HR‡, 121 RBI†, 112 runs†, .326†, GG
1968	*Denny McLain, Det	Pitcher	31†–6, 1.96 ERA, 280 K
1969	*Harmon Killebrew, Minn	Third base, First base	49 HR†, 140 RBI†, .276
1970	*Boog Powell, Balt	First base	35 HR, 114 RBI, .297
1971	Vida Blue, Oak	Pitcher	24–8, 1.82 ERA†, 8 SO†, 301 K
1972	Dick Allen, Chi	First base	37 HR†, 113 RBI†, .308
1973	*Reggie Jackson, Oak	Outfield	32 HR†, 117 RBI†, 99 runs†, .293
1974	Jeff Burroughs, Tex	Outfield	25 HR, 118 RBI†, .301
1975	*Fred Lynn, Bos	Outfield	21 HR, 105 RBI, 103 runs†, .331, GG
1976	*Thurman Munson, NY	Catcher	17 HR, 105 RBI, .302
1977	Rod Carew, Minn	First base	100 RBI, 128 runs†, 239 hits†, .388†
1978	Jim Rice, Bos	Outfield, DH	46 HR†, 139 RBI†, 213 hits†, .315
1979	*Don Baylor, Calif	Outfield, DH	36 HR, 139 RBI†, 120 runs†, .296
1980	*George Brett, KC	Third base	24 HR, 118 RBI, .390†
1981	*Rollie Fingers, Mil	Pitcher	6–3, 28 saves†, 1.04 ERA
1982	*Robin Yount, Mil	Shortstop	29 HR, 114 RBI, 210 hits†, .331, GG
1983	*Cal Ripken Jr., Balt	Shortstop	27 HR, 102 RBI, 121 runs†, 211 hits†, .318

Most Valuable Players *(Cont.)*
AMERICAN LEAGUE *(Cont.)*

Year	Name and Team	Position	Noteworthy
1984	*Willie Hernandez, Det	Pitcher	9–3, 32 saves, 1.92 ERA
1985	Don Mattingly, NY	First base	35 HR, 145 RBI†, 48 2B†, .324, GG
1986	*Roger Clemens, Bos	Pitcher	24†–4, 2.48 ERA†, 238 K
1987	George Bell, Tor	Outfield	47 HR, 134 RBI†, .308
1988	*Jose Canseco, Oak	Outfield	42 HR†, 124 RBI†, 40 SB, .307
1989	Robin Yount, Mil	Outfield	21 HR, 103 RBI, 101 runs, .318
1990	*Rickey Henderson, Oak	Outfield	28 HR, 119 runs†, 65 SB†, .325
1991	Cal Ripken Jr., Balt	Shortstop	34 HR, 114 RBI, .323
1992	Dennis Eckersley, Oak	Pitcher	7–1, 1.91 ERA, 51 saves
1993	Frank Thomas, Chi	First base	41 HR, 128 RBI, .317
1994	Frank Thomas, Chi	First base	38 HR, 101 RBI, .353
1995	*Mo Vaughn, Bos	First base	39 HR, 126 RBI, .300
1996	*Juan Gonzalez, Tex	Outfield	47 HR, 144 RBI, .314
1997	*Ken Griffey Jr., Sea	Outfield	56 HR†, 125 runs†, 393 TB†, 147 RBI†, .304
1998	*Juan Gonzalez, Tex	Outfield	45 HR, 157 RBI†, 50 2B†, .318
1999	*Ivan Rodriguez, Tex	Catcher	35 HR, 113 RBI, 116 runs, .332, GG
2000	*Jason Giambi, Oak	First Base	43 HR, 137 RBI, .333
2001	*Ichiro Suzuki, Sea	Outfield	.350†, 242 hits†, 127 runs, 56 SB†, GG
2002	*Miguel Tejada, Oak	Shortstop	34 HR, 131 RBI, .308
2003	Alex Rodriguez, Tex	Shortstop	47 HR†, 118 RBI, .600 SLG†, GG
2004	*Vladimir Guerrero, Ana	Outfield	39 HR, 126 RBI, .598 SLG
2005	*Alex Rodriguez, NY	Third Base	48 HR†, 130 RBI, .610 SLG†
2006	*Justin Morneau, Min	First Base	30 HR, 130 RBI, .321, 190 hits
2007	Alex Rodriguez, NY	Third Base	54 HR, 156 RBI, .314, 183 hits, 24 SB
2008	Dustin Pedroia, Bos	Second Base	17 HR, 118 runs, 213 hits, .326, 20 SB, GG
2009	*Joe Mauer, Min	Catcher	28 HR, 94 runs, 96 RBIs, 191 hits, .365, GG
2010	*Josh Hamilton, Tex	Outfield	32 HR, 100 RBI, 95 runs, .359†, .633 SLG†
2011	*Justin Verlander, Detroit	Pitcher	24 W†, 2.40 ERA†, 250 SO†, 251.0 IP†

*Played for pennant or, after 1968, division winner. †Led league. ‡Tied for league lead. Notes: 2B=doubles; 3B=triples; FA=fielding average; GG=won Gold Glove, award begun in 1957; K=strikeouts; O=shutouts; SB=stolen bases; TB=total bases.

Rookies of the Year

NATIONAL LEAGUE		AMERICAN LEAGUE	
1947*	Jackie Robinson, Bklyn (1B)	1949	Roy Sievers, StL (OF)
1948*	Alvin Dark, Bos (SS)	1950	Walt Dropo, Bos (1B)
1949	Don Newcombe, Bklyn (P)	1951	Gil McDougald, NY (3B)
1950	Sam Jethroe, Bos (OF)	1952	Harry Byrd, Phi (P)
1951	Willie Mays, NY (OF)	1953	Harvey Kuenn, Det (SS)
1952	Joe Black, Bklyn (P)	1954	Bob Grim, NY (P)
1953	Junior Gilliam, Bklyn (2B)	1955	Herb Score, Clev (P)
1954	Wally Moon, StL (OF)	1956	Luis Aparicio, Chi (SS)
1955	Bill Virdon, StL (OF)	1957	Tony Kubek, NY (OF, SS)
1956	Frank Robinson, Cin (OF)	1958	Albie Pearson, Wash (OF)
1957	Jack Sanford, Phi (P)	1959	Bob Allison, Wash (OF)
1958	Orlando Cepeda, SF (1B)	1960	Ron Hansen, Balt (SS)
1959	Willie McCovey, SF (1B)	1961	Don Schwall, Bos (P)
1960	Frank Howard, LA (OF)	1962	Tom Tresh, NY (SS)
1961	Billy Williams, Chi (OF)	1963	Gary Peters, Chi (P)
1962	Ken Hubbs, Chi (2B)	1964	Tony Oliva, Minn (OF)
1963	Pete Rose, Cin (2B)	1965	Curt Blefary, Balt (OF)
1964	Dick Allen, Phi (3B)	1966	Tommie Agee, Chi (OF)
1965	Jim Lefebvre, LA (2B)	1967	Rod Carew, Minn (2B)
1966	Tommy Helms, Cin (2B)	1968	Stan Bahnsen, NY (P)
1967	Tom Seaver, NY (P)	1969	Lou Piniella, KC (OF)
1968	Johnny Bench, Cin (C)	1970	Thurman Munson, NY (C)
1969	Ted Sizemore, LA (2B)	1971	Chris Chambliss, Clev (1B)
1970	Carl Morton, Mtl (P)	1972	Carlton Fisk, Bos (C)
1971	Earl Williams, Atl (C)	1973	Al Bumbry, Balt (OF)
1972	Jon Matlack, NY (P)	1974	Mike Hargrove, Tex (1B)
1973	Gary Matthews, SF (OF)	1975	Fred Lynn, Bos (OF)
1974	Bake McBride, StL (OF)	1976	Mark Fidrych, Det (P)
1975	John Montefusco, SF (P)	1977	Eddie Murray, Balt (DH)
1976	Pat Zachry, Cin (P)	1978	Lou Whitaker, Det (2B)
	Butch Metzger, SD (P)	1979	Alfredo Griffin, Tor (SS)
1977	Andre Dawson, Mtl (OF)		John Castino, Minn (3B)
1978	Bob Horner, Atl (3B)	1980	Joe Charboneau, Clev (OF)

*Just one selection for both leagues.

Rookies of the Year (Cont.)

NATIONAL LEAGUE (Cont.)		AMERICAN LEAGUE (Cont.)	
1979	Rick Sutcliffe, LA (P)	1981	Dave Righetti, NY (P)
1980	Steve Howe, LA (P)	1982	Cal Ripken Jr., Balt (SS)
1981	Fernando Valenzuela, LA (P)	1983	Ron Kittle, Chi (OF)
1982	Steve Sax, LA (2B)	1984	Alvin Davis, Sea (1B)
1983	Darryl Strawberry, NY (OF)	1985	Ozzie Guillen, Chi (SS)
1984	Dwight Gooden, NY (P)	1986	Jose Canseco, Oak (OF)
1985	Vince Coleman, StL (OF)	1987	Mark McGwire, Oak (1B)
1986	Todd Worrell, StL (P)	1988	Walt Weiss, Oak (SS)
1987	Benito Santiago, SD (C)	1989	Gregg Olson, Balt (P)
1988	Chris Sabo, Cin (3B)	1990	Sandy Alomar Jr, Clev (C)
1989	Jerome Walton, Chi (OF)	1991	Chuck Knoblauch, Minn (2B)
1990	David Justice, Atl (OF)	1992	Pat Listach, Mil (SS)
1991	Jeff Bagwell, Hou (3B)	1993	Tim Salmon, Calif (OF)
1992	Eric Karros, LA (1B)	1994	Bob Hamelin, KC (DH)
1993	Mike Piazza, LA (C)	1995	Marty Cordova, Minn (OF)
1994	Raul Mondesi, LA (OF)	1996	Derek Jeter, NY (SS)
1995	Hideo Nomo, LA (P)	1997	Nomar Garciaparra, Bos (SS)
1996	Todd Hollandsworth, LA (OF)	1998	Ben Grieve, Oak (OF)
1997	Scott Rolen, Phi (3B)	1999	Carlos Beltran, KC (OF)
1998	Kerry Wood, Chi (P)	2000	Kazuhiro Sasaki, Sea (P)
1999	Scott Williamson, Cin (P)	2001	Ichiro Suzuki, Sea (OF)
2000	Rafael Furcal, Atl (SS)	2002	Eric Hinske, Tor (3B)
2001	Albert Pujols, StL (OF)	2003	Angel Berroa, KC (SS)
2002	Jason Jennings, Col (P)	2004	Bobby Crosby, Oak (SS)
2003	Dontrelle Willis, Fla (P)	2005	Huston Street, Oak (P)
2004	Jason Bay, Pit (OF)	2006	Justin Verlander, Det (P)
2005	Ryan Howard, Phi (1B)	2007	Dustin Pedroia, Bos (2B)
2006	Hanley Ramirez, Fla (SS)	2008	Evan Longoria, TB (3B)
2007	Ryan Braun, Mil (OF)	2009	Andrew Bailey, Oak (P)
2008	Geovany Soto, Chi (C)	2010	Neftali Feliz, Tex (P)
2009	Chris Coghlan, Fla (OF)	2011	Jeremy Hellickson, TB (P)
2010	Buster Posey, SF (C)		
2011	Craig Kimbrel, Atl (P)		

2011 Gold Glove winners

NATIONAL LEAGUE		AMERICAN LEAGUE	
C	Yadier Molina, StL (4)	C	Matt Wieters, Bal
P	Clayton Kershaw, LA	P	Mark Buehrle, Chi (3)
1B	Joey Votto, Cin	1B	Adrian Gonzalez
2B	Brandon Phillips, Cin (3)	2B	Dustin Pedroia, Bos (2)
SS	Troy Tulowitzki, Col (2)	SS	Erick Aybar, LA
3B	Placido Polanco, Phi	3B	Adrian Beltre, Tex (3)
OF	Gerardo Parra, Ariz	OF	Alex Gordon, KC
OF	Matt Kemp, LA	OF	Jacoby Ellsbury, Bos
OF	Andre Ethier, LA	OF	Nick Markakis, Bal

Note: Number in parentheses indicates career totals.

2011 Silver Slugger winners

NATIONAL LEAGUE		AMERICAN LEAGUE	
C	Brian McCann, Atl (5)	C	Alex Avila, Det
P	Daniel Hudson, Ari	DH	David Ortiz, Bos (5)
1B	Prince Fielder, Mil (2)	1B	Adrian Gonzalez, Bos
2B	Brandon Phillips, Cin	2B	Robinson Cano, NY (3)
SS	Troy Tulowitzki, Col (2)	SS	Asdrubal Cabrera, Cle
3B	Aramis Ramirez, Chi	3B	Adrian Beltre, Tex (3)
OF	Matt Kemp, LA (2)	OF	Curtis Granderson, NY
OF	Ryan Braun, Mil (4)	OF	Jose Bautista, Tor (2)
OF	Justin Upton, Ari	OF	Jacoby Ellsbury, Bos

Note: Number in parentheses indicates career totals.

Cy Young Award

Year		W–L	Sv	ERA	Year		W–L	Sv	ERA
1956	....*Don Newcombe, Bklyn (NL)	27–7	0	3.06	1962	....Don Drysdale, LA (NL)	25–9	1	2.83
1957	....Warren Spahn, Mil (NL)	21–11	3	2.69	1963	....*Sandy Koufax, LA (NL)	25–5	0	1.88
1958	....Bob Turley, NY (AL)	21–7	1	2.97	1964	....Dean Chance, LA (AL)	20–9	4	1.65
1959	....Early Wynn, Chi (AL)	22–10	0	3.17	1965	....Sandy Koufax, LA (NL)	26–8	2	2.04
1960	....Vernon Law, Pitt (NL)	20–9	0	3.08	1966	....Sandy Koufax, LA (NL)	27–9	0	1.73
1961	....Whitey Ford, NY (AL)	25–4	0	3.21					

NATIONAL LEAGUE				AMERICAN LEAGUE			

Year		W–L	Sv	ERA	Year		W–L	Sv	ERA
1967	.....Mike McCormick, SF	22–10	0	2.85	1967	.....Jim Lonborg, Bos	22–9	0	3.16
1968	.....*Bob Gibson, StL	22–9	0	1.12	1968	.....*Denny McLain, Det	31–6	0	1.96
1969	.....Tom Seaver, NY	25–7	0	2.21	1969	.....Denny McLain, Det	24–9	0	2.80
1970	.....Bob Gibson, StL	23–7	0	3.12		Mike Cuellar, Balt	23–11	0	2.38
1971	.....Ferguson Jenkins, Chi	24–13	0	2.77	1970	.....Jim Perry, Minn	24–12	0	3.03
1972	.....Steve Carlton, Phi	27–10	0	1.97	1971	.....*Vida Blue, Oak	24–8	0	1.82
1973	.....Tom Seaver, NY	19–10	0	2.08	1972	.....Gaylord Perry, Clev	24–16	1	1.92
1974	.....Mike Marshall, LA	15–12	21	2.42	1973	.....Jim Palmer, Balt	22–9	1	2.40
1975	.....Tom Seaver, NY	22–9	0	2.38	1974	.....Catfish Hunter, Oak	25–12	0	2.49
1976	.....Randy Jones, SD	22–14	0	2.74	1975	.....Jim Palmer, Balt	23–11	1	2.09
1977	.....Steve Carlton, Phi	23–10	0	2.64	1976	.....Jim Palmer, Balt	22–13	0	2.51
1978	.....Gaylord Perry, SD	21–6	0	2.72	1977	.....Sparky Lyle, NY	13–5	26	2.17
1979	.....Bruce Sutter, Chi	6–6	37	2.23	1978	.....Ron Guidry, NY	25–3	0	1.74
1980	.....Steve Carlton, Phi	24–9	0	2.34	1979	.....Mike Flanagan, Balt	23–9	0	3.08
1981	.....Fernando Valenzuela, LA	13–7	0	2.48	1980	.....Steve Stone, Balt	25–7	0	3.23
1982	.....Steve Carlton, Phi	23–11	0	3.10	1981	.....*Rollie Fingers, Mil	6–3	28	1.04
1983	.....John Denny, Phi	19–6	0	2.37	1982	.....Pete Vuckovich, Mil	18–6	0	3.34
1984	.....†Rick Sutcliffe, Chi	16–1	0	2.69	1983	.....LaMarr Hoyt, Chi	24–10	0	3.66
1985	.....Dwight Gooden, NY	24–4	0	1.53	1984	.....*Willie Hernandez, Det	9–3	32	1.92
1986	.....Mike Scott, Hou	18–10	0	2.22	1985	.....Bret Saberhagen, KC	20–6	0	2.87
1987	.....Steve Bedrosian, Phi	5–3	40	2.83	1986	.....*Roger Clemens, Bos	24–4	0	2.48
1988	.....Orel Hershiser, LA	23–8	1	2.26	1987	.....Roger Clemens, Bos	20–9	0	2.97
1989	.....Mark Davis, SD	4–3	44	1.85	1988	.....Frank Viola, Minn	24–7	0	2.64
1990	.....Doug Drabek, Pitt	22–6	0	2.76	1989	.....Bret Saberhagen, KC	23–6	0	2.16
1991	.....Tom Glavine, Atl	20–11	0	2.55	1990	.....Bob Welch, Oak	27–6	0	2.95
1992	.....Greg Maddux, Chi	20–11	0	2.18	1991	.....Roger Clemens, Bos	18–10	0	2.62
1993	.....Greg Maddux, Atl	20–10	0	2.36	1992	.....*Dennis Eckersley, Oak	7–1	51	1.91
1994	.....Greg Maddux, Atl	16–6	0	1.56	1993	.....Jack McDowell, Chi	22–10	0	3.37
1995	.....Greg Maddux, Atl	19–2	0	1.63	1994	.....David Cone, KC	16–4	0	2.94
1996	.....John Smoltz, Atl	24–8	0	2.94	1995	.....Randy Johnson, Sea	18–2	0	2.48
1997	.....Pedro Martinez, Mtl	17–8	0	1.90	1996	.....Pat Hentgen, Tor	20–10	0	3.22
1998	.....Tom Glavine, Atl	20–6	0	2.47	1997	.....Roger Clemens, Tor	21–7	0	2.05
1999	.....Randy Johnson, Ari	17–9	0	2.48	1998	.....Roger Clemens, Tor	20–6	0	2.65
2000	.....Randy Johnson, Ari	19–7	0	2.64	1999	.....Pedro Martinez, Bos	23–4	0	1.55
2001	.....Randy Johnson, Ari	21–6	0	2.49	2000	.....Pedro Martinez, Bos	18–6	0	1.74
2002	.....Randy Johnson, Ari	24–5	0	2.32	2001	.....Roger Clemens, NY	20–3	0	3.51
2003	.....Eric Gagne, LA	2–3	55	1.20	2002	.....Barry Zito, Oak	23–5	0	2.75
2004	.....Roger Clemens, Hou	18–4	0	2.98	2003	.....Roy Halladay, Tor	22–7	0	3.25
2005	.....Chris Carpenter, StL	21–5	0	2.83	2004	.....Johan Santana, Min	20–6	0	2.61
2006	.....Brandon Webb, Ari	16–8	0	3.10	2005	.....Bartolo Colon, LA	21–8	0	3.48
2007	.....Jake Peavy, SD	19–6	0	2.54	2006	.....Johan Santana, Min	19–6	0	2.77
2008	.....Tim Lincecum, SF	18–5	0	2.62	2007	.....CC Sabathia, Cle	19–7	0	3.21
2009	.....Tim Lincecum, SF	15–7	0	2.48	2008	.....Cliff Lee, Cle	22–3	0	2.54
2010	.....Roy Halladay, Phi	21–10	0	2.44	2009	.....Zack Greinke, KC	16–8	0	2.16
2011	.....Clayton Kershaw, LA	21–5	0	2.28	2010	.....Felix Hernandez, Sea	13–12	0	2.27
					2011	.....*Justin Verlander, Det	24–5	0	2.40

*Won the MVP and Cy Young awards in the same season.
†NL games only. Sutcliffe pitched 15 games with Cleveland before being traded to the Cubs.

Career Individual Batting

GAMES

Pete Rose	3562
Carl Yastrzemski	3308
Hank Aaron	3298
Rickey Henderson	3081
Ty Cobb	3034
Eddie Murray	3026
Stan Musial	3026
Cal Ripken Jr.	3001
Willie Mays	2992
Barry Bonds	2986
Dave Winfield	2973
*Omar Vizquel	2968
Rusty Staub	2951
Brooks Robinson	2896
Robin Yount	2856
Craig Biggio	2850
Al Kaline	2834
Rafael Palmeiro	2831
Harold Baines	2830
Eddie Collins	2826
Reggie Jackson	2820
Frank Robinson	2808
Honus Wagner	2792

AT BATS

Pete Rose	14053
Hank Aaron	12364
Carl Yastrzemski	11988
Cal Ripken Jr.	11551
Ty Cobb	11434
Eddie Murray	11336
Robin Yount	11008
Dave Winfield	11003
Stan Musial	10972
Rickey Henderson	10961
Willie Mays	10881
Craig Biggio	10876
Paul Molitor	10835
Brooks Robinson	10654
*Omar Vizquel	10586
*Derek Jeter	10551
Rafael Palmeiro	10472
Honus Wagner	10430
George Brett	10349

RUNS

Rickey Henderson	2295
Ty Cobb	2246
Barry Bonds	2227
Hank Aaron	2174
Babe Ruth	2174
Pete Rose	2165
Willie Mays	2062
Cap Anson	1996
Stan Musial	1949
*Alex Rodriguez	1898
Lou Gehrig	1888
Tris Speaker	1882
*Derek Jeter	1868
Mel Ott	1859
Craig Biggio	1834
Frank Robinson	1829
Eddie Collins	1821
Carl Yastrzemski	1816
Ted Williams	1798
Paul Molitor	1782

BATTING AVERAGE (5,000 AB)

Ty Cobb	.367
Rogers Hornsby	.358
Ed Delahanty	.346
Tris Speaker	.345
Billy Hamilton	.344
Ted Williams	.344
Dan Brouthers	.342
Harry Heilmann	.342
Babe Ruth	.342
Willie Keeler	.341
Bill Terry	.341
Lou Gehrig	.340
George Sisler	.340
Jesse Burkett	.338
Tony Gwynn	.338
Nap Lajoie	.338
Al Simmons	.334
Cap Anson	.333
Eddie Collins	.333
Paul Waner	.333
Sam Thompson	.331
Heinie Manush	.330
Wade Boggs	.328
Rod Carew	.328
Honus Wagner	.327

HOME RUNS

Barry Bonds	762
Hank Aaron	755
Babe Ruth	714
Willie Mays	660
*Alex Rodriguez	647
Ken Griffey Jr.	630
*Jim Thome	612
Sammy Sosa	609
Frank Robinson	586
Mark McGwire	583
Harmon Killebrew	573
Rafael Palmeiro	569
Reggie Jackson	563
Manny Ramirez	555
Mike Schmidt	548
Mickey Mantle	536
Jimmie Foxx	534
Willie McCovey	521
Ted Williams	521
Frank Thomas	521
Ernie Banks	512
Eddie Mathews	512
Mel Ott	511
Gary Sheffield	509
Eddie Murray	504
Lou Gehrig	493
Fred McGriff	493
Stan Musial	475
Willie Stargell	475
*Albert Pujols	475

RUNS BATTED IN

Hank Aaron	2297
Babe Ruth	2213
Cap Anson	2076
Barry Bonds	1996
Lou Gehrig	1995
Stan Musial	1951
*Alex Rodriguez	1950
Ty Cobb	1937
Jimmie Foxx	1922
Eddie Murray	1917
Willie Mays	1903
Mel Ott	1860
Carl Yastrzemski	1844
Ted Williams	1839
Ken Griffey Jr.	1836
Rafael Palmeiro	1835
Dave Winfield	1833
Manny Ramirez	1831
Al Simmons	1827
Frank Robinson	1812
Honus Wagner	1732
Frank Thomas	1704
Reggie Jackson	1702
*Jim Thome	1699
Cal Ripken Jr.	1695
Gary Sheffield	1676

HITS

Pete Rose	4256
Ty Cobb	4191
Hank Aaron	3771
Stan Musial	3630
Tris Speaker	3515
Carl Yastrzemski	3419
Cap Anson	3418
Honus Wagner	3415
Paul Molitor	3319
Eddie Collins	3313
*Derek Jeter	3304
Willie Mays	3283
Eddie Murray	3255
Nap Lajoie	3251
Cal Ripken Jr.	3184
George Brett	3154
Paul Waner	3152
Robin Yount	3142
Tony Gwynn	3141
Dave Winfield	3110
Craig Biggio	3060
Rickey Henderson	3055
Rod Carew	3053
Lou Brock	3023
Rafael Palmeiro	3020
Wade Boggs	3010
Al Kaline	3007
Roberto Clemente	3000

* Active in 2012.

Career Individual Batting *(Cont.)*

DOUBLES

Tris Speaker	792
Pete Rose	746
Stan Musial	725
Ty Cobb	724
Craig Biggio	668
George Brett	665
Nap Lajoie	657
Carl Yastrzemski	646
Honus Wagner	640
Hank Aaron	624
Paul Molitor	605
Paul Waner	605
Cal Ripken Jr.	603
Barry Bonds	601
Luis Gonzalez	596
Rafael Palmeiro	585
Robin Yount	583
Cap Anson	581
Wade Boggs	578
Charlie Gehringer	574

TRIPLES

Sam Crawford	309
Ty Cobb	295
Honus Wagner	252
Jake Beckley	243
Roger Connor	233
Tris Speaker	222
Fred Clarke	220
Dan Brouthers	205
Joe Kelley	194
Paul Waner	191
Bid McPhee	188
Eddie Collins	187
Ed Delahanty	185
Sam Rice	184
Jesse Burkett	182
Ed Konetchy	182
Edd Roush	182
Buck Ewing	178
Rabbit Maranville	177
Stan Musial	177

BASES ON BALLS

Barry Bonds	2558
Rickey Henderson	2190
Babe Ruth	2062
Ted Williams	2021
Joe Morgan	1865
Carl Yastrzemski	1845
*Jim Thome	1747
Mickey Mantle	1733
Mel Ott	1708
Frank Thomas	1667
Eddie Yost	1614
Darrell Evans	1605
Stan Musial	1599
Pete Rose	1566
Harmon Killebrew	1559
*Chipper Jones	1512
Lou Gehrig	1508
Mike Schmidt	1507
Eddie Collins	1499
Gary Sheffield	1475
Willie Mays	1464
*Bobby Abreu	1456
Jimmie Foxx	1452

* Active in 2012.

SLUGGING AVERAGE (5,000 AB)

Babe Ruth	.690
Ted Williams	.634
Lou Gehrig	.632
Jimmie Foxx	.609
*Albert Pujols	.608
Barry Bonds	.607
Hank Greenberg	.605
Mark McGwire	.588
Manny Ramirez	.585
Joe Dimaggio	.579
Rogers Hornsby	.577
Larry Walker	.565
Albert Belle	.564
Johnny Mize	.562
*Miguel Cabrera	.561
Juan Gonzalez	.561
*Alex Rodriguez	.560
Stan Musial	.559
Willie Mays	.557
Mickey Mantle	.557

STOLEN BASES

Rickey Henderson	1406
Lou Brock	938
Billy Hamilton	912
Ty Cobb	892
Tim Raines	808
Vince Coleman	752
Eddie Collins	745
Max Carey	738
Honus Wagner	722
Joe Morgan	689
Willie Wilson	668
Bert Campaneris	649
Kenny Lofton	622
Otis Nixon	620
George Davis	616
Tom Brown	615
Dummy Hoy	594
*Juan Pierre	591
Maury Wills	586
George Van Haltren	583

ON-BASE PERCENTAGE (5,000 AB)

Ted Williams	.482
Babe Ruth	.474
Billy Hamilton	.455
Lou Gehrig	.447
Barry Bonds	.444
Rogers Hornsby	.434
Ty Cobb	.433
Jimmie Foxx	.428
Tris Speaker	.428
Eddie Collins	.424
Mickey Mantle	.421
Dan Brouthers	.420
Mickey Cochrane	.419
Frank Thomas	.419
*Todd Helton	.419
Edgar Martinez	.418
Stan Musial	.417
Ed Delahanty	.417
Clarence Childs	.416
Jesse Burkett	.415
Wade Boggs	.415
*Albert Pujols	.414
Mel Ott	.414

TOTAL BASES

Hank Aaron	6856
Stan Musial	6134
Willie Mays	6066
Barry Bonds	5976
Ty Cobb	5859
Babe Ruth	5793
Pete Rose	5752
Carl Yastrzemski	5539
*Alex Rodriguez	5414
Eddie Murray	5397
Rafael Palmeiro	5388
Frank Robinson	5373
Ken Griffey Jr.	5271
Dave Winfield	5221
Cal Ripken Jr.	5168
Tris Speaker	5101
Lou Gehrig	5060
George Brett	5044
Mel Ott	5041
Jimmie Foxx	4956
Ted Williams	4884

STRIKEOUTS

Reggie Jackson	2597
*Jim Thome	2548
Sammy Sosa	2306
*Alex Rodriguez	2032
*Adam Dunn	2031
Andres Galarraga	2003
Jose Canseco	1942
Willie Stargell	1936
Mike Cameron	1901
Mike Schmidt	1883
Fred McGriff	1882
Tony Perez	1867
*Bobby Abreu	1819
Dave Kingman	1816
Manny Ramirez	1813
Ken Griffey Jr.	1779
Bobby Bonds	1757
Craig Biggio	1753
*Andruw Jones	1748
Dale Murphy	1748
Carlos Delgado	1745
Lou Brock	1730
Jim Edmonds	1729
Mickey Mantle	1710

The 30–30 Club (minimum of 30 HR and 30 SB in single season)

Year		HR	SB	Year		HR	SB
1922	Kenny Williams, StL	39	37	1997	Jeff Bagwell, Hou	43	31
1956	Willie Mays, NYG	36	40	1997	Raul Mondesi, LA	30	32
1957	Willie Mays, NYG	35	38	1997	Barry Bonds, SF	40	37
1963	Hank Aaron, Mil	44	31	1998	Alex Rodriguez, Sea	42	46
1969	Bobby Bonds, SF	32	45	1998	Shawn Green, Tor	35	35
1970	Tommy Harper, Mil	31	38	1999	Jeff Bagwell, Hou	42	30
1973	Bobby Bonds, SF	39	43	1999	Raul Mondesi, LA	33	36
1975	Bobby Bonds, NYY	32	30	2000	Preston Wilson, Fla	31	36
1977	Bobby Bonds, Cal	37	41	2001	Vladimir Guerrero, Mtl	34	37
1978	Bobby Bonds, Chi/Tex	31	43	2001	Jose Cruz Jr., Tor	34	32
1983	Dale Murphy, Atl	36	30	2001	Bobby Abreu, Phi	31	36
1987	Joe Carter, Clev	32	31	2002	Alfonso Soriano, NYY	39	41
1987	Eric Davis, Cin	37	50	2002	Vladimir Guerrero, Mtl	39	40
1987	Darryl Strawberry, NYM	39	36	2003	Alfonso Soriano, NYY	38	35
1987	Howard Johnson, NYM	36	32	2004	Carlos Beltran, KC/Hou	38	42
1988	Jose Canseco, Oak	42	40	2004	Bobby Abreu, Phi	30	40
1989	Howard Johnson, NYM	36	41	2005	Alfonso Soriano, Tex	36	30
1990	Ron Gant, Atl	32	33	2006	Alfonso Soriano, Wash	46	41
1990	Barry Bonds, Pitt	33	52	2007	Brandon Phillips, Cin	30	32
1991	Ron Gant, Atl	32	34	2007	Jimmy Rollins, Phi	30	41
1991	Howard Johnson, NYM	38	30	2007	David Wright, NYM	30	34
1992	Barry Bonds, Pitt	34	39	2008	Grady Sizemore, Cle	33	38
1993	Sammy Sosa, ChiC	33	36	2008	Hanley Ramirez, Fla	33	35
1995	Barry Bonds, SF	33	31	2009	Ian Kinsler, Tex	31	31
1995	Sammy Sosa, ChiC	36	34	2011	Matt Kemp, LA	39	40
1996	Barry Bonds, SF	42	40	2011	Ryan Braun, Mil	33	33
1996	Ellis Burks, Col	40	32	2011	Jacoby Ellsbury, Bos	32	39
1996	Barry Larkin, Cin	33	36	2011	Ian Kinsler, Tex	32	30
1996	Dante Bichette, Col	31	31	2012	Mike Trout, LAA	30	49
1997	Larry Walker, Col	49	33	2012	Ryan Braun, Mil	41	30

Career Individual Pitching

GAMES

Jesse Orosco	1251
Mike Stanton	1178
John Franco	1119
Dennis Eckersley	1071
Hoyt Wilhelm	1070
Dan Plesac	1064
Mike Timlin	1058
*Mariano Rivera	1051
Kent Tekulve	1050
Trevor Hoffman	1035
Jose Mesa	1022
Lee Smith	1022
Roberto Hernandez	1010
Mike Jackson	1005
Goose Gossage	1002
Lindy McDaniel	987
Todd Jones	982
David Weathers	964
Rollie Fingers	944
Gene Garber	931
Eddie Guardado	908
Cy Young	906
Arthur Rhodes	900
Sparky Lyle	899
Jim Kaat	898
Tom Gordon	890

INNINGS PITCHED

Cy Young	7356.0
Pud Galvin	6003.1
Walter Johnson	5914.1
Phil Niekro	5404.1
Nolan Ryan	5386.0
Gaylord Perry	5350.1
Don Sutton	5282.1
Warren Spahn	5243.1
Steve Carlton	5217.1
Grover Alexander	5190.0
Kid Nichols	5056.1
Tim Keefe	5049.2
Greg Maddux	5008.1
Bert Blyleven	4970.0
Bobby Mathews	4956.0
Roger Clemens	4916.2
Mickey Welch	4802.0
Tom Seaver	4782.2
Christy Mathewson	4780.2
Tommy John	4710.1
Robin Roberts	4688.2
Early Wynn	4564.0
John Clarkson	4536.1
Charley Radbourn	4535.1
Tony Mullane	4531.1
Jim Kaat	4530.1

WINS

Cy Young	511
Walter Johnson	417
Grover Alexander	373
Christy Mathewson	373
Pud Galvin	365
Warren Spahn	363
Kid Nichols	361
Greg Maddux	355
Roger Clemens	354
Tim Keefe	342
Steve Carlton	329
John Clarkson	328
Eddie Plank	326
Nolan Ryan	324
Don Sutton	324
Phil Niekro	318
Gaylord Perry	314
Tom Seaver	311
Charley Radbourn	309
Mickey Welch	307
Tom Glavine	305
Randy Johnson	303
Lefty Grove	300
Early Wynn	300
Bobby Matthews	297
Tommy John	288

LOSSES

Cy Young	316
Pud Galvin	310
Nolan Ryan	292
Walter Johnson	279
Phil Niekro	274
Gaylord Perry	265
Don Sutton	256
Jack Powell	254
Eppa Rixey	251
Bert Blyleven	250
Bobby Mathews	248
Robin Roberts	245
Warren Spahn	245
Steve Carlton	244
Early Wynn	244
Jim Kaat	237
Frank Tanana	236
Gus Weyhing	232
Tommy John	231
Bob Friend	230
Ted Lyons	230
Greg Maddux	227
Ferguson Jenkins	226
Tim Keefe	225
Red Ruffing	225
Bob Newsom	222

WINNING PERCENTAGE**

Al Spalding	.795
Spud Chandler	.717
Whitey Ford	.690
Dave Foutz	.690
Bob Caruthers	.688
Pedro Martinez	.687
Don Gullett	.686
Lefty Grove	.680
Joe Wood	.672
Vic Raschi	.667
*Roy Halladay	.666
Larry Corcoran	.665
Christy Mathewson	.665
*Jered Weaver	.662
Sam Leever	.660
Roger Clemens	.658
Sal Maglie	.657
Dick McBride	.656
*Justin Verlander	.656
Sandy Koufax	.655
*Tim Hudson	.654
Johnny Allen	.654
*CC Sabathia	.652

SAVES

*Mariano Rivera	608
Trevor Hoffman	601
Lee Smith	478
John Franco	424
Billy Wagner	422
Dennis Eckersley	390
Jeff Reardon	367
Troy Percival	358
Randy Myers	347
Rollie Fingers	341
John Wetteland	330
*Francisco Cordero	329
Roberto Hernandez	326
Jose Mesa	321
Todd Jones	319
Rick Aguilera	318
Robb Nen	314
Tom Henke	311
Goose Gossage	310
Jeff Montgomery	304
Doug Jones	303
*Jason Isringhausen	300
Bruce Sutter	300
*Joe Nathan	298
*Francisco Rodriguez	294

* Active in 2012. ** Minumum 100 victories.

Career Individual Pitching (*Cont.*)

EARNED RUN AVERAGE (2,000 IP)

Ed Walsh	1.82
Addie Joss	1.89
Al Spalding	2.04
Three Finger Brown	2.06
John Ward	2.10
Christy Mathewson	2.13
Tommy Bond	2.14
Rube Waddell	2.16
Walter Johnson	2.17
Ed Reulbach	2.28
Will White	2.28
Eddie Plank	2.35
Larry Corcoran	2.36
Eddie Cicotte	2.38
Candy Cummings	2.39
Doc White	2.39
Nap Rucker	2.42
George Bradley	2.43
Jim McCormick	2.43
Chief Bender	2.46

SHUTOUTS

Walter Johnson	110
Grover Alexander	90
Christy Mathewson	79
Cy Young	76
Eddie Plank	69
Warren Spahn	63
Nolan Ryan	61
Tom Seaver	61
Bert Blyleven	60
Don Sutton	58
Pud Galvin	57
Ed Walsh	57
Bob Gibson	56
Three Finger Brown	55
Steve Carlton	55
Jim Palmer	53
Gaylord Perry	53
Juan Marichal	52
Rube Waddell	50
Vic Willis	50

COMPLETE GAMES

Cy Young	749
Pud Galvin	639
Tim Keefe	554
Walter Johnson	531
Kid Nichols	531
Mickey Welch	525
Bobby Mathews	525
Charley Radbourn	489
John Clarkson	485
Tony Mullane	468
Jim McCormick	466
Gus Weyhing	448
Grover Alexander	437
Christy Mathewson	434
Jack Powell	422
Eddie Plank	410
Will White	394
Amos Rusie	392
Vic Willis	388
Tommy Bond	386

STRIKEOUTS

Nolan Ryan	5714
Randy Johnson	4875
Roger Clemens	4672
Steve Carlton	4136
Bert Blyleven	3701
Tom Seaver	3640
Don Sutton	3574
Gaylord Perry	3534
Walter Johnson	3509
Greg Maddux	3371
Phil Niekro	3342
Ferguson Jenkins	3192
Pedro Martinez	3154
Bob Gibson	3117
Curt Schilling	3116
John Smoltz	3084
Jim Bunning	2855
Mickey Lolich	2832
Mike Mussina	2813
Cy Young	2803

BASES ON BALLS

Nolan Ryan	2795
Steve Carlton	1833
Phil Niekro	1809
Early Wynn	1775
Bob Feller	1764
Bobo Newsom	1732
Amos Rusie	1707
Charlie Hough	1665
Roger Clemens	1580
Gus Weyhing	1566
Red Ruffing	1541
Tom Glavine	1500
Randy Johnson	1497
Bump Hadley	1442
Warren Spahn	1434
Earl Whitehill	1431
Tony Mullane	1408
Sad Sam Jones	1396
Jack Morris	1390
Tom Seaver	1390
Gaylord Perry	1379

* Active in 2011.

Alltime Winningest Managers

CAREER

	W	L	Pct	Yrs		W	L	Pct	Yrs
Connie Mack	3755	3967	.486	53	Casey Stengel	1942	1868	.510	25
John McGraw	2810	1987	.586	33	Gene Mauch	1907	2044	.483	26
Tony LaRussa	2796	2419	.536	33	Bill McKechnie	1904	1737	.523	25
Bobby Cox	2571	2068	.554	29	Lou Piniella	1858	1737	.517	23
Joe Torre	2406	2051	.540	29	Ralph Houk	1627	1539	.514	20
Sparky Anderson	2238	1855	.547	26	*Jim Leyland	1715	1693	.503	21
Bucky Harris	2168	2228	.493	29	Fred Clarke	1609	1189	.575	19
Joe McCarthy	2155	1346	.616	24	*Dusty Baker	1600	1457	.523	19
Walter Alston	2063	1634	.558	23	Dick Williams	1592	1474	.519	21
Leo Durocher	2015	1717	.540	24	Tommy Lasorda	1589	1434	.526	20

REGULAR SEASON

	W	L	Pct	Yrs		W	L	Pct	Yrs
Connie Mack	3731	3948	.486	53	Casey Stengel	1905	1842	.508	25
John McGraw	2763	1948	.586	33	Gene Mauch	1902	2037	.483	26
Tony LaRussa	2728	2365	.536	33	Bill McKechnie	1896	1723	.524	25
Bobby Cox	2504	2001	.556	29	Lou Piniella	1835	1713	.517	23
Joe Torre	2326	1997	.538	29	*Jim Leyland	1676	1659	.503	21
Sparky Anderson	2194	1834	.545	26	Ralph Houk	1619	1531	.514	20
Bucky Harris	2157	2218	.493	29	Fred Clarke	1602	1181	.576	19
Joe McCarthy	2125	1333	.615	24	Tommy Lasorda	1599	1439	.526	21
Walter Alston	2040	1613	.558	23	*Dusty Baker	1581	1432	.525	19
Leo Durocher	2008	1709	.540	24	Dick Williams	1571	1451	.520	21

WORLD SERIES

	W	L	T	Pct	App	WS		W	L	T	Pct	App	WS
Casey Stengel	37	26	0	.587	10	7	Bucky Harris	11	10	0	.524	3	2
Joe McCarthy	30	13	0	.698	9	7	Billy Southworth	11	11	0	.500	4	2
John McGraw	26	28	2	.482	9	2	Earl Weaver	11	13	0	.458	4	1
Connie Mack	24	19	0	.558	8	5	Bobby Cox	11	18	0	.379	5	1
Joe Torre	21	11	0	.657	6	4	Whitey Herzog	10	11	0	.476	3	1
Walter Alston	20	20	0	.500	7	4	Terry Francona	8	0	0	1.000	2	2
Miller Huggins	18	15	1	.544	6	3	Bill Carrigan	8	2	0	.800	2	2
Sparky Anderson	16	12	0	.571	5	3	Cito Gaston	8	4	0	.667	2	2
Tony LaRussa	13	16	0	.448	6	3	*Bruce Bochy	8	5	0	.615	3	2
Tommy Lasorda	12	11	0	.522	4	2	Danny Murtaugh	8	6	0	.571	2	2
Dick Williams	12	14	0	.462	4	2	Tom Kelly	8	6	0	.571	2	2
Frank Chance	11	9	1	.548	4	2	Ralph Houk	8	8	0	.500	3	2

* Active in 2012.

Individual Batting Records (Single Season)

HITS

Ichiro Suzuki, 2004 262
George Sisler, 1920 257
Lefty O'Doul, 1929 254
Bill Terry, 1930 254
Al Simmons, 1925 253
Rogers Hornsby, 1922 250
Chuck Klein, 1930 250
Ty Cobb, 1911 248
George Sisler, 1922 246
Ichiro Suzuki, 2001 242

BATTING AVERAGE

Levi Meyerle, 1871 .... .492
Hugh Duffy, 1894 .... .440
Tip O'Neill, 1887 .... .435
Ross Barnes, 1872 .... .432
Cal McVey, 1871 .... .431
Ross Barnes, 1876 .... .429
Nap Lajoie, 1901 .... .426
Ross Barnes, 1873 .... .425
Willie Keeler, 1897 .... .424
Rogers Hornsby, 1924 ...... .424

DOUBLES

Earl Webb, 1931 67
George Burns, 1926 64
Joe Medwick, 1936 64
Hank Greenberg, 1934 63
Paul Waner, 1932 62
Charlie Gehringer, 1936 60
Tris Speaker, 1923 59
Chuck Klein, 1930 59
Todd Helton, 2000 59
Billy Herman, 1935 57
Billy Herman, 1936 57
Carlos Delgado, 2000 57

TOTAL BASES

Babe Ruth, 1921 457
Rogers Hornsby, 1922 450
Lou Gehrig, 1927 447
Chuck Klein, 1930 445
Jimmie Foxx, 1932 438
Stan Musial, 1948 429
Sammy Sosa, 2001 425
Hack Wilson, 1930 423
Chuck Klein, 1932 420
Lou Gehrig, 1930 419
Luis Gonzalez, 2001 419

TRIPLES

Chief Wilson, 1912 36
Dave Orr, 1886 31
Heinie Reitz, 1894 31
Perry Werden, 1893 29
Harry Davis, 1897 28
George Davis, 1893 27
Sam Thompson, 1894 27
Jimmy Williams, 1899 27
John Reilly,1890 26
George Treadway, 1894 26
Sam Crawford, 1914 26
Joe Jackson, 1912 26
Kiki Cuyler, 1925 26

HOME RUNS

Barry Bonds, 2001 73
Mark McGwire, 1998 70
Sammy Sosa, 1998 66
Mark McGwire, 1999 65
Sammy Sosa, 2001 64
Sammy Sosa, 1999 63
Roger Maris, 1961 61
Babe Ruth, 1927 60
Babe Ruth, 1921 59
Jimmie Foxx, 1932 58
Hank Greenberg, 1938 58
Mark McGwire, 1997 58
Ryan Howard, 2006 58

RUNS BATTED IN

Hack Wilson, 1930 191
Lou Gehrig, 1931 184
Hank Greenberg, 1937 183
Lou Gehrig, 1927 175
Jimmie Foxx, 1938 175
Lou Gehrig, 1930 174
Babe Ruth, 1921 171
Chuck Klein, 1930 170
Hank Greenberg, 1935 170
Jimmie Foxx, 1932 169

STRIKEOUTS

Mark Reynolds, 2009 223
Adam Dunn, 2012 222
Mark Reynolds, 2010 211
Drew Stubbs, 2011 205
Mark Reynolds, 2008 204
Ryan Howard, 2007 199
Ryan Howard, 2008 199
Adam Dunn, 2010 199
Jack Cust, 2008 197
Mark Reynolds, 2011 196
Adam Dunn, 2004 195
Curtis Granderson, 2012 195

RUNS

Billy Hamilton, 1894 192
Tom Brown, 1891 177
Babe Ruth, 1921 177
Tip O'Neill, 1887 167
Lou Gehrig, 1936 167
Billy Hamilton, 1895 166
Willie Keeler, 1894 165
Joe Kelley, 1894 165
Arlie Latham, 1887 163
Babe Ruth, 1928 163
Lou Gehrig, 1931 163

STOLEN BASES

Hugh Nicol, 1887 138
Rickey Henderson, 1982 130
Arlie Latham, 1887 129
Lou Brock, 1974 118
Charlie Comiskey, 1887 117
John Ward, 1887 111
Billy Hamilton, 1889 111
Billy Hamilton, 1891 111
Vince Coleman, 1985 110
Arlie Latham, 1888 109
Vince Coleman, 1987 109

BASES ON BALLS

Barry Bonds, 2004 232
Barry Bonds, 2002 198
Barry Bonds, 2001 177
Babe Ruth, 1923 170
Ted Williams, 1947 162
Ted Williams, 1949 162
Mark McGwire, 1998 162
Ted Williams, 1946 156
Eddie Yost, 1956 151
Barry Bonds,1996 151
Babe Ruth, 1920 150

SLUGGING AVERAGE

Barry Bonds, 2001 .... .863
Babe Ruth, 1920 .... .847
Babe Ruth, 1921 .... .846
Barry Bonds, 2004 .... .812
Barry Bonds, 2002 .... .799
Babe Ruth, 1927 .... .772
Lou Gehrig, 1927 .... .765
Babe Ruth, 1923 .... .764
Rogers Hornsby, 1925 .... .756
Mark McGwire, 1998 .... .752

Individual Pitching Records (Single Season)

GAME APPEARANCES

Mike Marshall, 1974 106
Kent Tekulve, 1979...............94
Salomon Torres, 2006 94
Mike Marshall, 1973 92
Pedro Feliciano, 2010...........92
Kent Tekulve, 1978...............91
Wayne Granger, 1969 90
Mike Marshall, 1979 90
Kent Tekulve, 1987...............90
Mark Eichhorn, 1987 89
Steve Kline, 2001 89
Paul Quantrill, 2003 89
Jim Brower, 2004...................89
Julian Tavarez, 2009 89

GAMES STARTED

Will White, 1879.....................75
Pud Galvin, 1883.....................75
Jim McCormick, 1880..............74
Charley Radbourn, 1884 73
Guy Hecker, 1884 73
Jim Galvin, 1884.....................72
John Clarkson, 1889...............72
Bobby Mathews, 1875............70
John Clarkson, 1885...............70
Bill Hutchison, 1892...............70

INNINGS PITCHED

Will White, 1878..................680.0
Charley Radbourn, 1884 ...678.2
Guy Hecker, 1884 ....670.2
Jim McCormick, 1880........657.2
Jim Galvin, 1883................656.1
Jim Galvin, 1884................636.1
Charley Radbourn, 1883 ..632.1
Bill Hutchison, 1892..........627.0
Bobby Mathews, 1875......626.2

WINS

Charley Radbourn, 1884 59
Al Spalding, 1875...................55
John Clarkson, 1885..............53
Al Spalding, 1874...................52
Guy Hecker, 1884 52
John Clarkson, 1889..............49
Charley Radbourn, 1883 48
Charlie Buffinton, 1884..........48
Al Spalding, 1876...................47
John Ward, 1879 47

LOSSES

John Coleman, 1883 48
Will White, 1880.....................42
Larry McKeon, 1884...............41
George Bradley, 1879............40
Jim McCormick, 1879.............40
Bobby Mathews, 1875............38
Henry Porter, 1888 37
Kid Carsey, 1891...................37
George Cobb, 1892 37

WINNING PERCENTAGE

Roy Face, 1959 947
Johnny Allen, 1937...............938
Greg Maddux, 1995 905
Randy Johnson, 1995 900
Ron Guidry, 1978 893
Freddie Fitzsimmons, 1940 .. .889
Lefty Grove, 1931..............886
Bob Stanley, 1978...............882
Preacher Roe, 1951 880
Cliff Lee, 2008 880
Fred Goldsmith, 1880...........875
Tom Seaver, 1981 875

SAVES

Francisco Rodriguez, 2008 ...62
Bobby Thigpen, 1990............57
John Smoltz, 2002.................55
Eric Gagne, 2003 55
Randy Myers, 1993 53
Trevor Hoffman, 1998............53
Mariano Rivera, 2004 53
Eric Gagne, 2002 52
Dennis Eckersley, 1992.........51
Rod Beck, 1998.....................51
Jim Johnson, 2012 51

EARNED RUN AVERAGE

Tim Keefe, 1880 ....0.86
Dutch Leonard, 1914 ....0.96
Three Finger Brown, 1906 ...1.04
Bob Gibson, 1968 ....1.12
Christy Mathewson, 1909...1.14
Walter Johnson, 1913.........1.14
Jack Pfiester, 1907 ....1.15
Addie Joss, 1908.................1.16
Carl Lundgren, 1907 ....1.17
Denny Driscoll, 1882 ....1.21

SHUTOUTS

Grover Alexander, 1916 16
George Bradley, 1876 16
Jack Coombs, 1910 13
Bob Gibson, 1968 13
Jim Galvin, 1884....................12
Ed Morris, 1886 12
Grover Alexander, 1915 12
Tommy Bond, 1879 11
Charles Radbourn, 1884 11
Dave Foutz, 1886 11
Christy Mathewson, 1908......11
Ed Walsh, 1908.....................11
Walter Johnson, 1913............11
Sandy Koufax, 1963 11
Dean Chance, 1964 11

COMPLETE GAMES

Will White, 1879.....................75
Charley Radbourn, 1884 73
Jim McCormick, 1880.............72
Pud Galvin, 1883....................72
Guy Hecker, 1884 72
Pud Galvin, 1884....................71
Bobby Mathews, 1875............69
John Clarkson, 1885...............68
John Clarkson, 1889...............68

STRIKEOUTS

Matt Kilroy, 1886.................513
Toad Ramsey, 1886 499
Hugh Daily, 1884.................483
Dupee Shaw, 1884...............451
Charley Radbourn, 1884 441
Charlie Buffinton, 1884........417
Guy Hecker, 1884 385
Nolan Ryan, 1973.................383
Sandy Koufax, 1965 382

BASES ON BALLS

Amos Rusie, 1890 289
Mark Baldwin, 1889..............274
Amos Rusie, 1892.................267
Amos Rusie, 1891.................262
Mark Baldwin, 1890..............249
Jack Stivetts, 1891 232
Mark Baldwin, 1891..............227
Phil Knell, 1891.....................226
Bob Barr, 1890 219

Manager of the Year

NATIONAL LEAGUE

1983 ....Tommy Lasorda, LA
1984 ....Jim Frey, Chi
1985 ....Whitey Herzog, StL
1986 ....Hal Lanier, Hou
1987 ....Buck Rodgers, Mtl
1988 ....Tommy Lasorda, LA
1989 ....Don Zimmer, Chi
1990 ....Jim Leyland, Pitt
1991 ....Bobby Cox, Atl
1992 ....Jim Leyland, Pitt
1993 ....Dusty Baker, SF
1994 ....Felipe Alou, Mtl
1995 ....Don Baylor, Col
1996 ....Bruce Bochy, SD
1997 ....Dusty Baker, SF
1998 ....Larry Dierker, Hou
1999 ....Jack McKeon, Cin

AMERICAN LEAGUE

1983 ....Tony LaRussa, Chi
1984 ....Sparky Anderson, Det
1985 ....Bobby Cox, Tor
1986 ....John McNamara, Bos
1987 ....Sparky Anderson, Det
1988 ....Tony LaRussa, Oak
1989 ....Frank Robinson, Balt
1990 ....Jeff Torborg, Chi
1991 ....Tom Kelly, Minn
1992 ....Tony LaRussa, Oak
1993 ....Gene Lamont, Chi
1994 ....Buck Showalter, NY
1995 ....Lou Piniella, Sea
1996 ....Joe Torre, NY/Johnny Oates, Tex
1997 ....Davey Johnson, Balt
1998 ....Joe Torre, NY
1999 ....Jimy Williams, Bos

Manager of the Year (*Cont.*)

NATIONAL LEAGUE		AMERICAN LEAGUE	
2000	Dusty Baker, SF	2000	Jerry Manuel, Chi
2001	Larry Bowa, Phi	2001	Lou Piniella, Sea
2002	Tony LaRussa, StL	2002	Mike Scioscia, Ana
2003	Jack McKeon, Fla	2003	Tony Pena, KC
2004	Bobby Cox, Atl	2004	Buck Showalter, Tex
2005	Bobby Cox, Atl	2005	Ozzie Guillen, Chi
2006	Joe Girardi, Fla	2006	Jim Leyland, Det
2007	Bob Melvin, Ari	2007	Eric Wedge, Cle
2008	Lou Piniella, Chi	2008	Joe Maddon, TB
2009	Jim Tracy, Col	2009	Mike Scioscia, LA
2010	Bud Black, SD	2010	Ron Gardenhire, Min
2011	Kirk Gibson, Ari	2011	Joe Maddon, TB

Individual Batting Records (Single Game)

MOST HITS

7	Wilbert Robinson, Balt	June 10, 1892
	Rennie Stennett, Pitt	Sept 16, 1975

MOST HOME RUNS

4	Bobby Lowe, Bos (N)	May 30, 1894
	Ed Delahanty, Phi	July 13, 1896
	Lou Gehrig, NY (A)	June 3, 1932
	Chuck Klein, Phi (N)	July 10, 1936
	Pat Seerey, Chi (A)	July 18, 1948
	Gil Hodges, Bklyn	Aug 31, 1950
	Joe Adcock, Mil (N)	July 31, 1954
	Rocky Colavito, Clev	June 10, 1959
	Willie Mays, SF	April 30, 1961
	Mike Schmidt, Phi	April 17, 1976
	Bob Horner, Atl	July 6, 1986
	Mark Whiten, StL	Sept 7, 1993
	Mike Cameron, Sea	May 2, 2002
	Shawn Green, LA	May 23, 2002
	Carlos Delgado, Tor	Sept 25, 2003
	Josh Hamilton, Tex	May 8, 2012

Note: All single-game hitting records for a nine-inning game.

MOST GRAND SLAMS

2	Tony Lazzeri, NY (A)	May 24, 1936
	Jim Tabor, Bos (A)	July 4, 1939
	Rudy York, Bos (A)	July 27, 1946
	Jim Gentile, Balt	May 9, 1961
	Tony Cloninger, Atl	July 3, 1966
	Jim Northrup, Det	June 24, 1968
	Frank Robinson, Balt	June 26, 1970
	Robin Ventura, Chi (A)	Sept 4, 1995
	Chris Hoiles, Balt	Aug 14, 1998
	Fernando Tatis, StL	Apr 23, 1999
	N. Garciaparra, Bos	May 10, 1999
	Bill Mueller, Bos	July 29, 2003
	Josh Willingham, Was	July 27, 2009

MOST RUNS

7	Guy Hecker, Lou	Aug 15, 1886

MOST RBIs

12	Jim Bottomley, StL	Sept 16, 1924
	Mark Whiten, StL	Sept 7, 1993

Individual Batting Records (Single Inning)

MOST RUNS

3	Tommy Burns, Chi (N)	Sept 6, 1883, 7th inning
	Ned Williamson, Chi (N)	Sept 6, 1883, 7th inning
	Sammy White, Bos (A)	June 18, 1953, 7th inning

MOST HITS

3	Tommy Burns, Chi (N)	Sept 6, 1883, 7th inning
	Fred Pfeiffer, Chi (N)	Sept 6, 1883, 7th inning

MOST HITS (*CONT.*)

	Ned Williamson, Chi (N)	Sept 6, 1883, 7th inning
	Gene Stephens, Bos (A)	June 18, 1953, 7th inning
	Johnny Damon, Bos (A),	June 27, 2003, 1st inning

MOST RBIs

8	Fernando Tatis, StL	Apr 23, 1999, 3rd inning

Individual Pitching Records (Single Game)

MOST INNINGS PITCHED

26	Leon Cadore, Bklyn	May 1, 1920, tie 1–1
	Joe Oeschger, Bos (N)	May 1, 1920, tie 1–1

MOST RUNS ALLOWED

24	Al Travers, Det	May 18, 1912

MOST HITS ALLOWED

36	Jack Wadsworth, Lou	Aug 17, 1894

MOST STRIKEOUTS

20	Roger Clemens, Bos	April 29, 1986
20	Roger Clemens, Bos	Sept 18, 1996
20	Kerry Wood, Chi (N)	May 6, 1998
20	Randy Johnson, Ariz	May 8, 2001

MOST WALKS ALLOWED

16	Bill George, NY (N)	May 30, 1887
	George Van Haltren, Chi (N)	June 27, 1887
	Henry Gruber, Clev	Apr 19, 1890
	Bruno Haas, Phi (A)	June 2, 1915

MOST WILD PITCHES

6	J.R. Richard, Hou	April 10, 1979
	Phil Niekro, Atl	Aug 14, 1979
	Bill Gullickson, Mtl	April 10, 1982

Individual Pitching Records (Single Inning)

MOST RUNS ALLOWED

13 .....Lefty O'Doul, Bos (A)   July 7, 1923

MOST WALKS ALLOWED

8 ....Dolly Gray, Wash   Aug 28, 1909

MOST WILD PITCHES

4	Walter Johnson, Wash	Sept 21, 1914
	Phil Niekro, Atl	Aug 14, 1979
	Kevin Gregg, Ana	July 25, 2004
	Ryan Madson, Phi	July 25, 2006

Miscellaneous Records

LONGEST GAME, BY INNINGS

26 .....Brooklyn 1, Boston 1   May 1, 1920

LONGEST NINE-INNING GAME, BY TIME

4:45...New York (A) 14, Boston 11   Aug 18, 2006

Baseball Hall of Fame

Players

	Position	Career	Selected		Position	Career	Selected
Hank Aaron	OF	1954–76	1982	Joe Cronin	SS	1926–45	1956
Grover Alexander	P	1911–30	1938	Candy Cummings	P	1872–77	1939
Roberto Alomar	2B	1988–2004	2011	Kiki Cuyler	OF	1921–38	1968
Cap Anson	1B	1876–97	1939	Ray Dandridge*	3B		1987
Luis Aparicio	SS	1956–73	1984	George Davis	SS	1890–1909	1998
Luke Appling	SS	1930–50	1964	Andre Dawson	OF	1976–96	2010
Richie Ashburn	OF	1948–62	1995	Leon Day*	P		1995
Earl Averill	OF	1929–41	1975	Dizzy Dean	P	1930–47	1953
Jose Mendez Baez*	P	1908–26	2006	Ed Delahanty	OF	1888–1903	1945
Frank Baker	3B	1908–22	1955	Bill Dickey	C	1928–46	1954
Dave Bancroft	SS	1915–30	1971	Martin Dihigo*	P-OF		1977
Ernie Banks	SS-1B	1953–71	1977	Joe DiMaggio	OF	1936–51	1955
Jake Beckley	1B	1888–1907	1971	Larry Doby	OF	1947–59	1998
Cool Papa Bell*	OF		1974	Bobby Doerr	2B	1937–51	1986
Johnny Bench	C	1967–83	1989	Don Drysdale	P	1956–69	1984
Chief Bender	P	1903–25	1953	Hugh Duffy	OF	1888–1906	1945
Yogi Berra	C	1946–65	1972	Dennis Eckersley	P	1975–98	2004
Bert Blyleven	P	1970–90; '92	2011	Johnny Evers	2B	1902–29	1939
Wade Boggs	3B	1982-99	2005	Buck Ewing	C	1880–97	1946
Jim Bottomley	1B	1922–37	1974	Red Faber	P	1914–33	1964
Lou Boudreau	SS	1938–52	1970	Bob Feller	P	1936–56	1962
Roger Bresnahan	C	1897–1915	1945	Rick Ferrell	C	1929–47	1984
George Brett	3B	1973–93	1999	Rollie Fingers	P	1968–85	1992
Lou Brock	OF	1961–79	1985	Carlton Fisk	C	1969–93	2000
Dan Brouthers	1B	1879–1904	1945	Elmer Flick	OF	1898–1910	1963
Ray Brown*	P	1930–48	2006	Whitey Ford	P	1950–67	1974
Three Finger Brown	P	1903–16	1949	Bill Foster*	P		1996
Willard Jesse Brown*	OF	1935–58	2006	Nellie Fox	2B	1947–65	1997
Jim Bunning	P	1955–71	1996	Jimmie Foxx	1B	1925–45	1951
Jesse Burkett	OF	1890–1905	1946	Frankie Frisch	2B	1919–37	1947
Roy Campanella	C	1948–57	1969	Pud Galvin	P	1879–92	1965
Rod Carew	1B-2B	1967–85	1991	Lou Gehrig	1B	1923–39	1939
Max Carey	OF	1910–29	1961	Charlie Gehringer	2B	1924–42	1949
Steve Carlton	P	1965–88	1994	Bob Gibson	P	1959–75	1981
Gary Carter	C	1974–92	2003	Josh Gibson*	C		1972
Orlando Cepeda	1B	1958–74	1999	Lefty Gomez	P	1930–43	1972
Frank Chance	1B	1898–1914	1946	Joe Gordon	2B	1938-43/46-50	2009
Oscar Charleston*	OF		1976	Goose Goslin	OF	1921–38	1968
Jack Chesbro	P	1899–1909	1946	Rich "Goose" Gossage	P	1972-94	2008
Fred Clarke	OF	1894–1915	1945	Ulysses F. Grant*	2B	1886–1903	2006
John Clarkson	P	1882–94	1963	Hank Greenberg	1B	1930–47	1956
Roberto Clemente	OF	1955–72	1973	Burleigh Grimes	P	1916–34	1964
Ty Cobb	OF	1905–28	1936	Lefty Grove	P	1925–41	1947
Mickey Cochrane	C	1925–37	1947	Tony Gwynn	OF	1982–2001	2007
Eddie Collins	2B	1906–30	1939	Chick Hafey	OF	1924–37	1971
Jimmy Collins	3B	1895–1908	1945	Jesse Haines	P	1918–37	1970
Earle Combs	OF	1924–35	1970	Billy Hamilton	OF	1888–1901	1961
Roger Connor	1B	1880–97	1976	Gabby Hartnett	C	1922–41	1955
Andrew Cooper*	P	1920–41	2006	Harry Heilmann	OF	1914–32	1952
Stan Coveleski	P	1912–28	1969	Rickey Henderson	OF	1979–2003	2009
Sam Crawford	OF	1899–1917	1957	Billy Herman	2B	1931–47	1975

Note: Career dates indicate first and last appearances in the majors. *Elected on the basis of their career in the Negro leagues.

Players (Cont.)

	Position	Career	Selected		Position	Career	Selected
Joseph Hill*	OF	1899–1925	2006	Jim Rice	OF	1974–89	2009
Harry Hooper	OF	1909–25	1971	Sam Rice	OF	1915–35	1963
Rogers Hornsby	2B	1915–37	1942	Cal Ripken Jr.	SS	1981–2001	2007
Waite Hoyt	P	1918–38	1969	Eppa Rixey	P	1912–33	1963
Carl Hubbell	P	1928–43	1947	Phil Rizzuto	SS	1941–56	1994
Catfish Hunter	P	1965–79	1987	Robin Roberts	P	1948–66	1976
Monte Irvin*	OF	1949–56	1973	Brooks Robinson	3B	1955–77	1983
Reggie Jackson	OF	1967–87	1993	Frank Robinson	OF	1956–76	1982
Travis Jackson	SS	1922–36	1982	Jackie Robinson	2B	1947–56	1962
Ferguson Jenkins	P	1965–83	1991	Joe (Bullet) Rogan*	P		1998
Hugh Jennings	SS	1891–1918	1945	Edd Roush	OF	1913–31	1962
Judy Johnson*	3B		1975	Red Ruffing	P	1924–47	1967
Walter Johnson	P	1907–27	1936	Amos Rusie	P	1889–1901	1977
Addie Joss	P	1902–10	1978	Babe Ruth	OF	1914–35	1936
Al Kaline	OF	1953–74	1980	Nolan Ryan	P	1966–93	1999
Tim Keefe	P	1880–93	1964	Ryne Sandberg	2B	1981–97	2005
Willie Keeler	OF	1892–1910	1939	Ron Santo	3B	1960–74	2012
George Kell	3B	1943–57	1983	Louis Santop*	C	1909–26	2006
Joe Kelley	OF	1891–1908	1971	Ray Schalk	C	1912–29	1955
George Kelly	1B	1915–32	1973	Mike Schmidt	3B	1972–89	1995
King Kelly	C	1878–93	1945	Red Schoendienst	2B	1945–63	1989
Harmon Killebrew	1B-3B	1954–75	1984	Tom Seaver	P	1967–86	1992
Ralph Kiner	OF	1946–55	1975	Joe Sewell	SS	1920–33	1977
Chuck Klein	OF	1928–44	1980	Al Simmons	OF	1924–44	1953
Sandy Koufax	P	1955–66	1972	George Sisler	1B	1915–30	1939
Nap Lajoie	2B	1896–1916	1937	Enos Slaughter	OF	1938–59	1985
Barry Larkin	SS	1986–2004	2012	Hilton Smith*	P		2001
Tony Lazzeri	2B	1926–39	1991	Ozzie Smith	SS	1978–96	2002
Bob Lemon	P	1941–58	1976	Duke Snider	OF	1947–64	1980
Buck Leonard*	1B		1977	Warren Spahn	P	1942–65	1973
Fred Lindstrom	3B	1924–36	1976	Al Spalding	P	1871–78	1939
Pop Lloyd*	SS-1B		1977	Tris Speaker	OF	1907–28	1937
Ernie Lombardi	C	1931–47	1986	Willie Stargell	OF-1B	1962–82	1988
Ted Lyons	P	1923–46	1955	Turkey Stearns*	CF		2000
James Mackey*	C	1920–47	2006	Don Sutton	P	1966–88	1998
Mickey Mantle	OF	1951–68	1974	Bruce Sutter	P	1976–88	2006
Heinie Manush	OF	1923–39	1964	George Suttles*	C	1923–44	2006
Rabbit Maranville	SS-2B	1912–35	1954	Benjamin Harrison Taylor*	P-1B	1908–29	2006
Juan Marichal	P	1960–75	1983	Bill Terry	1B	1923–36	1954
Rube Marquard	P	1908–25	1971	Sam Thompson	OF	1885–1906	1974
Eddie Mathews	3B	1952–68	1978	Joe Tinker	SS	1902–16	1946
Christy Mathewson	P	1900–16	1936	Cristóbal Torriente*	OF	1913–32	2006
Willie Mays	OF	1951–73	1979	Pie Traynor	3B	1920–37	1948
Bill Mazeroski	2B	1956–72	2001	Dazzy Vance	P	1915–35	1955
Tommy McCarthy	OF	1884–96	1946	Arky Vaughan	SS	1932–48	1985
Willie McCovey	1B	1959–80	1986	Rube Waddell	P	1897–1910	1946
Joe McGinnity	P	1899–1908	1946	Honus Wagner	SS	1897–1917	1936
Bid McPhee	2B	1882–99	2000	Bobby Wallace	SS	1894–1918	1953
Joe Medwick	OF	1932–48	1968	Ed Walsh	P	1904–17	1946
Johnny Mize	1B	1936–53	1981	Lloyd Waner	OF	1927–45	1967
Paul Molitor	3B	1978–98	2004	Paul Waner	OF	1926–45	1952
Joe Morgan	2B	1963–84	1990	John Ward	2B-P	1878–94	1964
Eddie Murray	1B	1977–97	2003	Mickey Welch	P	1880–92	1973
Stan Musial	OF-1B	1941–63	1969	Willie Wells*	SS	1924–49	1997
Hal Newhouser	P	1939–55	1992	Zach Wheat	OF	1909–27	1959
Kid Nichols	P	1890–1906	1949	Hoyt Wilhelm	P	1952–72	1985
Phil Niekro	P	1964–87	1997	Billy Williams	OF	1959–76	1987
Jim O'Rourke	OF	1876–1904	1945	Ted Williams	OF	1939–60	1966
Mel Ott	OF	1926–47	1951	Vic Willis	P	1898–1910	1995
Satchel Paige*	P	1948–65	1971	Ernest Judson Wilson*	3B	1922–45	2006
Jim Palmer	P	1965–84	1990	Hack Wilson	OF	1923–34	1979
Herb Pennock	P	1912–34	1948	Dave Winfield	OF	1973–95	2001
Tony Perez	1B	1964–86	2000	Early Wynn	P	1939–63	1972
Gaylord Perry	P	1962–83	1991	Carl Yastrzemski	OF	1961–83	1989
Eddie Plank	P	1901–17	1946	Cy Young	P	1890–1911	1937
Kirby Puckett	OF	1984–95	2001	Ross Youngs	OF	1917–26	1972
Charley Radbourn	P	1880–91	1939	Robin Yount	SS	1974–93	1999
Pee Wee Reese	SS	1940–58	1984				

*Elected on the basis of their career in the Negro leagues.

Pioneers/Executives

	Selected
Ed Barrow (manager-executive)	1953
Morgan Bulkeley (executive)	1937
Alexander Cartwright (executive)	1938
Henry Chadwick (writer-executive)	1938
Happy Chandler (commissioner)	1982
Charles Comiskey (manager-executive)	1939
Barney Dreyfuss (executive)	2008
Ford Frick (commissioner-executive)	1970
Warren Giles (executive)	1979
Pat Gillick (executive)	2011
Clark Griffith (executive)	1946
Will Harridge (executive)	1972
William Hulbert (executive)	1995
Ban Johnson (executive)	1937
Bowie Kuhn (commissioner)	2008
Kenesaw M. Landis (commissioner)	1944
Larry MacPhail Sr. (executive)	1978
Lee MacPhail Jr. (executive).	1998
Effa Manley (executive)	2006
Walter O'Malley (executive)	2008
Alex Pompez (executive)	2006
Cum Posey (player-manager-owner)	2006
Branch Rickey (manager-executive)	1967
Al Spalding (player-executive)	1939
Bill Veeck Jr. (owner)	1991
George Weiss (executive)	1971
Sol White (player-manager)	2006
J.L. Wilkinson (executive)	2006
George Wright (player-manager)	1937
Harry Wright (player-manager-executive)	1953
Tom Yawkey (executive)	1980

Managers

	Managed	Selected
Walter Alston	1954–76	1983
Sparky Anderson	1970–94	2000
Leo Durocher	1939–73	1994
Rube Foster	1907–26	1981
Ned Hanlon	1899–1907	1996
Bucky Harris	1924–56	1975
Miller Huggins	1913–29	1964
Tommy Lasorda	1977–96	1997
Al Lopez	1951–69	1977
Connie Mack	1894–1950	1937
Joe McCarthy	1926–50	1957
John McGraw	1899–1932	1937
Bill McKechnie	1915–46	1962
Wilbert Robinson	1902–31	1945
Frank Selee	1890–1905	1999
Billy Southworth	1929, 1940–51	2008
Casey Stengel	1934–65	1966
Earl Weaver	1968–82, 85–86	1996
Dick Williams	1967–69, 1971–88	2008
Whitey Herzog	1973–90	2010

Umpires

	Selected
Al Barlick	1989
Nestor Chylak	1999
Jocko Conlan	1974
Tom Connolly	1953
Billy Evans	1973
Cal Hubbard	1976
Bill Klem	1953
Bill McGowan	1992
Doug Harvey	2010

Notable Achievements

No-Hit Games, Nine Innings or More

NATIONAL LEAGUE

Date	Pitcher and Game
1876......July 15	George Bradley, StL vs Hart 2–0
1880......June 12	John Richmond, Wor vs Clev 1–0 (perfect game)
June 17	Monte Ward, Prov vs Buff 5–0 (perfect game)
Aug 19	Larry Corcoran, Chi vs Bos 6–0
Aug 20	Pud Galvin, Buff vs Wor 1–0
1882......Sept 20	Larry Corcoran, Chi vs Wor 5–0
Sept 22	Tim Lovett, Bklyn vs NY 4–0
1883......July 25	Hoss Radbourn, Prov vs Clev 8–0
Sept 13	Hugh Daily, Clev vs Phi 1–0
1884......June 27	Larry Corcoran, Chi vs Prov 6–0
Aug 4	Pud Galvin, Buff vs Det 18–0
1885......July 27	John Clarkson, Chi vs Prov 4–0
Aug 29	Charles Ferguson, Phi vs Prov 1–0
1891......July 31	Amos Rusie, NY vs Bklyn 6–0
June 22	Tom Lovett, Bklyn vs NY 4–0
1892......Aug 6	Jack Stivetts, Bos vs Bklyn 11–0
Aug 22	Alex Sanders, Lou vs Balt 6–2
Oct 15	Bumpus Jones, Cin vs Pitt 7–1 (first major league game)
1893......Aug 16	Bill Hawke, Balt vs Wash 5–0
1897......Sept 18	Cy Young, Clev vs Cin 6–0
1898......Apr 22	Ted Breitenstein, Cin vs Pitt 11–0
Apr 22	Jim Hughes, Balt vs Bos 8–0
July 8	Frank Donahue, Phi vs Bos 5–0
Aug 21	Walter Thornton, Chi vs Bklyn 2–0
1899......May 25	Deacon Phillippe, Lou vs NY 7–0
Aug 7	Vic Willis, Bos vs Wash 7–1
1900......July 12	Noodles Hahn, Cin vs Phi 4–0
1901......July 15	Christy Mathewson, NY vs StL 5–0
1903......Sept 18	Chick Fraser, Phi vs Chi 10–0
1904......June 11	Bob Wicker, Chi at NY 1–0 (hit in 10th; won in 12th)
1905......June 13	Christy Mathewson, NY vs Chi 1–0
1906......May 1	John Lush, Phi vs Bklyn 6–0
July 20	Mal Eason, Bklyn vs StL 2–0
Aug 1	Harry McIntire, Bklyn vs Pitt 0–1 (hit in 11th; lost in 13th)
1907......May 8	Frank Pfeffer, Bos vs Cin 6–0
Sept 20	Nick Maddox, Pitt vs Bklyn 2–1
1908......July 4	George Wiltse, NY vs Phi 1–0 (10 innings)
Sept 5	Nap Rucker, Bklyn vs Bos 6–0
1909......Apr 15	Leon Ames, NY vs Bklyn 0–3 (hit in 10th; lost in 13th)
1912......Sept 6	Jeff Tesreau, NY vs Phi 3–0
1914......Sept 9	George Davis, Bos vs Phi 7–0
1915......Apr 15	Rube Marquard, NY vs Bklyn 2–0
Aug 31	Jimmy Lavender, Chi vs NY 2–0
1916......June 16	Tom Hughes, Bos vs Pitt 2–0
1917......May 2	Jim Vaughn, Chi vs Cin 0–1 (hit in 10th; lost in 10th)
May 2	Fred Toney, Cin vs Chi 1–0 (10 innings)

No-Hit Games, Nine Innings or More *(Cont.)*

NATIONAL LEAGUE *(Cont.)*

Date	Pitcher and Game	Date	Pitcher and Game
1919......May 11	Hod Eller, Cin vs StL 6–0	1973......Aug 5	Phil Niekro, Atl vs SD 9–0
1922......May 7	Jesse Barnes, NY vs Phi 6–0	1975......Aug 24	Ed Halicki, SF vs NY 6–0
1924......July 17	Jesse Haines, StL vs Bos 5–0	1976......July 9	Larry Dierker, Hou vs Mtl 6–0
1925......Sept 13	Dazzy Vance, Bklyn vs Phi 10–1	Aug 9	John Candelaria, Pitt vs LA 2–0
1929......May 8	Carl Hubbell, NY vs Pitt 11–0	Sept 29	John Montefusco, SF vs Atl 9–0
1934......Sept 21	Paul Dean, StL vs Bklyn 3–0	1978......Apr 16	Bob Forsch, StL vs Phi 5–0
1938......June 11	Johnny Vander Meer, Cin vs Bos 3–0	June 16	Tom Seaver, Cin vs StL 4–0
June 15	Johnny Vander Meer, Cin vs Bklyn 6–0	1979......Apr 7	Ken Forsch, Hou vs Atl 6–0
1940......Apr 30	Tex Carleton, Bklyn vs Cin, 3–0	1980......June 27	Jerry Reuss, LA vs SF 8–0
1941......Aug 30	Lon Warneke, StL vs Cin 2–0	1981......May 10	Charlie Lea, Mtl vs SF 4–0
1944......Apr 27	Jim Tobin, Bos vs Bklyn 2–0	Sept 26	Nolan Ryan, Hou vs LA 5–0
May 15	Clyde Shoun, Cin vs Bos 1–0	1983......Sept 26	Bob Forsch, StL vs Mtl 3–0
1946......Apr 23	Ed Head, Bklyn vs Bos 5–0	1986......Sept 25	Mike Scott, Hou vs SF 2–0
1947......June 18	Ewell Blackwell, Cin vs Bos 6–0	1988......Sept 16	Tom Browning, Cin vs LA 1–0
1948......Sept 9	Rex Barney, Bklyn vs NY 2–0		(perfect game)
1950......Aug 11	Vern Bickford, Bos vs Bklyn 7–0	1990......June 29	Fernando Valenzuela, LA vs StL 6–0
1951......May 6	Cliff Chambers, Pitt vs Bos 3–0	Aug 15	Terry Mulholland, Phi vs SF 6–0
1952......June 19	Carl Erskine, Bklyn vs Chi 5–0	1991......May 23	Tommy Greene, Phi vs Mtl 2–0
1954......June 12	Jim Wilson, Mil vs Phi 2–0	July 26	Mark Gardner, Mtl vs LA 0–1
1955......May 12	Sam Jones, Chi vs Pitt 4–0		(hit in 10th, lost in 10th)
1956......May 12	Carl Erskine, Bklyn vs NY 3–0	July 28	Dennis Martinez, Mtl vs LA 2–0
Sept 25	Sal Maglie, Bklyn vs Phi 5–0		(perfect game)
1959......May 26	Harvey Haddix, Pitt vs Mil 0–1	Sept 11	Kent Mercker (6), Mark Wohlers (2),
	(hit in 13th; lost in 13th)		and Alejandro Pena (1), Atl vs SD 1–0
1960......May 15	Don Cardwell, Chi vs StL 4–0	1992......Aug 17	Kevin Gross, LA vs SF 2–0
Aug 18	Lew Burdette, Mil vs Phi 1–0	1993......Sept 8	Darryl Kile, Hou vs NY 7–1
Sept 16	Warren Spahn, Mil vs Phi 4–0	1994......Apr 8	Kent Mercker, Atl vs LA 6–0
1961......Apr 28	Warren Spahn, Mil vs SF 1–0	1995......June 3	Pedro Martinez, Mtl vs SD 1–0
1962......June 30	Sandy Koufax, LA vs NY 5–0		(perfect through nine, lost in 10th)
1963......May 11	Sandy Koufax, LA vs SF 8–0	July 14	Ramon Martinez, LA vs Fla 7–0
May 17	Don Nottebart, Hou vs Phi 4–1	1996......May 11	Al Leiter, Fla vs Col 11–0
June 15	Juan Marichal, SF vs Hou 1–0	Sept 17	Hideo Nomo, LA vs Col 9–0
1964......Apr 23	Ken Johnson, Hou vs Cin 0–1	1997......June 10	Kevin Brown, Fla vs SF 9–0
June 4	Sandy Koufax, LA vs Phi 3–0	July 12	Francisco Cordova (9) and
June 21	Jim Bunning, Phi vs NY 6–0		Ricardo Rincon (1), Pitt vs Col 3–0
	(perfect game)	1999......June 25	Jose Jimenez, StL vs Ariz 1–0
1965......June 14	Jim Maloney, Cin vs NY 0–1	2001......May 12	A.J. Burnett, Fla vs SD 3–0
	(hit in 11th; lost in 11th)	Sept 3	Bud Smith, StL vs SD 4–0
Aug 19	Jim Maloney, Cin vs Chi 1–0	2003......April 27	Kevin Millwood, Phi vs SF 1–0
	(10 innings)	June 11	R. Oswalt (1), P. Munro (2.2), K.
Sept 9	Sandy Koufax, LA vs Chi 1–0		Saarloos (1.1), B. Lidge (2), O. Dotel
	(perfect game)		(1), B. Wagner (1), Hou vs NYY 8–0
1967......June 18	Don Wilson, Hou vs Atl 2–0	April 27	Kevin Millwood, Phi vs SF 1–0
1968......July 29	George Culver, Cin vs Phi 6–1	2004......May 18	Randy Johnson, Ariz vs Atl 2–0
Sept 17	Gaylord Perry, SF vs StL 1–0		(perfect game)
Sept 18	Ray Washburn, StL vs SF 2–0	2006......Sept 6	Anibal Sanchez, Fla vs Ariz 2–0
1969......Apr 17	Bill Stoneman, Mtl vs Phi 7–0	2008......Sept 14	†Carlos Zambrano, Chi vs Hou 5–0
Apr 30	Jim Maloney, Cin vs Hou 10–0	2009......July 10	Jonathan Sanchez, SF vs SD 8–0
May 1	Don Wilson, Hou vs Cin 4–0	2010......Apr 17	Ubaldo Jimenez, Col vs Atl 4–0
Aug 19	Ken Holtzman, Chi vs Atl 3–0	May 29	Roy Halladay, Phi vs Fla 1–0
Sept 20	Bob Moose, Pitt vs NY 4–0		(perfect game)
1970......June 12	Dock Ellis, Pitt vs SD 2–0	June 26	‡Edwin Jackson, Ariz vs TB 1–0
July 20	Bill Singer, LA vs Phi 5–0	Oct 6	Roy Halladay, Phi vs Cin 4–0
1971......June 3	Ken Holtzman, Chi vs Cin 1–0		(NLDS)
June 23	Rick Wise, Phi vs Cin 4–0	2012......June 1	Johan Santana, NY vs. StL 8–0
Aug 14	Bob Gibson, StL vs Pitt 11–0	June 13	Matt Cain, SF vs. Hou 10–0
1972......Apr 16	Burt Hooton, Chi vs Phi 4–0	Sept 28	Homer Bailey, Cin vs. Pit 1–0
Sept 2	Milt Pappas, Chi vs SD 8–0		
Oct 2	Bill Stoneman, Mtl vs NY 7–0		

Note: Includes the games struck from the official record book on Sept. 4, 1991, when baseball's committee on statistical accuracy voted to define no-hitters as games of nine innings or more that end with a team getting no hits.

†Game played in Milwaukee due to weather-related closure of Houston's home field.

‡Interleague game.

No-Hit Games, Nine Innings or More (*Cont.*)

AMERICAN LEAGUE

Date	Pitcher and Game
1901......May 9	Earl Moore, Clev vs Chi 2–4 (hit in 10th; lost in 10th)
1902......Sept 20	Jimmy Callahan, Chi vs Det 3–0
1904......May 5	Cy Young, Bos vs Phi 3–0 (perfect game)
Aug 17	Jesse Tannehill, Bos vs Chi 6–0
1905......July 22	Weldon Henley, Phi vs StL 6–0
Sept 6	Frank Smith, Chi vs Det 15–0
Sept 27	Bill Dinneen, Bos vs Chi 2–0
1908......June 30	Cy Young, Bos vs NY 8–0
Sept 18	Bob Rhoades, Clev vs Bos 2–1
Sept 20	Frank Smith, Chi vs Phi 1–0
Oct 2	Addie Joss, Clev vs Chi 1–0 (perfect game)
1910......Apr 20	Addie Joss, Clev vs Chi 1–0
May 12	Chief Bender, Phi vs Clev 4–0
Aug 30	Tom Hughes, NY vs Clev 0–5 (hit in 10th; lost in 11th)
1911......July 29	Joe Wood, Bos vs StL 5–0
Aug 27	Ed Walsh, Chi vs Bos 5–0
1912......July 4	George Mullin, Det vs StL 7–0
Aug 30	Earl Hamilton, StL vs Det 5–1
1914......May 14	Jim Scott, Chi vs Wash 0–1 (hit in 10th; lost in 10th)
May 31	Joe Benz, Chi vs Clev 6–1
1916......June 21	George Foster, Bos vs NY 2–0
Aug 26	Joe Bush, Phi vs Clev 5–0
Aug 30	Dutch Leonard, Bos vs StL 4–0
1917......Apr 14	Ed Cicotte, Chi vs StL 11–0
Apr 24	George Mogridge, NY vs Bos 2–1
May 5	Ernie Koob, StL vs Chi 1–0
May 6	Bob Groom, StL vs Chi 3–0
June 23	Ernie Shore, Bos vs Wash 4–0 (perfect game)
1918......June 3	Dutch Leonard, Bos vs Det 5–0
1919......Sept 10	Ray Caldwell, Clev vs NY 3–0
1920......July 1	Walter Johnson, Wash vs Bos 1–0
1922.....,.Apr 30	Charlie Robertson, Chi vs Det 2–0 (perfect game)
1923......Sept 4	Sam Jones, NY vs Phi 2–0
Sept 7	Howard Ehmke, Bos vs Phi 4–0
1926......Aug 21	Ted Lyons, Chi vs Bos 6–0
1931......Apr 29	Wes Ferrell, Clev vs StL 9–0
Aug 8	Bob Burke, Wash vs Bos 5–0
1934......Sept 18	Bobo Newsom, StL vs Bos 1–2 (hit in 10th; lost in 10th)
1935......Aug 31	Vern Kennedy, Chi vs Clev 5–0
1937......June 1	Bill Dietrich, Chi vs StL 8–0
1938......Aug 27	Mtle Pearson, NY vs Clev 13–0
1940......Apr 16	Bob Feller, Clev vs Chi 1–0 (opening day)
1945......Sept 9	Dick Fowler, Phi vs StL 1–0
1946......Apr 30	Bob Feller, Clev vs NY 1–0
1947......July 10	Don Black, Clev vs Phi 3–0
Sep 3	Bill McCahan, Phi vs Wash 3–0
1948......June 30	Bob Lemon, Clev vs Det 2–0
1951......July 1	Bob Feller, Clev vs Det 2–1
July 12	Allie Reynolds, NY vs Clev 1–0
Sept 28	Allie Reynolds, NY vs Bos 8–0
1952......May 15	Virgil Trucks, Det vs Wash 1–0
Aug 25	Virgil Trucks, Det vs NY 1–0
1953......May 6	Bobo Holloman, StL vs Phi 6–0 (first major league start)
1956......July 14	Mel Parnell, Bos vs Chi 4–0
Oct 8	Don Larsen, NY (A) vs Bklyn (N) 2–0 (World Series) (perfect game)
1957......Aug 20	Bob Keegan, Chi vs Wash 6–0
1958......July 20	Jim Bunning, Det vs Bos 3–0
Sept 20	Hoyt Wilhelm, Balt vs NY 1–0
1962......May 5	Bo Belinsky, LA vs Balt 2–0
June 26	Earl Wilson, Bos vs LA 2–0
Aug 1	Bill Monbouquette, Bos vs Chi 1–0
Aug 26	Jack Kralick, Minn vs KC 1–0
1965......Sept 16	Dave Morehead, Bos vs Clev 2–0
1966......June 10	Sonny Siebert, Clev vs Wash 2–0
1967......Apr 30	Steve Barber (8⅔) and Stu Miller (⅓), Balt vs Det 1–2
Aug 25	Dean Chance, Minn vs Clev 2–1
Sept 10	Joel Horlen, Chi vs Det 6–0
1968......Apr 27	Tom Phoebus, Balt vs Bos 6–0
May 8	Jim (Catfish) Hunter, Oak vs Minn 4–0 (perfect game)
1969......Aug 13	Jim Palmer, Balt vs Oak 8–0
1970......July 3	Clyde Wright, Cal vs Oak 4–0
Sept 21	Vida Blue, Oak vs Minn 6–0
1973......Apr 27	Steve Busby, KC vs Det 3–0
May 15	Nolan Ryan, Cal vs KC 3–0
July 15	Nolan Ryan, Cal vs Det 6–0
July 30	Jim Bibby, Tex vs Oak 6–0
1974......June 19	Steve Busby, KC vs Mil 2–0
July 19	Dick Bosman, Clev vs Oak 4–0
Sept 28	Nolan Ryan, Cal vs Minn 4–0
1975......June 1	Nolan Ryan, Cal vs Balt 1–0
Sept 28	Vida Blue (5), Glenn Abbott and Paul Lindblad (1), Rollie Fingers (2), Oak vs Cal 5–0
1976......July 28	John Odom (5) and Francisco Barrios (4), Chi vs Oak 2–1
1977......May 14	Jim Colborn, KC vs Tex 6–0
May 30	Dennis Eckersley, Clev vs Cal 1–0
Sept 22	Bert Blyleven, Tex vs Cal 6–0
1981......May 15	Len Barker, Clev vs Tor 3–0 (perfect game)
1983......July 4	Dave Righetti, NY vs Bos 4–0
Sept 29	Mike Warren, Oak vs Chi 3–0
1984......Apr 7	Jack Morris, Det vs Chi 4–0
Sept 30	Mike Witt, Cal vs Tex 1–0 (perfect game)
1986......Sept 19	Joe Cowley, Chi vs Cal 7–1
1987......Apr 15	Juan Nieves, Mil vs Balt 7–0
1990......Apr 11	Mark Langston (7), Mike Witt (2), Cal vs Sea 1–0
June 2	Randy Johnson, Sea vs Det 2–0
June 11	Nolan Ryan, Tex vs Oak 5–0
June 29	Dave Stewart, Oak vs Tor 5–0
July 1	Andy Hawkins, NY vs Chi 0–4 (pitched eight of nine–innning game)
Sept 2	Dave Stieb, Tor vs Clev 3–0
1991......May 1	Nolan Ryan, Tex vs Tor 3–0
July 13	Bob Milacki (6), Mike Flanagan (1), Mark Williamson (1), and Gregg Olson (1), Balt vs Oak 2–0
Aug 11	Wilson Alvarez, Chi vs Balt 7–0
Aug 26	Bret Saberhagen, KC vs Chi 7–0
1993......Apr 22	Chris Bosio, Sea vs Bos 7–0
Sept 4	Jim Abbott, NY vs Clev 4–0
1994......Apr 27	Scott Erickson, Minn vs Mil 6–0
July 28	Kenny Rogers, Texas vs Cal 4–0 (perfect game)
1996......May 14	Dwight Gooden, NY vs Sea 2–0

No-Hit Games, Nine Innings or More *(Cont.)*
AMERICAN LEAGUE *(Cont.)*

Date		Pitcher and Game
1998	May 17	David Wells, NY vs Minn 4–0 (perfect game)
1999	July 18	David Cone, NY vs Mtl 6–0 (perfect game)
	Sept 11	Eric Milton, Minn vs Ana 7–0
2001	Apr 4	Hideo Nomo, Bos vs Balt 3–0
2002	Apr 27	Derek Lowe, Bos vs TB 10–0
2007	Apr 19	Mark Buehrle, Chi vs Tex, 6–0
	June 12	Justin Verlander, Det vs Mil 4–0
	Sep 1	Clay Buchholz, Bos vs Balt 10–0
2008	May 19	Jon Lester, Bos vs KC 7–0
2009	July 23	Mark Buehrle, Chi vs TB 5–0 (perfect game)
2010	May 9	Dallas Braden, Oak vs TB 4–0 (perfect game)
	July 26	Matt Garza, TB vs Det 5–0
2011	May 3	Francisco Liriano, Min vs Chi 1–0
	May 7	Justin Verlander, Det vs Tor 9–0
	July 27	Ervin Santana, LA vs Cle 3–1
2012	April 21	Philip Humber, Chi vs. Sea 4–0
	May 2	Jered Weaver, LA vs. Min 9–0
	Aug 15	Felix Hernandez, Sea vs. TB 1–0

Longest Hitting Streaks

NATIONAL LEAGUE

Player and Team	Year	G
Willie Keeler, Balt	1897	44
Pete Rose, Cin	1978	44
Bill Dahlen, Chi	1894	42
Tommy Holmes, Bos	1945	37
Billy Hamilton, Phi	1894	36
Jimmy Rollins, Phi	2005–06	36
Fred Clarke, Lou	1895	35
Luis Castillo, Fla	2002	35
Chase Utley, Phi	2006	35
Benito Santiago, SD	1987	34
George Davis, NY	1893	33
Rogers Hornsby, StL	1922	33
Dan Uggla, Atl	2011	33

AMERICAN LEAGUE

Player and Team	Year	G
Joe DiMaggio, NY	1941	56
George Sisler, StL	1922	41
Ty Cobb, Det	1911	40
Paul Molitor, Mil	1987	39
Ty Cobb, Det	1917	35
George Sisler, StL	1925	34
George McQuinn, StL	1938	34
Dom DiMaggio, Bos	1949	34
Hal Chase, NY	1907	33
Heinie Manush, Wash	1933	33

Triple Crown Hitters

NATIONAL LEAGUE

Player and Team	Year	HR	RBI	BA
Paul Hines, Prov	1878	4	50	.358
Hugh Duffy, Bos	1894	18	145	.438
Heinie Zimmerman*, Chi	1912	14	103	.372
Rogers Hornsby, StL	1922	42	152	.401
	1925	39	143	.403
Chuck Klein, Phi	1933	28	120	.368
Joe Medwick, StL	1937	31	154	.374

*Zimmerman ranked first in RBIs as calculated by Ernie Lanigan, but only third as calculated by Information Concepts Inc.

AMERICAN LEAGUE

Player and Team	Year	HR	RBI	BA
Nap Lajoie, Phi	1901	14	125	.422
Ty Cobb, Det	1909	9	115	.377
Jimmie Foxx, Phi	1933	48	163	.356
Lou Gehrig, NY	1934	49	165	.363
Ted Williams, Bos	1942	36	137	.356
	1947	32	114	.343
Mickey Mantle, NY	1956	52	130	.353
Frank Robinson, Balt	1966	49	122	.316
Carl Yastrzemski, Bos	1967	44	121	.326
Miguel Cabrera, Det	2012	44	139	.330

Triple Crown Pitchers

NATIONAL LEAGUE

Player and Team	Year	W	L	SO	ERA
Tommy Bond, Bos	1877	40	17	170	2.11
Hoss Radbourn, Prov	1884	60	12	441	1.38
Tim Keefe, NY	1888	35	12	333	1.74
John Clarkson, Bos	1889	49	19	284	2.73
Amos Rusie, NY	1894	36	13	195	2.78
Christy Mathewson, NY	1905	31	8	206	1.27
	1908	37	11	259	1.43
Grover Alexander, Phi	1915	31	10	241	1.22
	1916	33	12	167	1.55
	1917	30	13	201	1.86
Hippo Vaughn, Chi	1918	22	10	148	1.74
Dazzy Vance, Bklyn	1924	28	6	262	2.16
Bucky Walters, Cin	1939	27	11	137	2.29
Sandy Koufax, LA	1963	25	5	306	1.88
	1965	26	8	382	2.04
	1966	27	9	317	1.73
Steve Carlton, Phi	1972	27	10	310	1.97
Dwight Gooden, NY	1985	24	4	268	1.53
Randy Johnson, Ariz	2002	24	5	334	2.32
*Clayton Kershaw, LA	2011	21	5	248	2.28

AMERICAN LEAGUE

Player and Team	Year	W	L	SO	ERA
Cy Young, Bos	1901	33	10	158	1.62
Rube Waddell, Phi	1905	26	11	287	1.48
Walter Johnson, Wash	1913	36	7	303	1.09
	1918	23	13	162	1.27
	1924	23	7	158	2.72
Lefty Grove, Phi	1930	28	5	209	2.54
	1931	31	4	175	2.06
Lefty Gomez, NY	1934	26	5	158	2.33
	1937	21	11	194	2.33
Hal Newhouser, Det	1945	25	9	212	1.81
Roger Clemens, Tor	1997	21	7	292	2.05
	1998	20	6	271	2.64
Pedro Martinez, Bos	1999	23	4	313	2.07
*Johan Santana, Minn	2006	19	6	245	2.77
Justin Verlander, Det	2011	24	5	250	2.40

*Tied with another pitcher for most wins

Consecutive Games Played,
500 or More Games

Cal Ripken Jr.	2,632	Frank McCormick	652
Lou Gehrig	2,130	Sandy Alomar Sr.	648
Everett Scott	1,307	Eddie Brown	618
Steve Garvey	1,207	Roy McMillan	585
Miguel Tejada	1,152	George Pinckney	577
Billy Williams	1,117	Steve Brodie	574
Joe Sewell	1,103	Aaron Ward	565
Stan Musial	895	Alex Rodriguez	546
Eddie Yost	829	Candy LaChance	540
Gus Suhr	822	Buck Freeman	535
Nellie Fox	798	Fred Luderus	533
Pete Rose	745	Hideki Matsui	518
Dale Murphy	740	Clyde Milan	511
Richie Ashburn	730	Charlie Gehringer	511
Ernie Banks	717	Vada Pinson	508
Pete Rose	678	Tony Cuccinello	504
Earl Averill	673	Charlie Gehringer	504

Unassisted Triple Plays

Player and Team	Date	Pos	Opp	Opp Batter
Neal Ball, Clev	7-19-09	SS	Bos	Amby McConnell
Bill Wambsganss, Clev	10-10-20	2B	Bklyn	Clarence Mitchell
George Burns, Bos	9-14-23	1B	Clev	Frank Brower
Ernie Padgett, Bos	10-6-23	SS	Phi	Walter Holke
Glenn Wright, Pitt	5-7-25	SS	StL	Jim Bottomley
Jimmy Cooney, Chi	5-30-27	SS	Pitt	Paul Waner
Johnny Neun, Det	5-31-27	1B	Clev	Homer Summa
Ron Hansen, Wash	7-30-68	SS	Clev	Joe Azcue
Mickey Morandini, Phi	9-20-92	2B	Pitt	Jeff King
John Valentin, Bos	7-15-94	SS	Minn	Marc Newfield
Randy Velarde, Oak	5-29-00	2B	NYY	Shane Spencer
Rafael Furcal, Atl	8-10-03	SS	StL	Woody Williams
Troy Tulowitzki, Col	4-29-07	SS	Atl	Chipper Jones
Asdrubal Cabrera, Cle	5-12-08	2B	Tor	Lyle Overbay
Eric Bruntlett, Phi	8-23-09	2B	NYM	Jeff Francoeur

Year-by-Year Leaders

NATIONAL LEAGUE
Leading Batsmen

Year	Player and Team	BA	Year	Player and Team	BA
1900	Honus Wagner, Pitt	.381	1923	Rogers Hornsby, StL	.384
1901	Jesse Burkett, StL	.382	1924	Rogers Hornsby, StL	.424
1902	Ginger Beaumtl, Pitt	.357	1925	Rogers Hornsby, StL	.403
1903	Honus Wagner, Pitt	.355	1926	Bubbles Hargrave, Cin	.353
1904	Honus Wagner, Pitt	.349	1927	Paul Waner, Pitt	.380
1905	Cy Seymour, Cin	.377	1928	Rogers Hornsby, Bos	.387
1906	Honus Wagner, Pitt	.339	1929	Lefty O'Doul, Phi	.398
1907	Honus Wagner, Pitt	.350	1930	Bill Terry, NY	.401
1908	Honus Wagner, Pitt	.354	1931	Chick Hafey, StL	.349
1909	Honus Wagner, Pitt	.339	1932	Lefty O'Doul, Bklyn	.368
1910	Sherry Magee, Phi	.331	1933	Chuck Klein, Phi	.368
1911	Honus Wagner, Pitt	.334	1934	Paul Waner, Pitt	.362
1912	Heinie Zimmerman, Chi	.372	1935	Arky Vaughan, Pitt	.385
1913	Jake Daubert, Bklyn	.350	1936	Paul Waner, Pitt	.373
1914	Jake Daubert, Bklyn	.329	1937	Joe Medwick, StL	.374
1915	Larry Doyle, NY	.320	1938	Ernie Lombardi, Cin	.342
1916	Hal Chase, Cin	.339	1939	Johnny Mize, StL	.349
1917	Edd Roush, Cin	.341	1940	Debs Garms, Pitt	.355
1918	Zach Wheat, Bklyn	.335	1941	Pete Reiser, Bklyn	.343
1919	Edd Roush, Cin	.321	1942	Ernie Lombardi, Bos	.330
1920	Rogers Hornsby, StL	.370	1943	Stan Musial, StL	.357
1921	Rogers Hornsby, StL	.397	1944	Dixie Walker, Bklyn	.357
1922	Rogers Hornsby, StL	.401	1945	Phil Cavarretta, Chi	.355

NATIONAL LEAGUE *(Cont.)*
Leading Batsmen *(Cont.)*

Year	Player and Team	BA	Year	Player and Team	BA
1946	Stan Musial, St	.365	1980	Bill Buckner, Chi	.324
1947	Harry Walker, StL-Phi	.363	1981	Bill Madlock, Pitt	.341
1948	Stan Musial, StL	.376	1982	Al Oliver, Mtl	.331
1949	Jackie Robinson, Bklyn	.342	1983	Bill Madlock, Pitt	.323
1950	Stan Musial, StL	.346	1984	Tony Gwynn, SD	.351
1951	Stan Musial, StL	.355	1985	Willie McGee, StL	.353
1952	Stan Musial, StL	.336	1986	Tim Raines, Mtl	.334
1953	Carl Furillo, Bklyn	.344	1987	Tony Gwynn, SD	.370
1954	Willie Mays, NY	.345	1988	Tony Gwynn, SD	.313
1955	Richie Ashburn, Phi	.338	1989	Tony Gwynn, SD	.336
1956	Hank Aaron, Mil	.328	1990	Willie McGee, StL	.335
1957	Stan Musial, StL	.351	1991	Terry Pendleton, Atl	.319
1958	Richie Ashburn, Phi	.350	1992	Gary Sheffield, SD	.330
1959	Hank Aaron, Mil	.355	1993	Andres Galarraga, Col	.370
1960	Dick Groat, Pitt	.325	1994	Tony Gwynn, SD	.394
1961	Roberto Clemente, Pitt	.351	1995	Tony Gwynn, SD	.368
1962	Tommy Davis, LA	.346	1996	Tony Gwynn, SD	.353
1963	Tommy Davis, LA	.326	1997	Tony Gwynn, SD	.372
1964	Roberto Clemente, Pitt	.339	1998	Larry Walker, Col	.363
1965	Roberto Clemente, Pitt	.329	1999	Larry Walker, Col	.379
1966	Matty Alou, Pitt	.342	2000	Todd Helton, Col	.372
1967	Roberto Clemente, Pitt	.357	2001	Larry Walker, Col	.350
1968	Pete Rose, Cin	.335	2002	Barry Bonds, SF	.370
1969	Pete Rose, Cin	.348	2003	Albert Pujols, StL	.359
1970	Rico Carty, Atl	.366	2004	Barry Bonds, SF	.362
1971	Joe Torre, StL	.363	2005	Derrek Lee, Chi	.335
1972	Billy Williams, Chi	.333	2006	Freddy Sanchez, Pitt	.334
1973	Pete Rose, Cin	.338	2007	Matt Holliday, Col	.340*
1974	Ralph Garr, Atl	.353	2008	Chipper Jones, Atl	.364
1975	Bill Madlock, Chi	.354	2009	Hanley Ramirez, Fla	.342
1976	Bill Madlock, Chi	.339	2010	Carlos Gonzalez, Col	.336
1977	Dave Parker, Pitt	.338	2011	Jose Reyes, NY	.337
1978	Dave Parker, Pitt	.334	2012	Buster Posey, SF	.336
1979	Keith Hernandez, StL	.344			

*Includes one-game NL Wild Card tiebreaker.

Leaders in Runs Scored

Year	Player and Team	Runs	Year	Player and Team	Runs
1900	Roy Thomas, Phi	131	1925	Kiki Cuyler, Pitt	144
1901	Jesse Burkett, StL	139	1926	Kiki Cuyler, Pitt	113
1902	Honus Wagner, Pitt	105	1927	Lloyd Waner, Pitt	133
1903	Ginger Beaumont, Pitt	137		Rogers Hornsby, NY	133
1904	George Browne, NY	99	1928	Paul Waner, Pitt	142
1905	Mike Donlin, NY	124	1929	Rogers Hornsby, Chi	156
1906	Honus Wagner, Pitt	103	1930	Chuck Klein, Phi	158
	Frank Chance, Chi	103	1931	Bill Terry, NY	121
1907	Spike Shannon, NY	104		Chuck Klein, Phi	121
1908	Fred Tenney, NY	101	1932	Chuck Klein, Phi	152
1909	Tommy Leach, Pitt	126	1933	Pepper Martin, StL	122
1910	Sherry Magee, Phi	110	1934	Paul Waner, Pitt	122
1911	Jimmy Sheckard, Chi	121	1935	Augie Galan, Chi	133
1912	Bob Bescher, Cin	120	1936	Arky Vaughan, Pitt	122
1913	Tommy Leach, Chi	99	1937	Joe Medwick, StL	111
	Max Carey, Pitt	99	1938	Mel Ott, NY	116
1914	George Burns, NY	100	1939	Billy Werber, Cin	115
1915	Gavvy Cravath, Phi	89	1940	Arky Vaughan, Pitt	113
1916	George Burns, NY	105	1941	Pete Reiser, Bklyn	117
1917	George Burns, NY	103	1942	Mel Ott, NY	118
1918	Heinie Groh, Cin	88	1943	Arky Vaughan, Bklyn	112
1919	George Burns, NY	86	1944	Bill Nicholson, Chi	116
1920	George Burns, NY	115	1945	Eddie Stanky, Bklyn	128
1921	Rogers Hornsby, StL	131	1946	Stan Musial, StL	124
1922	Rogers Hornsby, StL	141	1947	Johnny Mize, NY	137
1923	Ross Youngs, NY	121	1948	Stan Musial, StL	135
1924	Frankie Frisch, NY	121	1949	Pee Wee Reese, Bklyn	132
	Rogers Hornsby, StL	121	1950	Earl Torgeson, Bos	120

NATIONAL LEAGUE *(Cont.)*
Leaders in Runs Scored *(Cont.)*

Year	Player and Team	Runs	Year	Player and Team	Runs
1951	Stan Musial, StL	124	1981	Mike Schmidt, Phi	78
	Ralph Kiner, Pitt	124	1982	Lonnie Smith, StL	120
1952	Stan Musial, StL	105	1983	Tim Raines, Mtl	133
	Solly Hemus, StL	105	1984	Ryne Sandberg, Chi	114
1953	Duke Snider, Bklyn	132	1985	Dale Murphy, Atl	118
1954	Stan Musial, StL	120	1986	Von Hayes, Phi	107
	Duke Snider, Bklyn	120		Tony Gwynn, SD	107
1955	Duke Snider, Bklyn	126	1987	Tim Raines, Mtl	123
1956	Frank Robinson, Cin	122	1988	Brett Butler, SF	109
1957	Hank Aaron, Mil	118	1989	Howard Johnson, NY	104
1958	Willie Mays, SF	121		Will Clark, SF	104
1959	Vada Pinson, Cin	131		Ryne Sandberg, Chi	104
1960	Bill Bruton, Mil	112	1990	Ryne Sandberg, Chi	116
1961	Willie Mays, SF	129	1991	Brett Butler, LA	112
1962	Frank Robinson, Cin	134	1992	Barry Bonds, Pitt	109
1963	Hank Aaron, Mil	121	1993	Lenny Dykstra, Phi	143
1964	Dick Allen, Phi	125	1994	Jeff Bagwell, Hou	104
1965	Tommy Harper, Cin	126	1995	Craig Biggio, Hou	123
1966	Felipe Alou, Atl	122	1996	Ellis Burks, Col	142
1967	Hank Aaron, Atl	113	1997	Craig Biggio, Hou	146
	Lou Brock, StL	113	1998	Sammy Sosa, Chi	134
1968	Glenn Beckert, Chi	98	1999	Jeff Bagwell, Hou	143
1969	Bobby Bonds, SF	120	2000	Jeff Bagwell, Hou	152
	Pete Rose, Cin	120	2001	Sammy Sosa, Chi	146
1970	Billy Williams, Chi	137	2002	Sammy Sosa, Chi	122
1971	Lou Brock, StL	126	2003	Albert Pujols, StL	137
1972	Joe Morgan, Cin	122	2004	Albert Pujols, StL	133
1973	Bobby Bonds, SF	131	2005	Albert Pujols, StL	129
1974	Pete Rose, Cin	110	2006	Chase Utley, Phi	131
1975	Pete Rose, Cin	112	2007	Jimmy Rollins, Phi	139
1976	Pete Rose, Cin	130	2008	Hanley Ramirez, Fla	125
1977	George Foster, Cin	124	2009	Albert Pujols, StL	124
1978	Ivan DeJesus, Chi	104	2010	Albert Pujols, StL	115
1979	Keith Hernandez, StL	116	2011	Matt Kemp, LA	115
1980	Keith Hernandez, StL	111	2012	Ryan Braun, Mil	108

Leaders in Hits

Year	Player and Team	Hits	Year	Player and Team	Hits
1900	Willie Keeler, Bklyn	208	1927	Paul Waner, Pitt	237
1901	Jesse Burkett, StL	228	1928	Freddy Lindstrom, NY	231
1902	Ginger Beaumont, Pitt	194	1929	Lefty O'Doul, Phi	254
1903	Ginger Beaumont, Pitt	209	1930	Bill Terry, NY	254
1904	Ginger Beaumont, Pitt	185	1931	Lloyd Waner, Pitt	214
1905	Cy Seymour, Cin	219	1932	Chuck Klein, Phi	226
1906	Harry Steinfeldt, Chi	176	1933	Chuck Klein, Phi	223
1907	Ginger Beaumont, Bos	187	1934	Paul Waner, Pitt	217
1908	Honus Wagner, Pitt	201	1935	Billy Herman, Chi	227
1909	Larry Doyle, NY	172	1936	Joe Medwick, StL	223
1910	Bobby Byrne, Pitt	178	1937	Joe Medwick, StL	237
	Honus Wagner, Pitt	178	1938	Frank McCormick, Cin	209
1911	Doc Miller, Bos	192	1939	Frank McCormick, Cin	209
1912	Heinie Zimmerman, Chi	207	1940	Stan Hack, Chi	191
1913	Gavvy Cravath, Phi	179		Frank McCormick, Cin	191
1914	Sherry Magee, Phi	171	1941	Stan Hack, Chi	186
1915	Larry Doyle, NY	189	1942	Enos Slaughter, StL	188
1916	Hal Chase, Cin	184	1943	Stan Musial, StL	220
1917	Heinie Groh, Cin	182	1944	Phil Cavarretta, Chi	197
1918	Charlie Hollocher, Chi	161		Stan Musial, StL	197
1919	Ivy Olson, Bklyn	164	1945	Tommy Holmes, Bos	224
1920	Rogers Hornsby, StL	218	1946	Stan Musial, StL	228
1921	Rogers Hornsby, StL	235	1947	Tommy Holmes, Bos	191
1922	Rogers Hornsby, StL	250	1948	Stan Musial, StL	230
1923	Frankie Frisch, NY	223	1949	Stan Musial, StL	207
1924	Rogers Hornsby, StL	227	1950	Duke Snider, Bklyn	199
1925	Jim Bottomley, StL	227	1951	Richie Ashburn, Phi	221
1926	Eddie Brown, Bos	201	1952	Stan Musial, StL	194

NATIONAL LEAGUE (Cont.)
Leaders in Hits (Cont.)

Year	Player and Team	Hits	Year	Player and Team	Hits
1953	Riche Ashburn, Phi	205	1984	Tony Gwynn, SD	213
1954	Don Mueller, NY	212	1985	Willie McGee, StL	216
1955	Ted Kluszewski, Cin	192	1986	Tony Gwynn, SD	211
1956	Hank Aaron, Mil	200	1987	Tony Gwynn, SD	218
1957	Red Schoendienst, NY-Mil	200	1988	Andres Galarraga, Mtl	184
1958	Richie Ashburn, Phi	215	1989	Tony Gwynn, SD	203
1959	Hank Aaron, Mil	223	1990	Brett Butler, SF	192
1960	Willie Mays, SF	190		Lenny Dykstra, Phi	192
1961	Vada Pinson, Cin	208	1991	Terry Pendleton, Atl	187
1962	Tommy Davis, LA	230	1992	Terry Pendleton, Atl	199
1963	Vada Pinson, Cin	204		Andy Van Slyke, Pitt	199
1964	Roberto Clemente, Pitt	211	1993	Lenny Dykstra, Phi	194
	Curt Flood, StL	211	1994	Tony Gwynn, SD	165
1965	Pete Rose, Cin	209	1995	Dante Bichette, Col	197
1966	Felipe Alou, Atl	218		Tony Gwynn, SD	197
1967	Roberto Clemente, Pitt	209	1996	Lance Johnson, NY	227
1968	Felipe Alou, Atl	210	1997	Tony Gwynn, SD	220
	Pete Rose, Cin	210	1998	Dante Bichette, Col	219
1969	Matty Alou, Pitt	231	1999	Luis Gonzalez, Ariz	206
1970	Pete Rose, Cin	205	2000	Todd Helton, Col	216
	Billy Williams, Chi	205	2001	Rich Aurilia, SF	206
1971	Joe Torre, StL	230	2002	Vladimir Guerrero	206
1972	Pete Rose, Cin	198	2003	Albert Pujols, StL	212
1973	Pete Rose, Cin	230	2004	Juan Pierre, Fla	221
1974	Ralph Garr, Atl	214	2005	Derrek Lee, Chi	199
1975	Dave Cash, Phi	213	2006	Juan Pierre, Chi	204
1976	Pete Rose, Cin	215	2007	Matt Holliday, Col	216*
1977	Dave Parker, Pitt	215	2008	Jose Reyes, NY	204
1978	Steve Garvey, LA	202	2009	Ryan Braun, Mil	203
1979	Garry Templeton, StL	211	2010	Carlos Gonzalez, Col	197
1980	Steve Garvey, LA	200	2011	Starlin Castro, Chi	207
1981	Pete Rose, Phi	140	2012	Andrew McCutchen, Pitt	194
1982	Al Oliver, Mtl	204			
1983	Jose Cruz, Hou	189		*Includes one-game NL Wild Card tiebreaker.	
	Andre Dawson, Mtl	189			

Home Run Leaders

Year	Player and Team	HR	Year	Player and Team	HR
1900	Herman Long, Bos	12	1924	Jack Fournier, Bklyn	27
1901	Sam Crawford, Cin	16	1925	Rogers Hornsby, StL	39
1902	Tommy Leach, Pitt	6	1926	Hack Wilson, Chi	21
1903	Jimmy Sheckard, Bklyn	9	1927	Hack Wilson, Chi	30
1904	Harry Lumley, Bklyn	9		Cy Williams, Phi	30
1905	Fred Odwell, Cin	9	1928	Jim Bottomley, StL	31
1906	Tim Jordan, Bklyn	12		Hack Wilson, Chi	31
1907	Dave Brain, Bos	10	1929	Chuck Klein, Phi	43
1908	Tim Jordan, Bklyn	12	1930	Hack Wilson, Chi	56
1909	Red Murray, NY	7	1931	Chuck Klein, Phi	31
1910	Fred Beck, Bos	10	1932	Chuck Klein, Phi	38
	Wildfire Schulte, Chi	10		Mel Ott, NY	38
1911	Wildfire Schulte, Chi	21	1933	Chuck Klein, Phi	28
1912	Heinie Zimmerman, Chi	14	1934	Ripper Collins, StL	35
1913	Gavvy Cravath, Phi	19		Mel Ott, NY	35
1914	Gavvy Cravath, Phi	19	1935	Wally Berger, Bos	34
1915	Gavvy Cravath, Phi	24	1936	Mel Ott, NY	33
1916	Dave Robertson, NY	12	1937	Joe Medwick, StL	31
	Cy Williams, Chi	12		Mel Ott, NY	31
1917	Gavvy Cravath, Phi	12	1938	Mel Ott, NY	36
	Dave Robertson, NY	12	1939	Johnny Mize, StL	28
1918	Gavvy Cravath, Phi	8	1940	Johnny Mize, StL	43
1919	Gavvy Cravath, Phi	12	1941	Dolph Camilli, Bklyn	34
1920	Cy Williams, Phi	15	1942	Mel Ott, NY	30
1921	George Kelly, NY	23	1943	Bill Nicholson, Chi	29
1922	Rogers Hornsby, StL	42	1944	Bill Nicholson, Chi	33
1923	Cy Williams, Phi	41	1945	Tommy Holmes, Bos	28

NATIONAL LEAGUE *(Cont.)*
Home Run Leaders *(Cont.)*

Year	Player and Team	HR	Year	Player and Team	HR
1946	Ralph Kiner, Pitt	23	1978	George Foster, Cin	40
1947	Ralph Kiner, Pitt	51	1979	Dave Kingman, Chi	48
	Johnny Mize, NY	51	1980	Mike Schmidt, Phi	48
1948	Ralph Kiner, Pitt	40	1981	Mike Schmidt, Phi	31
	Johnny Mize, NY	40	1982	Dave Kingman, NY	37
1949	Ralph Kiner, Pitt	54	1983	Mike Schmidt, Phi	40
1950	Ralph Kiner, Pitt	47	1984	Dale Murphy, Atl	36
1951	Ralph Kiner, Pitt	42		Mike Schmidt, Phi	36
1952	Ralph Kiner, Pitt	37	1985	Dale Murphy, Atl	37
	Hank Sauer, Chi	37	1986	Mike Schmidt, Phi	37
1953	Eddie Mathews, Mil	47	1987	Andre Dawson, Chi	49
1954	Ted Kluszewski, Cin	49	1988	Darryl Strawberry, NY	39
1955	Willie Mays, NY	51	1989	Kevin Mitchell, SF	47
1956	Duke Snider, Bklyn	43	1990	Ryne Sandberg, Chi	40
1957	Hank Aaron, Mil	44	1991	Howard Johnson, NY	38
1958	Ernie Banks, Chi	47	1992	Fred McGriff, SD	35
1959	Eddie Mathews, Mil	46	1993	Barry Bonds, SF	46
1960	Ernie Banks, Chi	41	1994	Matt Williams, SF	43
1961	Orlando Cepeda, SF	46	1995	Dante Bichette, Col	40
1962	Willie Mays, SF	49	1996	Andres Galarraga, Col	47
1963	Hank Aaron, Mil	44	1997	Larry Walker, Col	49
	Willie McCovey, SF	44	1998	Mark McGwire, StL	70
1964	Willie Mays, SF	47	1999	Mark McGwire, StL	65
1965	Willie Mays, SF	52	2000	Sammy Sosa, Chi	50
1966	Hank Aaron, Atl	44	2001	Barry Bonds, SF	73
1967	Hank Aaron, Atl	39	2002	Sammy Sosa, Chi	49
1968	Willie McCovey, SF	36	2003	Jim Thome, Phi	47
1969	Willie McCovey, SF	45	2004	Adrian Beltre, LA	48
1970	Johnny Bench, Cin	45	2005	Andruw Jones, Atl	51
1971	Willie Stargell, Pitt	48	2006	Ryan Howard, Phi	58
1972	Johnny Bench, Cin	40	2007	Prince Fielder, Mil	50
1973	Willie Stargell, Pitt	44	2008	Ryan Howard, Phi	48
1974	Mike Schmidt, Phi	36	2009	Albert Pujols, StL	47
1975	Mike Schmidt, Phi	38	2010	Albert Pujols, StL	42
1976	Mike Schmidt, Phi	38	2011	Matt Kemp, LA	39
1977	George Foster, Cin	52	2012	Ryan Braun, Mil	41

Runs Batted In Leaders

Year	Player and Team	RBI	Year	Player and Team	RBI
1900	Elmer Flick, Phi	110	1924	George Kelly, NY	136
1901	Honus Wagner, Pitt	126	1925	Rogers Hornsby, StL	143
1902	Honus Wagner, Pitt	91	1926	Jim Bottomley, StL	120
1903	Sam Mertes, NY	104	1927	Paul Waner, Pitt	131
1904	Bill Dahlen, NY	80	1928	Jim Bottomley, StL	136
1905	Cy Seymour, Cin	121	1929	Hack Wilson, Chi	159
1906	Jim Nealon, Pitt	83	1930	Hack Wilson, Chi	190
	Harry Steinfeldt, Chi	83	1931	Chuck Klein, Phi	121
1907	Sherry Magee, Phi	85	1932	Don Hurst, Phi	143
1908	Honus Wagner, Pitt	109	1933	Chuck Klein, Phi	120
1909	Honus Wagner, Pitt	100	1934	Mel Ott, NY	135
1910	Sherry Magee, Phi	123	1935	Wally Berger, Bos	130
1911	Wildfire Schulte, Chi	121	1936	Joe Medwick, StL	138
1912	Heinie Zimmerman, Chi	103	1937	Joe Medwick, StL	154
1913	Gavvy Cravath, Phi	128	1938	Joe Medwick, StL	122
1914	Sherry Magee, Phi	103	1939	Frank McCormick, Cin	128
1915	Gavvy Cravath, Phi	115	1940	Johnny Mize, StL	137
1916	Heinie Zimmerman, Chi-NY	83	1941	Dolph Camilli, Bklyn	120
1917	Heinie Zimmerman, NY	102	1942	Johnny Mize, NY	110
1918	Sherry Magee, Phi	76	1943	Bill Nicholson, Chi	128
1919	Hi Myers, Bklyn	73	1944	Bill Nicholson, Chi	122
1920	Rogers Hornsby, StL	94	1945	Dixie Walker, Bklyn	124
	George Kelly, NY	94	1946	Enos Slaughter, StL	130
1921	Rogers Hornsby, StL	126	1947	Johnny Mize, NY	138
1922	Rogers Hornsby, StL	152	1948	Stan Musial, StL	131
1923	Irish Meusel, NY	125	1949	Ralph Kiner, Pitt	127

NATIONAL LEAGUE (Cont.)
Runs Batted In Leaders (Cont.)

Year	Player and Team	RBI	Year	Player and Team	RBI
1950	Del Ennis, Phi	126	1983	Dale Murphy, Atl	121
1951	Monte Irvin, NY	121	1984	Gary Carter, Mtl	106
1952	Hank Sauer, Chi	121		Mike Schmidt, Phi	106
1953	Roy Campanella, Bklyn	142	1985	Dave Parker, Cin	125
1954	Ted Kluszewski, Cin	141	1986	Mike Schmidt, Phi	119
1955	Duke Snider, Bklyn	136	1987	Andre Dawson, Chi	137
1956	Stan Musial, StL	109	1988	Will Clark, SF	109
1957	Hank Aaron, Mil	132	1989	Kevin Mitchell, SF	125
1958	Ernie Banks, Chi	129	1990	Matt Williams, SF	122
1959	Ernie Banks, Chi	143	1991	Howard Johnson, NY	117
1960	Hank Aaron, Mil	126	1992	Darren Daulton, Phi	109
1961	Orlando Cepeda, SF	142	1993	Barry Bonds, SF	123
1962	Tommy Davis, LA	153	1994	Jeff Bagwell, Hou	116
1963	Hank Aaron, Mil	130	1995	Dante Bichette, Col	128
1964	Ken Boyer, StL	119	1996	Andres Galarraga, Col	150
1965	Deron Johnson, Cin	130	1997	Andres Galarraga, Col	140
1966	Hank Aaron, Atl	127	1998	Sammy Sosa, Chi	158
1967	Orlando Cepeda, StL	111	1999	Mark McGwire, StL	147
1968	Willie McCovey, SF	105	2000	Todd Helton, Col	147
1969	Willie McCovey, SF	126	2001	Sammy Sosa, Chi	160
1970	Johnny Bench, Cin	148	2002	Lance Berkman, Hou	128
1971	Joe Torre, StL	137	2003	Preston Wilson, Col	141
1972	Johnny Bench, Cin	125	2004	Vinny Castilla, Col	131
1973	Willie Stargell, Pitt	119	2005	Andruw Jones, Atl	128
1974	Johnny Bench, Cin	129	2006	Ryan Howard, Phi	149
1975	Greg Luzinski, Phi	120	2007	Matt Holliday, Col	137*
1976	George Foster, Cin	121	2008	Ryan Howard, Phi	146
1977	George Foster, Cin	149	2009	Prince Fielder, Mil	141
1978	George Foster, Cin	120		Ryan Howard, Phi	141
1979	Dave Winfield, SD	118	2010	Albert Pujols, StL	118
1980	Mike Schmidt, Phi	121	2011	Matt Kemp, LA	126
1981	Mike Schmidt, Phi	91	2012	Chase Headley, SD	115
1982	Dale Murphy, Atl	109			
	Al Oliver, Mtl	109			

*Includes one-game NL Wild Card tiebreaker.

Leading Base Stealers

Year	Player and Team	SB	Year	Player and Team	SB
1900	George Van Haltren, NY	45	1925	Max Carey, Pitt	46
	Patsy Donovan, StL	45	1926	Kiki Cuyler, Pitt	35
1901	Honus Wagner, Pitt	48	1927	Frankie Frisch, StL	48
1902	Honus Wagner, Pitt	43	1928	Kiki Cuyler, Chi	37
1903	Jimmy Sheckard, Bklyn	67	1929	Kiki Cuyler, Chi	43
	Frank Chance, Chi	67	1930	Kiki Cuyler, Chi	37
1904	Honus Wagner, Pitt	53	1931	Frankie Frisch, StL	28
1905	Billy Maloney, Chi	59	1932	Chuck Klein, Phi	20
	Art Devlin, NY	59	1933	Pepper Martin, StL	26
1906	Frank Chance, Chi	57	1934	Pepper Martin, StL	23
1907	Honus Wagner, Pitt	61	1935	Augie Galan, Chi	22
1908	Honus Wagner, Pitt	53	1936	Pepper Martin, StL	23
1909	Bob Bescher, Cin	54	1937	Augie Galan, Chi	23
1910	Bob Bescher, Cin	70	1938	Stan Hack, Chi	16
1911	Bob Bescher, Cin	80	1939	Stan Hack, Chi	17
1912	Bob Bescher, Cin	67		Lee Handley, Pitt	17
1913	Max Carey, Pitt	61	1940	Lonny Frey, Cin	22
1914	George Burns, NY	62	1941	Danny Murtaugh, Phi	18
1915	Max Carey, Pitt	36	1942	Pete Reiser, Bklyn	20
1916	Max Carey, Pitt	63	1943	Arky Vaughan, Bklyn	20
1917	Max Carey, Pitt	46	1944	Johnny Barrett, Pitt	28
1918	Max Carey, Pitt	58	1945	Red Schoendienst, StL	26
1919	George Burns, NY	40	1946	Pete Reiser, Bklyn	34
1920	Max Carey, Pitt	52	1947	Jackie Robinson, Bklyn	29
1921	Frankie Frisch, NY	49	1948	Richie Ashburn, Phi	32
1922	Max Carey, Pitt	51	1949	Jackie Robinson, Bklyn	37
1923	Max Carey, Pitt	51	1950	Sam Jethroe, Bos	35
1924	Max Carey, Pitt	49	1951	Sam Jethroe, Bos	35

NATIONAL LEAGUE *(Cont.)*
Leading Base Stealers *(Cont.)*

Year	Player and Team	SB	Year	Player and Team	SB
1952	Pee Wee Reese, Bklyn	30	1983	Tim Raines, Mtl	90
1953	Bill Bruton, Mil	26	1984	Tim Raines, Mtl	75
1954	Bill Bruton, Mil	34	1985	Vince Coleman, StL	110
1955	Bill Bruton, Mil	35	1986	Vince Coleman, StL	107
1956	Willie Mays, NY	40	1987	Vince Coleman, StL	109
1957	Willie Mays, NY	38	1988	Vince Coleman, StL	81
1958	Willie Mays, SF	31	1989	Vince Coleman, StL	65
1959	Willie Mays, SF	27	1990	Vince Coleman, StL	77
1960	Maury Wills, LA	50	1991	Marquis Grissom, Mtl	76
1961	Maury Wills, LA	35	1992	Marquis Grissom, Mtl	78
1962	Maury Wills, LA	104	1993	Chuck Carr, Fla	58
1963	Maury Wills, LA	40	1994	Craig Biggio, Hou	39
1964	Maury Wills, LA	53	1995	Quilvio Veras, Fla	56
1965	Maury Wills, LA	94	1996	Eric Young, Col	53
1966	Lou Brock, StL	74	1997	Tony Womack, Pitt	60
1967	Lou Brock, StL	52	1998	Tony Womack, Pitt	58
1968	Lou Brock, StL	62	1999	Tony Womack, Ariz	72
1969	Lou Brock, StL	53	2000	Luis Castillo, Fla	62
1970	Bobby Tolan, Cin	57	2001	Juan Pierre, Col	46
1971	Lou Brock, StL	64	2002	Luis Castillo, Fla	48
1972	Lou Brock, StL	63	2003	Juan Pierre, Fla	65
1973	Lou Brock, StL	70	2004	Scott Podsednik, Mil	70
1974	Lou Brock, StL	118	2005	Jose Reyes, NY	60
1975	Davey Lopes, LA	77	2006	Jose Reyes, NY	64
1976	Davey Lopes, LA	63	2007	Jose Reyes, NY	78
1977	Frank Taveras, Pitt	70	2008	Willy Taveras, Hou	68
1978	Omar Moreno, Pitt	71	2009	Michael Bourn, Hou	61
1979	Omar Moreno, Pitt	77	2010	Michael Bourn, Hou	52
1980	Ron LeFlore, Mtl	97	2011	Micheal Bourn, Hou/Atl	61
1981	Tim Raines, Mtl	71	2012	Everth Cabrera, SD	44
1982	Tim Raines, Mtl	78			

Leading Pitchers—Winning Percentage

Year	Pitcher and Team	W	L	Pct	Year	Pitcher and Team	W	L	Pct
1900	Jesse Tannehill, Pitt	20	6	.769	1930	Freddie Fitzsimmons, NY	19	7	.731
1901	Jack Chesbro, Pitt	21	10	.677	1931	Paul Derringer, StL	18	8	.692
1902	Jack Chesbro, Pitt	28	6	.824	1932	Lon Warneke, Chi	22	6	.786
1903	Sam Leever, Pitt	25	7	.781	1933	Ben Cantwell, Bos	20	10	.667
1904	Joe McGinnity, NY	35	8	.814	1934	Dizzy Dean, StL	30	7	.811
1905	Sam Leever, Pitt	20	5	.800	1935	Bill Lee, Chi	20	6	.769
1906	Ed Reulbach, Chi	19	4	.826	1936	Carl Hubbell, NY	26	6	.813
1907	Ed Reulbach, Chi	17	4	.810	1937	Carl Hubbell, NY	22	8	.733
1908	Ed Reulbach, Chi	24	7	.774	1938	Bill Lee, Chi	22	9	.710
1909	Howie Camnitz, Pitt	25	6	.806	1939	Paul Derringer, Cin	25	7	.781
	Christy Mathewson, NY	25	6	.806	1940	Freddie Fitzsimmons, Bklyn	16	2	.889
1910	King Cole, Chi	20	4	.833	1941	Elmer Riddle, Cin	19	4	.826
1911	Rube Marquard, NY	24	7	.774	1942	Larry French, Bklyn	15	4	.789
1912	Claude Hendrix, Pitt	24	9	.727	1943	Mort Cooper, StL	21	8	.724
1913	Bert Humphries, Chi	16	4	.800	1944	Ted Wilks, StL	17	4	.810
1914	Bill James, Bos	26	7	.788	1945	Harry Brecheen, StL	15	4	.789
1915	Grover Alexander, Phi	31	10	.756	1946	Murray Dickson, StL	15	6	.714
1916	Tom Hughes, Bos	16	3	.842	1947	Larry Jansen, NY	21	5	.808
1917	Ferdie Schupp, NY	21	7	.750	1948	Harry Brecheen, StL	20	7	.741
1918	Claude Hendrix, Chi	19	7	.731	1949	Preacher Roe, Bklyn	15	6	.714
1919	Dutch Ruether, Cin	19	6	.760	1950	Sal Maglie, NY	18	4	.818
1920	Burleigh Grimes, Bklyn	23	11	.676	1951	Preacher Roe, Bklyn	22	3	.880
1921	Bill Doak, StL	15	6	.714	1952	Hoyt Wilhelm, NY	15	3	.833
1922	Pete Donohue, Cin	18	9	.667	1953	Carl Erskine, Bklyn	20	6	.769
1923	Dolf Luque, Cin	27	8	.771	1954	Johnny Antonelli, NY	21	7	.750
1924	Emil Yde, Pitt	16	3	.842	1955	Don Newcombe, Bklyn	20	5	.800
1925	Bill Sherdel, StL	15	6	.714	1956	Don Newcombe, Bklyn	27	7	.794
1926	Ray Kremer, Pitt	20	6	.769	1957	Bob Buhl, Mil	18	7	.720
1927	Larry Benton, Bos-NY	17	7	.708	1958	Warren Spahn, Mil	22	11	.667
1928	Larry Benton, NY	25	9	.735		Lew Burdette, Mil	20	10	.667
1929	Charlie Root, Chi	19	6	.760	1959	Roy Face, Pitt	18	1	.947

Note: Percentages based on 15 or more victories.

NATIONAL LEAGUE (Cont.)

Leading Pitchers—Winning Percentage (Cont.)

Year	Pitcher and Team	W	L	Pct	Year	Pitcher and Team	W	L	Pct
1960	Ernie Broglio, StL	21	9	.700	1987	Dwight Gooden, NY	15	7	.682
1961	Johnny Podres, LA	18	5	.783	1988	David Cone, NY	20	3	.870
1962	Bob Purkey, Cin	23	5	.821	1989	Mike Bielecki, Chi	18	7	.720
1963	Ron Perranoski, LA	16	3	.842	1990	Doug Drabeck, Pitt	22	6	.786
1964	Sandy Koufax, LA	19	5	.792	1991	John Smiley, Pitt	20	8	.714
1965	Sandy Koufax, LA	26	8	.765		Jose Rijo, Cin	15	6	.714
1966	Juan Marichal, SF	25	6	.806	1992	Bob Tewksbury, StL	16	5	.762
1967	Dick Hughes, StL	16	6	.727	1993	Tom Glavine, Atl	22	6	.786
1968	Steve Blass, Pitt	18	6	.750	1994	Ken Hill, Mtl	16	5	.762
1969	Tom Seaver, NY	25	7	.781	1995	Greg Maddux, Atl	19	2	.905
1970	Bob Gibson, StL	23	7	.767	1996	John Smoltz, Atl	24	8	.750
1971	Don Gullett, Cin	16	6	.727	1997	Denny Neagle, Atl	20	5	.800
1972	Gary Nolan, Cin	15	5	.750	1998	John Smoltz, Atl	17	3	.850
1973	Tommy John, LA	16	7	.696	1999	Mike Hampton, Hou	22	4	.846
1974	Andy Messersmith, LA	20	6	.769	2000	Randy Johnson, Ariz	19	7	.730
1975	Don Gullett, Cin	15	4	.789	2001	Curt Schilling, Ariz	22	6	.786
1976	Steve Carlton, Phi	20	7	.741	2002	Randy Johnson, Ariz	24	5	.828
1977	John Candelaria, Pitt	20	5	.800	2003	Jason Schmidt, SF	17	5	.773
1978	Gaylord Perry, SD	21	6	.778	2004	Roger Clemens, Hou	18	4	.818
1979	Tom Seaver, Cin	16	6	.727	2005	Chris Carpenter, StL	21	5	.808
1980	Jim Bibby, Pitt	19	6	.760	2006	Carlos Zambrano, Chi	16	7	.695
1981*	Tom Seaver, Cin	14	2	.875	2007	Brad Penny, LA	16	4	.800
1982	Phil Niekro, Atl	17	4	.810	2008	Tim Lincecum, SF	18	5	.783
1983	John Denny, Phi	19	6	.760	2009	Chris Carpenter, StL	17	4	.810
1984	Rick Sutcliffe, Chi	16	1	.941	2010	Ubaldo Jimenez, Col	19	8	.704
1985	Orel Hershiser, LA	19	3	.864	2011	Ian Kennedy, Ari	21	4	.840
1986	Bob Ojeda, NY	18	5	.783	2012	Kyle Lohse, StL	16	3	.842

*1981 percentages based on 10 or more victories. All other years, percentages based on 15 or more victories.

Leading Pitchers—Earned Run Average

Year	Player and Team	ERA	Year	Player and Team	ERA
1900	Rube Waddell, Pitt	2.37	1932	Lon Warneke, Chi	2.37
1901	Jesse Tannehill, Pitt	2.18	1933	Carl Hubbell, NY	1.66
1902	Jack Taylor, Chi	1.33	1934	Carl Hubbell, NY	2.30
1903	Sam Leever, Pitt	2.06	1935	Cy Blanton, Pitt	2.59
1904	Joe McGinnity, NY	1.61	1936	Carl Hubbell, NY	2.31
1905	Christy Mathewson, NY	1.27	1937	Jim Turner, Bos	2.38
1906	Three Finger Brown, Chi	1.04	1938	Bill Lee, Chi	2.66
1907	Jack Pfiester, Chi	1.15	1939	Bucky Walters, Cin	2.29
1908	Christy Mathewson, NY	1.43	1940	Bucky Walters, Cin	2.48
1909	Christy Mathewson, NY	1.14	1941	Elmer Riddle, Cin	2.24
1910	George McQuillan, Phi	1.60	1942	Mort Cooper, StL	1.77
1911	Christy Mathewson, NY	1.99	1943	Howie Pollet, StL	1.75
1912	Jeff Tesreau, NY	1.96	1944	Ed Heusser, Cin	2.38
1913	Christy Mathewson, NY	2.06	1945	Hank Borowy, Chi	2.14
1914	Bill Doak, StL	1.72	1946	Howie Pollet, StL	2.10
1915	Grover Alexander, Phi	1.22	1947	Warren Spahn, Bos	2.33
1916	Grover Alexander, Phi	1.55	1948	Harry Brecheen, StL	2.24
1917	Grover Alexander, Phi	1.83	1949	Dave Koslo, NY	2.50
1918	Hippo Vaughn, Chi	1.74	1950	Jim Hearn, StL-NY	2.49
1919	Grover Alexander, Chi	1.72	1951	Chet Nichols, Bos	2.88
1920	Grover Alexander, Chi	1.91	1952	Hoyt Wilhelm, NY	2.43
1921	Bill Doak, StL	2.58	1953	Warren Spahn, Mil	2.10
1922	Rosy Ryan, NY	3.00	1954	Johnny Antonelli, NY	2.29
1923	Dolf Luque, Cin	1.93	1955	Bob Friend, Pitt	2.84
1924	Dazzy Vance, Bklyn	2.16	1956	Lew Burdette, Mil	2.71
1925	Dolf Luque, Cin	2.63	1957	Johnny Podres, Bklyn	2.66
1926	Ray Kremer, Pitt	2.61	1958	Stu Miller, SF	2.47
1927	Ray Kremer, Pitt	2.47	1959	Sam Jones, SF	2.82
1928	Dazzy Vance, Bklyn	2.09	1960	Mike McCormick, SF	2.70
1929	Bill Walker, NY	3.08	1961	Warren Spahn, Mil	3.01
1930	Dazzy Vance, Bklyn	2.61	1962	Sandy Koufax, LA	2.54
1931	Bill Walker, NY	2.26	1963	Sandy Koufax, LA	1.88

Note: Based on 10 complete games through 1950, then 154 innings until National League expanded in 1962, when it became 162 innings. In strike-shortened 1981, one inning per game required.

NATIONAL LEAGUE (Cont.)

Leading Pitchers—Earned Run Average (Cont.)

Year	Player and Team	ERA	Year	Player and Team	ERA
1964	Sandy Koufax, LA	1.74	1989	Scott Garrelts, SF	2.28
1965	Sandy Koufax, LA	2.04	1990	Danny Darwin, Hou	2.21
1966	Sandy Koufax, LA	1.73	1991	Dennis Martinez, Mtl	2.39
1967	Phil Niekro, Atl	1.87	1992	Bill Swift, SF	2.08
1968	Bob Gibson, StL	1.12	1993	Greg Maddux, Atl	2.36
1969	Juan Marichal, SF	2.10	1994	Greg Maddux, Atl	1.56
1970	Tom Seaver, NY	2.81	1995	Greg Maddux, Atl	1.63
1971	Tom Seaver, NY	1.76	1996	Kevin Brown, Fla	1.89
1972	Steve Carlton, Phi	1.98	1997	Pedro Martinez, Mtl	1.90
1973	Tom Seaver, NY	2.08	1998	Greg Maddux, Atl	1.98
1974	Buzz Capra, Atl	2.28	1999	Randy Johnson, Ariz	2.48
1975	Randy Jones, SD	2.24	2000	Kevin Brown, LA	2.58
1976	John Denny, StL	2.52	2001	Randy Johnson, Ariz	2.49
1977	John Candelaria, Pitt	2.34	2002	Randy Johnson, Ariz	2.32
1978	Craig Swan, NY	2.43	2003	Jason Schmidt, SF	2.34
1979	J.R. Richard, Hou	2.71	2004	Jake Peavy, SD	2.27
1980	Don Sutton, LA	2.21	2005	Roger Clemens, Hou	1.87
1981	Nolan Ryan, Hou	1.69	2006	Roy Oswalt, Hou	2.98
1982	Steve Rogers, Mtl	2.40	2007	Jake Peavy, SD	2.54*
1983	Atlee Hammaker, SF	2.25	2008	Johan Santana, NYM	2.53
1984	Alejandro Pena, LA	2.48	2009	Chris Carpenter, StL	2.24
1985	Dwight Gooden, NY	1.53	2010	Josh Johnson, Fla	2.30
1986	Mike Scott, Hou	2.22	2011	Clayton Kershaw, LA	2.28
1987	Nolan Ryan, Hou	2.76	2012	Clayton Kershaw, LA	2.53
1988	Joe Magrane, StL	2.18			

*Includes one-game NL Wild Card tiebreaker.

Leading Pitchers—Strikeouts

Year	Player and Team	SO	Year	Player and Team	SO
1900	Rube Waddell, Pitt	133	1937	Carl Hubbell, NY	159
1901	Noodles Hahn, Cin	233	1938	Clay Bryant, Chi	135
1902	Vic Willis, Bos	226	1939	Claude Passeau, Phi-Chi	137
1903	Christy Mathewson, NY	267		Bucky Walters, Cin	137
1904	Christy Mathewson, NY	212	1940	Kirby Higbe, Phi	137
1905	Christy Mathewson, NY	206	1941	Johnny Vander Meer, Cin	202
1906	Fred Beebe, Chi-StL	171	1942	Johnny Vander Meer, Cin	186
1907	Christy Mathewson, NY	178	1943	Johnny Vander Meer, Cin	174
1908	Christy Mathewson, NY	259	1944	Bill Voiselle, NY	161
1909	Orval Overall, Chi	205	1945	Preacher Roe, Pitt	148
1910	Christy Mathewson, NY	190	1946	Johnny Schmitz, Chi	135
1911	Rube Marquard, NY	237	1947	Ewell Blackwell, Cin	193
1912	Grover Alexander, Phi	195	1948	Harry Brecheen, StL	149
1913	Tom Seaton, Phi	168	1949	Warren Spahn, Bos	151
1914	Grover Alexander, Phi	214	1950	Warren Spahn, Bos	191
1915	Grover Alexander, Phi	241	1951	Warren Spahn, Bos	164
1916	Grover Alexander, Phi	167		Don Newcombe, Bkln	164
1917	Grover Alexander, Phi	200	1952	Warren Spahn, Bos	183
1918	Hippo Vaughn, Chi	148	1953	Robin Roberts, Phi	198
1919	Hippo Vaughn, Chi	141	1954	Robin Roberts, Phi	185
1920	Grover Alexander, Chi	173	1955	Sam Jones, Chi	198
1921	Burleigh Grimes, Bklyn	136	1956	Sam Jones, Chi	176
1922	Dazzy Vance, Bklyn	134	1957	Jack Sanford, Phi	188
1923	Dazzy Vance, Bklyn	197	1958	Sam Jones, StL	225
1924	Dazzy Vance, Bklyn	262	1959	Don Drysdale, LA	242
1925	Dazzy Vance, Bklyn	221	1960	Don Drysdale, LA	246
1926	Dazzy Vance, Bklyn	140	1961	Sandy Koufax, LA	269
1927	Dazzy Vance, Bklyn	184	1962	Don Drysdale, LA	232
1928	Dazzy Vance, Bklyn	200	1963	Sandy Koufax, LA	306
1929	Pat Malone, Chi	166	1964	Bob Veale, Pitt	250
1930	Bill Hallahan, StL	177	1965	Sandy Koufax, LA	382
1931	Bill Hallahan, StL	159	1966	Sandy Koufax, LA	317
1932	Dizzy Dean, StL	191	1967	Jim Bunning, Phi	253
1933	Dizzy Dean, StL	199	1968	Bob Gibson, StL	268
1934	Dizzy Dean, StL	195	1969	Ferguson Jenkins, Chi	273
1935	Dizzy Dean, StL	182	1970	Tom Seaver, NY	283
1936	Van Lingle Mungo, Bklyn	238	1971	Tom Seaver, NY	289

NATIONAL LEAGUE *(Cont.)*
Leading Pitchers—Strikeouts *(Cont.)*

Year	Player and Team	SO	Year	Player and Team	SO
1972	Steve Carlton, Phi	310	1993	Jose Rijo, Cin	227
1973	Tom Seaver, NY	251	1994	Andy Benes, SD	189
1974	Steve Carlton, Phi	240	1995	Hideo Nomo, LA	236
1975	Tom Seaver, NY	243	1996	John Smoltz, Atl	276
1976	Tom Seaver, NY	235	1997	Curt Schilling, Phi	319
1977	Phil Niekro, Atl	262	1998	Curt Schilling, Phi	300
1978	J.R. Richard, Hou	303	1999	Randy Johnson, Ariz	364
1979	J.R. Richard, Hou	313	2000	Randy Johnson, Ariz	347
1980	Steve Carlton, Phi	286	2001	Randy Johnson, Ariz	372
1981	Fernando Valenzuela, LA	180	2002	Randy Johnson, Ariz	334
1982	Steve Carlton, Phi	286	2003	Kerry Wood, Chi	266
1983	Steve Carlton, Phi	275	2004	Randy Johnson, Ariz	290
1984	Dwight Gooden, NY	276	2005	Jake Peavy, SD	216
1985	Dwight Gooden, NY	268	2006	Aaron Harang, Cin	216
1986	Mike Scott, Hou	306	2007	Jake Peavy, SD	240*
1987	Nolan Ryan, Hou	270	2008	Tim Lincecum, SF	265
1988	Nolan Ryan, Hou	228	2009	Tim Lincecum, SF	261
1989	Jose DeLeon, StL	201	2010	Tim Lincecum, SF	231
1990	David Cone, NY	233	2011	Clayton Kershaw, LA	248
1991	David Cone, NY	241	2012	R.A. Dickey, NY	230
1992	John Smoltz, Atl	215			

*Includes one-game NL Wild Card tiebreaker.

Leading Pitchers—Saves

Year	Player and Team	SV	Year	Player and Team	SV
1947	Hugh Casey, Bklyn	18	1980	Bruce Sutter, Chi	28
1948	Harry Gumpert, Cin	17	1981	Bruce Sutter, StL	25
1949	Ted Wilks, StL	9	1982	Bruce Sutter, StL	36
1950	Jim Konstanty, Phi	22	1983	Lee Smith, Chi	29
1951	Ted Wilks, StL, Pitt	13	1984	Bruce Sutter, StL	45
1952	Al Brazle, StL	16	1985	Jeff Reardon, Mtl	41
1953	Al Brazle, StL	18	1986	Todd Worrell, StL	36
1954	Jim Hughes, Bklyn	24	1987	Steve Bedrosian, Phi	40
1955	Jack Meyer, Phi	16	1988	John Franco, Cin	39
1956	Clem Labine, Bklyn	19	1989	Mark Davis, SD	44
1957	Clem Labine, Bklyn	17	1990	John Franco, NY	33
1958	Roy Face, Pitt	20	1991	Lee Smith, StL	47
1959	Lindy McDaniel, StL	15	1992	Lee Smith, StL	42
	Don McMahon, Mil	15	1993	Randy Myers, Chi	53
1960	Lindy McDaniel, StL	26	1994	John Franco, NY	30
1961	Roy Face, Pitt	17	1995	Randy Myers, Chi	38
	Stu Miller, SF	17	1996	Jeff Brantley, Cin	44
1962	Roy Face, Pitt	28		Todd Worrell, LA	44
1963	Lindy McDaniel, Chi	22	1997	Jeff Shaw, Cin	42
1964	Hal Woodeshick, Hou	23	1998	Trevor Hoffman, SD	53
1965	Ted Abernathy, Chi	31	1999	Ugueth Urbina, Mtl	41
1966	Phil Regan, LA	21	2000	Antonio Alfonseca, Fla	45
1967	Ted Abernathy, Cin	28	2001	Robb Nen, SF	45
1968	Phi Regan, Chi, LA	25	2002	John Smoltz, Atl	55
1969	Fred Gladding, Hou	29	2003	Eric Gagne, LA	55
1970	Wayne Granger, Cin	35	2004	Armando Benitez, Fla	47
1971	Dave Giusti, Pitt	30		Jason Isringhausen, StL	47
1972	Clay Carroll, Cin	37	2005	Chad Cordero, Wash	47
1973	Mike Marshall, Mtl	13	2006	Trevor Hoffman, SD	46
1974	Mike Marshall, LA	21	2007	Jose Valverde, Ariz	47
1975	Rawly Eastwick, Cin	22	2008	Jose Valverde, Hou	44
	Al Hrabosky, StL	22	2009	Heath Bell, SD	42
1976	Rawly Eastwick, Cin	26	2010	Brian Wilson, SF	48
1977	Rollie Fingers, SD	35	2011	John Axford, Mil	46
1978	Rollie Fingers, SD	37		Craig Kimbrel, Atl	46
1979	Bruce Sutter, Chi	37	2012	Jason Motte, StL	42
				Craig Kimbrel, Atl	42

AMERICAN LEAGUE
Leading Batsmen

Year	Player and Team	BA	Year	Player and Team	BA
1901	Nap Lajoie, Phi	.422	1957	Ted Williams, Bos	.388
1902	Ed Delahanty, Wash	.376	1958	Ted Williams, Bos	.328
1903	Nap Lajoie, Clev	.355	1959	Harvey Kuenn, Det	.353
1904	Nap Lajoie, Clev	.381	1960	Pete Runnels, Bos	.320
1905	Elmer Flick, Clev	.306	1961	Norm Cash, Det	.361
1906	George Stone, StL	.358	1962	Pete Runnels, Bos	.326
1907	Ty Cobb, Det	.350	1963	Carl Yastrzemski, Bos	.321
1908	Ty Cobb, Det	.324	1964	Tony Oliva, Minn	.323
1909	Ty Cobb, Det	.377	1965	Tony Oliva, Minn	.321
1910	Nap Lajoie, Clev†	.383	1966	Frank Robinson, Balt	.316
1911	Ty Cobb, Det	.420	1967	Carl Yastrzemski, Bos	.326
1912	Ty Cobb, Det	.410	1968	Carl Yastrzemski, Bos	.301
1913	Ty Cobb, Det	.390	1969	Rod Carew, Minn	.332
1914	Ty Cobb, Det	.368	1970	Alex Johnson, Cal	.329
1915	Ty Cobb, Det	.369	1971	Tony Oliva, Minn	.337
1916	Tris Speaker, Clev	.386	1972	Rod Carew, Minn	.318
1917	Ty Cobb, Det	.383	1973	Rod Carew, Minn	.350
1918	Ty Cobb, Det	.382	1974	Rod Carew, Minn	.364
1919	Ty Cobb, Det	.384	1975	Rod Carew, Minn	.359
1920	George Sisler, StL	.407	1976	George Brett, KC	.333
1921	Harry Heilmann, Det	.394	1977	Rod Carew, Minn	.388
1922	George Sisler, StL	.420	1978	Rod Carew, Minn	.333
1923	Harry Heilmann, Det	.403	1979	Fred Lynn, Bos	.333
1924	Babe Ruth, NY	.378	1980	George Brett, KC	.390
1925	Harry Heilmann, Det	.393	1981	Carney Lansford, Bos	.336
1926	Heinie Manush, Det	.378	1982	Willie Wilson, KC	.332
1927	Harry Heilmann, Det	.398	1983	Wade Boggs, Bos	.361
1928	Goose Goslin, Wash	.379	1984	Don Mattingly, NY	.343
1929	Lew Fonseca, Clev	.369	1985	Wade Boggs, Bos	.368
1930	Al Simmons, Phi	.381	1986	Wade Boggs, Bos	.357
1931	Al Simmons, Phi	.390	1987	Wade Boggs, Bos	.363
1932	Dale Alexander, Det-Bos	.367	1988	Wade Boggs, Bos	.366
1933	Jimmie Foxx, Phi	.356	1989	Kirby Puckett, Minn	.339
1934	Lou Gehrig, NY	.363	1990	George Brett, KC	.329
1935	Buddy Myer, Wash	.349	1991	Julio Franco, Tex	.341
1936	Luke Appling, Chi	.388	1992	Edgar Martinez, Sea	.343
1937	Charlie Gehringer, Det	.371	1993	John Olerud, Tor	.363
1938	Jimmie Foxx, Bos	.349	1994	Paul O'Neill, NY	.359
1939	Joe DiMaggio, NY	.381	1995	Edgar Martinez, Sea	.356
1940	Joe DiMaggio, NY	.352	1996	Alex Rodriguez, Sea	.358
1941	Ted Williams, Bos	.406	1997	Frank Thomas, Chi	.347
1942	Ted Williams, Bos	.356	1998	Bernie Williams, NY	.339
1943	Luke Appling, Chi	.328	1999	Nomar Garciaparra, Bos	.357
1944	Lou Boudreau, Clev	.327	2000	Nomar Garciaparra, Bos	.372
1945	Snuffy Stirnweiss, NY	.309	2001	Ichiro Suzuki, Sea	.350
1946	Mickey Vernon, Wash	.353	2002	Manny Ramirez, Bos	.349
1947	Ted Williams, Bos	.343	2003	Bill Mueller, Bos	.326
1948	Ted Williams, Bos	.369	2004	Ichiro Suzuki, Sea	.372
1949	George Kell, Det	.343	2005	Michael Young, Tex	.331
1950	Billy Goodman, Bos	.354	2006	Joe Mauer, Minn	.347
1951	Ferris Fain, Phi	.344	2007	Magglio Ordonez, Det	.363
1952	Ferris Fain, Phi	.327	2008	Joe Mauer, Minn	.330
1953	Mickey Vernon, Wash	.337	2009	Joe Mauer, Minn*	.365
1954	Bobby Avila, Clev	.341	2010	Josh Hamilton, Tex	.359
1955	Al Kaline, Det	.340	2011	Miguel Cabrera, Det	.344
1956	Mickey Mantle, NY	.353	2012	Miguel Cabrera, Det	.330

†League president Ban Johnson declared Ty Cobb batting champion with a .385 average, beating Lajoie's .384. However, subsequent research has led to the revision of Lajoie's average to .383 and Cobb's to .382.
*Includes one-game AL Central playoff tiebreaker.

AMERICAN LEAGUE *(Cont.)*

Leaders in Runs Scored

Year	Player and Team	Runs	Year	Player and Team	Runs
1901	Nap Lajoie, Phi	145	1959	Eddie Yost, Det	115
1902	Dave Fultz, Phi	110	1960	Mickey Mantle, NY	119
1903	Patsy Dougherty, Bos	108	1961	Mickey Mantle, NY	132
1904	Patsy Dougherty, Bos-NY	113		Roger Maris, NY	132
1905	Harry Davis, Phi	92	1962	Albie Pearson, LA	115
1906	Elmer Flick, Clev	98	1963	Bob Allison, Minn	99
1907	Sam Crawford, Det	102	1964	Tony Oliva, Minn	109
1908	Matty McIntyre, Det	105	1965	Zoilo Versalles, Minn	126
1909	Ty Cobb, Det	116	1966	Frank Robinson, Balt	122
1910	Ty Cobb, Det	106	1967	Carl Yastrzemski, Bos	112
1911	Ty Cobb, Det	147	1968	Dick McAuliffe, Det	95
1912	Eddie Collins, Phi	137	1969	Reggie Jackson, Oak	123
1913	Eddie Collins, Phi	125	1970	Carl Yastrzemski, Bos	125
1914	Eddie Collins, Phi	122	1971	Don Buford, Balt	99
1915	Ty Cobb, Det	144	1972	Bobby Murcer, NY	102
1916	Ty Cobb, Det	113	1973	Reggie Jackson, Oak	99
1917	Donie Bush, Det	112	1974	Carl Yastrzemski, Bos	93
1918	Ray Chapman, Clev	84	1975	Fred Lynn, Bos	103
1919	Babe Ruth, Bos	103	1976	Roy White, NY	104
1920	Babe Ruth, NY	158	1977	Rod Carew, Minn	128
1921	Babe Ruth, NY	177	1978	Ron LeFlore, Det	126
1922	George Sisler, StL	134	1979	Don Baylor, Cal	120
1923	Babe Ruth, NY	151	1980	Willie Wilson, KC	133
1924	Babe Ruth, NY	143	1981	Rickey Henderson, Oak	89
1925	Johnny Mostil, Chi	135	1982	Paul Molitor, Mil	136
1926	Babe Ruth, NY	139	1983	Cal Ripken, Balt	121
1927	Babe Ruth, NY	158	1984	Dwight Evans, Bos	121
1928	Babe Ruth, NY	163	1985	Rickey Henderson, NY	146
1929	Charlie Gehringer, Det	131	1986	Rickey Henderson, NY	130
1930	Al Simmons, Phi	152	1987	Paul Molitor, Mil	114
1931	Lou Gehrig, NY	163	1988	Wade Boggs, Bos	128
1932	Jimmie Foxx, Phi	151	1989	Wade Boggs, Bos	113
1933	Lou Gehrig, NY	138		Rickey Henderson, NY-Oak	113
1934	Charlie Gehringer, Det	134	1990	Rickey Henderson, Oak	119
1935	Lou Gehrig, NY	125	1991	Paul Molitor, Mil	133
1936	Lou Gehrig, NY	167	1992	Tony Philips, Det	114
1937	Joe DiMaggio, NY	151	1993	Rafael Palmeiro, Tex	124
1938	Hank Greenberg, Det	144	1994	Frank Thomas, Chi	106
1939	Red Rolfe, NY	139	1995	Albert Belle, Clev	121
1940	Ted Williams, Bos	134		Edgar Martinez, Sea	121
1941	Ted Williams, Bos	135	1996	Alex Rodriguez, Sea	141
1942	Ted Williams, Bos	141	1997	Ken Griffey Jr., Sea	125
1943	George Case, Wash	102	1998	Derek Jeter, NY	127
1944	Snuffy Stirnweiss, NY	125	1999	Roberto Alomar, Clev	138
1945	Snuffy Stirnweiss, NY	107	2000	Johnny Damon, KC	136
1946	Ted Williams, Bos	142	2001	Alex Rodriguez, Tex	133
1947	Ted Williams, Bos	125	2002	Alfonso Soriano, NY	128
1948	Tommy Henrich, NY	138	2003	Alex Rodriguez, Tex	124
1949	Ted Williams, Bos	150	2004	Vladimir Guerrero, Ana	124
1950	Dom DiMaggio, Bos	131	2005	Alex Rodriguez, NY	124
1951	Dom DiMaggio, Bos	113	2006	Grady Sizemore, Clev	134
1952	Larry Doby, Clev	104	2007	Alex Rodriguez, NY	143
1953	Al Rosen, Clev	115	2008	Dustin Pedroia, Bos	118
1954	Mickey Mantle, NY	129	2009	Dustin Pedroia, Bos	115
1955	Al Smith, Clev	123	2010	Mark Teixeira, NY	113
1956	Mickey Mantle, NY	132	2011	Curtis Granderson, NY	136
1957	Mickey Mantle, NY	121	2012	Mike Trout, LA	129
1958	Mickey Mantle, NY	127			

AMERICAN LEAGUE *(Cont.)*
Leaders in Hits

Year	Player and Team	Hits	Year	Player and Team	Hits
1901	Nap Lajoie, Phi	229	1956	Harvey Kuenn, Det	196
1902	Piano Legs Hickman, Bos-Clev	194	1957	Nellie Fox, Chi	196
1903	Patsy Dougherty, Bos	195	1958	Nellie Fox, Chi	187
1904	Nap Lajoie, Clev	211	1959	Harvey Kuenn, Det	198
1905	George Stone, StL	187	1960	Minnie Minoso, Chi	184
1906	Nap Lajoie, Clev	214	1961	Norm Cash, Det	193
1907	Ty Cobb, Det	212	1962	Bobby Richardson, NY	209
1908	Ty Cobb, Det	188	1963	Carl Yastrzemski, Bos	183
1909	Ty Cobb, Det	216	1964	Tony Oliva, Minn	217
1910	Nap Lajoie, Clev	227	1965	Tony Oliva, Minn	185
1911	Ty Cobb, Det	248	1966	Tony Oliva, Minn	191
1912	Ty Cobb, Det	227	1967	Carl Yastrzemski, Bos	189
1913	Joe Jackson, Clev	197	1968	Bert Campaneris, Oak	177
1914	Tris Speaker, Bos	193	1969	Tony Oliva, Minn	197
1915	Ty Cobb, Det	208	1970	Tony Oliva, Minn	204
1916	Tris Speaker, Clev	211	1971	Cesar Tovar, Minn	204
1917	Ty Cobb, Det	225	1972	Joe Rudi, Oak	181
1918	George Burns, Phi	178	1973	Rod Carew, Minn	203
1919	Ty Cobb, Det	191	1974	Rod Carew, Minn	218
	Bobby Veach, Det	191	1975	George Brett, KC	195
1920	George Sisler, StL	257	1976	George Brett, KC	215
1921	Harry Heilmann, Det	237	1977	Rod Carew, Minn	239
1922	George Sisler, StL	246	1978	Jim Rice, Bos	213
1923	Charlie Jamieson, Clev	222	1979	George Brett, KC	212
1924	Sam Rice, Wash	216	1980	Willie Wilson, KC	230
1925	Al Simmons, Phi	253	1981	Rickey Henderson, Oak	135
1926	George Burns, Clev	216	1982	Robin Yount, Mil	210
	Sam Rice, Wash	216	1983	Cal Ripken Jr., Balt	211
1927	Earle Combs, NY	231	1984	Don Mattingly, NY	207
1928	Heinie Manush, StL	241	1985	Wade Boggs, Bos	240
1929	Dale Alexander, Det	215	1986	Don Mattingly, NY	238
	Charlie Gehringer, Det	215	1987	Kirby Puckett, Minn	207
1930	Johnny Hodapp, Clev	225		Kevin Seitzer, KC	207
1931	Lou Gehrig, NY	211	1988	Kirby Puckett, Minn	234
1932	Al Simmons, Phi	216	1989	Kirby Puckett, Minn	215
1933	Heinie Manush, Wash	221	1990	Rafael Palmeiro, Tex	191
1934	Charlie Gehringer, Det	214	1991	Paul Molitor, Mil	216
1935	Joe Vosmik, Clev	216	1992	Kirby Puckett, Minn	210
1936	Earl Averill, Clev	232	1993	Paul Molitor, Tor	211
1937	Beau Bell, StL	218	1994	Kenny Lofton, Clev	160
1938	Joe Vosmik, Bos	201	1995	Lance Johnson, Chi	186
1939	Red Rolfe, NY	213	1996	Paul Molitor, Minn	225
1940	Doc Cramer, Bos	200	1997	Nomar Garciaparra, Bos	209
	Barney McCosky, Det	200	1998	Alex Rodriguez, Sea	213
	Rip Radcliff, StL	200	1999	Derek Jeter, NY	219
1941	Cecil Travis, Wash	218	2000	Darin Erstad, Ana	240
1942	Johnny Pesky, Bos	205	2001	Ichiro Suzuki, Sea	242
1943	Dick Wakefield, Det	200	2002	Alfonso Soriano, NY	209
1944	Snuffy Stirnweiss, NY	205	2003	Vernon Wells, Tor	215
1945	Snuffy Stirnweiss, NY	195	2004	Ichiro Suzuki, Sea	262
1946	Johnny Pesky, Bos	208	2005	Michael Young, Tex	221
1947	Johnny Pesky, Bos	207	2006	Ichiro Suzuki, Sea	224
1948	Bob Dillinger, StL	207	2007	Ichiro Suzuki, Sea	238
1949	Dale Mitchell, Clev	203	2008	Dustin Pedroia, Bos	213
1950	George Kell, Det	218		Ichiro Suzuki, Sea	213
1951	George Kell, Det	191	2009	Ichiro Suzuki, Sea	225
1952	Nellie Fox, Chi	192	2010	Ichiro Suzuki, Sea	214
1953	Harvey Kuenn, Det	209	2011	Adrian Gonzalez, Bos	213
1954	Nellie Fox, Chi	201		Michael Young, Tex	213
	Harvey Kuenn, Det	201	2012	Derek Jeter, NY	216
1955	Al Kaline, Det	200			

AMERICAN LEAGUE (Cont.)
Home Run Leaders

Year	Player and Team	HR	Year	Player and Team	HR
1901	Nap Lajoie, Phi	13		Harmon Killebrew, Wash	42
1902	Socks Seybold, Phi	16	1960	Mickey Mantle, NY	40
1903	Buck Freeman, Bos	13	1961	Roger Maris, NY	61
1904	Harry Davis, Phi	10	1962	Harmon Killebrew, Minn	48
1905	Harry Davis, Phi	8	1963	Harmon Killebrew, Minn	45
1906	Harry Davis, Phi	12	1964	Harmon Killebrew, Minn	49
1907	Harry Davis, Phi	8	1965	Tony Conigliaro, Bos	32
1908	Sam Crawford, Det	7	1966	Frank Robinson, Balt	49
1909	Ty Cobb, Det	9	1967	Harmon Killebrew, Minn	44
1910	Jake Stahl, Bos	10		Carl Yastrzemski, Bos	44
1911	Frank Baker, Phi	9	1968	Frank Howard, Wash	44
1912	Frank Baker, Phi	10	1969	Harmon Killebrew, Minn	49
	Tris Speaker, Bos	10	1970	Frank Howard, Wash	44
1913	Frank Baker, Phi	13	1971	Bill Melton, Chi	33
1914	Frank Baker, Phi	9	1972	Dick Allen, Chi	37
1915	Braggo Roth, Chi-Clev	7	1973	Reggie Jackson, Oak	32
1916	Wally Pipp, NY	12	1974	Dick Allen, Chi	32
1917	Wally Pipp, NY	9	1975	Reggie Jackson, Oak	36
1918	Babe Ruth, Bos	11		George Scott, Mil	36
	Tilly Walker, Phi	11	1976	Graig Nettles, NY	32
1919	Babe Ruth, Bos	29	1977	Jim Rice, Bos	39
1920	Babe Ruth, NY	54	1978	Jim Rice, Bos	46
1921	Babe Ruth, NY	59	1979	Gorman Thomas, Mil	45
1922	Ken Williams, StL	39	1980	Reggie Jackson, NY	41
1923	Babe Ruth, NY	41		Ben Oglivie, Mil	41
1924	Babe Ruth, NY	46	1981	Tony Armas, Oak	22
1925	Bob Meusel, NY	33		Dwight Evans, Bos	22
1926	Babe Ruth, NY	47		Bobby Grich, Cal	22
1927	Babe Ruth, NY	60		Eddie Murray, Balt	22
1928	Babe Ruth, NY	54	1982	Reggie Jackson, Cal	39
1929	Babe Ruth, NY	46		Gorman Thomas, Mil	39
1930	Babe Ruth, NY	49	1983	Jim Rice, Bos	39
1931	Babe Ruth, NY	46	1984	Tony Armas, Bos	43
	Lou Gehrig, NY	46	1985	Darrell Evans, Det	40
1932	Jimmie Foxx, Phi	58	1986	Jesse Barfield, Tor	40
1933	Jimmie Foxx, Phi	48	1987	Mark McGwire, Oak	49
1934	Lou Gehrig, NY	49	1988	Jose Canseco, Oak	42
1935	Jimmie Foxx, Phi	36	1989	Fred McGriff, Tor	36
	Hank Greenberg, Det	36	1990	Cecil Fielder, Det	51
1936	Lou Gehrig, NY	49	1991	Jose Canseco, Oak	44
1937	Joe DiMaggio, NY	46		Cecil Fielder, Det	44
1938	Hank Greenberg, Det	58	1992	Juan Gonzalez, Tex	43
1939	Jimmie Foxx, Bos	35	1993	Juan Gonzalez, Tex	46
1940	Hank Greenberg, Det	41	1994	Ken Griffey Jr., Sea	40
1941	Ted Williams, Bos	37	1995	Albert Belle, Clev	50
1942	Ted Williams, Bos	36	1996	Mark McGwire, Oak	52
1943	Rudy York, Det	34	1997	Ken Griffey Jr., Sea	56
1944	Nick Etten, NY	22	1998	Ken Griffey Jr., Sea	56
1945	Vern Stephens, StL	24	1999	Ken Griffey Jr., Sea	48
1946	Hank Greenberg, Det	44	2000	Troy Glaus, Ana	47
1947	Ted Williams, Bos	32	2001	Alex Rodriguez, Tex	52
1948	Joe DiMaggio, NY	39	2002	Alex Rodriguez, Tex	57
1949	Ted Williams, Bos	43	2003	Alex Rodriguez, Tex	47
1950	Al Rosen, Clev	37	2004	Manny Ramirez, Bos	43
1951	Gus Zernial, Chi-Phi	33	2005	Alex Rodriguez, NY	48
1952	Larry Doby, Clev	32	2006	David Ortiz, Bos	54
1953	Al Rosen, Clev	43	2007	Alex Rodriguez, NY	54
1954	Larry Doby, Clev	32	2008	Miguel Cabrera, Det	37
1955	Mickey Mantle, NY	37	2009	Carlos Pena, TB	39
1956	Mickey Mantle, NY	52		Mark Teixeira, NY	39
1957	Roy Sievers, Wash	42	2010	Jose Bautista, Tor	54
1958	Mickey Mantle, NY	42	2011	Jose Bautista, Tor	43
1959	Rocky Colavito, Clev	42	2012	Miguel Cabrera, Det	44

AMERICAN LEAGUE *(Cont.)*
Runs Batted In Leaders

Year	Player and Team	RBI	Year	Player and Team	RBI
1907	Ty Cobb, Det	116	1959	Jackie Jensen, Bos	112
1908	Ty Cobb, Det	108	1960	Roger Maris, NY	112
1909	Ty Cobb, Det	107	1961	Roger Maris, NY	142
1910	Sam Crawford, Det	120	1962	Harmon Killebrew, Minn	126
1911	Ty Cobb, Det	144	1963	Dick Stuart, Bos	118
1912	Frank Baker, Phi	133	1964	Brooks Robinson, Balt	118
1913	Frank Baker, Phi	126	1965	Rocky Colavito, Clev	108
1914	Sam Crawford, Det	104	1966	Frank Robinson, Balt	122
1915	Sam Crawford, Det	112	1967	Carl Yastrzemski, Bos	121
	Bobby Veach, Det	112	1968	Ken Harrelson, Bos	109
1916	Del Pratt, StL	103	1969	Harmon Killebrew, Minn	140
1917	Bobby Veach, Det	103	1970	Frank Howard, Wash	126
1918	Bobby Veach, Det	78	1971	Harmon Killebrew, Minn	119
1919	Babe Ruth, Bos	114	1972	Dick Allen, Chi	113
1920	Babe Ruth, NY	137	1973	Reggie Jackson, Oak	117
1921	Babe Ruth, NY	171	1974	Jeff Burroughs, Tex	118
1922	Ken Williams, StL	155	1975	George Scott, Mil	109
1923	Babe Ruth, NY	131	1976	Lee May, Balt	109
1924	Goose Goslin, Wash	129	1977	Larry Hisle, Minn	119
1925	Bob Meusel, NY	138	1978	Jim Rice, Bos	139
1926	Babe Ruth, NY	145	1979	Don Baylor, Cal	139
1927	Lou Gehrig, NY	175	1980	Cecil Cooper, Mil	122
1928	Babe Ruth, NY	142	1981	Eddie Murray, Balt	78
	Lou Gehrig, NY	142	1982	Hal McRae, KC	133
1929	Al Simmons, Phi	157	1983	Cecil Cooper, Mil	126
1930	Lou Gehrig, NY	174		Jim Rice, Bos	126
1931	Lou Gehrig, NY	184	1984	Tony Armas, Bos	123
1932	Jimmie Foxx, Phi	169	1985	Don Mattingly, NY	145
1933	Jimmie Foxx, Phi	163	1986	Joe Carter, Clev	121
1934	Lou Gehrig, NY	165	1987	George Bell, Tor	134
1935	Hank Greenberg, Det	170	1988	Jose Canseco, Oak	124
1936	Hal Trosky, Clev	162	1989	Ruben Sierra, Tex	119
1937	Hank Greenberg, Det	183	1990	Cecil Fielder, Det	132
1938	Jimmie Foxx, Bos	175	1991	Cecil Fielder, Det	133
1939	Ted Williams, Bos	145	1992	Cecil Fielder, Det	124
1940	Hank Greenberg, Det	150	1993	Albert Belle, Clev	129
1941	Joe DiMaggio, NY	125	1994	Kirby Puckett, Minn	112
1942	Ted Williams, Bos	137	1995	Albert Belle, Clev	126
1943	Rudy York, Det	118		Mo Vaughn, Bos	126
1944	Vern Stephens, StL	109	1996	Albert Belle, Clev	148
1945	Nick Etten, NY	111	1997	Ken Griffey Jr., Sea	147
1946	Hank Greenberg, Det	127	1998	Juan Gonzales, Tex	157
1947	Ted Williams, Bos	114	1999	Manny Ramirez, Clev	165
1948	Joe DiMaggio, NY	155	2000	Edgar Martinez, Sea	145
1949	Vern Stephens, Bos	159	2001	Bret Boone, Sea	141
	Ted Williams, Bos	159	2002	Alex Rodriguez, Tex	142
1950	Walt Dropo, Bos	144	2003	Carlos Delgado, Tor	145
	Vern Stephens, Bos	144	2004	Miguel Tejada, Balt	150
1951	Gus Zernial, Chi-Phi	129	2005	David Ortiz, Bos	148
1952	Al Rosen, Clev	105	2006	David Ortiz, Bos	137
1953	Al Rosen, Clev	145	2007	Alex Rodriguez, NY	156
1954	Larry Doby, Clev	126	2008	Josh Hamilton, Tex	130
1955	Ray Boone, Det	116	2009	Mark Teixeira, NY	122
	Jackie Jensen, Bos	116	2010	Miguel Cabrera, Det	126
1956	Mickey Mantle, NY	130	2011	Curtis Granderson, NY	119
1957	Roy Sievers, Wash	114	2012	Miguel Cabrera, Det	139
1958	Jackie Jensen, Bos	122			

Note: Runs Batted In not compiled before 1907; officially adopted in 1920.

AMERICAN LEAGUE *(Cont.)*
Leading Base Stealers

Year	Player and Team	SB	Year	Player and Team	SB
1901	Frank Isbell, Chi	48	1957	Luis Aparicio, Chi	28
1902	Topsy Hartsel, Phi	54	1958	Luis Aparicio, Chi	29
1903	Harry Bay, Clev	46	1959	Luis Aparicio, Chi	56
1904	Harry Bay, Clev	42	1960	Luis Aparicio, Chi	51
	Elmer Flick, Clev	42	1961	Luis Aparicio, Chi	53
1905	Danny Hoffman, Phi	46	1962	Luis Aparicio, Chi	31
1906	John Anderson, Wash	39	1963	Luis Aparicio, Balt	40
	Elmer Flick, Clev	39	1964	Luis Aparicio, Balt	57
1907	Ty Cobb, Det	49	1965	Bert Campaneris, KC	51
1908	Patsy Dougherty, Chi	47	1966	Bert Campaneris, KC	52
1909	Ty Cobb, Det	76	1967	Bert Campaneris, KC	55
1910	Eddie Collins, Phi	81	1968	Bert Campaneris, Oak	62
1911	Ty Cobb, Det	83	1969	Tommy Harper, Sea	73
1912	Clyde Milan, Wash	88	1970	Bert Campaneris, Oak	42
1913	Clyde Milan, Wash	75	1971	Amos Otis, KC	52
1914	Fritz Maisel, NY	74	1972	Bert Campaneris, Oak	52
1915	Ty Cobb, Det	96	1973	Tommy Harper, Bos	54
1916	Ty Cobb, Det	68	1974	Bill North, Oak	54
1917	Ty Cobb, Det	55	1975	Mickey Rivers, Cal	70
1918	George Sisler, StL	45	1976	Bill North, Oak	75
1919	Eddie Collins, Chi	33	1977	Freddie Patek, KC	53
1920	Sam Rice, Wash	63	1978	Ron LeFlore, Det	68
1921	George Sisler, StL	35	1979	Willie Wilson, KC	83
1922	George Sisler, StL	51	1980	Rickey Henderson, Oak	100
1923	Eddie Collins, Chi	49	1981	Rickey Henderson, Oak	56
1924	Eddie Collins, Chi	42	1982	Rickey Henderson, Oak	130
1925	John Mostil, Chi	43	1983	Rickey Henderson, Oak	108
1926	John Mostil, Chi	35	1984	Rickey Henderson, Oak	66
1927	George Sisler, StL	27	1985	Rickey Henderson, NY	80
1928	Buddy Myer, Bos	30	1986	Rickey Henderson, NY	87
1929	Charlie Gehringer, Det	27	1987	Harold Reynolds, Sea	60
1930	Marty McManus, Det	23	1988	Rickey Henderson, NY	93
1931	Ben Chapman, NY	61	1989	Rickey Henderson, NY-Oak	77
1932	Ben Chapman, NY	38	1990	Rickey Henderson, Oak	65
1933	Ben Chapman, NY	27	1991	Rickey Henderson, Oak	58
1934	Bill Werber, Bos	40	1992	Kenny Lofton, Clev	66
1935	Bill Werber, Bos	29	1993	Kenny Lofton, Clev	70
1936	Lyn Lary, StL	37	1994	Kenny Lofton, Clev	60
1937	Ben Chapman, Wash-Bos	35	1995	Kenny Lofton, Clev	54
	Bill Werber, Phi	35	1996	Kenny Lofton, Clev	75
1938	Frank Crosetti, NY	27	1997	Brian Hunter, Det	74
1939	George Case, Wash	51	1998	Rickey Henderson, Oak	66
1940	George Case, Wash	35	1999	Brian Hunter, Sea	44
1941	George Case, Wash	33	2000	Johnny Damon, KC	46
1942	George Case, Wash	44	2001	Ichiro Suzuki, Sea	56
1943	George Case, Wash	61	2002	Alfonso Soriano, NY	41
1944	Snuffy Stirnweiss, NY	55	2003	Carl Crawford, TB	55
1945	Snuffy Stirnweiss, NY	33	2004	Carl Crawford, TB	59
1946	George Case, Clev	28	2005	Chone Figgins, LA	62
1947	Bob Dillinger, StL	34	2006	Carl Crawford, TB	58
1948	Bob Dillinger, StL	28	2007	Carl Crawford, TB	50
1949	Bob Dillinger, StL	20		Brian Roberts, Balt	50
1950	Dom DiMaggio, Bos	15	2008	Jacoby Ellsbury, Bos	50
1951	Minnie Minoso, Clev-Chi	31	2009	Jacoby Ellsbury, Bos	70
1952	Minnie Minoso, Chi	22	2010	Juan Pierre, Chi	68
1953	Minnie Minoso, Chi	25	2011	Coco Crisp, Oak	49
1954	Jackie Jensen, Bos	22		Brett Gardner, NY	49
1955	Jim Rivera, Chi	25	2012	Mike Trout, LA	49
1956	Luis Aparicio, Chi	21			

AMERICAN LEAGUE (*Cont.*)

Leading Pitchers—Winning Percentage

Year	Pitcher and Team	W	L	Pct	Year	Pitcher and Team	W	L	Pct
1901	Clark Griffith, Chi	24	7	.774	1958	Bob Turley, NY	21	7	.750
1902	Bill Bernhard, Phi-Clev	18	5	.783	1959	Bob Shaw, Chi	18	6	.750
1903	Earl Moore, Clev	22	7	.759	1960	Jim Perry, Clev	18	10	.643
1904	Jack Chesbro, NY	41	12	.774	1961	Whitey Ford, NY	25	4	.862
1905	Jess Tannehill, Bos	22	9	.710	1962	Ray Herbert, Chi	20	9	.690
1906	Eddie Plank, Phi	19	6	.760	1963	Whitey Ford, NY	24	7	.774
1907	Wild Bill Donovan, Det	25	4	.862	1964	Wally Bunker, Balt	19	5	.792
1908	Ed Walsh, Chi	40	15	.727	1965	Mudcat Grant, Minn	21	7	.750
1909	George Mullin, Det	29	8	.784	1966	Sonny Siebert, Clev	16	8	.667
1910	Chief Bender, Phi	23	5	.821	1967	Joel Horlen, Chi	19	7	.731
1911	Chief Bender, Phi	17	5	.773	1968	Denny McLain, Det	31	6	.838
1912	Smoky Joe Wood, Bos	34	5	.872	1969	Jim Palmer, Balt	16	4	.800
1913	Walter Johnson, Wash	36	7	.837	1970	Mike Cuellar, Balt	24	8	.750
1914	Chief Bender, Phi	17	3	.850	1971	Dave McNally, Balt	21	5	.808
1915	Smoky Joe Wood, Bos	15	5	.750	1972	Catfish Hunter, Oak	21	7	.750
1916	Eddie Cicotte, Chi	15	7	.682	1973	Catfish Hunter, Oak	21	5	.808
1917	Reb Russell, Chi	15	5	.750	1974	Mike Cuellar, Balt	22	10	.688
1918	Sad Sam Jones, Bos	16	5	.762	1975	Mike Torrez, Balt	20	9	.690
1919	Eddie Cicotte, Chi	29	7	.806	1976	Bill Campbell, Minn	17	5	.773
1920	Jim Bagby, Clev	31	12	.721	1977	Paul Splittorff, KC	16	6	.727
1921	Carl Mays, NY	27	9	.750	1978	Ron Guidry, NY	25	3	.893
1922	Joe Bush, NY	26	7	.788	1979	Mike Caldwell, Mil	16	6	.727
1923	Herb Pennock, NY	19	6	.760	1980	Steve Stone, Balt	25	7	.781
1924	Walter Johnson, Wash	23	7	.767	1981*	Pete Vuckovich, Mil	14	4	.778
1925	Stan Coveleski, Wash	20	5	.800	1982	Pete Vuckovich, Mil	18	6	.750
1926	George Uhle, Clev	27	11	.711		Jim Palmer, Balt	15	5	.750
1927	Waite Hoyt, NY	22	7	.759	1983	Richard Dotson, Chi	22	7	.759
1928	General Crowder, StL	21	5	.808	1984	Doyle Alexander, Tor	17	6	.739
1929	Lefty Grove, Phi	20	6	.769	1985	Ron Guidry, NY	22	6	.786
1930	Lefty Grove, Phi	28	5	.848	1986	Roger Clemens, Bos	24	4	.857
1931	Lefty Grove, Phi	31	4	.886	1987	Roger Clemens, Bos	20	9	.690
1932	Johnny Allen, NY	17	4	.810	1988	Frank Viola, Minn	24	7	.774
1933	Lefty Grove, Phi	24	8	.750	1989	Bret Saberhagen, KC	23	6	.793
1934	Lefty Gomez, NY	26	5	.839	1990	Bob Welch, Oak	27	6	.818
1935	Eldon Auker, Det	18	7	.720	1991	Scott Erickson, Minn	20	8	.714
1936	Monte Pearson, NY	19	7	.731	1992	Mike Mussina, Balt	18	5	.783
1937	Johnny Allen, Clev	15	1	.938	1993	Jimmy Key, NY	18	6	.750
1938	Red Ruffing, NY	21	7	.750	1994	Jimmy Key, NY	17	4	.810
1939	Lefty Grove, Bos	15	4	.789	1995	Randy Johnson, Sea	18	2	.900
1940	Schoolboy Rowe, Det	16	3	.842	1996	Charles Nagy, Clev	17	5	.773
1941	Lefty Gomez, NY	15	5	.750	1997	Randy Johnson, Sea	20	4	.833
1942	Ernie Bonham, NY	21	5	.808	1998	David Wells, NY	18	4	.818
1943	Spud Chandler, NY	20	4	.833	1999	Pedro Martinez, Bos	23	4	.852
1944	Tex Hughson, Bos	18	5	.783	2000	Tim Hudson, Oak	20	6	.769
1945	Hal Newhouser, Det	25	9	.735	2001	Roger Clemens, NY	20	3	.870
1946	Boo Ferriss, Bos	25	6	.806	2002	Pedro Martinez, Bos	20	4	.833
1947	Allie Reynolds, NY	19	8	.704	2003	Roy Halladay, Tor	22	7	.759
1948	Jack Kramer, Bos	18	5	.783	2004	Curt Schilling, Bos	21	6	.778
1949	Ellis Kinder, Bos	23	6	.793	2005	Cliff Lee, Cle	18	5	.783
1950	Vic Raschi, NY	21	8	.724	2006	Roy Halladay, Tor	16	5	.762
1951	Bob Feller, Clev	22	8	.733	2007	Justin Verlander, Det	18	6	.750
1952	Bobby Shantz, Phi	24	7	.774	2008	Cliff Lee, Cle	22	3	.880
1953	Ed Lopat, NY	16	4	.800	2009	Felix Hernandez, Sea	19	5	.792
1954	Sandy Consuegra, Chi	16	3	.842	2010	David Price, TB	19	6	.760
1955	Tommy Byrne, NY	16	5	.762	2011	Justin Verlander, Det	24	5	.828
1956	Whitey Ford, NY	19	6	.760	2012	Jered Weaver, LA	20	5	.800
1957	Dick Donovan, Chi	16	6	.727		David Price, TB	20	5	.800
	Tom Sturdivant, NY	16	6	.727					

*1981 percentages based on 10 or more victories. Note: Percentages based on 15 or more victories in all other years.

AMERICAN LEAGUE *(Cont.)*
Leading Pitchers—Earned Run Average

Year	Player and Team	ERA	Year	Player and Team	ERA
1913	Walter Johnson, Wash	1.14	1963	Gary Peters, Chi	2.33
1914	Dutch Leonard, Bos	1.01	1964	Dean Chance, LA	1.65
1915	Smoky Joe Wood, Bos	1.49	1965	Sam McDowell, Clev	2.18
1916	Babe Ruth, Bos	1.75	1966	Gary Peters, Chi	1.98
1917	Eddie Cicotte, Chi	1.53	1967	Joe Horlen, Chi	2.06
1918	Walter Johnson, Wash	1.27	1968	Luis Tiant, Clev	1.60
1919	Walter Johnson, Wash	1.49	1969	Dick Bosman, Wash	2.19
1920	Bob Shawkey, NY	2.46	1970	Diego Segui, Oak	2.56
1921	Red Faber, Chi	2.47	1971	Vida Blue, Oak	1.82
1922	Red Faber, Chi	2.80	1972	Luis Tiant, Bos	1.91
1923	Stan Coveleski, Clev	2.76	1973	Jim Palmer, Balt	2.40
1924	Walter Johnson, Wash	2.72	1974	Catfish Hunter, Oak	2.49
1925	Stan Coveleski, Wash	2.84	1975	Jim Palmer, Balt	2.09
1926	Lefty Grove, Phi	2.51	1976	Mark Fidrych, Det	2.34
1927	Wilcy Moore, NY#	2.28	1977	Frank Tanana, Cal	2.54
1928	Garland Braxton, Wash	2.52	1978	Ron Guidry, NY	1.74
1929	Lefty Grove, Phi	2.81	1979	Ron Guidry, NY	2.78
1930	Lefty Grove, Phi	2.54	1980	Rudy May, NY	2.47
1931	Lefty Grove, Phi	2.06	1981	Steve McCatty, Oak	2.32
1932	Lefty Grove, Phi	2.84	1982	Rick Sutcliffe, Clev	2.96
1933	Monte Pearson, Clev	2.33	1983	Rick Honeycutt, Tex	2.42
1934	Lefty Gomez, NY	2.33	1984	Mike Boddicker, Balt	2.79
1935	Lefty Grove, Bos	2.70	1985	Dave Stieb, Tor	2.48
1936	Lefty Grove, Bos	2.81	1986	Roger Clemens, Bos	2.48
1937	Lefty Gomez, NY	2.33	1987	Jimmy Key, Tor	2.76
1938	Lefty Grove, Bos	3.07	1988	Allan Anderson, Minn	2.45
1939	Lefty Grove, Bos	2.54	1989	Bret Saberhagen, KC	2.16
1940	Bob Feller, Clev†	2.62	1990	Roger Clemens, Bos	1.93
1941	Thornton Lee, Chi	2.37	1991	Roger Clemens, Bos	2.62
1942	Ted Lyons, Chi	2.10	1992	Roger Clemens, Bos	2.41
1943	Spud Chandler, NY	1.64	1993	Kevin Appier, KC	2.56
1944	Dizzy Trout, Det	2.12	1994	Steve Ontiveros, Oak	2.65
1945	Hal Newhouser, Det	1.81	1995	Randy Johnson, Sea	2.48
1946	Hal Newhouser, Det	1.94	1996	Juan Guzman, Tor	2.93
1947	Spud Chandler, NY	2.46	1997	Roger Clemens, Tor	2.05
1948	Gene Bearden, Clev	2.43	1998	Roger Clemens, Tor	2.64
1949	Mel Parnell, Bos	2.78	1999	Pedro Martinez, Bos	2.07
1950	Early Wynn, Clev	3.20	2000	Pedro Martinez, Bos	1.74
1951	Saul Rogovin, Det-Chi	2.78	2001	Freddy Garcia, Sea	3.05
1952	Allie Reynolds, NY	2.07	2002	Pedro Martinez, Bos	2.26
1953	Ed Lopat, NY	2.43	2003	Pedro Martinez, Bos	2.22
1954	Mike Garcia, Clev	2.64	2004	Johan Santana, Minn	2.61
1955	Billy Pierce, Chi	1.97	2005	Kevin Millwood, Cle	2.86
1956	Whitey Ford, NY	2.47	2006	Johan Santana, Minn	2.77
1957	Bobby Shantz, NY	2.45	2007	John Lackey, LA	3.01
1958	Whitey Ford, NY	2.01	2008	Cliff Lee, Cle	2.54
1959	Hoyt Wilhelm, Balt	2.19	2009	Zack Greinke, KC	2.16
1960	Frank Baumann, Chi	2.68	2010	Felix Hernandez, Sea	2.27
1961	Dick Donovan, Wash	2.40	2011	Justin Verlander, Det	2.40
1962	Hank Aguirre, Det	2.21	2012	David Price, TB	2.56

Note: Based on 10 complete games through 1950, then 154 innings until the American League expanded in 1961, when it became 162 innings. In strike-shortened 1981, one inning per game required. Earned runs not tabulated in American League prior to 1913. #Wilcy Moore pitched only six complete games—he started 12—in 1927 but was recognized as leader because of 213 innings pitched. †Ernie Bonham, New York, had 1.91 ERA and 10 complete games in 1940 but appeared in only 12 games and 99 innings, and Bob Feller was recognized as the leader.

AMERICAN LEAGUE *(Cont.)*

Leading Pitchers—Strikeouts

Year	Player and Team	SO	Year	Player and Team	SO
1901	Cy Young, Bos	159	1957	Early Wynn, Clev	184
1902	Rube Waddell, Phi	210	1958	Early Wynn, Chi	179
1903	Rube Waddell, Phi	301	1959	Jim Bunning, Det	201
1904	Rube Waddell, Phi	349	1960	Jim Bunning, Det	201
1905	Rube Waddell, Phi	286	1961	Camilo Pascual, Minn	221
1906	Rube Waddell, Phi	203	1962	Camilo Pascual, Minn	206
1907	Rube Waddell, Phi	226	1963	Camilo Pascual, Minn	202
1908	Ed Walsh, Chi	269	1964	Al Downing, NY	217
1909	Frank Smith, Chi	177	1965	Sam McDowell, Clev	325
1910	Walter Johnson, Wash	313	1966	Sam McDowell, Clev	225
1911	Ed Walsh, Chi	255	1967	Jim Lonborg, Bos	246
1912	Walter Johnson, Wash	303	1968	Sam McDowell, Clev	283
1913	Walter Johnson, Wash	243	1969	Sam McDowell, Clev	279
1914	Walter Johnson, Wash	225	1970	Sam McDowell, Clev	304
1915	Walter Johnson, Wash	203	1971	Mickey Lolich, Det	308
1916	Walter Johnson, Wash	228	1972	Nolan Ryan, Cal	329
1917	Walter Johnson, Wash	188	1973	Nolan Ryan, Cal	383
1918	Walter Johnson, Wash	162	1974	Nolan Ryan, Cal	367
1919	Walter Johnson, Wash	147	1975	Frank Tanana, Cal	269
1920	Stan Coveleski, Clev	133	1976	Nolan Ryan, Cal	327
1921	Walter Johnson, Wash	143	1977	Nolan Ryan, Cal	341
1922	Urban Shocker, StL	149	1978	Nolan Ryan, Cal	260
1923	Walter Johnson, Wash	130	1979	Nolan Ryan, Cal	223
1924	Walter Johnson, Wash	158	1980	Len Barker, Clev	187
1925	Lefty Grove, Phi	116	1981	Len Barker, Clev	127
1926	Lefty Grove, Phi	194	1982	Floyd Bannister, Sea	209
1927	Lefty Grove, Phi	174	1983	Jack Morris, Det	232
1928	Lefty Grove, Phi	183	1984	Mark Langston, Sea	204
1929	Lefty Grove, Phi	170	1985	Bert Blyleven, Clev-Minn	206
1930	Lefty Grove, Phi	209	1986	Mark Langston, Sea	245
1931	Lefty Grove, Phi	175	1987	Mark Langston, Sea	262
1932	Red Ruffing, NY	190	1988	Roger Clemens, Bos	291
1933	Lefty Gomez, NY	163	1989	Nolan Ryan, Tex	301
1934	Lefty Gomez, NY	158	1990	Nolan Ryan, Tex	232
1935	Tommy Bridges, Det	163	1991	Roger Clemens, Bos	241
1936	Tommy Bridges, Det	175	1992	Randy Johnson, Sea	241
1937	Lefty Gomez, NY	194	1993	Randy Johnson, Sea	308
1938	Bob Feller, Clev	240	1994	Randy Johnson, Sea	204
1939	Bob Feller, Clev	246	1995	Randy Johnson, Sea	294
1940	Bob Feller, Clev	261	1996	Roger Clemens, Bos	257
1941	Bob Feller, Clev	260	1997	Roger Clemens, Tor	292
1942	Bobo Newsom, Wash	113	1998	Roger Clemens, Tor	271
	Tex Hughson, Bos	113	1999	Pedro Martinez, Bos	313
1943	Allie Reynolds, Clev	151	2000	Pedro Martinez, Bos	284
1944	Hal Newhouser, Det	187	2001	Hideo Nomo, Bos	220
1945	Hal Newhouser, Det	212	2002	Pedro Martinez, Bos	239
1946	Bob Feller, Clev	348	2003	Esteban Loaiza, Chi	207
1947	Bob Feller, Clev	196	2004	Johan Santana, Minn	265
1948	Bob Feller, Clev	164	2005	Johan Santana, Minn	238
1949	Virgil Trucks, Det	153	2006	Johan Santana, Minn	245
1950	Bob Lemon, Clev	170	2007	Scott Kazmir, TB	239
1951	Vic Raschi, NY	164	2008	A.J. Burnett, Tor	231
1952	Allie Reynolds, NY	160	2009	Justin Verlander, Det	269
1953	Billy Pierce, Chi	186	2010	Jered Weaver, LA	233
1954	Bob Turley, Balt	185	2011	Justin Verlander, Det	250
1955	Herb Score, Clev	245	2012	Justin Verlander, Det	239
1956	Herb Score, Clev	263			

AMERICAN (Cont.)
Leading Pitchers—Saves

FYear	Player and Team	SV	Year	Player and Team	SV
1947	Joe Page, NY	17	1981	Rollie Fingers, Mil	28
1948	Russ Christopher, Clev	17	1982	Dan Quisenberry, KC	35
1949	Joe Page, NY	29	1983	Dan Quisenberry, KC	35
1950	Mickey Harris, Wash	15	1984	Dan Quisenberry, KC	44
1951	Ellis Kinder, Bos	14	1985	Dan Quisenberry, KC	37
1952	Harry Dorish, Chi	11	1986	Dave Righetti, NY	46
1953	Ellis Kinder, Bos	27	1987	Tom Henke, Tor	34
1954	Johnny Sain, NY	22	1988	Dennis Eckersley, Oak	45
1955	Ray Narleski, Clev	19	1989	Jeff Russell, Tex	38
1956	George Zuverink, Bal	16	1990	Bobby Thigpen, Chi	57
1957	Bob Grim, NY	19	1991	Bryan Harvey, Cal	46
1958	Ryne Duren, NY	20	1992	Dennis Eckersley, Oak	51
1959	Turk Lown, Chi	15	1993	Jeff Montgomery, KC	45
1960	Mike Fornieles, Bos	14		Duane Ward, Tor	45
	Johnny Klippstein, Clev	14	1994	Lee Smith, Bal	33
1961	Luis Arroyo, NY	29	1995	Jose Mesa, Clev	46
1962	Dick Radatz, Bos	24	1996	John Wetteland, NY	43
1963	Stu Miller, Bal	27	1997	Randy Myers, Balt	45
1964	Dick Radatz, Bos	29	1998	Tom Gordon, Bos	46
1965	Ron Kline, Wash	29	1999	Mariano Rivera, NY	45
1966	Jack Aker, KC	32	2000	Todd Jones, Det	42
1967	Minnie Rojas, Cal	27	2001	Mariano Rivera, NY	50
1968	Al Worthington, Minn	18	2002	Eddie Guardado, Minn	45
1969	Ron Perranoski, Minn	31	2003	Keith Foulke, Oak	43
1970	Ron Perranoski, Minn	34	2004	Mariano Rivera, NY	53
1971	Ken Sanders, Mil	31	2005	Francisco Rodriguez, LA	45
1972	Sparky Lyle, NY	35		Bob Wickman, Cle	45
1973	John Hiller, Det	38	2006	Francisco Rodriguez, LA	47
1974	Terry Forster, Chi	24	2007	Joe Borowski, Cle	45
1975	Goose Gossage, Chi	26	2008	Francisco Rodriguez, LA	62
1976	Sparky Lyle, NY	23	2009	Brian Fuentes, LA	48
1977	Bill Campbell, Bos	31	2010	Rafael Soriano, TB	45
1978	Goose Gossage, NY	27	2011	Jose Valverde, Det	49
1979	Mike Marshall, Minn	32	2012	Jim Johnson, Bal	51
1980	Dan Quisenberry, KC	33			

The Commissioners of Baseball

Kenesaw Mountain Landis	Elected Nov. 12, 1920. Served until his death on Nov. 25, 1944.
Happy Chandler	Elected April 24, 1945. Served until July 15, 1951.
Ford Frick	Elected Sept. 20, 1951. Served until Nov. 16, 1965.
William Eckert	Elected Nov. 17, 1965. Served until Dec. 20, 1968.
Bowie Kuhn	Elected Feb. 8, 1969. Served until Sept. 30, 1984.
Peter Ueberroth	Elected March 3, 1984. Took office Oct. 1, 1984. Served through March 31, 1989.
A. Bartlett Giamatti	Elected Sept. 8, 1988. Took office April 1, 1989. Served until his death on Sept. 1, 1989.
Francis Vincent Jr.	Appointed Acting Commissioner Sept. 2, 1989. Elected Commissioner Sept. 13, 1989. Served through Sept. 7, 1992.
Allan H. (Bud) Selig	Elected chairman of the executive council and given the powers of interim commissioner on Sept. 9, 1992. Unanimously elected Commissioner July 9, 1998.

Pro Football

Eli Manning led the New York Giants to a 21–17 win over the New England Patriots in Super Bowl XLVI.

It's Déjà Vu For Big Blue

The New York Giants did just enough to survive the regular season, then marched through the playoffs en route to another victory over another dominant New England team in the Super Bowl

BY HANK HERSCH

THE SEASON THAT ALMOST wasn't ended with a team that almost didn't make the playoffs toppling a team that seemingly couldn't be beat—again. For the second time in five seasons quarterback Eli Manning guided the Giants on a fourth-quarter drive to defeat the Patriots, each comeback stamped by one brilliant completion. In Super Bowl XLII, it was his scrambling heave to David Tyree, who clamped the throw to his helmet; in Super Bowl XLVI, in Indianapolis, Manning thwarted double coverage with a 38-yard sideline rainbow to Mario Manningham, igniting an 88-yard touchdown drive for a 21–17 victory. "When somebody has your number there is nothing you can do about it," said New York defensive end Osi Umenyiora of his team's hold over the Pats. "Apparently we've found a way to beat an unbeatable team."

For the first half of 2011, it appeared the NFL's supply of high drama would be found only in boardrooms and on conference calls. For four-and-a-half months owners locked out players, the two sides waging a bitter battle over how to slice the highly lucrative

NFL pie. Finally, on July 21, owners voted 31–0 to approve a ten-year collective bargaining agreement in which players would receive 55% of the league's broadcast revenue (potentially $8 billion in 2014), 45% of all revenue from NFL ventures (merchandise, promotions) and 40% of local team revenues (tickets, stadium enhancements). Another concession to labor: The season would not expand from 16 to 18 games. Said one general manager, "I'm just surprised they didn't pass a rule saying we had to give the players juice boxes after every practice."

Once the season kicked off and deep into December, the streaking Packers were the story: The defending champs reeled off 13 straight wins, including a 38–35 defeat in Week 13 of the Giants, dropping New York to .500. Although Green Bay's roll ended in an unlikely 19–14 loss at Kansas City—the only blemish in a 15–1 finish—quarterback Aaron Rodgers showed that in many ways he was surpassing his peerless Packers predecessor, Brett Favre. The 28-year-old Rodgers passed for 4,643 yards with 45 touchdowns and just six interceptions for an unprecedented passer rating of 122.5. "He throws with velocity," says Green Bay

League MVP Rodgers had a season for the ages: 4,643 passing yards, 45 touchdowns and just six interceptions, for an astonishing passer rating of 122.5.

veteran receiver Greg Jennings. "You turn, and the ball is going to be there. His deep ball is better than Brett's. His accuracy running outside the pocket is second to none, almost better than when he's in the pocket, which is almost impossible."

How good was Rodgers? He was named MVP even though the Saints' Drew Brees set single-season records for passing yards (5,476, shattering Dan Marino's 27-year-old mark of 5,084), completions (468), completion percentage (71.2), 300-yard games (13) and consecutive 300-yard games (seven). Those numbers only reflected the league-

wide reliance on aerial attacks: Of the 693.7 total net yards per game in 2011—the NFL's alltime high—almost two thirds (459.4) came from the pass, leading to a record 11,356 points. Cam Newton, the No. 1 pick out of Auburn, made an instant contribution to that onslaught, setting a record by piling up 422 yards for the Panthers in his first start, en route to a 4,051-yard season and Rookie of the Year honors.

In fact, had Rodgers not sat out the season finale he might have joined Brees in the 5,000-yard club, along with the Lions' Matthew Stafford and 34-year-old Tom Brady of New England, who finished second with 5,235. The long-potent Pats offense—made even more dynamic by Rob Gronkowski, who set a record for TD catches by a tight end (17) in his second sea-

Tebow (in his signature pose) captured the heart of the nation with six fourth-quarter comeback wins.

on an 80-yard strike 11 seconds into OT for a 29–23 upset of the Steelers. But the following week Denver fell hard 45–10 to the Pats, who then reached their fifth Super Bowl in coach Bill Belichick's 12 seasons by edging the Ravens 23–20 when Baltimore kicker Billy Cundiff shanked a 32-yard field goal with 11 seconds remaining.

The Giants hardly seemed as charmed, winning two of their last three to scuffle into the postseason with a 9–7 mark. But they followed a 24–2 wild-card rout of the Falcons with a dominant 37–20 victory in Green Bay, where Manning threw three TDs, two to wideout Hakeem Nicks, who had seven catches for 165 yards. Against the 49ers in the NFC title game, Manning passed for two more scores and New York capitalized on a fumbled punt in overtime, with Lawrence Tynes kicking a 31-yarder for a 20–17 win. "I'm usually pretty cool, but there was something about tonight where I knew I was going to have to make a kick," Tynes said. "Hats off to Eli, offense, defense. Great win."

That left only New England in the Giants' way. Early in the third quarter Brady appeared to be having his way, completing a Super Bowl record 16 straight and guiding the Pats to a 17–9 lead. But New York's pass rush dug in, Patriots receiver Wes Welker made an uncharacteristic drop and Manning delivered the coup de grace on the field where his older brother Peyton had made so much magic. "We've won so many games like this, at the end," Giants coach Tom Coughlin said. "We talk about finishing all the time and winning the fourth quarter, being the stronger team. It happened again tonight."

son—was complemented by a refurbished defense littered with onetime wideouts and reclamation projects, such as stalwart linebacker Rob Ninkovich, a twice-released long snapper. Further fueling the 13–3 Patriots was their desire to ease the pain of owner Bob Kraft, whose wife of 48 years, Myra, died in July.

"Vince Wilfork used to kiss me coming off the field, and kiss my wife," Kraft said of the defensive tackle. "This year, he kisses me twice."

New England's mojo proved a match even for Tebowmania. Combining a charismatic personality, deep-seated Christian beliefs and a knack for dramatically muting critics of his awkward, southpaw delivery with TD passes—punctuated by his prayerful pose known as Tebowing—Tim Tebow became by some metrics the nation's most popular professional athlete in just his second season as a Broncos quarterback. The mania maxed out in the AFC wild-card round, when Tebow engineered his sixth fourth-quarter comeback and fourth overtime victory of 2011, connecting with Demaryius Thomas

FOR THE RECORD•2011–2012

2011 NFL Final Standings

American Football Conference

EAST DIVISION

	W	L	T	Pct	Pts	OP
New England	13	3	0	.813	513	342
NY Jets	8	8	0	.500	377	363
Miami	6	10	0	.375	329	313
Buffalo	6	10	0	.375	372	434

NORTH DIVISION

	W	L	T	Pct	Pts	OP
Baltimore	12	4	0	.750	378	266
*Pittsburgh	12	4	0	.750	325	227
*Cincinnati	9	7	0	.563	344	323
Cleveland	4	12	0	.250	218	307

SOUTH DIVISION

	W	L	T	Pct	Pts	OP
Houston	10	6	0	.625	381	278
Tennessee	9	7	0	.563	325	317
Jacksonville	5	11	0	.313	243	329
Indianapolis	2	14	0	.125	243	430

WEST DIVISION

	W	L	T	Pct	Pts	OP
Denver	8	8	0	.500	309	390
San Diego	8	8	0	.500	406	377
Oakland	8	8	0	.500	359	433
Kansas City	7	9	0	.438	212	338

National Football Conference

EAST DIVISION

	W	L	T	Pct	Pts	OP
NY Giants	9	7	0	.563	394	400
Philadelphia	8	8	0	.500	396	328
Dallas	8	8	0	.500	369	347
Washington	5	11	0	.313	288	367

NORTH DIVISION

	W	L	T	Pct	Pts	OP
Green Bay	15	1	0	.938	560	359
*Detroit	10	6	0	.625	474	387
Chicago	8	8	0	.500	353	341
Minnesota	3	13	0	.188	340	449

SOUTH DIVISION

	W	L	T	Pct	Pts	OP
New Orleans	13	3	0	.813	547	339
*Atlanta	10	6	0	.625	402	350
Carolina	6	10	0	.375	406	429
Tampa Bay	4	12	0	.250	287	494

WEST DIVISION

	W	L	T	Pct	Pts	OP
San Francisco	13	3	0	.813	380	229
Arizona	8	8	0	.500	312	348
Seattle	7	9	0	.438	321	315
St. Louis	2	14	0	.125	193	407

* Wild-card team.

2011–12 NFL Playoffs

AFC FIRST ROUND	AFC DIVISIONAL PLAYOFF	AFC CHAMPIONSHIP	NFC CHAMPIONSHIP	NFC DIVISIONAL PLAYOFF	NFC FIRST ROUND

SUPER BOWL XLVI
February 5, 2012
Indianapolis, Indiana

Houston 31
Cincinnati 10
Houston 13
Baltimore 20

New Orleans 32
San Francisco 17
New Orleans 45
Detroit 28

Baltimore 20

**NY GIANTS 21
New England 17**

San Francisco 36

Denver 29
Pittsburgh 23
Denver 10
New England 23

NY Giants 37

NY Giants 24
Atlanta 2

New England 45

NY Giants 20
Green Bay 20

NFL Playoff Recaps

AFC Wild Card Games

Cincinnati	7	3	0	0—10
Houston	7	10	7	7—31

FIRST QUARTER: Cincinnati: TD Benson 1 run (Nugent kick), 7:34.

Houston: TD Foster 8 run (Rackers kick), 4:47.

SECOND QUARTER: Cincinnati: FG Nugent 37, 7:09.

Houston: FG Rackers 39, 1:48.

Houston: TD Watts 29 interception return (Rackers kick), 0:52.

THIRD QUARTER: Houston: TD Johnson 40 pass from Yates (Rackers kick), 1:08.

FOURTH QUARTER: Houston: TD Foster 42 run (Rackers kick), 5:15.

A: 71,725.

Pittsburgh	6	0	7	10	0—23
Denver	0	20	0	3	6—29

FIRST QUARTER: Pittsburgh: FG Suisham 45, 11:14.

Pittsburgh: FG Suisham 38, 0:23.

SECOND QUARTER: Denver: TD Royal 30 pass from Tebow (Prater kick), 13:24.

Denver: TD Tebow 8 run (Prater kick), 10:36.

Denver: FG Prater 20, 7:30.

Denver: FG Prater 28, 1:05.

THIRD QUARTER: Pittsburgh: TD Wallace 1 run (Suisham kick), 4:29.

FOURTH QUARTER: Denver: FG Prater 35, 13:10.

Pittsburgh: FG Suisham 37, 9:59.

Pittsburgh: TD Cotchery 31 pass from Roethlisberger (Suisham kick), 3:48.

OVERTIME: Denver: TD Thomas 80 pass from Tebow, 14:49.

A: 75,970.

NFC Wild Card Games

Detroit	7	7	7	7—28
New Orleans	0	10	14	21—45

FIRST QUARTER: Detroit: TD Heller 10 pass from Stafford (Hanson kick), 10:58.

SECOND QUARTER: New Orleans: TD Sproles 2 run (Kasay kick), 14:01.

Detroit: TD Johnson 13 pass from Stafford (Hanson kick), 9:11.

New Orleans: FG Kasay 24, 0:00.

THIRD QUARTER: New Orleans: TD Henderson 41 pass from Brees (Kasay kick), 1:09.

New Orleans: TD Graham 3 pass from Brees (Kasay kick), 4:03.

Detroit: TD Stafford 1 run (Hanson kick), 1:08.

FOURTH QUARTER: New Orleans: TD Sproles 17 run (Kasay kick), 9:53.

New Orleans: TD Meachem 56 pass from Brees (Kasay kick), 7:29.

Detroit: TD Johnson 12 pass from Stafford (Hanson kick), 4:40.

New Orleans: TD Thomas 1 run (Kasay kick), 3:36.

A: 73,038.

Atlanta	0	2	0	0—2
NY Giants	0	7	10	7—24

SECOND QUARTER: Atlanta: Safety (intentional grounding on Manning in own end zone) 13:44.

NY Giants: TD Nicks 4 pass from Manning (Tynes kick), 2:47.

THIRD QUARTER: NY Giants: FG Tynes 22, 7:51.

NY Giants: TD Nicks 72 pass from Manning (Tynes kick), 2:44.

FOURTH QUARTER: NY Giants: TD Manningham 27 pass from Manning (Tynes kick), 9:55.

A: 79,909.

AFC Divisional Games

Denver	0	7	3	0—10
New England	14	21	7	3—45

FIRST QUARTER: New England: TD Welker 7 pass from Brady (Gostkowski kick), 13:09.

New England: TD Gronkowski 10 pass from Brady (Gostkowski kick), 6:42.

SECOND QUARTER: Denver: TD McGahee 5 run (Prater kick), 14:54.

New England: TD Gronkowski 12 pass from Brady (Gostkowski kick), 7:42.

New England: TD Branch 61 pass from Brady (Gostkowski kick), 1:57.

New England: TD Gronkowski 19 pass from Brady (Gostkowski kick), 0:05.

THIRD QUARTER: New England: TD Hernandez 17 pass from Brady (Gostkowski kick), 11:46.

Denver: FG Prater 41, 2:14.

FOURTH QUARTER: New England: FG Gostkowski 20, 12:39.

A: 68,756.

Houston	3	10	0	0—13
Baltimore	17	0	0	3—20

FIRST QUARTER: Houston: FG Rackers 40, 12:24.

Baltimore: TD Wilson 1 pass from Flacco (Cundiff kick), 9:51.

Baltimore: FG Cundiff 48, 6:02.

Baltimore: TD Boldin 10 pass from Flacco (Cundiff kick), 1:08.

SECOND QUARTER: Houston: FG Rackers 33, 11:42.

Houston: TD Foster 1 run (Rackers kick), 4:48.

FOURTH QUARTER: Baltimore: FG Cundiff 44, 2:52.

A: 71,547.

NFC Divisional Games

New Orleans	0	14	0	18—32
San Francisco	14	3	3	16—36

FIRST QUARTER: San Francisco: TD Davis 49 pass from Smith (Akers kick), 2:08.

San Francisco: TD Crabtree 4 pass from Smith (Akers kick), 0:41.

SECOND QUARTER: San Francisco: FG Akers 25, 14:12.

New Orleans: TD Graham 14 pass from Brees (Kasay kick), 9:32.

New Orleans: TD Colston 25 pass from Brees (Kasay kick), 4:09.

THIRD QUARTER: San Francisco: FG Akers 41, 10:36.

FOURTH QUARTER: New Orleans: FG Kasay 48, 13:08.

San Francisco: FG Akers 37, 7:36.

New Orleans: TD Sproles 44 pass from Brees (Kasay kick), 4:02.

San Francisco: TD Smith 28 run (2-pt. conversion failed), 2:11.

New Orleans: TD Graham 66 pass from Brees (Sproles pass from Brees for 2-pt. conversion), 1:37.

San Francisco: TD Davis 14 pass from Smith (Akers kick), 0:09.

A: 69,732.

NY Giants	10	10	0	17—37
Green Bay	3	7	3	7—20

FIRST QUARTER: NY Giants: FG Tynes 31, 8:33.

Green Bay: FG Crosby 47, 5:33.

NY Giants: TD Nicks 66 pass from Manning (Tynes kick), 3:47.

SECOND QUARTER: Green Bay: TD Kuhn 8 pass from Rodgers (Crosby kick), 14:54.

NY Giants: FG Tynes 23, 1:51.

NY Giants: TD Nicks 37 pass from Manning (Tynes kick), 0:00.

THIRD QUARTER: Green Bay: FG Crosby 35, 3:50.

FOURTH QUARTER: NY Giants: FG Tynes 23, 7:48.

NY Giants: TD Manningham 4 pass from Manning (Tynes kick), 6:48

Green Bay: TD Driver 16 pass from Rodgers (Crosby kick), 4:46.

NY Giants: TD Jacobs 14 run (Tynes kick), 2:36.

A: 72,080.

AFC Championship

Baltimore 0	10	10	0—20
New England 3	10	3	7—23

FIRST QUARTER: New England: FG Gostkowski 29, 5:49.

SECOND QUARTER: Baltimore: FG Cundiff 20, 14:21.

New England: TD Green-Ellis 7 run (Gostkowski kick), 10:35.

Baltimore: TD Pitta 6 pass from Flacco (Cundiff kick), 6:03.

New England: FG Gostkowski 35, 3:00.

THIRD QUARTER: New England: FG Gostkowski 24, 9:06.

Baltimore: TD T. Smith 29 pass from Flacco (Cundiff kick), 3:38.

Baltimore: FG Cundiff 39, 0:50.

FOURTH QUARTER: New England: TD Brady 1 run (Gostkowski kick), 11:29.

A: 68,756.

NFC Championship

NY Giants....................0	10	0	7	3—20
San Francisco 7	0	7	3	0—17

FIRST QUARTER: San Francisco: TD Davis 73 pass from Smith (Akers kick), 7:11.

SECOND QUARTER: NY Giants: TD Pascoe 6 pass from Manning (Tynes kick), 11:15.

NY Giants: FG Tynes 31, 0:02.

THIRD QUARTER: San Francisco: TD Davis 28 pass from Smith (Akers kick), 5:18.

FOURTH QUARTER: NY Giants: TD Manningham 17 pass from Manning (Tynes kick), 8:34.

San Francisco: FG Akers 25, 5:39.

OVERTIME: NY Giants: FG Tynes 31, 7:06.

A: 69,732.

Super Bowl XLVI Recap

New England 0	10	7	0—17
NY Giants 9	0	6	6—21

FIRST QUARTER: NY Giants: Safety (Brady called for intentional grounding in end zone), 8:52. **NY Giants 2–0.**

NY Giants: TD Cruz 2 pass from Manning (Tynes kick), 3:24. **NY Giants 9–0.**

SECOND QUARTER: New England FG Gostkowski 29, 13:48. **NY Giants 9–3.**

New England: TD Woodhead 4 pass from Brady (Gostkowski kick), 0:08. **New England 10–9.**

THIRD QUARTER: New England: TD Hernandez 12 pass from Brady (Gostkowski kick), 11:20. **New England 17–9.**

NY Giants: FG Tynes 38, 6:43. **New England 17–12.**

NY Giants: FG Tynes 33, 0:35. **New England 17–15.**

FOURTH QUARTER: NY Giants: TD Bradshaw 6 run (2-pt. conversion failed), 0:57. **NY Giants 21–17.**

A: 68,658.

Super Bowl XLVI Box Score

Team Statistics

	New England	NY Giants
FIRST DOWNS	21	26
Rushing	6	7
Passing	15	18
Penalty	0	1
THIRD DOWN EFF	6–12	5–11
FOURTH DOWN EFF	1–1	0–0
TOTAL NET YARDS	349	396
Total plays	62	71
Avg gain	5.6	5.6
NET YARDS RUSHING	83	114
Rushes	19	28
Avg per rush	4.4	4.1
NET YARDS PASSING	266	282
Completed–Att–Int	27–41–1	30–40–0
Yards per pass	6.2	6.6
Sacked–yards lost	2–10	3–14
Had intercepted	1	0
PUNTS–Avg	3–41.0	4–40.8
PENALTIES–Yds	5–28	4–24
FUMBLES–Lost	0–0	2–0
Time of Possession	22:55	37:05

Passing

NEW ENGLAND

	Comp	Att	Yds	Int	TD
Brady	27	41	276	1	2

NY GIANTS

	Comp	Att	Yds	Int	TD
Manning	30	40	296	0	1

Rushing

NEW ENGLAND

	No.	Yds	Lg	TD
Green-Ellis	10	44	17	0
Welker	2	21	11	0
Woodhead	7	18	6	0

NY GIANTS

	No.	Yds	Lg	TD
Bradshaw	17	72	24	1
Jacobs	9	37	11	0
Ware	1	6	6	0
Manning	1	-1	-1	0

Receiving

NEW ENGLAND

	No.	Yds	Lg	TD
Hernandez	8	67	12	1
Welker	7	60	19	0
Branch	3	45	19	0
Woodhead	4	42	19	1
Gronkowski	2	26	20	0
Ochocinco	1	21	21	0
Green-Ellis	2	15	8	0

NY GIANTS

	No.	Yds	Lg	TD
Nicks	10	109	19	0
Manningham	5	73	38	0
Pascoe	4	33	12	0
Cruz	4	25	8	1
Hynoski	2	19	13	0
Bradshaw	2	19	11	0
Ballard	2	10	9	0
Ware	1	8	8	0

Defense

NEW ENGLAND

	Tot. Tck	Solo	Int	Sack
Mayo	11	8	0	0
Spikes	11	8	0	0
McCourty	7	6	0	0
Chung	6	2	0	0
Molden	5	5	0	0
Arrington	5	4	0	0
Anderson	5	3	0	1.5
Ihedigbo	5	2	0	0
Ninkovich	4	3	0	.5
Moore	3	3	0	0
Wilfork	3	3	0	0
Slater	2	2	0	0
Warren	2	1	0	0
Ellis	2	0	0	0
White	2	0	0	0
Deaderick	1	1	0	1
Fletcher	1	1	0	0
Love	1	1	0	0
Gronkowski	1	1	0	0
Gostkowski	1	0	0	0

NY GIANTS

	Tot Tck	Solo	Int	Sack
Boley	10	9	0	0
Grant	6	5	0	0
Phillips	6	5	0	0
Blackburn	6	4	1	0
Tuck	3	3	0	2
Rolle	3	3	0	0
Williams	3	2	0	0
Ross	3	2	0	0
Pierre-Paul	2	2	0	0
Bernard	2	2	0	0
Paysinger	2	1	0	0
Joseph	2	1	0	0
Amukamara	1	1	0	0
Webster	1	1	0	0
Canty	1	1	0	0
Umenyiora	1	0	0	0

First Team

OFFENSE

Aaron Rodgers, Green Bay	Quarterback
Maurice Jones-Drew, Jacksonville	Running back
LeSean McCoy, Philadelphia	Running back
Vonta Leach, Baltimore	Fullback
Calvin Johnson, Detoit	Wide receiver
Wes Welker, New England	Wide receiver
Rob Gronkowski, New England	Tight end
Jason Peters, Philadelphia	Tackle
Joe Thomas, Cleveland	Tackle
Carl Nicks, New Orleans	Guard
Jahri Evans, New Orleans	Guard
Maurkice Pouncey, Pittsburgh	Center

DEFENSE

Jared Allen, Minnesota	Defensive end
Jason Pierre-Paul, N.Y. Giants	Defensive end
Haloti Ngata, Baltimore	Defensive tackle
Justin Smith, San Francisco	Defensive tackle
Terrell Suggs, Baltimore	Outside linebacker
DeMarcus Ware, Dallas	Outside linebacker
Patrick Willis, San Francisco	Inside linebacker
N. Bowman, San Francisco / D. Johnson, Kansas City (tie)	Inside linebacker
Charles Woodson, Green Bay	Cornerback
Darrelle Revis, N.Y. Jets	Cornerback
Troy Polamalu, Pittsburgh	Safety
Eric Weddle, San Diego	Safety

SPECIALISTS

David Akers, San Francisco	Kicker
Patrick Peterson, Arizona	Kick Returner
Andy Lee, San Francisco	Punter

Second Team

OFFENSE

Drew Brees, New Orleans	Quarterback
Ray Rice, Baltimore	Running back
Arian Foster, Houston	Running back
John Kuhn, Green Bay	Fullback
Jimmy Graham, New Orleans	Tight end
Larry Fitzgerald, Arizona	Wide receiver
Victor Cruz, New York Giants	Wide receiver
Duane Brown, Houston	Tackle
Joe Staley, San Francisco	Tackle
Marshal Yanda, Baltimore	Guard
Logan Mankins, New England	Guard
Ryan Kalil, Carolina / Nick Mangold, New York Jets (tie)	Center

DEFENSE

Justin Smith, San Francisco	Defensive end
Jason Babin, Philadelphia	Defensive end
Geno Atkins, Cincinnati	Defensive tackle
V. Wilfork, New England / R. Seymour, Oakland (tie)	Defensive tackle
Tamba Hali, Kansas City	Outside linebacker
Von Miller, Denver	Outside linebacker
Brian Cushing, Houston	Inside linebacker
London Fletcher, Washington	Inside linebacker
Johnathan Joseph, Houston	Cornerback
Carlos Rogers, San Francisco	Cornerback
Ed Reed, Baltimore	Safety
Earl Thomas, Seattle	Safety

SPECIALISTS

Sebastian Janikowski, Oakland	Kicker
Devin Hester, Chicago	Kick Returner
Shane Lechler, Oakland	Punter

BALTIMORE RAVENS (12-4)

35	PITTSBURGH	7
13	at Tennessee	26
37	at St. Louis	7
34	NY JETS	17
29	HOUSTON	14
7	at Jacksonville	12
30	ARIZONA	27
23	at Pittsburgh	20
17	at Seattle	22
31	CINCINNATI	24
16	SAN FRANCISCO	6
24	at Cleveland	10
24	INDIANAPOLIS	10
14	at San Diego	34
20	CLEVELAND	14
24	at Cincinnati	16
378		266

BUFFALO BILLS (6-10)

41	at Kansas City	7
38	OAKLAND	35
34	NEW ENGLAND	31
20	at Cincinnati	23
31	PHILADELPHIA	24
24	at NY Giants	27
23	WASHINGTON	0
11	NY JETS	27
7	at Dallas	44
8	at Miami	35
24	at NY Jets	28
17	TENNESSEE	23
10	at San Diego	37
23	MIAMI	30
40	DENVER	14
21	at New England	49
372		434

CINCINNATI BENGALS (9-7)

21	at Cleveland	17
22	at Denver	24
8	SAN FRANCISCO	13
23	BUFFALO	20
30	at Jacksonville	20
27	INDIANAPOLIS	17
34	at Seattle	12
24	at Tennessee	17
17	PITTSBURGH	24
24	at Baltimore	31
23	CLEVELAND	20
7	at Pittsburgh	35
19	HOUSTON	20
20	at St. Louis	13
23	ARIZONA	16
16	BALTIMORE	24
344		323

CLEVELAND BROWNS (4-12)

17	CINCINNATI	27
27	at Indianapolis	19
17	MIAMI	16
13	TENNESSEE	31
17	at Oakland	24
6	SEATTLE	3
10	at San Francisco	20
12	at Houston	30
12	ST. LOUIS	13
14	JACKSONVILLE	10
20	at Cincinnati	23
10	BALTIMORE	24
3	at Pittsburgh	14
17	at Arizona	20
14	at Baltimore	20
9	PITTSBURGH	13
218		307

DENVER BRONCOS (8-8)

20	OAKLAND	23
24	CINCINNATI	22
14	at Tennessee	17
23	at Green Bay	49
29	SAN DIEGO	49
18	at Miami	15
10	DETROIT	45
38	at Oakland	24
17	at Kansas City	10
17	NY JETS	13
16	at San Diego	13
35	at Minnesota	32
13	CHICAGO	10
23	NEW ENGLAND	41
14	at Buffalo	40
3	KANSAS CITY	7
309		390

HOUSTON TEXANS (10-6)

34	INDIANAPOLIS	7
23	at Miami	13
33	at New Orleans	40
17	PITTSBURGH	10
20	OAKLAND	25
14	at Baltimore	29
41	at Tennessee	7
24	JACKSONVILLE	14
30	CLEVELAND	12
37	at Tampa Bay	9
20	at Jacksonville	13
17	ATLANTA	10
20	at Cincinnati	19
13	CAROLINA	28
16	at Indianapolis	19
22	TENNESSEE	23
381		278

INDIANAPOLIS COLTS (2-14)

7	at Houston	34
19	CLEVELAND	27
20	PITTSBURGH	23
17	at Tampa Bay	24
24	KANSAS CITY	28
17	at Cincinnati	27
7	at New Orleans	62
10	at Tennessee	27
7	ATLANTA	31
3	JACKSONVILLE	17
19	CAROLINA	27
24	at New England	31
10	at Baltimore	24
27	TENNESSEE	13
19	HOUSTON	16
13	at Jacksonville	19
243		430

JACKSONVILLE JAGUARS (5-11)

16	TENNESSEE	14
3	at NY Jets	32
10	at Carolina	16
10	NEW ORLEANS	23
20	CINCINNATI	30
13	at Pittsburgh	17
12	BALTIMORE	7
14	at Houston	24
17	at Indianapolis	3
10	at Cleveland	24
13	HOUSTON	20
14	SAN DIEGO	38
41	TAMPA BAY	14
14	at Atlanta	41
17	at Tennessee	23
19	INDIANAPOLIS	13
243		329

KANSAS CITY CHIEFS (7-9)

7	BUFFALO	41
3	at Detroit	48
17	at San Diego	20
22	MINNESOTA	17
28	at Indianapolis	24
28	at Oakland	0
23	SAN DIEGO	20
3	MIAMI	31
10	DENVER	17
3	at New England	34
9	PITTSBURGH	13
10	at Chicago	3
10	at NY Jets	37
19	GREEN BAY	14
13	OAKLAND	16
7	at Denver	3
212		338

MIAMI DOLPHINS (6-10)

24	NEW ENGLAND	38	20	WASHINGTON	9
13	HOUSTON	23	35	BUFFALO	8
16	at Cleveland	17	19	at Dallas	20
16	at San Diego	26	34	OAKLAND	14
6	at NY Jets	24	10	PHILADELPHIA	26
15	DENVER	18	30	at Buffalo	23
17	at NY Giants	20	24	at New England	27
31	at Kansas City	3	19	NY JETS	17
			329		313

NEW ENGLAND PATRIOTS (13-3)

38	at Miami	24
35	SAN DIEGO	21
31	at Buffalo	34
31	at Oakland	19
30	NY JETS	21
20	DALLAS	16
17	at Pittsburgh	25
20	NY GIANTS	24
37	at NY Jets	16
34	KANSAS CITY	3
38	at Philadelphia	20
31	INDIANAPOLIS	24
34	at Washington	27
41	at Denver	23
27	MIAMI	24
49	BUFFALO	21
513		342

OAKLAND RAIDERS (8-8)

23	at Denver	20
35	at Buffalo	38
34	NY JETS	24
19	NEW ENGLAND	31
25	at Houston	20
24	CLEVELAND	17
0	KANSAS CITY	28
24	DENVER	38
24	at San Diego	17
27	at Minnesota	21
25	CHICAGO	20
14	at Miami	34
16	at Green Bay	46
27	DETROIT	28
16	at Kansas City	13
26	SAN DIEGO	38
359		433

SAN DIEGO CHARGERS (8-8)

24	MINNESOTA	17
21	at New England	35
20	KANSAS CITY	17
25	MIAMI	16
29	at Denver	24
21	at NY Jets	27
20	at Kansas City	23
38	GREEN BAY	45
17	OAKLAND	24
20	at Chicago	31
13	DENVER	16
38	at Jacksonville	14
37	BUFFALO	10
31	BALTIMORE	14
10	at Detroit	38
38	at Oakland	26
406		377

NEW YORK JETS (8-8)

27	DALLAS	24
32	JACKSONVILLE	3
24	at Oakland	34
17	at Baltimore	34
21	at New England	30
24	MIAMI	6
27	SAN DIEGO	21
27	at Buffalo	11
16	NEW ENGLAND	37
13	at Denver	17
28	BUFFALO	24
34	at Washington	19
37	KANSAS CITY	10
19	at Philadelphia	45
14	NY GIANTS	29
17	at Miami	19
377		363

PITTSBURGH STEELERS (12-4)

7	at Baltimore	35
24	SEATTLE	0
23	at Indianapolis	20
10	at Houston	17
38	TENNESSEE	17
17	JACKSONVILLE	13
32	at Arizona	20
25	NEW ENGLAND	17
20	BALTIMORE	23
24	at Cincinnati	17
13	at Kansas City	9
35	CINCINNATI	7
14	CLEVELAND	3
3	at San Francisco	20
27	ST. LOUIS	0
13	at Cleveland	9
325		227

TENNESSEE TITANS (9-7)

14	at Jacksonville	16
26	BALTIMORE	13
17	DENVER	14
31	at Cleveland	13
17	at Pittsburgh	38
7	HOUSTON	41
27	INDIANAPOLIS	10
17	CINCINNATI	24
30	at Carolina	3
17	at Atlanta	23
23	TAMPA BAY	17
23	at Buffalo	17
17	NEW ORLEANS	22
13	at Indianapolis	27
23	JACKSONVILLE	17
23	at Houston	22
325		317

2011 NFC Team-by-Team Results

ARIZONA CARDINALS (8-8)

28	CAROLINA	21
21	at Washington	22
10	at Seattle	13
27	NY GIANTS	31
10	at Minnesota	34
20	PITTSBURGH	32
27	at Baltimore	30
19	ST. LOUIS	13
21	at Philadelphia	17
7	at San Francisco	23
23	at St. Louis	20
19	DALLAS	13
21	SAN FRANCISCO	19
20	CLEVELAND	17
16	at Cincinnati	23
23	SEATTLE	20
312		348

ATLANTA FALCONS (10-6)

12	at Chicago	30
35	PHILADELPHIA	31
13	at Tampa Bay	16
30	at Seattle	28
14	GREEN BAY	25
31	CAROLINA	17
23	at Detroit	16
31	at Indianapolis	7
23	NEW ORLEANS	26
23	TENNESSEE	17
24	MINNESOTA	14
10	at Houston	17
31	at Carolina	23
41	JACKSONVILLE	14
16	at New Orleans	45
45	TAMPA BAY	24
402		350

CAROLINA PANTHERS (6-10)

21	at Arizona	28
23	GREEN BAY	30
16	JACKSONVILLE	10
29	at Chicago	34
27	NEW ORLEANS	30
17	at Atlanta	31
33	WASHINGTON	20
21	MINNESOTA	24
3	TENNESSEE	30
35	at Detroit	49
27	at Indianapolis	19
38	at Tampa Bay	19
23	ATLANTA	31
28	at Houston	13
48	TAMPA BAY	16
17	at New Orleans	45
406		429

CHICAGO BEARS (8-8)

30	ATLANTA	12
13	at New Orleans	30
17	GREEN BAY	27
34	CAROLINA	29
13	at Detroit	24
39	MINNESOTA	10
24	at Tampa Bay	18
30	at Philadelphia	24
37	DETROIT	13
31	SAN DIEGO	20
20	at Oakland	25
3	KANSAS CITY	10
10	at Denver	13
14	SEATTLE	38
21	at Green Bay	35
17	at Minnesota	13
353		341

DALLAS COWBOYS (8-8)

24	at NY Jets	27
27	at San Francisco	24
18	WASHINGTON	16
30	DETROIT	34
16	at New England	20
34	ST. LOUIS	7
7	at Philadelphia	34
23	SEATTLE	13
44	BUFFALO	7
27	at Washington	24
20	MIAMI	19
13	at Arizona	19
34	NY GIANTS	37
31	at Tampa Bay	15
7	PHILADELPHIA	20
14	at NY Giants	31
369		347

DETROIT LIONS (10-6)

27	at Tampa Bay	20
48	KANSAS CITY	3
26	at Minnesota	23
34	at Dallas	30
24	CHICAGO	13
19	SAN FRANCISCO	25
16	ATLANTA	23
45	at Denver	10
13	at Chicago	37
49	CAROLINA	35
15	GREEN BAY	27
17	at New Orleans	31
34	MINNESOTA	28
28	at Oakland	27
38	SAN DIEGO	10
41	at Green Bay	45
474		387

GREEN BAY PACKERS (15-1)

42	NEW ORLEANS	34
30	at Carolina	23
27	at Chicago	17
49	DENVER	23
25	at Atlanta	14
24	ST. LOUIS	3
33	at Minnesota	27
45	at San Diego	38
45	MINNESOTA	7
35	TAMPA BAY	26
27	at Detroit	15
38	at NY Giants	35
46	OAKLAND	16
14	at Kansas City	19
35	CHICAGO	21
45	DETROIT	41
560		359

MINNESOTA VIKINGS (3-13)

17	at San Diego	24
20	TAMPA BAY	24
23	DETROIT	26
17	at Kansas City	22
34	ARIZONA	10
10	at Chicago	39
27	GREEN BAY	33
24	at Carolina	21
7	at Green Bay	45
21	OAKLAND	27
14	at Atlanta	24
32	DENVER	35
28	at Detroit	34
20	NEW ORLEANS	42
33	at Washington	26
13	CHICAGO	17
340		449

NEW ORLEANS SAINTS (13-3)

34	at Green Bay	42
30	CHICAGO	13
40	HOUSTON	33
23	at Jacksonville	10
30	at Carolina	27
20	at Tampa Bay	26
62	INDIANAPOLIS	7
21	at St. Louis	31
27	TAMPA BAY	16
26	at Atlanta	23
49	NY GIANTS	24
31	DETROIT	17
22	at Tennessee	17
42	at Minnesota	20
45	ATLANTA	16
45	CAROLINA	17
547		339

NEW YORK GIANTS (9-7)

14	at Washington	28
28	ST LOUIS	16
29	at Philadelphia	16
31	at Arizona	27
25	SEATTLE	36
27	BUFFALO	24
20	MIAMI	17
24	at New England	20
20	at San Francisco	27
10	PHILADELPHIA	17
24	at New Orleans	49
35	GREEN BAY	38
37	at Dallas	34
10	WASHINGTON	23
29	at NY Jets	14
31	DALLAS	14
394		400

PHILADELPHIA EAGLES (8-8)

31	at St. Louis	13
31	at Atlanta	35
16	NY GIANTS	29
23	SAN FRANCISCO	24
24	at Buffalo	31
20	at Washington	13
34	DALLAS	7
24	CHICAGO	30
17	ARIZONA	21
17	at NY Giants	10
20	NEW ENGLAND	38
14	at Seattle	31
26	at Miami	10
45	NY JETS	19
20	at Dallas	7
34	WASHINGTON	10
396		328

SAN FRANCISCO 49ERS (13-3)

33	SEATTLE	17
24	DALLAS	27
13	at Cincinnati	8
24	at Philadelphia	23
48	TAMPA BAY	3
25	at Detroit	19
20	CLEVELAND	10
19	at Washington	11
27	NY GIANTS	20
23	ARIZONA	7
6	at Baltimore	16
26	ST. LOUIS	0
19	at Arizona	21
20	PITTSBURGH	3
19	at Seattle	17
34	at St. Louis	27
380		229

SEATTLE SEAHAWKS (7-9)

17	at San Francisco	33
0	at Pittsburgh	24
13	ARIZONA	10
28	ATLANTA	30
36	at NY Giants	25
3	at Cleveland	6
12	CINCINNATI	34
13	at Dallas	23
22	BALTIMORE	17
24	at St. Louis	7
17	WASHINGTON	23
31	PHILADELPHIA	14
30	ST. LOUIS	13
38	at Chicago	14
17	SAN FRANCISCO	19
20	at Arizona	23
321		**315**

ST. LOUIS RAMS (2-14)

13	PHILADELPHIA	31
16	at NY Giants	28
7	BALTIMORE	37
10	WASHINGTON	17
3	at Green Bay	24
7	at Dallas	34
31	NEW ORLEANS	21
13	at Arizona	19
13	at Cleveland	12
7	SEATTLE	24
20	ARIZONA	23
0	at San Francisco	26
13	at Seattle	30
13	CINCINNATI	20
0	at Pittsburgh	27
27	SAN FRANCISCO	34
193		**407**

TAMPA BAY BUCCANEERS (4-12)

20	DETROIT	27
24	at Minnesota	20
16	ATLANTA	13
24	INDIANAPOLIS	17
3	at San Francisco	48
26	NEW ORLEANS	20
18	CHICAGO	24
16	at New Orleans	27
9	HOUSTON	37
26	at Green Bay	35
17	at Tennessee	23
19	CAROLINA	38
14	at Jacksonville	41
15	DALLAS	31
16	at Carolina	48
24	at Atlanta	45
287		**494**

WASHINGTON REDSKINS (5-11)

28	NY GIANTS	14		9	at Miami	20
22	ARIZONA	21		24	DALLAS	27
16	at Dallas	18		23	at Seattle	17
17	at St. Louis	10		19	NY JETS	34
13	PHILADELPHIA	20		27	NEW ENGLAND	34
20	at Carolina	33		23	at NY Giants	10
0	at Buffalo	23		26	MINNESOTA	33
11	SAN FRANCISCO	19		10	at Philadelphia	34
				288		**367**

2011 NFL Individual Leaders

American Football Conference

Scoring

TOUCHDOWNS	TD	Rush	Rec	Ret	2PT	Pts	KICKING	FG	PAT	Pts
R. Gronkowski, NE	18	1	17	0	0	108	S. Gostkowski, NE	28	59	143
R. Rice, Bal	15	12	3	0	0	90	N. Rackers, Hou	32	39	135
A. Foster, Hou	12	10	2	0	0	72	M. Nugent, Cin	33	33	132
M. Jones-Drew, Jax	11	8	3	0	0	66	S. Janikowski, Oak	31	36	129
B. Green-Ellis, NE	11	11	0	0	0	66	B. Cundiff, Bal	28	38	122
M. Tolbert, SD	10	8	2	0	0	60	N. Novak, SD	27	41	122
W. Welker, NE	9	0	9	0	0	54	R. Bironas, Ten	29	34	121
V. Jackson, SD	9	0	9	0	0	54	D. Carpenter, Mia	29	26	113
R. Mendenhall, Pit	9	9	0	0	0	54	S. Suisham, Pit	23	36	105
E. Decker, Den	9	0	8	1	0	54	N. Folk, NYJ	19	44	101

Passing

	Att	Comp	Pct	Yds	Yds/Att	Lg	TD	Int	Rating Pts
Tom Brady, NE	611	401	65.6	5,235	8.57	99	39	12	105.6
Matt Schaub, Hou	292	178	61.0	2,479	8.49	80	15	6	96.8
Ben Roethlisberger, Pit	513	324	63.2	4,077	7.95	95	21	14	90.1
Philip Rivers, SD	582	366	62.9	4,624	7.95	58	27	20	88.7
Matt Moore, Mia	347	210	60.5	2,497	7.20	65	16	9	87.1
Matt Hasselbeck, Ten	518	319	61.6	3,571	6.89	80	18	14	82.4
Joe Flacco, Bal	542	312	57.6	3,610	6.66	74	20	12	80.9
Carson Palmer, Oak	328	199	60.7	2,753	8.39	78	13	16	80.5
Andy Dalton, Cin	516	300	58.1	3,398	6.59	84	20	13	80.4
Ryan Fitzpatrick, Buf	569	353	62.0	3,832	6.74	60	24	23	79.1

American Football Conference (Cont.)

Pass Receiving

RECEPTIONS	No.	Yds	Avg	Lg	TD	YARDS	Yds	No.	Avg	Lg	TD
Wes Welker, NE	122	1,569	12.9	99	9	Wes Welker, NE	1,569	122	12.9	99	9
Rob Gronkowski, NE	90	1,327	14.7	52	17	Rob Gronkowski, NE	1,327	90	14.7	52	17
Brandon Marshall, Mia	81	1,214	15.0	65	6	Brandon Marshall, Mia	1,214	81	15.0	65	6
Dwayne Bowe, KC	81	1,159	14.3	52	5	Mike Wallace, Pit	1,193	72	16.6	95	8
Aaron Hernandez, NE	79	910	11.5	46	7	Dwayne Bowe, KC	1,159	81	14.3	52	5
Ray Rice, Bal	76	704	9.3	52	3	Antonio Brown, Pit	1,108	69	16.1	79	2
Steve Johnson, Buf	76	1,004	13.2	55	7	Vincent Jackson, SD	1,106	60	18.4	58	9
Reggie Wayne, Ind	75	960	12.8	56	4	A.J. Green, Cin	1,057	65	16.3	58	7
Nate Washington, Ten	74	1,023	13.8	57	7	Nate Washington, Ten	1,023	74	13.8	57	7
Mike Wallace, Pit	72	1,193	16.6	95	8	Steve Johnson, Buf	1,004	76	13.2	55	7

Rushing

	Att	Yds	Avg	Lg	TD
M, Jones-Drew, Jax	343	1,606	4.7	56	8
Ray Rice, Bal	291	1,364	4.7	70	12
Arian Foster, Hou	278	1,224	4.4	43	10
Willis McGahee, Den	249	1,199	4.8	60	4
Ryan Mathews, SD	222	1,091	4.9	39	6
Reggie Bush, Mia	216	1,086	5.0	76	6
Cedric Benson, Cin	273	1,067	3.9	42	6
Shonn Greene, NYJ	253	1,054	4.2	31	6
Chris Johnson, Ten	262	1,047	4.0	48	4
Michael Bush, Oak	256	977	3.8	44	7

Interceptions

	No.	Yds	Lg	TD
Eric Weddle, SD	7	89	26	0
Kyle Arrington, NE	7	92	28	0
Matt Giordano, Oak	5	130	62	0
Lardarius Webb, Bal	5	81	73	1
11 tied with 4				

Sacks

Terrell Suggs, Bal	14.0
Tamba Hali, KC	12.0
Connor Barwin, Hou	11.5
Von Miller, Den	11.5
Antwan Barnes, SD	11.0
Andre Carter, NE	10.0
Mark Anderson, NE	10.0

Punting

	No.	Yds	Lng	Avg	Net Avg	Blk	In 20	TB	Ret	Ret Avg
Britton Colquitt, Den	101	4783	66	47.4	40.2	0	33	7	51	11.5
Pat McAfee, Ind	88	4102	64	46.6	39.6	1	21	3	48	11.5
Dustin Colquitt, KC	89	4084	68	45.9	40.1	0	27	5	36	11.4
Kevin Huber, Cin	91	4023	71	44.2	39.2	0	24	9	38	7.2
Shane Lechler, Oak	78	3960	80	50.8	40.9	0	27	9	44	13.5

Punt Returns

	No.	Yds	Avg	Lg	TD
Javier Arenas, KC	32	410	12.8	37	0
Davone Bess, Mia	37	442	11.9	25	0
Josh Cribbs, Cle	34	388	11.4	84	1
Jeremy Kerley, NYJ	29	317	10.9	53	0
Antonio Brown, Pit	30	325	10.8	60	1

Kickoff Returns

	No.	Yds	Avg	Lg	TD
Joe McKnight, NYJ	34	1073	31.6	107	1
Richard Goodman, SD	34	936	27.5	105	1
Antonio Brown, Pit	27	737	27.3	52	0
Josh Cribbs, Cle	39	974	25.0	63	0
Clyde Gates, Mia	34	843	24.8	77	0

National Football Conference

Scoring

TOUCHDOWNS	TD	Rush	Rec	Ret	2PT	Pts	KICKING	FG	PAT	Pts
L. McCoy, Phi	20	17	3	0	0	120	David Akers, SF	44	34	166
C. Johnson, Det	16	0	16	0	0	96	John Kasay, NO	28	63	147
J. Nelson, GB	15	0	15	0	0	90	Mason Crosby, GB	24	68	140
C. Newton, Car	14	14	0	0	0	84	Dan Bailey, Dal	32	39	135
A. Peterson, Min	13	12	1	0	0	78	Jason Hanson, Det	24	54	126
M. Lynch, Sea	13	12	1	0	0	78	Matt Bryant, Atl	27	45	126
A. Bradshaw, NYG	11	9	2	0	1	68	Robbie Gould, Chi	28	37	121
M. Turner, Atl	11	11	0	0	0	66	Graham Gano, Wash	31	25	118
L. Robinson, Dal	11	0	11	0	0	66	Alex Henery, Phi	24	46	118
J. Graham, NO	11	0	11	0	0	66	Olindo Mare, Car	22	44	110

National Football Conference (Cont.)

Passing

	Att	Comp	Pct	Yds	Yds/Att	Lg	TD	Int	Rating Pts
Aaron Rodgers, GB	502	343	68.3	4,643	9.25	93	45	6	122.5
Drew Brees, NO	657	468	71.2	5,476	8.34	79	46	14	110.6
Tony Romo, Dal	522	346	66.3	4,184	8.02	77	31	10	102.5
Matthew Stafford, Det	663	421	63.5	5,038	7.60	73	41	16	97.2
Eli Manning, NYG	589	359	61.0	4,933	8.38	99	29	16	92.9
Matt Ryan, Atl	566	347	61.3	4,177	7.38	80	29	12	92.2
Alex Smith, SF	445	273	61.3	3,144	7.07	56	17	5	90.7
Jay Cutler, Chi	314	182	58.0	2,319	7.39	56	13	7	85.7
Michael Vick, Phi	423	253	59.8	3,303	7.81	73	18	14	84.9
Cam Newton, Car	517	310	60.0	4,051	7.84	91	21	17	84.5

Pass Receiving

RECEPTIONS	No.	Yds	Avg	Lg	TD	YARDS	Yds	No.	Avg	Lg	TD
Roddy White, Atl	100	1,296	13.0	43	8	Calvin Johnson, Det	1,681	96	17.5	73	16
Jimmy Graham, NO	99	1,310	13.2	59	11	Victor Cruz, NYG	1,536	82	18.7	99	9
Calvin Johnson, Det	96	1,681	17.5	73	16	Larry Fitzgerald, Ari	1,411	80	17.6	73	8
Percy Harvin, Min	87	967	11.1	52	6	Steve Smith, Car	1,394	79	17.6	77	7
Darren Sproles, NO	86	710	8.3	39	7	Jimmy Graham, NO	1,310	99	13.2	59	11
B. Pettigrew, Det	83	777	9.4	27	5	Roddy White, Atl	1,296	100	13.0	43	8
Victor Cruz, NYG	82	1,536	18.7	99	9	Jordy Nelson, GB	1,263	68	18.6	93	15
Tony Gonzalez, Atl	80	875	10.9	30	7	Hakeem Nicks, NYG	1,192	76	15.7	68	7
Larry Fitzgerald, Ari	80	1,411	17.6	73	8	Marques Colston, NO	1,143	80	14.3	50	8
Marques Colston, NO	80	1,143	14.3	50	8	Percy Harvin, Min	967	87	11.1	52	6

Rushing

	Att	Yds	Avg	Lg	TD
M. Turner, Atl	301	1,340	4.5	81	11
L. McCoy, Phi	273	1,309	4.8	60	17
F. Gore, SF	282	1,211	4.3	55	8
M. Lynch, Sea	285	1,204	4.2	47	12
S. Jackson, StL	260	1,145	4.4	47	5
B. Wells, Ari	245	1,047	4.3	71	10
M. Forte, Chi	203	997	4.9	46	3
A. Peterson, Min	208	970	4.7	54	12
D. Murray, Dal	164	897	5.5	91	2
D. Williams, Car	155	836	5.4	74	7

Interceptions

	No.	Yds	Lg	TD
Charles Woodson, GB	7	63	30	1
Carlos Rogers, SF	6	106	31	1
Corey Webster, NYG	6	71	25	0
Brandon Browner, Sea	6	220	94	2
Dashon Goldson, SF	6	53	21	0

Sacks

Jared Allen, Min	22.0
DeMarcus Ware, Dal	19.5
Jason Babin, Phi	18.0
Jason Pierre-Paul, NYG	16.5
Aldon Smith, SF	14.0
Chris Long, StL	13.0
Julius Peppers, Chi	11.0
Chris Clemons, Sea	11.0
Trent Cole, Phi	11.0
Cliff Avril, Det	11.0

Punting

	No.	Yds	Lng	Avg	Net Avg	Blk	In 20	TB	Ret	Ret Avg
Andy Lee, SF	78	3970	68	50.9	44.6	1	28	9	39	8.1
Thomas Morstead, NO	46	2224	64	48.3	44.0	1	13	4	19	6.2
Jon Ryan, Sea	95	4431	77	46.6	39.3	0	34	8	47	11.5
Chris Kluwe, Min	77	3517	60	45.7	38.0	0	22	3	43	12.4
Steve Weatherford, NYG	82	3745	62	45.7	39.2	0	25	6	41	9.9

Punt Returns

	No.	Yds	Avg	Lg	TD
Devin Hester, Chi	28	454	16.2	82	2
Patrick Peterson, Ari	44	699	15.9	99	4
Ted Ginn, SF	38	466	12.3	55	1
Randall Cobb, GB	26	295	11.3	80	1
Leon Washington, Sea	41	464	11.3	37	0
Darren Sproles, NO	29	294	10.1	72	1
Eric Weems, Atl	32	315	9.8	42	0

Kickoff Returns

	No.	Yds	Avg	Lg	TD
Randall Cobb, GB	34	941	27.7	108	1
Ted Ginn, SF	29	800	27.6	102	1
Darren Sproles, NO	40	1089	27.2	92	0
Sammie Stroughter, TB	20	540	27.0	78	0
Kealoha Pilares, Car	23	590	25.7	101	1
Jerious Norwood, StL	24	611	25.5	47	0

AFC Total Offense

	Total Plays	Yds/Game	Pts/Game	1st Dwns/Game	Time of Poss
New England	1,082	428.0	32.1	24.9	28:47
San Diego	1,048	393.1	25.4	22.4	32:27
Oakland	1,015	379.5	22.4	20.5	29:55
Pittsburgh	1,015	372.3	20.3	21.3	32:33
Houston	1,046	372.1	23.8	20.1	32:40
Buffalo	992	351.5	23.2	19.6	30:11
Baltimore	1,036	338.7	23.6	19.5	30:35
Tennessee	984	335.1	20.3	17.6	27:54
Cincinnati	1,015	319.9	21.5	17.8	30:19
Miami	990	317.4	20.6	17.9	30:37
Denver	1,017	316.6	19.3	17.9	29:43
NY Jets	1,030	311.8	23.6	18.8	30:49
Kansas City	1,021	310.8	13.2	17.3	29:32
Cleveland	1,024	288.8	13.6	17.4	29:15
Indianapolis	951	286.8	15.2	16.1	26:13
Jacksonville	1,002	259.3	15.2	15.7	30:02

AFC Total Defense

	Opp Total Plays	Opp Yds/Game	Opp Yds/Play	Opp Pts/Game
Pittsburgh	964	271.8	4.5	14.2
Houston	960	285.7	4.8	17.4
Baltimore	1,002	288.9	4.6	16.6
NY Jets	993	312.1	5.0	22.7
Jacksonville	979	313.0	5.1	20.6
Cincinnati	1,009	316.2	5.0	20.2
Cleveland	1,035	332.4	5.1	19.2
Kansas City	991	333.3	5.4	21.1
Miami	1,043	345.1	5.3	19.6
San Diego	958	346.6	5.8	23.6
Tennessee	1,080	355.1	5.3	19.8
Denver	1,063	357.8	5.4	24.4
Indianapolis	1,062	370.9	5.6	26.9
Buffalo	1,003	371.1	5.9	27.1
Oakland	1,070	387.6	5.8	27.1
New England	1,064	411.1	6.2	21.4

NFC Total Offense

	Total Plays	Yds/Game	Pts/Game	1st Dwns/Game	Time of Poss
New Orleans	1,117	467.1	34.2	26.0	31:59
Green Bay	988	405.1	35.0	22.1	30:29
Philadelphia	1,036	399.1	24.8	22.2	31:20
Detroit	1,058	396.1	29.6	21.8	30:09
Carolina	999	389.8	25.4	21.6	30:16
NY Giants	1,028	385.1	24.6	20.7	29:30
Atlanta	1,073	376.6	25.1	21.8	32:18
Dallas	1,017	375.5	23.1	20.4	31:25
Washington	1,032	336.7	18.0	19.5	30:26
Minnesota	1,007	329.7	21.2	18.6	28:43
Arizona	993	324.5	19.5	17.9	28:43
Tampa Bay	966	319.2	17.9	17.3	29:07
Chicago	978	314.1	22.1	16.9	30:25
San Francisco	993	310.9	23.8	17.6	32:08
Seattle	1,003	303.8	20.1	16.6	28:23
St. Louis	1,013	283.6	12.1	16.7	28:11

NFC Total Defense

	Opp Total Plays	Opp Yds/Game	Opp Yds/Play	Opp Pts/Game
San Francisco	974	308.2	5.1	14.3
Philadelphia	982	324.9	5.3	20.5
Seattle	1,049	332.2	5.1	19.7
Atlanta	965	333.6	5.5	21.9
Washington	988	339.8	5.5	22.9
Dallas	972	343.2	5.6	21.7
Chicago	1,048	350.4	5.4	21.3
Arizona	1,095	355.1	5.2	21.8
Minnesota	1,027	358.2	5.6	28.1
St. Louis	1,033	358.4	5.6	25.4
Detroit	1,055	367.6	5.6	24.2
New Orleans	1,010	368.4	5.8	21.2
NY Giants	1,072	376.4	5.6	25.0
Carolina	972	377.6	6.2	26.8
Tampa Bay	1,002	394.4	6.3	30.9
Green Bay	1,049	411.6	6.3	22.4

Takeaways/Giveaways

American Football Conference

	Takeaways			Giveaways			Net Diff
	Int	Fum	Total	Int	Fum	Total	
New England	23	11	34	12	5	17	17
Houston	17	10	27	9	11	20	7
Jacksonville	17	11	28	15	8	23	5
Baltimore	15	11	26	12	12	24	2
Cleveland	9	11	20	13	6	19	1
Tennessee	11	12	23	14	8	22	1
Buffalo	20	11	31	25	5	30	1
Cincinnati	10	12	22	14	8	22	0
Kansas City	20	6	26	18	10	28	-2
NY Jets	19	12	31	18	16	34	-3
Oakland	18	8	26	23	7	30	-4
Miami	16	3	19	13	12	25	-6
San Diego	17	4	21	20	8	28	-7
Indianapolis	8	9	17	14	15	29	-12
Denver	9	9	18	13	17	30	-12
Pittsburgh	11	4	15	15	13	28	-13

National Football Conference

	Takeaways			Giveaways			Net Diff
	Int	Fum	Total	Int	Fum	Total	
San Francisco	23	15	38	5	5	10	28
Green Bay	31	7	38	8	6	14	24
Detroit	21	13	34	16	7	23	11
Seattle	22	9	31	14	9	23	8
Atlanta	19	10	29	13	8	21	8
NY Giants	20	11	31	16	8	24	7
Dallas	15	9	24	12	9	21	3
Chicago	20	11	31	20	9	29	2
Carolina	14	10	24	17	6	23	1
Minnesota	8	15	23	17	9	26	-3
New Orleans	9	7	16	14	5	19	-3
St. Louis	12	6	18	10	13	23	-5
Arizona	10	9	19	23	9	32	-13
Washington	13	8	21	24	11	35	-14
Philadelphia	15	9	24	25	13	38	-14
Tampa Bay	14	10	24	24	16	40	-16

Baltimore Ravens

SCORING

	TD						
	Rush	Rec	Ret	FG	PAT	2PT	Pts
Cundiff	0	0	0	28	38	0	122
Rice	12	3	0	0	0	0	90
Smith	0	7	0	0	0	0	42
Dickson	0	5	0	0	0	0	30
Boldin	0	3	0	0	0	0	18
Pitta	0	3	0	0	0	0	18

RUSHING

	No.	Yds	Avg	Lg	TD
Rice	291	1364	4.7	70	12
Williams	108	444	4.1	28	2
Flacco	39	88	2.3	33	1

PASSING

	Att	Comp	Pct Comp	Yds	Avg Gain	TD	Int	Rating Pts
Flacco	542	312	57.6	3610	6.7	20	12	80.9

RECEIVING

	No.	Yds	Avg	TD	Lg
Boldin	57	887	15.6	3	56
Smith	50	841	16.8	7	74
Rice	76	704	9.3	3	52
Dickson	54	528	9.8	5	25
Pitta	40	405	10.1	3	39

INTERCEPTIONS: Webb, 5

PUNTING

	No.	Yds	Avg	Net Avg	Blk	In 20	TB	Lg
Koch	73	3393	46.5	38.6	0	21	9	63

SACKS: Suggs, 14.0

Cincinnati Bengals

SCORING

	TD						
	Rush	Rec	Ret	FG	PAT	2PT	Pts
Nugent	0	0	0	33	33	0	132
Green	0	7	0	0	0	0	42
Benson	6	0	0	0	0	0	36
Gresham	0	6	0	0	0	0	36
Simpson	0	4	0	0	0	0	24
Caldwell	0	3	0	0	0	0	18
Scott	3	0	0	0	0	0	18

RUSHING

	No.	Yds	Avg	Lg	TD
Cedric Benson	273	1067	3.9	42	6
Bernard Scott	112	380	3.4	25	3
Andy Dalton	37	152	4.1	17	1

PASSING

	Att	Comp	Pct Comp	Yds	Avg Gain	TD	Int	Rating Pts
Dalton	516	300	58.1	3398	6.6	20	13	80.4

RECEIVING

	No.	Yds	Avg	Lg	TD
A.J. Green	65	1057	16.3	58	7
Jermaine Gresham	56	596	10.6	31	6
Jerome Simpson	50	725	14.5	84	4
Andre Caldwell	37	317	8.6	49	3
Andrew Hawkins	23	263	11.4	26	0
Brian Leonard	22	210	9.5	37	0
Cedric Benson	15	82	5.5	11	0

INTERCEPTIONS: Nelson, 4

PUNTING

	No.	Yds	Avg	Net Avg	Blk	In 20	TB	Lg
Huber	91	4023	44.2	39.2	0	24	9	71

SACKS: Atkins, 7.5

Buffalo Bills

SCORING

	TD						
	Rush	Rec	Ret	FG	PAT	2PT	Pts
Lindell	0	0	0	13	25	0	64
Rayner	0	0	0	10	13	0	43
St. Johnson	0	7	0	0	0	0	42
Jackson	6	0	0	0	0	0	36
Chandler	0	6	0	0	0	0	36
Spiller	4	2	0	0	0	0	36
Nelson	0	5	0	0	0	0	30

RUSHING

	No.	Yds	Avg	Lg	TD
Jackson	170	934	5.5	80	6
Spiller	107	561	5.2	38	4

PASSING

	Att	Comp	Pct Comp	Yds	Avg Gain	TD	Int	Rating Pts
Fitzpatrick	569	353	62.0	3832	6.7	24	23	79.1

RECEIVING

	No.	Yds	Avg	TD	Lg
St. Johnson	76	1004	13.2	7	55
Nelson	61	658	10.8	5	35
Jackson	39	442	11.3	0	49
Chandler	38	389	10.2	6	31
Spiller	39	269	6.9	2	19
Roosevelt	16	257	16.1	1	60
Smith	23	240	10.4	1	36
Jones	23	231	10.0	1	48

INTERCEPTIONS: Wilson, 4

PUNTING

	No.	Yds	Avg	Net Avg	Blk	In 20	TB	Lg
Moorman	72	3472	48.2	38.6	1	20	10	66

SACKS: Dareus, 5.5

Cleveland Browns

SCORING

	TD						
	Rush	Rec	Ret	FG	PAT	2PT	Pts
Dawson	0	0	0	24	20	0	92
Cribbs	0	4	1	0	0	0	30
Moore	0	4	0	0	0	0	24
Hillis	3	0	0	0	0	0	18

RUSHING

	No.	Yds	Avg	Lg	TD
Hillis	161	587	3.6	24	3
Ogbonnaya	73	334	4.6	40	1
Hardesty	88	266	3.0	19	0
McCoy	61	212	3.5	20	0

PASSING

	Att	Comp	Pct Comp	Yds	Avg Gain	TD	Int	Rating Pts
McCoy	463	265	57.2	2733	5.9	14	11	74.6
Wallace	107	55	51.4	567	5.3	2	2	65.4

RECEIVING

	No.	Yds	Avg	TD	Lg
Little	61	709	11.6	2	76
Cribbs	41	518	12.6	4	45
Watson	37	410	11.1	2	34
Massaquoi	31	384	12.4	2	56
Moore	34	324	9.5	4	33
Norwood	23	268	11.7	1	51

INTERCEPTIONS: Adams, 3

PUNTING

	No.	Yds	Avg	Net Avg	Blk	In 20	TB	Lg
Maynard	81	3282	40.5	36.7	0	32	1	63

SACKS: Sheard, 8.5

Denver Broncos

SCORING	Rush	TD Rec	Ret	FG	PAT	2PT	Pts
Prater	0	0	0	19	30	0	87
Decker	0	8	1	0	0	0	54
Tebow	6	0	0	0	0	2	40
McGahee	4	1	0	0	0	1	32
Thomas	0	4	0	0	0	0	24
Fells	0	3	0	0	0	0	18

RUSHING	No.	Yds	Avg	Lg	TD
McGahee	249	1199	4.8	60	4
Tebow	122	660	5.4	32	6
Ball	96	402	4.2	34	1

PASSING	Att	Comp	Pct Comp	Yds	Avg Gain	TD	Int	Rating Pts
Tebow	271	126	46.5	1729	6.4	12	6	72.9
Orton	155	91	58.7	979	6.3	8	7	75.7

RECEIVING	No.	Yds	Avg	TD	Lg
Decker	44	612	13.9	8	56
Thomas	32	551	17.2	4	47
Lloyd	19	283	14.9	0	44
Willis	18	267	14.8	1	42
Fells	19	256	13.5	3	32

INTERCEPTIONS: Goodman, Bailey, 2

PUNTING	No.	Yds	Avg	Net Avg	Blk	In 20	TB	Lg
B. Colquitt	101	4783	47.4	40.2	0	33	7	66

SACKS: Miller, 11.5

Indianapolis Colts

SCORING	Rush	TD Rec	Ret	FG	PAT	2PT	Pts
Vinatieri	0	0	0	23	24	0	93
Garcon	0	6	0	0	0	0	36
Brown	5	0	0	0	0	0	30
Wayne	0	4	0	0	0	0	24

RUSHING	No.	Yds	Avg	Lg	TD
Brown	134	645	4.8	80	5
Addai	118	433	3.7	16	1
Carter	101	377	3.7	42	2

PASSING	Att	Comp	Pct Comp	Yds	Avg Gain	TD	Int	Rating Pts
Painter	243	132	54.3	1541	6.3	6	9	66.6
Orlovsky	193	122	63.2	1201	6.2	6	4	82.4
Collins	98	48	49.0	481	4.9	2	1	65.9

RECEIVING	No.	Yds	Avg	TD	Lg
Wayne	75	960	12.8	4	56
Garcon	70	947	13.5	6	87
Collie	54	514	9.5	1	27
D. Clark	34	352	10.4	2	21
Tamme	19	177	9.3	1	29

INTERCEPTIONS: Lefeged, Powers, 2

PUNTING	No.	Yds	Avg	Net Avg	Blk	In 20	TB	Lg
McAfee	88	4102	46.6	39.6	1	21	3	64

SACKS: Mathis, 9.5

Houston Texans

SCORING	Rush	TD Rec	Ret	FG	PAT	2PT	Pts
Rackers	0	0	0	32	39	0	135
Foster	10	2	0	0	0	0	72
Dreessen	0	6	0	0	0	0	36
Tate	4	0	0	0	0	0	24
Walter	0	3	0	0	0	0	18
Daniels	0	3	0	0	0	0	18
Jones	0	2	1	0	0	0	18

RUSHING	No.	Yds	Avg	Lg	TD
Foster	278	1224	4.4	43	10
Tate	175	942	5.4	56	4
Ward	45	154	3.4	15	2

PASSING	Att	Comp	Pct Comp	Yds	Avg Gain	TD	Int	Rating Pts
Schaub	292	178	61.0	2479	8.5	15	6	96.8
Yates	134	82	61.2	949	7.1	3	3	80.7

RECEIVING	No.	Yds	Avg	TD	Lg
Daniels	54	677	12.5	3	34
Foster	53	617	11.6	2	78
Jones	31	512	16.5	2	80
Johnson	33	492	14.9	2	50
Walter	39	474	12.2	3	41
Dreessen	28	353	12.6	6	56

INTERCEPTIONS: Joseph, 4

PUNTING	No.	Yds	Avg	Net Avg	Blk	In 20	TB	Lg
Hartmann	58	2573	44.4	37.8	0	15	7	69

SACKS: Barwin, 11.5

Jacksonville Jaguars

SCORING	Rush	TD Rec	Ret	FG	PAT	2PT	Pts
Scobee	0	0	0	23	24	0	93
Jones-Drew	8	3	0	0	0	0	66
Hill	0	3	0	0	0	0	18
West	0	2	0	0	0	0	12

RUSHING	No.	Yds	Avg	Lg	TD
Jones-Drew	343	1606	4.7	56	8
Karim	63	130	2.1	14	0

PASSING	Att	Comp	Pct Comp	Yds	Avg Gain	TD	Int	Rating Pts
Gabbert	413	210	50.8	2214	5.4	12	11	65.4
McCown	56	30	53.6	296	5.3	0	4	39.0

RECEIVING	No.	Yds	Avg	TD	Lg
Lewis	39	460	11.8	0	62
Thomas	44	415	9.4	1	47
Jones-Drew	43	374	8.7	3	48
Hill	25	367	14.7	3	74
Dillard	29	292	10.1	1	25

INTERCEPTIONS: Posluszny, Landry, Coleman, Lowery, Trent, 2

PUNTING	No.	Yds	Avg	Net Avg	Blk	In 20	TB	Lg
Harris	72	3075	42.7	37.9	0	13	5	55
Turk	27	1072	39.7	32.8	0	7	5	65

SACKS: Mincey, 8.0

Kansas City Chiefs

SCORING

	Rush	TD Rec	Ret	FG	PAT	2PT	Pts
Succop	0	0	0	24	20	0	92
Bowe	0	5	0	0	0	0	30
McClain	1	1	0	0	0	0	12
Breaston	0	2	0	0	0	0	12
Battle	2	0	0	0	0	0	12
McCluster	1	1	0	0	0	0	12

RUSHING

	No.	Yds	Avg	Lg	TD
Battle	149	597	4.0	34	2
McCluster	114	516	4.5	32	1
Jones	153	478	3.1	26	0

PASSING

	Att	Comp	Pct Comp	Yds	Avg Gain	TD	Int	Rating Pts
Cassel	269	160	59.5	1713	6.4	10	9	76.6
Palko	134	80	59.7	796	5.9	2	7	59.8
Orton	97	59	60.8	779	8.0	1	2	81.1

RECEIVING

	No.	Yds	Avg	TD	Lg
Bowe	81	1159	14.3	5	52
Breaston	61	785	12.9	2	43
McCluster	46	328	7.1	1	49
Baldwin	21	254	12.1	1	39
Pope	24	247	10.3	1	39

INTERCEPTIONS: Flowers, Carr, 4

PUNTING

	No.	Yds	Avg	Net Avg	Blk	In 20	TB	Lg
D. Colquitt	89	4084	45.9	40.1	0	27	5	68

SACKS: Hali, 12.0

New England Patriots

SCORING

	Rush	TD Rec	Ret	FG	PAT	2PT	Pts
Gostkowski	0	0	0	28	59	0	143
Gronkowski	1	17	0	0	0	0	108
Green-Ellis	11	0	0	0	0	0	66
Welker	0	9	0	0	0	0	54
Hernandez	0	7	0	0	0	0	42
Branch	0	5	0	0	0	0	30
Brady	3	0	0	0	0	0	18

RUSHING

	No.	Yds	Avg	Lg	TD
Green-Ellis	181	667	3.7	18	11
Ridley	87	441	5.1	33	1
Woodhead	77	351	4.6	12	1

PASSING

	Att	Comp	Pct Comp	Yds	Avg Gain	TD	Int	Rating Pts
Brady	611	401	65.6	5235	8.6	39	12	105.6

RECEIVING

	No.	Yds	Avg	TD	Lg
Welker	122	1569	12.9	9	99
Gronkowski	90	1327	14.7	17	52
Hernandez	79	910	11.5	7	46
Branch	51	702	13.8	5	63
Ochocinco	15	276	18.4	1	53

INTERCEPTIONS: Arrington, 7

PUNTING

	No.	Yds	Avg	Net Avg	Blk	In 20	TB	Lg
Mesko	57	2648	46.5	41.5	0	24	3	65

SACKS: Carter, Anderson, 10.0

Miami Dolphins

SCORING

	Rush	TD Rec	Ret	FG	PAT	2PT	Pts
Carpenter	0	0	0	29	26	0	113
Bush	6	1	0	0	0	0	42
Marshall	0	6	0	0	0	0	36
Fasano	0	5	0	0	0	0	30
Graham	0	0	0	4	6	0	18
Bess	0	3	0	0	0	0	18
Clay	0	3	0	0	0	0	18

RUSHING

	No.	Yds	Avg	Lg	TD
Bush	216	1086	5.0	76	6
Thomas	165	581	3.5	28	0

PASSING

	Att	Comp	Pct Comp	Yds	Avg Gain	TD	Int	Rating Pts
Moore	347	210	60.5	2497	7.2	16	9	87.1
Henne	112	64	57.1	868	7.8	4	4	79.0

RECEIVING

	No.	Yds	Avg	TD	Lg
Marshall	81	1214	15.0	6	65
Hartline	35	549	15.7	1	41
Bess	51	537	10.5	3	41
Fasano	32	451	14.1	5	35
Bush	43	296	6.9	1	34
Clay	16	233	14.6	3	46

INTERCEPTIONS: Davis, 4

PUNTING

	No.	Yds	Avg	Net Avg	Blk	In 20	TB	Lg
Fields	78	3810	48.8	41.1	0	32	7	70

SACKS: Wake, 8.5

New York Jets

SCORING

	Rush	TD Rec	Ret	FG	PAT	2PT	Pts
Folk	0	0	0	19	44	0	101
Burress	0	8	0	0	0	0	48
Holmes	0	8	0	0	0	0	48
Sanchez	6	0	0	0	0	0	36
Greene	6	0	0	0	0	0	36
Keller	0	5	0	0	0	0	30
Tomlinson	1	2	0	0	0	0	18

RUSHING

	No.	Yds	Avg	Lg	TD
Greene	253	1054	4.2	31	6
Tomlinson	75	280	3.7	20	1

PASSING

	Att	Comp	Pct Comp	Yds	Avg Gain	TD	Int	Rating Pts
Sanchez	543	308	56.7	3474	6.4	26	18	78.2

RECEIVING

	No.	Yds	Avg	TD	Lg
Keller	65	815	12.5	5	41
Holmes	51	654	12.8	8	38
Burress	45	612	13.6	8	30
Tomlinson	42	449	10.7	2	74
Kerley	29	314	10.8	1	38
Greene	30	211	7.0	0	36

INTERCEPTIONS: Harris, Revis, Cromartie, 4

PUNTING

	No.	Yds	Avg	Net Avg	Blk	In 20	TB	Lg
Conley	92	3926	42.7	38.8	0	32	6	63

SACKS: Maybin, 6.0

Oakland Raiders

SCORING	Rush	Rec	Ret	FG	PAT	2PT	Pts
		TD					
Janikowski	0	0	0	31	36	0	129
Bush	7	1	0	0	0	0	48
Moore	1	5	0	0	0	0	36
McFadden	4	1	0	0	0	0	30
Heyward-Bey	0	4	0	0	0	0	24
Boss	0	3	0	0	0	0	18

RUSHING	No.	Yds	Avg	Lg	TD
Bush	256	977	3.8	44	7
McFadden	113	614	5.4	70	4

PASSING	Att	Comp	Pct Comp	Yds	Avg Gain	TD	Int	Rating Pts
Palmer	328	199	60.7	2753	8.4	13	16	80.5
Campbell	165	100	60.6	1170	7.1	6	4	84.2
Boller	28	15	53.6	161	5.8	0	3	31.1

RECEIVING	No.	Yds	Avg	TD	Lg
Heyward-Bey	64	975	15.2	4	58
Moore	33	618	18.7	5	78
Bush	37	418	11.3	1	55
Boss	28	368	13.1	3	35
Reece	27	301	11.1	2	47
Ford	19	279	14.7	1	41
Schilens	23	271	11.8	2	30
Murphy	15	241	16.1	0	47

INTERCEPTIONS: Giordano, 5

PUNTING	No.	Yds	Avg	Net Avg	Blk	In 20	TB	Lg
Lechler	78	3960	50.8	40.9	0	27	9	80

SACKS: Kelly, 7.5

Pittsburgh Steelers

SCORING	Rush	Rec	Ret	FG	PAT	2PT	Pts
		TD					
Suisham	0	0	0	23	36	0	105
Mendenhall	9	0	0	0	0	0	54
Wallace	0	8	0	0	0	0	48
Redman	3	0	0	0	0	0	18
Brown	0	2	1	0	0	0	18

RUSHING	No.	Yds	Avg	Lg	TD
Mendenhall	228	928	4.1	68	9
Redman	110	479	4.4	27	3

PASSING	Att	Comp	Pct Comp	Yds	Avg Gain	TD	Int	Rating Pts
Roethlisberger	513	324	63.2	4077	7.9	21	14	90.1
Batch	24	15	62.5	208	8.7	0	1	72.9

RECEIVING	No.	Yds	Avg	TD	Lg
Wallace	72	1193	16.6	8	95
Brown	69	1108	16.1	2	79
Miller	51	631	12.4	2	39
Ward	46	381	8.3	2	31
Sanders	22	288	13.1	2	32
Cotchery	16	237	14.8	2	36

INTERCEPTIONS: Polamalu, Gay, Taylor, 2

PUNTING	No.	Yds	Avg	Net Avg	Blk	In 20	TB	Lg
Kapinos	34	1530	45.0	38.3	0	10	1	59
Sepulveda	25	1153	46.1	40.6	1	8	5	66

SACKS: Harrison, Woodley, 9.0

San Diego Chargers

SCORING	Rush	Rec	Ret	FG	PAT	2PT	Pts
		TD					
Novak	0	0	0	27	41	0	122
Tolbert	8	2	0	0	0	0	60
Jackson	0	9	0	0	0	0	54
Gates	0	7	0	0	0	0	42
Mathews	6	0	0	0	0	0	36
Floyd	0	5	0	0	0	0	30
Brown	0	2	0	0	0	0	12

RUSHING	No.	Yds	Avg	Lg	TD
Mathews	222	1091	4.9	39	6
Tolbert	121	490	4.1	40	8

PASSING	Att	Comp	Pct Comp	Yds	Avg Gain	TD	Int	Rating Pts
Rivers	582	366	62.9	4624	7.9	27	20	88.7

RECEIVING	No.	Yds	Avg	TD	Lg
Jackson	60	1106	18.4	9	58
Floyd	43	856	19.9	5	52
Gates	64	778	12.2	7	38
Mathews	50	455	9.1	0	42
Tolbert	54	433	8.0	2	27
Brown	19	329	17.3	2	31
McMichael	30	271	9.0	0	30
Crayton	23	248	10.8	1	26

INTERCEPTIONS: Weddle, 7

PUNTING	No.	Yds	Avg	Net Avg	Blk	In 20	TB	Lg
Scifres	47	2234	47.5	39.7	0	17	2	71

SACKS: Barnes, 11.0

Tennessee Titans

SCORING	Rush	Rec	Ret	FG	PAT	2PT	Pts
		TD					
Bironas	0	0	0	29	34	0	121
Washington	1	7	0	0	0	0	48
Williams	0	5	0	0	0	0	30
Johnson	4	0	0	0	0	0	24
Cook	0	3	0	0	0	0	18
Britt	0	3	0	0	0	0	18

RUSHING	No.	Yds	Avg	Lg	TD
Johnson	262	1047	4.0	48	4
Ringer	59	185	3.1	25	1

PASSING	Att	Comp	Pct Comp	Yds	Avg Gain	TD	Int	Rating Pts
Hasselbeck	518	319	61.6	3571	6.9	18	14	82.4
Locker	66	34	51.5	542	8.2	4	0	99.4

RECEIVING	No.	Yds	Avg	TD	Lg
Washington	74	1023	13.8	7	57
Cook	49	759	15.5	3	80
Williams	45	592	13.2	5	54
Hawkins	47	470	10.0	1	32
Johnson	57	418	7.3	0	34
Britt	17	289	17.0	3	80

INTERCEPTIONS: Griffin, McCourty, 2

PUNTING	No.	Yds	Avg	Net Avg	Blk	In 20	TB	Lg
Kern	86	3747	43.6	39.4	0	31	7	64

SACKS: Klug, 7.0

Arizona Cardinals

SCORING	Rush	TD Rec	Ret	FG	PAT	2PT	Pts
Feely	0	0	0	19	33	0	90
Wells	10	0	0	0	0	0	60
Fitzgerald	0	8	0	0	0	0	48
Doucet	0	5	0	0	0	0	30
Peterson	0	0	4	0	0	0	24
King	0	3	0	0	0	0	18

RUSHING	No.	Yds	Avg	Lg	TD
Wells	245	1047	4.3	71	10
Stephens-Howling	43	167	3.9	39	0

PASSING	Att	Comp	Pct Comp	Yds	Avg Gain	TD	Int	Rating Pts
Kolb	253	146	57.7	1955	7.7	9	8	81.1
Skelton	275	151	54.9	1913	7.0	11	14	68.9
Bartel	22	10	45.5	86	3.9	1	1	52.5

RECEIVING	No.	Yds	Avg	TD	Lg
Fitzgerald	80	1411	17.6	8	73
Doucet	54	689	12.8	5	70
Roberts	51	586	11.5	2	45
Heap	24	283	11.8	1	28
King	27	271	10.0	3	48

INTERCEPTIONS: Marshall, 3

PUNTING	No.	Yds	Avg	Net Avg	Blk	In 20	TB	Lg
Zastudil	87	3929	45.2	37.5	0	24	5	66

SACKS: Campbell, 8.0

Atlanta Falcons

SCORING	Rush	TD Rec	Ret	FG	PAT	2PT	Pts
Bryant	0	0	0	27	45	0	126
Turner	11	0	0	0	0	0	66
White	0	8	0	0	0	0	48
Jones	0	8	0	0	0	0	48
Gonzalez	0	7	0	0	0	0	42
Mughelli	0	2	0	0	0	0	12
Ryan	2	0	0	0	0	0	12
Rodgers	1	1	0	0	0	0	12

RUSHING	No.	Yds	Avg	Lg	TD
Turner	301	1340	4.5	81	11
Rodgers	57	205	3.6	13	1

PASSING	Att	Comp	Pct Comp	Yds	Avg Gain	TD	Int	Rating Pts
Ryan	566	347	61.3	4177	7.4	29	12	92.2
Redman	28	18	64.3	188	6.7	0	1	68.8

RECEIVING	No.	Yds	Avg	TD	LG
R. White	100	1296	13.0	8	43
Jones	54	959	17.8	8	80
Gonzalez	80	875	10.9	7	30
H. Douglas	39	498	12.8	1	49

INTERCEPTIONS: DeCoud, 4

PUNTING	No.	Yds	Avg	Net Avg	Blk	In 20	TB	Lg
Bosher	70	2990	42.7	39.4	1	27	4	59

SACKS: Abraham, 9.5

Carolina Panthers

SCORING	Rush	TD Rec	Ret	FG	PAT	2PT	Pts
Mare	0	0	0	22	44	0	110
Newton	14	0	0	0	0	0	84
Smith	0	7	0	0	0	1	44
Williams	7	0	0	0	0	0	42
Olsen	0	5	0	0	0	1	32
Stewart	4	1	0	0	0	0	30
Shockey	0	4	0	0	0	0	24
LaFell	0	3	0	0	0	0	18

RUSHING	No.	Yds	Avg	Lg	TD
Williams	155	836	5.4	74	7
Stewart	142	761	5.4	32	4
Newton	126	706	5.6	49	14

PASSING	Att	Comp	Pct Comp	Yds	Avg Gain	TD	Int	Rating Pts
Newton	517	310	60.0	4051	7.8	21	17	84.5

RECEIVING	No.	Yds	Avg	TD	Lg
Smith	79	1394	17.6	7	77
LaFell	36	613	17.0	3	91
Olsen	45	540	12.0	5	44
Naanee	44	467	10.6	1	28
Shockey	37	455	12.3	4	29
Stewart	47	413	8.8	1	26

INTERCEPTIONS: Gamble, 3

PUNTING	No.	Yds	Avg	Net Avg	Blk	In 20	TB	Lg
Baker	66	2819	42.7	34.1	0	19	5	56

SACKS: C. Johnson, 9.0

Chicago Bears

SCORING	Rush	TD Rec	Ret	FG	PAT	2PT	Pts
Gould	0	0	0	28	37	0	121
Barber	6	0	0	0	0	0	36
Davis	0	5	0	0	0	0	30
Hester	0	1	3	0	0	0	24
Forte	3	1	0	0	0	0	24
Sanzenbacher	0	3	0	0	0	0	18

RUSHING	No.	Yds	Avg	Lg	TD
Forte	203	997	4.9	46	3
Barber	114	422	3.7	29	6
Bell	79	337	4.3	26	0

PASSING	Att	Comp	Pct Comp	Yds	Avg Gain	TD	Int	Rating Pts
Cutler	314	182	58.0	2319	7.4	13	7	85.7
Hanie	102	51	50.0	613	6.0	3	9	41.8
McCown	55	35	63.6	414	7.5	2	4	68.3

RECEIVING	No.	Yds	Avg	TD	Lg
Knox	37	727	19.6	2	81
Williams	37	507	13.7	2	25
Forte	52	490	9.4	1	56
Bennett	24	381	15.9	1	49
Hester	26	369	14.2	1	53
Sanzenbacher	27	276	10.2	3	22

INTERCEPTIONS: Moore, 4

PUNTING	No.	Yds	Avg	Net Avg	Blk	In 20	TB	Lg
Podlesh	89	3903	43.9	40.4	0	21	4	70

SACKS: Peppers, 11.0

Dallas Cowboys

SCORING	Rush	Rec	Ret	FG	PAT	2PT	Pts
Bailey	0	0	0	32	39	0	135
Robinson	0	11	0	0	0	0	66
Bryant	0	9	0	0	0	0	54
Austin	0	7	0	0	0	0	42
Witten	0	5	0	0	0	0	30

RUSHING	No.	Yds	Avg	Lg	TD
Murray	164	897	5.5	91	2
Jones	127	575	4.5	40	1

PASSING	Att	Comp	Pct Comp	Yds	Avg Gain	TD	Int	Rating Pts
Romo	522	346	66.3	4184	8.0	31	10	102.5
McGee	38	24	63.2	182	4.8	1	0	83.4

RECEIVING	No.	Yds	Avg	TD	Lg
Witten	79	942	11.9	5	64
Bryant	63	928	14.7	9	50
Robinson	54	858	15.9	11	74
Austin	43	579	13.5	7	53
Jones	33	221	6.7	0	27

INTERCEPTIONS: Newman, Lee, 4

PUNTING	No.	Yds	Avg	Net Avg	Blk	In 20	TB	Lg
McBriar	58	2542	43.8	36.7	1	21	7	68
Jones	10	426	42.6	40.5	0	4	1	54

SACKS: Ware, 19.5

Green Bay Packers

SCORING	Rush	Rec	Ret	FG	PAT	2PT	Pts
Crosby	0	0	0	24	68	0	140
Nelson	0	15	0	0	0	0	90
Jennings	0	9	0	0	0	0	54
Finley	0	8	0	0	0	0	48
Jones	0	7	0	0	0	0	42
Driver	0	6	0	0	0	0	36
Kuhn	4	2	0	0	0	0	36

RUSHING	No.	Yds	Avg	Lg	TD
Starks	133	578	4.3	40	1
Grant	134	559	4.2	47	2
Rodgers	60	257	4.3	25	3

PASSING	Att	Comp	Pct Comp	Yds	Avg Gain	TD	Int	Rating Pts
Rodgers	502	343	68.3	4643	9.2	45	6	122.5
Flynn	49	33	67.3	518	10.6	6	2	124.8

RECEIVING	No.	Yds	Avg	TD	Lg
Nelson	68	1263	18.6	15	93
Jennings	67	949	14.2	9	79
Finley	55	767	13.9	8	41
Jones	38	635	16.7	7	70
Driver	37	445	12.0	6	35
Cobb	25	375	15.0	1	61
Grant	19	268	14.1	1	80

INTERCEPTIONS: Woodson, 7

PUNTING	No.	Yds	Avg	Net Avg	Blk	In 20	TB	Lg
Masthay	55	2506	45.6	38.6	0	23	4	71

SACKS: Matthews, 6.0

Detroit Lions

SCORING	Rush	Rec	Ret	FG	PAT	2PT	Pts
Hanson	0	0	0	24	54	0	126
Johnson	0	16	0	0	0	0	96
Smith	4	3	0	0	0	0	42
Scheffler	0	6	0	0	0	1	38
Young	0	6	0	0	0	1	38
Pettigrew	0	5	0	0	0	0	30

RUSHING	No.	Yds	Avg	Lg	TD
Best	84	390	4.6	88	2
Smith	72	356	4.9	43	4
Morris	80	316	4.0	31	1

PASSING	Att	Comp	Pct Comp	Yds	Avg Gain	TD	Int	Rating Pts
Stafford	663	421	63.5	5038	7.6	41	16	97.2

RECEIVING	No.	Yds	Avg	TD	Lg
Johnson	96	1681	17.5	16	73
Pettigrew	83	777	9.4	5	27
Burleson	73	757	10.4	3	47
Young	48	607	12.6	6	57
Scheffler	26	347	13.3	6	36
Best	27	287	10.6	1	60

INTERCEPTIONS: Houston, 5

PUNTING	No.	Yds	Avg	Net Avg	Blk	In 20	TB	Lg
Donahue	49	2093	42.7	35.6	0	13	4	60
Graham	28	1235	44.1	38.7	0	10	3	58

SACKS: Avril, 11.0

Minnesota Vikings

SCORING	Rush	Rec	Ret	FG	PAT	2PT	Pts
Longwell	0	0	0	22	38	0	104
Peterson	12	1	0	0	0	0	78
Harvin	2	6	1	0	0	0	54
Gerhart	1	3	0	0	0	0	24
Shiancoe	0	3	0	0	0	0	18
Jenkins	0	3	0	0	0	0	18
Rudolph	0	3	0	0	0	0	18

RUSHING	No.	Yds	Avg	Lg	TD
Peterson	208	970	4.7	54	12
Gerhart	109	531	4.9	67	1
Harvin	52	345	6.6	39	2

PASSING	Att	Comp	Pct Comp	Yds	Avg Gain	TD	Int	Rating Pts
Ponder	291	158	54.3	1853	6.4	13	13	70.1
McNabb	156	94	60.3	1026	6.6	4	2	82.9
Webb	63	34	54.0	376	6.0	3	2	74.6

RECEIVING	No.	Yds	Avg	TD	Lg
Harvin	87	967	11.1	6	52
Aromashodu	26	468	18.0	1	60
Jenkins	38	466	12.3	3	72
Shiancoe	36	409	11.4	3	37
Rudolph	26	249	9.6	3	41

INTERCEPTIONS: Sanford, 2

PUNTING	No.	Yds	Avg	Net Avg	Blk	In 20	TB	Lg
Kluwe	77	3517	45.7	38.0	0	22	3	60

SACKS: Allen, 22.0

New Orleans Saints

SCORING	Rush	Rec	Ret	FG	PAT	2PT	Pts
Kasay	0	0	0	28	63	0	147
Graham	0	11	0	0	0	0	66
Sproles	2	7	1	0	0	0	60
Moore	0	8	0	0	0	2	52
Colston	0	8	0	0	0	0	48
Meachem	0	6	0	0	0	0	36
Thomas	5	1	0	0	0	0	36
Ingram	5	0	0	0	0	0	30
Collins	2	2	0	0	0	0	24

RUSHING	No.	Yds	Avg	Lg	TD
Sproles	87	603	6.9	36	2
Thomas	110	562	5.1	33	5
Ingram	122	474	3.9	35	5
Ivory	79	374	4.7	35	1

PASSING	Att	Comp	Pct Comp	Yds	Avg Gain	TD	Int	Rating Pts
Brees	657	468	71.2	5476	8.3	46	14	110.6

RECEIVING	No.	Yds	Avg	TD	Lg
Graham	99	1310	13.2	11	59
Colston	80	1143	14.3	8	50
Sproles	86	710	8.3	7	39
Moore	52	627	12.1	8	47
Meachem	40	620	15.5	6	67
Henderson	32	503	15.7	2	79
Thomas	50	425	8.5	1	57

INTERCEPTIONS: Robinson, 4

PUNTING	No.	Yds	Avg	Net Avg	Blk	In 20	TB	Lg
Morstead	46	2224	48.3	44.0	1	13	4	64

SACKS: Harper, 7.5

Philadelphia Eagles

SCORING	Rush	Rec	Ret	FG	PAT	2PT	Pts
McCoy	17	3	0	0	0	0	120
Henery	0	0	0	24	46	0	118
Celek	0	5	0	0	0	0	30
Maclin	0	5	0	0	0	0	30
Jackson	0	4	0	0	0	0	24

RUSHING	No.	Yds	Avg	Lg	TD
McCoy	273	1309	4.8	60	17
Vick	76	589	7.8	53	1

PASSING	Att	Comp	Pct Comp	Yds	Avg Gain	TD	Int	Rating Pts
Vick	423	253	59.8	3303	7.8	18	14	84.9
Young	114	66	57.9	866	7.6	4	9	60.8

RECEIVING	No.	Yds	Avg	TD	Lg
Jackson	58	961	16.6	4	62
Maclin	63	859	13.6	5	59
Celek	62	811	13.1	5	73
Avant	52	679	13.1	1	35
McCoy	48	315	6.6	3	26
Cooper	16	315	19.7	1	58

INTERCEPTIONS: Coleman, 4

PUNTING	No.	Yds	Avg	Net Avg	Blk	In 20	TB	Lg
Henry	66	2830	42.9	37.5	1	19	9	60

SACKS: Babin, 18.0

New York Giants

SCORING	Rush	Rec	Ret	FG	PAT	2PT	Pts
Tynes	0	0	0	19	43	0	100
Bradshaw	9	2	0	0	0	1	68
Cruz	0	9	0	0	0	0	54
Jacobs	7	1	0	0	0	1	50
Nicks	0	7	0	0	0	0	42
Manningham	0	4	0	0	0	0	24
Ballard	0	4	0	0	0	0	24

RUSHING	No.	Yds	Avg	Lg	TD
Bradshaw	171	659	3.9	37	9
Jacobs	152	571	3.8	28	7

PASSING	Att	Comp	Pct Comp	Yds	Avg Gain	TD	Int	Rating Pts
Manning	589	359	61.0	4933	8.4	29	16	92.9

RECEIVING	No.	Yds	Avg	TD	Lg
Cruz	82	1536	18.7	9	99
Nicks	76	1192	15.7	7	68
Ballard	38	604	15.9	4	41
Manningham	39	523	13.4	4	47
Bradshaw	34	267	7.9	2	26

INTERCEPTIONS: Webster, 6

PUNTING	No.	Yds	Avg	Net Avg	Blk	In 20	TB	Lg
Weatherford	82	3745	45.7	39.2	0	25	6	62

SACKS: Pierre-Paul, 16.5

St. Louis Rams

SCORING	Rush	Rec	Ret	FG	PAT	2PT	Pts
Brown	0	0	0	21	18	0	81
Jackson	5	1	0	0	0	0	36
Lloyd	0	5	0	0	0	0	30
Alexander	0	2	0	0	0	0	12

RUSHING	No.	Yds	Avg	Lg	TD
Jackson	260	1145	4.4	47	5
Williams	87	361	4.1	23	1

PASSING	Att	Comp	Pct Comp	Yds	Avg Gain	TD	Int	Rating Pts
Bradford	357	191	53.5	2164	6.1	6	6	70.5
Feeley	97	53	54.6	548	5.6	1	2	66.0
Clemens	91	48	52.7	546	6.0	2	1	73.8

RECEIVING	No.	Yds	Avg	TD	Lg
Lloyd	51	683	13.4	5	37
Gibson	36	431	12.0	1	34
Alexander	26	431	16.6	2	68
Kendricks	28	352	12.6	0	45
Jackson	42	333	7.9	1	50
Salas	27	264	9.8	0	21
Pettis	27	256	9.5	0	35

INTERCEPTIONS: Gordy, 3

PUNTING	No.	Yds	Avg	Net Avg	Blk	In 20	TB	Lg
Jones	105	4652	44.3	37.3	1	29	9	65

SACKS: Long, 13.0

San Francisco 49ers

SCORING	Rush	TD Rec	Ret	FG	PAT	2PT	Pts
Akers	0	0	0	44	34	0	166
Gore	8	0	0	0	0	0	48
Davis	0	6	0	0	0	0	36
Crabtree	0	4	0	0	0	1	26
Walker	0	3	0	0	0	0	18
Williams	0	3	0	0	0	0	18

RUSHING	No.	Yds	Avg	Lg	TD
Gore	282	1211	4.3	55	8
Hunter	112	473	4.2	44	2

PASSING	Att	Comp	Pct Comp	Yds	Avg Gain	TD	Int	Rating Pts
Smith	445	273	61.3	3144	7.1	17	5	90.7

RECEIVING	No.	Yds	Avg	TD	Lg
Crabtree	72	874	12.1	4	52
Davis	67	792	11.8	6	44
Williams	20	241	12.1	3	56
Ginn	19	220	11.6	0	26
Morgan	15	220	14.7	1	30
Walker	19	198	10.4	3	29

INTERCEPTIONS: Goldson, Rogers, 6

PUNTING	No.	Yds	Avg	Net Avg	Blk	In 20	TB	Lg
Lee	78	3970	50.9	44.6	1	28	9	68

SACKS: Smith, 14.0

Tampa Bay Buccaneers

SCORING	Rush	TD Rec	Ret	FG	PAT	2PT	Pts
Barth	0	0	0	26	23	0	101
Briscoe	0	6	0	0	0	0	36
Blount	5	0	0	0	0	0	30
Freeman	4	0	0	0	0	0	24
Benn	0	3	0	0	0	0	18
Williams	0	3	0	0	0	0	18
Parker	0	3	0	0	0	0	18
Winslow	0	2	0	0	0	2	16

RUSHING	No.	Yds	Avg	Lg	TD
Blount	184	781	4.2	54	5
Freeman	55	238	4.3	25	4
Graham	37	206	5.6	34	0

PASSING	Att	Comp	Pct Comp	Yds	Avg Gain	TD	Int	Rating Pts
Freeman	551	346	62.8	3592	6.5	16	22	74.6
Johnson	36	19	52.8	246	6.8	1	2	60.6

RECEIVING	No.	Yds	Avg	TD	Lg
Williams	65	771	11.9	3	42
Winslow	75	763	10.2	2	37
Parker	40	554	13.9	3	51
Benn	30	441	14.7	3	65
Briscoe	35	387	11.1	6	46
Lumpkin	41	291	7.1	0	16

INTERCEPTIONS: Barber, 3

PUNTING	No.	Yds	Avg	Net Avg	Blk	In 20	TB	Lg
Koenen	67	3023	45.1	40.3	0	24	3	65

SACKS: Clayborn, 7.5

Seattle Seahawks

SCORING	Rush	TD Rec	Ret	FG	PAT	2PT	Pts
Hauschka	0	0	0	25	34	0	109
Lynch	12	1	0	0	0	0	78
Baldwin	0	4	0	0	0	0	24
Tate	0	3	0	0	0	0	18
Browner	0	0	2	0	0	0	12
Robinson	0	1	1	0	0	0	12
Obomanu	0	2	0	0	0	0	12
Rice	0	2	0	0	0	0	12

RUSHING	No.	Yds	Avg	Lg	TD
Lynch	285	1204	4.2	47	12
Washington	53	248	4.7	48	1

PASSING	Att	Comp	Pct Comp	Yds	Avg Gain	TD	Int	Rating Pts
Jackson	450	271	60.2	3091	6.9	14	13	79.2
Whitehurst	56	27	48.2	298	5.3	1	1	62.9

RECEIVING	No.	Yds	Avg	TD	Lg
Baldwin	51	788	15.5	4	55
Rice	32	484	15.1	2	52
Obomanu	37	436	11.8	2	55
Tate	35	382	10.9	3	33
Williams	18	236	13.1	1	55
Miller	25	233	9.3	0	28
Lynch	28	212	7.6	1	26

INTERCEPTIONS: Browner, 6

PUNTING	No.	Yds	Avg	Net Avg	Blk	In 20	TB	Lg
Ryan	95	4431	46.6	39.3	0	34	8	77

SACKS: Clemons, 11.0

Washington Redskins

SCORING	Rush	TD Rec	Ret	FG	PAT	2PT	Pts
Gano	0	0	0	31	25	0	118
Gaffney	0	5	0	0	0	0	30
Moss	0	4	0	0	0	0	24
Davis	0	3	0	0	0	0	18
Helu	2	1	0	0	0	0	18

RUSHING	No.	Yds	Avg	Lg	TD
Helu	151	640	4.2	28	2
Royster	56	328	5.9	28	0
Hightower	84	321	3.8	22	1

PASSING	Att	Comp	Pct Comp	Yds	Avg Gain	TD	Int	Rating Pts
Grossman	458	265	57.9	3151	6.9	16	20	72.4
Beck	132	80	60.6	858	6.5	2	4	72.1

RECEIVING	No.	Yds	Avg	TD	Lg
Gaffney	68	947	13.9	5	45
Davis	59	796	13.5	3	42
Moss	46	584	12.7	4	49
Helu	49	379	7.7	1	47
Stallworth	22	309	14.0	2	51

INTERCEPTIONS: Hall, Atogwe, 3

PUNTING	No.	Yds	Avg	Net Avg	Blk	In 20	TB	Lg
Rocca	66	2842	43.1	39.0	0	28	1	63

SACKS: Orakpo, 9.0

First two rounds of the 76th annual NFL Draft, held April 26, 2012 in New York City.

First Round

Team	Selection	Position
1. ....Indianapolis	Andrew Luck, Stanford	QB
2. ....Washington	Robert Griffin III, Baylor	QB
3. ....Cleveland	Trent Richardson, Alabama	RB
4. ....Minnesota	Matt Kalil, USC	OT
5. ....Jacksonville Jaguars	Justin Blackmon, Oklahoma State	WR
6. ....Dallas Cowboys	Morris Claiborne, LSU	CB
7. ....Tampa Bay Buccaneers	Mark Barron, Alabama	DB
8. ....Miami Dolphins	Ryan Tannehill, Texas A&M	QB
9. ....Carolina Panthers	Luke Kuechly, Boston College	LB
10. ....Buffalo Bills	Stephon Gilmore, South Carolina	CB
11. ....Kansas City Chiefs	Dontari Poe, Memphis	NT
12. ....Philadelphia Eagles	Fletcher Cox, Mississippi State	DT
13. ....Arizona Cardinals	Michael Floyd, Notre Dame	WR
14. ....St. Louis Rams	Michael Brockers, LSU	DT
15. ....Seattle Seahawks	Bruce Irvin, West Virginia	DE
16. ....New York Jets	Quinton Coples, North Carolina	DE
17. ....Cincinnati Bengals	Dre Kirkpatrick, Alabama	CB
18. ....San Diego Chargers	Melvin Ingram, South Carolina	LB
19. ....Chicago Bears	Shea McClellin, Boise State	DE
20. ....Tennessee Titans	Kendall Wright, Baylor	WR
21. ....New England Patriots	Chandler Jones, Syracuse	DE
22. ....Cleveland Browns	Brandon Weeden, Oklahoma State	QB
23. ....Detroit Lions	Riley Reiff, Iowa	T
24. ....Pittsburgh Steelers	David DeCastro, Stanford	G
25. ....New England Patriots	Dont'a Hightower, Alabama	LB
26. ....Houston Texans	Whitney Mercilus, Illinois	LB
27. ....Cincinnati Bengals	Kevin Zeitler, Wisconsin	G
28. ....Green Bay Packers	Nick Perry, USC	LB
29. ....Minnesota Vikings	Harrison Smith, Notre Dame	DB
30. ....San Francisco 49ers	A.J. Jenkins, Illinois	WR
31. ....Tampa Bay Buccaneers	Doug Martin, Boise State	RB
32. ....New York Giants	David Wilson, Virginia Tech	RB

Second Round

Team	Selection	Position
33. ....St. Louis Rams	Brian Quick, Appalachian State	WR
34. ....Indianapolis Colts	Coby Fleener, Stanford	TE
35. ....Baltimore Ravens	Courtney Upshaw, Alabama	LB
36. ....Denver Broncos	Derek Wolfe, Cincinnati	DT
37. ....Cleveland Browns	Mitchell Schwartz, California	T
38. ....Jacksonville Jaguars	Andre Branch, Clemson	DE
39. ....St. Louis Rams	Janoris Jenkins, North Alabama	CB
40. ....Carolina Panthers	Amini Silatolu, Midwestern State	G
41. ....Buffalo Bills	Cordy Glenn, Georgia	T
42. ....Miami Dolphins	Jonathan Martin, Stanford	T
43. ....New York Jets	Stephen Hill, Georgia Tech	WR
44. ....Kansas City Chiefs	Jeff Allen, Illinois	T
45. ....Chicago Bears	Alshon Jeffery, South Carolina	WR
46. ....Philadelphia Eagles	Mychal Kendricks, California	LB
47. ....Seattle Seahawks	Bobby Wagner, Utah State	LB
48. ....New England Patriots	Tavon Wilson, Illinois	FS
49. ....San Diego Chargers	Kendall Reyes, Connecticut	DE
50. ....St. Louis Rams	Isaiah Pead, Cincinnati	RB
51. ....Green Bay Packers	Jerel Worthy, Michigan State	DE
52. ....Tennessee Titans	Zach Brown, North Carolina	LB
53. ....Cincinnati Bengals	Devon Still, Penn State	DT
54. ....Detroit Lions	Ryan Broyles, Oklahoma	WR
55. ....Atlanta Falcons	Peter Konz, Wisconsin	G
56. ....Pittsburgh Steelers	Mike Adams, Ohio State	T
57. ....Denver Broncos	Brock Osweiler, Arizona State	QB
58. ....Tampa Bay Buccaneers	Lavonte David, Nebraska	LB
59. ....Philadelphia Eagles	Vinny Curry, Marshall	DE
60. ....Baltimore Ravens	Kelechi Osemele, Iowa State	T
61. ....San Francisco 49ers	LaMichael James, Oregon	RB
62. ....Green Bay Packers	Casey Hayward, Vanderbilt	CB
63. ....New York Giants	Rueben Randle, LSU	WR

Regular Season Results

WEST DIVISION	W	L	T	Pts	PF	PA
†British Columbia	11	7	0	22	511	385
*Edmonton	11	7	0	22	427	401
*Calgary	11	7	0	22	511	476
Saskatchewan	5	13	0	10	346	482

EAST DIVISION	W	L	T	Pts	PF	PA
†Winnipeg	10	8	0	20	432	432
*Montreal	10	8	0	20	515	468
*Hamilton	8	10	0	16	481	478
Toronto	6	12	0	12	397	498

†Clinched division title.

*Clinched playoff berth.

Playoff Results

DIVISION SEMI-FINALS

Nov. 13, 2011

Hamilton 52, MONTREAL 44
EDMONTON 33, Calgary 19

DIVISION FINALS

Nov. 20, 2011

WINNIPEG 19, Hamilton 3
BRITISH COLUMBIA 40, Edmonton 23
Home team in caps.

2011 Grey Cup Championship

Nov. 27, 2011, Vancouver, British Columbia

Winnipeg	0	6	3	14—23
British Columbia	11	3	10	10—34

FIRST QUARTER: BC: TD Harris 19 run (McCallum convert), 6:54.

BC: FG McCallum 22, 3:42.

BC: Single McCallum 57 punt, 0:48.

SECOND QUARTER: BC: FG McCallum 16, 4:44.

Winnipeg: FG Palardy 33, 2:41.

Winnipeg: FG Palardy 15, 0:33.

THIRD QUARTER: Winnipeg: FG Palardy 33, 10:25.

BC: FG McCallum 22, 2:59.

BC: TD Johnson 66 pass from Lulay (McCallum convert), 0:30.

FOURTH QUARTER: BC: TD Bruce 6 pass from Lulay (McCallum convert), 7:13.

Winnipeg: TD Carr 45 pass from Pierce (Palardy convert), 3:51.

Winnipeg: TD Edwards 13 pass from Pierce (Palardy convert), 1:52

BC: FG McCallum 34, 1:20.

A: 54,313.

Season-by-Season NFL Final Standings

1920*

	W	L	T	Pct	Pts	OP
Akron Pros	8	0	3	1.000	151	7
Decatur Staleys	10	1	2	.909	164	21
Buffalo All-Americans	9	1	1	.900	258	32
Chicago Cardinals	6	2	1	.750	101	29
Rock Island Independents	6	2	2	.750	201	49
Dayton Triangles	5	2	2	.714	150	54
Rochester Jeffersons	6	3	2	.667	156	57
Canton Bulldogs	7	4	2	.636	208	57
Detroit Heralds	2	3	3	.400	53	82
Cleveland Tigers	2	4	2	.333	28	46
Chicago Tigers	2	5	1	.286	49	63
Hammond Pros	2	5	0	.286	41	154
Columbus Panhandles	2	6	2	.250	41	121
Muncie Flyers	0	1	0	.000	0	45

*no official standings kept

1921

	W	L	T	Pct	Pts	OP
Buffalo All-Americans	9	1	2	.900	211	29
Chicago Staleys	9	1	1	.900	128	53
Akron Pros	8	3	1	.727	148	31
Canton Bulldogs	5	2	3	.714	106	55
Rock Island Independents	4	2	1	.667	65	30
Evansville Crimson Giants	3	2	0	.600	89	46
Green Bay Packers	3	2	1	.600	70	55
Chicago Cardinals	3	3	2	.500	54	53
Dayton Triangles	4	4	1	.500	96	54
Rochester Jeffersons	2	3	0	.400	85	76
Cleveland Tigers	3	5	0	.375	95	58
Washington Senators	1	2	0	.333	21	43
Cincinnati Celts	1	3	0	.250	14	117
Hammond Pros	1	3	1	.250	17	45
Minneapolis Marines	1	3	0	.250	37	41
Detroit Tigers	1	5	1	.167	19	109
Columbus Panhandles	1	8	0	.111	47	222
Muncie Flyers	0	2	0	.000	0	28
Louisville Brecks	0	2	0	.000	0	27
New York Giants	0	2	0	.000	0	72
Tonawanda Kardex	0	1	0	.000	0	45

1922

	W	L	T	Pct	Pts	OP
Canton Bulldogs	10	0	2	1.000	184	15
Chicago Bears	9	3	0	.750	123	44
Chicago Cardinals	8	3	0	.727	96	50
Toledo Maroons	5	2	2	.714	94	59
Rock Island Independents	4	2	1	.667	154	27
Racine Legion	6	4	1	.600	122	56
Dayton Triangles	4	3	1	.571	80	62
Green Bay Packers	4	3	3	.571	70	54
Buffalo All-Americans	5	4	1	.556	87	41
Akron Pros	3	5	2	.375	146	95
Milwaukee Badgers	2	4	3	.333	51	71
Oorang Indians	3	6	0	.333	69	190
Minneapolis Marines	1	3	0	.250	19	40
Louisville Brecks	1	3	0	.250	13	140
Evansville Crimson Giants	0	3	0	.000	6	88
Rochester Jeffersons	0	4	1	.000	13	76
Hammond Pros	0	5	1	.000	0	69
Columbus Panhandles	0	8	0	.000	24	174

1923

	W	L	T	Pct	Pts	OP
Canton Bulldogs	11	0	1	1.000	246	19
Chicago Bears	9	2	1	.818	123	35
Green Bay Packers	7	2	1	.778	85	34
Milwaukee Badgers	7	2	3	.778	100	49
Cleveland Indians	3	1	3	.750	52	49
Chicago Cardinals	8	4	0	.667	139	37
Duluth Kelleys	4	3	0	.571	35	33
Buffalo All-Americans	5	4	3	.556	94	43
Columbus Tigers	5	4	1	.556	119	35
Racine Legion	4	4	2	.500	86	76
Toledo Maroons	3	3	2	.500	35	66
Rock Island Independents	2	3	2	.400	83	62
Minneapolis Marines	2	5	1	.286	48	80
St. Louis All-Stars	1	4	2	.200	14	32
Hammond Pros	1	5	1	.167	14	59
Dayton Triangles	1	6	1	.143	16	95
Akron Pros	1	6	0	.143	25	74
Oorang Indians	1	10	0	.091	24	235
Louisville Brecks	0	3	0	.000	0	90
Rochester Jeffersons	0	4	0	.000	6	141

1924

	W	L	T	Pct	Pts	OP
Cleveland Bulldogs	7	1	1	.875	229	60
Chicago Bears	6	1	4	.857	136	55
Frankfort Yellow Jackets	11	2	1	.846	326	109
Duluth Kelleys	5	1	0	.833	56	16
Rock Island Independents	5	2	2	.714	81	15
Green Bay Packers	7	4	0	.636	108	38
Racine Legion	4	3	3	.571	69	47
Chicago Cardinals	5	4	1	.556	90	67
Buffalo Bisons	6	5	0	.545	120	140
Columbus Tigers	4	4	0	.500	91	68
Hammond Pros	2	2	1	.500	18	45
Milwaukee Badgers	5	8	0	.385	142	188
Akron Pros	2	6	0	.250	59	132
Dayton Triangles	2	6	0	.250	45	148
Kansas City Blues	2	7	0	.222	46	124
Kenosha Maroons	0	4	1	.000	12	117
Minneapolis Marines	0	6	0	.000	14	108
Rochester Jeffersons	0	7	0	.000	14	179

1925

	W	L	T	Pct	Pts	OP
Chicago Cardinals	11	2	1	.846	230	65
Pottsville Maroons	10	2	0	.833	280	45
Detroit Panthers	8	2	2	.800	118	42
New York Giants	8	4	0	.667	122	67
Akron Pros	4	2	2	.650	65	51
Frankfort Yellow Jackets	13	7	0	.643	196	189
Chicago Bears	9	5	3	.625	158	96
Rock Island Independents	5	3	3	.615	99	58
Green Bay Packers	8	5	0	.545	151	120
Providence Steam Roller	6	5	1	.500	131	108
Canton Bulldogs	4	4	0	.385	50	73
Cleveland Bulldogs	5	8	1	.286	75	134
Kansas City Cowboys	2	5	1	.200	68	106
Hammond Pros	1	4	0	.143	23	87

1925 *(Cont.)*

	W	L	T	Pct	Pts	OP
Buffalo Bisons	1	6	2	.143	33	113
Duluth Kelleys	0	3	0	.000	6	25
Rochester Jeffersons	0	6	1	.000	26	91
Milwaukee Badgers	0	6	0	.000	7	191
Dayton Triangles	0	7	1	.000	3	84
Columbus Tigers	0	9	0	.000	28	124

1926

	W	L	T	Pct	Pts	OP
Frankfort Yellow Jackets	14	1	2	.765	223	43
Chicago Bears	12	1	3	.844	216	63
Pottsville Maroons	10	2	2	.714	155	29
Kansas City Cowboys	8	3	0	.727	76	54
Green Bay Packers	7	3	3	.462	144	68
Los Angeles Buccaneers	6	3	1	.600	67	57
NY Giants	8	4	1	.583	140	45
Duluth Eskimos	6	5	3	.429	114	81
Buffalo Rangers	4	4	2	.400	53	62
Chicago Cardinals	5	6	1	.417	67	86
Providence Steam Roller	5	7	1	.417	94	96
Detroit Panthers	4	6	2	.500	115	52
Hartford Blues	3	7	0	.300	57	99
Brooklyn Lions	3	8	0	.273	60	150
Milwaukee Badgers	2	7	0	.222	41	66
Akron Indians	1	4	3	.125	23	89
Dayton Triangles	1	4	1	.167	15	82
Racine Tornadoes	1	4	0	.200	8	92
Columbus Tigers	1	6	0	.143	26	93
Canton Bulldogs	1	9	3	.077	46	172
Hammond Pros	0	4	0	.000	3	56
Louisville Colonels	0	4	0	.000	0	108

1927

	W	L	T	Pct	Pts	OP
NY Giants	11	1	1	.917	197	20
Green Bay Packers	7	2	1	.778	113	43
Chicago Bears	9	3	2	.750	149	98
Cleveland Bulldogs	8	4	1	.667	209	107
Providence Steam Roller	8	5	1	.615	105	88
New York Yankees	7	8	1	.467	142	174
Frankfort Yellow Jackets	6	9	3	.400	152	166
Pottsville Maroons	5	8	0	.385	80	163
Chicago Cardinals	3	7	1	.300	69	134
Dayton Triangles	1	6	1	.143	15	57
Duluth Eskimos	1	8	0	.111	68	134
Buffalo Bisons	0	5	0	.000	8	123

1928

	W	L	T	Pct	Pts	OP
Providence Steam Roller	8	1	1	.889	128	36
Frankfort Yellow Jackets	11	3	1	.786	169	84
Detroit Wolverines	7	2	1	.778	189	76
Green Bay Packers	6	4	3	.600	120	92
Chicago Bears	7	5	1	.583	182	85
NY Giants	4	7	2	.364	79	137
NY Yankees	4	8	1	.333	104	179
Pottsville Maroons	2	8	0	.200	74	134
Chicago Cardinals	1	5	0	.167	7	107
Dayton Triangles	0	7	0	.000	9	131

1929

	W	L	T	Pct	Pts	OP
Green Bay Packers	12	0	1	1.000	198	22
NY Giants	13	1	1	.929	312	86
Frankfort Yellow Jackets	10	4	5	.714	139	128
Chicago Cardinals	6	6	1	.500	154	83
Boston Bulldogs	4	4	0	.500	98	73
Staten Island Stapletons	3	6	3	.429	89	62
Providence Steam Roller	4	5	2	.400	107	117
Orange Tornadoes	3	6	4	.375	32	90
Chicago Bears	4	9	2	.308	119	227
Buffalo Bisons	1	7	1	.125	48	142
Minneapolis Red Jackets	1	9	0	.100	48	185
Dayton Triangles	0	6	0	.000	7	136

1930

	W	L	T	Pct	Pts	OP
Green Bay Packers	10	3	1	.769	234	111
NY Giants	13	4	0	.765	308	98
Chicago Bears	9	4	1	.692	169	71
Brooklyn Dodgers	7	4	1	.636	154	59
Providence Steam Roller	6	4	1	.600	90	125
Staten Island Stapletons	5	5	2	.500	95	112
Chicago Cardinals	5	6	2	.455	128	132
Portsmouth Spartans	5	6	3	.455	176	161
Frankfort Yellow Jackets	4	13	1	.222	113	321
Minneapolis Red Jackets	1	7	1	.125	27	165
Newark Tornadoes	1	10	1	.091	51	190

1931

	W	L	T	Pct	Pts	OP
Green Bay Packers	12	2	0	.857	318	94
Portsmouth Spartans	11	3	0	.786	161	77
Chicago Bears	8	5	0	.615	145	92
Chicago Cardinals	5	4	0	.556	120	128
NY Giants	7	6	1	.538	161	127
Providence Steam Roller	4	4	3	.500	78	127
Staten Island Stapletons	4	6	1	.400	79	118
Cleveland Indians	2	8	0	.200	45	137
Brooklyn Dodgers	2	12	0	.143	64	199
Frankfort Yellow Jackets	1	6	1	.143	13	85

1932

	W	L	T	Pct	Pts	OP
Chicago Bears	7	1	6	.875	160	44
Green Bay Packers	10	3	1	.769	152	63
Portsmouth Spartans	6	2	4	.750	116	71
Boston Braves	4	4	2	.500	55	79
NY Giants	4	6	2	.400	93	113
Brooklyn Dodgers	3	9	0	.250	63	131
Chiago Cardinals	2	6	2	.250	72	114
Staten Island Stapletons	2	7	3	.222	77	173

1933

EAST	W	L	T	Pct	Pts	OP
NY Giants	11	3	0	.786	244	101
Brooklyn Dodgers	5	4	1	.556	93	54
Boston Redskins	5	5	2	.500	103	97
Philadelphia Eagles	3	5	1	.375	77	158
Pittsburgh Pirates	3	6	2	.333	67	208

1933 *(Cont.)*

WEST	W	L	T	Pct	Pts	OP
Chicago Bears	10	2	1	.833	133	82
Portsmouth Spartans	6	5	0	.545	128	87
Green Bay Packers	5	7	1	.417	170	107
Cincinnati Reds	3	6	1	.333	38	110
Chicago Cardinals	1	9	1	.100	52	101

1934

EAST	W	L	T	Pct	Pts	OP
NY Giants	8	5	0	.615	147	107
Boston Redskins	6	6	0	.500	107	93
Brooklyn Dodgers	4	7	0	.364	60	153
Philadelphia Eagles	4	7	0	.364	127	85
Pittsburgh Pirates	2	10	0	.167	51	206

WEST	W	L	T	Pct	Pts	OP
Chicago Bears	13	0	0	1.000	286	86
Detroit Lions	10	3	0	.769	238	59
Green Bay Packers	7	6	0	.538	156	112
Chicago Cardinals	5	6	0	.455	80	84
St. Louis Gunners	1	2	0	.333	27	61
Cincinnati Reds	0	8	0	.000	10	243

1935

EAST	W	L	T	Pct	Pts	OP
NY Giants	9	3	0	.750	180	96
Brooklyn Dodgers	5	6	1	.455	90	141
Pittsburgh Pirates	4	8	0	.333	99	209
Boston Redskins	2	8	1	.200	65	122
Philadelphia Eagles	2	9	0	.182	60	179

WEST	W	L	T	Pct	Pts	OP
Detroit Lions	7	3	2	.700	191	111
Green Bay Packers	8	4	0	.667	181	96
Chicago Bears	6	4	2	.600	192	106
Chicago Cardinals	6	4	2	.600	99	97

1936

EAST	W	L	T	Pct	Pts	OP
Boston Redskins	7	5	0	.583	149	110
Pittsburgh Pirates	6	6	0	.500	98	187
NY Giants	5	6	1	.455	115	163
Brooklyn Dodgers	3	8	1	.273	92	161
Philadelphia Eagles	1	11	0	.083	51	206

WEST	W	L	T	Pct	Pts	OP
Green Bay	10	1	1	.909	248	118
Chicago Bears	9	3	0	.750	222	94
Detroit Lions	8	4	0	.667	235	102
Chicago Cardinals	3	8	1	.273	74	143

1937

EAST	W	L	T	Pct	Pts	OP
Washington Redskins	8	3	0	.727	195	120
NY Giants	6	3	2	.667	128	109
Pittsburgh Pirates	4	7	0	.364	122	145
Brooklyn Dodgers	3	7	1	.300	82	174
Philadelphia Eagles	2	8	1	.200	86	177

1937 *(Cont.)*

WEST	W	L	T	Pct	Pts	OP
Chicago Bears	9	1	1	.900	201	100
Green Bay Packers	7	4	0	.636	220	122
Detroit Lions	7	4	0	.636	180	105
Chicago Cardinals	5	5	1	.500	135	165
Cleveland Rams	1	10	0	.091	75	207

1938

EAST	W	L	T	Pct	Pts	OP
NY Giants	8	2	1	.800	194	79
Washington Redskins	6	3	2	.667	148	154
Brooklyn Dodgers	4	4	3	.500	131	161
Philadelphia Eagles	5	6	0	.455	154	164
Pittsburgh Pirates	2	9	0	.182	79	169

WEST	W	L	T	Pct	Pts	OP
Green Bay Packers	8	3	0	.727	223	118
Detroit Lions	7	4	0	.636	119	108
Chicago Bears	6	5	0	.545	194	148
Cleveland Rams	4	7	0	.364	131	215
Chicago Cardinals	2	9	0	.182	111	168

1939

EAST	W	L	T	Pct	Pts	OP
NY Giants	9	1	1	.168	168	85
Washington Redskins	8	2	1	.242	242	94
Brooklyn Dodgers	4	6	1	.108	108	219
Philadelphia Eagles	1	9	1	.105	105	200
Pittsburgh Pirates	1	9	1	.114	114	216

WEST	W	L	T	Pct	Pts	OP
Green Bay Packers	9	2	0	.818	233	153
Chicago Bears	8	3	0	.727	298	157
Detroit Lions	6	5	0	.545	145	150
Cleveland Rams	5	5	1	.195	195	164
Chicago Cardinals	1	10	0	.091	84	254

1940

EAST	W	L	T	Pct	Pts	OP
Washington Redskins	9	2	0	.818	245	142
Brooklyn Dodgers	8	2	0	.800	179	110
NY Giants	6	4	1	.545	131	133
Pittsburgh Pirates	2	7	2	.182	67	174
Philadelphia Eagles	1	10	0	.091	121	200

WEST	W	L	T	Pct	Pts	OP
Chicago Bears	8	3	0	.727	238	152
Green Bay Packers	6	4	1	.600	238	155
Detroit Lions	5	5	1	.500	120	177
Cleveland Rams	4	6	1	.400	181	191
Chicago Cardinals	2	7	2	.222	139	222

1941

EAST	W	L	T	Pct	Pts	OP
NY Giants	8	3	0	.727	238	114
Brooklyn Dodgers	7	4	0	.636	158	127
Washington	6	5	0	.545	176	174
Philadelphia	2	8	1	.200	119	218
Pittsburgh Steelers	1	9	1	.100	103	276

1941 *(Cont.)*

WEST	W	L	T	Pct	Pts	OP
Green Bay	10	1	0	.909	258	120
Chicago Bears	10	1	0	.909	396	147
Detroit	4	6	1	.400	121	195
Chicago Cardinals	3	7	1	.300	127	197
Cleveland Rams	2	9	0	.182	116	244

1942

EAST	W	L	T	Pct	Pts	OP
Washington	10	1	0	.909	227	102
Pittsburgh Steelers	7	4	0	.636	167	119
NY Giants	5	5	1	.500	155	139
Brooklyn Dodgers	3	8	0	.273	100	168
Philadelphia	2	9	0	.182	134	239

WEST	W	L	T	Pct	Pts	OP
Chicago Bears	11	0	0	1.000	376	84
Green Bay	8	2	1	.800	300	215
Cleveland Rams	5	6	0	.455	150	207
Chicago Cardinals	3	8	0	.273	98	209
Detroit	0	11	0	.000	38	263

1943

EAST	W	L	T	Pct	Pts	OP
Washington	6	3	1	.667	229	137
NY Giants	6	3	1	.667	197	170
Phi/Pitt Eagles/Steelers	5	4	1	.556	225	230
Brooklyn Dodgers	2	8	0	.200	65	234

WEST	W	L	T	Pct	Pts	OP
Chicago Bears	8	1	1	.889	303	157
Green Bay	7	2	1	.778	264	172
Detroit	3	6	1	.333	178	218
Chicago Cardinals	0	10	0	.000	95	238

1944

EAST	W	L	T	Pct	Pts	OP
NY Giants	8	1	1	.889	206	75
Philadelphia	7	1	2	.875	267	131
Washington	6	3	1	.667	169	180
Boston Yanks	2	8	0	.200	82	233
Brooklyn Tigers	0	10	0	.000	69	166

WEST	W	L	T	Pct	Pts	OP
Green Bay	8	2	0	.800	238	141
Chicago Bears	6	3	1	.667	258	172
Detroit	6	3	1	.667	216	151
Cleveland Rams	4	6	0	.400	188	224
Chi/Pitt Cards/Steelers	0	10	0	.000	116	336

1945

EAST	W	L	T	Pct	Pts	OP
Washington	8	2	0	.800	209	121
Philadelphia	7	3	0	.700	272	133
NY Giants	3	6	1	.333	179	198
Bos/Bkn Yanks/Tigers	3	6	1	.333	123	211
Pittsburgh	2	8	0	.200	79	220

WEST	W	L	T	Pct	Pts	OP
Cleveland Rams	9	1	0	.900	244	136
Detroit	7	3	0	.700	195	194
Green Bay	6	4	0	.600	258	173
Chicago Bears	3	7	0	.300	192	235
Chicago Cardinals	1	9	0	.100	98	228

1946

EAST	W	L	T	Pct	Pts	OP
NY Giants	7	3	1	.700	236	162
Philadelphia	6	5	0	.545	231	220
Washington	5	5	1	.500	171	191
Pittsburgh	5	5	1	.500	136	117
Boston Yanks	2	8	1	.200	189	273

WEST	W	L	T	Pct	Pts	OP
Chicago Bears	8	2	1	.800	289	193
LA Rams	6	4	1	.600	277	257
Chicago Cardinals	6	5	0	.545	260	198
Green Bay	6	5	0	.545	148	158
Detroit	1	10	0	.091	142	310

1947

EAST	W	L	T	Pct	Pts	OP
Pittsburgh	8	4	0	.667	240	259
Philadelphia	8	4	0	.667	308	242
Boston Yanks	4	7	1	.364	168	256
Washington	4	8	0	.333	295	367
NY Giants	2	8	2	.200	190	309

WEST	W	L	T	Pct	Pts	OP
Chicago Cardinals	9	3	0	.750	306	231
Chicago Bears	8	4	0	.667	363	241
Green Bay	6	5	1	.542	274	210
LA Rams	6	6	0	.500	259	214
Detroit Lions	3	9	0	.250	231	305

1948

EAST	W	L	T	Pct	Pts	OP
Philadelphia	9	2	1	.818	376	156
Washington	7	5	0	.583	291	287
Pittsburgh	4	8	0	.333	200	243
NY Giants	4	8	0	.333	297	388
Boston Yanks	3	9	0	.250	174	372

WEST	W	L	T	Pct	Pts	OP
Chicago Cardinals	11	1	0	.917	395	226
Chicago Bears	10	2	0	.833	375	151
LA Rams	6	5	1	.545	327	269
Green Bay	3	9	0	.250	154	290
Detroit Lions	2	10	0	.167	200	407

1949

EAST	W	L	T	Pct	Pts	OP
Philadelphia	11	1	0	.917	364	134
Pittsburgh	6	5	1	.545	224	214
NY Giants	6	6	0	.500	287	298
Washington	4	7	1	.364	268	339
NY Bulldogs	1	10	1	.091	153	368

WEST	W	L	T	Pct	Pts	OP
LA Rams	8	2	2	.800	360	239
Chicago Bears	9	3	0	.750	332	218
Chicago Cardinals	6	5	1	.545	360	301
Detroit Lions	4	8	0	.333	237	259
Green Bay	2	10	0	.167	114	329

1950

EAST

	W	L	T	Pct	Pts	OP
Cleveland Browns	10	2	0	.833	310	144
NY Giants	10	2	0	.833	268	150
Philadelphia	6	6	0	.500	254	141
Pittsburgh	6	6	0	.500	180	195
Chicago Cardinals	5	7	0	.417	233	287
Washington	3	9	0	.250	232	326

WEST

	W	L	T	Pct	Pts	OP
Chicago Bears	9	3	0	.750	279	207
LA Rams	9	3	0	.750	466	309
New York Yanks	7	5	0	.583	366	367
Detroit	6	6	0	.500	321	285
San Francisco 49ers	3	9	0	.250	213	300
Green Bay	3	9	0	.250	244	406
Baltimore Colts	1	11	0	.067	213	462

1951

AMERICAN

	W	L	T	Pct	Pts	OP
Cleveland	11	1	0	.917	331	152
NY Giants	9	2	1	.818	254	161
Washington	5	7	0	.417	183	296
Pittsburgh	4	7	1	.364	183	235
Philadelphia	4	8	0	.333	234	264
Chicago Cardinals	3	9	0	.250	210	287

NATIONAL

	W	L	T	Pct	Pts	OP
LA Rams	8	4	0	.667	392	261
Detroit Lions	7	4	1	.636	336	259
San Francisco 49ers	7	4	1	.636	255	205
Chicago Bears	7	5	0	.583	286	282
Green Bay	3	9	0	.250	254	375
NY Yanks	1	9	2	.100	241	382

1952

AMERICAN

	W	L	T	Pct	Pts	OP
Cleveland	8	4	0	.667	310	213
Philadelphia	7	5	0	.583	252	271
NY Giants	7	5	0	.583	234	231
Pittsburgh	5	7	0	.417	300	273
Washington	4	8	0	.333	240	287
Chicago Cardinals	4	8	0	.333	172	221

NATIONAL

	W	L	T	Pct	Pts	OP
Detroit	9	3	0	.750	344	192
LA Rams	9	3	0	.750	349	234
San Francisco	7	5	0	.583	285	221
Green Bay	6	6	0	.500	295	312
Chicago Bears	5	7	0	.417	245	326
Dallas Texans	1	11	0	.083	182	427

1953

EAST

	W	L	T	Pct	Pts	OP
Cleveland	11	1	0	.917	348	162
Philadelphia	7	4	1	.636	352	215
Washington	6	5	1	.545	208	215
Pittsburgh	5	7	0	.417	211	272
NY Giants	4	8	0	.333	188	277
Chicago Cardinals	1	10	1	.091	190	337

1953 *(Cont.)*

WEST

	W	L	T	Pct	Pts	OP
Detroit	10	2	0	.833	271	205
San Francisco	9	3	0	.750	372	237
LA Rams	8	3	1	.727	366	236
Chicago Bears	3	8	1	.273	218	262
Baltimore Colts	3	9	0	.250	182	350
Green Bay	2	9	1	.182	200	338

1954

EAST

	W	L	T	Pct	Pts	OP
Cleveland	9	3	0	.750	336	162
Philadelphia	7	4	1	.636	284	230
NY Giants	7	5	0	.583	293	184
Pittsburgh	5	7	0	.417	219	263
Washington	3	9	0	.250	207	432
Chicago Cardinals	2	10	0	.167	183	347

WEST

	W	L	T	Pct	Pts	OP
Detroit	9	2	1	.818	337	189
Chicago Bears	8	4	0	.667	301	279
San Francisco	7	4	1	.636	313	251
LA Rams	6	5	1	.545	314	285
Green Bay	4	8	0	.333	234	251
Baltimore	3	9	0	.250	131	279

1955

EAST

	W	L	T	Pct	Pts	OP
Cleveland	9	2	1	.818	349	218
Washington	8	4	0	.667	246	222
NY Giants	6	5	1	.545	267	223
Philadelphia	4	7	1	.364	248	231
Chicago Cardinals	4	7	1	.364	224	252
Pittsburgh	4	8	0	.333	195	285

WEST

	W	L	T	Pct	Pts	OP
LA Rams	8	3	1	.727	260	231
Chicago Bears	8	4	0	.667	294	251
Green Bay	6	6	0	.500	258	276
Baltimore	5	6	1	.455	214	239
San Francisco	4	8	0	.333	216	298
Detroit	3	9	0	.250	230	275

1956

EAST

	W	L	T	Pct	Pts	OP
NY Giants	8	3	1	.727	264	197
Chicago Cardinals	7	5	0	.583	240	182
Washington	6	6	0	.500	183	225
Pittsburgh	5	7	0	.417	217	250
Cleveland	5	7	0	.417	167	177
Philadelphia	3	8	1	.273	143	215

WEST

	W	L	T	Pct	Pts	OP
Chicago Bears	9	2	1	.818	269	169
Detroit	9	3	0	.750	300	188
San Francisco	5	6	1	.455	233	284
Baltimore	5	7	0	.417	270	322
Green Bay	4	8	0	.333	264	342
LA Rams	4	8	0	.333	291	307

1957

EAST

	W	L	T	Pct	Pts	OP
Cleveland	9	2	1	.818	269	169
NY Giants	7	5	0	.583	251	211
Pittsburgh	6	6	0	.500	155	178
Washington	5	6	1	.455	251	230
Philadelphia	4	8	0	.333	173	224
Chicago Cardinals	3	9	0	.250	200	299

WEST

	W	L	T	Pct	Pts	OP
San Francisco	8	4	0	.667	260	264
Detroit	8	4	0	.667	251	231
Baltimore	7	5	0	.583	303	235
LA Rams	6	6	0	.500	307	278
Chicago Bears	5	7	0	.417	203	211
Green Bay	3	9	0	.250	218	311

1958

EAST

	W	L	T	Pct	Pts	OP
Cleveland	9	3	0	.750	302	217
NY Giants	9	3	0	.750	246	183
Pittsburgh	7	4	1	.636	261	230
Washington	4	7	1	.364	214	268
Chicago Cardinals	2	9	1	.182	261	356
Philadelphia	2	9	1	.182	235	306

WEST

	W	L	T	Pct	Pts	OP
Baltimore	9	3	0	.750	381	203
LA Rams	8	4	0	.667	344	278
Chicago Bears	8	4	0	.667	298	230
San Francisco	6	6	0	.500	257	324
Detroit	4	7	1	.364	261	276
Green Bay	1	10	1	.091	193	382

1959

EAST

	W	L	T	Pct	Pts	OP
NY Giants	10	2	0	.833	284	167
Philadelphia	7	5	0	.583	268	278
Cleveland	7	5	0	.583	270	214
Pittsburgh	6	5	1	.545	257	216
Washington	3	9	0	.250	185	350
Chicago Cardinals	2	10	0	.167	231	324

WEST

	W	L	T	Pct	Pts	OP
Baltimore	9	3	0	.750	374	251
Chicago Bears	8	4	0	.667	246	196
Green Bay	7	5	0	.583	248	240
San Francisco	7	5	0	.583	255	237
Detroit	3	8	1	.273	203	275
LA Rams	2	10	0	.167	242	315

1960

NFL EAST

	W	L	T	Pct	Pts	OP
Philadelphia	10	2	0	.833	321	246
Cleveland	8	3	1	.727	362	217
NY Giants	6	4	2	.600	271	261
St. Louis Cardinals	6	5	1	.545	288	230
Pittsburgh	5	6	1	.455	240	275
Washington	1	9	2	.100	178	309

1960 *(Cont.)*

NFL WEST

	W	L	T	Pct	Pts	OP
Green Bay	8	4	0	.667	332	209
Detroit	7	5	0	.583	239	212
San Francisco	7	5	0	.583	208	205
Baltimore	6	6	0	.500	288	234
Chicago Bears	5	6	1	.455	194	299
LA Rams	4	7	1	.364	265	297
Dallas Cowboys	0	11	1	.000	177	369

AFL EAST

	W	L	T	Pct	Pts	OP
Houston Oilers	10	4	0	.714	379	285
NY Titans	7	7	0	.500	382	399
Buffalo Bills	5	8	1	.385	296	303
Boston Patriots	5	9	0	.357	286	349

AFL WEST

	W	L	T	Pct	Pts	OP
Los Angeles Chargers	10	4	0	.714	373	336
Dallas Texans	8	6	0	.571	361	253
Oakland Raiders	6	8	0	.429	319	388
Denver Broncos	4	9	1	.308	309	393

1961

NFL EAST

	W	L	T	Pct	Pts	OP
NY Giants	10	3	1	.769	368	220
Philadelphia	10	4	0	.714	361	297
Cleveland	8	5	1	.615	319	270
St. Louis Cardinals	7	7	0	.500	279	267
Pittsburgh	6	8	0	.429	295	287
Dallas Cowboys	4	9	1	.308	236	380
Washington	1	12	1	.077	174	392

NFL WEST

	W	L	T	Pct	Pts	OP
Green Bay	11	3	0	.786	391	223
Detroit	8	5	1	.615	270	258
Baltimore	8	6	0	.571	302	307
Chicago	8	6	0	.571	326	302
San Francisco	7	6	1	.538	346	272
LA Rams	4	10	0	.286	263	407
Minnesota Vikings	3	11	0	.214	285	407

AFL EAST

	W	L	T	Pct	Pts	OP
Houston Oilers	10	3	1	.769	513	242
Boston Patriots	9	4	1	.692	413	313
New York Titans	7	7	0	.500	301	390
Buffalo Bills	6	8	0	.429	294	342

AFL WEST

	W	L	T	Pct	Pts	OP
San Diego Chargers	12	2	0	.857	396	219
Dallas Texans	6	8	0	.429	334	343
Denver	3	11	0	.214	251	432
Oakland	2	12	0	.143	237	458

1962

NFL EAST

	W	L	T	Pct	Pts	OP
NY Giants	12	2	0	.857	398	283
Pittsburgh	9	5	0	.642	312	363
Cleveland	7	6	1	.538	291	257
Washington	5	7	2	.417	305	376
Dallas Cowboys	5	8	1	.385	398	402
St. Louis Cardinals	4	9	1	.308	287	361
Philadelphia	3	10	1	.231	282	356

1962 (*Cont.*)

NFL WEST	W	L	T	Pct	Pts	OP
Green Bay	13	1	0	.929	415	148
Detroit	11	3	0	.786	315	177
Chicago	9	5	0	.643	321	287
Baltimore	7	7	0	.500	293	288
San Francisco	6	8	0	.429	282	331
Minnesota	2	11	1	.154	254	410
LA Rams	1	12	1	.077	220	334

AFL EAST	W	L	T	Pct	Pts	OP
Houston	11	3	0	.786	387	270
Boston	9	4	1	.692	346	295
Buffalo	7	6	1	.538	309	272
NY Titans	5	9	0	.357	278	423

AFL WEST	W	L	T	Pct	Pts	OP
Dallas Texans	11	3	0	.786	389	233
Denver	6	7	0	.462	323	313
San Diego	4	9	0	.308	293	362
Oakland	1	13	0	.071	213	370

1963

NFL EAST	W	L	T	Pct	Pts	OP
NY Giants	11	3	0	.786	448	280
Cleveland	10	4	0	.714	343	262
St. Louis	9	5	0	.643	341	283
Pittsburgh	7	4	3	.636	321	295
Dallas Cowboys	4	10	0	.286	305	378
Washington	3	11	0	.214	279	398
Philadelphia	2	10	2	.214	242	381

NFL WEST	W	L	T	Pct	Pts	OP
Chicago	11	1	2	.917	301	144
Green Bay	11	2	1	.846	369	206
Baltimore	8	6	0	.571	316	285
Minnesota	5	8	1	.385	309	390
Detroit	5	8	1	.385	32	265
LA Rams	5	9	0	.357	210	350
San Francisco	2	12	0	.143	198	391

AFL EAST	W	L	T	Pct	Pts	OP
Boston	7	6	1	.538	327	257
Buffalo	7	6	1	.538	304	291
Houston	6	8	0	.429	302	372
NY Jets	5	8	1	.385	249	399

AFL WEST	W	L	T	Pct	Pts	OP
San Diego	11	3	0	.786	399	255
Oakland	10	4	0	.714	363	282
Kansas City Chiefs	5	7	2	.417	347	263
Denver	2	11	1	.154	301	473

1964

NFL EAST	W	L	T	Pct	Pts	OP
Cleveland	10	3	1	.769	415	293
St. Louis	9	3	2	.750	357	331
Philadelphia	6	8	0	.429	312	313
Washington	6	8	0	.429	307	305
Dallas	5	8	1	.385	250	289
Pittsburgh	5	9	0	.357	253	315
NY Giants	2	10	2	.167	241	399

1964 (*Cont.*)

NFL WEST	W	L	T	Pct	Pts	OP
Baltimore	12	2	0	.857	428	225
Green Bay	8	5	1	.615	342	245
Minnesota	8	5	1	.615	355	296
Detroit	7	5	2	.583	280	260
LA Rams	5	7	2	.417	283	339
Chicago	5	9	0	.357	260	379
San Francisco	4	10	0	.286	236	330

AFL EAST	W	L	T	Pct	Pts	OP
Buffalo	12	2	0	.857	400	242
Boston	10	3	1	.769	365	297
NY Jets	5	8	1	.385	278	315
Houston	4	10	0	.286	310	355

AFL WEST	W	L	T	Pct	Pts	OP
San Diego	8	5	1	.615	341	300
Kansas City	7	7	0	.500	366	306
Oakland	5	7	2	.417	303	350
Denver	2	11	1	.154	240	438

1965

NFL EAST	W	L	T	Pct	Pts	OP
Cleveland	11	3	0	.786	363	325
NY Giants	7	7	0	.500	270	338
Dallas	7	7	0	.500	325	280
Washington	6	8	0	.429	257	301
St. Louis	5	9	0	.357	296	309
Philadelphia	5	9	0	.357	363	359
Pittsburgh	2	12	0	.143	202	397

NFL WEST	W	L	T	Pct	Pts	OP
Green Bay	10	3	1	.769	316	224
Baltimore	9	3	1	.769	389	263
Chicago	9	5	0	.643	409	275
San Francisco	7	6	1	.538	421	402
Minnesota	7	6	0	.500	383	362
Detroit	6	7	1	.462	257	295
LA Rams	4	10	0	.286	269	328

AFL EAST	W	L	T	Pct	Pts	OP
Buffalo	10	3	1	.769	313	226
NY Jets	5	8	1	.385	285	303
Boston	4	8	2	.333	244	302
Houston	4	10	0	.286	298	429

AFL WEST	W	L	T	Pct	Pts	OP
San Diego	9	2	3	.818	340	227
Oakland	8	5	1	.615	298	239
Kansas City	7	5	2	.583	322	285
Denver	4	10	0	.286	303	392

1966

NFL EAST	W	L	T	Pct	Pts	OP
Dallas	10	3	1	.769	445	239
Cleveland	9	5	0	.643	403	259
Philadelphia	9	5	0	.643	326	340
St. Louis	8	5	1	.625	264	265
Washington	7	7	0	.500	351	355
Pittsburgh	5	8	1	.385	316	347
Atlanta Falcons	3	11	0	.214	204	437
NY Giants	1	12	1	.077	263	501

1966 *(Cont.)*

NFL WEST	W	L	T	Pct	Pts	OP
Green Bay	12	2	0	.857	335	163
Baltimore	9	5	0	.643	314	226
LA Rams	8	6	0	.571	289	212
San Francisco	6	6	2	.500	320	325
Chicago	5	7	2	.417	234	272
Detroit	4	9	1	.308	206	317
Minnesota	4	9	1	.308	292	304

AFL EAST	W	L	T	Pct	Pts	OP
Buffalo	9	4	1	.692	358	255
Boston	8	4	2	.677	315	283
NY Jets	6	6	2	.500	322	312
Houston	3	11	0	.214	335	396
Miami Dolphins	3	11	0	.214	213	362

AFL WEST	W	L	T	Pct	Pts	OP
Kansas City	11	2	1	.846	448	276
Oakland	8	5	1	.615	315	288
San Diego	7	6	1	.538	335	284
Denver	4	10	0	.286	196	381

1967

NFL CAPITOL	W	L	T	Pct	Pts	OP
Dallas	9	5	0	.643	342	268
Philadelphia	6	7	1	.462	351	409
Washington	5	6	3	.455	347	353
New Orleans Saints	3	11	0	.214	233	379

NFL CENTURY	W	L	T	Pct	Pts	OP
Cleveland	9	5	0	.643	334	297
NY Giants	7	7	0	.500	369	379
St. Louis	6	7	1	.462	333	356
Pittsburgh	4	9	1	.308	281	320

NFL COASTAL	W	L	T	Pct	Pts	OP
LA Rams	11	1	2	.917	398	196
Baltimore	11	1	2	.917	394	198
San Francisco	7	7	0	.500	273	337
Atlanta	1	12	1	.077	175	422

NFL CENTRAL	W	L	T	Pct	Pts	OP
Green Bay	9	4	1	.692	332	209
Chicago	7	6	1	.538	239	218
Detroit	5	7	2	.417	260	259
Minnesota	3	8	3	.273	233	294

AFL EAST	W	L	T	Pct	Pts	OP
Houston	9	4	1	.692	258	199
NY Jets	8	5	1	.615	371	329
Buffalo	4	10	0	.286	237	285
Miami	4	10	0	.286	219	407
Boston	3	10	1	.231	280	389

AFL WEST	W	L	T	Pct	Pts	OP
Oakland	13	1	0	.929	468	233
Kansas City	9	5	0	.643	408	254
San Diego	8	5	1	.615	360	352
Denver	3	11	0	.214	256	409

1968

NFL CAPITOL	W	L	T	Pct	Pts	OP
Dallas	12	2	0	.857	431	186
NY Giants	7	7	0	.500	294	325
Washington	5	9	0	.357	249	358
Philadelphia	2	12	0	.143	202	351

1968 *(Cont.)*

NFL CENTURY	W	L	T	Pct	Pts	OP
Cleveland	10	4	0	.714	394	273
St. Louis	9	4	1	.692	325	289
New Orleans	4	9	1	.308	246	327
Pittsburgh	2	11	1	.154	244	397

NFL COASTAL	W	L	T	Pct	Pts	OP
Baltimore	13	1	0	.929	402	144
LA Rams	10	3	1	.769	312	200
San Francisco	7	6	1	.538	303	310
Atlanta	2	12	0	.143	202	351

NFL CENTRAL	W	L	T	Pct	Pts	OP
Minnesota	8	6	0	.571	282	242
Chicago	7	7	0	.500	250	333
Green Bay	6	7	1	.462	281	227
Detroit	4	8	2	.333	207	241

AFL EAST	W	L	T	Pct	Pts	OP
NY Jets	11	3	0	.786	419	280
Houston	7	7	0	.500	303	248
Miami	5	8	1	.385	276	355
Boston	4	10	0	.286	229	406
Buffalo	1	12	1	.077	199	367

AFL WEST	W	L	T	Pct	Pts	OP
Oakland	12	2	0	.857	453	233
Kansas City	12	2	0	.857	371	170
San Diego	9	5	0	.643	382	310
Denver	5	9	0	.357	255	404
Cincinnati Bengals	3	11	0	.214	215	329

1969

NFL CAPITOL	W	L	T	Pct	Pts	OP
Dallas	11	2	1	.846	369	223
Washington	7	5	2	.583	307	319
New Orleans	5	9	0	.357	311	393
Philadelphia	4	9	1	.308	279	377

NFL CENTURY	W	L	T	Pct	Pts	OP
Cleveland	10	3	1	.769	351	300
NY Giants	6	8	0	.429	264	298
St. Louis	4	9	1	.308	314	389
Pittsburgh	1	13	0	.071	218	404

NFL COASTAL	W	L	T	Pct	Pts	OP
LA Rams	11	3	0	.786	320	243
Baltimore	7	5	2	.615	307	319
Atlanta	6	8	0	.429	276	268
San Francisco	4	8	2	.333	277	319

NFL CENTRAL	W	L	T	Pct	Pts	OP
Minnesota	12	2	0	.857	379	133
Detroit	9	4	1	.692	259	188
Green Bay	8	6	0	.571	269	221
Chicago	1	13	0	.071	210	339

AFL EAST	W	L	T	Pct	Pts	OP
NY Jets	10	4	0	.714	353	269
Houston	6	6	2	.500	278	279
Buffalo	4	10	0	.286	230	359
Boston	4	10	0	.286	266	316
Miami	3	10	1	.231	233	332

1969 (*Cont.*)

AFL WEST

	W	L	T	Pct	Pts	OP
Oakland	12	1	1	.923	377	242
Kansas City	11	3	0	.786	359	177
San Diego	8	6	0	.571	288	276
Denver	5	8	1	.385	297	344
Cincinnati	4	9	1	.308	280	367

1970

AFC EAST

	W	L	T	Pct	Pts	OP
Baltimore	11	2	1	.846	321	234
Miami	10	4	0	.714	297	228
NY Jets	4	10	0	.286	255	286
Buffalo	3	10	1	.231	204	337
Boston	2	12	0	.143	149	361

AFC CENTRAL

	W	L	T	Pct	Pts	OP
Cincinnati	8	6	0	.571	312	255
Cleveland	7	7	0	.500	286	265
Pittsburgh	5	9	0	.357	210	272
Houston	3	10	1	.231	217	352

AFC WEST

	W	L	T	Pct	Pts	OP
Oakland	8	4	2	.667	300	293
Kansas City	7	5	2	.583	272	244
San Diego	5	6	3	.455	282	278
Denver	5	8	1	.385	253	264

NFC EAST

	W	L	T	Pct	Pts	OP
Dallas	10	4	0	.714	299	221
NY Giants	9	5	0	.643	301	270
St. Louis	8	5	1	.615	325	228
Washington	6	8	0	.429	297	314
Philadelphia	3	10	1	.231	241	332

NFC CENTRAL

	W	L	T	Pct	Pts	OP
Minnesota	12	2	0	.857	335	143
Detroit	10	4	0	.714	347	202
Green Bay	6	8	0	.429	196	293
Chicago	6	8	0	.429	256	261

NFC WEST

	W	L	T	Pct	Pts	OP
San Francisco	10	3	1	.769	352	267
LA Rams	9	4	1	.692	325	202
Atlanta	4	8	2	.333	206	261
New Orleans	2	11	1	.154	172	347

1971

AFC EAST

	W	L	T	Pct	Pts	OP
Miami	10	3	1	.769	315	174
Baltimore	10	4	0	.714	313	140
New England Patriots	6	8	0	.429	238	325
NY Jets	6	8	0	.429	212	299
Buffalo	1	13	0	.071	184	394

AFC CENTRAL

	W	L	T	Pct	Pts	OP
Cleveland	9	5	0	.643	285	273
Pittsburgh	6	8	0	.429	246	292
Houston	4	9	1	.308	251	330
Cincinnati	4	10	0	.286	284	265

AFC WEST

	W	L	T	Pct	Pts	OP
Kansas City	10	3	1	.769	302	208
Oakland	8	4	2	.667	344	278
San Diego	6	8	0	.429	311	341
Denver	4	9	1	.308	203	275

1971 (*Cont.*)

NFC EAST

	W	L	T	Pct	Pts	OP
Dallas	11	3	0	.786	406	222
Washington	9	4	1	.692	276	190
Philadelphia	6	7	1	.462	221	302
St. Louis	4	9	1	.308	231	279
NY Giants	4	10	0	.286	228	362

NFC CENTRAL

	W	L	T	Pct	Pts	OP
Minnesota	11	3	0	.786	245	139
Detroit	7	6	1	.538	341	286
Chicago	6	8	0	.429	185	276
Green Bay	4	8	2	.333	274	298

NFC WEST

	W	L	T	Pct	Pts	OP
San Francisco	9	5	0	.643	300	216
LA Rams	8	5	1	.615	313	260
Atlanta	7	6	1	.538	274	277
New Orleans	4	8	2	.333	266	347

1972

AFC EAST

	W	L	T	Pct	Pts	OP
Miami	14	0	0	1.000	385	171
NY Jets	7	7	0	.500	367	324
Baltimore	5	9	0	.357	235	252
Buffalo	4	9	1	.321	257	377
New England	3	11	0	.214	192	446

AFC CENTRAL

	W	L	T	Pct	Pts	OP
Pittsburgh	11	3	0	.786	343	175
Cleveland	10	4	0	.714	268	249
Cincinnati	8	6	0	.571	299	229
Houston	1	13	0	.071	164	380

AFC WEST

	W	L	T	Pct	Pts	OP
Oakland	10	3	1	.750	365	248
Kansas City	8	6	0	.571	287	254
Denver	5	9	0	.357	325	350
San Diego	4	9	1	.321	264	344

NFC EAST

	W	L	T	Pct	Pts	OP
Washington	11	3	0	.786	336	218
Dallas	10	4	0	.286	319	240
NY Giants	8	6	0	.571	331	247
St. Louis	4	9	1	.321	193	303
Philadelphia	2	11	1	.179	145	352

NFC CENTRAL

	W	L	T	Pct	Pts	OP
Green Bay	10	4	0	.714	304	226
Detroit	8	5	1	.607	339	290
Minnesota	7	7	0	.500	301	252
Chicago	4	9	1	.321	225	275

NFC WEST

	W	L	T	Pct	Pts	OP
San Francisco	8	5	1	.607	353	249
Atlanta	7	7	0	.500	269	274
LA Rams	6	7	1	.464	291	286
New Orleans	2	11	1	.179	215	361

1973

AFC EAST

	W	L	T	Pct	Pts	OP
Miami	12	2	0	.857	343	150
Buffalo	9	5	0	.643	259	230
New England	5	9	0	.357	258	300
Baltimore	4	10	0	.286	226	341
NY Jets	4	10	0	.286	240	306

1973 *(Cont.)*

AFC CENTRAL	W	L	T	Pct	Pts	OP
Pittsburgh	10	4	0	.714	347	210
Cincinnati	10	4	0	.714	286	231
Cleveland	7	5	2	.571	234	255
Houston	1	13	0	.071	199	447

AFC WEST	W	L	T	Pct	Pts	OP
Oakland	9	4	1	.679	292	175
Kansas City	7	5	2	.571	231	192
Denver	7	5	2	.571	354	296
San Diego	2	11	1	.179	188	386

NFC EAST	W	L	T	Pct	Pts	OP
Washington	10	4	0	.714	325	198
Dallas	10	4	0	.714	325	198
Philadelphia	5	8	1	.393	310	393
St. Louis	4	9	1	.321	286	365
NY Giants	2	11	1	.179	226	362

NFC CENTRAL	W	L	T	Pct	Pts	OP
Minnesota	12	2	0	.857	296	168
Detroit	6	7	1	.464	271	247
Green Bay	5	7	2	.429	202	259
Chicago	3	11	0	.214	195	334

NFC WEST	W	L	T	Pct	Pts	OP
LA Rams	12	2	0	.857	388	178
Atlanta	9	5	0	.643	318	224
New Orleans	5	9	0	.357	163	312
San Francisco	5	9	0	.357	262	319

1974

AFC EAST	W	L	T	Pct	Pts	OP
Miami	11	3	0	.786	327	216
Buffalo	9	5	0	.643	264	244
NY Jets	7	7	0	.500	279	300
New England	7	7	0	.500	348	289
Baltimore	2	12	0	.143	190	329

AFC CENTRAL	W	L	T	Pct	Pts	OP
Pittsburgh	10	3	1	.750	305	189
Houston	7	7	0	.500	236	282
Cincinnati	7	7	0	.500	283	259
Cleveland	4	10	0	.283	251	344

AFC WEST	W	L	T	Pct	Pts	OP
Oakland	12	2	0	.857	355	228
Denver	7	6	1	.536	302	294
Kansas City	5	9	0	.357	233	293
San Diego	5	9	0	.357	212	285

NFC EAST	W	L	T	Pct	Pts	OP
Washington	10	4	0	.714	320	196
St. Louis	10	4	0	.714	285	218
Dallas	8	6	0	.571	297	235
Philadelphia	7	7	0	.500	242	217
NY Giants	2	12	0	.143	195	299

NFC CENTRAL	W	L	T	Pct	Pts	OP
Minnesota	10	4	0	.714	310	195
Detroit	7	7	0	.500	256	270
Green Bay	6	8	0	.429	210	206
Chicago	4	10	0	.286	152	279

1974 *(Cont.)*

NFC WEST	W	L	T	Pct	Pts	OP
LA Rams	10	4	0	.714	263	181
San Francisco	6	8	0	.429	226	236
New Orleans	5	9	0	.357	166	263
Atlanta	3	11	0	.214	111	271

1975

AFC EAST	W	L	T	Pct	Pts	OP
Miami	10	4	0	.714	357	222
Baltimore	10	4	0	.714	395	269
Buffalo	8	6	0	.571	420	355
NY Jets	3	11	0	.214	258	433
New England	3	11	0	.214	258	358

AFC CENTRAL	W	L	T	Pct	Pts	OP
Pittsburgh	12	2	0	.857	373	162
Cincinnati	11	3	0	.786	340	246
Houston	10	4	0	.714	293	226
Cleveland	3	11	0	.214	218	372

AFC WEST	W	L	T	Pct	Pts	OP
Oakland	11	3	0	.786	375	255
Denver	6	8	0	.429	254	307
Kansas City	5	9	0	.357	282	341
San Diego	2	12	0	.143	189	345

NFC EAST	W	L	T	Pct	Pts	OP
St. Louis	11	3	0	.786	356	276
Dallas	10	4	0	.714	350	268
Washington	8	6	0	.571	325	276
NY Giants	5	9	0	.357	216	306
Philadelphia	4	10	0	.286	225	302

NFC CENTRAL	W	L	T	Pct	Pts	OP
Minnesota	12	2	0	.857	377	180
Detroit	7	7	0	.500	245	262
Green Bay	4	10	0	.286	226	285
Chicago	4	10	0	.286	191	379

NFC WEST	W	L	T	Pct	Pts	OP
LA Rams	12	2	0	.857	312	135
San Francisco	5	9	0	.357	255	286
Atlanta	4	10	0	.286	240	289
New Orleans	2	12	0	.143	165	360

1976

AFC EAST	W	L	T	Pct	Pts	OP
Baltimore	11	3	0	.786	417	246
New England	11	3	0	.786	376	236
Miami	6	8	0	.429	263	264
NY Jets	3	11	0	.214	169	383
Buffalo	2	12	0	.143	246	363

AFC CENTRAL	W	L	T	Pct	Pts	OP
Cincinnati	10	4	0	.714	335	210
Pittsburgh	10	4	0	.714	342	138
Cleveland	9	5	0	.643	267	287
Houston	5	9	0	.357	222	273

AFC WEST	W	L	T	Pct	Pts	OP
Oakland	13	1	0	.929	350	237
Denver	9	5	0	.643	315	206
San Diego	6	8	0	.429	248	285
Kansas City	5	9	0	.357	290	376
Tampa Bay Buccaneers	0	14	0	.000	125	412

1976 *(Cont.)*

NFC EAST	W	L	T	Pct	Pts	OP
Dallas	11	3	0	.786	296	194
Washington	10	4	0	.714	291	217
St. Louis	10	4	0	.714	309	267
Philadelphia	4	10	0	.286	165	286
NY Giants	3	11	0	.214	170	250

NFC CENTRAL	W	L	T	Pct	Pts	OP
Minnesota	11	2	1	.821	305	176
Chicago	7	7	0	.500	253	216
Detroit	6	8	0	.429	218	299
Green Bay	5	9	0	.357	218	299

NFC WEST	W	L	T	Pct	Pts	OP
LA Rams	10	3	1	.750	351	190
San Francisco	8	6	0	.571	270	190
Atlanta	4	10	0	.286	172	312
New Orleans	4	10	0	.286	253	346
Seattle Seahawks	2	12	0	.143	229	429

1977

AFC EAST	W	L	T	Pct	Pts	OP
Miami	10	4	0	.714	313	197
Baltimore	10	4	0	.714	295	221
New England	9	5	0	.643	279	217
Buffalo	3	11	0	.214	160	313
NY Jets	3	11	0	.214	191	313

AFC CENTRAL	W	L	T	Pct	Pts	OP
Pittsburgh	9	5	0	.643	283	243
Houston	8	6	0	.571	299	230
Cincinnati	8	6	0	.571	238	235
Cleveland	6	8	0	.429	269	267

AFC WEST	W	L	T	Pct	Pts	OP
Denver	12	2	0	.857	274	148
Oakland	11	3	0	.786	351	230
San Diego	7	7	0	.500	222	205
Seattle	5	9	0	.357	282	373
Kansas City	2	12	0	.143	225	349

NFC EAST	W	L	T	Pct	Pts	OP
Dallas	12	2	0	.857	345	212
Washington	9	5	0	.643	196	189
St. Louis	7	7	0	.500	272	287
NY Giants	5	9	0	.357	181	265
Philadelphia	5	9	0	.357	220	207

NFC CENTRAL	W	L	T	Pct	Pts	OP
Chicago	9	5	0	.643	255	253
Minnesota	9	5	0	.643	231	227
Detroit	6	8	0	.429	183	252
Green Bay	4	10	0	.286	134	219
Tampa Bay	2	12	0	.143	103	223

NFC WEST	W	L	T	Pct	Pts	OP
LA Rams	10	4	0	.714	302	146
Atlanta	7	7	0	.500	179	129
San Francisco	5	9	0	.357	220	260
New Orleans	3	11	0	.214	232	336

1978

AFC EAST	W	L	T	Pct	Pts	OP
New England	11	5	0	.688	358	286
Miami	11	5	0	.688	372	254
NY Jets	8	8	0	.500	359	364
Buffalo	5	11	0	.313	302	354
Baltimore	5	11	0	.313	239	421

AFC CENTRAL	W	L	T	Pct	Pts	OP
Pittsburgh	14	2	0	.875	356	195
Houston	10	6	0	.625	283	298
Cleveland	8	8	0	.500	334	356
Cincinnati	4	12	0	.250	252	284

AFC WEST	W	L	T	Pct	Pts	OP
Denver	10	6	0	.625	282	198
Seattle	9	7	0	.563	345	358
Oakland	9	7	0	.563	311	283
San Diego	9	7	0	.563	355	309
Kansas City	4	12	0	.250	243	327

NFC EAST	W	L	T	Pct	Pts	OP
Dallas	12	4	0	.750	384	208
Philadelphia	9	7	0	.563	270	250
Washington	8	8	0	.500	273	283
St. Louis	6	10	0	.375	248	296
NY Giants	6	10	0	.375	264	298

NFC CENTRAL	W	L	T	Pct	Pts	OP
Green Bay	8	7	1	.531	249	269
Minnesota	8	7	1	.531	294	306
Detroit	7	9	0	.438	290	300
Chicago	7	9	0	.438	253	274
Tampa Bay	5	11	0	.313	241	259

NFC WEST	W	L	T	Pct	Pts	OP
LA Rams	12	4	0	.750	316	245
Atlanta	9	7	0	.563	240	290
New Orleans	7	9	0	.438	281	298
San Francisco	2	14	0	.125	219	350

1979

AFC EAST	W	L	T	Pct	Pts	OP
Miami	10	6	0	.625	341	257
New England	9	7	0	.563	411	326
NY Jets	8	8	0	.500	337	383
Buffalo	7	9	0	.438	268	279
Baltimore	5	11	0	.313	271	351

AFC CENTRAL	W	L	T	Pct	Pts	OP
Pittsburgh	12	4	0	.750	416	262
Houston	11	5	0	.688	362	331
Cleveland	9	7	0	.563	359	352
Cincinnati	4	12	0	.250	337	421

AFC WEST	W	L	T	Pct	Pts	OP
San Diego	12	4	0	.750	411	246
Denver	10	6	0	.625	289	262
Seattle	9	7	0	.563	378	372
Oakland	9	7	0	.563	365	337
Kansas City	7	9	0	.438	238	262

NFC EAST	W	L	T	Pct	Pts	OP
Dallas	11	5	0	.688	371	313
Philadelphia	11	5	0	.688	339	282
Washington	10	6	0	.625	348	295
NY Giants	6	10	0	.375	237	323
St. Louis	5	11	0	.313	307	358

1979 *(Cont.)*

NFC CENTRAL

	W	L	T	Pct	Pts	OP
Chicago	10	6	0	.625	306	249
Tampa Bay	10	6	0	.625	273	237
Minnesota	7	9	0	.438	259	337
Green Bay	5	11	0	.313	246	316
Detroit	2	14	0	.125	219	365

NFC WEST

	W	L	T	Pct	Pts	OP
LA Rams	9	7	0	.563	323	309
New Orleans	8	8	0	.500	370	360
Atlanta	6	10	0	.375	300	388
San Francisco	2	14	0	.125	308	416

1980

AFC EAST

	W	L	T	Pct	Pts	OP
Buffalo	11	5	0	.688	320	260
New England	10	6	0	.625	441	325
Miami	8	8	0	.500	266	305
Baltimore	7	9	0	.438	355	387
NY Jets	4	12	0	.250	302	395

AFC CENTRAL

	W	L	T	Pct	Pts	OP
Cleveland	11	5	0	.688	357	310
Houston	11	5	0	.688	295	251
Pittsburgh	9	7	0	.563	352	313
Cincinnati	6	10	0	.375	244	312

AFC WEST

	W	L	T	Pct	Pts	OP
San Diego	11	5	0	.688	418	327
Oakland	11	5	0	.688	364	306
Denver	8	8	0	.500	310	323
Kansas City	8	8	0	.500	319	336
Seattle	4	12	0	.250	291	408

NFC EAST

	W	L	T	Pct	Pts	OP
Dallas	12	4	0	.750	454	311
Philadelphia	12	4	0	.750	384	222
Washington	6	10	0	.375	261	293
St. Louis	5	11	0	.313	299	350
NY Giants	4	12	0	.250	249	425

NFC CENTRAL

	W	L	T	Pct	Pts	OP
Detroit	9	7	0	.563	334	272
Minnesota	9	7	0	.563	317	308
Chicago	7	9	0	.438	304	264
Tampa Bay	5	10	1	.344	271	341
Green Bay	5	10	1	.344	231	371

NFC WEST

	W	L	T	Pct	Pts	OP
Atlanta	12	4	0	.750	405	272
LA Rams	11	5	0	.688	424	289
San Francisco	6	10	0	.375	320	415
New Orleans	1	15	0	.063	291	487

1981

AFC EAST

	W	L	T	Pct	Pts	OP
Miami	11	4	1	.719	345	275
NY Jets	10	5	1	.656	355	287
Buffalo	10	6	0	.625	311	276
Baltimore	2	14	0	.125	259	533
New England	2	14	0	.125	322	370

AFC CENTRAL

	W	L	T	Pct	Pts	OP
Cincinnati	12	4	0	.750	421	304
Pittsburgh	8	8	0	.500	356	297
Houston	7	9	0	.438	281	355
Cleveland	5	11	0	.313	276	375

1981 *(Cont.)*

AFC WEST

	W	L	T	Pct	Pts	OP
Denver	10	6	0	.625	321	289
San Diego	10	6	0	.625	478	390
Kansas City	9	7	0	.563	343	290
Oakland	7	9	0	.438	273	343
Seattle	6	10	0	.375	322	388

NFC EAST

	W	L	T	Pct	Pts	OP
Dallas	12	4	0	.750	367	277
Philadelphia	10	6	0	.625	368	221
NY Giants	9	7	0	.563	295	257
Washington	8	8	0	.500	347	349
St. Louis	7	9	0	.438	315	407

NFC CENTRAL

	W	L	T	Pct	Pts	OP
Tampa Bay	9	7	0	.563	315	268
Detroit	8	8	0	.500	397	322
Green Bay	8	8	0	.500	324	361
Minnesota	7	9	0	.438	325	369
Chicago	6	10	0	.375	253	324

NFC WEST

	W	L	T	Pct	Pts	OP
San Francisco	13	3	0	.813	357	250
Atlanta	7	9	0	.438	426	355
LA Rams	6	10	0	.375	303	351
New Orleans	4	12	0	.250	207	378

1982

AFC EAST

	W	L	T	Pct	Pts	OP
Miami	7	2	0	.778	198	131
NY Jets	6	3	0	.667	245	166
New England	5	4	0	.556	143	157
Buffalo	4	5	0	.444	150	154
Baltimore	0	8	1	.056	113	236

AFC CENTRAL

	W	L	T	Pct	Pts	OP
Cincinnati	7	2	0	.778	232	177
Pittsburgh	6	3	0	.667	204	146
Cleveland	4	5	0	.444	140	182
Houston	1	8	0	.111	136	245

AFC WEST

	W	L	T	Pct	Pts	OP
LA Raiders	8	1	0	.889	260	200
San Diego	6	3	0	.667	288	221
Seattle	4	5	0	.444	127	147
Kansas City	3	6	0	.333	176	184
Denver	2	7	0	.222	148	226

NFC EAST

	W	L	T	Pct	Pts	OP
Washington	8	1	0	.889	190	128
Dallas	6	3	0	.667	226	145
St. Louis	5	4	0	.556	135	170
NY Giants	4	5	0	.444	164	160
Philadelphia	3	6	0	.333	191	195

NFC CENTRAL

	W	L	T	Pct	Pts	OP
Green Bay	5	3	1	.611	226	169
Tampa Bay	5	4	0	.556	158	178
Minnesota	5	4	0	.556	187	198
Detroit	4	5	0	.444	181	176
Chicago	3	6	0	.333	141	174

NFC WEST

	W	L	T	Pct	Pts	OP
Atlanta	5	4	0	.556	183	199
New Orleans	4	5	0	.444	129	160
San Francisco	3	6	0	.333	209	206
LA Rams	2	7	0	.222	200	250

1983

AFC EAST
	W	L	T	Pct	Pts	OP
Miami	12	4	0	.750	389	250
Buffalo	8	8	0	.500	283	351
New England	8	8	0	.500	274	289
Baltimore	7	9	0	.438	264	354
NY Jets	7	9	0	.438	313	331

AFC CENTRAL
	W	L	T	Pct	Pts	OP
Pittsburgh	10	6	0	.625	355	303
Cleveland	9	7	0	.563	356	342
Cincinnati	7	9	0	.438	346	302
Houston	2	14	0	.125	288	460

AFC WEST
	W	L	T	Pct	Pts	OP
LA Raiders	12	4	0	.750	442	338
Seattle	9	7	0	.563	403	397
Denver	9	7	0	.563	302	327
San Diego	6	10	0	.375	358	462
Kansas City	6	10	0	.375	386	367

NFC EAST
	W	L	T	Pct	Pts	OP
Washington	14	2	0	.875	541	332
Dallas	12	4	0	.750	479	360
St. Louis	8	7	1	.531	374	428
Philadelphia	5	11	0	.313	233	322
NY Giants	3	12	1	.219	267	347

NFC CENTRAL
	W	L	T	Pct	Pts	OP
Detroit	9	7	0	.563	47	286
Minnesota	8	8	0	.500	316	348
Chicago	8	8	0	.500	311	301
Green Bay	8	8	0	.500	429	439
Tampa Bay	2	14	0	.125	241	380

NFC WEST
	W	L	T	Pct	Pts	OP
San Francisco	10	6	0	.625	432	293
LA Rams	9	7	0	.563	361	344
New Orleans	8	8	0	.500	319	337
Atlanta	7	9	0	.438	370	389

1984

AFC EAST
	W	L	T	Pct	Pts	OP
Miami	14	2	0	.875	513	298
New England	9	7	0	.563	362	352
NY Jets	7	9	0	.438	332	364
Indianapolis Colts	4	12	0	.250	239	414
Buffalo	2	14	0	.125	250	454

AFC CENTRAL
	W	L	T	Pct	Pts	OP
Pittsburgh	9	7	0	.563	387	310
Cincinnati	8	8	0	.500	339	339
Cleveland	5	11	0	.313	250	297
Houston	3	13	0	.188	240	437

AFC WEST
	W	L	T	Pct	Pts	OP
Denver	13	3	0	.813	353	241
Seattle	12	4	0	.750	418	282
LA Raiders	11	5	0	.313	368	278
Kansas City	8	8	0	.500	314	324
San Diego	7	9	0	.438	394	413

NFC EAST
	W	L	T	Pct	Pts	OP
Washington	11	5	0	.688	426	310
NY Giants	9	7	0	.563	299	301
Dallas	9	7	0	.563	308	308
St. Louis	9	7	0	.563	423	345
Philadelphia	6	9	1	.406	278	320

1984 *(Cont.)*

NFC CENTRAL
	W	L	T	Pct	Pts	OP
Chicago	10	6	0	.625	325	248
Green Bay	8	8	0	.500	390	309
Tampa Bay	6	10	0	.375	335	380
Detroit	4	11	1	.281	283	408
Minnesota	3	13	0	.188	276	484

NFC WEST
	W	L	T	Pct	Pts	OP
San Francisco	15	1	0	.938	475	227
LA Rams	10	6	0	.625	346	316
New Orleans	7	9	0	.438	298	361
Atlanta	4	12	0	.250	281	382

1985

AFC EAST
	W	L	T	Pct	Pts	OP
Miami	12	4	0	.750	428	320
New England	11	5	0	.688	362	290
NY Jets	11	5	0	.688	393	264
Indianapolis	5	11	0	.313	320	386
Buffalo	2	14	0	.125	200	381

AFC CENTRAL
	W	L	T	Pct	Pts	OP
Cleveland	8	8	0	.500	287	294
Cincinnati	7	9	0	.438	441	437
Pittsburgh	7	9	0	.438	379	355
Houston	5	11	0	.313	284	412

AFC WEST
	W	L	T	Pct	Pts	OP
LA Raiders	12	4	0	.750	354	308
Denver	11	5	0	.688	380	329
Seattle	8	8	0	.500	349	303
San Diego	8	8	0	.500	467	435
Kansas City	6	10	0	.375	317	360

NFC EAST
	W	L	T	Pct	Pts	OP
Washington	10	6	0	.625	297	312
NY Giants	10	6	0	.625	399	283
Dallas	10	6	0	.625	357	333
Philadelphia	7	9	0	.438	286	310
St. Louis	5	11	0	.313	278	414

NFC CENTRAL
	W	L	T	Pct	Pts	OP
Chicago	15	1	0	.938	456	198
Green Bay	8	8	0	.500	337	355
Detroit	7	9	0	.438	307	366
Minnesota	7	9	0	.438	346	359
Tampa Bay	2	14	0	.125	294	448

NFC WEST
	W	L	T	Pct	Pts	OP
LA Rams	11	5	0	.688	340	277
San Francisco	10	6	0	.625	411	263
New Orleans	5	11	0	.313	294	401
Atlanta	4	12	0	.250	282	452

1986

AFC EAST
	W	L	T	Pct	Pts	OP
New England	11	5	0	.688	412	307
NY Jets	10	6	0	.625	364	386
Miami	8	8	0	.500	430	405
Buffalo	4	12	0	.250	287	348
Indianapolis	3	13	0	.188	299	400

AFC CENTRAL
	W	L	T	Pct	Pts	OP
Cleveland	12	4	0	.750	391	310
Cincinnati	10	6	0	.625	409	394
Pittsburgh	6	10	0	.375	307	336
Houston	5	11	0	.313	274	329

1986 *(Cont.)*

AFC WEST

	W	L	T	Pct	Pts	OP
Denver	11	5	0	.688	378	327
Kansas City	10	6	0	.625	358	326
Seattle	10	6	0	.625	366	293
LA Raiders	8	8	0	.500	323	346
San Diego	4	12	0	.250	335	396

NFC EAST

	W	L	T	Pct	Pts	OP
NY Giants	14	2	0	.875	371	236
Washington	12	4	0	.750	368	296
Dallas	7	9	0	.438	346	337
Philadelphia	5	10	1	.344	256	312
St. Louis	4	11	1	.281	518	351

NFC CENTRAL

	W	L	T	Pct	Pts	OP
Chicago	14	2	0	.875	352	187
Minnesota	9	7	0	.563	398	271
Detroit	5	11	0	.313	277	326
Green Bay	4	12	0	.250	254	418
Tampa Bay	2	14	0	.125	239	473

NFC WEST

	W	L	T	Pct	Pts	OP
San Francisco	10	5	1	.656	374	247
LA Rams	10	6	0	.625	309	267
Atlanta	7	8	1	.469	280	280
New Orleans	7	9	0	.438	288	287

1987

AFC EAST

	W	L	T	Pct	Pts	OP
Indianapolis	9	6	0	.643	300	238
Miami	8	7	0	.533	362	335
New England	8	7	0	.533	320	293
Buffalo	7	8	0	.467	320	293
NY Jets	6	9	0	.400	334	360

AFC CENTRAL

	W	L	T	Pct	Pts	OP
Cleveland	10	5	0	.700	390	239
Houston	9	6	0	.600	345	349
Pittsburgh	8	7	0	.533	285	299
Cincinnati	4	11	0	.267	285	370

AFC WEST

	W	L	T	Pct	Pts	OP
Denver	10	4	1	.667	379	288
Seattle	9	6	0	.600	371	314
San Diego	8	7	0	.563	253	317
LA Raiders	5	10	0	.333	301	289
Kansas City	4	11	0	.267	276	388

NFC EAST

	W	L	T	Pct	Pts	OP
Washington	11	4	0	.733	379	285
Dallas	7	8	0	.467	340	348
St. Louis	7	8	0	.467	362	368
Philadelphia	7	8	0	.467	337	380
NY Giants	6	9	0	.400	280	312

NFC CENTRAL

	W	L	T	Pct	Pts	OP
Chicago	11	4	0	.733	356	282
Minnesota	8	7	0	.533	336	335
Green Bay	5	9	1	.367	255	300
Tampa Bay	4	11	0	.267	286	360
Detroit	4	11	0	.267	269	384

NFC WEST

	W	L	T	Pct	Pts	OP
San Francisco	13	2	0	.867	459	253
New Orleans	12	3	0	.800	422	283
LA Rams	6	9	0	.400	317	361
Atlanta	3	12	0	.200	205	436

1988

AFC EAST

	W	L	T	Pct	Pts	OP
Buffalo	12	4	0	.750	329	237
New England	9	7	0	.563	250	284
Indianapolis	9	7	0	.563	354	315
NY Jets	8	7	1	.531	372	354
Miami	6	10	0	.375	319	380

AFC CENTRAL

	W	L	T	Pct	Pts	OP
Cincinnati	12	4	0	.750	448	329
Cleveland	10	6	0	.625	304	288
Houston	10	6	0	.625	424	365
Pittsburgh	5	1	0	.313	336	421

AFC WEST

	W	L	T	Pct	Pts	OP
Seattle	9	7	0	.563	339	329
Denver	8	8	0	.500	327	352
LA Raiders	7	9	0	.438	325	369
San Diego	6	10	0	.375	231	332
Kansas City	4	11	1	.281	254	320

NFC EAST

	W	L	T	Pct	Pts	OP
NY Giants	10	6	0	.625	359	304
Philadelphia	10	6	0	.625	379	319
Phoenix Cardinals	7	9	0	.438	344	398
Washington	7	9	0	.438	345	387
Dallas	3	13	0	.188	265	381

NFC CENTRAL

	W	L	T	Pct	Pts	OP
Chicago	12	4	0	.750	312	215
Minnesota	11	5	0	.688	406	233
Tampa Bay	5	11	0	.313	261	350
Detroit	4	12	0	.250	220	313
Green Bay	4	12	0	.250	240	315

NFC WEST

	W	L	T	Pct	Pts	OP
New Orleans	10	6	0	.625	312	283
San Francisco	10	6	0	.625	369	294
LA Rams	10	6	0	.625	407	293
Atlanta	5	11	0	.313	244	315

1989

AFC EAST

	W	L	T	Pct	Pts	OP
Buffalo	9	7	0	.563	407	317
Miami	8	8	0	.500	331	379
Indianapolis	8	8	0	.500	298	301
New England	5	11	0	.313	297	391
NY Jets	4	12	0	.250	253	411

AFC CENTRAL

	W	L	T	Pct	Pts	OP
Cleveland	9	6	1	.594	334	254
Houston	9	7	0	.563	365	412
Pittsburgh	9	7	0	.563	265	326
Cincinnati	8	8	0	.500	404	285

AFC WEST

	W	L	T	Pct	Pts	OP
Denver	11	5	0	.688	362	226
Kansas City	8	7	1	.531	318	286
LA Raiders	8	8	0	.500	315	297
Seattle	7	9	0	.438	241	327
San Diego	6	10	0	.375	266	290

NFC EAST

	W	L	T	Pct	Pts	OP
NY Giants	12	4	0	.750	348	252
Philadelphia	11	5	0	.688	342	274
Washington	10	6	0	.625	386	308
Phoenix	5	11	0	.313	258	377
Dallas	1	15	0	.063	204	393

1989 *(Cont.)*

NFC CENTRAL

	W	L	T	Pct	Pts	OP
Green Bay	10	6	0	.625	362	356
Minnesota	10	6	0	.625	351	275
Detroit	7	9	0	.438	312	364
Chicago	6	10	0	.375	358	377
Tampa Bay	5	11	0	.313	320	419

NFC WEST

	W	L	T	Pct	Pts	OP
San Francisco	14	2	0	.875	442	253
LA Rams	11	5	0	.688	426	344
New Orleans	9	7	0	.563	386	301
Atlanta	3	13	0	.188	279	437

1990

AFC EAST

	W	L	T	Pct	Pts	OP
Buffalo	13	3	0	.813	428	263
Miami	12	4	0	.750	336	242
Indianapolis	7	9	0	.438	281	353
NY Jets	6	10	0	.375	295	345
New England	1	15	0	.063	181	446

AFC CENTRAL

	W	L	T	Pct	Pts	OP
Pittsburgh	9	7	0	.563	292	240
Cincinnati	9	7	0	.563	360	352
Houston	9	7	0	.563	405	307
Cleveland	3	13	0	.188	228	462

AFC WEST

	W	L	T	Pct	Pts	OP
LA Raiders	12	4	0	.750	337	268
Kansas City	11	5	0	.688	369	257
Seattle	9	7	0	.563	306	286
San Diego	6	10	0	.375	315	281
Denver	5	11	0	.313	331	374

NFC EAST

	W	L	T	Pct	Pts	OP
NY Giants	13	3	0	.813	335	211
Washington	10	6	0	.625	381	301
Philadelphia	10	6	0	.625	396	299
Dallas	7	9	0	.438	244	308
Phoenix	5	11	0	.313	268	396

NFC CENTRAL

	W	L	T	Pct	Pts	OP
Chicago	11	5	0	.688	348	280
Green Bay	6	10	0	.375	271	347
Minnesota	6	10	0	.375	351	326
Detroit	6	10	0	.375	373	413
Tampa Bay	6	10	0	.375	264	367

NFC WEST

	W	L	T	Pct	Pts	OP
San Francisco	14	2	0	.875	353	239
New Orleans	8	8	0	.500	274	275
LA Rams	5	11	0	.313	345	412
Atlanta	5	11	0	.313	348	365

1991

AFC EAST

	W	L	T	Pct	Pts	OP
Buffalo	13	3	0	.813	458	318
Miami	8	8	0	.500	343	349
NY Jets	8	8	0	.500	314	293
New England	6	10	0	.375	211	305
Indianapolis	1	15	0	.063	143	381

AFC CENTRAL

	W	L	T	Pct	Pts	OP
Houston	11	5	0	.688	386	251
Pittsburgh	7	9	0	.438	292	344
Cleveland	6	10	0	.375	293	298
Cincinnati	3	13	0	.188	263	435

1991 *(Cont.)*

AFC WEST

	W	L	T	Pct	Pts	OP
Denver	12	4	0	.750	304	235
Kansas City	10	6	0	.625	322	252
LA Raiders	9	7	0	.563	298	297
Seattle	7	9	0	.438	276	261
San Diego	4	12	0	.250	274	342

NFC EAST

	W	L	T	Pct	Pts	OP
Washington	14	2	0	.875	485	224
Dallas	11	5	0	.688	342	310
Philadelphia	10	6	0	.625	285	244
NY Giants	8	8	0	.500	281	297
Phoenix	4	12	0	.250	196	344

NFC CENTRAL

	W	L	T	Pct	Pts	OP
Detroit	12	4	0	.750	339	295
Chicago	11	5	0	.688	299	269
Minnesota	8	8	0	.500	301	306
Green Bay	4	12	0	.250	273	313
Tampa Bay	3	13	0	.188	199	365

NFC WEST

	W	L	T	Pct	Pts	OP
New Orleans	11	5	0	.688	341	211
Atlanta	10	6	0	.625	361	338
San Francisco	10	6	0	.625	393	239
LA Rams	3	13	0	.188	234	390

1992

AFC EAST

	W	L	T	Pct	Pts	OP
Buffalo	11	5	0	.688	381	283
Miami	11	5	0	.688	340	281
Indianapolis	9	7	0	.563	216	302
NY Jets	4	12	0	.250	220	315
New England	2	14	0	.125	205	363

AFC CENTRAL

	W	L	T	Pct	Pts	OP
Pittsburgh	11	5	0	.688	299	225
Houston	10	6	0	.625	352	258
Cleveland	7	9	0	.438	272	275
Cincinnati	5	11	0	.313	274	364

AFC WEST

	W	L	T	Pct	Pts	OP
San Diego	11	5	0	.688	335	241
Kansas City	10	6	0	.625	348	282
Denver	8	8	0	.500	262	329
LA Raiders	7	9	0	.438	249	281
Seattle	2	14	0	.125	140	312

NFC EAST

	W	L	T	Pct	Pts	OP
Dallas	13	3	0	.813	409	243
Philadelphia	11	5	0	.688	354	245
Washington	9	7	0	.563	300	255
NY Giants	6	10	0	.375	306	367
Phoenix	4	12	0	.250	243	332

NFC CENTRAL

	W	L	T	Pct	Pts	OP
Minnesota	11	5	0	.688	374	249
Green Bay	9	7	0	.563	276	296
Tampa Bay	5	11	0	.313	267	365
Detroit	5	11	0	.313	273	332
Chicago	5	11	0	.313	295	361

NFC WEST

	W	L	T	Pct	Pts	OP
San Francisco	14	2	0	.875	431	236
New Orleans	12	4	0	.750	330	202
Atlanta	6	10	0	.375	327	414
LA Rams	6	10	0	.375	313	383

1993

AFC EAST

	W	L	T	Pct	Pts	OP
Buffalo	12	4	0	.750	329	242
Miami	9	7	0	.563	349	351
NY Jets	8	8	0	.500	270	247
New England	5	11	0	.313	238	286
Indianapolis	4	12	0	.250	189	378

AFC CENTRAL

	W	L	T	Pct	Pts	OP
Houston	12	4	0	.750	368	238
Pittsburgh	9	7	0	.563	308	281
Cleveland	7	9	0	.438	304	307
Cincinnati	3	13	0	.188	187	319

AFC WEST

	W	L	T	Pct	Pts	OP
Kansas City	11	5	0	.688	328	291
LA Raiders	10	6	0	.625	306	326
Denver	9	7	0	.563	373	284
San Diego	8	8	0	.500	322	290
Seattle	6	10	0	.375	280	314

NFC EAST

	W	L	T	Pct	Pts	OP
Dallas	12	4	0	.750	376	229
NY Giants	11	5	0	.688	288	205
Philadelphia	8	8	0	.500	293	315
Phoenix	7	9	0	.438	326	269
Washington	4	12	0	.250	230	345

NFC CENTRAL

	W	L	T	Pct	Pts	OP
Detroit	10	6	0	.625	298	292
Green Bay	9	7	0	.563	340	282
Minnesota	9	7	0	.563	277	290
Chicago	7	9	0	.438	234	230
Tampa Bay	5	11	0	.313	237	375

NFC WEST

	W	L	T	Pct	Pts	OP
San Francisco	10	6	0	.625	473	295
New Orleans	8	8	0	.500	317	343
Atlanta	6	10	0	.375	316	385
LA Rams	5	11	0	.313	221	367

1994

AFC EAST

	W	L	T	Pct	Pts	OP
Miami	10	6	0	.625	389	327
New England	10	6	0	.625	351	312
Indianapolis	8	8	0	.500	307	320
Buffalo	7	9	0	.438	340	356
NY Jets	6	10	0	.375	264	320

AFC CENTRAL

	W	L	T	Pct	Pts	OP
Pittsburgh	12	4	0	.750	316	234
Cleveland	11	5	0	.688	340	204
Cincinnati	3	13	0	.188	276	406
Houston	2	14	0	.125	226	352

AFC WEST

	W	L	T	Pct	Pts	OP
San Diego	11	5	0	.688	384	306
LA Raiders	9	7	0	.563	303	327
Kansas City	9	7	0	.563	319	298
Denver	7	9	0	.438	347	396
Seattle	6	10	0	.375	287	323

1994 *(Cont.)*

NFC EAST

	W	L	T	Pct	Pts	OP
Dallas	12	4	0	.750	414	248
NY Giants	9	7	0	.563	279	305
Arizona Cardinals	8	8	0	.500	235	267
Philadelphia	7	9	0	.438	308	308
Washington	3	13	0	.188	320	412

NFC CENTRAL

	W	L	T	Pct	Pts	OP
Minnesota	10	6	0	.625	356	314
Green Bay	9	7	0	.563	382	287
Detroit	9	7	0	.563	357	342
Chicago	9	7	0	.563	271	307
Tampa Bay	6	10	0	.375	251	351

NFC WEST

	W	L	T	Pct	Pts	OP
San Francisco	13	3	0	.813	505	296
New Orleans	7	9	0	.438	348	407
Atlanta	7	9	0	.438	317	385
LA Rams	4	12	0	.250	286	365

1995

AFC EAST

	W	L	T	Pct	Pts	OP
Buffalo	10	6	0	.625	350	335
Miami	9	7	0	.563	398	332
Indianapolis	9	7	0	.563	331	316
New England	6	10	0	.375	294	377
NY Jets	3	13	0	.188	233	384

AFC CENTRAL

	W	L	T	Pct	Pts	OP
Pittsburgh	11	5	0	.688	407	327
Houston	7	9	0	.438	348	324
Cincinnati	7	9	0	.438	349	374
Cleveland	5	11	0	.313	289	356
Jacksonville Jaguars	4	12	0	.250	275	404

AFC WEST

	W	L	T	Pct	Pts	OP
Kansas City	13	3	0	.813	358	241
San Diego	9	7	0	.563	321	323
Oakland Raiders	8	8	0	.500	348	332
Denver	8	8	0	.500	388	345
Seattle	8	8	0	.500	363	366

NFC EAST

	W	L	T	Pct	Pts	OP
Dallas	12	4	0	.750	435	291
Philadelphia	10	6	0	.625	318	338
Washington	6	10	0	.375	326	359
NY Giants	5	11	0	.313	290	340
Arizona	4	12	0	.250	275	422

NFC CENTRAL

	W	L	T	Pct	Pts	OP
Green Bay	11	5	0	.688	404	314
Detroit	10	6	0	.625	436	336
Chicago	9	7	0	.563	392	360
Minnesota	8	8	0	.500	412	385
Tampa Bay	7	9	0	.438	238	335

NFC WEST

	W	L	T	Pct	Pts	OP
San Francisco	11	5	0	.688	457	258
Atlanta	9	7	0	.563	362	349
St. Louis Rams	7	9	0	.438	309	418
Carolina Panthers	7	9	0	.438	289	325
New Orleans	7	9	0	.438	319	348

1996

AFC EAST

	W	L	T	Pct	Pts	OP
New England	11	5	0	.688	418	313
Buffalo	10	6	0	.625	319	266
Indianapolis	9	7	0	.563	317	334
Miami	8	8	0	.500	339	325
NY Jets	1	15	0	.063	279	454

AFC CENTRAL

	W	L	T	Pct	Pts	OP
Pittsburgh	10	6	0	.625	344	257
Jacksonville	9	7	0	.563	325	334
Houston	8	8	0	.500	345	319
Cincinnati	8	8	0	.500	372	369
Baltimore Ravens	4	12	0	.250	371	441

AFC WEST

	W	L	T	Pct	Pts	OP
Denver	13	3	0	.813	391	275
Kansas City	9	7	0	.563	297	300
San Diego	8	8	0	.500	310	376
Seattle	7	9	0	.438	317	375
Oakland	7	9	0	.438	340	293

NFC EAST

	W	L	T	Pct	Pts	OP
Dallas	10	6	0	.625	286	250
Philadelphia	10	6	0	.625	363	341
Washington	9	7	0	.563	364	312
Arizona	7	9	0	.438	300	397
NY Giants	6	10	0	.375	242	297

NFC CENTRAL

	W	L	T	Pct	Pts	OP
Green Bay	13	3	0	.813	456	210
Minnesota	9	7	0	.563	298	315
Chicago	7	9	0	.438	283	305
Tampa Bay	6	10	0	.375	221	293
Detroit	5	11	0	.313	302	368

NFC WEST

	W	L	T	Pct	Pts	OP
San Francisco	12	4	0	.750	398	257
Carolina	12	4	0	.750	367	218
St. Louis	6	10	0	.375	303	409
New Orleans	3	13	0	.188	229	339
Atlanta	3	13	0	.188	309	461

1997

AFC EAST

	W	L	T	Pct	Pts	OP
New England	10	6	0	.625	369	289
Miami	9	7	0	.563	339	327
NY Jets	9	7	0	.563	348	287
Buffalo	6	10	0	.375	255	367
Indianapolis	3	13	0	.188	313	401

AFC CENTRAL

	W	L	T	Pct	Pts	OP
Jacksonville	11	5	0	.688	394	318
Pittsburgh	11	5	0	.688	372	307
Tennessee Oilers	8	8	0	.500	333	310
Cincinnati	7	9	0	.438	355	405
Baltimore	6	9	1	.375	326	345

AFC WEST

	W	L	T	Pct	Pts	OP
Kansas City	13	3	0	.813	375	232
Denver	12	4	0	.750	472	287
Seattle	8	8	0	.500	365	362
Oakland	4	12	0	.250	324	419
San Diego	4	12	0	.250	266	425

1997 *(Cont.)*

NFC EAST

	W	L	T	Pct	Pts	OP
NY Giants	10	5	1	.656	307	265
Washington	8	7	1	.531	327	289
Philadelphia	6	9	1	.406	317	372
Dallas	6	10	0	.375	304	314
Arizona	4	12	0	.250	283	379

NFC CENTRAL

	W	L	T	Pct	Pts	OP
Green Bay	13	3	0	.813	422	282
Tampa Bay	10	6	0	.625	299	263
Detroit	9	7	0	.563	379	306
Minnesota	9	7	0	.563	354	359
Chicago	4	12	0	.250	263	421

NFC WEST

	W	L	T	Pct	Pts	OP
San Francisco	13	3	0	.813	375	265
Carolina	7	9	0	.438	265	314
Atlanta	7	9	0	.438	320	361
New Orleans	6	10	0	.375	237	327
St. Louis	5	11	0	.313	299	359

1998

AFC EAST

	W	L	T	Pct	Pts	OP
NY Jets	12	4	0	.750	416	266
Miami	10	6	0	.625	321	265
Buffalo	10	6	0	.625	400	333
New England	9	7	0	.563	337	329
Indianapolis	3	13	0	.188	310	444

AFC CENTRAL

	W	L	T	Pct	Pts	OP
Jacksonville	11	5	0	.688	392	338
Tennessee	8	8	0	.500	330	320
Pittsburgh	7	9	0	.438	263	303
Baltimore	6	10	0	.375	269	335
Cincinnati	3	13	0	.188	268	452

AFC WEST

	W	L	T	Pct	Pts	OP
Denver	14	2	0	.875	501	309
Oakland	8	8	0	.500	288	356
Seattle	8	8	0	.500	372	310
Kansas City	7	9	0	.438	327	363
San Diego	5	11	0	.313	241	342

NFC EAST

	W	L	T	Pct	Pts	OP
Dallas	10	6	0	.625	381	275
Arizona	9	7	0	.563	325	378
NY Giants	8	8	0	.500	287	309
Washington	6	10	0	.375	319	421
Philadelphia	3	13	0	.188	161	344

NFC CENTRAL

	W	L	T	Pct	Pts	OP
Minnesota	15	1	0	.938	556	296
Green Bay	11	5	0	.688	408	319
Tampa Bay	8	8	0	.500	314	295
Detroit	5	11	0	.313	306	378
Chicago	4	12	0	.250	276	368

NFC WEST

	W	L	T	Pct	Pts	OP
Atlanta	14	2	0	.875	442	289
San Francisco	12	4	0	.750	479	328
New Orleans	6	10	0	.375	305	359
Carolina	4	12	0	.250	336	413
St. Louis	4	12	0	.250	285	378

1999

AFC EAST

	W	L	T	Pct	Pts	OP
Indianapolis	13	3	0	.813	423	333
Buffalo	11	5	0	.688	320	229
Miami	9	7	0	.563	326	336
NY Jets	8	8	0	.500	309	309
New England	8	8	0	.500	299	284

AFC CENTRAL

	W	L	T	Pct	Pts	OP
Jacksonville	14	2	0	.875	396	217
Tennessee Titans	13	3	0	.813	392	324
Baltimore	8	8	0	.500	324	277
Pittsburgh	6	10	0	.375	317	320
Cincinnati	4	12	0	.250	283	460
Cleveland Browns	2	14	0	.125	217	437

AFC WEST

	W	L	T	Pct	Pts	OP
Seattle	9	7	0	.563	338	298
Kansas City	9	7	0	.563	390	322
Oakland	8	8	0	.500	390	329
San Diego	8	8	0	.500	269	316
Denver	6	10	0	.375	314	318

NFC EAST

	W	L	T	Pct	Pts	OP
Washington	10	6	0	.625	443	377
Dallas	8	8	0	.500	352	276
NY Giants	7	9	0	.438	299	358
Arizona	6	10	0	.375	245	382
Philadelphia	5	11	0	.313	272	357

NFC CENTRAL

	W	L	T	Pct	Pts	OP
Tampa Bay	11	5	0	.688	270	235
Minnesota	10	6	0	.625	399	335
Green Bay	8	8	0	.500	357	341
Detroit	8	8	0	.500	322	323
Chicago	6	10	0	.375	272	341

NFC WEST

	W	L	T	Pct	Pts	OP
St. Louis	13	3	0	.813	526	242
Carolina	8	8	0	.500	421	381
Atlanta	5	11	0	.313	285	380
San Francisco	4	12	0	.250	295	453
New Orleans	3	13	0	.188	260	434

2000

AFC EAST

	W	L	T	Pct	Pts	OP
Miami	11	5	0	.688	323	226
Indianapolis	10	6	0	.625	429	326
NY Jets	9	7	0	.563	321	321
Buffalo	8	8	0	.500	315	350
New England	5	11	0	.313	276	338

AFC CENTRAL

	W	L	T	Pct	Pts	OP
Tennessee	13	3	0	.813	346	191
Baltimore	12	4	0	.750	333	165
Pittsburgh	9	7	0	.563	321	255
Jacksonville	7	9	0	.438	367	327
Cincinnati	4	12	0	.250	185	359
Cleveland	3	13	0	.188	161	419

AFC WEST

	W	L	T	Pct	Pts	OP
Oakland	12	4	0	.750	479	299
Denver	11	5	0	.688	485	369
Kansas City	7	9	0	.438	355	354
Seattle	6	10	0	.375	320	405
San Diego	1	15	0	.063	269	440

NFC EAST

	W	L	T	Pct	Pts	OP
NY Giants	12	4	0	.750	328	246
Philadelphia	11	5	0	.688	351	245
Washington	8	8	0	.500	281	269
Dallas	5	11	0	.313	294	361
Arizona	3	13	0	.188	210	443

NFC CENTRAL

	W	L	T	Pct	Pts	OP
Minnesota	11	5	0	.688	397	371
Tampa Bay	10	6	0	.625	388	269
Green Bay	9	7	0	.563	353	323
Detroit	9	7	0	.563	307	307
Chicago	5	11	0	.313	216	355

NFC WEST

	W	L	T	Pct	Pts	OP
New Orleans	10	6	0	.625	354	306
St. Louis	10	6	0	.625	540	471
Carolina	7	9	0	.438	310	310
San Francisco	6	10	0	.375	388	422
Atlanta	4	12	0	.250	252	413

2001

AFC EAST

	W	L	T	Pct	Pts	OP
New England	11	5	0	.688	371	272
Miami	11	5	0	.688	344	290
NY Jets	10	6	0	.625	413	486
Indianapolis	6	10	0	.375	413	486
Buffalo	3	13	0	.188	265	420

AFC CENTRAL

	W	L	T	Pct	Pts	OP
Pittsburgh	13	3	0	.813	352	212
Baltimore	10	6	0	.625	303	265
Cleveland	7	9	0	.438	285	319
Tennessee	7	9	0	.438	336	388
Jacksonville	6	10	0	.375	294	286
Cincinnati	6	10	0	.375	226	309

AFC WEST

	W	L	T	Pct	Pts	OP
Oakland	10	6	0	.625	399	327
Seattle	9	7	0	.563	301	324
Denver	8	8	0	.500	340	339
Kansas City	6	10	0	.375	320	344
San Diego	5	11	0	.313	332	321

NFC EAST

	W	L	T	Pct	Pts	OP
Philadelphia	11	5	0	.688	343	208
Washington	8	8	0	.500	256	303
NY Giants	7	9	0	.438	294	321
Arizona	7	9	0	.438	295	343
Dallas	5	11	0	.313	246	338

NFC CENTRAL

	W	L	T	Pct	Pts	OP
Chicago	13	3	0	.813	338	203
Green Bay	12	4	0	.750	390	266
Tampa Bay	9	7	0	.563	324	280
Minnesota	5	11	0	.313	290	390
Detroit	2	14	0	.125	270	424

NFC WEST

	W	L	T	Pct	Pts	OP
St. Louis	14	2	0	.875	503	273
San Francisco	12	4	0	.750	409	282
Atlanta	7	9	0	.438	291	377
New Orleans	7	9	0	.438	333	409
Carolina	1	15	0	.938	253	410

2002

AFC EAST	W	L	T	Pct	Pts	OP
New England	9	7	0	.563	384	346
Miami	9	7	0	.563	378	301
NY Jets	9	7	0	.563	359	336
Buffalo	8	8	0	.500	379	397

AFC NORTH	W	L	T	Pct	Pts	OP
Pittsburgh	10	5	1	.656	390	345
Cleveland	9	7	0	.563	344	320
Baltimore	7	9	0	.438	316	354
Cincinnati	2	14	0	.125	279	456

AFC SOUTH	W	L	T	Pct	Pts	OP
Tennessee	11	5	0	.688	367	324
Indianapolis	10	6	0	.625	349	313
Jacksonville	6	10	0	.375	328	315
Houston Texans	4	12	0	.250	213	356

AFC WEST	W	L	T	Pct	Pts	OP
Oakland	11	5	0	.688	450	304
Denver	9	7	0	.563	392	344
Kansas City	8	8	0	.500	467	399
San Diego	8	8	0	.500	333	367

NFC EAST	W	L	T	Pct	Pts	OP
Philadelphia	12	4	0	.750	415	241
NY Giants	10	6	0	.625	320	279
Washington	7	9	0	.438	307	365
Dallas	5	11	0	.313	217	329

NFC NORTH	W	L	T	Pct	Pts	OP
Green Bay	12	4	0	.750	398	328
Minnesota	6	10	0	.375	390	442
Chicago	4	12	0	.250	281	379
Detroit	3	13	0	.188	306	451

NFC SOUTH	W	L	T	Pct	Pts	OP
Tampa Bay	12	4	0	.750	346	196
Atlanta	9	6	1	.594	402	314
New Orleans	9	7	0	.563	432	388
Carolina	7	9	0	.438	258	302

NFC WEST	W	L	T	Pct	Pts	OP
San Francisco	10	6	0	.625	367	351
St. Louis	7	9	0	.438	316	367
Seattle	7	9	0	.438	355	369
Arizona	5	11	0	.313	262	417

2003

AFC EAST	W	L	T	Pct	Pts	OP
New England	14	2	0	.875	348	238
Miami	10	6	0	.625	311	261
Buffalo	6	10	0	.375	243	279
NY Jets	6	10	0	.375	283	299

AFC NORTH	W	L	T	Pct	Pts	OP
Baltimore	10	6	0	.625	391	281
Cincinnati	8	8	0	.500	346	384
Pittsburgh	6	10	0	.375	300	327
Cleveland	5	11	0	.313	254	322

AFC SOUTH	W	L	T	Pct	Pts	OP
Indianapolis	12	4	0	.750	447	336
Tennessee	12	4	0	.750	435	324
Houston	5	11	0	.313	255	380
Jacksonville	5	11	0	.313	276	331

2003 (*Cont.*)

AFC WEST	W	L	T	Pct	Pts	OP
Kansas City	13	3	0	.813	484	332
Denver	10	6	0	.625	381	301
Oakland	4	12	0	.250	270	379
San Diego	4	12	0	.250	313	441

NFC EAST	W	L	T	Pct	Pts	OP
Philadelphia	12	4	0	.750	374	287
Dallas	10	6	0	.625	289	260
Washington	5	11	0	.313	287	372
NY Giants	4	12	0	.250	243	387

NFC NORTH	W	L	T	Pct	Pts	OP
Green Bay	10	6	0	.625	442	307
Minnesota	9	7	0	.563	416	353
Chicago	7	9	0	.438	283	346
Detroit	5	11	0	.313	270	379

NFC SOUTH	W	L	T	Pct	Pts	OP
Carolina	11	5	0	.688	325	304
New Orleans	8	8	0	.500	340	326
Tampa Bay	7	9	0	.438	301	264
Atlanta	5	11	0	.313	299	422

NFC WEST	W	L	T	Pct	Pts	OP
St. Louis	12	4	0	.750	447	328
Seattle	10	6	0	.625	404	327
San Francisco	7	9	0	.438	384	337
Arizona	4	12	0	.250	225	452

2004

AFC EAST	W	L	T	Pct	Pts	OP
New England	14	2	0	.875	437	260
NY Jets	10	6	0	.625	333	261
Buffalo	9	7	0	.562	395	284
Miami	4	12	0	.250	275	354

AFC NORTH	W	L	T	Pct	Pts	OP
Pittsburgh	15	1	0	.938	372	251
Baltimore	9	7	0	.562	317	268
Cincinnati	8	8	0	.500	374	372
Cleveland	4	12	0	.250	275	354

AFC SOUTH	W	L	T	Pct	Pts	OP
Indianapolis	12	4	0	.750	522	351
Jacksonville	9	7	0	.562	261	280
Houston	7	9	0	.438	309	339
Tennessee	5	11	0	.312	344	439

AFC WEST	W	L	T	Pct	Pts	OP
San Diego	12	4	0	.750	446	313
Denver	10	6	0	.625	381	304
Kansas City	7	9	0	.438	483	435
Oakland	5	11	0	.312	320	442

NFC EAST	W	L	T	Pct	Pts	OP
Philadelphia	13	3	0	.812	386	260
NY Giants	6	10	0	.375	303	347
Dallas	6	10	0	.375	293	405
Washington	6	10	0	.375	240	265

NFC NORTH	W	L	T	Pct	Pts	OP
Green Bay	10	6	0	.625	424	380
Minnesota	8	8	0	.500	405	395
Detroit	6	10	0	.375	296	350
Chicago	5	11	0	.312	231	331

2004 *(Cont.)*

NFC SOUTH

	W	L	T	Pct	Pts	OP
Atlanta	11	5	0	.688	340	337
New Orleans	8	8	0	.500	348	405
Carolina	7	9	0	.438	355	339
Tampa Bay	5	11	0	.312	301	304

NFC WEST

	W	L	T	Pct	Pts	OP
Seattle	9	7	0	.562	371	373
St. Louis	8	8	0	.500	319	392
Arizona	6	10	0	.375	284	322
San Francisco	2	14	0	.125	259	452

2005

AFC EAST

	W	L	T	Pct	Pts	OP
New England	10	6	0	.625	379	338
Miami	9	7	0	.562	318	317
Buffalo	5	11	0	.312	271	367
NY Jets	4	12	0	.250	240	355

AFC NORTH

	W	L	T	Pct	Pts	OP
Cincinnati	11	5	0	.688	421	350
Pittsburgh	11	5	0	.688	389	258
Cleveland	6	10	0	.375	232	301
Baltimore	6	10	0	.375	265	299

AFC SOUTH

	W	L	T	Pct	Pts	OP
Indianapolis	14	2	0	.875	439	247
Jacksonville	12	4	0	.750	361	269
Tennessee	4	12	0	.250	299	421
Houston	2	14	0	.125	260	431

AFC WEST

	W	L	T	Pct	Pts	OP
Denver	13	3	0	.812	395	258
Kansas City	10	6	0	.625	403	325
San Diego	9	7	0	.562	418	312
Oakland	4	12	0	.250	290	383

NFC EAST

	W	L	T	Pct	Pts	OP
NY Giants	11	5	0	.688	422	314
Washington	10	6	0	.625	359	293
Dallas	9	7	0	.562	325	308
Philadelphia	6	10	0	.375	310	388

NFC NORTH

	W	L	T	Pct	Pts	OP
Chicago	11	5	0	.688	260	202
Minnesota	9	7	0	.562	306	344
Detroit	5	11	0	.312	254	345
Green Bay	4	12	0	.250	298	344

NFC SOUTH

	W	L	T	Pct	Pts	OP
Carolina	11	5	0	.688	391	259
Tampa Bay	11	5	0	.688	300	274
Atlanta	8	8	0	.500	351	341
New Orleans	3	13	0	.188	235	398

NFC WEST

	W	L	T	Pct	Pts	OP
Seattle	13	3	0	.812	452	271
St. Louis	6	10	0	.375	363	429
Arizona	5	11	0	.312	311	387
San Francisco	4	12	0	.250	239	428

2006

AFC EAST

	W	L	T	Pct	Pts	OP
New England	12	4	0	.750	385	237
NY Jets	10	6	0	.625	316	295
Buffalo	7	9	0	.438	300	311
Miami	6	10	0	.375	260	283

AFC NORTH

	W	L	T	Pct	Pts	OP
Baltimore	13	3	0	.812	353	201
Cincinnati	8	8	0	.500	373	331
Pittsburgh	8	8	0	.500	353	315
Cleveland	4	12	0	.250	238	356

AFC SOUTH

	W	L	T	Pct	Pts	OP
Indianapolis	12	4	0	.750	427	360
Tennessee	8	8	0	.500	324	400
Jacksonville	8	8	0	.500	371	274
Houston	6	10	0	.375	267	366

AFC WEST

	W	L	T	Pct	Pts	OP
San Diego	14	2	0	.875	492	303
Kansas City	9	7	0	.562	331	315
Denver	9	7	0	.562	319	305
Oakland	2	14	0	.125	168	332

NFC EAST

	W	L	T	Pct	Pts	OP
Philadelphia	10	6	0	.625	398	328
Dallas	9	7	0	.562	425	350
NY Giants	8	8	0	.500	355	362
Washington	5	11	0	.312	307	376

NFC NORTH

	W	L	T	Pct	Pts	OP
Chicago	13	3	0	.812	427	255
Green Bay	8	8	0	.500	301	366
Minnesota	6	10	0	.375	282	327
Detroit	3	13	0	.188	305	398

NFC SOUTH

	W	L	T	Pct	Pts	OP
New Orleans	10	6	0	.625	413	322
Carolina	8	8	0	.500	270	305
Atlanta	7	9	0	.438	292	328
Tampa Bay	4	12	0	.250	211	353

NFC WEST

	W	L	T	Pct	Pts	OP
Seattle	9	7	0	.562	335	341
St. Louis	8	8	0	.500	367	381
San Francisco	7	9	0	.438	298	412
Arizona	5	11	0	.312	314	389

2007

AFC EAST

	W	L	T	Pct	Pts	OP
New England	16	0	0	1.000	589	274
Buffalo	7	9	0	.438	252	354
NY Jets	4	12	0	.250	268	355
Miami	1	15	0	.063	267	437

AFC NORTH

	W	L	T	Pct	Pts	OP
Pittsburgh	10	6	0	.625	393	269
Cleveland	10	6	0	.625	402	382
Cincinnati	7	9	0	.438	380	385
Baltimore	5	11	0	.313	275	384

AFC SOUTH

	W	L	T	Pct	Pts	OP
Indianapolis	13	3	0	.813	450	262
Jacksonville	11	5	0	.688	411	304
Tennessee	10	6	0	.625	301	297
Houston	8	8	0	.500	379	384

2007 *(Cont.)*

AFC WEST

	W	L	T	Pct	Pts	OP
San Diego	11	5	0	.688	412	284
Denver	7	9	0	.438	320	409
Kansas City	4	12	0	.250	226	335
Oakland	4	12	0	.250	286	398

NFC EAST

	W	L	T	Pct	Pts	OP
Dallas	13	3	0	.813	455	325
NY Giants	10	6	0	.625	373	351
Washington	9	7	0	.563	334	310
Philadelphia	8	8	0	.500	336	300

NFC NORTH

	W	L	T	Pct	Pts	OP
Green Bay	13	3	0	.813	435	291
Minnesota	8	8	0	.500	365	311
Detroit	7	9	0	.438	346	444
Chicago	7	9	0	.438	334	348

NFC SOUTH

	W	L	T	Pct	Pts	OP
Tampa Bay	9	7	0	.563	334	270
Carolina	7	9	0	.438	267	347
New Orleans	7	9	0	.438	379	388
Atlanta	4	12	0	.250	259	414

NFC WEST

	W	L	T	Pct	Pts	OP
Seattle	10	6	0	.625	393	291
Arizona	8	8	0	.500	404	399
San Francisco	5	11	0	.313	219	364
St. Louis	3	13	0	.188	263	438

2008

AFC EAST

	W	L	T	Pct	Pts	OP
Miami	11	5	0	.688	345	317
New England	11	5	0	.688	410	309
NY Jets	9	7	0	.563	405	356
Buffalo	7	9	0	.438	336	342

AFC NORTH

	W	L	T	Pct	Pts	OP
Pittsburgh	12	4	0	.750	347	223
*Baltimore	11	5	0	.688	385	244
Cincinnati	4	11	1	.281	204	364
Cleveland	4	12	0	.250	232	350

AFC SOUTH

	W	L	T	Pct	Pts	OP
Tennessee	13	3	0	.813	375	234
Indianapolis	12	4	0	.750	377	298
Houston	8	8	0	.500	366	394
Jacksonville	5	11	0	.313	302	367

AFC WEST

	W	L	T	Pct	Pts	OP
San Diego	8	8	0	.500	439	347
Denver	8	8	0	.500	370	448
Oakland	5	11	0	.313	263	388
Kansas City	2	14	0	.125	291	440

NFC EAST

	W	L	T	Pct	Pts	OP
NY Giants	12	4	0	.750	427	294
Philadelphia	9	6	1	.594	416	289
Dallas	9	7	0	.563	362	365
Washington	8	8	0	.500	265	296

NFC NORTH

	W	L	T	Pct	Pts	OP
Minnesota	10	6	0	.625	379	333
Chicago	9	7	0	.563	375	350
Green Bay	6	10	0	.375	419	380
Detroit	0	16	0	.000	268	517

2008 *(Cont.)*

NFC SOUTH

	W	L	T	Pct	Pts	OP
Carolina	12	4	0	.750	414	329
Atlanta	11	5	0	.688	391	325
Tampa Bay	9	7	0	.563	361	323
New Orleans	8	8	0	.500	463	393

NFC WEST

	W	L	T	Pct	Pts	OP
Arizona	9	7	0	.563	427	426
San Francisco	7	9	0	.438	339	381
Seattle	4	12	0	.250	294	392
St. Louis	2	14	0	.125	232	465

2009

AFC EAST

	W	L	T	Pct	Pts	OP
New England	10	6	0	.625	427	285
NY Jets	9	7	0	.563	348	236
Miami	7	9	0	.438	360	390
Buffalo	6	10	0	.375	258	326

AFC NORTH

	W	L	T	Pct	Pts	OP
Cincinnati	10	6	0	.625	305	291
Baltimore	9	7	0	.563	391	261
Pittsburgh	9	7	0	.563	368	324
Cleveland	5	11	0	.313	245	375

AFC SOUTH

	W	L	T	Pct	Pts	OP
Indianapolis	14	2	0	.875	416	307
Houston	9	7	0	.563	388	333
Tennessee	8	8	0	.500	354	402
Jacksonville	7	9	0	.438	290	380

AFC WEST

	W	L	T	Pct	Pts	OP
San Diego	13	3	0	.813	454	320
Denver	8	8	0	.500	326	324
Oakland	5	11	0	.313	379	379
Kansas City	4	12	0	.250	424	424

NFC EAST

	W	L	T	Pct	Pts	OP
Dallas	11	5	0	.688	361	250
Philadelphia	11	5	0	.688	429	337
NY Giants	8	8	0	.500	402	427
Washington	4	12	0	.250	266	336

NFC NORTH

	W	L	T	Pct	Pts	OP
Minnesota	12	4	0	.750	470	312
Green Bay	11	5	0	.688	461	297
Chicago	7	9	0	.438	327	375
Detroit	2	14	0	.125	262	494

NFC SOUTH

	W	L	T	Pct	Pts	OP
New Orleans	13	3	0	.813	510	341
Atlanta	9	7	0	.563	363	325
Carolina	8	8	0	.500	315	308
Tampa Bay	3	13	0	.188	244	400

NFC WEST

	W	L	T	Pct	Pts	OP
Arizona	10	6	0	.625	375	325
San Francisco	8	8	0	.500	330	281
Seattle	5	11	0	.313	280	390
St. Louis	1	15	0	.063	175	436

2010

AFC EAST
	W	L	T	Pct	Pts	OP
New England	14	2	0	.875	518	313
NY Jets	11	5	0	.688	367	304
Miami	7	9	0	.438	273	333
Buffalo	4	12	0	.250	283	425

AFC NORTH
	W	L	T	Pct	Pts	OP
Pittsburgh	12	4	0	.750	375	232
Baltimore	12	4	0	.750	357	270
Cincinnati	5	11	0	.313	271	332
Cleveland	4	12	0	.250	322	395

AFC SOUTH
	W	L	T	Pct	Pts	OP
Indianapolis	10	6	0	.625	435	388
Jacksonville	8	8	0	.500	353	419
Houston	6	10	0	.375	390	427
Tennessee	6	10	0	.375	356	336

AFC WEST
	W	L	T	Pct	Pts	OP
Kansas City	10	6	0	.625	366	326
San Diego	9	7	0	.563	441	322
Oakland	8	8	0	.500	410	371
Denver	4	12	0	.250	344	471

NFC EAST
	W	L	T	Pct	Pts	OP
Philadelphia	10	6	0	.625	439	377
NY Giants	10	6	0	.625	394	347
Dallas	6	10	0	.375	394	436
Washington	6	10	0	.375	302	377

NFC NORTH
	W	L	T	Pct	Pts	OP
Chicago	11	5	0	.688	334	286
Green Bay	10	6	0	.625	388	240
Detroit	6	10	0	.375	362	369
Minnesota	6	10	0	.375	281	348

NFC SOUTH
	W	L	T	Pct	Pts	OP
Atlanta	13	3	0	.813	414	288
New Orleans	11	5	0	.688	384	307
Tampa Bay	10	6	0	.625	341	318
Carolina	2	14	0	.125	196	408

NFC WEST
	W	L	T	Pct	Pts	OP
Seattle	7	9	0	.438	310	407
St. Louis	7	9	0	.438	289	328
San Francisco	6	10	0	.375	305	346
Arizona	5	11	0	.313	289	434

2011

AFC EAST
	W	L	T	Pct	Pts	OP
New England	13	3	0	.813	513	342
NY Jets	8	8	0	.500	377	363
Miami	6	10	0	.375	329	313
Buffalo	6	10	0	.375	372	434

AFC NORTH
	W	L	T	Pct	Pts	OP
Baltimore	12	4	0	.750	378	266
Pittsburgh	12	4	0	.750	325	227
Cincinnati	9	7	0	.563	344	323
Cleveland	4	12	0	.250	218	307

AFC SOUTH
	W	L	T	Pct	Pts	OP
Houston	10	6	0	.625	381	278
Tennessee	9	7	0	.563	325	317
Jacksonville	5	11	0	.313	243	329
Indianapolis	2	14	0	.125	243	430

2011 *(Cont.)*

AFC WEST
	W	L	T	Pct	Pts	OP
Denver	8	8	0	.500	309	390
San Diego	8	8	0	.500	406	377
Oakland	8	8	0	.500	359	433
Kansas City	7	9	0	.438	212	338

NFC EAST
	W	L	T	Pct	Pts	OP
NY Giants	9	7	0	.563	394	400
Philadelphia	8	8	0	.500	396	328
Dallas	8	8	0	.500	369	347
Washington	5	11	0	.313	288	367

NFC NORTH
	W	L	T	Pct	Pts	OP
Green Bay	15	1	0	.938	560	359
Detroit	10	6	0	.625	474	387
Chicago	8	8	0	.500	353	341
Minnesota	3	13	0	.188	340	449

NFC SOUTH
	W	L	T	Pct	Pts	OP
New Orleans	13	3	0	.813	547	339
Atlanta	10	6	0	.625	402	350
Carolina	6	10	0	.375	406	429
Tampa Bay	4	12	0	.250	287	494

NFC WEST
	W	L	T	Pct	Pts	OP
San Francisco	13	3	0	.813	380	229
Arizona	8	8	0	.500	312	348
Seattle	7	9	0	.438	321	315
St. Louis	2	14	0	.125	193	407

Results

Date	Winner (Share)	Loser (Share)	Score	Site (Attendance)
I 1-15-67	Green Bay ($15,000)	Kansas City ($7,500)	35–10	Los Angeles (61,946)
II 1-14-68	Green Bay ($15,000)	Oakland ($7,500)	33–14	Miami (75,546)
III 1-12-69	NY Jets ($15,000)	Baltimore ($7,500)	16–7	Miami (75,389)
IV 1-11-70	Kansas City ($15,000)	Minnesota ($7,500)	23–7	New Orleans (80,562)
V 1-17-71	Baltimore ($15,000)	Dallas ($7,500)	16–13	Miami (79,204)
VI 1-16-72	Dallas ($15,000)	Miami ($7,500)	24–3	New Orleans (81,023)
VII 1-14-73	Miami ($15,000)	Washington ($7,500)	14–7	Los Angeles (90,182)
VIII 1-13-74	Miami ($15,000)	Minnesota ($7,500)	24–7	Houston (71,882)
IX 1-12-75	Pittsburgh ($15,000)	Minnesota ($7,500)	16–6	New Orleans (80,997)
X 1-18-76	Pittsburgh ($15,000)	Dallas ($7,500)	21–17	Miami (80,187)
XI 1-9-77	Oakland ($15,000)	Minnesota ($7,500)	32–14	Pasadena (103,438)
XII 1-15-78	Dallas ($18,000)	Denver ($9,000)	27–10	New Orleans (76,400)
XIII 1-21-79	Pittsburgh ($18,000)	Dallas ($9,000)	35–31	Miami (79,484)
XIV 1-20-80	Pittsburgh ($18,000)	Los Angeles ($9,000)	31–19	Pasadena (103,985)
XV 1-25-81	Oakland ($18,000)	Philadelphia ($9,000)	27–10	New Orleans (76,135)
XVI 1-24-82	San Francisco ($18,000)	Cincinnati ($9,000)	26–21	Pontiac, Mich. (81,270)
XVII 1-30-83	Washington ($36,000)	Miami ($18,000)	27–17	Pasadena (103,667)
XVIII 1-22-84	LA Raiders ($36,000)	Washington ($18,000)	38–9	Tampa (72,920)
XIX 1-20-85	San Francisco ($36,000)	Miami ($18,000)	38–16	Stanford, Calif. (84,059)
XX 1-26-86	Chicago ($36,000)	New England ($18,000)	46–10	New Orleans (73,818)
XXI 1-25-87	NY Giants ($36,000)	Denver ($18,000)	39–20	Pasadena (101,063)
XXII 1-31-88	Washington ($36,000)	Denver ($18,000)	42–10	San Diego (73,302)
XXIII 1-22-89	San Francisco ($36,000)	Cincinnati ($18,000)	20–16	Miami (75,129)
XXIV 1-28-90	San Francisco ($36,000)	Denver ($18,000)	55–10	New Orleans (72,919)
XXV 1-27-91	NY Giants ($36,000)	Buffalo ($18,000)	20–19	Tampa (73,813)
XXVI 1-26-92	Washington ($36,000)	Buffalo ($18,000)	37–24	Minneapolis (63,130)
XXVII 1-31-93	Dallas ($36,000)	Buffalo ($18,000)	52–17	Pasadena (98,374)
XXVIII 1-30-94	Dallas ($38,000)	Buffalo ($23,500)	30–13	Atlanta (72,817)
XXIX 1-29-95	San Francisco ($42,000)	San Diego ($26,000)	49–26	Miami (74,107)
XXX 1-28-96	Dallas ($42,000)	Pittsburgh ($27,000)	27–17	Tempe, Ariz. (76,347)
XXXI 1-26-97	Green Bay ($48,000)	New England ($29,000)	35–21	New Orleans (72,301)
XXXII 1-25-98	Denver ($48,000)	Green Bay ($27,500)	31–24	San Diego (68,912)
XXXIII 1-31-99	Denver ($53,000)	Atlanta ($32,500)	34–19	Miami (74,803)
XXXIV 1-30-00	St. Louis ($58,000)	Tennessee ($33,000)	23–16	Atlanta (72,625)
XXXV 1-28-01	Baltimore ($58,000)	NY Giants ($34,500)	34–7	Tampa (71,921)
XXXVI 2-3-02	New England ($63,000)	St. Louis ($34,500)	20–17	New Orleans (72,922)
XXXVII 1-26-03	Tampa Bay ($64,000)	Oakland ($35,000)	48–21	San Diego (67,603)
XXXVIII ...2-1-04	New England ($64,000)	Carolina ($35,000)	32–29	Houston (71,525)
XXXIX 2-6-05	New England ($68,000)	Philadelphia ($36,500)	24–21	Jacksonville (78,125)
XL 2-5-06	Pittsburgh ($73,000)	Seattle ($38,000)	21–10	Detroit (68,206)
XLI 2-4-07	Indianapolis ($78,000)	Chicago ($40,000)	29–17	Miami (74,512)
XLII 2-3-08	NY Giants ($78,000)	New England ($40,000)	17–14	Glendale, Ariz. (71,101)
XLIII 2-1-09	Pittsburgh ($78,000)	Arizona ($40,000)	27–23	Tampa (70,774)
XLIV 2-7-10	New Orleans ($83,000)	Indianapolis ($42,000)	31–17	Miami (74,059)
XLV 2-6-11	Green Bay ($83,000)	Pittsburgh ($42,000)	31–25	Arlington, Tex. (103,219)
XLVI 2-5-12	NY Giants ($88,000)	New England ($44,000)	21–17	Indianapolis (68,658)

Most Valuable Players

Super Bowl	Player/ Team	Position	Super Bowl	Player/ Team	Position
I ....Bart Starr, GB		QB	XXI ....Phil Simms, NYG		QB
II ....Bart Starr, GB		QB	XXII ....Doug Williams, Wash		QB
III ....Joe Namath, NYJ		QB	XXIII ....Jerry Rice, SF		WR
IV ....Len Dawson, KC		QB	XXIV ....Joe Montana, SF		QB
V ....Chuck Howley, Dal		LB	XXV ....Ottis Anderson, NYG		RB
VI ....Roger Staubach, Dal		QB	XXVI ....Mark Rypien, Wash		QB
VII ....Jake Scott, Mia		S	XXVII ....Troy Aikman, Dal		QB
VIII ....Larry Csonka, Mia		RB	XXVIII ....Emmitt Smith, Dal		RB
IX ....Franco Harris, Pit		RB	XXIX ....Steve Young, SF		QB
X ....Lynn Swann, Pit		WR	XXX ....Larry Brown, Dal		CB
XI ....Fred Biletnikoff, Oak		WR	XXXI ....Desmond Howard, GB		KR
XII ....Randy White/Harvey Martin, Dal		DT/DE	XXXII ....Terrell Davis, Den		RB
XIII, XIV ....Terry Bradshaw, Pit		QB	XXXIII ....John Elway, Den		QB
XV ....Jim Plunkett, Oak		QB	XXXIV ....Kurt Warner, StL		QB
XVI ....Joe Montana, SF		QB	XXXV ....Ray Lewis, Balt		LB
XVII ....John Riggins, Wash		RB	XXXVI ....Tom Brady, NE		QB
XVIII ....Marcus Allen, LA Rai		RB	XXXVII ....Dexter Jackson, TB		S
XIX ....Joe Montana, SF		QB	XXXVIII ....Tom Brady, NE		QB
XX ....Richard Dent, Chi		DE	XXXIX ....Deion Branch, NE		WR

Most Valuable Players *(Cont.)*

Super Bowl	Player/ Team	Position	Super Bowl	Player/ Team	Position
XL	Hines Ward, Pit	WR	XLIV	Drew Brees, NO	QB
XLI	Peyton Manning, Ind	QB	XLV	Aaron Rodgers, GB	QB
XLII	Eli Manning, NYG	QB	XLVI	Eli Manning, NYG	QB
XLIII	Santonio Holmes, Pit	WR			

Composite Standings, by Wins

	W	L	Pct	Pts	Opp Pts
Pittsburgh Steelers	6	2	.750	193	164
San Francisco 49ers	5	0	1.000	188	89
Dallas Cowboys	5	3	.625	221	132
Green Bay Packers	4	1	.800	158	101
New York Giants	4	1	.800	104	104
Oakland/LA Raiders	3	2	.600	132	114
Washington Redskins	3	2	.600	122	103
New England Patriots	3	4	.429	138	186
Baltimore/Indianapolis Colts	2	2	.500	69	77
Miami Dolphins	2	3	.400	74	103
Denver Broncos	2	4	.333	115	206
Tampa Bay Buccaneers	1	0	1.000	48	21
Baltimore Ravens	1	0	1.000	34	7
New Orleans Saints	1	0	1.000	34	17
New York Jets	1	0	1.000	16	7
Chicago Bears	1	1	.500	63	39
Kansas City Chiefs	1	1	.500	33	42
Los Angeles/St. Louis Rams	1	2	.333	59	67
Carolina Panthers	0	1	.000	29	32
San Diego Chargers	0	1	.000	26	49
Arizona Cardinals	0	1	.000	23	27
Atlanta Falcons	0	1	.000	19	34
Tennessee Titans	0	1	.000	16	23
Seattle Seahawks	0	1	.000	10	21
Cincinnati Bengals	0	2	.000	37	46
Philadelphia Eagles	0	2	.000	31	51
Buffalo Bills	0	4	.000	73	139
Minnesota Vikings	0	4	.000	34	95

Career Leaders

Passing

	GP	Att	Comp	Pct Comp	Yds	Avg Gain/ Att	TD	Pct TD	Int	Pct Int	Lg	Rating Pts
Joe Montana, SF	4	122	83	68.0	1142	9.36	11	9.0	0	0.0	44	127.8
Jim Plunkett, Oak/LA Rai.	2	46	29	63.0	433	9.41	4	8.7	0	0.0	t80	122.8
Terry Bradshaw, Pit	4	84	49	58.3	932	11.10	9	10.7	4	4.8	t75	112.8
Troy Aikman, Dal	3	80	56	70.0	689	8.61	5	6.3	1	1.3	t56	111.9
Bart Starr, GB	2	47	29	61.7	452	9.62	3	6.4	1	2.1	62	106.0
Brett Favre, GB	2	69	39	56.5	502	7.28	5	7.2	1	1.4	t81	97.6
Roger Staubach, Dal	4	97	61	62.9	734	7.57	8	8.2	4	4.1	t45	96.3
Eli Manning, NY Giants	2	74	49	66.2	551	7.45	3	4.1	1	1.4	45	96.2
Kurt Warner, StL, Ari	3	133	83	62.4	1156	8.69	6	4.5	3	2.3	t73	95.9
Tom Brady, NE	5	197	127	64.5	1277	6.48	9	4.6	2	1.0	52	93.8
Peyton Manning, Ind	2	83	58	67.5	580	6.99	2	2.4	2	2.4	t53	85.4

Note: Minimum 40 attempts.

Rushing Yards

	GP	Yds	Att	Avg	Lg	TD
Franco Harris, Pit	4	354	101	3.5	25	4
Larry Csonka, Mia	3	297	57	5.2	49	2
Emmitt Smith, Dal	3	289	70	4.1	38	5
Terrell Davis, Den	2	259	55	4.7	27	3
John Riggins, Was	2	230	64	3.6	43	2
Timmy Smith, Was	1	204	22	9.3	58	2
Thurman Thomas, Buf	4	204	52	3.9	31	4
Roger Craig, SF	3	201	52	3.9	18	2
Marcus Allen, LA Rai	1	191	20	9.6	t74	2
Antowain Smith, NE	2	175	44	4.0	17	1

t-scored touchdown

Receptions

	GP	No.	Yds	Avg	Lg	TD
Jerry Rice, SF	4	33	589	17.9	t48	8
Andre Reed, Buf	4	27	323	12.0	40	0
Deion Branch, NE	3	24	321	13.4	52	1
Roger Craig, SF	3	20	212	10.6	40	2
Thurman Thomas, Buf	4	20	144	7.2	24	0
Wes Welker, NE	2	18	163	9.1	19	0
Jay Novacek, Dal	3	17	148	8.7	23	2
Joseph Addai, Ind	2	17	124	7.3	17	0
Lynn Swann, Pit	4	16	364	22.8	t74	3
Michael Irvin, Dal	3	16	256	16.0	25	2
Troy Brown, NE	3	16	182	11.4	23	0

Single-Game Leaders

Scoring

	Pts
Roger Craig: XIX, San Francisco vs Miami (1 rush, 2 rec)	18
Jerry Rice: XXIV, San Francisco vs Denver (3 rec); XXIX, SF vs San Diego (3 rec)	18
Ricky Watters: XXIX, San Francisco vs San Diego (1 rush, 2 rec)	18
Terrell Davis: XXXII, Denver vs Green Bay (3 rec)	18

Rushing Yards

	Yds
Timmy Smith: XXII, Washington vs Denver	204
Marcus Allen: XVIII, LA Raiders vs Washington	191
John Riggins: XVII, Washington vs Miami	166
Franco Harris: IX, Pittsburgh vs Minnesota	158
Terrell Davis: XXXII, Denver vs Green Bay	157
Larry Csonka: VIII, Miami vs Minnesota	145
Clarence Davis: XI, Oakland vs Minnesota	137
Thurman Thomas: XXV, Buffalo vs NY Giants	135
Emmitt Smith: XXVIII, Dallas vs Buffalo	132
Michael Pittman: XXXVII, Tampa Bay vs Oakland	124

Receptions

	No.
Wes Welker: XLII, New England vs NY Giants	11
Deion Branch: XXXIX, New England vs Phila.	11
Jerry Rice: XXIII, San Francisco vs Cincinnati	11
Dan Ross: XVI, Cincinnati vs San Francisco	11
Joseph Addai: XLI, Indianapolis vs Chicago	10
Deion Branch: XXXVIII, New England vs Carolina	10
Andre Hastings: XXX, Pittsburgh vs Dallas	10
Jerry Rice: XXIX, San Francisco vs San Diego	10
Tony Nathan: XIX, Miami vs San Francisco	10
Hakeem Nicks: XLVI, NY Giants vs. New England	10

Touchdown Passes

	No.
Steve Young: XXIX, San Francisco vs San Diego	6
Joe Montana: XXIV, San Francisco vs Denver	5
Troy Aikman: XXVII, Dallas vs Buffalo	4
Doug Williams: XXII, Washington vs Denver	4
Terry Bradshaw: XIII, Pittsburgh vs Dallas	4
Nine tied with three.	

Passing Yards

	Yds
Kurt Warner: XXXIV, St. Louis vs Tennessee	414
Kurt Warner: XLIII, Arizona vs Pittsburgh	377
Kurt Warner: XXXVI, St. Louis vs New England	365
Joe Montana: XXIII, San Francisco vs Cincinnati	357
Donovan McNabb, XXXIX, Phila. vs. New England	357
Tom Brady: XXXVIII, New England vs Carolina	354
Doug Williams: XXII, Washington vs Denver	340
John Elway: XXXIII, Denver vs Atlanta	336
Peyton Manning: XLIV, Indianapolis vs New Orl'ns	333
Joe Montana: XIX, San Francisco vs Miami	331
Steve Young: XXIX, San Francisco vs San Diego	325
Jake Delhomme: XXXVIII Carolina vs New England	323
Terry Bradshaw: XIII, Pittsburgh vs Dallas	318
Dan Marino: XIX, Miami vs San Francisco	318

Receiving Yards

	Yds
Jerry Rice: XXIII, San Francisco vs Cincinnati	215
Ricky Sanders: XXII, Washington vs Denver	193
Isaac Bruce: XXXIV, St. Louis vs Tennessee	162
Lynn Swann: X, Pittsburgh vs Dallas	161
Andre Reed: XXVII, Buffalo vs Dallas	152
Rod Smith: XXXIII, Denver vs Atlanta	152
Jerry Rice: XXIX, San Francisco vs San Diego	149
Jerry Rice: XXIV, San Francisco vs Denver	148
Deion Branch: XXXVIII, New England vs Carolina	143

Super Bowl History Recaps*

I - 1967

Green Bay	7	7	14	7—35
Kansas City	0	10	0	0—10

FIRST QUARTER: GB: McGee 37 pass from Starr (Chandler kick), 8:56. **Green Bay 7-0.**

SECOND QUARTER: KC: McClinton 7 pass from Dawson (Mercer kick), 4:20. **7-7.**
GB: Taylor 14 run (Chandler kick), 10:23. **Green Bay 14-7.**
KC: FG Mercer 31, 14:06. **Green Bay 14-10.**

THIRD QUARTER: GB: Pitts 5 run (Chandler kick), 2:27. **Green Bay 21-10.**
GB: McGee 13 pass from Starr (Chandler kick), 14:09. **Green Bay 28-10.**

FOURTH QUARTER: GB: Pitts 1 run (Chandler kick), 8:25. **Green Bay 35-10.**
A: 61,946.

II - 1968

Green Bay	3	13	10	7—33
Oakland	0	7	0	7—14

FIRST QUARTER: GB: FG Chandler 39 5:07. **Green Bay 3-0.**

SECOND QUARTER: GB: FG Chandler, 20, 3:08. **Green Bay 6-0.**
GB: Dowler 62 pass from Starr (Chandler kick), 4:10. **Green Bay 13-0.**

SECOND QUARTER (CONT.): Oak: Miller 23 pass from Lamonica (Blanda kick), 8:45. **Green Bay 13-7.**
GB: FG Chandler 43, 14:59. **Green Bay 16-7.**

THIRD QUARTER: GB: Anderson 2 run (Chandler kick), 9:06. **Green Bay 23-7.**
GB: FG Chandler 31, 14:58. **Green Bay 26-7.**

FOURTH QUARTER:
GB: Adderley 60 int return (Chandler kick), 3:57. **Green Bay 33-7.**
Oak: Miller 23 pass from Lamonica (Blanda kick), 5:47. **Green Bay 33-14.**
A: 75,546.

*From 1967 to 1999, Super Bowl scoring times indicate the time elapsed in each quarter. Starting in 2000, times listed give the time remaining in each quarter.

III - 1969

NY Jets	0	7	6	3—16
Baltimore	0	0	0	7—7

SECOND QUARTER: Jets: Snell 4 run (Turner kick), 5:57. **Jets: 7-0.**

THIRD QUARTER: Jets: FG Turner 32, 4:52. **Jets: 10-0.** Jets: FG Turner 30, 11:02. **Jets: 13-0.**

FOURTH QUARTER: Jets: FG Turner 9, 1:34. **Jets: 16-0.** Balt: Hill 1 run (Michaels kick), 11:41. **Jets: 16-7.** A: 75,389.

IV - 1970

Kansas City	3	13	7	0—23
Minnesota	0	0	7	0—7

FIRST QUARTER: KC: FG Stenerud 48, 8:08. **Kansas City 3-0.**

SECOND QUARTER: KC: FG Stenerud 32, 1:40. **Kansas City 6-0.** KC: FG Stenerud 25, 7:08. **Kansas City 9-0.** KC: Garrett 5 run (Stenerud kick), 9:26. **Kansas City 16-0.**

THIRD QUARTER: Minn: Osborn 4 run (Cox kick), 10:28. **Kansas City 16-7.** KC: Taylor 46 pass from Dawson (Stenerud kick), 13:38. **Kansas City 23-7.** A: 80,562.

V - 1971

Baltimore	0	6	0	10—16
Dallas	3	10	0	0—13

FIRST QUARTER: Dal: FG Clark 14, 9:28. **Dallas 3-0.**

SECOND QUARTER: Dal: FG Clark 30, 0:08. **Dallas 6-0.** Balt: Mackey 75 pass from Unitas (kick blocked). 0:50. **6-6.** Dal: Thomas 7 pass from Morton (Clark kick), 7:07. **Dallas 13-6.**

FOURTH QUARTER: Balt: Nowatzke 2 run (O'Brien kick), 7:25. **13-13.** Balt: FG O'Brien 32, 14:55. **Baltimore 16-13.** A: 79,204.

VI - 1972

Dallas	3	7	7	7—24
Miami	0	3	0	0—3

FIRST QUARTER: Dal: FG Clark 9, 13:37. **Dallas 3-0.**

SECOND QUARTER: Dal: Alworth 7 pass from Staubach (Clark kick), 13:45. **Dallas 10-0.** Mia: FG Yepremian, 31, 14:56. **Dallas 10-3.**

THIRD QUARTER: Dal: D. Thomas 3 run (Clark kick), 5:17. **Dallas 17-3.**

FOURTH QUARTER: Dal: Ditka 7 pass from Staubach (Clark kick), 3:18. **Dallas 24-3.** A: 81,023.

VII - 1973

Miami	7	7	0	0—14
Washington	0	0	0	7—7

FIRST QUARTER: Mia: Twilley 28 pass from Griese (Yepremian kick), 14:59. **Miami 7-0.**

SECOND QUARTER: Mia: Kiick 1 run (Yepremian kick), 14:42. **Miami 14-0.**

FOURTH QUARTER: Wash: Bass 49 fumble recovery return (Knight kick), 12:53. **Miami 14-7.** A: 90,182.

VIII - 1974

Miami	14	3	7	0—24
Minnesota	0	0	0	7—7

FIRST QUARTER: Mia: Csonka 5 run (Yepremian kick), 5:27. **Miami 7-0.** Mia: Kiick 1 run (Yepremian kick), 13:38. **Miami 14-0.**

SECOND QUARTER: Mia: FG Yepremian 28, 8:58. **Miami 17-0.**

THIRD QUARTER: Mia: Csonka 2 run (Yepremian kick), 6:16. **Miami 24-0.**

FOURTH QUARTER: Minn: Tarkenton 4 run (Cox kick), 1:35. **Miami 24-7.** A: 71,882.

IX - 1975

Pittsburgh	0	2	7	7—16
Minnesota	0	0	0	6—6

SECOND QUARTER: Pit: White tackled Tarkenton for safety, 7:49. **Pittsburgh 2-0.**

THIRD QUARTER: Pit: Harris 9 run (Gerela kick), 1:35. **Pittsburgh 9-0.**

FOURTH QUARTER: Minn: T. Brown recovered blocked punt in end zone (kick failed), 4:27. **Pittsburgh 9-6.** Pit: L. Brown 4 pass from Bradshaw (Gerela kick), 11:29. **Pittsburgh 16-6.** A: 80,997.

X - 1976

Pittsburgh	7	0	0	14—21
Dallas	7	3	0	7—17

FIRST QUARTER: Dal: D. Pearson 29 pass from Staubach (Fritsch kick), 4:36. **Dallas 7-0.** Pit: Grossman 7 pass from Bradshaw (Gerela kick), 9:03. **7-7.**

SECOND QUARTER: Dal: FG Fritsch 36, 0:15. **Dallas 10-7.**

FOURTH QUARTER: Pit: Harrison blocked Hoopes's punt for safety, 3:32. **Dallas 10-9.** Pit: FG Gerela 36, 6:19. **Pittsburgh 12-10.** Pit: FG Gerela 18, 8:32. **Pittsburgh 15-10.** Pit: Swann 64 pass from Bradshaw (kick failed), 11:58. **Pittsburgh 21-10.** Dal: P. Howard 34 pass from Staubach (Fritsch kick), 13:12. **Pittsburgh 21-17.** A: 80,187.

XI - 1977

Oakland	0	16	3	13—32
Minnesota	0	0	7	7—14

SECOND QUARTER: Oak: FG Mann, 24, 0:48. **Oakland 3-0.** Oak: Casper 1 pass from Stabler (Mann kick), 7:50. **Oakland 10-0.** Oak: Banaszak 1 run (kick failed), 11:27. **Oakland 16-0.**

THIRD QUARTER: Oak: FG Mann, 40, 9:44. **Oakland 19-0.** Min: S. White 8 pass from Tarkenton (Cox kick), 14:13. **Oakland 19-7.**

FOURTH QUARTER: Oak: Banaszak 2 run (Mann kick), 7:21. **Oakland 26-7.** Oak: Brown 75 int return (kick failed), 9:17. **Oakland 32-7.** Min: Voigt 13 pass from Lee (Cox kick), 14:35. **Oakland 32-14.** A: 103,438.

XII - 1978

Dallas	10	3	7	7—27
Denver	0	0	10	0—10

FIRST QUARTER: Dal: Dorsett 3 run (Herrera kick), 10:31. **Dallas 7-0.**
Dal: FG Herrera 35, 13:29. **Dallas 10-0.**

SECOND QUARTER: Dal: FG Herrera 43, 3:44.
Dallas 13-0.

THIRD QUARTER: Den: FG Turner 47, 2:28. **Dallas 13-3.**
Dal: Johnson 45 pass from Staubach (Herrera kick), 8:01. **Dallas 20-3.**
Den: Lytle 1 run (Turner kick), 9:21. **Dallas 20-10.**

FOURTH QUARTER: Dal: Richards 29 pass from Newhouse (Herrera kick), 7:56. **Dallas 27-10.**
A: 76,400.

XIII - 1979

Pittsburgh	7	14	0	14—35
Dallas	7	7	3	14—31

FIRST QUARTER: Pit: Stallworth 28 pass from Bradshaw (Gerela kick), 5:13. **Pittsburgh 7-0.**
Dal: Hill 39 pass from Staubach (Septien kick), 15:00. **7-7.**

SECOND QUARTER: Dal: Hegman 37 fumble recovery return (Septien kick), 2:52. **Dallas 14-7.**
Pit: Stallworth 75 pass from Bradshaw (Gerela kick), 4:35. **14-14.**
Pit: Bleier 7 pass from Bradshaw (Gerela kick), 14:34. **Pittsburgh 21-14.**

THIRD QUARTER: Dal: FG Septien 27, 12:24.
Pittsburgh 21-17.

FOURTH QUARTER: Pit: Harris 22 run (Gerela kick), 7:50.
Pittsburgh 28-17.
Pit: Swann 18 pass from Bradshaw (Gerela kick), 8:09. **Pittsburgh 35-17.**
Dal: DuPree 7 pass from Staubach (Septien kick), 12:33. **Pittsburgh 35-24.**
Dal: B. Johnson 4 pass from Staubach (Septien kick), 14:38. **Pittsburgh 35-31.**

A: 79,484.

XIV - 1980

Pittsburgh	3	7	7	14—31
LA Rams	7	6	6	0—19

FIRST QUARTER: Pit: FG Bahr, 41, 7:29. **Pittsburgh 3-0.**
LA: Bryant 1 run (Corral kick), 12:16. **LA Rams 7-3.**

SECOND QUARTER: Pit: Harris 1 run (Bahr kick), 2:08.
Pittsburgh 10-7.
LA: FG Corral 31, 7:39. **10-10.**
LA: FG Corral 45, 14:46. **LA Rams 13-10.**

THIRD QUARTER: Pit: Swann 47 pass from Bradshaw (Bahr kick), 2:48. **Pittsburgh 17-13.**
LA: Smith 24 pass from McCutcheon (kick failed), 4:45. **LA Rams 19-17.**

FOURTH QUARTER: Pit: Stallworth 73 pass from Bradshaw (Bahr kick), 2:56. **Pittsburgh 24-19.**
Pit: Harris 1 run (Bahr kick), 13:11. **Pittsburgh 31-19.**
A: 103,985.

XV - 1981

Oakland	14	0	10	3—27
Philadelphia	0	3	0	7—10

FIRST QUARTER: Oak: Branch 2 pass from Plunkett (Bahr kick), 6:04. **Oakland 7-0.**
Oak: King 80 pass from Plunkett (Bahr kick), 14:51. **Oakland 14-0.**

SECOND QUARTER: Phi: FG Franklin 30, 4:32.
Oakland 14-3.

THIRD QUARTER: Oak: Branch 29 pass from Plunkett (Bahr kick), 2:36. **Oakland 21-3.**
Oak: FG Bahr 46, 10:25. **Oakland 24-3.**

FOURTH QUARTER: Phi: Krepfle 8 pass from Jaworski (Franklin kick), 1:01. **Oakland 24-10.**
Oak: FG Bahr, 35, 6:31. **Oakland 27-10.**
A: 76,135.

XVI - 1982

San Francisco	7	13	0	6—26
Cincinnati	0	0	7	14—21

FIRST QUARTER: SF: Montana 1 run (Wersching kick), 9:08. **San Francisco 7-0.**

SECOND QUARTER: SF: E. Cooper 11 pass from Montana (Wersching kick), 8:07. **San Francisco 14-0.**
SF: FG Wersching 22, 14:45. **San Francisco 17-0.**
SF: FG Wersching 26, 14:58. **San Francisco 20-0.**

THIRD QUARTER: Cin: Anderson 5 run (Breech kick), 3:35. **San Francisco 20-7.**

FOURTH QUARTER: Cin: Ross 4 pass from Anderson (Breech kick), 4:54. **San Francisco 20-14.**
SF: FG Wersching 40, 9:35. **San Francisco 23-14.**
SF: FG Wersching 23, 13:03. **San Francisco 26-14.**
Cin: Ross 3 pass from Anderson (Breech kick), 14:44. **San Francisco 26-21.**
A: 81,270.

XVII - 1983

Washington	0	10	3	14—27
Miami	7	10	0	0—17

FIRST QUARTER: Mia: Cefalo 76 pass from Woodley (Von Schamann kick), 6:49. **Miami 7-0.**

SECOND QUARTER: Wash: FG Moseley 31, 0:21.
Miami 7-3.
Mia: FG Von Schamann 20, 9:00. **Miami 10-3.**
Wash: Garrett 4 pass from Theismann (Moseley kick), 13:09. **10-10.**
Mia: Walker 98 kick return (Von Schamann kick), 13:22. **Miami 17-10.**

THIRD QUARTER: Wash: FG Moseley 20, 6:51.
Miami 17-13.

FOURTH QUARTER: Wash: Riggins 43 run (Moseley kick), 4:59. **Washington 20-17.**
Wash: Brown 6 pass from Theismann (Moseley kick), 13:05. **Washington 27-17.**
A: 103,667.

XVIII - 1984

LA Raiders	7	14	14	3—38
Washington	0	3	6	0—9

FIRST QUARTER: LA: Jensen 0 blocked punt return (Bahr kick), 4:52. **LA Raiders 7-0.**

SECOND QUARTER: LA: Branch 12 pass from Plunkett (Bahr kick), 5:46. **LA Raiders 14-0.**
Wash: FG Moseley 24, 11:55. **LA Raiders 14-3.**
LA: Squirek 5 int return (Bahr kick), 14:53.
LA Raiders 21-3.

THIRD QUARTER: Wash: Riggins 1 run (kick blocked), 4:08. **LA Raiders 21-9.**
LA: Allen 5 run (Bahr kick), 7:54. **LA Raiders 28-9.**
LA: Allen 74 run (Bahr kick), 15:00. **LA Raiders 35-9.**

FOURTH QUARTER: LA: FG Bahr 21, 12:36.
LA Raiders 38-9.
A: 72,920.

XIX - 1985

San Francisco	7	21	10	0—38
Miami	10	6	0	0—16

FIRST QUARTER: Mia: FG Von Schamann 37, 7:36.
Miami 3-0.
SF: Monroe 33 pass from Montana (Wersching kick), 11:48. **San Francisco 7-3.**
Mia: D. Johnson 2 pass from Marino (Von Schamann kick), 14:15. **Miami 10-7.**

SECOND QUARTER: SF: Craig 8 pass from Montana (Wersching kick), 3:26. **San Francisco 14-10.**
SF: Montana 6 run (Wersching kick), 8:02.
San Francisco 21-10.
SF: Craig 2 run (Wersching kick), 12:55.
San Francisco 28-10.
Mia: FG Von Schamann 31, 14:48.
San Francisco 28-13.
Mia: FG Von Schamann 30, 15:00.
San Francisco 28-16.

THIRD QUARTER: SF: FG Wersching 27, 4:48.
San Francisco 31-16.
SF: Craig 16 pass from Montana (Wersching kick), 8:42. **San Francisco 38-16.**
A: 84,059.

XX - 1986

Chicago	13	10	21	2—46
New England	3	0	0	7—10

FIRST QUARTER: NE: FG Franklin 36, 1:19.
New England 3-0.
Chi: FG Butler 28, 5:40. **3-3.**
Chi: FG Butler 24, 13:34. **Chicago 6-3.**
Chi: Suhey 11 run (Butler kick), 14:37. **Chicago 13-3.**

SECOND QUARTER: Chi: McMahon 2 run (Butler kick), 7:36. **Chicago 20-3.**
Chi: FG Butler 24, 15:00. **Chicago 23-3.**

THIRD QUARTER: Chi: McMahon 1 run (Butler kick), 7:38. **Chicago 30-3.**
Chi: Phillips 28 int return (Butler kick), 8:44. **Chicago 37-3.**
Chi: Perry 1 run (Butler kick), 11:38. **Chicago 44-3.**

FOURTH QUARTER: NE: Fryar 8 pass from Grogan (Franklin kick), 1:46. **Chicago 44-10.**
Chi: Waechter safety, 9:24. **Chicago 46-10.**
A: 73,818.

XXI - 1987

NY Giants	7	2	17	13—39
Denver	10	0	0	10—20

FIRST QUARTER: Den: FG Karlis 48, 4:09. **Denver 3-0.**
NYG: Mowatt 6 pass from Simms (Allegre kick), 9:33.
NY Giants 7-3.
Den: Elway 4 run (Karlis kick), 12:54. **Denver 10-7.**

SECOND QUARTER: NYG: Martin safety, 12:14.
Denver 10-9.

THIRD QUARTER: NYG: Bavaro 13 pass from Simms (Allegre kick), 4:52. **NY Giants 16-10.**
NYG: FG Allegre 21, 11:06. **NY Giants 19-10.**
NYG: Morris 1 run (Allegre kick), 14:36.
NY Giants 26-10.

FOURTH QUARTER: NYG: McConkey 6 pass from Simms (Allegre kick), 4:04. **NY Giants 33-10.**
Den: FG Karlis 28, 8:59. **NY Giants 33-13.**
NYG: Anderson 2 run (kick failed), 11:42.
NY Giants 39-13.
Den: Johnson 47 pass from Elway (Karlis kick), 12:54. **NY Giants 39-20.**
A: 101,063.

XXII - 1988

Washington	0	35	0	7—42
Denver	10	0	0	0—10

FIRST QUARTER: Den: Nattiel 56 pass from Elway (Karlis kick), 1:57. **Denver 7-0.**
Den: FG Karlis 24, 5:51. **Denver 10-0.**

SECOND QUARTER: Wash: Sanders 80 pass from D. Williams (Haji-Sheikh kick), 0:53. **Denver 10-7.**
Wash: Clark 27 pass from D. Williams (Haji-Sheikh kick), 4:45. **Washington 14-10.**
Wash: Smith 58 run (Haji-Sheikh kick), 8:33.
Washington 21-10.
Wash: Sanders 50 pass from D. Williams (Haji-Sheikh kick), 11:18. **Washington 28-10.**
Wash: Didier 8 pass from D. Williams (Haji-Sheikh kick), 13:56. **Washington 35-10.**

FOURTH QUARTER: Wash: Smith 4 run (Haji-Sheikh kick), 1:51. **Washington 42-10.**
A: 73,302.

XXIII - 1989

San Francisco	3	0	3	14—20
Cincinnati	0	3	10	3—16

FIRST QUARTER: SF: FG Cofer 41, 11:46.
San Francisco 3-0.

SECOND QUARTER: Cin: FG Breech 34, 13:41. **3-3.**

THIRD QUARTER: Cin: FG Breech 43, 9:15.
Cincinnati 6-3.
SF: FG Cofer 32, 14:10. **6-6.**
Cin: Jennings 93 kick return (Breech kick), 14:26.
Cincinnati 13-6.

FOURTH QUARTER: SF: Rice 14 pass from Montana (Cofer kick), 0:57. **13-13.**
Cin: FG Breech 40, 11:40. **Cincinnati 16-13.**
SF: Taylor 10 pass from Montana (Cofer kick), 14:26.
San Francisco 20-16.
A: 75,129.

XXIV - 1990

San Francisco	13	14	14	14—55
Denver	3	0	7	0—10

FIRST QUARTER: SF: Rice 20 pass from Montana (Cofer kick), 4:54. **San Francisco 7-0.**
Den: FG Treadwell 42, 8:13. **San Francisco 7-3.**
SF: Jones 7 pass from Montana (kick failed), 14:57. **San Francisco 13-3.**

SECOND QUARTER: SF: Rathman 1 run (Cofer kick), 7:45. **San Francisco 20-3.**
SF: Rice 38 pass from Montana (Cofer kick), 14:26. **San Francisco 27-3.**

THIRD QUARTER: SF: Rice 28 pass from Montana (Cofer kick), 2:12. **San Francisco 34-3.**
SF: Taylor 35 pass from Montana (Cofer kick), 5:16. **San Francisco 41-3.**
Den: Elway 3 run (Treadwell kick), 8:07. **San Francisco 41-10.**

FOURTH QUARTER: SF: Rathman 3 run (Cofer kick), 0:03. **San Francisco 48-10.**
SF: Craig 1 run (Cofer kick), 1:13. **San Francisco 55-10.**
A: 72,919.

XXV - 1991

NY Giants	3	7	7	3—20
Buffalo	3	9	0	7—19

FIRST QUARTER: NYG: FG Bahr 28, 7:46. **NY Giants 3-0.**
Buff: FG Norwood 23, 9:09. **3-3.**

SECOND QUARTER: Buff: D. Smith 1 run (Norwood kick), 2:30. **Buffalo 10-3.**
Buff: B. Smith safety 0, 6:33. **Buffalo 12-3.**
NYG: Baker 14 pass from Hostetler (Bahr kick), 14:35. **Buffalo 12-10.**

THIRD QUARTER: NYG: Anderson 1 run (Bahr kick), 9:29. **NY Giants 17-12.**

FOURTH QUARTER: Buff: Thomas 31 run (Norwood kick), 0:08. **Buffalo 19-17.**
NYG: FG Bahr 21, 7:40. **NY Giants 20-19.**
A: 73,813.

XXVI - 1992

Washington	0	17	14	6—37
Buffalo	0	0	10	14—24

SECOND QUARTER: Wash: FG Lohmiller 34, 1:58. **Washington 3-0.**
Wash: Byner 10 pass from Rypien (Lohmiller kick), 5:06. **Washington 10-0.**
Wash: Riggs 1 run (Lohmiller kick), 7:43. **Washington 17-0.**

THIRD QUARTER: Wash: Riggs 2 run (Lohmiller kick), 0:16. **Washington 24-0.**
Buff: FG Norwood 21, 3:01. **Washington 24-3.**
Buff: Thomas 1 run (Norwood kick), 9:02. **Washington 24-10.**
Wash: Clark 30 pass from Rypien (Lohmiller kick), 13:36. **Washington 31-10.**

FOURTH QUARTER: Wash: FG Lohmiller 25, 0:06. **Washington 34-10.**
Wash: FG Lohmiller 39, 3:24. **Washington 37-10.**
Buff: Metzelaars 2 pass from Kelly (Norwood kick), 9:01. **Washington 37-17.**
Buff: Beebe 4 pass from Kelly (Norwood kick), 11:05. **Washington 37-24.**
A: 63,130.

XXVII - 1993

Dallas	14	14	3	21—52
Buffalo	7	3	7	0—17

FIRST QUARTER: Buff: Thomas 2 run (Christie kick), 5:00. **Buffalo 7-0.**
Dal: Novacek 23 pass from Aikman (Elliott kick), 13:24. **7-7.**
Dal: J.Jones 2 fumble return (Elliott kick), 13:39. **Dallas 14-7.**

SECOND QUARTER: Buff: FG Christie 21, 11:36. **Dallas 14-10.**
Dal: Irvin 19 pass from Aikman (Elliott kick)13:06. **Dallas 21-10.**
Dal: Irvin 18 pass from Aikman (Elliott kick), 13:24. **Dallas 28-10.**

THIRD QUARTER: Dal: FG Elliott 20, 6:39. **Dallas 31-10.**
Buff: Beebe 40 pass from Reich (Christie kick), 15:00. **Dallas 31-17.**

FOURTH QUARTER: Dal: Harper 45 pass from Aikman (Elliott kick), 4:56. **Dallas 38-17.**
Dal: E. Smith 10 run (Elliott kick), 6:48. **Dallas 45-17.**
Dal: Norton 9 fumble return (Elliott kick), 7:29. **Dallas 52-17.**
A: 98,374.

XXVIII - 1994

Dallas	6	0	14	10—30
Buffalo	3	10	0	0—13

FIRST QUARTER: Dal: FG Murray 41, 2:19. **Dallas 3-0.**
Buff: FG Christie 54: 4:41. **3-3.**
Dal: FG Murray 24, 11:05. **Dallas 6-3.**

SECOND QUARTER: Buff: Thomas 4 run (Christie kick), 2:34. **Buffalo 10-6.**
Buff: FG Christie 28, 15:00. **Buffalo 13-6.**

THIRD QUARTER: Dal: Washington fumble return (Murray kick), 0:55. **13-13.**
Dal: Smith15 run (Murray kick), 0:55. **Dallas 20-13.**

FOURTH QUARTER: Dal: Smith1 run (Murray kick), 5:10. **Dallas 27-13.**
Dal: FG Murray 20, 12:10. **Dallas 30-13.**
A: 72,817.

XXIX - 1995

San Francisco	14	14	14	7—49
San Diego	7	3	8	8—26

FIRST QUARTER: SF: Rice 44 pass from Young (Brien kick), 1:24. **San Francisco 7-0.**
SF: Watters 51 pass from Young (Brien kick, 4:55. **San Francisco 14-0.**
SD: Means 1 run (Carney kick), 12:16. **San Francisco 14-7.**

SECOND QUARTER: SF: Floyd 5 pass from Young (Brien kick), 1:58. **San Francisco 21-7.**
SF: Watters 8 pass from Young (Brien kick), 10:16. **San Francisco 28-7.**
SD: FG Carney 31, 13:16. **San Francisco 28-10.**

THIRD QUARTER: SF: Watters 9 run (Brien kick), 5:25. **San Francisco 35-10.**
SF: Rice 15 pass from Young (Brien kick), 11:42. **San Francisco 42-10.**

XXIX - 1995 *(Cont.)*

THIRD QUARTER *(CONT.)***:** SD: Coleman 98 kickoff return (Humphries 2-pt conv pass to Seay), 11:59. **San Francisco 42-18.**

FOURTH QUARTER: SF: Rice 7 pass from Young (Brien kick), 1:11. **San Francisco 49-18.** SD: Martin 30 pass from Humphries (Humphries 2 pt-conv pass to Pupunu), 12:35. **San Francisco 49-26.**

A: 74,107.

XXX - 1996

Dallas	10	3	7	7—27
Pittsburgh	0	7	0	10—17

FIRST QUARTER: Dal: FG Boniol 42, 2:55. **Dallas 3-0.** Dal: Novacek 3 pass from Aikman (Boniol kick), 9:37. **Dallas 10-0.**

SECOND QUARTER: Dal: FG Boniol 35, 8:57. **Dallas 13-0.** Pit: Thigpen 6 pass from O'Donnell (N. Johnson kick), 14:47. **Dallas 13-7.**

THIRD QUARTER: Dal: E. Smith 1 run (Boniol kick), 8:18. **Dallas 20-7.**

FOURTH QUARTER: Pit: FG N. Johnson 46, 3:40. **Dallas 20-10.** Pit: Morris 1 run (N. Johnson kick), 8:24. **Dallas 20-17.** Dal: E. Smith 4 run (Boniol kick), 11:17. **Dallas 27-17.**

A: 76,347.

XXXI - 1997

Green Bay	10	17	8	0—35
New England	14	0	7	0—21

FIRST QUARTER: GB: Rison 54 pass from Favre (Jacke kick), 3:32. **Green Bay 7-0.** GB: FG Jacke 37, 6:18. **Green Bay 10-0.** NE: Byars 1 pass from Bledsoe (Vinatieri kick), 8:25. **Green Bay 10-7.** NE: Coates 4 pass from Bledsoe (Vinatieri kick), 12:27. **New England 14-10.**

SECOND QUARTER: GB: Freeman 81 pass from Favre (Jacke kick), 0:56. **Green Bay 17-14.** GB: FG Jacke 31, 6:45. **Green Bay 20-14.** GB: Favre 2 run (Jacke kick), 13:49. **Green Bay 27-14.**

THIRD QUARTER: NE: Martin 18 run (Vinatieri kick), 11:33. **Green Bay 27-21.** GB: Howard 99 kickoff return (Favre 2 pt conv pass to Chmura), 11:50. **Green Bay 35-21.**

A: 72,301.

XXXII - 1998

Denver	7	10	7	7—31
Green Bay	7	7	3	7—24

FIRST QUARTER: GB: Freeman 22 pass from Favre (Longwell kick), 4:02. **Green Bay 7-0.** Den: Davis 1 run (Elam kick), 9:21. **7-7.**

SECOND QUARTER: Den: Elway 1 run (Elam kick), 0:05. **Denver 14-7.** Den: FG Elam 51, 2:39. **Denver 17-7.** GB: Chmura 6 pass from Favre (Longwell kick), 14:48. **Denver 17-14.**

XXXII - 1998 *(Cont.)*

THIRD QUARTER: GB: FG Longwell 27, 3:01. **17-17.** Den: Davis 1 run (Elam kick), 14:26. **Denver 24-17.**

FOURTH QUARTER: GB: Freeman 13 pass from Favre (Longwell kick), 1:28. **24-24.** Den: Davis 1 run (Elam kick), 13:15. **Denver 31-24.** A: 68,912.

XXXIII - 1999

Denver	7	10	0	17—34
Atlanta	3	3	0	13—19

FIRST QUARTER: Atl: FG Andersen 32, 5:25. **Atlanta 3-0.** Den: Griffith 1 run (Elam kick), 11:05. **Denver 7-3.**

SECOND QUARTER: Den: FG Elam 26, 5:43. **Denver 10-3.** Den: Smith 80 pass from Elway (Elam kick), 10:06. **Denver 17-3.** Atl: FG Andersen 28, 12:35. **Denver 17-6.**

FOURTH QUARTER: Den: Griffith 1 run (Elam kick), 0:04. **Denver 24-6.** Den: Elway 3 run (Elam kick), 3:40. **Denver 31-6.** Atl: Dwight 94 kickoff return (Andersen kick), 3:59. **Denver 31-13.** Den: FG Elam 37, 7:52. **Denver 34-13.** Atl: Mathis 3 pass from Chandler (2-pt conv failed), 12:56. **Denver 34-19.**

A: 74,803.

XXXIV - 2000

St. Louis	3	6	7	7—23
Tennessee	0	0	6	10—16

FIRST QUARTER: StL: FG Wilkins 27, 3:00. **St. Louis 3-0.**

SECOND QUARTER: StL: FG Wilkins 29, 4:16. **St. Louis 6-0.** StL: FG Wilkins 28, 0:15. **St. Louis 9-0.**

THIRD QUARTER: StL: Holt 9 pass from Warner (Wilkins kick), 7:20. **St. Louis 16-0.** Tenn: George 1 run (2-pt conv failed), 0:14. **St. Louis 16-6.**

FOURTH QUARTER: Tenn: George 2 run (Del Greco kick), 7:21. **St. Louis 16-13.** Tenn: FG Del Greco 43, 2:15. **16-16.** StL: Bruce 73 pass from Warner, 1:54. **St. Louis 23-16.**

A: 72,265.

XXXV - 2001

Baltimore	7	3	14	10—34
NY Giants	0	0	7	0—7

FIRST QUARTER: Balt: Stokely 38 pass from Dilfer (Stover kick), 6:50. **Baltimore 7-0.**

SECOND QUARTER: Balt: FG Stover 47, 1:41. **Baltimore 10-0.**

THIRD QUARTER: Balt: Starks 49 int return (Stover kick), 3:49. **Baltimore 17-0.** NYG: Dixon 97 kickoff return (Daluiso kick), 3:31. **Baltimore 17-7.** Balt: Je. Lewis 84 kickoff return (Stover kick), 3:13. **Baltimore 24-7.**

XXXV - 2001 *(Cont.)*

FOURTH QUARTER: Balt: Ja. Lewis 3 run (Stover kick), 8:45. **Baltimore 31-7.**
Balt: FG Stover 34, 5:28. **Baltimore 34-7.**
A: 71,921.

XXXVI - 2002

New England	0	14	3	3—20
St. Louis	3	0	0	14—17

FIRST QUARTER: StL: FG Wilkins 50, 3:50. **St. Louis 3-0.**

SECOND QUARTER: NE: Law 47 int return (Vinatieri kick), 8:49. **New England 7-3.**
NE: Patten 8 pass from Brady (Vinatieri kick), 0:31. **New England 14-3.**

THIRD QUARTER: NE: FG Vinatieri 37, 1:18. **New Eng. 17-3.**

FOURTH QUARTER: StL: Warner 2 run (Wilkins kick), 9:31. **New England 17-10.**
StL: Proehl 26 pass from Warner (Wilkins kick), 1:30. **17-17.**
NE: FG Vinatieri 48, 0:00. **New England 20-17.**
A: 72,922.

XXXVII - 2003

Tampa Bay	3	17	14	14—48
Oakland	3	0	6	12—21

FIRST QUARTER: Oak: FG Janikowski 40, 10:20. **Oakland 3-0.**
TB: FG Gramatica 31, 7:51. **3-3.**

SECOND QUARTER: TB: FG Gramatica 43, 11:16. **Tampa Bay 6-3.**
TB: Alstott 2 run (Gramatica kick), 6:24. **Tampa Bay 13-3.**
TB: McCardell 5 pass from B. Johnson (Gramatica kick), 0:30. **Tampa Bay 20-3.**

THIRD QUARTER: TB: McCardell 8 pass from B. Johnson (Gramatica kick), 5:30. **Tampa Bay 27-3.**
TB: Smith 44 int. return (Gramatica kick), 4:47. **Tampa Bay 34-3.**
Oak: Porter 39 pass from Gannon (2-pt conv failed), 2:14. **Tampa Bay 34-9.**

FOURTH QUARTER: Oak: Johnson 13 return of blocked punt (2-pt. conversion failed), 14:14. **Tampa Bay 34-15.**
Oak: Rice 48 pass from Gannon (2-pt conv failed), 6:06. **Tampa Bay 34-21.**
TB: Brooks 44 int. return (Gramatica kick), 1:18. **Tampa Bay 41-21.**
TB: Smith 50 int. return (Gramatica kick), 0:02. **Tampa Bay 48-21.**
A: 67,603.

XXXVIII - 2004

New England	0	14	0	18—32
Carolina	0	10	0	19—29

SECOND QUARTER: NE: Branch 5 pass from Brady (Vinatieri kick), 3:11. **New England 7-0.**
Car: Smith 39 pass from Delhomme (Kasay kick), 1:17. **7-7.**
NE: Givens 5 pass from Brady (Vinatieri kick), 0:28. **New England 14-7.**
Car: FG Kasay 50, 0:00. **New England 14-10.**

XXXVIII - 2004 *(Cont.)*

FOURTH QUARTER: NE: Smith 2 run (Vinatieri kick), 14:49. **New England 21-10.**
Car: Foster 33 run (2-pt conv failed), 12:49. **New England 21-16.**
Car: Muhammad 85 pass from Delhomme (2-pt conv failed), 7:13. **Carolina 22-21.**
NE: Vrabel 1 pass from Brady (Faulk ran for 2-pt conv), 2:51. **New England 29-22.**
Car: Proehl 12 pass from Delhomme (Kasay kick), 1:18. **29-29.**
NE: FG Vinatieri 41, 0:04. **New England 32-29.**
A: 71,525.

XXXIX - 2005

New England	0	7	7	10—24
Philadelphia	0	7	7	7—21

SECOND QUARTER: Phil: Smith 6 pass from McNabb (Akers kick), 10:05. **Philadelphia 7-0.**
NE: Givens 4 pass from Brady (Vinatieri kick), 1:10. **7-7.**

THIRD QUARTER: NE: Vrabel 2 pass from Brady (Vinatieri kick), 11:04. **New England 14-7.**
Phil: Westbrook 10 pass from McNabb (Akers kick), 3:35. **14-14.**

FOURTH QUARTER: NE: Dillon 2 run (Vinatieri kick), 13:44. **New England 21-14.**
NE: FG Vinatieri 22, 8:40. **New England 24-14.**
Phil: Lewis 30 pass from McNabb (Akers kick), 1:48. **New England 24-21.**

A: 78,125.

XL - 2006

Pittsburgh	0	7	7	7—21
Seattle	3	0	7	0—10

FIRST QUARTER: Sea: FG Brown 47, 0:22. **Seattle 3-0.**

SECOND QUARTER: Pit: Roethlisberger 1 run (Reed kick), 1:55. **Pittsburgh 7-3.**

THIRD QUARTER: Pit: Parker 75 run (Reed kick) , 14:38. **Pittsburgh 14-3.**
Sea: Stevens 16 pass from Hasselbeck (Brown kick), 6:45. **Pittsburgh 14-10.**

FOURTH QUARTER: Pit: Ward 43 pass from Randle El (Reed kick), 8:56. **Pittsburgh 21-10.**

A: 68,206.

XLI - 2007

Indianapolis	6	10	6	7—29
Chicago	14	0	3	0—17

FIRST QUARTER: Chi: TD Hester 92 kick return (Gould kick)14:46. **Chicago 7-0.**
Ind: TD Wayne 53 pass from Manning, 6:50 (Vinatieri kick failed). **Chicago 7-6.**
Chi: TD Muhammad 4 pass from Grossman (Gould kick), 4:34. **Chicago 14-6.**

SECOND QUARTER: Ind: FG Vinatieri 29, 11:17. **Chicago 14-9.**
Ind: TD Rhodes 1 run (Vinatieri kick), 6:09. **Indianapolis 16-14.**

THIRD QUARTER: Indi FG Vinatieri 24, 7:26. **Indianapolis 19-14.**
Ind: FG Vinatieri 20, 3:16. **Indianapolis 22-14.**
Chi: FG Gould 44, 1:14. **Indianapolis 22-17.**

XLI - 2007 *(Cont.)*

FOURTH QUARTER: Ind: TD Hayden 56 interception return (Vinatieri kick) 11:44. **Indianapolis 29-17.**
A: 74,512.

XLII - 2008

NY Giants	3	0	0	14—17
New England	0	7	0	7—14

FIRST QUARTER: NYG: FG Tynes 32, 5:01. **NY Giants 3-0.**

SECOND QUARTER: NE: TD Maroney 1 run (Gostkowski kick), 14:57. **New England 7-3.**

FOURTH QUARTER: NYG: TD Tyree 5 pass from Manning (Tynes kick), 11:05. **NY Giants 10-7.**
NE: TD Moss 6 pass from Brady (Gostkowski kick), 2:42. **New England 14-10.**
NYG: TD Burress 13 pass from Manning (Tynes kick), 0:35. **NY Giants 17-14.**
A: 71,101.

XLIII - 2009

Pittsburgh	3	14	3	7—27
Arizona	0	7	0	16—23

FIRST QUARTER: Pit: FG Reed 18, 9:45. **Pittsburgh 3-0.**

SECOND QUARTER: Pit: Russell 1 run (Reed kick), 14:01. **Pittsburgh 10-0.**
Ari: Patrick 1 pass from Warner (Rackers kick), 8:34. **Pittsburgh 10-7.**
Pit: Harrison 100 Int return (Rackers kick), 0:00. **Pittsburgh 17-7.**

THIRD QUARTER: Pit: FG Reed 21, 2:11. **Pittsburgh 20-7.**

FOURTH QUARTER: Ari: Fitzgerald 1 pass from Warner (Rackers kick), 7:33. **Pittsburgh 20-14.**
Ari: Safety (Hartwig offensive holding penalty in end zone), 2:58. **Pittsburgh 20-16.**
Ari: Fitzgerald 64 pass from Warner (Rackers kick), 2:37. **Arizona 23-20.**
Pit: Holmes 6 pass from Roethlisberger (Reed kick), 0:35. **Pittsburgh 27-23.**
A: 70,774.

XLIV - 2010

New Orleans	0	6	10	15—31
Indianapolis	10	0	7	0—17

FIRST QUARTER: Ind: FG Stover 38, 7:29. **Indianapolis 3-0.**
Ind: TD Garcon 19 pass from Manning (Stover kick), 0:36. **Indianapolis 10-0.**

SECOND QUARTER: NO: FG Hartley 46, 9:34. **Indianapolis 10-3.**
NO: FG Hartley 44, 0:00. **Indianapolis 10-6.**

THIRD QUARTER: NO: TD Thomas 16 pass from Brees (Hartley kick), 11:41. **New Orleans 13-10.**
Ind: TD Addai 4 run (Stover kick), 6:15. **Indianapolis 17-13.**
NO: FG Hartley 47, 2:01. **Indianapolis 17-16.**

FOURTH QUARTER: NO: TD Shockey 2 pass from Brees (Moore 2 pass from Brees for 2-pt conv), 5:42. **New Orleans 24-17.**
NO: TD Porter 74 interception return (Hartley kick), 3:12. **New Orleans 31-17.**
A: 74,059.

XLV - 2011

Pittsburgh	0	10	7	8—25
Green Bay	14	7	0	10—31

FIRST QUARTER: GB: TD Nelson 29 pass from Rodgers (Crosby kick), 3:44. **Green Bay 7-0.**
GB TD Collins 37 interception return (Crosby kick), 3:20. **Green Bay 14-0.**

SECOND QUARTER: Pit: FG Suisham 33, 11:08. **Green Bay 14-3.**
GB: TD Jennings 21 pass from Rodgers (Crosby kick), 2:24. **Green Bay 21-3.**
Pit: TD Ward 8 pass from Roethlisberger (Suisham kick), 0:39. **Green Bay 21-10.**

THIRD QUARTER: Pit: TD Mendenhall 8 run (Suisham kick), 10:19. **Green Bay 21-17.**

FOURTH QUARTER: GB: TD Jennings 8 pass from Rodgers (Crosby kick), 11:57. **Green Bay 28-17.**
Pit: TD Wallace 25 pass from Roethlisberger (Randle El 2 pass for 2-pt. conv), 7:34.
Green Bay 28-25.
GB: FG Crosby 23, 2:07. **Green Bay 31-25.**
A: 103,219.

XLVI - 2012

New England	0	10	7	0—17
NY Giants	9	0	6	6—21

FIRST QUARTER: NYG: Safety (Brady called for intentional grounding in end zone), 8:52. **NY Giants 2-0.**
NYG: TD Cruz 2 pass from Manning (Tynes kick), 3:24. **NY Giants 9-0.**

SECOND QUARTER: NE FG Gostkowski 29, 13:48. **NY Giants 9-3.**
NE: TD Woodhead 4 pass from Brady (Gostkowski kick), 0:08. **New England 10-9.**

THIRD QUARTER: NE: TD Hernandez 12 pass from Brady (Gostkowski kick), 11:20. **New England 17-9.**
NYG: FG Tynes 38, 6:43. **New England 17-12.**
NYG: FG Tynes 33, 0:35. **New England 17-15.**

FOURTH QUARTER: NYG: TD Bradshaw 6 run (2-pt conv failed), 0:57. **NY Giants 21-17.**
A: 68,658.

1933
NFL championship Chicago Bears 23, NY Giants 21
1934
NFL championship NY Giants 30, Chicago Bears 13
1935
NFL championship Detroit 26, NY Giants 7
1936
NFL championship Green Bay 21, Boston 6
1937
NFL championship Washington 28, Chicago Bears 21
1938
NFL championship NY Giants 23, Green Bay 17
1939
NFL championship Green Bay 27, NY Giants 0
1940
NFL championship Chicago Bears 73, Washington 0
1941
W. div. playoff Chicago Bears 33, Green Bay 14
NFL championship Chicago Bears 37, NY Giants 9
1942
NFL championship Washington 14, Chicago Bears 6
1943
E. div. playoff Washington 28, NY Giants 0
NFL championship Chicago Bears 41, Washington 21
1944
NFL championship Green Bay 14, NY Giants 7
1945
NFL championship Cleveland 15, Washington 14
1946
NFL championship Chicago Bears 24, NY Giants 14
1947
E. div. playoff Philadelphia 21, Pittsburgh 0
NFL championship Chi Cardinals 28, Philadelphia 21
1948
NFL championship Philadelphia 7, Chi Cardinals 0
1949
NFL championship Philadelphia 14, Los Angeles 0
1950
Am. Conf. playoff Cleveland 8, NY Giants 3
Nat. Conf. playoff Los Angeles 24, Chicago Bears 14
NFL championship Cleveland 30, Los Angeles 28
1951
NFL championship Los Angeles 24, Cleveland 17
1952
Nat. Conf. playoff Detroit 31, Los Angeles 21
NFL championship Detroit 17, Cleveland 7
1953
NFL championship Detroit 17, Cleveland 16
1954
NFL championship Cleveland 56, Detroit 10
1955
NFL championship Cleveland 38, Los Angeles 14
1956
NFL championship NY Giants 47, Chicago Bears 7
1957
W. Conf. playoff Detroit 31, San Francisco 27
NFL championship Detroit 59, Cleveland 14
1958
E. Conf. playoff NY Giants 10, Cleveland 0
NFL championship Baltimore 23, NY Giants 17
1959
NFL championship Baltimore 31, NY Giants 16

1960
NFL championship Philadelphia 17, Green Bay 13
AFL championship Houston 24, LA Chargers 16
1961
NFL championship Green Bay 37, NY Giants 0
AFL championship Houston 10, San Diego 3
1962
NFL championship Green Bay 16, NY Giants 7
AFL championship Dallas Texans 20, Houston 17
1963
NFL championship Chicago 14, NY Giants 10
AFL E. div. playoff Boston 26, Buffalo 8
AFL championship San Diego 51, Boston 10
1964
NFL championship Cleveland 27, Baltimore 0
AFL championship Buffalo 20, San Diego 7
1965
NFL W. Conf. Green Bay 13, Baltimore 10
playoff
NFL championship Green Bay 23, Cleveland 12
AFL championship Buffalo 23, San Diego 0
1966
NFL championship Green Bay 34, Dallas 27
AFL championship Kansas City 31, Buffalo 7
1967
NFL E. Conf. Dallas 52, Cleveland 14
championship
NFL W. Conf. Green Bay 28, Los Angeles 7
championship
NFL championship Green Bay 21, Dallas 17
AFL championship Oakland 40, Houston 7
1968
NFL E. Conf. Cleveland 31, Dallas 20
championship
NFL W. Conf. Baltimore 24, Minnesota 14
championship
NFL championship Baltimore 34, Cleveland 0
AFL W. div. playoff Oakland 41, Kansas City 6
AFL championship NY Jets 27, Oakland 23
1969
NFL E. Conf. Cleveland 38, Dallas 14
championship
NFL W. Conf. Minnesota 23, Los Angeles 20
championship
NFL championship Minnesota 27, Cleveland 7
AFL div. playoffs Kansas City 13, NY Jets 6
Oakland 56, Houston 7
AFL championship Kansas City 17, Oakland 7
1970
AFC div. playoffs Baltimore 17, Cincinnati 0
Oakland 21, Miami 14
AFC championship Baltimore 27, Oakland 17
NFC div. playoffs Dallas 5, Detroit 0
San Francisco 17, Minnesota 14
NFC championship Dallas 17, San Francisco 10
1971
AFC div. playoffs Miami 27, Kansas City 24
Baltimore 20, Cleveland 3
AFC championship Miami 21, Baltimore 0
NFC div. playoffs Dallas 20, Minnesota 12
San Francisco 24, Washington 20
NFC championship Dallas 14, San Francisco 3
1972
AFC div. playoffs Pittsburgh 13, Oakland 7
Miami 20, Cleveland 14
AFC championship Miami 21, Pittsburgh 17

1972 *(Cont.)*

NFC div. playoffs	Dallas 30, San Francisco 28
	Washington 16, Green Bay 3
NFC championship	Washington 26, Dallas 3

1973

AFC div. playoffs	Oakland 33, Pittsburgh 14
	Miami 34, Cincinnati 16
AFC championship	Miami 27, Oakland 10
NFC div. playoffs	Minnesota 27, Washington 20
	Dallas 27, Los Angeles 16
NFC championship	Minnesota 27, Dallas 10

1974

AFC div. playoffs	Oakland 28, Miami 26
	Pittsburgh 32, Buffalo 14
AFC championship	Pittsburgh 24, Oakland 13
NFC div. playoffs	Minnesota 30, St Louis 14
	Los Angeles 19, Washington 10
NFC championship	Minnesota 14, Los Angeles 10

1975

AFC div. playoffs	Pittsburgh 28, Baltimore 10
	Oakland 31, Cincinnati 28
AFC championship	Pittsburgh 16, Oakland 10
NFC div. playoffs	Los Angeles 35, St Louis 23
	Dallas 17, Minnesota 14
NFC championship	Dallas 37, Los Angeles 7

1976

AFC div. playoffs	Oakland 24, New England 21
	Pittsburgh 40, Baltimore 14
AFC championship	Oakland 24, Pittsburgh 7
NFC div. playoffs	Minnesota 35, Washington 20
	Los Angeles 14, Dallas 12
NFC championship	Minnesota 24, Los Angeles 13

1977

AFC div. playoffs	Denver 34, Pittsburgh 21
	Oakland 37, Baltimore 31
AFC championship	Denver 20, Oakland 17
NFC div. playoffs	Dallas 37, Chicago 7
	Minnesota 14, Los Angeles 7
NFC championship	Dallas 23, Minnesota 6

1978

AFC 1st-rd. playoff	Houston 17, Miami 9
AFC div. playoffs	Houston 31, New England 14
	Pittsburgh 33, Denver 10
AFC championship	Pittsburgh 34, Houston 5
NFC 1st-rd. playoff	Atlanta 14, Philadelphia 13
NFC div. playoffs	Dallas 27, Atlanta 20
	Los Angeles 34, Minnesota 10
NFC championship	Dallas 28, Los Angeles 0

1979

AFC 1st-rd. playoff	Houston 13, Denver 7
AFC div. playoffs	Houston 17, San Diego 14
	Pittsburgh 34, Miami 14
AFC championship	Pittsburgh 27, Houston 13
NFC 1st-rd. playoff	Philadelphia 27, Chicago 17
NFC div. playoffs	Tampa Bay 24, Philadelphia 17
	Los Angeles 21, Dallas 19
NFC championship	Los Angeles 9, Tampa Bay 0

1980

AFC 1st-rd. playoff	Oakland 27, Houston 7
AFC div. playoffs	San Diego 20, Buffalo 14
	Oakland 14, Cleveland 12
AFC championship	Oakland 34, San Diego 27
NFC 1st-rd. playoff	Dallas 34, Los Angeles 13
NFC div. playoffs	Philadelphia 31, Minnesota 16
	Dallas 30, Atlanta 27
NFC championship	Philadelphia 20, Dallas 7

1981

AFC 1st-rd. playoff	Buffalo 31, NY Jets 27
AFC div. playoffs	San Diego 41, Miami 38
	Cincinnati 28, Buffalo 21
AFC championship	Cincinnati 27, San Diego 7
NFC 1st-rd. playoff	NY Giants 27, Philadelphia 21
NFC div. playoffs	Dallas 38, Tampa Bay 0
	San Francisco 38, NY Giants 24
NFC championship	San Francisco 28, Dallas 27

1982

AFC 1st-rd. playoffs	Miami 28, New England 13
	LA Raiders 27, Cleveland 10
	NY Jets 44, Cincinnati 17
	San Diego 31, Pittsburgh 28
AFC div. playoffs	NY Jets 17, LA Raiders 14
	Miami 34, San Diego 13
AFC championship	Miami 14, NY Jets 0
NFC 1st-rd. playoffs	Washington 31, Detroit 7
	Green Bay 41, St Louis 16
	Minnesota 30, Atlanta 24
	Dallas 30, Tampa Bay 17
NFC div. playoffs	Washington 21, Minnesota 7
	Dallas 37, Green Bay 26
NFC championship	Washington 31, Dallas 17

1983

AFC 1st-rd. playoff	Seattle 31, Denver 7
AFC div. playoffs	Seattle 27, Miami 20
	LA Raiders 38, Pittsburgh 10
AFC championship	LA Raiders 30, Seattle 14
NFC 1st-rd. playoff	LA Rams 24, Dallas 17
NFC div. playoffs	San Francisco 24, Detroit 23
	Washington 51, LA Rams 7
NFC championship	Washington 24, San Francisco 21

1984

AFC 1st-rd. playoff	Seattle 13, LA Raiders 7
AFC div. playoffs	Miami 31, Seattle 10
	Pittsburgh 24, Denver 17
AFC championship	Miami 45, Pittsburgh 28
NFC 1st-rd. playoff	NY Giants 16, LA Rams 13
NFC div. playoffs	San Francisco 21, NY Giants 10
	Chicago 23, Washington 19
NFC championship	San Francisco 23, Chicago 0

1985

AFC 1st-rd. playoff	New England 26, NY Jets 14
AFC div. playoffs	Miami 24, Cleveland 21
	New England 27, LA Raiders 20
AFC championship	New England 31, Miami 14
NFC 1st-rd. playoff	NY Giants 17, San Francisco 3
NFC div. playoffs	LA Rams 20, Dallas 0
	Chicago 21, NY Giants 0
NFC championship	Chicago 24, LA Rams 0

1986

AFC 1st-rd. playoff	NY Jets 35, Kansas City 15
AFC div. playoffs	Cleveland 23, NY Jets 20
	Denver 22, New England 17
AFC championship	Denver 23, Cleveland 20
NFC 1st-rd. playoff	Washington 19, LA Rams 7
NFC div playoffs	Washington 27, Chicago 13
	NY Giants 49, San Francisco 3
NFC championship	NY Giants 17, Washington 0

1987

AFC 1st-rd. playoff	Houston 23, Seattle 20
AFC div. playoffs	Cleveland 38, Indianapolis 21
	Denver 34, Houston 10
AFC championship	Denver 38, Cleveland 33
NFC 1st-rd. playoff	Minnesota 44, New Orleans 10
NFC div playoffs	Minnesota 36, San Francisco 24
	Washington 21, Chicago 17
NFC championship	Washington 17, Minnesota 10

1988

AFC 1st-rd. playoff	Houston 24, Cleveland 23
AFC div. playoffs	Cincinnati 21, Seattle 13
	Buffalo 17, Houston 10
AFC championship	Cincinnati 21, Buffalo 10
NFC 1st-rd. playoff	Minnesota 28, LA Rams 17
NFC div. playoffs	Chicago 20, Philadelphia 12
	San Francisco 34, Minnesota 9
NFC championship	San Francisco 28, Chicago 3

1989

AFC 1st-rd. playoff	Pittsburgh 26, Houston 23
AFC div. playoffs	Cleveland 34, Buffalo 30
	Denver 24, Pittsburgh 23
AFC championship	Denver 37, Cleveland 21
NFC 1st-rd. playoff	LA Rams 21, Philadelphia 7
NFC div. playoffs	LA Rams 19, NY Giants 13
	San Francisco 41, Minnesota 13
NFC championship	San Francisco 30, LA Rams 3

1990

AFC 1st-rd. playoffs	Miami 17, Kansas City 16
	Cincinnati 41, Houston 14
AFC div. playoffs	Buffalo 44, Miami 34
	LA Raiders 20, Cincinnati 10
AFC championship	Buffalo 51, LA Raiders 3
NFC 1st-rd. playoffs	Chicago 16, New Orleans 6
	Washington 20, Philadelphia 6
NFC div. playoffs	NY Giants 31, Chicago 3
	San Francisco 28, Washington 10
NFC championship	NY Giants 15, San Francisco 13

1991

AFC 1st-rd. playoffs	Houston 17, NY Jets 10
	Kansas City 10, LA Raiders 6
AFC div. playoffs	Denver 26, Houston 24
	Buffalo 37, Kansas City 14
AFC championship	Buffalo 10, Denver 7
NFC 1st-rd. playoffs	Atlanta 27, New Orleans 20
	Dallas 17, Chicago 13
NFC div. playoffs	Washington 24, Atlanta 7
	Detroit 38, Dallas 6
NFC championship	Washington 41, Detroit 10

1992

AFC 1st-rd. playoffs	San Diego 17, Kansas City 0
	Buffalo 41, Houston 38 (OT)
AFC div. playoffs	Buffalo 24, Pittsburgh 3
	Miami 31, San Diego 0
AFC championship	Buffalo 29, Miami 10
NFC 1st-rd. playoffs	Washington 24, Minnesota 7
	Philadelphia 36, New Orleans 20
NFC div. playoffs	San Francisco 20, Washington 13
	Dallas 34, Philadelphia 10
NFC championship	Dallas 30, San Francisco 20

1993

AFC 1st-rd. playoffs	LA Raiders 42, Denver 24
	Kansas City 27, Pittsburgh 24 (OT)
AFC div. playoffs	Buffalo 29, LA Raiders 23
	Kansas City 28, Houston 20
AFC championship	Buffalo 30, Kansas City 13
NFC 1st-rd. playoffs	NY Giants 17, Minnesota 10
	Green Bay 28, Detroit 24
NFC div. playoffs	San Francisco 44, NY Giants 3
	Dallas 27, Green Bay 17
NFC championship	Dallas 38, San Francisco 21

1994

AFC 1st-rd. playoffs	Miami 27, Kansas City 17
	Cleveland 20, New England 13
AFC div. playoffs	San Diego 22, Miami 21
	Pittsburgh 29, Cleveland 9
AFC championship	San Diego 17, Pittsburgh 13
NFC 1st-rd. playoffs	Green Bay 16, Detroit 12
	Chicago 35, Minnesota 18

1994 *(Cont.)*

NFC div. playoffs	Dallas 35, Green Bay 9
	San Francisco 44, Chicago 15
NFC championship	San Francisco 38, Dallas 28

1995

AFC 1st-rd. playoffs	Buffalo 37, Miami 22
	Indianapolis 35, San Diego 20
AFC div. playoffs	Pittsburgh 40, Buffalo 21
	Indianapolis 10, Kansas City 7
AFC championship	Pittsburgh 20, Indianapolis 16
NFC 1st-rd. playoffs	Philadelphia 58, Detroit 37
	Green Bay 37, Atlanta 20
NFC div. playoffs	Dallas 30, Philadelphia 11
	Green Bay 27, San Francisco 17
NFC championship	Dallas 38, Green Bay 27

1996

AFC 1st-rd. playoffs	Jacksonville 30, Buffalo 27
	Pittsburgh 42, Indianapolis 14
AFC div. playoffs	Jacksonville 30, Denver 27
	New England 28, Pittsburgh 3
AFC championship	New England 20, Jacksonville 6
NFC 1st-rd. playoffs	Dallas 40, Minnesota 15
	San Francisco 14, Philadelphia 0
NFC div. playoffs	Green Bay 35, San Francisco 14
	Carolina 26, Dallas 17
NFC championship	Green Bay 30, Carolina 13

1997

AFC 1st-rd. playoffs	Denver 42, Jacksonville 17
	New England 17, Miami 3
AFC div. playoffs	Denver 14, Kansas City 0
	Pittsburgh 7, New England 6
AFC championship	Denver 24, Pittsburgh 21
NFC 1st-rd. playoffs	Minnesota 23, NY Giants 22
	Tampa Bay 20, Detroit 10
NFC div. playoffs	Green Bay 21, Tampa Bay 7
	San Francisco 38, Minnesota 22
NFC championship	Green Bay 23, San Francisco 10

1998

AFC 1st-rd. playoffs	Miami 24, Buffalo 17
	Jacksonville 25, New England 10
AFC div. playoffs	Denver 38, Miami 3
	NY Jets 34, Jacksonville 24
AFC championship	Denver 23, NY Jets 10
NFC 1st-rd. playoffs	Arizona 20, Dallas 7
	San Francisco 30, Green Bay 27
NFC div. playoffs	Atlanta 20, San Francisco 18
	Minnesota 41, Arizona 21
NFC championship	Atlanta 30, Minnesota 27 (OT)

1999

AFC 1st-rd. playoffs	Tennessee 22, Buffalo 16
	Miami 20, Seattle 17
AFC div. playoffs	Jacksonville 62, Miami 7
	Tennessee 19, Indianapolis 16
AFC championship	Tennessee 33, Jacksonville 14
NFC 1st-rd. playoffs	Washington 27, Detroit 13
	Minnesota 27, Dallas 10
NFC div. playoffs	Tampa Bay 14, Washington 13
	St Louis 49, Minnesota 37
NFC championship	St Louis 11, Tampa Bay 6

2000

AFC 1st-rd. playoffs	Baltimore 21, Denver 3
	Miami 23, Indianapolis 17 (OT)
AFC div. playoffs	Baltimore 24, Tennessee 10
	Oakland 27, Miami 0
AFC championship	Baltimore 16, Oakland 3
NFC 1st-rd. playoffs	New Orleans 31, St. Louis 28
	Philadelphia 21, Tampa Bay 3
NFC div. playoffs	NY Giants 20, Philadelphia 10
	Minnesota 34, New Orleans 16
NFC championship	NY Giants 41, Minnesota 0

2001

AFC 1st-rd. playoffs	Oakland 38, NY Jets 24
	Baltimore 20, Miami 3
AFC div. playoffs	New England 16, Oakland 13 (OT)
	Pittsburgh 27, Baltimore 10
AFC championship	New England 24, Pittsburgh 17
NFC 1st-rd. playoffs	Philadelphia 31, Tampa Bay 9
	Green Bay 25, San Francisco 15
NFC div. playoffs	Philadelphia 33, Chicago 19
	St. Louis 45, Green Bay 17
NFC championship	St. Louis 29, Philadelphia 24

2002

AFC 1st-rd. playoffs	NY Jets 41, Indianapolis 0
	Pittsburgh 36, Cleveland 33
AFC div. playoffs	Tennessee 34, Pittsburgh 31 (OT)
	Oakland 30, NY Jets 10
AFC championship	Oakland 41, Tennessee 24
NFC 1st-rd. playoffs	Atlanta 27, Green Bay 7
	San Francisco 39, NY Giants 38
NFC div. playoffs	Philadelphia 20, Atlanta 6
	Tampa Bay 31, San Francisco 6
NFC championship	Tampa Bay 27, Philadelphia 10

2003

AFC 1st-rd. playoffs	Tennessee 20, Baltimore 17
	Indianapolis 41, Denver 10
AFC div. playoffs	New England 17, Tennessee 14
	Indianapolis 38, Kansas City 31
AFC championship	New England 24, Indianapolis 14
NFC 1st-rd. playoffs	Carolina 29, Dallas 10
	Green Bay 37, Seattle 31 (OT)
NFC div. playoffs	Carolina 29, St. Louis 23
	Philadelphia 20, Green Bay 17 (OT)
NFC championship	Carolina 14, Philadelphia 3

2004

AFC 1st-rd. playoffs	Indianapolis 49, Denver 24
	NY Jets 20, San Diego 17
AFC div. playoffs	New England 20, Indianapolis 3
	Pittsburgh 20, NY Jets 17
AFC championship	New England 41, Pittsburgh 27
NFC 1st-rd. playoffs	Minnesota 31, Green Bay 17
	St. Louis 27, Seattle 20
NFC div. playoffs	Atlanta 47, St. Louis 17
	Philadelphia 27, Minnesota 14
NFC championship	Philadelphia 27, Atlanta 10

2005

AFC 1st-rd. playoffs	Pittsburgh 31, Cincinnati 17
	New England 28, Jacksonville 3
AFC div. playoffs	Pittsburgh 21, Indianapolis 18
	Denver 27, New England 13
AFC championship	Pittsburgh 34, Denver 17
NFC 1st-rd. playoffs	Washington 17, Tampa Bay 10
	Carolina 23, NY Giants 0
NFC div. playoffs	Seattle 20, Washington 10
	Carolina 29, Chicago 21
NFC championship	Seattle 34, Carolina 14

2006

AFC 1st-rd. playoffs	Indianapolis 23, Kansas City 8
	New England 37, NY Jets 16
AFC div. playoffs	Indianapolis 15, Baltimore 6
	New England 24, San Diego 21
AFC championship	Indianapolis 38, New England 34
NFC 1st-rd. playoffs	Seattle 21, Dallas 20
	Philadelphia 23, NY Giants 20
NFC div. playoffs	Chicago 27, Seattle 24
	New Orleans 27, Philadelphia 24
NFC championship	Chicago 39, New Orleans 14

2007

AFC 1st-rd. playoffs	Jacksonville 31, Pittsburgh 29
	San Diego 17, Tennessee 6
AFC div. Playoffs	New England 31, Jacksonville 20
	San Diego 28, Indianapolis 24
AFC championship	New England 21, San Diego 12
NFC 1st-rd. playoffs	Seattle 35, Washington 14
	NY Giants 24, Tampa Bay 14
NFC div. Playoffs	NY Giants 21, Dallas 17
	Green Bay 42, Seattle 20
NFC championship	NY Giants 23, Green Bay 20 (OT)

2008

AFC 1st-rd. playoffs	Baltimore 27, Miami 9
	San Diego 23, Indianapolis 17 (OT)
AFC div. Playoffs	Baltimore 13, Tennessee 10
	Pittsburgh 35, San Diego 24
AFC championship	Pittsburgh 23, Baltimore 14
NFC 1st-rd. playoffs	Philadelphia 26, Minnesota 14
	Arizona 30, Atlanta 24
NFC div. Playoffs	Philadelphia 23, NY Giants 11
	Arizona 33, Carolina 13
NFC championship	Arizona 32, Philadelphia 25

2009

AFC 1st-rd. playoffs	NY Jets 24, Cincinnati 14
	Baltimore 33, New England 14
AFC div. Playoffs	NY Jets 17, San Diego 14
	Indianapolis 20, Baltimore 3
AFC championship	Indianapolis 30, NY Jets 17
NFC 1st-rd. playoffs	Dallas 34, Philadelphia 14
	Arizona 51, Green Bay 45 (OT)
NFC div. Playoffs	Minnesota 34, Dallas 3
	New Orleans 45, Arizona 14
NFC championship	New Orleans 31, Minnesota 28 (OT)

2010

AFC 1st-rd. playoffs	NY Jets 17, Indianapolis 16
	Baltimore 30, Kansas City 17
AFC div. Playoffs	NY Jets 28, New England 21
	Pittsburgh 31, Baltimore 24
AFC championship	Pittsburgh 24, NY Jets 19
NFC 1st-rd. playoffs	Seattle 41, New Orleans 36
	Green Bay 21, Philadelphia 16
NFC div. Playoffs	Chicago 35, Seattle 24
	Green Bay 48, Atlanta 21
NFC championship	Green Bay 21, Chicago 14

2011

AFC 1st-rd. playoffs	Houston 31, Cincinnati 10
	Denver 29, Pittsburgh 23
AFC div. Playoffs	New England 45, Denver 10
	Baltimore 20, Houston 13
AFC championship	New England 23, Baltimore 20
NFC 1st-rd. playoffs	New Orleans 45, Detroit 28
	NY Giants 24, Atlanta 2
NFC div. Playoffs	San Francisco 36, New Orleans 32
	NY Giants 37, Green Bay 20
NFC championship	NY Giants 20, San Francisco 17

Career Leaders

Scoring

	Yrs	TD	FG	PAT	Pts
Morten Andersen	25	0	565	849	2,544
Gary Anderson	23	0	538	820	2,434
John Carney	23	0	478	628	2,062
†Jason Hanson	20	0	463	627	2,016
Matt Stover	20	0	471	591	2,004
George Blanda	26	9	335	943	2,002
Jason Elam	17	0	436	675	1,983
†John Kasay	20	0	461	587	1,970
†Adam Vinatieri	16	0	387	589	1,752
Norm Johnson	18	0	366	638	1,736
Nick Lowery	18	0	383	562	1,711
Jan Stenerud	19	0	373	580	1,699
†Ryan Longwell	15	0	361	604	1,687
Lou Groza	21	1	264	810	1,608
Eddie Murray	19	0	352	538	1,594
Al Del Greco	17	0	347	543	1,584
†Olindo Mare	15	0	350	480	1,530
†David Akers	14	0	338	477	1,491
Steve Christie	15	0	336	468	1,476
Pat Leahy	18	0	304	558	1,470

Note: Adam Vinatieri completed one two-point conversion in 1998.

Rushing

	Yrs	Att	Yds	Avg	Lg	TD
Emmitt Smith	15	4,409	18,355	4.2	75	164
Walter Payton	13	3,838	16,726	4.4	76	110
Barry Sanders	10	3,062	15,269	5.0	85	99
Curtis Martin	11	3,518	14,101	4.0	70	90
†LaD. Tomlinson	11	3,174	13,684	4.3	85	144
Jerome Bettis	13	3,479	13,662	3.9	71	91
Eric Dickerson	11	2,996	13,259	4.4	85	90
Tony Dorsett	12	2,936	12,739	4.3	99	77
Jim Brown	9	2,359	12,312	5.2	80	106
Marshall Faulk	12	2,836	12,279	4.3	71	100
Edgerrin James	11	3,028	12,246	4.0	72	80
Marcus Allen	16	3,022	12,243	4.1	61	123
Franco Harris	13	2,949	12,120	4.1	75	91
Thurman Thomas	13	2,877	12,074	4.2	80	66
†Fred Taylor	13	2,534	11,695	4.6	80	66
John Riggins	14	2,916	11,352	3.9	66	104
Corey Dillon	10	2,618	11,241	4.3	96	82
O.J. Simpson	11	2,404	11,236	4.7	94	61
Warrick Dunn	12	2,669	10,967	4.1	90	49
Ricky Watters	10	2,622	10,643	4.1	57	78

Touchdowns

	Yrs	Rush	Rec	Ret	Total TD
Jerry Rice	20	10	197	1	208
Emmitt Smith	15	164	11	0	175
†LaDainian Tomlinson	11	145	17	0	162
Terrell Owens	15	3	153	0	156
Randy Moss	13	0	153	1	154
Marcus Allen	16	123	21	1	145
Marshall Faulk	12	100	36	0	136
Cris Carter	16	0	130	1	131
Marvin Harrison	13	0	128	0	128
Jim Brown	9	106	20	0	126

	Yrs	Rush	Rec	Ret	Total TD
Walter Payton	13	110	15	0	125
John Riggins	14	104	12	0	116
Lenny Moore	12	63	48	2	113
Shaun Alexander	9	100	12	0	112
Barry Sanders	10	99	10	0	109
Tim Brown	17	1	100	4	105
Don Hutson	11	3	99	3	105
Steve Largent	14	1	100	0	101
Curtis Martin	12	90	10	0	100
Franco Harris	13	91	9	0	100

Combined Yards Gained

	Yrs	Total	Rush	Rec	Int Ret	Punt Ret	Kickoff Ret	Fum Ret
Jerry Rice	20	23,546	645	22,895	0	0	6	0
Brian Mitchell	14	23,330	1,967	2,336	0	4,999	14,014	14
Walter Payton	13	21,803	16,726	4,538	0	0	539	0
Emmitt Smith	15	21,583	18,355	3,224	0	0	0	4
Tim Brown	17	19,682	190	14,934	0	3,320	1,235	3
Marshall Faulk	12	19,190	12,279	6,875	0	0	18	18
†LaDainian Tomlinson	11	18,456	13,684	4,772	0	0	0	0
Barry Sanders	10	18,308	15,269	2,921	0	0	118	0
Herschel Walker	12	18,168	8,225	4,859	0	0	5,084	0
Marcus Allen	16	17,654	12,243	5,411	0	0	0	0
Curtis Martin	11	17,430	14,101	3,329	0	0	0	0
Tiki Barber	10	17,359	10,449	5,183	0	1,181	544	2
Eric Metcalf	13	17,230	2,392	5,572	0	3,453	5,813	0
†Derrick Mason	15	17,150	3	12,061	0	1,590	3,496	0
Thurman Thomas	13	16,532	12,074	4,458	0	0	0	0
Tony Dorsett	12	16,293	12,739	3,554	0	0	0	0
Terrell Owens	15	16,263	251	15,934	0	0	78	0
Henry Ellard	16	15,718	50	13,777	0	1,527	364	0
Warrick Dunn	12	15,664	10,967	4,339	0	48	310	0
Edgerrin James	11	15,610	12,246	3,364	0	0	0	0

†Active in 2011.

Career Leaders (Cont.)

Passing

PASSER RATING*

	Yrs	Att	Comp	Pct Comp	Yds	Avg Gain	TD	Pct TD	Int	Pct Int	Rating Pts
†Aaron Rodgers	7	2,113	1,381	65.4	17,366	8.2	132	6.2	38	1.8	104.1
†Tony Romo	8	2,592	1,672	64.5	20,834	8.0	149	5.7	72	2.8	96.9
Steve Young	15	4,149	2,667	64.3	33,124	8.0	232	5.6	107	2.6	96.8
†Tom Brady	12	5,321	3,397	63.8	39,979	7.5	300	5.6	115	2.2	96.4
†Philip Rivers	8	3,037	1,930	63.5	24,285	8.0	163	5.4	78	2.6	95.5
Peyton Manning	13	7,210	4,682	64.9	54,828	7.6	399	5.5	198	2.7	94.9
†Drew Brees	11	5,479	3,613	65.9	40,742	7.4	281	5.1	146	2.7	94.0
Kurt Warner	12	4,070	2,666	65.5	32,344	7.9	208	5.1	128	3.1	93.7
Joe Montana	15	5,391	3,409	63.2	40,551	7.5	273	5.2	139	2.6	92.3
†Matt Schaub	8	2,279	1,466	64.3	17,936	7.9	98	4.3	58	2.5	92.2
†Ben Roethlisberger	8	3,313	2,090	63.1	26,579	8.0	165	5.0	100	3.0	92.1
Chad Pennington	11	2,471	1,632	66.0	17,823	7.2	102	4.1	64	2.6	90.1
†Matt Ryan	4	2,022	1,232	60.9	14,238	7.0	95	4.7	46	2.3	88.4
Daunte Culpepper	11	3,199	2,016	63.0	24,123	7.6	149	4.7	106	3.3	87.8
Jeff Garcia	11	3,676	2,264	61.6	25,537	6.9	161	4.4	83	2.3	87.5
Otto Graham	10	2,626	1,464	55.8	23,584	9.0	174	6.6	135	5.1	86.6
Dan Marino	17	8,358	4,967	59.4	61,361	7.3	420	5.0	252	3.0	86.4
†Carson Palmer	8	3,545	2,223	62.7	25,447	7.2	167	4.7	116	3.3	86.3
Brett Favre	20	10,169	6,300	62.0	71,838	7.1	508	5.0	336	3.3	86.0
Trent Green	11	3,740	2,266	60.6	28,475	7.6	162	4.3	114	3.0	86.0
†Joe Flacco	4	1,958	1,190	60.8	13,816	7.1	80	4.1	46	2.3	86.0
David Garrard	9	2,281	1,406	61.6	16,003	7.0	89	3.9	54	2.4	85.8
†Donovan McNabb	13	5,374	3,170	59.0	37,276	6.9	234	4.4	117	2.2	85.6
Rich Gannon	18	4,206	2,533	60.2	28,743	6.8	180	4.3	104	2.3	84.7
†Jay Cutler	6	2,521	1,541	61.1	18,283	7.3	117	4.6	86	3.4	84.5

*1,500 or more attempts. The passer ratings are based on performance standards established for completion percentage, interception percentage, touchdown percentage and average gain. Passers are allocated points according to how their marks compare with those standards.

PASSING YARDS

	Yrs	Att	Comp	Pct Comp	Yds			Yrs	Att	Comp	Pct Comp	Yds
Brett Favre	20	10,169	6,300	62.0	71,838		†Tom Brady	12	5,321	3,397	63.8	39,979
Dan Marino	17	8,358	4,967	59.4	61,361		Dave Krieg	19	5,311	3,105	58.5	38,147
Peyton Manning	13	7,210	4,682	64.9	54,828		Boomer Esiason	14	5,205	2,969	57.0	37,920
John Elway	16	7,250	4,123	56.9	51,475		†Donovan McNabb	13	5,374	3,170	59.0	37,276
Warren Moon	17	6,823	3,988	58.5	49,325		Jim Kelly	11	4,779	2,874	60.1	35,467
Fran Tarkenton	18	6,467	3,686	57.0	47,003		Jim Everett	12	4,923	2,841	57.7	34,837
Vinny Testaverde	21	6,701	3,787	56.5	46,233		Jim Hart	19	5,076	2,593	51.1	34,665
Drew Bledsoe	14	6,717	3,839	57.2	44,611		Steve DeBerg	17	4,746	2,924	61.6	34,241
Dan Fouts	15	5,604	3,297	58.8	43,040		John Hadl	16	4,687	2,363	50.4	33,503
†Kerry Collins	17	6,261	3,487	55.7	40,922		Phil Simms	14	4,647	2,576	55.4	33,462
†Drew Brees	11	5,479	3,613	65.9	40,742		†Matt Hasselbeck	13	4,797	2,891	60.3	33,150
Joe Montana	15	5,391	3,409	63.2	40,551		Steve Young	15	4,149	2,667	64.3	33,124
Johnny Unitas	18	5,186	2,830	54.6	40,239							

PASSING TOUCHDOWNS

	No.		No.		No.
Brett Favre	508	Dave Krieg	261	Steve Young	232
Dan Marino	420	Sonny Jurgensen	255	John Brodie	214
Peyton Manning	399	Dan Fouts	254	Terry Bradshaw	212
Fran Tarkenton	342	Drew Bledsoe	251	Jim Hart	209
John Elway	300	Boomer Esiason	247	Kurt Warner	208
†Tom Brady	300	John Hadl	244	†Kerry Collins	208
Warren Moon	291	*Y.A. Tittle	242	Randall Cunningham	207
Johnny Unitas	290	Len Dawson	239	Jim Everett	203
†Drew Brees	281	Jim Kelly	237	Roman Gabriel	201
Vinny Testaverde	275	George Blanda	236	Phil Simms	199
Joe Montana	273	†Donovan McNabb	234	Ken Anderson	197

* Includes 30 TDs with Baltimore Colts (1948–49) in All-American Football Conference.

† Active in 2011.

Career Leaders *(Cont.)*

Receiving

RECEPTIONS

	Yrs	No.	Yds	Avg	Lg	TD		Yrs	No.	Yds	Avg	Lg	TD
Jerry Rice	20	1,549	22,895	14.8	96	197	†Reggie Wayne	11	862	11,708	13.6	71	73
†Tony Gonzalez	15	1,149	13,338	11.6	73	95	Muhsin Muhammad	14	860	11,438	13.3	72	62
Marvin Harrison	12	1,102	14,580	13.2	80	128	Irving Fryar	17	851	12,785	15.0	80	84
Cris Carter	16	1,101	13,899	12.6	80	130	Rod Smith	12	849	11,389	13.4	85	68
Tim Brown	17	1,094	14,934	13.7	80	100	Larry Centers	14	827	6,797	8.2	54	28
Terrell Owens	15	1,078	15,934	14.8	98	153	Steve Largent	14	819	13,089	16.0	74	100
Isaac Bruce	16	1,024	15,208	14.9	80	91	Shannon Sharpe	15	815	10,060	12.3	82	62
†Hines Ward	14	1,000	12,083	12.1	85	85	Henry Ellard	16	814	13,777	16.9	81	65
Randy Moss	13	954	14,858	15.6	82	153	Keyshawn Johnson	11	814	10,571	13.0	76	64
Andre Reed	16	951	13,198	13.9	83	87	Marshall Faulk	11	767	6,875	9.0	85	36
†Derrick Mason	15	943	12,061	12.8	79	66	†Chad Ochocinco	11	766	11,059	14.4	82	67
Art Monk	16	940	12,721	13.5	79	68	James Lofton	16	764	14,004	18.3	80	75
Torry Holt	11	920	13,382	14.5	85	74	Eric Moulds	12	764	9,995	13.1	84	49
Keenan McCardell	17	883	11,373	12.9	76	63	Michael Irvin	12	750	11,904	15.9	87	65
Jimmy Smith	13	862	12,287	14.3	75	67	Charlie Joiner	18	750	12,146	16.2	87	65

YARDS

Jerry Rice	22,895	Torry Holt	13,382	†Hines Ward 12,083
Terrell Owens	15,934	†Tony Gonzalez	13,338	†Derrick Mason 12,061
Isaac Bruce	15,208	Andre Reed	13,198	Michael Irvin 11,904
Tim Brown	14,934	Steve Largent	13,089	Don Maynard 11,834
Randy Moss	14,858	Irving Fryar	12,785	Muhsin Muhammad 11,438
Marvin Harrison	14,580	Art Monk	12,721	†Reggie Wayne 11,708
James Lofton	14,004	Jimmy Smith	12,287	Rod Smith 11,389
Cris Carter	13,899	Charlie Joiner	12,146	Keenan McCardell 11,373
Henry Ellard	13,777			

Sacks

Bruce Smith	200.0	†Jason Taylor	139.5
Reggie White	198.0	John Randle	137.5
Kevin Greene	160.0	Richard Dent	137.5
Chris Doleman	150.5	Leslie O'Neal	132.5
Michael Strahan	141.5	Lawrence Taylor	132.5

Note: Stat officially compiled since 1982.

Interceptions

	Yrs	No.	Yds	Avg	Lg	TD
Paul Krause	16	81	1,185	14.6	81	3
Emlen Tunnell	14	79	1,282	16.2	55	4
Rod Woodson	17	71	1,483	20.9	98	12
Dick (Night Train) Lane	14	68	1,207	17.8	80	5
Ken Riley	15	65	596	9.2	66	5
Ronnie Lott	14	63	730	8.5	63	5
Darren Sharper	14	63	1,412	22.4	99	11
Dick LeBeau	14	62	762	12.3	70	3
Dave Brown	15	62	698	11.3	90	5
Emmitt Thomas	13	58	937	16.2	73	5

Punting

	Yrs	No.	Yds	Avg	Lg	Blk
†Shane Lechler	12	933	44,389	47.6	80	3
†Andy Lee	8	723	33,069	45.7	82	3
†Brandon Fields	5	377	17,227	45.7	71	2
†Donnie Jones	8	648	29,379	45.3	80	3
†Mat McBriar	8	494	22,369	45.3	75	3
Sammy Baugh	16	338	15,245	45.1	85	9
†Jon Ryan	6	483	21,713	45.0	77	3
†Mike Scifres	9	492	22,044	44.8	71	5
Tommy Davis	11	511	22,833	44.7	82	2
†Dustin Colquitt	7	574	25,494	44.4	81	3
†Chris Kluwe	7	551	24,446	44.4	70	1
†Brett Kern	4	273	12,109	44.4	68	0

Punt Returns

	Yrs	No.	Yds	Avg	Lg	TD
†Devin Hester	6	206	2,654	12.9	89	12
George McAfee	8	112	1,431	12.8	74	2
Jack Christiansen	8	85	1,084	12.8	89	8
Claude Gibson	5	110	1,381	12.6	85	3
Bill Dudley	9	124	1,515	12.2	96	3
Rick Upchurch	9	248	3,008	12.1	92	8
†Roscoe Parrish	7	135	1,622	12.0	82	3
Desmond Howard	11	244	2,895	11.9	95	8
†Eddie Royal	4	81	967	11.9	85	2
Billy Johnson	14	282	3,317	11.8	87	6

Note: 75 or more returns.

Kickoff Returns

	Yrs	No.	Yds	Avg	Lg	TD
Gale Sayers	7	91	2,781	30.6	103	6
Lynn Chandnois	7	92	2,720	29.6	93	3
Abe Woodson	9	193	5,538	28.7	105	5
Claude (Buddy) Young	6	90	2,514	27.9	104	2
Travis Williams	5	102	2,801	27.5	105	6
Joe Arenas	7	139	3,798	27.3	96	1
Clifton Smith	3	75	2,038	27.2	97	1
Clarence Davis	7	79	2,140	27.1	76	0
†Danieal Manning	6	114	3,067	26.9	83	1
Steve Van Buren	7	76	2,030	26.7	98	3
Lenny Lyles	12	81	2,161	26.7	103	3

Note: 75 or more returns.

† Active in 2011.

Single-Season Leaders

Scoring

POINTS

	Year	TD	PAT	FG	Pts
†LaDainian Tomlinson, SD	2006	31	0	0	186
Paul Hornung, GB	1960	15	41	15	176
Shaun Alexander, Sea	2005	28	0	0	168
†David Akers, SF	2011	0	34	44	166
Gary Anderson, Min	1998	0	59	35	164
Jeff Wilkins, StL	2003	0	46	39	163
Priest Holmes, KC	2003	27	0	0	162
Mark Moseley, Was	1983	0	62	33	161
Marshall Faulk, StL	2000	26	2	0	160
Mike Vanderjagt, Ind	2003	0	46	37	157
Gino Cappelletti, Bos	1964	7	37	25	155
Emmitt Smith, Dal	1995	25	0	0	150
Chip Lohmiller, Was	1991	0	56	31	149
†Stephen Gostkowski, NE	2008	0	40	36	148
†Jay Feely, NYG	2005	0	43	35	148

Note: Faulk's and Cappelletti's totals include two-point conversions.

TOUCHDOWNS

	Year	Rush	Rec	Ret	Total
†LaDainian Tomlinson, SD	2006	28	3	0	31
Shaun Alexander, Sea	2005	27	1	0	28
Priest Holmes, KC	2003	27	0	0	27
Marshall Faulk, StL	2000	18	8	0	26
Emmitt Smith, Dal	1995	25	0	0	25
Priest Holmes, KC	2002	21	3	0	24
John Riggins, Was	1983	24	0	0	24
Randy Moss, NE	2007	0	23	0	23
Terrell Davis, Den	1998	21	2	0	23
Jerry Rice, SF	1987	1	22	0	23
O.J. Simpson, Buf	1975	16	7	0	23

FIELD GOALS

	Year	FGA	FGM
†David Akers	2011	52	44
†Neil Rackers, Ari	2005	42	40
Jeff Wilkins, StL	2003	42	39
†Olindo Mare, Mia	1999	46	39
Mike Vanderjagt, Ind	2003	37	37
†John Kasay, Car	1996	45	37
†Stephen Gostkowski, NE	2008	40	36
Al Del Greco, Ten	1998	39	36
Cary Blanchard, Ind	1996	40	36

Rushing

YARDS GAINED

	Year	Att	Yds	Avg
Eric Dickerson, LA Rams	1984	379	2,105	5.6
Jamal Lewis, Bal	2003	387	2,066	5.3
Barry Sanders, Det	1997	335	2,053	6.1
Terrell Davis, Den	1998	392	2,008	5.1
†Chris Johnson, Ten	2009	358	2,006	5.6
O.J. Simpson, Buf	1973	332	2,003	6.0
Earl Campbell, Hou	1980	373	1,934	5.2
Ahman Green, GB	2003	355	1,883	5.3
Barry Sanders, Det	1994	331	1,883	5.7
Shaun Alexander, Sea	2005	370	1,880	5.1
Jim Brown, Cle	1963	291	1,863	6.4
Tiki Barber, NYG	2005	357	1,860	5.2
†Ricky Williams, Mia	2002	383	1,853	4.8
Walter Payton, Chi	1977	339	1,852	5.5
Jamal Anderson, Atl	1998	410	1,846	4.5

AVERAGE GAIN

	Year	Avg
†Michael Vick, Atl	2006	8.45
Beattie Feathers, Chi	1934	8.44
Randall Cunningham, Phi	1990	7.98
†Michael Vick, Atl	2004	7.50
†Michael Vick, Atl	2002	6.88

Minimum 100 attempts.

TOUCHDOWNS

	Year	No.
†LaDainian Tomlinson, SD	2006	28
Shaun Alexander, Sea	2005	27
Priest Holmes, KC	2003	27
Emmitt Smith, Dal	1995	25
John Riggins, Was	1983	24

Passing

YARDS GAINED

	Year	Att	Comp	Pct	Yds
†Drew Brees, NO	2011	657	468	71.2	5,476
†Tom Brady, NE	2011	611	401	65.6	5,235
Dan Marino, Mia	1984	564	362	64.2	5,084
†Drew Brees, NO	2008	635	413	65.0	5,069
†Matthew Stafford, Det	2011	663	421	63.5	5,038
†Eli Manning, NYG	2011	589	359	61.0	4,933
Kurt Warner, StL	2001	546	375	68.7	4,830
†Tom Brady, NE	2007	578	398	68.9	4,806
Dan Fouts, SD	1981	609	360	59.1	4,802
†Matt Schaub, Hou	2009	583	396	67.9	4,770
Dan Marino, Mia	1986	623	378	60.7	4,746
D. Culpepper, Min	2004	548	379	69.2	4,717
Dan Fouts, SD	1980	589	348	59.1	4,715
†Philip Rivers, SD	2010	541	357	66.0	4,710
Peyton Manning, Ind	2010	679	450	66.3	4,700

PASSER RATING

	Year	Rat.
†Aaron Rodgers, GB	2011	122.5
Peyton Manning, Ind	2004	121.1
†Tom Brady, NE	2007	117.2
Steve Young, SF	1994	112.8
Joe Montana, SF	1989	112.4
†Tom Brady, NE	2010	111.0
Daunte Culpepper, Min	2004	110.9

TOUCHDOWNS

	Year	No.
†Tom Brady, NE	2007	50
Peyton Manning, Ind	2004	49
Dan Marino, Mia	1984	48
†Drew Brees, NO	2011	46
†Aaron Rodgers, GB	2011	45
Dan Marino, Mia	1986	44
Kurt Warner, StL	1999	41
†Matthew Stafford, Det	2011	41
Daunte Culpepper, Min	2004	39
Brett Favre, GB	1996	39

† Active in 2011.

Single-Season Leaders *(Cont.)*

Receiving

RECEPTIONS

	Year	No.	Yds
Marvin Harrison, Ind	2002	143	1,722
Herman Moore, Det	1995	123	1,686
†Wes Welker, NE	2009	123	1,348
Cris Carter, Min	1994	122	1,256
Jerry Rice, SF	1995	122	1,848
Cris Carter, Min	1995	122	1,371
Isaac Bruce, StL	1995	119	1,781
Torry Holt, StL	2003	117	1,696
Jimmy Smith, Jac	1999	116	1,636
Marvin Harrison, Ind	1999	115	1,663
†Roddy White, Atl	2010	115	1,389
†Andre Johnson, Hou	2008	115	1,575
Rod Smith, Den	2001	113	1,343

YARDS GAINED

	Year	Yds
Jerry Rice, SF	1995	1,848
Isaac Bruce, StL	1995	1,781
Charley Hennigan, Hou	1961	1,746
Marvin Harrison, Ind	2002	1,722
Torry Holt, StL	2003	1,696

TOUCHDOWNS

	Year	No.
Randy Moss, NE	2007	23
Jerry Rice, SF	1987	22
Mark Clayton, Mia	1984	18
Sterling Sharpe, GB	1994	18

Nine players tied with 17.

All-Purpose Yards

	Year	Run	Rec	Ret	Ttl Yds
†Darren Sproles, NO	2011	603	710	1,383	2,696
†Derrick Mason, Ten	2000	1	895	1,794	2,690
Michael Lewis, NO	2002	15	200	2,432	2,647
†Fred Jackson, Buf	2009	1,062	371	1,083	2,516
†Josh Cribbs, Cle	2009	381	135	1,994	2,510
†Chris Johnson, Ten	2009	2,006	503	0	2,509
Lionel James, SD	1985	516	1,027	992	2,535
Brian Mitchell, Was	1994	311	236	1,930	2,477
Dante Hall, KC	2003	73	423	1,950	2,446
Mack Herron, NE	1974	824	474	1,146	2,444
Gale Sayers, Chi	1966	1,231	447	762	2,440
Terry Metcalf, StL Cards	1975	816	378	1,245	2,439
Marshall Faulk, StL	1999	1,381	1,048	0	2,429
Timmy Brown, Phi	1963	841	487	1,097	2,425
MarTay Jenkins, Ari	2000	-4	219	2,187	2,402

Punting

	Year	No.	Yds	Avg
Sammy Baugh, Was	1940	35	1,799	51.4
†Shane Lechler, Oak	2009	96	4,909	51.1
†Andy Lee, SF	2011	78	3,970	50.9
†Shane Lechler, Oak	2011	78	3,960	50.8
†Donnie Jones, StL	2008	82	4,100	50.0
†Shane Lechler, Oak	2007	73	3,585	49.1
†Mat McBriar, Dal	2008	24	1,175	49.0
Yale Lary, Det	1963	35	1,713	48.9
†Shane Lechler, Oak	2008	90	4,391	48.8
†Brandon Fields, Mia	2011	78	3,810	48.8

Interceptions

	Year	No.
Dick (Night Train) Lane, LA Rams	1952	14
Lester Hayes, Oak	1980	13
Spec Sanders, NY Yanks	1950	13
Dan Sandifer, Was	1948	13

Nine tied with 12.

Sacks

	Year	No.
Michael Strahan, NYG	2001	22.5
Mark Gastineau, NYJ	1984	22.0
†Jared Allen, Min	2011	22.0
Chris Doleman, Min	1989	21.0
Reggie White, Phi	1987	21.0
Lawrence Taylor, NYG	1986	20.5
†DeMarcus Ware, Dal	2008	20.0
Derrick Thomas, KC	1990	20.0
Tim Harris, GB	1989	19.5
†DeMarcus Ware, Dal	2011	19.5

Three tied with 19.0.

Punt Returns

	Year	Avg
Jack Christiansen, Det	1952	21.5
Red Cochran, Chi Cards	1949	20.9
Jerry Davis, Chi Cards	1948	20.9
Bob Hayes, Dal	1968	20.8
Billy Grimes, GB	1950	19.1
Jack Christiansen, Det	1951	19.1

Minimum of 15 returns.

Kickoff Returns

	Year	Avg
Travis Williams, GB	1967	41.1
Gale Sayers, Chi	1967	37.7
Ollie Matson, Chi Cards	1958	35.5
Jim Duncan, Balt Colts	1970	35.4
Lynn Chandnois, Pit	1952	35.2

Minimum of 14 returns.

Single-Game Leaders

Scoring

POINTS

	Date	Pts
Ernie Nevers, Chi Cards vs Chi	11-28-29	40
Gale Sayers, Chi vs SF	12-12-65	36
Dub Jones, Clev vs Chi	11-25-51	36
Paul Hornung, GB vs Balt Colts	10-8-61	33

On Thanksgiving Day, 1929, Nevers scored all the Cardinals' points on six rushing TDs and four PATs. The Cards defeated Red Grange and the Bears, 40–6. Jones and Sayers each rushed for four touchdowns and scored two more on returns in their teams' victories. Hornung scored four touchdowns and kicked 6 PATs and a field goal in a 45-7 win over the Colts.

FIELD GOALS

	Date	No.
†Rob Bironas, Ten vs Hou	10-21-07	8
†Shayne Graham, Cin vs Balt	11-11-07	7
†Billy Cundiff, Dal vs NYG (OT)	9-15-03	7
Chris Boniol, Dal vs GB	11-18-96	7
Rich Karlis, Min vs LA Rams (OT)	11-5-89	7
Jim Bakken, StL Cards vs Pit	9-24-67	7

Bironas was 8 for 8.

Bakken was 7 for 9; Cundiff was 7 for 8; and Karlis, Boniol, and Graham went 7 for 7.

† Active in 2011.

Single-Game Leaders *(Cont.)*

Scoring *(Cont.)*

TOUCHDOWNS

	Date	No.
Gale Sayers, Chi vs SF	12-12-65	6
Dub Jones, Clev vs Chi	11-25-51	6
Ernie Nevers, Chi Cards vs Chi	11-28-29	6
Clinton Portis, Den vs KC	12-07-03	5
Shaun Alexander, Sea vs Min	9-29-02	5
James Stewart, Jac vs Phil	10-12-97	5
Ricky Watters, SF vs NY Giants	1-15-94	5
Jerry Rice, SF vs Atl	10-14-90	5
Kellen Winslow, SD vs Oak	11-22-81	5
Paul Hornung, GB vs Balt Colts	12-12-65	5
Jim Brown, Clev vs Balt Colts	11-1-59	5
Bob Shaw, Chi Cards vs Balt Colts	10-2-50	5

Rushing

YARDS GAINED

	Date	Yds
†Adrian Peterson, Min vs SD	11-4-07	296
Jamal Lewis, Balt vs Cle	9-14-03	295
Jerome Harrison, Cle vs KC	12-20-09	286
Corey Dillon, Cin vs Den	10-22-00	278
Walter Payton, Chi vs Min	11-20-77	275
O.J. Simpson, Buf vs Det	11-25-76	273

CARRIES

	Date	No.
Jamie Morris, Wash vs Cin	12-17-88	45
Rudi Johnson, Cin vs Hou	11-9-03	43
James Wilder, TB vs GB	9-30-84	43
Butch Woolfolk, NYG vs Phil	11-20-83	43
†Ricky Williams, Mia vs Buf	9-21-03	42
Terrell Davis, Den vs Buf (OT)	10-26-97	42
James Wilder, TB vs Pit	10-30-83	42

TOUCHDOWNS

	Date	No.
Ernie Nevers, Chi Cards vs Chi	11-28-29	6
Clinton Portis, Den vs KC	12-7-03	5
James Stewart, Jac vs Phil	10-12-97	5
Ricky Watters, SF vs. NY Giants	1-15-94	5
Jim Brown, Clev vs Balt Colts	11-1-59	5
Jimmie Conzelman, RI vs Evansville	10-15-22	5

Passing

YARDS GAINED

	Date	Yds
N. Van Brocklin, Rams vs NY Yanks	9-28-51	554
Warren Moon, Hou vs KC	12-16-90	527
Boomer Esiason, Ariz vs Wash	11-10-96	522
Dan Marino, Mia vs NYJ	10-23-88	521
†Matthew Stafford, Det vs. GB	1-1-12	520

COMPLETIONS

	Date	No.
Drew Bledsoe, NE vs Min	11-13-94	45
Rich Gannon, Oak vs Pit	9-15-02	43
Vinny Testaverde, NYJ vs Sea	12-6-98	42
Richard Todd, NYJ vs SF	9-21-80	42
†Tony Romo, Dal vs NYG	12-06-09	41
Warren Moon, Hou vs Dal	11-10-91	41
†Colt McCoy, Cle vs. Tenn	10-2-11	40
Peyton Manning, Ind vs Hou	9-12-10	40
Kurt Warner, Ari vs NYJ	9-28-08	40
Marc Bulger, StL Rams vs NYG	10-02-05	40
†Billy Volek, Tenn vs. Oak	12-19-04	40
Brad Johnson, TB vs Chi	11-18-01	40
Phil Simms, NYG vs Cin	10-13-85	40
Ken Anderson, Cin vs SD	12-20-82	40

TOUCHDOWNS

	Date	No.
Joe Kapp, Min vs Balt Colts	9-28-69	7
Y. A. Tittle, NYG vs Wash	10-28-62	7
Adrian Burk, Phil vs Wash	10-17-54	7
Sid Luckman, Chi vs NYG	11-14-43	7
Twenty-six tied at 6		

Receiving

YARDS GAINED

	Date	Yds
Flipper Anderson, LA Rams vs NO	11-26-89	336
Stephone Paige, KC vs SD	12-22-85	309
Jim Benton, Clev vs Det	11-22-45	303
Cloyce Box, Det vs Balt Colts	12-3-50	302
Jimmy Smith, Jax vs Balt Ravens	9-10-00	291

RECEPTIONS

	Date	No.
†Brandon Marshall, Den vs Ind	12-13-09	21
Terrell Owens, SF vs Chi	12-17-00	20
†Brandon Marshall, Den vs SD	9-14-08	18
Tom Fears, Rams vs GB	12-3-50	18
Clark Gaines, NYJ vs SF	9-21-80	17
†Wes Welker, NE vs. Buf	9-25-11	16
Troy Brown, NE vs KC	9-22-02	16
Keenan McCardell, Jax vs Rams	10-20-96	16
Jerry Rice, SF vs Rams	11-20-94	16
Sonny Randle, StL Cards vs NYG	11-4-62	16

† Active in 2011.

Single-Game Leaders (Cont.)

Receiving (Cont.)
TOUCHDOWNS

	Date	No.
Jerry Rice, SF vs Atl	10-14-90	5
Kellen Winslow, SD vs Oak	11-22-81	5
Bob Shaw, Chi Cards vs Balt Colts	10-2-50	5

All-Purpose Yards

	Date	Yds
Glyn Milburn, Den vs Sea	12-10-95	404
†Adrian Peterson, Minn vs. Chi	10-14-07	361
Michael Lewis, NO vs. Wash	10-13-02	356
Tyrone Hughes, NO vs. LA Rams	10-23-94	347
Lionel James, SD vs LA Rai	11-10-85	345

Longest Plays

RUSHING	Opponent	Year	Yds
Tony Dorsett, Dal	Min	1983	99
Ahman Green, GB	Den	2003	98
Bob Gage, Pit	Chi	1949	97
Andy Uram, GB	Chi Cards	1939	97
Corey Dillon, Cin	Det	2001	96
Garrison Hearst, SF	NYJ	1998	96
Jim Spavital, Balt Colts	GB	1950	96
Bob Hoernschemeyer, Det	NY Yanks	1950	96

PASSING	Opponent	Year	Yds
†Eli Manning to Victor Cruz, NYG	NYJ	2011	99
†Tom Brady to Wes Welker, NE	Mia	2011	99
Gus Frerotte to Bernard Berrian, Min	Chi	2008	99
Jeff Garcia to Andre Davis, Clev	Cin	2004	99
Trent Green to Marc Boerigter, KC	SD	2002	99
Brett Favre to Robert Brooks, GB	Chi	1995	99
Stan Humphries to Tony Martin, SD	Sea	1994	99
Ron Jaworski to Mike Quick, Phil	Atl	1985	99
Jim Plunkett to Cliff Branch, LA Raiders	Wash	1983	99
Sonny Jurgensen to Gerry Allen, Wash	Chi	1968	99
Karl Sweetan to Pat Studstill, Det	Balt Colts	1966	99
George Izo to Bobby Mitchell, Wash	Clev	1963	99
Frank Filchock to Andy Farkas, Wash	Pit	1939	99

FIELD GOALS	Opponent	Year	Yds
†Sebastian Janikowski, Oak	Den	2011	63
Tom Dempsey, NO	Det	1970	63
Jason Elam, Den	Jac	1998	63
†Matt Bryant, TB	Phi	2006	62
†Sebastian Janikowski, Oak	Cle	2009	61

PUNTS	Opponent	Year	Yds
Steve O'Neal, NYJ	Den	1969	98
Joe Lintzenich, Chi	NYG	1931	94
Shawn McCarthy, NE	Buf	1991	93
Randall Cunningham, Phil	NYG	1989	91

INTERCEPTION RETURNS	Opponent	Year	Yds
†Ed Reed, Balt	Phi	2008	107
†Ed Reed, Balt	Clev	2004	106
Louis Oliver, Mia	Buf	1992	103
Vencie Glenn, SD	Den	1987	103

FUMBLE RETURNS	Opponent	Year	Yds
Aeneas Williams, Ari	Was	2000	104
Jack Tatum, Oak	GB	1972	104
Travis Davis, Pit	Car	1999	102
Chris Martin, KC	Mia	1991	100

KICKOFF RETURNS	Opponent	Year	Yds
†Randall Cobb, GB	NO	2011	108
Ellis Hobbs, NE	NYJ	2007	108
†Joe McKnight, NYJ	Bal	2011	107
†Brad Smith, NYJ	Ind	2009	106
Roy Green, StL Cards	Dal	1979	106
Noland Smith, NYJ	Den	1967	106
Al Carmichael, GB	Chi	1956	106
Nine players tied at 105.			

PUNT RETURNS	Opponent	Year	Yds
Robert Bailey, LA Rams	NO	1994	103
†Patrick Peterson, Ari	StL	2011	99
Gil LeFebvre, Cin	Brooklyn	1933	98
Charlie West, Min	Wash	1968	98
Dennis Morgan, Dal	StL Cards	1974	98
Terance Mathis, NYJ	Dal	1990	98
Greg Pruitt, LA Raiders	Was	1983	97
†Bryan McCann, Dal	Det	2010	97

MISSED FIELD GOAL RETURNS	Opponent	Year	Yds
†Antonio Cromartie, SD	Min	2007	109
†Devin Hester, Chi	NYG	2006	108
†Nathan Vasher, Chi	SF	2005	108
Chris McAlister, Balt	Den	2002	107
Aaron Glenn, NYJ	Ind	1998	104

† Active in 2011.

Rushing

Year	Player, Team	Att	Yards	Avg	TD
1932	Cliff Battles, Bos	148	576	3.9	3
1933	Jim Musick, Bos	173	809	4.7	5
1934	Beattie Feathers, Chi	119	1,004	8.4	8
1935	Doug Russell, Chi Cards	140	499	3.6	0
1936	Alphonse Leemans, NY	206	830	4.0	2
1937	Cliff Battles, Wash	216	874	4.0	5
1938	Byron White, Pit	152	567	3.7	4
1939	Bill Osmanski, Chi	121	699	5.8	7
1940	Byron White, Det	146	514	3.5	5
1941	Clarence Manders, Bklyn	111	486	4.4	5
1942	Bill Dudley, Pit	162	696	4.3	5
1943	Bill Paschal, NY	147	572	3.9	10
1944	Bill Paschal, NY	196	737	3.8	9
1945	Steve Van Buren, Phil	143	832	5.8	15
1946	Bill Dudley, Pit	146	604	4.1	3
1947	Steve Van Buren, Phil	217	1,008	4.6	13
1948	Steve Van Buren, Phil	201	945	4.7	10
1949	Steve Van Buren, Phil	263	1,146	4.4	11
1950	Marion Motley, Clev	140	810	5.8	3
1951	Eddie Price, NY	271	971	3.6	7
1952	Dan Towler, LA	156	894	5.7	10
1953	Joe Perry, SF	192	1,018	5.3	10
1954	Joe Perry, SF	173	1,049	6.1	8
1955	Alan Ameche, Balt	213	961	4.5	9
1956	Rick Casares, Chi	234	1,126	4.8	12
1957	Jim Brown, Clev	202	942	4.7	9
1958	Jim Brown, Clev	257	1,527	5.9	17
1959	Jim Brown, Clev	290	1,329	4.6	14
1960	Jim Brown, Clev, NFL	215	1,257	5.8	9
	Abner Haynes,				
	Dallas Texans, AFL	156	875	5.6	9
1961	Jim Brown, Clev, NFL	305	1,408	4.6	8
	Billy Cannon, Hou, AFL	200	948	4.7	6
1962	Jim Taylor, GB, NFL	272	1,474	5.4	19
	Cookie Gilchrist, Buf, AFL	214	1,096	5.1	13
1963	Jim Brown, Clev, NFL	291	1,863	6.4	12
	Clem Daniels, Oak, AFL	215	1,099	5.1	3
1964	Jim Brown, Clev, NFL	280	1,446	5.2	7
	Cookie Gilchrist, Buf, AFL	230	981	4.3	6
1965	Jim Brown, Clev, NFL	289	1,544	5.3	17
	Paul Lowe, SD, AFL	222	1,121	5.0	7
1966	Jim Nance, Bos, AFL	299	1,458	4.9	11
	Gale Sayers, Chi, NFL	229	1,231	5.4	8
1967	Jim Nance, Bos, AFL	269	1,216	4.5	7
	Leroy Kelly, Clev, NFL	235	1,205	5.1	11
1968	Leroy Kelly, Clev, NFL	248	1,239	5.0	16
	Paul Robinson, Cin, AFL	238	1,023	4.3	8
1969	Gale Sayers, Chi, NFL	236	1,032	4.4	8
	Dickie Post, SD, AFL	182	873	4.8	6
1970	Larry Brown, Wash, NFC	237	1,125	4.7	5
	Floyd Little, Den, AFC	209	901	4.3	3
1971	Floyd Little, Den, AFC	284	1,133	4.0	6
	John Brockington,				
	GB, NFC	216	1,105	5.1	4
1972	O.J. Simpson, Buf, AFC	292	1,251	4.3	6
	Larry Brown, Wash, NFC	285	1,216	4.3	8
1973	O.J. Simpson, Buf, AFC	332	2,003	6.0	12
	John Brockington,				
	GB, NFC	265	1,144	4.3	3
1974	Otis Armstrong,				
	Den, AFC	263	1,407	5.3	9
	Lawrence McCutcheon,				
	LA, NFC	236	1,109	4.7	3
1975	O.J. Simpson, Buf, AFC	329	1,817	5.5	16
	Jim Otis, StL, NFC	269	1,076	4.0	5
1976	O.J. Simpson, Buf, AFC	290	1,503	5.2	8
	Walter Payton, Chi, NFC	311	1,390	4.5	13
1977	Walter Payton, Chi, NFC	339	1,852	5.5	14
	Mark van Eeghen,				
	Oak, AFC	324	1,273	3.9	7
1978	Earl Campbell, Hou, AFC	302	1,450	4.8	13
	Walter Payton, Chi, NFC	333	1,395	4.2	11
1979	Earl Campbell, Hou, AFC	368	1,697	4.6	19
	Walter Payton, Chi, NFC	369	1,610	4.4	14
1980	Earl Campbell, Hou, AFC	373	1,934	5.2	13
	Walter Payton, Chi, NFC	317	1,460	4.6	6
1981	George Rogers, NO, NFC	378	1,674	4.4	13
	Earl Campbell, Hou, AFC	361	1,376	3.8	10
1982	Freeman McNeil,				
	NYJ, AFC	151	786	5.2	6
	Tony Dorsett, Dal, NFC	177	745	4.2	5
1983	Eric Dickerson, LA, NFC	390	1,808	4.6	18
	Curt Warner, Sea, AFC	335	1,449	4.3	13
1984	Eric Dickerson, LA, NFC	379	2,105	5.6	14
	Earnest Jackson,				
	SD, AFC	296	1,179	4.0	8
1985	Marcus Allen, LA, AFC	380	1,759	4.6	11
	Gerald Riggs, Atl, NFC	397	1,719	4.3	10
1986	Eric Dickerson, LA, NFC	404	1,821	4.5	11
	Curt Warner, Sea, AFC	319	1,481	4.6	13
1987	Charles White, LA, NFC	324	1,374	4.2	11
	Eric Dickerson, Ind, AFC	223	1,011	4.5	5
1988	Eric Dickerson, Ind, AFC	388	1,659	4.3	14
	Herschel Walker,				
	Dal, NFC	361	1,514	4.2	5
1989	Christian Okoye, KC, AFC	370	1,480	4.0	12
	Barry Sanders, Det, NFC	280	1,470	5.3	14
1990	Barry Sanders, Det, NFC	255	1,304	5.1	13
	Thurman Thomas,				
	Buf, AFC	271	1,297	4.8	11
1991	Emmitt Smith, Dal, NFC	365	1,563	4.3	12
	Thurman Thomas,				
	Buf, AFC	288	1,407	4.9	7
1992	Emmitt Smith, Dal, NFC	373	1,713	4.6	18
	Barry Foster, Pit, AFC	390	1,690	4.3	11
1993	Emmitt Smith, Dal, NFC	283	1,486	5.3	9
	Thurman Thomas,				
	Buf, AFC	355	1,315	3.7	6
1994	Barry Sanders, Det, NFC	331	1,883	5.7	7
	Chris Warren, Sea, AFC	333	1,545	4.6	9
1995	Emmitt Smith, Dal, NFC	377	1,773	4.7	25
	Curtis Martin, NE, AFC	368	1,487	4.0	14
1996	Barry Sanders, Det, NFC	307	1,553	5.1	11
	Terrell Davis, Den, AFC	345	1,538	4.5	13
1997	Barry Sanders, Det, NFC	335	2,053	6.1	11
	Terrell Davis, Den, AFC	369	1,750	4.7	15
1998	Terrell Davis, Den, AFC	392	2,008	5.1	21
	Jamal Anderson, Atl, NFC	410	1,846	4.5	14
1999	Edgerrin James, Ind, AFC	369	1,553	4.2	13
	Stephen Davis, Wash, NFC	290	1,405	4.8	17
2000	Edgerrin James, Ind, AFC	387	1,709	4.4	13
	Robert Smith, Min, NFC	295	1,521	5.2	7
2001	Priest Holmes, Kan, AFC	327	1,555	4.8	8
	Stephen Davis, Wash, NFC	356	1,432	4.0	5
2002	Ricky Williams, Mia, AFC	383	1,853	4.8	16
	Deuce McAllister,				
	NO, NFC	325	1,388	4.3	13

Rushing *(Cont.)*

Year	Player, Team	Att	Yards	Avg	TD
2003	Jamal Lewis, Balt, AFC	387	2,066	5.3	14
	Ahman Green, GB, NFC	355	1,883	5.3	15
2004	Curtis Martin NY Jets, AFC	371	1,697	4.6	12
	Shaun Alexander, Sea, NFC	353	1,696	4.8	16
2005	Shaun Alexander, Sea, NFC	370	1,880	5.1	27
	Larry Johnson, KC, AFC	336	1,750	5.2	20
2006	LaDainian Tomlinson, SD, AFC	348	1,815	5.2	28
	Frank Gore, SF, NFC	312	1,695	5.4	8
2007	LaDainian Tomlinson, SD, AFC	315	1,474	4.7	15
	Adrian Peterson, Min, NFC	238	1,341	5.6	12
2008	Adrian Peterson, Min, NFC	363	1,760	4.8	10
	Thomas Jones, NYJ, AFC	290	1,312	4.5	13
2009	Chris Johnson, Ten, AFC	358	2,006	5.6	14
	Steven Jackson, StL, NFC	324	1,416	4.4	4
2010	Arian Foster, Hou, AFC	327	1,616	4.9	16
	Michael Turner, Atl, NFC	334	1,371	4.1	12
2011	M. Jones-Drew, Jax, AFC	343	1,606	4.7	8
	Michael Turner, Atl, NFC	301	1,340	4.5	11

Passing

Year	Player, Team	Att	Comp	Yards	TD	Int
1932	Arnie Herber, GB	101	37	639	9	9
1933	Harry Newman, NYG	136	53	973	11	17
1934	Arnie Herber, GB	115	42	799	8	12
1935	Ed Danowski, NYG	113	57	794	10	9
1936	Arnie Herber, GB	173	77	1,239	11	13
1937	Sammy Baugh, Wash	171	81	1,127	8	14
1938	Ed Danowski, NYG	129	70	848	7	8
1939	Parker Hall, Clev	208	106	1,227	9	13
1940	Sammy Baugh, Wash	177	111	1,367	12	10
1941	Cecil Isbell, GB	206	117	1,479	15	11
1942	Cecil Isbell, GB	268	146	2,021	24	14
1943	Sammy Baugh, Wash	239	133	1,754	23	19
1944	Frank Filchock, Wash	147	84	1,139	13	9
1945	Sid Luckman, Chi	217	117	1,725	14	10
1946	Bob Waterfield, LA	251	127	1,747	18	17
1947	Sammy Baugh, Wash	354	210	2,938	25	15
1948	Tommy Thompson, Phil	246	141	1,965	25	11
1949	Sammy Baugh, Wash	255	145	1,903	18	14
1950	Norm Van Brocklin, LA	233	127	2,061	18	14
1951	Bob Waterfield, LA	176	88	1,566	13	10
1952	Norm Van Brocklin, LA	205	113	1,736	14	17
1953	Otto Graham, Clev	258	167	2,722	11	9
1954	Norm Van Brocklin, LA	260	139	2,637	13	21
1955	Otto Graham, Clev	185	98	1,721	15	8
1956	Ed Brown, Chi	168	96	1,667	11	12
1957	Tommy O'Connell, Clev	110	63	1,229	9	8
1958	Eddie LeBaron, Wash	145	79	1,365	11	10
1959	Charlie Conerly, NYG	194	113	1,706	14	4
1960	Jack Kemp, LA, AFL	406	211	3,018	20	25
	Milt Plum, Clev, NFL	250	151	2,297	21	5
1961	George Blanda, Hou, AFL	362	187	3,330	36	22
	Milt Plum, Clev, NFL	302	177	2,416	18	10
1962	Len Dawson, Dal, AFL	310	189	2,759	29	17
	Bart Starr, GB, NFL	285	178	2,438	12	9
1963	Y.A. Tittle, NY, NFL	367	221	3,145	36	14
	Tobin Rote, SD, AFL	286	170	2,510	20	17
1964	Len Dawson, KC, AFL	354	199	2,879	30	18
	Bart Starr, GB, NFL	272	163	2,144	15	4
1965	Rudy Bukich, Chi, NFL	312	176	2,641	20	9
	John Hadl, SD, AFL	348	174	2,798	20	21
1966	Bart Starr, GB, NFL	251	156	2,257	14	3
	Len Dawson, KC, AFL	284	159	2,527	26	10
1967	Sonny Jurgensen, Wash, NFL	508	288	3,747	31	16
	Daryle Lamonica, Oak, AFL	425	220	3,228	30	20
1968	Len Dawson, KC, AFL	224	131	2,109	17	9
	Earl Morrall, Balt, NFL	317	182	2,909	26	17
1969	S. Jurgensen, Wash, NFL	442	274	3,102	22	15
	Greg Cook, Cin, AFL	197	106	1,854	15	11
1970	John Brodie, SF, NFC	378	223	2,941	24	10
	Daryle Lamonica, Oak, AFC	356	179	2,516	22	15
1971	Roger Staubach, Dal, NFC	211	126	1,882	15	4
	Bob Griese, Mia, AFC	263	145	2,089	19	9
1972	Norm Snead, NY, NFC	325	196	2,307	17	12
	Earl Morrall, Mia, AFC	150	83	1,360	11	7

Year	Player, Team		Yards	TD	Int	
1973	Roger Staubach, Dal, NFC	62.6	2,428	23	15	94.6
	Ken Stabler, Oak, AFC	62.7	1,997	14	10	88.3
1974	Ken Anderson, Cin, AFC	64.9	2,667	18	10	95.7
	Sonny Jurgensen, Wash, NFC	64.1	1,185	11	5	94.5
1975	Ken Anderson, Cin, AFC	60.5	3,169	21	11	93.9
	Fran Tarkenton, Min, NFC	64.2	2,994	25	13	91.8
1976	Ken Stabler, Oak, AFC	66.7	2,737	27	17	103.4
	James Harris, LA, NFC	57.6	1,460	8	6	89.6

Passing* *(Cont.)*

*Since 1973, the annual passing NFL leaders have been determined by a passer rating system that compares individual performances to a fixed performance standard. Before 1973, total passing yards gained was used.

Year	Player, Team	Comp%	Yds	TD	Int	Rating
1977	Bob Griese, Mia, AFC	58.6	2,252	22	13	87.8
	Roger Staubach, Dal, NFC	58.2	2,620	18	9	87.0
1978	Roger Staubach, Dal, NFC	55.9	3,190	25	16	84.9
	Terry Bradshaw, Pit, AFC	56.3	2,915	28	20	84.7
1979	Roger Staubach, Dal, NFC	57.9	3,586	27	11	92.3
	Dan Fouts, SD, AFC	62.6	4,082	24	24	82.6
1980	Brian Sipe, Clev, AFC	60.8	4,132	30	14	91.4
	Ron Jaworski, Phi, NFC	57.0	3,529	27	12	91.0
1981	Ken Anderson, Cin, AFC	62.6	3,754	29	10	98.4
	Joe Montana, SF, NFC	63.7	3,565	19	12	88.4
1982	Ken Anderson, Cin, AFC	70.6	2,495	12	9	95.3
	Joe Theismann, Wash, NFC	63.9	2,033	13	9	91.3
1983	Steve Bartkowski, Atl, NFC	63.4	3,167	22	5	97.6
	Dan Marino, Mia AFC	58.4	2,210	20	6	96.0
1984	Dan Marino, Mia, AFC	64.2	5,084	48	17	108.9
	Joe Montana, SF, NFC	64.6	3,630	28	10	102.9
1985	Ken O'Brien, NY, AFC	60.9	3,888	25	8	96.2
	Joe Montana, SF, NFC	61.3	3,653	27	13	91.3
1986	Tommy Kramer, Min, NFC	55.9	3,000	24	10	92.6
	Dan Marino, Mia, AFC	60.7	4,746	44	23	92.5
1987	Joe Montana, SF, NFC	66.8	3,054	31	13	102.1
	Bernie Kosar, Clev, AFC	61.9	3,033	22	9	95.4
1988	Boomer Esiason, Cin, AFC	57.5	3,572	28	14	97.4
	Wade Wilson, Min, NFC	61.4	2,746	15	9	91.5
1989	Joe Montana, SF, NFC	70.2	3,521	26	8	112.4
	Boomer Esiason, Cin, AFC	56.7	3,525	28	11	92.1
1990	Jim Kelly, Buf, AFC	63.3	2,829	24	9	101.2
	Phil Simms, NY, NFC	59.2	2,284	15	4	92.7
1991	Steve Young, SF, NFC	64.5	2,517	17	8	101.8
	Jim Kelly, Buf, AFC	64.1	3,844	33	17	97.6
1992	Steve Young, SF, NFC	66.7	3,465	25	7	107.0
	Warren Moon, Hou, AFC	64.7	2,521	18	12	89.3
1993	Steve Young, SF, NFC	68.0	4,023	29	16	101.5
	John Elway, Den, AFC	63.2	4,030	25	10	92.8
1994	Steve Young, SF, NFC	70.3	3,969	35	10	112.8
	Dan Marino, Mia, AFC	62.0	4,453	30	17	89.2
1995	Brett Favre, GB, NFC	62.9	4,413	38	13	99.5
	Jim Harbaugh, Ind, AFC	61.2	2,575	17	5	100.7
1996	John Elway, Den, AFC	61.6	3,328	26	14	89.2
	Steve Young, SF, NFC	67.7	2,410	14	6	97.2
1997	Steve Young, SF, NFC	67.7	3,029	19	6	104.7
	Mark Brunell, Jax, AFC	60.7	3,281	18	7	91.2
1998	Randall Cunningham, Min, NFC	60.9	3,704	34	10	106.0
	Vinny Testaverde, NYJ, AFC	61.5	3,256	29	7	101.6
1999	Kurt Warner, StL, NFC	65.1	4,353	41	13	109.2
	Peyton Manning, Ind, AFC	62.1	4,135	26	15	90.7
2000	Trent Green, StL, NFC	60.4	2,063	16	5	101.8
	Brian Griese, Den, AFC	64.3	2,688	19	4	102.9
2001	Kurt Warner, StL, NFC	68.7	4,830	36	22	101.4
	Rich Gannon, Oak, AFC	65.8	3,828	27	9	95.5
2002	Brad Johnson, TB, NFC	62.3	3,049	22	6	92.9
	Chad Pennington, NY, AFC	68.9	3,120	22	6	104.2
2003	Steve McNair, Ten, AFC	62.5	3,215	24	7	100.4
	Daunte Culpepper, Min, NFC	65.0	3,479	25	11	96.4
2004	Peyton Manning, Ind, AFC	67.6	4,557	49	10	121.1
	Daunte Culpepper, Min, NFC	69.2	4,717	39	11	110.9
2005	Peyton Manning, Ind, AFC	67.3	3,747	28	10	104.1
	Matt Hasselbeck, GB, NFC	65.5	3,459	24	9	98.2
2006	Peyton Manning, Ind, AFC	65.0	4,397	31	9	101.0
	Drew Brees, NO, NFC	64.3	4,418	26	11	96.2

Passing (Cont.)

Year	Player, Team	Comp%	Yds	TD	Int	Rating
2007	Tom Brady, NE, AFC	68.9	4,806	50	8	117.2
	Tony Romo, Dal, NFC	64.4	4,211	36	19	97.4
2008	Philip Rivers, SD, AFC	65.3	4,009	34	11	105.5
	Kurt Warner, Ari, NFC	67.1	4,583	30	14	96.9
2009	Drew Brees, NO, NFC	70.6	4,388	34	11	109.6
	Philip Rivers, SD, AFC	65.2	4,254	28	9	104.4
2010	Tom Brady, NE, AFC	65.9	3,900	36	4	111.0
	Aaron Rodgers, GB, NFC	65.7	3,922	28	11	101.2
2011	Tom Brady, NE, AFC	65.6	5,235	39	12	105.6
	Aaron Rodgers, GB, NFC	68.3	4,643	45	6	122.5

Pass Receiving†

Year	Player, Team	No.	Yds	Avg	TD
1932	Ray Flaherty, NY	21	350	16.7	3
1933	John Kelly, Brooklyn	22	246	11.2	3
1934	Joe Carter, Phil	16	238	14.9	4
	Morris Badgro, NY	16	206	12.9	1
1935	Tod Goodwin, NY	26	432	16.6	4
1936	Don Hutson, GB	34	536	15.8	8
1937	Don Hutson, GB	41	552	13.5	7
1938	Gaynell Tinsley, Chi Cards	41	516	12.6	1
1939	Don Hutson, GB	34	846	24.9	6
1940	Don Looney, Phil	58	707	12.2	4
1941	Don Hutson, GB	58	738	12.7	10
1942	Don Hutson, GB	74	1,211	16.4	17
1943	Don Hutson, GB	47	776	16.5	11
1944	Don Hutson, GB	58	866	14.9	9
1945	Don Hutson, GB	47	834	17.7	9
1946	Jim Benton, LA	63	981	15.6	6
1947	Jim Keane, Chi	64	910	14.2	10
1948	Tom Fears, LA	51	698	13.7	4
1949	Tom Fears, LA	77	1,013	13.2	9
1950	Tom Fears, LA	84	1,116	13.3	7
1951	Elroy Hirsch, LA	66	1,495	22.7	17
1952	Mac Speedie, Clev	62	911	14.7	5
1953	Pete Pihos, Phil	63	1,049	16.7	10
1954	Pete Pihos, Phil	60	872	14.5	10
	Billy Wilson, SF	60	830	13.8	5
1955	Pete Pihos, Phil	62	864	13.9	7
1956	Billy Wilson, SF	60	889	14.8	5
1957	Billy Wilson, SF	52	757	14.6	6
1958	Raymond Berry, Balt	56	794	14.2	9
	Pete Retzlaff, Phil	56	766	13.7	2
1959	Raymond Berry, Balt	66	959	14.5	14
1960	Lionel Taylor, Den, AFL	92	1,235	13.4	12
	Raymond Berry, Balt, NFL	74	1,298	17.5	10
1961	Lionel Taylor, Den, AFL	100	1,176	11.8	4
	Jim Phillips, LA, NFL	78	1,092	14.0	5
1962	Lionel Taylor, Den, AFL	77	908	11.8	4
	Bobby Mitchell, Wash, NFL	72	1,384	19.2	11
1963	Lionel Taylor, Den, AFL	78	1,101	14.1	10
	Bobby Joe Conrad, St. Louis, NFL	73	967	13.2	10
1964	Charley Hennigan, Houston, AFL	101	1,546	15.3	8
	Johnny Morris, Chi, NFL	93	1,200	12.9	10
1965	Lionel Taylor, Den, AFL	85	1,131	13.3	6
	Dave Parks, SF, NFL	80	1,344	16.8	12
1966	Lance Alworth, SD, AFL	73	1,383	18.9	13
	Charley Taylor, Wash, NFL	72	1,119	15.5	12
1967	George Sauer, NY, AFL	75	1,189	15.9	6
	Charley Taylor, Wash, NFL	70	990	14.1	9
1968	Clifton McNeil, SF, NFL	71	994	14.0	7
	Lance Alworth, SD, AFL	68	1,312	19.3	10
1969	Dan Abramowicz, NO, NFL	73	1,015	13.9	7
	Lance Alworth, SD, AFL	64	1,003	15.7	4
1970	Dick Gordon, Chi, NFC	71	1,026	14.5	13
	Marlin Briscoe, Buf, AFC	57	1,036	18.2	8
1971	Fred Biletnikoff, Oak, AFC	61	929	15.2	9
	Bob Tucker, NY, NFC	59	791	13.4	4
1972	Harold Jackson, Phil, NFC	62	1,048	16.9	4
	Fred Biletnikoff, Oak, AFC	58	802	13.8	7
1973	Harold Carmichael, Phil, NFC	67	1,116	16.7	9
	Fred Willis, Hou, AFC	57	371	6.5	1
1974	Lydell Mitchell, Balt, AFC	72	544	7.6	2
	Charles Young, Phil, NFC	63	696	11.0	3
1975	Chuck Foreman, Min, NFC	73	691	9.5	9
	Reggie Rucker, Clev, AFC	60	770	12.8	3
	Lydell Mitchell, Balt, AFC	60	544	9.1	4
1976	MacArthur Lane, KC, AFC	66	686	10.4	1
	Drew Pearson, Dal, NFC	58	806	13.9	6
1977	Lydell Mitchell, Balt, AFC	71	620	8.7	4
	Ahmad Rashad, Min, NFC	51	681	13.4	2
1978	Rickey Young, Min, NFC	88	704	8.0	5
	Steve Largent, Sea, AFC	71	1,168	16.5	8
1979	Joe Washington, Balt, AFC	82	750	9.1	3
	Ahmad Rashad, Min, NFC	80	1,156	14.5	9
1980	Kellen Winslow, SD, AFC	89	1,290	14.5	9
	Earl Cooper, SF, NFC	83	567	6.8	4
1981	Kellen Winslow, SD, AFC	88	1,075	12.2	10
	Dwight Clark, SF, NFC	85	1,105	13.0	4

†Most catches.

Pass Receiving† *(Cont.)*

Year	Player, Team	No.	Yds	Avg	TD
1982	Dwight Clark, SF, NFC	60	913	15.2	5
	Kellen Winslow, SD, AFC	54	721	13.4	6
1983	Todd Christensen, LA, AFC	92	1,247	13.6	12
	Roy Green, StL, NFC	78	1,227	15.7	14
	Charlie Brown, Wash, NFC	78	1,225	15.7	8
	Earnest Gray, NY, NFC	78	1,139	14.6	5
1984	Art Monk, Wash, NFC	106	1,372	12.9	7
	Ozzie Newsome, Clev, AFC	89	1,001	11.2	5
1985	Roger Craig, SF, NFC	92	1,016	11.0	6
	Lionel James, SD, AFC	86	1,027	11.9	6
1986	Todd Christensen, LA, AFC	95	1,153	12.1	8
	Jerry Rice, SF, NFC	86	1,570	18.3	15
1987	J.T. Smith, StL Card, NFC	91	1,117	12.3	8
	Al Toon, NY, AFC	68	976	14.4	5
1988	Al Toon, NY, AFC	93	1,067	11.5	5
	Henry Ellard, LA, NFC	86	1,414	16.4	10
1989	Sterling Sharpe, GB, NFC	90	1,423	15.8	12
	Andre Reed, Buf, AFC	88	1,312	14.9	9
1990	Jerry Rice, SF, NFC	100	1,502	15.0	13
	Haywood Jeffires, Hou, AFC	74	1,048	14.2	8
	Drew Hill, Hou, AFC	74	1,019	13.8	5
1991	Haywood Jeffires, Hou, AFC	100	1,181	11.8	7
	Michael Irvin, Dal, NFC	93	1,523	16.4	8
1992	Sterling Sharpe, GB, NFC	108	1,461	13.5	13
	Haywood Jeffires, Hou, AFC	90	913	10.1	9
1993	Sterling Sharpe, GB, NFC	112	1,274	11.4	11
	Reggie Langhorne, Ind, AFC	85	1,038	12.2	3
1994	Cris Carter, Min, NFC	122	1,256	10.3	7
	Ben Coates, NE, AFC	96	1,174	12.2	7
1995	Herman Moore, Det, NFC	123	1,686	13.7	14
	Carl Pickens, Cin, AFC	99	1,234	12.5	17
1996	Jerry Rice, SF, NFC	108	1,254	11.6	8
	Carl Pickens, Cin, AFC	100	1,180	11.8	12
1997	Herman Moore, Det, NFC	104	1,293	12.4	8
	Tim Brown, Oak, AFC	104	1,408	13.5	5
1998	Frank Sanders, Ariz, NFC	89	1,145	12.9	3
	O.J. McDuffie, Mia, AFC	90	1,050	11.7	7
1999	Muhsin Muhammad, Car, NFC	96	1,253	13.1	8
	Jimmy Smith, Jax, AFC	116	1,636	14.1	6
2000	Muhsin Muhammad, Car, NFC	102	1,183	11.6	6
	Marvin Harrison, Ind, AFC	102	1,413	13.9	14
2001	Rod Smith, Den, AFC	113	1,343	11.9	11
	Keyshawn Johnson, TB, NFC	106	1,266	11.9	1
2002	Marvin Harrison, Ind, AFC	143	1,722	12.0	11
	Randy Moss, Min, NFC	106	1,347	12.7	7
2003	LaDainian Tomlinson, SD, AFC	100	725	7.3	4
	Torry Holt, StL, NFC	117	1,696	14.5	12
2004	Tony Gonzalez, KC, AFC	102	1,258	12.3	7
	Joe Horn, NO, NFC	94	1,399	14.9	11
2005	Chad Johnson, Cin, AFC	97	1,432	14.8	9
	Steve Smith, Car, NFC	103	1,563	15.2	12
2006	Chad Johnson, Cin, AFC	87	1,369	15.7	7
	Roy Williams, Det, NFC	82	1,310	16.0	7
2007	Reggie Wayne, Ind, AFC	104	1,510	14.5	10
	Larry Fitzgerald, Ari, NFC	100	1,409	14.1	10
2008	Andre Johnson, Hou, AFC	115	1,575	13.7	8
	Larry Fitzgerald, Ari, NFC	96	1,431	14.9	12
2009	Wes Welker, NE, AFC	123	1,348	11.0	4
	Steve Smith, NYG, NFC	107	1,220	11.4	7
2010	Roddy White, Atl, NFC	115	1,389	12.1	10
	Reggie Wayne, Ind, AFC	111	1,355	12.2	6
2011	Wes Welker, NE, AFC	122	1,569	12.9	9
	Rod White, Atl, NFC	100	1,296	13.0	8

†Most catches.

Scoring

Year	Player, Team	TD	FG	PAT	TP
1932	Earl Clark, Portsmouth	6	3	10	55
1933	Ken Strong, NY	6	5	13	64
	Glenn Presnell, Ports	6	6	10	64
1934	Jack Manders, Chi	3	10	31	79
1935	Earl Clark, Det	6	1	16	55
1936	Earl Clark, Det	7	4	19	73
1937	Jack Manders, Chi	5	18	15	69
1938	Clarke Hinkle, GB	7	3	7	58
1939	Andy Farkas, Wash	11	0	2	68
1940	Don Hutson, GB	7	0	15	57
1941	Don Hutson, GB	12	1	20	95
1942	Don Hutson, GB	17	1	33	138
1943	Don Hutson, GB	12	3	36	117
1944	Don Hutson, GB	9	0	31	85
1945	Steve Van Buren, Phil	18	0	2	110
1946	Ted Fritsch, GB	10	9	13	100
1947	Pat Harder, Chicago Cards	7	7	39	102
1948	Pat Harder, Chicago Cards	6	7	53	110
1949	Pat Harder, Chicago Cards	8	3	45	102
	Gene Roberts, NY	17	0	0	102
1950	Doak Walker, Det	11	8	38	128
1951	Elroy Hirsch, LA	17	0	0	102
1952	Gordy Soltau, SF	7	6	34	94
1953	Gordy Soltau, SF	6	10	48	114
1954	Bobby Walston, Phi	11	4	36	114
1955	Doak Walker, Det	7	9	27	96
1956	Bobby Layne, Det	5	12	33	99
1957	Sam Baker, Was	1	14	29	77
	Lou Groza, Cle	0	15	32	77
1958	Jim Brown, Cle	18	0	0	108

Scoring *(Cont.)*

Year	Player, Team	TD	FG	PAT	TP	Year	Player, Team	TD	FG	PAT	TP
1959	Paul Hornung, GB	7	7	31	94	1989	Mike Cofer, SF, NFC	0	29	49	136
1960	Paul Hornung, GB, NFL	15	15	41	176		David Treadwell, Den, AFC	0	27	39	120
	Gene Mingo, Den, AFL	6	18	33	123	1990	Nick Lowery, KC, AFC	0	34	37	139
1961	Gino Cappelletti, Bos, AFL	8	17	48	147		Chip Lohmiller, Was, NFC	0	30	41	131
	Paul Hornung, GB, NFL	10	15	41	146	1991	Chip Lohmiller, Was, NFC	0	31	56	149
1962	Gene Mingo, Den, AFL	4	27	32	137		Pete Stoyanovich, Mia, AFC	0	31	28	121
	Jim Taylor, GB, NFL	19	0	0	114	1992	Pete Stoyanovich, Mia, AFC	0	30	34	124
1963	Gino Cappelletti, Bos, AFL	2	22	35	113		Morten Anderson, NO, NFC	0	29	33	120
	Don Chandler, NY, NFL	0	18	52	106		Chip Lohmiller, Was, NFC	0	30	30	120
1964	Gino Cappelletti, Bos, AFL	7	25	36	155	1993	Jeff Jaeger, Rai, AFC	0	35	27	132
	Lenny Moore, Balt, NFL	20	0	0	120		Jason Hanson, Det, NFC	0	34	28	130
1965	Gale Sayers, Chi, NFL	22	0	0	132	1994	John Carney, SD, AFC	0	34	33	135
	Gino Cappelletti, Bos, AFL	9	17	27	132		Fuad Reveiz, Min, NFC	0	34	30	132
1966	Gino Cappelletti, Bos, AFL	6	16	35	119		Emmitt Smith, Dal, NFC	22	0	0	132
	Bruce Gossett, LA, NFL	0	28	29	113	1995	Emmitt Smith, Dal, NFC	25	0	0	150
1967	Jim Bakken, StL, NFL	0	27	36	117		Norm Johnson, Pit, AFC	0	34	39	141
	George Blanda, Oak, AFL	0	20	56	116	1996	John Kasay, Car, NFC	0	37	34	145
1968	Jim Turner, NY, AFL	0	34	43	145		Cary Blanchard, Ind, AFC	0	36	27	135
	Leroy Kelly, Clev, NFL	20	0	0	120	1997	Richie Cunningham, Dal, NFC	0	34	24	126
1969	Jim Turner, NY, AFL	0	32	33	129		Mike Hollis, Jax, AFC	0	41	31	134
	Fred Cox, Min, NFL	0	26	43	121	1998	Gary Anderson, Min, NFC	0	35	59	164
1970	Fred Cox, Min, NFC	0	30	35	125		Steve Christie, Buf, AFC	0	33	41	140
	Jan Stenerud, KC, AFC	0	30	26	116	1999	Jeff Wilkins, StL, NFC	0	20	64	124
1971	Garo Yepremian, Mia, AFC	0	28	33	117		Mike Vanderjagt, Ind, AFC	0	34	43	145
	Curt Knight, Was, NFC	0	29	27	114	2000	Marshall Faulk, StL, NFC	26	0	0	160
1972	Chester Marcol, GB, NFC	0	33	29	128		Matt Stover, Balt, AFC	0	35	30	135
	Bobby Howfield, NY AFC	0	27	40	121	2001	Marshall Faulk, StL, NFC	21	0	0	128
1973	David Ray, LA, NFC	0	30	40	130		Mike Vanderjagt, Ind, AFC	0	28	41	125
	Roy Gerela, Pit, AFC	0	29	36	123	2002	Jay Feely, Atl, NFC	0	32	42	138
1974	Chester Marcol, GB, NFC	0	25	19	94		Priest Holmes, KC, AFC	24	0	0	144
	Roy Gerela, Pit, AFC	0	20	33	93	2003	Jeff Wilkins StL, NFC	0	39	46	163
1975	O.J. Simpson, Buf, AFC	23	0	0	138		Priest Holmes, KC, AFC	27	0	0	162
	Chuck Foreman, Min, NFC	22	0	0	132	2004	Adam Vinatieri, NE, AFC	0	31	48	141
1976	Toni Linhart, Balt, AFC	0	20	49	109		David Akers, Phi, NFC	0	27	41	122
	Mark Moseley, Wash, NFC	0	22	31	97	2005	Shayne Graham, Cin, AFC	0	28	47	131
1977	Errol Mann, Oak, AFC	0	20	39	99		Shaun Alexander, Sea, NFC	28	0	0	168
	Walter Payton, Chi, NFC	16	0	0	96	2006	LaDainian Tomlinson, SD, AFC	31	0	0	186
1978	Frank Corral, LA, NFC	0	29	31	118		Robbie Gould, Chi, NFC	0	32	47	143
	Pat Leahy, NY, AFC	0	22	41	107	2007	Randy Moss, NE, AFC	23	0	0	138
1979	John Smith, NE, AFC	0	23	46	115		Mason Crosby, GB, NFC	0	31	48	141
	Mark Moseley, Was, NFC	0	25	39	114	2008	Stephen Gostkowski, NE, AFC	0	36	40	148
1980	John Smith, NE, AFC	0	26	51	129		David Akers, Phi, NFC	0	33	45	144
	Ed Murray, Det, NFC	0	27	35	116	2009	Nate Kaeding, SD, AFC	0	32	50	146
1981	Ed Murray, Det, NFC	0	25	46	121		David Akers, Phi, NFC	0	32	43	139
	Rafael Septien, Dal, NFC	0	27	40	121	2010	David Akers, Phi, NFC	0	32	47	143
	Jim Breech, Cin, AFC	0	22	49	115		Sebastian Janikowski, Oak, AFC	0	33	43	142
	Nick Lowery, KC, AFC	0	26	37	115	2011	Stephen Gostkowski, NE, AFC	0	28	59	143
1982	Marcus Allen, LA, AFC	14	0	0	84		David Akers, SF, NFC	0	44	34	166
	Wendell Tyler, LA, NFC	13	0	0	78						
1983	Mark Moseley, Was, NFC	0	33	62	161						
	Gary Anderson, Pit, AFC	0	27	38	119						
1984	Ray Wersching, SF, NFC	0	25	56	131						
	Gary Anderson, Pit, AFC	0	24	45	117						
1985	Kevin Butler, Chi, NFC	0	31	51	144						
	Gary Anderson, Pit, AFC	0	33	40	139						
1986	Tony Franklin, NE, AFC	0	32	44	140						
	Kevin Butler, Chi, NFC	0	28	36	120						
1987	Jerry Rice, SF, NFC	23	0	0	138						
	Jim Breech, Cin, AFC	0	24	25	97						
1988	Scott Norwood, Buf, AFC	0	32	33	129						
	Mike Cofer, SF, NFC	0	27	40	121						

Interceptions

Year	Player, Team	Int	Yds	Year	Player, Team	Int	Yds
1940	Clarence Parker, Brooklyn	6	146	1975	Mel Blount, Pit, AFC	11	121
	Kent Ryan, Det	6	65		Paul Krause, Min, NFC	10	201
	Don Hutson, GB	6	24	1976	Monte Jackson, LA, NFC	10	173
1941	Marshall Goldberg, Chicago Card	7	54		Ken Riley, Cin, AFC	9	141
	Art Jones, Pit	7	35	1977	Lyle Blackwood, Balt, AFC	10	163
1942	Clyde Turner, Chicago Bears	8	96		Rolland Lawrence, Atl, NFC	7	138
1943	Sammy Baugh, Wash	11	112	1978	Thom Darden, Clev, AFC	10	200
1944	Howard Livingston, NYG	9	172		Ken Stone, StL, NFC	9	139
1945	Ray Zimmerman, Phil	7	90		Willie Buchanon, GB, NFC	9	93
1946	Bill Dudley, Pittsburgh	10	242	1979	Mike Reinfeldt, Hou, AFC	12	205
1947	Frank Reagan, NYG	10	203		Lemar Parrish, Wash, NFC	9	65
	Frank Seno, Bos	10	100	1980	Lester Hayes, Oak, AFC	13	273
1948	Dan Sandifier, Wash	13	258		Nolan Cromwell, LA, NFC	8	140
1949	Bob Nussbaumer, Chicago Car	12	157	1981	Everson Walls, Dal, NFC	11	133
1950	Orban Sanders, NY Yanks	13	199		John Harris, Sea, AFC	10	155
1951	Otto Schnellbacher, NYG	11	194	1982	Everson Walls, Dal, NFC	7	61
1952	Dick Lane, LA	14	298		Ken Riley, Cin, AFC	5	88
1953	Jack Christiansen, Det	12	238		Bobby Jackson, NYJ, AFC	5	84
1954	Dick Lane, Chicago Card	10	181		Dwayne Woodruff, Pit, AFC	5	53
1955	Will Sherman, LA	11	101		Donnie Shell, Pit, AFC	5	27
1956	Lindon Crow, Chicago Card	11	170	1983	Mark Murphy, Wash, NFC	9	127
1957	Milt Davis, Balt	10	219		Ken Riley, Cin, AFC	8	89
	Jack Christiansen, Det	10	137		Vann McElroy, LA, AFC	8	68
	Jack Butler, Pit	10	85	1984	Ken Easley, Sea, AFC	10	126
1958	Jim Patton, NYG	11	183		Tom Flynn, GB, NFC	9	106
1959	Dean Derby, Pit	7	127	1985	Everson Walls, Dal, NFC	9	31
	Milt Davis, Balt	7	119		Albert Lewis, KC, AFC	8	59
	Don Shinnick, Balt	7	70		Eugene Daniel, Ind, AFC	8	53
1960	Goose Gonsoulin, Den, AFL	11	98	1986	Ronnie Lott, SF, NFC	10	134
	Dave Baker, SF, NFL	10	96		Deron Cherry, KC, AFC	9	150
	Jerry Norton, StL, NFL	10	96	1987	Barry Wilburn, Wash, NFC	9	135
1961	Billy Atkins, Buf, AFL	10	158		Mike Prior, Ind, AFC	6	57
	Dick Lynch, NYG, NFL	9	60		Mark Kelso, Buf, AFC	6	25
1962	Lee Riley, NY Titans, AFL	11	122		Keith Bostic, Hou, AFC	6	-14
	Willie Wood, GB, NFL	9	132	1988	Scott Case, Atl, NFC	10	47
1963	Fred Glick, Hous, AFL	12	180		Erik McMillan, NYJ, AFC	8	168
	Dick Lynch, NYG, NFL	9	251	1989	Felix Wright, Clev, AFC	9	91
	Roosevelt Taylor, Chi, NFL	9	172		Eric Allen, Phil, NFC	8	38
1964	Dainard Paulson, NYJ, AFL	12	157	1990	Mark Carrier, Chi, NFC	10	39
	Paul Krause, Wash, NFL	12	140		Richard Johnson, Hou, AFC	8	100
1965	W. K. Hicks, Hous, AFL	9	156	1991	Ronnie Lott, LA, AFC	8	52
	Bobby Boyd, Balt, NFL	9	78		Ray Crockett, Det, NFC	6	141
1966	Larry Wilson, StL, NFL	10	180		Deion Sanders, Atl, NFC	6	119
	Johnny Robinson, KC, AFL	10	136		Aeneas Williams, Phoenix, NFC	6	60
	Bobby Hunt, KC, AFL	10	113		Tim McKyer, Atl, NFC	6	24
1967	Lem Barney, Det, NFL	10	232	1992	Henry Jones, Buf, AFC	8	263
	Dave Whitsell, NO, NFL	10	178		Audray McMillian, Min, NFC	8	157
	Miller Farr, Hous, AFL	10	264	1993	Eugene Robinson, Sea, AFC	9	80
	Tom Janik, Buf, AFL	10	222		Nate Odomes, Buf, AFC	9	65
	Dick Westmoreland, Mia, AFL	10	127		Deion Sanders, Atl, NFC	7	91
1968	Dave Grayson, Oak, AFL	10	195	1994	Eric Turner, Clev, AFC	9	199
	Willie Williams, NYG, NFL	10	103		Aeneas Williams, Ariz, NFC	9	89
1969	Mel Renfro, Dal, NFL	10	118	1995	Orlando Thomas, Min, NFC	9	108
	Emmitt Thomas, KC, AFL	9	146		Willie Williams, Pit, AFC	9	122
1970	Johnny Robinson, KC, AFC	10	155	1996	Tyrone Braxton, Den, AFC	9	128
	Dick LeBeau, Det, NFC	9	96		Keith Lyle, StL, NFC	9	152
1971	Bill Bradley, Phil, NFC	11	248	1997	Ryan McNeil, StL, NFC	9	127
	Ken Houston, Hou, AFC	9	220		Mark McMillian, KC, AFC	8	274
1972	Bill Bradley, Phil, NFC	9	73		Darryl Williams, Sea, AFC	8	172
	Mike Sensibaugh, KC, AFC	8	65	1998	Ty Law, NE, AFC	9	133
1973	Dick Anderson, Mia, AFC	8	163		Kwamie Lassiter, Ariz, NFC	8	80
	Mike Wagner, Pit, AFC	8	134	1999	Rod Woodson, Balt, AFC	7	195
	Bobby Bryant, Min, NFC	7	105		Sam Madison, Mia, AFC	7	164
1974	Emmitt Thomas, KC, AFC	12	214		James Hasty, KC, AFC	7	98
	Ray Brown, Atl, NFC	8	164		Donnie Abraham, TB, NFC	7	115
					Troy Vincent, Phil, NFC	7	91

Interceptions *(Cont.)*

Year	Player, Team	Int	Yds
2000	Darren Sharper, GB, NFC	9	109
	Samari Rolle, Ten, AFC	7	140
	Brian Walker, Mia, AFC	7	80
2001	Ronde Barber, TB, NFC	10	86
	Anthony Henry, Clev, AFC	10	177
2002	Rod Woodson, Oak, AFC	8	225
	Brian Kelly, TB, NFC	8	68
2003	Brian Russell, Min, NFC	9	185
	Tony Parrish, SFo, NFC	9	202
	Patrick Surtain, Mia, AFC	7	59
	Ed Reed, Balt, AFC	7	132
	Marcus Coleman, Hou, AFC	7	95
2004	Ed Reed, Balt, AFC	9	358
	Chris Gamble, Car, NFC	6	15
	Ken Lucas, Sea, NFC	6	46
2005	Ty Law, NYJ, AFC	10	195
	Deltha O'Neal, Cin, AFC	10	103
	Darren Sharper, Min, NFC	9	276
2006	Champ Bailey, Den, AFC	10	162
	Asante Samuel, NE, AFC	10	120
	Walt Harris, SF, NFC	8	84
	Charles Woodson, GB, NFC	8	61
2007	Antonio Cromartie, SD, AFC	10	144
	O. J. Atogwe, StL, NFC	8	125
2008	Ed Reed, Balt, AFC	9	264
	Nick Collins, GB, NFC	7	295
	Charles Woodson, GB, NFC	7	169
2009	Darren Sharper, NO, NFC	9	376
	Charles Woodson, GB, NFC	9	179
	Asante Samuel, Phi, NFC	9	117
	Jairus Byrd, Buf, AFC	9	118
2010	Ed Reed, Bal, AFC	8	183
	Asante Samuel, Phi, NFC	7	70
2011	Eric Weddle, SD, AFC	7	89
	Charles Woodson, GB, NFC	7	63

Sacks*

Year	Player, Team	Sacks
1982	Doug Martin, Min, NFC	11.5
	Jesse Baker, Hou, AFC	7.5
1983	Mark Gastineau, NYJ, AFC	19.0
	Fred Dean, SF, NFC	17.5
1984	Mark Gastineau, NYJ, AFC	22.0
	Richard Dent, Chi, NFC	17.5
1985	Richard Dent, Chi, NFC	17.0
	Andre Tippett, NE, AFC	16.5
1986	Lawrence Taylor, NYG, NFC	20.5
	Sean Jones, LA, AFC	15.5
1987	Reggie White, Phil, NFC	21.0
	Andre Tippett, NE, AFC	12.5
1988	Reggie White, Phil, NFC	18.0
	G. Townsend, LA, AFC	11.5
1989	Chris Doleman, Min, NFC	21.0
	Lee Williams, SD, AFC	14.0
1990	Derrick Thomas, KC, AFC	20.0
	Charles Haley, SF, NFC	16.0
1991	Pat Swilling, NO, NFC	17.0
	William Fuller, Hou, AFC	15.0
1992	Clyde Simmons, Phil, NFC	19.0
	Leslie O'Neal, SD, AFC	17.0
1993	Neil Smith, KC, AFC	15.0
	Renaldo Turnbull, NO, NFC	13.0
	Reggie White, GB, NFC	13.0
1994	Kevin Greene, Pit, AFC	14.0
	Ken Harvey, Wash, NFC	13.5
	John Randle, Min, NFC	13.5
1995	Bryce Paup, Buf, AFC	17.5
	William Fuller, Phil, NFC	13.0
	Wayne Martin, NO, NFC	13.0
1996	Kevin Greene, Car, NFC	14.5
	Michael McCrary, Sea, AFC	13.5
	Bruce Smith, Buf, AFC	13.5
1997	John Randle, Min, NFC	15.5
	Bruce Smith, Buf, AFC	14.0
1998	Michael Sinclair, Sea, AFC	16.5
	Reggie White, GB, NFC	16.0
1999	Kevin Carter, StL, NFC	17.0
	Jevon Kearse, Ten, AFC	14.5
2000	La'Roi Glover, NO, NFC	17.0
	Trace Armstrong, Mia, AFC	16.5
2001	Michael Strahan, NYG, NFC	22.5
	Peter Boulware, Balt, AFC	15.0
2002	Jason Taylor, Mia, AFC	18.5
	Simeon Rice, TB, NFC	15.5
2003	Michael Strahan, NYG, NFC	18.5
	Adewale Ogunleye, Mia, AFC	15.0
2004	Dwight Freeney, Ind, AFC	16.0
	Bertrand Berry, Ariz, NFC	14.5
2005	Derrick Burgess, Oak, AFC	16.0
	Osi Umenyiora, NYG, NFC	14.5
2006	Shawne Merriman, SD, AFC	17.0
	Aaron Kampman, GB, NFC	15.5
2007	Jared Allen, KC, AFC	15.5
	Patrick Kerney, Sea, NFC	14.5
2008	DeMarcus Ware, Dal, NFC	20.0
	Joey Porter, Mia, AFC	17.5
2009	Elvis Dumervil, Den, AFC	17.0
	Jared Allen, Min, NFC	14.5
2010	DeMarcus Ware, Dal, NFC	15.5
	Tamba Hali, KC, AFC	14.5
2011	Terrell Suggs, Bal, AFC	14.0
	Jared Allen, Min, NFC	22.0

*Sacks were not kept as an official NFL statistic until 1982.

Date	Result
1-15-39	NY Giants 13, Pro All-Stars 10
1-14-40	Green Bay 16, NFL All-Stars 7
12-29-40	Chi Bears 28, NFL All-Stars 14
1-4-42	Chi Bears 35, NFL All-Stars 24
12-27-42	NFL All-Stars 17, Washington 14
1-14-51	A. Conf. 28, N. Conf. 27
1-12-52	N. Conf. 30, A. Conf. 13
1-10-53	N. Conf. 27, A. Conf. 7
1-17-54	East 20, West 9
1-16-55	West 26, East 19
1-15-56	East 31, West 30
1-13-57	West 19, East 10
1-12-58	West 26, East 7
1-11-59	East 28, West 21
1-17-60	West 38, East 21
1-15-61	West 35, East 31
1-7-62	AFL West 47, East 27
1-14-62	NFL West 31, East 30
1-13-63	AFL West 21, East 14
1-13-63	NFL East 30, West 20
1-12-64	NFL West 31, East 17
1-19-64	AFL West 27, East 24
1-10-65	NFL West 34, East 14

Date	Result
1-16-65	AFL West 38, East 14
1-15-66	AFL All-Stars 30, Buffalo 19
1-15-66	NFL East 36, West 7
1-21-67	AFL East 30, West 23
1-22-67	NFL East 20, West 10
1-21-68	AFL East 25, West 24
1-21-68	NFL West 38, East 20
1-19-69	AFL West 38, East 25
1-19-69	NFL West 10, East 7
1-17-70	AFL West 26, East 3
1-18-70	NFL West 16, East 13
1-24-71	NFC 27, AFC 6
1-23-72	AFC 26, NFC 13
1-21-73	AFC 33, NFC 28
1-20-74	AFC 15, NFC 13
1-20-75	NFC 17, AFC 10
1-26-76	NFC 23, AFC 20
1-17-77	AFC 24, NFC 14
1-23-78	NFC 14, AFC 13
1-29-79	NFC 13, AFC 7
1-27-80	NFC 37, AFC 27
2-1-81	NFC 21, AFC 7
1-31-82	AFC 16, NFC 13
2-6-83	NFC 20, AFC 19
1-29-84	NFC 45, AFC 3
1-27-85	AFC 22, NFC 14
2-2-86	NFC 28, AFC 24

Date	Result
2-1-87	AFC 10, NFC 6
2-7-88	AFC 15, NFC 6
1-29-89	NFC 34, AFC 3
2-4-90	NFC 27, AFC 21
2-3-91	AFC 23, NFC 21
2-2-92	NFC 21, AFC 15
2-7-93	AFC 23, NFC 20
2-6-94	NFC 17, AFC 3
2-5-95	AFC 41, NFC 13
2-4-96	NFC 20, AFC 13
2-2-97	AFC 26, NFC 23
2-1-98	AFC 29, NFC 24
2-7-99	AFC 23, NFC 10
2-6-00	NFC 51, AFC 31
2-4-01	AFC 38, NFC 17
2-10-02	AFC 38, NFC 30
2-2-03	AFC 45, NFC 20
2-8-04	NFC 55, AFC 52
2-13-05	AFC 38, NFC 27
2-12-06	NFC 23, AFC 17
2-10-07	AFC 31, NFC 28
2-10-08	NFC 42, AFC 30
2-8-09	NFC 30, AFC 21
1-31-10	AFC 41, NFC 34
1-30-11	NFC 55, AFC 41
1-29-12	AFC 59, NFC 41

Date	Result (Attendance)
8-31-34	Chi Bears 0, All-Stars 0 (79,432)
8-29-35	Chi Bears 5, All-Stars 0 (77,450)
9-2-36	All-Stars 7, Detroit 7 (76,000)
9-1-37	All-Stars 6, Green Bay 0 (84,560)
8-31-38	All-Stars 28, Washington 16 (74,250)
8-30-39	NY Giants 9, All-Stars 0 (81,456)
8-29-40	Green Bay 45, All-Stars 28 (84,567)
8-28-41	Chi Bears 37, All-Stars 13 (98,203)
8-28-42	Chi Bears 21, All-Stars 0 (101,100)
8-25-43	All-Stars 27, Washington 7 (48,471)
8-30-44	Chi Bears 24, All-Stars 21 (48,769)
8-30-45	Green Bay 19, All-Stars 7 (92,753)
8-23-46	All-Stars 16, Los Angeles 0 (97,380)
8-22-47	All-Stars 16, Chi Bears 0 (105,840)
8-20-48	Chi Cardinals 28, All-Stars 0 (101,220)
8-12-49	Philadelphia 38, All-Stars 0 (93,780)
8-11-50	All-Stars 17, Philadelphia 7 (88,885)
8-17-51	Cleveland 33, All-Stars 0 (92,180)
8-15-52	Los Angeles 10, All-Stars 7 (88,316)
8-14-53	Detroit 24, All-Stars 10 (93,818)
8-13-54	Detroit 31, All-Stars 6 (93,470)

Date	Result (Attendance)
8-12-55	All-Stars 30, Cleveland 27 (75,000)
8-10-56	Cleveland 26, All-Stars 0 (75,000)
8-9-57	NY Giants 22, All-Stars 12 (75,000)
8-15-58	All-Stars 35, Detroit 19 (70,000)
8-14-59	Baltimore 29, All-Stars 0 (70,000)
8-12-60	Baltimore 32, All-Stars 7 (70,000)
8-4-61	Philadelphia 28, All-Stars 14 (66,000)
8-3-62	Green Bay 42, All-Stars 20 (65,000)
8-2-63	All-Stars 20, Green Bay 17 (65,000)
8-7-64	Chicago 28, All-Stars 17 (65,000)
8-6-65	Cleveland 24, All-Stars 16 (68,000)
8-5-66	Green Bay 38, All-Stars 0 (72,000)
8-4-67	Green Bay 27, All-Stars 0 (70,934)
8-2-68	Green Bay 34, All-Stars 17 (69,917)
8-1-69	NY Jets 26, All-Stars 24 (74,208)
7-31-70	Kansas City 24, All-Stars 3 (69,940)
7-30-71	Baltimore 24, All-Stars 17 (52,289)
7-28-72	Dallas 20, All-Stars 7 (54,162)
7-27-73	Miami 14, All-Stars 3 (54,103)
1974	No game
8-1-75	Pittsburgh 21, All-Stars 14 (54,562)
7-23-76	Pittsburgh 24, All-Stars 0 (52,895)

*Discontinued.

Most Career Wins

Coach	Yrs	Teams	Regular Season W	L	T	Pct	Career W	L	T	Pct
Don Shula	33	Balt Colts, Dolphins	328	156	6	.676	347	173	6	.665
George Halas	40	Bears	318	148	31	.671	324	151	31	.671
Tom Landry	29	Cowboys	250	162	6	.605	270	178	6	.601
Curly Lambeau	33	Packers, Chi Cards, Redskins	226	132	22	.624	229	134	22	.623
*Paul Brown	25	Browns, Bengals	213	104	9	.672	222	116	9	.668
Chuck Noll	23	Steelers	193	148	1	.566	209	156	1	.572
M. Schottenheimer	20	Browns, Chiefs, Redskins, Chargers	200	126	1	.613	205	139	1	.596
Dan Reeves	23	Broncos, NY Giants, Falcons	190	165	2	.535	201	174	2	.536
Chuck Knox	22	LA Rams, Bills, Seahawks	186	147	1	.558	193	158	1	.550
†Bill Belichick	17	Browns, Patriots	175	97	0	.643	192	104	0	.649
Bill Parcells	18	NY Giants, Patriots, NY Jets, Cowboys	172	130	1	.569	183	138	1	.570
Mike Holmgren	17	Packers, Seahawks	161	111	0	.592	174	122	0	.588
Joe Gibbs	15	Redskins	154	94	0	.621	171	101	0	.629
Bud Grant	18	Vikings	158	96	5	.620	168	108	5	.607
†Mike Shanahan	18	Raiders, Broncos, Redskins	157	119	0	.569	165	124	0	.571
Bill Cowher	14	Steelers	149	90	1	.623	161	99	1	.619
Marv Levy	17	Chiefs, Bills	143	112	0	.561	154	120	0	.562
†Tom Coughlin	16	Jaguars, NY Giants	142	114	0	.555	154	121	0	.560
Steve Owen	23	NY Giants	151	100	17	.595	153	108	17	.581
Tony Dungy	13	Buccaneers, Ind Colts	139	69	0	.668	148	79	0	.652
Jeff Fisher	17	Hou/Tenn Oilers, Tenn Titans	142	120	0	.542	147	126	0	.563
Hank Stram	17	Chiefs, Saints	131	97	10	.571	136	100	10	.573

Top Winning Percentages

	W	L	T	Pct		W	L	T	Pct
Vince Lombardi	105	35	6	.740	*Paul Brown	222	112	9	.660
John Madden	112	39	7	.731	Tony Dungy	148	79	0	.652
George Allen	118	54	5	.681	George Seifert	124	67	0	.650
George Halas	324	151	31	.671	†Bill Belichick	192	104	0	.649
Don Shula	347	173	6	.665	Joe Gibbs	171	101	0	.629

Note: Minimum 100 victories.

†Active in 2011. *Includes a 52–4–3 (5–0 playoff) record with Browns in AAFC and a 7–20–1 record with Bengals in AFL.

Pro Football Most Valuable Players

Year	Player/ Team	Position	Year	Player/ Team	Position
1938	Mel Hein, NYG (NFL)	C		Lou Groza, Clev (TSN)	OT/K
1939	Parker Hall, Clev (NFL)	HB	1955	Otto Graham, Clev (UP, TSN)	QB
1940	Ace Parker, Brooklyn (NFL)	QB		Harlon Hill, Chi Bears (NEA)	E
1941	Don Hutson, GB (NFL)	E	1956	Frank Gifford, NYG (UP, NEA, TSN)	HB
1942	Don Hutson, GB (NFL)	E	1957	Y.A. Tittle, SF (TSN)	QB
1943	Sid Luckman, Chi Bears (NFL)	QB		Jim Brown, Clev (AP, TSN)	FB
1944	Frank Sinkwich, Det (NFL)	HB		John Unitas, Balt (NEA)	QB
1945	Bob Waterfield, Clev (NFL)	QB	1958	Jim Brown, Clev (UP, AP, NEA, TSN)	FB
1946	Bill Dudley, Pit (NFL)	HB	1959	John Unitas, Balt (UP, MCP, TSN)	QB
	Glenn Dobbs, Brooklyn (AAFC)	HB		Charley Conerly, NYG (AP, NEA)	QB
1947	No Selection (NFL)		1960	Norm Van Brocklin, Phil, NFL (UP, AP, NEA, TSN, MCP)	QB
	Otto Graham, Clev (AAFC)	QB		Joe Schmidt, Det, NFL (UP- tie)	LB
1948	No Selection (NFL)			Abner Haynes, Dal Texans, AFL (UP, TSN)	HB
	Otto Graham, Clev (AAFC-tie)	QB	1961	Paul Hornung, GB, NFL (UP, AP, TSN, MCP)	HB
	Frankie Albert, SF (AAFC-tie)	QB		Y.A. Tittle, NYG, NFL (MCP)	QB
1949	No Selection (NFL)			George Blanda, Hous, AFL (UP, TSN)	QB
1950	No Selection (NFL)		1962	Y.A. Tittle, NYG, NFL (UP, TSN)	QB
1951	Otto Graham, Clev (UP)	QB		Jim Taylor, GB, NFL (AP, NEA)	FB
1952	No Selection (NFL)			Andy Robustelli, NYG, NFL (MCP)	DE
1953	Otto Graham, Clev (UP)	QB		Cookie Gilchrist, Buf, AFL (UP)	FB
1954	Joe Perry, SF (UP)	FB		Len Dawson, Dal Texans, AFL (TSN)	QB
			1963	Jim Brown, Clev, NFL (UP, NEA (tie), MCP)	FB
				Y.A. Tittle, NYG, NFL (AP, NEA (tie), TSN)	QB
				Lance Alworth, SD, AFL (UP)	WR

Year	Player/Team	Position	Year	Player/Team	Position
	Clem Daniels, Oak, AFL (TSN)	HB		(PFWAA, AP, NEA)	
1964	Johnny Unitas, Balt,	QB		Eric Dickerson, LA Rams (TSN)	RB
	NFL (UP, AP, TSN, MCP)			John Riggins, Washington (MCP)	RB
	Lenny Moore, Balt, NFL (NEA)	HB	1984	Dan Marino, Miami	QB
	Gino Cappelletti, Boston, AFL (UP, TSN)	WR		(PFWAA, AP, NEA, MCP, TSN)	
1965	Jim Brown, Clev, NFL (UP, AP, TSN, NEA)	FB	1985	Marcus Allen, LA Raiders	RB
	Pete Retzlaff, Phil, NFL (MCP)	TE		(PFWAA, AP, TSN)	
	Jack Kemp, Buf, AFL (UP)	QB		Walter Payton, Chi Bears (NEA, MCP)	RB
	Paul Lowe, SD, AFL (TSN)	RB	1986	Lawrence Taylor, NYG	LB
1966	Bart Starr, GB, NFL (UP, AP, NEA, TSN)	QB		(PFWAA, AP, MCP, TSN)	
	Don Meredith, Dal, NFL (MCP)	QB		Phil Simms, NYG (NEA)	QB
	Jim Nance, Boston, AFL (UP, AP, TSN)	FB	1987	Jerry Rice, SF (PFWAA, NEA, MCP, TSN)	WR
1967	Johnny Unitas, Balt,	QB		John Elway, Den (AP)	QB
	NFL (UP, AP, NEA, TSN, MCP)		1988	Boomer Esiason, Cin (PFWAA, AP, TSN)	QB
	Daryl Lamonica, Oak, AFL (UP, AP, TSN)	QB		Roger Craig, SF (NEA)	RB
1968	Earl Morrall, Balt,	QB		Randall Cunningham, Phil (MCP)	QB
	NFL (UP, AP, NEA, TSN, PFW)		1989	Joe Montana, SF	QB
	Leroy Kelly, Clev, AFL (MCP)	HB		(PFWAA, AP, NEA, MCP, TSN)	
	Joe Namath, NY Jets, AFL (UP, TSN, PFW)	QB	1990	Randall Cunningham, Phil (PFWAA)	QB
1969	Roman Gabriel, LA Rams, NFL (UP, AP,			Joe Montana, SF (AP)	QB
	NEA, MCP, TSN, PFW)	QB		Jerry Rice, SF (TSN)	WR
	Daryle Lamonica, Oak, AFL (UP, TSN, PFW)	QB	1991	Thurman Thomas, Buf (PFWAA, AP, TSN)	RB
	Joe Namath, NY Jets, AFL (AP)	QB		Barry Sanders, Det (MCP)	RB
1970	John Brodie, SF (AP, NEA)	QB	1992	Steve Young, SF (PFWAA, AP, MCP, TSN)	QB
	George Blanda, Oak (MCP)	QB/K	1993	Emmitt Smith, Dal (PFWAA, AP, MCP, TSN)	RB
1971	Alan Page, Min (AP)	DT	1994	Steve Young, SF (PFWAA, AP, MCP, TSN)	QB
	Bob Griese, Miami (NEA)	QB	1995	Brett Favre, GB (PFWAA, AP, MCP, TSN)	QB
	Roger Staubach, Dal (MCP)	QB	1996	Brett Favre, GB (PFWAA, AP, MCP, TSN)	QB
1972	Larry Brown, Wash (AP, NEA, MCP)	RB	1997	Brett Favre, GB (AP – tie)	QB
1973	O.J. Simpson, Buf (AP, NEA, MCP)	RB		Barry Sanders, Det	RB
1974	Ken Stabler, Oak (AP, NEA)	QB		(PFWAA, AP (tie), MCP, TSN)	
	Merlin Olsen, LA Rams (MCP)	DT	1998	Terrell Davis, Den (PFWAA, AP, TSN)	RB
1975	Fran Tarkenton, Min	QB		Randall Cunningham, Min (MCP)	QB
	(PFWA, AP, NEA, MCP)		1999	Kurt Warner, StL (AP, PFWAA, MCP)	QB
1976	Bert Jones, Balt (PFWA, AP, NEA)	QB	2000	Marshall Faulk, StL (AP, PFWAA)	QB
	Ken Stabler, Oak (MCP)	QB		Rich Gannon, Oak (MCP)	QB
1977	Walter Payton, Chi (PFWA, AP, NEA)	RB	2001	Kurt Warner, StL (AP)	QB
	Bob Griese, Miami (MCP)	QB		Marshall Faulk, StL (PFWAA, MCP, TSN)	RB
1978	Earl Campbell, Hous (PFWA, NEA)	RB	2002	Rich Gannon, Oak (AP)	QB
	Terry Bradshaw, Pit (AP, MCP)	QB	2003	Peyton Manning, Ind (AP - tie)	QB
1979	Earl Campbell, Hou	RB		Steve McNair, Ten (AP - tie)	QB
	(PFWA, AP, NEA, MCP)		2004	Peyton Manning, Ind (AP)	QB
1980	Brian Sipe, Clev (PFWA, AP, TSN)	QB	2005	Shaun Alexander, Sea (AP)	RB
	Earl Campbell, Hou (NEA)	RB	2006	LaDainian Tomlinson, SD (AP)	RB
	Ron Jaworski, Phil (MCP)	QB	2007	Tom Brady, NE (AP)	QB
1981	Ken Anderson, Cin	QB	2008	Peyton Manning, Ind (AP)	QB
	(PFWA, AP, NEA, TSN, MCP)		2009	Peyton Manning, Ind (AP)	QB
1982	Dan Fouts, SD (PFWA, NEA)	QB	2010	Tom Brady, NE (AP)	QB
	Mark Moseley, Wash (AP, TSN)	K	2011	Aaron Rodgers, GB (AP)	QB
	Joe Theismann, Wash (MCP)	QB			
1983	Joe Theismann, Wash	QB			

NOTE: AP-Associated Press, UP-United Press, PFW-*Pro Football Weekly*; TSN-*The Sporting News*; PFWAA-Pro Football Writers Association of America; PFWA-Pro Football Writers of America; MCP-Maxwell Club of Philadelphia, NEA-Newspaper Enterprise Association.

The NFL began awarding its MVP award, the Joe F. Carr Trophy (Carr was league president from 1921-39), in 1938, and continued to do so until 1946. Since that time, the NFL's Most Valuable Players and Players of the Year have been named by a variety of sources, among them, the United Press, the Associated Press, the Maxwell Club of Philadelphia, and the Pro Football Writers Association of America as well as magazines such as *Pro Football Weekly* and *The Sporting News*.

Pro Football Rookies of the Year

Year	Player/ Team	Position
1955	Alan Ameche, Balt (UP, TSN)	FB
1956	Lenny Moore, Balt (UP)	HB
	J.C. Caroline, Chi Bears (TSN)	DB
1957	Jim Brown, Clev (UP, AP, TSN)	FB
1958	Jimmy Orr, Pit (UP, AP)	OE
	Bobby Mitchell, Cleveland (TSN)	HB
1959	Nick Pietrosante, Det (AP, TSN)	FB
	Boyd Dowler, GB (UP)	OE
1960	Gail Cogdill, Det, NFL (AP, UP, TSN)	OE
	Abner Haynes, Dal Texans, AFL (UP, TSN)	HB
1961	Mike Ditka, Chi Bears, NFL (AP, UP, TSN)	OE
	Earl Faison, SD, AFL (UP, TSN)	DE
1962	Ronnie Bull, Chi Bears, NFL (AP, UP, TSN)	HB
	Curtis McClinton, Dal, AFL (UP, TSN)	FB
1963	Paul Flatley, Min, NFL (AP, UP, TSN)	OE
	Billy Joe, Den, AFL (UP, TSN)	FB
1964	Charley Taylor, Wash, NFL (AP, UP, TSN, NEA)	HB
	Matt Snell, NYJ, AFL (UP, TSN)	FB
1965	Gale Sayers, Chi, NFL (AP, UP, TSN, NEA)	HB
	Joe Namath, NYJ, AFL (UP, TSN)	QB
1966	Johnny Roland, StL, NFL (UP)	HB
	Tommy Nobis, Atl, NFL (AP, TSN, NEA)	LB
	Bobby Burnett, Buf, AFL (UP, TSN)	HB
1967	Mel Farr, Det, NFL (AP-Off, UP, TSN, NEA)	HB
	Lem Barney, Det NFL (AP-Def)	CB
	George Webster, Hous, AFL (UP)	LB
	Dickie Post, SD, AFL (TSN)	HB
1968	Earl McCullouch, Det, NFL (AP-Off, UP, TSN, NEA)	OE
	Claude Humphrey NFL (AP-Def)	DE
	Paul Robinson, Cin, AFL (UP, TSN)	HB
1969	Calvin Hill, Dal, NFL (AP-Off, UP, TSN, NEA)	HB
	Joe Greene NFL (AP-Def)	DT
	Greg Cook, Cin, AFL (UP)	QB
	Carl Garrett, Boston, AFL (TSN)	HB
1970	Raymond Chester, Oak (NEA)	TE
	Dennis Shaw Buf (AP-Off, UP-AFC)	QB
	Bruce Taylor, DB SF (AP-Def, UP-NFC)	DB
1971	Jim Plunkett NE (UP-AFC)	QB
	John Brockington GB (AP-Off, UP-NFC)	RB
	Isiah Robertson, SF (AP-Def)	LB
1972	Franco Harris, Pit (AP-Off, PFW, UP-AFC)	RB
	Chester Marcol, GB (UP-NFC)	PK
	Willie Buchanan, GB (AP-Def)	CB
1973	Chuck Foreman, Min (AP-Off, PFW)	RB
	Wally Chambers, Chi (AP-Def)	DT
	Bobbie Clark, Cin (UP-AFC)	RB
	Charle Young Phil (UP-NFC)	TE
1974	Don Woods, SD (AP-Off, PFW, UP-AFC)	RB
	John Hicks, NYG (UP-NFC)	G
	Jack Lambert, Pit (AP-Def)	LB
1975	Steve Bartkowski, Atl (PFW)	QB
	Robert Brazile, Hous (AP-Def, UP-AFC)	LB
	Mike Thomas, Wash (AP-Off, UP-NFC)	RB
1976	Mike Haynes, NE (AP-Def, UP-AFC)	DB
	Sammy White, Min (AP-Off, UP-NFC)	WR
1977	Tony Dorsett, Dal (NEA, AP-Off, UP-NFC)	RB
	A.J. Duhe, Mia (AP-Def, UP-AFC)	DE
1978	Earl Campbell, Hous Oilers (NEA, PFWA, AP-Off, UP-AFC)	RB
	Al "Bubba" Baker, Det (AP-Def, UP-NFC)	DE

Year	Player/ Team	Position
1979	Ottis Anderson, StL Card (NEA, PFWA, AP-Off, UP-NFC)	RB
	Jerry Butler, Buf (UP-AFC)	WR
	Jim Haslett, Buf (AP-Def)	LB
1980	Billy Sims, Det (NEA, TSN, PFWA, AP-Off, UP-NFC)	RB
	Joe Cribbs Buf (UP-AFC)	RB
	Buddy Curry, Atl (AP-Def tie)	LB
	Al Richardson, Atl (AP-Def tie)	LB
1981	Lawrence Taylor, NYG (NEA, AP-Def)	LB
	George Rogers, NO (TSN, PFWA, AP-Off, UP-NFC)	RB
	Joe Delaney, KC (UP-AFC)	RB
1982	Marcus Allen, LA Raiders (NEA, TSN, PFWA, AP-Off, UP-AFC)	RB
	Jim McMahon, Chi (UP-NFC)	QB
	Chip Banks, Cle (AP-Def)	LB
1983	Eric Dickerson, LA Rams (NEA, PFWA, AP-Off, UP-NFC)	RB
	Dan Marino, Mia (TSN)	QB
	Curt Warner, Sea (UP-AFC)	RB
	Vernon Maxwell, Balt (AP-Def)	LB
1984	Louis Lipps, Pit (NEA, TSN, PFWA, AP-Off, UP-AFC)	WR
	Paul McFadden, Phil (UP-NFC)	PK
	Bill Maas, KC (AP-Def)	DT
1985	Eddie Brown, Cin (NEA, TSN, AP-Off, PFWA)	WR
	Kevin Mack, Clev (UP-AFC)	RB
	Jerry Rice, SF (UP-NFC)	WR
	Duane Bickett, Ind (AP-Def)	LB
1986	Reuben Mayes, NO (NEA, TSN, PFWA, AP-Off, UP-NFC)	RB
	Leslie O'Neal, SD (AP-Def, UP-AFC)	DE
1987	Shane Conlan, Buf (PFWA, AP-Def, UP-AFC)	LB
	Bo Jackson, LA Raiders (NEA)	RB
	Robert Awalt, StL Card (TSN, UP-NFC)	TE
	Troy Stradford, Mia (AP-Off)	RB
1988	John Stephens, NE (NEA, AP-Off, PFWA)	RB
	Keith Jackson, Phil (TSN, UP-NFC)	TE
	Eric McMillan, NYJ (AP-Def)	S
1989	Barry Sanders, Det (NEA, TSN, PFWA, AP-Off, UP-NFC)	RB
	Derrick Thomas, KC (AP-Def, UP-AFC)	LB
1990	Mark Carrier, Chi (PFWA, UP-NFC, AP-Def)	S
	Emmitt Smith, Dal (AP-Off)	RB
	Richmond Webb, Mia (TSN, UP-AFC)	OT
1991	Mike Croel, Den (PFWA, TSN, AP-Def, UP-AFC)	LB
	Lawrence Dawsey, TB (UP-NFC)	WR
	Leonard Russell, NE (AP-Off)	RB
1992	Dale Carter, KC (PFWA, AP-Def, UP-AFC)	CB
	Carl Pickens, Cin (AP-Off)	WR
	Santana Dotson, TB (TSN)	DE
	Robert Jones, Dal (UP-NFC)	LB
1993	Jerome Bettis, LA Rams (PFWA, TSN, AP-Off, UP-NFC)	RB
	Rick Mirer, Sea (UP-AFC)	QB
	Dana Stubblefield, SF (AP-Def)	DT
1994	Marshall Faulk, Ind (PFWA, TSN, AP-Off, UP-NFC)	RB
	Bryant Young, SF (UP-NFC)	DT
	Tim Bowens, Mia (AP-Def)	DT
1995	Curtis Martin, NE (PFWA, TSN, AP-Off, UP-AFC)	RB
	Rashaan Salaam, Chi (UP-NFC)	RB
	Hugh Douglas, NYJ (AP-Def)	DE

Pro Football Rookies of the Year *(Cont.)*

Year	Player/ Team	Position	Year	Player/ Team	Position
1996	Eddie George, Ten (AP, PFWA, AP-Off, TSN)	RB	2004	Ben Roethlisberger, Pit (AP-Off)	QB
	Terry Glenn, NE (UP-AFC)	WR		Jonathan Vilma, NYJ (AP-Def)	LB
	Simeon Rice, Ariz (AP-Def, UP-NFC)	DE	2005	Carnell Williams, TB (AP-Off)	RB
1997	Warrick Dunn, TB (PFWA, AP-Off, TSN)	RB		Shawne Merriman, SD (AP-Def)	LB
	Peter Boulware, Balt (AP-Def)	LB	2006	Vince Young, Ten (AP-Off)	QB
1998	Randy Moss, Min (PFWA, AP-Off, TSN)	WR		DeMeco Ryans, Hou (AP-Def)	LB
	Charles Woodson, LA Raiders (AP-Def)	CB	2007	Adrian Peterson, Min (AP-Off)	RB
1999	Edgerrin James, Ind (AP-Off, TSN)	RB		Patrick Willis, SF (AP-Def)	LB
	Jevon Kearse, Ten (AP-Def)	DE	2008	Matt Ryan, Atl (AP-Off)	QB
2000	Mike Anderson, Den (AP-Off, TSN)	RB		Jerod Mayo, NE (AP-Def)	LB
	Brian Urlacher, Chi (AP-Def)	LB	2009	Percy Harvin, Min (AP-Off)	WR
2001	Anthony Thomas, Chi (AP-Off)	RB		Brian Cushing, Hou (AP-Def)	LB
	Kendrell Bell, Pit (AP-Def)	LB	2010	Sam Bradford, StL (AP-Off)	QB
2002	Clinton Ports, Den (AP-Off)	RB		Ndamukong Suh, Det (AP-Def)	DT
	Julius Peppers, Car (AP-Def)	DE	2011	Cam Newton, Car (AP-Off)	QB
2003	Anquan Boldin, Ariz (AP-Off)	WR		Von Miller, Den (AP-Def)	LB
	Terrell Suggs, Bal (AP-Def)	LB			

NOTE: AP-Associated Press, UP-United Press, PFW-*Pro Football Weekly*, TSN-*The Sporting News*, PFWAA-Pro Football Writers Association of America, PFWA-Pro Football Writers of America, MCP-Maxwell Club of Philadelphia, NEA-Newspaper Enterprise Association

Starting in 1960, the United Press annually awarded two Rookie of the Year awards, one to an AFL player and one to a NFL player. After the AFL-NFL merger, the UP kept the two-award format for the AFC and NFC. The UP stopped awarding RoY awards after the 1996 season.

Starting in 1967, the Associated Press began announcing two annual Rookie of the Year awards as well. One went to the best offensive rookie in the NFL, the other to the best defensive rookie.

Alltime Number-One Draft Choices

Year	Team	Selection	Position
1936	Philadelphia	Jay Berwanger, Chicago	HB
1937	Philadelphia	Sam Francis, Nebraska	FB
1938	Cleveland	Corbett Davis, Indiana	FB
1939	Chicago Cardinals	Ki Aldrich, Texas Christian	C
1940	Chicago Cardinals	George Cafego, Tennessee	HB
1941	Chicago Bears	Tom Harmon, Michigan	HB
1942	Pittsburgh	Bill Dudley, Virginia	HB
1943	Detroit	Frank Sinkwich, Georgia	HB
1944	Boston	Angelo Bertelli, Notre Dame	QB
1945	Chicago Cardinals	Charley Trippi, Georgia	HB
1946	Boston	Frank Dancewicz, Notre Dame	QB
1947	Chicago Bears	Bob Fenimore, Oklahoma A&M	HB
1948	Washington	Harry Gilmer, Alabama	QB
1949	Philadelphia	Chuck Bednarik, Pennsylvania	C
1950	Detroit	Leon Hart, Notre Dame	E
1951	New York Giants	Kyle Rote, SMU	HB
1952	Los Angeles	Bill Wade, Vanderbilt	QB
1953	San Francisco	Harry Babcock, Georgia	E
1954	Cleveland	Bobby Garrett, Stanford	QB
1955	Baltimore	George Shaw, Oregon	QB
1956	Pittsburgh	Gary Glick, Colorado A&M	DB
1957	Green Bay	Paul Hornung, Notre Dame	HB
1958	Chicago Cardinals	King Hill, Rice	QB
1959	Green Bay	Randy Duncan, Iowa	QB
1960	Los Angeles	Billy Cannon, LSU	RB
1961	Minnesota	Tommy Mason, Tulane	RB
	Buffalo (AFL)	Ken Rice, Auburn	G
1962	Washington	Ernie Davis, Syracuse	RB
	Oakland (AFL)	Roman Gabriel, North Carolina St	QB
1963	LA Rams	Terry Baker, Oregon St	QB
	Kansas City (AFL)	Buck Buchanan, Grambling	DT
1964	San Francisco	Dave Parks, Texas Tech	E
	Boston (AFL)	Jack Concannon, Boston College	QB
1965	NY Giants	Tucker Frederickson, Auburn	RB
	Houston (AFL)	Lawrence Elkins, Baylor	E
1966	Atlanta	Tommy Nobis, Texas	LB
	Miami (AFL)	Jim Grabowski, Illinois	RB

Year	Team	Selection	Position
1967	Baltimore	Bubba Smith, Michigan St	DT
1968	Minnesota	Ron Yary, USC	T
1969	Buffalo (AFL)	O.J. Simpson, USC	RB
1970	Pittsburgh	Terry Bradshaw, Louisiana Tech	QB
1971	New England	Jim Plunkett, Stanford	QB
1972	Buffalo	Walt Patulski, Notre Dame	DE
1973	Houston	John Matuszak, Tampa	DE
1974	Dallas	Ed Jones, Tennessee St	DE
1975	Atlanta	Steve Bartkowski, California	QB
1976	Tampa Bay	Lee Roy Selmon, Oklahoma	DE
1977	Tampa Bay	Ricky Bell, USC	RB
1978	Houston	Earl Campbell, Texas	RB
1979	Buffalo	Tom Cousineau, Ohio St	LB
1980	Detroit	Billy Sims, Oklahoma	RB
1981	New Orleans	George Rogers, South Carolina	RB
1982	New England	Kenneth Sims, Texas	DT
1983	Baltimore	John Elway, Stanford	QB
1984	New England	Irving Fryar, Nebraska	WR
1985	Buffalo	Bruce Smith, Virginia Tech	DE
1986	Tampa Bay	Bo Jackson, Auburn	RB
1987	Tampa Bay	Vinny Testaverde, Miami (Fla.)	QB
1988	Atlanta	Aundray Bruce, Auburn	LB
1989	Dallas	Troy Aikman, UCLA	QB
1990	Indianapolis	Jeff George, Illinois	QB
1991	Dallas	Russell Maryland, Miami (Fla.)	DT
1992	Indianapolis	Steve Emtman, Washington	DT
1993	New England	Drew Bledsoe, Washington St	QB
1994	Cincinnati	Dan Wilkinson, Ohio St	DT
1995	Cincinnati	Ki-Jana Carter, Penn St	RB
1996	New York Jets	Keyshawn Johnson, USC	WR
1997	St Louis	Orlando Pace, Ohio St	OT
1998	Indianapolis	Peyton Manning, Tennessee	QB
1999	Cleveland	Tim Couch, Kentucky	QB
2000	Cleveland	Courtney Brown, Penn St	DE
2001	Atlanta	Michael Vick, Virginia Tech	QB
2002	Houston	David Carr, Fresno St	QB
2003	Cincinnati	Carson Palmer, USC	QB
2004	San Diego	Eli Manning, Mississippi	QB
2005	San Francisco	Alex Smith, Utah	QB
2006	Houston	Mario Williams, North Carolina St	DE
2007	Oakland	JaMarcus Russell, LSU	QB
2008	Miami	Jake Long, Michigan	OT
2009	Detroit	Matthew Stafford, Georgia	QB
2010	St. Louis	Sam Bradford, Oklahoma	QB
2011	Carolina	Cam Newton, Auburn	QB
2012	Indianapolis	Andrew Luck, Stanford	QB

From 1947 through 1958, the first selection in the draft was a bonus pick, awarded to the winner of a random draw. That club, in turn, forfeited its last-round draft choice. The winner of the bonus choice was eliminated from future draws. The system was abolished after 1958, by which time all clubs had received a bonus choice.

Members of the Pro Football Hall of Fame

Herb Adderley	Raymond Berry	Nick Buoniconti	Lou Creekmur
Troy Aikman	Elvin Bethea	Dick Butkus	Larry Csonka
George Allen	Charles W. Bidwill Sr.	Jack Butler	Al Davis
Marcus Allen	Fred Biletnikoff	Earl Campbell	Willie Davis
Lance Alworth	George Blanda	Tony Canadeo	Dermontti Dawson
Doug Atkins	Mel Blount	Joe Carr	Len Dawson
Morris (Red) Badgro	Terry Bradshaw	Harry Carson	Fred Dean
Lem Barney	Bob (the Boomer) Brown	Dave Casper	Joe DeLamielleure
Cliff Battles	Jim Brown	Guy Chamberlin	Richard Dent
Sammy Baugh	Paul Brown	Jack Christiansen	Eric Dickerson
Chuck Bednarik	Roosevelt Brown	Earl (Dutch) Clark	Dan Dierdorf
Bert Bell	Willie Brown	George Connor	Mike Ditka
Bobby Bell	Junious (Buck) Buchanan	Jimmy Conzelman	Chris Doleman

Art Donovan
Tony Dorsett
John (Paddy) Driscoll
Bill Dudley
Albert Glen (Turk) Edwards
Carl Eller
John Elway
Weeb Ewbank
Marshall Faulk
Tom Fears
Jim Finks
Ray Flaherty
Len Ford
Dan Fortmann
Dan Fouts
Benny Friedman
Frank Gatski
Bill George
Joe Gibbs
Frank Gifford
Sid Gillman
Otto Graham
Harold (Red) Grange
Bud Grant
Darrell Green
Joe Greene
Forrest Gregg
Bob Griese
Russ Grimm
Lou Groza
Joe Guyon
George Halas
Jack Ham
Dan Hampton
Chris Hanburger
John Hannah
Franco Harris
Bob Hayes
Mike Haynes
Ed Healey
Mel Hein
Ted Hendricks
Wilbur (Pete) Henry
Arnie Herber
Bill Hewitt
Gene Hickerson
Clarke Hinkle
Elroy (Crazylegs) Hirsch
Paul Hornung
Ken Houston
Robert (Cal) Hubbard
Sam Huff
Lamar Hunt
Don Hutson
Michael Irvin
Rickey Jackson
Jimmy Johnson
John Henry Johnson
Charlie Joiner
David (Deacon) Jones
Stan Jones
Henry Jordan
Sonny Jurgensen
Jim Kelly
Leroy Kelly

Cortez Kennedy
Walt Kiesling
Frank (Bruiser) Kinard
Paul Krause
Earl (Curly) Lambeau
Jack Lambert
Tom Landry
Dick (Night Train) Lane
Jim Langer
Willie Lanier
Steve Largent
Yale Lary
Dante Lavelli
Bobby Layne
Dick LeBeau
Alphonse (Tuffy) Leemans
Marv Levy
Bob Lilly
Floyd Little
Larry Little
James Lofton
Vince Lombardi
Howie Long
Ronnie Lott
Sid Luckman
William Roy (Link) Lyman
Tom Mack
John Mackey
John Madden
Tim Mara
Wellington Mara
Gino Marchetti
Dan Marino
George Preston Marshall
Curtis Martin
Ollie Matson
Bruce Matthews
Don Maynard
George McAfee
Mike McCormack
Randall McDaniel
Tommy McDonald
Hugh McElhenny
John (Blood) McNally
Mike Michalske
Wayne Millner
Bobby Mitchell
Ron Mix
Art Monk
Joe Montana
Warren Moon
Lenny Moore
Marion Motley
Mike Munchak
Anthony Munoz
George Musso
Bronko Nagurski
Joe Namath
Earle (Greasy) Neale
Ernie Nevers
Ozzie Newsome
Ray Nitschke
Chuck Noll
Leo Nomellini
Merlin Olsen

Jim Otto
Steve Owen
Alan Page
Clarence (Ace) Parker
Jim Parker
Walter Payton
Joe Perry
Pete Pihos
Fritz Pollard
John Randle
Hugh (Shorty) Ray
Dan Reeves
Mel Renfro
Jerry Rice
Les Richter
John Riggins
Jim Ringo
Willie Roaf
Andy Robustelli
Art Rooney
Dan Rooney
Pete Rozelle
Bob St. Clair
Ed Sabol
Barry Sanders
Charlie Sanders
Deion Sanders
Gale Sayers
Joe Schmidt
Tex Schramm
Lee Roy Selmon
Shannon Sharpe
Billy Shaw
Art Shell
Don Shula
O.J. Simpson
Mike Singletary
Jackie Slater
Bruce Smith
Emmitt Smith
Jackie Smith
John Stallworth
Bart Starr
Roger Staubach
Ernie Stautner
Jan Stenerud
Dwight Stephenson
Hank Stram
Ken Strong
Joe Stydahar
Lynn Swann
Fran Tarkenton
Charley Taylor
Jim Taylor
Lawrence Taylor
Derrick Thomas
Emmitt Thomas
Thurman Thomas
Jim Thorpe
Andre Tippett
Y.A. Tittle
George Trafton
Charley Trippi
Emlen Tunnell
Clyde (Bulldog) Turner

Johnny Unitas
Gene Upshaw
Norm Van Brocklin
Steve Van Buren
Doak Walker
Bill Walsh
Paul Warfield
Bob Waterfield
Mike Webster
Roger Wehrli
Arnie Weinmeister
Randy White
Reggie White
Dave Wilcox
Bill Willis
Larry Wilson
Ralph Wilson
Kellen Winslow
Alex Wojciechowicz
Willie Wood
Rod Woodson
Rayfield Wright
Ron Yary
Steve Young
Jack Youngblood
Gary Zimmerman

Canadian Football League Grey Cup

Year	Results	Site	Attendance
1909	U of Toronto 26, Parkdale 6	Toronto	3,807
1910	U of Toronto 16, Hamilton Tigers 7	Hamilton	12,000
1911	U of Toronto 14, Toronto 7	Toronto	13,687
1912	Hamilton Alerts 11, Toronto 4	Hamilton	5,337
1913	Hamilton Tigers 44, Parkdale 2	Hamilton	2,100
1914	Toronto 14, U of Toronto 2	Toronto	10,500
1915	Hamilton Tigers 13, Toronto RAA 7	Toronto	2,808
1916–19	No game	—	—
1920	U of Toronto 16, Toronto 3	Toronto	10,088
1921	Toronto 23, Edmonton 0	Toronto	9,558
1922	Queen's U 13, Edmonton 1	Kingston	4,700
1923	Queen's U 54, Regina 0	Toronto	8,629
1924	Queen's U 11, Balmy Beach 3	Toronto	5,978
1925	Ottawa Senators 24, Winnipeg 1	Ottawa	6,900
1926	Ottawa Senators 10, Toronto U 7	Toronto	8,276
1927	Balmy Beach 9, Hamilton Tigers 6	Toronto	13,676
1928	Hamilton Tigers 30, Regina 0	Hamilton	4,767
1929	Hamilton Tigers 14, Regina 3	Hamilton	1,906
1930	Balmy Beach 11, Regina 6	Toronto	3,914
1931	Montreal AAA 22, Regina 0	Montreal	5,112
1932	Hamilton Tigers 25, Regina 6	Hamilton	4,806
1933	Toronto 4, Sarnia 3	Sarnia	2,751
1934	Sarnia 20, Regina 12	Toronto	8,900
1935	Winnipeg 18, Hamilton Tigers 12	Hamilton	6,405
1936	Sarnia 26, Ottawa RR 20	Toronto	5,883
1937	Toronto 4, Winnipeg 3	Toronto	11,522
1938	Toronto 30, Winnipeg 7	Toronto	18,778
1939	Winnipeg 8, Ottawa 7	Ottawa	11,738
1940	Ottawa 8, Balmy Beach 2	Toronto	4,998
1940	Ottawa 12, Balmy Beach 5	Ottawa	1,700
1941	Winnipeg 18, Ottawa 16	Toronto	19,065
1942	Toronto RCAF 8, Winnipeg RCAF 5	Toronto	12,455
1943	Hamilton F Wild 23, Winnipeg RCAF 14	Toronto	16,423
1944	Montreal St H-D Navy 7, Hamilton F Wild 6	Hamilton	3,871
1945	Toronto 35, Winnipeg 0	Toronto	18,660
1946	Toronto 28, Winnipeg 6	Toronto	18,960
1947	Toronto 10, Winnipeg 9	Toronto	18,885
1948	Calgary 12, Ottawa 7	Toronto	20,013
1949	Montreal Als 28, Calgary 15	Toronto	20,087
1950	Toronto 13, Winnipeg 0	Toronto	27,101
1951	Ottawa 21, Saskatchewan 14	Toronto	27,341
1952	Toronto 21, Edmonton 11	Toronto	27,391
1953	Hamilton Ticats 12, Winnipeg 6	Toronto	27,313
1954	Edmonton 26, Montreal 25	Toronto	27,321
1955	Edmonton 34, Montreal 19	Vancouver	39,417
1956	Edmonton 50, Montreal 27	Toronto	27,425
1957	Hamilton 32, Winnipeg 7	Toronto	27,051
1958	Winnipeg 35, Hamilton 28	Vancouver	36,567
1959	Winnipeg 21, Hamilton 7	Toronto	33,133
1960	Ottawa 16, Edmonton 6	Vancouver	38,102
1961	Winnipeg 21, Hamilton 14	Toronto	32,651
1962	Winnipeg 28, Hamilton 27	Toronto	32,655
1963	Hamilton 21, British Columbia 10	Vancouver	36,545
1964	British Columbia 34, Hamilton 24	Toronto	32,655
1965	Hamilton 22, Winnipeg 16	Toronto	32,655
1966	Saskatchewan 29, Ottawa 14	Vancouver	36,553
1967	Hamilton 24, Saskatchewan 1	Ottawa	31,358
1968	Ottawa 24, Calgary 21	Toronto	32,655
1969	Ottawa 29, Saskatchewan 11	Montreal	33,172
1970	Montreal 23, Calgary 10	Toronto	32,669
1971	Calgary 14, Toronto 11	Vancouver	34,484
1972	Hamilton 13, Saskatchewan 10	Hamilton	33,993
1973	Ottawa 22, Edmonton 18	Toronto	36,653
1974	Montreal 20, Edmonton 7	Vancouver	34,450
1975	Edmonton 9, Montreal 8	Calgary	32,454
1976	Ottawa 23, Saskatchewan 20	Toronto	53,467
1977	Montreal 41, Edmonton 6	Montreal	68,318
1978	Edmonton 20, Montreal 13	Toronto	54,695

Canadian Football League Grey Cup *(Cont.)*

Year	Results	Site	Attendance
1979	Edmonton 17, Montreal 9	Montreal	65,113
1980	Edmonton 48, Hamilton 10	Toronto	54,661
1981	Edmonton 26, Ottawa 23	Montreal	52,478
1982	Edmonton 32, Toronto 16	Toronto	54,741
1983	Toronto 18, British Columbia 17	Vancouver	59,345
1984	Winnipeg 47, Hamilton 17	Edmonton	60,081
1985	British Columbia 37, Hamilton 24	Montreal	56,723
1986	Hamilton 39, Edmonton 15	Vancouver	59,621
1987	Edmonton 38, Toronto 36	Vancouver	59,478
1988	Winnipeg 22, British Columbia 21	Ottawa	50,604
1989	Saskatchewan 43, Hamilton 40	Toronto	54,088
1990	Winnipeg 50, Edmonton 11	Vancouver	46,968
1991	Toronto 36, Calgary 21	Winnipeg	51,985
1992	Calgary 24, Winnipeg 10	Toronto	45,863
1993	Edmonton 33, Winnipeg 23	Calgary	50,035
1994	British Columbia 26, Baltimore 23	Vancouver	55,097
1995	Baltimore 37, Calgary 20	Regina, Saskatchewan	52,564
1996	Toronto 43, Edmonton 37	Hamilton, Ontario	38,595
1997	Toronto 47, Saskatchewan 23	Edmonton	60,431
1998	Calgary 26, Hamilton 24	Winnipeg	34,157
1999	Hamilton 32, Calgary 21	Vancouver	45,118
2000	British Columbia 28, Montreal 26	Calgary	43,822
2001	Calgary 27, Winnipeg 19	Montreal	65,255
2002	Montreal 25, Edmonton 16	Edmonton	62,531
2003	Edmonton 34, Montreal 22	Regina, Saskatchewan	50,909
2004	Toronto 27, British Columbia 19	Ottawa	51,242
2005	Edmonton 38, Montreal 35 (OT)	Vancouver	59,157
2006	British Columbia 25, Montreal 14	Winnipeg	44,786
2007	Saskatchewan 23, Winnipeg 19	Toronto	52,230
2008	Calgary 22, Montreal 14	Montreal	66,308
2009	Montreal 28, Saskatchewan 27	Calgary	46,020
2010	Montreal 21, Saskatchewan 18	Edmonton	63,317
2011	British Columbia 34, Winnipeg 23	Vancouver	54,313

In 1909, Earl Grey, the Governor-General of Canada, donated a trophy for the Rugby Football Championship of Canada. The trophy, which subsequently became known as the Grey Cup, was originally open only to teams registered with the Canada Rugby Union. Since 1954, it has been awarded to the winner of the Canadian Football League's championship game.

AMERICAN FOOTBALL LEAGUE I

Year	Champion	Record
1926	Philadelphia Quakers	7-2

AMERICAN FOOTBALL LEAGUE II

Year	Champion	Record
1936	Boston Shamrocks	8-3
1937	LA Bulldogs	8-0

AMERICAN FOOTBALL LEAGUE III

Year	Champion	Record
1940	Columbus Bullies	8-1-1
1941	Columbus Bullies	5-1-2

ALL-AMERICAN FOOTBALL CONFERENCE

Year	Championship Game
1946	Cleveland 14, NY Yankees 9
1947	Cleveland 14, NY Yankees 3
1948	Cleveland 49, Buffalo 7
1949	Cleveland 21, San Francisco 7

WORLD FOOTBALL LEAGUE

Year	World Bowl Championship
1974	Birmingham 22, Florida 21
1975	Disbanded midseason

UNITED STATES FOOTBALL LEAGUE

Year	Championship Game
1983	Michigan 24, Philadelphia 22
1984	Philadelphia 23, Arizona 3
1985	Baltimore 28, Oakland 24

X FOOTBALL LEAGUE

Year	Championship Game
2001	Los Angeles 38, San Francisco 6

NFL EUROPE*

Year	Champion	Record
1991	London	9-1-0
1992	Sacramento	8-2-0
1995	Frankfurt	6-4-0
1996	Scotland	7-3-0
1997	Barcelona	5-5-0
1998	Rhein	7-3-0
1999	Frankfurt	6-4-0
2000	Rhein	7-3-0
2001	Berlin	6-4-0
2002	Berlin	6-4-0
2003	Frankfurt	6-4-0
2004	Berlin	9-1-0
2005	Amsterdam	6-4-0
2006	Frankfurt	7-3-0
2007	Hamburg	7-3-0

*Known as the World League of American Football until 1998. League folded after the 2007 season.

UNITED FOOTBALL LEAGUE

Year	Championship Game
2009	Las Vegas 20, Florida 17
2010	Las Vegas 23, Florida 20
2011	Virginia 17, Las Vegas 3

GREG NELSON

College Football

Baylor quarterback Robert Griffin III threw for 3,988 yards and ran for 644 more en route to the Heisman

Bama Wins, BCS Loses

Anchored by Nick Saban's typically stifling defense, Alabama won the national title fair and square, but its second meeting with LSU seemed less than satisfying

B.J. SCHECTER

THE TIPPING POINT OF THE BCS era finally came. What finally pushed the BCS over the edge wasn't a straightforward, blatant controversy like in past years, but a feeling that enough was enough. There was little doubt that LSU and Alabama were the two best teams in the nation in 2011. Both teams had dominant defenses and enough talent to fill NFL rosters. But LSU and Alabama had already played in a November contest that was dubbed the Game of the Century and failed miserably to live up to the hype, as LSU gutted out a 9-6 victory in a defensive slugfest. Seeing the Tigers and Crimson Tide meet again for the national title, as good as they both were, was just . . . unsatisfying.

And that perfectly sums up the BCS Era. Often the convoluted computer formula that no one seemed to understand produced a true No. 1 vs. No. 2 matchup, but there were always controversies and the system didn't produce the drama that has made the NCAA basketball tournament an annual must-see event. The media and fans have long clamored for a playoff, but each year the idea has been shot down by tone deaf conference commissioners and school presidents. Finally, after the SEC was guaranteed to win its sixth straight national title, there was a prevailing feeling that something had to be done. A four-team playoff was agreed upon starting in the 2014 season. Plenty of details still need to get worked out, but one thing is certain: soon the BCS will be gone.

That's not to minimize what Alabama accomplished during the 2011 season. The Crimson Tide were the best team from start to finish and came up big in the biggest game of the season, getting revenge against LSU with a 21–0 victory in the national championship game in New Orleans. Bolstered by a dominant defense and workhorse running back Trent Richardson, Nick Saban's squad was a deserving champion, but there was a sentiment that Alabama had its chance at LSU during the regular season. What about one-loss Oklahoma State or Stanford?

Alabama entered the season with heavy hearts after a tornado in April ravaged Tuscaloosa, killing hundreds and causing millions in property damage. The storm barely missed the University of Alabama campus, but it affected the entire community nonetheless, including several football players. Crimson Tide long snapper Carson Tinker took cover in a walk-in closet with his girlfriend, Ashley Harrison, but she was ripped from his arms and thrown 100 yards.

Saban's brilliant defensive scheme and a ball-controlling ground game led by Richardson (above), who rushed for 96 yards, helped Alabama dominate LSU in the BCS title game.

She died of a broken neck. Football has always been a religion and a tremendous source of pride for Alabamians, but now it took on even greater meaning. Rooting for the Crimson Tide allowed the victims of the tornado a momentary escape from the tragedy and offered them hope.

Everywhere the players went in town they were greeted with "Roll Tide!" but this time it seemed to have a larger purpose. As Tuscaloosa slowly tried to clean up from the physical and emotional devastation, residents found an even deeper connection with the Alabama players, who embraced the extra responsibility and rolled through the early part of the season

with more determination than ever. The 9-6 loss to LSU at home in November—Alabama outplayed LSU but missed four field goals and couldn't get the ball into the end zone—was a temporary blip as the Crimson Tide continued to win impressively enough to move back to No. 2 in the polls and earn a shot in the BCS national championship game.

Saban may have lost two straight to his nemesis, LSU's Les Miles, but with 43 days to prepare for the title game it wasn't a fair fight. A defensive mastermind, Saban drew up the perfect game plan and stifled LSU, holding the Tigers to 92 yards of total offense and just five first downs. LSU crossed midfield only once. Meanwhile, Alabama's offense—led by A.J. McCarron, who completed 23 of 34 passes for 234 yards—finally kicked into gear and kicker Jeremy Shelley made five field goals. With

© DAN WOZNIAK/SOUTHCREEK/ZUMAPRESS.COM

win the Heisman and carried that distinction for most of the season. But when Luck didn't deliver any spectacular performances, Griffin stepped up and grabbed the award. Luck would end up being the No. 1 pick in the draft (Griffin went No. 2), but RG3 earned the award as the nation's most outstanding player.

"It's a transformative moment for Baylor football and the university," said Baylor athletic director Ian McCaw. "The Baylor Brand has been changed based on what's happened this fall."

Oklahoma State has quickly established itself as a premier brand name in college football. Backed by mega booster T. Boone Pickens, the Cowboys have among the best facilities in the nation, and coach Mike Gundy has installed a high-powered, big-play offense. Oklahoma State nearly earned a spot in the title game, but a mid-November loss at Iowa State on the night after tragedy struck the school again when a plane crash claimed the lives of two women's basketball coaches, set the Cowboys back. Still, many believed that Oklahoma State deserved a shot at LSU, especially after the Cowboys blew out Oklahoma 44-10 in their annual Bedlam game behind the spectacular duo of quarterback Brandon Weeden and receiver Justin Blackmon. Instead, Oklahoma State earned an invitation to the Fiesta Bowl, where the Cowboys rallied for a thrilling 41-38 victory over Stanford.

In the end, any debate was moot as Alabama thoroughly dominated LSU and proved it was the nation's best team. Years from now the Crimson Tide will not only be remembered for lifting a storm-ravaged community and possessing one of the best college defenses in history. They'll also be known as the team that pushed the BCS over the edge.

five minutes remaining, the Tide finally cracked the end zone as Richardson went off tackle left for a 34-yard touchdown.

Afterward, as the Crimson Tide celebrated on the Superdome turf and in their locker room, they remembered the victims of the tornado and what it did to their state. "This isn't a win for just us, it's a win for Tuscaloosa and all of Alabama," said Carson. "We've been through so much this year, and I'm at a loss for words to describe what I feel. Just happy."

Baylor quarterback Robert Griffin III made fans across the country happy every time he took the field. With blazing speed and jaw-dropping athleticism, Griffin carried Baylor to its best season in school history, throwing for 3,998 yards and 36 touchdowns and rushing for another 644 yards and nine TDs. From a season-opening 50-48 victory over TCU to a wild 67-56 win over Washington in the Alamo Bowl, Griffin captivated the nation with highlight-reel plays and his ability to make something out of nothing as he led the Bears to a surprising 10-3 record. Stanford's Andrew Luck entered the season as the odds on favorite to

FOR THE RECORD • 2011—2012

Final Polls

Associated Press

	Record	Pts	Head Coach	SI Preseason Rank
1. Alabama (55)	12-1	1495	Nick Saban	1
2. LSU (1)	13-1	1425	Les Miles	3
3. Oklahoma State (4)	12-1	1399	Mike Gundy	13
4. Oregon	12-2	1250	Chip Kelly	5
5. Arkansas	11-2	1198	Bobby Petrino	10
6. USC	10-2	1181	Lane Kiffin	20
7. Stanford	11-2	1167	David Shaw	4
8. Boise State	12-1	1127	Chris Petersen	8
9. South Carolina	11-2	1013	Steve Spurrier	7
10. Wisconsin	11-3	905	Bret Bielema	12
11. Michigan State	11-3	873	Mark Dantonio	14
12. Michigan	11-2	839	Brady Hoke	*
13. Baylor	10-3	780	Art Briles	*
14. TCU	11-2	653	Gary Patterson	18
15. Kansas State	10-3	621	Bill Snyder	*
16. Oklahoma	10-3	572	Bob Stoops	2
17. West Virginia	10-3	547	Dana Holgorsen	23
18. Houston	13-1	518	Tony Levine	*
19. Georgia	10-4	439	Mark Richt	*
20. Southern Miss	12-2	411	Larry Fedora	*
21. Virginia Tech	11-3	329	Frank Beamer	16
22. Clemson	10-4	188	Dabo Swinney	*
23. Florida State	9-4	154	Jimbo Fisher	6
24. Nebraska	9-4	143	Bo Pelini	9
25. Cincinnati	10-3	103	Butch Jones	*

Note: As voted by a panel of 60 sportswriters and broadcasters following bowl games (first-place votes in parentheses).
*Not ranked in preseason top 25.

USA Today/Coaches

	Pts	SI Preseason Rank			Pts	SI Preseason Rank
1 Alabama (59)	1475	1	14 Houston		673	*
2 LSU	1404	3	15 Oklahoma		610	2
3 Oklahoma State	1367	13	16 Kansas State		602	*
4 Oregon	1290	5	17 Virginia Tech		574	16
5 Arkansas	1188	10	18 West Virginia		554	23
6 Boise State	1162	8	19 Southern Miss		429	*
7 Stanford	1106	4	20 Georgia		345	*
8 South Carolina	1084	7	21 Cincinnati		248	*
9 Michigan	925	*	22 Clemson		237	*
10 Michigan State	912	14	23 Florida State		205	6
11 Wisconsin	911	12	24 Nebraska		144	9
12 Baylor	775	*	25 Brigham Young		79	*
13 TCU	710	18				

Note: Voted by a panel of 59 FBS (I-A) head coaches; 25 points for 1st, 24 for 2nd, etc. (first-place votes in parentheses).
*Not ranked in preseason top 25.

Bowls and Playoffs

NCAA Football Bowl Subdivision (I-A) Bowl Results

Date	Bowl	Result	Payout/Team ($)	Attendance
12-17-11	New Mexico	Temple 37, Wyoming 15	750,000	25,762
12-17-11	Famous Idaho Potato	Ohio 24, Utah St 23	750,000	28,076
12-17-11	New Orleans	LA-Lafayette 32, San Diego St 30	500,000	42,841
12-20-11	St. Petersburg	Marshall 20, Florida Int'l 10	500,000	20,072
12-21-11	Poinsettia	TCU 31, Louisiana Tech 24	500,000	24,607
12-22-11	Las Vegas	Boise St 56, Arizona St 24	1.1 million	35,720
12-24-11	Hawaii	Southern Miss 24, Nevada 17	750,000	32,630
12-26-11	Independence	Missouri 41, North Carolina 24	1.15 million	41,728
12-27-11	Little Caesars	Purdue 37, W Michigan 32	750,000	46,177
12-27-11	Belk	North Carolina St 31, Louisville 24	1.7 million	58,427
12-28-11	Military	Toledo 42, Air Force 41	862,500	25,042
12-28-11	Holiday	Texas 21, California 10	2.15 million	56,313
12-29-11	Champs Sports	Florida St 18, Notre Dame 14	2.325 million	68,305

NCAA Football Bowl Subdivision (I-A) Bowl Results *(Cont.)*

Date	Bowl	Result	Payout/Team($)	Attendance
12-29-11	Alamo	Baylor 67, Washington 56	3.175 million	65,256
12-30-11	Armed Forces	BYU 24, Tulsa 21	600,000	30,258
12-30-11	Pinstripe	Rutgers 27, Iowa St 13	1.8 million	38,328
12-30-11	Music City	Mississippi St 23, Wake Forest 17	1.837 million	55,208
12-30-11	Insight	Oklahoma 31, Iowa 14	3.35 million	54,247
12-31-11	Meineke Car Care	Texas A&M 33, Northwestern 22	1.7 million	68,395
12-31-11	Sun	Utah 30, Georgia Tech 27	2 million	48,123
12-31-11	Fight Hunger	Illinois 20, UCLA 14	837,500	29,878
12-31-11	Liberty	Cincinnati 31, Vanderbilt 24	1.7 million	57,103
12-31-11	Chick-fil-A	Auburn 43, Virginia 24	3.97 million (ACC) 2.93 million (SEC)	72,919
01-02-12	Outback	Michigan St 33, Georgia 30	3.5 million	49,429
01-02-12	Ticket City	Houston 30, Penn St 14	1.1 million	46,817
01-02-12	Capital One	South Carolina 30, Nebraska 13	4.6 million	61,351
01-02-12	Gator	Florida 24, Ohio St 17	2.7 million	61,312
01-02-12	Rose	Oregon 45, Wisconsin 38	17 million	91,245
01-02-12	Fiesta	Oklahoma St 41, Stanford 38	17 million	69,927
01-03-12	Sugar	Michigan 23, Virginia Tech 20	17 million	64,512
01-04-12	Orange	West Virginia 70, Clemson 33	17 million	67,563
01-06-12	Cotton	Arkansas 29, Kansas State 16	3.625 million	80,956
01-07-12	Compass	SMU 28, Pittsburgh 6	900,000 (SEC) 600,000 (Big East)	29,726
01-08-12	GoDaddy.com	Northern Illinois 38, Arkansas St 20	750,000	38,734
01-09-12	BCS Championship	Alabama 21, LSU 0	18 million	78,237

NCAA FCS (I-AA) Championship Box Score

Sam Houston St	0	6	0	0—6
North Dakota St	3	0	7	7—17

FIRST QUARTER
North Dakota St: FG Jastram 19, 0:03.

SECOND QUARTER
Sam Houston St: FG Alaniz 24, 2:18.
Sam Houston St: FG Alaniz 31, 0:40.

THIRD QUARTER
North Dakota St: TD McNorton 39 pass from Jensen (Jastram kick), 12:47.

FOURTH QUARTER
North Dakota St: TD Jensen 1 run (Jastram kick), 8:45.

	SAM HOUSTON ST	NORTH DAKOTA ST
First downs	12	9
Rushes-net yards	42-95	34-115
Net passing yards	115	120
Comp/Att/Int	12-32-2	10-20-1
Punts/total yards	7-329	10-442
Fumbles-lost	0-0	1-1
Penalties-yards	3-15	4-35
Time of possession	33:05	26:55

1-7-12, Frisco, Texas; Att: 20,586.

Small College Championship Summaries

NCAA DIVISION II

First round: Kutztown 17, Concord 14; California (PA) 44, Elizabeth City St 0; Minnesota-Duluth 30, Saginaw Valley 27; NW Missouri St 35, Missouri West 29; Wayne St (MI) 48, St. Cloud St 38; North Alabama 43, West Alabama 27; N Greenville 63, Albany St (GA) 14; Washburn 52, Abilene Christian 49.

Second Round: N Greenville 58, Mars Hill 32; New Haven 44, Kutztown 37; NW Missouri St 38, Midwestern St 31; Wayne St (MI) 38, Nebraska-Kearney 26; Winston-Salem 35, California (PA) 28; Pittsburg St 31, Washburn 22; Delta St 42, North Alabama 14; Minnesota-Duluth 24, Colorado St-Pueblo 21 .

Quarterfinals: Winston-Salem 27, New Haven 7; Wayne St (MI) 31, Minnesota-Duluth 25; Pittsburg St 41, NW Missouri St 16; Delta St 28, N Greenville 23.

Semifinals: Pittsburg St 49, Delta St 23; Wayne St (MI) 21, Winston-Salem 14.

NCAA DIVISION II

Championship: 12-17-11, Florence, Ala., Att: 7,276.

Wayne St (MI)	14	0	0	7—21
Pittsburg St	10	17	0	8—35

NCAA DIVISION III

First round: Wabash 38, IL College 20; St. John Fisher 23, Johns Hopkins 12; Mount Union 47, Benedictine 7; Centre 51, Hampden-Sydney 41; Franklin 24, Thomas More 21; Salisbury 62, W New England 24; Delaware Valley 62, Norwich 10; Wesley 35, Hobart 28; Kean 34, Christopher Newport 10; Monmouth (IL) 33, Illinois Wesleyan 27; McMurry 25, Trinity (TX) 16; Mary Hardin-Baylor 34, Redlands 13; UW-Whitewater 59, Albion 0; St. Thomas (MN) 48, St. Scholastica 2; North Central 59, U of Dubuque 13; Linfield 30, Cal Lutheran 27.

NCAA DIVISION III (CONT.)

Second Round: Wabash 29, North Central 28; Mount Union 30, Centre 10; Salisbury 49, Kean 47; St. John Fisher 27, Delaware Valley 14; Wesley 49, Linfield 34; Mary Hardin-Baylor 49, McMurry 20; UW-Whitewater 41, Franklin 14; St. Thomas (MN) 38, Monmouth (IL) 10.
Quarterfinals: Mount Union 20, Wabash 8; Wesley 27, Mary Hardin-Baylor 24; UW-Whitewater 34, Salisbury 14; St. Thomas (MN) 45, St. John Fisher 10.
Semifinals: UW-Whitewater 20, St. Thomas (MN) 0; Mount Union 28, Wesley 21.

NCAA DIVISION III

Championship: 12-16-11, Salem, Virginia, Att: 3,784

Mount Union	0	0	0	10—10
UW-Whitewater	0	3	7	3—13

NAIA CHAMPIONSHIP

Championship: 12-17-11, Rome, Georgia, Att: 6,000

Carroll (Mont)	0	14	6	0—20
St. Xavier (Ill.)	10	7	7	0—24

Awards

Heisman Memorial Trophy

Player, School	Class	Pos	1st	2nd	3rd	Total
Robert Griffin III, Baylor	Jr.	QB	405	168	136	1,687
Andrew Luck, Stanford	Sr.	QB	247	250	166	1,407
Trent Richardson, Alabama	Jr.	RB	138	207	150	978
Montee Ball, Wisconsin	Jr.	RB	22	83	116	348

Note: Former Heisman winners and the media vote, with ballots allowing for three names (3 points for 1st, 2 for 2nd, 1 for 3rd).

Other Awards

Maxwell Award (Player)	Andrew Luck, Stanford, QB
Sporting News Player of the Year	Robert Griffin III, Baylor, QB
Walter Camp Player of the Year	Andrew Luck, Stanford, QB
Chuck Bednarik Award (Defense)	Tyrann Mathieu, LSU, CB
Vince Lombardi/Rotary Award (Lineman/LB)	Luke Kuechly, Boston College, LB
Outland Trophy (Interior Lineman)	Barrett Jones, Alabama, OT
Davey O'Brien Award (QB)	Robert Griffin III, Baylor, QB
Unitas Golden Arm Award (Senior QB)	Andrew Luck, Stanford, QB
Doak Walker Award (RB)	Trent Richardson, Alabama, RB
Biletnikoff Award (WR)	Justin Blackmon, Oklahoma St, WR
Butkus Award (Linebacker)	Luke Kuechly, Boston College, LB
Jim Thorpe Award (Defensive Back)	Morris Claiborne, LSU, CB
Associated Press Player of the Year	Robert Griffin III, Baylor, QB
Walter Payton Award (FCS Player)	Bo Levi Mitchell, Eastern Washington, QB
Harlon Hill Trophy (Div. II Player)	Jonas Randolph, Mars Hill, RB
Gagliardi Trophy (Div. III Player)	Michael Zweifel, Dubuque, WR

Coaches' Awards

Home Depot Award	Les Miles, LSU
Eddie Robinson Award (FCS)	Rob Ambrose, Towson
Bobby Dodd Award	Dabo Swinney, Clemson
Bear Bryant Award	Mike Gundy, Oklahoma St

AFCA COACHES OF THE YEAR

FBS (Division I-A)	Les Miles, LSU
FCS (Division I-AA)	Willie Fritz, Sam Houston St
Division II	Paul Winters, Wayne St
Division III	Lance Leipold, UW-Whitewater
NAIA	Mike Feminis, St. Xavier

Associated Press First Team All-America

OFFENSE

QB........Robert Griffin III, Baylor, Jr.
RB........Trent Richardson, Alabama, Jr.
RB........Montee Ball, Wisconsin, Jr.
WR......Justin Blackmon, Oklahoma St, Jr.
WR......Robert Woods, USC, So.
TE........Dwayne Allen, Clemson, Jr.
OG......David DeCastro, Stanford, Sr.
OG......Kevin Zeitler, Wisconsin, Sr.
OT........Barrett Jones, Alabama, Sr.
OT........Matt Kalil, USC, Jr.
C..........David Molk, Michigan, Sr.
K..........Randy Bullock, Texas A&M, Sr.
All-P ....Sammy Watkins, Clemson, Fr.

DEFENSE

DT ....Devon Still, Penn St, Sr.
DT ....Jerel Worthy, Michigan St, Jr.
DE ....Melvin Ingram, South Carolina, Sr.
DE ....Whitney Mercilus, Illinois, Jr.
LB ....Luke Kuechly, Boston College, Jr.
LB ....Jarvis Jones, Georgia, So.
LB ....Dont'a Hightower, Alabama, Jr.
CB........Morris Claiborne, LSU, Jr.
CB........Tyrann Mathieu, LSU, So.
S ....Mark Barron, Alabama, Sr.
S ....Bacarri Rambo, Georgia, Jr.
P............Brad Wing, LSU, Fr.

Football Bowl Subdivision (I-A)

ATLANTIC COAST CONFERENCE

ATLANTIC

	Conference		Full Season		
ATLANTIC	W	L	W	L	Pct
Clemson	6	2	10	4	.714
Florida St.	5	3	9	4	.692
Wake Forest	5	3	6	7	.462
N. Carolina St.	4	4	8	5	.615
Boston College	3	5	4	8	.333
Maryland	1	7	2	10	.167

COASTAL

COASTAL	W	L	W	L	Pct
Virginia Tech	7	2	11	3	.786
Georgia Tech	5	3	8	5	.615
Virginia	5	3	8	5	.615
North Carolina	3	5	7	6	.538
Miami (Fla.)	3	5	6	6	.500
Duke	1	7	3	9	.250

BIG EAST CONFERENCE

	Conference		Full Season		
	W	L	W	L	Pct
Cincinnati	5	2	10	3	.769
West Virginia	5	2	10	3	.769
Louisville	5	2	7	6	.538
Rutgers	4	3	9	4	.692
Pittsburgh	4	3	6	7	.462
Connecticut	3	4	5	7	.417
South Florida	1	6	5	7	.417
Syracuse	1	6	5	7	.417

BIG TEN CONFERENCE

LEGENDS

	Conference		Full Season		
LEGENDS	W	L	W	L	Pct
Michigan St.	7	2	11	3	.786
Michigan	6	2	11	2	.846
Nebraska	5	3	9	4	.692
Iowa	4	4	7	6	.538
Northwestern	3	5	6	7	.462
Minnesota	2	6	3	9	.250

LEADERS

LEADERS	W	L	W	L	Pct
Wisconsin	7	2	11	3	.786
Penn St.	6	2	9	4	.692
Purdue	4	4	7	6	.538
Ohio St.	3	5	6	7	.462
Illinois	2	6	7	6	.538
Indiana	0	8	1	11	.083

BIG 12 CONFERENCE

	Conference		Full Season		
	W	L	W	L	Pct
Oklahoma State	8	1	12	1	.923
Kansas State	7	2	10	3	.769
Baylor	6	3	10	3	.769
Oklahoma	6	3	10	3	.769
Missouri	5	4	8	5	.615
Texas	4	5	8	5	.615
Texas A&M	4	5	7	6	.538
Iowa State	3	6	6	7	.462
Texas Tech	2	7	5	7	.417
Kansas	0	9	2	10	.167

Football Bowl Subdivision (I-A) *(Cont.)*

CONFERENCE USA

EAST

	Conference		Full Season		
EAST	W	L	W	L	Pct
Southern Miss	6	2	12	2	.857
Marshall	5	3	7	6	.538
East Carolina	4	4	5	7	.417
UCF	3	5	5	7	.417
UAB	3	5	3	9	.250
Memphis	1	7	2	10	.167

WEST

WEST	W	L	W	L	Pct
Houston	8	0	13	1	.929
Tulsa	7	1	8	5	.615
Southern Methodist	5	3	8	5	.615
Rice	3	5	4	8	.333
UTEP	2	6	5	7	.417
Tulane	1	7	2	11	.154

MID-AMERICAN ATHLETIC CONFERENCE

EAST

	Conference		Full Season		
EAST	W	L	W	L	Pct
Ohio	6	2	10	4	.714
Temple	5	3	9	4	.692
Kent State	4	4	5	7	.417
Bowling Green	3	5	5	7	.417
Miami (OH)	3	5	4	8	.333
Buffalo	2	6	3	9	.250
Akron	0	8	1	11	.083

WEST

WEST	W	L	W	L	Pct
Northern Illinois	7	1	11	3	.786
Toledo	7	1	9	4	.692
Western Michigan	5	3	7	6	.538
Ball State	4	4	6	6	.500
Eastern Michigan	4	4	6	6	.500
Central Michigan	2	6	3	9	.250

MOUNTAIN WEST CONFERENCE

	Conference		Full Season		
	W	L	W	L	Pct
TCU	7	0	11	2	.846
Boise State	6	1	12	1	.923
Wyoming	5	2	8	5	.615
San Diego State	4	3	8	5	.615
Air Force	3	4	7	6	.538
Colorado State	1	6	3	9	.250
UNLV	1	6	2	10	.167
New Mexico	1	6	1	11	.083

PACIFIC 12 CONFERENCE

NORTH

	Conference		Full Season		
NORTH	W	L	W	L	Pct
Oregon	8	1	12	2	.857
Stanford	8	1	11	2	.846
Washington	5	4	7	6	.538
California	4	5	7	6	.538
Oregon State	3	6	3	9	.250
Washington State	2	7	4	8	.333

SOUTH

SOUTH	W	L	W	L	Pct
*USC	7	2	10	2	.833
UCLA	5	4	6	8	.429
Arizona State	4	5	6	7	.462
Utah	4	5	8	5	.615
Colorado	2	7	3	10	.231
Arizona	2	7	4	8	.333

*Barred from bowl eligibility by the NCAA for rules violations.

Football Bowl Subdivision (I-A) (*Cont.*)

SOUTHEASTERN CONFERENCE

EAST	Conference		Full Season		
	W	L	W	L	Pct
Georgia	7	1	10	4	.714
South Carolina	6	2	11	2	846
Florida	3	5	7	6	.538
Vanderbilt	2	6	6	7	.462
Kentucky	2	6	5	7	.417
Tennessee	1	7	5	7	.417
WEST					
LSU	8	0	13	1	.929
Alabama	7	1	12	1	.923
Arkansas	6	2	11	2	.846
Auburn	4	4	8	5	.615
Mississippi State	2	6	7	6	.538
Ole Miss	0	8	2	10	.167

SUN BELT CONFERENCE

	Conference		Full Season		
	W	L	W	L	Pct
Arkansas State	8	0	10	3	.769
Western Kentucky	7	1	7	5	.583
Louisiana-Lafayette	6	2	9	4	.692
Florida International	5	3	8	5	.615
North Texas	4	4	5	7	.417
Louisiana-Monroe	3	5	4	8	.333
Troy	2	6	3	9	.250
Middle Tennessee	1	7	2	10	.167
Florida Atlantic	0	8	1	11	.083

WESTERN ATHLETIC CONFERENCE

	Conference		Full Season		
	W	L	W	L	Pct
Louisiana Tech	6	1	8	5	.615
Utah State	5	2	7	6	.538
Nevada	5	2	7	6	.538
San Jose State	3	4	5	7	.417
Fresno State	3	4	4	9	.308
Hawaii	3	4	6	7	.462
New Mexico State	2	5	4	9	.308
Idaho	1	6	2	10	.167

INDEPENDENTS

	Full Season		
	W	L	Pct
Brigham Young	10	3	.769
Notre Dame	8	5	.615
Navy	5	7	.417
Army	3	9	.250

Football Championship Subdivision (I-AA)

BIG SKY CONFERENCE

	Conference		Full Season		
	W	L	W	L	Pct
Montana	7	1	11	3	.786
Montana State	7	1	10	3	.769
Portland State	5	3	7	4	.636
Eastern Washington	5	3	6	5	.545
Weber State	5	3	5	6	.455
Northern Arizona	3	5	4	7	.364
Sacramento State	3	5	4	7	.364
Idaho State	1	7	2	9	.182
Northern Colorado	0	8	0	11	.000

BIG SOUTH CONFERENCE

	Conference		Full Season		
	W	L	W	L	Pct
Stony Brook	6	0	9	4	.692
Liberty	5	1	7	4	.636
Coastal Carolina	3	3	7	4	.636
Presbyterian	3	3	4	7	.364
Gardner-Webb	2	4	4	7	.364
VMI	2	4	2	9	.182
Charleston Southern	0	6	0	11	.000

COLONIAL CONFERENCE

	Conference		Full Season		
	W	L	W	L	Pct
Towson	7	1	9	3	.750
Old Dominion	6	2	10	3	.769
Maine	6	2	9	4	.692
New Hampshire	6	2	8	4	.667
Delaware	5	3	7	4	.636
James Madison	5	3	8	5	.615
Massachusetts	3	5	5	6	.455
William & Mary	3	5	5	6	.455
Rhode Island	2	6	3	8	.273
Villanova	1	7	2	9	.182
Richmond	0	8	3	8	.273

GREAT WEST

	Conference		Full Season		
	W	L	W	L	Pct
North Dakota	3	1	8	3	.727
Cal Poly	3	1	6	5	.545
South Dakota	2	2	6	5	.545
Southern Utah	1	3	6	5	.545
UC Davis	1	3	4	7	.364

IVY LEAGUE

	Conference		Full Season		
	W	L	W	L	Pct
Harvard	7	0	9	1	.900
Brown	4	3	7	3	.700
Dartmouth	4	3	5	5	.500
Pennsylvania	4	3	5	5	.500
Yale	4	3	5	5	.500
Cornell	3	4	5	5	.500
Columbia	1	6	1	9	.100
Princeton	1	6	1	9	.100

Football Champ. Subdivision (I-AA) *(Cont.)*

MID-EASTERN ATHLETIC CONFERENCE

	Conference		Full Season		
	W	L	W	L	Pct
Norfolk State	7	1	9	3	.750
Bethune-Cookman	6	2	8	3	.727
South Carolina State	6	2	7	4	.636
Florida A&M	5	3	7	4	.636
Hampton	5	3	7	4	.636
Howard	4	4	5	6	.455
Morgan State	4	4	5	6	.455
North Carolina A&T	4	4	5	6	.455
Delaware State	1	7	3	8	.273
North Carolina Central	1	7	2	9	.182
Savannah State	1	7	1	10	.091

MISSOURI VALLEY CONFERENCE

	Conference		Full Season		
	W	L	W	L	Pct
North Dakota State	7	1	14	1	.933
Northern Iowa	7	1	10	3	.769
Illinois State	5	3	7	4	.636
Indiana State	4	4	6	5	.545
South Dakota State	4	4	5	6	.455
Youngstown State	4	4	6	5	.545
Southern Illinois	2	6	4	7	.364
Missouri State	2	6	2	9	.182
Western Illinois	1	7	2	9	.182

NORTHEAST CONFERENCE

	Conference		Full Season		
	W	L	W	L	Pct
Duquesne	7	1	9	2	.818
Albany	7	1	8	4	.667
Bryant University	5	3	7	4	.636
Monmouth	4	4	5	6	.455
Wagner	4	4	4	7	.364
Sacred Heart	3	5	5	6	.455
Central Connecticut St	3	5	4	7	.364
Robert Morris	2	6	2	9	.182
St. Francis (PA)	1	7	2	9	.182

OHIO VALLEY CONFERENCE

	Conference		Full Season		
	W	L	W	L	Pct
Jacksonville St	6	2	7	4	.636
Tennessee Tech	6	2	7	4	.636
Eastern Kentucky	6	2	7	5	.583
Murray State	5	3	7	4	.636
Tennessee State	4	4	5	6	.455
Tennessee-Martin	4	4	5	6	.455
Austin Peay	2	6	3	8	.273
Southeast Missouri St	2	6	3	8	.273
Eastern Illinois	1	7	2	9	.182

PATRIOT LEAGUE

	Conference		Full Season		
	W	L	W	L	Pct
Lehigh	6	0	11	2	.846
Georgetown	4	2	8	3	.727
Holy Cross	4	2	6	5	.545
Bucknell	3	3	6	5	.545
Colgate	2	4	5	6	.455
Lafayette	2	4	4	7	.364
Fordham	0	6	1	10	.091

Football Champ. Subdivision (I-AA) *(Cont.)*

PIONEER LEAGUE

	Conference		Full Season		
	W	L	W	L	Pct
Drake	7	1	9	2	.818
San Diego	7	1	9	2	.818
Jacksonville	6	2	7	4	.636
Campbell	5	3	6	5	.545
Dayton	4	4	6	5	.545
Butler	3	5	5	6	.455
Marist	3	5	4	7	.364
Davidson	2	6	4	7	.364
Morehead State	2	6	3	8	.273
Valparaiso	1	7	1	10	.091

SOUTHERN CONFERENCE

	Conference		Full Season		
	W	L	W	L	Pct
Georgia Southern	7	1	11	3	.786
Wofford	6	2	8	4	.667
Appalachian State	6	2	8	4	.667
Furman	5	3	6	5	.545
Samford	4	4	6	5	.545
Chattanooga	3	5	5	6	.455
Elon	3	5	5	6	.455
Citadel	2	6	4	7	.364
Western Carolina	0	8	1	10	.091

SOUTHLAND CONFERENCE

	Conference		Full Season		
	W	L	W	L	Pct
Sam Houston State	7	0	14	1	.933
Central Arkansas	6	1	9	4	.692
Stephen F. Austin	5	2	6	5	.545
McNeese State	4	3	6	5	.545
Northwestern State	3	4	5	6	.455
Lamar	2	5	4	7	.364
SE Louisiana	1	6	3	8	.273
Nicholls State	0	7	1	10	.091

SOUTHWESTERN ATHLETIC CONFERENCE

	Conference		Full Season		
EAST	W	L	W	L	Pct
Jackson State	7	2	9	2	.818
Alabama State	7	2	8	3	.727
Alabama A&M	7	2	8	4	.667
Alcorn State	1	8	2	8	.200
Mississippi Valley St	1	8	1	10	.091
WEST					
Grambling State	6	3	8	4	.667
Arkansas-Pine Bluff	5	4	6	5	.545
Prairie View A&M	5	4	5	6	.455
Southern University	4	5	4	7	.364
Texas Southern	2	7	4	7	.364

INDEPENDENTS

	Full Season		
	W	L	Pct
Texas State	6	6	.500
UTSA	4	6	.400
Georgia State	3	8	.273

Football Bowl Subdivision (I-A)

SCORING

	Class	GP	TD	XP	FG	Pts	Pts/Game
Montee Ball, Wisconsin	Jr.	14	39	0	0	234	16.71
Bernard Pierce, Temple	Jr.	12	27	0	0	162	13.50
Collin Klein, Kansas St.	Jr.	13	27	0	0	162	12.46
Joseph Randle, Oklahoma St.	So.	13	26	0	0	156	12.00
Quinn Sharp, Oklahoma St.	Jr.	13	0	79	22	145	11.15
Trent Richardson, Alabama	Jr.	13	24	0	0	144	11.08
Randy Bullock, Texas A&M	Sr.	13	0	55	29	142	10.92
Robert Turbin, Utah St.	Jr.	13	23	00	0	138	10.62
Zach Line, SMU	Jr.	10	17	0	0	102	10.20
Terrance Ganaway, Baylor	Sr.	13	22	0	0	132	10.15
LaMichael James, Oregon	Jr.	12	20	0	0	120	10.00
Mike Hunnicutt, Oklahoma	Fr.	12	0	55	21	118	9.83
Jordan Williamson, Stanford	So.	10	0	54	13	93	9.30
Danny Hrapmann, Southern Miss.	Sr.	14	0	61	23	130	9.29
Matt Hogan, Houston	Jr.	14	0	91	13	130	9.29

FIELD GOALS

	Class	GP	FGA	FG	Pct	FG/Game
Randy Bullock, Texas A&M	Sr.	13	33	29	.879	2.23
Jens Alvernik, San Jose St.	Sr.	9	25	18	.720	2.00
Caleb Sturgis, Florida	Jr.	12	26	22	.846	1.83
Dave Teggart, Connecticut	Sr.	12	28	22	.786	1.83
Matt Weller, Ohio	Jr.	14	34	25	.735	1.79

TOTAL OFFENSE

			Rushing		Passing			Total Offense	
	Class	GP	Car	Net	Att	Yds	Tot. Yds	Yds/Play	Yds/Game
Case Keenum, Houston	Sr.	14	57	35	603	5631	5666	8.58	404.71
Robert Griffin III, Baylor	Jr.	13	179	699	402	4293	4992	8.59	384.00
Brandon Weeden, Oklahoma St.	Sr.	13	17	-102	564	4727	4625	7.96	355.77
Nick Foles, Arizona	Sr.	12	43	-103	560	4334	4231	7.02	352.58
Alex Carder, Western Mich.	Jr.	12	128	270	502	3873	4143	6.58	345.25
Landry Jones, Oklahoma	Jr.	13	32	-24	562	4463	4439	7.47	341.46
Seth Doege, Texas Tech	Jr.	12	54	46	581	4004	4050	6.38	337.50
Geno Smith, West Virginia	Jr.	13	56	-33	526	4385	4352	7.48	334.77
Chandler Harnish, Northern Ill.	Sr.	14	194	1379	384	3216	4595	7.95	328.21
Ryan Aplin, Arkansas St.	Jr.	13	161	588	476	3588	4176	6.56	321.23

RUSHING

	Class	GP	Car	Yds	TD	Avg	Yds/Game
LaMichael James, Oregon	Jr.	12	247	1805	18	7.31	150.42
Bobby Rainey, Western Ky.	Sr.	12	369	1695	13	4.59	141.25
Montee Ball, Wisconsin	Jr.	14	307	1923	33	6.26	137.36
Ronnie Hillman, San Diego St.	So.	13	311	1711	19	5.50	131.62
Trent Richardson, Alabama	Jr.	13	283	1679	21	5.93	129.15
Bernard Pierce, Temple	Jr.	12	273	1481	27	5.42	123.42
Zach Line, SMU	Jr.	10	208	1224	17	5.88	122.40
David Wilson, Virginia Tech	Jr.	14	290	1709	9	5.89	122.07
Robbie Rouse, Fresno St.	Jr.	13	329	1549	13	4.71	119.15
Terrance Ganaway, Baylor	Sr.	13	250	1547	21	6.19	119.00

PASSING EFFICIENCY

	Class	GP	Att	Comp	Pct Comp	Yds	Yds/Att	TD	Int	Rating Pts
Russell Wilson, Wisconsin	Sr.	14	309	225	72.82	3175	10.28	33	4	191.78
Robert Griffin III, Baylor	Jr.	13	402	291	72.39	4293	10.68	37	6	189.48
Kellen Moore, Boise St.	Sr.	13	439	326	74.26	3800	8.66	43	9	175.19
Case Keenum, Houston	Sr.	14	603	428	70.98	5631	9.34	48	5	174.03
Andrew Luck, Stanford	Sr.	13	404	288	71.29	3517	8.71	37	10	169.69
Terrance Owens, Toledo	Jr.	12	230	166	72.17	2022	8.79	18	3	169.24
Keith Price, Washington	So.	13	362	242	66.85	3063	8.46	33	11	161.93
Matt Barkley, Southern California	Jr.	12	446	308	69.06	3528	7.91	39	7	161.22
Brandon Weeden, Oklahoma St.	Sr.	13	564	408	72.34	4727	8.38	37	13	159.78
Bryn Renner North Carolina	So.	13	350	239	68.29	3086	8.82	26	13	159.44

Note: Minimum 15 attempts per game.

Football Bowl Subdivision (I-A) *(Cont.)*

RECEPTIONS PER GAME

	Class	GP	No.	Yds	TD	Rec/G
Jordan White, Western Mich.	Sr.	13	140	1911	17	10.77
Eric Page, Toledo	Jr.	13	125	1182	10	9.62
Justin Blackmon, Oklahoma St.	Jr.	13	121	1522	18	9.31
Robert Woods, Southern California	So.	12	111	1292	15	9.25
Mohamed Sanu, Rutgers	Jr.	13	115	1206	7	8.85

RECEIVING YARDS PER GAME

	Class	GP	No.	Yds	TD	Yds/Game
Jordan White, Western Mich.	Sr.	13	140	1911	17	147.00
Nick Harwell, Miami (OH)	So.	11	97	1425	9	129.55
Kendall Wright, Baylor	Sr.	13	108	1663	14	127.92
Patrick Edwards, Houston	Sr.	14	89	1752	20	125.14
Justin Blackmon, Oklahoma St.	Jr.	13	121	1522	18	117.08

ALL-PURPOSE RUNNING

	Class	GP	Rush	Rec	PR	KOR	Total Yds	Yds/Game
Tavon Austin, West Virginia	Jr.	13	182	1186	268	938	2574	198.00
Taveon Rogers, New Mexico St.	Sr.	12	-10	1048	0	1318	2356	196.33
LaMichael James, Oregon	Jr.	12	1805	210	139	21	2175	181.25
Sammy Watkins, Clemson	Fr.	13	231	1219	12	826	2288	176.00
Eric Page, Toledo	Jr.	13	10	1182	196	856	2244	172.62

INTERCEPTIONS

	Class	GP	No.	Int/Game
David Amerson, N Carolina St.	So.	13	13	1.00
Bacarri Rambo, Georgia	Jr.	13	8	.62
Phillip Thomas, Syracuse	Jr.	10	6	.60
Casey Hayward, Vanderbilt	Sr.	13	7	.54
Nigel Malone, Kansas St.	Jr.	13	7	.54
Larry Parker, San Diego St.	Sr.	13	7	.54

PUNT RETURNS

	Class	No.	Yds	TD	Avg
Dustin Harris, Texas A&M	Jr.	18	335	1	18.61
Joe Adams, Arkansas	Sr.	19	321	4	16.89
Jared Abbrederis, Wisconsin	So.	20	315	1	15.75
Tyrann Mathieu, LSU	So.	27	421	2	15.59
Devon Wylie, Fresno St.	Sr.	29	446	2	15.38

Note: Minimum 1.2 punt returns per game.

PUNTING

	Class	No.	Avg Y/Pt
Shawn Powell, Florida St.	Sr.	57	47.04
Bobby Cowan, Idaho	Jr.	88	46.41
Quinn Sharp, Oklahoma St.	Jr.	47	46.28
Ian Campbell, UTEP	Jr.	48	46.13
Ryan Allen, Louisiana Tech	Jr.	83	46.12

Note: Minimum of 3.6 punts per game.

KICKOFF RETURNS

	Class	No.	Yds	TD	Avg
Raheem Mostert, Purdue	Fr.	25	837	1	33.48
John Evans, Western Ky.	Fr.	18	579	1	32.17
Luther Ambrose, La.-Monroe	Sr.	26	811	2	31.19
Jeremy Deering, Rutgers	So.	17	530	1	31.18
Rannell Hall, UCF	Fr.	23	714	0	31.04

Note: Minimum of 1.2 kickoff returns per game.

Football Championship Subdivision (I-AA)

SCORING

	Class	GP	TD	XP	FG	Pts	Pts/Game
Terrance West, Towson	Fr.	11	29	0	0	174	15.82
Nicholas Edwards, Eastern Wash.	Jr.	11	19	0	0	114	10.36
Andre Broadous, Cal Poly	Jr.	11	18	0	0	108	9.82
Tim Flanders, Sam Houston St.	So.	15	24	0	0	144	9.60
Eric Breitenstein, Wofford	Jr.	12	19	0	0	114	9.50

FIELD GOALS

	Class	GP	FGA	FG	Pct	FG/Game
Zach Brown, Portland St.	Jr.	11	27	24	.889	2.18
Cameron Yaw, Samford	Jr.	11	28	23	.821	2.09
Jordan Wiggs, Stephen F. Austin	Fr.	10	24	17	.708	1.70
Jason Cunningham, Montana St.	Sr.	13	31	22	.710	1.69
Ryan Estep, Norfolk St.	Sr.	12	22	20	.909	1.67

TOTAL OFFENSE

			Rushing		Passing			Total Offense	
	Class	GP	Car	Net	Att	Yds	Total Yds	Yds/Play	Yds/Game
Bo Levi Mitchell, Eastern Wash.	Sr.	11	55	-5	503	4009	4004	7.18	364.00
Casey Therriault, Jackson St.	Sr.	11	94	103	453	3808	3911	7.15	355.55
Chris Lum, Lehigh	Sr.	13	61	121	543	4378	4499	7.45	346.08
Jeff Mathews, Cornell	So.	10	49	-138	368	3412	3274	7.85	327.40
Casey Brockman, Murray St.	Jr.	11	94	194	477	3276	3470	6.08	315.45

RUSHING

	Class	GP	Car	Yds	Avg	TD	Yds/Game
Shakir Bell, Indiana St.	So.	11	230	1670	7.26	14	151.82
Nick Schwieger, Dartmouth	Sr.	10	241	1310	5.44	10	131.00
Matt Denham, Eastern Ky.	Jr.	12	254	1570	6.18	9	130.83
Zach Bauman, Northern Ariz.	So.	11	271	1435	5.30	15	130.45
Jonathan Grimes, William & Mary	Sr.	11	288	1431	4.97	10	130.09

PASSING EFFICIENCY

	Class	GP	Att	Comp	Pct Comp	Yds	Yds/Att	TD	Int	Rating Pts
Chris Forcier, Furman	Sr.	11	231	148	64.07	2265	9.81	23	8	172.36
Kyle Essington, Stony Brook	Jr.	13	203	111	54.68	1919	9.45	20	4	162.66
Jeff Mathews, Cornell	So.	10	368	250	67.93	3412	9.27	25	11	162.26
Kurt Hess, Youngstown St.	So.	11	288	187	64.93	2468	8.57	26	8	161.15
Cary Grossart, Northern Ariz.	Jr.	11	299	197	65.89	2745	9.18	16	7	155.98

Note: Minimum 15 attempts per game.

RECEPTIONS PER GAME

	Class	GP	No.	Yds	TD	Rec/G
Aaron Mellette, Elon	Jr.	11	113	1639	12	10.27
Rodrick Rumble, Idaho St.	Jr.	11	112	1348	9	10.18
Lanny Funsten, Davidson	Jr.	11	100	1107	8	9.09
Nicholas Edwards, Eastern Wash.	Jr.	11	95	1250	19	8.64
Tre Gray, Richmond	Sr.	11	95	1187	4	8.64

RECEIVING YARDS PER GAME

	Class	GP	No.	Yds	TD	Yds/Game
Aaron Mellette, Elon	Jr.	11	113	1639	12	149.00
Ryan Spadola, Lehigh	Jr.	12	96	1614	11	134.50
Rodrick Rumble, Idaho St.	Jr.	11	112	1348	9	122.55
Nicholas Edwards, Eastern Wash.	Jr.	11	95	1250	19	113.64
Shane Savage, Cornell	Sr.	10	65	1080	12	108.00

ALL-PURPOSE RUNNING

	Class	GP	Rush	Rec	PR	KOR	Total Yds	Yds/Game
Jonathan Grimes, William & Mary	Sr.	11	1431	262	0	817	2510	228.18
Kenny James, San Diego	So.	11	1149	334	0	828	2311	210.09
Brock Jackolski, Stony Brook	Sr.	13	1418	114	55	854	2441	187.77
Fabian Truss, Samford	So.	10	847	137	0	790	1774	177.40
Kyle Harbridge, Saint Francis (PA)	Jr.	11	1430	164	0	356	1950	177.27

Football Championship Subdivision (I-AA) (Cont.)

INTERCEPTIONS

	Class	GP	No.	Yds	TD	Int/G
Bryce Robertson, Bucknell	Sr.	11	13	184	0	1.18
Kejuan Riley, Alabama St.	Jr.	11	9	140	0	.82
D. Swanson, S Houston St.	Jr.	15	8	117	0	.53
C. Houston, New Hampshire	So.	12	6	45	0	.50
James Pitts, Villanova	Sr.	10	5	26	1	.50
Marcus Williams, N Dakota St.	So.	15	7	174	3	.47

PUNTING

	Class	No.	Avg
David Harrington, Idaho St.	Sr.	56	48.70
Jonathan Plisco, Old Dominion	Jr.	51	46.12
Patrick Murray, Fordham	Jr.	49	44.08
Billy Janssen, Drake	Sr.	50	43.30
Cass Couey, Citadel	Sr.	40	42.98

Division II

SCORING

	Class	GP	TD	XP	FG	Pts	Pts/Game
Joe Glendening, Hillsdale	Jr.	10	31	0	0	186	18.60
Rashaad Slowley, Southern Conn. St.	Sr.	10	29	0	0	174	17.40
Daronte McNeill, Elizabeth City St.	Jr.	12	23	0	0	140	11.67
David Carter, Morehouse	Jr.	10	19	0	0	114	11.40
James Franklin, Northwest Mo. St.	So.	14	25	0	0	150	10.71

Note: McNeill's total includes one two-point conversion.

FIELD GOALS

	Class	GP	FGA	FG	Pct	FG/Game
Greg Zuerlein, Mo. Western St.	Sr.	10	24	23	.958	2.30
Kyle Major, Colorado St.-Pueblo	Sr.	12	30	22	.733	1.83
Dan Fisher, Bloomsburg	So.	11	21	17	.810	1.55
Shawn Leo, West Chester	So.	10	20	15	.750	1.50
Danny Padilla, Minn. St. Mankato	Jr.	11	20	16	.800	1.45
Gregg Berkshire, Ashland	Sr.	11	28	16	.571	1.45

TOTAL OFFENSE

			Rushing		Passing		Total Offense		
	Class	GP	Car	Net	Att	Yds	Total Yds	Yds/Play	Yds/Game
Adam Neugebauer, W Va. Wesleyan	Sr.	11	54	-94	521	4111	4017	6.99	365.18
Mitchell Gale, Abilene Christian	Jr.	11	66	97	458	3823	3920	7.48	356.36
Tommy Corwin, Central Mo.	Sr.	12	64	187	479	3798	3985	7.34	332.08
Dane Simoneau, Washburn	Sr.	13	41	-27	482	4089	4062	7.77	312.46
Jake Spitzlberger, Neb.-Kearney	Sr.	12	186	1075	327	2656	3731	7.27	310.92

RUSHING

	Class	GP	Car	Yds	TD	Yds/Game
Jonas Randolph, Mars Hill	Sr.	11	366	2170	18	197.27
Joe Glendening, Hillsdale	Jr.	10	325	1600	27	160.00
Rashaad Slowley, Southern Conn. St.	Sr.	10	274	1584	27	158.40
David Carter, Morehouse	Jr.	10	235	1495	19	149.50
Travis Daniels, UNC Pembroke	Sr.	11	292	1631	15	148.27

PASSING EFFICIENCY

				Pct				Rating
	Class	GP	Att	Comp	Comp	Yds	TD	Int	Pts
Heath Parling, Grand Valley St.	So.	11	249	154	61.85	2415	34	10	180.35
Ryan Osiecki, New Haven	Jr.	13	341	224	65.69	3336	36	12	175.67
Jonathon Jennings, Saginaw Valley	So.	11	309	210	67.96	2924	29	9	172.59
Kevin Morton, Kutztown	Jr.	12	316	198	62.66	2680	32	11	160.35
Willy Korn, North Greenville	Sr.	14	289	178	61.59	2525	27	8	160.28

Note: Minimum 15 attempts per game.

RECEPTIONS PER GAME

	Class	GP	No.	Yds	TD	Rec/Game
Jon Meadows, West Va. Wesleyan	Sr.	11	99	1275	10	9.00
Deonte' Gist, Tusculum	Sr.	10	81	900	4	8.10
Trevor Kennedy, Mercyhurst	Sr.	11	88	1389	15	8.00
Landon Zerkel, Mo. Southern St.	Jr.	10	77	1047	6	7.70
Darian Dale, Eastern N.M.	Sr.	11	84	798	6	7.64

RECEIVING YARDS PER GAME

	Class	GP	No.	Yds	TD	Yds/Game
Trevor Kennedy, Mercyhurst	Sr.	11	88	1389	15	126.27
Trey McVay, Northeastern St.	Sr.	12	81	1514	15	126.17
Isaiah Voegeli, Merrimack	Jr.	10	59	1251	14	125.10
Jon Meadowsy, West Va. Wesleyan	Sr.	11	99	1275	10	115.91
Landon Zerkel, Mo. Southern St.	Jr.	10	77	1047	6	104.70

Division II (Cont.)

INTERCEPTIONS

	Class	GP	No.	Yds	Int/Game
Joshua Scales, Fayetteville St.	So.	8	7	113	.88
Alex Dinolfi, Kutztown	Jr.	13	11	96	.85
Bryce Peila, Western Ore.	Jr.	11	9	243	.82
Clarence Laster, SW Okla.	Sr.	11	8	244	.73
Derek Lohmann, Emporia St.	Jr.	11	8	155	.73
Brandon Watters, Slippery Rock	Sr.	11	8	87	.73

PUNTING

	Class	No.	Avg
Taylor Accardi, Colorado Mines	Jr.	51	48.55
Randy Weich, Wayne St. (NE)	Jr.	59	45.14
Ethan Kosjer, Fort Hays St.	Sr.	62	44.39
Scott Groner, Mo. Western St.	Jr.	50	43.86
Marquette King, Fort Valley St.	Sr.	60	43.03

Note: Minimum 3.6 punts per game.

Division III

SCORING

	Class	GP	TD	XP	FG	Pts	Pts/Game
Josh Carter, Springfield	Sr.	10	27	0	0	170	17.00
Michael Zweifel, Dubuque	Sr.	11	26	0	0	156	14.18
John Borsellino, Benedictine (IL)	Jr.	11	22	0	0	132	12.00
Ben Guiles, Lebanon Valley	Sr.	11	22	0	0	132	12.00
Melikke Van Alstyne, Framingham St.	So.	11	21	0	0	130	11.82

Note: Carter's total includes four two-point conversions; Van Alstyne's total includes two two-point conversions.

FIELD GOALS

	Class	GP	FGA	FG	Pct	FG/Game
Allen Cain, Texas Lutheran	Jr.	10	21	17	.810	1.70
Dylan Rushe, Endicott	So.	11	26	17	.654	1.55
Jacob Gahart, Ripon	Jr.	10	16	15	.938	1.50
Ryan Zipf, Allegheny	Sr.	10	22	15	.682	1.50
Eric Kindler, Wis.-Whitewater	So.	15	31	22	.710	1.47

TOTAL OFFENSE

			Rushing		Passing		Total Offense		
	Class	GP	Car	Net	Att	Yds	Total Yds	Yds/Play	Yds/Game
McCallum Foote, Middlebury	So.	7	15	-23	364	2420	2397	6.32	342.43
Travis Lane, Hampden-Sydney	Sr.	11	78	103	487	3648	3751	6.64	341.00
Michael Bates, Illinois Col.	Fr.	11	123	458	423	3129	3587	6.57	326.09
Keith Welch, Lewis & Clark	So.	9	157	740	287	2181	2921	6.58	324.56
Wyatt Hanus, Dubuque	Jr.	11	55	19	363	3490	3509	8.39	319.00

RUSHING

	Class	GP	Car	Yds	TD	Yds/Game
Luke Sweeney, Pomona-Pitzer	Jr.	8	298	1419	10	177.38
Shawn Morris, Birmingham-So.	Jr.	9	169	1449	17	161.00
Chris D'Andrea, Montclair St.	Sr.	10	248	1583	15	158.30
Johrone Bunch, Mount Ida	Sr.	10	286	1582	14	158.20
Josh Carter, Springfield	Sr.	10	196	1490	27	149.00

PASSING EFFICIENCY

					Pct				Rating
	Class	GP	Att	Comp	Comp	Yds	TD	Int	Pts
Alex Thiry, St. Scholastica	Sr.	11	227	160	70.48	2608	37	3	218.14
Wyatt Hanus, Dubuque	Jr.	11	363	265	73.00	3490	44	8	189.36
Alex Tanney, Monmouth (IL)	Sr.	12	393	281	71.50	3867	38	8	181.99
Shane McSweeny, Wesley	Sr.	14	310	200	64.52	3019	33	10	175.00
Phil Konopka, Endicott	Sr.	11	300	200	66.67	2701	27	9	165.99

Note: Minimum 15 attempts per game.

RECEPTIONS PER GAME

	Class	GP	No.	Yds	TD	Rec/Game
Michael Zweifel, Dubuque	Sr.	11	140	1915	25	12.73
Adam Kniffin, Puget Sound	Jr.	9	95	995	12	10.56
Mike Blodgett, Monmouth (IL)	Sr.	12	126	1867	18	10.50
Kyle Vance, Hampden-Sydney	Sr.	11	103	1391	16	9.36
Robert Seer, Grinnell	Sr.	10	84	1152	18	8.40

RECEIVING YARDS PER GAME

	Class	GP	No.	Yds	TD	Yds/Game
Michael Zweifel, Dubuque	Sr.	11	140	1915	25	174.09
Mike Blodgett, Monmouth (IL)	Sr.	12	126	1867	18	155.58
Kevin Davis, Lake Forest	Sr.	10	77	1286	11	128.60
Wes Schmidgall, Eureka	Sr.	10	73	1274	16	127.40
Kyle Vance, Hampden-Sydney	Sr.	11	103	1391	16	126.45

Division III *(Cont.)*

INTERCEPTIONS

	Class	GP	No.	Yds	Int/G
Demetreus Johnson, Coe	Jr.	10	8	144	.80
Bobby Fischer, Saint John's (MN)	Jr.	10	7	243	.70
Sam Thompson, Carnegie Mellon	Jr.	10	7	108	.70
J. Haulcy-Bateman, Cal Lutheran	Sr.	10	7	67	.70
Tyler Barrett, Trinity (TX)	Sr.	11	7	99	.64
Zach Autenreib, Thomas More	Jr.	11	7	87	.64
Zach Morgan, Hampden-Sydney	So.	11	7	34	.64

PUNTING

	Class	No.	Avg
Cote Schacherl, Howard Payne	Sr.	64	43.91
Kyle Trella, Trinity (TX)	Jr.	62	42.65
Christian Hallingstad, Wis.-La Crosse	Jr.	64	42.56
Jimmy Adranly, Chapman	Sr.	30	42.43
Patrick Garrett, Carnegie Mellon	Sr.	47	41.72

Note: Minimum 3.6 per game.

2011 NCAA FBS (I-A) Team Leaders

Offense

SCORING

	GP	Pts	Avg
Houston	14	690	49.29
Oklahoma St.	13	633	48.69
Oregon	14	645	46.07
Baylor	13	589	45.31
Boise St.	13	575	44.23
Wisconsin	14	618	44.14
Stanford	13	561	43.15
Toledo	13	549	42.23
TCU	13	531	40.85
Oklahoma	13	514	39.54

RUSHING

	GP	Car	Yds	Avg	TD	Yds/Game
Army	12	740	4158	5.62	35	346.50
Georgia Tech	13	717	4114	5.74	45	316.46
Air Force	13	723	4092	5.66	43	314.77
Navy	12	694	3747	5.40	34	312.25
Oregon	14	629	4189	6.66	42	299.21
Utah St.	13	623	3675	5.90	37	282.69
Temple	13	636	3335	5.24	38	256.54
Nevada	13	628	3218	5.12	29	247.54
Missouri	13	589	3172	5.39	30	244.00
Baylor	13	576	3063	5.32	37	235.62

PASSING

	GP	Att	Comp	Int	Pct Comp	Yds	Yds/Gm	TD
Houston	14	682	479	6	70.23	6301	450.07	54
Oklahoma St.	13	595	428	13	71.93	5034	387.23	40
Arizona	12	577	398	15	68.98	4449	370.75	29
Baylor	13	424	307	6	72.41	4569	351.46	40
Oklahoma	13	583	365	16	62.61	4542	349.38	29
West Virginia	13	542	353	9	65.13	4509	346.85	32
Texas Tech	12	600	409	10	68.17	4145	345.42	31
Western Mich.	13	554	369	16	66.61	4385	337.31	40
Washington St.	12	492	297	12	60.37	3867	322.25	30
Arizona St.	13	527	333	13	63.19	4117	316.69	27

TOTAL OFFENSE

	GP	Plays	Yds	Avg	TD	Yds/Game
Houston	14	1102	8387	7.61	93	599.07
Baylor	13	1000	7632	7.63	80	587.08
Oklahoma St.	13	987	7148	7.24	81	549.85
Oregon	14	1015	7319	7.21	88	522.79
Oklahoma	13	1052	6660	6.33	63	512.31
Nevada	13	1037	6587	6.35	53	506.69
Texas A&M	13	1044	6373	6.10	60	490.23
Stanford	13	935	6361	6.80	73	489.31
Boise St.	13	969	6257	6.46	81	481.31
Toledo	13	980	6257	6.38	72	481.31

Defense

OPPONENTS' SCORING

	GP	Pts	Avg
Alabama	13	106	8.15
LSU	14	158	11.29
Temple	13	181	13.92
Florida St.	13	196	15.08
Penn St.	13	218	16.77
Michigan	13	226	17.38
Virginia Tech	14	247	17.64
Rutgers	13	238	18.31
UCF	12	220	18.33
Michigan St.	14	257	18.36

TOTAL DEFENSE

	GP	Plays	Yds	Avg Y/Play	Avg Y/G
Alabama	13	720	2387	3.32	183.62
LSU	14	897	3661	4.08	261.50
South Carolina	13	835	3480	4.17	267.69
Florida St.	13	859	3575	4.16	275.00
Georgia	14	870	3881	4.46	277.21
Michigan St.	14	903	3884	4.30	277.43
Illinois	13	842	3720	4.42	286.15
Florida	13	848	3894	4.59	299.54
UCF	12	732	3640	4.97	303.33
Virginia Tech	14	865	4265	4.93	304.64

OPPONENTS' RUSHING

	GP	Car	Yds	Avg	TD	Yds/G
Alabama	13	386	938	2.43	3	72.15
Florida St.	13	458	1075	2.35	8	82.69
Connecticut	12	385	1028	2.67	11	85.67
Stanford	13	364	1149	3.16	16	88.38
LSU	14	460	1261	2.74	7	90.07
Cincinnati	13	456	1251	2.74	10	96.23
Texas	13	409	1251	3.06	15	96.23
La.-Monroe	12	386	1200	3.11	13	100.00
Michigan St.	14	502	1407	2.80	11	100.50
Louisville	13	435	1307	3.00	11	100.54

TURNOVER MARGIN

		Turnovers Gained			Turnovers Lost			
	GP	Fum	Int	Total	Fum	Int	Total	Mar/G
Oklahoma St.	13	20	24	44	10	13	23	1.62
LSU	14	12	18	30	5	5	10	1.43
Toledo	13	16	14	30	7	7	14	1.23
Houston	14	10	21	31	9	6	15	1.14
Wisconsin	14	10	16	26	5	5	10	1.14
N Carolina St.	13	12	27	39	13	12	25	1.08
Kent St.	12	17	14	31	10	9	19	1.00
Memphis	12	18	12	30	10	8	18	1.00
Cincinnati	13	17	16	33	7	14	21	.92
Kansas St.	13	9	18	27	9	6	15	.92
San Diego St.	13	13	15	28	8	8	16	.92
Wyoming	13	18	13	31	8	11	19	.92

OPPONENTS' PASSING EFFICIENCY

	GP	Att	Comp	Pct Comp	Int	Pct Int	Yds	Yds/Att	TD	Pct TD	Rating Pts
Alabama	13	334	164	49.10	13	3.89	1449	4.34	6	1.80	83.69
South Carolina	13	346	174	50.29	19	5.49	1712	4.95	14	4.05	94.22
LSU	14	437	229	52.40	18	4.12	2400	5.49	7	1.60	95.58
Georgia	14	430	218	50.70	20	4.65	2464	5.73	12	2.79	98.74
Rutgers	13	355	184	51.83	19	5.35	2240	6.31	8	2.25	101.57
Penn St.	13	427	238	55.74	14	3.28	2478	5.80	12	2.81	107.20
Southern Miss.	14	535	308	57.57	19	3.55	3142	5.87	14	2.62	108.44
UCF	12	385	208	54.03	9	2.34	2334	6.06	12	3.12	110.56
Vanderbilt	13	398	216	54.27	19	4.77	2499	6.28	16	4.02	110.73
Texas	13	456	258	56.58	12	2.63	2728	5.98	13	2.85	110.98

FOR THE RECORD•Year by Year

NCAA Football Bowl Subdivision* National Champions

Year	Champion	Record	Bowl Game	Head Coach
1883	Yale	8-0-0	No bowl	Ray Tompkins (Captain)
1884	Yale	9-0-0	No bowl	Eugene L. Richards (Captain)
1885	Princeton	9-0-0	No bowl	Charles DeCamp (Captain)
1886	Yale	9-0-1	No bowl	Robert N. Corwin (Captain)
1887	Yale	9-0-0	No bowl	Harry W. Beecher (Captain)
1888	Yale	13-0-0	No bowl	Walter Camp
1889	Princeton	10-0-0	No bowl	Edgar Poe (Captain)
1890	Harvard	11-0-0	No bowl	George A. Stewart/George C. Adams
1891	Yale	13-0-0	No bowl	Walter Camp
1892	Yale	13-0-0	No bowl	Walter Camp
1893	Princeton	11-0-0	No bowl	Tom Trenchard (Captain)
1894	Yale	16-0-0	No bowl	William C. Rhodes
1895	Pennsylvania	14-0-0	No bowl	George Woodruff
1896	Princeton	10-0-1	No bowl	Garrett Cochran
1897	Pennsylvania	15-0-0	No bowl	George Woodruff
1898	Harvard	11-0-0	No bowl	W. Cameron Forbes
1899	Harvard	10-0-1	No bowl	Benjamin H. Dibblee
1900	Yale	12-0-0	No bowl	Malcolm McBride
1901	Michigan	11-0-0	Won Rose	Fielding Yost
1902	Michigan	11-0-0	Won Rose	Fielding Yost
1903	Princeton	11-0-0	No bowl	Art Hillebrand
1904	Pennsylvania	12-0-0	No bowl	Carl Williams
1905	Chicago	11-0-0	No bowl	Amos Alonzo Stagg
1906	Princeton	9-0-1	No bowl	Bill Roper
1907	Yale	9-0-1	No bowl	Bill Knox
1908	Pennsylvania	11-0-1	No bowl	Sol Metzger
1909	Yale	10-0-0	No bowl	Howard Jones
1910	Harvard	8-0-1	No bowl	Percy Houghton
1911	Princeton	8-0-2	No bowl	Bill Roper
1912	Harvard	9-0-0	No bowl	Percy Houghton
1913	Harvard	9-0-0	No bowl	Percy Houghton
1914	Army	9-0-0	No bowl	Charley Daly
1915	Cornell	9-0-0	No bowl	Al Sharpe
1916	Pittsburgh	8-0-0	No bowl	Pop Warner
1917	Georgia Tech	9-0-0	No bowl	John Heisman
1918	Pittsburgh	4-1-0	No bowl	Pop Warner
1919	Harvard	9-0-1	Won Rose	Bob Fisher
1920	California	9-0-0	Won Rose	Andy Smith
1921	Cornell	8-0-0	No bowl	Gil Dobie
1922	Cornell	8-0-0	No bowl	Gil Dobie
1923	Illinois	8-0-0	No bowl	Bob Zuppke
1924	Notre Dame	10-0-0	Won Rose	Knute Rockne
1925	Alabama (H)	10-0-0	Won Rose	Wallace Wade
	Dartmouth (D)	8-0-0	No bowl	Jesse Hawley
1926	Alabama (H)	9-0-1	Tied Rose	Wallace Wade
	Stanford (D)(H)	10-0-1	Tied Rose	Pop Warner
1927	Illinois	7-0-1	No bowl	Bob Zuppke
1928	Georgia Tech (H)	10-0-0	Won Rose	Bill Alexander
	USC (D)	9-0-1	No bowl	Howard Jones
1929	Notre Dame	9-0-0	No bowl	Knute Rockne
1930	Notre Dame	10-0-0	No bowl	Knute Rockne
1931	USC	10-1-0	Won Rose	Howard Jones
1932	USC (H)	10-0-0	Won Rose	Howard Jones
	Michigan (D)	8-0-0	No bowl	Harry Kipke
1933	Michigan	7-0-1	No bowl	Harry Kipke
1934	Minnesota	8-0-0	No bowl	Bernie Bierman
1935	Minnesota (H)	8-0-0	No bowl	Bernie Bierman
	SMU (D)	12-1-0	Lost Rose	Matty Bell
1936	Minnesota	7-1-0	No bowl	Bernie Bierman
1937	Pittsburgh	9-0-1	No bowl	Jock Sutherland
1938	TCU (AP)	11-0-0	Won Sugar	Dutch Meyer
	Notre Dame (D)	8-1-0	No bowl	Elmer Layden
1939	USC (D)	8-0-2	Won Rose	Howard Jones
	Texas A&M (AP)	11-0-0	Won Sugar	Homer Norton

*In 2007, the NCAA renamed Division I-A as the "Football Bowl Subdivision" and Division I-AA as the "Football Championship Subdivision."

Year	Champion	Record	Bowl Game	Head Coach
1940	Minnesota	8-0-0	No bowl	Bernie Bierman
1941	Minnesota	8-0-0	No bowl	Bernie Bierman
1942	Ohio St	9-1-0	No bowl	Paul Brown
1943	Notre Dame	9-1-0	No bowl	Frank Leahy
1944	Army	9-0-0	No bowl	Red Blaik
1945	Army	9-0-0	No bowl	Red Blaik
1946	Notre Dame	8-0-1	No bowl	Frank Leahy
1947	Notre Dame	9-0-0	No bowl	Frank Leahy
	Michigan*	10-0-0	Won Rose	Fritz Crisler
1948	Michigan	9-0-0	No bowl	Bennie Oosterbaan
1949	Notre Dame	10-0-0	No bowl	Frank Leahy
1950	Oklahoma	10-1-0	Lost Sugar	Bud Wilkinson
1951	Tennessee	10-1-0	Lost Sugar	Bob Neyland
1952	Michigan St	9-0-0	No bowl	Biggie Munn
1953	Maryland	10-1-0	Lost Orange	Jim Tatum
1954	Ohio St	10-0-0	Won Rose	Woody Hayes
	UCLA (UPI)	9-0-0	No bowl	Red Sanders
1955	Oklahoma	11-0-0	Won Orange	Bud Wilkinson
1956	Oklahoma	10-0-0	No bowl	Bud Wilkinson
1957	Auburn	10-0-0	No bowl	Shug Jordan
	Ohio St (UPI)	9-1-0	Won Rose	Woody Hayes
1958	LSU	11-0-0	Won Sugar	Paul Dietzel
1959	Syracuse	11-0-0	Won Cotton	Ben Schwartzwalder
1960	Minnesota	8-2-0	Lost Rose	Murray Warmath
1961	Alabama	11-0-0	Won Sugar	Bear Bryant
1962	USC	11-0-0	Won Rose	John McKay
1963	Texas	11-0-0	Won Cotton	Darrell Royal
1964	Alabama	10-1-0	Lost Orange	Bear Bryant
1965	Alabama	9-1-1	Won Orange	Bear Bryant
	Michigan St (UPI)	10-1-0	Lost Rose	Duffy Daugherty
1966	Notre Dame	9-0-1	No bowl	Ara Parseghian
1967	USC	10-1-0	Won Rose	John McKay
1968	Ohio St	10-0-0	Won Rose	Woody Hayes
1969	Texas	11-0-0	Won Cotton	Darrell Royal
1970	Nebraska	11-0-1	Won Orange	Bob Devaney
	Texas (UPI)	10-1-0	Lost Cotton	Darrell Royal
1971	Nebraska	13-0-0	Won Orange	Bob Devaney
1972	USC	12-0-0	Won Rose	John McKay
1973	Notre Dame	11-0-0	Won Sugar	Ara Parseghian
	Alabama (UPI)	11-1-0	Lost Sugar	Bear Bryant
1974	Oklahoma	11-0-0	No bowl	Barry Switzer
	USC (UPI)	10-1-1	Won Rose	John McKay
1975	Oklahoma	11-1-0	Won Orange	Barry Switzer
1976	Pittsburgh	12-0-0	Won Sugar	Johnny Majors
1977	Notre Dame	11-1-0	Won Cotton	Dan Devine
1978	Alabama	11-1-0	Won Sugar	Bear Bryant
	USC (UPI)	12-1-0	Won Rose	John Robinson
1979	Alabama	12-0-0	Won Sugar	Bear Bryant
1980	Georgia	12-0-0	Won Sugar	Vince Dooley
1981	Clemson	12-0-0	Won Orange	Danny Ford
1982	Penn St	11-1-0	Won Sugar	Joe Paterno
1983	Miami (Fla.)	11-1-0	Won Orange	Howard Schnellenberger
1984	BYU	13-0-0	Won Holiday	LaVell Edwards
1985	Oklahoma	11-1-0	Won Orange	Barry Switzer
1986	Penn St	12-0-0	Won Fiesta	Joe Paterno
1987	Miami (Fla.)	12-0-0	Won Orange	Jimmy Johnson
1988	Notre Dame	12-0-0	Won Fiesta	Lou Holtz
1989	Miami (Fla.)	11-1-0	Won Sugar	Dennis Erickson
1990	Colorado	11-1-1	Won Orange	Bill McCartney
	Georgia Tech (UPI)	11-0-1	Won Citrus	Bobby Ross
1991	Miami (Fla.)	12-0-0	Won Orange	Dennis Erickson
	Washington (CNN)	12-0-0	Won Rose	Don James
1992	Alabama	13-0-0	Won Sugar	Gene Stallings
1993	Florida St	12-1-0	Won Orange	Bobby Bowden
1994	Nebraska	13-0-0	Won Orange	Tom Osborne
1995	Nebraska	12-0-0	Won Fiesta	Tom Osborne
†1996	Florida	12–1	Won Sugar	Steve Spurrier
1997	Michigan	12–0	Won Rose	Lloyd Carr
	Nebraska (ESPN)	13–0	Won Orange	Tom Osborne

Year	Champion	Record	Bowl Game	Head Coach
1998	Tennessee	13–0	Won Fiesta	Phillip Fulmer
1999	Florida St	12–0	Won Sugar	Bobby Bowden
2000	Oklahoma	13–0	Won Orange	Bob Stoops
2001	Miami (Fla.)	12–0	Won Rose	Larry Coker
2002	Ohio St	14–0	Won Fiesta	Jim Tressel
2003	LSU	13–1	Won Sugar	Nick Saban
	USC	12–1	Won Rose	Pete Carroll
§2004	Vacated			
2005	Texas	13–0	Won Rose	Mack Brown
‡2006	Florida	13–1	Won BCS Nat'l Championship	Urban Meyer
2007	LSU	12–2	Won BCS Nat'l Championship	Les Miles
2008	Florida	13–1	Won BCS Nat'l Championship	Urban Meyer
2009	Alabama	14–0	Won BCS Nat'l Championship	Nick Saban
2010	Auburn	14–0	Won BCS Nat'l Championship	Gene Chizik
2011	Alabama	12–1	Won BCS Nat'l Championship	Nick Saban

*The AP, which had voted Notre Dame No. 1, took a second vote, giving the national title to Michigan after its 49–0 win over USC in the Rose Bowl. Note: Selectors: Helms Athletic Foundation (H) 1883–1935, The Dickinson System (D) 1924–40, The Associated Press (AP) 1936–2005, United Press International (UPI) 1958–90, *USA Today*/CNN (CNN) 1991–96, and *USA Today*/ESPN (ESPN) 1997–2005. †In 1996 the NCAA introduced overtime to break ties. ‡In 2006, the BCS established a separate national championship game in addition to its existing four-bowl structure. §USC's 2005 Orange Bowl victory and 2004 national championship were vacated in 2010 due to rules violations.

Results of Major Bowl Games

Rose Bowl

1-1-02 ....Michigan 49, Stanford 0	1-1-57 ....Iowa 35, Oregon St 19
1-1-16 ....Washington St 14, Brown 0	1-1-58 ....Ohio St 10, Oregon 7
1-1-17 ....Oregon 14, Pennsylvania 0	1-1-59 ....Iowa 38, California 12
1-1-18 ....Mare Island 19, Camp Lewis 7	1-1-60 ....Washington 44, Wisconsin 8
1-1-19 ....Great Lakes 17, Mare Island 0	1-2-61 ....Washington 17, Minnesota 7
1-1-20 ....Harvard 7, Oregon 6	1-1-62 ....Minnesota 21, UCLA 3
1-1-21 ....California 28, Ohio St 0	1-1-63 ....USC 42, Wisconsin 37
1-2-22 ....Washington & Jefferson 0, California 0	1-1-64 ....Illinois 17, Washington 7
1-1-23 ....USC 14, Penn St 3	1-1-65 ....Michigan 34, Oregon St 7
1-1-24 ....Navy 14, Washington 14	1-1-66 ....UCLA 14, Michigan St 12
1-1-25 ....Notre Dame 27, Stanford 10	1-2-67 ....Purdue 14, USC 13
1-1-26 ....Alabama 20, Washington 19	1-1-68 ....USC 14, Indiana 3
1-1-27 ....Alabama 7, Stanford 7	1-1-69 ....Ohio St 27, USC16
1-2-28 ....Stanford 7, Pittsburgh 6	1-1-70 ....USC 10, Michigan 3
1-1-29 ....Georgia Tech 8, California 7	1-1-71 ....Stanford 27, Ohio St 17
1-1-30 ....USC47, Pittsburgh 14	1-1-72 ....Stanford 13, Michigan 12
1-1-31 ....Alabama 24, Washington St 0	1-1-73 ....USC 42, Ohio St 17
1-1-32 ....USC 21, Tulane 12	1-1-74 ....Ohio St 42, USC 21
1-2-33 ....USC 35, Pittsburgh 0	1-1-75 ....USC 18, Ohio St 17
1-1-34 ....Columbia 7, Stanford 0	1-1-76 ....UCLA 23, Ohio St 10
1-1-35 ....Alabama 29, Stanford 13	1-1-77 ....USC 14, Michigan 6
1-1-36 ....Stanford 7, Southern Methodist 0	1-2-78 ....Washington 27, Michigan 20
1-1-37 ....Pittsburgh 21, Washington 0	1-1-79 ....USC 17, Michigan 10
1-1-38 ....California 13, Alabama 0	1-1-80 ....USC 17, Ohio St 16
1-2-39 ....USC 7, Duke 3	1-1-81 ....Michigan 23, Washington 6
1-1-40 ....USC 14, Tennessee 0	1-1-82 ....Washington 28, Iowa 0
1-1-41 ....Stanford 21, Nebraska 13	1-1-83 ....UCLA 24, Michigan 14
1-1-42 ....Oregon St 20, Duke 16	1-2-84 ....UCLA 45, Illinois 9
1-1-43 ....Georgia 9, UCLA 0	1-1-85 ....USC 20, Ohio St 17
1-1-44 ....USC 29, Washington 0	1-1-86 ....UCLA 45, Iowa 28
1-1-45 ....USC 25, Tennessee 0	1-1-87 ....Arizona St 22, Michigan 15
1-1-46 ....Alabama 34, USC 14	1-1-88 ....Michigan St 20, USC 17
1-1-47 ....Illinois 45, UCLA 14	1-2-89 ....Michigan 22, USC 14
1-1-48 ....Michigan 49, USC 0	1-1-90 ....USC 17, Michigan 10
1-1-49 ....Northwestern 20, California 14	1-1-91 ....Washington 46, Iowa 34
1-2-50 ....Ohio St 17, California 14	1-1-92 ....Washington 34, Michigan 14
1-1-51 ....Michigan 14, California 6	1-1-93 ....Michigan 38, Washington 31
1-1-52 ....Illinois 40, Stanford 7	1-1-94 ....Wisconsin 21, UCLA 16
1-1-53 ....USC 7, Wisconsin 0	1-2-95 ....Penn St 38, Oregon 20
1-1-54 ....Michigan St 28, UCLA 20	1-1-96 ....USC 41, Northwestern 32
1-1-55 ....Ohio St 20, USC 7	1-1-97 ....Ohio St 20, Arizona St 17
1-2-56 ....Michigan St 17, UCLA 14	1-1-98 ....Michigan 21, Washington St 16
	1-1-99 ....Wisconsin 38, UCLA 31

Rose Bowl *(Cont.)*

1-1-00..............Wisconsin 17, Stanford 9
1-1-01..............Washington 34, Purdue 24
1-3-02..............Miami 37, Nebraska 14
1-1-03..............Oklahoma 34, Washington St 14
1-1-04..............USC 28, Michigan 14
1-1-05..............Texas 38, Michigan 37
1-4-06..............Texas 41, USC 38
1-1-07..............USC 32, Michigan 18
1-1-08..............USC 49, Illinois 17
1-1-09..............USC 38, Penn St 24
1-1-10..............Ohio St 26, Oregon 17
1-1-11..............TCU 21, Wisconsin 19
1-2-12..............Oregon 45, Wisconsin 38

City: Pasadena. Stadium: Rose Bowl, capacity 96,576.
Playing Sites: Tournament Park (1902, 1916–22), Rose Bowl
(1923–41, since 1943), Duke Stadium, Durham, NC (1942).

Orange Bowl

1-1-35..............Bucknell 26, Miami (Fla.) 0
1-1-36..............Catholic 20, Mississippi 19
1-1-37..............Duquesne 13, Mississippi St 12
1-1-38..............Auburn 6, Michigan St 0
1-2-39..............Tennessee 17, Oklahoma 0
1-1-40..............Georgia Tech 21, Missouri 7
1-1-41..............Mississippi St 14, Georgetown 7
1-1-42..............Georgia 40, TCU 26
1-1-43..............Alabama 37, Boston College 21
1-1-44..............LSU 19, Texas A&M 14
1-1-45..............Tulsa 26, Georgia Tech 12
1-1-46..............Miami (Fla.) 13, Holy Cross 6
1-1-47..............Rice 8, Tennessee 0
1-1-48..............Georgia Tech 20, Kansas 14
1-1-49..............Texas 41, Georgia 28
1-2-50..............Santa Clara 21, Kentucky 13
1-1-51..............Clemson 15, Miami (Fla.) 14
1-1-52..............Georgia Tech 17, Baylor 14
1-1-53..............Alabama 61, Syracuse 6
1-1-54..............Oklahoma 7, Maryland 0
1-1-55..............Duke 34, Nebraska 7
1-2-56..............Oklahoma 20, Maryland 6
1-1-57..............Colorado 27, Clemson 21
1-1-58..............Oklahoma 48, Duke 21
1-1-59..............Oklahoma 21, Syracuse 6
1-1-60..............Georgia 14, Missouri 0
1-2-61..............Missouri 21, Navy 14
1-1-62..............LSU 25, Colorado 7
1-1-63..............Alabama 17, Oklahoma 0
1-1-64..............Nebraska 13, Auburn 7
1-1-65..............Texas 21, Alabama 17
1-1-66..............Alabama 39, Nebraska 28
1-2-67..............Florida 27, Georgia Tech 12
1-1-68..............Oklahoma 26, Tennessee 24
1-1-69..............Penn St 15, Kansas 14
1-1-70..............Penn St 10, Missouri 3
1-1-71..............Nebraska 17, LSU 12
1-1-72..............Nebraska 38, Alabama 6
1-1-73..............Nebraska 40, Notre Dame 6
1-1-74..............Penn St 16, LSU 9
1-1-75..............Notre Dame 13, Alabama 11
1-1-76..............Oklahoma 14, Michigan 6
1-1-77..............Ohio St 27, Colorado 10
1-2-78..............Arkansas 31, Oklahoma 6
1-1-79..............Oklahoma 31, Nebraska 24
1-1-80..............Oklahoma 24, Florida St 7
1-1-81..............Oklahoma 18, Florida St 17
1-1-82..............Clemson 22, Nebraska 15
1-1-83..............Nebraska 21, LSU 20
1-2-84..............Miami (Fla.) 31, Nebraska 30
1-1-85..............Washington 28, Oklahoma 17

Orange Bowl *(Cont.)*

1-1-86..............Oklahoma 25, Penn St 10
1-1-87..............Oklahoma 42, Arkansas 8
1-1-88..............Miami (Fla.) 20, Oklahoma 14
1-2-89..............Miami (Fla.) 23, Nebraska 3
1-1-90..............Notre Dame 21, Colorado 6
1-1-91..............Colorado 10, Notre Dame 9
1-1-92..............Miami (Fla.) 22, Nebraska 0
1-1-93..............Florida St 27, Nebraska 14
1-1-94..............Florida St 18, Nebraska 16
1-1-95..............Nebraska 24, Miami (Fla.) 17
1-1-96..............Florida St 31, Notre Dame 26
12-31-96..........Nebraska 41, Virginia Tech 21
1-2-98..............Nebraska 42, Tennessee 17
1-2-99..............Florida 31, Syracuse 10
1-1-00..............Michigan 35, Alabama 34 (ot)
1-3-01..............Oklahoma 13, Florida St 2
1-2-02..............Florida 56, Maryland 23
1-2-03..............USC 38, Iowa 17
1-1-04..............Miami (Fla.) 16, Florida St 15
1-4-05..............*Vacated
1-3-06..............Penn State 26, Florida State 23 (3OT)
1-2-07..............Louisville 24, Wake Forest 13
1-3-08..............Kansas 24, Virginia Tech 21
1-1-09..............Virginia Tech 20, Cincinnati 7
1-5-10..............Iowa 24, Georgia Tech 14
1-3-11..............Stanford 40, Virginia Tech12
1-4-12..............West Virginia 70, Clemson 33

City: Miami. Stadium: Pro Player Stadium, capacity 75,192.
Playing Sites: Orange Bowl (1935–96), Pro Player Stadium
(1996–2005), Dolphin(s) Stadium (2005–09), Land Shark
Stadium (2010). *USC's 2005 Orange Bowl victory was
vacated in 2010 due to rules violations.

Sugar Bowl

1-1-35..............Tulane 20, Temple 14
1-1-36..............TCU 3, LSU 2
1-1-37..............Santa Clara 21, LSU 14
1-1-38..............Santa Clara 6, LSU 0
1-2-39..............TCU 15, Carnegie Tech 7
1-1-40..............Texas A&M 14, Tulane 13
1-1-41..............Boston Col 19, Tennessee 13
1-1-42..............Fordham 2, Missouri 0
1-1-43..............Tennessee 14, Tulsa 7
1-1-44..............Georgia Tech 20, Tulsa 18
1-1-45..............Duke 29, Alabama 26
1-1-46..............Oklahoma St 33, St. Mary's (Ca.) 13
1-1-47..............Georgia 20, North Carolina 10
1-1-48..............Texas 27, Alabama 7
1-1-49..............Oklahoma 14, North Carolina 6
1-2-50..............Oklahoma 35, LSU 0
1-1-51..............Kentucky 13, Oklahoma 7
1-1-52..............Maryland 28, Tennessee 13
1-1-53..............Georgia Tech 24, Mississippi 7
1-1-54..............Georgia Tech 42, W Virginia 19
1-1-55..............Navy 21, Mississippi 0
1-2-56..............Georgia Tech 7, Pittsburgh 0
1-1-57..............Baylor 13, Tennessee 7
1-1-58..............Mississippi 39, Texas 7
1-1-59..............LSU 7, Clemson 0
1-1-60..............Mississippi 21, LSU 0
1-2-61..............Mississippi 14, Rice 6
1-1-62..............Alabama 10, Arkansas 3
1-1-63..............Mississippi 17, Arkansas 13
1-1-64..............Alabama 12, Mississippi 7
1-1-65..............LSU 13, Syracuse 10
1-1-66..............Missouri 20, Florida 18
1-2-67..............Alabama 34, Nebraska 7
1-1-68..............LSU 20, Wyoming 13
1-1-69..............Arkansas 16, Georgia 2

Sugar Bowl *(Cont.)*

1-1-70 ....Mississippi 27, Arkansas 22
1-1-71 ....Tennessee 34, Air Force 13
1-1-72 ....Oklahoma 40, Auburn 22
12-31-72 ....Oklahoma 14, Penn St 0
12-31-73 ....Notre Dame 24, Alabama 23
12-31-74 ....Nebraska 13, Florida 10
12-31-75 ....Alabama 13, Penn St 6
1-1-77 ....Pittsburgh 27, Georgia 3
1-2-78 ....Alabama 35, Ohio St 6
1-1-79 ....Alabama 14, Penn St 7
1-1-80 ....Alabama 24, Arkansas 9
1-1-81 ....Georgia 17, Notre Dame 10
1-1-82 ....Pittsburgh 24, Georgia 20
1-1-83 ....Penn St 27, Georgia 23
1-2-84 ....Auburn 9, Michigan 7
1-1-85 ....Nebraska 28, LSU 10
1-1-86 ....Tennessee 35, Miami (Fla.) 7
1-1-87 ....Nebraska 30, LSU 15
1-1-88 ....Syracuse 16, Auburn 16
1-2-89 ....Florida St 13, Auburn 7
1-1-90 ....Miami (Fla.) 33, Alabama 25
1-1-91 ....Tennessee 23, Virginia 22
1-1-92 ....Notre Dame 39, Florida 28
1-1-93 ....Alabama 34, Miami (Fla.) 13
1-1-94 ....Florida 41, West Virginia 7
1-2-95 ....Florida St 23, Florida 17
12-31-95 ....Virginia Tech 28, Texas 10
1-2-97 ....Florida 52, Florida St 20
1-1-98 ....Florida St 31, Ohio St 14
1-1-99 ....Ohio St 24, Texas A&M 14
1-4-00 ....Florida St 46, Virginia Tech 29
1-2-01 ....Miami (Fla.) 37, Florida 20
1-1-02 ....LSU 47, Illinois 34
1-1-03 ....Georgia 26, Florida St 13
1-4-04 ....LSU 21, Oklahoma 14
1-3-05 ....Auburn 16, Virginia Tech 13
1-2-06 ....West Virginia 38, Georgia 35
1-3-07 ....LSU 41, Notre Dame 14
1-1-08 ....Georgia 41, Hawaii 10
1-2-09 ....Utah 31, Alabama 17
1-1-10 ....Florida 51, Cincinnati 24
1-4-11 ....Vacated
1-3-12 ....Michigan 23, Virginia Tech 20

City: New Orleans. Stadium: Louisiana Superdome, capacity 76,791. Playing Sites: Tulane Stadium (1935–74), Louisiana Superdome (since 1975). Due to Hurricane Katrina, 2006 Sugar Bowl played in Atlanta's Georgia Dome.

Cotton Bowl

1-1-37 ....TCU 16, Marquette 6
1-1-38 ....Rice 28, Colorado 14
1-2-39 ....St. Mary's (Ca.) 20, Texas Tech 13
1-1-40 ....Clemson 6, Boston Col 3
1-1-41 ....Texas A&M 13, Fordham 12
1-1-42 ....Alabama 29, Texas A&M 21
1-1-43 ....Texas 14, Georgia Tech 7
1-1-44 ....Texas 7, Randolph Field 7
1-1-45 ....Oklahoma St 34, TCU 0
1-1-46 ....Texas 40, Missouri 27
1-1-47 ....Arkansas 0, LSU 0
1-1-48 ....Southern Methodist 13, Penn St 13
1-1-49 ....Southern Methodist 21, Oregon 13
1-2-50 ....Rice 27, North Carolina 13
1-1-51 ....Tennessee 20, Texas 14
1-1-52 ....Kentucky 20, TCU 7
1-1-53 ....Texas 16, Tennessee 0
1-1-54 ....Rice 28, Alabama 6
1-1-55 ....Georgia Tech 14, Arkansas 6

Cotton Bowl *(Cont.)*

1-2-56 ....Mississippi 14, TCU 13
1-1-57 ....TCU 28, Syracuse 27
1-1-58 ....Navy 20, Rice 7
1-1-59 ....TCU 0, Air Force 0
1-1-60 ....Syracuse 23, Texas 14
1-2-61 ....Duke 7, Arkansas 6
1-1-62 ....Texas 12, Mississippi 7
1-1-63 ....LSU 13, Texas 0
1-1-64 ....Texas 28, Navy 6
1-1-65 ....Arkansas 10, Nebraska 7
1-1-66 ....LSU 14, Arkansas 7
12-31-66 ....Georgia 24, Southern Methodist 9
1-1-68 ....Texas A&M 20, Alabama 16
1-1-69 ....Texas 36, Tennessee 13
1-1-70 ....Texas 21, Notre Dame 17
1-1-71 ....Notre Dame 24, Texas 11
1-1-72 ....Penn St 30, Texas 6
1-1-73 ....Texas 17, Alabama 13
1-1-74 ....Nebraska 19, Texas 3
1-1-75 ....Penn St 41, Baylor 20
1-1-76 ....Arkansas 31, Georgia 10
1-1-77 ....Houston 30, Maryland 21
1-2-78 ....Notre Dame 38, Texas 10
1-1-79 ....Notre Dame 35, Houston 34
1-1-80 ....Houston 17, Nebraska 14
1-1-81 ....Alabama 30, Baylor 2
1-1-82 ....Texas 14, Alabama 12
1-1-83 ....SMU 7, Pittsburgh 3
1-2-84 ....Georgia 10, Texas 9
1-1-85 ....Boston Col 45, Houston 28
1-1-86 ....Texas A&M 36, Auburn 16
1-1-87 ....Ohio St 28, Texas A&M 12
1-1-88 ....Texas A&M 35, Notre Dame 10
1-2-89 ....UCLA 17, Arkansas 3
1-1-90 ....Tennessee 31, Arkansas 27
1-1-91 ....Miami (Fla.) 46, Texas 3
1-1-92 ....Florida St 10, Texas A&M 2
1-1-93 ....Notre Dame 28, Texas A&M 3
1-1-94 ....Notre Dame 24, Texas A&M 21
1-2-95 ....USC 55, Texas Tech 14
1-1-96 ....Colorado 38, Oregon 6
1-1-97 ....BYU 19, Kansas St 15
1-1-98 ....UCLA 29, Texas A&M 23
1-1-99 ....Texas 38, Mississippi St 11
1-1-00 ....Arkansas 27, Texas 6
1-1-01 ....Kansas St 35, Tennessee 21
1-1-02 ....Oklahoma 10, Arkansas 3
1-1-03 ....Texas 35, LSU 20
1-2-04 ....Mississippi 31, Oklahoma St 28
1-1-05 ....Tennessee 38, Texas A&M 7
1-2-06 ....Alabama 13, Texas Tech 10
1-1-07 ....Auburn 17, Nebraska 14
1-1-08 ....Missouri 38, Arkansas 7
1-2-09 ....Mississippi 47, Texas Tech 34
1-2-10 ....Mississippi 21, Oklahoma St 7
1-7-11 ....LSU 41, Texas A&M 24
1-6-12 ....Arkansas 29, Kansas State 16

City: Dallas. Stadium: Cotton Bowl (1937–2009), capacity 88,175. Cowboys Stadium (2010–), capacity 71,167.

Sun Bowl

1-1-36 ....Hardin-Simmons 14, New Mexico St 14
1-1-37 ....Hardin-Simmons 34, UTEP 6
1-1-38 ....W Virginia 7, Texas Tech 6
1-2-39 ....Utah 26, New Mexico 0
1-1-40 ....Catholic 0, Arizona St 0
1-1-41 ....Case Reserve 26, Arizona St 13
1-1-42 ....Tulsa 6, Texas Tech 0

Sun Bowl *(Cont.)*

1-1-43..............2nd Air Force 13, Hardin-Simmons 7
1-1-44..............Southwestern (Tex.) 7, New Mexico 0
1-1-45..............Southwestern (Tex.) 35, New Mexico 0
1-1-46..............New Mexico 34, Denver 24
1-1-47..............Cincinnati 18, Virginia Tech 6
1-1-48..............Miami (OH) 13, Texas Tech 12
1-1-49..............W Virginia 21, UTEP 12
1-2-50..............UTEP 33, Georgetown 20
1-1-51..............W Texas St 14, Cincinnati 13
1-1-52..............Texas Tech 25, Pacific 14
1-1-53..............Pacific 26, Southern Miss 7
1-1-54..............UTEP 37, Southern Miss 14
1-1-55..............UTEP 47, Florida St 20
1-2-56..............Wyoming 21, Texas Tech 14
1-1-57..............George Washington 13, UTEP 0
1-1-58..............Louisville 34, Drake 20
12-31-58..........Wyoming 14, Hardin-Simmons 6
12-31-59..........New Mexico St 28, N Texas 8
12-31-60..........New Mexico St 20, Utah St 13
12-30-61..........Villanova 17, Wichita St 9
12-31-62..........W Texas St 15, Ohio 14
12-31-63..........Oregon 21, Southern Methodist 14
12-26-64..........Georgia 7, Texas Tech 0
12-31-65..........UTEP 13, TCU 12
12-24-66..........Wyoming 28, Florida St 20
12-30-67..........UTEP 14, Mississippi 7
12-28-68..........Auburn 34, Arizona 10
12-20-69..........Nebraska 45, Georgia 6
12-19-70..........Georgia Tech 17, Texas 9
12-18-71..........LSU 33, Iowa St 15
12-30-72..........North Carolina 32, Texas Tech 28
12-29-73..........Missouri 34, Auburn 17
12-28-74..........Mississippi St 26, North Carolina 24
12-26-75..........Pittsburgh 33, Kansas 19
1-2-77..............Texas A&M 37, Florida 14
12-31-77..........Stanford 24, LSU 14
12-23-78..........Texas 42, Maryland 0
12-22-79..........Washington 14, Texas 7
12-27-80..........Nebraska 31, Mississippi St 17
12-26-81..........Oklahoma 40, Houston 14
12-25-82..........North Carolina 26, Texas 10
12-24-83..........Alabama 28, Southern Methodist 7
12-22-84..........Maryland 28, Tennessee 27
12-28-85..........Georgia 13, Arizona 13
12-25-86..........Alabama 28, Washington 6
12-25-87..........Oklahoma St 35, W Virginia 33
12-24-88..........Alabama 29, Army 28
12-30-89..........Pittsburgh 31, Texas A&M 28
12-31-90..........Michigan St 17, USC 16
12-31-91..........UCLA 6, Illinois 3
12-31-92..........Baylor 20, Arizona 15
12-24-93..........Oklahoma 41, Texas Tech 10
12-30-94..........Texas 35, North Carolina 31
12-29-95..........Iowa 38, Washington 18
12-31-96..........Stanford 38, Michigan St 0
12-31-97..........Arizona St 17, Iowa 7
12-31-98..........TCU 28, USC 19
12-31-99..........Oregon 24, Minnesota 20
12-29-00..........Wisconsin 21, UCLA 20
12-31-01..........Washington St 33, Purdue 27
12-31-02..........Purdue 34, Washington 24
12-31-03..........Minnesota 31, Oregon 30
12-31-04..........Arizona State 27, Purdue 23
12-30-05..........UCLA 50, Northwestern 39
12-29-06..........Oregon State 39, Missouri 38
12-31-07..........Oregon 56, South Florida 21
12-31-08..........Oregon St 3, Pittsburgh 0
12-31-09..........Oklahoma 31, Stanford 27

Sun Bowl *(Cont.)*

12-31-10..........Notre Dame 33, Miami (Fla.) 17
12-31-11..........Utah 30, Georgia Tech 27
City: El Paso. Stadium: Sun Bowl, capacity 51,270.
Name Changes: Sun Bowl (1936–86; 94–), John Hancock
Sun Bowl (1987–88), John Hancock Bowl (1989–93).
Playing Sites: Kidd Field (1936–62), Sun Bowl (since 1963).

Gator Bowl

1-1-46..............Wake Forest 26, South Carolina 14
1-1-47..............Oklahoma 34, North Carolina St 13
1-1-48..............Maryland 20, Georgia 20
1-1-49..............Clemson 24, Missouri 23
1-2-50..............Maryland 20, Missouri 7
1-1-51..............Wyoming 20, Washington & Lee 7
1-1-52..............Miami (Fla.) 14, Clemson 0
1-1-53..............Florida 14, Tulsa 13
1-1-54..............Texas Tech 35, Auburn 13
12-31-54..........Auburn 33, Baylor 13
12-31-55..........Vanderbilt 25, Auburn 13
12-29-56..........Georgia Tech 21, Pittsburgh 14
12-28-57..........Tennessee 3, Texas A&M 0
12-27-58..........Mississippi 7, Florida 3
1-2-60..............Arkansas 14, Georgia Tech 7
12-31-60..........Florida 13, Baylor 12
12-30-61..........Penn St 30, Georgia Tech 15
12-29-62..........Florida 17, Penn St 7
12-28-63..........North Carolina 35, Air Force 0
1-2-65..............Florida St 36, Oklahoma 19
12-31-65..........Georgia Tech 31, Texas Tech 21
12-31-66..........Tennessee 18, Syracuse 12
12-30-67..........Penn St 17, Florida St 17
12-28-68..........Missouri 35, Alabama 10
12-27-69..........Florida 14, Tennessee 13
1-2-71..............Auburn 35, Mississippi 28
12-31-71..........Georgia 7, North Carolina 3
12-30-72..........Auburn 24, Colorado 3
12-29-73..........Texas Tech 28, Tennessee 19
12-30-74..........Auburn 27, Texas 3
12-29-75..........Maryland 13, Florida 0
12-27-76..........Notre Dame 20, Penn St 9
12-30-77..........Pittsburgh 34, Clemson 3
12-29-78..........Clemson 17, Ohio St 15
12-28-79..........North Carolina 17, Michigan 15
12-29-80..........Pittsburgh 37, South Carolina 9
12-28-81..........North Carolina 31, Arkansas 27
12-30-82..........Florida St 31, W Virginia 12
12-30-83..........Florida 14, Iowa 6
12-28-84..........Oklahoma St 21, South Carolina 14
12-30-85..........Florida St 34, Oklahoma St 23
12-27-86..........Clemson 27, Stanford 21
12-31-87..........LSU 30, South Carolina 13
1-1-89..............Georgia 34, Michigan St 27
12-30-89..........Clemson 27, W Virginia 7
1-1-91..............Michigan 35, Mississippi 3
12-29-91..........Oklahoma 48, Virginia 14
12-31-92..........Florida 27, North Carolina St 10
12-31-93..........Alabama 24, North Carolina 10
12-30-94..........Tennessee 45, Virginia Tech 23
1-1-96..............Syracuse 41, Clemson 0
1-1-97..............North Carolina 20, W Virginia 13
1-1-98..............North Carolina 42, Virginia Tech 13
1-1-99..............Georgia Tech 35, Notre Dame 28
1-1-00..............Miami 27, Georgia Tech 13
1-1-01..............Virginia Tech 41, Clemson 20
1-1-02..............Florida St 30, Virginia Tech 17
1-1-03..............North Carolina St 28, Notre Dame 6
1-1-04..............Maryland 41, W Virginia 7
1-1-05..............Florida State 30, W Virginia 18
1-2-06..............Virginia Tech 35, Louisville 24

Gator Bowl *(Cont.)*

1-1-07..............W Virginia 38, Georgia Tech 35
1-1-08..............Texas Tech 31, Virginia 28
1-1-09..............Nebraska 26, Clemson 21
1-1-10..............Florida St 33, W Virginia 21
1-1-11..............Mississippi St 52, Michigan 14
1-2-12..............Florida 24, Ohio State 17

City: Jacksonville, FL. Stadium: Gator Bowl Stadium (1946-1993); Ben Hill Griffin Stadium (1994); Alltel Stadium (1997–2007), Jacksonville Municipal Stadium (1995–96, 2008–), capacity 76,976.

Capital One Bowl

1-1-47..............Catawba 31, Maryville (Tenn.) 6
1-1-48..............Catawba 7, Marshall 0
1-1-49..............Murray St 21, Sul Ross St 21
1-2-50..............St. Vincent 7, Emory & Henry 6
1-1-51..............Morris Harvey 35, Emory & Henry 14
1-1-52..............Stetson 35, Arkansas St 20
1-1-53..............E Texas St 33, Tennessee Tech 0
1-1-54..............E Texas St 7, Arkansas St 7
1-1-55..............NE-Omaha 7, Eastern Kentucky 6
1-2-56..............Juniata 6, Missouri Valley 6
1-1-57..............W Texas St 20, Southern Miss 13
1-1-58..............E Texas St 10, Southern Miss 9
12-27-58..........E Texas St 26, Missouri Valley 7
1-1-60..............Middle Tennessee St 21, Presbyterian 12
12-30-60..........Citadel 27, Tennessee Tech 0
12-29-61..........Lamar 21, Middle Tennessee St 14
12-22-62..........Houston 49, Miami (Ohio) 21
12-28-63..........Western Kentucky 27, Coast Guard 0
12-12-64..........E Carolina 14, Massachusetts 13
12-11-65..........E Carolina 31, Maine 0
12-10-66..........Morgan St 14, W Chester 6
12-16-67..........TN-Martin 25, W Chester 8
12-27-68..........Richmond 49, Ohio 42
12-26-69..........Toledo 56, Davidson 33
12-28-70..........Toledo 40, William & Mary 12
12-28-71..........Toledo 28, Richmond 3
12-29-72..........Tampa 21, Kent St 18
12-22-73..........Miami (Ohio) 16, Florida 7
12-21-74..........Miami (Ohio) 21, Georgia 10
12-20-75..........Miami (Ohio) 20, South Carolina 7
12-18-76..........Oklahoma St 49, BYU 21
12-23-77..........Florida St 40, Texas Tech 17
12-23-78..........North Carolina St 30, Pittsburgh 17
12-22-79..........LSU 34, Wake Forest 10
12-20-80..........Florida 35, Maryland 20
12-19-81..........Missouri 19, Southern Miss 17
12-18-82..........Auburn 33, Boston Col 26
12-17-83..........Tennessee 30, Maryland 23
12-22-84..........Georgia 17, Florida St 17
12-28-85..........Ohio St 10, BYU 7
1-1-87..............Auburn 16, USC 7
1-1-88..............Clemson 35, Penn St 10
1-2-89..............Clemson 13, Oklahoma 6
1-1-90..............Illinois 31, Virginia 21
1-1-91..............Georgia Tech 45, Nebraska 21
1-1-92..............California 37, Clemson 13
1-1-93..............Georgia 21, Ohio State 14
1-1-94..............Penn State 31, Tennessee 13
1-2-95..............Alabama 24, Ohio St 17
1-1-96..............Tennessee 20, Ohio St 14
1-1-97..............Tennessee 48, Northwestern 28
1-1-98..............Florida 21, Penn St 6
1-1-99..............Michigan 45, Arkansas 31
1-1-00..............Michigan St 37, Florida 34
1-1-01..............Michigan 31, Auburn 28
1-1-02..............Tennessee 45, Michigan 17
1-1-03..............Auburn 13, Penn St 9

Capital One Bowl *(Cont.)*

1-1-04..............Georgia 34, Purdue 27 (OT)
1-1-05..............Iowa 30, LSU 25
1-2-06..............Wisconsin 24, Auburn 10
1-1-07..............Wisconsin 17, Arkansas 14
1-1-08..............Michigan 41, Florida 35
1-1-09..............Georgia 24, Michigan St 12
1-1-10..............Penn St 19, LSU 17
1-1-11..............Alabama 49, Michigan St 7
1-2-12..............South Carolina 30, Nebraska 13

City: Orlando, FL. Stadium: Florida Citrus Bowl, capacity 70,000. Name Change: Tangerine Bowl (1947–82). Florida Citrus Bowl (1983–2007). Playing Sites: Tangerine Bowl (1947–72, 1974–82); Florida Field, Gainesville (1973); Orlando Stadium/Florida Citrus Bowl-Orlando (1983–2007).

Liberty Bowl

12-19-59..........Penn St 7, Alabama 0
12-17-60..........Penn St 41, Oregon 12
12-16-61..........Syracuse 15, Miami (Fla.) 14
12-15-62..........Oregon St 6, Villanova 0
12-21-63..........Mississippi St 16, North Carolina St 12
12-19-64..........Utah 32, W Virginia 6
12-18-65..........Mississippi 13, Auburn 7
12-10-66..........Miami (Fla.) 14, Virginia Tech 7
12-16-67..........North Carolina St 14, Georgia 7
12-14-68..........Mississippi 34, Virginia Tech 17
12-13-69..........Colorado 47, Alabama 33
12-12-70..........Tulane 17, Colorado 3
12-20-71..........Tennessee 14, Arkansas 13
12-18-72..........Georgia Tech 31, Iowa St 30
12-17-73..........North Carolina St 31, Kansas 18
12-16-74..........Tennessee 7, Maryland 3
12-22-75..........USC 20, Texas A&M 0
12-20-76..........Alabama 36, UCLA 6
12-19-77..........Nebraska 21, North Carolina 17
12-23-78..........Missouri 20, LSU 15
12-22-79..........Penn St 9, Tulane 6
12-27-80..........Purdue 28, Missouri 25
12-30-81..........Ohio St 31, Navy 28
12-29-82..........Alabama 21, Illinois 15
12-29-83..........Notre Dame 19, Boston Col 18
12-27-84..........Auburn 21, Arkansas 15
12-27-85..........Baylor 21, LSU 7
12-29-86..........Tennessee 21, Minnesota 14
12-29-87..........Georgia 20, Arkansas 17
12-28-88..........Indiana 34, South Carolina 10
12-28-89..........Mississippi 42, Air Force 29
12-27-90..........Air Force 23, Ohio St 11
12-29-91..........Air Force 38, Mississippi St 15
12-31-92..........Mississippi 13, Air Force 0
12-28-93..........Louisville 18, Michigan St 7
12-31-94..........Illinois 30, E Carolina 0
12-30-95..........East Carolina 19, Stanford 13
12-27-96..........Syracuse 30, Houston 17
12-31-97..........Southern Miss 41, Pittsburgh 7
12-31-98..........Tulane 41, BYU 27
12-31-99..........Southern Miss 23, Colorado St 17
12-29-01..........Colorado St 22, Louisville 17
12-31-01..........Louisville 28, BYU 10
12-31-02..........TCU 17, Colorado St 3
12-31-03..........Utah 17, Southern Mississippi 0
12-31-04..........Louisville 44, Boise State 40
12-31-05..........Tulsa 31, Fresno State 24
12-29-06..........South Carolina 44, Houston 36
12-29-07..........Mississippi St 10, Central Florida 3
1-2-09..............Kentucky 25, East Carolina 19
1-2-10..............Arkansas 20, East Carolina 17

Liberty Bowl *(Cont.)*

12-31-10 ....Central Florida 10, Georgia 6
12-31-11 ....Cincinnati 31, Vanderbilt 24
City: Memphis (since 1965). Stadium: Liberty Bowl
Memorial Stadium, capacity 62,921.
Playing Sites: Philadelphia (Municipal Stadium, 1959–63),
Atlantic City (Convention Center, 1964).

Bluebonnet Bowl

12-19-59 ....Clemson 23, TCU 7
12-17-60 ....Texas 3, Alabama 3
12-16-61 ....Kansas 33, Rice 7
12-22-62 ....Missouri 14, Georgia Tech 10
12-21-63 ....Baylor 14, LSU 7
12-19-64 ....Tulsa 14, Mississippi 7
12-18-65 ....Tennessee 27, Tulsa 6
12-17-66 ....Texas 19, Mississippi 0
12-23-67 ....Colorado 31, Miami (Fla.) 21
12-31-68 ....Southern Methodist 28, Oklahoma 27
12-31-69 ....Houston 36, Auburn 7
12-31-70 ....Alabama 24, Oklahoma 24
12-31-71 ....Colorado 29, Houston 17
12-30-72 ....Tennessee 24, LSU 17
12-29-73 ....Houston 47, Tulane 7
12-23-74 ....North Carolina St 31, Houston 31
12-27-75 ....Texas 38, Colorado 21
12-31-76 ....Nebraska 27, Texas Tech 24
12-31-77 ....USC 47, Texas A&M 28
12-31-78 ....Stanford 25, Georgia 22
12-31-79 ....Purdue 27, Tennessee 22
12-31-80 ....North Carolina 16, Texas 7
12-31-81 ....Michigan 33, UCLA 14
12-31-82 ....Arkansas 28, Florida 24
12-31-83 ....Oklahoma St 24, Baylor 14
12-31-84 ....West Virginia 31, TCU 14
12-31-85 ....Air Force 24, Texas 16
12-31-86 ....Baylor 21, Colorado 9
12-31-87 ....Texas 32, Pittsburgh 27
City: Houston. Playing sites: Rice Stadium (1959–67;
1985–86), Astrodome (1968–84, 1987).
Name change: Astro-Bluebonnet Bowl (1968–84). Bowl
was discontinued after 1987.

Chick-fil-A Bowl

12-3-68 ....LSU 31, Florida St 27
12-30-69 ....W Virginia 14, South Carolina 3
12-30-70 ....Arizona St 48, North Carolina 26
12-30-71 ....Mississippi 41, Georgia Tech 18
12-29-72 ....North Carolina St 49, W Virginia 13
12-28-73 ....Georgia 17, Maryland 16
12-28-74 ....Vanderbilt 6, Texas Tech 6
12-31-75 ....W Virginia 13, North Carolina St 10
12-31-76 ....Kentucky 21, North Carolina 0
12-31-77 ....North Carolina St 24, Iowa St 14
12-25-78 ....Purdue 41, Georgia Tech 21
12-31-79 ....Baylor 24, Clemson 18
1-2-81 ....Miami (Fla.) 20, Virginia Tech 10
12-31-81 ....W Virginia 26, Florida 6
12-31-82 ....Iowa 28, Tennessee 22
12-30-83 ....Florida St 28, North Carolina 3
12-31-84 ....Virginia 27, Purdue 24
12-31-85 ....Army 31, Illinois 29
12-31-86 ....Virginia Tech 25, North Carolina St 24
1-2-88 ....Tennessee 27, Indiana 22
12-31-88 ....North Carolina St 28, Iowa 23
12-30-89 ....Syracuse 19, Georgia 18
12-29-90 ....Auburn 27, Indiana 23
1-1-92 ....E. Carolina 37, North Carolina St 34
1-2-93 ....North Carolina 21, Mississippi St 17
12-31-93 ....Clemson 14, Kentucky 13

Chick-fil-A Bowl *(Cont.)*

1-1-95 ....North Carolina St 28, Mississippi St 24
12-30-95 ....Virginia 34, Georgia 27
12-28-96 ....LSU 10, Clemson 7
1-2-98 ....Auburn 21, Clemson 17
12-31-98 ....Georgia 35, Virginia 33
12-30-99 ....Mississippi St 17, Clemson 7
12-29-00 ....LSU 28, Georgia Tech 14
12-31-01 ....North Carolina 16, Auburn 10
12-31-02 ....Maryland 30, Tennessee 3
1-2-04 ....Clemson 27, Tennessee 14
12-31-04 ....Miami (Fla.) 27, Florida 10
12-30-05 ....LSU 40, Miami (Fla.) 3
12-30-06 ....Georgia 31, Virginia Tech 24
12-31-07 ....Auburn 23, Clemson 20 (OT)
12-31-08 ....LSU 38, Georgia Tech 3
12-31-09 ....Virginia Tech 37, Tennessee 14
12-31-10 ....Florida St 26, South Carolina 17
12-31-11 ....Auburn 43, Virginia 24
City: Atlanta. Stadium: Georgia Dome, capacity 71,500.
Name change: Peach Bowl (1968–2005). Playing Sites:
Grant Field (1968–70), Atlanta–Fulton County Stadium
(1971–92), Georgia Dome (since 1993).

Fiesta Bowl

12-27-71 ....Arizona St 45, Florida St 38
12-23-72 ....Arizona St 49, Missouri 35
12-21-73 ....Arizona St 28, Pittsburgh 7
12-28-74 ....Oklahoma St 16, BYU 6
12-26-75 ....Arizona St 17, Nebraska 14
12-25-76 ....Oklahoma 41, Wyoming 7
12-25-77 ....Penn St 42, Arizona St 30
12-25-78 ....Arkansas 10, UCLA 10
12-25-79 ....Pittsburgh 16, Arizona 10
12-26-80 ....Penn St 31, Ohio St 19
1-1-82 ....Penn St 26, USC 10
1-1-83 ....Arizona St 32, Oklahoma 21
1-2-84 ....Ohio St 28, Pittsburgh 23
1-1-85 ....UCLA 39, Miami (Fla.) 37
1-1-86 ....Michigan 27, Nebraska 23
1-2-87 ....Penn St 14, Miami (Fla.) 10
1-1-88 ....Florida St 31, Nebraska 28
1-2-89 ....Notre Dame 34, W Virginia 21
1-1-90 ....Florida St 41, Nebraska 17
1-1-91 ....Louisville 34, Alabama 7
1-1-92 ....Penn St 42, Tennessee 17
1-1-93 ....Syracuse 26, Colorado 22
1-1-94 ....Arizona 29, Miami (Fla.) 0
1-2-95 ....Colorado 41, Notre Dame 24
1-2-96 ....Nebraska 62, Florida 24
1-1-97 ....Penn St 38, Texas 15
12-31-97 ....Kansas St 35, Syracuse 18
1-4-99 ....Tennessee 23, Florida St 16
1-2-00 ....Nebraska 31, Tennessee 21
1-1-01 ....Oregon St 41, Notre Dame 9
1-1-02 ....Oregon 38, Colorado 16
1-3-03 ....Ohio St 31, Miami (Fla.) 24 [2 OT]
1-2-04 ....Ohio St 35, Kansas St 28
1-1-05 ....Utah 35, Pittsburgh 7
1-2-06 ....Ohio St 34, Notre Dame 20
1-1-07 ....Boise St 43, Oklahoma 42
1-2-08 ....West Virginia 48, Oklahoma 28
1-5-09 ....Texas 24, Ohio St 21
1-4-10 ....Boise St 17, TCU 10
1-1-11 ....Oklahoma 48, Connecticut 20
1-2-12 ....Oklahoma St 41, Stanford 38
Stadium: Sun Devil Stadium, Tempe, Ariz. (1971–2006),
capacity 73,471. University of Phoenix Stadium,
Glendale, Ariz. (2007–), capacity 72,200.

Independence Bowl

12-13-76 ....McNeese St 20, Tulsa 16
12-17-77 ....Louisiana Tech 24, Louisville 14
12-16-78 ....E Carolina 35, Louisiana Tech 13
12-15-79 ....Syracuse 31, McNeese St 7
12-13-80 ....Southern Miss 16, McNeese St 14
12-12-81 ....Texas A&M 33, Oklahoma St 16
12-11-82 ....Wisconsin 14, Kansas St 3
12-10-83 ....Air Force 9, Mississippi 3
12-15-84 ....Air Force 23, Virginia Tech 7
12-21-85 ....Minnesota 20, Clemson 13
12-20-86 ....Mississippi 20, Texas Tech 17
12-19-87 ....Washington 24, Tulane 12
12-23-88 ....Southern Miss 38, UTEP 18
12-16-89 ....Oregon 27, Tulsa 24
12-15-90 ....Louisiana Tech 34, Maryland 34
12-29-91 ....Georgia 24, Arkansas 15
12-31-92 ....Wake Forest 39, Oregon 35
12-31-93 ....Virginia Tech 45, Indiana 20
12-28-94 ....Virginia 20, TCU 10
12-29-95 ....LSU 45, Michigan St 26
12-31-96 ....Auburn 32, Army 29
12-28-97 ....LSU 27, Notre Dame 9
12-31-98 ....Mississippi 35, Texas Tech 18
12-31-99 ....Mississippi 27, Oklahoma 25
12-31-00 ....Mississippi St 43, Texas A&M 41
12-27-01 ....Alabama 14, Iowa St 13
12-27-02 ....Mississippi 27, Nebraska 23
12-31-03 ....Arkansas 27, Missouri 14
12-28-04 ....Iowa State 17, Miami (Ohio) 13
12-30-05 ....Missouri 38, South Carolina 31
12-28-06 ....Oklahoma State 34, Alabama 31
12-30-07 ....Alabama 30, Colorado 24
12-28-08 ....Louisiana Tech 17, Northern Ill. 10
12-28-09 ....Georgia 44, Texas A&M 20
12-27-10 ....Air Force 14, Georgia Tech 7
12-26-11 ....Missouri 41, North Carolina 24

City: Shreveport, LA. Stadium: Independence Stadium, capacity 50,459.

All-American Bowl

12-22-77 ....Maryland 17, Minnesota 7
12-20-78 ....Texas A&M 28, Iowa St 12
12-29-79 ....Missouri 24, South Carolina 14
12-27-80 ....Arkansas 34, Tulane 15
12-31-81 ....Mississippi St 10, Kansas 0
12-31-82 ....Air Force 36, Vanderbilt 28
12-22-83 ....W Virginia 20, Kentucky 16
12-29-84 ....Kentucky 20, Wisconsin 19
12-31-85 ....Georgia Tech 17, Michigan St 14
12-31-86 ....Florida St 27, Indiana 13
12-22-87 ....Virginia 22, BYU 16
12-29-88 ....Florida 14, Illinois 10
12-28-89 ....Texas Tech 49, Duke 21
12-28-90 ....North Carolina St 31, Southern Miss 27

City: Birmingham, AL. Stadium: Legion Field.
Name Change: Hall of Fame Classic (1977–84). Bowl was discontinued after 1990.

Holiday Bowl

12-22-78 ....Navy 23, BYU 16
12-21-79 ....Indiana 38, BYU 37
12-19-80 ....BYU 46, SMU 45
12-18-81 ....BYU 38, Washington St 36
12-17-82 ....Ohio St 47, BYU 17
12-23-83 ....BYU 21, Missouri 17
12-21-84 ....BYU 24, Michigan 17
12-22-85 ....Arkansas 18, Arizona St 17
12-30-86 ....Iowa 39, San Diego St 38
12-30-87 ....Iowa 20, Wyoming 19

Holiday Bowl *(Cont.)*

12-30-88 ....Oklahoma St 62, Wyoming 14
12-29-89 ....Penn St 50, BYU 39
12-29-90 ....Texas A&M 65, BYU 14
12-30-91 ....Iowa 13, BYU 13
12-30-92 ....Hawaii 27, Illinois 17
12-30-93 ....Ohio St 28, BYU 21
12-30-94 ....Michigan 24, Colorado St 14
12-29-95 ....Kansas St 54, Colorado St 21
12-30-96 ....Colorado 33, Washington 21
12-29-97 ....Colorado St 35, Missouri 24
12-30-98 ....Arizona 23, Nebraska 20
12-29-99 ....Kansas St 24, Washington 20
12-29-00 ....Oregon 35, Texas 30
12-28-01 ....Texas 47, Washington 43
12-27-02 ....Kansas St 34, Arizona St 27
12-30-03 ....Washington St 28, Texas 20
12-30-04 ....Texas Tech 45, California 31
12-29-05 ....Oklahoma 17, Oregon 14
12-28-06 ....California 45, Texas A&M 10
12-27-07 ....Texas 52, Arizona St 34
12-30-08 ....Oregon 42, Oklahoma St 31
12-30-09 ....Nebraska 33, Arizona 0
12-30-11 ....Washington 19, Nebraska 7
12-28-11 ....Texas 21, California 10

City: San Diego. Stadium: Qualcomm Stadium, capacity 70,000.

Las Vegas Bowl

12-19-81 ....Toledo 27, San Jose St 25
12-18-82 ....Fresno St 29, Bowling Green 28
12-17-83 ....Northern Illinois 20,
................................Cal St–Fullerton 13
12-15-84 ....UNLV 30, Toledo 13*
12-14-85 ....Fresno St 51, Bowling Green 7
12-13-86 ....San Jose St 37, Miami (Ohio) 7
12-12-87 ....Eastern Michigan 30, San Jose St 27
12-10-88 ....Fresno St 35, Western Michigan 30
12-9-89 ....Fresno St 27, Ball St 6
12-8-90 ....San Jose St 48, Central Michigan 24
12-14-91 ....Bowling Green 28, Fresno St 21
12-18-92 ....Bowling Green 35, Nevada 34
12-17-93 ....Utah St 42, Ball St 33
12-15-94 ....UNLV 52, Central Michigan 24
12-14-95 ....Toledo 40, Nevada 37
12-19-96 ....Nevada 18, Ball St 15
12-19-97 ....Oregon 41, Air Force 13
12-19-98 ....North Carolina 20, San Diego St 13
12-18-99 ....Utah 17, Fresno St 16
12-21-00 ....UNLV 31, Arkansas 14
12-25-01 ....Utah 10, USC 6
12-25-02 ....UCLA 27, New Mexico 13
12-24-03 ....Oregon St 55, New Mexico 14
12-23-04 ....Wyoming 24, UCLA, 21
12-22-05 ....California 35, BYU 28
12-21-06 ....BYU 38, Oregon 8
12-22-07 ....BYU 17, UCLA 16
12-20-08 ....Arizona 31, BYU 21
12-22-09 ....BYU 44, Oregon St 20
12-22-10 ....Boise St 26, Utah 3
12-22-11 ....Boise St 56, Arizona St 24

* Toledo won later by forfeit. City: Las Vegas (since 1992). Stadium: Sam Boyd Silver Bowl Stadium, capacity 40,000. Name change: California Bowl (1981–91). Playing sites: Fresno, CA (Bulldog Stadium, 1981–91), Las Vegas.

Aloha Bowl

12-25-82 ....Washington 21, Maryland 20
12-26-83 ....Penn St 13, Washington 10
12-29-84 ....Southern Methodist 27, Notre Dame 20
12-28-85 ....Alabama 24, USC 3
12-27-86 ....Arizona 30, North Carolina 21
12-25-87 ....UCLA 20, Florida 16
12-25-88 ....Washington St 24, Houston 22
12-25-89 ....Michigan St 33, Hawaii 13
12-25-90 ....Syracuse 28, Arizona 0
12-25-91 ....Georgia Tech 18, Stanford 17
12-25-92 ....Kansas 23, BYU 20
12-25-93 ....Colorado 41, Fresno St 30
12-25-94 ....Boston College 12, Kansas St 7
12-25-95 ....Kansas 51, UCLA 30
12-25-96 ....Navy 42, California 38
12-25-97 ....Washington 51, Michigan St 23
12-25-98 ....Colorado 51, Oregon 43
12-25-99 ....Wake Forest 23, Arizona St 3
12-25-00 ....Boston College 31, Arizona St 17

City: Honolulu. Stadium: Aloha Stadium. Bowl was discontinued after 2000.

Freedom Bowl

12-16-84 ....Iowa 55, Texas 17
12-30-85 ....Washington 20, Colorado 17
12-30-86 ....UCLA 31, BYU 10
12-30-87 ....Arizona St 33, Air Force 28
12-29-88 ....BYU 20, Colorado 17
12-30-89 ....Washington 34, Florida 7
12-29-90 ....Colorado St 32, Oregon 31
12-30-91 ....Tulsa 28, San Diego St 17
12-29-92 ....Fresno St 24, USC 7
12-30-93 ....USC 28, Utah 21
12-29-94 ....Utah 16, Arizona 13

City: Anaheim. Stadium: Anaheim Stadium. Bowl was discontinued after 1994.

Outback Bowl

12-23-86 ....Boston College 27, Georgia 24
1-2-88 ....Michigan 28, Alabama 24
1-2-89 ....Syracuse 23, LSU 10
1-1-90 ....Auburn 31, Ohio St 14
1-1-91 ....Clemson 30, Illinois 0
1-1-92 ....Syracuse 24, Ohio St 17
1-1-93 ....Tennessee 38, Boston College 23
1-1-94 ....Michigan 42, North Carolina St 7
1-2-95 ....Wisconsin 34, Duke 20
1-1-96 ....Penn St 43, Auburn 14
1-1-97 ....Alabama 17, Michigan 14
1-1-98 ....Georgia 33, Wisconsin 6
1-1-99 ....Penn St 26, Kentucky 14
1-1-00 ....Georgia 28, Purdue 25
1-1-01 ....South Carolina 24, Ohio St 7
1-1-02 ....South Carolina 31, Ohio St 28
1-1-03 ....Michigan 38, Florida 30
1-1-04 ....Iowa 37, Florida 17
1-1-05 ....Georgia 24, Wisconsin 21
1-2-06 ....Florida 31, Iowa 24
1-1-07 ....Penn State 20, Tennessee 10
1-1-08 ....Tennessee 21, Wisconsin 17
1-1-09 ....Iowa 31, South Carolina 10
1-1-10 ....Auburn 38, Northwestern 35
1-1-11 ....Florida 37, Penn St 24
1-2-12 ....Michigan St 33, Georgia 30

City: Tampa. Stadium: Raymond James Stadium, capacity 75,000. Name change: Hall of Fame Bowl (1986–95).

Insight Bowl

12-31-89 ....Arizona 17, North Carolina St 10
12-31-90 ....California 17, Wyoming 15
12-31-91 ....Indiana 24, Baylor 0
12-29-92 ....Washington St 31, Utah 28
12-29-93 ....Kansas St 52, Wyoming 17
12-29-94 ....BYU 31, Oklahoma 6
12-27-95 ....Texas Tech 55, Air Force 41
12-27-96 ....Wisconsin 38, Utah 10
12-27-97 ....Arizona 20, New Mexico 14
12-26-98 ....Missouri 34, W Virginia 31
12-31-99 ....Colorado 62, Boston College 28
12-28-00 ....Iowa St 37, Pittsburgh 29
12-29-01 ....Syracuse 26, Kansas St 3
12-26-02 ....Pittsburgh 38, Oregon St 13
12-26-03 ....California 52, Virginia Tech 49
12-28-04 ....Oregon State 38, Notre Dame 21
12-27-05 ....Arizona State 45, Rutgers 40
12-29-06 ....Texas Tech 44, Minnesota 41
12-31-07 ....Oklahoma St 49, Indiana 33
12-31-08 ....Kansas 42, Minnesota 21
12-31-09 ....Iowa St 14, Minnesota 13
12-28-10 ....Iowa 27, Missouri 24
12-30-11 ....Oklahoma 31, Iowa 14

City: Tucson. Stadium: Arizona Stadium, capacity 55,883. Name change: Copper Bowl (1989–97), Insight.com Bowl (1998–2000).

Tangerine Bowl

12-28-90 ....Florida St 24, Penn St 17
12-28-91 ....Alabama 30, Colorado 25
1-1-93 ....Stanford 24, Penn St 3
1-1-94 ....Boston College 31, Virginia 13
1-2-95 ....South Carolina 24, W Virginia 21
12-30-95 ....North Carolina 20, Arkansas 10
12-27-96 ....Miami (Fla.) 31, Virginia 21
12-29-97 ....Georgia Tech 35, W Virginia 30
12-29-98 ....Miami (Fla.) 46, North Carolina St 23
12-30-99 ....Illinois 62, Virginia 21
12-28-00 ....North Carolina St 38, Minnesota 30
12-20-01 ....Pittsburgh 34, North Carolina St 19
12-23-02 ....Texas Tech 55, Clemson 15
12-22-03 ....North Carolina 56, Kansas 26

City: Miami. Stadium: Pro Player Stadium, capacity 75,192. Name change: Blockbuster Bowl (1990–93), Carquest Bowl (1994–97), Micron PC Bowl (1998–2001). Bowl was discontinued after 2003.

Alamo Bowl

12-31-93 ....California 37, Iowa 3
12-31-94 ....Washington St 10, Baylor 3
12-28-95 ....Texas A&M 22, Michigan 20
12-29-96 ....Iowa 27, Texas Tech 0
12-30-97 ....Purdue 33, Oklahoma St 20
12-29-98 ....Purdue 37, Kansas St 34
12-28-99 ....Penn St 24, Texas A&M 0
12-30-00 ....Nebraska 66, Northwestern 17
12-29-01 ....Iowa 16, Texas Tech 13
12-28-02 ....Wisconsin 31, Colorado 28 (OT)
12-29-03 ....Nebraska 17, Michigan St 3
12-29-04 ....Ohio State 33, Oklahoma State 7
12-28-05 ....Nebraska 32, Michigan 28
12-30-06 ....Texas 26, Iowa 24
12-29-07 ....Penn St 24, Texas A&M 17
12-29-08 ....Missouri 30, Northwestern 23
1-2-10 ....Texas Tech 41, Michigan St 31
12-29-10 ....Oklahoma St 36, Arizona 10
12-29-11 ....Baylor 67, Washington 56

City: San Antonio, TX. Stadium: Alamodome, capaciity 67,000.

1936

		Record	Coach
1.	Minnesota	7-1-0	Bernie Bierman
2.	LSU	9-0-1	Bernie Moore
3.	Pittsburgh	7-1-1	Jock Sutherland
4.	Alabama	8-0-1	Frank Thomas
5.	Washington	7-1-1	Jimmy Phelan
6.	Santa Clara	7-1-0	Buck Shaw
7.	Northwestern	7-1-0	Pappy Waldorf
8.	Notre Dame	6-2-1	Elmer Layden
9.	Nebraska	7-2-0	Dana X. Bible
10.	Pennsylvania	7-1-0	Harvey Harman
11.	Duke	9-1-0	Wallace Wade
12.	Yale	7-1-0	Ducky Pond
13.	Dartmouth	7-1-1	Red Blaik
14.	Duquesne	7-2-0	John Smith
15.	Fordham	5-1-2	Jim Crowley
16.	TCU	8-2-2	Dutch Meyer
17.	Tennessee	6-2-2	Bob Neyland
18.	Arkansas	7-3-0	Fred Thomsen
19.	Navy	6-3-0	Tom Hamilton
20.	Marquette	7-1-0	Frank Murray

1937

		Record	Coach
1.	Pittsburgh	9-0-1	Jock Sutherland
2.	California	9-0-1	Stub Allison
3.	Fordham	7-0-1	Jim Crowley
4.	Alabama	9-0-0	Frank Thomas
5.	Minnesota	6-2-0	Bernie Bierman
6.	Villanova	8-0-1	Clipper Smith
7.	Dartmouth	7-0-2	Red Blaik
8.	LSU	9-1-0	Bernie Moore
9.	Notre Dame	6-2-1	Elmer Layden
	Santa Clara	8-0-0	Buck Shaw
11.	Nebraska	6-1-2	Biff Jones
12.	Yale	6-1-1	Ducky Pond
13.	Ohio St	6-2-0	Francis Schmidt
14.	Holy Cross	8-0-2	Eddie Anderson
	Arkansas	6-2-2	Fred Thomsen
16.	TCU	4-2-2	Dutch Meyer
17.	Colorado	8-0-0	Bunnie Oakes
18.	Rice	5-3-2	Jimmy Kitts
19.	North Carolina	7-1-1	Ray Wolf
20.	Duke	7-2-1	Wallace Wade

1938

		Record	Coach
1.	TCU	10-0-0	Dutch Meyer
2.	Tennessee	10-0-0	Bob Neyland
3.	Duke	9-0-0	Wallace Wade
4.	Oklahoma	10-0-0	Tom Stidham
5.	#Notre Dame	8-1-0	Elmer Layden
6.	Carnegie Tech	7-1-0	Bill Kern
7.	USC	8-2-0	Howard Jones
8.	Pittsburgh	8-2-0	Jock Sutherland
9.	Holy Cross	8-1-0	Eddie Anderson
10.	Minnesota	6-2-0	Bernie Bierman
11.	Texas Tech	10-0-0	Pete Cawthon
12.	Cornell	5-1-1	Carl Snavely
13.	Alabama	7-1-1	Frank Thomas
14.	California	10-1-0	Stub Allison
15.	Fordham	6-1-2	Jim Crowley
16.	Michigan	6-1-1	Fritz Crisler
17.	Northwestern	4-2-2	Pappy Waldorf

1938 (Cont.)

		Record	Coach
18.	Villanova	8-0-1	Clipper Smith
19.	Tulane	7-2-1	Red Dawson
20.	Dartmouth	7-2-0	Red Blaik

#Selected No. 1 by the Dickinson System.

1939

		Record	Coach
1.	Texas A&M	10-0-0	Homer Norton
2.	Tennessee	10-0-0	Bob Neyland
3.	#USC	7-0-2	Howard Jones
4.	Cornell	8-0-0	Carl Snavely
5.	Tulane	8-0-1	Red Dawson
6.	Missouri	8-1-0	Don Faurot
7.	UCLA	6-0-4	Babe Horrell
8.	Duke	8-1-0	Wallace Wade
9.	Iowa	6-1-1	Eddie Anderson
10.	Duquesne	8-0-1	Buff Donelli
11.	Boston College	9-1-0	Frank Leahy
12.	Clemson	8-1-0	Jess Neely
13.	Notre Dame	7-2-0	Elmer Layden
14.	Santa Clara	5-1-3	Buck Shaw
15.	Ohio St	6-2-0	Francis Schmidt
16.	Georgia Tech	7-2-0	Bill Alexander
17.	Fordham	6-2-0	Jim Crowley
18.	Nebraska	7-1-1	Biff Jones
19.	Oklahoma	6-2-1	Tom Stidham
20.	Michigan	6-2-0	Fritz Crisler

#Selected No. 1 by the Dickinson System.

1940

		Record	Coach
1.	Minnesota	8-0-0	Bernie Bierman
2.	Stanford	9-0-0	C. Shaughnessy
3.	Michigan	7-1-0	Fritz Crisler
4.	Tennessee	10-0-0	Bob Neyland
5.	Boston College	10-0-0	Frank Leahy
6.	Texas A&M	8-1-0	Homer Norton
7.	Nebraska	8-1-0	Biff Jones
8.	Northwestern	6-2-0	Pappy Waldorf
9.	Mississippi St	9-0-1	Allyn McKeen
10.	Washington	7-2-0	Jimmy Phelan
11.	Santa Clara	6-1-1	Buck Shaw
12.	Fordham	7-1-0	Jim Crowley
13.	Georgetown	8-1-0	Jack Hagerty
14.	Pennsylvania	6-1-1	George Munger
15.	Cornell	6-2-0	Carl Snavely
16.	SMU	8-1-1	Matty Bell
17.	Hard.-Simmons	9-0-0	Abe Woodson
18.	Duke	7-2-0	Wallace Wade
19.	Lafayette	9-0-0	Hooks Mylin
20.	—		

Only 19 teams selected.

1941

		Record	Coach
1.	Minnesota	8-0-0	Bernie Bierman
2.	Duke	9-0-0	Wallace Wade
3.	Notre Dame	8-0-1	Frank Leahy
4.	Texas	8-1-1	Dana X. Bible
5.	Michigan	6-1-1	Fritz Crisler
6.	Fordham	7-1-0	Jim Crowley
7.	Missouri	8-1-0	Don Faurot
8.	Duquesne	8-0-0	Buff Donelli

Note: Except where indicated with an asterisk, the polls from 1936 through 1964 were taken before the bowl games and those from 1965 through the present were taken after the bowl games.

1941 *(Cont.)*

		Record	Coach
9.	Texas A&M	9-1-0	Homer Norton
10.	Navy	7-1-1	Swede Larson
11.	Northwestern	5-3-0	Pappy Waldorf
12.	Oregon St	7-2-0	Lon Stiner
13.	Ohio St	6-1-1	Paul Brown
14.	Georgia	8-1-1	Wally Butts
15.	Pennsylvania	7-1-1	George Munger
16.	Mississippi St	8-1-1	Allyn McKeen
17.	Mississippi	6-2-1	Harry Mehre
18.	Tennessee	8-2-0	John Barnhill
19.	Washington St	6-4-0	Babe Hollingbery
20.	Alabama	8-2-0	Frank Thomas

1942

		Record	Coach
1.	Ohio St	9-1-0	Paul Brown
2.	Georgia	10-1-0	Wally Butts
3.	Wisconsin	8-1-1	H. Stuhldreher
4.	Tulsa	10-0-0	Henry Frnka
5.	Georgia Tech	9-1-0	Bill Alexander
6.	Notre Dame	7-2-2	Frank Leahy
7.	Tennessee	8-1-1	John Barnhill
8.	Boston College	8-1-0	Denny Myers
9.	Michigan	7-3-0	Fritz Crisler
10.	Alabama	7-3-0	Frank Thomas
11.	Texas	8-2-0	Dana X. Bible
12.	Stanford	6-4-0	Marchie Schwartz
13.	UCLA	7-3-0	Babe Horrell
14.	William & Mary	9-1-1	Carl Voyles
15.	Santa Clara	7-2-0	Buck Shaw
16.	Auburn	6-4-1	Jack Meagher
17.	Washington St	6-2-2	Babe Hollingbery
18.	Mississippi St	8-2-0	Allyn McKeen
19.	Minnesota	5-4-0	George Hauser
	Holy Cross	5-4-1	Ank Scanlon
	Penn St	6-1-1	Bob Higgins

1943

		Record	Coach
1.	Notre Dame	9-1-0	Frank Leahy
2.	Iowa Pre-Flight	9-1-0	Don Faurot
3.	Michigan	8-1-0	Fritz Crisler
4.	Navy	8-1-0	Billick Whelchel
5.	Purdue	9-0-0	Elmer Burnham
6.	Great Lakes	10-2-0	Tony Hinkle
7.	Duke	8-1-0	Eddie Cameron
8.	Del Monte P-F	7-1-0	Bill Kern
9.	Northwestern	6-2-0	Pappy Waldorf
10.	March Field	9-1-0	Paul Schissler
11.	Army	7-2-1	Red Blaik
12.	Washington	4-0-0	Ralph Welch
13.	Georgia Tech	7-3-0	Bill Alexander
14.	Texas	7-1-0	Dana X. Bible
15.	Tulsa	6-0-1	Henry Frnka
16.	Dartmouth	6-1-0	Earl Brown
17.	Bainbridge NTS	7-0-0	Joe Maniaci
18.	Colorado College	7-0-0	Hal White
19.	Pacific	7-2-0	Amos A. Stagg
20.	Pennsylvania	6-2-1	George Munger

1944

		Record	Coach
1.	Army	9-0-0	Red Blaik
2.	Ohio St	9-0-0	Carroll Widdoes
3.	Randolph Field	11-0-0	Frank Tritico
4.	Navy	6-3-0	Oscar Hagberg
5.	Bainbridge NTS	9-0-0	Joe Maniaci
6.	Iowa Pre-Flight	10-1-0	Jack Meagher

1944 *(Cont.)*

		Record	Coach
7.	USC	7-0-2	Jeff Cravath
8.	Michigan	8-2-0	Fritz Crisler
9.	Notre Dame	8-2-0	Ed McKeever
10.	March Field	7-1-2	Paul Schissler
11.	Duke	5-4-0	Eddie Cameron
12.	Tennessee	8-0-1	John Barnhill
13.	Georgia Tech	8-2-0	Bill Alexander
	Norman P-F	6-0-0	John Gregg
15.	Illinois	5-4-1	Ray Eliot
16.	El Toro Marines	8-1-0	Dick Hanley
17.	Great Lakes	9-2-1	Paul Brown
18.	Fort Pierce	9-0-0	Hamp Pool
19.	St. Mary's P-F	4-4-0	Jules Sikes
20.	2nd Air Force	7-2-1	Bill Reese

1945

		Record	Coach
1.	Army	9-0-0	Red Blaik
2.	Alabama	9-0-0	Frank Thomas
3.	Navy	7-1-1	Oscar Hagberg
4.	Indiana	9-0-1	Bo McMillan
5.	Oklahoma A&M	8-0-0	Jim Lookabaugh
6.	Michigan	7-3-0	Fritz Crisler
7.	St. Mary's (CA)	7-1-0	Jimmy Phelan
8.	Pennsylvania	6-2-0	George Munger
9.	Notre Dame	7-2-1	Hugh Devore
10.	Texas	9-1-0	Dana X. Bible
11.	USC	7-3-0	Jeff Cravath
12.	Ohio St	7-2-0	Carroll Widdoes
13.	Duke	6-2-0	Eddie Cameron
14.	Tennessee	8-1-0	John Barnhill
15.	LSU	7-2-0	Bernie Moore
16.	Holy Cross	8-1-0	John DeGrosa
17.	Tulsa	8-2-0	Henry Frnka
18.	Georgia	8-2-0	Wally Butts
19.	Wake Forest	4-3-1	Peahead Walker
20.	Columbia	8-1-0	Lou Little

1946

		Record	Coach
1.	Notre Dame	8-0-1	Frank Leahy
2.	Army	9-0-1	Red Blaik
3.	Georgia	10-0-0	Wally Butts
4.	UCLA	10-0-0	B. LaBrucherie
5.	Illinois	7-2-0	Ray Eliot
6.	Michigan	6-2-1	Fritz Crisler
7.	Tennessee	9-1-0	Bob Neyland
8.	LSU	9-1-0	Bernie Moore
9.	North Carolina	8-1-1	Carl Snavely
10.	Rice	8-2-0	Jess Neely
11.	Georgia Tech	8-2-0	Bobby Dodd
12.	Yale	7-1-1	Howard Odell
13.	Pennsylvania	6-2-0	George Munger
14.	Oklahoma	7-3-0	Jim Tatum
15.	Texas	8-2-0	Dana X. Bible
16.	Arkansas	6-3-1	John Barnhill
17.	Tulsa	9-1-0	J.O. Brothers
18.	North Carolina St	8-2-0	Beattie Feathers
19.	Delaware	9-0-0	Bill Murray
20.	Indiana	6-3-0	Bo McMillan

1947

		Record	Coach
1.	Notre Dame	9-0-0	Frank Leahy
2.	#Michigan	9-0-0	Fritz Crisler
3.	SMU	9-0-1	Matty Bell
4.	Penn St	9-0-0	Bob Higgins
5.	Texas	9-1-0	Blair Cherry

1947 *(Cont.)*

		Record	Coach
6.	Alabama	8-2-0	Red Drew
7.	Pennsylvania	7-0-1	George Munger
8.	USC	7-1-1	Jeff Cravath
9.	North Carolina	8-2-0	Carl Snavely
10.	Georgia Tech	9-1-0	Bobby Dodd
11.	Army	5-2-2	Red Blaik
12.	Kansas	8-0-2	George Sauer
13.	Mississippi	8-2-0	Johnny Vaught
14.	William & Mary	9-1-0	Rube McCray
15.	California	9-1-0	Pappy Waldorf
16.	Oklahoma	7-2-1	Bud Wilkinson
17.	North Carolina St	5-3-1	Beattie Feathers
18.	Rice	6-3-1	Jess Neely
19.	Duke	4-3-2	Wallace Wade
20.	Columbia	7-2-0	Lou Little

#The AP, which had voted Notre Dame No. 1 before the bowl games, took a second vote, giving the title to Michigan after its 49–0 win over USC in the Rose Bowl.

1948

		Record	Coach
1.	Michigan	9-0-0	Bennie Oosterbaan
2.	Notre Dame	9-0-1	Frank Leahy
3.	North Carolina	9-0-1	Carl Snavely
4.	California	10-0-0	Pappy Waldorf
5.	Oklahoma	9-1-0	Bud Wilkinson
6.	Army	8-0-1	Red Blaik
7.	Northwestern	7-2-0	Bob Voigts
8.	Georgia	9-1-0	Wally Butts
9.	Oregon	9-1-0	Jim Aiken
10.	SMU	8-1-1	Matty Bell
11.	Clemson	10-0-0	Frank Howard
12.	Vanderbilt	8-2-1	Red Sanders
13.	Tulane	9-1-0	Henry Frnka
14.	Michigan St	6-2-2	Biggie Munn
15.	Mississippi	8-1-0	Johnny Vaught
16.	Minnesota	7-2-0	Bernie Bierman
17.	William & Mary	6-2-2	Rube McCray
18.	Penn St	7-1-1	Bob Higgins
19.	Cornell	8-1-0	Lefty James
20.	Wake Forest	6-3-0	Peahead Walker

1949

		Record	Coach
1.	Notre Dame	10-0-0	Frank Leahy
2.	Oklahoma	10-0-0	Bud Wilkinson
3.	California	10-0-0	Pappy Waldorf
4.	Army	9-0-0	Red Blaik
5.	Rice	9-1-0	Jess Neely
6.	Ohio St	6-1-2	Wes Fesler
7.	Michigan	6-2-1	Bennie Oosterbaan
8.	Minnesota	7-2-0	Bernie Bierman
9.	LSU	8-2-0	Gaynell Tinsley
10.	Pacific	11-0-0	Larry Siemering
11.	Kentucky	9-2-0	Bear Bryant
12.	Cornell	8-1-0	Lefty James
13.	Villanova	8-1-0	Jim Leonard
14.	Maryland	8-1-0	Jim Tatum
15.	Santa Clara	7-2-1	Len Casanova
16.	North Carolina	7-3-0	Carl Snavely
17.	Tennessee	7-2-1	Bob Neyland
18.	Princeton	6-3-0	Charlie Caldwell
19.	Michigan St	6-3-0	Biggie Munn
20.	Missouri	7-3-0	Don Faurot
	Baylor	8-2-0	Bob Woodruff

1950

		Record	Coach
1.	Oklahoma	10-0-0	Bud Wilkinson
2.	Army	8-1-0	Red Blaik
3.	Texas	9-1-0	Blair Cherry
4.	Tennessee	10-1-0	Bob Neyland
5.	California	9-0-1	Pappy Waldorf
6.	Princeton	9-0-0	Charlie Caldwell
7.	Kentucky	10-1-0	Bear Bryant
8.	Michigan St	8-1-0	Biggie Munn
9.	Michigan	5-3-1	Bennie Oosterhaan
10.	Clemson	8-0-1	Frank Howard
11.	Washington	8-2-0	Howard Odell
12.	Wyoming	9-0-0	Bowden Wyatt
13.	Illinois	7-2-0	Ray Eliot
14.	Ohio St	6-3-0	Wes Fesler
15.	Miami (Fla.)	9-0-1	Andy Gustafson
16.	Alabama	9-2-0	Red Drew
17.	Nebraska	6-2-1	Bill Glassford
18.	Washington & Lee	8-2-0	George Barclay
19.	Tulsa	9-1-1	J.O. Brothers
20.	Tulane	6-2-1	Henry Frnka

1951

		Record	Coach
1.	Tennessee	10-0-0	Bob Neyland
2.	Michigan St	9-0-0	Biggie Munn
3.	Maryland	9-0-0	Jim Tatum
4.	Illinois	8-0-1	Ray Eliot
5.	Georgia Tech	10-0-1	Bobby Dodd
6.	Princeton	9-0-0	Charlie Caldwell
7.	Stanford	9-1-0	Chuck Taylor
8.	Wisconsin	7-1-1	Ivy Williamson
9.	Baylor	8-1-1	George Sauer
10.	Oklahoma	8-2-0	Bud Wilkinson
11.	TCU	6-4-0	Dutch Meyer
12.	California	8-2-0	Pappy Waldorf
13.	Virginia	8-1-0	Art Guepe
14.	San Francisco	9-0-0	Joe Kuharich
15.	Kentucky	7-4-0	Bear Bryant
16.	Boston University	6-4-0	Buff Donelli
17.	UCLA	5-3-1	Red Sanders
18.	Washington St	7-3-0	Forest Evashevski
19.	Holy Cross	8-2-0	Eddie Anderson
20.	Clemson	7-2-0	Frank Howard

1952

		Record	Coach
1.	Michigan St	9-0-0	Biggie Munn
2.	Georgia Tech	11-0-0	Bobby Dodd
3.	Notre Dame	7-2-1	Frank Leahy
4.	Oklahoma	8-1-1	Bud Wilkinson
5.	USC	9-1-0	Jess Hill
6.	UCLA	8-1-0	Red Sanders
7.	Mississippi	8-0-2	Johnny Vaught
8.	Tennessee	8-1-1	Bob Neyland
9.	Alabama	9-2-0	Red Drew
10.	Texas	8-2-0	Ed Price
11.	Wisconsin	6-2-1	Ivy Williamson
12.	Tulsa	8-1-1	J.O. Brothers
13.	Maryland	7-2-0	Jim Tatum
14.	Syracuse	7-2-0	Ben Schwartzwalder
15.	Florida	7-3-0	Bob Woodruff
16.	Duke	8-2-0	Bill Murray
17.	Ohio St	6-3-0	Woody Hayes
18.	Purdue	4-3-2	Stu Holcomb
19.	Princeton	8-1-0	Charlie Caldwell
20.	Kentucky	5-4-2	Bear Bryant

1953

		Record	Coach
1.	Maryland	10-0-0	Jim Tatum
2.	Notre Dame	9-0-1	Frank Leahy
3.	Michigan St	8-1-0	Biggie Munn
4.	Oklahoma	8-1-1	Bud Wilkinson
5.	UCLA	8-1-0	Red Sanders
6.	Rice	8-2-0	Jess Neely
7.	Illinois	7-1-1	Ray Eliot
8.	Georgia Tech	8-2-1	Bobby Dodd
9.	Iowa	5-3-1	Forest Evashevski
10.	W Virginia	8-1-0	Art Lewis
11.	Texas	7-3-0	Ed Price
12.	Texas Tech	10-1-0	DeWitt Weaver
13.	Alabama	6-2-3	Red Drew
14.	Army	7-1-1	Red Blaik
15.	Wisconsin	6-2-1	Ivy Williamson
16.	Kentucky	7-2-1	Bear Bryant
17.	Auburn	7-2-1	Shug Jordan
18.	Duke	7-2-1	Bill Murray
19.	Stanford	6-3-1	Chuck Taylor
20.	Michigan	6-3-0	Bennie Oosterbaan

1954

		Record	Coach
1.	Ohio St	9-0-0	Woody Hayes
2.	#UCLA	9-0-0	Red Sanders
3.	Oklahoma	10-0-0	Bud Wilkinson
4.	Notre Dame	9-1-0	Terry Brennan
5.	Navy	7-2-0	Eddie Erdelatz
6.	Mississippi	9-1-0	Johnny Vaught
7.	Army	7-2-0	Red Blaik
8.	Maryland	7-2-1	Jim Tatum
9.	Wisconsin	7-2-0	Ivy Williamson
10.	Arkansas	8-2-0	Bowden Wyatth
11.	Miami (Fla.)	8-1-0	Andy Gustafson
12.	W Virginia	8-1-0	Art Lewis
13.	Auburn	7-3-0	Shug Jordan
14.	Duke	7-2-1	Bill Murray
15.	Michigan	6-3-0	Bennie Oosterbaan
16.	Virginia Tech	8-0-1	Frank Moseley
17.	USC	8-3-0	Jess Hill
18.	Baylor	7-3-0	George Sauer
19.	Rice	7-3-0	Jess Neely
20.	Penn St	7-2-0	Rip Engle

#Selected No. 1 by UPI.

1955

		Record	Coach
1.	Oklahoma	10-0-0	Bud Wilkinson
2.	Michigan St	8-1-0	Duffy Daugherty
3.	Maryland	10-0-0	Jim Tatum
4.	UCLA	9-1-0	Red Sanders
5.	Ohio St	7-2-0	Woody Hayes
6.	TCU	9-1-0	Abe Martin
7.	Georgia Tech	8-1-1	Bobby Dodd
8.	Auburn	8-1-1	Shug Jordan
9.	Notre Dame	8-2-0	Terry Brennan
10.	Mississippi	9-1-0	Johnny Vaught
11.	Pittsburgh	7-3-0	John Michelosen
12.	Michigan	7-2-0	Bennie Oosterbaan
13.	USC	6-4-0	Jess Hill
14.	Miami (Fla.)	6-3-0	Andy Gustafson
15.	Miami (Ohio)	9-0-0	Ara Parseghian
16.	Stanford	6-3-1	Chuck Taylor
17.	Texas A&M	7-2-1	Bear Bryant
18.	Navy	6-2-1	Eddie Erdelatz
19.	W Virginia	8-2-0	Art Lewis
20.	Army	6-3-0	Red Blaik

1956

		Record	Coach
1.	Oklahoma	10-0-0	Bud Wilkinson
2.	Tennessee	10-0-0	Bowden Wyatt
3.	Iowa	8-1-0	Forest Evashevski
4.	Georgia Tech.	9-1-0	Bobby Dodd
5.	Texas A&M	9-0-1	Bear Bryant
6.	Miami (Fla.)	8-1-1	Andy Gustafson
7.	Michigan	7-2-0	Bennie Oosterbaan
8.	Syracuse	7-1-0	Ben Schwartzwalder
9.	Michigan St	7-2-0	Duffy Daugherty
10.	Oregon St	7-2-1	Tommy Prothro
11.	Baylor	8-2-0	Sam Boyd
12.	Minnesota	6-1-2	Murray Warmath
13.	Pittsburgh	7-2-1	John Michelosen
14.	TCU	7-3-0	Abe Martin
15.	Ohio St	6-3-0	Woody Hayes
16.	Navy	6-1-2	Eddie Erdelatz
17.	Geo Washington	7-1-1	Gene Sherman
18.	USC	8-2-0	Jess Hill
19.	Clemson	7-1-2	Frank Howard
20.	Colorado	7-2-1	Dallas Ward
	Penn St	6-2-1	Rip Engle

1957

		Record	Coach
1.	Auburn	10-0-0	Shug Jordan
2.	#Ohio St	8-1-0	Woody Hayes
3.	Michigan St	8-1-0	Duffy Daugherty
4.	Oklahoma	9-1-0	Bud Wilkinson
5.	Navy	8-1-1	Eddie Erdelatz
6.	Iowa	7-1-1	Forest Evashevski
7.	Mississippi	8-1-1	Johnny Vaught
8.	Rice	7-3-0	Jess Neely
9.	Texas A&M	8-2-0	Bear Bryant
10.	Notre Dame	7-3-0	Terry Brennan
11.	Texas	6-3-1	Darrell Royal
12.	Arizona St	10-0-0	Dan Devine
13.	Tennessee	7-3-0	Bowden Wyatt
14.	Mississippi St	6-2-1	Wade Walker
15.	North Carolina St	7-1-2	Earle Edwards
16.	Duke	6-2-2	Bill Murray
17.	Florida	6-2-1	Bob Woodruff
18.	Army	7-2-0	Red Blaik
19.	Wisconsin	6-3-0	Milt Brunt
20.	VMI	9-0-1	John McKenna

#Selected No. 1 by UPI.

1958

		Record	Coach
1.	LSU	10-0-0	Paul Dietzel
2.	Iowa	7-1-1	Forest Evashevski
3.	Army	8-0-1	Red Blaik
4.	Auburn	9-0-1	Shug Jordan
5.	Oklahoma	9-1-0	Bud Wilkinson
6.	Air Force	9-0-1	Ben Martin
7.	Wisconsin	7-1-1	Milt Bruhn
8.	Ohio St	6-1-2	Woody Hayes
9.	Syracuse	8-1-0	Ben Schwartzwalder
10.	TCU	8-2-0	Abe Martin
11.	Mississippi	8-2-0	Johnny Vaught
12.	Clemson	8-2-0	Frank Howard
13.	Purdue	6-1-2	Jack Mollenkopf
14.	Florida	6-3-1	Bob Woodruff
15.	South Carolina	7-3-0	Warren Giese

1958 *(Cont.)*

	Record	Coach
16. California	7-3-0	Pete Elliott
17. Notre Dame	6-4-0	Terry Brennan
18. SMU	6-4-0	Bill Meek
19. Oklahoma St	7-3-0	Cliff Speegle
20. Rutgers	8-1-0	John Stiegman

1959

	Record	Coach
1. Syracuse	10-0-0	Ben Schwartzwalder
2. Mississippi	9-1-0	Johnny Vaught
3. LSU	9-1-0	Paul Dietzel
4. Texas	9-1-0	Darrell Royal
5. Georgia	9-1-0	Wally Butts
6. Wisconsin	7-2-0	Milt Bruhn
7. TCU	8-2-0	Abe Martin
8. Washington	9-1-0	Jim Owens
9. Arkansas	8-2-0	Frank Broyles
10. Alabama	7-1-2	Bear Bryant
11. Clemson	8-2-0	Frank Howard
12. Penn St	8-2-0	Rip Engle
13. Illinois	5-3-1	Ray Eliot
14. USC	8-2-0	Don Clark
15. Oklahoma	7-3-0	Bud Wilkinson
16. Wyoming	9-1-0	Bob Devaney
17. Notre Dame	5-5-0	Joe Kuharich
18. Missouri	6-4-0	Dan Devine
19. Florida	5-4-1	Bob Woodruff
20. Pittsburgh	6-4-0	John Michelosen

1960

	Record	Coach
1. Minnesota	8-1-0	Murray Warmath
2. Mississippi	9-0-1	Johnny Vaught
3. Iowa	8-1-0	Forest Evashevski
4. Navy	9-1-0	Wayne Hardin
5. Missouri	9-1-0	Dan Devine
6. Washington	9-1-0	Jim Owens
7. Arkansas	8-2-0	Frank Broyles
8. Ohio St	7-2-0	Woody Hayes
9. Alabama	8-1-1	Bear Bryant
10. Duke	7-3-0	Bill Murray
11. Kansas	7-2-1	Jack Mitchell
12. Baylor	8-2-0	John Bridgers
13. Auburn	8-2-0	Shug Jordan
14. Yale	9-0-0	Jordan Oliver
15. Michigan St	6-2-1	Duffy Daugherty
16. Penn St	6-3-0	Rip Engle
17. New Mexico St	10-0-0	Warren Woodson
18. Florida	8-2-0	Ray Graves
19. Syracuse	7-2-0	Ben Schwartzwalder
Purdue	4-4-1	Jack Mollenkopf

1961

	Record	Coach
1. Alabama	10-0-0	Bear Bryant
2. Ohio St	8-0-1	Woody Hayes
3. Texas	9-1-0	Darrell Royal
4. LSU	9-1-0	Paul Dietzel
5. Mississippi	9-1-0	Johnny Vaught
6. Minnesota	7-2-0	Murray Warmath
7. Colorado	9-1-0	Sonny Grandelius
8. Michigan St	7-2-0	Duffy Daugherty
9. Arkansas	8-2-0	Frank Broyles
10. Utah St	9-0-1	John Ralston
11. Missouri	7-2-1	Dan Devine
12. Purdue	6-3-0	Jack Mollenkopf

1961 *(Cont.)*

	Record	Coach
13. Georgia Tech	7-3-0	Bobby Dodd
14. Syracuse	7-3-0	Ben Schwartzwalder
15. Rutgers	9-0-0	John Bateman
16. UCLA	7-3-0	Bill Barnes
17. Rice	7-3-0	Jess Neely
Penn St	7-3-0	Rip Engle
Arizona	8-1-1	Jim LaRue
20. Duke	7-3-0	Bill Murray

1962

	Record	Coach
1. USC	10-0-0	John McKay
2. Wisconsin	8-1-0	Milt Bruhn
3. Mississippi	9-0-0	Johnny Vaught
4. Texas	9-0-1	Darrell Royal
5. Alabama	9-1-0	Bear Bryant
6. Arkansas	9-1-0	Frank Broyles
7. LSU	8-1-1	Charlie McClendon
8. Oklahoma	8-2-0	Bud Wilkinson
9. Penn St	9-1-0	Rip Engle
10. Minnesota	6-2-1	Murray Warmath
11–20: UPI		
11. Georgia Tech	7-2-1	Bobby Dodd
12. Missouri	7-1-2	Dan Devine
13. Ohio St	6-3-0	Woody Hayes
14. Duke	8-2-0	Bill Murray
Washington	7-1-2	Jim Owens
16. Northwestern	7-2-0	Ara Parseghian
Oregon St	8-2-0	Tommy Prothro
18. Arizona St	7-2-1	Frank Kush
Miami (Fla.)	7-3-0	Andy Gustafson
Illinois	2-7-0	Pete Elliott

1963

	Record	Coach
1. Texas	10-0-0	Darrell Royal
2. Navy	9-1-0	Wayne Hardin
3. Illinois	7-1-1	Pete Elliott
4. Pittsburgh	9-1-0	John Michelosen
5. Auburn	9-1-0	Shug Jordan
6. Nebraska	9-1-0	Bob Devaney
7. Mississippi	7-0-2	Johnny Vaught
8. Alabama	8-2-0	Bear Bryant
9. Oklahoma	8-2-0	Bud Wilkinson
10. Michigan St	6-2-1	Duffy Daugherty
11–20: UPI		
11. Mississippi St	6-2-2	Paul Davis
12. Syracuse	8-2-0	Ben Schwartzwalder
13. Arizona St	8-1-0	Frank Kush
14. Memphis St	9-0-1	Billy J. Murphy
15. Washington	6-4-0	Jim Owens
16. Penn St	7-3-0	Rip Engle
USC	7-3-0	John McKay
Missouri	7-3-0	Dan Devine
19. North Carolina	8-2-0	Jim Hickey
20. Baylor	7-3-0	John Bridgers

1964

	Record	Coach
1. Alabama	10-0-0	Bear Bryant
2. Arkansas	10-0-0	Frank Broyles
3. Notre Dame	9-1-0	Ara Parseghian
4. Michigan	8-1-0	Bump Elliott
5. Texas	9-1-0	Darrell Royal
6. Nebraska	9-1-0	Bob Devaney
7. LSU	7-2-1	Charlie McClendon

1964 *(Cont.)*

		Record	Coach
8.	Oregon St	8-2-0	Tommy Prothro
9.	Ohio St	7-2-0	Woody Hayes
10.	USC	7-3-0	John McKay

11–20: UPI

		Record	Coach
11.	Florida St	8-1-0	Bill Peterson
12.	Syracuse	7-3-0	Ben Schwartzwalder
13.	Princeton	9-0-0	Dick Colman
14.	Penn St	6-4-0	Rip Engle
	Utah	8-2-0	Ray Nagel
16.	Illinois	6-3-0	Pete Elliott
	New Mexico	9-2-0	Bill Weeks
18.	Tulsa	8-2-0	Glenn Dobbs
19.	Missouri	6-3-1	Dan Devine
20.	Mississippi	5-4-1	Johnny Vaught
	Michigan St	4-5-1	Duffy Daugherty

1965

		Record	Coach
1.	Alabama	9-1-1	Bear Bryant
2.	#Michigan St	10-1-0	Duffy Daugherty
3.	Arkansas	10-1-0	Frank Broyles
4.	UCLA	8-2-1	Tommy Prothro
5.	Nebraska	10-1-0	Bob Devaney
6.	Missouri	8-2-1	Dan Devine
7.	Tennessee	8-1-2	Doug Dickey
8.	LSU	8-3-0	Charlie McClendon
9.	Notre Dame	7-2-1	Ara Parseghian
10.	USC	7-2-1	John McKay

11–20: UPI

		Record	Coach
11.	Texas Tech	8-2-0	J.T. King
12.	Ohio St	7-2-0	Woody Hayes
13.	Florida	7-3-0	Ray Graves
14.	Purdue	7-2-1	Jack Mollenkopf
15.	Georgia	6-4-0	Vince Dooley
16.	Tulsa	8-2-0	Glenn Dobbs
17.	Mississippi	6-4-0	Johnny Vaught
18.	Kentucky	6-4-0	Charlie Bradshaw
19	Syracuse	7-3-0	Ben Schwartzwalder
20.	Colorado	6-2-2	Eddie Crowder

#Selected No. 1 by UPI.

1966

		Record	Coach
1.	Notre Dame	9-0-1	Ara Parseghian
2.	Michigan St	9-0-1	Duffy Daugherty
3.	Alabama	10-0-0	Bear Bryant
4.	Georgia	9-1-0	Vince Dooley
5.	UCLA	9-1-0	Tommy Prothro
6.	Nebraska	9-1-0	Bob Devaney
7.	Purdue	8-2-0	Jack Mollenkopf
8.	Georgia Tech	9-1-0	Bobby Dodd
9.	Miami (Fla.)	7-2-1	Charlie Tate
10.	SMU	8-2-0	Hayden Fry

11–20: UPI

		Record	Coach
11.	Florida	8-2-0	Ray Graves
12.	Mississippi	8-2-0	Johnny Vaught
13.	Arkansas	8-2-0	Frank Broyles
14.	Tennessee	7-3-0	Doug Dickey
15.	Wyoming	9-1-0	Lloyd Eaton
16.	Syracuse	8-2-0	Ben Schwartzwalder
17.	Houston	8-2-0	Bill Yeoman
18.	USC	7-3-0	John McKay
19.	Oregon St	7-3-0	Dee Andros
20.	Virginia Tech	8-1-1	Jerry Claiborne

1967

		Record	Coach
1.	USC	9-1-0	John McKay
2.	Tennessee	9-1-0	Doug Dickey
3.	Oklahoma	9-1-0	Chuck Fairbanks
4.	Indiana	9-1-0	John Pont
5.	Notre Dame	8-2-0	Ara Parseghian
6.	Wyoming	10-0-0	Lloyd Eaton
7.	Oregon St	7-2-1	Dee Andros
8.	Alabama	8-1-1	Bear Bryant
9.	Purdue	8-2-0	Jack Mollenkopf
10.	Penn St	8-2-0	Joe Paterno

11–20: UPI†

		Record	Coach
11.	UCLA	7-2-1	Tommy Prothro
12.	Syracuse	8-2-0	Ben Schwartzwalder
13.	Colorado	8-2-0	Eddie Crowder
14.	Minnesota	8-2-0	Murray Warmath
15.	Florida St	7-2-1	Bill Peterson
16.	Miami (Fla.)	7-3-0	Charlie Tate
17.	North Carolina St	8-2-0	Earle Edwards
18.	Georgia	7-3-0	Vince Dooley
19.	Houston	9-2-0	Bill Yeoman
20.	Arizona St	8-2-0	Frank Kush

†UPI ranked Penn St 11th and did not rank Alabama,
which was on probation.

1968

		Record	Coach
1.	Ohio St	10-0-0	Woody Hayes
2.	Penn St	11-0-0	Joe Paterno
3.	Texas	9-1-1	Darrell Royal
4.	USC	9-1-1	John McKay
5.	Notre Dame	7-2-1	Ara Parseghian
6.	Arkansas	10-1-0	Frank Broyles
7.	Kansas	9-2-0	Pepper Rodgers
8.	Georgia	8-1-2	Vince Dooley
9.	Missouri	8-3-0	Dan Devine
10.	Purdue	8-2-0	Jack Mollenkopf
11.	Oklahoma	7-4-0	Chuck Fairbanks
12.	Michigan	8-2-0	Bump Elliott
13.	Tennessee	8-2-1	Doug Dickey
14.	SMU	8-3-0	Hayden Fry
15.	Oregon St	7-3-0	Dee Andros
16.	Auburn	7-4-0	Shug Jordan
17.	Alabama	8-3-0	Bear Bryant
18.	Houston	6-2-2	Bill Yeoman
19.	LSU	8-3-0	Charlie McClendon
20.	Ohio	10-1-0	Bill Hess

1969

		Record	Coach
1.	Texas	11-0-0	Darrell Royal
2.	Penn St	11-0-0	Joe Paterno
3.	USC	10-0-1	John McKay
4.	Ohio St	8-1-0	Woody Hayes
5.	Notre Dame	8-2-1	Ara Parseghian
6.	Missouri	9-2-0	Dan Devine
7.	Arkansas	9-2-0	Frank Broyles
8.	Mississippi	8-3-0	Johnny Vaught
9.	Michigan	8-3-0	Bo Schembechler
10.	LSU	9-1-0	Charlie McClendon
11.	Nebraska	9-2-0	Bob Devaney
12.	Houston	9-2-0	Bill Yeoman
13.	UCLA	8-1-1	Tommy Prothro
14.	Florida	9-1-1	Ray Graves
15.	Tennessee	9-2-0	Doug Dickey
16.	Colorado	8-3-0	Eddie Crowder

1969 *(Cont.)*

	Record	Coach
17. W Virginia	10-0-1	Jim Carlen
18. Purdue	8-2-0	Jack Mollenkopf
19. Stanford	7-2-1	John Ralston
20. Auburn	8-3-0	Shug Jordan

1970

	Record	Coach
1. Nebraska	11-0-1	Bob Devaney
2. Notre Dame	10-1-0	Ara Parseghian
3. #Texas	10-1-0	Darrell Royal
4. Tennessee	11-0-1	Bill Battle
5. Ohio St	9-1-0	Woody Hayes
6. Arizona St	11-0-0	Frank Kush
7. LSU	9-3-0	Charlie McClendon
8. Stanford	9-3-0	John Ralston
9. Michigan	9-1-0	Bo Schembechler
10. Auburn	9-2-0	Shug Jordan
11. Arkansas	9-2-0	Frank Broyles
12. Toledo	12-0-0	Frank Lauterbur
13. Georgia Tech	9-3-0	Bud Carson
14. Dartmouth	9-0-0	Bob Blackman
15. USC	6-4-1	John McKay
16. Air Force	9-3-0	Ben Martin
17. Tulane	8-4-0	Jim Pittman
18. Penn St	7-3-0	Joe Paterno
19. Houston	8-3-0	Bill Yeoman
20. Oklahoma	7-4-1	Chuck Fairbanks
Mississippi	7-4-0	Johnny Vaught

#Selected No. 1 by UPI.

1971

	Record	Coach
1. Nebraska	13-0-0	Bob Devaney
2. Oklahoma	11-1-0	Chuck Fairbanks
3. Colorado	10-2-0	Eddie Crowder
4. Alabama	11-1-0	Bear Bryant
5. Penn St	11-1-0	Joe Paterno
6. Michigan	11-1-0	Bo Schembechler
7. Georgia	11-1-0	Vince Dooley
8. Arizona St	11-1-0	Frank Kush
9. Tennessee	10-2-0	Bill Battle
10. Stanford	9-3-0	John Ralston
11. LSU	9-3-0	Charlie McClendon
12. Auburn	9-2-0	Shug Jordan
13. Notre Dame	8-2-0	Ara Parseghian
14. Toledo	12-0-0	John Murphy
15. Mississippi	10-2-0	Billy Kinard
16. Arkansas	8-3-1	Frank Broyles
17. Houston	9-3-0	Bill Yeoman
18. Texas	8-3-0	Darrell Royal
19. Washington	8-3-0	Jim Owens
20. USC	6-4-1	John McKay

1972

	Record	Coach
1. USC	12-0-0	John McKay
2. Oklahoma	11-1-0	Chuck Fairbanks
3. Texas	10-1-0	Darrell Royal
4. Nebraska	9-2-1	Bob Devaney
5. Auburn	10-1-0	Shug Jordan
6. Michigan	10-1-0	Bo Schembechler
7. Alabama	10-2-0	Bear Bryant
8. Tennessee	10-2-0	Bill Battle
9. Ohio St	9-2-0	Woody Hayes
10. Penn St	10-2-0	Joe Paterno

1972 *(Cont.)*

	Record	Coach
11. LSU	9-2-1	Charlie McClendon
12. North Carolina	11-1-0	Bill Dooley
13. Arizona St	10-2-0	Frank Kush
14. Notre Dame	8-3-0	Ara Parseghian
15. UCLA	8-3-0	Pepper Rodgers
16. Colorado	8-4-0	Eddie Crowder
17. North Carolina St	8-3-1	Lou Holtz
18. Louisville	9-1-0	Lee Corso
19. Washington St	7-4-0	Jim Sweeney
20. Georgia Tech	7-4-1	Bill Fulch

1973

	Record	Coach
1. Notre Dame	11-0-0	Ara Parseghian
2. Ohio St	10-0-1	Woody Hayes
3. Oklahoma	10-0-1	Barry Switzer
4. #Alabama	11-1-0	Bear Bryant
5. Penn St	12-0-0	Joe Paterno
6. Michigan	10-0-1	Bo Schembechler
7. Nebraska	9-2-1	Tom Osborne
8. USC	9-2-1	John McKay
9. Arizona St	11-1-0	Frank Kush
Houston	11-1-0	Bill Yeoman
11. Texas Tech	11-1-0	Jim Carlen
12. UCLA	9-2-0	Pepper Rodgers
13. LSU	9-3-0	Charlie McClendon
14. Texas	8-3-0	Darrell Royal
15. Miami (Ohio)	11-0-0	Bill Mallory
16. North Carolina St	9-3-0	Lou Holtz
17. Missouri	8-4-0	Al Onofrio
18. Kansas	7-4-1	Don Fambrough
19. Tennessee	8-4-0	Bill Battle
20. Maryland	8-4-0	Jerry Claiborne
Tulane	9-3-0	Bennie Ellender

#Selected No. 1 by UPI.

1974

	Record	Coach
1. Oklahoma	11-0-0	Barry Switzer
2. #USC	10-1-1	John McKay
3. Michigan	10-1-0	Bo Schembechler
4. Ohio St	10-2-0	Woody Hayes
5. Alabama	11-1-0	Bear Bryant
6. Notre Dame	10-2-0	Ara Parseghian
7. Penn St	10-2-0	Joe Paterno
8. Auburn	10-2-0	Shug Jordan
9. Nebraska	9-3-0	Tom Osborne
10. Miami (Ohio)	10-0-1	Dick Crum
11. North Carolina St	9-2-1	Lou Holtz
12. Michigan St	7-3-1	Denny Stolz
13. Maryland	8-4-0	Jerry Claiborne
14. Baylor	8-4-0	Grant Teaff
15. Florida	8-4-0	Doug Dickey
16. Texas A&M	8-3-0	Emory Ballard
17. Mississippi St	9-3-0	Bob Tyler
Texas	8-4-0	Darrell Royal
19. Houston	8-3-1	Bill Yeoman
20. Tennessee	7-3-2	Bill Battle

#Selected No. 1 by UPI

1975

	Record	Coach
1. Oklahoma	11-1-0	Barry Switzer
2. Arizona St	12-0-0	Frank Kush
3. Alabama	11-1-0	Bear Bryant
4. Ohio St	11-1-0	Woody Hayes

1975 *(Cont.)*

		Record	Coach
5.	UCLA	9-2-1	Dick Vermeil
6.	Texas	10-2-0	Darrell Royal
7.	Arkansas	10-2-0	Frank Broyles
8.	Michigan	8-2-2	Bo Schembechler
9.	Nebraska	10-2-0	Tom Osborne
10.	Penn St	9-3-0	Joe Paterno
11.	Texas A&M	10-2-0	Emory Bellard
12.	Miami (Ohio)	11-1-0	Dick Crum
13.	Maryland	9-2-1	Jerry Claiborne
14.	California	8-3-0	Mike White
15.	Pittsburgh	8-4-0	Johnny Majors
16.	Colorado	9-3-0	Bill Mallory
17.	USC	8-4-0	John McKay
18.	Arizona	9-2-0	Jim Young
19.	Georgia	9-3-0	Vince Dooley
20.	W Virginia	9-3-0	Bobby Bowden

1976

		Record	Coach
1.	Pittsburgh	12-0-0	Johnny Majors
2.	USC	11-1-0	John Robinson
3.	Michigan	10-2-0	Bo Schembechler
4.	Houston	10-2-0	Bill Yeoman
5.	Oklahoma	9-2-1	Barry Switzer
6.	Ohio St	9-2-1	Woody Hayes
7.	Texas A&M	10-2-0	Emory Bellard
8.	Maryland	11-1-0	Jerry Claiborne
9.	Nebraska	9-3-1	Tom Osborne
10.	Georgia	10-2-0	Vince Dooley
11.	Alabama	9-3-0	Bear Bryant
12.	Notre Dame	9-3-0	Dan Devine
13.	Texas Tech	10-2-0	Steve Sloan
14.	Oklahoma St	9-3-0	Jim Stanley
15.	UCLA	9-2-1	Terry Donahue
16.	Colorado	8-4-0	Bill Mallory
17.	Rutgers	11-0-0	Frank Burns
18.	Kentucky	9-3-0	Fran Curci
19.	Iowa St	8-3-0	Earle Bruce
20.	Mississippi St	9-2-0	Bob Tyler

1977

		Record	Coach
1.	Notre Dame	11-1-0	Dan Devine
2.	Alabama	11-1-0	Bear Bryant
3.	Arkansas	11-1-0	Lou Holtz
4.	Texas	11-1-0	Fred Akers
5.	Penn St	11-1-0	Joe Paterno
6.	Kentucky	10-1-0	Fran Curci
7.	Oklahoma	10-2-0	Barry Switzer
8.	Pittsburgh	9-2-1	Jackie Sherrill
9.	Michigan	10-2-0	Bo Schembechler
10.	Washington	10-2-0	Don James
11.	Ohio St	9-3-0	Woody Hayes
12.	Nebraska	9-3-0	Tom Osborne
13.	USC	8-4-0	John Robinson
14.	Florida St	10-2-0	Bobby Bowden
15.	Stanford	9-3-0	Bill Walsh
16.	San Diego St	10-1-0	Claude Gilbert
17.	North Carolina	8-3-1	Bill Dooley
18.	Arizona St	9-3-0	Frank Kush
19.	Clemson	8-3-1	Charley Pell
20.	BYU	9-2-0	LaVell Edwards

1978

		Record	Coach
1.	Alabama	11-1-0	Bear Bryant
2.	#USC	12-1-0	John Robinson
3.	Oklahoma	11-1-0	Barry Switzer

1978 *(Cont.)*

		Record	Coach
4.	Penn St	11-1-0	Joe Paterno
5.	Michigan	10-2-0	Bo Schembechler
6.	Clemson	11-1-0	Charley Pell
7.	Notre Dame	9-3-0	Dan Devine
8.	Nebraska	9-3-0	Tom Osborne
9.	Texas	9-3-0	Fred Akers
10.	Houston	9-3-0	Bill Yeoman
11.	Arkansas	9-2-1	Lou Holtz
12.	Michigan St	8-3-0	Darryl Rogers
13.	Purdue	9-2-1	Jim Young
14.	UCLA	8-3-1	Terry Donahue
15.	Missouri	8-4-0	Warren Powers
16.	Georgia	9-2-1	Vince Dooley
17.	Stanford	8-4-0	Bill Walsh
18.	North Carolina St	9-3-0	Bo Rein
19.	Texas A&M	8-4-0	Emory Bellard/ Tom Wilson
20.	Maryland	9-3-0	Jerry Claiborne

#Selected No. 1 by UPI.

1979

		Record	Coach
1.	Alabama	12-0-0	Bear Bryant
2.	USC	11-0-1	John Robinson
3.	Oklahoma	11-1-0	Barry Switzer
4.	Ohio St	11-1-0	Earle Bruce
5.	Houston	11-1-0	Bill Yeoman
6.	Florida St	11-1-0	Bobby Bowden
7.	Pittsburgh	11-1-0	Jackie Sherrill
8.	Arkansas	10-2-0	Lou Holtz
9.	Nebraska	10-2-0	Tom Osborne
10.	Purdue	10-2-0	Jim Young
11.	Washington	10-1-0	Don James
12.	Texas	9-3-0	Fred Akers
13.	BYU	11-1-0	LaVell Edwards
14.	Baylor	8-4-0	Grant Teaff
15.	North Carolina	8-3-1	Dick Crum
16.	Auburn	8-3-0	Doug Barfield
17.	Temple	10-2-0	Wayne Hardin
18.	Michigan	8-4-0	Bo Schembechler
19.	Indiana	8-4-0	Lee Corso
20.	Penn St	8-4-0	Joe Paterno

1980

		Record	Coach
1.	Georgia	12-0-0	Vince Dooley
2.	Pittsburgh	11-1-0	Jackie Sherrill
3.	Oklahoma	10-2-0	Barry Switzer
4.	Michigan	10-2-0	Bo Schembechler
5.	Florida St	10-2-0	Bobby Bowden
6.	Alabama	10-2-0	Bear Bryant
7.	Nebraska	10-2-0	Tom Osborne
8.	Penn St	10-2-0	Joe Paterno
9.	Notre Dame	9-2-1	Dan Devine
10.	North Carolina	11-1-0	Dick Crum
11.	USC	8-2-1	John Robinson
12.	BYU	12-1-0	LaVell Edwards
13.	UCLA	9-2-0	Terry Donahue
14.	Baylor	10-2-0	Grant Teaff
15.	Ohio St	9-3-0	Earle Bruce
16.	Washington	9-3-0	Don James
17.	Purdue	9-3-0	Jim Young
18.	Miami (Fla.)	9-3-0	H. Schnellenberger
19.	Mississippi St	9-3-0	Emory Bellard
20.	SMU	8-4-0	Ron Meyer

1981

		Record	Coach
1.	Clemson	12-0-0	Danny Ford
2.	Texas	10-1-1	Fred Akers
3.	Penn St	10-2-0	Joe Paterno
4.	Pittsburgh	11-1-0	Jackie Sherrill
5.	SMU	10-1-0	Ron Meyer
6.	Georgia	10-2-0	Vince Dooley
7.	Alabama	9-2-1	Bear Bryant
8.	Miami (Fla.)	9-2-0	H. Schnellenberger
9.	North Carolina	10-2-0	Dick Crum
10.	Washington	10-2-0	Don James
11.	Nebraska	9-3-0	Tom Osborne
12.	Michigan	9-3-0	Bo Schembechler
13.	BYU	11-2-0	LaVell Edwards
14.	USC	9-3-0	John Robinson
15.	Ohio St	9-3-0	Earle Bruce
16.	Arizona St	9-2-0	Darryl Rogers
17.	W Virginia	9-3-0	Don Nehlen
18.	Iowa	8-4-0	Hayden Fry
19.	Missouri	8-4-0	Warren Powers
20.	Oklahoma	7-4-1	Barry Switzer

1982

		Record	Coach
1.	Penn St	11-1-0	Joe Paterno
2.	SMU	11-0-1	Bobby Collins
3.	Nebraska	12-1-0	Tom Osborne
4.	Georgia	11-1-0	Vince Dooley
5.	UCLA	10-1-1	Terry Donahue
6.	Arizona St	10-2-0	Darryl Rogers
7.	Washington	10-2-0	Don James
8.	Clemson	9-1-1	Danny Ford
9.	Arkansas	9-2-1	Lou Holtz
10.	Pittsburgh	9-3-0	Foge Fazio
11.	LSU	8-3-1	Jerry Stovall
12.	Ohio St	9-3-0	Earle Bruce
13.	Florida St	9-3-0	Bobby Bowden
14.	Auburn	9-3-0	Pat Dye
15.	USC	8-3-0	John Robinson
16.	Oklahoma	8-4-0	Barry Switzer
17.	Texas	9-3-0	Fred Akers
18.	North Carolina	8-4-0	Dick Crum
19.	W Virginia	9-3-0	Don Nehlen
20.	Maryland	8-4-0	Bobby Ross

1983

		Record	Coach
1.	Miami (Fla.)	11-1-0	H. Schnellenberger
2.	Nebraska	12-1-0	Tom Osborne
3.	Auburn	11-1-0	Pat Dye
4.	Georgia	10-1-1	Vince Dooley
5.	Texas	11-1-0	Fred Akers
6.	Florida	9-2-1	Charlie Pell
7.	BYU	11-1-0	LaVell Edwards
8.	Michigan	9-3-0	Bo Schembechler
9.	Ohio St	9-3-0	Earle Bruce
10.	Illinois	10-2-0	Mike White
11.	Clemson	9-1-1	Danny Ford
12.	SMU	10-2-0	Bobby Collins
13.	Air Force	10-2-0	Ken Hatfield
14.	Iowa	9-3-0	Hayden Fry
15.	Alabama	8-4-0	Ray Perkins
16.	W Virginia	9-3-0	Don Nehlen
17.	UCLA	7-4-1	Terry Donahue
18.	Pittsburgh	8-3-1	Foge Fazio
19.	Boston College	9-3-0	Jack Bicknell
20.	E Carolina	8-3-0	Ed Emory

1984

		Record	Coach
1.	BYU	13-0-0	LaVell Edwards
2.	Washington	11-1-0	Don James
3.	Florida	9-1-1	Chas Pell (0-1-1)
			Galen Hall (9-0)
4.	Nebraska	10-2-0	Tom Osborne
5.	Boston College	10-2-0	Jack Bicknell
6.	Oklahoma	9-2-1	Barry Switzer
7.	Oklahoma St	10-2-0	Pat Jones
8.	SMU	10-2-0	Bobby Collins
9.	UCLA	9-3-0	Terry Donahue
10.	USC	10-3-0	Ted Tollner
11.	South Carolina	10-2-0	Joe Morrison
12.	Maryland	9-3-0	Bobby Ross
13.	Ohio St	9-3-0	Earle Bruce
14.	Auburn	9-4-0	Pat Dye
15.	LSU	8-3-1	Bill Arnsparger
16.	Iowa	8-4-1	Hayden Fry
17.	Florida St	7-3-2	Bobby Bowden
18.	Miami (Fla.)	8-5-0	Jimmy Johnson
19.	Kentucky	9-3-0	Jerry Claiborne
20.	Virginia	8-2-2	George Welsh

1985

		Record	Coach
1.	Oklahoma	11-1-0	Barry Switzer
2.	Michigan	10-1-1	Bo Schembechler
3.	Penn St	11-1-0	Joe Paterno
4.	Tennessee	9-1-2	Johnny Majors
5.	Florida	9-1-1	Galen Hall
6.	Texas A&M	10-2-0	Jackie Sherrill
7.	UCLA	9-2-1	Terry Donahue
8.	Air Force	12-1-0	Fisher DeBerry
9.	Miami (Fla.)	10-2-0	Jimmy Johnson
10.	Iowa	10-2-0	Hayden Fry
11.	Nebraska	9-3-0	Tom Osborne
12.	Arkansas	10-2-0	Ken Hatfield
13.	Alabama	9-2-1	Ray Perkins
14.	Ohio St	9-3-0	Earle Bruce
15.	Florida St	9-3-0	Bobby Bowden
16.	BYU	11-3-0	LaVell Edwards
17.	Baylor	9-3-0	Grant Teaff
18.	Maryland	9-3-0	Bobby Ross
19.	Georgia Tech	9-2-1	Bill Curry
20.	LSU	9-2-1	Bill Arnsparger

1986

		Record	Coach
1.	Penn St	12-0-0	Joe Paterno
2.	Miami (Fla.)	11-1-0	Jimmy Johnson
3.	Oklahoma	11-1-0	Barry Switzer
4.	Arizona St	10-1-1	John Cooper
5.	Nebraska	10-2-0	Tom Osborne
6.	Auburn	10-2-0	Pat Dye
7.	Ohio St	10-3-0	Earle Bruce
8.	Michigan	11-2-0	Bo Schembechler
9.	Alabama	10-3-0	Ray Perkins
10.	LSU	9-3-0	Bill Arnsparger
11.	Arizona	9-3-0	Larry Smith
12.	Baylor	9-3-0	Grant Teaff
13.	Texas A&M	9-3-0	Jackie Sherrill
14.	UCLA	8-3-1	Terry Donahue
15.	Arkansas	9-3-0	Ken Hatfield
16.	Iowa	9-3-0	Hayden Fry
17.	Clemson	8-2-2	Danny Ford
18.	Washington	8-3-1	Don James
19.	Boston College	9-3-0	Jack Bicknell
20.	Virginia Tech	9-2-1	Bill Dooley

1987

		Record	Coach
1.	Miami (Fla.)	12-0-0	Jimmy Johnson
2.	Florida St.	11-1-0	Bobby Bowden
3.	Oklahoma	11-1-0	Barry Switzer
4.	Syracuse	11-0-1	Dick MacPherson
5.	LSU	10-1-1	Mike Archer
6.	Nebraska	10-2-0	Tom Osborne
7.	Auburn	9-1-2	Pat Dye
8.	Michigan St.	9-2-1	George Perles
9.	UCLA	10-2-0	Terry Donahue
10.	Texas A&M	10-2-0	Jackie Sherrill
11.	Oklahoma St	10-2-0	Pat Jones
12.	Clemson	10-2-0	Danny Ford
13.	Georgia	9-3-0	Vince Dooley
14.	Tennessee	10-2-1	Johnny Majors
15.	South Carolina	8-4-0	Joe Morrison
16.	Iowa	10-3-0	Hayden Fry
17.	Notre Dame	8-4-0	Lou Holtz
18.	USC	8-4-0	Larry Smith
19.	Michigan	8-4-0	Bo Schembechler
20.	Arizona St	7-4-1	John Cooper

1988

		Record	Coach
1.	Notre Dame	12-0-0	Lou Holtz
2.	Miami (Fla.)	11-1-0	Jimmy Johnson
3.	Florida St.	11-1-0	Bobby Bowden
4.	Michigan	9-2-1	Bo Schembechler
5.	West Virginia	11-1-0	Don Nehlen
6.	UCLA	10-2-0	Terry Donahue
7.	USC	10-2-0	Larry Smith
8.	Auburn	10-2-0	Pat Dye
9.	Clemson	10-2-0	Danny Ford
10.	Nebraska	11-2-0	Tom Osborne
11.	Oklahoma St	10-2-0	Pat Jones
12.	Arkansas	10-2-0	Ken Hatfield
13.	Syracuse	10-2-0	Dick MacPherson
14.	Oklahoma	9-3-0	Barry Switzer
15.	Georgia	9-3-0	Vince Dooley
16.	Washington St	9-3-0	Dennis Erickson
17.	Alabama	9-3-0	Bill Curry
18.	Houston	9-3-0	Jack Pardee
19.	LSU	8-4-0	Mike Archer
20.	Indiana	8-3-1	Bill Mallor

†1989

		Record	Coach
1.	Miami (Fla.)	11-1-0	Dennis Erickson
2.	Notre Dame	12-1-0	Lou Holtz
3.	Florida St.	10-2-0	Bobby Bowden
4.	Colorado	11-1-0	Bill McCartney
5.	Tennessee	11-1-0	Johnny Majors
6.	Auburn	10-2-0	Pat Dye
7.	Michigan	10-2-0	Bo Schembechler
8.	USC	9-2-1	Larry Smith
9.	Alabama	10-2-0	Bill Curry
10.	Illinois	10-2-0	John Mackovic
11.	Nebraska	10-2-0	Tom Osborne
12.	Clemson	10-2-0	Danny Ford
13.	Arkansas	10-2-0	Ken Hatfield
14.	Houston	9-2-0	Jack Pardee
15.	Penn St	8-3-1	Joe Paterno
16.	Michigan St	8-4-0	George Perles
17.	Pittsburgh	8-3-1	Mike Gottfried
18.	Virginia	10-3-0	George Welsh
19.	Texas Tech	9-3-0	Spike Dykes

†In 1989 the AP expanded its final poll to 25 teams.

1989 (Cont.)

		Record	Coach
20.	Texas A&M	8-4-0	R.C. Slocum
21.	W Virginia	8-3-1	Don Nehlen
22.	BYU	10-3-0	LaVell Edwards
23.	Washington	8-4-0	Don James
24.	Ohio St	8-4-0	John Cooper
25.	Arizona	8-4-0	Dick Tomey

1990

		Record	Coach
1.	Colorado	11-1-1	Bill McCartney
2.	#Ga. Tech (UPI)	11-0-1	Bobby Ross
3.	Miami (Fla.)	10-2-0	Dennis Erickson
4.	Florida St.	10-2-0	Bobby Bowden
5.	Washington	10-2-0	Don James
6.	Notre Dame	9-3-0	Lou Holtz
7.	Michigan	9-3-0	Gary Moeller
8.	Tennessee	9-2-2	Johnny Majors
9.	Clemson	10-2-0	Ken Hatfield
10.	Houston	10-1-0	John Jenkins
11.	Penn St	9-3-0	Joe Paterno
12.	Texas	10-2-0	David McWilliams
13.	Florida	9-2-0	Steve Spurrier
14.	Louisville	10-1-1	H. Schnellenberger
15.	Texas A&M	9-3-1	R.C. Slocum
16.	Michigan St	8-3-1	George Perles
17.	Oklahoma	8-3-0	Gary Gibbs
18.	Iowa	8-4-0	Hayden Fry
19.	Auburn	8-3-1	Pat Dye
20.	USC	8-4-1	Larry Smith
21.	Mississippi	9-3-0	Billy Brewer
22.	BYU	10-3-0	LaVell Edwards
23.	Virginia	8-4-0	George Wells
24.	Nebraska	9-3-0	Tom Osborne
25.	Illinois	8-4-0	John Mackovic

1991

		Record	Coach
1.	Miami (Fla.)	12-0-0	Dennis Erickson
2.	#Washington	12-0-0	Don James
3.	Penn St	11-2-0	Joe Paterno
4.	Florida St.	11-2-0	Bobby Bowden
5.	Alabama	11-1-0	Gene Stallings
6.	Michigan	10-2-0	Gary Moeller
7.	Florida	10-2-0	Steve Spurrier
8.	California	10-2-0	Bruce Snyder
9.	E Carolina	11-1-0	Bill Lewis
10.	Iowa	10-1-1	Hayden Fry
11.	Syracuse	10-2-0	Paul Pasqualoni
12.	Texas A&M	10-2-0	R.C. Slocum
13.	Notre Dame	10-3-0	Lou Holtz
14.	Tennessee	9-3-0	Johnny Majors
15.	Nebraska	9-2-1	Tom Osborne
16.	Oklahoma	9-3-0	Gary Gibbs
17.	Georgia	9-3-0	Ray Goff
18.	Clemson	9-2-1	Ken Hatfield
19.	UCLA	9-3-0	Terry Donahue
20.	Colorado	8-3-1	Bill McCartney
21.	Tulsa	10-2-0	David Rader
22.	Stanford	8-4-0	Dennis Green
23.	BYU	8-3-2	LaVell Edwards
24.	North Carolina St	9-3-0	Dick Sheridan
25.	Air Force	10-3-0	Fisher DeBerry

#Selected No. 1 by USA Today/CNN.

1992

		Record	Coach
1.	Alabama	13-0-0	Gene Stallings
2.	Florida St	11-1-0	Bobby Bowden
3.	Miami	11-1-0	Dennis Erickson
4.	Notre Dame	10-1-1	Lou Holtz
5.	Michigan	9-0-3	Gary Moeller
6.	Syracuse	10-2-0	Paul Pasqualoni
7.	Texas A&M	12-1-0	R.C. Slocum
8.	Georgia	10-2-0	Ray Goff
9.	Stanford	10-3-0	Bill Walsh
10.	Florida	9-4-0	Steve Spurrier
11.	Washington	9-3-0	Don James
12.	Tennessee	9-3-0	Johnny Majors
13.	Colorado	9-2-1	Bill McCartney
14.	Nebraska	9-3-0	Tom Osborne
15.	Washington St	9-3-0	Mike Price
16.	Mississippi	9-3-0	Billy Brewer
17.	North Carolina St	9-3-1	Dick Sheridan
18.	Ohio St	8-3-1	John Cooper
19.	North Carolina	9-3-0	Mack Brown
20.	Hawaii	11-2-0	Bob Wagner
21.	Boston College	8-3-1	Tom Coughlin
22.	Kansas	8-4-0	Glen Mason
23.	Mississippi St	7-5-0	Jackie Sherrill
24.	Fresno St	9-4-0	Jim Sweeney
25.	Wake Forest	8-4-0	Bill Dooley

1993

		Record	Coach
1.	Florida St	12-1-0	Bobby Bowden
2.	Notre Dame	11-1-0	Lou Holtz
3.	Nebraska	11-1-0	Tom Osborne
4.	Auburn	11-0-0	Terry Bowden
5.	Florida	11-2-0	Steve Spurrier
6.	Wisconsin	10-1-1	Barry Alvarez
7.	W Virginia	11-1-0	Don Nehlen
8.	Penn St	10-2-0	Joe Paterno
9.	Texas A&M	10-2-0	R.C. Slocum
10.	Arizona	10-2-0	Dick Tomey
11.	Ohio St	10-1-1	John Cooper
12.	Tennessee	9-2-1	Phil Fulmer
13.	Boston College	9-3-0	Tom Coughlin
14.	Alabama	9-3-1	Gene Stallings
15.	Miami	9-3-0	Dennis Erickson
16.	Colorado	8-3-1	Bill McCartney
17.	Oklahoma	9-3-0	Gary Gibbs
18.	UCLA	8-4-0	Terry Donahue
19.	North Carolina	10-3-0	Mack Brown
20.	Kansas St	9-2-1	Bill Snyder
21.	Michigan	8-4-0	Gary Moeller
22.	Virginia Tech	9-3-0	Frank Beamer
23.	Clemson	9-3-0	Ken Hatfield
24.	Louisville	9-3-0	H. Schnellenberger
25.	California	9-4-0	Keith Gilbertson

1994

		Record	Coach
1.	Nebraska	13-0-0	Tom Osborne
2.	Penn St	12-0-0	Joe Paterno
3.	Colorado	11-1-0	Bill McCartney
4.	Florida St	10-1-1	Bobby Bowden
5.	Alabama	12-1-0	Gene Stallings
6.	Miami (Fla.)	10-2-0	Dennis Erickson
7.	Florida	10-2-1	Steve Spurrier
8.	Texas A&M	10-0-1	R.C. Slocum
9.	Auburn	9-1-1	Terry Bowden

1994 (Cont.)

		Record	Coach
10.	Utah	10-2-0	Ron McBride
11.	Oregon	9-4-0	Rich Brooks
12.	Michigan	8-4-0	Gary Moeller
13.	USC	8-3-1	John Robinson
14.	Ohio St	9-4-0	John Cooper
15.	Virginia	9-3-0	George Welsh
16.	Colorado St	10-2-0	Sonny Lubick
17.	North Carolina St	9-3-0	Mike O'Cain
18.	BYU	10-3-0	LaVell Edwards
19.	Kansas St	9-3-0	Bill Snyder
20.	Arizona	8-4-0	Dick Tomey
21.	Washington St	8-4-0	Mike Price
22.	Tennessee	8-4-0	Phillip Fulmer
23.	Boston College	7-4-1	Dan Henning
24.	Mississippi St	8-4-0	Jackie Sherrill
25.	Texas	8-4-0	John Mackovic

1995

		Record	Coach
1.	Nebraska	12-0-0	Tom Osborne
2.	Florida	12-1-0	Steve Spurrier
3.	Tennessee	11-1-0	Phillip Fulmer
4.	Florida St	10-2-0	Bobby Bowden
5.	Colorado	10-2-0	Rick Neuheisel
6.	Ohio St	11-2-0	John Cooper
7.	Kansas St	10-2-0	Bill Snyder
8.	Northwestern	10-2-0	Gary Barnett
9.	Kansas	10-2-0	Glen Mason
10.	Virginia Tech	10-2-0	Frank Beamer
11.	Notre Dame	9-3-0	Lou Holtz
12.	USC	9-2-1	John Robinson
13.	Penn St	9-3-0	Joe Paterno
14.	Texas	10-2-1	John Mackovic
15.	Texas A&M	9-3-0	R.C. Slocum
16.	Virginia	9-4-0	George Welsh
17.	Michigan	9-4-0	Lloyd Carr
18.	Oregon	9-3-0	Mike Bellotti
19.	Syracuse	9-3-0	Paul Pasqualoni
20.	Miami (Fla.)	8-3-0	Butch Davis
21.	Alabama	8-3-0	Gene Stallings
22.	Auburn	8-4-0	Terry Bowden
23.	Texas Tech	9-3-0	Spike Dykes
24.	Toledo	11-0-1	Gary Pinkel
25.	Iowa	8-4-0	Hayden Fry

*1996

		Record	Coach
1.	Florida	12-1	Steve Spurrier
2.	Ohio St	11-1	John Cooper
3.	Florida St	11-1	Bobby Bowden
4.	Arizona St	11-1	Bruce Snyder
5.	BYU	14-1	LaVell Edwards
6.	Nebraska	11-2	Tom Osborne
7.	Penn St	11-2	Joe Paterno
8.	Colorado	10-2	Rick Neuheisel
9.	Tennessee	10-2	Phillip Fulmer
10.	North Carolina	10-2	Mack Brown
11.	Alabama	10-3	Gene Stallings
12.	LSU	10-2	Gerry DiNardo
13.	Virginia Tech	10-2	Frank Beamer
14.	Miami (Fla.)	9-3	Butch Davis
15.	Northwestern	9-3	Gary Barnett
16.	Washington	9-3	Jim Lambright
17.	Kansas St	9-3	Bill Snyder
18.	Iowa	9-3	Hayden Fry

†In 1989 the AP expanded its final poll to 25 teams.

*In 1996 the NCAA introduced overtime to break ties.

1996 (Cont.)

	Record	Coach
19. Notre Dame	8–3	Lou Holtz
20. Michigan	8–4	Lloyd Carr
21. Syracuse	9–3	Paul Pasqualoni
22. Wyoming	10–2	Joe Tiller
23. Texas	8–5	John Mackovic
24. Auburn	8–4	Terry Bowden
25. Army	10–2	Bob Sutton

1997

	Record	Coach
1. Michigan	12–0	Lloyd Carr
#2. Nebraska	13–0	Tom Osborne
3. Florida St	11–1	Bobby Bowden
4. Florida	10–2	Steve Spurrier
5. UCLA	10–2	Bob Toledo
6. North Carolina	11–1	Mack Brown
7. Tennessee	11–2	Phillip Fulmer
8. Kansas St	11–1	Bill Snyder
9. Washington St	10–2	Mike Price
10. Georgia	10–2	Jim Donnan
11. Auburn	10–3	Terry Bowden
12. Ohio St	10–3	John Cooper
13. LSU	9–3	Gerry DiNardo
14. Arizona St	8–3	Bruce Snyder
15. Purdue	9–3	Joe Tiller
16. Penn St	9–3	Joe Paterno
17. Colorado St	11–2	Sonny Lubick
18. Washington	8–4	Jim Lambright
19. Southern Mississippi	9–3	Jeff Bower
20. Texas A&M	9–4	R.C. Slocum
21. Syracuse	9–4	Paul Pasqualoni
22. Mississippi	8–4	Tommy Tuberville
23. Missouri	7–5	Larry Smith
24. Oklahoma St	8–4	Bob Simmons
25. Georgia Tech	7–5	George O'Leary

#Selected No. 1 by USA Today/CNN.

1998

	Record	Coach
1. Tennessee	13–0	Phillip Fulmer
2. Ohio St	11–1	John Cooper
3. Florida St	11–2	Bobby Bowden
4. Arizona	12–1	Dick Tomey
5. Florida	10–2	Steve Spurrier
6. Wisconsin	11–1	Barry Alvarez
7. Tulane	12–0	Tommy Bowden
8. UCLA	10–2	Bob Toledo
9. Georgia Tech	10–2	George O'Leary
10. Kansas St	11–2	Bill Snyder
11. Texas A&M	11–3	R.C. Slocum
12. Michigan	10–3	Lloyd Carr
13. Air Force	12–1	Fisher DeBerry
14. Georgia	9–3	Jim Donnan
15. Texas	9–3	Mack Brown
16. Arkansas	9–3	Houston Nutt
17. Penn St	9–3	Joe Paterno
18. Virginia	9–3	George Welsh
19. Nebraska	9–4	Frank Solich
20. Miami (Fla.)	9–3	Butch Davis
21. Missouri	8–4	Larry Smith
22. Notre Dame	9–3	Bob Davie
23. Virginia Tech	9–3	Frank Beamer
24. Purdue	9–4	Joe Tiller
25. Syracuse	8–4	Paul Pasqualoni

1999

	Record	Coach
1. Florida St	12–0	Bobby Bowden
2. Virginia Tech	11–1	Frank Beamer
3. Nebraska	12–1	Frank Solich
4. Wisconsin	10–2	Barry Alvarez
5. Michigan	10–2	Lloyd Carr
6. Kansas St	11–1	Bill Snyder
7. Michigan St	10–2	Nick Saban
8. Alabama	10–3	Mike DuBose
9. Tennessee	9–3	Phillip Fulmer
10. Marshall	13–0	Bob Pruett
11. Penn St	10–3	Joe Paterno
12. Florida	9–4	Steve Spurrier
13. Mississippi St	10–2	Jackie Sherrill
14. Southern Miss	9–3	Jeff Bower
15. Miami (Fla.)	9–4	Butch Davis
16. Georgia	8–4	Jim Donnan
17. Arkansas	8–4	Houston Nutt
18. Minnesota	8–4	Glen Mason
19. Oregon	9–3	Mike Bellotti
20. Georgia Tech	8–4	Goerge O'Leary
21. Texas	9–5	Mack Brown
22. Mississippi	8–4	David Cutcliffe
23. Texas A&M	8–4	R.C. Slocum
24. Illinois	8–4	Ron Turner
25. Purdue	7–5	Joe Tiller

2000

	Record	Coach
1. Oklahoma	13–0	Bob Stoops
2. Miami (Fla.)	11–1	Butch Davis
3. Washington	11–1	Rick Neuheisel
4. Oregon St	11–1	Dennis Erickson
5. Florida St	11–2	Bobby Bowden
6. Virginia Tech	11–1	Frank Beamer
7. Oregon	10–2	Mike Belotti
8. Nebraska	10–2	Frank Solich
9. Kansas St	11–3	Bill Snyder
10. Florida	10–3	Steve Spurrier
11. Michigan	9–3	Lloyd Carr
12. Texas	9–3	Mack Brown
13. Purdue	8–4	Joe Tiller
14. Colorado St	10–2	Sonny Lubeck
15. Notre Dame	9–3	Bob Davie
16. Clemson	9–3	Tommy Bowden
17. Georgia Tech	9–3	George O'Leary
18. Auburn	9–4	Tommy Tuberville
19. South Carolina	8–4	Lou Holtz
20. Georgia	8–4	Jim Donnan
21. TCU	10–2	Dennis Franchione
22. LSU	8–4	Nick Saban
23. Wisconsin	9–4	Barry Alvarez
24. Mississippi St	8–4	Jackie Sherrill
25. Iowa St	9–3	Dan McCarney

2001

	Record	Coach
1. Miami (Fla.)	12–0	Larry Coker
2. Oregon	11–1	Mike Belotti
3. Florida	10–2	Steve Spurrier
4. Tennessee	11–2	Phillip Fulmer
5. Texas	11–2	Mack Brown
6. Oklahoma	11–2	Bob Stoops
7. LSU	10–3	Nick Saban
8. Nebraska	11–2	Frank Solich
9. Colorado	10–3	Gary Barnett
10. Washington St	10–2	Mike Price

2001 *(Cont.)*

		Record	Coach
11.	Maryland	10–2	Ralph Friedgen
12.	Illinois	10–2	Ron Turner
13.	South Carolina	9–3	Lou Holtz
14.	Syracuse	10–3	Paul Pasqualoni
15.	Florida St	8–4	Bobby Bowden
16.	Stanford	9–3	Tyrone Willingham
17.	Louisville	11–2	John Smith
18.	Virginia Tech	8–4	Frank Beamer
19.	Washington	8–4	Rick Neuheisel
20.	Michigan	8–4	Lloyd Carr
21.	Boston College	8–4	Tom O'Brien
22.	Georgia	8–4	Mark Richt
23.	Toledo	10–2	Tom Amstutz
24.	Georgia Tech	8–5	George O'Leary
25.	BYU	12–2	Gary Crowton

2002

		Record	Coach
1.	Ohio St	14–0	Jim Tressel
2.	Miami (Fla.)	12–1	Larry Coker
3.	Georgia	13–1	Mark Richt
4.	USC	11–2	Pete Carroll
5.	Oklahoma	12–2	Bob Stoops
6.	Texas	11–2	Mack Brown
7.	Kansas St	11–2	Bill Snyder
8.	Iowa	11–2	Kirk Ferentz
9.	Michigan	10–3	Lloyd Carr
10.	Washington St	10–3	Mike Price
11.	Alabama	10–3	Dennis Franchione
12.	North Carolina St	11–3	Chuck Amato
13.	Maryland	11–3	Ralph Friedgen
14.	Auburn	9–4	Tommy Tuberville
15.	Boise St	12–1	Dan Hawkins
16.	Penn St	9–4	Joe Paterno
17.	Notre Dame	10–3	Tyrone Willingham
18.	Virginia Tech	10–4	Frank Beamer
19.	Pittsburgh	9–4	Walt Harris
20.	Colorado	9–5	Gary Barnett
21.	Florida St	9–5	Bobby Bowden
22.	Virginia	9–5	Al Groh
23.	TCU	10–2	Gary Patterson
24.	Marshall	11–2	Bob Pruett
25.	W Virginia	9–4	Rich Rodriguez

2003

		Record	Coach
1.	USC	12–1	Pete Carroll
#2.	LSU	13–1	Nick Saban
3.	Oklahoma	12–2	Bob Stoops
4.	Ohio St	11–2	Jim Tressel
5.	Miami (Fla.)	11–2	Larry Coker
6.	Michigan	10–3	Lloyd Carr
7.	Georgia	11–3	Mark Richt
8.	Iowa	10–3	Kirk Ferentz
9.	Washington St	10–3	Bill Doba
10.	Miami (Ohio)	13–1	Terry Hoeppner
11.	Florida St	10–3	Bobby Bowden
12.	Texas	10–3	Mack Brown
13.	Kansas St	11–4	Bill Snyder
	Mississippi	10–3	David Cutcliffe
15.	Tennessee	10–3	Phillip Fulmer
16.	Boise St	13–1	Dan Hawkins
17.	Maryland	10–3	Ralph Friedgen
18.	Nebraska	10–3	Frank Solich/Bo Pelini
	Purdue	9–4	Joe Tiller
20.	Minnesota	10–3	Glen Mason
21.	Utah	10–2	Urban Meyer

2003 *(Cont.)*

		Record	Coach
22.	Clemson	9–4	Tommy Bowden
23.	Bowling Green	11–3	Gregg Brandon
24.	Florida	8–5	Ron Zook
25.	TCU	11–2	Gary Patterson

#Selected No. 1 by *USA Today*/CNN.

2004

		Record	Coach
1.	*Vacated		
2.	Auburn	13–0	Tommy Tuberville
3.	Oklahoma	12–1	Bob Stoops
4.	Utah	12–0	Kyle Whittingham
5.	Texas	11–1	Mack Brown
6.	Louisville	11–1	Bobby Petrino
7.	Georgia	10–2	Mark Richt
8.	Iowa	10–2	Kirk Ferentz
9.	California	10–2	Jeff Tedford
10.	Virginia Tech	10–3	Frank Beamer
11.	Miami (Fla.)	9–3	Larry Coker
12.	Boise St	11–1	Dan Hawkins
13.	Tennessee	10–3	Phillip Fulmer
14.	Michigan	9–3	Lloyd Carr
15.	Florida St	8–5	Bobby Bowden
16.	LSU	9–3	Les Miles
17.	Wisconsin	9–3	Barry Alvarez
18.	Texas Tech	8–4	Mike Leach
19.	Arizona St	9–3	Dirk Koetter
20.	Ohio St	8–4	Jim Tressel
21.	Boston College	9–3	Tom O'Brien
22.	Fresno St	9–3	Pat Hill
23.	Virginia	8–4	Al Groh
24.	Navy	10–2	Paul Johnson
25.	Pittsburgh	8–4	Walt Harris

*USC was stripped of its 2004 BCS victory in 2010.

2005

		Record	Coach
1.	Texas	13–0	Mack Brown
2.	*Vacated		
3.	Penn St	11–1	Joe Paterno
4.	Ohio St	10–2	Jim Tressel
5.	Texas	11–1	Mack Brown
6.	LSU	11–2	Les Miles
7.	Virginia Tech	10–3	Frank Beamer
8.	Alabama	10–2	Mike Shula
9.	Notre Dame	9–3	Charlie Weis
10.	Georgia	10–3	Mark Richt
11.	TCU	11–1	Gary Patterson
12.	Florida	9–3	Urban Meyer
	Oregon	10–2	Mike Bellotti
14.	Auburn	9–3	Tommy Tuberville
15.	Wisconsin	9–3	Barry Alvarez
15.	Michigan	9–3	Lloyd Carr
16.	UCLA	10–2	Karl Dorrell
17.	Miami (Fla.)	9–3	Larry Coker
18.	Boston College	9–3	Tom O'Brien
19.	Louisville	9–3	Bobby Petrino
20.	Texas Tech	9–3	Mike Leach
21.	Clemson	8–4	Tommy Bowden
22.	Oklahoma	8–4	Bob Stoops
23.	Florida St	8–5	Bobby Bowden
24.	Nebraska	8–4	Bill Callahan
25.	California	8–4	Jeff Tedford

*USC was stripped of its 2005 season victories in 2010.

2006

		Record	Coach
1.	Florida	13-1	Urban Meyer
2.	Ohio St	12-1	Jim Tressel
3.	LSU	11-2	Les Miles
4.	USC	11-2	Pete Carroll
5.	Boise St	13-0	Chris Petersen
6.	Louisville	12-1	Steve Kragthorpe
7.	Wisconsin	12-1	Bret Bielema
8.	Michigan	11-2	Lloyd Carr
9.	Auburn	11-2	Tommy Tuberville
10.	W Virginia	11-2	Rich Rodriguez
11.	Oklahoma	11-3	Bob Stoops
12.	Rutgers	11-2	Greg Schiano
13.	Texas	10-3	Mack Brown
14.	California	10-3	Jeff Tedford
15.	Arkansas	10-4	Houston Nutt
16.	BYU	11-2	Bronco Mendenhall
17.	Notre Dame	10-3	Charlie Weis
18.	Wake Forest	11-3	Jim Grobe
19.	Virginia Tech	10-3	Frank Beamer
20.	Boston College	10-3	Jeff Jagodzinski
21.	Oregon St	10-4	Mike Riley
22.	TCU	11-2	Gary Patterson
23.	Georgia	9-4	Mark Richt
24.	Penn St	9-4	Joe Paterno
25.	Tennessee	9-4	Phillip Fulmer

2007

		Record	Coach
1.	LSU	12-2	Les Miles
2.	Georgia	11-2	Mark Richt
3.	USC	11-2	Pete Carroll
4.	Missouri	12-2	Gary Pinkell
5.	Ohio St	11-2	Jim Tressel
6.	W Virginia	11-2	Rich Rodriguez
7.	Kansas	12-1	Mark Mangino
8.	Oklahoma	11-3	Bob Stoops
9.	Virginia Tech	11-3	Frank Beamer
10.	Texas	10-3	Mack Brown
	Boston College	11-3	Jeff Jagodzinski
12.	Tennessee	10-4	Philip Fulmer
13.	Florida	9-4	Urban Meyer
14.	BYU	11-2	Bronco Mendenhall
15.	Auburn	9-4	Tommy Tuberville
16.	Arizona St	10-3	Dennis Erickson
17.	Cincinnati	10-3	Brian Kelly
18.	Michigan	9-4	Lloyd Carr
19.	Hawaii	12-1	June Jones
20.	Illinois	9-4	Ron Zook
21.	Clemson	9-4	Tommy Bowden
22.	Texas Tech	9-4	Mike Leach
23.	Oregon	9-4	Mike Bellotti
24.	Wisconsin	9-4	Bret Bielema
25.	Oregon St	9-4	Mike Riley

2008

		Record	Coach
1.	Florida	12-1	Urban Meyer
2.	Utah	12-0	Kyle Whittingham
3.	USC	11-1	Pete Carroll
4.	Texas	11-1	Mack Brown
5.	Olahoma	12-1	Bob Stoops
6.	Alabama	12-2	Nick Saban
7.	TCU	10-2	Gary Patterson
8.	Penn St	11-1	Joe Paterno
9.	Ohio State	10-2	Jim Tressel

2008 *(Cont.)*

		Record	Coach
10.	Oregon	9-3	Mike Bellotti
11.	Boise St	12-0	Chris Petersen
12.	Texas Tech	11-1	Mike Leach
13.	Georgia	9-3	Mike Richt
14.	Mississippi	8-4	Houston Nutt
15.	Virginia Tech	9-4	Frank Beamer
16.	Oklahoma St	9-3	Mike Gundy
17.	Cincinnati	11-2	Brian Kelly
18.	Oregon St	8-4	Mike Riley
19.	Missouri	9-4	Gary Pinkel
20.	Iowa	8-4	Kirk Ferentz
21.	Florida St	8-4	Bobby Bowden
22.	Georgia Tech	9-3	Paul Johnson
23.	W Virginia	8-4	Bill Stewart
24.	Michigan St	9-3	Mark Dantonio
25.	BYU	10-2	Bronco Mendenhall

2009

		Record	Coach
1.	Alabama	14-0	Nick Saban
2.	Texas	13-1	Mack Brown
3.	Florida	13-1	Urban Meyer
4.	Boise St	14-0	Chris Petersen
5.	Ohio St	11-2	Jim Tressel
6.	TCU	12-1	Gary Patterson
7.	Iowa	11-2	Mark Mangino
8.	Cincinnati	12-1	Brian Kelly
9.	Penn St	11-2	Joe Paterno
10.	Virginia Tech	10-3	Frank Beamer
11.	Oregon	10-3	Chip Kelly
12.	BYU	11-2	Bronco Mendenhall
13.	Georgia Tech	11-3	Paul Johnson
14.	Nebraska	10-4	Bo Pelini
15.	Pittsburgh	10-3	Dave Wannstedt
16.	Wisconsin	10-3	Bret Bielema
17.	LSU	9-4	Les Miles
18.	Utah	10-3	Kyle Whittingham
19.	Miami (Fla.)	9-4	Randy Shannon
20.	Mississippi	9-4	Houston Nutt
21.	Texas Tech	9-4	Mike Leach
22.	USC	9-4	Pete Carroll
23.	Central Michigan	12-2	Butch Jones
24.	Clemson	9-5	Dabo Swinney
25.	W Virginia	9-4	Bill Stewart

2010

		Record	Coach
1.	Auburn	14-0	Gene Chizik
2.	TCU	13-0	Gary Patterson
3.	Oregon	12-1	Chip Kelly
4.	Stanford	12-1	Jim Harbaugh
5.	Ohio St	12-1	Jim Tressel
6.	Oklahoma	12-2	Bob Stoops
7.	Wisconsin	11-2	Bret Bielema
8.	LSU	11-2	Les Miles
9.	Boise St	12-1	Chris Petersen
10.	Alabama	10-3	Nick Saban
11.	Nevada	13-1	Chris Ault
12.	Arkansas	10-3	Bobby Petrino
13.	Oklahoma St	11-2	Mike Gundy
14.	Michigan St	11-2	Mark Dantonio
15.	Mississippi St	9-4	Dan Mullen

2010 *(Cont.)*

		Record	Coach
16.	Virginia Tech	11-3	Frank Beamer
17.	Florida St	10-4	Jimbo Fisher
18.	Missouri	10-3	Gary Pinkel
19.	Texas A&M	9-4	Mike Sherman
20.	Nebraska	10-4	Bo Pelini
21.	Central Florida	11-3	George O'Leary
22.	South Carolina	9-5	Steve Spurrier
23.	Maryland	9-4	Ralph Friedgen
24.	Tulsa	10-3	Todd Graham
25.	North Carolina St	9-4	Todd O'Brien

2011

		Record	Coach
1.	Alabama	12-1	Nick Saban
2.	LSU	13-1	Les Miles
3.	Oklahoma State	12-1	Mike Gundy
4.	Oregon	12-2	Chip Kelly
5.	Arkansas	11-2	Bobby Petrino
6.	USC	10-2	Lane Kiffin
7.	Stanford	11-2	David Shaw
8.	Boise State	12-1	Chris Peterseny
9.	South Carolina	11-2	Steve Spurrier
10.	Wisconsin	11-3	Bret Bielema
11.	Michigan State	11-3	Mark Dantonio
12.	Michigan	11-2	Brady Hoke
13.	Baylor	10-3	Art Briles
14.	TCU	11-2	Gary Patterson
15.	Kansas State	10-3	Bill Snyder
16.	Oklahoma	10-3	Bob Stoops
17.	W Virginia	10-3	Dana Holgorsen
18.	Houston	13-1	Tony Levine
19.	Georgia	10-4	Mark Richt
20.	Southern Miss	12-2	Larry Fedora
21.	Virginia Tech	11-3	Frank Beamer
22.	Clemson	10-4	Dabo Swinney
23.	Florida State	9-4	Jimbo Fisher
24.	Nebraska	9-4	Bo Pelini
25.	Cincinnati	10-3	Butch Jones

NCAA Divisional Championships

Football Championship Subdivision (Div. I-AA)

Year	Winner	Runner-Up	Score
1978	Florida A&M	Massachusetts	35–28
1979	Eastern Kentucky	Lehigh	30–7
1980	Boise St	Eastern Kentucky	31–29
1981	Idaho St	Eastern Kentucky	34–23
1982	Eastern Kentucky	Delaware	17–14
1983	Southern Illinois	Western Carolina	43–7
1984	Montana St	Louisiana Tech	19–6
1985	Georgia Southern	Furman	44–42
1986	Georgia Southern	Arkansas St	48–21
1987	NE Louisiana	Marshall	43–42
1988	Furman	Georgia Southern	17–12
1989	Georgia Southern	Stephen F. Austin St	37–34
1990	Georgia Southern	Nevada-Reno	36–13
1991	Youngstown St	Marshall	25–17
1992	Marshall	Youngstown St	31–28
1993	Youngstown St	Marshall	17–5
1994	Youngstown St	Boise St	28–14
1995	Montana	Marshall	22–20
1996	Marshall	Montana	49–29
1997	Youngstown St	McNesse St	10–9
1998	Massachusetts	Georgia Southern	55–43
1999	Georgia Southern	Youngstown St	59–24
2000	Georgia Southern	Montana	27–25
2001	Montana	Furman	13–6
2002	Western Kentucky	McNeese St	34–14
2003	Delaware	Colgate	40–0
2004	James Madison	Montana	31–21
2005	Appalachian St	Northern Iowa	21–16
2006	Appalachian St	Massachusetts	28–17
2007	Appalachian St	Delaware	49–21
2008	Richmond	Montana	24–7
2009	Villanova	Montana	23–21
2010	Eastern Washington	Delaware	20–19
2011	North Dakota St	Sam Houston St	17–6

Division II

Year	Winner	Runner-Up	Score
1973	Louisiana Tech	Western Kentucky	34–0
1974	Central Michigan	Delaware	54–14
1975	Northern Michigan	Western Kentucky	16–14
1976	Montana St	Akron	24–13
1977	Lehigh	Jacksonville St	33–0
1978	Eastern Illinois	Delaware	10–9
1979	Delaware	Youngstown St	38–21
1980	Cal Poly SLO	Eastern Illinois	21–13
1981	SW Texas St	North Dakota St	42–13
1982	SW Texas St	UC–Davis	34–9
1983	North Dakota St	Central St (Ohio)	41–21
1984	Troy St	North Dakota St	18–17
1985	North Dakota St	North Alabama	35–7
1986	North Dakota St	South Dakota	27–7
1987	Troy St	Portland St	31–17
1988	North Dakota St	Portland St	35–21
1989	Mississippi College	Jacksonville St	3–0
1990	N Dakota St	Indiana (Pa.)	51–11
1991	Pittsburg St	Jacksonville St	23–6
1992	Jacksonville St	Pittsburg St	17–13
1993	North Alabama	Indiana (Pa.)	41–34
1994	North Alabama	Texas A&M–Kingsville	16–10
1995	North Alabama	Pittsburg St	27–7
1996	Northern Colorado	Carson-Newman	23–14
1997	Northern Colorado	New Haven	51–0
1998	NW Missouri St	Carson-Newman	24–6
1999	NW Missouri St	Carson-Newman	58–52 (OT)
2000	Delta St	Bloomsburg	63–34
2001	Grand Valley St	North Dakota	17–14

Division II *(Cont.)*

Year	Winner	Runner-Up	Score
2002	Grand Valley St	Valdosta St	31–24
2003	Grand Valley St	North Dakota	10–3
2004	Valdosta State	Pittsburg State	36–31
2005	Grand Valley St	NW Missouri St	21–17
2006	Grand Valley St	NW Missouri St	17–14
2007	Valdosta St	NW Missouri St	25–20
2008	Minnesota-Duluth	NW Missouri St	21–14
2009	NW Missouri St	Grand Valley St	30–23
2010	Minnesota-Duluth	Delta St	20–17
2011	Pittsburg St	Wayne St	35–21

Division III

Year	Winner	Runner-Up	Score
1973	Wittenberg	Juniata	41–0
1974	Central (Iowa)	Ithaca	10–8
1975	Wittenberg	Ithaca	28–0
1976	St. John's (Minn.)	Towson St	31–28
1977	Widener	Wabash	39–36
1978	Baldwin-Wallace	Wittenberg	24–10
1979	Ithaca	Wittenberg	14–10
1980	Dayton	Ithaca	63–0
1981	Widener	Dayton	17–10
1982	West Georgia	Augustana (Ill.)	14–0
1983	Augustana (Ill.)	Union (N.Y.)	21–17
1984	Augustana (Ill.)	Central (Iowa)	21–12
1985	Augustana (Ill.)	Ithaca	20–7
1986	Augustana (Ill.)	Salisbury St	31–3
1987	Wagner	Dayton	19–3
1988	Ithaca	Central (Iowa)	39–24
1989	Dayton	Union (N.Y.)	17–7
1990	Allegheny	Lycoming	21–14 (OT)
1991	Ithaca	Dayton	34–20
1992	UW-LaCrosse	Washington & Jefferson	16–12
1993	Mount Union	Rowan	34–24
1994	Albion	Washington & Jefferson	38–15
1995	UW-LaCrosse	Rowan	36–7
1996	Mount Union	Rowan	56–24
1997	Mount Union	Lycoming	61–12
1998	Mount Union	Rowan	44–24
1999	Pacific Lutheran	Rowan	42–13
2000	Mount Union	St. John's (Minn.)	10–7
2001	Mount Union	Bridgewater	30–27
2002	Mount Union	Trinity (Tex.)	48–7
2003	St. John's (Minn.)	Mount Union	24–6
2004	Linfield	Mary Hardin-Baylor	28–21
2005	Mount Union	UW-Whitewater	35–28
2006	Mount Union	UW-Whitewater	35–16
2007	UW-Whitewater	Mount Union	31–21
2008	Mount Union	UW-Whitewater	31–26
2009	UW-Whitewater	Mount Union	38–28
2010	UW-Whitewater	Mount Union	31–21
2011	UW-Whitewater	Mount Union	13–10

NAIA Divisional Championships

Division I

Year	Winner	Runner-Up	Score
1956	St. Joseph's (Ind.)/Montana St		0–0
1957	Pittsburg St (Kan.)	Hillsdale	27–26
1958	NE Oklahoma	Northern Arizona	19–13
1959	Texas A&I	Lenoir-Rhyne	20–7
1960	Lenoir-Rhyne	Humboldt St	15–14
1961	Pittsburg St (Kan.)	Linfield	12–7
1962	Central St (Okla.)	Lenoir-Rhyne	28–13
1963	St. John's (Minn.)	Prairie View	33–27

Division I *(Cont.)*

Year	Winner	Runner-Up	Score
1964	Concordia-Moorhead/ Sam Houston St		7–7
1965	St. John's (Minn.)	Linfield	33–0
1966	Waynesburg	UW-Whitewater	42–21
1967	Fairmont St	Eastern Washington	28–21
1968	Troy St (Mich.)	Texas A&I	43–35
1969	Texas A&I	Concordia-Moorhead (Minn.)	32–7
1970	Texas A&I	Wofford	48–7
1971	Livingston (Ala.)	Arkansas Tech	14–12
1972	E Texas St	Carson-Newman	21–18
1973	Abilene Christian	Elon	42–14
1974	Texas A&I	Henderson St	34–23
1975	Texas A&I	Salem (W.V.)	37–0
1976	Texas A&I	Central Arkansas	26–0
1977	Abilene Christian	SW Oklahoma	24–7
1978	Angelo St	Elon	34–14
1979	Texas A&I	Central St (Okla.)	20–14
1980	Elon	NE Oklahoma	17–10
1981	Elon	Pittsburg St	3–0
1982	Central St (Okla.)	Mesa	14–11
1983	Carson-Newman	Mesa	36–28
1984	Carson-Newman/Central Arkansas		19–19
1985	Central Arkansas/Hillsdale		10–10
1986	Carson-Newman	Cameron	17–0
1987	Cameron	Carson-Newman	30–2
1988	Carson-Newman	Adams St (Col.)	56–21
1989	Carson-Newman	Emporia St	34–20
1990	Central St (Ohio)	Mesa St	38–16
1991	Central Arkansas	Central St (Ohio)	19–16
1992	Central St (Ohio)	Gardner-Webb	19–16
1993	East Central (Okla.)	Glenville St	49–35
1994	Northeastern St (Okla.)	Arkansas–Pine Bluff	13–12
1995	Central St (Ohio)	Northeastern St (Okla.)	37–7
1996	SW Oklahoma St	Montana Tech	33–31
1997	Findlay	Willamette	14–7
1998	Azusa Pacific	Olivet Nazarene	17–14
1999	Northwestern Oklahoma St	Georgetown (Ky.)	34–26
2000	Georgetown (Ky.)	Northwestern Oklahoma St	20–0
2001	Georgetown (Ky.)	Sioux Falls (S.D.)	49–27
2002	Carroll (Mont.)	Georgetown (Ky.)	28–7
2003	Carroll (Mont.)	Northwestern Oklahoma St	41–28
2004	Carroll (Mont.)	St. Francis (Ind.)	15–13
2005	Carroll (Mont.)	St. Francis (Ind.)	27–10
2006	Sioux Falls (S.D.)	St. Francis (Ind.)	23–19
2007	Carroll (Mont.)	Sioux Falls (S.D.)	17–9
2008	Sioux Falls (S.D.)	Carroll (Mont.)	23–7
2009	Sioux Falls (S.D.)	Lindenwood	25–22
2010	Carroll (Mont.)	Sioux Falls (S.D.)	10–7
2011	St. Xavier (Ill.)	Carroll (Mont.)	24-20

Division II†

Year	Winner	Runner-Up	Score
1970	Westminster (Pa.)	Anderson	21–16
1971	California Lutheran	Westminster (Pa.)	30–14
1972	Missouri Southern	Northwestern (Iowa)	21–14
1973	Northwestern (Iowa)	Glenville St	10–3
1974	Texas Lutheran	Missouri Valley	42–0
1975	Texas Lutheran	California Lutheran	34–8
1976	Westminster (Pa.)	Redlands	20–13
1977	Westminster (Pa.)	California Lutheran	17–9
1978	Concordia-Moorhead (Minn.)	Findlay	7–0
1979	Findlay	Northwestern (Iowa)	51–6
1980	Pacific Lutheran	Wilmington (Ohio)	38–10
1981	Austin Coll./Conc.-Moorhead (Minn.)		24–24
1982	Linfield	William Jewell	33–15
1983	Northwestern (Iowa)	Pacific Lutheran	25–21

†In 1997 the NAIA consolidated its two divisions into one.

†Division II *(Cont.)*

Year	Winner	Runner-Up	Score
1984	Linfield	Northwestern (Iowa)	33–22
1985	UW-La Crosse	Pacific Lutheran	24–7
1986	Linfield	Baker	17–0
1987	Pacific Lutheran	UW-Stevens Point*	16–16
1988	Westminster (Pa.)	UW-La Crosse	21–14
1989	Westminster (Pa.)	UW-La Crosse	51–30
1990	Peru St	Westminster (Pa.)	17–7
1991	Georgetown (Ky.)	Pacific Lutheran	28–20
1992	Findlay	Linfield	26–13
1993	Pacific Lutheran	Westminster (Pa.)	50–20
1994	Westminster (Pa.)	Pacific Lutheran	27–7
1995	Findlay	Central Washington	21–21
1996	Sioux Falls (S.D.)	Western Washington	47–25

*Forfeited 1987 season due to use of an ineligible player. †In 1997 the NAIA consolidated its two divisions into one.

Awards

Heisman Memorial Trophy

Awarded to the best college player by the Downtown Athletic Club of New York City. The trophy is named after John W. Heisman, who coached Georgia Tech to the national championship in 1917 and later served as DAC athletic director.

Year	Winner, College, Position	Winner's Season Statistics	Runner-Up, College
1935	Jay Berwanger, Chicago, HB	Rush: 119 Yds: 577 TD: 6	Monk Meyer, Army
1936	Larry Kelley, Yale, E	Rec: 17 Yds: 372 TD: 6	Sam Francis, Nebraska
1937	Clint Frank, Yale, HB	Rush: 157 Yds: 667 TD: 11	Byron White, Colorado
1938	†Davey O'Brien, TCU, QB	Att/Comp: 194/110 Yds: 1733 TD: 19	Marshall Goldberg, Pittsburgh
1939	Nile Kinnick, Iowa, HB	Rush: 106 Yds: 374 TD: 5	Tom Harmon, Michigan
1940	Tom Harmon, Michigan, HB	Rush: 191 Yds: 852 TD: 16	John Kimbrough, Texas A&M
1941	†Bruce Smith, Minnesota, HB	Rush: 98 Yds: 480 TD: 6	Angelo Bertelli, Notre Dame
1942	Frank Sinkwich, Georgia, HB	Att/Comp: 166/84 Yds: 1392 TD: 10	Paul Governali, Columbia
1943	Angelo Bertelli, Notre Dame, QB	Att/Comp: 36/25 Yds: 511 TD: 10	Bob Odell, Pennsylvania
1944	Les Horvath, Ohio State, QB	Rush: 163 Yds: 924 TD: 12	Glenn Davis, Army
1945	*†Doc Blanchard, Army, FB	Rush: 101 Yds: 718 TD: 13	Glenn Davis, Army
1946	Glenn Davis, Army, HB	Rush: 123 Yds: 712 TD: 7	Charley Trippi, Georgia
1947	†John Lujack, Notre Dame, QB	Att/Comp: 109/61 Yds: 777 TD: 9	Bob Chappius, Michigan
1948	*Doak Walker, SMU, HB	Rush: 108 Yds: 532 TD: 8	Charlie Justice, North Carolina
1949	†Leon Hart, Notre Dame, E	Rec: 19 Yds: 257 TD: 5	Charlie Justice, North Carolina
1950	*Vic Janowicz, Ohio St, HB	Att/Comp: 77/32 Yds: 561 TD: 12	Kyle Rote, SMU
1951	Dick Kazmaier, Princeton, HB	Rush: 149 Yds: 861 TD: 9	Hank Lauricella, Tennessee
1952	Billy Vessels, Oklahoma, HB	Rush: 167 Yds: 1072 TD: 17	Jack Scarbath, Maryland
1953	John Lattner, Notre Dame, HB	Rush: 134 Yds: 651 TD: 6	Paul Giel, Minnesota
1954	Alan Ameche, Wisconsin, FB	Rush: 146 Yds: 641 TD: 9	Kurt Burris, Oklahoma
1955	Howard Cassady, Ohio St, HB	Rush: 161 Yds: 958 TD: 15	Jim Swink, TCU
1956	Paul Hornung, Notre Dame, QB	Att/Comp: 111/59 Yds: 917 TD: 3	Johnny Majors, Tennessee
1957	John David Crow, Texas A&M, HB	Rush: 129 Yds: 562 TD: 10	Alex Karras, Iowa
1958	Pete Dawkins, Army, HB	Rush: 78 Yds: 428 TD: 6	Randy Duncan, Iowa
1959	Billy Cannon, LSU, HB	Rush: 139 Yds: 598 TD: 6	Rich Lucas, Penn St
1960	Joe Bellino, Navy, HB	Rush: 168 Yds: 834 TD: 18	Tom Brown, Minnesota
1961	Ernie Davis, Syracuse, HB	Rush: 150 Yds: 823 TD: 15	Bob Ferguson, Ohio St
1962	Terry Baker, Oregon St, QB	Att/Comp: 203/112 Yds: 1738 TD: 15	Jerry Stovall, LSU
1963	*Roger Staubach, Navy, QB	Att/Comp: 161/107 Yds: 1474 TD: 7	Billy Lothridge, Georgia Tech
1964	John Huarte, Notre Dame, QB	Att/Comp: 205/114 Yds: 2062 TD: 16	Jerry Rhome, Tulsa
1965	Mike Garrett, USC, HB	Rush: 267 Yds: 1440 TD: 16	Howard Twilley, Tulsa
1966	Steve Spurrier, Florida, QB	Att/Comp: 291/179 Yds: 2012 TD: 1	Bob Griese, Purdue
1967	Gary Beban, UCLA, QB	Att/Comp: 156/87 Yds: 1359 TD: 8	O.J. Simpson, USC
1968	O.J. Simpson, USC, HB	Rush: 383 Yds: 1880 TD: 23	Leroy Keyes, Purdue

Heisman Memorial Trophy *(Cont.)*

Year	Winner, College, Position	Winner's Season Statistics	Runner-Up, College
1969	Steve Owens, Oklahoma, FB	Rush: 358 Yds: 1523 TD: 23	Mike Phipps, Purdue
1970	Jim Plunkett, Stanford, QB	Att/Comp: 358/191 Yds: 2715 TD: 18	Joe Theismann, Notre Dame
1971	Pat Sullivan, Auburn, QB	Att/Comp: 281/162 Yds: 2012; 20 TD	Ed Marinaro, Cornell
1972	Johnny Rodgers, Nebraska, FL	Rec: 55 Yds: 942 TD: 17	Greg Pruitt, Oklahoma
1973	John Cappelletti, Penn St, HB	Rush: 286 Yds: 1522 TD: 17	John Hicks, Ohio St
1974	*Archie Griffin, Ohio St, HB	Rush: 256 Yds: 1695 TD: 12	Anthony Davis, USC
1975	Archie Griffin, Ohio St, HB	Rush: 262 Yds: 1450 TD: 4	Chuck Muncie, California
1976	†Tony Dorsett, Pittsburgh, HB	Rush: 370 Yds: 2150 TD: 23	Ricky Bell, USC
1977	Earl Campbell, Texas, FB	Rush: 267 Yds: 1744 TD: 19	Terry Miller, Oklahoma St
1978	*Billy Sims, Oklahoma, HB	Rush: 231 Yds: 1762 TD: 20	Chuck Fusina, Penn St
1979	Charles White, USC, HB	Rush: 332 Yds: 1803 TD: 19	Billy Sims, Oklahoma
1980	George Rogers, South Carolina, HB	Rush: 324 Yds: 1894 TD: 14	Hugh Green, Pittsburgh
1981	Marcus Allen, USC, HB	Rush: 433 Yds: 2427 TD: 23	Herschel Walker, Georgia
1982	*Herschel Walker, Georgia, HB	Rush: 335 Yds: 1752 TD: 17	John Elway, Stanford
1983	Mike Rozier, Nebraska, HB	Rush: 275 Yds: 2148 TD: 29	Steve Young, BYU
1984	Doug Flutie, Boston College, QB	Att/Comp: 396/233 Yds: 3454 TD: 27	Keith Byars, Ohio St
1985	Bo Jackson, Auburn, HB	Rush: 278 Yds: 1786 TD: 17	Chuck Long, Iowa
1986	Vinny Testaverde, Miami (Fla.), QB	Att/Comp: 276/175 Yds: 2557 TD: 26	Paul Palmer, Temple
1987	Tim Brown, Notre Dame, WR	Rec: 39 Yds: 846 TD: 7	Don McPherson, Syracuse
1988	*Barry Sanders, Oklahoma St, RB	Rush: 344 Yds: 2628 TD: 39	Rodney Peete, USC
1989	*Andre Ware, Houston, QB	Att/Comp: 578/365 Yds: 4699 TD: 46	Anthony Thompson, Indiana
1990	*Ty Detmer, BYU, QB	Att/Comp: 562/361 Yds: 5188 TD: 41	Raghib Ismail, Notre Dame
1991	*Desmond Howard, Michigan, WR	Rec: 61 Yds: 950 TD: 23	Casey Weldon, Florida St
1992	Gino Torretta, Miami (FL), QB	Att/Comp: 402/228 Yds: 3060 TD: 19	Marshall Faulk, San Diego St
1993	†Charlie Ward, Florida St, QB	Att/Comp: 380/264 Yds: 3032 TD: 27	Heath Shuler, Tennessee
1994	Rashaan Salaam, Colorado, RB	Rush: 298 Yds: 2055 TD: 24	Ki-Jana Carter, Penn St
1995	Eddie George, Ohio State, RB	Rush: 303 Yds: 1826 TD: 23	Tommie Frazier, Nebraska
1996	†Danny Wuerffel, Florida, QB	Att/Comp: 360/207 Yds: 3625 TD: 39	Troy Davis, Iowa St
1997	†Charles Woodson, Michigan, CB/ WR	7 interceptions; Rec: 11 Yds: 231 TD: 4	Peyton Manning, Tennessee
1998	Ricky Williams, Texas, RB	Rush: 361 Yds: 2124 TD: 28	Michael Bishop, Kansas St
1999	Ron Dayne, Wisconsin, RB	Rush: 303 Yds: 1834 TD: 19	Joe Hamilton, Georgia Tech
2000	Chris Weinke, Florida St, QB	Att/Comp: 431/266 Yds: 4167 TD: 33	Josh Heupel, Oklahoma
2001	Eric Crouch, Nebraska, QB	Att/Comp: 189/105 Yds: 1510 TD: 7; Rush: 1115 Yds, 18 TD	Rex Grossman, Florida
2002	Carson Palmer, USC, QB	Att/Comp: 450/228 Yds: 3639 TD: 32	Brad Banks, Iowa
2003	Jason White, Oklahoma, QB	Pct. Comp: 64; 3744 Yds; TD: 40	Larry Fitzgerald, Pittsburgh
2004	*†Matt Leinart, USC, QB	Att/Comp: 269/412 Yds: 2990 TD: 28	Adrian Peterson, Oklahoma
2005	**Vacated		Vince Young, Texas
2006	Troy Smith, Ohio State, QB	Att/Comp: 311/203 Yds: 2542 TD: 30	Darren McFadden, Arkansas
2007	^Tim Tebow, Florida, QB	Att/Comp: 350/234 Yds: 3286 TD: 32	Darren McFadden, Arkansas
2008	^Sam Bradford, Oklahoma, QB	Att/Comp: 483/328 Yds: 4720 TD: 50	Colt McCoy, Texas
2009	^†Mark Ingram, Alabama, RB	Rush: 249 Yds:1,542 TD: 15	Toby Gerhart, Stanford
2010	*†Cam Newton, Auburn, QB	Att/Comp: 280/185 Yds: 2854 TD: 30 Rush:1473 Yds TD: 20	Andrew Luck, Stanford
2011	Robert Griffin III, Baylor	Att/Comp: 402/291 Yds: 4293 TD :37 Rush: 699 Yds TD: 10	Andrew Luck, Stanford

*Juniors; ^Sophomore; (all others seniors). †Winners who played for national championship teams the same year.
Note: Former Heisman winners and national media cast votes, with ballots allowing for three names (3 points for first, 2 for second and 1 for third). **In September 2010, Reggie Bush forfeited the 2005 Heisman Trophy he won while at USC.

Maxwell Award

Given to the outstanding college player of the year by the Maxwell Club of Philadelphia.

Year	Player, College, Position	Year	Player, College, Position
1937	Clint Frank, Yale, HB	1975	Archie Griffin, Ohio St, RB
1938	Davey O'Brien, TCU, QB	1976	Tony Dorsett, Pittsburgh, RB
1939	Nile Kinnick, Iowa, HB	1977	Ross Browner, Notre Dame, DE
1940	Tom Harmon, Michigan, HB	1978	Chuck Fusina, Penn St, QB
1941	Bill Dudley, Virginia, HB	1979	Charles White, USC, RB
1942	Paul Governali, Columbia, QB	1980	Hugh Green, Pittsburgh, DE
1943	Bob Odell, Pennsylvania, HB	1981	Marcus Allen, USC, RB
1944	Glenn Davis, Army, HB	1982	Herschel Walker, Georgia, RB
1945	Doc Blanchard, Army, FB	1983	Mike Rozier, Nebraska, RB
1946	Charley Trippi, Georgia, HB	1984	Doug Flutie, Boston College, QB
1947	Doak Walker, SMU, HB	1985	Chuck Long, Iowa, QB
1948	Chuck Bednarik, Pennsylvania, C	1986	Vinny Testaverde, Miami (Fla.), QB
1949	Leon Hart, Notre Dame, E	1987	Don McPherson, Syracuse, QB
1950	Reds Bagnell, Pennsylvania, HB	1988	Barry Sanders, Oklahoma St, RB
1951	Dick Kazmaier, Princeton, HB	1989	Anthony Thompson, Indiana, RB
1952	John Lattner, Notre Dame, HB	1990	Ty Detmer, BYU, QB
1953	John Lattner, Notre Dame, HB	1991	Desmond Howard, Michigan, WR
1954	Ron Beagle, Navy, E	1992	Gino Torretta, Miami (Fla.), QB
1955	Howard Cassady, Ohio St, HB	1993	Charlie Ward, Florida St, QB
1956	Tommy McDonald, Oklahoma, HB	1994	Kerry Collins, Penn St, QB
1957	Bob Reifsnyder, Navy, T	1995	Eddie George, Ohio St, RB
1958	Pete Dawkins, Army, HB	1996	Danny Wuerffel, Florida, QB
1959	Rich Lucas, Penn St, QB	1997	Peyton Manning, Tennessee, QB
1960	Joe Bellino, Navy, HB	1998	Ricky Williams, Texas, RB
1961	Bob Ferguson, Ohio St, FB	1999	Ron Dayne, Wisconsin, RB
1962	Terry Baker, Oregon St, QB	2000	Drew Brees, Purdue, QB
1963	Roger Staubach, Navy, QB	2001	Ken Dorsey, Miami (Fla.), QB
1964	Glenn Ressler, Penn St, C	2002	Larry Johnson, Penn St, RB
1965	Tommy Nobis, Texas, LB	2003	Eli Manning, Mississippi, QB
1966	Jim Lynch, Notre Dame, LB	2004	Jason White, Oklahoma, QB
1967	Gary Beban, UCLA, QB	2005	Vince Young, Texas, QB
1968	O.J. Simpson, USC, RB	2006	Brady Quinn, Notre Dame, QB
1969	Mike Reid, Penn St, DT	2007	Tim Tebow, Florida, QB
1970	Jim Plunkett, Stanford, QB	2008	Tim Tebow, Florida, QB
1971	Ed Marinaro, Cornell, RB	2009	Colt McCoy, Texas, QB
1972	Brad Van Pelt, Michigan St, DB	2010	Cam Newton, Auburn, QB
1973	John Cappelletti, Penn St, RB	2011	Andrew Luck, Stanford, QB
1974	Steve Joachim, Temple, QB		

Davey O'Brien National Quarterback Award

Given to the top quarterback in the nation by the Davey O'Brien Educational and Charitable Trust of Fort Worth. Named for TCU Hall of Fame quarterback Davey O'Brien (1936–38).

Year	Player, College	Year	Player, College
1981	Jim McMahon, BYU	1997	Peyton Manning, Tennessee
1982	Todd Blackledge, Penn St	1998	Michael Bishop, Kansas St
1983	Steve Young, BYU	1999	Joe Hamilton, Georgia Tech
1984	Doug Flutie, Boston College	2000	Chris Weinke, Florida St
1985	Chuck Long, Iowa	2001	Eric Crouch, Nebraska
1986	Vinny Testaverde, Miami (Fla.)	2002	Brad Banks, Iowa
1987	Don McPherson, Syracuse	2003	Jason White, Oklahoma
1988	Troy Aikman, UCLA	2004	Jason White, Oklahoma
1989	Andre Ware, Houston	2005	Vince Young, Texas
1990	Ty Detmer, BYU	2006	Troy Smith, Ohio St
1991	Ty Detmer, BYU	2007	Tim Tebow, Florida
1992	Gino Torretta, Miami (Fla.)	2008	Sam Bradford, Oklahoma
1993	Charlie Ward, Florida St	2009	Colt McCoy, Texas
1994	Kerry Collins, Penn St	2010	Cam Newton, Auburn
1995	Danny Wuerffel, Florida	2011	Robert Griffin III, Baylor
1996	Danny Wuerffel, Florida		

Note: Originally honored the outstanding football player in the Southwest as follows: 1977—Earl Campbell, Texas, RB; 1978—Billy Sims, Oklahoma, RB; 1979—Mike Singletary, Baylor, LB; 1980—Mike Singletary, Baylor, LB.

Vince Lombardi/Rotary Award

Given to the outstanding college lineman or linebacker, the award is sponsored by the Rotary Club of Houston.

Year	Player, College, Position	Year	Player, College, Position
1970	Jim Stillwagon, Ohio St, MG	1991	Steve Emtman, Washington, DT
1971	Walt Patulski, Notre Dame, DE	1992	Marvin Jones, Florida St, LB
1972	Rich Glover, Nebraska, MG	1993	Aaron Taylor, Notre Dame, OT
1973	John Hicks, Ohio St, OT	1994	Warren Sapp, Miami (Fla.), DT
1974	Randy White, Maryland, DT	1995	Orlando Pace, Ohio St, OT
1975	Lee Roy Selmon, Oklahoma, DT	1996	Orlando Pace, Ohio St, OT
1976	Wilson Whitley, Houston, DT	1997	Grant Wistrom, Nebraska, DE
1977	Ross Browner, Notre Dame, DE	1998	Dat Nguyen, Texas A&M, LB
1978	Bruce Clark, Penn St, DT	1999	Corey Moore, Virginia Tech, DE
1979	Brad Budde, USC, G	2000	Jamal Reynolds, Florida St, DE
1980	Hugh Green, Pittsburgh, DE	2001	Julius Peppers, North Carolina, DE
1981	Kenneth Sims, Texas, DT	2002	Terrell Suggs, Arizona St, DL
1982	Dave Rimington, Nebraska, C	2003	Tommie Harris, Oklahoma, DT
1983	Dean Steinkuhler, Nebraska, G	2004	David Pollack, Georgia, DE
1984	Tony Degrate, Texas, DT	2005	A.J. Hawk, Ohio St, LB
1985	Tony Casillas, Oklahoma, NG	2006	LaMarr Woodley, Michigan, DE
1986	Cornelius Bennett, Alabama, LB	2007	Glenn Dorsey, LSU, DT
1987	Chris Spielman, Ohio St, LB	2008	Brian Orakpo, Texas, DE
1988	Tracy Rocker, Auburn, DT	2009	Ndamukong Suh, Nebraska, DT
1989	Percy Snow, Michigan St, LB	2010	Nick Fairley, Auburn, DT
1990	Chris Zorich, Notre Dame, NG	2011	Luke Kuechly, Boston College, LB

Outland Trophy

Given to the outstanding interior lineman, selected by the Football Writers Association of America.

Year	Player, College, Position	Year	Player, College, Position
1946	George Connor, Notre Dame, T	1979	Jim Ritcher, North Carolina St, C
1947	Joe Steffy, Army, G	1980	Mark May, Pittsburgh, OT
1948	Bill Fischer, Notre Dame, G	1981	Dave Rimington, Nebraska, C
1949	Ed Bagdon, Michigan St, G	1982	Dave Rimington, Nebraska, C
1950	Bob Gain, Kentucky, T	1983	Dean Steinkuhler, Nebraska, G
1951	Jim Weatherall, Oklahoma, T	1984	Bruce Smith, Virginia Tech, DT
1952	Dick Modzelewski, Maryland, T	1985	Mike Ruth, Boston College, NG
1953	J.D. Roberts, Oklahoma, G	1986	Jason Buck, BYU, DT
1954	Bill Brooks, Arkansas, G	1987	Chad Hennings, Air Force, DT
1955	Calvin Jones, Iowa, G	1988	Tracy Rocker, Auburn, DT
1956	Jim Parker, Ohio St, G	1989	Mohammed Elewonibi, BYU, G
1957	Alex Karras, Iowa, T	1990	Russell Maryland, Miami (Fla.), DT
1958	Zeke Smith, Auburn, G	1991	Steve Emtman, Washington, DT
1959	Mike McGee, Duke, T	1992	Will Shields, Nebraska, G
1960	Tom Brown, Minnesota, G	1993	Rob Waldrop, Arizona, NG
1961	Merlin Olsen, Utah St, T	1994	Zach Wiegert, Nebraska, G
1962	Bobby Bell, Minnesota, T	1995	Jonathan Ogden, UCLA, OT
1963	Scott Appleton, Texas, T	1996	Orlando Pace, Ohio St, OT
1964	Steve DeLong, Tennessee, T	1997	Aaron Taylor, Nebraska, G
1965	Tommy Nobis, Texas, G	1998	Kris Farris, UCLA, OL
1966	Loyd Phillips, Arkansas, T	1999	Chris Samuels, Alabama, OL
1967	Ron Yary, USC, T	2000	John Henderson, Tennessee, DT
1968	Bill Stanfill, Georgia, T	2001	Bryant McKinnie, Miami (Fla.), OT
1969	Mike Reid, Penn St, DT	2002	Rien Long, Washington St, DL
1970	Jim Stillwagon, Ohio St, MG	2003	Robert Gallery, Iowa, OT
1971	Larry Jacobson, Nebraska, DT	2004	Jammal Brown, Oklahoma, OT
1972	Rich Glover, Nebraska, MG	2005	Greg Eslinger, Minnesota, C
1973	John Hicks, Ohio St, OT	2006	Joe Thomas, Wisconsin, OT
1974	Randy White, Maryland, DE	2007	Glenn Dorsey, LSU, DT
1975	Lee Roy Selmon, Oklahoma, DT	2008	Andre Smith, Alabama, OT
1976	Ross Browner, Notre Dame, DE	2009	Ndamukong Suh, Nebraska, DT
1977	Brad Shearer, Texas, DT	2010	Gabe Carimi, Wisconsin, OT
1978	Greg Roberts, Oklahoma, G	2011	Barrett Jones, Alabama, OT

Butkus Award

Given to the top collegiate linebacker, the award was established by the Downtown Athletic Club of Orlando and named for college Hall of Famer Dick Butkus of Illinois.

Year	Player, College	Year	Player, College
1985	Brian Bosworth, Oklahoma	1999	LaVar Arrington, Penn St
1986	Brian Bosworth, Oklahoma	2000	Dan Morgan, Miami (Fla.)
1987	Paul McGowan, Florida St	2001	Rocky Calmus, Oklahoma
1988	Derrick Thomas, Alabama	2002	E.J. Henderson, Maryland
1989	Percy Snow, Michigan St	2003	Teddy Lehman, Oklahoma
1990	Alfred Williams, Colorado	2004	Derrick Johnson, Texas
1991	Erick Anderson, Michigan	2005	Paul Posluszny, Penn State
1992	Marvin Jones, Florida St	2006	Patrick Willis, Mississippi
1993	Trev Alberts, Nebraska	2007	James Laurinaitis, Ohio St
1994	Dana Howard, Illinois	2008	Aaron Curry, Wake Forest
1995	Kevin Hardy, Illinois	2009	Rolando McClain, Alabama
1996	Matt Russell, Colorado	2010	Von Miller, Texas A&M
1997	Andy Katzenmoyer, Ohio St	2011	Luke Kuechly, Boston College
1998	Chris Claiborne, USC		

Jim Thorpe Award

Given to the best defensive back of the year, the award is presented by the Jim Thorpe Athletic Club of Oklahoma City.

Year	Player, College	Year	Player, College
1986	Thomas Everett, Baylor	1999	Tyrone Carter, Minnesota
1987	Bennie Blades, Miami (Fla.)	2000	Jamar Fletcher, Wisconsin
	Rickey Dixon, Oklahoma	2001	Roy Williams, Oklahoma
1988	Deion Sanders, Florida St	2002	Terence Newman, Kansas St
1989	Mark Carrier, USC	2003	Derrick Strait, Oklahoma
1990	Darryl Lewis, Arizona	2004	Carlos Rogers, Auburn
1991	Terrell Buckley, Florida St	2005	Michael Huff, Texas
1992	Deon Figures, Colorado	2006	Aaron Ross, Texas
1993	Antonio Langham, Alabama	2007	Antoine Cason, Arizona
1994	Chris Hudson, Colorado	2008	Malcolm Jenkins, Ohio St
1995	Greg Myers, Colorado St	2009	Eric Berry, Tennessee
1996	Lawrence Wright, Florida	2010	Patrick Peterson, LSU
1997	Charles Woodson, Michigan	2011	Morris Claiborne, LSU
1998	Antoine Winfield, Ohio St		

Walter Payton Player of the Year Award

Given to the top FCS (I-AA) player, voted by Div. I-AA sports information directors.

Year	Player, College, Position	Year	Player, College, Position
1987	Kenny Gamble, Colgate, RB	2000	Louis Ivory, Furman, RB
1988	Dave Meggett, Towson St, RB	2001	Brian Westbrook, Villanova, RB
1989	John Friesz, Idaho, QB	2002	Tony Romo, Eastern Ilinois, QB
1990	Walter Dean, Grambling, RB	2003	Jamaal Branch, Colgate, RB
1991	Jamie Martin, Weber St, QB	2004	Lang Campbell, William & Mary, QB
1992	Michael Payton, Marshall, QB	2005	Erik Meyer, Eastern Washington, QB
1993	Doug Nussmeier, Idaho, QB	2006	Ricky Santos, New Hampshire, QB
1994	Steve McNair, Alcorn St, QB	2007	Jayson Foster, Georgia Southern, QB
1995	Dave Dickenson, Montana, QB	2008	Armanti Edwards, Appalachian St, QB
1996	Archie Amerson, Northern Arizona, RB	2009	Armanti Edwards, Appalachian St, QB
1997	Brian Finneran, Villanova, WR	2010	Jeremy Moses, Stephen F. Austin, QB
1998	Jerry Azumah, New Hampshire, RB	2011	Bo Levi Mitchell, Eastern Washington, QB
1999	Adrian Peterson, Georgia Southern, RB		

Career

SCORING

Most Points Scored: 468—Travis Prentice, Miami (Ohio), 1996–99
Most Points Scored per Game: 12.1—Marshall Faulk, San Diego St, 1991–93
Most Touchdowns Scored: 78—Travis Prentice, Miami (Ohio), 1996–99 (73 rushing, 5 receiving)
Most Touchdowns Scored per Game: 2.0—Marshall Faulk, San Diego St, 1991–93
Most Touchdowns Scored, Rushing: 73—Travis Prentice, Miami (Ohio), 1996–99
Most Touchdowns Scored, Passing: 155—Case Keenum, Houston, 2007–11; 131—Colt Brennan, Hawaii, 2005–07 (3 years)
Most Touchdowns Scored, Receiving: 60—Jarrett Dillard, Rice, 2005–08
Most Touchdowns Scored, Interception Returns: 5—Ken Thomas, San Jose St, 1979–82; Jackie Walker, Tennessee, 1969–71; Deltha O'Neal, California, 1996–99; Darrent Williams, Okla St, 2001–04
Most Touchdowns Scored, Punt Returns: 8—Wes Welker, Texas Tech, 2000–03; Antonio Perkins, Oklahoma, 2001–04
Most Touchdowns Scored, Kickoff Returns: 7—C.J. Spiller, Clemson, 2006–09

TOTAL OFFENSE

Most Plays: 2,587—Timmy Chang, Hawaii, 2000–04
Most Plays per Game: 50.1—Kliff Kingsbury, Texas Tech, 1999–2002
Most Yards Gained: 20,114—Case Keenum, Houston, 2007–11 (897 rushing, 19,217 passing)
Most Yards Gained per Game: 387.9—Colt Brennan, Hawaii, 2005–07
Most 300+ Yard Games: 40—Case Keenum, Houston, 2007–11

RUSHING

Most Rushes: 1,215—Steve Bartalo, Colorado St, 1983–86 (4,813 yds)
Most Rushes per Game: 34.0—Ed Marinaro, Cornell, 1969–71
Most Yards Gained: 6,397—Ron Dayne, Wisconsin, 1996–99
Most Yards Gained per Game: 174.6—Ed Marinaro, Cornell, 1969–71
Most 100+ Yard Games: 34—DeAngelo Williams, Memphis, 2002–05
Most 200+ Yard Games: 11—Marcus Allen, USC, 1978–81; Ricky Williams, Texas, 1995–98; Ron Dayne, Wisconsin, 1996–99

SPECIAL TEAMS

Highest Punt Return Average: 23.6—Jack Mitchell, Oklahoma, 1946–48
††Highest Kickoff Return Average: 35.1—Anthony Davis, Southern California, 1972–74
Highest Average Yards per Punt: 46.3—Todd Sauerbrun, West Virginia, 1991–93 (150–199 punts). 45.3—Ryan Plackemeier, Wake Forest, 2002–05 (200-250 punts). 45.2—Daniel Sepulveda, Baylor, 2003–06 (250+ punts).

†Minimum 200 receptions.
‡Minimum 275 plays.
††Minimum 1.2 returns per game and 30 returns.

PASSING

Highest Passing Efficiency Rating: 175.6—Sam Bradford, Oklahoma, 2007–09 (min. 325 comp.)
Most Passes Attempted: 2,436—Timmy Chang, Hawaii, 2000–04
Most Passes Attempted per Game: 47.0—Tim Rattay, Louisiana Tech, 1997–99
Most Passes Completed: 1,546—Case Keenum, Houston, 2007–11
Most Passes Completed per Game: 31.2—Graham Harrell, Texas Tech, 2005–08
Highest Completion Percentage: 70.4—Colt Brennan, Hawaii, 2005–07
Most Yards Gained: 19,217—Case Keenum, Houston, 2007–11
Most Yards Gained per Game: 386.2—Tim Rattay, Louisiana Tech, 1997–99 (3 years); 351.0—Graham Harrell, Texas Tech, 2005–08 (4 years)

RECEIVING

Most Passes Caught: 349—Ryan Broyles, Oklahoma, 2008-11 (4,586 yards)
Most Passes Caught per Game: 10.5—Emmanuel Hazard, Houston, 1989–90
Most Yards Gained: 5,005—Trevor Insley, Nevada, 1996–99
Most Yards Gained per Game: 140.9—Alex Van Dyke, Nevada, 1994–95
†Highest Average Gain per Reception: 19.0—Ryan Yarborough, Wyoming, 1990–93

ALL-PURPOSE RUNNING

Most Plays: 1,347—Steve Bartalo, Colorado St, 1983-86 (1,215 rushes, 132 receptions)
Most Yards Gained: 7,796—Damaris Johnson, Tulsa, 2008–11 (1,062 rushing, 2,746 receiving, 3,417 KO returns)
Most Yards Gained per Game: 237.8—Ryan Benjamin, Pacific, 1990–92
‡Highest Average Gain per Play: 17.4—Anthony Carter, Michigan, 1979–82

INTERCEPTIONS

Most Passes Intercepted: 29—Al Brosky, Illinois, 1950–52
Most Passes Intercepted per Game: 1.1—Al Brosky, Illinois, 1950–52
Most Yards on Interception Returns: 501—Terrell Buckley, Florida St, 1989–91
Highest Average Gain per Interception: 26.5—Tom Pridemore, West Virginia, 1975–77

Single Season

SCORING

Most Points Scored: 234—Barry Sanders, Oklahoma St, 1988; Montee Ball, Wisconsin, 2011
Most Points Scored per Game: 21.3—Barry Sanders, Oklahoma St, 1988
Most Touchdowns Scored: 39—Barry Sanders, Oklahoma St, 1988; Montee Ball, Wisconsin, 2011
Most Touchdowns Scored, Rushing: 37—Barry Sanders, Oklahoma St, 1988
Most Touchdowns Scored, Passing: 58—Colt Brennan, Hawaii, 2006
Most Touchdowns Scored, Receiving: 27—Troy Edwards, Louisiana Tech, 1998
Most Touchdowns Scored, Interception Returns: 4—Deltha O'Neal, California, 1999
Most Touchdowns Scored, Punt Returns: 5—Chad Owens, Hawaii, 2004
Most Touchdowns Scored, Kickoff Returns: 5—Ashlan Davis, Tulsa, 2004

TOTAL OFFENSE

Most Plays: 814—Kliff Kingsbury, Texas Tech, 2002
Most Yards Gained: 5,976—B.J. Symons, Texas Tech, 2003
Most Yards Gained per Game: 474.6—David Klingler, Houston, 1990
Most 300+ Yard Games: 14—Colt Brennan, Hawaii, 2006; Paul Smith, Tulsa, 2007

RUSHING

Most Rushes: 450—Kevin Smith, Central Florida, 2007
Most Rushes per Game: 39.6—Ed Marinaro, Cornell, 1971
Most Yards Gained: 2,628—Barry Sanders, Oklahoma St, 1988
Most Yards Gained per Game: 238.9—Barry Sanders, Oklahoma St, 1988
Most 100+ Yard Games: 13—Shonn Greene, Iowa, 2008

PASSING

Highest Passing Efficiency Rating: 191.78—Russell Wilson, Wisconsin, 2011
Most Passes Attempted: 719—B.J. Symons, Texas Tech, 2003
Most Passes Attempted per Game: 58.5—David Klingler, Houston, 1990
Most Passes Completed: 512—Graham Harrell, Texas Tech, 2007

PASSING *(Cont.)*

Most Passes Completed per Game: 39.4—Graham Harrell, Texas Tech, 2007
Highest Completion Percentage: 76.7—Colt McCoy, Texas, 2008
Most Yards Gained: 5,140—David Klingler, Houston, 1990 (11 games); 5,336—B.J. Symons, Texas Tech, 2003 (12 games); 5,833—B.J. Symons, Texas Tech, 2003 (13-plus games)
Most Yards Gained per Game: 467.3—David Klingler, Houston, 1990

RECEIVING

Most Passes Caught: 155—Freddie Barnes, Bowling Green, 2009
Most Passes Caught per Game: 13.4—Howard Twilley, Tulsa, 1965
Most Yards Gained: 2,060—Trevor Insley, Nevada, 1999
Most Yards Gained per Game: 187.3—Trevor Insley, Nevada, 1999
Highest Average Gain per Reception: 31.9—Brennan Marion, Tulsa, 2007 (min. 30 receptions)

ALL-PURPOSE RUNNING

Most Plays: 432—Marcus Allen, USC, 1981
Most Yards Gained: 3,250—Barry Sanders, Oklahoma St, 1988
Most Yards Gained per Game: 295.5—Barry Sanders, Oklahoma St, 1988
Highest Average Gain per Play: 21.2—Taveon Rogers, New Mexico St, 2011 (min.100 plays)

INTERCEPTIONS

Most Passes Intercepted: 14—Al Worley, Washington, 1968
Most Yards on Interception Returns: 302—Charles Phillips, USC, 1974
Highest Average Gain per Interception: 51.8—Norm Thompson, Utah, 1969

SPECIAL TEAMS

Highest Punt Return Average: 28.5—Maurice Drew, UCLA, 2005
Highest Kickoff Return Average: 40.1—Paul Allen, BYU, 1961
Highest Average Yards per Punt: 50.3—Chad Kessler, LSU, 1997 (min. 36 punts)

Single Game

SCORING

Most Points Scored: 48—Howard Griffith, Illinois, 1990 (vs Southern Illinois)
Most Field Goals: 7—Dale Klein, Nebraska, 1985 (vs Missouri); Mike Prindle, Western Michigan, 1984 (vs Marshall)
Most Extra Points (Kick): 13—Derek Mahoney, Fresno St, 1991 (vs New Mexico); Terry Leiweke, Houston, 1968 (vs Tulsa)
Most Extra Points (2-Pts): 6—Jim Pilot, New Mexico St, 1961 (vs Hardin-Simmons), all 6 rush

PASSING

Most Passes Completed: 58—Andy Schmitt, Eastern Michigan, 2008 (vs Central Michigan)
Most Yards Gained: 716—David Klingler, Houston, 1990 (vs Arizona St)
Most Touchdown Passes: 11—David Klingler, Houston, 1990 [vs Eastern Washington (I-AA)]

TOTAL OFFENSE

Most Yards Gained: 732—David Klingler, Houston, 1990 (vs Arizona St); (716 pass, 16 rush)

RUSHING

Most Yards Gained: 406—LaDainian Tomlinson, TCU, 1999 (vs UTEP)
Most Touchdowns Rushed: 8—Howard Griffith, Illinois, 1990 (vs Southern Illinois)

RECEIVING

Most Passes Caught: 23—Randy Gatewood, UNLV, 1994 (vs Idaho); Tyler Jones, Eastern Michigan, 2008 (vs Central Michigan)
Most Yards Gained: 405—Troy Edwards, Louisiana Tech, 1998 (vs Nebraska)
Most Touchdown Catches: 7—Rashaun Woods, Oklahoma St, 2003 (vs SMU)

Career

SCORING

Most Points Scored: 544—Brian Westbrook, Villanova, 1997–98, 2000-01
Most Touchdowns Scored: 89—Brian Westbrook, Villanova, 1997–98, 2000-01
Most Touchdowns Scored, Rushing: 84—Adrian Peterson, Georgia Southern, 1998–2001
Most Touchdowns Scored, Passing: 140—Bruce Eugene, Grambling St, 2001–05
Most Touchdowns Scored, Receiving: 58—David Ball, New Hampshire, 2003–06

RUSHING

Most Rushes: 1,240—Jordan Scott, Colgate, 2005–08
Most Rushes per Game: 38.2—Arnold Mickens, Butler, 1994–95
Most Yards Gained: 6,559—Adrian Peterson, Georgia Southern, 1998–2001
Most Yards Gained per Game: 190.7—Arnold Mickens, Butler, 1994–95 (2 years); 164.5—Adrian Peterson, Georgia Southern, 1998–2000 (3 years); 156.2—Adrian Peterson, Georgia Southern, 1998–2001 (4 years)

PASSING

Highest Passing Efficiency Rating: 176.7—Josh Johnson, San Diego, 2004–07
Most Passes Attempted: 1,893—Jeremy Moses, Stephen F. Austin, 2007–10
Most Passes Completed: 1,184—Jeremy Moses, Stephen F. Austin, 2007–10
Most Passes Completed per Game: 26.9—Jeremy Moses, Stephen F. Austin, 2007–10
Highest Completion Percentage: 69.6—Eric Sanders, Northern Iowa, 2004–07
Most Yards Gained: 14,496—Steve McNair, Alcorn St, 1991–94
Most Yards Gained per Game: 350.0—Neil Lomax, Portland St, 1978–80

RECEIVING

Most Passes Caught: 395—Terrell Hudgins, Elon, 2006–09
Most Yards Gained: 5,250—Terrell Hudgins, Elon, 2006–09
Most Yards Gained per Game: 116.7—Terrell Hudgins, Elon, 2006–09 (min. 3,000 yds)
Highest Average Gain per Reception: 22.0—Dedric Ward, Northern Iowa, 1993–96 (min. 125 rec.)

Single Season

SCORING

Most Points Scored: 234—Omar Cuff, Delaware, 2007
Most Touchdowns Scored: 39—Omar Cuff, Delaware, 2007 (15 games)
Most Touchdowns Scored, Rushing: 35—Omar Cuff, Delaware, 2007
Most Touchdowns Scored, Passing: 56—Willie Totten, Mississippi Valley St, 1984; Bruce Eugene, Grambling St, 2005
Most Touchdowns Scored, Receiving: 27—Jerry Rice, Mississippi Valley St, 1984

PASSING

Highest Passing Efficiency Rating: 204.6—Shawn Knight, William & Mary, 1993
Most Passes Attempted: 598—Jeremy Moses, Stephen F. Austin, 2008
Most Passes Completed: 385—Brett Gordon, Villanova, 2002; Jeremy Moses, Stephen F. Austin, 2009
Most Passes Completed per Game: 32.4—Willie Totten, Mississippi Valley St, 1984
Highest Completion Percentage: 75.2—Eric Sanders, Northern Iowa, 2007
Most Yards Gained: 4,863—Steve McNair, Alcorn St, 1994
Most Yards Gained per Game: 455.7—Willie Totten, Mississippi Valley St, 1984

RUSHING

Most Rushes: 450—Jamaal Branch, Colgate, 2003
Most Rushes per Game: 40.9—Arnold Mickens, Butler, 1994
Most Yards Gained: 2,326—Jamaal Branch, Colgate, 2003
Most Yards Gained per Game: 225.5—Arnold Mickens, Butler, 1994

RECEIVING

Most Passes Caught: 123—Terrell Hudgins, Elon, 2009
Most Yards Gained: 1,712—Eddie Conti, Delaware, 1998
Most Yards Gained per Game: 168.2—Jerry Rice, Mississippi Valley St, 1984
Highest Average Gain per Reception: 28.9—Mikhael Ricks, Stephen F. Austin, 1997; (min. 35 receptions); 20.7—Golden Tate, Tennessee St, 1983 (min 60 receptions)

Single Game

SCORING

Most Points Scored: 42—Omar Cuff, Delaware, 2007 (vs William & Mary); Jesse Burton, McNeese St, 1998 (vs Southern Utah); Archie Amerson, Northern Arizona, 1996 (vs Weber St)
Most Field Goals: 8—Goran Lingmerth, Northern Arizona, 1986 (vs Idaho)

RUSHING

Most Yards Gained: 437—Maurice Hicks, North Carolina A&T, 2001 (vs Morgan St)
Most Touchdowns Rushed: 7—Archie Amerson, Northern Arizona, 1996 (vs Weber St)

PASSING

Most Passes Completed: 57—Jeremy Moses, Stephen F. Austin, 2008, (vs. Sam Houston St)
Most Yards Gained: 624—Jamie Martin, Weber St, 1991 (vs Idaho St)
Most Touchdown Passes: 9—Willie Totten, Mississippi Valley St, 1984 (vs Kentucky St); Drew Hubel, Portland St, 2007 (vs Weber St)

RECEIVING

Most Passes Caught: 24—Chas Gessner, Brown, 2002, (vs Rhode Island); Jerry Rice, Mississippi Valley St, 1983 (vs Southern–Birmingham)
Most Yards Gained: 376—Kassim Osgood, Cal Poly, 2000 (vs Northern Iowa)
Most Touchdown Catches: 6—Cos DeMatteo, Chattanooga, 2000 (vs Mississippi Valley St)

NCAA Division II Individual Records

Career

SCORING

Most Points Scored: 656—Germaine Rice, Pittsburg St, 2003–06
Most Touchdowns Scored: 109—Germaine Rice, Pittsburg St, 2003–06; Danny Woodhead, Chadron St 2004–07
Most Touchdowns Scored, Rushing: 107—Germaine Rice, Pittsburg St, 2003–06
Most Touchdowns Scored, Passing: 148—Jimmy Terwilliger, East Stroudsburg, 2003–06
Most Touchdowns Scored, Receiving: 78—Dallas Mall, Bentley, 2001–04

RUSHING

Most Rushes: 1,271—Xavier Omon, NW Missouri St, 2004–07
Most Rushes per Game: 29.8—Bernie Peeters, Luther, 1968–71
Most Yards Gained: 7,962—Danny Woodhead, Chadron St, 2004–07
Most Yards Gained per Game: 183.4—Anthony Gray, Western New Mexico, 1997–98

PASSING

Highest Passing Efficiency Rating: 170.7—Jimmy Terwilliger, East Stroudsburg, 2003–06 (Min. 750 comps.)
Most Passes Attempted: 1,898—Andrew Webb, Fort Lewis, 2000–03

PASSING *(Cont.)*

Most Passes Completed: 1,119—Steven Gachette, Southwest Baptist, 2007–10
Most Passes Completed per Game: 25.9—Evan Gray, Missouri S&T*, 2003–05
Highest Completion Percentage: 70.2—Troy Weatherhead, Hillsdale, 2006–10 (min. 1,000 att.)
Most Yards Gained: 14,733—Zach Amedro, West Liberty, 2007–10
Most Yards Gained per Game: 334.8—Zach Amedro, West Liberty, 2007–10

RECEIVING

Most Passes Caught: 323—Clarence Coleman, Ferris St, 1998–2001
Most Yards Gained: 4,983—Clarence Coleman, Ferris St, 1998–2001
Most Yards Gained per Game: 160.8—Chris George, Glenville St, 1993–94
Highest Average Gain per Reception: 23.2—Romar Crenshaw, SE Oklahoma, 2000–03 (min. 135 receptions)

*Missouri S&T was formerly known as Missouri-Rolla.

Single Season

SCORING

Most Points Scored: 228—Xavier Odom, Northwest Missouri St, 2007; Danny Woodhead, Chadron St, 2006

Most Touchdowns Scored: 38—Xavier Omon, NW Missouri St, 2007; Danny Woodhead, Chadron St, 2006

Most Touchdowns Scored, Rushing: 37—Xavier Omon, NW Missouri St, 2007

Most Touchdowns Scored, Passing: 54—Dusty Bonner, Valdosta St, 2000

Most Touchdowns Scored, Receiving: 35—David Kircus, Grand Valley St, 2002

RUSHING

Most Rushes: 385—Joe Gough, Wayne St (Mich.), 1994

Most Rushes per Game: 38.6—Mark Perkins, Hobart, 1968

Most Yards Gained: 2,756—Danny Woodhead, Chadron St, 2006

Most Yards Gained per Game: 222.0—Anthony Gray, Western New Mexico, 1997

PASSING

Highest Passing Efficiency Rating: 221.6—Curt Anes, Grand Valley St, 2001 (min. 100 comp.); 196.5—Dusty Bonner, Valdosta St, 2001 (min. 200 comp.)

Most Passes Attempted: 670—Eric Czerniewski, Central Missouri, 2010

Most Passes Completed: 447—Eric Czerniewski, Central Missouri, 2010

Most Passes Completed per Game: 40.4—J.J. Harp, Eastern New Mexico, 2009

Highest Completion Percentage: 76.9—Troy Weatherhead, Hillsdale, 2010 (min. 250 att.)

Most Yards Gained: 5,207—Eric Czerniewski, Central Missouri, 2010

Most Yards Gained per Game: 437.3—J.J. Harp, Eastern New Mexico, 2009

RECEIVING

Most Passes Caught: 143—Nick Smart, Southwest Baptist, 2007

Most Yards Gained: 1,876—Chris George, Glenville St, 1993

Most Yards Gained per Game: 187.6—Chris George, Glenville St, 1993

Highest Average Gain per Reception: 32.5—Tyrone Johnson, Western St, 1991 (min. 30 receptions)

Single Game

SCORING

Most Points Scored: 48—Paul Zaeske, North Park, 1968 (vs North Central [Ill.]); Junior Wolf, Okla. Panhandle St, 1958 (vs St. Mary [Ks.])

Most Field Goals: 6—Steve Huff, Central Missouri St, 1985 (vs SE Missouri St); Austin Wellock, Ashland, 2002 (vs. Wayne St)

RUSHING

Most Yards Gained: 418—Jarom Freeman, Southern Connecticut St, 2007 (vs Bryant)

Most Touchdowns Rushed: 8—Junior Wolf, Okla. Panhandle St, 1958 (vs St. Mary [Ks.])

PASSING

Most Passes Completed: 64—J.J. Harp, Eastern New Mexico, 2009 (vs SE Oklahoma)

Most Yards Gained: 695—J.J. Harp, Eastern New Mexico, 2009 (vs SE Oklahoma)

Most Touchdowns Passed: 10—Bruce Swanson, North Park, 1968 (vs North Central [Ill.])

RECEIVING

Most Passes Caught: 23—Chris George, Glenville St, 1994 (vs W.V. Wesleyan); Barry Wagner, Alabama A&M, 1989 (vs Clark Atlanta)

Most Yards Gained: 401—Kevin Ingram, West Chester, 1998 (vs Clarion)

Most Touchdown Catches: 8—Paul Zaeske, North Park, 1968 (vs North Central [Ill.])

NCAA Division III Individual Records

Career

SCORING

Most Points Scored: 780—Nate Kmic, Mount Union, 2005–08

Most Touchdowns Scored: 130—Nate Kmic, Mount Union, 2005–08

Most Touchdowns Scored, Rushing: 125—Nate Kmic, Mount Union, 2005–08

Most Touchdowns Scored, Passing: 148—Justin Peery, Westminster (Mo.), 1996–99

Most Touchdowns Scored, Receiving: 75—Scott Pingel, Westminster (Mo.), 1996–99

RUSHING

Most Rushes: 1,324—Levell Coppage, Wis.-Whitewater, 2008-11

Most Rushes per Game: 32.7—Chris Sizemore, Bridgewater (Va.), 1972–74

RUSHING (*Cont.*)

Most Yards Gained: 8,074—Nate Kmic, Mount Union, 2005–08

Most Yards Gained per Game: 187.1—Tony Sutton, Wooster, 2002–04

PASSING

Highest Passing Efficiency Rating: 194.2—Greg Micheli, Mount Union, 2005–08 (min. 325 comps.)

Most Passes Attempted: 1,982—Josh Vogelbach, Guilford, 2005–08

Most Passes Completed: 1,205—Alex Tanney, Monmouth (IL), 2007-11

Most Passes Completed per Game: 29.7—Josh Vogelbach, Guilford, 2005–08

Highest Completion Percentage: 74.1—Greg Micheli, Mount Union, 2005–08 (min. 750 att.)

Career *(Cont.)*

PASSING *(Cont.)*

Most Yards Gained: 14,249—Alex Tanney, Monmouth (IL), 2007-11
Most Yards Gained per Game: 358.9—Brett Elliott, Linfield, 2004–05

RECEIVING

Most Passes Caught: 463—Michael Zweifel, Wis.-River Falls/Dubuque
Most Yards Gained: 6,108—Scott Pingel, Westminster (Mo.), 1996–99
Most Yards Gained per Game: 156.6—Scott Pingel, Westminster (Mo.), 1996–99
Highest Average Gain per Reception: 23.4—Michael Coleman, Widener, 1998–2001

Single Season

SCORING

Most Points Scored: 264—Nate Kmic, Mount Union, 2008
Most Points Scored per Game: 20.8—James Regan, Pomona-Pitzer, 1997
Most Touchdowns Scored: 44—Nate Kmic, Mount Union, 2008
Most Touchdowns Scored, Rushing: 43—Nate Kmic, Mount Union, 2008
Most Touchdowns Scored, Passing: 61—Brett Elliott, Linfield, 2004
Most Touchdowns Scored, Receiving: 26—Scott Pingel, Westminster (Mo.), 1998; Jack Phelan, Hartwick, 2008

RUSHING

Most Rushes: 463—Dante Washington, Carthage, 2004
Most Rushes per Game: 38.0—Mike Birosak, Dickinson, 1989
Most Yards Gained: 2,790—Nate Kmic, Mount Union, 2008
Most Yards Gained per Game: 238.5—Dante Brown, Marietta, 1996

PASSING

Highest Passing Efficiency Rating: 225.0—Mike Simpson, Eureka, 1994
Most Passes Attempted: 575—Brett Dietz, Hanover, 2003
Most Passes Completed: 360—Brett Dietz, Hanover, 2003
Most Passes Completed per Game: 32.9—Justin Peery, Westminster (Mo.), 1999
Highest Completion Percentage: 75.0—Greg Micheli, Mount Union, 2008
Most Yards Gained: 4,595—Brett Elliott, Linfield, 2004
Most Yards Gained per Game: 450.1—Justin Peery, Westminster (Mo.), 1998

RECEIVING

Most Passes Caught: 140—Michael Zweifel, Dubuque, 2011
Most Yards Gained: 2,157—Scott Pingel, Westminster, (Mo.), 1998
Most Yards Gained per Game: 215.7—Scott Pingel, Westminster, (Mo.), 1998
Highest Average Gain per Reception: 26.9—Marty Redlawsk, Concordia (Ill.), 1985 (min. 35 receptions)

Single Game

SCORING

Most Points Scored: 48—Carey Bender, Coe, 1994 (vs Beloit)
Most Field Goals: 6—Jim Hever, Rhodes, 1984 (vs Millsaps)

PASSING

Most Passes Completed: 56—Brandon Luczak, Kalamazoo, 2009 (vs Hope)
Most Yards Gained: 731—Zamir Amin, Menlo, 2000 (vs California Lutheran)
Most Touchdown Passes: 9—Joe Zarlinga, Ohio Northern, 1998 (vs Capital)

RUSHING

Most Yards Gained: 441—Dante Brown, Marietta, 1996 (vs Baldwin-Wallace)
Most Touchdowns Rushed: 8—Carey Bender, Coe, 1994 (vs Beloit)

RECEIVING

Most Passes Caught: 25—Daniel Passafiume, Hanover, 2009 (vs Franklin)
Most Yards Gained: 418—Lewis Howes, Principia, 2002 (vs Martin Luther)
Most Touchdown Catches: 7—Matt Perceval, Wesleyan (Conn.), 1998 (vs Middlebury)

Career

Scoring

POINTS (KICKERS)

	Years	Pts
Kyle Brotzman, Boise St	2007–10	439
Art Carmody, Louisville	2004–07	433
‡Kevin Kelly, Penn St	2005–08	425
Roman Anderson, Houston	1988–91	423
Blair Walsh, Georgia	2008–11	412

‡includes one TD and one 2-pt. conversion (rush)

POINTS (NON-KICKERS)

	Years	Pts
Travis Prentice, Miami (Ohio)	1996–99	468
Ricky Williams, Texas	1995–98	452
Taurean Henderson, Texas Tech	2002–05	414
Brock Forsey, Boise St	1999–02	408
Cedric Benson, Texas	2001–04	404

POINTS PER GAME (NON-KICKERS)

	Years	Pts/Game
Marshall Faulk, San Diego St	1991–93	12.1
Ed Marinaro, Cornell	1969–71	11.8
Bill Burnett, Arkansas	1968–70	11.3
Steve Owens, Oklahoma	1967–69	11.2
Eddie Talboom, Wyoming	1948–50	10.8

Total Offense

YARDS GAINED

	Years	Yds
Case Keenum, Houston	2007–11	20,114
Timmy Chang, Hawaii	2000–04	16,910
Dan LeFevour, Central Michigan	2006–09	15,853
Graham Harrell, Texas Tech	2005–08	15,599
Colt McCoy, Texas	2006–09	14,824
Kellen Moore, Boise St	2008–11	14,534

YARDS PER GAME

	Years	Yds/Game
Colt Brennan, Hawaii	2005–07	387.9
Tim Rattay, Louisiana Tech	1997–99	382.4
Case Keenum, Houston	2007–11	352.9
Graham Harrell, Texas Tech	2005–08	346.6
Chase Holbrook, New Mexico St	2005–08	321.4

Rushing

YARDS GAINED

	Years	Yds
Ron Dayne, Wisconsin	1996–99	6,397
Ricky Williams, Texas	1995–98	6,279
Tony Dorsett, Pittsburgh	1973–76	6,082
DeAngelo Williams, Memphis	2002–05	6,026
Charles White, USC	1976–79	5,598
Travis Prentice, Miami (Ohio)	1996–99	5,596

YARDS PER GAME

	Years	Yds/Game
Ed Marinaro, Cornell	1969–71	174.6
O.J. Simpson, USC	1967–68	164.4
Herschel Walker, Georgia	1980–82	159.4
Garrett Wolfe, Northern Illinois	2004–06	156.5
LeShon Johnson, Northern Illinois	1992–93	150.6

TOUCHDOWNS RUSHING

	Years	TD
Travis Prentice, Miami (Ohio)	1996–99	73
Ricky Williams, Texas	1995–98	72
Anthony Thompson, Indiana	1986–89	64
Cedric Benson, Texas	2001–04	64
Ron Dayne, Wisconsin	1996–99	63

Passing

PASSING EFFICIENCY

	Years	Rating
Sam Bradford, Oklahoma	2007–09	175.6
Tim Tebow, Florida	2006–09	170.8
Kellen Moore, Boise St	2008–11	169.0
Ryan Dinwiddie, Boise St	2000–03	168.9
Colt Brennan, Hawaii	2005–07	167.7

Note: Minimum 500 completions.

YARDS GAINED

	Years	Yds
Case Keenum, Houston	2007–11	19,217
Timmy Chang, Hawaii	2000–04	17,072
Graham Harrell, Texas Tech	2005–08	15,793
Ty Detmer, BYU	1988–91	15,031
Kellen Moore, Boise St	2008–11	14,667

COMPLETIONS

	Years	Comp
Case Keenum, Houston	2007–11	1,546
Graham Harrell, Texas Tech	2005–08	1,403
Timmy Chang, Hawaii	2000–04	1,388
Kliff Kingsbury, Texas Tech	1999–02	1,231
Dan LeFevour, Central Michigan	2006–09	1,171

TOUCHDOWNS PASSING

	Years	TD
Case Keenum, Houston	2007–11	155
Kellen Moore, Boise St	2008–11	142
Graham Harrell, Texas Tech	2005–08	134
Colt Brennan, Hawaii	2005–07	131
Ty Detmer, BYU	1988–91	121

Receiving

CATCHES

	Years	No.
Ryan Broyles, Oklahoma	2008–11	349
Tyron Carrier, Houston	2008–11	320
Taylor Stubblefield, Purdue	2001–04	316
Josh Davis, Marshall	2001–04	306
Jordan White, W Michigan	2007–11	306
Eric Page, Toledo	2009–11	306

CATCHES PER GAME

	Years	No./Game
Emmanuel Hazard, Houston	1989–90	10.5
Alex Van Dyke, Nevada	1994–95	10.3
Howard Twilley, Tulsa	1963–65	10.0
Jason Phillips, Houston	1987–88	9.4
Michael Crabtree, Texas Tech	2007–08	8.9

YARDS GAINED

	Years	Yds
Trevor Insley, Nevada	1996–99	5,005
Ryan Broyles, Oklahoma	2008–11	4,586
Marcus Harris, Wyoming	1993–96	4,518
Patrick Edwards, Houston	2008–11	4,507
Rashaun Woods, Oklahoma St	2000–03	4,414

TOUCHDOWN CATCHES

	Years	TD
Jarrett Dillard, Rice	2005–08	60
Troy Edwards, Louisiana Tech	1996–98	50
Darius Watts, Marshall	2000–03	47
Ryan Broyles, Oklahoma	2008–11	45
Patrick Edwards, Houston	2008–11	43
Aaron Turner, Pacific	1989–92	43

Career (*Cont.*)

All-Purpose Running

YARDS GAINED	Years	Yds
Damaris Johnson, Tulsa	2008–10	7,796
Brandon West, Western Michigan	2006–09	7,764
C.J. Spiller, Clemson	2006–09	7,588
DeAngelo Williams, Memphis	2002–05	7,573
T.Y. Hilton, FIU	2008–11	7,498

YARDS PER GAME	Years	Yds/Game
Ryan Benjamin, Pacific	1990–92	237.8
Sheldon Canley, San Jose St	1988–90	205.8
Jeremy Maclin, Missouri	2007–08	200.3
Damaris Johnson, Tulsa	2008–10	194.9
Howard Stevens, Louisville	1971–72	193.7

Interceptions

PLAYER/SCHOOL	Years	Int
Al Brosky, Illinois	1950–52	29
John Provost, Holy Cross	1972–74	27
Martin Bayless, Bowling Green	1980–83	27
Tom Curtis, Michigan	1967–69	25
Tony Thurman, Boston College	1981–84	25
Tracy Saul, Texas Tech	1989–92	25

Punting Average

PLAYER/SCHOOL	Years	Avg
Daniel Sepulveda, Baylor	2003–06	45.24
Shane Lechler, Texas A&M	1996–99	44.69
Bill Smith, Mississippi	1983–86	44.33
Jim Arnold, Vanderbilt	1979–82	43.94
Bryan Anger, California	2008–11	43.74

Note: Minimum 250 punts.

Punt Return Average

PLAYER/SCHOOL	Years	Avg
Jack Mitchell, Oklahoma	1946–48	23.6
Gene Gibson, Cincinnati	1949–50	20.5
Eddie Macon, Pacific	1949–51	18.9
Jackie Robinson, UCLA	1939–40	18.8
Dan Shelton, Illinois	2001–04	17.9

Note: Minimum 30 returns.

Kickoff Return Average

PLAYER/SCHOOL	Years	Avg
Anthony Davis, USC	1972–74	35.1
Eric Booth, Southern Miss	1994–97	32.4
Overton Curtis, Utah St	1957–58	31.0
Justin Miller, Clemson	2001–04	30.7
Fred Montgomery, New Mexico St	1991–92	30.5
Bryan Williams, Akron	2005–08	30.5

Note: Minimum 30 returns.

Single Season

Scoring

POINTS	Year	Pts
Barry Sanders, Oklahoma St	1988	234
Montee Ball, Wisconsin	2011	234
Brock Forsey, Boise St	2002	192
Troy Edwards, Louisiana Tech	1998	186
Kevin Smith, Central Florida	2007	180

FIELD GOALS	Year	FG
Billy Bennett, Georgia	2003	31
Leigh Tiffin, Alabama	2009	30
John Lee, UCLA	1984	29
John Sullivan, New Mexico	2007	29
Randy Bullock, Texas A&M	2011	29

All-Purpose Running

YARDS GAINED	Year	Yds
Barry Sanders, Oklahoma St	1988	3,250
Ryan Benjamin, Pacific	1991	2,995
Chris Johnson, East Carolina	2007	2,960
Jeremy Maclin, Missouri	2008	2,833
Kevin Smith, Central Florida	2007	2,809

YARDS PER GAME	Year	Yds/Game
Barry Sanders, Oklahoma St	1988	295.5
Ryan Benjamin, Pacific	1991	249.6
Byron (Whizzer) White, Colorado	1937	246.3
Mike Pringle, Fullerton St	1989	244.6
Paul Palmer, Temple	1986	239.4

*Active player.

Total Offense

YARDS GAINED	Year	Yds
B.J. Symons, Texas Tech	2003	5,976
Colt Brennan, Hawaii	2006	5,915
Case Keenum, Houston	2009	5,829
Case Keenum, Houston	2011	5,666
Graham Harrell, Texas Tech	2007	5,614

Total Offense (*Cont.*)

YARDS PER GAME	Year	Yds/Game
David Klingler, Houston	1990	474.6
B.J. Symons, Texas Tech	2003	459.7
Graham Harrell, Texas Tech	2007	431.8
Andre Ware, Houston	1989	423.7
Colt Brennan, Hawaii	2006	422.5

Rushing

YARDS GAINED	Year	Yds
Barry Sanders, Oklahoma St	1988	2,628
Kevin Smith, Central Florida	2007	2,567
Marcus Allen, USC	1981	2,342
Troy Davis, Iowa St	1996	2,185
LaDainian Tomlinson, TCU	2000	2,158

YARDS PER GAME	Year	Yds/Game
Barry Sanders, Oklahoma St	1988	238.9
Marcus Allen, USC	1981	212.9
Ed Marinaro, Cornell	1971	209.0
Troy Davis, Iowa St	1996	198.6
LaDainian Tomlinson, TCU	2000	196.2

TOUCHDOWNS RUSHING	Year	TD
Barry Sanders, Oklahoma St	1988	37
Montee Ball, Wisconsin	2011	33
Mike Rozier, Nebraska	1983	29
Kevin Smith, Central Florida	2007	29
Willis McGahee, Miami (Fla.)	2002	28
Toby Gerhart, Stanford	2009	28

Passing

PASSING EFFICIENCY	Year	Rating
Russell Wilson, Wisconsin	2011	191.8
Robert Griffin III, Baylor	2011	189.5
Colt Brennan, Hawaii	2006	186.0
Shaun King, Tulane	1998	183.3
Kellen Moore, Boise St	2010	182.6

Single Season *(Cont.)*

Passing *(Cont.)*

YARDS GAINED

	Year	Yds
B.J. Symons, Texas Tech	2003	5,833
Graham Harrell, Texas Tech	2007	5,705
Case Keenum, Houston	2009	5,671
Case Keenum, Houston	2011	5,631
Colt Brennan, Hawaii	2006	5,549

COMPLETIONS

	Year	Att	Comp
Graham Harrell, Texas Tech	2007	713	512
Case Keenum, Houston	2009	700	492
Kliff Kingsbury, Texas Tech	2002	712	479
B.J. Symons, Texas Tech	2003	719	470
Graham Harrell, Texas Tech	2008	626	442

TOUCHDOWNS PASSING

	Year	TD
Colt Brennan, Hawaii	2006	58
David Klingler, Houston	1990	54
B.J. Symons, Texas Tech	2003	52
Sam Bradford, Oklahoma	2008	50
Graham Harrell, Texas Tech	2007	48
Case Keenum, Houston	2011	48

Receiving

CATCHES

	Year	GP	No.
Freddie Barnes, Bowling Green	2009	13	155
Emmanuel Hazard, Houston	1989	11	142
Troy Edwards, Louisiana Tech	1998	12	140
Jordan White, W Michigan	2011	13	140
Nate Burleson, Nevada	2002	12	138

Receiving *(Cont.)*

CATCHES

	Year	GP	No.
Howard Twilley, Tulsa	1965	10	134
Trevor Insley, Nevada	1999	11	134
Michael Crabtree, Texas Tech	2008	13	134

CATCHES PER GAME

	Year	No.	No./Game
Howard Twilley, Tulsa	1965	134	13.4
Emmanuel Hazard, Houston	1989	142	12.9
Trevor Insley, Nevada	1999	134	12.2
Freddie Barnes, Bowling Green	2009	155	11.9
Alex Van Dyke, Nevada	1995	129	11.7
Troy Edwards, Louisiana Tech	1998	140	11.7

YARDS GAINED

	Year	Yds
Trevor Insley, Nevada	1999	2,060
Troy Edwards, Louisiana Tech	1998	1,996
Michael Crabtree, Texas Tech	2007	1,962
Jordan White, W Michigan	2011	1,911
Greg Salas, Hawaii	2010	1,889

TOUCHDOWN CATCHES

	Year	TD
Troy Edwards, Louisiana Tech	1998	27
Randy Moss, Marshall	1997	25
Emmanuel Hazard, Houston	1989	22
Larry Fitzgerald, Pittsburgh	2003	22
Michael Crabtree, Texas Tech	2007	22

Single Game

Scoring

POINTS

	Opponent	Year	Pts
Howard Griffith, Illinois	Southern Illinois	1990	48
Marshall Faulk, San Diego St.	Pacific	1991	44
Jim Brown, Syracuse	Colgate	1956	43
Fred Wendt, UTEP*	New Mexico St	1948	42
Arnold Boykin, Mississippi	Mississippi St	1951	42
Rashaun Woods, Okla. St	SMU	2003	42

*UTEP was Texas Mines in 1948.

FIELD GOALS

	Opponent	Year	FG
Dale Klein, Nebraska	Missouri	1985	7
Mike Prindle, Western Michigan	Marshall	1984	7

Note: 15 tied with 6.

Klein's distances were 32-22-43-44-29-43-43.
Prindle's distances were 32-44-42-23-48-41-27.

Total Offense

YARDS GAINED

	Opponent	Year	Yds
David Klingler, Houston	Arizona St	1990	732
Matt Vogler, TCU	Houston	1990	696
B.J. Symons, Texas Tech	Mississippi	2003	681
Brian Lindgren, Idaho	Middle Tenn St	2001	657
Graham Harrell, Texas Tech	Oklahoma St	2007	643
David Klingler, Houston	TCU	1990	625
Scott Mitchell, Utah	Air Force	1988	625

Passing

YARDS GAINED

	Opponent	Year	Yds
David Klingler, Houston	Arizona St	1990	716
Matt Vogler, TCU	Houston	1990	690
B.J. Symons, Texas Tech	Mississippi	2003	661
Graham Harrell, Texas Tech	Oklahoma St	2007	646
Cody Hodges, Texas Tech	Kansas St	2005	643

Passing *(Cont.)*

COMPLETIONS

	Opponent	Year	Comp
Andy Schmitt, E. Michigan	Central Mich.	2008	58
Case Keenum, Houston	East Carolina	2009	56
Drew Brees, Purdue	Wisconsin	1998	55
Rusty LaRue, Wake Forest	Duke	1995	55
Case Keenum, Houston	UTEP	2009	51
Andy Schmitt, E. Michigan	Temple	2008	50
Rusty LaRue, Wake Forest	No.Carolina St	1995	50

Note: Five tied with 49.

TOUCHDOWNS PASSING

	Opponent	Year	TD
David Klingler, Houston	E. Wash	1990	11

Note: Klingler's TD passes were for 5-48-29-7-3-7-40-10-7-8-51 yards, respectively.

Rushing

YARDS GAINED

	Opponent	Year	Yds
LaDainian Tomlinson, TCU	UTEP	1999	406
Tony Sands, Kansas	Missouri	1991	396
Marshall Faulk, San Diego St.	Pacific	1991	386
Troy Davis, Iowa St	Missouri	1996	378
Anthony Thompson, Indiana	Wisconsin	1989	377
Robbie Mixon, Cent. Mich.	Eastern Mich	2002	377

TOUCHDOWNS RUSHING

	Opponent	Year	TD
Howard Griffith, Illinois	Southern Illinois	1990	8

Note: Griffith's TD runs were for 5-51-7-41-5-18-5-3 yards, respectively.

Single Game (Cont.)

Receiving

CATCHES	Opponent	Year	No.
Tyler Jones, E. Michigan. ...Central Mich.		2008	23
Randy Gatewood, UNLV.....Idaho		1994	23
Freddie Barnes, Bowl. Green..Kent St		2009	22
Jay Miller, BYU ....New Mexico		1973	22
Troy Edwards, La. Tech......Nebraska		1998	21
Chris Daniels, Purdue.........Michigan St		1999	21

Note: Three tied with 20.

Receiving (Cont.)

YARDS GAINED	Opponent	Year	Yds
Troy Edwards, Louisiana Tech..Nebraska		1998	405
Randy Gatewood, UNLV.........Idaho		1994	363
Chuck Hughes, UTEP*............North Texas		1965	349
Donnie Avery, Houston ....Rice		2007	346
Casey Fitzgerald, North Texas .SMU		2007	327

*UTEP was Texas Western in 1965.

TOUCHDOWN CATCHES	Opponent	Year	TD
Rashaun Woods, Okla. St .....SMU		2003	7
Tim Delaney, San Diego St ...New Mex. St		1969	6

Longest Plays (since 1941)

PASSING	Opponent	Year	Yds
Fred Owens to Jack Ford, Portland.................St. Mary's (Ca.)		1947	99
Bo Burris to Warren McVea, Houston.................Washington St		1966	99
Colin Clapton to Eddie Jenkins, Holy Cross ....Boston Univ.		1970	99
Terry Peel to Robert Ford, Houston.................Syracuse		1970	99
Terry Peel to Robert Ford, Houston.................San Diego St		1972	99
Cris Collinsworth to Derrick Gaffney, Florida ....Rice		1977	99
Scott Ankrom to James Maness, TCU.........................Rice		1984	99
Gino Toretta to Horace Copeland, Miami (Fla.).............Arkansas		1991	99
John Paci to Thomas Lewis, Indiana ....Penn St		1993	99
Troy DeGar to Wes Caswell, Tulsa ....Oklahoma		1996	99
Drew Brees to Vinny Sutherland, Purdue ....Northwestern		1999	99
Dan Urban to Justin McCariens, Northern Illinois ....Ball St		2000	99
Jason Johnson to Brandon Marshall, Arizona.......................Idaho		2001	99
Dondrial Pinkins to Troy Williamson, South Carolina ....Virginia		2003	99
Jim Sorgi to Lee Evans, Wisconsin.................Akron		2003	99
Giovanni Vizza to Casey Fitzgerald, North Texas ....La.-Monroe		2007	99
Jeff Tuel to Johnny Forzani, Washington St.............Arizona St		2009	99

RUSHING	Opponent	Year	Yd
Gale Sayers, Kansas ....Nebraska		1963	99
Max Anderson, Arizona St....Wyoming		1967	99
Ralph Thompson, West Texas St.......................Wichita St		1970	99
Kelsey Finch, Tennessee......Florida		1977	99
Eric Vann, Kansas ....Oklahoma		1997	99
Terry Caulley, Connecticut ...Army		2006	99
Broderick Green, Arkansas ..E. Michigan		2009	99
Ronnie Hillman, San Diego St ..Wyoming		2011	99

Eleven tied at 98 yards.

FIELD GOALS	Opponent	Year	Yds
Steve Little, Arkansas ....Texas		1977	67
Russell Erxleben, Texas.........Rice		1977	67
Joe Williams, Wichita St ....Southern Ill.		1978	67
Martin Gramatica, Kansas St...Northern Ill.		1998	65
Tony Franklin, Texas A&M .....Baylor		1976	65

PUNTS	Opponent	Year	Yds
Pat Brady, Nevada* ....Loyola (Ca.)		1950	99
George O'Brien, Wisconsin ...Iowa		1952	96
John Hadl, Kansas.......:.........Oklahoma		1959	94
Carl Knox, TCU ....Oklahoma St		1947	94
Preston Johnson, SMU ....Pittsburgh		1940	94

*Nevada was Nevada-Reno in 1950.

FOOTBALL BOWL SUBDIVISION (I-A) WINNINGEST TEAMS
Alltime Winning Percentage

	Yrs	W	L	T	Pct	GP	Bowl Record
Michigan	132	895	310	36	.736	1,241	20-21-0
Notre Dame	123	853	300	42	.731	1,195	15-16-0
Boise St	44	377	146	2	.720	525	8-4-0
Oklahoma	117	821	307	53	.718	1,181	27-17-1
Texas	119	858	330	33	.716	1,221	26-22-2
Ohio St	122	825	316	53	.713	1,194	20-23-0
Alabama	117	814	320	43	.710	1,177	33-22-3
Southern Cal	118	779	313	54	.703	1,146	31-15-0
Nebraska	122	846	349	40	.701	1,235	24-25-0
Tennessee	115	794	347	53	.687	1,194	25-24-0
Florida St	65	473	235	17	.664	725	22-14-2
Penn St	125	715	361	41	.658	1,117	21-14-2
LSU	118	733	390	47	.647	1,170	22-20-1
Georgia	118	747	400	54	.644	1,201	26-18-3
Miami (Fla.)	86	574	326	19	.635	919	18-16-0
Auburn	119	711	405	47	.632	1,163	22-13-2
Florida	105	669	385	40	.630	1,094	20-19-0
Miami (Ohio)	123	664	402	44	.618	1,110	7-3-0
Washington	122	670	418	50	.611	1,138	15-15-1
South Florida	15	108	69	0	.610	177	4-2-0
Arizona St	99	561	356	24	.609	941	12-12-1
Virginia Tech	118	689	435	46	.609	1,170	9-15-0
Central Michigan	111	576	375	36	.602	987	2-4-0
West Virginia	119	701	457	45	.601	1,203	14-17-0
Texas A&M	117	681	450	48	.598	1,179	14-19

Note: Includes bowl and playoff games.

Alltime Victories

Michigan	895	LSU	733	Colorado	674
Texas	858	Penn St.	715	Washington	670
Notre Dame	853	Auburn	711	Florida	669
Nebraska	846	West Virginia	701	Miami (Ohio)	664
Ohio St	825	Syracuse	691	Clemson	657
Oklahoma	821	Virginia Tech	689	Navy	656
Alabama	814	Georgia Tech	687	California	655
Tennessee	794	Texas A&M	681	Army	652
Southern Cal	779	Arkansas	680	Minnesota	646
Georgia	747	Pittsburgh	677	North Carolina	646

NUMBER ONE VS NUMBER TWO

The No. 1 and No. 2 teams, according to the Associated Press Poll, have met 33 times, including 13 bowl games, since the poll's inception in 1936. The No. 1 teams have a 20-11-2 record in these matchups. Notre Dame (4-3-2) has played in nine of the games.

Date	Results	Stadium
10-9-43	No. 1 Notre Dame 35, No. 2 Michigan 12	Michigan (Ann Arbor)
11-20-43	No. 1 Notre Dame 14, No. 2 Iowa Pre-Flight 13	Notre Dame (South Bend)
12-2-44	No. 1 Army 23, No. 2 Navy 7	Municipal (Baltimore)
11-10-45	No. 1 Army 48, No. 2 Notre Dame 0	Yankee (New York)
12-1-45	No. 1 Army 32, No. 2 Navy 13	Municipal (Philadelphia)
11-9-46	No. 1 Army 0, No. 2 Notre Dame 0	Yankee (New York)
1-1-63	No. 1 USC 42, No. 2 Wisconsin 37 (Rose Bowl)	Rose Bowl (Pasadena)
10-12-63	No. 2 Texas 28, No. 1 Oklahoma 7	Cotton Bowl (Dallas)
1-1-64	No. 1 Texas 28, No. 2 Navy 6 (Cotton Bowl)	Cotton Bowl (Dallas)
11-19-66	No. 1 Notre Dame 10, No. 2 Michigan St 10	Spartan (East Lansing)
9-28-68	No. 1 Purdue 37, No. 2 Notre Dame 22	Notre Dame (South Bend)
1-1-69	No. 1 Ohio St 27, No. 2 USC 16 (Rose Bowl)	Rose Bowl (Pasadena)
12-6-69	No. 1 Texas 15, No. 2 Arkansas 14	Razorback (Fayetteville)
11-25-71	No. 1 Nebraska 35, No. 2 Oklahoma 31	Owen Field (Norman)
1-1-72	No. 1 Nebraska 38, No. 2 Alabama 6 (Orange Bowl)	Orange Bowl (Miami)
1-1-79	No. 2 Alabama 14, No. 1 Penn St 7 (Sugar Bowl)	Sugar Bowl (New Orleans)
9-26-81	No. 1 USC 28, No. 2 Oklahoma 24	Coliseum (Los Angeles)
1-1-83	No. 2 Penn St 27, No. 1 Georgia 23 (Sugar Bowl)	Sugar Bowl (New Orleans)
10-19-85	No. 1 Iowa 12, No. 2 Michigan 10	Kinnick (Iowa City)
9-27-86	No. 2 Miami (Fla.) 28, No. 1 Oklahoma 16	Orange Bowl (Miami)
1-2-87	No. 2 Penn St 14, No. 1 Miami (Fla.) 10 (Fiesta Bowl)	Sun Devil (Tempe)
11-21-87	No. 2 Oklahoma 17, No. 1 Nebraska 7	Memorial (Lincoln)

NUMBER ONE VS NUMBER TWO *(Cont.)*

Date	Results	Stadium
1-1-88	No. 2 Miami (Fla.) 20, No. 1 Oklahoma 14 (Orange Bowl)	Orange Bowl (Miami)
11-26-88	No. 1 Notre Dame 27, No. 2 USC 10	Coliseum (Los Angeles)
9-16-89	No. 1 Notre Dame 24, No. 2 Michigan 19	Michigan (Ann Arbor)
11-16-91	No. 2 Miami (Fla.) 17, No. 1 Florida St 16	Doak Campbell (Tallahassee)
1-1-93	No. 2 Alabama 34, No. 1 Miami (Fla.) 13 (Sugar Bowl)	Superdome (New Orleans)
11-13-93	No. 2 Notre Dame 31, No. 1 Florida St 24	Notre Dame (South Bend)
1-1-94	No. 1 Florida St 18, No. 2 Nebraska 16 (Orange Bowl)	Orange Bowl (Miami)
1-2-96	No. 1 Nebraska 62, No. 2 Florida 24 (Fiesta Bowl)	Sun Devil (Tempe)
11-30-96	No. 2 Florida St 24, No. 1 Florida 21	Doak Campbell (Tallahassee)
1-4-99	No. 1 Tennessee 23, No. 2 Florida St 16 (Fiesta Bowl)	Sun Devil (Tempe)
1-4-00	No. 1 Florida St 46, No. 2 Virginia Tech 29 (Sugar Bowl)	Superdome (New Orleans)
1-3-03	No. 2 Ohio St 31, No. 1 Miami (Fla.) 24 [2OT] (Fiesta Bowl)	Sun Devil (Tempe)
1-5-06	No. 2 Texas 41, No. 1 USC 38 (Rose Bowl)	Rose Bowl (Pasadena)
9-9-06	No. 1 Ohio St 24, No. 2 Texas 7	Texas Memorial (Austin)
11-18-06	No. 1 Ohio St 42, No. 2 Michigan 39	Ohio (Columbus)
1-8-07	No. 2 Florida 41, No. 1 Ohio St 14 (BCS Championship)	Univ. of Phoenix (Glendale)
1-7-08	No. 2 LSU 38, No. 1 Ohio St. 24 (BCS Championship)	Superdome (New Orleans)
12-6-08	No. 2 Florida 31, No. 1 Alabama 20 (SEC Championship)	Georgia Dome (Atlanta)
1-8-09	No. 1 Florida 24, No. 2 Oklahoma 14 (BCS Championship)	Dolphins Stadium (Miami)
12-5-09	No. 1 Florida 13, No. 2 Alabama 32 (SEC Championship)	Georgia Dome (Atlanta)
1-7-10	No. 1 Alabama 37, No. 2 Texas 21 (BCS Championship)	Rose Bowl (Pasadena)
1-10-11	No. 1 Auburn 22, No. 2 Oregon 19 (BCS Championship)	Univ. of Phoenix (Glendale)
11-5-11	No. 1 LSU 9, No. 2 Alabama 6	Alabama (Tuscaloosa)
1-9-12	No. 2 Alabama 21, No. 1 LSU 0 (BCS Championship)	Superdome (New Orleans)

Note: No. 1 USC's Orange Bowl victory over No. 2 Oklahoma on Jan. 4, 2005 was vacated in 2010 for rules violations.

LONGEST FBS (I-A) WINNING STREAKS

Wins	Team	Yrs	Ended by	Score
47	Oklahoma	1953–57	Notre Dame	7–0
39	Washington	1908–14	Oregon St	0–0
37	Yale	1890–93	Princeton	6–0
37	Yale	1887–89	Princeton	10–0
35	Toledo	1969–71	Tampa	21–0
34	Miami	2000–03	Ohio St	31–24 (2 OT)
34	Pennsylvania	1894–96	Lafayette	6–4
31	Oklahoma	1948–50	Kentucky	13–7
31	Pittsburgh	1914–18	Cleveland Naval Reserve	10–9
31	Pennsylvania	1896–98	Harvard	10–0
30	Texas	1968–70	Notre Dame	24–11

LONGEST FBS (I-A) UNBEATEN STREAKS

No.	W	T	Team	Yrs	Ended by	Score
63	59	4	Washington	1907–17	California	27–0
56	55	1	Michigan	1901–05	Chicago	2–0
50	46	4	California	1920–25	Olympic Club	15–0
48	47	1	Oklahoma	1953–57	Notre Dame	7–0
48	47	1	Yale	1885–89	Princeton	10–0
47	42	5	Yale	1879–85	Princeton	6–5
44	42	2	Yale	1894–96	Princeton	24–6
42	39	3	Yale	1904–08	Harvard	4–0
39	37	2	Notre Dame	1946–50	Purdue	28–14
37	36	1	Oklahoma	1972–75	Kansas	23–3
37	37	0	Yale	1890–93	Princeton	6–0
35	35	0	Toledo	1969–71	Tampa	21–0
35	34	1	Minnesota	1903–05	Wisconsin	16–12
34	34	0	Miami (Fla.)	2000–03	Ohio St	31–24 (2 OT)
34	33	1	Nebraska	1912–16	Kansas	7–3
34	34	0	Pennsylvania	1894–96	Lafayette	6–4
34	32	2	Princeton	1884–87	Harvard	12–0
34	29	5	Princeton	1877–82	Harvard	1–0
33	30	3	Tennessee	1926–30	Alabama	18–6
33	31	2	Georgia Tech	1914–18	Pittsburgh	32–0
33	30	3	Harvard	1911–15	Cornell	10–0
32	31	1	Nebraska	1969–71	UCLA	20–17
32	30	2	Army	1944–47	Columbia	21–20
32	31	1	Harvard	1898–1900	Yale	28–0

Note: Includes bowl games.

LONGEST FBS (I-A) LOSING STREAKS

Losses		Seasons	Ended Against	Score
34	Northwestern	1979–82	Northern Illinois	31–6
28	Virginia	1958–61	William & Mary	21–6
28	Kansas St	1945–48	Arkansas St	37–6
27	New Mexico St	1988–90	Cal St–Fullerton	43–9
27	Eastern Michigan	1980–82	Kent St	9–7

MOST-PLAYED FBS (I-A) RIVALRIES

GP	Opponents (Series Leader Listed First)	Record	First Game	GP	Opponents (Series Leader Listed First)	Record	First Game
121	Minnesota–Wisconsin	59-54-8	1890	109	Kansas–Kansas St	65-39-5	1902
120	Missouri–Kansas	56-55-9	1891	108	Michigan–Ohio St	58-44-6	1897
118	Texas–Texas A&M	76-37-5	1894	108	Mississippi–Mississippi St	60-42-6	1901
117	Nebraska–Kansas	91-23-3	1892	107	Baylor–TCU	50-50-7	1899
116	Miami (Ohio)–Cincinnati	59-50-7	1888	107	Tennessee–Kentucky	74-24-9	1893
116	North Carolina–Virginia	59-53-4	1892	106	Georgia–Georgia Tech	62-39-5	1893
115	Auburn–Georgia	54-53-8	1892	106	Texas–Oklahoma	59-42-5	1900
115	Oregon–Oregon St	59-46-10	1894	106	Oklahoma–Oklahoma St	82-17-7	1904
114	Purdue–Indiana	71-37-6	1891	105	Nebraska–Iowa St	86-17-2	1896
114	Stanford–California	57-46-11	1892	105	Tennessee–Vanderbilt	73-27-2	1888
112	Navy–Army	56-49-7	1890				
109	Utah–Utah St	77-28-4	1892				
109	Clemson–South Carolina	65-40-4	1896				

NCAA Coaches' Records

ALLTIME WINNINGEST FBS (I-A) COACHES
By Percentage

Coach (Alma Mater)	Colleges Coached	Yrs	W	L	T	Pct
Knute Rockne (Notre Dame '14)†	Notre Dame 1918–30	13	105	12	5	.881
Frank W. Leahy (Notre Dame '31)†	Boston College 1939–40; Notre Dame 1941–43, 1946–53	13	107	13	9	.864
George W. Woodruff (Yale 1889)†	Pennsylvania 1892–01; Illinois 1903; Carlisle 1905	12	142	25	2	.846
Barry Switzer (Arkansas '60)	Oklahoma 1973–88	16	157	29	4	.837
Tom Osborne (Hastings '59)†	Nebraska 1973–97	25	255	49	3	.836
Percy D. Haughton (Harvard 1899)†	Cornell 1899–1900; Harvard 1908–16; Columbia 1923–24	13	97	17	6	.833
Fielding Yost (West Virginia 1895)†	Ohio Wesleyan 1897; Nebraska 1898; Kansas 1899; Stanford 1900; Michigan 1901–23, 1925–26	29	198	35	12	.833
Bob Neyland (Army '16)†	Tennessee 1926–34, 1936–40, 1946–52	21	173	31	12	.829
Bud Wilkinson (Minnesota '37)†	Oklahoma 1947–63	17	145	29	4	.826
Urban Meyer (Cincinnati '86)	Bowling Green 2001–02; Utah 2003–04; Florida 2005–10	10	104	23	0	.819
Jock Sutherland (Pittsburgh '18)†	Lafayette 1919–23; Pittsburgh 1924–38	20	144	28	14	.812
Bob Devaney (Alma [Mich] '39)†	Wyoming 1957–61; Nebraska 1962–72	16	136	30	7	.806
*Bob Stoops (Iowa '83)	Oklahoma 1999–	13	139	34	0	.803
Frank W. Thomas (Notre Dame '23)†	Tenn.-Chattanooga 1925–28; Alabama 1931–42, 1944–46	19	141	33	9	.795
Henry L. Williams (Yale 1891)†	Army 1891; Minnesota 1900–21	23	141	34	12	.786
*Gary Patterson (Kansas St '83)	TCU 2000–	12	109	30	0	.784
Gil Dobie (Minnesota '02)†	North Dakota St 1906–07; Washington 1908-16; Navy 1917–19; Cornell 1920–35; Boston College 1936–38	33	180	45	15	.781
Paul "Bear" Bryant (Alabama '36)†	Maryland 1945; Kentucky 1946–53; Alabama 1958–82	38	323	85	17	.780
Fred Folsom (Dartmouth 1895)	Colorado 1895–99, 1901–02; Dartmouth 1903–06; Colorado 1908–15	19	106	28	6	.779
Bo Schembechler (Miami [Ohio] '51)	Miami (Ohio) 1963–68; Michigan 1969–89	27	234	65	8	.775

*Active in 2011. †Hall of Fame member.

Note: Minimum 10 years as head coach at Division I institutions; record at four-year colleges only; bowl games included; ties computed as half won, half lost.

ALLTIME WINNINGEST FBS (I-A) COACHES *(Cont.)*

By Victories

	Yrs	W	L	T	Pct		Yrs	W	L	T	Pct
Bobby Bowden	44	377	129	4	.743	Bo Schembechler	27	234	65	8	.775
Paul (Bear) Bryant	38	323	85	17	.780	Hayden Fry	37	232	178	10	.564
Glenn (Pop) Warner	44	319	106	32	.733	†Jim Tressel	25	229	79	2	.742
Amos Alonzo Stagg	57	314	199	35	.605	*Mack Brown	27	227	113	1	.667
*††Joe Paterno	46	298	136	3	.685	*Chris Ault	26	226	103	1	.686
LaVell Edwards	29	257	100	3	.718	Jess Neely	40	207	176	19	.539
Tom Osborne	25	255	49	3	.836	Warren Woodson	31	203	95	14	.673
*Frank Beamer	31	251	121	4	.673	Don Nehlen	30	202	128	8	.609
Lou Holtz	33	249	132	7	.651	Vince Dooley	25	201	77	10	.715
Woody Hayes	33	238	72	10	.759	Eddie Anderson	39	201	128	15	.606
						Jim Sweeney	27	200	154	4	.564

*Active in 2011. Record at four-year colleges only.
†One bowl win and 11 regular-season victories from Tressel's totals were vacated in 2010. ††Six bowl wins and 105 regular-season victories were vacated in 2012.

Most Bowl Victories

	W	L	T		W	L	T
Bobby Bowden	21	10	1	Barry Alvarez	8	3	0
*Joe Paterno	18	12	1	Terry Donahue	8	4	1
Paul (Bear) Bryant	15	12	2	Barry Switzer	8	5	0
Lou Holtz	12	8	2	Jackie Sherrill	8	6	0
Tom Osborne	12	13	0	Philip Fulmer	8	7	0
*Mack Brown	12	7	0	Darrell Royal	8	7	1
Don James	10	5	0	Vince Dooley	8	10	2
John Vaught	10	8	0	*Frank Beamer	8	11	0
Bobby Dodd	9	4	0	*Tom O'Brien	8	2	0
Johnny Majors	9	7	0	*Steve Spurrier	8	10	0
John Robinson	8	1	0				

WINNINGEST ACTIVE* FBS (I-A) COACHES

By Percentage

Coach, College	Yrs	W	L	T	Pct.	Bowls		
						W	L	T
Chris Petersen, Boise St	6	73	6	0	.924	4	2	0
Bob Stoops, Oklahoma	13	139	34	0	.803	7	6	0
Gary Patterson, TCU	12	109	30	0	.784	7	4	0
Bret Bielema, Wisconsin	6	60	19	0	.759	2	4	0
Bobby Petrino, Arkansas	8	75	26	0	.743	4	3	0
Mark Richt, Georgia	11	106	38	0	.736	7	4	0
Brian Kelly, Cincinnati	21	187	67	2	.734	3	2	0
Bronco Mendenhall, BYU	7	66	24	0	.733	5	2	0
Les Miles, LSU	11	103	39	0	.725	6	4	0
Kyle Whittingham, Utah	8	66	25	0	.725	7	1	0
Steve Spurrier, South Carolina	22	197	75	2	.723	8	10	0
Nick Saban, Alabama	16	141	54	1	.722	7	6	0
Paul Johnson, Georgia Tech	15	140	58	0	.707	2	6	0
Chris Ault, Nevada	27	226	103	1	.686	2	7	0
Joe Paterno, Penn St	46	298	136	3	.685	18	12	1
Frank Beamer, Virginia Tech	31	251	121	4	.673	8	11	0
Mack Brown, Texas	28	227	113	1	.667	12	7	0
Mike Gundy, Oklahoma St	7	59	30	0	.663	4	2	0
Bill Snyder, Kansas St	20	159	83	0	.656	5	7	0
Dennis Erickson, Arizona St	23	179	96	1	.650	5	7	0

#Bowl games included. Ties computed as half win, half loss. Note: Minimum five years as Div. I-A head coach at four-year colleges only.

By Victories

Joe Paterno, Penn St	298	Larry Blakeney, Troy	164
Frank Beamer, Viginia Tech	251	Bill Snyder, Kansas St	159
Mack Brown, Texas	227	Howard Schnellenberger, Fla. Atlantic	158
Chris Ault, Nevada	226	Gary Pinkel, Missouri	158
Steve Spurrier, South Carolina	197	Paul Pasqualoni, Connecticut	146
Brian Kelly, Cincinnati	187	Nick Saban, Alabama	141
Dennis Erickson, Arizona St	179	Paul Johnson, Georgia Tech	140
Mike Price, UTEP	174	Bob Stoops, Oklahoma	139

*Active in 2011.

WINNINGEST ACTIVE* FCS (I-AA) COACHES
By Percentage

Coach, College	Yrs	W	L	T	Pct
Al Bagnoli, Pennsylvania	30	227	76	0	.749
Chris Hatcher, Murray St	12	107	36	0	.748
Joe Taylor, Florida A&M	29	229	89	4	.717
Rod Broadway, NC A&T	9	73	29	0	.716
Buddy Pough, South Carolina St	10	83	33	0	.716
K.C. Keeler, Delaware	19	169	67	1	.715
Mark Farley, UNI	11	99	40	0	.712
Danny Rocco, Richmond	6	47	20	0	.701
Matt Viator, McNeese St	6	45	20	0	.692
Doug Williams, Grambling	8	63	30	0	.677
Doug Biddle, Colgate	16	125	61	0	.672
Rick Comegy, Jackson St	20	149	77	0	.659
Chuck Priore, Stony Brook	12	76	40	0	.655
Ron Caragher, San Diego	5	36	19	0	.655
Rob Ash, Montana St	32	215	119	5	.642

By Victories

Bob Ford, Albany St (N.Y.)	255	Mike Ayers, Wofford	173
Jerry Moore, Appalachian St	234	K.C. Keeler, Delaware	169
Joe Taylor, Florida A&M	229	Tim Murphy, Harvard	152
Al Bagnoli, Pennsylvania	227	Rick Comegy, Jackson St	149
Andy Talley, Villanova	217	Tim Walsh, Cal Poly	134
Rob Ash, Montana St	215	Matt Ballard, Morehead St	132
Jimmye Laycock, William & Mary	213	Dick Biddle, Colgate	125
Walt Hameline, Wagner	204		

WINNINGEST ACTIVE* DIVISION II COACHES
By Percentage

Coach, College	Yrs	W	L	T	Pct
Willie Slater, Tuskegee	6	53	13	0	.803
Ken Sparks, Carson-Newman	32	299	80	2	.787
John Luckhardt, California (PA)	27	225	70	2	.761
Danny Hale, Bloomsburg	24	203	67	1	.751
David Dean, Valdosta St	5	42	15	0	.737
Bob Nielson, Minn. Duluth	19	160	57	1	.736
Tom Sawyer, Winona St	16	130	54	0	.707
Rich Freeman, Morehouse	5	36	15	0	.706
Bill Zwaan, West Chester	15	124	52	0	.705
Darrell Morris, Neb.-Kearney	12	92	39	0	.702
Mike White, Albany St. (GA)	12	93	40	0	.699
Bill Maskill, Midwestern St	12	92	40	0	.697
Bryan Collins, LIU Post	14	107	47	0	.695
Scott Browning, Edinboro	6	45	23	0	.662
Monte Cater, Shepherd	31	211	108	2	.660

Ties computed as half win, half loss. Playoff games included.

Note: Minimum five years as a college head coach; record at four-year colleges only.

By Victories

Ken Sparks, Carson-Newman	299	Rob Smith, Humboldt St	133
Dennis Douds, East Stroudsburg	232	Tom Sawyer, Winona St	130
John Luckhardt, California (Pa.)	225	Bobby Wallace, North Alabama	127
Monte Cater, Shepherd	211	Bill Zwaan, West Chester	124
Danny Hale, Bloomsburg	203	Keith Otterbein, Hillsdale	124
Richard Cavanagh, Southern Connecticut St	163	Jerry Partridge, Missouri Western St	112
George Mihalik, Slippery Rock	161	Don Carthel, West Texas A&M	112
Bob Nielson, Minnesota-Duluth	160	Art Wilkins, American International	112

*Active in 2011.

WINNINGEST ACTIVE* DIVISION III COACHES
By Percentage

Coach, College	Yrs	W	L	T	Pct
Lance Leipold, Wis.-Whitewater	5	72	3	0	.960
Larry Kehres, Mount Union	26	317	24	3	.926
Jeff Devanney, Trinity (CT)	6	41	7	0	.854
Mike Sirianni, Wash. & Jeff.	9	85	18	0	.825
Joe Fincham, Wittenberg	16	144	33	0	.814
Rick Willis, Wartburg	13	113	27	0	.807
Pete Fredenburg, Mary Hardin-Baylor	14	133	33	0	.801
Jeff McMartin, Central (IA)	8	68	18	0	.791
Joe Smith, Linfield	6	68	18	0	.791
John Thorne, North Central (IL)	10	88	24	0	.786
John Gagliardi, Saint John's (MN)	63	484	133	11	.779
Mike Drass, Wesley	19	166	47	1	.778
Jim Purtill, St. Norbert	14	114	33	1	.774
Mike Swider, Wheaton (IL)	16	132	39	0	.772
Jim Hilvert, Thomas More	5	43	13	0	.768

Ties computed as half won, half lost. Playoff games included.
Note: Minimum five years as a college head coach; record at four-year colleges only.

By Victories

John Gagliardi, St John's (Minn.)	484	Larry Kindborn, Washington-St.Louis	171
Larry Kehres, Mount Union	317	Barry Streeter, Gettysburg	167
Rick Giancola, Montclair St.	209	Mike Drass, Wesley	166
Eric Hamilton, The College of New Jersey	208	Steve Johnson, Bethel (Minn.)	164
Michael DeLong, Springfield	177	Norm Eash, Illinois Wesleyan	158
Rich Lackner, Carnegie Mellon	175	Mike Maynard, Redlands	151
Steve Mohr, Trinity (Texas)	174	Brien Cullen, Worcester St	150
Vic Wallace, Rockford	174		

NAIA Coaches' Records

WINNINGEST ACTIVE* NAIA COACHES
By Percentage

Coach, College	Yrs	W	L	T	Pct
Mike Van Diest, Carroll (Mont.)	12	144	20	0	.878
Bill Cronin, Georgetown (Ky.)	14	133	34	0	.796
Steve Ryan, Morningside (Ia.)	9	76	28	0	.731
John Bland, Cumberlands (Ky.)	5	40	15	0	.727
Hank Biesiot, Dickinson St (N.D.)	35	251	96	1	.723
Mike Feminis, St. Xavier (Ill.)	12	102	40	0	.718
Paul Troth, Missouri Valley	14	106	49	0	.684
Kevin Donley, St. Francis (Ind.)	33	246	114	1	.683
Monty Lewis, Friends (Ks.)	18	118	55	0	.682
Mike Cochran, Southern Nazarene (Okla.)	10	75	36	0	.676
Keith Barefield, Northwestern Oklahoma St.	14	96	47	2	.669
Mike Gardner, Malone (Ohio)	7	49	27	0	.645
Larry Wilcox, Benedictine (Ks.)	32	220	123	0	.641
Kent Kessinger, Ottawa (Ks.)	7	41	32	0	.562
Phil Jones, Shorter (Ga.)	6	37	29	0	.561

Playoff games included.

Note: Minimum five years as a collegiate head coach and includes record against four-year institutions only.

By Victories

Hank Biesiot, Dickinson St (N.D.)	251	Paul Troth, Missouri Valley	106
Kevin Donley, St. Francis (Ind.)	246	Mike Feminis, St. Xavier (Ill.)	102
Larry Wilcox, Benedictine (Kan.)	220	Keith Barefield, Northwestern Oklahoma St	96
Mike Van Diest, Carroll (Mont.)	144	Brian Keller, Nebraska Wesleyan	83
Bill Cronin, Georgetown (Ky.)	133	Dennis McCulloch, Valley City State (N.D.)	78
Monty Lewis, Friends (Ks.)	118	Steve Ryan, Morningside (Iowa)	76
Dave Dallas, Kansas Wesleyan	117	Andy Lambert, Sterling (Ks.)	75
		Mike Cochran, Southern Nazarene (Okla.)	75

*Active in 2011.

LeBron James led the Miami Heat to the NBA title in a dominant five-game final series against Oklahoma City

GREG NELSON

Pro Basketball

Redemption At Last

Reviled by the millions who rooted for him to lose after he exited Cleveland for Miami in 2010, LeBron James is now the transcendent champion of the NBA

BY CHRIS MANNIX

LEBRON JAMES FOLDED HIM-self into a seat on the dais, the Larry O'Brien trophy to his right, the NBA Finals MVP trophy to his left, a toothy smile creasing the center of his face. After nine years, two teams and unprecedented scrutiny that comes with being a mega star in the social media age, James had finally climbed the mountaintop, winning the 2012 NBA championship, and, for a moment, he allowed the moment to wash over him. "I dreamed about this opportunity and this moment for a long time," said James. "My dream has become a reality now, and it's the best feeling I've ever had."

If the 2010–11 season was about validation for James, who left a hero's role in Cleveland for a villainous one in Miami, only, much to the delight of everyone outside of South Florida, to fall short in the Finals, this one was about redemption. James and the Heat were still reviled, sure, but not in the same way they were last season, when in a smoky ceremony on South Beach, James, Dwyane Wade and Chris Bosh declared Miami the team of the decade. This Heat team was more humble,

more reserved, more focused on basketball. And from opening night, it showed.

The Heat started the '11-'12 season fast, knocking off Dallas and Boston in the first two games, winning five of its first six, eight of its first nine and losing just twice in the month of February. The lockout that cost the league the first two months of the season and shrunk an 82-game schedule down to 66 did little to slow Miami, which utilized young legs and improved depth provided by free agent signee Shane Battier and rookie Norris Cole to run opponents off the floor.

It didn't slow Chicago much, either, which picked up right where it left off in 2011, piling up wins on the back of a stingy defense (league-best 88.2 points allowed per game) and flawless offensive execution. Even without reigning MVP Derrick Rose—who missed 26 games with a variety of injuries—the Bulls were a machine, winning 50 games and compiling the best win differential in the league (8.2).

Out west, the dismantling of the Mavericks—who declined to offer long-term deals to Tyson Chandler, J.J. Barea and Caron Butler—opened the door for Oklahoma City to leap to the next level. Since 2009, the

GREG NELSON

Thunder has been a How-To guide to building a winner: They followed a 23-win 2008–09 season by winning 50-games in 2009–10 and advancing to the conference finals in 2010–11. With a young core of Kevin Durant, Russell Westbrook, James Harden and Serge Ibaka, Oklahoma City boasted a scary-good future.

That future appeared to become the present early on, as the Thunder won 12 of its first 14 games to take command of the conference. With the Mavericks struggling and the Lakers adjusting to new coach Mike Brown, only the Spurs stood as serious challengers. San Antonio was the same as it ever was: same stalwart coach (Gregg Popovich), same even keeled leader (Tim Duncan), same strong supporting cast (Tony Parker,

While the 2011–12 season ultimately belonged to James, the superstar-in-waiting is Durant, who electrified the nation with his league-leading 29 points per game.

Manu Ginobili). A draft-day deal added rookie Kawhi Leonard to the fold, giving the Spurs the defensive minded presence at small forward they had been lacking since Bruce Bowen retired.

Both the Thunder and Spurs stormed through the early rounds of the playoffs, Oklahoma City wiping out Dallas (4-0) and the Lakers (4-1) while San Antonio swept the Jazz and the Clippers. After dropping the first two games against San Antonio, the Thunder stormed back, winning four straight, closing out the series with an

Chicago superstar Derrick Rose was dogged by injury all season, and when he went down in the first round of the playoffs, the Bulls were done.

ter at the trade deadline but thanks to a little luck (a season-ending ACL injury to Rose in the first round) and the grittiness of 36-year old Kevin Garnett, who slid over and played center for the first time in his career, Boston was back. The Celtics storybook season appeared to be on the verge of a final chapter, too, after Boston stunned Miami in Game 5 and headed home with a chance to clinch. But there was James again, erupting for 45 points, 15 rebounds and five assists, single-handedly evening the series. In Game 7, James mercilessly poured in 11 of his 31 points in the fourth quarter, sending Miami back to the Finals and closing the curtain on Boston's Big Three.

emphatic 107-99 win in Game 6. Durant, who picked up his third straight scoring title in the regular season, was unstoppable, totaling 34 points, 14 rebounds and five assists in the clincher.

Back east, the Heat rolled over New York in the first round before meeting a hungry young Indiana team. The Pacers surged to a 2–1 series lead early, battering Miami—which lost Chris Bosh for the series to an abdominal injury in Game 1—in the paint with Roy Hibbert and David West. But in Game 4 there was James who, after reclaiming the MVP award in the regular season, put on an MVP-performance, tallying 40-points, 18-rebounds and nine assists, helping the Heat even the series. Two games later, they won it.

Miami faced more adversity against Boston. The Celtics nearly broke up the ros-

The anticipated contest against the Thunder was less a series than a coronation. Oklahoma City was talented, but not ready, much like Miami wasn't a year ago. The Thunder took Game 1 at home but could not hold off James, Wade and Bosh, who combined for 72 points in Miami's narrow 100-96 win in Game 2. At home, the Heat locked in, winning Game 3, surviving a 43-point onslaught from Westbrook to take Game 4 and closing the series with a 121–106 rout in Game 5. As James leaped into his teammates' arms, years of disappointment and frustration dissolved in the celebration. "I did it the right way," said James. "I didn't shortcut anything. I put a lot of hard work and dedication in it, and hard work pays off. It's a great moment for myself."

NBA Final Standings

Western Conference
NORTHWEST DIVISION

Team	W	L	Pct	GB
†Oklahoma City	47	19	.712	—
*Denver	38	28	.576	9
*Utah	36	30	.545	11
Portland	28	38	.424	19
Minnesota	26	40	.394	21

PACIFIC DIVISION

Team	W	L	Pct	GB
†LA Lakers	41	25	.621	—
*LA Clippers	40	26	.606	1
Phoenix	33	33	.500	8
Golden State	23	43	.348	18
Sacramento	22	44	.333	19

SOUTHWEST DIVISION

Team	W	L	Pct	GB
‡San Antonio	50	16	.758	—
*Memphis	41	25.	.621	9
*Dallas	36	30	.545	14
Houston	34	32	.515	16
New Orleans	21	45	.318	29

Eastern Conference
ATLANTIC DIVISION

Team	W	L	Pct	GB
†Boston	39	27	.591	—
*New York	36	30	.545	3
*Philadelphia	35	31	.530	4
Toronto	23	43	.348	16
New Jersey	22	44	.333	17

CENTRAL DIVISION

Team	W	L	Pct	GB
‡Chicago	50	16	.758	—
*Indiana	42	24	.636	8
Milwaukee	31	35	.470	19
Detroit	25	41	.379	25
Cleveland	21	45	.318	29

SOUTHEAST DIVISION

Team	W	L	Pct	GB
†Miami	46	20	.697	—
*Atlanta	40	26	.606	6
*Orlando	37	29	.561	9
Washington	20	46	.303	26
Charlotte	7	59	.106	39

†Clinched division title.   *Clinched playoff berth.   ‡Clinched conference title.

2012 NBA Playoffs

WESTERN CONFERENCE

1st ROUND — SEMIFINALS — FINALS

1-San Antonio
8-Utah
San Antonio (4–0)
San Antonio (4–0)

4-Memphis
5-LA Clippers
LA Clippers (4–3)
Okla. City (4–2)

3-LA Lakers
6-Denver
LA Lakers (4–3)
Okla. City (4–1)

2-Okla. City
7-Dallas
Okla. City (4–0)

NBA FINALS

MIAMI (4–1)

EASTERN CONFERENCE

FINALS — SEMIFINALS — 1st ROUND

Philadelphia (4–2)
Boston (4–3)
Boston (4–2)
Chicago-1
Philadephia-8
Boston-4
Atlanta-5

Miami (4–3)
Indiana (4–1)
Miami (4–2)
Miami (4–1)
Indiana-3
Orlando-6
Miami-2
New York-7

2012 NBA Playoff Results

Eastern Conference First Round

Game 1......Philadelphia	91	at Chicago	103
Game 2......Philadelphia	109	at Chicago	92
Game 3......Chicago	74	at Philadelphia	79
Game 4......Chicago	82	at Philadelphia	89
Game 5......Philadelphia	69	at Chicago	77
Game 6......Chicago	78	at Philadelphia	79

Philadelphia won series 4–2.

Game 1......New York	67	at Miami	100
Game 2......New York	94	at Miami	104
Game 3......Miami	87	at New York	70
Game 4......Miami	87	at New York	89
Game 5......New York	94	at Miami	106

Miami won series 4–1.

Game 1......Orlando	81	at Indiana	77
Game 2......Orlando	78	at Indiana	93
Game 3......Indiana	97	at Orlando	74
Game 4......Indiana	101	at Orlando	99
Game 5......Orlando	87	at Indiana	105

Indiana won series 4–1.

Game 1......Atlanta	83	at Boston	74
Game 2......Atlanta	80	at Boston	87
Game 3......Boston	90	at Atlanta	84
Game 4......Boston	101	at Atlanta	79
Game 5......Atlanta	87	at Boston	86
Game 6......Boston	83	at Atlanta	80

Boston won series 4–2.

Western Conference First Round

Game 1......Utah	91	at San Antonio	106
Game 2......Utah	83	at San Antonio	114
Game 3......San Antonio	102	at Utah	90
Game 4......San Antonio	87	at Utah	81

San Antonio won series 4–0.

Game 1......Denver	88	at LA Lakers	103
Game 2......Denver	100	at LA Lakers	104
Game 3......LA Lakers	84	at Denver	99
Game 4......LA Lakers	92	at Denver	88
Game 5......Denver	102	at LA Lakers	99
Game 6......LA Lakers	96	at Denver	113
Game 7......Denver	87	at LA Lakers	96

LA Lakers won series 4–3.

Game 1......LA Clippers	99	at Memphis	98
Game 2......LA Clippers	98	at Memphis	105
Game 3......Memphis	86	at LA Clippers	87
Game 4......Memphis	97	at LA Clippers	101
Game 5......LA Clippers	80	at Memphis	92
Game 6......Memphis	90	at LA Clippers	88
Game 7......LA Clippers	82	at Memphis	72

LA Clippers won series 4–3.

Game 1......Dallas	98	at Okla. City	99
Game 2......Dallas	99	at Okla. Cty	102
Game 3......Okla. City	95	at Dallas	79
Game 4......Okla. City	103	at Dallas	97

Oklahoma City won series 4–0.

Eastern Conference Semifinals

Game 1......Philadelphia	91	at Boston	92
Game 2......Philadelphia	82	at Boston	81
Game 3......Boston	107	at Philadelphia	91
Game 4......Boston	83	at Philadelphia	92
Game 5......Philadelphia	85	at Boston	101
Game 6......Boston	75	at Philadelphia	82
Game 7......Philadelphia	75	at Boston	85

Boston won series 4–3.

Game 1......Indiana	86	at Miami	95
Game 2......Indiana	78	at Miami	75
Game 3......Miami	75	at Indiana	94
Game 4......Miami	101	at Indiana	93
Game 5......Indiana	83	at Miami	115
Game 6......Miami	105	at Indiana	93

Miami won series 4–2.

Western Conference Semifinals

Game 1......LA Clippers	92	at San Antonio	108
Game 2......LA Clippers	88	at San Antonio	105
Game 3......San Antonio	96	at LA Clippers	86
Game 4......San Antonio	102	at LA Clippers	99

San Antonio won series 4–0.

Game 1......LA Lakers	90	at Okla. City	114
Game 2......LA Lakers	75	at Okla. City	77
Game 3......Okla. City	96	at LA Lakers	99
Game 4......Okla. City	103	at LA Lakers	100
Game 5......LA Lakers	90	at Okla. City	106

Oklahoma City won series 4–1.

Eastern Conference Finals

Game 1......Boston	79	at Miami	93
Game 2......Boston	111	at Miami	115*
Game 3......Miami	91	at Boston	101
Game 4......Miami	91	at Boston	93*
Game 5......Boston	94	at Miami	90
Game 6......Miami	98	at Boston	79
Game 7......Boston	88	at Miami	101

Miami won series 4–3.

Western Conference Finals

Game 1......Okla. City	98	at San Antonio	101
Game 2......Okla. City	111	at San Antonio	120
Game 3......San Antonio	82	at Okla. City	102
Game 4......San Antonio	103	at Okla. City	109
Game 5......Okla. City	108	at San Antonio	103
Game 6......San Antonio	99	at Okla. City	107

Oklahoma City won series 4–2.

NBA Finals

Game 1......Miami	94	at Okla. City	105
Game 2......Miami	100	at Okla. City	96
Game 3......Okla. City	85	at Miami	91
Game 4......Okla. City	98	at Miami	104
Game 5......Okla. City	106	at Miami	121

Miami won series 4–1.

*Overtime game.

MIAMI HEAT

Player	GP	Mpg	FG%	3FG%	FT%	Reb./per game Off.	Total	Apg	Spg	Bpg	TOpg	Ppg
LeBron James	5	44.0	.472	.188	.826	3.0	10.2	7.4	1.6	0.4	3.8	28.6
Dwyane Wade	5	40.6	.435	.400	.775	1.2	6.0	5.2	1.4	1.2	2.8	22.6
Chris Bosh	5	36.6	.452	.400	.882	3.0	9.4	0.2	0.6	1.2	1.0	14.6
Shane Battier	5	37.4	.613	.577	.714	0.4	3.4	0.4	0.8	0.0	0.2	11.6
Mario Chalmers	5	36.6	.442	.348	.857	0.2	2.6	4.0	1.8	0.4	2.0	10.4
Mike Miller	5	8.8	.563	.636	1.000	0.2	1.8	0.4	0.2	0.2	0.0	6.2
Norris Cole	4	11.0	.333	.429	.000	0.0	1.0	0.0	0.0	0.0	0.2	3.3
Terrel Harris	1	3.0	.000	.000	.750	0.0	1.0	0.0	0.0	0.0	0.0	3.0
James Jones	4	10.8	.500	.400	1.000	0.25	1.5	0.0	0.3	0.0	0.5	2.8
Udonis Haslem	5	16.2	.400	.000	.833	1.6	4.4	0.4	0.0	0.4	1.0	2.6
Joel Anthony	1	2.0	.000	.000	.000	0.0	0.0	0.0	0.0	0.0	0.0	0.0
Juwan Howard	1	3.0	.000	.000	.000	0.0	0.0	0.0	0.0	0.0	0.0	0.0
Ronny Turiaf	1	3.0	.000	.000	.000	0.0	1.0	0.0	0.0	0.0	0.0	0.0
Avg/Total	5	239.8	.464	.429	.824	9.8	40.2	18.0	6.6	3.8	11.5	102.0

OKLAHOMA CITY THUNDER

Player	GP	Mpg	FG%	3FG%	FT%	Reb./per game Off.	Total	Apg	Spg	Bpg	TOpg	Ppg
Kevin Durant	5	42.6	.548	.394	.839	1.2	6.0	2.2	1.4	1.0	3.8	30.6
Russell Westbrook	5	42.2	.433	.136	.824	0.8	6.4	6.6	1.0	0.4	2.2	27.0
James Harden	5	32.8	.375	.318	.792	0.8	4.8	3.6	1.2	0.0	2.4	12.4
Serge Ibaka	5	26.4	.424	.000	.636	1.6	5.2	0.8	0.4	2.0	0.2	7.0
Derek Fisher	5	25.6	.423	.357	1.000	0.2	1.6	0.8	1.0	0.0	0.0	5.6
Kendrick Perkins	5	23.2	.429	.000	.750	2.4	6.8	0.0	0.2	0.6	1.2	4.8
Thabo Sefolosha	5	26.0	.296	.182	.833	0.6	2.0	1.0	1.4	0.8	0.4	4.6
Nick Collison	5	16.6	.600	.000	.000	2.2	4.6	0.6	0.6	0.2	0.4	3.6
Royal Ivey	1	3.0	1.000	1.000	.000	0.0	0.0	0.0	0.0	0.0	0.0	6.0
Cole Aldrich	1	5.0	1.000	.000	.000	0.0	1.0	0.0	0.0	0.0	0.0	2.0
Daequan Cook	3	3.7	.333	.000	.000	0.0	0.0	0.3	0.0	0.0	0.0	0.7
Lazar Hayward	1	5.0	.500	.000	.000	0.0	2.0	0.0	0.0	0.0	0.0	2.0
Avg/Total	5	240.2	.455	.305	.773	9.8	38.0	15.8	7.2	5.0	11.0	98.0

NBA Finals Game Box Scores

Game 1

MIAMI 94

Player	Min	FG M-A	FT M-A	Reb O-T	A	PF	S	TO	TP
L. James	46	11-24	7-9	1-9	4	1	4	4	30
S. Battier	42	6-9	1-2	2-4	0	3	1	0	17
U. Haslem	29	2-6	0-0	3-11	0	5	0	1	4
D. Wade	42	7-19	5-5	1-4	8	3	1	3	19
M. Chalmers	35	5-7	0-0	0-2	6	4	0	1	12
C. Bosh	34	4-11	1-2	0-5	0	2	0	1	10
M. Miller	10	1-2	0-0	0-0	2	1	0	0	2
J. Anthony	2	0-0	0-0	0-0	0	0	0	0	0
Totals	240	36-78	14-18	7-35	20	19	6	10	94

Percentages: FG—.462, FT—.778. 3-pt goals: 8–19, .421 (James 1–3, Battier 4–6, Wade 0–2, Chalmers 2–4, Bosh 1–3, Miller 0–1). Blocked shots: 1 (Chalmers).

Technical foul: Battier

OKLAHOMA CITY 105

Player	Min	FG M-A	FT M-A	Reb O-T	A	PF	S	TO	TP
K. Durant	46	12-20	8-9	1-8	4	2	0	2	36
S. Ibaka	27	5-10	0-1	1-6	1	2	1	0	10
K. Perkins	25	2-2	0-0	2-7	0	0	0	2	4
T. Sefolosha	28	2-5	5-6	0-1	2	3	2	1	9
R. Westbrook	42	10-24	7-9	1-8	11	1	1	2	27
N. Collison	21	4-5	0-0	5-10	0	3	1	2	8
J. Harden	22	2-6	0-0	0-0	3	4	0	1	5
D. Fisher	25	3-5	0-0	0-3	1	1	0	0	6
D. Cook	3	0-0	0-2	0-0	0	0	0	0	0
Totals	240	40-77	20-27	10-43	22	16	5	10	105

Percentages: FG—.519, FT—.741. 3-pt goals: 5–17, .294 (Durant 4–8, Sefolosha 0–2, Westbrook 0–4, Harden 1–2, Fisher 0–1). Blocked shots: 3 (Durant, Perkins, Sefolosha).

Technical foul: Westbrook

A: 18,203. Officials: M. McCutchen, D. Stafford, E. Malloy.

Game 2

MIAMI 100

Player	Min	FG M-A	FT M-A	Reb O-T	A	PF	S	TO	TP
L. James	42	10-22	12-12	2-8	5	4	1	2	32
S. Battier	42	6-8	0-0	0-1	1	3	0	0	17
C. Bosh	40	6-13	4-5	7-15	1	3	1	2	16
D. Wade	39	10-20	4-6	1-6	5	2	0	3	24
M. Chalmers	39	1-7	0-0	0-4	1	2	3	3	3
U. Haslem	16	1-2	0-0	1-4	0	3	0	2	2
J. Jones	6	1-1	0-0	0-0	0	0	0	0	2
N. Cole	13	1-3	0-0	0-1	0	3	0	1	2
M. Miller	1	0-0	2-2	0-1	0	1	0	0	2
Totals	240	36-76	22-25	11-40	13	21	5	13	100

Percentages: FG—.474, FT—.880. 3-pt goals: 6-14, .429 (James 0-2, Battier 5-7, Bosh 0-1, Chalmers 1-3, Cole 0-1). Blocked shots: 4 (Bosh 2, Wade, Haslem).

OKLAHOMA CITY 96

Player	Min	FG M-A	FT M-A	Reb O-T	A	PF	S	TO	TP
K. Durant	38	12-22	4-6	0-3	1	5	2	2	32
S. Ibaka	29	2-5	3-4	2-4	1	2	0	0	7
K. Perkins	20	1-5	2-2	4-8	0	3	0	3	4
T. Sefolosha	37	1-5	0-0	2-5	2	2	2	1	3
R. Westbrook	42	10-26	5-7	2-8	7	3	1	2	27
J. Harden	35	7-11	5-7	0-4	2	3	1	2	21
N. Collison	15	0-0	0-0	0-3	1	3	1	0	0
D. Fisher	24	1-5	0-0	0-1	0	1	2	0	2
Totals	240	34-79	19-26	10-36	14	22	9	10	96

Percentages: FG—.430, FT—.731. 3-pt goals: 9-26, .346 (Durant 4-10, Sefolosha 1-3, Westbrook 2-6, Harden 2-3, Fisher 0-4). Blocked shots: 9 (Durant, Ibaka 5, Perkins, Sefolosha 2).

A: 18,203. Officials: D. Crawford, T. Brothers, T. Washington.

Game 3

OKLAHOMA CITY 85

Player	Min	FG M-A	FT M-A	Reb O-T	A	PF	S	TO	TP
K. Durant	39	11-19	2-4	2-6	0	5	1	5	25
S. Ibaka	22	2-5	1-2	0-5	0	2	0	0	5
K. Perkins	34	3-5	4-6	6-12	0	3	0	0	10
T. Sefolosha	27	3-8	0-0	1-2	1	3	3	2	6
R. Westbrook	39	8-18	2-2	0-5	4	2	0	2	19
J. Harden	34	2-10	5-7	1-6	6	4	2	2	9
D. Fisher	28	3-8	1-1	0-0	0	2	2	0	9
N. Collison	13	1-3	0-2	1-2	0	4	1	0	2
D. Cook	3	0-1	0-0	0-0	0	0	0	0	0
Totals	240	33-77	15-24	11-38	11	25	9	11	85

Percentages: FG—.429, FT—.625. 3-pt goals: 4-18, .222 (Durant 1-4, Sefolosha 0-2, Westbrook 1-4, Harden 0-4, Fisher 2-3, Cook 0-1). Blocked shots: 8 (Durant 2, Ibaka 2, Perkins, Sefolosha, Westbrook 2).

Technical Foul: Brooks (coach)

MIAMI 91

Player	Min	FG M-A	FT M-A	Reb O-T	A	PF	S	TO	TP
L. James	44	11-23	6-8	5-14	3	1	0	4	29
S. Battier	35	2-2	3-3	0-3	0	3	1	0	9
C. Bosh	37	3-12	4-4	4-11	0	1	0	1	10
D. Wade	45	8-22	9-11	2-7	7	4	2	5	25
M. Chalmers	40	1-8	0-0	0-3	3	2	2	1	2
M. Miller	6	1-2	2-2	1-2	0	3	0	0	4
N. Cole	6	0-2	0-0	0-0	0	2	0	0	0
U. Haslem	14	1-1	4-4	2-3	0	2	0	1	6
J. Jones	12	1-2	3-3	0-2	0	1	1	0	6
Totals	240	28-74	31-35	14-45	13	19	6	12	91

Percentages: FG—.378, FT—.886. 3-pt goals: 4-13, .308 (James 1-4, Battier 2-2, Chalmers 0-3, Miller 0-1, Cole 0-1, Jones 1-2). Blocked shots: 5 (Bosh 2, Chalmers, Miller, Haslem).

A: 20,003. Officials: J. Crawford, J. Capers, K. Mauer.

Game 4

OKLAHOMA CITY 98

Player	Min	FG M-A	FT M-A	Reb O-T	A	PF	S	TO	TP
K. Durant	46	9-19	9-9	1-2	3	2	3	2	28
S. Ibaka	27	2-4	0-0	1-7	2	3	1	1	4
K. Perkins	18	2-5	0-0	0-3	0	2	0	0	4
T. Sefolosha	27	2-7	0-0	0-2	0	1	0	0	5
R. Westbrook	45	20-32	3-3	1-7	5	3	1	4	43
N. Collison	17	3-4	0-0	3-4	1	1	0	0	6
J. Harden	37	2-10	3-4	2-10	2	5	1	4	8
D. Fisher	22	0-1	0-0	0-0	0	2	1	0	0
Totals	240	40-82	15-16	8-35	13	20	6	11	98

Percentages: FG—.488, FT—.938. 3-pt goals: 3-16, .188. (Durant 1-5, Sefolosha 1-3, Westbrook 0-3, Harden 1-5). Blocked shots: 2 (Ibaka, Collison)

MIAMI 104

Player	Min	FG M-A	FT M-A	Reb O-T	A	PF	S	TO	TP
L. James	44	10-20	5-8	3-9	12	2	2	3	26
S. Battier	40	1-4	1-2	0-5	0	4	1	0	4
C. Bosh	37	6-12	1-4	1-9	0	2	1	1	13
D. Wade	42	8-19	7-9	0-5	3	2	2	2	25
M. Chalmers	34	9-15	4-5	0-2	3	3	2	1	25
M. Miller	3	0-1	0-0	0-1	0	0	0	0	0
N. Cole	8	3-6	0-0	0-2	0	1	0	0	8
U. Haslem	11	0-0	0-0	1-3	1	0	0	1	0
J. Jones	20	1-2	0-0	0-2	0	4	0	1	3
Totals	240	38-79	18-25	9-40	19	18	8	9	104

Percentages: FG—.481, FT—.720. 3-pt goals: 10-26, .385 (James 1-4, Battier 1-4, Wade 2-3, Chalmers 3-9, Miller 0-1, Cole 2-3, Jones 1-2). Blocked shots: 2 (Wade 2).

A: 20,003. Officials: S. Foster, M. Callahan, B. Kennedy.

Game 5

OKLAHOMA CITY 106

Player	Min	FG M-A	FT M-A	Reb O-T	A	PF	S	TO	TP
K. Durant	43	13-24	3-3	2–11	3	5	2	7	32
S. Ibaka	26	3-9	3-4	4–4	0	3	0	0	9
K. Perkins	20	1-4	0-0	0–4	0	5	1	1	2
T. Sefolosha	9	0-2	0-0	0–0	0	2	0	0	0
R. Westbrook	43	4-20	11-13	0–4	6	3	2	2	19
J. Harden	36	5-11	6-6	1–4	5	2	2	3	19
N. Collison	17	1-3	0-0	2–4	1	3	0	0	2
D. Fisher	29	4-7	0-0	1–4	3	4	0	0	11
D. Cook	5	1-2	0-0	0–0	1	1	0	0	2
C. Aldrich	5	1-1	0-0	0–1	0	0	0	0	2
L. Hayward	5	1-2	0-0	0–2	0	1	0	0	2
R. Ivey	3	2-2	0-0	0–0	0	0	0	0	6
Totals	240	36-87	23-26	10–38	19	29	7	13	106

Percentages: FG—.414, FT—.885. 3-pt goals: 11–28, .393 (Durant 3–6, Sefolosha 0–1, Westbrook 0–5, Harden 3–8, Fisher 3–6, Ivey 2–2). Blocked shots: 3 (Durant, Ibaka 2).

MIAMI 121

Player	Min	FG M-A	FT M-A	Reb O-T	A	PF	S	TO	TP
L. James	44	9-19	8-9	4–11	13	2	1	6	26
S. Battier	29	4-8	0-0	0–4	1	4	1	1	11
C. Bosh	34	9-14	5-5	0–7	0	1	1	0	24
D. Wade	35	7-12	6-9	2–8	3	4	2	1	20
M. Chalmers	34	3-6	2-2	1–2	7	3	2	4	10
M. Miller	23	7-11	2-2	0–5	0	4	1	0	23
U. Haslem	11	0-1	1-2	1–1	1	1	0	0	1
N. Cole	17	1-4	0-0	0–1	0	2	0	0	3
J. Jones	5	0-1	0-0	0–0	0	0	0	1	0
J. Howard	3	0-1	0-0	0–0	0	0	0	0	0
R. Turiaf	3	0-0	0-0	0–1	0	0	0	0	0
T. Harris	3	0-0	3-4	0–1	0	0	0	0	3
Totals	240	40-77	27-33	8–41	25	21	8	13	121

Percentages: FG—.519, FT—.818. 3-pt goals: 14–26, .538 (James 0–3, Battier 3–7, Bosh 1–1, Chalmers 2–4, Miller 7–8, Cole 1–2, Jones 0–1). Blocked shots: 7 (James 2, Bosh 2, Wade 3).

A: 20,003. Officials: D. Crawford, M. McCutchen, D. Stafford.

2011-12 All-NBA Teams

FIRST TEAM	SECOND TEAM	THIRD TEAM
F LeBron James, Mia	F Kevin Love, Min	F Carmelo Anthony, NYK
F Kevin Durant, OKC	F Blake Griffin, LAC	F Dirk Nowitzki, Dal
C Dwight Howard, Orl	C Andrew Bynum, LAL	C Tyson Chandler, NYK
G Kobe Bryant, LAL	G Tony Parker, SA	G Dwyane Wade, Mia
G Chris Paul, LAC	G Russell Westbrook, OKC	G Rajon Rondo, Bos

All-Rookie Teams

FIRST TEAM	SECOND TEAM
Kyrie Irving, Cle	Chandler Parsons, Hou
Ricky Rubio, Min	Isaiah Thomas, Sac
Kenneth Faried, Den	MarShon Brooks, NJ
Klay Thompson, GS	Derrick Williams, Min
Iman Shumpert, NYK	Tristan Thompson, Cle
Kawhi Leonard, SA	
Brandon Knight, Det	

All-Defensive Teams

	FIRST TEAM		SECOND TEAM
F	LeBron James, Mia	F	Kevin Garnett, Bos
F	Serge Ibaka, OKC	F	Luol Deng, Chi
C	Dwight Howard, Orl	C	Tyson Chandler, NYK
G	Chris Paul, LAC	G	Rajon Rondo, Bos
G	Tony Allen, Mem	G	Kobe Bryant, LAL

2011-12 NBA Regular Season Individual Leaders

Scoring

	GP	Pts	Avg
Kevin Durant, OKC	66	1,850	28.0
Kobe Bryant, LAL	58	1,616	27.9
LeBron James, Mia	62	1,683	27.1
Kevin Love, Min	55	1,432	26.0
Russell Westbrook, OKC	66	1,558	23.6
Carmelo Anthony, NYK	55	1,245	22.6
LaMarcus Aldridge, Por	55	1,191	21.7
Dirk Nowitzki, Dal	62	1,342	21.6
Deron Williams, NJ	55	1,154	21.0
Blake Griffin, LAC	66	1,368	20.7

Assists

	GP	Ast	Avg
Rajon Rondo, Bos	53	620	11.7
Steve Nash, Phx	62	664	10.7
Chris Paul, LAC	60	543	9.1
Jose Calderon, Tor	53	468	8.8
Deron Williams, NJ	55	481	8.7
Ricky Rubio, Min	41	336	8.2
John Wall, Was	66	530	8.0
Tony Parker, SA	60	463	7.7
Andre Miller, Den	66	441	6.7
Ty Lawson, Den	61	401	6.6

Free-Throw Percentage

	FTA	FTM	Pct
Jamal Crawford, Por	206	191	.927
JJ Redick, Orl	157	143	.911
Dirk Nowitzki, Dal	355	318	.896
Kevin Martin, Hou	179	160	.894
Steve Nash, Phx	142	127	.894
Luke Ridnour, Min	119	106	.891
Ryan Anderson, Orl	171	150	.877
D.J. Augustin, Cha	120	105	.875
Andrea Bargnani, Tor	173	151	.873
Danny Granger, Ind	291	254	.873

Steals

	GP	Steals	Avg
Chris Paul, LAC	60	152	2.53
Mike Conley, Mem	62	136	2.19
LeBron James, Mia	62	115	1.86
Paul Millsap, Utah	64	118	1.84
Tony Allen, Mem	58	104	1.79
Andre Iguodala, Phi	62	107	1.73
Iman Shumpert, NYK	59	101	1.71
Russell Westbrook, OKC	66	112	1.7
Paul George, Ind	66	108	1.64
Jeff Teague, Atl	66	106	1.61

Rebounds

	GP	Reb	Avg
Dwight Howard, Orl	54	785	14.5
Kevin Love, Min	55	734	13.3
Andrew Bynum, LAL	60	709	11.8
DeMarcus Cousins, Sac	64	703	11.0
Kris Humphries, NJ	62	681	11.0
Blake Griffin, LAC	66	717	10.9
Pau Gasol, LAL	65	678	10.4
Marcin Gortat, Phx	66	659	10.0
Tyson Chandler, NYK	62	612	9.9
Joakim Noah, Chi	64	629	9.8

Field-Goal Percentage

	FGM	FGA	Pct
Dwight Howard, Orl	416	726	.573
Nikola Pekovic, Min	256	454	.564
Andrew Bynum, LAL	444	796	.558
JaVale McGee, Den	307	552	.556
Marcin Gortat, Phx	427	769	.555
Blake Griffin, LAC	561	1,022	.549
Serge Ibaka, OKC	262	490	.535
DeJuan Blair, SA	269	504	.534
Carlos Boozer, Chi	448	842	.532
Steve Nash, Phx	295	555	.532

Three-Point Field-Goal Percentage

	3FGM	3FGA	Pct
Steve Novak, NYK	133	282	.472
Stephen Curry, GS	55	121	.455
Ersan Ilyasova, Mil	51	112	.455
Ray Allen, Bos	106	234	.453
Mike Miller, Mia	53	117	.453
Brandon Rush, GS	99	219	.452
Willie Green, Atl	50	113	.442
Jordan Farmar, NJ	55	125	.440
Danny Green, SA	102	234	.436
Kyle Korver, Chi	118	271	.435

Blocked Shots

	GP	BS	Avg
Serge Ibaka, OKC	66	241	3.65
JaVale McGee, Den	61	132	2.16
Dwight Howard, Orl	54	116	2.15
DeAndre Jordan, LAC	66	134	2.03
Roy Hibbert, Ind	65	128	1.97
Andrew Bynum, LAL	60	116	1.93
Marc Gasol, Mem	65	121	1.86
Bismack Biyombo, Cha	63	115	1.83
Josh Smith, Atl	66	115	1.74
Samuel Dalembert, Hou	65	111	1.71

2011-12 NBA Regular Season Team Statistics

Offense

Team	FG Pct	3FG Pct	FT Pct	Rebound Avg Off	Total	A	TO	Stl	Scoring Avg
Denver Nuggets	47.6	33.2	73.5	11.2	43.1	24.0	15.0	8.2	104.1
San Antonio Spurs	47.8	39.3	74.8	10.4	43.0	23.2	13.2	7.4	103.7
Oklahoma City Thunder	47.1	35.8	80.6	11.0	43.7	18.6	16.0	7.6	103.1
Utah Jazz	45.6	32.3	75.4	13.1	44.2	21.8	13.6	8.3	99.7
Milwaukee Bucks	44.3	34.5	77.4	12.4	42.5	23.5	13.7	8.3	99.0
Sacramento Kings	43.6	31.6	73.6	13.4	42.9	19.3	13.8	8.5	98.8
Miami Heat	46.9	35.9	77.5	10.4	41.6	20.0	14.7	8.9	98.5
Phoenix Suns	45.8	34.3	75.7	10.9	41.7	22.5	13.5	6.5	98.4
Houston Rockets	44.9	35.9	78.3	11.7	42.2	21.3	13.8	7.5	98.1
New York Knicks	44.3	33.6	74.1	11.3	41.7	20.1	15.3	9.4	97.9
Minnesota Timberwolves	43.3	33.2	77.1	12.1	43.7	19.6	14.7	6.6	97.9
Golden State Warriors	45.7	38.8	77.0	9.7	39.2	22.3	13.4	8.0	97.8
Indiana Pacers	43.8	36.8	78.3	12.5	43.9	18.6	13.2	7.9	97.7
Los Angeles Clippers	45.5	35.7	68.0	12.1	41.6	21.0	12.4	8.4	97.6
Los Angeles Lakers	45.7	32.6	75.7	12.1	46.2	22.5	14.6	5.9	97.3
Portland Trail Blazers	44.3	34.6	79.6	11.1	40.7	20.4	13.8	8.0	97.2
Atlanta Hawks	45.4	37.0	74.0	9.9	41.2	22.4	13.3	8.1	96.6
Chicago Bulls	45.2	37.5	72.2	13.9	46.7	23.1	13.4	6.9	96.4
Dallas Mavericks	44.3	34.0	77.1	10.1	42.8	20.9	13.5	8.6	95.8
Memphis Grizzlies	44.7	32.6	75.9	12.6	42.1	19.6	13.9	9.6	95.0
Orlando Magic	44.1	37.5	66.0	11.2	42.5	20.0	14.1	6.8	94.2
Philadelphia 76ers	44.8	36.2	74.2	10.7	43.2	22.0	10.7	8.0	93.6
Washington Wizards	44.1	32.0	72.7	11.7	41.7	19.1	14.6	8.0	93.6
New Jersey Nets	42.5	34.2	77.7	11.9	40.3	19.9	14.3	7.5	93.1
Cleveland Cavaliers	42.2	34.6	71.6	12.7	42.3	19.8	14.6	7.1	93.0
Boston Celtics	46.0	36.7	77.8	7.7	38.8	23.6	14.1	7.6	91.9
Detroit Pistons	43.8	34.6	75.2	11.7	40.3	18.7	14.6	7.0	90.9
Toronto Raptors	44.0	34.0	77.0	10.6	42.0	20.9	14.5	6.5	90.7
New Orleans Hornets	45.1	33.3	75.7	11.0	41.1	20.7	14.6	7.4	89.6
Charlotte Bobcats	41.4	29.5	74.6	10.3	39.0	20.1	13.6	6.0	87.0

Defense (Opponents' Statistics)

Team	FG Pct	3FG Pct	FT Pct	Rebound Avg. Off	Total	A	TO	Stl	Scoring Avg
Chicago Bulls	42.1	32.5	74.0	11.4	40.0	18.9	12.6	7.4	88.2
Boston Celtics	41.9	30.8	76.0	11.8	43.2	18.7	14.7	7.8	89.3
Philadelphia 76ers	42.7	33.4	75.2	10.7	43.7	19.6	13.2	5.9	89.4
Miami Heat	43.4	36.3	72.5	11.0	39.8	19.7	15.8	8.3	92.5
Memphis Grizzlies	44.4	34.5	76.4	11.1	40.7	19.3	16.3	7.9	93.0
Atlanta Hawks	44.4	34.4	75.3	10.8	42.3	20.5	14.4	7.5	93.2
New Orleans Hornets	44.4	31.7	75.9	11.1	40.0	20.9	13.2	7.9	93.4
Orlando Magic	44.9	34.7	77.2	10.1	41.3	20.5	12.7	7.5	93.4
Toronto Raptors	43.6	32.8	74.4	10.3	40.5	20.1	14.6	7.2	94.0
Indiana Pacers	43.5	35.1	72.9	12.0	42.3	19.6	14.4	6.6	94.4
New York Knicks	44.2	35.9	73.7	10.9	41.9	18.9	16.2	8.1	94.7
Dallas Mavericks	43.5	34.6	75.0	11.0	43.9	20.5	14.0	8.5	94.8
Los Angeles Clippers	44.7	36.5	74.6	10.8	39.8	20.7	14.1	6.0	95.0
Detroit Pistons	46.2	35.5	76.6	10.7	40.7	22.5	13.8	8.5	95.7
Los Angeles Lakers	43.7	34.8	74.2	11.5	41.0	21.9	10.9	8.4	95.9
San Antonio Spurs	45.2	35.3	75.6	10.3	41.2	19.6	13.2	7.4	96.5
Oklahoma City Thunder	42.7	34.2	76.8	12.7	41.3	19.9	13.6	8.2	96.9
Portland Trail Blazers	46.3	36.3	74.7	11.1	42.3	21.1	14.1	7.6	97.8
Houston Rockets	45.6	32.5	76.6	11.1	41.8	20.0	14.1	7.5	97.9
Washington Wizards	45.3	35.0	75.8	12.3	43.5	21.5	14.6	7.9	98.4
Phoenix Suns	45.5	35.2	76.2	12.2	43.4	21.5	13.5	8.0	98.6
Milwaukee Bucks	44.9	35.1	76.9	12.3	44.7	21.7	15.4	7.6	98.7
Utah Jazz	45.3	34.0	75.4	11.0	41.2	20.5	14.1	7.5	99.0
New Jersey Nets	47.2	37.5	74.0	11.8	42.6	23.3	13.8	8.0	99.1
Minnesota Timberwolves	45.5	34.0	75.5	11.7	43.4	21.6	12.9	8.3	100.1
Cleveland Cavaliers	46.7	36.2	74.8	11.4	42.8	23.1	13.4	7.9	100.2
Charlotte Bobcats	47.5	35.6	75.0	11.8	45.0	23.3	13.0	7.6	100.9
Denver Nuggets	45.6	38.4	75.9	11.1	40.3	23.2	14.9	7.9	101.2
Golden State Warriors	45.3	36.5	74.7	13.2	45.9	23.1	14.3	7.6	101.2
Sacramento Kings	47.6	35.5	76.2	12.4	45.0	23.8	14.8	7.9	104.4

NBA Team-by-Team Statistical Leaders

Atlanta Hawks

Player	GP	MPG	FG%	3Pt%	FT%	OFF	DEF	Total	APG	SPG	BPG	TO	PF	PPG
			Field Goals			Rebounds Per Game								
Joe Johnson	60	35.5	.454	.388	.849	0.90	2.80	3.70	3.9	0.80	0.22	1.93	1.25	18.8
Josh Smith	66	35.3	.458	.257	.630	2.10	7.50	9.60	3.9	1.41	1.74	2.48	2.61	18.8
Jeff Teague	66	33.1	.476	.342	.757	0.30	2.10	2.40	4.9	1.61	0.56	2.03	2.20	12.6
Al Horford	11	31.6	.553	.000	.733	2.40	4.60	7.00	2.2	0.91	1.27	1.45	1.91	12.4
Marvin Williams	57	26.3	.432	.389	.788	1.30	3.80	5.20	1.2	0.82	0.32	0.68	1.47	10.2
Zaza Pachulia	58	28.3	.499	.000	.741	2.70	5.20	7.90	1.4	0.95	0.50	1.40	2.97	7.8
Willie Green	53	17.4	.471	.442	.857	0.30	1.20	1.50	0.8	0.43	0.11	0.62	1.40	7.6
Kirk Hinrich	48	25.8	.414	.346	.781	0.20	1.90	2.10	2.8	0.79	0.23	1.21	2.08	6.6
Ivan Johnson	56	16.7	.513	.333	.720	1.20	2.90	4.00	0.6	0.77	0.32	1.23	2.07	6.4
Jannero Pargo	50	13.4	.415	.384	.950	0.20	1.30	1.50	1.9	0.40	0.04	0.98	1.28	5.6
Tracy McGrady	52	16.1	.437	.455	.675	0.40	2.50	3.00	2.1	0.31	0.29	1.02	0.67	5.3
Vladimir Radmanovic	49	15.4	.376	.370	.759	0.70	2.20	2.90	1.1	0.43	0.31	0.71	1.27	4.5
Jerry Stackhouse	30	9.1	.370	.342	.913	0.20	0.60	0.80	0.5	0.33	0.10	0.43	0.40	3.6
Jason Collins	30	10.3	.400	.000	.467	0.40	1.20	1.60	0.3	0.13	0.10	0.33	1.13	1.3
Erick Dampier	15	5.5	.125	.000	.000	0.70	1.00	1.70	0.3	0.07	0.33	0.20	0.60	0.1
Hawks	**66**	**244.9**	**.454**	**.370**	**.740**	**9.88**	**31.30**	**41.18**	**22.4**	**8.12**	**4.59**	**13.96**	**17.85**	**96.6**
Opponents	**66**	**244.9**	**.444**	**.344**	**.753**	**10.79**	**31.50**	**42.29**	**20.5**	**7.49**	**4.74**	**15.14**	**19.14**	**93.2**

Boston Celtics

Player	GP	MPG	FG%	3Pt%	FT%	OFF	DEF	Total	APG	SPG	BPG	TO	PF	PPG
			Field Goals			Rebounds Per Game								
Paul Pierce	61	34.0	.443	.366	.852	0.6	4.6	5.2	4.5	1.1	0.4	2.8	2.4	19.4
Kevin Garnett	60	31.1	.503	.333	.857	1.1	7.1	8.2	2.9	0.9	1.0	1.8	2.4	15.8
Ray Allen	46	34.0	.458	.453	.915	0.3	2.8	3.1	2.4	1.1	0.2	1.5	1.8	14.2
Brandon Bass	59	31.7	.479	.000	.810	1.6	4.6	6.2	0.9	0.6	0.9	1.1	2.3	12.5
Rajon Rondo	53	36.9	.448	.238	.597	1.2	3.7	4.8	11.7	1.8	0.1	3.6	1.9	11.9
Avery Bradley	64	21.4	.498	.407	.795	0.5	1.3	1.8	1.4	0.7	0.2	1.2	1.7	7.6
Mickael Pietrus	42	21.9	.385	.335	.645	0.4	2.7	3.1	0.6	0.5	0.2	0.8	1.9	6.9
Chris Wilcox	28	17.2	.598	.000	.615	1.4	3.0	4.4	0.4	0.4	0.3	1.1	2.3	5.4
Jermaine O'Neal	25	22.8	.433	.000	.677	1.5	3.9	5.4	0.4	0.3	1.7	0.8	3.2	5.0
Keyon Dooling	46	14.4	.405	.333	.742	0.1	0.8	0.8	1.1	0.3	0.0	0.7	1.2	4.0
Sean Williams	3	14.0	.333	.000	1.000	1.3	2.7	4.0	1.0	1.0	1.0	1.0	1.3	3.7
JaJuan Johnson	36	8.3	.446	.000	.667	0.6	1.1	1.6	0.2	0.1	0.4	0.4	0.7	3.2
Marquis Daniels	38	12.7	.364	.000	.739	0.4	1.3	1.7	1.2	0.6	0.2	0.7	0.9	3.2
Greg Stiemsma	55	13.9	.545	.000	.707	0.9	2.3	3.2	0.5	0.7	1.5	0.6	2.6	2.9
E'Twaun Moore	38	8.7	.381	.378	1.000	1.0	0.8	0.9	0.9	0.3	0.1	0.6	0.9	2.9
Ryan Hollins	15	10.7	.643	.000	.300	0.6	1.1	1.7	0.2	0.1	0.3	0.7	1.5	2.8
Sasha Pavlovic	45	11.7	.391	.293	.375	0.1	1.5	1.6	0.4	0.4	0.3	0.4	1.2	2.7
Celtics	**66**	**241.5**	**.460**	**.367**	**.778**	**7.7**	**31.1**	**38.8**	**23.6**	**7.5**	**5.5**	**14.8**	**19.9**	**91.8**
Opponents	**66**	**241.5**	**.419**	**.308**	**.760**	**11.8**	**31.4**	**43.2**	**18.7**	**7.8**	**4.6**	**15.7**	**18.4**	**89.3**

Charlotte Bobcats

Player	GP	MPG	FG%	3Pt%	FT%	OFF	DEF	Total	APG	SPG	BPG	TO	PF	PPG
			Field Goals			Rebounds Per Game								
Gerald Henderson	55	33.3	.459	0.234	.760	1.20	2.90	4.10	2.3	0.89	0.36	1.82	2.33	15.1
Corey Maggette	32	27.5	.373	0.364	.856	0.70	3.30	3.90	1.2	0.72	0.03	1.84	2.59	15.0
Kemba Walker	66	27.2	.366	0.305	.789	0.50	3.10	3.50	4.4	0.91	0.30	1.80	1.20	12.1
D.J. Augustin	48	29.3	.376	0.341	.875	0.50	1.80	2.30	6.4	0.75	0.02	2.29	1.35	11.1
Byron Mullens	65	22.5	.425	0.235	.821	1.50	3.60	5.00	0.9	0.32	0.80	1.14	2.11	9.3
Reggie Williams	33	22.6	.416	0.308	.725	0.80	2.00	2.80	1.8	0.61	0.09	1.00	1.03	8.3
Derrick Brown	65	22.2	.518	0.250	.667	1.50	2.20	3.60	1.0	0.74	0.18	0.85	1.48	8.1
DJ White	58	18.9	.493	1.000	.705	0.90	2.70	3.60	0.8	0.29	0.40	0.74	1.62	6.8
Tyrus Thomas	54	18.8	.367	0.333	.759	0.90	2.80	3.70	0.6	0.67	1.11	0.98	2.67	5.6
Bismack Biyombo	63	23.1	.464	0.000	.483	1.80	4.00	5.80	0.4	0.32	1.83	1.13	2.30	5.2
Cory Higgins	38	11.1	.325	0.200	.700	0.20	0.70	0.90	0.9	0.13	0.16	1.03	1.05	3.9
Matt Carroll	53	11.2	.331	0.186	.789	0.20	0.90	1.10	0.7	0.30	0.13	0.45	0.98	2.7
Eduardo Najera	22	12.3	.375	0.276	.500	0.50	1.80	2.30	0.5	0.86	0.18	0.32	1.82	2.6
Jamario Moon	8	15.4	.292	0.200	1.000	0.30	2.50	2.80	0.6	0.13	0.63	1.00	0.63	2.3
DeSagana Diop	27	12.0	.357	0.000	.167	1.20	1.90	3.10	0.9	0.22	0.48	0.70	1.33	1.1
Bobcats	**66**	**240.8**	**.414**	**.295**	**.746**	**10.26**	**28.70**	**38.96**	**20.1**	**6.02**	**5.47**	**14.50**	**18.92**	**87.0**
Opponents	**66**	**240.8**	**.475**	**.356**	**.750**	**11.79**	**33.23**	**45.02**	**23.3**	**7.56**	**5.73**	**13.49**	**20.32**	**100.9**

Chicago Bulls

Player	GP	MPG	FG%	3Pt%	FT%	OFF	DEF	Total	APG	SPG	BPG	TO	PF	PPG
			Field Goals			**Rebounds Per Game**								
Derrick Rose	39	35.3	.435	.312	.812	0.70	2.70	3.40	7.9	0.90	0.72	3.05	1.33	21.8
Luol Deng	54	39.4	.412	.367	.770	1.40	5.10	6.50	2.9	1.04	0.67	1.78	1.50	15.3
Carlos Boozer	66	29.5	.532	.000	.693	1.70	6.80	8.50	1.9	0.95	0.36	1.74	2.55	15.0
Richard Hamilton	28	24.9	.452	.370	.784	0.70	1.60	2.40	3.0	0.43	0.04	1.75	2.00	11.6
Joakim Noah	64	30.4	.508	.000	.748	3.80	6.00	9.80	2.5	0.64	1.44	1.44	2.53	10.2
C.J. Watson	49	23.7	.368	.393	.808	0.40	1.70	2.10	4.1	0.92	0.16	1.98	2.10	9.7
Kyle Korver	65	22.6	.432	.435	.833	0.40	2.00	2.40	1.7	0.55	0.23	0.82	1.69	8.1
Taj Gibson	63	20.4	.495	.000	.622	2.10	3.10	5.30	0.7	0.43	1.29	0.95	2.08	7.7
John Lucas III	49	14.8	.399	.393	.875	0.40	1.10	1.60	2.2	0.39	0.02	0.86	0.86	7.5
Ronnie Brewer	66	24.8	.427	.275	.560	1.10	2.40	3.50	2.1	1.09	0.32	0.89	0.97	6.9
Mike James	11	10.9	.408	.600	.875	0.20	0.70	0.90	2.6	0.36	0.18	1.27	1.82	4.8
Omer Asik	66	14.7	.506	.000	.456	1.90	3.40	5.30	0.5	0.45	1.03	1.03	1.83	3.1
Jimmy Butler	42	8.5	.405	.182	.768	0.50	0.80	1.30	0.3	0.26	0.12	0.33	0.48	2.6
Brian Scalabrine	28	4.4	.467	.143	.500	0.30	0.50	0.80	0.5	0.18	0.21	0.32	0.32	1.1
Bulls	66	241.5	.452	.375	.722	13.86	32.80	46.67	23.1	6.91	5.88	13.99	17.26	96.3
Opponents	66	241.5	.421	.325	.740	11.36	28.62	39.99	18.9	7.42	5.20	13.27	17.67	88.2

Cleveland Cavaliers

Player	GP	MPG	FG%	3Pt%	FT%	OFF	DEF	Total	APG	SPG	BPG	TO	PF	PPG
			Field Goals			**Rebounds Per Game**								
Kyrie Irving	51	30.5	.469	.399	.872	0.90	2.90	3.70	5.4	1.06	0.39	3.14	2.16	18.5
Antawn Jamison	65	33.1	.403	.341	.683	1.90	4.40	6.30	2.0	0.78	0.66	1.38	2.52	17.2
Anderson Varejao	25	31.4	.514	.000	.672	4.40	7.10	11.50	1.7	1.40	0.68	1.80	2.48	10.8
Alonzo Gee	63	29.0	.412	.321	.788	1.60	3.50	5.10	1.8	1.32	0.27	1.81	2.37	10.6
Tristan Thompson	60	23.7	.439	.000	.552	3.10	3.40	6.50	0.5	0.45	1.03	1.35	2.23	8.2
Daniel Gibson	35	26.2	.351	.396	.791	0.30	2.60	2.90	2.2	0.74	0.46	1.29	1.97	7.5
Anthony Parker	51	25.1	.433	.362	.625	0.20	2.50	2.70	2.4	0.75	0.14	0.98	1.27	7.2
Omri Casspi	65	20.6	.403	.315	.685	1.00	2.50	3.50	1.0	0.57	0.32	0.98	1.77	7.1
Manny Harris	26	17.5	.400	.333	.695	0.40	2.30	2.70	1.2	0.50	0.23	1.04	1.08	6.7
D.J. Kennedy	2	29.5	.417	.500	.000	0.50	3.00	3.50	1.5	1.00	0.00	1.50	3.50	6.0
*Donald Sloan	33	20.3	.399	.080	.767	0.50	1.50	2.00	3.2	0.39	0.09	1.48	0.00	5.5
Samardo Samuels	54	15.3	.455	.000	.701	1.20	2.20	3.30	0.4	0.37	0.37	1.04	2.09	5.4
Semih Erden	28	11.9	.527	.000	.512	0.70	1.90	2.60	0.3	0.36	0.18	0.57	2.14	3.5
Luke Harangody	21	11.0	.354	.238	.750	1.00	1.60	2.50	0.3	0.29	0.14	0.19	0.81	2.9
*Luke Walton	30	12.1	.369	.350	.000	0.40	1.20	1.60	1.2	0.17	0.03	0.90	0.00	1.8
Cavaliers	66	241.9	.422	.346	.716	12.74	29.53	42.27	19.8	7.06	3.97	15.41	19.95	93.0
Opponents	66	241.9	.467	.362	.748	11.39	31.41	42.80	23.1	7.94	6.20	13.89	20.92	100.2

Dallas Mavericks

Player	GP	MPG	FG%	3Pt%	FT%	OFF	DEF	Total	APG	SPG	BPG	TO	PF	PPG
			Field Goals			**Rebounds Per Game**								
Dirk Nowitzki	62	33.5	.457	.368	.896	0.70	6.00	6.70	2.2	0.68	0.48	1.89	2.08	21.6
Jason Terry	63	31.7	.430	.378	.883	0.30	2.10	2.40	3.6	1.16	0.17	2.02	1.10	15.1
Shawn Marion	63	30.5	.446	.294	.750	2.30	5.10	7.40	2.1	1.06	0.57	1.56	1.38	10.6
Vince Carter	61	25.3	.411	.361	.826	0.50	2.80	3.40	2.3	0.92	0.41	1.38	2.20	10.1
Delonte West	44	24.1	.461	.355	.886	0.30	2.00	2.30	3.2	1.32	0.25	1.73	1.52	9.6
Rodrigue Beaubois	53	21.7	.422	.288	.841	0.40	2.50	2.80	2.9	1.06	0.53	1.32	1.85	8.9
Brandan Wright	49	16.1	.618	.000	.634	1.30	2.30	3.60	0.3	0.45	1.29	0.43	1.24	6.9
Lamar Odom	50	20.5	.352	.252	.592	0.70	3.40	4.20	1.7	0.40	0.36	1.04	1.94	6.6
Jason Kidd	48	28.7	.363	.354	.786	0.30	3.80	4.10	5.5	1.71	0.21	1.90	1.73	6.2
Ian Mahinmi	61	18.7	.546	.000	.639	1.80	3.00	4.70	0.2	0.62	0.51	0.82	2.89	5.8
Brendan Haywood	54	21.2	.518	.000	.469	2.60	3.40	6.00	0.4	0.44	1.00	0.85	2.24	5.2
Dominique Jones	33	8.1	.397	.125	.784	0.30	1.10	1.30	1.3	0.30	0.15	0.85	0.85	2.7
Yi Jianlian	30	6.8	.378	.300	.667	0.40	1.20	1.60	0.2	0.23	0.27	0.47	0.77	2.6
Kelenna Azubuike	3	6.0	.375	.333	.000	0.00	0.00	0.00	0.0	0.33	0.00	1.33	0.33	2.3
Brian Cardinal	44	6.3	.255	.204	.833	0.10	0.70	0.80	0.4	0.18	0.05	0.18	0.86	1.0
Mavericks	66	243.4	.443	.339	.771	10.08	32.68	42.76	20.9	8.56	5.11	14.03	18.58	95.8
Opponents	66	243.4	.435	.346	.750	10.99	32.92	43.91	20.5	8.50	4.02	14.71	18.38	94.8

* mid-season trade

Denver Nuggets

Player	GP	MPG	Field Goals			Rebounds Per Game			APG	SPG	BPG	TO	PF	PPG
			FG%	3Pt%	FT%	OFF	DEF	Total						
Ty Lawson	61	34.8	.488	.365	.824	0.90	2.80	3.70	6.6	1.34	0.10	2.44	1.54	16.4
Arron Afflalo	62	33.6	.471	.398	.798	0.60	2.50	3.20	2.4	0.58	0.21	1.37	2.16	15.2
Danilo Gallinari	43	31.4	.414	.328	.871	0.70	4.00	4.70	2.7	0.98	0.53	1.58	2.00	14.6
Al Harrington	64	27.5	.446	.333	.676	1.10	5.00	6.10	1.4	0.91	0.19	1.75	2.83	14.2
*JaVale McGee	61	25.2	.556	.000	.461	2.70	5.10	7.80	0.5	0.57	2.16	1.43	0.00	11.3
Kenneth Faried	46	22.5	.586	.000	.665	3.10	4.60	7.70	0.8	0.74	1.02	1.17	2.52	10.2
Andre Miller	66	27.4	.438	.217	.811	0.80	2.50	3.30	6.7	0.95	0.14	2.68	2.02	9.7
Wilson Chandler	8	26.9	.392	.250	.833	0.80	4.40	5.10	2.1	0.75	0.75	2.25	2.25	9.4
Corey Brewer	59	21.8	.434	.260	.692	0.70	1.80	2.50	1.5	1.22	0.29	0.95	1.92	8.9
Rudy Fernandez	31	22.9	.440	.328	.698	0.30	1.80	2.10	2.4	1.00	0.10	1.29	1.19	8.6
Kosta Koufos	48	16.5	.599	.000	.600	2.00	3.40	5.40	0.3	0.50	0.85	0.69	2.00	5.5
Timofey Mozgov	44	15.6	.526	.000	.684	1.20	2.90	4.10	0.5	0.34	0.95	1.20	1.95	5.4
Chris Andersen	32	15.2	.546	.000	.610	1.50	3.10	4.60	0.2	0.59	1.44	0.53	1.63	5.3
Jordan Hamilton	26	9.9	.432	.362	.400	0.40	2.00	2.40	0.8	0.15	0.12	0.62	0.58	4.4
Julyan Stone	22	8.1	.419	.182	.727	0.20	0.90	1.10	1.7	0.36	0.27	0.50	0.82	1.6
Nuggets	**66**	**243.0**	**.476**	**.332**	**.735**	**11.18**	**31.89**	**43.08**	**24.0**	**8.18**	**5.00**	**15.38**	**19.65**	**104.1**
Opponents	**66**	**243.0**	**.456**	**.383**	**.759**	**11.06**	**29.21**	**40.27**	**23.2**	**7.94**	**6.65**	**15.58**	**22.00**	**101.2**

Detroit Pistons

Player	GP	MPG	Field Goals			Rebounds Per Game			APG	SPG	BPG	TO	PF	PPG
			FG%	3Pt%	FT%	OFF	DEF	Total						
Greg Monroe	66	31.5	.521	.000	.739	3.60	6.00	9.70	2.3	1.26	0.70	2.44	2.73	15.4
Rodney Stuckey	55	29.9	.429	.317	.834	0.70	1.90	2.60	3.8	0.80	0.18	1.93	2.25	14.8
Brandon Knight	66	32.3	.415	.380	.759	0.50	2.70	3.20	3.8	0.74	0.15	2.59	2.33	12.8
Tayshaun Prince	63	33.1	.421	.356	.774	1.10	3.30	4.50	2.4	0.43	0.52	1.17	1.22	12.7
Ben Gordon	52	26.9	.442	.429	.860	0.30	2.10	2.30	2.4	0.65	0.21	2.21	2.19	12.5
Jonas Jerebko	64	22.9	.468	.302	.806	1.50	3.30	4.80	0.7	0.64	0.33	1.03	2.53	8.7
Charlie Villanueva	13	13.8	.385	.333	.857	0.70	3.00	3.70	0.5	0.54	0.38	0.54	1.92	7.0
Jason Maxiell	65	22.6	.478	.000	.547	1.90	3.20	5.10	0.6	0.49	0.77	1.09	2.32	6.5
Will Bynum	36	14.3	.381	.241	.766	0.30	1.30	1.60	1.8	0.64	0.06	1.50	1.69	5.7
Austin Daye	41	14.7	.322	.210	.814	0.30	1.90	2.20	0.8	0.54	0.51	0.98	1.51	4.7
Damien Wilkins	60	15.4	.394	.304	.630	0.40	1.30	1.70	0.7	0.48	0.22	0.50	1.42	3.2
Walker Russell	28	12.8	.347	.308	.636	0.30	0.70	0.90	2.1	0.64	0.04	1.18	1.04	3.0
Vernon Macklin	23	5.9	.543	.000	.571	0.60	0.90	1.50	0.2	0.17	0.17	0.13	0.39	2.0
Ben Wallace	62	15.8	.395	.250	.340	1.30	3.00	4.30	0.7	0.76	0.82	0.55	0.97	1.4
Pistons	**66**	**241.9**	**.438**	**.346**	**.752**	**11.74**	**28.52**	**40.26**	**18.7**	**6.97**	**4.21**	**15.65**	**19.59**	**90.9**
Opponents	**66**	**241.9**	**.462**	**.355**	**.765**	**10.65**	**30.08**	**40.73**	**22.5**	**8.53**	**5.27**	**14.53**	**19.44**	**95.7**

Golden State Warriors

Player	GP	MPG	Field Goals			Rebounds Per Game			APG	SPG	BPG	TO	PF	PPG
			FG%	3Pt%	FT%	OFF	DEF	Total						
David Lee	57	37.2	.503	.000	.782	3.00	6.60	9.60	2.8	0.95	0.39	2.61	3.14	20.1
Stephen Curry	26	28.2	.490	.455	.809	0.60	2.80	3.40	5.3	1.50	0.31	2.50	2.38	14.7
Klay Thompson	66	24.4	.443	.414	.868	0.40	2.10	2.40	2.0	0.74	0.30	1.56	2.35	12.5
Nate Robinson	51	23.4	.424	.365	.832	0.30	1.70	2.00	4.5	1.16	0.04	1.47	2.31	11.2
Dorell Wright	61	27.0	.422	.360	.816	1.00	3.60	4.60	1.5	0.95	0.43	0.84	1.59	10.3
Brandon Rush	65	26.4	.501	.452	.793	0.50	3.40	3.90	1.4	0.54	0.89	1.05	0.98	9.8
*Richard Jefferson	63	27.7	.416	.420	.694	0.40	3.10	3.50	1.4	0.59	0.30	0.79	0.00	9.2
Charles Jenkins	51	17.5	.447	.150	.872	0.20	1.20	1.30	3.3	0.65	0.12	1.18	1.67	5.8
Jeremy Tyler	42	13.5	.421	.000	.558	1.30	2.00	3.30	0.4	0.38	0.48	0.86	2.00	4.9
Dominic McGuire	64	17.6	.448	.000	.736	1.10	2.70	3.80	1.7	0.69	0.56	0.88	1.63	3.5
Mikki Moore	7	16.9	.450	.000	.857	1.00	2.10	3.10	0.7	0.43	0.43	1.00	3.43	3.4
*Mickell Gladness	26	9.7	.424	.000	.500	0.50	1.70	2.20	0.2	0.15	0.77	0.27	0.00	2.2
Chris Wright	24	7.8	.511	.000	.774	0.80	1.10	1.90	0.2	0.29	0.54	0.33	0.92	2.9
Andris Biedrins	47	15.7	.609	.000	.111	1.00	2.80	3.70	0.3	0.49	0.96	0.30	2.66	1.7
Warriors	**66**	**241.1**	**.457**	**0.388**	**0.770**	**9.70**	**29.50**	**39.20**	**22.3**	**8.00**	**5.49**	**13.86**	**21.36**	**97.8**
Opponents	**66**	**241.1**	**.453**	**0.365**	**0.747**	**13.17**	**32.68**	**45.85**	**23.1**	**7.56**	**4.97**	**14.82**	**16.59**	**101.2**

* mid-season trade

Houston Rockets

Player	GP	MPG	FG%	3Pt%	FT%	OFF	DEF	Total	APG	SPG	BPG	TO	PF	PPG
			Field Goals			Rebounds Per Game								
Kevin Martin	40	31.6	.413	.347	.894	.30	2.30	2.70	2.8	.70	.08	1.75	1.80	17.1
Luis Scola	66	31.3	.491	.000	.773	1.80	4.60	6.50	2.1	.53	.36	2.32	3.20	15.5
Kyle Lowry	47	32.1	.409	.374	.864	.80	3.70	4.60	6.6	1.55	.30	2.77	2.80	14.3
Goran Dragic	66	26.5	.462	.337	.805	.80	1.70	2.50	5.3	1.29	.15	2.38	2.50	11.7
Courtney Lee	58	30.3	.433	.401	.826	.40	2.30	2.70	1.5	1.17	.38	1.10	1.80	11.4
Chase Budinger	58	22.4	.442	.402	.771	.70	3.10	3.70	1.3	.50	.12	.95	1.10	9.6
C. Parsons	63	28.6	.452	.337	.551	1.40	3.30	4.80	2.1	1.16	.46	1.29	2.30	9.5
P. Patterson	64	23.2	.440	.000	.702	1.80	2.70	4.50	.8	.42	.56	.77	1.80	7.7
S. Dalembert	65	22.2	.506	.000	.796	2.40	4.60	7.00	.5	.57	1.71	1.26	2.50	7.5
*Marcus Camby	59	22.9	.446	.400	.453	2.70	6.30	9.00	1.8	.85	1.44	.97	2.10	4.9
Earl Boykins	8	13.9	.333	.222	.867	.00	1.40	1.40	2.1	.13	.00	.88	.60	4.9
*C. Fortson	10	9.5	.344	.231	.667	.60	.90	1.50	1.0	.30	.00	1.00	.50	3.5
Jeff Adrien	8	7.9	.438	.000	.583	.60	2.10	2.80	.1	.00	.25	.25	1.60	2.6
Marcus Morris	17	7.4	.296	.118	.750	.30	.60	.90	.2	.12	.12	.24	.70	2.4
Greg Smith	8	8.6	.636	.000	.000	.60	1.90	2.50	.1	.25	.63	.13	2.10	1.8
Rockets	**66**	**243.4**	**.449**	**.359**	**.782**	**11.7**	**30.5**	**42.2**	**21.3**	**7.5**	**4.8**	**14.5**	**20.4**	**98.1**
Opponents	**66**	**243.4**	**.456**	**.325**	**.766**	**11.0**	**30.7**	**41.8**	**20.0**	**7.5**	**5.2**	**14.7**	**18.4**	**97.9**

Indiana Pacers

Player	GP	MPG	FG%	3Pt%	FT%	OFF	DEF	Total	APG	SPG	BPG	TO	PF	PPG
			Field Goals			Rebounds Per Game								
Danny Granger	62	33.3	.416	.381	.873	1.30	3.70	5.00	1.8	1.00	0.65	1.77	2.32	18.7
David West	66	29.2	.487	.222	.807	1.80	4.80	6.60	2.1	0.79	0.70	1.41	2.42	12.8
Roy Hibbert	65	29.8	.497	.000	.711	3.30	5.50	8.80	1.7	0.49	1.97	1.97	3.00	12.8
Paul George	66	29.7	.440	.385	.802	0.80	4.80	5.60	2.4	1.64	0.58	1.77	2.89	12.1
*L. Barbosa	21.6	.425	.382	.815	0.50	1.50	2.00	1.5	0.88	0.11	1.47	0.00	11.1	
Darren Collison	60	31.3	.440	.362	.830	0.50	2.60	3.10	4.8	0.82	0.23	1.90	1.68	10.3
George Hill	50	25.5	.442	.367	.778	0.60	2.40	3.00	2.9	0.84	0.34	1.04	1.96	9.6
T. Hansbrough	66	21.8	.405	.000	.813	1.70	2.70	4.40	0.5	0.82	0.14	0.98	2.41	9.3
Dahntay Jones	65	16.2	.409	.429	.838	0.40	1.40	1.80	1.0	0.35	0.17	0.71	1.83	5.3
A.J. Price	44	12.9	.339	.295	.800	0.30	1.10	1.40	2.0	0.45	0.05	0.73	0.68	3.9
Lou Amundson	12.6	.430	.000	.427	1.60	2.10	3.70	0.2	0.45	0.73	0.75	2.08	3.5	
Kyrylo Fesenko	3	5.7	.400	.000	.667	0.70	2.30	3.00	0.3	0.67	0.00	0.00	0.67	2.7
L. Stephenson	42	10.5	.376	.133	.471	0.30	1.00	1.30	1.1	0.50	0.12	0.86	0.71	2.5
Jeff Foster	11	12.8	.500	.000	.667	1.60	2.20	3.80	0.4	0.73	0.09	0.64	2.36	2.3
J. Pendergraph	20	5.3	.417	.000	.571	0.60	1.10	1.60	0.2	0.15	0.10	0.10	0.80	1.7
Pacers	**66**	**242.3**	**.438**	**.368**	**.782**	**12.52**	**31.36**	**43.88**	**18.6**	**7.92**	**5.41**	**14.02**	**21.67**	**97.7**
Opponents	**66**	**242.3**	**.435**	**.351**	**.729**	**12.03**	**30.27**	**42.30**	**19.6**	**6.56**	**6.03**	**14.92**	**21.64**	**94.4**

Los Angeles Clippers

Player	GP	MPG	FG%	3Pt%	FT%	OFF	DEF	Total	APG	SPG	BPG	TO	PF	PPG
			Field Goals			Rebounds Per Game								
Blake Griffin	66	36.2	.549	.125	.521	3.3	7.6	10.9	3.2	0.8	0.7	2.3	3.3	20.7
Chris Paul	60	36.4	.478	.371	.861	0.7	2.9	3.6	9.1	2.5	0.1	2.1	2.3	19.8
Chauncey Billups	20	30.4	.364	.384	.895	0.2	2.3	2.5	4.0	0.5	0.2	1.9	2.0	15.0
Mo Williams	52	28.3	.426	.389	.900	0.4	1.5	1.9	3.1	1.0	0.1	1.7	2.0	13.2
Caron Butler	63	29.7	.425	.358	.813	0.7	3.0	3.7	1.2	0.8	0.1	1.2	2.0	12.0
Randy Foye	65	25.9	.398	.386	.859	0.4	1.7	2.1	2.2	0.7	0.4	1.1	2.0	11.0
Nick Young	22	23.5	.394	.353	.821	0.5	1.1	1.6	0.5	0.6	0.3	1.1	2.3	9.7
DeAndre Jordan	66	27.2	.632	.000	.525	3.1	5.2	8.3	0.3	0.5	2.0	1.1	2.9	7.4
Kenyon Martin	42	22.4	.441	.231	.370	1.2	3.1	4.3	0.4	1.0	1.0	0.8	2.5	5.2
Courtney Fortson	4	11.5	.417	.250	.667	1.0	1.0	2.0	1.3	0.0	0.0	1.3	0.8	4.3
Eric Bledsoe	40	16.9	.389	.200	.636	0.6	1.1	1.6	1.7	0.8	0.4	1.2	1.5	3.3
Bobby Simmons	28	14.9	.311	.333	.571	0.6	1.4	2.0	0.4	0.5	0.1	0.4	1.5	2.9
Trey Thompkins	24	5.0	.393	.308	.714	0.2	0.8	1.0	0.1	0.1	0.1	0.3	0.4	2.4
Ryan Gomes	32	13.3	.326	.138	.727	0.4	1.5	1.9	0.4	0.5	0.0	0.5	1.1	2.3
Reggie Evans	56	13.8	.472	.000	.507	1.8	3.1	4.8	0.3	0.6	0.1	0.8	2.1	1.9
Brian Cook	16	7.6	.224	.185	1.000	0.3	1.2	1.4	0.1	0.1	0.3	0.3	1.6	1.9
Travis Leslie	10	4.5	.357	.000	.444	0.6	0.3	0.9	0.5	0.2	0.2	0.2	0.4	1.4
Solomon Jones	10	9.6	.125	.000	.800	1.1	0.6	1.7	0.2	0.4	0.5	0.5	1.2	0.6
Clippers	**66**	**241.9**	**.455**	**.357**	**.680**	**12.1**	**29.4**	**41.6**	**21.0**	**8.4**	**4.8**	**13.3**	**21.2**	**97.5**
Opponents	**66**	**241.9**	**.447**	**.365**	**.746**	**10.8**	**29.0**	**39.8**	**20.7**	**6.0**	**4.5**	**14.6**	**21.2**	**95.0**

* mid-season trade

Los Angeles Lakers

Player	GP	MPG	FG%	3Pt%	FT%	OFF	DEF	Total	APG	SPG	BPG	TO	PF	PPG
Kobe Bryant	58	38.5	.430	.303	.845	1.10	4.30	5.40	4.6	1.19	0.31	3.52	1.81	27.9
Andrew Bynum	60	35.2	.558	.200	.692	3.20	8.60	11.80	1.4	0.45	1.93	2.53	1.73	18.7
Pau Gasol	65	37.4	.501	.259	.782	2.80	7.60	10.40	3.6	0.57	1.35	2.18	1.95	17.4
Ramon Sessions	64	26.7	.428	.443	.782	0.50	2.80	3.30	5.5	0.69	0.05	2.20	0.00	11.3
Matt Barnes	63	22.9	.452	.333	.742	1.50	3.90	5.50	2.0	0.56	0.76	1.16	2.41	7.8
Metta World Peace	64	26.9	.394	.296	.617	1.10	2.30	3.40	2.2	1.08	0.42	1.08	2.14	7.7
Steve Blake	53	23.3	.377	.335	.778	0.20	1.40	1.60	3.3	0.74	0.04	1.36	1.42	5.2
*Jordan Hill	39	14.1	.497	.000	.638	1.60	3.20	4.80	0.4	0.36	0.69	0.79	0.00	5.0
Andrew Goudelock	40	10.5	.391	.373	.917	0.10	0.70	0.80	1.5	0.10	0.00	0.53	0.80	4.4
Devin Ebanks	24	16.5	.416	.000	.657	1.10	1.20	2.30	0.5	0.46	0.25	0.75	1.08	4.0
Troy Murphy	59	16.2	.450	.418	.667	0.70	2.60	3.20	0.9	0.25	0.27	0.44	1.66	3.2
Josh McRoberts	50	14.4	.475	.429	.639	1.20	2.20	3.40	1.0	0.30	0.36	0.62	1.48	2.8
Darius Morris	19	8.9	.429	.444	.667	0.10	0.70	0.80	1.1	0.11	0.00	1.00	0.84	2.4
Christian Eyenga	7	14.7	.240	.333	.500	0.60	1.40	2.00	0.7	0.43	0.71	0.43	0.00	2.4
Lakers	66	243.4	.457	.326	.756	12.11	34.11	46.21	22.5	5.91	5.32	15.11	16.80	97.3
Opponents	66	243.4	.437	.348	.742	11.49	29.49	40.97	21.9	8.42	4.58	11.29	20.18	95.9

Memphis Grizzlies

Player	GP	MPG	FG%	3Pt%	FT%	OFF	DEF	Total	APG	SPG	BPG	TO	PF	PPG
Rudy Gay	65	37.3	.455	.312	.791	2.00	4.40	6.40	2.3	1.46	0.85	2.48	2.12	19.0
Marc Gasol	65	36.5	.482	.083	.748	1.80	7.10	8.90	3.1	0.95	1.86	1.86	3.09	14.6
Mike Conley	62	35.1	.433	.377	.861	0.40	2.20	2.50	6.5	2.19	0.18	2.02	2.15	12.7
O.J. Mayo	66	26.8	.408	.364	.773	0.50	2.70	3.20	2.6	1.08	0.35	1.88	2.08	12.6
Zach Randolph	28	26.3	.463	.250	.659	2.80	5.30	8.00	1.7	0.75	0.14	1.43	2.04	11.6
*Lester Hudson	16	20.9	.383	.250	.829	0.40	2.40	2.90	2.3	0.88	0.19	2.00	0.00	10.9
Tony Allen	58	26.3	.469	.308	.800	1.70	2.30	4.00	1.4	1.79	0.57	1.62	2.45	9.8
Marreese Speights	60	22.4	.453	.000	.771	2.20	4.00	6.20	0.8	0.35	0.48	1.23	2.45	8.8
Dante Cunningham	64	17.6	.516	.000	.652	1.40	2.40	3.80	0.6	0.66	0.53	0.45	1.53	5.2
Gilbert Arenas	17	12.4	.406	.333	.700	0.10	0.90	1.10	1.1	0.65	0.06	0.71	2.06	4.2
Quincy Pondexter	64	15.7	.452	.301	.623	0.90	1.10	2.00	0.6	0.42	0.08	0.47	1.41	4.2
Jeremy Pargo	44	9.6	.333	.263	.593	0.30	0.60	0.80	1.3	0.34	0.01	1.05	1.05	2.9
Josh Selby	28	8.5	.347	.133	.786	0.10	0.50	0.50	1.1	0.25	0.00	1.04	0.61	2.3
Hamed Haddadi	35	5.9	.542	.000	.692	0.80	1.20	2.00	0.2	0.03	0.74	0.60	1.23	2.0
Grizzlies	66	241.5	.447	.326	.759	12.59	29.46	42.05	19.5	9.56	5.23	14.47	19.94	95.0
Opponents	66	241.5	.444	.345	.764	11.05	29.61	40.65	19.3	7.85	5.50	17.12	19.32	93.0

Miami Heat

Player	GP	MPG	FG%	3Pt%	FT%	OFF	DEF	Total	APG	SPG	BPG	TO	PF	PPG
LeBron James	62	37.5	.531	.362	.771	1.5	6.4	7.9	6.2	1.9	0.8	3.4	1.5	27.1
Dwyane Wade	49	33.2	.497	.268	.791	1.5	3.3	4.8	4.6	1.7	1.3	2.6	2.2	22.1
Chris Bosh	57	35.2	.487	.286	.821	1.6	6.3	7.9	1.8	0.9	0.8	2.1	2.2	18.0
Mario Chalmers	64	28.5	.448	.388	.792	0.3	2.4	2.7	3.5	1.5	0.2	2.2	2.6	9.8
Norris Cole	65	19.4	.393	.276	.776	0.3	1.1	1.4	2.0	0.7	0.0	1.6	1.9	6.8
Mike Miller	39	19.3	.435	.453	.400	0.6	2.7	3.3	1.1	0.4	0.2	0.8	1.5	6.1
Udonis Haslem	64	24.8	.423	.000	.814	1.8	5.5	7.3	0.7	0.5	0.4	0.9	2.2	6.0
Shane Battier	65	23.1	.387	.339	.622	0.9	1.5	2.4	1.3	1.0	0.5	0.6	1.6	4.8
Terrel Harris	22	14.5	.349	.205	.667	0.8	1.5	2.3	1.2	0.4	0.1	1.1	1.5	3.6
James Jones	51	13.1	.380	.404	.833	0.1	0.8	1.0	0.4	0.3	0.2	0.2	0.9	3.6
Ronny Turiaf	13	17.0	.533	.000	.591	1.5	3.0	4.5	0.4	0.6	1.1	0.6	2.5	3.5
Joel Anthony	64	21.1	.559	.000	.690	1.6	2.3	3.9	0.1	0.6	1.3	0.7	2.0	3.4
Dexter Pittman	35	8.6	.468	.000	.643	0.8	1.3	2.0	0.3	0.2	0.2	0.5	2.1	3.0
Eddy Curry	14	5.9	.462	.000	.750	0.3	0.6	0.9	0.1	0.0	0.1	0.7	1.2	2.1
Juwan Howard	28	6.8	.309	.000	.800	0.6	1.0	1.7	0.4	0.1	0.0	0.7	0.6	1.5
Mickell Gladness	8	3.5	.333	.000	.000	0.1	1.3	1.4	0.3	0.1	0.1	0.4	1.0	0.3
Heat	66	242.6	.469	.359	.775	10.4	31.2	41.6	20.0	8.9	5.4	15.2	19.4	98.5
Opponents	66	242.6	.434	.363	.725	11.0	28.7	39.8	20.6	8.3	4.2	16.8	20.5	92.5

* mid-season trade

Milwaukee Bucks

Player	GP	MPG	FG%	3Pt%	FT%	OFF	DEF	Total	APG	SPG	BPG	TO	PF	PPG
*Monta Ellis	58	36.6	0.433	0.308	0.796	0.30	3.10	3.40	6.0	1.47	0.31	3.05	0.00	20.4
Brandon Jennings	66	35.3	0.418	0.332	0.808	0.70	2.70	3.40	5.5	1.58	0.33	2.21	1.73	19.1
Drew Gooden	56	26.2	0.437	0.291	0.846	2.30	4.20	6.50	2.6	0.82	0.61	1.95	2.00	13.7
Ersan Ilyasova	60	27.6	0.492	0.455	0.781	3.30	5.50	8.80	1.2	0.70	0.73	1.27	2.22	13.0
Mike Dunleavy	55	26.3	0.474	0.399	0.811	0.50	3.20	3.70	2.1	0.15	0.15	1.05	1.58	12.3
Carlos Delfino	54	28.5	0.402	0.360	0.792	0.40	3.50	3.90	2.3	1.46	0.19	1.22	1.83	9.0
Luc Mbah a Moute	43	23.5	0.510	0.250	0.641	1.80	3.50	5.30	0.7	0.93	0.51	0.91	2.16	7.7
Beno Udrih	59	18.3	0.440	0.288	0.709	0.40	1.30	1.70	3.8	0.63	0.02	1.31	1.17	5.9
*Ekpe Udoh	61	21.1	0.431	0.000	0.754	1.60	2.50	4.20	0.9	0.66	1.67	0.87	0.00	5.6
Shaun Livingston	58	18.8	0.469	0.667	0.785	0.70	1.40	2.10	2.1	0.47	0.34	1.14	1.36	5.5
Tobias Harris	42	11.4	0.467	0.261	0.815	0.70	1.70	2.40	0.5	0.31	0.17	0.74	1.07	5.0
Jon Leuer	46	12.1	0.508	0.333	0.750	1.00	1.60	2.60	0.5	0.30	0.37	0.39	1.46	4.7
Larry Sanders	52	12.4	0.467	0.000	0.474	1.20	1.90	3.10	0.6	0.62	1.46	0.83	2.56	3.6
Jon Brockman	35	6.8	0.333	0.000	0.467	0.90	1.20	2.10	0.3	0.11	0.03	0.29	0.94	1.1
Bucks	66	240.4	0.443	0.345	0.774	12.42	30.05	42.47	23.5	8.30	5.08	14.08	19.29	99.0
Opponents	66	240.4	0.449	0.351	0.769	12.32	32.39	44.71	21.7	7.56	4.50	15.89	19.36	98.7

Minnesota Timberwolves

Player	GP	MPG	FG%	3Pt%	FT%	OFF	DEF	Total	APG	SPG	BPG	TO	PF	PPG
Kevin Love	55	39.0	.448	.372	.824	4.10	9.20	13.30	2.0	0.85	0.51	2.33	2.76	26.0
Nikola Pekovic	47	26.9	.564	.000	.743	3.90	3.50	7.40	0.7	0.62	0.66	1.85	2.09	13.9
Luke Ridnour	53	33.0	.440	.322	.891	0.40	2.30	2.70	4.8	1.06	0.30	1.81	2.57	12.1
Michael Beasley	47	23.1	.445	.376	.642	0.80	3.60	4.40	1.0	0.38	0.40	1.70	1.77	11.5
Jose Barea	41	25.2	.400	.371	.776	0.30	2.40	2.80	5.7	0.51	0.00	2.51	1.49	11.3
Ricky Rubio	41	34.2	.357	.340	.803	0.50	3.70	4.20	8.2	2.22	0.20	3.20	2.37	10.6
Derrick Williams	66	21.5	.412	.268	.697	1.20	3.50	4.70	0.6	0.45	0.47	1.17	1.44	8.8
Anthony Randolph	34	15.2	.470	.000	.762	1.20	2.40	3.60	0.6	0.38	1.03	1.18	1.65	7.4
Martell Webster	47	24.3	.423	.339	.792	0.90	2.70	3.60	0.9	0.66	0.36	0.98	1.83	6.9
Wayne Ellington	51	19.1	.404	.324	.800	0.30	1.70	1.90	0.6	0.51	0.20	0.51	1.10	6.1
Wesley Johnson	65	22.6	.398	.314	.706	0.40	2.40	2.70	0.9	0.54	0.74	0.92	1.77	6.0
Darko Milicic	29	16.3	.454	.000	.432	1.20	2.10	3.30	0.6	0.31	0.86	1.10	2.03	4.6
Anthony Tolliver	51	17.3	.390	.248	.745	1.00	2.00	3.00	0.4	0.35	0.37	0.69	1.69	4.1
Malcolm Lee	19	12.8	.390	.200	.824	0.50	0.90	1.40	1.6	0.42	0.21	0.89	1.16	3.3
Brad Miller	15	9.7	.333	.467	.833	0.30	1.10	1.40	1.2	0.27	0.13	0.80	0.67	2.3
Timberwolves	66	241.5	.433	.332	.771	12.08	31.65	43.73	19.5	6.61	4.44	15.17	18.36	97.9
Opponents	66	241.5	.455	.340	.755	11.68	31.76	43.44	21.5	8.32	5.71	13.26	21.74	100.1

New Jersey Nets

Player	GP	MPG	FG%	3Pt%	FT%	OFF	DEF	Total	APG	SPG	BPG	TO	PF	PPG
Deron Williams	55	36.3	.407	.336	.843	.40	2.90	3.30	8.7	1.22	.36	3.98	2.20	21.0
Brook Lopez	5	27.2	.494	.000	.625	1.60	2.00	3.60	1.2	.20	.80	1.20	1.60	19.2
*Gerald Wallace	58	35.8	.454	.307	.800	1.50	5.20	6.70	2.8	1.47	.62	1.91	2.50	13.8
Kris Humphries	62	34.9	.481	.000	.752	3.80	7.20	11.00	1.5	.81	1.19	1.92	2.80	13.8
Gerald Green	31	25.2	.481	.391	.754	.50	3.00	3.50	1.1	.90	.55	1.77	2.60	12.9
MarShon Brooks	56	29.4	.428	.313	.764	1.30	2.30	3.60	2.3	.93	.27	2.11	2.10	12.6
Anthony Morrow	62	26.4	.413	.371	.933	.50	1.50	2.00	1.0	.74	.15	1.13	1.40	12.0
Jordan Farmar	39	21.3	.467	.440	.905	.20	1.40	1.60	3.3	.62	.05	1.74	1.30	10.4
*Armon Johnson	9	13.8	.465	.333	1.000	.10	1.30	1.40	1.2	.56	.00	.67	1.00	5.2
Sundiata Gaines	57	13.9	.376	.341	.615	.50	1.40	1.90	2.2	.96	.04	.91	1.00	5.1
Damion James	7	24.3	.371	.000	.667	1.00	3.70	4.70	.4	1.00	1.00	1.71	2.40	4.9
Jordan Williams	43	14.8	.507	.000	.652	1.50	2.10	3.60	.3	.49	.35	.53	1.40	4.6
Shelden Williams	58	22.0	.478	.000	.731	2.40	3.60	6.00	.6	.81	.67	1.14	2.60	4.6
Johan Petro	59	15.6	.419	1.000	.838	1.20	2.60	3.80	.8	.36	.39	.64	2.10	4.2
Keith Bogans	5	18.8	.381	.250	.400	1.00	1.20	2.20	.6	.40	.00	.60	3.00	4.2
D. Stevenson	51	18.8	.285	.283	.563	.10	1.80	2.00	.8	.37	.08	.37	1.20	2.9
Andre Emmett	6	7.5	.571	.000	.625	.30	.70	1.00	.2	.33	.17	.33	.30	2.2
Larry Owens	7	10.7	.364	.400	.750	.30	1.60	1.90	.6	.00	.14	.29	1.40	1.9
Jerry Smith	5	9.2	.214	.167	.000	.40	1.00	1.40	.8	1.00	.00	.00	1.00	1.4
Dennis Horner	8	2.8	.250	.000	.750	.30	.40	.60	.0	.00	.00	.13	.10	.6
Nets	66	240.8	.425	.342	.777	11.9	28.5	40.3	19.9	7.5	3.9	15.1	19.2	93.1
Opponents	66	240.8	.472	.374	.740	11.8	30.8	42.6	23.3	8.0	5.0	14.3	19.3	99.1

* mid-season trade

New Orleans Hornets

Player	GP	MPG	FG%	3Pt%	FT%	OFF	DEF	Total	APG	SPG	BPG	TO	PF	PPG
Eric Gordon	9	34.4	.450	.250	.754	.20	2.60	2.80	3.4	1.44	.44	2.67	2.20	20.6
Jarrett Jack	45	34.0	.456	.348	.872	.50	3.40	3.90	6.3	.69	.20	2.36	2.10	15.6
Chris Kaman	47	29.2	.446	.000	.785	1.90	5.90	7.70	2.1	.53	1.64	2.74	2.30	13.1
Carl Landry	41	24.4	.503	.000	.799	1.90	3.30	5.20	.9	.32	.29	1.56	2.20	12.5
Marco Belinelli	66	29.8	.417	.377	.783	.30	2.30	2.60	1.5	.73	.08	1.05	1.70	11.8
Trevor Ariza	41	32.9	.417	.333	.775	1.00	4.20	5.20	3.3	1.68	.61	1.85	1.80	10.8
Jason Smith	40	23.7	.520	.111	.702	1.80	3.10	4.90	.9	.53	1.03	1.00	2.60	9.9
Emeka Okafor	27	28.9	.533	.000	.514	2.60	5.30	7.90	.9	.59	.96	1.37	2.70	9.9
Greivis Vasquez	66	25.8	.430	.319	.821	.30	2.30	2.60	5.4	.91	.12	2.24	1.90	8.9
Jerome Dyson	9	20.0	.396	.125	.778	.20	1.90	2.10	2.0	1.22	.22	2.22	2.10	7.4
Al-Farouq Aminu	66	22.4	.411	.277	.754	1.40	3.20	4.70	1.0	.89	.52	1.38	2.10	6.0
Gustavo Ayon	54	20.1	.536	.000	.619	1.60	3.30	4.90	1.4	.98	.85	.85	2.20	5.9
*Xavier Henry	45	16.9	.395	.412	.612	.50	1.80	2.40	.8	.58	.18	.78	1.30	5.3
Darryl Watkins	5	19.6	.500	.000	.500	1.60	3.80	5.40	.6	1.00	.80	1.60	2.80	4.6
DaJuan Summers	15	13.9	.431	.313	.778	.50	1.00	1.50	.7	.47	.00	.53	2.10	4.5
Lance Thomas	42	15.0	.452	.000	.839	1.20	1.80	3.00	.3	.24	.17	.57	1.90	4.0
*Solomon Jones	21	13.9	.393	.000	.826	1.50	1.20	2.80	.4	.43	.52	.86	2.00	3.2
*Chris Johnson	27	6.5	.488	.000	.789	.60	.90	1.50	.1	.22	.33	.56	1.20	2.0
Trey Johnson	11	5.5	.571	.000	1.000	.30	.80	1.10	.4	.09	.00	.45	.90	1.9
Carldell Johnson	15	7.9	.314	.267	.333	.10	.50	.60	1.5	.53	.00	.47	.70	1.8
Jeff Foote	4	9.8	.333	.000	.000	.30	1.30	1.50	.0	.00	.25	.50	1.30	1.0
Hornets	**66**	**241.5**	**.451**	**.333**	**.757**	**11.0**	**30.2**	**41.1**	**20.7**	**7.4**	**4.8**	**15.5**	**20.1**	**89.6**
Opponents	**66**	**241.5**	**.444**	**.317**	**.759**	**11.1**	**28.9**	**40.0**	**20.9**	**7.9**	**5.8**	**13.9**	**18.7**	**93.4**

New York Knicks

Player	GP	MPG	FG%	3Pt%	FT%	OFF	DEF	Total	APG	SPG	BPG	TO	PF	PPG
Carmelo Anthony	55	34.1	.430	.335	.804	1.6	4.7	6.3	3.6	1.1	0.4	2.6	2.8	22.6
Amare Stoudemire	47	32.8	.483	.238	.765	2.3	5.6	7.8	1.1	0.8	1.0	2.4	2.9	17.5
Jeremy Lin	35	26.9	.446	.320	.798	0.5	2.5	3.1	6.2	1.6	0.3	3.6	2.2	14.6
J.R. Smith	35	27.6	.407	.347	.709	0.8	3.1	3.9	2.4	1.5	0.2	1.3	2.5	12.5
Tyson Chandler	62	33.2	.679	.000	.689	3.4	6.5	9.9	0.9	0.9	1.4	1.6	3.0	11.3
Iman Shumpert	59	28.9	.401	.306	.798	0.7	2.4	3.2	2.8	1.7	0.1	1.9	2.9	9.5
Landry Fields	66	28.7	.460	.256	.562	0.9	3.3	4.2	2.6	1.2	0.3	1.5	1.5	8.8
Steve Novak	54	18.9	.478	.472	.846	0.2	1.8	1.9	0.2	0.3	0.2	0.4	1.1	8.8
Toney Douglas	38	17.3	.324	.231	.846	0.4	1.5	1.9	2.0	0.8	0.0	1.5	1.4	6.2
Baron Davis	29	20.5	.370	.306	.667	0.4	1.5	1.9	4.7	1.2	0.1	2.6	2.1	6.1
Bill Walker	32	19.4	.398	.319	.850	0.3	2.2	2.5	1.2	0.6	0.2	1.1	2.6	5.9
Jared Jeffries	39	18.7	.410	.188	.681	1.8	2.1	3.9	0.7	0.7	0.6	0.7	2.3	4.4
Josh Harrellson	37	14.6	.423	.339	.615	1.3	2.6	3.9	0.3	0.6	0.5	0.5	1.3	4.4
Renaldo Balkman	14	8.2	.500	.222	.727	0.4	1.4	1.9	0.4	0.3	0.2	0.4	1.0	3.0
Mike Bibby	39	14.3	.282	.318	.750	0.1	1.4	1.5	2.1	0.5	0.1	0.5	1.2	2.6
Jerome Jordan	21	5.1	.515	.000	.800	0.7	0.6	1.3	0.2	0.0	0.3	0.1	0.7	2.0
Dan Gadzuric	2	6.5	.000	.000	.000	0.5	2.0	2.5	0.0	0.5	0.5	0.5	2.0	0.0
Knicks	**66**	**241.5**	**.443**	**.336**	**.741**	**11.3**	**30.5**	**41.7**	**20.1**	**9.4**	**4.2**	**16.0**	**21.1**	**97.8**
Opponents	**66**	**241.5**	**.442**	**.359**	**.736**	**10.9**	**31.0**	**41.8**	**18.9**	**8.1**	**5.1**	**17.0**	**22.8**	**94.7**

Oklahoma City Thunder

Player	GP	MPG	FG%	3Pt%	FT%	OFF	DEF	Total	APG	SPG	BPG	TO	PF	PPG
Kevin Durant	66	38.6	.496	.387	.860	0.60	7.40	8.00	3.5	1.33	1.17	3.76	2.02	28.0
Russell Westbrook	66	35.3	.457	.316	.823	1.50	3.10	4.60	5.5	1.70	0.32	3.62	2.23	23.6
James Harden	62	31.4	.491	.390	.846	0.50	3.60	4.10	3.7	1.00	0.24	2.21	2.42	16.8
Serge Ibaka	66	27.2	.535	.333	.661	2.90	4.60	7.50	0.4	0.50	3.65	1.20	2.71	9.1
*Derek Fisher	63	23.9	.371	.321	.851	0.20	1.70	1.90	2.7	0.81	0.06	1.16	0.00	5.6
Daequan Cook	57	17.4	.368	.346	.636	0.20	1.90	2.10	0.3	0.39	0.19	0.28	1.21	5.5
Kendrick Perkins	65	26.8	.489	.000	.652	1.80	4.70	6.60	1.2	0.38	1.12	1.82	2.91	5.1
Thabo Sefolosha	42	21.8	.432	.437	.884	0.50	2.50	3.00	1.1	0.88	0.40	0.95	1.86	4.8
Nick Collison	63	20.7	.597	.000	.710	1.90	2.50	4.30	1.3	0.52	0.44	0.97	2.43	4.5
Eric Maynor	9	15.2	.359	.353	.000	0.30	1.10	1.40	2.4	0.56	0.00	1.22	1.44	4.2
Reggie Jackson	45	11.1	.321	.210	.862	0.30	0.90	1.20	1.6	0.56	0.02	0.80	0.69	3.1
Nazr Mohammed	63	11.0	.467	.000	.565	0.90	1.80	2.70	0.2	0.32	0.59	0.41	1.60	2.7
Cole Aldrich	26	6.7	.524	.000	.929	0.50	1.30	1.80	0.1	0.31	0.62	0.35	0.85	2.2
Royal Ivey	34	10.4	.356	.340	.125	0.00	0.70	0.70	0.3	0.41	0.00	0.26	1.06	2.1
Lazar Hayward	26	5.4	.342	.286	.583	0.10	0.50	0.60	0.2	0.12	0.04	0.35	0.69	1.4
Thunder	**66**	**242.3**	**.471**	**.358**	**.806**	**11.00**	**32.68**	**43.68**	**18.5**	**7.55**	**8.17**	**16.35**	**20.48**	**103.1**
Opponents	**66**	**242.3**	**.427**	**.342**	**.768**	**12.65**	**28.62**	**41.27**	**19.9**	**8.21**	**4.86**	**14.20**	**20.03**	**96.9**

* mid-season trade

Orlando Magic

Player	GP	MPG	Field Goals FG%	3Pt%	FT%	Rebounds OFF	DEF	Total	APG	SPG	BPG	TO	PF	PPG
Dwight Howard	54	38.3	.573	.000	.491	3.70	10.80	14.50	1.9	1.50	2.15	3.24	2.94	20.6
Ryan Anderson	61	32.2	.439	.393	.877	3.70	4.00	7.70	0.9	0.82	0.43	0.93	2.39	16.1
Jameer Nelson	57	29.9	.427	.377	.807	0.50	2.70	3.20	5.7	0.67	0.09	2.37	2.28	11.9
J.J. Redick	65	27.2	.425	.418	.911	0.30	2.00	2.30	2.5	0.42	0.09	1.05	1.42	11.6
Jason Richardson	54	29.5	.408	.368	.594	0.70	2.90	3.60	2.0	0.98	0.41	1.11	1.69	11.6
Hedo Turkoglu	53	31.2	.415	.353	.705	0.50	3.30	3.80	4.4	0.85	0.32	2.68	2.62	10.9
Glen Davis	61	23.4	.421	.143	.683	1.80	3.70	5.40	0.8	0.70	0.31	1.23	1.74	9.3
Von Wafer	33	14.2	.452	.359	.704	0.20	1.20	1.40	0.9	0.30	0.09	1.06	0.79	5.9
Q. Richardson	48	18.0	.376	.347	.833	0.30	2.30	2.60	0.8	0.58	0.13	0.60	1.54	4.5
Chris Duhon	63	19.5	.419	.420	.810	0.20	1.40	1.60	2.4	0.56	0.14	1.29	1.13	3.8
Daniel Orton	16	11.7	.567	.000	.440	1.20	1.30	2.40	0.3	0.50	0.56	0.44	1.88	2.8
Earl Clark	45	12.4	.367	.000	.724	0.80	2.00	2.80	0.4	0.27	0.71	0.56	1.60	2.7
*Ish Smith	26	9.0	.383	.333	.700	0.30	1.10	1.30	1.6	0.58	0.08	0.50	0.00	2.8
DeAndre Liggins	17	6.8	.480	.000	.474	0.40	0.50	0.90	0.3	0.35	0.00	0.59	0.35	1.9
Justin Harper	14	6.0	.290	.154	.000	0.20	0.60	0.90	0.1	0.14	0.21	0.43	0.36	1.4
Magic	**66**	**241.9**	**.441**	**.375**	**.660**	**11.24**	**31.21**	**42.46**	**20.0**	**6.83**	**4.17**	**14.91**	**17.70**	**94.2**
Opponents	**66**	**241.9**	**.449**	**.347**	**.772**	**10.11**	**31.23**	**41.33**	**20.5**	**7.50**	**4.14**	**13.14**	**19.82**	**93.4**

Philadelphia 76ers

Player	GP	MPG	Field Goals FG%	3Pt%	FT%	Rebounds OFF	DEF	Total	APG	SPG	BPG	TO	PF	PPG
Louis Williams	64	26.3	.407	.362	.812	0.50	2.00	2.40	3.5	0.83	0.28	1.11	1.41	14.9
Jrue Holiday	65	33.8	.432	.380	.783	0.90	2.40	3.30	4.5	1.58	0.28	2.08	2.11	13.5
Thaddeus Young	63	27.9	.507	.250	.771	2.20	3.00	5.20	1.2	1.02	0.65	0.87	2.02	12.8
Andre Iguodala	62	35.6	.454	.394	.617	0.90	5.20	6.10	5.5	1.73	0.48	1.85	1.48	12.4
Elton Brand	60	28.9	.494	.000	.733	2.40	4.70	7.20	1.6	0.97	1.62	1.08	2.93	11.0
Spencer Hawes	37	24.9	.489	.250	.727	2.10	5.20	7.30	2.6	0.43	1.30	1.49	2.70	9.6
Evan Turner	65	26.4	.446	.224	.676	0.40	5.40	5.80	2.8	0.62	0.31	1.62	1.80	9.4
Jodie Meeks	66	24.9	.409	.365	.906	0.30	2.20	2.40	0.8	0.61	0.05	0.44	1.24	8.4
Nikola Vucevic	51	15.9	.450	.375	.529	1.70	3.10	4.80	0.6	0.39	0.67	0.65	2.18	5.5
Xavier Silas	2	19.5	.267	.167	.667	1.00	1.00	2.00	1.5	0.00	0.00	1.50	2.50	5.5
Lavoy Allen	41	15.2	.473	.000	.786	1.10	3.00	4.20	0.8	0.32	0.44	0.49	1.78	4.1
*Sam Young	35	10.7	.354	.294	.731	0.60	1.20	1.80	0.4	0.49	0.17	0.46	0.00	3.3
Craig Brackins	14	6.3	.273	.333	.500	0.40	0.70	1.10	0.6	0.00	0.07	0.29	0.43	1.6
Tony Battie	27	10.9	.373	.000	1.000	0.30	2.20	2.50	0.6	0.15	0.22	0.15	0.96	1.6
Sixers	**66**	**241.1**	**.448**	**.362**	**.742**	**10.67**	**32.49**	**43.15**	**22.0**	**7.97**	**5.15**	**11.18**	**17.53**	**93.6**
Opponents	**66**	**241.1**	**.427**	**.334**	**.752**	**10.70**	**33.05**	**43.74**	**19.6**	**5.92**	**4.79**	**13.91**	**16.21**	**89.4**

Phoenix Suns

Player	GP	MPG	Field Goals FG%	3Pt%	FT%	Rebounds OFF	DEF	Total	APG	SPG	BPG	TO	PF	PPG
Marcin Gortat	66	32.0	.555	.000	.649	2.80	7.20	10.00	0.9	0.73	1.50	1.36	2.15	15.4
Jared Dudley	65	31.1	.485	.383	.726	1.50	3.20	4.60	1.7	0.75	0.29	1.11	1.65	12.7
Steve Nash	62	31.6	.532	.390	.894	0.40	2.60	3.00	10.7	0.61	0.13	3.69	0.85	12.5
Shannon Brown	59	23.7	.420	.362	.808	0.60	2.00	2.70	1.2	0.75	0.25	1.08	1.12	11.0
Channing Frye	64	26.1	.416	.346	.890	1.10	4.80	5.90	1.4	0.60	1.09	0.98	2.75	10.5
Grant Hill	49	28.1	.446	.264	.761	0.60	2.90	3.50	2.2	0.84	0.59	1.33	1.80	10.2
Michael Redd	51	15.1	.400	.318	.793	0.30	1.20	1.50	0.6	0.25	0.00	0.73	0.57	8.2
Markieff Morris	63	19.5	.399	.347	.717	1.10	3.30	4.40	1.0	0.65	0.67	1.11	2.84	7.4
Hakim Warrick	35	14.4	.411	.100	.768	0.90	1.70	2.60	0.9	0.23	0.09	1.03	1.00	6.4
Sebastian Telfair	60	14.9	.412	.314	.791	0.30	1.20	1.50	2.3	0.68	0.20	1.13	2.00	6.1
Robin Lopez	64	14.0	.461	.000	.714	1.40	1.90	3.30	0.3	0.28	0.94	0.67	2.00	5.4
Ronnie Price	36	14.4	.377	.295	.800	0.50	1.10	1.60	1.9	0.94	0.08	1.28	2.00	3.6
Josh Childress	34	14.4	.485	.000	.000	0.90	1.90	2.80	1.0	0.41	0.18	0.26	1.12	2.9
Suns	**66**	**240.0**	**.458**	**.343**	**.757**	**10.86**	**30.83**	**41.70**	**22.5**	**6.53**	**5.55**	**14.06**	**18.68**	**98.4**
Opponents	**66**	**240.0**	**.455**	**.352**	**.762**	**12.15**	**31.27**	**43.42**	**21.5**	**7.97**	**4.36**	**14.08**	**19.59**	**98.6**

* mid-season trade

Portland Trail Blazers

Player	GP	MPG	FG%	3Pt%	FT%	OFF	DEF	Total	APG	SPG	BPG	TO	PF	PPG
			Field Goals			Rebounds								
LaMarcus Aldridge	55	36.3	.512	.182	.814	2.70	5.30	8.00	2.4	.93	.82	2.02	2.80	21.7
Jamal Crawford	60	26.9	.384	.308	.927	.30	1.70	2.00	3.2	.92	.23	1.85	1.20	14.0
Nicolas Batum	59	30.4	.451	.391	.836	1.40	3.20	4.60	1.4	.97	1.02	1.53	1.80	13.9
Wesley Matthews	66	33.8	.412	.383	.860	.80	2.50	3.40	1.7	1.45	.23	1.11	2.20	13.7
Raymond Felton	60	31.8	.407	.305	.806	.50	2.00	2.50	6.5	1.30	.17	2.83	2.00	11.4
*J.J. Hickson	54	23.0	.467	.000	.642	2.50	3.70	6.20	.8	.56	.65	1.30	1.60	8.4
Luke Babbitt	40	13.4	.410	.430	.850	.40	2.00	2.40	.4	.25	.10	.68	1.20	5.1
*Jonny Flynn	29	14.3	.351	.294	.744	.30	1.10	1.30	3.3	.21	.07	1.24	.80	4.5
Nolan Smith	44	12.3	.372	.289	.714	.40	.90	1.30	1.4	.41	.07	.95	1.30	3.8
Elliot Williams	24	6.2	.500	.296	.333	.30	.50	.80	.3	.25	.13	.21	.80	3.7
Craig Smith	47	9.9	.504	.000	.717	.70	1.60	2.30	.4	.34	.11	.51	1.20	3.3
Kurt Thomas	53	15.2	.465	.000	.700	.70	2.80	3.50	.9	.45	.58	.58	2.30	3.0
Joel Przybilla	27	16.6	.458	.000	.611	1.10	4.00	5.10	.2	.15	.59	.81	2.40	2.0
*Hasheem Thabeet	20	7.0	.524	.000	.650	.80	1.30	2.10	.0	.05	.50	.40	1.00	1.8
Trail Blazers	66	241.9	.443	.346	.796	11.1	29.5	40.7	20.4	8.0	4.9	14.2	19.0	97.2
Opponents	66	241.9	.463	.363	.747	11.1	31.2	42.3	21.1	7.6	4.8	14.9	19.8	97.8

Sacramento Kings

Player	GP	MPG	FG%	3Pt%	FT%	OFF	DEF	Total	APG	SPG	BPG	TO	PF	PPG
			Field Goals			Rebounds								
Marcus Thornton	51	34.9	.438	.345	.865	1.60	2.00	3.70	1.9	1.39	0.24	1.65	2.18	18.7
DeMarcus Cousins	64	30.5	.448	.143	.702	4.10	6.80	11.00	1.6	1.45	1.17	2.66	4.02	18.1
Tyreke Evans	63	34.3	.453	.202	.779	1.00	3.60	4.60	4.5	1.33	0.46	2.71	2.16	16.5
Isaiah Thomas	65	25.5	.448	.379	.832	0.70	1.80	2.60	4.1	0.82	0.12	1.62	1.86	11.5
Jason Thompson	64	25.9	.535	.000	.602	2.60	4.30	6.90	1.2	0.67	0.69	1.06	2.33	9.1
Jimmer Fredette	61	18.6	.386	.361	.833	0.30	0.90	1.20	1.8	0.49	0.05	1.10	1.20	7.6
John Salmons	46	27.2	.409	.295	.644	0.40	2.50	2.90	2.0	0.80	0.15	0.98	1.67	7.5
*Terrence Williams	30	18.3	.429	.348	.587	0.40	3.00	3.40	2.2	0.67	0.23	1.43	0.00	7.1
Donte Greene	53	14.7	.406	.238	.800	0.40	2.20	2.50	0.6	0.34	0.55	0.60	1.26	5.4
Francisco Garcia	49	16.3	.376	.290	.800	0.20	1.80	2.00	0.6	0.73	0.76	0.45	1.49	4.8
Travis Outlaw	39	12.8	.343	.267	.674	0.50	1.10	1.60	0.4	0.49	0.54	0.51	0.87	4.3
Chuck Hayes	54	19.2	.429	.000	.667	1.30	3.00	4.30	1.4	0.67	0.31	0.93	2.06	3.2
Hassan Whiteside	18	6.1	.444	.000	.417	0.90	1.30	2.20	0.0	0.17	0.83	0.28	0.67	1.6
Tyler Honeycutt	11	5.9	.333	.333	.600	0.20	0.70	0.90	0.5	0.27	0.20	0.13	0.20	1.3
Kings	66	241.1	.436	.316	.736	13.36	29.50	42.86	19.3	8.50	4.89	14.42	19.50	98.8
Opponents	66	241.1	.476	.355	.762	12.35	32.64	44.99	23.8	7.85	6.41	15.36	19.89	104.4

San Antonio Spurs

Player	GP	MPG	FG%	3Pt%	FT%	OFF	DEF	Total	APG	SPG	BPG	TO	PF	PPG
			Field Goals			Rebounds								
Tony Parker	60	32.0	.480	.230	.799	0.40	2.50	2.90	7.7	0.95	0.08	2.55	1.25	18.3
Tim Duncan	58	28.2	.492	.000	.695	1.90	7.10	9.00	2.3	0.66	1.52	1.67	1.69	15.4
Manu Ginobili	34	23.3	.526	.413	.871	0.50	2.90	3.40	4.4	0.71	0.35	1.88	1.65	12.9
Patty Mills	16	16.3	.485	.429	1.000	0.30	1.50	1.80	2.4	0.63	0.06	1.63	0.88	10.3
Gary Neal	56	21.5	.436	.419	.781	0.20	1.90	2.10	2.1	0.48	0.04	1.07	1.34	9.9
*Stephen Jackson	47	25.8	.374	.288	.825	0.50	3.00	3.50	2.5	1.15	0.28	2.19	0.00	9.8
DeJuan Blair	64	21.3	.534	.000	.613	2.40	3.10	5.50	1.2	0.92	0.19	1.44	2.63	9.5
Tiago Splitter	59	19.0	.618	.000	.691	1.60	3.60	5.20	1.1	0.36	0.80	1.47	2.27	9.3
Danny Green	66	23.1	.442	.436	.790	0.80	2.60	3.50	1.3	0.88	0.70	1.02	1.62	9.1
Kawhi Leonard	64	24.0	.493	.376	.773	1.60	3.50	5.10	1.1	1.33	0.38	0.69	1.38	7.9
Matt Bonner	65	20.4	.440	.420	.762	0.40	2.80	3.30	0.9	0.23	0.32	0.22	1.05	6.6
*Boris Diaw	57	25.0	.444	.313	.629	1.20	3.70	4.90	3.6	0.60	0.44	1.96	0.06	6.4
Derrick Byars	2	18.5	.273	.000	1.000	3.00	2.50	5.50	0.5	1.00	0.00	0.00	1.00	5.0
James Anderson	51	11.8	.379	.279	.750	0.30	1.20	1.50	0.8	0.16	0.04	0.59	0.69	3.7
Cory Joseph	29	9.2	.314	.200	.647	0.20	0.70	0.90	1.2	0.24	0.10	0.41	0.55	2.0
Spurs	66	241.5	.478	.393	.748	10.35	32.62	42.97	23.2	7.42	4.44	13.56	17.32	103.7
Opponents	66	241.5	.452	.353	.756	10.30	30.89	41.20	19.6	7.41	5.00	13.73	18.85	96.5

* mid-season trade

Toronto Raptors

Player	GP	MPG	FG%	3Pt%	FT%	OFF	DEF	Total	APG	SPG	BPG	TO	PF	PPG
Andrea Bargnani	31	33.3	.432	.296	.873	0.80	4.80	5.50	2.0	0.58	0.48	2.23	1.68	19.5
DeMar DeRozan	63	35.0	.422	.261	.810	0.60	2.70	3.30	2.0	0.76	0.27	1.95	2.57	16.7
Jerryd Bayless	31	22.7	.424	.423	.852	0.30	1.90	2.10	3.8	0.77	0.13	1.71	2.26	11.4
Jose Calderon	53	33.9	.457	.371	.882	0.40	2.70	3.00	8.8	0.89	0.06	1.96	1.77	10.5
Linas Kleiza	49	21.6	.402	.346	.810	0.90	3.20	4.10	0.9	0.47	0.08	1.31	2.43	9.7
Alan Anderson	17	27.1	.387	.393	.853	0.50	1.50	2.00	1.5	0.29	0.18	1.47	2.06	9.6
James Johnson	62	25.2	.450	.317	.704	1.20	3.50	4.70	2.0	1.15	1.35	1.63	2.85	9.1
Amir Johnson	64	24.3	.576	.400	.690	2.30	4.00	6.40	1.2	0.52	1.08	1.47	3.27	7.1
Gary Forbes	48	14.9	.413	.349	.725	0.60	1.60	2.10	1.1	0.50	0.08	1.13	1.17	6.6
Ed Davis	66	23.2	.513	.000	.670	2.00	4.60	6.60	0.9	0.61	0.95	1.02	2.36	6.3
*Ben Uzoh	18	20.6	.354	.000	.579	1.10	2.70	3.70	3.4	0.94	0.17	1.06	0.00	4.5
Aaron Gray	49	16.6	.516	.000	.532	1.70	4.00	5.70	0.6	0.45	0.35	1.04	2.59	3.9
Solomon Alabi	14	8.7	.361	.000	.875	1.10	2.30	3.40	0.2	0.14	0.64	0.36	0.79	2.4
Jamaal Magloire	34	11.0	.378	.000	.259	0.70	2.60	3.30	0.2	0.12	0.29	0.65	1.94	1.2
Raptors	**66**	**241.9**	**.440**	**.340**	**.770**	**10.56**	**31.42**	**41.99**	**20.9**	**6.50**	**4.86**	**15.17**	**23.21**	**90.7**
Opponents	**66**	**241.9**	**.435**	**.328**	**.744**	**10.26**	**30.26**	**40.52**	**20.1**	**7.24**	**4.88**	**13.18**	**18.39**	**94.0**

Utah Jazz

Player	GP	MPG	FG%	3Pt%	FT%	OFF	DEF	Total	APG	SPG	BPG	TO	PF	PPG
Al Jefferson	61	34.0	.492	.250	.774	2.20	7.40	9.60	2.2	0.77	1.66	1.02	2.54	19.2
Paul Millsap	64	32.8	.495	.226	.792	2.80	6.00	8.80	2.3	1.84	0.81	1.75	3.47	16.6
Gordon Hayward	66	30.5	.456	.346	.832	0.90	2.60	3.50	3.1	0.80	0.62	1.65	1.61	11.8
Devin Harris	63	27.6	.445	.362	.746	0.20	1.60	1.80	5.0	1.02	0.21	1.94	2.16	11.3
C.J. Miles	56	20.4	.381	.307	.794	0.50	1.60	2.10	1.2	0.82	0.32	0.95	2.18	9.1
Derrick Favors	65	21.2	.499	.000	.649	2.40	4.10	6.50	0.7	0.58	1.00	1.58	2.23	8.8
Josh Howard	43	23.0	.399	.243	.773	0.90	2.80	3.70	1.2	0.74	0.23	1.23	2.12	8.7
Alec Burks	59	15.9	.429	.333	.727	1.00	1.30	2.20	0.9	0.46	0.08	0.86	1.42	7.2
Raja Bell	34	23.4	.466	.391	.840	0.20	1.30	1.40	1.1	0.38	0.06	0.62	2.29	6.4
Enes Kanter	66	13.2	.496	.000	.667	1.60	2.60	4.20	0.1	0.27	0.35	0.82	1.32	4.6
*DeMarre Carroll	24	14.5	.410	.368	.875	1.20	1.00	2.20	0.8	0.50	0.04	0.46	0.00	4.5
Jamaal Tinsley	37	13.7	.404	.270	.765	0.20	1.10	1.20	3.3	0.46	0.22	1.41	1.27	3.7
Earl Watson	50	20.7	.338	.192	.674	0.60	1.80	2.40	4.3	1.08	0.44	1.70	2.10	3.0
Blake Ahearn	4	7.5	.286	.222	.000	0.00	0.50	0.50	0.3	0.00	0.00	1.25	1.00	2.5
Jeremy Evans	29	7.5	.643	.000	.500	0.70	1.10	1.70	0.4	0.21	0.83	0.17	0.79	2.1
Jazz	**66**	**244.9**	**.456**	**.323**	**.754**	**13.05**	**31.14**	**44.18**	**21.8**	**8.26**	**5.83**	**14.18**	**21.83**	**99.7**
Opponents	**66**	**244.9**	**.453**	**.340**	**.754**	**11.03**	**30.12**	**41.15**	**20.5**	**7.49**	**5.68**	**14.67**	**20.70**	**99.0**

Washington Wizards

Player	GP	MPG	FG%	3Pt%	FT%	OFF	DEF	Total	APG	SPG	BPG	TO	PF	PPG
John Wall	66	36.2	.423	.071	.789	0.70	3.80	4.50	8.0	1.44	0.86	3.86	2.08	16.3
Jordan Crawford	64	27.4	.400	.289	.793	0.70	1.90	2.60	3.0	0.92	0.08	2.20	1.73	14.7
*Nene	39	28.5	.537	.000	.673	1.60	5.80	7.50	2.1	1.08	0.97	2.46	0.00	13.7
Cartier Martin	17	23.0	.440	.387	.579	0.70	2.70	3.40	0.6	0.65	0.12	0.76	2.06	9.3
Andray Blatche	26	24.1	.380	.286	.673	1.60	4.20	5.80	1.1	0.77	0.65	1.42	2.08	8.5
Trevor Booker	50	25.2	.531	.500	.602	2.40	4.10	6.50	0.8	0.96	0.86	1.16	2.76	8.4
James Singleton	12	21.8	.547	.222	.933	2.10	4.70	6.80	1.3	0.75	0.67	0.83	2.25	8.2
Kevin Seraphin	57	20.6	.531	.000	.671	1.80	3.10	4.90	0.6	0.33	1.33	1.16	2.33	7.9
Rashard Lewis	28	26.0	.385	.239	.838	1.20	2.70	3.90	1.0	0.82	0.36	1.14	1.75	7.8
Maurice Evans	24	14.3	.402	.378	.769	0.30	0.70	1.00	0.4	0.58	0.00	0.42	1.50	4.9
Jan Vesely	57	18.9	.537	.000	.532	1.80	2.60	4.40	0.8	0.68	0.56	1.05	2.74	4.7
Chris Singleton	66	21.7	.372	.346	.682	0.70	2.90	3.50	0.7	1.06	0.45	0.58	2.67	4.6
Shelvin Mack	64	12.2	.400	.286	.712	0.20	1.30	1.40	2.0	0.44	0.03	0.75	0.78	3.6
Morris Almond	4	16.8	.353	.333	.333	0.30	1.80	2.00	0.5	1.75	0.00	0.25	1.50	3.5
*Brian Cook	32	8.6	.316	.200	.900	0.30	1.70	2.00	0.3	0.19	0.16	0.34	0.00	2.5
Wizards	**66**	**240.4**	**.441**	**.320**	**.727**	**11.74**	**29.92**	**41.67**	**19.1**	**7.99**	**6.32**	**15.27**	**21.29**	**93.6**
Opponents	**66**	**240.4**	**.453**	**.350**	**.758**	**12.29**	**31.24**	**43.53**	**21.5**	**7.88**	**4.55**	**15.21**	**18.65**	**98.4**

* mid-season trade

2012 NBA Draft

The 2012 NBA Draft was held on June 28, 2012 in Newark, New Jersey.

First Round

1. NO—Anthony Davis, Kentucky
2. CHA—Michael Kidd-Gilchrist, Kentucky
3. WAS—Bradley Beal, Florida
4. CLE—Dion Waiters, Syracuse
5. SAC—Thomas Robinson, Kansas
6. POR—Damian Lilard, Weber State (from Brooklyn)
7. GS—Harrison Barnes, North Carolina
8. TOR—Terrence Ross, Washington
9. DET—Andre Drummond, Connecticut
10. NO—Austin Rivers, Duke (from Minnesota via LA Clippers)
11. POR—Meyers Leonard, Illinois
12. HOU—Jeremy Lamb, Connecticut (from Milwaukee)
13. PHX—Kendall Marshall, North Carolina
14. MIL—John Henson, North Carolina (from Houston)
15. PHI—Maurice Harkless, St John's
16. HOU—Royce White, Iowa State (from NY)
17. DAL—Tyler Zeller, North Carolina
18. HOU—Terrence Jones, Kentucky (from Minnesota via Utah)
19. ORL—Andrew Nicholson, St Bonaventure
20. DEN—Evan Fournier, France
21. BOS—Jared Sullinger, Ohio St

First Round *(Cont.)*

22. BOS—Fab Melo, Syracuse (from LA Clippers via Okla. City)
23. ATL—John Jenkins, Vanderbilt
24. CLE—Jared Cunningham, Oregon St
25. MEM—Tony Wroten, Washington
26. IND—Miles Plumlee, Duke
27. MIA—Arnett Moultrie, Mississippi St
28. OKC—Perry Jones, Baylor
29. CHI—Marquis Teague, Kentucky
30. GS—Festus Ezeli, Vanderbilt (from San Antonio)

Second Round

31. CHA—Jeff Taylor, Vanderbilt
32. WAS—Tomas Satoransky, Spain
33. CLE—Bernard James, Florida St
34. CLE—Jae Crowder, Marquette (from New Orleans via Miami)
35. GS—Draymond Green, Michigan St (from Brooklyn)
36. SAC—Orlando Johnson, UCSB
37. TOR—Quincy Apy, Baylor
38. DEN—Quincy Miller, Baylor (from Golden State via New York)
39. DET—Khris Middleton, Texas
40. POR—Will Barton, Memphis (from Minnesota via Houston)
41. POR—Tyshawn Taylor, Kansas
42. MIL—Doron Lamb, Kentucky

Second Round *(Cont.)*

43. ATL—Mike Scott, Virginia (from Phoenix)
44. DET—Kim English, Missouri (from Houston)
45. PHI—Justin Hamiton, LSU
46. NO—Darius Miller, Kentucky (from Washington via Dallas)
47. UTAH—Kevin Murphy, Tennessee Tech
48. NYK—Kostas Papanikolaou, Greece
49. ORL—Kyle O'Quinn, Norfolk St
50. DEN—Izzet Turkyllmaz, Turkey
51. BOS—Kris Joseph, Syracuse
52. GS—Ognjen Kuzmic, Spain (from Atlanta)
53. LAC—Furkan Aldemir, Turkey
54. PHI—Tornike Shengelia, Belgium (from Memphis)
55. DAL—Darius Johnson-Odom, Marquette (from LA Lakers)
56. TOR—Tomislav Zubcic, Croatia (from Indiana)
57. BRO—Ilkan Karaman, Turkey (from Miami)
58. MIN—Robbie Hummel, Purdue (from Okla. City)
59. SAS—Marcus Denmon, Missouri
60. LAL—Robert Sacre, Gonzaga (from Chicago via Milwaukee and Brooklyn)

Women's National Basketball Association

2012 Final Regular Season Standings

WESTERN CONFERENCE

Team	W	L	Pct	GB
†Minnesota	27	7	.794	—
*Los Angeles	24	10	.706	3.0
*San Antonio	21	13	.618	6.0
*Seattle	16	18	.471	11.0
Tulsa	9	25	.265	18.0
Phoenix	7	27	0.206	20.0

EASTERN CONFERENCE

Team	W	L	Pct	GB
†Connecticut	25	9	.735	—
*Indiana	22	12	.647	3.0
*Atlanta	19	15	.559	6.0
*New York	15	19	.441	10.0
Chicago	14	20	.412	11.0
Washington	5	29	0.147	20.0

†Clinched conference title. *Clinched playoff berth.

2012 Playoffs

WESTERN CONFERENCE SEMI-FINALS

Game 1......Seattle 70   at Minneapolis 78
Game 2......Minneapolis 70   at Seattle 86
Game 3......Seattle 72   at Minneapolis 73
        Minneapolis won series 2–1.

Game 1......San Antonio 86   at Los Angeles 93
Game 2......Los Angeles 101   at San Antonio 94
        Los Angeles won series 2–0.

WESTERN CONFERENCE FINALS

Game 1......Los Angeles 77   at Minnesota 94
Game 2......Minnesota 80   at Los Angeles 79
        Minnesota won series 2–0.

EASTERN CONFERENCE SEMI-FINALS

Game 1......New York 60   at Connecticut 65
Game 2......Connecticut 75   at New York 62
        Connecticut won series 2–0.

Game 1......Atlanta 75   at Indiana 66
Game 2......Indiana 103   at Atlanta 88
Game 3......Atlanta 64   at Indiana 75
        Indiana won series 2–1.

EASTERN CONFERENCE FINALS

Game 1......Indiana 64   at Connecticut 76
Game 2......Connecticut 76   at Indiana 78
Game 3......Indiana 87   at Connecticut 71
        Indiana won series 2–1.

WNBA FINALS

Game 1..........Indiana 76   at Minnesota 70
Game 2..........Indiana 71   at Minnesota 83
Game 3..........Minnesota 59   at Indiana 76
Game 4..........Minnesota 78   at Indiana 87
        Minnesota won series 3–1.
202 WNBA Finals MVP: Tamika Catchings, Indiana

NBA Champions

Season	Winner	Series	Runner-Up	Winning Coach	Finals MVP
1946–47	Philadelphia	4–1	Chicago	Eddie Gottlieb	—
1947–48	Baltimore	4–2	Philadelphia	Buddy Jeannette	—
1948–49	Minneapolis	4–2	Washington	John Kundla	—
1949–50	Minneapolis	4–2	Syracuse	John Kundla	—
1950–51	Rochester	4–3	New York	Les Harrison	—
1951–52	Minneapolis	4–3	New York	John Kundla	—
1952–53	Minneapolis	4–1	New York	John Kundla	—
1953–54	Minneapolis	4–3	Syracuse	John Kundla	—
1954–55	Syracuse	4–3	Ft Wayne	Al Cervi	—
1955–56	Philadelphia	4–1	Ft Wayne	George Senesky	—
1956–57	Boston	4–3	St Louis	Red Auerbach	—
1957–58	St Louis	4–2	Boston	Alex Hannum	—
1958–59	Boston	4–0	Minneapolis	Red Auerbach	—
1959–60	Boston	4–3	St Louis	Red Auerbach	—
1960–61	Boston	4–1	St Louis	Red Auerbach	—
1961–62	Boston	4–3	LA Lakers	Red Auerbach	—
1962–63	Boston	4–2	LA Lakers	Red Auerbach	—
1963–64	Boston	4–1	San Francisco	Red Auerbach	—
1964–65	Boston	4–1	LA Lakers	Red Auerbach	—
1965–66	Boston	4–3	LA Lakers	Red Auerbach	—
1966–67	Philadelphia	4–2	San Francisco	Alex Hannum	—
1967–68	Boston	4–2	LA Lakers	Bill Russell	—
1968–69	Boston	4–3	LA Lakers	Bill Russell	Jerry West, LA
1969–70	New York	4–3	LA Lakers	Red Holzman	Willis Reed, NY
1970–71	Milwaukee	4–0	Baltimore	Larry Costello	Kareem Abdul-Jabbar, Mil
1971–72	LA Lakers	4–1	New York	Bill Sharman	Wilt Chamberlain, LA
1972–73	New York	4–1	LA Lakers	Red Holzman	Willis Reed, NY
1973–74	Boston	4–3	Milwaukee	Tommy Heinsohn	John Havlicek, Bos
1974–75	Golden State	4–0	Washington	Al Attles	Rick Barry, GS
1975–76	Boston	4–2	Phoenix	Tommy Heinsohn	JoJo White, Bos
1976–77	Portland	4–2	Philadelphia	Jack Ramsay	Bill Walton, Port
1977–78	Washington	4–3	Seattle	Dick Motta	Wes Unseld, Wash
1978–79	Seattle	4–1	Washington	Lenny Wilkens	Dennis Johnson, Sea
1979–80	LA Lakers	4–2	Philadelphia	Paul Westhead	Magic Johnson, LA
1980–81	Boston	4–2	Houston	Bill Fitch	Cedric Maxwell, Bos
1981–82	LA Lakers	4–2	Philadelphia	Pat Riley	Magic Johnson, LA
1982–83	Philadelphia	4–0	LA Lakers	Billy Cunningham	Moses Malone, Phil
1983–84	Boston	4–3	LA Lakers	K.C. Jones	Larry Bird, Bos
1984–85	LA Lakers	4–2	Boston	Pat Riley	Kareem Abdul-Jabbar, LA
1985–86	Boston	4–2	Houston	K.C. Jones	Larry Bird, Bos
1986–87	LA Lakers	4–2	Boston	Pat Riley	Magic Johnson, LA
1987–88	LA Lakers	4–3	Detroit	Pat Riley	James Worthy, LA
1988–89	Detroit	4–0	LA Lakers	Chuck Daly	Joe Dumars, Det
1989–90	Detroit	4–1	Portland	Chuck Daly	Isiah Thomas, Det
1990–91	Chicago	4–1	LA Lakers	Phil Jackson	Michael Jordan, Chi
1991–92	Chicago	4–2	Portland	Phil Jackson	Michael Jordan, Chi
1992–93	Chicago	4–2	Phoenix	Phil Jackson	Michael Jordan, Chi
1993–94	Houston	4–3	New York	Rudy Tomjanovich	Hakeem Olajuwon, Hou
1994–95	Houston	4–0	Orlando	Rudy Tomjanovich	Hakeem Olajuwon, Hou
1995–96	Chicago	4–2	Seattle	Phil Jackson	Michael Jordan, Chi
1996–97	Chicago	4–2	Utah	Phil Jackson	Michael Jordan, Chi
1997–98	Chicago	4–2	Utah	Phil Jackson	Michael Jordan, Chi
1998–99	San Antonio	4–1	New York	Gregg Popovich	Tim Duncan, SA
1999–00	LA Lakers	4–2	Indiana	Phil Jackson	Shaquille O'Neal, LA
2000–01	LA Lakers	4–1	Philadelphia	Phil Jackson	Shaquille O'Neal, LA
2001–02	LA Lakers	4–0	New Jersey	Phil Jackson	Shaquille O'Neal, LA
2002–03	San Antonio	4–2	New Jersey	Gregg Popovich	Tim Duncan, SA
2003–04	Detroit	4–1	LA Lakers	Larry Brown	Chauncey Billups, Det
2004–05	San Antonio	4–3	Detroit	Gregg Popovich	Tim Duncan, SA
2005–06	Miami	4–2	Dallas	Pat Riley	Dwyane Wade, Mia
2006–07	San Antonio	4–0	Cleveland	Gregg Popovich	Tony Parker, SA
2007–08	Boston	4–2	LA Lakers	Doc Rivers	Paul Pierce, Bos
2008–09	LA Lakers	4–2	Orlando	Phil Jackson	Kobe Bryant, LA
2009–10	LA Lakers	4–3	Boston	Phil Jackson	Kobe Bryant, LA
2010–11	Dallas	4–2	Miami	Rick Carlisle	Dirk Nowitzki, Dal
2011–12	Miami	4–1	Oklahoma City	Erik Spoelstra	LeBron James, Mia

Regular Season Most Valuable Player: Maurice Podoloff Trophy

Season	Player, Team	GP	Field Goals FGM	Pct	3-Pt FG FGM	Pct	Free Throws FTM	Pct	Rebounds Off	Total	A	Stl	BS	Avg
1955–56	Bob Pettit, StL	72	646	42.9	–	–	557	73.6	–	1,164	189	–	–	25.7
1956–57	Bob Cousy, Bos	64	478	37.8	–	–	363	82.1	–	309	478	–	–	20.6
1957–58	Bill Russell, Bos	69	456	44.2	–	–	230	51.9	–	1,564	202	–	–	16.6
1958–59	Bob Pettit, StL	72	719	43.8	–	–	667	75.9	–	1,182	221	–	–	29.2
1959–60	Wilt Chamberlain, Phil	72	1,065	46.1	–	–	577	58.2	–	1,941	168	–	–	37.6
1960–61	Bill Russell, Bos	78	532	42.6	–	–	258	55.0	–	1,868	264	–	–	16.9
1961–62	Bill Russell, Bos	76	575	45.7	–	–	286	59.5	–	1,891	341	–	–	18.9
1962–63	Bill Russell, Bos	78	511	43.2	–	–	287	55.5	–	1,843	348	–	–	16.8
1963–64	Oscar Robertson, Cin	79	840	48.3	–	–	800	85.3	–	783	868	–	–	31.4
1964–65	Bill Russell, Bos	78	429	43.8	–	–	244	57.3	–	1,878	410	–	–	14.1
1965–66	Wilt Chamberlain, Phil	79	1,074	54.0	–	–	501	51.3	–	1,943	414	–	–	33.5
1966–67	Wilt Chamberlain, Phil	81	785	68.3	–	–	386	44.1	–	1,957	630	–	–	24.1
1967–68	Wilt Chamberlain, Phil	82	819	59.5	–	–	354	38.0	–	1,952	702	–	–	24.3
1968–69	Wes Unseld, Balt	82	427	47.6	–	–	277	60.5	–	1,491	213	–	–	13.8
1969–70	Willis Reed, NY	81	702	50.7	–	–	351	75.6	–	1,126	161	–	–	21.7
1970–71	Lew Alcindor*, Mil	82	1,063	57.7	–	–	470	69.0	–	1,311	272	–	–	31.7
1971–72	Kareem Abdul-Jabbar, Mil	81	1,159	57.4	–	–	504	68.9	–	1,346	370	–	–	34.8
1972–73	Dave Cowens, Bos	82	740	45.2	–	–	204	77.9	–	1,329	333	–	–	20.5
1973–74	Kareem Abdul-Jabbar, Mil	81	948	53.9	–	–	295	70.2	287	1,178	386	112	283	27.0
1974–75	Bob McAdoo, Buff	82	1,095	51.2	–	–	641	80.5	307	1,155	179	92	174	34.5
1975–76	Kareem Abdul-Jabbar, LAL	82	914	52.9	–	–	447	70.3	272	1,383	413	119	338	37.7
1976–77	Kareem Abdul-Jabbar, LAL	82	888	57.9	–	–	376	70.1	266	1,090	319	101	261	26.2
1977–78	Bill Walton, Port	58	460	52.2	–	–	177	72.0	118	766	291	60	146	18.9
1978–79	Moses Malone, Hou	82	716	54.0	–	–	599	73.9	587	1,444	147	79	119	24.8
1979–80	Kareem Abdul-Jabbar, LAL	82	835	60.4	0	00.0	364	76.5	190	886	371	81	280	24.8
1980–81	Julius Erving, Phil	82	794	52.1	4	22.2	422	78.7	244	657	364	173	147	24.6
1981–82	Moses Malone, Hou	81	945	51.9	0	00.0	630	76.2	558	1,188	142	76	125	31.1
1982–83	Moses Malone, Phil	78	654	50.1	0	00.0	600	76.1	445	1,194	101	89	157	24.5
1983–84	Larry Bird, Bos	79	758	49.2	18	24.7	374	88.8	181	796	520	144	69	24.2
1984–85	Larry Bird, Bos	80	918	52.2	56	42.7	403	88.2	164	842	531	129	98	28.7
1985–86	Larry Bird, Bos	82	796	49.6	82	42.3	441	89.6	190	805	557	166	51	25.8
1986–87	Magic Johnson, LAL	80	683	52.2	8	20.5	535	84.8	122	504	977	138	36	23.9
1987–88	Michael Jordan, Chi	82	1,069	53.5	7	13.2	723	84.1	139	449	485	259	131	35.0
1988–89	Magic Johnson, LAL	77	579	50.9	59	31.4	513	91.1	111	607	988	138	22	22.5
1989–90	Magic Johnson, LAL	79	546	48.0	106	38.4	567	89.0	128	522	907	132	34	22.3
1990–91	Michael Jordan, Chi	82	990	53.9	29	31.2	571	85.1	118	492	453	223	83	31.5
1991–92	Michael Jordan, Chi	80	943	51.9	27	27.0	491	83.2	91	511	489	182	75	30.1
1992–93	Charles Barkley, Phx	76	716	52.0	67	30.5	445	76.5	237	928	385	119	74	25.6
1993–94	Hakeem Olajuwon, Hou	80	894	52.8	8	42.1	388	71.6	229	955	287	128	297	27.3
1994–95	David Robinson, SA	81	788	53.0	6	30.0	656	77.4	234	877	236	134	262	27.6
1995–96	Michael Jordan, Chi	82	916	49.5	111	42.7	548	83.4	148	543	352	180	42	30.4
1996–97	Karl Malone, Utah	82	864	55.0	0	00.0	521	75.5	193	809	368	113	48	27.4
1997–98	Michael Jordan, Chi	82	881	46.5	30	23.8	565	78.4	130	475	283	141	45	28.7
1998–99	Karl Malone, Utah	49	393	49.3	0	00.0	378	78.8	107	463	201	62	28	23.8
1999–00	Shaquille O'Neal, LAL	79	956	57.4	0	00.0	432	52.4	336	1078	299	36	239	29.7
2000–01	Allen Iverson, Phil	71	762	42.0	98	32.0	585	81.4	50	273	325	78	20	31.1
2001–02	Tim Duncan, SA	82	764	50.8	1	10.0	560	79.9	268	1042	307	61	203	25.5
2002–03	Tim Duncan, SA	81	714	51.3	6	27.3	450	71.0	260	1045	316	55	237	23.3
2003–04	Kevin Garnett, Minn	82	804	49.9	11	25.6	368	79.1	245	1139	409	120	178	24.2
2004–05	Steve Nash, Phx	75	430	50.2	94	43.1	211	88.7	80	330	861	74	6	26.0
2005–06	Steve Nash, Phx	79	541	51.2	150	43.9	257	92.1	47	333	826	61	12	18.8
2006–07	Dirk Nowitzki, Dal	78	673	50.2	72	41.6	498	90.4	122	693	263	52	62	24.6
2007–08	Kobe Bryant, LAL	82	775	45.9	150	36.1	623	84.0	94	517	441	151	40	28.3
2008–09	LeBron James, Cle	81	789	48.9	132	34.4	594	78.0	106	613	587	137	93	28.4
2009–10	LeBron James, Cle	76	768	50.3	129	33.3	756	76.7	71	554	651	125	77	29.7
2010–11	Derrick Rose, Chi	81	711	44.5	128	33.2	476	85.8	81	330	623	85	51	25.0
2011–12	LeBron James, Mia	62	621	53.1	54	36.2	387	77.1	94	492	387	115	50	27.1

*Alcindor changed his name to Kareem Abdul-Jabbar after the 1970–71 season.

Coach of the Year: Arnold (Red) Auerbach Trophy

1962–63...Harry Gallatin, StL
1963–64...Alex Hannum, SF
1964–65...Red Auerbach, Bos
1965–66...Dolph Schayes, Phil
1966–67...Johnny Kerr, Chi
1967–68...Richie Guerin, StL
1968–69...Gene Shue, Balt
1969–70...Red Holzman, NY
1970–71...Dick Motta, Chi
1971–72...Bill Sharman, LA
1972–73...Tom Heinsohn, Bos
1973–74...Ray Scott, Det
1974–75...Phil Johnson, KC-Oma
1975–76...Bill Fitch, Clev
1976–77...Tom Nissalke, Hou
1977–78...Hubie Brown, Atl
1978–79...Cotton Fitzsimmons, KC

1979–80...Bill Fitch, Bos
1980–81...Jack McKinney, Ind
1981–82...Gene Shue, Wash
1982–83...Don Nelson, Mil
1983–84...Frank Layden, Utah
1984–85...Don Nelson, Mil
1985–86...Mike Fratello, Atl
1986–87...Mike Schuler, Port
1987–88...Doug Moe, Den
1988–89...Cotton Fitzsimmons, Phx
1989–90...Pat Riley, LAL
1990–91...Don Chaney, Hou
1991–92...Don Nelson, GS
1992–93...Pat Riley, NY
1993–94...Lenny Wilkens, Atl
1994–95...Del Harris, LAL
1995–96...Phil Jackson, Chi

1996–97...Pat Riley, Mia
1997–98...Larry Bird, Ind
1998–99...Mike Dunleavy, Port
1999–00...Glenn (Doc) Rivers, Orl
2000–01...Larry Brown, Phil
2001–02...Rick Carlisle, Det
2002–03...Gregg Popovich, SA
2003–04...Hubie Brown, Mem
2004–05...Mike D'Antoni, Phx
2005–06...Avery Johnson, Dal
2006–07...Sam Mitchell, Tor
2007–08...Byron Scott, NO
2008–09...Mike Brown, Cle
2009–10...Scott Brooks, OKC
2010–11...Tom Thibodeau, Chi
2011–12...Gregg Popovich, SA

Note: Award named after Auerbach in 1986.

Rookie of the Year: Eddie Gottlieb Trophy

1952–53...Don Meineke, FW
1953–54...Ray Felix, Balt
1954–55...Bob Pettit, Mil
1955–56...Maurice Stokes, Roch
1956–57...Tom Heinsohn, Bos
1957–58...Woody Sauldsberry, Phil
1958–59...Elgin Baylor, Minn
1959–60...Wilt Chamberlain, Phil
1960–61...Oscar Robertson, Cin
1961–62...Walt Bellamy, Chi
1962–63...Terry Dischinger, Chi
1963–64...Jerry Lucas, Cin
1964–65...Willis Reed, NY
1965–66...Rick Barry, SF
1966–67...Dave Bing, Det
1967–68...Earl Monroe, Balt
1968–69...Wes Unseld, Balt
1969–70...K. Abdul-Jabbar, Mil
1970–71...Dave Cowens, Bos
    Geoff Petrie, Port

1971–72...Sidney Wicks, Port
1972–73...Bob McAdoo, Buff
1973–74...Ernie DiGregorio, Buf
1974–75...Keith Wilkes, GS
1975–76...Alvan Adams, Phx
1976–77...Adrian Dantley, Buf
1977–78...Walter Davis, Phx
1978–79...Phil Ford, KC
1979–80...Larry Bird, Bos
1980–81...Darrell Griffith, Utah
1981–82...Buck Williams, NJ
1982–83...Terry Cummings, SD
1983–84...Ralph Sampson, Hou
1984–85...Michael Jordan, Chi
1985–86...Patrick Ewing, NY
1986–87...Chuck Person, Ind
1987–88...Mark Jackson, NY
1988–89...Mitch Richmond, GS
1989–90...David Robinson, SA
1990–91...Derrick Coleman, NJ
1991–92...Larry Johnson, Cha

1992–93...Shaquille O'Neal, Orl
1993–94...Chris Webber, GS
1994–95...Grant Hill, Det
    Jason Kidd, Dal
1995–96...Damon Stoudamire, Tor
1996–97...Allen Iverson, Phil
1997–98...Tim Duncan, SA
1998–99...Vince Carter, Tor
1999–00...Elton Brand, Chi
    Steve Francis, Hou
2000–01..Mike Miller, Orl
2001–02..Pau Gasol, Mem
2002–03..Amare Stoudemire, Phx
2003–04..LeBron James, Clev
2004–05..Emeka Okafor, Cha
2005–06..Chris Paul, NO
2006–07..Brandon Roy, Port
2007–08..Kevin Durant, Sea
2008–09..Derrick Rose, Chi
2009–10..Tyreke Evans, Sac
2010–11..Blake Griffin, LAC
2011–12..Kyrie Irving, Cle

Defensive Player of the Year

1982–83...Sidney Moncrief, Mil
1983–84...Sidney Moncrief, Mil
1984–85...Mark Eaton, Utah
1985–86...Alvin Robertson, SA
1986–87...Michael Cooper, LAL
1987–88...Michael Jordan, Chi
1988–89...Mark Eaton, Utah
1989–90...Dennis Rodman, Det
1990–91...Dennis Rodman, Det
1991–92...David Robinson, SA

1992–93...Hakeem Olajuwon, Hou
1993–94...Hakeem Olajuwon, Hou
1994–95...Dikembe Mutombo, Den
1995–96...Gary Payton, Sea
1996–97...Dikembe Mutombo, Atl
1997–98...Dikembe Mutombo, Atl
1998–99...Alonzo Mourning, Mia
1999–00...Alonzo Mourning, Mia
2000–01...Dikembe Mutombo, Phil/Atl
2001–02...Ben Wallace, Det

2002–03...Ben Wallace, Det
2003–04...Ron Artest, Ind
2004–05...Ben Wallace, Det
2005–06...Ben Wallace, Det
2006–07...Marcus Camby, Den
2007–08...Kevin Garnett, Bos
2008–09...Dwight Howard, Orl
2009–10...Dwight Howard, Orl
2010–11...Dwight Howard, Orl
2011–12...Tyson Chandler, NY

Sixth Man Award

1982–83...Bobby Jones, Phil
1983–84...Kevin McHale, Bos
1984–85...Kevin McHale, Bos
1985–86...Bill Walton, Bos
1986–87...Ricky Pierce, Mil
1987–88...Roy Tarpley, Dal
1988–89...Eddie Johnson, Phx
1989–90...Ricky Pierce, Mil
1990–91...Detlef Schrempf, Ind
1991–92...Detlef Schrempf, Ind

1992–93...Cliff Robinson, Port
1993–94...Dell Curry, Cha
1994–95...Anthony Mason, NY
1995–96...Tony Kukoc, Chi
1996–97...John Starks, NY
1997–98...Danny Manning, Phx
1998–99...Darrell Armstrong, Orl
1999–00...Rodney Rogers, Phx
2000–01...Aaron McKie, Phil
2001–02...Corliss Williamson, Det

2002–03...Bobby Jackson, Sac
2003–04...Antawn Jamison, Dal
2004–05...Ben Gordon, Chi
2005–06...Mike Miller, Mem
2006–07...Leandro Barbosa, Phx
2007–08...Manu Ginobli, SA
2008–09...Jason Terry, Dal
2009–10...Jamal Crawford, Atl
2010–11...Lamar Odom, LAL
2011–12...James Harden, OKC

J. Walter Kennedy Citizenship Award

1974–75...Wes Unseld, Wash	1986–87...Isiah Thomas, Det	1999–00...Vlade Divac, Sac
1975–76...Slick Watts, Sea	1987–88...Alex English, Den	2000–01...Dikembe Mutombo, Phi
1976–77...Dave Bing, Wash	1988–89...Thurl Bailey, Utah	2001–02...Alonzo Mourning, Mia
1977–78...Bob Lanier, Det	1989–90...Glenn (Doc) Rivers, Atl	2002–03...David Robinson, SA
1978–79...Calvin Murphy, Hou	1990–91...Kevin Johnson, Phx	2003–04...Reggie Miller, Ind
1979–80...Austin Carr, Cle	1991–92...Magic Johnson, LAL	2004–05...Eric Snow, Clev
1980–81...Mike Glenn, NY	1992–93...Terry Porter, Port	2005–06...Kevin Garnett, Min
1981–82...Kent Benson, Det	1993–94...Joe Dumars, Det	2006–07...Luol Deng, Chi
1982–83...Julius Erving, Phi	1994–95...Joe O'Toole, Atl	2007–08...Grant Hill, Phx
1983–84...Frank Layden, Utah	1995–96...Chris Dudley, Port	2008–09...Dikembe Mutombo, Hou
1984–85...Dan Issel, Den	1996–97...P.J. Brown, Mia	2009–10...Samuel Dalembert, Phi
1985–86...Michael Cooper, LAL	1997–98...Steve Smith, Atl	2010–11...Ron Artest, LAL
Rory Sparrow, NY	1998–99...Brian Grant, Port	2011–12...Pau Gasol, LAL

Most Improved Player

1985–86...Alvin Robertson, SA	1994–95...Dana Barros, Phil	2003–04...Zach Randolph, Port
1986–87...Dale Ellis, Sea	1995–96...Gheorghe Muresan, Wash	2004–05...Bobby Simmons, LAC
1987–88...Kevin Duckworth, Port	1996–97...Isaac Austin, Mia	2005–06...Boris Diaw, Phx
1988–89...Kevin Johnson, Phx	1997–98...Alan Henderson, Atl	2006–07...Monta Ellis, GS
1989–90...Rony Seikaly, Mia	1998–99...Darrell Armstrong, Orl	2007–08...Hedo Turkoglu, Orl
1990–91...Scott Skiles, Orl	1999–00...Jalen Rose, Ind	2008–09...Danny Granger, Ind
1991–92...Pervis Ellison, Wash	2000–01...Tracy McGrady, Orl	2009–10...Aaron Brooks, Hou
1992–93...Mahmoud Abdul-Rauf, Den	2001–02...Jermaine O'Neal, Ind	2010–11...Kevin Love, Min
1993–94...Don MacLean, Wash	2002–03...Gilbert Arenas, GS	2011–12...Ryan Anderson, Orl

Executive of the Year

1972–73...Joe Axelson, KC-Oma	1986–87...Stan Kasten, Atl	2000–01...Geoff Petrie, Sac
1973–74...Eddie Donovan, Buf	1987–88...Jerry Krause, Chi	2001–02...Rod Thorn, NJ
1974–75...Dick Vertlieb, GS	1988–89...Jerry Colangelo, Phx	2002–03...Joe Dumars, Det
1975–76...Jerry Colangelo, Phx	1989–90...Bob Bass, SA	2003–04...Jerry West, Mem
1976–77...Ray Patterson, Hou	1990–91...Bucky Buckwalter, Port	2004–05...Bryan Colangelo, Phx
1977–78...Angelo Drossos, SA	1991–92...Wayne Embry, Clev	2005–06...Elgin Baylor, LAC
1978–79...Bob Ferry, Wash	1992–93...Jerry Colangelo, Phx	2006–07...Bryan Colangelo, Tor
1979–80...Red Auerbach, Bos	1993–94...Bob Whitsitt, Sea	2007–08...Danny Ainge, Bos
1980–81...Jerry Colangelo, Phx	1994–95...Jerry West, LAL	2008–09...Mark Warkentien, Den
1981–82...Bob Ferry, Wash	1995–96...Jerry Krause, Chi	2009–10...John Hammond, Mil
1982–83...Zollie Volchok, Sea	1996–97...Bob Bass, Cha	2010–11...Gar Forman, Chi
1983–84...Frank Layden, Utah	1997–98...Wayne Embry, Clev	Pat Riley, Mia
1984–85...Vince Boryla, Den	1998–99...Geoff Petrie, Sac	2011–12...Larry Bird, Ind
1985–86...Stan Kasten, Atl	1999–00...John Gabriel, Orl	

NBA Alltime Individual Leaders

Scoring

MOST POINTS, CAREER

	Pts	Avg
Kareem Abdul-Jabbar	38,387	24.6
Karl Malone	36,928	25.0
Michael Jordan	32,292	30.1
Wilt Chamberlain	31,419	30.1
*Kobe Bryant	29,484	25.4
Shaquille O'Neal	28,596	23.7
Moses Malone	27,409	20.6
Elvin Hayes	27,313	21.0
Hakeem Olajuwon	26,946	21.8
Oscar Robertson	26,710	25.7

*Active in 2011–12.

HIGHEST SCORING AVERAGE, CAREER

Michael Jordan	30.1	1,072 games
Wilt Chamberlain	30.1	1,045 games
*LeBron James	27.7	689 games
Elgin Baylor	27.4	846 games
Jerry West	27.0	932 games
Allen Iverson	26.7	914 games
Bob Pettit	26.4	792 games
George Gervin	26.2	791 games
Oscar Robertson	25.7	1,040 games
*Kobe Bryant	25.4	1,161 games

*Active in 2011–12. Note: Minimum 400 games.

MOST POINTS, SEASON

Wilt Chamberlain, Phil	4,029	1961–62
Wilt Chamberlain, SF	3,586	1962–63
Michael Jordan, Chi	3,041	1986–87
Wilt Chamberlain, Phil	3,033	1960–61
Wilt Chamberlain, SF	2,948	1963–64
Michael Jordan, Chi	2,868	1987–88
Kobe Bryant, LA	2,832	2005–06
Bob McAdoo, Buff	2,831	1974–75
Kareem Abdul-Jabbar, Mil	2,822	1971–72
Rick Barry, SF	2,775	1966–67
Michael Jordan, Chi	2,753	1989–90

HIGHEST SCORING AVERAGE, SEASON

Wilt Chamberlain, Phil	50.4	1961–62
Wilt Chamberlain, SF	44.8	1962–63
Wilt Chamberlain, Phil	38.4	1960–61
Wilt Chamberlain, Phil	37.6	1959–60
Michael Jordan, Chi	37.1	1986–87
Wilt Chamberlain, SF	36.9	1963–64
Rick Barry, SF	35.6	1966–67
Kobe Bryant, LA	35.4	2005–06
Michael Jordan, Chi	35.0	1987–88
Kareem Abdul-Jabbar, LA	34.8	1971–72
Elgin Baylor, LA	34.8	1960–61

Note: Minimum 70 games.

Scoring *(Cont.)*

MOST POINTS, SINGLE GAME

Player, Team	Opp	Date
100 ....Wilt Chamberlain, Phil	NY	3/2/62
81 ....Kobe Bryant, LAL	Tor	1/22/06
78 ....Wilt Chamberlain, Phil	LAL	12/8/61
73 ....Wilt Chamberlain, Phil	Chi	1/13/62
73 ....Wilt Chamberlain, SF	NY	11/16/62
73 ....David Thompson, Den	Det	4/9/78
72 ....Wilt Chamberlain, SF	LAL	11/3/62
71 ....David Robinson, SA	LAC	4/24/94
71 ....Elgin Baylor, LAL	NY	11/15/60
70 ....Wilt Chamberlain, SF	Syr	3/10/63

Field-Goal Percentage

Highest FG Percentage, Career: .599—Artis Gilmore

Highest FG Percentage, Season: .727—Wilt Chamberlain, LA Lakers, 1972–73 (426/586)

Free Throws

HIGHEST FREE-THROW PERCENTAGE, CAREER

Mark Price............................	.904
*Steve Nash.........................	.904
Rick Barry	.900
*Peja Stojakovic	.895
*Ray Allen	.8939
*Chauncey Billups	.8937

Note: Minimum 1200 free throws made. *Active 2011–12.

HIGHEST FREE-THROW PERCENTAGE, SEASON

Jose Calderon, Tor	.981	2008–09
Calvin Murphy, Hou	.958	1980–81
Mahmoud Abdul-Rauf, Den...	.956	1993–94
Ray Allen, Bos	.952	2008–09
Jeff Hornacek, Utah.............	.950	1999–00

MOST FREE THROWS MADE, CAREER

	No.	Yrs	Pct
Karl Malone........................	9,787	19	.742
Moses Malone	8,531	19	.769
Oscar Robertson	7,694	14	.838
*Kobe Bryant	7,407	16	.838
Michael Jordan	7,327	15	.835

Three-Point Field Goals

Most Three-Point Field-Goals, Career: 2,718—Ray Allen*

Highest Three-Point Field-Goal Percentage, Career: .454—Steve Kerr

Most Three-Point Field Goals, Season: 269—Ray Allen, Sea, 2005–06

Highest Three-Point Field-Goal Percentage, Season: .536—Kyle Korver, Utah, 2009–10

Most Three-Point Field Goals, Game: 12—Kobe Bryant, LA Lakers vs Seattle, 1/7/03; Donyell Marshall, Toronto vs. Philadelphia, 3/13/05

Note: First season of three-point field goal: 1979–80.

*Active 2011–12.

Steals

Most Steals, Career: 3,265—John Stockton

Most Steals, Season: 301—Alvin Robertson, San Antonio, 1985–86

Most Steals, Game: 11—Kendall Gill, New Jersey vs Miami, 4/3/99; Larry Kenon, San Antonio vs Kansas City, 12/26/76

Rebounds

MOST REBOUNDS, CAREER

	No.	Yrs	Avg
Wilt Chamberlain	23,924	14	22.9
Bill Russell	21,620	13	22.5
Kareem Abdul-Jabbar	17,440	20	11.2
Elvin Hayes......................	16,279	16	12.5
Moses Malone	16,212	19	12.2
Karl Malone	14,968	19	10.1
Robert Parish....................	14,715	21	9.1
Nate Thurmond.................	14,464	14	15.0
Walt Bellamy	14,241	14	13.7
Wes Unseld	13,769	13	14.0

MOST REBOUNDS, SEASON

Wilt Chamberlain, Phil	2,149	1960–61
Wilt Chamberlain, Phil	2,052	1961–62
Wilt Chamberlain, Phil	1,957	1966–67
Wilt Chamberlain, Phil	1,952	1967–68
Wilt Chamberlain, SF	1,946	1962–63
Wilt Chamberlain, Phil	1,943	1965–66
Wilt Chamberlain, Phil	1,941	1959–60
Bill Russell, Bos	1,930	1963–64
Bill Russell, Bos	1,878	1964–65
Bill Russell, Bos	1,868	1960–61

MOST REBOUNDS, GAME

Player, Team	Opp	Date
55 ....Wilt Chamberlain, Phil	Bos	11/24/60
51 ....Bill Russell, Bos	Syr	02/05/60
49 ....Bill Russell, Bos	Phil	11/16/57
49 ....Bill Russell, Bos	Det	03/11/65
45 ....Wilt Chamberlain, Phil	Syr	02/06/60
45 ....Wilt Chamberlain, Phil	LA	01/21/61

Assists

MOST ASSISTS, CAREER

John Stockton..	15,806
*Jason Kidd..	11,842
Mark Jackson..	10,334
Magic Johnson	10,141
*Steve Nash..	9,916

*Active in 2011–12.

MOST ASSISTS, SEASON

John Stockton, Utah..................	1,164	1990–91
John Stockton, Utah..................	1,134	1989–90
John Stockton, Utah..................	1,128	1987–88
John Stockton, Utah..................	1,126	1991–92
Isiah Thomas, Det	1,123	1984–85

MOST ASSISTS, GAME: 30—Scott Skiles, Orlando vs Denver, 12/30/90

Blocked Shots

MOST BLOCKED SHOTS, CAREER

Hakeem Olajuwon	3,830
Dikembe Mutombo	3,289
Kareem Abdul-Jabbar	3,189
Mark Eaton	3,064
David Robinson	2,954

MOST BLOCKED SHOTS, SEASON

Mark Eaton, Utah	456	1984–85
Manute Bol, Wash	397	1985–86
Elmore Smith, LAL.......................	393	1973–74
Hakeem Olajuwon, Hou	376	1989–90
Mark Eaton, Utah	369	1985–86

MOST BLOCKED SHOTS, GAME: 17—Elmore Smith, LA Lakers vs Portland, 10/28/73

Scoring
MOST POINTS, CAREER

	Pts	App.	Avg
Michael Jordan	5,987	13	33.4
Kareem Abdul-Jabbar	5,762	18	24.3
*Kobe Bryant	5,640	15	25.6
Shaquille O'Neal	5,250	17	24.3
Karl Malone	4,761	19	24.7
Jerry West	4,457	13	29.1
*Tim Duncan	4,233	14	22.3
Larry Bird	3,897	12	23.8
John Havlicek	3,776	13	22.0
Hakeem Olajuwon	3,755	15	25.9
Magic Johnson	3,701	13	19.5
Scottie Pippen	3,642	16	17.5
Elgin Baylor	3,623	12	27.0
Wilt Chamberlain	3,607	13	22.5
*Dirk Nowitzki	3,321	12	25.9

*Active 2011–12.

†HIGHEST SCORING AVERAGE, CAREER

	Avg	Games
Michael Jordan	33.4	179
Allen Iverson	29.7	71
Jerry West	29.1	153
*LeBron James	28.5	115
*Kevin Durant	28.1	43
Elgin Baylor	27.0	134
George Gervin	27.0	59
Hakeem Olajuwon	25.9	145
*Dirk Nowitzki	25.9	128
*Kobe Bryant	25.6	220
Bob Pettit	25.5	88
Dominique Wilkins	25.4	55
*Dwyane Wade	25.2	110
*Tracy McGrady	25.2	44
*Carmelo Anthony	24.9	54

†Minimum of 25 games. *Active 2011–12.

MOST POINTS, GAME

	Player, Team	Opp	Date
†63	Michael Jordan, Chi	Bos	4/20/86
61	Elgin Baylor, LAL	Bos	4/14/62
56	Wilt Chamberlain, Phil	Syr	3/22/62
56	Michael Jordan, Chi	Mia	4/29/92
56	Charles Barkley, Phx	GS	5/4/94
55	Rick Barry, SF	Phil	4/18/67
55	Michael Jordan, Chi	Cle	5/1/88
55	Michael Jordan, Chi	Phx	6/16/93
55	Michael Jordan, Chi	Was	4/27/97
55	Allen Iverson, Phi	NO	4/20/03

†Double overtime game.

John Stockton	19
Karl Malone	19
Kareem Abdul-Jabbar	18
Shaquille O'Neal	17
Robert Horry	16
Robert Parish	16
Scottie Pippen	16
Terry Porter	16

Rebounds
MOST REBOUNDS, CAREER

	No.	App.	Avg
Bill Russell	4,104	13	24.9
Wilt Chamberlain	3,913	13	24.5
Shaquille O'Neal	2,508	17	11.6
Kareem Abdul-Jabbar	2,481	18	10.5
*Tim Duncan	2,308	14	12.1
Karl Malone	2,062	19	10.7

*Active 2011–12.

MOST REBOUNDS, GAME

	Player, Team	Opp	Date
41	Wilt Chamberlain, Phil	Bos	4/5/67
40	Bill Russell, Bos	Phil	3/23/58
40	Bill Russell, Bos	StL	3/29/60
†40	Bill Russell, Bos	LA	4/18/62

†Overtime game. Three tied at 39.

Assists
MOST ASSISTS, CAREER

	No.	Games
Magic Johnson	2,346	190
John Stockton	1,839	182
*Jason Kidd	1,239	146
Larry Bird	1,062	164
*Steve Nash	1,052	118
Scottie Pippen	1,048	208
*Kobe Bryant	1,040	220

*Active 2011–12.

MOST ASSISTS, GAME

	Player, Team	Opp	Date
24	Magic Johnson, LAL	Phx	5/15/84
24	John Stockton, Utah	LAL	5/17/88
23	Magic Johnson, LAL	Port	5/3/85
23	John Stockton, Utah	Port	4/25/96
23	Steve Nash, Phx	LAL	4/24/07

Games played

Robert Horry	244
Kareem Abdul-Jabbar	237
*Derek Fisher	229
*Kobe Bryant	220
Shaquille O'Neal	216
Scottie Pippen	208
Danny Ainge	193
Karl Malone	193
Magic Johnson	190
*Tim Duncan	190

*Active 2011–12.

Appearances

Dolph Schayes	15
Clyde Drexler	15
Jerome Kersey	15
Hakeem Olajuwon	15
Tree Rollins	15
*Kobe Bryant	15

*Active 2011–12.

NBA Regular Season Leaders

Scoring

1946–47	Joe Fulks, Phil	1389	1979–80	George Gervin, SA	33.1
1947–48	Max Zaslofsky, Chi	1007	1980–81	Adrian Dantley, Utah	30.7
1948–49	George Mikan, Min	1698	1981–82	George Gervin, SA	32.3
1949–50	George Mikan, Min	1865	1982–83	Alex English, Den	28.4
1950–51	George Mikan, Min	1932	1983–84	Adrian Dantley, Utah	30.6
1951–52	Paul Arizin, Phil	1674	1984–85	Bernard King, NY	32.9
1952–53	Neil Johnston, Phil	1564	1985–86	Dominique Wilkins, Atl	30.3
1953–54	Neil Johnston, Phil	1759	1986–87	Michael Jordan, Chi	37.1
1954–55	Neil Johnston, Phil	1631	1987–88	Michael Jordan, Chi	35.0
1955–56	Bob Pettit, StL	1849	1988–89	Michael Jordan, Chi	32.5
1956–57	Paul Arizin, Phil	1817	1989–90	Michael Jordan, Chi	33.6
1957–58	George Yardley, Det	2001	1990–91	Michael Jordan, Chi	31.5
1958–59	Bob Pettit, StL	2105	1991–92	Michael Jordan, Chi	30.1
1959–60	Wilt Chamberlain, Phil	2707	1992–93	Michael Jordan, Chi	32.6
1960–61	Wilt Chamberlain, Phil	3033	1993–94	David Robinson, SA	29.8
1961–62	Wilt Chamberlain, Phil	4029	1994–95	Shaquille O'Neal, Orl	29.3
1962–63	Wilt Chamberlain, SF	3586	1995–96	Michael Jordan, Chi	30.4
1963–64	Wilt Chamberlain, SF	2948	1996–97	Michael Jordan, Chi	29.6
1964–65	Wilt Chamberlain, SF-Phil	2534	1997–98	Michael Jordan, Chi	28.7
1965–66	Wilt Chamberlain, Phil	2649	1998–99	Allen Iverson, Phil	26.8
1966–67	Rick Barry, SF	2775	1999–00	Shaquille O'Neal, LAL	29.7
1967–68	Dave Bing, Det	2142	2000–01	Allen Iverson, Phil	31.1
1968–69	Elvin Hayes, SD	2327	2001–02	Allen Iverson, Phil	31.4
1969–70	Jerry West, LAL	*31.2	2002–03	Tracy McGrady, Orl	32.1
1970–71	Kareem Abdul-Jabbar, Mil	31.7	2003–04	Tracy McGrady, Orl	28.0
1971–72	Kareem Abdul-Jabbar, Mil	34.8	2004–05	Allen Iverson, Phil	30.7
1972–73	Nate Archibald, KC-Oma	34.0	2005–06	Kobe Bryant, LAL	35.4
1973–74	Bob McAdoo, Buff	30.6	2006–07	Kobe Bryant, LAL	31.6
1974–75	Bob McAdoo, Buff	34.5	2007–08	LeBron James, Cle	30.0
1975–76	Bob McAdoo, Buff	31.1	2008–09	Dwyane Wade, Mia	30.2
1976–77	Pete Maravich, NO	31.1	2009–10	Kevin Durant, OKC	30.1
1977–78	George Gervin, SA	27.2	2010–11	Kevin Durant, OKC	27.7
1978–79	George Gervin, SA	29.6	2011–12	Kevin Durant, OKC	28.0

*Based on per game average since 1969–70.

Rebounding

1950–51	Dolph Schayes, Syr	1080	1981–82	Moses Malone, Hou	14.7
1951–52	Larry Foust, FW	880	1982–83	Moses Malone, Phil	15.3
	Mel Hutchins, Mil	880	1983–84	Moses Malone, Phil	13.4
1952–53	George Mikan, Min	1007	1984–85	Moses Malone, Phil	13.1
1953–54	Harry Gallatin, NY	1098	1985–86	Bill Laimbeer, Den	13.1
1954–55	Neil Johnston, Phil	1085	1986–87	Charles Barkley, Phil	14.6
1955–56	Bob Pettit, StL	1164	1987–88	Michael Cage, LAC	13.0
1956–57	Maurice Stokes, Roch	1256	1988–89	Hakeem Olajuwon, Hou	13.5
1957–58	Bill Russell, Bos	1564	1989–90	Hakeem Olajuwon, Hou	14.0
1958–59	Bill Russell, Bos	1612	1990–91	David Robinson, SA	13.0
1959–60	Wilt Chamberlain, Phil	1941	1991–92	Dennis Rodman, Det	18.7
1960–61	Wilt Chamberlain, Phil	2149	1992–93	Dennis Rodman, Det	18.3
1961–62	Wilt Chamberlain, Phil	2052	1993–94	Dennis Rodman, SA	17.3
1962–63	Wilt Chamberlain, SF	1946	1994–95	Dennis Rodman, SA	16.8
1963–64	Bill Russell, Bos	1930	1995–96	Dennis Rodman, Chi	14.9
1964–65	Bill Russell, Bos	1878	1996–97	Dennis Rodman, Chi	16.1
1965–66	Wilt Chamberlain, Phil	1943	1997–98	Dennis Rodman, Chi	15.0
1966–67	Wilt Chamberlain, Phil	1957	1998–99	Chris Webber, Sac	13.0
1967–68	Wilt Chamberlain, Phil	1952	1999–00	Dikembe Mutombo, Atl	14.1
1968–69	Wilt Chamberlain, LAL	1712	2000–01	Dikembe Mutombo, Atl	13.5
1969–70	Elvin Hayes, SD	*16.9	2001–02	Ben Wallace, Det	13.0
1970–71	Wilt Chamberlain, LAL	18.2	2002–03	Ben Wallace, Det	15.4
1971–72	Wilt Chamberlain, LAL	19.2	2003–04	Kevin Garnett, Min	13.9
1972–73	Wilt Chamberlain, LAL	18.6	2004–05	Kevin Garnett, Min	13.5
1973–74	Elvin Hayes, Capital (Wash.)	18.1	2005–06	Kevin Garnett, Min	12.7
1974–75	Wes Unseld, Wash	14.8	2006–07	Kevin Garnett, Min	12.8
1975–76	Kareem Abdul-Jabbar, LAL	16.9	2007–08	Dwight Howard, Orl	14.2
1976–77	Bill Walton, Port	14.4	2008–09	Dwight Howard, Orl	13.8
1977–78	Len Robinson, NO	15.7	2009–10	Dwight Howard, Orl	12.7
1978–79	Moses Malone, Hou	17.6	2010–11	Kevin Love, Min	15.2
1979–80	Swen Nater, SD	15.0	2011–12	Dwight Howard, Orl	14.5
1980–81	Moses Malone, Hou	14.8			

*Based on per game average since 1969–70.

Assists

1946–47	Ernie Calverly, Prov	202
1947–48	Howie Dallmar, Phil	120
1948–49	Bob Davies, Roch	321
1949–50	Dick McGuire, NY	386
1950–51	Andy Phillip, Phil	414
1951–52	Andy Phillip, Phil	539
1952–53	Bob Cousy, Bos	547
1953–54	Bob Cousy, Bos	518
1954–55	Bob Cousy, Bos	557
1955–56	Bob Cousy, Bos	642
1956–57	Bob Cousy, Bos	478
1957–58	Bob Cousy, Bos	463
1958–59	Bob Cousy, Bos	557
1959–60	Bob Cousy, Bos	715
1960–61	Oscar Robertson, Cin	690
1961–62	Oscar Robertson, Cin	899
1962–63	Guy Rodgers, SF	825
1963–64	Oscar Robertson, Cin	868
1964–65	Oscar Robertson, Cin	861
1965–66	Oscar Robertson, Cin	847
1966–67	Guy Rodgers, Chi	908
1967–68	Wilt Chamberlain, Phil	702
1968–69	Oscar Robertson, Cin	772
1969–70	Lenny Wilkens, Sea	*9.1
1970–71	Norm Van Lier, Cin	10.1
1971–72	Jerry West, LAL	9.7
1972–73	Nate Archibald, KC-Oma	11.4
1973–74	Ernie DiGregorio, Buf	8.2
1974–75	Kevin Porter, Wash	8.0
1975–76	Don Watts, Sea	8.1
1976–77	Don Buse, Ind	8.5
1977–78	Kevin Porter, NJ-Det	10.2
1978–79	Kevin Porter, Det	13.4
1979–80	Micheal Ray Richardson, NY	10.1
1980–81	Kevin Porter, Wash	9.1
1981–82	Johnny Moore, SA	9.6
1982–83	Magic Johnson, LAL	10.5
1983–84	Magic Johnson, LAL	13.1
1984–85	Isiah Thomas, Det	13.9
1985–86	Magic Johnson, LAL	12.6
1986–87	Magic Johnson, LAL	12.2
1987–88	John Stockton, Utah	13.8
1988–89	John Stockton, Utah	13.6
1989–90	John Stockton, Utah	14.5
1990–91	John Stockton, Utah	14.2
1991–92	John Stockton, Utah	13.7
1992–93	John Stockton, Utah	12.0
1993–94	John Stockton, Utah	12.6
1994–95	John Stockton, Utah	12.3
1995–96	John Stockton, Utah	11.2
1996–97	Mark Jackson, Ind	11.4
1997–98	Rod Strickland, Wash	10.5
1998–99	Jason Kidd, Phx	10.8
1999–00	Jason Kidd, Phx	10.1
2000–01	Jason Kidd, Phx	9.8
2001–02	Andre Miller, Cle	10.9
2002–03	Jason Kidd, NJ	8.9
2003–04	Jason Kidd, NJ	9.2
2004–05	Steve Nash, Phx	11.5
2005–06	Steve Nash, Phx	10.5
2006–07	Steve Nash, Phx	11.6
2007–08	Chris Paul, NO	11.6
2008–09	Chris Paul, NO	11.0
2009–10	Steve Nash, Phx	11.0
2010–11	Steve Nash, Phx	11.4
2011–12	Rajon Rondo, Bos	11.7

*Based on per game average since 1969–70.

Free-Throw Percentage

1946–47	Fred Scolari, Wash	81.1
1947–48	Bob Feerick, Wash	78.8
1948–49	Bob Feerick, Wash	85.9
1949–50	Max Zaslofsky, Chi	84.3
1950–51	Joe Fulks, Phil	85.5
1951–52	Bob Wanzer, Roch	90.4
1952–53	Bill Sharman, Bos	85.0
1953–54	Bill Sharman, Bos	84.4
1954–55	Bill Sharman, Bos	89.7
1955–56	Bill Sharman, Bos	86.7
1956–57	Bill Sharman, Bos	90.5
1957–58	Dolph Schayes, Syr	90.4
1958–59	Bill Sharman, Bos	93.2
1959–60	Dolph Schayes, Syr	89.3
1960–61	Bill Sharman, Bos	92.1
1961–62	Dolph Schayes, Syr	89.7
1962–63	Larry Costello, Syr	88.1
1963–64	Oscar Robertson, Cin	85.3
1964–65	Larry Costello, Phil	87.7
1965–66	Larry Siegfried, Bos	88.1
1966–67	Adrian Smith, Cin	90.3
1967–68	Oscar Robertson, Cin	87.3
1968–69	Larry Siegfried, Bos	86.4
1969–70	Flynn Robinson, Mil	89.8
1970–71	Chet Walker, Chi	85.9
1971–72	Jack Marin, Balt	89.4
1972–73	Rick Barry, GS	90.2
1973–74	Ernie DiGregorio, Buf	90.2
1974–75	Rick Barry, GS	90.4
1975–76	Rick Barry, GS	92.3
1976–77	Ernie DiGregorio, Buf	94.5
1977–78	Rick Barry, GS	92.4
1978–79	Rick Barry, Hou	94.7
1979–80	Rick Barry, Hou	93.5
1980–81	Calvin Murphy, Hou	95.8
1981–82	Kyle Macy, Phx	89.9
1982–83	Calvin Murphy, Hou	92.0
1983–84	Larry Bird, Bos	88.8
1984–85	Kyle Macy, Phx	90.7
1985–86	Larry Bird, Bos	89.6
1986–87	Larry Bird, Bos	91.0
1987–88	Jack Sikma, Mil	92.2
1988–89	Magic Johnson, LAL	91.1
1989–90	Larry Bird, Bos	93.0
1990–91	Reggie Miller, Ind	91.8
1991–92	Mark Price, Clev	94.7
1992–93	Mark Price, Clev	94.8
1993–94	Mahmoud Abdul-Rauf, Den	95.6
1994–95	Spud Webb, Atl	93.4
1995–96	Mahmoud Abdul-Rauf, Den	93.0
1996–97	Mark Price, GS	90.6
1997–98	Chris Mullin, Ind	93.9
1998–99	Reggie Miller, Ind	91.5
1999–00	Jeff Hornacek, Utah	95.0
2000–01	Reggie Miller, Ind	92.8
2001–02	Reggie Miller, Ind	91.1
2002–03	Allan Houston, NY	91.9
2003–04	Peja Stojakovic, Sac	92.7
2004–05	Reggie Miller, Ind	93.3
2005–06	Steve Nash, Phx	92.1
2006–07	Kyle Korver, Phil	91.4
2007–08	Peja Stojakovic, NO	92.9
2008–09	Jose Calderon, Tor	98.1
2009–10	Steve Nash, Phx	93.8
2010–11	Stephen Curry, GS	93.4
2011–12	Jamal Crawford, Por	92.7

Field-Goal Percentage

1946–47	Bob Feerick, Wash	40.1	1979–80	Cedric Maxwell, Bos	60.9
1947–48	Bob Feerick, Wash	34.0	1980–81	Artis Gilmore, Chi	67.0
1948–49	Arnie Risen, Roch	42.3	1981–82	Artis Gilmore, Chi	65.2
1949–50	Alex Groza, Ind	47.8	1982–83	Artis Gilmore, SA	62.6
1950–51	Alex Groza, Ind	47.0	1983–84	Artis Gilmore, SA	63.1
1951–52	Paul Arizin, Phil	44.8	1984–85	James Donaldson, LAC	63.7
1952–53	Neil Johnston, Phil	45.2	1985–86	Steve Johnson, SA	63.2
1953–54	Ed Macauley, Bos	48.6	1986–87	Kevin McHale, Bos	60.4
1954–55	Larry Foust, FW	48.7	1987–88	Kevin McHale, Bos	60.4
1955–56	Neil Johnston, Phil	45.7	1988–89	Dennis Rodman, Det	59.5
1956–57	Neil Johnston, Phil	44.7	1989–90	Mark West, Phx	62.5
1957–58	Jack Twyman, Cin	45.2	1990–91	Buck Williams, Port	60.2
1958–59	Ken Sears, NY	49.0	1991–92	Buck Williams, Port	60.4
1959–60	Ken Sears, NY	47.7	1992–93	Cedric Ceballos, Phx	57.6
1960–61	Wilt Chamberlain, Phil	50.9	1993–94	Shaquille O'Neal, Orl	59.9
1961–62	Walt Bellamy, Chi	51.9	1994–95	Chris Gatling, GS	63.3
1962–63	Wilt Chamberlain, SF	52.8	1995–96	Gheorghe Muresan, Wash	58.4
1963–64	Jerry Lucas, Cin	52.7	1996–97	Gheorghe Muresan, Wash	60.4
1964–65	Wilt Chamberlain, SF-Phil	51.0	1997–98	Shaquille O'Neal, LAL	58.4
1965–66	Wilt Chamberlain, Phil	54.0	1998–99	Shaquille O'Neal, LAL	57.6
1966–67	Wilt Chamberlain, Phil	68.3	1999–00	Shaquille O'Neal, LAL	57.4
1967–68	Wilt Chamberlain, Phil	59.5	2000–01	Shaquille O'Neal, LAL	57.2
1968–69	Wilt Chamberlain, LAL	58.3	2001–02	Shaquille O'Neal, LAL	57.9
1969–70	Johnny Green, Cin	55.9	2002–03	Eddy Curry, Chi	58.5
1970–71	Johnny Green, Cin	58.7	2003–04	Shaquille O'Neal, LAL	58.4
1971–72	Wilt Chamberlain, LAL	64.9	2004–05	Shaquille O'Neal, Mia	60.1
1972–73	Wilt Chamberlain, LAL	72.7	2005–06	Shaquille O'Neal, Mia	60.0
1973–74	Bob McAdoo, Buf	54.7	2006–07	Mikki Moore, NJ	60.9
1974–75	Don Nelson, Bos	53.9	2007–08	Andris Biedrins, GS	62.6
1975–76	Wes Unseld, Wash	56.1	2008–09	Erick Dampier, Dal	65.0
1976–77	Kareem Abdul-Jabbar, LAL	57.9	2009–10	Erick Dampier, Dal	62.4
1977–78	Bobby Jones, Den	57.8	2010–11	Nene Hilario, Den	61.5
1978–79	Cedric Maxwell, Bos	58.4	2011–12	Dwight Howard, Orl	57.3

Three-Point Field-Goal Percentage

1979–80	Fred Brown, Sea	44.3	1995–96	Tim Legler, Wash	52.2
1980–81	Brian Taylor, SD	38.3	1996–97	Glen Rice, Cha	47.0
1981–82	Campy Russell, NY	43.9	1997–98	Dale Ellis, Sea	46.0
1982–83	Mike Dunleavy, SA	34.5	1998–99	Dell Curry, Cha	47.6
1983–84	Darrell Griffith, Utah	36.1	1999–00	Hubert Davis, Dal	49.1
1984–85	Byron Scott, LAL	43.3	2000–01	Brent Barry, Sea	47.6
1985–86	Craig Hodges, Mil	45.1	2001–02	Steve Smith, SA	47.2
1986–87	Kiki Vandeweghe, Por	48.1	2002–03	Bruce Bowen, SA	44.1
1987–88	Craig Hodges, Mil-Phx	49.1	2003–04	Anthony Peeler, Sac	48.2
1988–89	Jon Sundvold, Mia	52.2	2004–05	Fred Hoiberg, Min	48.3
1989–90	Steve Kerr, Clev	50.7	2005–06	Richard Hamilton, Det	45.8
1990–91	Jim Les, Sac	46.1	2006–07	Jason Kapono, Mia	51.4
1991–92	Dana Barros, Sea	44.6	2007–08	Jason Kapono, Tor	48.3
1992–93	Chris Mullin, GS	45.1	2008–09	Anthony Morrow, GS	46.7
1993–94	Tracy Murray, Por	45.9	2009–10	Mike Miller, Wash	48.0
1994–95	Steve Kerr, Chi	52.4	2010–11	Matt Bonner, SA	45.7
			2011–12	Steve Novak, NY	47.2

Steals

1973–74	Larry Steele, Por	2.68	1986–87	Alvin Robertson, SA	3.21
1974–75	Rick Barry, GS	2.85	1987–88	Michael Jordan, Chi	3.16
1975–76	Don Watts, Sea	3.18	1988–89	John Stockton, Utah	3.21
1976–77	Don Buse, Ind	3.47	1989–90	Michael Jordan, Chi	2.77
1977–78	Ron Lee, Phx	2.74	1990–91	Alvin Robertson, Mil	3.04
1978–79	M.L. Carr, Det	2.46	1991–92	John Stockton, Utah	2.98
1979–80	Micheal Ray Richardson, NY	3.23	1992–93	Michael Jordan, Chi	2.83
1980–81	Magic Johnson, LAL	3.43	1993–94	Nate McMillan, Sea	2.96
1981–82	Magic Johnson, LAL	2.67	1994–95	Scottie Pippen, Chi	2.94
1982–83	Micheal Ray Richardson, GS-NJ	2.84	1995–96	Gary Payton, Sea	2.85
1983–84	Rickey Green, Utah	2.65	1996–97	Mookie Blaylock, Atl	2.72
1984–85	Micheal Ray Richardson, NJ	2.96	1997–98	Mookie Blaylock, Atl	2.61
1985–86	Alvin Robertson, SA	3.67	1998–99	Kendall Gill, NJ	2.68

Steals *(Cont.)*

1999–00	Eddie Jones, Cha	2.67	2006–07	Baron Davis, GS	2.14
2000–01	Allen Iverson, Phil	2.51	2007–08	Chris Paul, NO	2.71
2001–02	Allen Iverson, Phil	2.80	2008–09	Chris Paul, NO	2.77
2002–03	Allen Iverson, Phil	2.74	2009–10	Rajon Rondo, Bos	2.33
2003–04	Baron Davis, NO	2.36	2010–11	Chris Paul, NO	2.35
2004–05	Larry Hughes, Wash	2.89	2011–12	Chris Paul, LAC	2.53
2005–06	Gerald Wallace, Cha	2.51			

Blocked Shots

1973–74	Elmore Smith, LAL	4.85	1993–94	Dikembe Mutombo, Den	4.10
1974–75	Kareem Abdul-Jabbar, Mil	3.26	1994–95	Dikembe Mutombo, Den	3.91
1975–76	Kareem Abdul-Jabbar, LAL	4.12	1995–96	Dikembe Mutombo, Den	4.49
1976–77	Bill Walton, Port	3.25	1996–97	Shawn Bradley, NJ	3.40
1977–78	George Johnson, NJ	3.38	1997–98	Marcus Camby, Tor	3.65
1978–79	Kareem Abdul-Jabbar, LAL	3.95	1998–99	Alonzo Mourning, Mia	3.91
1979–80	Kareem Abdul-Jabbar, LAL	3.41	1999–00	Alonzo Mourning, Mia	3.72
1980–81	George Johnson, SA	3.39	2000–01	Theo Ratliff, Phil/Atl	3.74
1981–82	George Johnson, SA	3.12	2001–02	Ben Wallace, Det	3.48
1982–83	Wayne Rollins, Atl	4.29	2002–03	Theo Ratliff, Atl	3.23
1983–84	Mark Eaton, Utah	4.28	2003–04	Theo Ratliff, Port	3.61
1984–85	Mark Eaton, Utah	5.56	2004–05	Andrei Kirilenko, Utah	3.32
1985–86	Manute Bol, Wash	4.96	2005–06	Marcus Camby, Den	3.29
1986–87	Mark Eaton, Utah	4.06	2006–07	Marcus Camby, Den	3.30
1987–88	Mark Eaton, Utah	3.71	2007–08	Marcus Camby, Den	3.61
1988–89	Manute Bol, GS	4.31	2008–09	Dwight Howard, Orl	2.92
1989–90	Hakeem Olajuwon, Hou	4.59	2009–10	Dwight Howard, Orl	2.78
1990–91	Hakeem Olajuwon, Hou	3.95	2010–11	Andrew Bogut, Mil	2.58
1991–92	David Robinson, SA	4.49	2011–12	Serge Ibaka, OKC	3.65
1992–93	Hakeem Olajuwon, Hou	4.17			

NBA All-Star Game Results

Year	Result	Site	Winning Coach	Most Valuable Player
1951	East 111, West 94	Boston	Joe Lapchick	Ed Macauley, Bos
1952	East 108, West 91	Boston	Al Cervi	Paul Arizin, Phil
1953	West 79, East 75	Ft Wayne	John Kundla	George Mikan, Min
1954	East 98, West 93 (OT)	New York	Joe Lapchick	Bob Cousy, Bos
1955	East 100, West 91	New York	Al Cervi	Bill Sharman, Bos
1956	West 108, East 94	Rochester	Charley Eckman	Bob Pettit, StL
1957	East 109, West 97	Boston	Red Auerbach	Bob Cousy, Bos
1958	East 130, West 118	St Louis	Red Auerbach	Bob Pettit, StL
1959	West 124, East 108	Detroit	Ed Macauley	B. Pettit, StL/ E. Baylor, Min
1960	East 125, West 115	Philadelphia	Red Auerbach	Wilt Chamberlain, Phil
1961	West 153, East 131	Syracuse	Paul Seymour	Oscar Robertson, Cin
1962	West 150, East 130	St Louis	Fred Schaus	Bob Pettit, StL
1963	East 115, West 108	Los Angeles	Red Auerbach	Bill Russell, Bos
1964	East 111, West 107	Boston	Red Auerbach	Oscar Robertson, Cin
1965	East 124, West 123	St Louis	Red Auerbach	Jerry Lucas, Cin
1966	East 137, West 94	Cincinnati	Red Auerbach	Adrian Smith, Cin
1967	West 135, East 120	San Francisco	Fred Schaus	Rick Barry, SF
1968	East 144, West 124	New York	Alex Hannum	Hal Greer, Phil
1969	East 123, West 112	Baltimore	Gene Shue	Oscar Robertson, Cin
1970	East 142, West 135	Philadelphia	Red Holzman	Willis Reed, NY
1971	West 108, East 107	San Diego	Larry Costello	Lenny Wilkens, Sea
1972	West 112, East 110	Los Angeles	Bill Sharman	Jerry West, LA
1973	East 104, West 84	Chicago	Tom Heinsohn	Dave Cowens, Bos
1974	West 134, East 123	Seattle	Larry Costello	Bob Lanier, Det
1975	East 108, West 102	Phxnix	K.C. Jones	Walt Frazier, NY
1976	East 123, West 109	Philadelphia	Tom Heinsohn	Dave Bing, Wash
1977	West 125, East 124	Milwaukee	Larry Brown	Julius Erving, Phil
1978	East 133, West 125	Atlanta	Billy Cunningham	Randy Smith, Buff
1979	West 134, East 129	Detroit	Lenny Wilkens	David Thompson, Den
1980	East 144, West 135 (OT)	Washington	Billy Cunningham	George Gervin, SA
1981	East 123, West 120	Cleveland	Billy Cunningham	Nate Archibald, Bos
1982	East 120, West 118	New Jersey	Bill Fitch	Larry Bird, Bos
1983	East 132, West 123	Los Angeles	Billy Cunningham	Julius Erving, Phil
1984	East 154, West 145 (OT)	Denver	K.C. Jones	Isiah Thomas, Det
1985	West 140, East 129	Indiana	Pat Riley	Ralph Sampson, Hou

Year	Result	Site	Winning Coach	Most Valuable Player
1986	East 139, West 132	Dallas	K.C. Jones	Isiah Thomas, Det
1987	West 154, East 149 (OT)	Seattle	Pat Riley	Tom Chambers, Sea
1988	East 138, West 133	Chicago	Mike Fratello	Michael Jordan, Chi
1989	West 143, East 134	Houston	Pat Riley	Karl Malone, Utah
1990	East 130, West 113	Miami	Chuck Daly	Magic Johnson, LAL
1991	East 116, West 114	Charlotte	Chris Ford	Charles Barkley, Phil
1992	West 153, East 113	Orlando	Don Nelson	Magic Johnson, LAL
1993	West 135, East 132	Salt Lake City	Paul Westphal	K. Malone/J. Stockton, Utah
1994	East 127, West 118	Minneapolis	Lenny Wilkens	Scottie Pippen, Chi
1995	West 139, East 112	Phoenix	Paul Westphal	Mitch Richmond, Sac
1996	East 129, West 118	San Antonio	Phil Jackson	Michael Jordan, Chi
1997	East 132, West 120	Cleveland	Doug Collins	Glen Rice, Cha
1998	East 135, West 114	New York	Larry Bird	Michael Jordan, Chi
1999	Cancelled due to lockout.			
2000	West 137, East 126	Oakland	Phil Jackson	S. O'Neal, LAL/T. Duncan, SA
2001	East 111, West 110	Washington	Larry Brown	Allen Iverson, Phi
2002	West 135, East 120	Philadelphia	Don Nelson	Kobe Bryant, LAL
2003	West 155, East 145 (2OT)	Atlanta	Rick Adelman	Kevin Garnett, Min
2004	West 136, East 132	Los Angeles	Flip Saunders	Shaquille O'Neal, LAL
2005	East 125, West 115	Denver	Stan Van Gundy	Allen Iverson, Phi
2006	East 122, West 120	Houston	Flip Saunders	LeBron James, Cle
2007	West 153, East 132	Las Vegas	Mike D'Antoni	Kobe Bryant, LAL
2008	East 134, West 128	New Orleans	Doc Rivers	LeBron James, Cle
2009	West 146, West 119	Phoenix	Phil Jackson	K. Bryant, LAL/S. O'Neal, Phx
2010	East 141, West 139	Dallas	Stan Van Gundy	Dwyane Wade, Mia
2011	West 148, East 143	Los Angeles	Gregg Popovich	Kobe Bryant, LAL
2012	West 152, East 149	Orlando	Scott Brooks	Kevin Durant, OKC

Members of the Basketball Hall of Fame

Contributors

Senda Abbott (1984)
Don Barksdale (2012)
Clair F. Bee (1967)
Danny Biasone (2000)
Hubie Brown (2005)
Walter A. Brown (1965)
John W. Bunn (1964)
Jerry Buss (2010)
Jerry Colangelo (2004)
William Davidson (2008)
Bob Douglas (1971)
Al Duer (1981)
Wayne Embry (1999)
Clifford Fagan (1983)
Harry A. Fisher (1973)
Larry Fleisher (1991)
Dave Gavitt (2006)
Edward Gottlieb (1971)
Luther H. Gulick (1959)

Lester Harrison (1979)
Chick Hearn (2003)
Ferenc Hepp (1980)
Edward J. Hickox (1959)
Paul D. (Tony) Hinkle (1965)
Ned Irish (1964)
R. William Jones (1964)
J. Walter Kennedy (1980)
Phil Knight (2012)
Meadowlark Lemon (2003)
Emil S. Liston (1974)
Earl Lloyd (2003)
Bill Mokray (1965)
Ralph Morgan (1959)
Frank Morgenweck (1962)
James Naismith (1959)
C.M. Newton (2000)
John J. O'Brien (1961)
Larry O'Brien (1991)

Harold G. Olsen (1959)
Maurice Podoloff (1973)
H.V. Porter (1960)
William A. Reid (1963)
Elmer Ripley (1972)
Lynn W. St. John (1962)
Tom (Satch) Sanders (2011)
Abe Saperstein (1970)
Arthur A. Schabinger (1961)
Amos Alonzo Stagg (1959)
Boris Stankovic (1991)
Edward Steitz (1983)
Chuck Taylor (1968)
Bertha F. Teague (1984)
Oswald Tower (1959)
Arthur L. Trester (1961)
Dick Vitale (2008)
Clifford Wells (1971)
Lou Wilke (1982)
Fred Zollner (1999)

Players

Kareem Abdul-Jabbar (1995)
Nate (Tiny) Archibald (1991)
Paul J. Arizin (1977)
Charles Barkley (2006)
Thomas B. Barlow (1980)
Rick Barry (1987)
Elgin Baylor (1976)
John Beckman (1972)
Walt Bellamy (1993)
Sergei Belov (1992)
Dave Bing (1990)
Larry Bird (1998)
Carol Blazejowski (1994)
Bennie Borgmann (1961)
Bill Bradley (1982)

Joseph Brennan (1974)
Al Cervi (1984)
Wilt Chamberlain (1978)
Charles (Tarzan) Cooper (1976)
Cynthia Cooper (2010)
Kresimir Cosic (1996)
Bob Cousy (1970)
Dave Cowens (1991)
Joan Crawford (1997)
Billy Cunningham (1986)
Denise Curry (1997)
Drazen Dalipagic (2004)
Mel Daniels (2012)
Adrian Dantley (2008)
Bob Davies (1969)

Forrest S. DeBernardi (1961)
Dave DeBusschere (1982)
H.G. (Dutch) Dehnert (1968)
Anne Donovan (1995)
Clyde Drexler (2004)
Joe Dumars (2006)
Teresa Edwards (2011)
Paul Endacott (1971)
Alex English (1997)
Julius Erving (1993)
Patrick Ewing (2008)
Harold (Bud) Foster (1964)
Walter (Clyde) Frazier (1987)
Max (Marty) Friedman (1971)
Joe Fulks (1977)

Players *(Cont.)*

Lauren (Laddie) Gale (1976)
Harry (the Horse) Gallatin (1991)
William Gates (1989)
George Gervin (1996)
Artis Gilmore (2011)
Tom Gola (1975)
Gail Goodrich (1996)
Hal Greer (1981)
Robert (Ace) Gruenig (1963)
Clifford O. Hagan (1977)
Victor Hanson (1960)
Lusia Harris-Stewart (1992)
John Havlicek (1983)
Connie Hawkins (1992)
Elvin Hayes (1990)
Marques Haynes (1998)
Tom Heinsohn (1986)
Nat Holman (1964)
Robert J. Houbregs (1987)
Bailey Howell (1997)
Chuck Hyatt (1959)
Dan Issel (1993)
Harry (Buddy) Jeannette (1994)
Dennis Johnson (2010)
Earvin (Magic) Johnson (2002)
Gus Johnson (2010)
William C. Johnson (1976)
D. Neil Johnston (1990)
K.C. Jones (1989)
Sam Jones (1983)
Michael Jordan (2009)
Edward (Moose) Krause (1975)
Bob Kurland (1961)
Bob Lanier (1992)
Joe Lapchick (1966)
Nancy Lieberman-Cline (1996)
Clyde Lovellette (1988)
Jerry Lucas (1979)

Angelo (Hank) Luisetti (1959)
C. Edward Macauley (1960)
Karl Malone (2010)
Moses Malone (2001)
Peter P. Maravich (1987)
Hortencia Marcari (2005)
Slater Martin (1981)
Bob McAdoo (2000)
Katrina McClain (2012)
Branch McCracken (1960)
Jack McCracken (1962)
Bobby McDermott (1988)
Dick McGuire (1993)
Kevin McHale (1999)
Dino Meneghin (2003)
Ann Meyers (1993)
George L. Mikan (1959)
Vern Mikkelsen (1995)
Cheryl Miller (1995)
Reggie Miller (2012)
Earl Monroe (1990)
Chris Mullin (2011)
Calvin Murphy (1993)
Charles (Stretch) Murphy (1960)
Hakeem Olajuwon (2008)
H.O. (Pat) Page (1962)
Robert Parish (2003)
Maciel (Ubiratan) Pereira (2010)
Drazen Petrovic (2002)
Bob Pettit (1970)
Andy Phillip (1961)
Scottie Pippen (2010)
Jim Pollard (1977)
Frank Ramsey (1981)
Willis Reed (1981)
Arnie Risen (1998)
Oscar Robertson (1979)
David Robinson (2009)

Dennis Rodman (2011)
John S. Roosma (1961)
Bill Russell (1974)
John (Honey) Russell (1964)
Arvydas Sabonis (2011)
Ralph Sampson (2012)
Adolph Schayes (1972)
Ernest J. Schmidt (1973)
John J. Schommer (1959)
Barney Sedran (1962)
Uljana Semjonova (1993)
Bill Sharman (1975)
Christian Steinmetz (1961)
Lusia Harris Stewart (1992)
John Stockton (2009)
Maurice Stokes (2004)
Reece (Goose) Tatum (2011)
Isiah Thomas (2000)
David Thompson (1996)
John A. (Cat) Thompson (1962)
Nate Thurmond (1984)
Jack Twyman (1982)
Wes Unseld (1988)
Robert (Fuzzy) Vandivier (1974)
Edward A. Wachter (1961)
Chet Walker (2012)
Bill Walton (1993)
Robert F. Wanzer (1987)
Jerry West (1979)
Nera White (1992)
Lenny Wilkens (1989)
Jamaal Wilkes (2012)
Dominique Wilkins (2006)
Lynette Woodard (2004)
John R. Wooden (1960)
James Worthy (2003)
George (Bird) Yardley (1996)

Coaches

Lidia Alexeeva (2012)
Forest C. (Phog) Allen (1959)
Harold Anderson (1984)
Red Auerbach (1968)
Geno Auriemma (2006)
Leon Barmore (2003)
Sam Barry (1978)
Ernest A. Blood (1960)
Jim Boeheim (2005)
Larry Brown (2002)
Jim Calhoun (2005)
Howard G. Cann (1967)
H. Clifford Carlson (1959)
Lou Carnesecca (1992)
Ben Carnevale (1969)
Pete Carril (2007)
Everett Case (1981)
Van Chancellor (2007)
John Chaney (2001)
Jody Conradt (1998)
Denny Crum (1994)
Chuck Daly (1994)
Everett S. Dean (1966)
Antonio Diaz-Miguel (1997)

Edgar A. Diddle (1971)
Bruce Drake (1972)
Pedro Ferrandiz (2007)
Sandro Gamba (2006)
Clarence Gaines (1981)
Jack Gardner (1983)
Amory T. (Slats) Gill (1967)
Aleksandr Gomelsky (1995)
Sue Gunter (2005)
Alex Hannum (1998)
Marv Harshman (1984)
Don Haskins (1997)
Edgar S. Hickey (1978)
Howard A. Hobson (1965)
Red Holzman (1986)
Bob Hurley Sr. (2010)
Hank Iba (1968)
Phil Jackson (2007)
Alvin F. (Doggie) Julian (1967)
Frank W. Keaney (1960)
George E. Keogan (1961)
Bob Knight (1991)
Mike Krzyzewski (2001)
John Kundla (1995)

Ward L. Lambert (1960)
Harry Litwack (1975)
Kenneth D. Loeffler (1964)
A.C. (Dutch) Lonborg (1972)
John B. McLendon (1978)
Arad A. McCutchan (1980)
Herb Magee (2011)
Al McGuire (1992)
Frank McGuire (1976)
Walter E. Meanwell (1959)
Raymond J. Meyer (1978)
Ralph Miller (1988)
Billie Moore (1999)
Don Nelson (2012)
Peter F. Newell (1978)
Aleksandar Nikolic (1998)
Mirko Novosel (2007)
Lute Olson (2002)
Jack Ramsay (1992)
Pat Riley (2008)
Cesare Rubini (1994)
Adolph F. Rupp (1968)
Cathy Rush (2008)
Leonard D. Sachs (1961)

Note: Year of election in parentheses.

Coaches (Cont.)

Bill Sharman (2004)
Everett F. Shelton (1979)
Jerry Sloan (2009)
Dean Smith (1982)
C. Vivian Stringer (2009)
Pat Summitt (2000)

Fred R. Taylor (1985)
John Thompson (1999)
Tara VanDerveer (2011)
Margaret Wade (1984)
Stanley H. Watts (1985)
Lenny Wilkens (1998)

Roy Williams (2007)
Tex Winter (2011)
John R. Wooden (1972)
Morgan Wooten (2000)
Phil Woolpert (1992)
Kay Yow (2002)

Referees

James E. Enright (1978)
George T. Hepbron (1960)
George Hoyt (1961)
Matthew P. Kennedy (1959)
Lloyd Leith (1982)
Zigmund J. Mihalik (1985)
Hank Nichols (2012)

John P. Nucatola (1977)
Ernest C. Quigley (1961)
Marvin Rudolph (2007)
J. Dallas Shirley (1979)
Earl Strom (1995)
David Tobey (1961)
David H. Walsh (1961)

Teams

1960 USA Olympic Team (2010)
1966 Texas Western (2007)
1992 USA Olympic "Dream" Team
 (2010)
All American Redheads (2012)
Buffalo Germans (1961)
First Team (1959)
Harlem Globetrotters (2002)
New York Renaissance (1963)
Original Celtics (1959)

Note: Year of election in parentheses.

American Basketball Association (ABA)

Champions

Year	Champion	Series	Runner-up	Winning Coach
1968	Pittsburgh Pipers	4–3	New Orleans Bucs	Vince Cazetta
1969	Oakland Oaks	4–1	Indiana Pacers	Alex Hannum
1970	Indiana Pacers	4–2	Los Angeles Stars	Bob Leonard
1971	Utah Stars	4–3	Kentucky Colonels	Bill Sharman
1972	Indiana Pacers	4–2	New York Nets	Bob Leonard
1973	Indiana Pacers	4–3	Kentucky Colonels	Bob Leonard
1974	New York Nets	4–1	Utah Stars	Kevin Loughery
1975	Kentucky Colonels	4–1	Indiana Pacers	Hubie Brown
1976	New York Nets	4–2	Denver Nuggets	Kevin Loughery

ABA Postseason Awards

Most Valuable Player

1967–68	Connie Hawkins, Pitt
1968–69	Mel Daniels, Ind
1969–70	Spencer Haywood, Den
1970–71	Mel Daniels, Ind
1971–72	Artis Gilmore, Ken
1972–73	Billy Cunningham, Car
1973–74	Julius Erving, NY
1974–75	Julius Erving, NY
	George McGinnis, Ind
1975–76	Julius Erving, NY

Rookie of the Year

1967–68	Mel Daniels, Minn
1968–69	Warren Armstrong, Oak
1969–70	Spencer Haywood, Den
1970–71	Dan Issel, Ken
	Charlie Scott, Vir
1971–72	Artis Gilmore, Ken
1972–73	Brian Taylor, NY
1973–74	Swen Nater, SA
1974–75	Marvin Barnes, StL
1975–76	David Thompson, Den

Coach of the Year

1967–68	Vince Cazetta, Pitt
1968–69	Alex Hannum, Oak
1969–70	Joe Belmont, Den
	Bill Sharman, LA
1970–71	Al Bianchi, Vir
1971–72	Tom Nissalke, Dal
1972–73	Larry Brown, Car
1973–74	Babe McCarthy, Ken
	Joe Mullaney, Utah
1974–75	Larry Brown, Den
1975–76	Larry Brown, Den

ABA Season Leaders

Scoring

		GP	Pts	Avg
1967–68	Connie Hawkins, Pitt	70	1875	26.8
1968–69	Rick Barry, Oak	35	1190	34.0
1969–70	Spencer Haywood, Den	84	2519	30.0
1970–71	Dan Issel, Ken	83	2480	29.9
1971–72	Charlie Scott, Vir	79	2637	33.4
1972–73	Julius Erving, Vir	71	2268	31.9
1973–74	Julius Erving, NY	84	2299	27.4
1974–75	George McGinnis, Ind	79	2353	29.8
1975–76	Julius Erving, NY	84	2462	29.3

Rebounds

1967–68	Mel Daniels, Minn	15.6
1968–69	Mel Daniels, Ind	16.5
1969–70	Spencer Haywood, Den	19.5
1970–71	Mel Daniels, Ind	18.0
1971–72	Artis Gilmore, Ken	17.8
1972–73	Artis Gilmore, Ken	17.6
1973–74	Artis Gilmore, Ken	18.3
1974–75	Swen Nater, SA	16.4
1975–76	Artis Gilmore, Ken	15.5

Assists

1967–68	Larry Brown, NO	6.5
1968–69	Larry Brown, Oak	7.1
1969–70	Larry Brown, Wash	7.1
1970–71	Bill Melchionni, NY	8.3
1971–72	Bill Melchionni, NY	8.4
1972–73	Bill Melchionni, NY	7.4
1973–74	Al Smith, Den	8.2
1974–75	Mack Calvin, Den	7.7
1975–76	Don Buse, Ind	8.2

Steals

1973–74	Ted McClain, Car	2.98
1974–75	Brian Taylor, NY	2.80
1975–76	Don Buse, Ind	4.12

Blocked Shots

1973–74	Caldwell Jones, SD	4.00
1974–75	Caldwell Jones, SD	3.24
1975–76	Billy Paultz, SA	3.05

World Championship of Basketball

Year	Winner	Runner-Up	Score	Site
1950	Argentina	United States	†	Buenos Aires
1954	United States	Brazil	†	Rio de Janeiro
1959	Brazil	United States	†	Santiago, Chile
1963	Brazil	Yugoslavia	†	Rio de Janeiro
1967	Soviet Union	Yugoslavia	†	Montevideo, Uruguay
1970	Yugoslavia	Brazil	†	Ljubljana, Yugoslavia
1974	Soviet Union	Yugoslavia	†	San Juan
1978	Yugoslavia	Soviet Union	82–81 (OT)	Manila
1982	Soviet Union	United States	95–94	Cali, Colombia
1986	United States	Soviet Union	87–85	Madrid
1990	Yugoslavia	Soviet Union	92–75	Buenos Aires
*1994	United States	Russia	137–91	Toronto
†1998	Yugoslavia	Russia	64–62	Athens
2002	Yugoslavia	Argentina	84–77 (OT)	Indianapolis
2006	Spain	Greece	70–47	Saitama, Japan
2010	United States	Turkey	81–64	Turkey

*U.S. professionals began competing in 1994.†In 1998, a labor dispute resulted in a boycott of the World Championship by NBA stars; the U.S. roster was filled by members of the CBA and European professional leagues and college players.
†Result determined by overall record in final round of competition.

Anthony Davis dominated on defense in Kentucky's 67–59 win over Kansas for the NCAA championship

College Basketball

Kentucky Kings

Led by three one-and-done freshmen, including Player of the Year Anthony Davis, Kentucky stormed to the national championship against Kansas

BY B.J. SCHECTER

THE NCAA TOURNAMENT IS such a dazzling event because of the emotion, drama and intrigue that it produces. Each year a different set of Cinderellas steps forward, brackets are busted and new darlings emerge. The unpredictability of the tournament is a large part of what makes it so great. The best teams often don't win it all and many of the nation's best players in any given year end up watching the championship game like the rest of us. From the opening tip of the 2011–12 season, Kentucky was clearly the best team, with another band of fantastic freshmen and a slick coach who year after year gathers the best recruiting classes but until now had failed to win a national title.

This Kentucky team, John Calipari's third since jumping from Memphis (where he nearly won a national title with Derrick Rose) to the Bluegrass State, was unique because in addition to another talented crop of freshmen, two key members from the previous class decided to stay for a second season. Led by fantastic freshmen Anthony Davis and Michael Kidd-Gilchrist, the Wildcats started three freshmen and two sophomores. Kentucky rolled through the regular season with relative ease, its lone loss (after

a hard-fought one-point win over North Carolina) coming on a buzzer-beating three-pointer at Indiana in December. Following that defeat the Wildcats reeled off 24 straight victories until losing to Vanderbilt in the SEC Tournament final. Calipari seemed relieved that his team lost their final game before the NCAA tournament because it took some of the pressure off the Wildcats and allowed him to impress upon his young 'Cats that they weren't unbeatable.

"My comment to them [was]: Maybe I'll have your attention now, and you're really going to focus in and listen to what I'm saying, how we're going to have to play these next few weekends," Calipari said. "I'm fine now. We get this off our plate. We don't have to worry about a win streak. Let's just go play this tournament."

And did Kentucky ever play. The Wildcats rolled through the early rounds, easily marching through Western Kentucky, Iowa State, a rematch with Indiana, and Baylor to reach the Final Four. There, in New Orleans, Kentucky met Louisville in what was otherwise known as Armageddon in the Bluegrass State. Louisville is the biggest city in the state and is everything the rest of Kentucky isn't: bustling, sophisticated and a little bit edgy. But the University of Louisville

The highly touted Buckeyes, led by their dominant center, Sullinger (0), ran out of gas in Kansas' 64–62 comeback victory in the Final Four semifinal.

has always had an inferiority complex toward the state flagship university. In the week leading up to the Final Four showdown, the state of Kentucky was on red alert. Offices became battlegrounds, families were torn apart. In the strangest of strange stories, two dialysis patients, aged 69 and 72, had to be separated because they were arguing too vehemently over the game.

The action on the court wasn't nearly as riveting as the contentiousness off it. Kentucky controlled the game from start to finish and advanced to the championship game with a never-in-doubt 69–61 victory. In the final, Kentucky met Kansas, which came from behind to beat Jared Sullinger and Ohio State, 64–62. The Jayhawks were the perfect foil for Calipari. In 2008, when he was at Memphis, Calipari and the Tigers appeared to be on their way to a

national championship, holding a nine-point lead over Kansas with 2:12 remaining. Then it unraveled as Kansas furiously came back and sent the game into overtime on a Mario Chalmers three-pointer at the buzzer. The Jayhawks went on to win the game and the never-can-win-the-big-one label followed Calipari ever since. Like his first Final Four appearance at UMass, the one with Memphis was vacated by the NCAA (though Calipari was never implicated of any wrongdoing). This was Calipari's chance at redemption. This time he would finally shed the good-recruiter-can't-coach label.

Even Calipari's harshest critics had to acknowledge the extraordinary job he did coaching this team. He knew exactly when to push his young squad, when to lay off and when to motivate. These Wildcats were supremely talented, but they also played well together, had a killer instinct and were clearly, dare we say, well coached.

The Young 'Cats were also unflappable and withstood everything any team threw at

CSM/LANDOV

Griner savored the moment as she cut down the nets after Baylor's victory over Notre Dame, which capped the Bears' unprecedented 40–0 season.

them. At the center of it all was the 6' 10" Davis, the Player of the Year and someone who could dominate a game without scoring a point. Davis proved that against Kansas by going scoreless for most of the game, but dominating in every other way. Davis ended up with just one field goal (on 1-for-10 shooting), but had 16 rebounds, six blocks and three steals. Kentucky jumped out to a 16-point lead, but then stepped off the gas and saw its advantage cut to seven with 3:52 remaining. The Superdome was rocking and it looked like déjà vu all over again. But freshman point guard Marquis Teague hit a huge three-pointer and added some clutch free throws as Kentucky maintained control and held on for a 67–59 victory.

"I wanted everybody to see we were the best team this season," said Calipari after his team cut down the nets. "We were the best team. I wanted this to be one for the ages."

The Baylor women were a team for the ages indeed, going wire-to-wire to win the national title and become the first Division I team to go 40-0. Backed by 6' 8" junior center Brittney Griner, the Bears dominated every opponent and blew out Notre Dame 80–61 in the title game. As usual, Griner

stood above the rest with 26 points, 13 rebounds and three blocks, but afterward Irish coach Muffet McGraw created a stir when she said Griner was "one of a kind. I think she's like a guy playing with women."

McGraw's comments immediately lit up Twitter and she was forced to quickly clarify them in a statement, but she didn't mean them to be derogatory. They were clearly a compliment and fortunately they were taken that way by Griner. What McGraw was trying to say—and perhaps what she should have said—was the Griner is on a different level than everyone else. She competes on both ends of the court, can score, pass, block shocks and, heck, even dunk. Nobody in the women's game can match here one-on-one.

After she cut down the nets with her teammates, Griner reflected on what she and Baylor had just accomplished. "Looking back when we get older, I'm always going to remember this moment, always going to remember confetti falling and being here with my team," she said.

It would be hard to imagine Griner topping what she did in 2012, just like it would be hard to imagine Calipari and Kentucky replicating their feat. But the rest of the nation should beware: Griner has one more year of eligibility and Calipari will usher in another top recruiting class. Their dominance could well continue.

NCAA Men's Championship Game Box Score

Kentucky 67

	Min	FG M-A	FT M-A	Reb O-T	A	PF	TP
T. Jones, F	29	4-7	1-2	1-7	0	4	9
Kidd-Gilchrist	35	4-7	3-4	2-6	1	2	11
D. Lamb	35	7-12	5-6	1-2	3	2	22
A. Davis	36	1-10	4-6	4-16	5	2	6
M. Teague	34	5-14	2-3	1-2	3	2	14
E. Vargas	3	0-0	0-0	0-0	0	1	0
D. Miller	25	2-5	0-0	1-6	0	2	5
K. Wiltjer	3	0-1	0-0	0-0	0	0	0
Totals		23-56	15-21	10-39	12	15	67

Kansas 59

	Min	FG M-A	FT M-A	Reb O-T	A	PF	TP
T. Robinson	36	6-17	6-7	5-17	1	2	18
J. Withey	32	2-8	1-1	3-7	1	2	5
T. Taylor	36	8-17	2-3	1-4	3	1	19
T. Releford	30	1-6	1-2	0-1	1	5	4
E. Johnson	36	5-13	0-0	1-2	2	1	13
C. Teahan	17	0-1	0-0	0-0	1	1	0
K. Young	11	0-0	0-2	0-3	0	4	0
J. Wesley	2	0-0	0-0	0-0	0	0	0
Totals		22-62	10-15	10-34	9	16	59

Percentages: FG-.411, FT-.714. 3-Point Goals: 6–14, .429 (T. Jones 0-1, M. Kidd-Gilchrist 0-1, D. Lamb 3-6, M. Teague 2-3, D. Miller 1-2, K. Wiltjer 0-1). Team Rebounds: 0. Blocked Shots: 11 (T. Jones 2, M. Kidd-Gilchrist 1, A. Davis 6, D. Miller 2). Turnovers: 11 (T. Jones 2, M. Kidd-Gilchrist 1, D. Lamb 1, A. Davis 3, M. Teague 2, D. Miller 2). Steals: 4 (T. Jones 1, A. Davis 3). Technical Fouls: None.

Percentages: FG-.355, FT-.667. 3-Point Goals: 5–11, .455 (T. Taylor 1-1, T. Releford 1-2, E. Johnson 3-7, C. Teahan 0-1). Team Rebounds: 0. Blocked Shots: 5 (J. Withey 4, K. Young 1). Turnovers: 9 (T. Robinson 1, J. Withey 1, T. Taylor 5, E. Johnson 2). Steals: 6 (J. Withey 2, T. Taylor 1, T. Releford 1, E. Johnson 1, C. Teahan 1). Technical Fouls: None.

Halftime: Kentucky 41, Kansas 27.

Final Four Most Outstanding Player: Anthony Davis, Kentucky.

Officials: Verne Harris, Mark Whitehead, Mike Stuart. A: 70,913

Final ESPN/USA Today Top 25 Coaches Poll

1. Kentucky (31)	37-2	
2. Kansas	32-6	
3. Ohio State	31-8	
4. Louisville	30-10	
5. Syracuse	34-3	
6. North Carolina	32-6	
7. Michigan State	29-8	
8. Baylor	30-8	
9. Florida	26-11	
10. Marquette	27-8	
11. Missouri	30-5	
12. Wisconsin	26-10	
13. Indiana	27-9	
14. Duke	27-7	
15. Florida State	25-10	
16. Murray State	31-2	
17. Georgetown	24-9	
18. Cincinnati	26-11	
19. Vanderbilt	25-11	
20. North Carolina State	24-13	
21. Creighton	29-6	
22. Michigan	24-10	
23. New Mexico	28-7	
24. Xavier	23-13	
25. Ohio	29-8	

Note: First-place votes in parenthesis

National Invitation Tournament Scores

First round: Washington 82, UT-Arlington 72; Northwestern 76, Akron 74; Oregon 96, LSU 74; Iowa 84, Dayton 72; Tennessee 65, Savannah St 51; Middle Tennessee 86, Marshall 78; Minnesota 70, La Salle 61; Miami 66, Valparaiso 50; Seton Hall 63, Stony Brook 61; UMass 101, Mississippi St 96 (2OT); Drexel 81, UCF 56; Northern Iowa 67, St. Joseph's 65; Bucknell 65, Arizona 54; Nevada 68, Oral Roberts 59; Stanford 76, Cleveland St 65; Illinois St 96, Mississippi 93 (2OT).

Second round: Washington 76, Northwestern 55; Oregon 108, Iowa 97; Middle Tennessee 71, Tennessee 64; Minnesota 78, Miami 60; UMass 77, Seton Hall 67; Drexel 65, Northern Iowa 63; Nevada 75, Bucknell 67; Stanford 92, Illinois St 88 (OT).

Quarterfinals: Washington 90, Oregon 86; Minnesota 78, Middle Tennessee 72; UMass 72, Drexel 70; Stanford 84, Nevada 56.

Semifinals: Minnesota 68, Washington 67 (OT); Stanford 84, UMass 74.

Championship Game: Stanford 75, Minnesota 51.

2012 NCAA Basketball Men's Division I Tournament

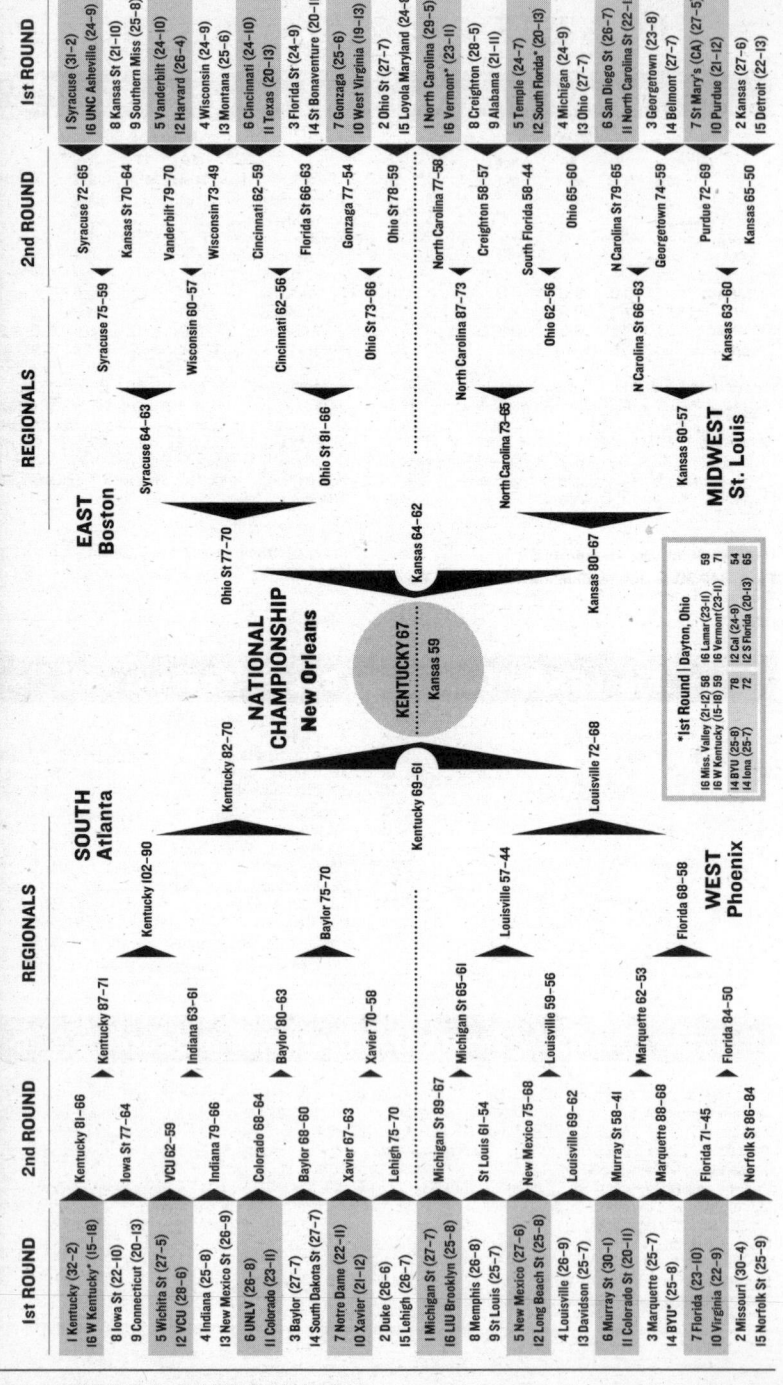

1st ROUND

I Syracuse (31–2)
16 UNC Asheville (24–9)
8 Kansas St (21–10)
9 Southern Miss (25–8)
5 Vanderbilt (24–10)
12 Harvard (26–4)
4 Wisconsin (24–9)
13 Montana (25–6)
6 Cincinnati (24–10)
11 Texas (20–13)
3 Florida St (24–9)
14 St Bonaventure (20–11)
7 Gonzaga (25–6)
10 West Virginia (19–13)
15 Loyola Maryland (24–8)

I North Carolina (29–5)
16 Vermont* (23–11)
8 Creighton (28–5)
9 Alabama (21–11)
5 Temple (24–7)
12 South Florida* (20–13)
4 Michigan (24–9)
13 Ohio (27–7)
6 San Diego St (26–7)
11 North Carolina St (22–12)
3 Georgetown (23–8)
14 Belmont (27–7)
7 St Mary's (CA) (27–5)
10 Purdue (21–12)
2 Kansas (27–6)
15 Detroit (22–13)

2nd ROUND

Syracuse 72–65
Kansas St 70–64
Vanderbilt 79–70
Wisconsin 73–49
Cincinnati 62–59
Florida St 66–63
Gonzaga 77–54
Ohio St 78–59

North Carolina 77–58
Creighton 58–57
South Florida 58–44
Ohio 65–60
N Carolina St 79–65
Georgetown 74–59
Purdue 72–69
Kansas 65–50

REGIONALS

Syracuse 75–59
Wisconsin 60–57
Cincinnati 62–56
Ohio St 73–66

North Carolina 87–73
Ohio 62–56
N Carolina St 66–63
Kansas 63–60

EAST
Boston

Syracuse 64–63
Ohio St 81–66

North Carolina 73–65
Kansas 60–57

MIDWEST
St. Louis

Ohio St 77–70
Kansas 64–62

Kansas 80–67

NATIONAL CHAMPIONSHIP
New Orleans

KENTUCKY 67
Kansas 59

Kentucky 82–70

Louisville 72–68

SOUTH
Atlanta

Kentucky 102–90
Baylor 75–70

Louisville 57–44
Florida 68–58

WEST
Phoenix

Kentucky 69–61
Louisville 69–61

Kentucky 87–71
Indiana 63–61
Baylor 80–63
Xavier 70–58

Michigan St 65–61
New Mexico 75–68
Louisville 59–56
Marquette 62–53
Florida 84–50

2nd ROUND

Kentucky 81–66
Iowa St 77–64
VCU 62–59
Indiana 79–66
Colorado 68–64
Baylor 68–60
Xavier 67–63
Lehigh 75–70

Michigan St 89–67
St Louis 61–54
New Mexico 75–68
Louisville 69–62
Murray St 58–41
Marquette 88–68
Florida 71–45
Norfolk St 86–84

1st ROUND

I Kentucky (32–2)
16 W Kentucky* (15–18)
8 Iowa St (22–10)
9 Connecticut (20–13)
5 Wichita St (27–5)
12 VCU (28–6)
4 Indiana (25–8)
13 New Mexico St (26–9)
6 UNLV (26–8)
11 Colorado (23–11)
3 Baylor (27–7)
14 South Dakota St (27–7)
7 Notre Dame (22–11)
10 Xavier (21–12)
2 Duke (26–6)
15 Lehigh (26–7)

I Michigan St (27–7)
16 LIU Brooklyn (25–8)
8 Memphis (26–8)
9 St Louis (25–7)
5 New Mexico (27–6)
12 Long Beach St (25–8)
4 Louisville (26–9)
13 Davidson (25–7)
6 Murray St (30–1)
11 Colorado St (20–11)
3 Marquette (25–7)
14 BYU* (25–8)
7 Florida (23–10)
10 Virginia (22–9)
2 Missouri (30–4)
15 Norfolk St (25–9)

*1st Round | Dayton, Ohio

16 Miss. Valley (21–12)	16 Lamar (23–11)	59
16 W Kentucky (15–18)	59	16 Vermont (23–11)	71
14 BYU (25–8)	78	12 Cal (24–9)	54
14 Iona (25–7)	72	12 S Florida (20–13)	65

America East

	Conference			All Games		
	W	L	Pct	W	L	Pct
Stony Brook	14	2	.875	22	9	.710
*Vermont	13	3	.813	23	11	.676
Boston University	12	2	.750	16	16	.500
Albany	9	7	.563	19	14	.576
New Hampshire	7	9	.438	13	16	.448
Hartford	7	9	.438	9	22	.290
Maine	6	10	.375	12	17	.414
UMBC	3	13	.188	4	26	.133
Binghamton	1	15	.063	2	29	.065

Atlantic Coast

	Conference			All Games		
	W	L	Pct	W	L	Pct
North Carolina	14	2	.875	29	5	.853
Duke	13	3	.813	27	6	.818
*Florida State	12	4	.750	24	9	.727
N Carolina State	9	7	.563	22	12	.647
Virginia	9	7	.563	22	9	.710
Miami (FL)	9	7	.563	19	12	.613
Clemson	8	8	.500	16	15	.516
Maryland	6	10	.375	17	15	.531
Wake Forest	4	12	.250	13	18	.419
Virginia Tech	4	12	.250	16	17	.485
Georgia Tech	4	12	.250	11	20	.355
Boston College	4	12	.250	9	22	.290

Atlantic Sun

	Conference			All Games		
	W	L	Pct	W	L	Pct
*Belmont	16	2	.889	27	7	.794
Mercer	13	5	.722	22	11	.667
USC Upstate	13	5	.722	20	12	.625
E Tennessee St	10	8	.556	17	14	.548
North Florida	10	8	.556	16	16	.500
Florida Gulf Coast	8	10	.444	15	17	.469
Lipscomb	8	10	.444	13	18	.419
Stetson	6	12	.333	9	20	.310
Jacksonville	6	12	.333	8	22	.267
Kennesaw State	0	18	.000	3	28	.097

Atlantic 10

	Conference			All Games		
	W	L	Pct	W	L	Pct
Temple	13	3	.813	24	7	.774
Saint Louis	12	4	.750	25	7	.781
*St. Bonaventure	10	6	.625	20	11	.645
Xavier	10	6	.625	21	12	.636
Saint Joseph's	9	7	.563	20	13	.606
Dayton	9	7	.563	20	12	.625
La Salle	9	7	.563	21	12	.636
Massachusetts	9	7	.563	22	11	.667
Duquesne	7	9	.438	16	15	.516
Richmond	7	9	.438	16	16	.500
Charlotte	5	11	.313	13	17	.433
George Washington	5	11	.313	10	21	.323
Rhode Island	4	12	.250	7	24	.226
Fordham	3	13	.188	10	19	.345

Big East

	Conference			All Games		
	W	L	Pct	W	L	Pct
Syracuse	17	1	.944	31	2	.939
Marquette	14	4	.778	25	7	.781
Notre Dame	13	5	.722	22	11	.667
Cincinnati	12	6	.667	24	10	.706
South Florida	12	6	.667	20	13	.606
Georgetown	12	6	.667	23	8	.742
*Louisville	10	8	.556	26	9	.743
West Virginia	9	9	.500	19	13	.594
Seton Hall	8	10	.444	20	12	.625
Connecticut	8	10	.444	20	13	.606
Rutgers	6	12	.333	14	18	.438
St. John's	6	12	.333	13	19	.406
Pittsburgh	5	13	.278	17	16	.515
Villanova	5	13	.278	13	19	.406
Providence	4	14	.222	15	17	.469
DePaul	3	15	.167	12	19	.387

Big Sky

	Conference			All Games		
	W	L	Pct	W	L	Pct
*Montana	15	1	.938	25	6	.806
Weber State	14	2	.875	24	6	.800
Portland State	10	6	.625	17	15	.531
Eastern Washington	8	8	.500	15	17	.469
Montana State	7	9	.438	12	17	.414
Idaho State	7	9	.438	9	21	.300
Sacramento State	5	11	.313	10	18	.357
Northern Colorado	5	11	.313	9	19	.321
Northern Arizona	1	15	.063	5	24	.172

Big South

	Conference			All Games		
	W	L	Pct	W	L	Pct
*UNC Asheville	16	2	.889	24	9	.727
Coastal Carolina	12	6	.667	19	11	.633
Charleston Southern	11	7	.611	19	12	.613
Campbell	11	7	.611	17	15	.531
Liberty	9	9	.500	14	18	.438
Virginia Military	8	10	.444	17	16	.515
High Point	8	10	.444	13	18	.419
Presbyterian	8	10	.444	14	15	.483
Winthrop	8	10	.444	12	20	.375
Gardner-Webb	6	12	.333	12	20	.375
Radford	2	16	.111	6	26	.188

Big 10

	Conference			All Games		
	W	L	Pct	W	L	Pct
*Michigan State	13	5	.722	27	7	.794
Ohio State	13	5	.722	27	7	.794
Michigan	13	5	.722	24	9	.727
Wisconsin	12	6	.667	24	9	.727
Indiana	11	7	.611	25	8	.758
Purdue	10	8	.556	21	12	.636
Northwestern	8	10	.444	18	13	.581
Iowa	8	10	.444	17	16	.515
Minnesota	6	12	.333	19	14	.576
Illinois	6	12	.333	15	11	.535
Nebraska	4	14	.222	12	18	.400
Penn State	4	14	.222	12	20	.375

Note: Standings based on regular-season conference play only; overall records include all tournament play.
*Conference tournament winner.

Big 12

	Conference			All Games		
	W	L	Pct	W	L	Pct
Kansas	16	2	.889	27	6	.818
*Missouri	14	4	.778	30	4	.882
Baylor	12	6	.667	27	7	.794
Iowa State	12	6	.667	22	10	.688
Kansas State	10	8	.556	21	10	.677
Texas	9	9	.500	20	13	.606
Oklahoma State	7	11	.389	15	18	.455
Oklahoma	5	13	.278	15	16	.484
Texas A&M	4	14	.222	14	18	.438
Texas Tech	1	17	.056	8	23	.258

Big West

	Conference			All Games		
	W	L	Pct	W	L	Pct
*Long Beach State	15	1	.938	25	8	.758
Cal State Fullerton	12	4	.750	21	9	.700
UC Santa Barbara	12	4	.750	20	10	.667
Cal Poly	8	8	.500	18	15	.545
UC Riverside	7	9	.438	14	17	.452
UC Irvine	6	10	.375	12	20	.375
Pacific	6	10	.375	11	19	.367
Cal St Northridge	3	13	.188	7	21	.250
UC Davis	3	13	.188	5	26	.161

Colonial

	Conference			All Games		
	W	L	Pct	W	L	Pct
Drexel	16	2	.889	27	6	.818
*VCU	15	3	.833	28	6	.824
George Mason	14	4	.778	24	9	.727
Old Dominion	13	5	.722	20	13	.606
Delaware	12	6	.667	18	13	.581
Georgia State	11	7	.611	21	11	.656
Northeastern	9	9	.500	14	17	.452
James Madison	5	13	.278	12	20	.375
NC-Wilmington	5	13	.278	10	21	.323
William & Mary	4	14	.222	6	26	.188
Hofstra	3	15	.167	10	22	.313
Towson	1	17	.056	1	31	.031

Conference USA

	Conference			All Games		
	W	L	Pct	W	L	Pct
*Memphis	13	3	.813	26	8	.765
Southern Miss	11	5	.688	25	8	.758
Tulsa	10	6	.625	17	14	.548
UCF	10	6	.625	22	10	.688
Marshall	9	7	.563	21	13	.618
UAB	9	7	.563	15	16	.484
Rice	8	8	.500	17	15	.531
UTEP	7	9	.438	15	17	.469
Houston	7	9	.438	15	15	.500
East Carolina	5	11	.313	15	16	.484
Southern Methodist	4	12	.250	13	19	.406
Tulane	3	13	.188	15	16	.484

Great West**

	Conference			All Games		
	W	L	Pct	W	L	Pct
Utah Valley	9	1	.900	20	12	.625
*North Dakota	6	4	.600	17	14	.548
N.J.I.T.	5	5	.500	15	17	.469
Texas-Pan American	5	5	.500	11	21	.344
Houston Baptist	3	7	.300	10	20	.333
Chicago State	2	8	.200	4	26	.133

Horizon League

	Conference			All Games		
	W	L	Pct	W	L	Pct
Valparaiso	14	4	.778	22	11	.667
Cleveland State	12	6	.667	22	10	.688
*Detroit	11	7	.611	22	13	.629
Milwaukee	11	7	.611	20	13	.606
Butler	11	7	.611	20	14	.588
Youngstown State	10	8	.556	16	15	.516
Green Bay	10	8	.556	15	15	.500
Wright State	7	11	.389	13	19	.406
Illinois-Chicago	3	15	.167	8	22	.267
Loyola (IL)	1	17	.056	7	23	.233

Ivy League†

	Conference			All Games		
	W	L	Pct	W	L	Pct
Harvard	12	2	.857	26	4	.867
Pennsylvania	11	3	.786	19	12	.613
Princeton	10	4	.714	19	11	.633
Yale	9	5	.643	19	9	.679
Cornell	7	7	.500	12	16	.429
Columbia	4	10	.286	15	15	.500
Brown	2	12	.143	8	23	.258
Dartmouth	1	13	.071	5	25	.167

Metro Atlantic

	Conference			All Games		
	W	L	Pct	W	L	Pct
Iona	15	3	.833	25	7	.781
*Loyola (MD)	13	5	.722	24	8	.750
Manhattan	12	6	.667	20	12	.625
Fairfield	12	6	.667	19	14	.576
Rider	10	8	.556	13	19	.406
Siena	8	10	.444	14	17	.452
Niagara	8	10	.444	14	19	.424
Marist	7	11	.389	14	18	.438
St. Peter's	4	14	.222	5	26	.161
Canisius	1	17	.056	5	25	.167

Mid-American

	Conference			All Games		
	W	L	Pct	W	L	Pct
EAST						
Akron	13	3	.813	22	11	.667
Buffalo	12	4	.750	19	10	.655
*Ohio	11	5	.688	27	7	.794
Kent State	10	6	.625	21	11	.656
Bowling Green	9	7	.563	16	15	.516
Miami (OH)	5	11	.313	9	21	.300
WEST						
Eastern Michigan	9	7	.563	14	18	.438
Toledo	7	9	.438	18	16	.529
Ball State	6	10	.375	15	15	.500
Western Michigan	6	10	.375	14	20	.412
Central Michigan	5	11	.313	11	21	.344
Northern Illinois	3	13	.188	5	26	.161

*Conference tournament winner.
**No automatic bid for conference tournament winner.
†Does not hold end-of-season conference tournament.

Mid-Eastern Athletic

	Conference			All Games		
	W	L	Pct	W	L	Pct
Savannah State	14	2	.875	21	11	.656
*Norfolk State	13	3	.813	25	9	.735
Delaware State	12	4	.750	15	14	.517
Bethune-Cookman	11	5	.688	18	17	.514
N Carolina Central	10	6	.625	17	15	.531
Coppin State	9	7	.563	14	16	.467
North Carolina A&T	7	9	.438	12	20	.375
Hampton	6	10	.375	12	21	.364
Howard	6	10	.375	10	21	.323
Morgan State	6	10	.375	9	20	.310
Florida A&M	6	10	.375	10	23	.303
MD-Eastern Shore	4	12	.250	7	23	.233
S Carolina State	0	16	.000	5	26	.161

Missouri Valley

	Conference			All Games		
	W	L	Pct	W	L	Pct
Wichita State	16	2	.889	27	5	.844
*Creighton	14	4	.778	28	5	.848
Illinois State	9	9	.500	20	13	.606
Evansville	9	9	.500	16	15	.516
Northern Iowa	9	9	.500	19	13	.594
Drake	9	9	.500	17	15	.531
Missouri State	9	9	.500	16	16	.500
Indiana State	8	10	.444	18	14	.563
Southern Illinois	5	13	.278	8	23	.258
Bradley	2	16	.111	7	25	.219

Mountain West

	Conference			All Games		
	W	L	Pct	W	L	Pct
*New Mexico	10	4	.714	27	6	.818
San Diego State	10	4	.714	26	7	.788
UNLV	9	5	.643	26	8	.765
Colorado State	8	6	.571	20	11	.645
TCU	7	7	.500	17	14	.548
Wyoming	6	8	.429	20	11	.645
Air Force	3	11	.214	13	16	.448
Boise State	3	11	.214	13	17	.433

Northeast

	Conference			All Games		
	W	L	Pct	W	L	Pct
Long Island	16	2	.889	27	6	.818
*LIU Brooklyn	16	2	.889	25	8	.758
Wagner	15	3	.833	25	6	.806
Robert Morris	13	5	.722	24	10	.706
St. Francis (NY)	12	6	.667	15	15	.500
Quinnipiac	10	8	.556	18	13	.581
Monmouth	10	8	.556	12	20	.375
Central Conn State	10	8	.556	13	16	.448
Sacred Heart	8	10	.444	14	18	.438
Mount St. Mary's	6	12	.333	8	21	.276
St. Francis (PA)	5	13	.278	6	23	.207
Fairleigh Dickinson	2	16	.111	3	26	.103
Bryant University	1	17	.056	2	28	.067

Ohio Valley

	Conference			All Games		
	W	L	Pct	W	L	Pct
*Murray State	15	1	.938	30	1	.968
Tennessee State	11	5	.688	20	12	.625
Morehead State	10	6	.625	18	15	.545
Tennessee Tech	9	7	.563	19	13	.594
SE Missouri State	9	7	.563	15	16	.484
Jacksonville State	8	8	.500	15	18	.455
Austin Peay	8	8	.500	12	20	.375
Eastern Kentucky	7	9	.438	16	16	.500
SIU-Edwardsville	6	10	.375	10	17	.370
Eastern Illinois	5	11	.313	12	17	.414
Tennessee-Martin	0	16	.000	4	27	.129

Pac 12

	Conference			All Games		
	W	L	Pct	W	L	Pct
Washington	14	4	.778	21	10	.677
California	13	5	.722	24	9	.727
Oregon	13	5	.722	22	9	.710
Arizona	12	6	.667	23	11	.676
UCLA	11	7	.611	19	14	.576
*Colorado	11	7	.611	23	11	.676
Stanford	10	8	.556	21	11	.656
Washington State	7	11	.389	15	16	.484
Oregon State	7	11	.389	19	14	.576
Arizona State	6	12	.333	10	21	.323
Utah	3	15	.167	6	25	.194
USC	1	17	.056	6	26	.188

Patriot League

	Conference			All Games		
	W	L	Pct	W	L	Pct
Bucknell	12	2	.857	24	9	.727
*Lehigh	11	3	.786	26	7	.788
American U	10	4	.714	20	11	.645
Holy Cross	9	5	.643	15	14	.517
Lafayette	7	7	.500	13	18	.419
Army	5	9	.357	12	18	.400
Colgate	2	12	.143	8	22	.267
Navy	0	14	.000	3	26	.103

Southeastern

	Conference			All Games		
	W	L	Pct	W	L	Pct
Kentucky	16	0	1.000	32	2	.941
Tennessee	10	6	.625	18	14	.563
*Vanderbilt	10	6	.625	24	10	.706
Florida	10	6	.625	23	10	.697
Alabama	9	7	.563	21	11	.656
Mississippi State	8	8	.500	21	11	.656
Ole Miss	8	8	.500	20	13	.606
LSU	7	9	.438	18	14	.563
Arkansas	6	10	.375	18	14	.563
Auburn	5	11	.313	15	16	.484
Georgia	5	11	.313	15	17	.469
South Carolina	2	14	.125	10	21	.323

*Conference tournament winner.

Southern

NORTH	Conference			All Games		
	W	L	Pct	W	L	Pct
UNC Greensboro	10	8	.556	13	19	.406
Elon	9	9	.500	15	16	.484
Western Carolina	8	10	.444	17	18	.486
Samford	8	10	.444	11	19	.367
Appalachian State	7	11	.389	13	18	.419
Chattanooga	5	13	.278	11	21	.344
SOUTH						
*Davidson	16	2	.889	25	7	.781
Wofford	12	6	.667	19	13	.594
Georgia Southern	12	6	.667	15	15	.500
Charleston	10	8	.556	19	12	.613
Furman	8	10	.444	15	16	.484
Citadel	3	15	.167	6	24	.200

Southland

EAST	Conference			All Games		
	W	L	Pct	W	L	Pct
*Lamar	11	5	.688	23	11	.676
McNeese State	10	6	.625	17	15	.531
Northwestern State	8	8	.500	16	16	.500
Nicholls State	6	10	.375	10	20	.333
SE Louisiana	5	11	.313	12	17	.414
Central Arkansas	3	13	.188	8	21	.276
WEST						
Texas-Arlington	15	1	.938	24	8	.750
Stephen F. Austin	12	4	.750	20	12	.625
UTSA	10	6	.625	18	14	.563
Sam Houston State	7	9	.438	13	19	.406
Texas State	5	11	.313	13	17	.433
Texas A&M-CC	4	12	.250	6	24	.200

Southwestern Athletic

	Conference			All Games		
	W	L	Pct	W	L	Pct
*Miss Valley St	17	1	.944	21	12	.636
Southern University	13	5	.722	17	14	.548
Texas Southern	12	6	.667	15	18	.455
Prairie View A&M	10	8	.556	14	18	.438
Arkansas-Pine Bluff	9	9	.500	11	22	.333
Alabama State	9	9	.500	12	19	.387
Alcorn State	6	12	.333	10	22	.313
Alabama A&M	5	13	.278	7	21	.250
Jackson State	5	13	.278	7	24	.226
Grambling State	4	14	.222	4	24	.143

Summit League

	Conference			All Games		
	W	L	Pct	W	L	Pct
Oral Roberts	17	1	.944	27	6	.818
*South Dakota St	15	3	.833	27	7	.794
Oakland	11	7	.611	17	15	.531
Western Illinois	9	9	.500	18	14	.563
North Dakota St	9	9	.500	17	13	.567
Southern Utah	8	10	.444	14	17	.452
IUPUI	7	11	.389	14	18	.438
IPFW	5	13	.278	11	19	.367
South Dakota	5	13	.278	10	18	.357
UMKC	4	14	.222	10	21	.323

Sun Belt

EAST	Conference			All Games		
	W	L	Pct	W	L	Pct
Middle Tennessee	14	2	.875	25	6	.806
South Alabama	8	8	.500	17	12	.586
*Western Kentucky	7	9	.438	15	18	.455
Florida Atlantic	7	9	.438	11	19	.367
Troy	5	11	.313	10	18	.357
Florida International	5	11	.313	8	21	.276
WEST						
Ark-Little Rock	12	4	.750	15	16	.484
Denver	11	5	.688	22	9	.710
Louisiana-Lafayette	10	6	.625	16	15	.516
North Texas	9	7	.563	18	14	.563
Arkansas State	6	10	.375	14	20	.412
Louisiana-Monroe	2	14	.125	3	26	.103

West Coast

	Conference			All Games		
	W	L	Pct	W	L	Pct
*Saint Mary's	14	2	.875	27	5	.844
Gonzaga	13	3	.813	25	6	.806
Brigham Young	12	4	.750	25	8	.758
Loyola Marymount	11	5	.688	19	12	.613
San Francisco	8	8	.500	20	13	.606
San Diego	7	9	.438	13	18	.419
Pepperdine	4	12	.250	10	19	.345
Portland	3	13	.188	7	24	.226
Santa Clara	0	16	.000	8	22	.267

Western Athletic

	Conference			All Games		
	W	L	Pct	W	L	Pct
Nevada	13	1	.929	26	6	.813
*New Mexico St	10	4	.714	26	9	.743
Idaho	9	5	.643	18	13	.581
Utah State	8	6	.571	17	15	.531
Louisiana Tech	6	8	.429	18	16	.529
Hawaii	6	8	.429	16	16	.500
Fresno State	3	11	.214	13	20	.394
San Jose State	1	13	.071	9	22	.290

Independents

	All Games		
	W	L	Pct
Cal State Bakersfield	16	14	.533
Seattle	12	15	.444
Longwood	10	21	.323

*Conference tournament winner.

Scoring

	Class	GP	FG	3FG	FT	Pts	Avg
Reggie Hamilton, Oakland	Sr.	36	281	118	262	942	26.2
Damian Lillard, Weber St.	Jr.	32	231	94	228	784	24.5
Doug McDermott, Creighton	So.	35	307	54	133	801	22.9
Shane Gibson, Sacred Heart	Jr.	32	253	87	112	705	22.0
C.J. McCollum, Lehigh	Jr.	35	254	60	198	766	21.9
Terrell Stoglin, Maryland	So.	32	220	91	159	690	21.6
Gerardo Suero, Albany (NY)	Jr.	32	220	29	220	689	21.5
Nate Wolters, South Dakota St.	Jr.	34	250	33	188	721	21.2
Frank Gaines, IPFW	Jr.	30	207	49	172	635	21.2
Kevin Murphy, Tennessee Tech	Sr.	33	239	79	124	681	20.6
Colt Ryan, Evansville	Jr.	32	199	74	184	656	20.5
Nick Barbour, High Point	Sr.	31	185	108	155	633	20.4
Alex Young, IUPUI	Sr.	32	219	59	156	653	20.4
J'Covan Brown, Texas	Jr.	34	223	80	157	683	20.1
John Shurna, Northwestern	Sr.	33	228	95	110	661	20.0
Kevin Jones, West Virginia	Sr.	33	260	34	103	657	19.9
Mike Moore, Hofstra	Sr.	32	200	81	156	637	19.9
John Jenkins, Vanderbilt	Jr.	35	217	134	128	696	19.9
Dominique Morrison, Oral Roberts	Sr.	34	215	55	189	674	19.8
Orlando Johnson, UC Santa Barbara	Sr.	31	207	70	127	611	19.7
Darryl Partin, Boston U.	Sr.	32	218	69	123	628	19.6
Antwan Carter, Longwood	Sr.	31	245	23	88	601	19.4
Charles Odum, Portland St.	Sr.	32	192	38	190	612	19.1
George Beamon, Manhattan	Jr.	33	210	61	145	626	19.0
Isaiah Canaan, Murray St.	Jr.	33	187	98	154	626	19.0

FIELD-GOAL PERCENTAGE

	Class	GP	FG	FGA	Pct
Ricardo Ratliffe, Missouri	Sr.	35	210	303	69.3
Mike Glover, Iona	Sr.	33	239	375	63.7
Anthony Davis, Kentucky	Fr.	40	210	337	62.3
Cody Zeller, Indiana	Fr.	36	200	321	62.3
Scott Eatherton, St. Francis (PA)	So.	29	162	264	61.4
Eric Griffin, Campbell	Sr.	31	177	290	61.0
Doug McDermott, Creighton	So.	35	307	511	60.1
Mike Groselle, Citadel	Jr.	30	198	335	59.1
Trey McCorkle, IPFW	Sr.	29	152	258	58.9
Kelvin Martin, Charleston So.	Sr.	31	187	318	58.8

Note: Minimum 5 made per game.

REBOUNDS

	Class	GP	Reb	Avg
O.D. Anosike, Siena	Jr.	31	388	12.5
Thomas Robinson, Kansas	Jr.	39	463	11.9
Andre Roberson, Colorado	So.	36	401	11.1
Drew Gordon, New Mexico	Sr.	35	388	11.1
Jamelle Hagins, Delaware	Jr.	32	354	11.1
Kevin Jones, West Virginia	Sr.	33	360	10.9
Rob Jones, St. Mary's (CA)	Sr.	33	357	10.8
Wendell McKines, New Mexico St.	Sr.	35	374	10.7
Draymond Green, Michigan St.	Sr.	37	394	10.6
Mike Moser, UNLV	So.	35	369	10.5
Cameron Moore, UAB	Sr.	31	325	10.5
Arnett Moultrie, Mississippi St.	Jr.	30	314	10.5

FREE-THROW PERCENTAGE

	Class	GP	FT	FTA	Pct
Robby Ptacek, Cent Conn. St.	Sr.	29	126	137	92.0
E.J. Singler, Oregon	Jr.	34	110	121	90.9
Scott Christopherson, Iowa St.	Sr.	34	93	103	90.3
Brian Barbour, Columbia	Jr.	30	146	162	90.1
Austin Morgan, Yale	Jr.	29	90	100	90.0
Marcus Denmon, Missouri	Sr.	35	120	134	89.6
Maalik Wayns, Villanova	Jr.	29	141	158	89.2
Bryce Cotton, Providence	So.	32	90	101	89.1
Darien Brothers, Richmond	Jr.	32	106	119	89.1
Four McGlynn, Vermont	Fr.	36	96	108	88.9
Logan Aronhalt, Albany (NY)	Jr.	30	80	90	88.9

Note: Minimum 2.5 made per game.

ASSISTS

	Class	GP	Ast	Avg
Scott Machado, Iona	Sr.	33	327	9.9
Kendall Marshall, North Carolina	So.	36	351	9.8
Jesse Sanders, Liberty	Sr.	32	255	8.0
Vincent Council, Providence	Jr.	31	231	7.5
Jason Brickman, LIU Brooklyn	So.	34	249	7.3
Jeremiah Ostrowski, Hawaii	Sr.	25	175	7.0
Dylan Garrity, Sacramento St.	Fr.	28	193	6.9
Jordan Theodore, Seton Hall	Sr.	34	226	6.6
Kaylon Williams, Milwaukee	Sr.	33	215	6.5
M. Dellavedova, St. Mary's (CA)	Jr.	33	212	6.4

*Includes games played in tournaments.

THREE-POINT FIELD-GOAL PERCENTAGE

	Class	GP	3FG	3FGA	Avg
Nick Barbour, High Point	Sr.	31	108	223	48.4
Drew Hanlen, Belmont	Sr.	35	94	195	48.2
Reggie Chamberlain, UMKC	Sr.	31	97	206	47.1
L. Galloway, St. Joseph's	So.	34	90	193	46.6
Ceola Clark, Western Ill.	Sr.	32	86	186	46.2
Isaiah Canaan, Murray St.	Jr.	33	98	215	45.6
Brady Heslip, Baylor	So.	38	100	220	45.5
Brian Sullivan, Miami (OH)	Fr.	30	79	176	44.9
John Shurna, Northwestern	Sr.	33	95	216	44.0
Deremy Geiger, Idaho	Sr.	33	87	198	43.9
John Jenkins, Vanderbilt	Jr.	35	134	305	43.9

Note: Minimum 2.5 made per game

BLOCKED SHOTS

	Class	GP	BS	Avg
Anthony Davis, Kentucky	Fr.	40	186	4.65
William Mosley, Northwestern St.	Sr.	32	130	4.06
Damian Eargle, Youngstown St.	Jr.	31	116	3.74
Jeff Withey, Kansas	Jr.	39	140	3.59
C.J. Aiken, Saint Joseph's	So.	34	120	3.53
Eric Buckner, Georgia St.	Sr.	34	118	3.47
Darrius Garrett, Richmond	Sr.	32	107	3.34
Gorgui Dieng, Louisville	So.	40	128	3.20
Jamelle Hagins, Delaware	Jr.	32	95	2.97
Alec Brown, Green Bay	So.	30	89	2.97

THREE-POINT FIELD GOALS MADE PER GAME

	Class	GP	3FG	Avg
John Jenkins, Vanderbilt	Jr.	35	134	3.83
Nick Barbour, High Point	Sr.	31	108	3.48
Travis Bader, Oakland	So.	36	124	3.44
Keaton Cole, Western Carolina	Sr.	35	116	3.31
Reggie Hamilton, Oakland	Sr.	36	118	3.28
Keiton Page, Oklahoma St.	Sr.	32	103	3.22
Reggie Chamberlain, UMKC	Sr.	31	97	3.13
Zach Filzen, Buffalo	Sr.	31	97	3.13
Omar Strong, Texas Southern	Jr.	33	102	3.09
Parker Smith, North Florida	Jr.	32	96	3.00
Andrew Ferry, Cornell	Sr.	28	84	3.00

STEALS

	Class	GP	Stl	Avg
Anthony Nelson, Niagara	Sr.	29	98	3.4
Josh Slater, Lipscomb	Sr.	30	93	3.1
Jay Threatt, Delaware St	Jr.	30	93	3.1
T. J. McConnell, Duquesne	Fr.	32	91	2.8
Jared Cunningham, Oregon St	So.	30	85	2.8
Iman Shumpert, Georgia Tech	Jr.	31	85	2.7
Jackson Emery, BYU	Sr.	37	101	2.7
Devin Gibson, Tex.-San Antonio	Sr.	34	91	2.7
Will Cherry, Montana	So.	30	79	2.6
Akeem Bennett, St. Francis (N.Y.)	Sr.	29	76	2.6

Single-Game Highs

POINTS

50........Kevin Murphy, Tennessee Tech, January 30, 2012 (vs. SIU Edwardsville)
46........Parker Smith, North Florida, February 20, 2012 (vs Mercer)
44........Nick Barbour, High Point, Febuary 22, 2012 (vs Campbell)
44........Doug McDermott, Creighton, January 7, 2012 (vs Bradley)

Five tied with 43

REBOUNDS

24........Cameron Moore, UAB, December 28, 2011 (vs George Washington)
23........Andrew Nicholson, St. Bonaventure, February 11, 2012 (vs Duquesne)

Six tied with 22

ASSISTS

16........Jason Brickman, LIU, February 18, 2012 (vs Brooklyn)
16 ....Dylan Garrity, Sacramento St, February 9, 2012 (vs Montana St.)
16 ....Kendall Marshall, North Carolina, February 4, 2012 (vs Maryland)
16 ....Scott Machado, Iona, January 12, 2012 (vs Manhattan)
16 ....Keegan Bell, Chattanooga, December 29, 2011 (vs Longwood)
16 ....Jesse Sanders, Liberty, December 20, 2011 (vs Montreat)
16 ....Kendall Marshall, North Carolina, December 10, 2011 (vs Long Beach St.)

Ten tied with15.

THREE-POINT FIELD GOALS

11 ....Parker Smith, North Florida, Febuary 20, 2012 (vs. Mercer)
10........Travis Bader, Oakland, January 26, 2012 (vs South Dakota St)
10........Sean Armand, Iona, January 3, 2012 (vs Siena)
10 ....Jim Mower, Lafayette, November 22, 2011 (vs Fairleigh Dickinson)

Twelve tied with 9.

STEALS

9..........Lasan Kromah, George Washington, December 28, 2011 (vs UAB)

Nine tied with 8.

BLOCKED SHOTS

11 ....Alec Brown, Green Bay, January 14, 2012 (vs Wright St.)
10........Jeff Withey, Kansas, March 23, 2012 (vs North Carolina St.)
10 ....Kenny Gabriel, Auburn, January 2, 2012 (vs Bethune-Cookman)
10 ....Fab Melo, Syracuse, December 28, 2011 (vs Seton Hall)
10 ....Peter 'PJ' Roberson, Grambling, November 26, 2011

SCORING OFFENSE

	GP	W	L	Pts	Avg
Iona	33	25	7	2736	82.9
LIU Brooklyn	34	25	8	2769	81.4
North Carolina	38	29	5	3091	81.3
Belmont	35	27	7	2831	80.9
UNC Asheville	34	24	9	2745	80.7
Missouri	35	30	4	2814	80.4
Oakland	36	17	15	2875	79.9
VMI	33	17	16	2631	79.7
Creighton	35	28	5	2772	79.2
Oregon St.	36	19	14	2841	78.9

SCORING DEFENSE

	GP	W	L	Pts	Avg
Wisconsin	36	24	9	1915	53.2
Virginia	32	22	9	1735	54.2
Stephen F. Austin	32	20	12	1741	54.4
Harvard	31	26	4	1724	55.6
Drexel	36	27	6	2020	56.1
Wyoming	33	20	11	1855	56.2
South Florida	36	20	13	2037	56.6
Saint Louis	34	25	7	1960	57.6
Alabama	33	21	11	1918	58.1
Eastern Mich.	32	14	18	1878	58.7

SCORING MARGIN

	Off	Def	Mar
Kentucky	77.4	60.6	16.8
Ohio St.	74.7	59.8	14.9
Wichita St.	77.1	62.4	14.7
North Carolina	81.3	67.1	14.3
Missouri	80.4	66.3	14.1
New Mexico	72.7	59.3	13.4
Belmont	80.9	67.5	13.4
Syracuse	74.1	61.0	13.1
Murray St.	73.1	60.6	12.5
Michigan St.	71.6	59.3	12.3

FIELD-GOAL PERCENTAGE

	FGM	FGA	Pct
Missouri	981	1945	50.4
Creighton	975	1935	50.4
Iona	1021	2033	50.2
Middle Tenn.	882	1782	49.5
Indiana	949	1928	49.2
Memphis	933	1899	49.1
North Dakota St.	805	1649	48.8
Denver	728	1493	48.8
Kentucky	1096	2248	48.8
Coastal Carolina	853	1753	48.7

FIELD-GOAL PERCENTAGE DEFENSE

	Opp FG	Opp FGA	Opp Pct
Kentucky	889	2379	37.4
Michigan St.	751	1982	37.9
Kansas	826	2176	38.0
Georgia St.	702	1847	38.0
Florida St.	749	1965	38.1
Louisville	857	2233	38.4
New Mexico	731	1903	38.4
Syracuse	795	2064	38.5
Connecticut	785	2034	38.6
Memphis	751	1945	38.6

FREE-THROW PERCENTAGE

	FT	FTA	Pct
Weber St.	538	661	81.4
Dayton	484	623	77.7
IUPUI	495	638	77.6
Bucknell	532	687	77.4
Lehigh	590	768	76.8
Colorado St.	526	685	76.8
Missouri	335	437	76.7
Nebraska	559	730	76.6
UNC Asheville	682	893	76.4
Evansville	572	749	76.4

THREE-POINT FIELD GOALS MADE PER GAME

	GP	3FG	Avg
Florida	37	357	9.6
Coppin St.	30	289	9.6
Oakland	36	335	9.3
Lafayette	31	283	9.1
Northwestern	33	297	9.0
Troy	28	250	8.9
Weber St.	32	285	8.9
Eastern Wash.	32	283	8.8
Belmont	35	309	8.8
Youngstown St.	31	270	8.7

REBOUNDING MARGIN

	GP	Reb	Opp Reb	Margin Avg
North Carolina	38	1711	1313	10.5
Quinnipiac	32	1384	1057	10.2
New Mexico St.	36	1433	1126	8.5
Stony Brook	32	1203	936	8.3
Michigan St.	37	1403	1106	8.0
South Alabama	29	1152	933	7.6
Stephen F. Austin	32	1128	892	7.4
St. Mary's (CA)	33	1211	973	7.2
Ohio St.	39	1440	1159	7.2
Marshall	35	1388	1143	7.0

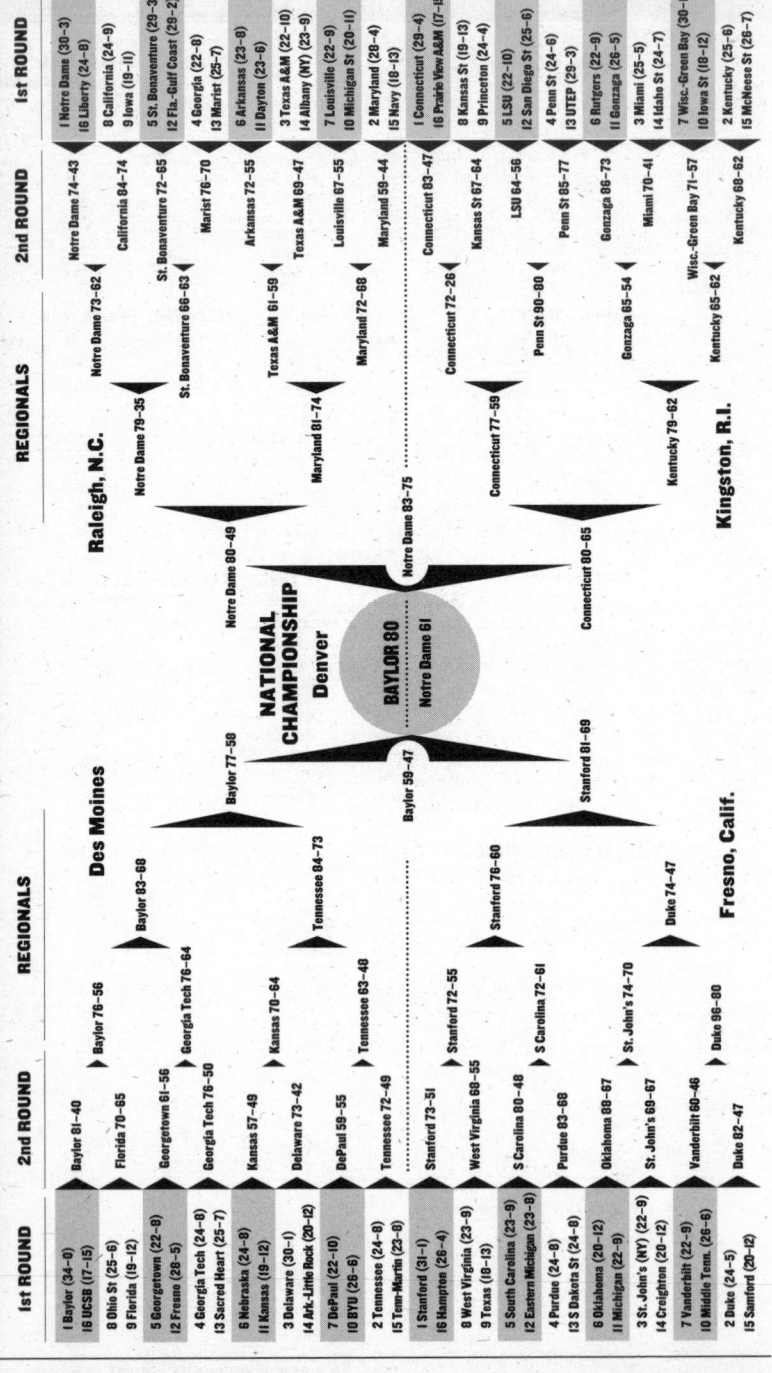

2012 NCAA Basketball Women's Division I Tournament

1st ROUND

1 Baylor (34–0)
16 UCSB (17–15)
8 Ohio St (25–6)
9 Florida (19–12)
5 Georgetown (22–8)
12 Fresno (28–5)
4 Georgia Tech (24–8)
13 Sacred Heart (25–7)
6 Nebraska (24–8)
11 Kansas (19–12)
3 Delaware (30–1)
14 Ark-Little Rock (20–12)
7 DePaul (22–10)
10 BYU (26–6)
2 Tennessee (24–8)
15 Tenn-Martin (23–8)

1 Stanford (31–1)
16 Hampton (26–4)
8 West Virginia (23–9)
9 Texas (18–13)
5 South Carolina (23–9)
12 Eastern Michigan (23–8)
4 Purdue (24–8)
13 S Dakota St (24–8)
6 Oklahoma (20–12)
11 Michigan (22–8)
3 St. John's (NY) (22–9)
14 Creighton (20–12)
7 Vanderbilt (22–9)
10 Middle Tenn. (26–6)
2 Duke (24–5)
15 Samford (20–12)

1 Notre Dame (30–3)
16 Liberty (24–8)
8 California (24–9)
9 Iowa (19–11)
5 St. Bonaventure (29–3)
12 Fla.-Gulf Coast (29–2)
4 Georgia (22–8)
13 Marist (25–7)
6 Arkansas (23–8)
11 Dayton (23–6)
3 Texas A&M (22–10)
14 Albany (NY) (23–9)
10 Louisville (22–9)
10 Michigan St (20–11)
2 Maryland (28–4)
15 Navy (18–13)

1 Connecticut (29–4)
16 Prairie View A&M (17–15)
8 Kansas St (19–13)
9 Princeton (24–4)
5 LSU (22–10)
12 San Diego St (25–6)
4 Penn St (24–6)
13 UTEP (29–3)
6 Rutgers (22–9)
11 Gonzaga (26–5)
3 Miami (25–5)
14 Idaho St (24–7)
7 Wisc.-Green Bay (30–1)
10 Iowa St (18–12)
2 Kentucky (25–6)
15 McNeese St (26–7)

2nd ROUND

Baylor 81–40
Florida 70–65
Georgetown 61–56
Georgia Tech 76–50
Kansas 57–49
Delaware 73–42
DePaul 59–55
Tennessee 72–49

Stanford 73–51
West Virginia 68–55
S Carolina 80–48
Purdue 83–68
Oklahoma 88–67
St. John's 69–67
Vanderbilt 60–46
Duke 82–47

Notre Dame 74–43
California 84–74
St. Bonaventure 72–65
Marist 76–70
Arkansas 72–55
Texas A&M 69–47
Louisville 67–55
Maryland 59–44

Connecticut 83–47
Kansas St 67–64
LSU 64–56
Penn St 85–77
Gonzaga 86–73
Miami 70–41
Wisc.-Green Bay 71–57
Kentucky 68–62

REGIONALS

Des Moines

Baylor 76–56
Georgia Tech 76–64
Kansas 70–64
Tennessee 84–73

Stanford 72–55
S Carolina 72–61
St. John's 74–70
Duke 96–80

Raleigh, N.C.

Notre Dame 79–35
St. Bonaventure 66–63
Texas A&M 61–59
Louisville 67–55

Connecticut 83–47
Kansas 67–64
Penn St 90–80
Gonzaga 65–54

2nd ROUND

Baylor 83–68
Tennessee 63–48

Stanford 76–60
Duke 74–47

Notre Dame 70–35
Maryland 81–74

Connecticut 72–26
Kentucky 79–62

REGIONALS

Fresno, Calif.

Baylor 77–58
Stanford 81–69

Kingston, R.I.

Notre Dame 80–49
Connecticut 80–65

Baylor 59–47
Notre Dame 83–75

NATIONAL CHAMPIONSHIP

Denver

BAYLOR 80
Notre Dame 61

Baylor 80

	Min	FG M-A	FT M-A	Reb O-T	A	PF	TP
B. Griner	39	11-16	4-6	1-13	1	1	26
D. Williams	28	5-7	2-2	4-6	2	1	12
K. Hayden	29	3-11	0-0	2-4	5	1	8
J. Madden	35	0-2	0-0	1-6	5	3	0
O. Sims	38	6-16	5-5	4-7	4	5	19
T. Condrey	14	2-3	2-2	0-5	2	1	6
A. Field	1	0-0	0-0	0-0	0	0	0
L. Palmer	1	0-0	1-2	0-0	0	0	1
B. Pope	12	2-3	4-4	4-4	1	1	8
M. Robertson	2	0-0	0-0	0-0	0	0	0
S. Agbuke	1	0-0	0-0	0-0	0	0	0
Totals		**29-58**	**18-21**	**16-45**	**20**	**13**	**80**

Percentages: FG-.500, FT-.857, 3-pt goals: 4–11, .364 (K. Hayden 2-3, J. Madden 0-2, O. Sims 2-6). Blocked shots: 6 (B. Griner 5, J. Madden 1). Turnovers: 9 (B. Griner 2, D. Williams 2, K. Hayden 1, J. Madden 1, O. Sims 2, B. Pope 1). Steals: 2 (O. Sims 2). Technical Fouls: None.

Halftime: Baylor 34, Notre Dame 28.

Notre Dame 61

	Min	FG M-A	FT M-A	Reb O-T	A	PF	TP
D. Peters	15	3-5	1-2	3-3	1	4	7
B. Mallory	33	1-3	0-0	1-6	2	0	3
N. Novosel	30	0-11	5-8	1-1	2	1	5
S. Diggins	37	7-17	4-4	1-2	3	3	20
K. McBride	25	5-13	1-1	0-3	3	3	11
F. Miller	5	0-0	0-0	0-0	0	1	0
K. Turner	7	2-5	0-0	0-0	1	0	6
N. Achonwa	27	3-5	1-1	3-6	1	4	7
A. Braker	1	0-0	0-0	0-1	0	0	0
W. Holloway	1	0-0	0-0	0-0	0	0	0
M. Wright	19	1-3	0-0	0-2	0	2	2
Totals		**22-62**	**12-16**	**9-24**	**13**	**19**	**61**

Percentages: FG-.335, FT-.750, 3-pt goals: 5–13, .385 (B. Mallory 1–2, N. Novosel 0–2, S. Diggins 2–5, K. Turner 2-4). Blocked shots: 4 (D. Peters 1, S. Diggins 1, N. Achonwa 1, M. Wright 1). Turnovers: 7 (D. Peters 1, N. Novosel 2, K. McBride 2, N. Achonwa 1, M. Wright 1). Steals: 6 (B. Mallory 2, S. Diggins 2, K. Turner 1, N. Achonwa 1). Technical Fouls: None.

Final Four Most Outstanding Player: Brittney Griner, Baylor.

Officials: Dee Kantner, Tina Napier, Lisa Jones.
A: 19,028

NCAA Women's Division I Individual Leaders

SCORING

Player and Team	Class	GP	TFG	3FG	FT	Pts	Avg
Elena Delle Donne, Delaware	Jr.	33	325	52	225	927	28.1
Kevi Luper, Oral Roberts	Jr.	30	273	48	120	714	23.8
Tavelyn James, Eastern Michigan	Sr.	32	261	79	160	761	23.8
Heather Butler, UT Martin	So.	32	266	99	129	760	23.8
Kristina Santiago, Cal Poly	Sr.	29	274	4	128	680	23.4
Jerica Coley, FIU	So.	34	270	46	208	794	23.4
Brittney Griner, Baylor	Jr.	40	358	1	212	929	23.2
Nnemkadi Ogwumike, Stanford	Sr.	36	307	4	191	809	22.5
Courtney Hurt, VCU	Sr.	34	287	23	160	757	22.3
Alex Cowling, Loyola Marymount	Jr.	30	231	44	160	666	22.2
Dequesha McClanahan, Winthrop	So.	31	230	42	151	653	21.1
Taleia Moton, George Mason	Sr.	31	230	35	147	642	20.7
Tayler Hill, Ohio St.	Jr.	32	215	82	141	653	20.4
Brittany Hedderson, Buffalo	Sr.	31	237	58	99	631	20.4
Brittany Johnson, San Jose St.	Sr.	30	217	11	158	603	20.1
Whiquitta Tobar, Alabama A&M	Sr.	28	165	23	202	555	19.8
Samantha Prahalis, Ohio St.	Sr.	31	216	62	119	613	19.8
Jasmine Newsome, UT Martin	So.	32	207	60	152	626	19.6
Julie Wojta, Green Bay	Sr.	33	252	29	111	644	19.5
Maggie Lucas, Penn St.	So.	33	202	82	156	642	19.5
Brianne Ryan, Eastern Wash.	Sr.	30	212	70	84	578	19.3
Whitney Hanley, Austin Peay	Sr.	31	218	55	104	595	19.2
Ashley Palmer, LIU Brooklyn	Sr.	31	220	16	139	595	19.2
Shante Evans, Hofstra	Jr.	31	220	0	154	594	19.2
Anna Martin, DePaul	Jr.	34	235	64	114	648	19.1

FIELD-GOAL PERCENTAGE

Player and Team	Class	GP	FG	FGA	Pct
Tianna Hawkins, Maryland	Jr.	36	187	300	62.3
Brittney Griner, Baylor	Jr.	40	358	588	60.9
Regina Rogers, Washington	Sr.	33	219	375	58.4
Chiney Ogwumike, Stanford	So.	37	215	369	58.3
Shareta Brown, Detroit	Fr.	34	213	381	55.9
Kristina Santiago, Cal Poly	Sr.	29	274	494	55.5
Morgan Johnson, Iowa	Jr.	31	179	326	54.9
Nnemkadi Ogwumike, Stanford	Sr.	36	307	561	54.7
Ebony Rowe, Middle Tenn.	So.	33	222	407	54.5
Jasmine Hassell, Georgia	Jr.	31	164	302	54.3

Note: Minimum 5 FG per game.

REBOUNDS

Player and Team	Class	GP	Reb	Avg
Courtney Hurt, VCU	Sr.	34	447	13.1
S. Thomas, Sam Houston St.	Jr.	30	377	12.6
Ashar Harris, Morehead St.	Jr.	29	361	12.4
Cheyenne Parker, High Point	So.	33	403	12.2
Rachael Hackbarth, Drake	Sr.	34	401	11.8
Kylie Kuhns, Sacramento St.	Jr.	31	360	11.6
Avery Warley, Liberty	Sr.	33	381	11.5
Megan Herbert, Central Ark.	Jr.	31	350	11.3
Jessica Kuster, Rice	So.	30	334	11.1
Markel Walker, UCLA	Jr.	23	252	11.0

FREE-THROW PERCENTAGE

Player and Team	Class	GP	FT	FTA	Pct
Abby Oliver, Richmond	Sr.	32	106	113	93.8
Chassidy Fussell, Texas	So.	32	86	95	90.5
Jill Young, South Dakota St.	Sr.	33	86	95	90.5
Sam Martin, Colorado St.	So.	30	82	91	90.1
C. VanBrocklin, Portland St.	Jr.	29	109	121	90.1
Devyn Christensen, Utah St.	Jr.	31	97	108	89.8
Ashley Durham, Canisius	Jr.	30	114	128	89.1
Elena Delle Donne, Delaware	Jr.	33	225	253	88.9
Michelle Kurowski, UMBC	Sr.	32	88	99	88.9
Chantell Alford, Boston U.	Jr.	32	94	106	88.7
Brooke Jackson, Utah St.	Sr.	31	86	97	88.7

Note: Minimum 2.5 made per game.

ASSISTS

Player and Team	Class	GP	Ast	Avg
Angel Goodrich, Kansas	Jr.	34	250	7.4
Dequesha McClanahan, Winthrop	So.	31	224	7.2
Jamierra Faulkner, Southern Miss.	So.	29	209	7.2
Haley Steed, BYU	Sr.	33	237	7.2
Jericka Jenkins, Hampton	Sr.	31	221	7.1
Chene Cooper, Eastern Wash.	Sr.	30	208	6.9
Tiffany Bias, Oklahoma St.	So.	34	229	6.7
Chelsea Hopkins, San Diego St.	Jr.	32	209	6.5
Emiko Smith, Denver	Jr.	31	200	6.5
Samantha Prahalis, Ohio St.	Sr.	31	194	6.3

THREE-POINT FIELD-GOAL PERCENTAGE

Player and Team	Class	GP	3FG	3FGA	Pct
Courtney Ingersoll, Toledo	Sr.	34	96	217	44.2
Heather Butler, UT Martin	So.	32	99	234	42.3
Tayler Hill, Ohio St.	Jr.	32	82	196	41.8
Jill Young, South Dakota St.	Sr.	33	83	199	41.7
Christina Foggie, Vanderbilt	So.	33	91	219	41.6
Ashlee Burns, Cal Poly	Sr.	32	71	172	41.3
Alyssa Shoji, Santa Clara	Sr.	30	99	240	41.3
Maggie Lucas, Penn St.	So.	33	82	200	41.0
Megan Zullo, Massachusetts	Sr.	28	65	160	40.6
Monica Albano, Loyola Chicago	Jr.	27	58	143	40.6

Note: Minimum 2.0 made per game.

BLOCKED SHOTS

Player and Team	Class	GP	BS	Avg
Brittney Griner, Baylor	Jr.	40	206	5.15
Danielle Fiacco, Lafayette	So.	30	112	3.73
Adobi Agbasi, Md. Eastern Shore	Sr.	29	108	3.72
Cheyenne Parker, High Point	So.	33	121	3.67
Elizabeth Williams, Duke	Fr.	33	116	3.52
Patricia Bright, Oregon St.	Jr.	33	115	3.48
Brittany Carnago, Oakland	So.	25	82	3.28
Ashley Adams, Ohio St.	So.	32	96	3.00
Christine Flores, Missouri	Sr.	31	93	3.00
Gloria Brown, UTEP	Sr.	33	97	2.94

NCAA Men's Division II Individual Leaders

SCORING

Player and Team	Class	GP	TFG	3FG	FT	Pts	Avg
Sammy Emile, Mars Hill	Sr.	28	199	64	239	701	25.0
Trevin Parks, Johnson C. Smith	Jr.	27	193	65	161	612	22.7
James Ellisor, Bemidji St.	Sr.	31	251	34	144	680	21.9
Steve Custis, Fairmont St.	Sr.	26	193	41	141	568	21.8
Dwight Tolbert, Lander	Sr.	27	202	91	94	589	21.8
Marcus Coleman, Washington Adventist	Sr.	28	223	29	134	609	21.8
Stefan Bonneau, C.W. Post	Sr.	29	217	79	116	629	21.7
D.J. Rivera, Montevallo	Sr.	35	268	55	164	755	21.6
Keane Thomann, Mo. Southern St.	Sr.	30	257	0	132	646	21.5
Greg Rice, Central St. (OH)	Sr.	28	232	31	107	602	21.5
Raymont McElroy, West Va. Wesleyan	Sr.	31	231	71	133	666	21.5
Keon Moore, Catawba	So.	26	179	64	134	556	21.4
Isaac Thornton, Fairmont St.	Jr.	27	222	39	94	577	21.4
Tyshawn Good, Belmont Abbey	Jr.	27	175	56	168	574	21.3
Evan Yates, Ashland	Jr.	26	198	0	146	542	20.8
Chad Moore, Shepherd	Jr.	28	209	7	157	582	20.8

REBOUNDS

Player and Team	Class	GP	Reb	Avg
Garret Kerr, USciences	Fr.	25	325	13.0
Cory Quimby, Dominican (NY)	Jr.	28	320	11.4
Argelix Gil, Concordia (NY)	Jr.	27	308	11.4
Evan Yates, Ashland	Jr.	26	295	11.3
Marcus Goode, Benedict	Jr.	30	338	11.3
Michael Fakuade, Ill.-Springfield	Sr.	24	263	11.0
Ryan Aquino, Georgia College	Sr.	27	282	10.4
Paul Harrison, North Greenville	Sr.	27	281	10.4
Matt Morris, Fort Lewis	Sr.	27	275	10.2
Chad Moore, Shepherd	Jr.	28	280	10.0

ASSISTS

Player and Team	Class	GP	Ast	Avg
Josh Magette, Ala.-Huntsville	Sr.	33	295	8.9
PJ Turner, Davis & Elkins	Sr.	25	209	8.4
Corey Wright, Lander	Jr.	27	220	8.1
Ryan Rozsnaki, Assumption	Jr.	28	225	8.0
Lionel Foster, West Tex. A&M	Sr.	24	180	7.5
Ben Siefert, Wheeling Jesuit	Jr.	32	224	7.0
Ahmad Harris, Bloomfield	Jr.	34	232	6.8
Nigel Munson, Dist. Columbia	Sr.	28	181	6.5
Jamie Newton, Wash. Adventist	Sr.	28	179	6.4
Dory Hines, Mount Olive	So.	29	173	6.0

FIELD-GOAL PERCENTAGE

Player and Team	Class	GP	FG	FGA	Pct
Zach Roddenberry, Harding	Jr.	27	157	224	70.1
Kevin Kotzur, St. Mary's (TX)	Jr.	28	220	335	65.7
Jack Osborn, Adams St.	Jr.	28	143	218	65.6
Obi Ukwuoma, Wheeling Jesuit	Sr.	32	164	251	65.3
Donald Sims, West Tex. A&M	Jr.	28	164	255	64.3
K. Thomann, Mo. Southern St.	Sr.	30	257	406	63.3
K. Olafeso, Concordia-St. Paul	Sr.	26	160	254	63.0
Taylor Rohde, Alaska Anchorage	Sr.	30	222	354	62.7
Patrick Grubbs, Pitt.-Johnstown	Jr.	29	192	310	61.9
C.J. Hester, West Liberty	Fr.	34	206	336	61.3
Evan Yates, Ashland	Jr.	26	198	323	61.3

Note: Minimum 5 made per game.

FREE-THROW PERCENTAGE

Player and Team	Class	GP	FT	FTA	Pct
A. Brown, Tex. A&M-Kingsville	Jr.	26	124	129	96.1
Kyle Caiola, Findlay	Sr.	31	150	161	93.2
Nate Barnes, Alderson-Broaddus	Sr.	28	80	87	92.0
Brett Beland, Saginaw Valley	Jr.	26	72	79	91.1
Jim Connolly, Philadelphia U.	Jr.	25	90	99	90.9
K. Bohanon, Alderson-Broaddus	Jr.	28	82	91	90.1
Sterling Council, S.C. Aiken	Sr.	29	100	111	90.1
Brett Putz, St. Cloud St.	Sr.	29	80	89	89.9
Ronnie Steward, Ashland	Jr.	27	71	79	89.9
John Allen, Western Wash.	Jr.	36	94	105	89.5

Note: Minimum 2.5 made per game.

NCAA Women's Division II Individual Leaders

SCORING

Player and Team	Class	GP	TFG	3FG	FT	Pts	Avg
Jaymee Carnes, North Ga.	So.	25	214	16	180	624	25.0
Lydia Bridenbaugh, West Virginia Wesleyan	Sr.	31	226	54	202	708	22.8
Satoria Bell, Newman	Sr.	29	239	30	148	656	22.6
Jessica Koch, Mo. Western St.	Sr.	27	204	48	139	595	22.0
Mack Lankford, Abilene Christian	So.	21	140	40	131	451	21.5
Kaitlin Snyder, Fairmont St.	Jr.	28	213	70	105	601	21.5
Kari Daugherty, Ashland	Jr.	35	284	44	132	744	21.3
Jolysa Brown, Concord	Sr.	29	213	0	179	605	20.9
Brittany Cox, Pfeiffer	Jr.	26	172	84	112	540	20.8
Dayshalee Salaman, Lincoln Memorial	Sr.	27	184	46	143	557	20.6
Michaela Hawley, Florida Southern	Sr.	31	227	6	159	619	20.0
Christine Wooding, Philadelphia U.	Sr.	29	187	8	193	575	19.8
Porsha Morgan, Erskine	Sr.	27	191	38	113	533	19.7
Kristin Turner, Indianapolis	Jr.	30	203	76	99	581	19.4
Jamie Kauffman, West Virginia Wesleyan	Sr.	31	231	1	129	592	19.1

REBOUNDS

Player and Team	Class	GP	Reb	Avg
Kari Daugherty, Ashland	Jr.	35	492	14.1
Erika Rousculp, Charleston (WV)	So.	28	378	13.5
C. Blakemore, Concordia (NY)	Sr.	26	340	13.1
Mauri Wells, Armstrong	So.	26	338	13.0
Mishae Miles, Glenville St.	Sr.	30	365	12.2
Jolysa Brown, Concord	Sr.	29	352	12.1
Dana Hicks, Catawba	Sr.	29	344	11.9
Hannah Heeter, Clarion	Fr.	24	284	11.8
Jewel White, Franklin Pierce	Jr.	30	354	11.8
Briauna Hagins, Florida Tech	Sr.	29	340	11.7

ASSISTS

Player and Team	Class	GP	Ast	Avg
Christine Duffy, Southern N.H.	Sr.	29	241	8.3
Cambria Smith, Texas Woman's	Sr.	27	196	7.3
Roselis Silva, Arkansas Tech	Jr.	26	174	6.7
Danyele Hoffman, BYU-Hawaii	Fr.	26	164	6.3
Chelsea Carlisle, UC San Diego	Jr.	33	201	6.1
Tammy Acosta, Tex. Permian Basin	Sr.	25	147	5.9
Christina Whitelaw, Colo. Christian	So.	33	191	5.8
Simone Williams, Mercy	Sr.	26	150	5.8
Symone Wilkerson, Albany St. (GA)	Sr.	28	157	5.6
Nicole Pendarvis, Cameron	Sr.	26	144	5.5
Kelley Sundberg, Gannon	So.	29	159	5.5

FIELD-GOAL PERCENTAGE

Player and Team	Class	GP	FG	FGA	Pct
Sumiya Darden, SW Okla.	Sr.	29	170	283	60.1
Hannah Heeter, Clarion	Fr.	24	144	243	59.3
L. Cochran, Lincoln Memorial	Sr.	27	174	296	58.8
Nikki Fredrickson, Mercyhurst	Sr.	26	146	251	58.2
Shaquanda Wiggins, Central Mo.	Jr.	23	136	234	58.1
Jewel White, Franklin Pierce	Jr.	30	171	296	57.8
Michaela Hawley, Fla. Southern	Sr.	31	227	394	57.6
Sloane Sorrell, Southern N.H.	Jr.	29	186	323	57.6
Mishae Miles, Glenville St.	Sr.	30	153	266	57.5
Hailey Garrett, Fairmont St.	Fr.	28	175	305	57.4

Note: Minimum 5 FG per game.

FREE-THROW PERCENTAGE

Player and Team	Class	GP	FT	FTA	Pct
Peyton Adamson, Tarleton St.	So.	32	97	105	92.4
Heather Robben, Emporia St.	Sr.	32	154	168	91.7
Kendal Baxter, Tusculum	Jr.	28	75	82	91.5
Emily Bayly, Le Moyne	Jr.	25	68	75	90.7
Angie Jetvig, Minn. St. Moorhead	Sr.	27	128	144	88.9
Shelby Miller, Maryville (MO)	Fr.	31	96	108	88.9
Mary Louise Dixon, Stonehill	So.	27	87	98	88.8
Tyler Carlson, Mars Hill	So.	26	79	89	88.8
Coreen Hennessy, Saint Michael's	Sr.	27	86	97	88.7
Tricia Principe, Ferris St.	Sr.	30	104	118	88.1

Note: Minimum 2.5 made per game.

NCAA Men's Division III Individual Leaders

SCORING

Player and Team	Class	GP	TFG	3FG	FT	Pts	Avg
Lamonte Thomas, Johnson & Wales (RI)	Sr.	22	245	59	202	751	34.1
DaQuan Brooks, Western Conn. St.	Sr.	28	257	100	201	815	29.1
Matt Addison, Hardin-Simmons	Sr.	26	234	79	197	744	28.6
Jerome Alexander, John Jay	Sr.	25	237	16	169	659	26.4
Griffin Lentsch, Grinnell	Jr.	23	202	102	96	602	26.2
Aris Wurtz, Ripon	Sr.	22	194	46	115	549	25.0
Raymond Askew, Albertus Magnus	Sr.	30	241	14	231	727	24.2
Jake Schwarz, Lakeland	Jr.	28	218	75	144	655	23.4
Raysean Johnson, D'Youville	Sr.	26	194	34	178	600	23.1
Tim Brady, Ohio Wesleyan	Sr.	28	209	34	178	630	22.5
AJ Matthews, Farmingdale St.	Jr.	27	239	0	127	605	22.4
Nathan Roeder, North Central (MN)	Jr.	24	175	51	135	536	22.3
Taeshon Johnson, Southern Vt.	Sr.	24	204	7	119	534	22.3
Chris Davis, Wis.-Whitewater	Sr.	31	258	60	113	689	22.2
Tyshawn Russell, Brooklyn	Sr.	29	219	33	169	640	22.1

REBOUNDS

Player and Team	Class	GP	Reb	Avg
AJ Matthews, Farmingdale St.	Jr.	27	439	16.3
Matt Pepdjonovic, Suffolk	Sr.	25	340	13.6
David Palmer, Pitt.-Greensburg	Jr.	24	313	13.0
Winston Douglas, Medgar Evers	Jr.	29	376	13.0
Simon Smith, Stevens	Sr.	28	336	12.0
Theo Robinson, Emmanuel (MA)	So.	26	305	11.7
Joshua Ford, Mitchell	So.	23	269	11.7
Aaron Van Klaveren, Cal Lutheran	Sr.	24	273	11.4
Will Hanley, Bowdoin	Sr.	25	284	11.4
Spencer Liddic, Muhlenberg	Sr.	27	303	11.2

ASSISTS

Player and Team	Class	GP	Ast	Avg
Sean Rossi, Ithaca	Jr.	28	259	9.3
Jerald Williams, Lycoming	Jr.	27	227	8.4
Williams Montgomery, Rust	Sr.	25	198	7.9
Austin Claunch, Emory	Sr.	25	180	7.2
Jason Rosenberg, Rowan	So.	26	177	6.8
Cory Lemons, Cabrini	Jr.	32	206	6.4
Michael Horton, Beloit	Sr.	23	145	6.3
Woody Redding, Rutgers-Camden	So.	25	156	6.2
Omer Haim, Yeshiva	Sr.	21	131	6.2
Josh Regal, Lakeland	Sr.	28	172	6.1
DaQuan Brooks, Western Conn. St.	Sr.	28	170	6.1

FIELD-GOAL PERCENTAGE

Player and Team	Class	GP	FG	FGA	Pct
Kenneth Hardnett, Keystone	Sr.	27	197	302	65.2
Travis Clark, Lake Forest	Sr.	24	187	291	64.3
John Coleman, Clarkson	Fr.	25	157	245	64.1
Kendall Hinze, Wilkes	Sr.	26	147	230	63.9
James Lazarcik, Beloit	So.	23	116	182	63.7
Brian Clark, Salem St.	Sr.	28	215	342	62.9
Matt Lorello, Geneva	Jr.	26	164	261	62.8
Simon Smith, Stevens	Sr.	28	190	305	62.6
A. Van Klaveren, Cal Lutheran	Sr.	24	140	225	62.2
Javon Williams, Lasell	Sr.	27	208	335	62.1

Note: Minimum 5 made per game.

FREE-THROW PERCENTAGE

Player and Team	Class	GP	FT	FTA	Pct
Ryan Martin, Keene St.	So.	27	112	122	91.8
Joey Kizel, Middlebury	So.	30	114	125	91.2
Tyler Schmidt, Augsburg	Jr.	26	72	79	91.1
Aaron Toomey, Amherst	So.	28	182	200	91.0
Markeith Wilson, Rust	Sr.	25	78	86	90.7
Derek Raridon, North Central (IL)	Jr.	28	107	118	90.7
Matt Johnson, Chicago	Sr.	25	131	147	89.1
Chris Davis, Wis.-Whitewater	Sr.	31	113	127	89.0
J. DiBartolomeo, Rochester (NY)	Jr.	25	129	145	89.0
Julian Lott, Blackburn	Sr.	24	64	72	88.9

Note: Minimum 2.5 made per game.

SCORING

Player and Team	Class	GP	TFG	3FG	FT	Pts	Avg
Karin Bird, Thomas (ME)	Sr.	20	145	35	165	490	24.5
Megan Rahn, Meredith	So.	25	178	39	211	606	24.2
Amy Fahey, Fitchburg St.	So.	25	210	0	170	590	23.6
Naimah Clemons, Kean	Jr.	24	224	23	83	554	23.1
Caty Eeten, Eureka	So.	26	197	10	190	594	22.8
Olivia Lett, Ill. Wesleyan	Sr.	33	251	50	167	719	21.8
Gretchen Owens, Linfield	Sr.	25	190	36	119	535	21.4
April Smith, Wm. Paterson	Sr.	29	232	10	143	617	21.3
Sabrina Jarmolinski, St. Elizabeth	Sr.	26	222	28	76	548	21.1
Elizabeth Sunderhaus, Cedar Crest	Sr.	22	164	15	116	459	20.9
Deanna Purcell, Rivier	Fr.	28	197	21	164	579	20.7
Becky Hebert, Fredonia St.	So.	23	181	21	89	472	20.5
Meghan Nowak, Eastern	Fr.	26	194	24	119	531	20.4
Taylor DeSanty, Colby-Sawyer	Jr.	30	224	74	89	611	20.4
Kathleen Payne, Plattsburgh St.	So.	24	168	32	108	476	19.8

REBOUNDS

Player and Team	Class	GP	Reb	Avg
Catherine O'Connell, Newbury	Jr.	27	404	15.0
Rebecca Yoshor, Yeshiva	So.	18	262	14.6
Ashley Roser, Wells	So.	20	287	14.4
Rebecca Goreham, Fitchburg St.	Sr.	23	318	13.8
Kayla Skiffington, Bay Path	So.	18	247	13.7
Jamie Tate, Hendrix	So.	26	355	13.7
Yvanna Jack, Medgar Evers	Sr.	22	290	13.2
Keneisha Milton, Wheelock	Jr.	22	287	13.0
Margaux Pickell, Polytechnic (NY)	Sr.	25	324	13.0
Holly Phelps, East Tex. Baptist	Sr.	23	296	12.9

FIELD-GOAL PERCENTAGE

Player and Team	Class	GP	FG	FGA	Pct
L. Oliver, Richard Stockton	Sr.	30	155	254	61.0
Callie Halama, Wis.-Eau Claire	Sr.	27	141	235	60.0
Sada Wheeler, Piedmont	Jr.	26	194	328	59.1
April Smith, Wm. Paterson	Sr.	29	232	395	58.7
Emily Peel, Carnegie Mellon	Jr.	25	146	250	58.4
B. Ygarza, East. Mennonite	So.	26	131	226	58.0
Claire Ramonas, Regis (MA)	So.	27	146	253	57.7
Sarah Collins, Babson	Jr.	28	197	343	57.4
Khassandrae Brown, Eureka	Sr.	26	156	272	57.4
Carissa Verkaik, Calvin	Jr.	30	225	396	56.8

Note: Minimum 5 made per game.

ASSISTS

Player and Team	Class	GP	Ast	Avg
Aja Wallpher, York (PA)	So.	30	219	7.3
Amanda De La Cruz, Lehman	Sr.	25	173	6.9
Cailin Bullett, Colby-Sawyer	Jr.	30	197	6.6
Maggie Prewitt, Centre	Sr.	30	191	6.4
Meghan Tait, Washington Col.	Sr.	25	153	6.1
S. Slonski, Western Conn. St.	Sr.	24	141	5.9
Katelyn Fischer, Marymount (VA)	Jr.	27	154	5.7
Lacey Phillips, Ozarks (AR)	Sr.	26	148	5.7
Kaitlyn Birrell, Salve Regina	Jr.	29	165	5.7
Savannah Morgan, Emory	So.	25	142	5.7
Alissa Lamey, Rowan	Sr.	26	147	5.7

THREE-POINT FIELD-GOAL PERCENTAGE

Player and Team	Class	GP	3FG	3FGA	Pct
Sarah Albert, Marian (WI)	So.	26	62	125	49.6
Maria Mackey, Northland	Sr.	25	72	150	48.0
Kayla Blom, Dominican (IL)	Sr.	23	67	143	46.9
Chelsea Paul, Green Mountain	Jr.	23	51	110	46.4
Kori Wiedt, Mount Union	Sr.	30	84	182	46.2
Nicole Garland, Southern Me.	Sr.	28	78	174	44.8
Allison Long, Thomas More	Jr.	29	77	176	43.8
Maureen Hirt, Kenyon	So.	27	85	195	43.6
Shea Rasmussen, Neb. Wesleyan	Sr.	25	70	165	42.4
Stephanie Reiter, Wartburg	Sr.	27	73	173	42.2

Note: Minimum 2.5 made per game.

NCAA Men's Division I Championship Results

NCAA Final Four Results

Year	Winner	Score	Runner-up	Third Place	Fourth Place	Winning Coach
1939	Oregon	46–33	Ohio St	*Oklahoma	*Villanova	Howard Hobson
1940	Indiana	60–42	Kansas	*Duquesne	*USC	Branch McCracken
1941	Wisconsin	39–34	Washington St	*Pittsburgh	*Arkansas	Harold Foster
1942	Stanford	53–38	Dartmouth	*Colorado	*Kentucky	Everett Dean
1943	Wyoming	46–34	Georgetown	*Texas	*DePaul	Everett Shelton
1944	Utah	42–40 (OT)	Dartmouth	*Iowa St	*Ohio St	Vadal Peterson
1945	Oklahoma St	49–45	NYU	*Arkansas	*Ohio St	Hank Iba
1946	Oklahoma St	43–40	North Carolina	Ohio St	California	Hank Iba
1947	Holy Cross	58–47	Oklahoma	Texas	CCNY	Alvin Julian
1948	Kentucky	58–42	Baylor	Holy Cross	Kansas St	Adolph Rupp
1949	Kentucky	46–36	Oklahoma St	Illinois	Oregon St	Adolph Rupp
1950	CCNY	71–68	Bradley	North Carolina St	Baylor	Nat Holman
1951	Kentucky	68–58	Kansas St	Illinois	Oklahoma St	Adolph Rupp
1952	Kansas	80–63	St. John's (N.Y.)	Illinois	Santa Clara	Forrest Allen
1953	Indiana	69–68	Kansas	Washington	LSU	Branch McCracken
1954	La Salle	92–76	Bradley	Penn St	USC	Kenneth Loeffler
1955	San Francisco	77–63	La Salle	Colorado	Iowa	Phil Woolpert
1956	San Francisco	83–71	Iowa	Temple	SMU	Phil Woolpert
1957	North Carolina	54–53 (3OT)	Kansas	San Francisco	Michigan St	Frank McGuire
1958	Kentucky	84–72	Seattle	Temple	Kansas St	Adolph Rupp
1959	California	71–70	West Virginia	Cincinnati	Louisville	Pete Newell
1960	Ohio St	75–55	California	Cincinnati	NYU	Fred Taylor
1961	Cincinnati	70–65 (OT)	Ohio St	Vacated‡	Utah	Edwin Jucker
1962	Cincinnati	71–59	Ohio St	Wake Forest	UCLA	Edwin Jucker
1963	Loyola (Ill.)	60–58 (OT)	Cincinnati	Duke	Oregon St	George Ireland
1964	UCLA	98–83	Duke	Michigan	Kansas St	John Wooden
1965	UCLA	91–80	Michigan	Princeton	Wichita St	John Wooden
1966	UTEP	72–65	Kentucky	Duke	Utah	Don Haskins
1967	UCLA	79–64	Dayton	Houston	North Carolina	John Wooden
1968	UCLA	78–55	North Carolina	Ohio St	Houston	John Wooden
1969	UCLA	92–72	Purdue	Drake	North Carolina	John Wooden
1970	UCLA	80–69	Jacksonville	New Mexico St	St. Bonaventure	John Wooden
1971	UCLA	68–62	Vacated‡	Vacated‡	Kansas	John Wooden
1972	UCLA	81–76	Florida St	North Carolina	Louisville	John Wooden
1973	UCLA	87–66	Memphis St	Indiana	Providence	John Wooden
1974	North Carolina St	76–64	Marquette	UCLA	Kansas	Norm Sloan
1975	UCLA	92–85	Kentucky	Louisville	Syracuse	John Wooden
1976	Indiana	86–68	Michigan	UCLA	Rutgers	Bob Knight
1977	Marquette	67–59	North Carolina	UNLV	UNC-Charlotte	Al McGuire
1978	Kentucky	94–88	Duke	Arkansas	Notre Dame	Joe Hall
1979	Michigan St	75–64	Indiana St	DePaul	Penn	Jud Heathcote
1980	Louisville	59–54	Vacated‡	Purdue	Iowa	Denny Crum
1981	Indiana	63–50	North Carolina	Virginia	LSU	Bob Knight
1982	North Carolina	63–62	Georgetown	*Houston	*Louisville	Dean Smith
1983	North Carolina St	54–52	Houston	*Georgia	*Louisville	Jim Valvano
1984	Georgetown	84–75	Houston	*Kentucky	*Virginia	John Thompson
1985	Villanova	66–64	Georgetown	St. John's (N.Y.)	Vacated‡	Rollie Massimino
1986	Louisville	72–69	Duke	*Kansas	*LSU	Denny Crum
1987	Indiana	74–73	Syracuse	*UNLV	*Providence	Bob Knight
1988	Kansas	83–79	Oklahoma	*Arizona	*Duke	Larry Brown
1989	Michigan	80–79 (OT)	Seton Hall	*Duke	*Illinois	Steve Fisher
1990	UNLV	103–73	Duke	*Arkansas	*Georgia Tech	Jerry Tarkanian
1991	Duke	72–65	Kansas	*UNLV	*North Carolina	Mike Krzyzewski
1992	Duke	71–51	Michigan	*Cincinnati	*Indiana	Mike Krzyzewski
1993	North Carolina	77–71	Michigan	*Kansas	*Kentucky	Dean Smith
1994	Arkansas	76–72	Duke	*Arizona	*Florida	Nolan Richardson
1995	UCLA	89–78	Arkansas	*North Carolina	*Oklahoma St	Jim Harrick
1996	Kentucky	76–67	Syracuse	Vacated‡	Mississippi St	Rick Pitino
1997	Arizona	84–79 (OT)	Kentucky	Vacated‡	*North Carolina	Lute Olson
1998	Kentucky	78–69	Utah	*Stanford	*North Carolina	Tubby Smith
1999	Connecticut	77–74	Duke	*Michigan St	*Ohio St	Jim Calhoun
2000	Michigan St	89–76	Florida	*Wisconsin	*North Carolina	Tom Izzo
2001	Duke	82–72	Arizona	*Maryland	*Michigan St	Mike Krzyzewski

NCAA Final Four Results *(Cont.)*

Year	Winner	Score	Runner-up	Third Place	Fourth Place	Winning Coach
2002	Maryland	64–52	Indiana	*Kansas	*Oklahoma	Gary Williams
2003	Syracuse	81–78	Kansas	*Marquette	*Texas	Jim Boeheim
2004	Connecticut	82–73	Georgia Tech	*Oklahoma St	*Duke	Jim Calhoun
2005	North Carolina	75-70	Illinois	*Louisville	*Michigan St	Roy Williams
2006	Florida	73–57	UCLA	*George Mason	*LSU	Billy Donovan
2007	Florida	84–75	Ohio St	*UCLA	*Georgetown	Billy Donovan
2008	Kansas	75–68 (OT)	Vacated‡	*UCLA	*North Carolina	Bill Self
2009	North Carolina	89–72	Michigan St	*Villanova	*Connecticut	Roy Williams
2010	Duke	61–59	Butler	*West Virginia	*Michigan St	Mike Krzyzewski
2011	Connecticut	53–41	Butler	*Kentucky	*VCU	Jim Calhoun
2012	Kentucky	67–59	Kansas	*Ohio State	*Louisville	John Calipari

*Tied for third place. ‡Student-athletes representing St. Joseph's (Pa.) in 1961, Villanova in 1971, Western Kentucky in 1971, UCLA in 1980, Memphis State in 1985, Massachusetts in 1996, Minnesota in 1997 and Memphis in 2008 were declared ineligible subsequent to the tournament. Under NCAA rules, the teams' and ineligible student-athletes' records were deleted, and the teams' places in the standings were vacated.

NCAA Final Four Most Outstanding Players

			Field Goals		3-Pt FG		Free Throws						
Year	Winner, School	GP	FGM	Pct	FGA	FGM	FTM	Pct	Reb	Asst	Stl	BS	Avg
1939	None selected												
1940	Marv Huffman, Indiana	2	7	—	—	—	4	—	—	—	—	—	9.0
1941	John Kotz, Wisconsin	2	8	—	—	—	6	—	—	—	—	—	11.0
1942	Howard Dallmar, Stanford	2	8	—	—	—	4	66.7	—	—	—	—	10.0
1943	Ken Sailors, Wyoming	2	10	—	—	—	8	72.7	—	—	—	—	14.0
1944	Arnie Ferrin, Utah	2	11	—	—	—	6	—	—	—	—	—	14.0
1945	Bob Kurland, Oklahoma St	2	16	—	—	—	5	—	—	—	—	—	18.5
1946	Bob Kurland, Oklahoma St	2	21	—	—	—	10	66.7	—	—	—	—	26.0
1947	George Kaftan, Holy Cross	2	18	—	—	—	12	70.6	—	—	—	—	24.0
1948	Alex Groza, Kentucky	2	16	—	—	—	5	—	—	—	—	—	18.5
1949	Alex Groza, Kentucky	2	19	—	—	—	14	—	—	—	—	—	26.0
1950	Irwin Dambrot, CCNY	2	12	42.9	—	—	4	50.0	—	—	—	—	14.0
1951	None selected												
1952	Clyde Lovellette, Kansas	2	24	—	—	—	18	—	—	—	—	—	33.0
1953	*B.H. Horn, Kansas	2	17	—	—	—	17	—	—	—	—	—	25.5
1954	Tom Gola, La Salle	2	12	—	—	—	14	—	—	—	—	—	19.0
1955	Bill Russell, San Francisco	2	19	—	—	—	9	—	—	—	—	—	23.5
1956	*Hal Lear, Temple	2	32	—	—	—	16	—	—	—	—	—	40.0
1957	*Wilt Chamberlain, Kansas	2	18	51.4	—	—	19	70.4	25	—	—	—	32.5
1958	*Elgin Baylor, Seattle	2	18	34.0	—	—	12	75.0	41	—	—	—	24.0
1959	*Jerry West, West Virginia	2	22	66.7	—	—	22	68.8	25	—	—	—	33.0
1960	Jerry Lucas, Ohio St	2	16	66.7	—	—	3	100.0	23	—	—	—	17.5
1961	*Jerry Lucas, Ohio St	2	20	71.4	—	—	16	94.1	25	—	—	—	28.0
1962	Paul Hogue, Cincinnati	2	23	63.9	—	—	12	63.2	38	—	—	—	29.0
1963	Art Heyman, Duke	2	18	41.0	—	—	15	68.2	19	—	—	—	25.5
1964	Walt Hazzard, UCLA	2	11	55.0	—	—	8	66.7	10	—	—	—	15.0
1965	*Bill Bradley, Princeton	2	34	63.0	—	—	19	95.0	24	—	—	—	43.5
1966	*Jerry Chambers, Utah	2	25	53.2	—	—	20	83.3	35	—	—	—	35.0
1967	Lew Alcindor, UCLA	2	14	60.9	—	—	11	45.8	38	—	—	—	19.5
1968	Lew Alcindor, UCLA	2	22	62.9	—	—	9	90.0	34	—	—	—	26.5
1969	Lew Alcindor, UCLA	2	23	67.7	—	—	16	64.0	41	—	—	—	31.0
1970	Sidney Wicks, UCLA	2	15	71.4	—	—	9	60.0	34	—	—	—	19.5
1971	*†Howard Porter, Villanova	2	20	48.8	—	—	7	77.8	24	—	—	—	23.5
1972	Bill Walton, UCLA	2	20	69.0	—	—	17	73.9	41	—	—	—	28.5
1973	Bill Walton, UCLA	2	28	82.4	—	—	2	40.0	30	—	—	—	29.0
1974	David Thompson, NC St	2	19	51.4	—	—	11	78.6	17	—	—	—	24.5
1975	Richard Washington, UCLA	2	23	54.8	—	—	8	72.7	20	—	—	—	27.0
1976	Kent Benson, Indiana	2	17	50.0	—	—	7	63.6	18	—	—	—	20.5
1977	Butch Lee, Marquette	2	11	34.4	—	—	8	100.0	6	2	1	1	15.0
1978	Jack Givens, Kentucky	2	28	65.1	—	—	8	66.7	17	4	1	3	32.0
1979	Earvin Johnson, Michigan St	2	17	68.0	—	—	19	86.4	17	3	0	2	26.5
1980	Darrell Griffith, Louisville	2	23	62.2	—	—	11	68.8	7	15	0	2	28.5
1981	Isiah Thomas, Indiana	2	14	56.0	—	—	9	81.8	4	9	3	4	18.5
1982	James Worthy, North Carolina	2	20	74.1	—	—	2	28.6	8	9	0	4	21.0
1983	*Akeem Olajuwon, Houston	2	16	55.2	—	—	4	64.3	40	3	2	5	20.5
1984	Patrick Ewing, Georgetown	2	8	57.1	—	—	2	100.0	18	1	1	15	9.0
1985	Ed Pinckney, Villanova	2	8	57.1	—	—	12	75.0	15	6	3	0	14.0

*Not a member of the championship-winning team.   †Record later vacated.

NCAA Final Four Most Outstanding Players (Cont.)

Year	Winner, School	GP	Field Goals		3-Pt FG		Free Throws		Reb	Ast	Stl	BS	Avg
			FGM	Pct	FGA	FGM	FTM	Pct					
1986	Pervis Ellison, Louisville	2	15	60.0	—	—	6	75.0	24	2	3	1	18.0
1987	Keith Smart, Indiana	2	14	63.6	1	0	7	77.8	7	7	0	2	17.5
1988	Danny Manning, Kansas	2	25	55.6	1	0	6	66.7	17	4	8	9	28.0
1989	Glen Rice, Michigan	2	24	49.0	16	7	4	100.0	16	1	0	3	29.5
1990	Anderson Hunt, UNLV	2	19	61.3	16	9	2	50.0	4	9	1	1	24.5
1991	Christian Laettner, Duke	2	12	54.5	1	1	21	91.3	17	2	1	2	23.0
1992	Bobby Hurley, Duke	2	10	41.7	12	7	8	80.0	3	11	0	3	17.5
1993	Donald Williams, North Carolina	2	15	65.2	14	10	10	100.0	4	2	2	0	25.0
1994	Corliss Williamson, Arkansas	2	21	50.0	0	0	10	71.4	21	8	4	3	26.0
1995	Ed O'Bannon, UCLA	2	16	45.7	8	3	10	76.9	25	3	7	1	22.5
1996	Tony Delk, Kentucky	2	15	41.7	16	8	6	54.6	9	2	3	2	22.0
1997	Miles Simon, Arizona	2	17	45.9	10	3	17	77.3	8	6	0	1	27.0
1998	Jeff Sheppard, Kentucky	2	16	55.2	10	4	7	77.8	10	7	4	0	21.5
1999	Richard Hamilton, Connecticut	2	20	51.3	7	3	8	72.7	12	4	2	1	25.5
2000	Mateen Cleaves, Michigan St	2	8	44.4	4	3	10	83.3	6	5	2	0	14.5
2001	Shane Battier, Duke	2	13	50.0	12	5	12	70.6	19	8	2	6	21.5
2002	Juan Dixon, Maryland	2	16	59.3	15	7	12	80.0	8	5	7	0	25.5
2003	Carmelo Anthony, Syracuse	2	19	54.3	6	9	9	81.1	24	8	4	0	26.5
2004	Emeka Okafor, Connecticut	2	17	65.4	0	0	8	53.3	22	2	1	4	21.0
2005	Sean May, North Carolina	2	19	65.5	0	0	10	71.4	17	5	1	2	24.0
2006	Joakim Noah, Florida	2	12	60.0	1	0	4	100.0	17	5	2	10	14.0
2007	Corey Brewer, Florida	2	9	47.3	13	7	7	87.5	10	2	3	5	16.0
2008	Mario Chalmers, Kansas	2	10	43.5	9	3	6	75.0	7	6	7	0	14.5
2009	Wayne Ellington, North Carolina	2	14	53.8	11	8	3	75.0	13	4	0	0	19.5
2010	Kyle Singler, Duke	2	15	34.1	10	6	4	100.0	18	7	3	2	20.0
2011	Kemba Walker, Connecticut	2	11	32.4	9	1	11	84.6	15	7	3	1	17.0
2012	Anthony Davis, Kentucky	2	8	44.4	0	0	8	66.6	30	7	4	11	12.0

Best NCAA Tournament Single-Game Scoring Performances

Player and Team	Year	Round	FG	3FG	FT	TP
Austin Carr, Notre Dame vs Ohio	1970	1st	25	—	11	61
Bill Bradley, Princeton vs Wichita St	1965	C*	22	—	14	58
Oscar Robertson, Cincinnati vs Arkansas	1958	C	21	—	14	56
Austin Carr, Notre Dame vs Kentucky	1970	2nd	22	—	8	52
Austin Carr, Notre Dame vs TCU	1971	1st	20	—	12	52
David Robinson, Navy vs Michigan	1987	1st	22	0	6	50
Elvin Hayes, Houston vs Loyola (Ill.)	1968	1st	20	—	9	49
Hal Lear, Temple vs SMU	1956	C*	17	—	14	48
Austin Carr, Notre Dame vs Houston	1971	C	17	—	13	47
Dave Corzine, DePaul vs Louisville	1978	2nd	18	—	10	46

C=regional third place; C*=third-place game.

NIT Championship Results

Year	Winner	Score	Runner-up	Year	Winner	Score	Runner-up
1938	Temple	60–36	Colorado	1958	Xavier (Ohio)	78–74 (OT)	Dayton
1939	Long Island U.	44–32	Loyola (Ill.)	1959	St. John's (N.Y.)	76–71 (OT)	Bradley
1940	Colorado	51–40	Duquesne	1960	Bradley	88–72	Providence
1941	Long Island U.	56–42	Ohio U	1961	Providence	62–59	St. Louis
1942	West Virginia	47–45	W. Kentucky	1962	Dayton	73–67	St. John's (N.Y.)
1943	St. John's (N.Y.)	48–27	Toledo	1963	Providence	81–66	Canisius
1944	St. John's (N.Y.)	47–39	DePaul	1964	Bradley	86–54	New Mexico
1945	DePaul	71–54	Bowling Green	1965	St. John's (N.Y.)	55–51	Villanova
1946	Kentucky	46–45	Rhode Island	1966	BYU	97–84	NYU
1947	Utah	49–45	Kentucky	1967	Southern Illinois	71–56	Marquette
1948	St. Louis	65–52	NYU	1968	Dayton	61–48	Kansas
1949	San Francisco	48–47	Loyola (Ill.)	1969	Temple	89–76	Boston College
1950	CCNY	69–61	Bradley	1970	Marquette	65–53	St. John's (N.Y.)
1951	BYU	62–43	Dayton	1971	North Carolina	84–66	Georgia Tech
1952	La Salle	75–64	Dayton	1972	Maryland	100–69	Niagara
1953	Seton Hall	58–46	St. John's (N.Y.)	1973	Virginia Tech	92–91 (OT)	Notre Dame
1954	Holy Cross	71–62	Duquesne	1974	Purdue	97–81	Utah
1955	Duquesne	70–58	Dayton	1975	Princeton	80–69	Providence
1956	Louisville	93–80	Dayton	1976	Kentucky	71–67	UNC-Charlotte
1957	Bradley	84–83	Memphis St	1977	St. Bonaventure	94–91	Houston

NIT Championship Results *(Cont.)*

Year	Winner	Score	Runner-up	Year	Winner	Score	Runner-up
1978	Texas	101–93	North Carolina St	1996	Nebraska	60–56	St. Joseph's
1979	Indiana	53–52	Purdue	1997	Michigan	82–73	Florida St
1980	Virginia	58–55	Minnesota	1998	Minnesota	79–72	Penn St
1981	Tulsa	86–84 (OT)	Syracuse	1999	California	61–60	Clemson
1982	Bradley	67–58	Purdue	2000	Wake Forest	71–61	Notre Dame
1983	Fresno St	69–60	DePaul	2001	Tulsa	79–60	Alabama
1984	Michigan	83–63	Notre Dame	2002	Memphis	72–62	South Carolina
1985	UCLA	65–62	Indiana	2003	St. John's	70–67	Georgetown
1986	Ohio St	73–63	Wyoming	2004	Michigan	62–55	Rutgers
1987	Southern Miss	84–80	La Salle	2005	South Carolina	60–57	Saint Joseph's
1988	Connecticut	72–67	Ohio St	2006	South Carolina	76–64	Michigan
1989	St. John's (N.Y.)	73–65	St. Louis	2007	West Virginia	78–73	Clemson
1990	Vanderbilt	74–72	St. Louis	2008	Ohio St	92–85	Massachusetts
1991	Stanford	78–72	Oklahoma	2009	Penn St	69–63	Baylor
1992	Virginia	81–76	Notre Dame	2010	Dayton	79–68	North Carolina
1993	Minnesota	62–61	Georgetown	2011	Wichita St	66–57	Alabama
1994	Villanova	80–73	Vanderbilt	2012	Stanford	75–51	Minnesota
1995	Virginia Tech	65–64 (OT)	Marquette				

NCAA Men's Division I Season Leaders

Scoring Average

Year	Player and Team	Ht	Class	GP	FG	3FG	FT	Pts	Avg
1949	Murray Wier, Iowa	5-9	Sr.	19	152	—	95	399	21.0
1950	Tony Lavelli, Yale	6-3	Sr.	30	228	—	215	671	22.4
1951	Paul Arizin, Villanova	6-3	Sr.	29	260	—	215	735	25.3
1952	Bill Mlkvy, Temple	6-4	Sr.	25	303	—	125	731	29.2
1953	Clyde Lovellette, Kansas	6-9	Sr.	28	315	—	165	795	28.4
1954	Frank Selvy, Furman	6-3	Jr.	25	272	—	194	738	29.5
1955	Frank Selvy, Furman	6-3	Sr.	29	427	—	355	1209	41.7
1956	Darrell Floyd, Furman	6-1	Jr.	25	344	—	209	897	35.9
1957	Darrell Floyd, Furman	6-1	Sr.	28	339	—	268	946	33.8
1958	Grady Wallace, South Carolina	6-4	Sr.	29	336	—	234	906	31.2
1959	Oscar Robertson, Cincinnati	6-5	So.	28	352	—	280	984	35.1
1960	Oscar Robertson, Cincinnati	6-5	Jr.	30	331	—	316	978	32.6
1961	Oscar Robertson, Cincinnati	6-5	Sr.	30	369	—	273	1011	33.7
1962	Frank Burgess, Gonzaga	6-1	Sr.	26	304	—	234	842	32.4
1963	Billy McGill, Utah	6-9	Sr.	26	394	—	221	1009	38.8
1964	Nick Werkman, Seton Hall	6-3	Jr.	22	221	—	208	650	29.5
1965	Howard Komives, Bowling Green	6-1	Sr.	23	292	—	260	844	36.7
1966	Rick Barry, Miami (Fla.)	6-7	Sr.	26	340	—	293	973	37.4
1967	Dave Schellhase, Purdue	6-4	Sr.	24	284	—	213	781	32.5
1968	Jim Walker, Providence	6-3	Sr.	28	323	—	205	851	30.4
1969	Pete Maravich, LSU	6-5	So.	26	432	—	274	1138	43.8
1970	Pete Maravich, LSU	6-5	Jr.	26	433	—	282	1148	44.2
1971	Pete Maravich, LSU	6-5	Sr.	31	522	—	337	1381	44.5
1972	Johnny Neumann, Mississippi	6-6	So.	23	366	—	191	923	40.1
1973	Dwight Lamar, SW Louisiana	6-1	Jr.	29	429	—	196	1054	36.3
1974	William Averitt, Pepperdine	6-1	Sr.	25	352	—	144	848	33.9
1975	Larry Fogle, Canisius	6-5	So.	25	326	—	183	835	33.4
1976	Bob McCurdy, Richmond	6-7	Sr.	26	321	—	213	855	32.9
1977	Marshall Rodgers, Tex.-Pan American	6-2	Sr.	25	361	—	197	919	36.8
1978	Freeman Williams, Portland St	6-4	Jr.	26	417	—	176	1010	38.8
1979	Freeman Williams, Portland St	6-4	Sr.	27	410	—	149	969	35.9
1990	Lawrence Butler, Idaho St	6-3	Sr.	27	310	—	192	812	30.1
1981	Tony Murphy, Southern-Birmingham	6-3	Sr.	29	377	—	178	932	32.1
1982	Zam Fredrick, South Carolina	6-2	Sr.	27	300	—	181	781	28.9
1983	Harry Kelly, Texas Southern	6-7	Jr.	29	336	—	190	862	29.7
1984	Harry Kelly, Texas Southern	6-7	Sr.	29	333	—	169	835	28.8
1985	Joe Jakubick, Akron	6-5	Sr.	27	304	—	206	814	30.1
1986	Xavier McDaniel, Wichita St	6-8	Sr.	31	351	—	142	844	27.2
1987	Terrance Bailey, Wagner	6-2	Jr.	29	321	—	212	854	29.4
1988	Kevin Houston, Army	5-11	Sr.	29	311	63	268	953	32.9
1989	Hersey Hawkins, Bradley	6-3	Sr.	31	377	87	284	1125	36.3
1990	Hank Gathers, Loyola Marymount	6-7	Jr.	31	419	0	177	1015	32.7
1991	Bo Kimble, Loyola Marymount	6-5	Sr.	32	404	92	231	1131	35.3

Scoring Average (Cont.)

Year	Player and Team	Ht	Class	GP	FG	3FG	FT	Pts	Avg
1992	Kevin Bradshaw, U.S. Int'l	6-6	Sr.	28	358	60	278	1054	37.6
1993	Brett Roberts, Morehead St	6-8	Sr.	29	278	66	193	815	28.1
1994	Greg Guy, Tex.-Pan American	6-1	Jr.	19	189	67	111	556	29.3
1995	Glenn Robinson, Purdue	6-8	Jr.	34	368	79	215	1030	30.3
1996	Kurt Thomas, TCU	6-9	Sr.	27	288	3	202	781	28.9
1997	Kevin Granger, Texas Southern	6-3	Sr.	24	194	30	230	648	27.0
1998	Charles Jones, LIU-Brooklyn	6-3	Jr.	30	338	109	118	903	30.1
1999	Charles Jones, LIU-Brooklyn	6-3	Sr.	30	326	116	101	869	29.0
2000	Alvin Young, Niagara	6-3	Sr.	29	253	65	157	728	25.1
2001	Courtney Alexander, Fresno St	6-6	Sr.	27	252	58	107	669	24.8
2002	Ronnie McCollum, Centenary	6-4	Sr.	27	244	85	214	787	29.1
2003	Jason Conley, Virginia Military	6-5	Fr.	28	285	79	171	820	29.3
2004	Ruben Douglas, New Mexico	6-5	Sr.	28	218	94	253	783	28.0
2005	Keydren Clark, St. Peter's	5-9	So.	29	233	112	197	775	26.7
2006	Keydren Clark, St. Peter's	5-9	Jr.	28	230	109	152	721	25.8
2007	Adam Morrison, Gonzaga	6-8	Jr.	33	306	74	240	926	28.1
2008	Reggie Williams, Virginia Military Institute	6-5	Jr.	33	338	76	176	928	28.1
2009	Stephen Curry, Davidson	6-3	Jr.	34	312	130	220	974	28.6
2010	Aubrey Coleman, Houston	6-4	Sr.	35	305	51	235	896	25.6
2011	Jimmer Fredette, BYU	6-2	Sr.	37	346	124	252	1068	28.9
2012	Reggie Hamilton, Oakland	5-11	Sr.	36	281	118	262	942	26.2

Rebounds

Year	Player and Team	Ht	Class	GP	Reb	Avg
1952	Ernie Beck, Pennsylvania	6-4	So.	27	556	20.6
1953	Bill Hannon, Army	6-3	So.	17	355	20.9
1954	Ed Conlin, Fordham	6-5	So.	26	612	23.5
1955	Art Quimby, Connecticut	6-5	Jr.	26	588	22.6
1956	Charlie Slack, Marshall	6-5	Jr.	21	538	25.6
1957	Joe Holup, George Washington	6-6	Sr.	26	604	†.256
1958	Elgin Baylor, Seattle	6-6	Jr.	25	508	†.235
1959	Alex Ellis, Niagara	6-5	Sr.	25	536	†.262
1960	Leroy Wright, Pacific	6-8	Jr.	26	652	†.238
1961	Leroy Wright, Pacific	6-8	Sr.	17	380	†.234
1961	Jerry Lucas, Ohio St	6-8	Jr.	27	470	†.198
1963	Jerry Lucas, Ohio St	6-8	Sr.	28	499	†.211
1964	Paul Silas, Creighton	6-7	Sr.	27	557	20.6
1965	Bob Pelkington, Xavier (Ohio)	6-7	Sr.	26	567	21.8
1966	Toby Kimball, Connecticut	6-8	Sr.	23	483	21.0
1967	Jim Ware, Oklahoma City	6-8	Sr.	29	607	20.9
1968	Dick Cunningham, Murray St	6-10	Jr.	22	479	21.8
1969	Neal Walk, Florida	6-10	Jr.	25	494	19.8
1970	Spencer Haywood, Detroit	6-8	So.	22	472	21.5
1971	Artis Gilmore, Jacksonville	7-2	Jr.	28	621	22.2
1972	Artis Gilmore, Jacksonville	7-2	Sr.	26	603	23.2
1973	Kermit Washington, American	6-8	Jr.	23	455	19.8
1974	Kermit Washington, American	6-8	Sr.	22	439	20.0
1975	Marvin Barnes, Providence	6-9	Sr.	32	597	18.7
1976	John Irving, Hofstra	6-9	So.	21	323	15.4
1977	Sam Pellom, Buffalo	6-8	So.	26	420	16.2
1978	Glenn Mosley, Seton Hall	6-8	Sr.	29	473	16.3
1979	Ken Williams, North Texas St	6-7	Sr.	28	411	14.7
1980	Monti Davis, Tennessee St	6-7	Jr.	26	421	16.2
1981	Larry Smith, Alcorn St	6-8	Sr.	26	392	15.1
1982	Darryl Watson, Miss. Valley St	6-7	Sr.	27	379	14.0
1983	LaSalle Thompson, Texas	6-10	Jr.	27	365	13.5
1984	Xavier McDaniel, Wichita St	6-7	So.	28	403	14.4
1985	Akeem Olajuwon, Houston	7-0	Jr.	37	500	13.5
1986	Xavier McDaniel, Wichita St	6-7	Sr	31	460	14.8
1987	David Robinson, Navy	6-11	Jr.	35	455	13.0
1988	Jerome Lane, Pittsburgh	6-6	So.	33	444	13.5
1989	Kenny Miller, Loyola (Ill.)	6-9	Fr.	29	395	13.6
1990	Hank Gathers, Loyola (Calif.)	6-7	Jr.	31	426	13.7
1991	Anthony Bonner, St. Louis	6-8	Sr.	33	456	13.8
1992	Shaquille O'Neal, LSU	7-1	So.	28	411	14.7
1993	Popeye Jones, Murray St	6-8	Sr.	30	431	14.4

Rebounds *(Cont.)*

Year	Player and Team	Ht	Class	GP	Reb	Avg
1994	Warren Kidd, Middle Tenn. St	6-9	Sr.	26	386	14.8
1995	Jerome Lambert, Baylor	6-8	Jr.	24	355	14.8
1996	Kurt Thomas, TCU	6-9	Sr.	27	393	14.6
1997	Marcus Mann, Miss. Valley St	6-8	Sr.	29	394	13.6
1998	Tim Duncan, Wake Forest	6-11	Sr.	31	457	14.7
1999	Ryan Perryman, Dayton	6-7	Sr.	33	412	12.5
2000	Ian McGinnis, Dartmouth	6-8	So.	26	317	12.2
2001	Darren Phillips, Fairfield	6-7	Sr.	29	405	14.0
2002	Chris Marcus, Western Kentucky	7-1	Jr.	31	374	12.1
2003	Jeremy Bishop, Quinnipiac	6-6	J..	29	347	12.0
2004	Brandon Hunter, Ohio	6-7	Sr.	30	378	12.6
2005	Paul Millsap, Louisiana Tech	6-7	Fr.	30	374	12.5
2006	Paul Millsap, Louisiana Tech	6-8	So.	29	360	12.4
2007	Paul Millsap, Louisiana Tech	6-8	Jr.	33	438	13.3
2008	Rashad Jones-Jennings, Ark.-Little Rock	6-8	Sr.	30	392	13.3
2009	Blake Griffin, Oklahoma	6-10	So.	35	504	14.4
2010	Artsiom Parakhouski, Radford	6-11	Sr.	31	414	13.4
2011	Kenneth Faried, Morehead St	6-8	Sr.	35	508	14.5
2012	O.D. Anosike, Siena	6-8	Jr.	31	388	12.5

†From 1956–1962, title was based on highest individual recoveries out of total by both teams in all games.

Assists

Year	Player and Team	Class	GP	Ast	Avg
1985	Craig Lathen, Ill.-Chicago	Jr.	29	274	9.45
1986	Rob Weingard, Hofstra	Sr.	24	228	9.50
1987	Mark Jackson, St. John's (N.Y.)	Jr.	36	328	9.11
1988	Avery Johnson, Southern-Birm.	Jr.	31	333	10.74
1989	Avery Johnson, Southern-Birm.	Sr.	30	399	13.30
1990	Glenn Williams, Holy Cross	Sr.	28	278	9.93
1991	Todd Lehmann, Drexel	Sr.	28	260	9.29
1992	Chris Corchiani, North Carolina St	Sr.	31	299	9.65
1993	Van Usher, Tennessee Tech	Sr.	29	254	8.76
1994	Sam Crawford, New Mexico St	Sr.	34	310	9.12
1995	Jason Kidd, California	So.	30	272	9.06
1996	Nelson Haggerty, Baylor	Sr.	28	284	10.10
1997	Raimonds Miglinieks, UC-Irvine	Sr.	27	230	8.52
1998	Kenny Mitchell, Dartmouth	Sr.	26	203	7.81
1999	Ahlon Lewis, Arizona St	Sr.	32	294	9.19
2000	Doug Gottlieb, Oklahoma St	Jr.	34	299	8.79
2001	Mark Dickel, UNLV	Sr.	31	280	9.03
2002	Markus Carr, CSU-Northridge	Jr.	32	286	8.94
2003	T.J. Ford, Texas	Fr.	33	273	8.27
2004	Martell Bailey, Ill.-Chicago	Jr.	30	244	8.13
2005	Greg Davis, Troy St	Sr.	31	256	8.26
2006	Damitrius Coleman, Mercer	Jr.	28	224	8.00
	Will Funn, Portland St	Sr.	28	224	8.00
2007	Jared Jordan, Marist	Jr.	29	247	8.52
2008	Jared Jordan, Marist	Sr.	31	274	8.83
2009	Johnathon Jones, Oakland	Jr.	36	290	8.06
2010	Ronald Moore, Siena	Sr.	34	261	7.68
2011	Aaron Johnson, UAB	Sr.	31	239	7.71
2012	Scott Machado, Iona	Sr.	33	327	9.9

Blocked Shots

Year	Player and Team	Class	GP	BS	Avg
1986	David Robinson, Navy	Jr.	35	207	5.91
1987	David Robinson, Navy	Sr.	32	144	4.50
1988	Rodney Blake, St. Joseph's (Pa.)	Sr.	29	116	4.00
1989	Alonzo Mourning, Georgetown	Fr.	34	169	4.97
1990	Kenny Green, Rhode Island	Sr.	26	124	4.77
1991	Shawn Bradley, BYU	Fr.	34	177	5.21
1992	Shaquille O'Neal, LSU	Jr.	30	157	5.23
1993	Theo Ratliff, Wyoming	Jr.	28	124	4.43
1994	Grady Livingston, Howard	Jr.	26	115	4.42
1995	Keith Closs, Central Conn. St	Fr.	26	139	5.35
1996	Keith Closs, Central Conn. St	So.	28	178	6.36
1997	Adonal Foyle, Colgate	Jr.	28	180	6.43
1998	Jerome James, Florida A&M	Sr.	27	125	4.63
1999	Tarvis Williams, Hampton	So.	27	135	5.00
2000	Ken Johnson, Ohio St	Sr.	30	161	5.37
2001	Tarvis Williams, Hampton	Sr	32	147	4.59
2002	Wojciech Myrda, La.-Monroe	Sr.	32	172	5.38
2003	Emeka Okafor, Connecticut	So.	33	156	4.73
2004	Anwar Ferguson, Houston	Sr.	27	111	4.11
2005	Deng Gai, Fairfield	Sr.	30	165	5.50
2006	Shawn James, Northeastern	So.	30	196	6.53
2007	Mickell Gladness, Ala.-A&M	Jr.	30	188	6.26
2008	Jarvis Varnado, Mississippi St	So.	34	157	4.62
2009	Jarvis Varnado, Mississippi St	Jr.	36	170	4.72
2010	Hassan Whiteside, Marshall	Fr.	34	182	5.35
2011	William Mosley, Northwestern St	Jr.	32	156	4.88
2012	Anthony Davis, Kentucky	Fr.	40	186	4.65

Steals

Year	Player and Team	Class	GP	Stl	Avg
1987	Darron Brittman, Chicago St	Sr.	28	139	4.96
1988	Tony Fairley, Charleston South.	Sr.	28	114	4.07
1989	Aldwin Ware, Florida A&M	Sr.	29	142	4.90
1990	Kenny Robertson, Cleveland St	Jr.	28	111	3.96
1991	Ronn McMahon, E. Washington	Sr.	29	130	4.48
1992	Van Usher, Tennessee Tech	Jr.	28	104	3.71
1993	Victor Snipes, NE Illinois	So.	25	86	3.44
1994	Jason Kidd, California	Fr.	29	110	3.80
1995	Shawn Griggs, SW Louisiana	Sr.	30	120	4.00
1996	Roderick Anderson, Texas	Sr.	30	101	3.37
1997	Pointer Williams, McNeese St	Sr.	27	118	4.37
1998	Joel Hoover, Md.-Eastern Shore	Fr.	28	90	3.21
1999	Bonzi Wells, Ball St	Sr.	29	103	3.55
2000	Shawnta Rogers, George Wash.	Sr.	29	103	3.55
2001	Carl Williams, Liberty	Sr.	28	107	3.82
2002	Greedy Daniels, TCU	Jr.	25	108	4.32
2003	Desmond Cambridge, Ala. A&M	Sr.	29	160	5.52
2004	Alexis McMillan, Stetson	Sr.	22	87	3.95
2005	Marques Green, St. Bonaventure	Sr.	27	107	3.96
2006	Obie Trotter, Alabama A&M	Jr.	32	125	3.91
2007	Tim Smith, East Tennessee St	Sr.	28	95	3.39
2008	Travis Holmes, Virg. Mil. Inst.	So.	33	111	3.36
2009	Chavis Holmes, Virg. Mil. Inst.	Sr.	31	105	3.39
2010	Jay Threatt, Delaware St	So.	29	82	2.83
2011	Anthony Nelson, Niagara	Sr.	29	98	3.38
2012	Fuquan Edwin, Seton Hall	So.	34	102	3.00

Single Game Records

SCORING HIGHS VS DIVISION I OPPONENT

Pts	Player and Team vs Opponent	Date
72	Kevin Bradshaw, U.S. Int'l vs Loyola Marymount	1-5-91
69	Pete Maravich, LSU vs Alabama	2-7-70
68	Calvin Murphy, Niagara vs Syracuse	12-7-68
66	Jay Handlan, Washington & Lee vs Furman	2-17-51
66	Pete Maravich, LSU vs Tulane	2-10-69
66	Anthony Roberts, Oral Roberts vs North Carolina A&T	2-19-77
65	Anthony Roberts, Oral Roberts vs Oregon	3-9-77
65	Scott Haffner, Evansville vs Dayton	2-18-89
64	Pete Maravich, LSU vs Kentucky	2-21-70
63	Johnny Neumann, Mississippi vs LSU	1-30-71
63	Hersey Hawkins, Bradley vs Detroit	2-22-88

SCORING HIGHS VS NON-DIVISION I OPPONENT

Pts	Player and Team vs Opponent	Date
100	Frank Selvy, Furman vs Newberry	2-13-54
85	Paul Arizin, Villanova vs Philadelphia NAMC	2-12-49
81	Freeman Williams, Portland St vs Rocky Mountain	2-3-78
73	Bill Mlkvy, Temple vs Wilkes	3-3-51
71	Freeman Williams, Portland St vs S. Oregon	2-9-77

REBOUNDING HIGHS ALL-TIME

Reb	Player and Team vs Opponent	Date
51	Bill Chambers, William & Mary vs Virginia	2-14-53
43	Charlie Slack, Marshall vs Morris Harvey	1-12-54
42	Tom Heinsohn, Holy Cross vs Boston College	3-1-55
40	Art Quimby, Connecticut vs Boston University	1-11-55
39	Maurice Stokes, St. Francis (Pa.) vs John Carroll	1-28-55
39	Dave DeBusschere, Detroit vs C. Michigan	1-30-60
39	Keith Swagerty, Pacific vs UC-Santa Barbara	3-5-65

REBOUNDING HIGHS SINCE 1973*

Reb	Player and Team vs Opponent	Date
35	Larry Abney, Fresno St vs SMU	2-17-00
34	David Vaughn, Oral Roberts vs Brandeis	1-8-73
32	Jervaughn Scales, Southern-Birm. vs Grambling	2-7-94
32	Durand Macklin, LSU vs Tulane	11-26-76
31	Jim Bradley, Northern Illinois vs UW-Milwaukee	2-19-73
31	Calvin Natt, NE Louisiana vs Georgia Southern	12-29-76

ASSISTS

Asst	Player and Team vs Opponent	Date
22	Tony Fairley, Baptist vs Armstrong St	2-9-87
22	Avery Johnson, Southern-Birm. vs Texas Southern	1-25-88
22	Sherman Douglas, Syracuse vs Providence	1-28-89
21	Kelvin Scarborough, New Mexico vs Hawaii	2-13-87
21	Anthony Manuel, Bradley vs UC-Irvine	12-19-87
21	Avery Johnson, Southern-Birm. vs Alabama St	1-16-88

STEALS

Stl	Player and Team vs Opponent	Date
13	Mookie Blaylock, Oklahoma vs Centenary	12-12-87
13	Mookie Blaylock, Oklahoma vs Loyola Marymount	12-17-88
12	Kenny Robertson, Cleveland St vs Wagner	12-3-88
12	Terry Evans, Oklahoma vs Florida A&M	1-27-93
12	Richard Duncan, Middle Tenn. St vs Eastern Kentucky	2-20-99
12	Greedy Daniels, Texas Christian vs Ark.–Pine Bluff	12-30-00
12	Jehiel Lewis, Navy vs Bucknell	1-12-02
12	Carldell Johnson, Ala.-Birmingham vs. South Carolina St	11-27-05

BLOCKED SHOTS

BS	Player and Team vs Opponent	Date
16	Mickell Gladness, Alabama A&M vs Texas Southern	2-24-07
14	David Robinson, Navy vs UNC–Wilmington	1-4-86
14	Shawn Bradley, BYU vs Eastern Kentucky	12-7-90
14	Roy Rogers, Alabama vs Georgia	2-10-96
14	Loren Woods, Arizona vs Oregon	2-3-00
14	Darrius Garrett, Richmond vs Massachusetts	1-13-10

Eleven players tied with 13

Single Season Records

POINTS

Player and Team	Year	GP	FG	3FG	FT	Pts
Pete Maravich, LSU	1970	31	522	—	337	1381
Elvin Hayes, Houston	1968	33	519	—	176	1214
Frank Selvy, Furman	1954	29	427	—	355	1209
Pete Maravich, LSU	1969	26	433	—	282	1148
Pete Maravich, LSU	1968	26	432	—	274	1138
Bo Kimble, Loyola Marymount	1990	32	404	92	231	1131
Hersey Hawkins, Bradley	1988	31	377	87	284	1125
Austin Carr, Notre Dame	1970	29	444	—	218	1106
Austin Carr, Notre Dame	1971	29	430	—	241	1101
Otis Birdsong, Houston	1977	36	452	—	186	1090

SCORING AVERAGE

Player and Team	Year	GP	FG	FT	Pts	Avg
Pete Maravich, LSU	1970	31	522	337	1381	44.5
Pete Maravich, LSU	1969	26	433	282	1148	44.2
Pete Maravich, LSU	1968	26	432	274	1138	43.8
Frank Selvy, Furman	1954	29	427	355	1209	41.7
Johnny Neumann, Mississippi	1971	23	366	191	923	40.1
Freeman Williams, Portland St	1977	26	417	176	1010	38.8
Billy McGill, Utah	1962	26	394	221	1009	38.8
Calvin Murphy, Niagara	1968	24	337	242	916	38.2
Austin Carr, Notre Dame	1970	29	444	218	1106	38.1
Austin Carr, Notre Dame	1971	29	430	241	1101	38.0

REBOUNDS

Player and Team	Year	GP	Reb	Player and Team	Year	GP	Reb
Walt Dukes, Seton Hall	1953	33	734	Artis Gilmore, Jacksonville	1970	28	621
Leroy Wright, Pacific	1959	26	652	Tom Gola, La Salle	1955	31	618
Tom Gola, La Salle	1954	30	652	Ed Conlin, Fordham	1953	26	612
Charlie Tyra, Louisville	1956	29	645	Art Quimby, Connecticut	1955	25	611
Paul Silas, Creighton	1964	29	631	Bill Russell, San Francisco	1956	29	609
Elvin Hayes, Houston	1968	33	624	Jim Ware, Oklahoma City	1966	29	607

REBOUND AVERAGE ALL-TIME

Player and Team	Year	GP	Reb	Avg
Charlie Slack, Marshall	1955	21	538	25.6
Leroy Wright, Pacific	1959	26	652	25.1
Art Quimby, Connecticut	1955	25	611	24.4
Charlie Slack, Marshall	1956	22	520	23.6
Ed Conlin, Fordham	1953	26	612	23.5

REBOUND AVERAGE SINCE 1973*

Player and Team	Year	GP	Reb	Avg
Kermit Washington, American	1973	22	439	20.0
Marvin Barnes, Providence	1973	30	571	19.0
Marvin Barnes, Providence	1974	32	597	18.7
Pete Padgett, Nev.-Reno	1973	26	462	17.8
Jim Bradley, Northern Illinois	1973	24	426	17.8

ASSISTS

Player and Team	Year	GP	Asst	Player and Team	Year	GP	Asst
Mark Wade, UNLV	1987	38	406	Mark Jackson, St. John's (N.Y.)	1986	32	328
Avery Johnson, Southern-Birm	1988	30	399	Scott Machado, Iona	2012	33	327
Anthony Manuel, Bradley	1988	31	373	Sherman Douglas, Syracuse	1989	38	326
Kendall Marshall, North Carolina	2012	36	351	Sam Crawford, New Mex. St	1993	34	310
Avery Johnson, Southern-Birm	1987	31	333	Greg Anthony, UNLV	1991	35	310
				Reid Gettys, Houston	1984	37	309

ASSIST AVERAGE

Player and Team	Year	GP	Asst	Avg	Player and Team	Year	GP	Asst	Avg
Avery Johnson, Southern-Birm.	1988	30	399	13.3	Scott Machado, Iona	2012	33	327	9.9
Anthony Manuel, Bradley	1988	31	373	12.0	Kendall Marshall, North Carolina	2012	36	351	9.75
Avery Johnson, Southern-Birm.	1987	31	333	10.7	Chris Corchiani, North Carolina St.	1991	31	299	9.6
Mark Wade, UNLV	1987	38	406	10.7	Tony Fairley, Charleston South.†	1987	28	270	9.6
Nelson Haggerty, Baylor	1995	28	284	10.1	Tyrone Bogues, Wake Forest	1987	29	276	9.5
Glenn Williams, Holy Cross	1989	28	278	9.9	Ron Weingard, Hofstra	1985	24	228	9.5

*Freshmen became eligible for varsity play in 1973. †Formerly Baptist College.

Single Season Records *(Cont.)*

FIELD-GOAL PERCENTAGE

Player and Team	Year	GP	FG	FGA	Pct
Steve Johnson, Oregon St	1981	28	235	315	74.6
Dwayne Davis, Florida	1989	33	179	248	72.2
Keith Walker, Utica	1985	27	154	216	71.3
Steve Johnson, Oregon St	1980	30	211	297	71.0
Adam Mark, Belmont	2002	26	150	212	70.8
Oliver Miller, Arkansas	1991	38	254	361	70.4
Alan Williams, Princeton	1987	25	163	232	70.3
Mark McNamara, California	1982	27	231	329	70.2
Warren Kidd, Middle Tennessee St	1991	30	173	247	70.0
Pete Freeman, Akron	1991	28	175	250	70.0

Based on qualifiers for NCAA annual championship.

FREE-THROW PERCENTAGE

Player and Team	Year	GP	FT	FTA	Pct
Blake Ahearn, SW Missouri St†	2004	33	117	120	97.5
Ryan Toolson, Utah Valley St.	2006	29	96	99	97.0
Derek Raivio, Gonzaga	2006	33	146	152	96.1
Craig Collins, Penn St	1985	27	94	98	95.9
A.J. Graves, Butler	2006	32	137	143	95.8
J.J. Redick, Duke	2004	37	143	150	95.3
Steve Drabyn, Belmont	2003	29	78	82	95.1
Donald Sims, Appalachian St	2009	37	175	184	95.1
Rod Foster, UCLA	1982	27	95	100	95.0
Clay McKnight, Pacific	2000	24	74	78	94.9
Matt Logie, Lehigh	2003	28	91	96	94.8

THREE-POINT FIELD-GOAL PERCENTAGE

Player and Team	Year	GP	3FG	3FGA	Pct
Glenn Tropf, Holy Cross	1988	29	52	82	63.4
Sean Wightman, Western Michigan	1992	30	48	76	63.2
Keith Jennings, East Tennessee St	1991	33	84	142	59.2
Dave Calloway, Monmouth (N.J.)	1989	28	48	82	58.5
Steve Kerr, Arizona	1988	38	114	199	57.3
Reginald Jones, Prairie View	1987	28	64	112	57.1
Jim Cantamessa, Siena	1998	29	66	117	56.4
Joel Tribelhorn, Colorado St	1989	33	76	135	56.3
Mike Joseph, Bucknell	1988	28	65	116	56.0
Brian Jackson, Evansville	1995	27	53	95	55.8

Based on qualifiers for annual championship.

STEALS

Player and Team	Year	GP	Stl
Desmond Cambridge, Alabama A&M	2002	29	160
Mookie Blaylock, Oklahoma	1988	39	150
Aldwin Ware, Florida A&M	1988	29	142
Darron Brittman, Chicago St	1986	28	139
John Linehan, Providence	2002	31	139

BLOCKED SHOTS

Player and Team	Year	GP	BS
David Robinson, Navy	1986	35	207
Shawn James, Northeastern	2005	30	196
Mickell Gladness, Alabama A&M	2006	30	188
Anthony Davis, Kentucky	2012	40	186
Hassan Whiteside, Marshall	2010	34	182

STEAL AVERAGE

Player and Team	Year	GP	Stl	Avg
D. Cambridge, Alabama A&M	2002	29	160	5.52
Darron Brittman, Chicago St	1986	28	139	4.96
Aldwin Ware, Florida A&M	1988	29	142	4.90
John Linehan, Providence	2002	31	139	4.48
Ronn McMahon, E. Washington	1990	29	130	4.48

BLOCKED-SHOT AVERAGE

Player and Team	Year	GP	BS	Avg
Shawn James, Northeastern	2005	30	196	6.53
Adonal Foyle, Colgate	1997	28	180	6.43
Keith Closs, Central Conn. St	1996	28	178	6.36
Mickell Gladness, Alabama A&M	2006	30	188	6.26
David Robinson, Navy	1986	35	207	5.91

†Southwest Missouri State changed name to Missouri State after 2004–05 season.
Based on qualifiers for annual championship.

Career Records

POINTS

Player and Team	Ht	Final Year	GP	FG	3FG*	FT	Pts
Pete Maravich, LSU	6-5	1970	83	1387	—	893	3667
Freeman Williams, Portland St.	6-4	1978	106	1369	—	511	3249
Lionel Simmons, La Salle	6-7	1990	131	1244	56	673	3217
Alphonso Ford, Mississippi Valley St	6-2	1993	109	1121	333	590	3165
Harry Kelly, Texas Southern	6-7	1983	110	1234	—	598	3066
Keydren Clark, St. Peter's	5-9	2006	118	967	435	689	3058
Hersey Hawkins, Bradley	6-3	1988	125	1100	118	690	3008
Oscar Robertson, Cincinnati	6-5	1960	88	1052	—	869	2973
Danny Manning, Kansas	6-10	1988	147	1216	10	509	2951
Alfredrick Hughes, Loyola (Ill.)	6-5	1985	120	1226	—	462	2914
Elvin Hayes, Houston	6-8	1968	93	1215	—	454	2884
Tyler Hansbrough, North Carolina	6-9	2009	142	939	12	982	2872
Larry Bird, Indiana St.	6-9	1979	94	1154	—	542	2850
Otis Birdsong, Houston	6-4	1977	116	1176	—	480	2832
Kevin Bradshaw, Bethune-Cookman, U.S. Int'l	6-6	1991	111	1027	132	618	2804
Allan Houston, Tennessee	6-6	1993	128	902	346	651	2801
J.J. Redick, Duke	6-4	2006	139	825	457	662	2769
Hank Gathers, USC, Loyola Marymount	6-7	1990	117	1127	0	469	2723
Reggie Lewis, Northeastern	6-7	1987	122	1043	30 (1)	592	2708
Daren Queenan, Lehigh	6-5	1988	118	1024	29	626	2703

*Listed is the number of three-pointers scored since it became the national rule in 1987; the number in the parentheses is number scored prior to 1987—these counted as three points in the game but counted as two-pointers in the national rankings. The three-pointers in the parentheses are not included in total points.

SCORING AVERAGE

Player and Team	Final Year	GP	FG	FT	Pts	Avg
Pete Maravich, LSU	1968	83	1387	893	3667	44.2
Austin Carr, Notre Dame	1971	74	1017	526	2560	34.6
Oscar Robertson, Cincinnati	1960	88	1052	869	2973	33.8
Calvin Murphy, Niagara	1970	77	947	654	2548	33.1
Dwight Lamar, SW Louisiana	1973	57	768	326	1862	32.7
Frank Selvy, Furman	1954	78	922	694	2538	32.5
Rick Mount, Purdue	1970	72	910	503	2323	32.3
Darrell Floyd, Furman	1956	71	868	545	2281	32.1
Nick Werkman, Seton Hall	1964	71	812	649	2273	32.0
Willie Humes, Idaho St.	1971	48	565	380	1510	31.5
William Averitt, Pepperdine	1973	49	615	311	1541	31.4
Elgin Baylor, Coll. of Idaho, Seattle	1958	80	956	588	2500	31.3
Elvin Hayes, Houston	1968	93	1215	454	2884	31.0
Freeman Williams, Portland St.	1978	106	1369	511	3249	30.7
Larry Bird, Indiana St.	1979	94	1154	542	2850	30.3

Career Records *(Cont.)*

REBOUNDS ALL-TIME

Player and Team	Final Year	GP	Reb
Tom Gola, La Salle	1955	118	2201
Joe Holup, George Washington	1956	104	2030
Charlie Slack, Marshall	1956	88	1916
Ed Conlin, Fordham	1955	102	1884
Dickie Hemric, Wake Forest	1955	104	1802

REBOUNDS SINCE 1973*

Player and Team	Final Year	GP	Reb
Kenneth Faried, Morehead St	2011	136	1673
Tim Duncan, Wake Forest	1997	128	1570
Derrick Coleman, Syracuse	1990	143	1537
Malik Rose, Drexel	1996	120	1514
Ralph Sampson, Virginia	1983	132	1511

ASSISTS

Player and Team	Final Year	GP	Asst
Bobby Hurley, Duke	1993	140	1076
Chris Corchiani, North Carolina St	1991	124	1038
Ed Cota, North Carolina	2000	138	1030
Keith Jennings, East Tennessee St	1991	127	983
Steve Blake, Maryland	2003	138	972

FIELD-GOAL PERCENTAGE

Player and Team	Final Year	FG	FGA	Pct
Steve Johnson, Oregon St	1981	828	1222	67.8
Michael Bradley, Kentucky/Villanova	2001	441	651	67.7
Murray Brown, Florida St	1980	566	847	66.8
Lee Campbell, SW Missouri St	1990	411	618	66.5
Warren Kidd, Middle Tennessee St	1993	496	747	66.4

Note: Minimum 400 field goals and 4 FG made per game.

FREE-THROW PERCENTAGE

Player and Team	Final Year	FT	FTA	Pct
Blake Ahearn, Missouri St	2007	435	460	94.6
Derek Raivio, Gonzaga	2007	343	370	92.7
Gary Buchanan, Villanova	2003	324	355	91.3
J.J. Redick, Duke	2006	662	726	91.2
Greg Starrick, Kentucky/Southern Illinois	1972	341	375	90.9

Note: Minimum 300 free throws made.

*Freshmen became eligible for varsity play in 1973.

Career Records *(Cont.)*

THREE-POINT FIELD GOALS MADE

Player and Team	Final Year	GP	3FG
J.J. Redick, Duke	2006	139	457
David Holston, Chicago St	2009	119	450
Keydren Clark, St. Peter's	2006	118	435
Chris Lofton, Tennessee	2008	128	431
Stephen Curry, Davidson	2009	104	414

THREE-POINT FIELD-GOAL PERCENTAGE

Player and Team	Final Year	3FG	3FGA	Pct
Tony Bennett, UW–Green Bay	1992	290	584	49.7
Stephen Sir, San Diego St/Northern Ariz.	2007	323	689	46.9
David Olson, Eastern Illinois	1992	262	562	46.6
Jaycee Carroll, Utah St	2008	369	793	46.5
Ross Land, Northern Arizona	2000	308	664	46.4

Note: Minimum 200 3-point field goals and 2.0 3-point field goals per game.

STEALS

Player and Team	Final Year	GP	Stl
John Linehan, Providence	2002	122	385
Eric Murdock, Providence	1991	117	376
Pepe Sanchez, Temple	2000	116	365
Cookie Belcher, Nebraska	2001	131	353
Kevin Braswell, Georgetown	2002	128	349

BLOCKED SHOTS

Player and Team	Final Year	GP	BS
Jarvis Varnado, Mississipi St	2010	141	564
Wojciech Myrda, La.-Monroe	2002	115	535
Adonal Foyle, Colgate	1997	87	492
Tim Duncan, Wake Forest	1997	128	481
William Mosley, Northwestern St	2012	124	460
Alonzo Mourning, Georgetown	1992	120	453

Division I Team Alltime Wins

Team	First Year	Yrs	W	L
Kentucky	1903	109	2090	649
Kansas	1899	114	2070	806
North Carolina	1911	102	2065	734
Duke	1906	107	1971	834
Syracuse	1901	111	1844	822
Temple	1895	116	1790	982
St. John's (N.Y.)	1908	105	1737	915
UCLA	1920	93	1728	769
Notre Dame	1898	107	1723	939
Pennsylvania	1897	112	1697	998
Indiana	1901	112	1690	959
Utah	1909	104	1670	918
Illinois	1906	107	1667	897
Brigham Young	1903	110	1666	1014
Washington	1896	110	1665	1079

Division I Alltime Winning Percentage

Team	First Year	Yrs	W	L	Pct
Kentucky	1903	109	2090	649	.763
North Carolina	1911	102	2065	734	.738
Kansas	1898	114	2070	806	.720
UNLV	1959	54	1133	456	.713
Duke	1906	107	1971	834	.703
Syracuse	1901	111	1844	822	.692
UCLA	1920	93	1728	769	.692
Western Kentucky	1915	93	1655	828	.667
Louisville	1912	98	1662	864	.658
St. John's (N.Y.)	1908	105	1737	915	.655
Illinois	1906	107	1667	897	.650
Notre Dame	1898	107	1723	939	.647
Temple	1895	116	1790	982	.646
Utah	1909	104	1670	918	.645
Arizona	1905	107	1618	892	.645
Missouri State	1909	100	1564	870	.643

Note: Minimum of 25 years in Division I.

NCAA Men's Division I Winning Streaks

Longest—Full Season

Team	Games	Years	Ended by
UCLA	88	1971–74	Notre Dame (71–70)
San Francisco	60	1955–57	Illinois (62–33)
UCLA	47	1966–68	Houston (71–69)
UNLV	45	1990–91	Duke (79–77)
Texas	44	1913–17	Rice (24–18)
Seton Hall	43	1939–41	LIU-Brooklyn (49–26)
LIU-Brooklyn	43	1935–37	Stanford (45–31)
UCLA	41	1968–69	USC (46–44)
Marquette	39	1970–71	Ohio St (60–59)
Cincinnati	37	1962–63	Wichita St (65–64)
North Carolina	37	1957–58	West Virginia (75–64)

Longest—Regular Season

Team	Games	Years	Ended by
UCLA	76	1971–74	Notre Dame (71–70)
Indiana	57	1975–77	Toledo (59–57)
Marquette	56	1970–72	Detroit (70–49)
Kentucky	54	1952–55	Georgia Tech (59–58)
San Francisco	51	1955–57	Illinois (62–33)
Pennsylvania	48	1970–72	Temple (57–52)
Ohio State	47	1960–62	Wisconsin (86–67)
Texas	44	1913–17	Rice (24–18)
UCLA	43	1966–68	Houston (71–69)
LIU-Brooklyn	43	1935–37	Stanford (45–31)
Seton Hall	42	1939–41	LIU-Brooklyn (49–26)

Longest—Home Court

Team	Games	Years	Team	Games	Years
Kentucky	129	1943–55	Lamar	80	1978–84
St. Bonaventure	99	1948–61	Long Beach St	75	1968–74
UCLA	98	1970–76	UNLV	72	1974–78
Cincinnati	86	1957–64	Arizona	71	1987–92
Marquette	81	1967–73	Cincinnati	68	1972–78
Arizona	81	1945–51	Western Kentucky	67	1949–55

Active Coaches*

WINS

Coach and Team	W
Mike Krzyzewski, Duke	.927
Jim Boeheim, Syracuse	.890
Jim Calhoun, Connecticut	.877
Bob Huggins, West Virginia	.710
Roy Williams, North Carolina	.675
Bo Ryan, Wisconsin	.651
Mike Montgomery, California	.634
Cliff Ellis, Coastal Carolina	.633
Rick Pitino, Louisville	.627
Stew Morrill, Utah St.	.563

WINNING PERCENTAGE

Coach and Team	Yrs	W	L	Pct
Roy Williams, North Carolina	24	675	169	.800
Mark Few, Gonzaga	13	342	90	.792
Dave Rose, BYU	7	185	54	.781
Thad Matta, Ohio St	12	323	96	.771
John Calipari, Kentucky	20	505	153	.767
Bo Ryan, Wisconsin	28	651	204	.761
Mike Krzyzewski, Duke	37	927	291	.761
Jamie Dixon, Pittsburgh	9	238	77	.756
Bill Self, Kansas	19	476	158	.751
Jim Boeheim, Syracuse	36	890	304	.745

Note: Minimum 5 years as a Division I head coach; includes record at 4-year colleges only.

Note: Minimum 5 years as a Division I head coach; includes record at 4-year colleges only.

Alltime Winningest Men's Division I Coaches

WINS

Coach	W
*Mike Krzyzewski (Army, Duke)	.927
Bob Knight (Army, Indiana, Texas Tech)	.902
*Jim Boeheim (Syracuse)	.890
Dean Smith (North Carolina)	.879
*Jim Calhoun (Northeastern, Connecticut)	.877
Adolph Rupp (Kentucky)	.876
Jim Phelan (Mt. St. Mary's)	.830
Eddie Sutton (Creighton, Arkansas, Kentucky, Oklahoma St)	.804
Lefty Driesell (Davidson, Maryland, James Madison, Georgia St)	.786
Lute Olson (Long Beach St, Iowa, Arizona)	.780
Lou Henson (Hardin-Simmons, New Mexico St, Illinois, New Mexico St)	.779
Henry Iba (NW Missouri St, Colorado, Oklahoma St)	.764
Ed Diddle (Western Kentucky)	.759
Phog Allen (Baker, Kansas, Haskell, Central Missouri St, Kansas)	.746
John Chaney (Cheyney St, Temple)	.741
Jerry Tarkanian (Long Beach St, UNLV, Fresno St)	.729
Norm Stewart (Northern Iowa, Missouri)	.728
Ray Meyer (DePaul)	.724
Don Haskins (Oklahoma St, UTEP)	.719
*Bob Huggins (Walsh, Akron, Cincinnati, Kansas St, West Virginia)	.710
Denny Crum (UCLA, Louisville)	.675
*Roy Williams (Kansas, North Carolina)	.675
Gary Williams (American, Boston College, Ohio St, Maryland)	.668
John Wooden (Indiana St, UCLA)	.664
Ralph Miller (Wichita St, Iowa, Oregon St)	.657
*Bo Ryan (UW-Platteville, Milwaukee, Wisconsin)	.651
Tom Penders (Tufts, Columbia, Fordham, URI, Texas, George Wash., Houston)	.648
Gene Bartow (C. Missouri St, Valparaiso, Memphis, Illinois, UCLA, UAB)	.647
Billy Tubbs (Lamar, Southwestern [Tex.], Oklahoma, TCU)	.641
Homer Drew (Bethel Coll., Indiana-South Bend, Valparaiso)	.640
Marv Harshman (Pacific Lutheran, Washington St, Washington)	.637

Note: Minimum 10 head coaching seasons in Division I.

*Active in 2011–12.

Alltime Winningest Men's Division I Coaches *(Cont.)*
WINNING PERCENTAGE

Coach (Team, Years)	Yrs	W	L	Pct
Clair Bee (Rider 1929–31, LIU-Brooklyn 1932–45, 1946–51)	21	412	87	.826
Adolph Rupp (Kentucky 1931–72)	41	876	190	.822
John Wooden (Indiana St 1946–48, UCLA 1948–75)	29	664	162	.804
*Roy Williams (Kansas 1989–2003, North Carolina 2003–)	24	675	169	.800
John Kresse (College of Charleston 1980–2002)	23	560	143	.797
*Mark Few (Gonzaga 1999–)	13	342	90	.792
Jerry Tarkanian (Long Beach St 1969–73, UNLV 1974–92, Fresno St 1995–2002)	31	729	201	.784
Francis Schmidt (Tulsa 1916–17, Arkansas 1924–29, TCU 1930–34)	17	258	72	.782
Dean Smith (North Carolina 1962–97)	36	879	254	.776
*Thad Matta (Butler 2001, Xavier 2002–04, Ohio St 2005–)	12	323	96	.771
*John Calipari (Massachusetts 1989–96, Memphis 2001–09, Kentucky 2009–)	20	505	153	.767
Jack Ramsay (St. Joseph's [Pa.] 1956–66)	11	231	71	.765
Frank Keaney (Rhode Island 1921–48)	28	401	124	.764
George Keogan (St. Louis 1916, Allegheny 1919, Valparaiso 1920–21, Notre Dame 1924–43)	27	414	127	.764
*Bo Ryan (UW-Platteville 1984–99, UW-Milwaukee 1999–2001, Wisconsin 2001–)	28	651	204	.761
Bruce Pearl (UW-Milwaukee 2001–05, Tennessee 2005–11)	19	462	145	.761
Vic Bubas (Duke 1960–69)	10	213	67	.761
*Mike Krzyzewski (Army 1976–80, Duke 1981–)	37	927	291	.761
Harry Fisher (Columbia 1907–16, Army 1922–23, 1925)	16	189	60	.759
Fred Bennion (Brigham Young 1909–10, Utah 1911-14, Montana St 1915-19)	11	95	31	.756
*Bill Self (Oral Roberts 1993–97, Tulsa 1997–2000, Illinois 2000–03, Kansas 2003–)	19	476	158	.751
Charles (Chick) Davies (Duquesne 1925–43, 1947–48)	21	314	106	.748
Ray Mears (Wittenberg 1957–62, Tennessee 1963–77)	21	399	135	.747
Edward McNichol (Penn 1921-30)	10	186	63	.747
*Jim Boeheim (Syracuse 1977–)	36	890	304	.745
Al McGuire (Belmont Abbey 1958–64, Marquette 1965–77)	20	406	142	.741
Phog Allen (Baker 1906–08, Haskell 1909, Cent. Mo. St 1913–19, Kansas 1908–09, 1920–56)	50	746	264	.739
Everett Case (North Carolina St 1947–65)	19	377	134	.738
Lute Olson (Long Beach St 1973–74, Iowa 1974–83, Arizona 1983–)	34	780	280	.736

*Active in 2011–12. Note: Minimum 10 years head coaching in Division I.

NCAA Women's Division I Winningest Coaches

Alltime Winningest Women's Division I Coaches
WINNING PERCENTAGE

Coach (Team, Years)	Yrs	W	L	Pct
Leon Barmore (Louisiana Tech 1983–02)	20	576	87	.869
*Geno Auriemma (Connecticut 1986–)	26	771	124	.861
*Pat Summitt (Tennessee 1975–)	37	1071	199	.843
*Tara VanDerveer (Idaho 1979-80, Ohio St 1981–85, Stanford 1986–95, 1997–)	32	826	198	.807
*Kim Mulkey (Baylor 2001–)	11	298	79	.790
Bill Sheahan (Mt. St. Mary's 1982–98)	17	372	104	.782
*Wes Moore (Maryville 1988–93, Francis Marion 1996–98, Chattanooga 1999–)	22	507	155	.766
*Robin Selvig (Montana 1979–)	33	758	233	.765
*Gail Goestenkors (Duke 1993–07, Texas 2007–)	19	479	148	.764
*Carey Green (Liberty 1999–)	12	286	94	.753

Note: Minimum 10 head coaching seasons in Division I.
*Active in 2010–11.

Alltime Winningest Women's Division I Coaches

	W
*Pat Summitt (Tennessee)	1,071
Jody Conradt (Sam Houston St, Tex.-Arlington, Texas)	900
*C. Vivian Stringer (Cheyney St, Iowa, Rutgers)	863
*Sylvia Hatchell (Francis Marion, North Carolina)	859
*Tara VanDerveer (Idaho, Ohio St, Stanford)	826
*Andy Landers (Georgia)	773
*Geno Auriemma (Connecticut)	771
*Robin Selvig (Montana)	758
*Jim Foster (St. Joseph's, Vanderbilt, Ohio St)	740
*Debbie Ryan (Virginia)	739
Kay Yow (Elon, North Carolina St)	737

Note: Minimum 10 head coaching seasons in Division I.
*Active in 2010–11.

Year	Winner	Score	Runner-up	Winning Coach
1982	Louisiana Tech	76–62	Cheyney	Sonja Hogg/Leon Barmore
1983	USC	69–67	Louisiana Tech	Linda Sharp
1984	USC	72–61	Tennessee	Linda Sharp
1985	Old Dominion	70–65	Georgia	Marianne Stanley
1986	Texas	97–81	USC	Jody Conradt
1987	Tennessee	67–44	Louisiana Tech	Pat Summitt
1988	Louisiana Tech	56–54	Auburn	Leon Barmore
1989	Tennessee	76–60	Auburn	Pat Summitt
1990	Stanford	88–81	Auburn	Tara VanDerveer
1991	Tennessee	70–67 (OT)	Virginia	Pat Summitt
1992	Stanford	78–62	Western Kentucky	Tara VanDerveer
1993	Texas Tech	84–82	Ohio State	Marsha Sharp
1994	North Carolina	60–59	Louisiana Tech	Sylvia Hatchell
1995	Connecticut	70–64	Tennessee	Geno Auriemma
1996	Tennessee	83–65	Georgia	Pat Summitt
1997	Tennessee	68–59	Old Dominion	Pat Summitt
1998	Tennessee	93–75	Louisiana Tech	Pat Summitt
1999	Purdue	62–45	Duke	Carolyn Peck
2000	Connecticut	71–52	Tennessee	Geno Auriemma
2001	Notre Dame	68–66	Purdue	Muffet McGraw
2002	Connecticut	82–70	Oklahoma	Geno Auriemma
2003	Connecticut	73–68	Tennessee	Geno Auriemma
2004	Connecticut	70–61	Tennessee	Geno Auriemma
2005	Baylor	84–62	Michigan St	Kim Mulkey-Robinson
2006	Maryland	78–75	Duke	Brenda Frese
2007	Tennessee	59–46	Rutgers	Pat Summitt
2008	Tennessee	64–48	Stanford	Pat Summitt
2009	Connecticut	76–54	Louisville	Geno Auriemma
2010	Connecticut	53–47	Stanford	Geno Auriemma
2011	Texas A&M	76–70	Notre Dame	Gary Blair
2012	Baylor	80–61	Notre Dame	Kim Mulkey

Single-Game Records

SCORING HIGHS

Pts	Player and Team vs Opponent	Year
60	Cindy Brown, Long Beach St vs San Jose St	1987
58	Kim Perrot, SW Louisiana vs SE Louisiana	1990
58	Lorri Bauman, Drake vs SW Missouri St*	1984
56	Jackie Stiles, SW Missouri St vs Evansville	2000
55	Patricia Hoskins, Mississippi Valley St vs Southern-Birm.	1989
55	Patricia Hoskins, Mississippi Valley St vs Alabama St	1989
54	Anjinea Hopson, Grambling vs Jackson St	1994
54	Mary Lowry, Baylor vs Texas	1994
54	Wanda Ford, Drake vs SW Missouri St*	1986
54	Elena Delle Donne, Delaware vs James Madison	2010
54	Briana Williams, Mercer vs. S.C. Upstate	2012

Three tied with 53.

REBOUNDS

Reb	Player and Team vs Opponent	Year
40	Deborah Temple, Delta St vs UAB	1983
37	Rosina Pearson, Bethune-Cookman vs Florida Memorial	1985
33	Maureen Formico, Pepperdine vs Loyola (Calif.)	1985
32	Lachelle Lyles, Southeast Missouri St. vs Tennessee St.	2006
31	Darlene Beale, Howard vs South Carolina St	1987
30	Cindy Bonforte, Wagner vs Queens (N.Y.)	1983
30	Kayone Hankins, New Orleans vs. Nicholls St	1994
30	Wanda Ford, Drake vs Eastern Illinois	1985
30	Jennifer Butler, Massachusetts vs Florida	2003

Three tied with 29.

*School changed name to Missouri State after 2004–05 season.

Single Game Records *(Cont.)*
ASSISTS

Asst	Player and Team vs Opponent	Year
23	Michelle Burden, Kent St vs Ball St	1991
22	Shawn Monday, Tennessee Tech vs Morehead St	1988
22	Veronica Pettry, Loyola (Ill.) vs Detroit	1989
22	Tine Freil, Pacific vs Wichita St	1991
21	Tine Freil, Pacific vs Fresno St	1992
21	Amy Bauer, Wisconsin vs Detroit	1989
21	Neacole Hall, Alabama St vs Southern-Birm.	1989

Six tied with 20.

Single Season Records
POINTS

Player and Team	Year	GP	FG	3FG	FT	Pts
Jackie Stiles, SW Missouri St*	2001	35	365	65	267	1062
Cindy Brown, Long Beach St	1987	35	362	—	250	974
Genia Miller, CSU-Fullerton	1991	33	376	0	217	969
Sheryl Swoopes, Texas Tech	1993	34	356	32	211	955
Alysha Clark, Middle Tennessee St	2008	34	343	12	237	935
Elena Delle Donne, Delaware	2012	33	325	52	225	927
Andrea Congreaves, Mercer	1992	28	353	77	142	925
Wanda Ford, Drake	1986	30	390	—	139	919
Chamique Holdsclaw, Tennessee	1998	39	370	9	166	915
Andrea Riley, Oklahoma St	2010	34	296	78	239	909
Barbara Kennedy, Clemson	1982	31	392	—	124	908
Patricia Hoskins, Mississippi Valley St	1989	27	345	13	205	908

SEASON SCORING AVERAGE

Player and Team	Year	GP	FG	3FG	FT	Pts	Avg
Patricia Hoskins, Mississippi Valley St	1989	27	345	13	205	908	33.6
Andrea Congreaves, Mercer	1992	28	353	77	142	925	33.0
Deborah Temple, Delta St	1984	28	373	—	127	873	31.2
Andrea Congreaves, Mercer	1993	26	302	51	150	805	31.0
Wanda Ford, Drake	1986	30	390	—	139	919	30.6
Anucha Browne, Northwestern	1985	28	341	—	173	855	30.5
LeChandra LeDay, Grambling	1988	28	334	36	146	850	30.4
Jackie Stiles, SW Missouri St*	2001	35	365	65	267	1062	30.3
Kim Perrot, SW Louisiana	1990	28	308	95	128	839	30.0
Tina Hutchinson, San Diego St	1984	30	383	—	132	898	29.9
Jan Jensen, Drake	1991	30	358	6	166	888	29.6
Genia Miller, CSU-Fullerton	1991	33	376	0	217	969	29.4
Barbara Kennedy, Clemson	1982	31	392	—	124	908	29.3
LaTaunya Pollard, Long Beach St	1983	31	376	—	155	907	29.3
Lisa McMullen, Alabama St	1991	28	285	126	119	815	29.1

REBOUNDS

Player and Team	Year	GP	Reb	Player and Team	Year	GP	Reb
Courtney Paris, Oklahoma	2006	36	539	Anne Donovan, Old Dominion	1983	35	504
Wanda Ford, Drake	1985	30	534	Courtney Paris, Oklahoma	2009	37	503
Lachelle Lyles, SE Missouri St.	2006	30	517	Darlene Jones, Miss Valley St.	1983	31	487
Courtney Paris, Oklahoma	2007	33	526	Melanie Simpson, Okla. City	1982	37	481
Wanda Ford, Drake	1986	30	506	R. Pearson, Beth.-Cookman	1985	26	480

REBOUND AVERAGE

Player and Team	Year	GP	Reb	Avg
Rosina Pearson, Bethune-Cookman	1985	26	480	18.5
Wanda Ford, Drake	1985	30	534	17.8
Katie Beck, East Tennessee St	1988	25	441	17.6
DeShawne Blocker, East Tennessee St	1994	26	450	17.3
Lachelle Lyles, SE Missouri St.	2006	31	527	17.0
Patricia Hoskins, Mississippi Valley St	1987	28	476	17.0
Wanda Ford, Drake	1986	30	506	16.9
Patricia Hoskins, Mississippi Valley St	1989	27	440	16.3
Joy Kellogg, Oklahoma City	1984	23	373	16.2
Deborah Mitchell, Mississippi Coll.	1983	28	447	16.0
Courtney Paris, Oklahoma	2007	33	526	15.9

*School changed name to Missouri State after 2004–05 season

Single Season Records *(Cont.)*

FIELD-GOAL PERCENTAGE

Player and Team	Year	GP	FG	FGA	Pct
Myndee Larsen, Southern Utah	1998	28	249	344	72.4
Chantelle Anderson, Vanderbilt	2001	34	292	404	72.3
Deneka Knowles, SE Louisiana	1996	26	199	276	72.1
Crystal Langhorne, Maryland	2006	32	202	280	72.1
Barbara Farris, Tulane	1998	27	151	210	71.9
Renay Adams, Tennessee Tech	1991	30	185	258	71.7
Carolyn Swords, Boston College	2011	33	240	336	71.4
Regina Days, Georgia Southern	1986	27	234	332	70.5
Kim Wood, UW-Green Bay	1994	27	188	271	69.4
Kelly Lyons, Old Dominion	1990	31	308	444	69.4

Based on NCAA qualifiers for annual championship.

FREE-THROW PERCENTAGE

Player and Team	Year	GP	FT	FTA	Pct
Adrienne Squire, Penn St	2006	29	80	83	96.4
Shanna Zolman, Tennessee	2004	35	88	92	95.7
Ginny Doyle, Richmond	1992	29	96	101	95.0
Jill Marano, La Salle	2003	29	88	93	94.6
Sue Bird, Connecticut	2002	39	98	104	94.2
Paula Corder-King, SE Missouri St	1999	28	111	118	94.1
Abby Oliver, Richmond	2012	32	106	113	93.8
Kandi Brown, Morehead St	2003	28	104	111	93.7
Linda Cyborski, Delaware	1991	29	74	79	93.7
Kandi Brown, Morehead St	2002	29	74	79	93.7

Based on NCAA qualifiers for annual championship.

Career Records

POINTS

Player and Team	Yrs	GP	Pts
Jackie Stiles, SW Missouri St*	1997–01	129	3393
Patricia Hoskins, Mississippi Valley St	1985–89	110	3122
Lorri Bauman, Drake	1981–84	120	3115
Maya Moore, Connecticut	2007–11	154	3036
Chamique Holdsclaw, Tennessee	1995–99	148	3025
Cheryl Miller, USC	1983–86	128	3018
Cindy Blodgett, Maine	1994–98	118	3005
LaToya Thomas, Mississippi St	1999–2003	125	2981
Valorie Whiteside, Appalachian St	1984–88	116	2944
Kelly Mazzante, Penn St	2000–04	133	2919

SCORING AVERAGE

Player and Team	Yrs	GP	FG	3FG	FT	Pts	Avg
Patricia Hoskins, Mississippi Valley St	1985–89	110	1196	24	706	3122	28.4
Sandra Hodge, New Orleans	1981–84	107	1194	—	472	2860	26.7
Jackie Stiles, SW Missouri St*	1997–01	129	1160	221	852	3393	26.3
Lorri Bauman, Drake	1981–84	120	1104	—	907	3115	26.0
Andrea Congreaves, Mercer	1989–93	108	1107	153	429	2796	25.9
Cindy Blodgett, Maine	1994–98	118	1055	219	676	3005	25.5
Valorie Whiteside, Appalachian St	1984–88	116	1153	0	638	2944	25.4
Joyce Walker, LSU	1981–84	117	1259	—	388	2906	24.8
Tarcha Hollis, Grambling	1989–91	84	891	3	246	2031	24.2
Korie Hlede, Duquesne	1994–98	109	1045	162	379	2631	24.1
Karen Pelphrey, Marshall	1983–86	114	1175	—	396	2746	24.1
Erma Jones, Bethune-Cookman	1982–84	87	961	—	173	2095	24.1

*School changed name to Missouri State after 2004–05 season

Year	Winner	Score	Runner-up	Third Place	Fourth Place
1957	Wheaton (Ill.)	89–65	Kentucky Wesleyan	Mt. St. Mary's (Md.)	CSU-Los Angeles
1958	South Dakota	75–53	St. Michael's	Evansville	Wheaton (Ill.)
1959	Evansville	83–67	SW Missouri St	North Carolina A&T	CSU-Los Angeles
1960	Evansville	90–69	Chapman	Kentucky Wesleyan	Cornell College
1961	Wittenberg	42–38	SE Missouri St	South Dakota	Mt. St. Mary's (Md.)
1962	Mt. St. Mary's (Md.)	58–57 (OT)	CSU-Sacramento	Southern Illinois	Nebraska Wesleyan
1963	South Dakota St	44–42	Wittenberg	Oglethorpe	Southern Illinois
1964	Evansville	72–59	Akron	North Carolina A&T	Northern Iowa
1965	Evansville	85–82 (OT)	Southern Illinois	North Dakota	St. Michael's
1966	Kentucky Wesleyan	54–51	Southern Illinois	Akron	North Dakota
1967	Winston-Salem	77–74	SW Missouri St	Kentucky Wesleyan	Illinois St
1968	Kentucky Wesleyan	63–52	Indiana St	Trinity (Tex.)	Ashland
1969	Kentucky Wesleyan	75–71	SW Missouri St	†Vacated	Ashland
1970	Philadelphia Textile	76–65	Tennessee St	UC-Riverside	Buffalo St
1971	Evansville	97–82	Old Dominion	†Vacated	Kentucky Wesleyan
1972	Roanoke	84–72	Akron	Tennessee St	Eastern Mich
1973	Kentucky Wesleyan	78–76 (OT)	Tennessee St	Assumption	Brockport St
1974	Morgan St	67–52	SW Missouri St	Assumption	New Orleans
1975	Old Dominion	76–74	New Orleans	Assumption	Tenn.-Chattanooga
1976	Puget Sound	83–74	Tenn.-Chattanooga	Eastern Illinois	Old Dominion
1977	Tenn.-Chattanooga	71–62	Randolph-Macon	North Alabama	Sacred Heart
1978	Cheyney	47–40	UW-Green Bay	Eastern Illinois	Central Florida
1979	North Alabama	64–50	UW-Green Bay	Cheyney	Bridgeport
1980	Virginia Union	80–74	New York Tech	Florida Southern	North Alabama
1981	Florida Southern	73–68	Mt. St. Mary's (Md.)	Cal Poly-SLO	UW-Green Bay
1982	District of Columbia	73–63	Florida Southern	Kentucky Wesleyan	CSU-Bakersfield
1983	Wright St	92–73	District of Columbia	*CSU-Bakersfield	*Morningside
1984	Central Missouri St	81–77	St. Augustine's	*Kentucky Wesleyan	*N Alabama
1985	Jacksonville St	74–73	South Dakota St	*Kentucky Wesleyan	*Mt. St. Mary's (Md.)
1986	Sacred Heart	93–87	SE Missouri St	*Cheyney	*Florida Southern
1987	Kentucky Wesleyan	92–74	Gannon	*Delta St	*Eastern Montana
1988	Lowell	75–72	Ak.-Anchorage	Florida Southern	Troy St
1989	North Carolina Central	73–46	SE Missouri St	UC-Riverside	Jacksonville St
1990	Kentucky Wesleyan	93–79	CSU-Bakersfield	North Dakota	Morehouse
1991	North Alabama	79–72	Bridgeport (Conn.)	*CSU-Bakersfield	*Virginia Union
1992	Virginia Union	100–75	Bridgeport (Conn.)	*CSU-Bakersfield	*California (Pa.)
1993	CSU-Bakersfield	85–72	Troy St (Ala.)	*New Hampshire Coll	*Wayne St (Mich.)
1994	CSU-Bakersfield	92–86	Southern Indiana	*New Hampshire Coll	*Washburn
1995	Southern Indiana	71–63	UC-Riverside	*Norfolk St	*Indiana (Pa.)
1996	Fort Hays St	70–63	Northern Kentucky	*California (Pa.)	*Virginia Union
1997	CSU-Bakersfield	57–56	Northern Kentucky	*Lynn	*Salem-Teikyo
1998	UC-Davis	83–77	Kentucky Wesleyan	*St. Rose	*Virginia Union
1999	Kentucky Wesleyan	75–60	Metropolitan St	*Truman St	*Florida Southern
2000	Metropolitan St	97–79	Kentucky Wesleyan	*Missouri Southern	*Seattle Pacific
2001	Kentucky Wesleyan	72–63	Washburn	*Western Washington	*Tampa
2002	Metropolitan St	80–72	Kentucky Wesleyan	*Shaw	*Indiana (Pa.)
2003	Northeastern St (Okla.)	75–64	†Vacated	*Bowie St	*Queens (N.Y.)
2004	Kennesaw St	84–59	Southern Indiana	*Humboldt St	*Metropolitan St
2005	Virginia Union	63–58	Bryant	*Lynn	*Tarleton St
2006	Winona St (Minn.)	73–61	Virginia Union	*Seattle Pacific	*Stonehill
2007	Barton	77–75	Winona St (Minn.)	*CSU-San Bernardino	*Central Missouri
2008	Winona St (Minn.)	87–76	Augusta St	*Bentley	*Ak.-Anchorage
2009	Findlay	56–53 (OT)	Cal Poly.-Pomona	*Augusta St	*Central Missouri
2010	Cal Poly	65–53	Indiana Univ. (Pa.)	*Bentley	*St. Cloud St
2011	Bellarmine	71–68	BYU-Hawaii	*Minnesota St-Mankato	*West Liberty
2012	Western Washington	72–65	Montevallo	*Stonehill	*Bellarmine

*Indicates tied for third. †Student-athletes representing American International in 1969, Southwestern Louisiana in 1971, and Kentucky Wesleyan in 2003 were declared ineligible subsequent to the tournament. Under NCAA rules, the teams' and ineligible student-athletes' records were deleted, and the teams' places in the final standings were vacated.

NCAA Men's Division II Alltime Individual Leaders

SINGLE-GAME SCORING HIGHS

Pts	Player and Team vs Opponent	Date
113	Bevo Francis, Rio Grande vs Hillsdale	1954
84	Bevo Francis, Rio Grande vs Alliance	1954
82	Bevo Francis, Rio Grande vs Bluffton	1954
80	Paul Crissman, USC vs Pacific Christian	1966
77	William English, Winston-Salem vs Fayetteville St	1968

Single Season Records
SCORING AVERAGE

Player and Team	Year	GP	FG	FT	Pts	Avg
Bevo Francis, Rio Grande	1954	27	444	367	1255	46.5
Earl Glass, Mississippi Industrial	1963	19	322	171	815	42.9
Earl Monroe, Winston-Salem	1967	32	509	311	1329	41.5
John Rinka, Kenyon	1970	23	354	234	942	41.0
Willie Shaw, Lane	1964	18	303	121	727	40.4

REBOUND AVERAGE

Player and Team	Year	GP	Reb	Avg
Tom Hart, Middlebury	1955	22	649	29.5
Tom Hart, Middlebury	1956	21	620	29.5
Frank Stronczek, American Int'l	1966	26	717	27.6
R.C. Owens, College of Idaho	1954	25	677	27.1
Maurice Stokes, St. Francis (Pa.)	1954	26	689	26.5

ASSISTS

Player and Team	Year	GP	Asst
Steve Ray, Bridgeport	1989	32	400
Steve Ray, Bridgeport	1990	33	385
Tony Smith, Pfeiffer	1992	35	349
Luke Cooper, Alaska Anchorage	2008	35	310
Rob Paternostro, New Hamp. Coll.	1995	33	309
Jim Ferrer, Bentley	1989	31	309

ASSIST AVERAGE

Player and Team	Year	GP	Asst	Avg
Steve Ray, Bridgeport	1989	32	400	12.5
Steve Ray, Bridgeport	1990	33	385	11.7
Demetri Beekman, Assumption	1993	23	264	11.5
Ernest Jenkins, N.M.-Highlands	1995	27	291	10.8
Brian Gregory, Oakland	1989	28	300	10.7
Zack Whiting, Chaminade	2007	27	289	10.7

FIELD-GOAL PERCENTAGE

Player and Team	Year	Pct
Garret Siler, Augusta St	2009	78.9
Garret Siler, Augusta St	2008	76.2
Todd Linder, Tampa	1987	75.2
Maurice Stafford, North Alabama	1984	75.0
Matthew Cornegay, Tuskegee	1982	74.8

FREE-THROW PERCENTAGE

Player and Team	Year	Pct
Paul Cluxton, Northern Kentucky	1997	100.0
Jake Linton, Saint Martin's	2008	96.4
Ashton Brown, Tex. A&M-Kingsville	2012	96.1
Tomas Rimkus, Pace	1997	95.6
C.J. Cowgill, Chaminade	2001	95.0

Career Records
POINTS

Player and Team	Yrs	Pts
Travis Grant, Kentucky St	1969–72	4045
Bob Hopkins, Grambling	1953–56	3759
Tony Smith, Pfeiffer	1989–92	3350
Earnest Lee, Clark Atlanta	1984–87	3298
Joe Miller, Alderson-Broaddus	1954–57	3294

CAREER SCORING AVERAGE

Player and Team	Yrs	GP	Pts	Avg
Travis Grant, Kentucky St	1969–72	121	4045	33.4
John Rinka, Kenyon	1967–70	99	3251	32.8
Florindo Vieira, Quinnipiac	1954–57	69	2263	32.8
Willie Shaw, Lane	1961–64	76	2379	31.3
Mike Davis, Virginia Union	1966–69	89	2758	31.0

Note: Minimum 1,400 points.

REBOUND AVERAGE

Player and Team	Yrs	GP	Reb	Avg
Tom Hart, Middlebury	1953, 55–56	63	1738	27.6
Maurice Stokes, St. Francis (Pa.)	1953–55	72	1812	25.2
Frank Stronczek, American Int'l	1965–67	62	1549	25.0
Bill Thieben, Hofstra	1954–56	76	1837	24.2
Hank Brown, Lowell Tech	1965–67	49	1129	23.0

Note: Minimum 800 rebounds.

Career Records (Cont.)

ASSISTS

Player and Team	Yrs	Asst
Demetri Beekman, Assumption	1990–93	1044
Adam Kaufman, Edinboro	1998–01	936
Rob Paternostro, New Hamp. Coll.	1992–95	919
Luke Cooper, Alaska-Anchorage	2005–08	880
Josh Magette, Ala.-Huntsville	2009–12	878

ASSIST AVERAGE

Player and Team	Yrs	GP	Asst	Avg
Steve Ray, Bridgeport	1989–90	65	785	12.1
Demetri Beekman, Assumption	1990–93	119	1044	8.8
D.J. Ferguson, Flagler	2009–11	79	679	8.6
Ernest Jenkins, N.M.-Highlands	1992–95	84	699	8.3
Zack Whiting, Chaminade	2004–07	86	703	8.2

Note: Minimum 550 Assists.

FIELD-GOAL PERCENTAGE

Player and Team	Yrs	Pct
Garrett Siler, Augusta St	2006–09	74.5
Todd Linder, Tampa	1984–87	70.8
Tom Schurfranz, Bellarmine	1989–92	70.2
Chad Scott, California (Pa.)	1991–94	70.0
Ed Phillips, Alabama A&M	1968–71	68.9

Note: Minimum 400 FGM.

FREE-THROW PERCENTAGE

Player and Team	Yrs	Pct
Paul Cluxton, Northern Kentucky	1994–97	93.5
Jake Linton, St. Martin's	2006–09	92.4
Kent Andrews, McNeese St	1967–69	91.6
Kyle Caiola, Findlay	2011–12	91.2
Nathan Hyde, Findlay	2008–11	90.1

Note: Minimum 250 FTM.

NCAA Men's Division III Championship Results

Year	Winner	Score	Runner-up	Third Place	Fourth Place
1975	LeMoyne-Owen	57–54	Glassboro St	Augustana (Ill.)	Brockport St
1976	Scranton	60–57	Wittenberg	Augustana (Ill.)	Plattsburgh St
1977	Wittenberg	79–66	Oneonta St	Scranton	Hamline
1978	North Park	69–57	Widener	Albion	Stony Brook
1979	North Park	66–62	Potsdam St	Franklin & Marshall	Centre
1980	North Park	83–76	Upsala	Wittenberg	Longwood
1981	Potsdam St	67–65 (OT)	Augustana (Ill.)	Ursinus	Otterbein
1982	Wabash	83–62	Potsdam St	Brooklyn	CSU-Stanislaus
1983	Scranton	64–63	Wittenberg	Roanoke	UW–Whitewater
1984	UW–Whitewater	103–86	Clark (Mass.)	DePauw	Upsala
1985	North Park	72–71	Potsdam St	Nebraska Wesleyan	Widener
1986	Potsdam St	76–73	LeMoyne-Owen	Nebraska Wesleyan	Jersey City St
1987	North Park	106–100	Clark (Mass.)	Wittenberg	Stockton St
1988	Ohio Wesleyan	92–70	Scranton	Nebraska Wesleyan	Hartwick
1989	UW–Whitewater	94–86	Trenton St	Southern Maine	Centre
1990	Rochester	43–42	DePauw	Washington (Md.)	Calvin
1991	UW–Platteville	81–74	Franklin & Marshall	Otterbein	Ramapo (N.J.)
1992	Calvin	62–49	Rochester	UW–Platteville	Jersey City St
1993	Ohio Northern	71–68	Augustana	Mass.–Dartmouth	Rowan
1994	Lebanon Valley Coll	66–59 (OT)	NYU	Wittenberg	St Thomas (Minn.)
1995	UW–Platteville	69–55	Manchester	Rowan	Trinity (Conn.)
1996	Rowan	100–93	Hope (Mich.)	Illinois Wesleyan	Franklin & Marshall
1997	Illinois Wesleyan	89–86	Nebraska Wesleyan	Williams	Alvernia
1998	UW–Platteville	69–56	Hope (Mich.)	Williams	Wilkes
1999	UW–Platteville	76–75 (2 OT)	Hampden-Sydney	William Paterson	Connecticut Coll.
2000	Calvin	79–74	UW–Eau Claire	Salem St	Franklin & Marshall
2001	Catholic	76–62	William Paterson	Illinois Wesleyan	Ohio Northern
2002	Otterbein	102–83	Elizabethtown	Carthage	Rochester
2003	Williams	67–65	Gustavus Adolphus	Wooster	Hampden Sydney
2004	UW–Stevens Point	84–82	Williams	John Carroll	Amherst
2005	UW–Stevens Point	73–49	Rochester	Calvin	York
2006	Virginia Wesleyan	59–56	Wittenberg	Illinois Wesleyan	Amherst
2007	Amherst	80–67	Virginia Wesleyan	Washington (Mo.)	Wooster
2008	Washington-St. Louis	90–86	Amherst	Hope	Ursinus
2009	Washington-St. Louis	61–52	Richard Stockton	Guilford	Franklin & Marshall
2010	UW-Stevens Point	78–73	Williams	*Guilford	*Randolph Macon
2011	St. Thomas (Minn.)	78–54	Wooster	*Middlebury	*Williams
2012	Wisconsin-Whitewater	63–60	Cabrini	*Illinois Wesleyan	*MIT

*Indicates tied for third. In 2010, the NCAA eliminated the consolation game to determine third place.

SINGLE-GAME SCORING HIGHS

Pts	Player and Team vs Opponent	Year
89	Griffin Lentsch, Grinnell vs. Principia	2012
77	Jeff Clement, Grinnell vs Illinois College	1998
69	Sami Wylie, Lincoln (Pa.) vs Ohio St-Marion	2007
69	Steve Diekmann, Grinnell vs Simpson	1995
64	Tim Russell, Albertus Magnus	2005
63	Ryan Hodges, Cal-Lutheran	2005
63	Joe DeRoche, Thomas vs St. Joseph's (Me.)	1988
62	Shannon Lilly, Bishop vs Southwest Assembly of God	1983
62	Nick Pelotte, Plymouth St	2005
62	Kyle Myrick, Lincoln (Pa.) vs. Penn St.-Abington	2006

Three tied at 61.

Single Season Records

SCORING AVERAGE

Player and Team	Year	GP	FG	FT	Pts	Avg
Steve Diekmann, Grinnell	1995	20	223	162	745	37.3
Rickey Sutton, Lyndon St	1976	14	207	93	507	36.2
Shannon Lilly, Bishop	1983	26	345	218	908	34.9
Dana Wilson, Husson	1974	20	288	122	698	34.9
Rickey Sutton, Lyndon St	1977	16	223	112	558	34.9

REBOUND AVERAGE

Player and Team	Year	GP	Reb	Avg
Joe Manley, Bowie St	1976	29	579	20.0
Fred Petty, New Hampshire Coll.	1974	22	436	19.8
Larry Williams, Pratt	1977	24	457	19.0
Larry Parker, Plattsburgh St	1975	23	430	18.7
harles Greer, Thomas	1977	17	318	18.7

ASSISTS

Player and Team	Year	GP	Asst
Robert James, Kean	1989	29	391
Tennyson Whitted, Ramapo	2002	29	319
Ricky Spicer, UW-Whitewater	1989	31	295
Joe Marcotte, New Jersey Tech	1995	30	292
Andre Bolton, Chris. Newport	1996	30	289

ASSIST AVERAGE

Player and Team	Year	GP	Asst	Avg
Robert James, Kean	1989	29	391	13.5
Albert Kirchner, Mt. St. Vincent	1990	24	267	11.1
Tennyson Whitted, Ramapo	2002	29	319	11.0
Ron Torgalski, Hamilton	1989	26	275	10.6
David Arsenault, Grinnell	2008	21	219	10.4

FIELD-GOAL PERCENTAGE

Player and Team	Year	Pct
Travis Weiss, St. John's (Minn.)	1994	76.6
Brian Schmitting, Ripon	2006	76.3
Pete Metzelaars, Wabash	1982	75.3
Tony Rychlec, Mass. Maritime	1981	74.9
Tony Rychlec, Mass. Maritime	1982	73.1

FREE-THROW PERCENTAGE

Player and Team	Year	Pct
Korey Coon, Illinois Wesleyan	2000	96.3
Ryan Martin, Keene St	2011	96.1
Ryan Junghans, Hood	2008	95.9
Nick Wilkins, Coe	2003	95.7
Chanse Young, Manchester	1998	95.6

Career Records

POINTS

Player and Team	Yrs	Pts
Andre Foreman, Salisbury St	1989–92	2940
Willie Chandler, Misericordia	2000–03	2898
John Grotberg, Grinnell	2006–09	2848
Lamonte Thomas, Johnson & Wales (RI)	2009–12	2740
Lamont Strothers, Chris. Newport	1988–91	2709

SCORING AVERAGE

Player and Team	Yrs	GP	Avg
Dwain Govan, Bishop	1974–75	55	32.8
Dave Russell, Shepherd	1974–75	60	30.6
Kyle Myrick, Lincoln (Pa.)	2005–06	57	30.2
Rickey Sutton, Lyndon St	1976–79	80	29.7
John Grotberg, Grinnell	2006–09	96	29.7

Note: Minimum 1,400 points.

REBOUND AVERAGE

Player and Team	Yrs	GP	Reb	Avg
Larry Parker, Plattsburgh St	1975–78	85	1482	17.4
Charles Greer, Thomas	1975–77	58	926	16.0
Willie Parr, LeMoyne-Owen	1974–76	76	1182	15.6
Michael Smith, Hamilton	1989–92	107	1632	15.2
Dave Kufeld, Yeshiva	1977–80	81	1222	15.1

Note: Minimum 800 rebounds.

ASSIST AVERAGE

Player and Team	Yrs	Avg
David Arsenault, Grinnell	2006–09	9.4
Phil Dixon, Shenandoah	1993–96	8.6
Tennyson Whitted, Ramapo	2000–03	8.5
Steve Artis, Chris. Newport	1990–93	8.1
David Genovese, Mt. St. Vincent	1992–95	7.5

Note: Minimum 550 Assists.

Hockey

Playoff MVP Jonathan Quick was almost unbeatable during L.A.'s run to its first Stanley Cup

Kings Rule

Drew Doughty and Jonathan Quick helped the high-flying Los Angeles Kings dominate the Stanley Cup playoffs, but a lockout looms for next season

BY MARK BEECH

IT'S NOT OFTEN THAT THE STANLEY Cup finals can be described as low profile—especially when the series is contested in and around the country's two biggest media markets—but that was certainly the case last spring when the Kings defeated the Devils in six games for the NHL championship. The 2012 finals did not feature an Original Six team, which would have added historical heft and boosted the Cup's appeal. Likewise, there was no historical animosity between the two clubs and the players seemed to spend much of the series trying hard to be polite to one another. Television ratings were low. Buzz was almost non-existent.

This was understandable to an extent. New Jersey, despite a rich playoff legacy, plays second banana in the New York area to the lights of Manhattan and the rival Rangers. And Los Angeles? Well, the Kings' problems have more to do with apathy than geography. Throughout the club's run through the playoffs, the L.A. media made screw-up after screw-up while trying to plug the hometown team. During a report on the Western Conference finals, one TV station displayed the logo for the Sacramento Kings. A sports anchor referred to goalie Jonathan Quick as Jonathan Swift, and another bungled the pronunciation of the surnames for two players—center Anze Kopitar and defenseman Drew Doughty—

during one confused report. Forget the entire USA, the Kings are low profile in their own city.

Says Hall of Famer Luc Robitaille, L.A.'s president of business operations, "Thirteen million people here. We're not a city. We're a country."

A country, however, that has the good fortune to be home to a defenseman like Doughty, who though he lost out on the Conn Smythe Trophy to Kings goalie Jonathan Quick as the playoff MVP, had perhaps the most to do with the team's first Stanley Cup in its 45 years of existence. He seemed to be everywhere during the King's dismantling of the Devils: breaking up New Jersey's vaunted forecheck; controlling the Los Angeles attack; and scoring crucial goals, none more memorable than the gorgeous end-to end job he unleashed in a Game 2 victory. "If you look at the subtle things he does with his hands and his feet to create the room for that move, most people don't understand it," says Kings assistant G.M. Ron Hextall of Doughty's goal. "Drew probably doesn't understand it either."

"Doughty's got patience," said Devils defenseman Mark Fayne during the Cup finals. "He sells plays without doing anything. A quick look-off maybe, and he makes a play. Most guys you move at will make a play to get rid of the puck. He just stands there."

Such encomiums could not have been used to describe the start to Doughty's season, which was, to put it bluntly, miserable. He began the season by holding out for a bigger contract, eventually signing an eight-year, $56-million deal on Sept. 30—just 48 hours before L.A. boarded a plane for Europe, where they opened the season. The upshot was that Doughty, 22, began the season out of condition and out of sync. Two years after a 59-point season that earned him Norris-Trophy consideration, the six-foot, 212-pound blueliner scored just eight points in his first 25 games. The Kings, not coincidentally, began the season with a 13-13-4 record. It wasn't until January, by the time Doughty had played himself into shape, that they began to play like a Cup contender.

Doughty and the Kings weren't alone in their early-season struggles. The entire league began in a bit of a fog, with hockey's best player, Sidney Crosby, still sidelined with the aftereffects of a concussion that he had suffered in January 2011. The Penguins center was rumored to be close to returning to the ice, but the only impact he had on the game to start was the rules changes the league had instituted over the offseason to deal with the rising rate of head injuries. Hits to the head didn't completely leave the game, but suspensions for hits to the head became prevalent, with Brendan Shanahan, the NHL's newly minted dean of discipline, explaining each in a series of web videos that did their best to make the punishment process transparent.

Crosby, 25, came back in spectacular fashion, scoring a pair of goals in a 5–0 victory over the Islanders on Nov. 21. He scored 12 points in his first eight games, but

DAMIAN STROHMEYER

Doughty's holdout hampered the Kings early on, but by playoffs time, he was a dominant force for L.A.

an apparent elbow from the Bruins' David Krejci sent him back to the bench for another extended rest. Crosby did not return until March 15. He finished the season with 37 points in 22 games.

In Crosby's absence, Pittsburgh center Evgeni Malkin stepped up to win the Hart Trophy as NHL MVP. The gifted 6' 3", 195-pound Russian scored 50 goals and led the league with 109 points, filling the hole left by Crosby as the best player in all of hockey. Dominant and dynamic, Malkin, 26, led the Penguins to within a point of the Rangers as Eastern Conference champions. "[He] can dominate because he understands the spatial part of the game so well," says Pittsburgh coach Dan Bylsma.

It was odd to see Malkin assume the mantle of the world's best player in the absence of Crosby. For years, it was assumed that Crosby's chief rival for that honor was Malkin's countryman, Alex Ovechkin. The Capitals' 26-year-old winger, however, struggled through a second straight 30-goal season, and his point production dropped from 85 in 2010–11 to 65 in '11–12. Part of

JIM McISAAC

year before, had spent much of the season alienating fans and teammates. First by refusing to go with the team to the traditional visit to the White House to meet the president—he explained in a post on his Facebook page that he disagreed with the policies of President Obama—and then later by abruptly announcing that he would not play the 2012–13 season. In another Facebook posting, Thomas said that he wanted to focus on "friends, family and faith," and refused to promise that he would ever play again. "What does this portend for the future?" he wrote. "We'll see. . . . God's will be done." It is likely that, if he plays hockey again, it will not be in a Bruins sweater.

That sort of open-ended conclusion was a fitting one for the NHL, which entered the offseason uncertain about its own future. The league's collective bargaining agreement with the players must be renewed before the 2012–13 season, and the owners are adamant that they want a new deal. The NHL could be headed for its second lockout in less than a decade.

At issue is the question of hockey related revenue. That split favors the players, 57% to 43%, even though the players accepted a 24% salary rollback as part of the last CBA. Now the owners are looking for more. "Players understand what happened last time," says players' association head Donald Fehr. "Nobody you represent . . . starts with the proposition that that's what I'd like to do—I'd like to negotiate a worse deal than what I have."

Both sides seem far apart in their positions, and it seems more and more likely that the season will not begin on time. It's a stark reminder that the fun part of the game came to an end with Doughty's dazzling run through the Stanley Cup finals. Now the game is being played for keeps. And it's deadly serious.

the reason for his decline was the coaching change that Ovechkin helped engineer early in the season. With the club struggling, Capitals general manager George McPhee abruptly fired coach Bruce Boudreau and hired franchise legend Dale Hunter, a conservative, defensive-minded taskmaster.

"The first couple of years, anytime [Ovechkin] stepped on the ice he was full bore—go, go, go," says Washington assistant goaltending coach Olaf Kolzig. "I think he's gotten away from that. He's not looking for the easy play, but he's not taking the bull by the horns like he did. And I think Dale will probably get that back out of him."

While Ovechkin never did regain his scoring touch, he and the Capitals did make a surprising run into the second round of the playoffs, defeating defending Stanley-Cup champion Boston in seven games in Round 1. The postseason success was made possible in part by Ovechkin accepting a reduced role on the ice—he would often ride the bench late in games in favor of more defensive-minded players. "It's most important thing right now, guys," he told reporters. "Just win the series and win the game. If you gonna talk about my game time and all that kind of stuff, it's not a season—it's the playoffs. How I said before, you have to suck it up and play for team."

For the Bruins, the team that Washington beat, the offseason began much earlier than it had the year before. To some in Beantown, that may have been a relief. Goalie Tim Thomas, everybody's favorite player from the

FOR THE RECORD•2011–2012

2011-12 NHL Final Regular Season Standings

Western Conference

CENTRAL DIVISION

	GP	W	L	OTL	Pts	GF	GA
†St Louis	82	49	22	11	109	210	165
*Nashville	82	48	26	8	104	237	210
*Detroit	82	48	28	6	102	248	203
*Chicago	82	45	26	11	101	248	238
Columbus	82	29	46	7	65	202	262

NORTHWEST DIVISION

	GP	W	L	OTL	Pts	GF	GA
‡Vancouver	82	51	22	9	111	249	198
Calgary	82	37	29	16	90	202	226
Colorado	82	41	35	6	88	208	220
Minnesota	82	35	36	11	81	177	226
Edmonton	82	32	40	10	74	212	239

PACIFIC DIVISION

	GP	W	L	OTL	Pts	GF	GA
†Phoenix	82	42	27	13	97	216	204
*San Jose	82	43	29	10	96	228	210
*Los Angeles	82	40	27	15	95	194	179
Dallas	82	42	35	5	89	211	222
Anaheim	82	34	36	12	80	204	231

OTL=overtime loss; worth 1 pt.

Eastern Conference

NORTHEAST DIVISION

	GP	W	L	OTL	Pts	GF	GA
†Boston	82	49	29	4	102	269	202
*Ottawa	82	41	31	10	92	249	240
Buffalo	82	39	32	11	89	218	230
Toronto	82	35	37	10	80	231	264
Montreal	82	31	35	16	78	212	226

ATLANTIC DIVISION

	GP	W	L	OTL	Pts	GF	GA
‡NY Rangers	82	51	24	7	109	226	187
*Pittsburgh	82	51	25	6	108	282	221
*Philadelphia	82	47	26	9	103	264	232
*New Jersey	82	48	28	6	102	228	209
NY Islanders	82	34	37	11	79	203	255

SOUTHEAST DIVISION

	GP	W	L	OTL	Pts	GF	GA
†Florida	82	38	26	18	94	203	227
*Washington	82	42	32	8	92	222	230
Tampa Bay	82	38	36	8	84	235	281
Winnipeg	82	37	35	10	84	225	246
Carolina	82	33	33	16	82	213	243

‡Conference winner. †Division winner. *Playoff team.

2012 Stanley Cup Playoffs

WESTERN CONFERENCE

QUARTERFINALS | SEMIFINALS | CONFERENCE FINAL

1-Vancouver
8-Los Angeles — Los Angeles (4–1)
Los Angeles (4–0)
2-St Louis
7-San Jose — St Louis (4–1)
Los Angeles (4–1)
3-Phoenix
6-Chicago — Phoenix (4–2)
Phoenix (4–1)
4-Nashville
5-Detroit — Nashville (4–1)

STANLEY CUP

Los Angeles (4–2)

EASTERN CONFERENCE

CONFERENCE FINAL | SEMIFINALS | QUARTERFINALS

NY Rangers (4–3)
NY Rangers-1
Ottawa-8
NY Rangers (4–3)
Washington (4–3)
Boston-2
Washington-7
New Jersey (4–2)
New Jersey (4–3)
Florida-3
New Jersey-6
New Jersey (4–1)
Philadelphia (4–2)
Pittsburgh-4
Philadelphia-5

Note: Playoff teams are re-seeded after quarterfinals

Stanley Cup Playoff Results

Conference Quarterfinals

EASTERN CONFERENCE

Game 1	Ottawa	2	at NY Rangers	4
Game 2	Ottawa	3	at NY Rangers	2
Game 3	NY Rangers	1	at Ottawa	0
Game 4	NY Rangers	2	at Ottawa	3*

*Overtime game.

Game 5	Ottawa	2	at NY Rangers	0
Game 6	NY Rangers	3	at Ottawa	2
Game 7	Ottawa	1	at NY Rangers	2

NY Rangers won series 4–3.

HOCKEY **319**

Conference Quarterfinals *(Cont.)*

EASTERN CONFERENCE *(CONT.)*

Game 1	Washington	0	at Boston	1
Game 2	Washington	2	at Boston	1*
Game 3	Boston	4	at Washington	3
Game 4	Boston	1	at Washington	2
Game 5	Washington	4	at Boston	3
Game 6	Boston	4	at Washington	3*
Game 7	Washington	2	at Boston	1*

Washington won series 4–3.

Game 1	New Jersey	3	at Florida	2
Game 2	New Jersey	2	at Florida	4
Game 3	Florida	4	at New Jersey	3
Game 4	Florida	0	at New Jersey	4
Game 5	New Jersey	0	at Florida	3
Game 6	Florida	2	at New Jersey	3
Game 7	New Jersey	3	at Florida	2**

New Jersey won series 4–3.

Game 1	Philadelphia	4	at Pittsburgh	3*
Game 2	Philadelphia	8	at Pittsburgh	5
Game 3	Pittsburgh	4	at Philadelphia	8
Game 4	Pittsburgh	10	at Philadelphia	3
Game 5	Philadelphia	2	at Pittsburgh	3
Game 6	Pittsburgh	1	at Philadelphia	5

Philadelphia won series 4–2.

WESTERN CONFERENCE

Game 1	Los Angeles	4	at Vancouver	2
Game 2	Los Angeles	4	at Vancouver	2
Game 3	Vancouver	0	at Los Angeles	1
Game 4	Vancouver	3	at Los Angeles	1
Game 5	Los Angeles	2	at Vancouver	1*

Los Angeles won series 4–1.

Game 1	Chicago	2	at Phoenix	3*
Game 2	Chicago	4	at Phoenix	3*
Game 3	Phoenix	3	at Chicago	2*
Game 4	Phoenix	3	at Chicago	2*
Game 5	Chicago	2	at Phoenix	1*
Game 6	Phoenix	4	at Chicago	0

Phoenix won series 4–2.

Game 1	San Jose	3	at St Louis	2**
Game 2	San Jose	0	at St Louis	3
Game 3	St Louis	4	at San Jose	3
Game 4	St Louis	2	at San Jose	1
Game 5	San Jose	1	at St Louis	3

St Louis won series 4–1.

Game 1	Detroit	2	at Nashville	3
Game 2	Detroit	3	at Nashville	2
Game 3	Nashville	3	at Detroit	2
Game 4	Nashville	3	at Detroit	1
Game 5	Detroit	1	at Nashville	2

Nashville won series 4–1.

Conference Semifinals

EASTERN CONFERENCE

Game 1	Washington	1	at NY Rangers	3
Game 2	Washington	3	at NY Rangers	2
Game 3	NY Rangers	2	at Washington	1***
Game 4	NY Rangers	2	at Washington	3
Game 5	Washington	2	at NY Rangers	3**
Game 6	NY Rangers	1	at Washington	2
Game 7	Washington	1	at NY Rangers	2

NY Rangers won series 4–3.

Game 1	New Jersey	3	at Philadelphia	4*
Game 2	New Jersey	4	at Philadelphia	1
Game 3	Philadelphia	3	at New Jersey	4*
Game 4	Philadelphia	2	at New Jersey	4
Game 5	New Jersey	3	at Philadelphia	1

New Jersey won series 4–1.

WESTERN CONFERENCE

Game 1	Los Angeles	3	at St Louis	1
Game 2	Los Angeles	5	at St Louis	2
Game 3	St Louis	2	at Los Angeles	4
Game 4	St Louis	1	at Los Angeles	3

Los Angeles won series 4–0.

Game 1	Nashville	3	at Phoenix	4*
Game 2	Nashville	3	at Phoenix	5
Game 3	Phoenix	0	at Nashville	2
Game 4	Phoenix	1	at Nashville	0
Game 5	Nashville	1	at Phoenix	2

Phoenix won series 4–1.

Eastern Conference Finals

Game 1	New Jersey	0	at NY Rangers	3
Game 2	New Jersey	3	at NY Rangers	2
Game 3	NY Rangers	3	at New Jersey	0
Game 4	NY Rangers	1	at New Jersey	4
Game 5	New Jersey	5	at NY Rangers	3
Game 6	NY Rangers	2	at New Jersey	3

New Jersey won series 4–2.

Western Conference Finals

Game 1	Los Angeles	4	at Phoenix	2
Game 2	Los Angeles	4	at Phoenix	0
Game 3	Phoenix	1	at Los Angeles	2
Game 4	Phoenix	2	at Los Angeles	0
Game 5	Los Angeles	4	at Phoenix	3*

Los Angeles won series 4–1.

Stanley Cup Final

Game 1	Los Angeles	2	at New Jersey	1*
Game 2	Los Angeles	2	at New Jersey	1*
Game 3	New Jersey	0	at Los Angeles	4
Game 4	New Jersey	3	at Los Angeles	1
Game 5	Los Angeles	1	at New Jersey	2
Game 6	New Jersey	1	at Los Angeles	6

Los Angeles won series 4–2.

*Overtime game. **Double overtime game. ***Triple overtime game.

Stanley Cup Final Box Scores

Game 1

```
Los Angeles...................1    0    0    1——2
New Jersey....................0    1    0    0——1
```

FIRST PERIOD

Scoring: Los Angeles, 1, Fraser (Nolan), 9:56. Penalties: Los Angeles, 1, Brown (goaltender interference), 12:19.

SECOND PERIOD

Scoring: New Jersey, 1, Volchenkov (Elias, Clarkson), 18:48. Penalties: Los Angeles, 1, Stoll (tripping), 8:31, New Jersey, 1, Zubrus (elbowing), 13:23.

THIRD PERIOD

Scoring and Penalties: None.

OVERTIME

Scoring: Los Angeles, 1, Kopitar (Williams, Doughty), 8:13.

Shots on goal: LA 5–9–8–3—25; NJ 5–3–7–2—17.

Power-play opportunities: LA 0–1, NJ 0–2.

Goalies: LA, Quick (17 shots, 16 saves); NJ, Brodeur (25 shots, 23 saves).

Referees: O'Halloran, Watson. Linesmen: Amell, Murray.

A: 17,625.

Game 2

```
Los Angeles...................1    0    0    1——2
New Jersey....................0    0    1    0——1
```

FIRST PERIOD

Scoring: Los Angeles, 1, Doughty (unassisted), 7:49. Penalties: Los Angeles, 2, Greene (cross checking), 2:54, Mitchell (cross checking), 7:56.

SECOND PERIOD

Penalties: New Jersey, 1, Greene (tripping), 9:29; Los Angeles, 1, King (high-sticking), 13:38.

THIRD PERIOD

Scoring: New Jersey, 1, R. Carter (Zidlicky, Bernier), 2:59. Penalties: New Jersey, 1, Zubrus (interference), 16:55; Los Angeles, 1, Doughty (hooking), 17:46.

OVERTIME

Scoring: Los Angeles, 1, J. Carter (Penner, Martinez), 13:42.

Shots on goal: LA 6–9–6–11–0—32; NJ 11–9–10–3—33.

Power-play opportunities: LA 0–2, NJ 0–4.

Goalies: LA, Quick (33 shots, 32 saves); NJ, Brodeur (32 shots, 30 saves).

Referees: O'Rourke, Rooney. Linesmen: Racicot, Morin.

A: 17,625.

Game 3

```
New Jersey ....................0    0    0——0
Los Angeles ...................0    2    2——4
```

FIRST PERIOD

Penalties: Los Angeles, 2, Richards (elbowing), 14:35, Carter (high-stick, double minor), 15:36; New Jersey, 1, Zidlicky (tripping), 16:57.

SECOND PERIOD

Scoring: Los Angeles, 2, Martinez (King, Lewis), 5:40, Kopitar (Brown, Williams), 15:07. Penalties: Los Angeles, 3, Kopitar (holding), 6:16, Penner (goaltender interference), 9:41, Gagne (slashing), 18:30.

THIRD PERIOD

Scoring: Los Angeles, 2, J. Carter (Richards, Mitchell), 4:15, Williams (Doughty, Kopitar), 6:47. Penalties: New Jersey, 2, Fayne (cross checking), 3:29, Zidlicky (high-sticking), 5:30.

Shots on goal: NJ 7–9–6—22; LA 6–9–6—21.

Power-play opportunities: NJ 0–6, LA 2–2.

Goalies: NJ, Brodeur (21 shots, 17 saves). LA, Quick (22 shots, 22 saves).

Referees: O'Halloran, Watson. Linesmen: Amell, Murray.

A: 18,764.

Game 4

```
New Jersey ...............................0    0    3 — 3
Los Angeles ...........................0    0    1 — 1
```

FIRST PERIOD

Penalties: New Jersey, 2, Parise (tripping), 3:02, Salvador (interference), 19:15; Los Angeles 2, Stoll (hooking), 5:53, Brown (tripping), 7:58.

SECOND PERIOD

Penalties: New Jersey, 1, Salvador (interference), 8:19.

THIRD PERIOD

Scoring: New Jersey 3, Elias (Salvador, Zubrus), 7:56, Henrique (Clarkson, Ponikarovsky), 15:29, Kovalchuk (Zajac, Salvador), 19:40; Los Angeles, 1, Doughty (Richards, Kopitar), 8:56. Penalties: New Jersey, 1, Clarkson (boarding), 8:52; Los Angeles, 1, Mitchell (high-sticking), 17:10.

Shots on goal: NJ 8–3–13—24; LA 7–7–8—22.

Power-play opportunities: NJ 0–3, LA 1–4.

Goalies: NJ, Brodeur (22 shots, 21 saves), LA, Quick (23 shots, 21 saves).

Referees: O'Rourke, Rooney. Linesmen: Morin, Racicot.

A: 18,867.

Game 5

```
Los Angeles..............................0    1    0 — 1
New Jersey ...............................1    1    0 — 2
```

FIRST PERIOD

Scoring: New Jersey, 1, Parise (none), 12:45. Penalties: Los Angeles, 1, Mitchell (interference), 11:00.

SECOND PERIOD

Scoring: Los Angeles, 1, Williams (Greene), 3:26; New Jersey, 1, Salvador (Ponikarovsky, Zajac), 9:05. Penalties: New Jersey, 2, Fayne (delay of game), 9:33, Salvador (high-sticking), 18:38.

THIRD PERIOD

Penalties: Los Angeles, 2, Brown (holding stick), 5:51, Penner (roughing), 18:24; New Jersey, 1, Ponikarovsky (roughing), 18:24.

Shots on goal: LA 7–10–9—26; NJ 4–12–3—19.

Power-play opportunities: LA 0–2, NJ 1–2.

Goalies: LA, Quick (19 shots, 17 saves). NJ, Brodeur (26 shots, 25 saves).

Referees: O'Halloran, Watson. Linesmen: Amell, Murray.

A: 17,625.

Game 6

```
New Jersey ...............................0    1    0 — 1
Los Angeles ...........................3    1    2 — 6
```

FIRST PERIOD

Scoring: Los Angeles, 3, Brown (Doughty, Richards), 11:03, Carter (Brown, Richards), 12:45, Lewis (King, Doughty), 15:01. Penalties: New Jersey, 3, Volchenkov (hooking), 3:01, Bernier (boarding, major), 10:10, Bernier (game misconduct), 10:10.

SECOND PERIOD

Scoring: Los Angeles, 1, Carter (Brown, Kopitar), 1:30; New Jersey, 1, Henrique (Sykora, Ponikarovsky), 18:45. Penalties: New Jersey, 4, Salvador (high-sticking, double minor), 6:00, Carter (roughing), 14:23, Carter (misconduct, 10 min), 14:23, Clarkson (misconduct, 10 min), 18:19; Los Angeles, 1, Penner (roughing), 19:43.

THIRD PERIOD

Scoring: Los Angeles, 2, Lewis (King, Stoll), 16:15, Greene (none), 16:30. Penalties: Los Angeles, 2, Brown (tripping), 6:55, Brown (charging), 6:55; New Jersey, 2, Sykora (roughing), 6:55, Zidlicky (tripping), 8:06.

Shots on goal: NJ 4–6–8—18; LA 13–8–4—25.

Power-play opportunities: NJ 0–2, LA 3–9.

Goalies : NJ, Brodeur (25 shots, 19 saves), LA, Quick (18 shots, 17 saves).

Referees: O'Rourke, Rooney. Linesmen: Morin, Amell.

A: 18,858.

Individual 2012 Playoff Leaders

Scoring

POINTS

Player and Team	GP	G	Ast	Pts	+/-	PM	Player and Team	GP	G	Ast	Pts	+/-	PM
Anze Kopitar, LA	20	8	12	20	+16	9	Travis Zajac, NJ	24	7	7	14	-6	4
Dustin Brown, LA	20	8	12	20	+16	34	Bryce Salvador, NJ	24	4	10	14	+9	26
Ilya Kovalchuk, NJ	23	8	11	19	-7	6	Jeff Carter, LA	20	8	5	13	+0	4
Claude Giroux, Phi	10	8	9	17	+2	13	Danny Briere, Phi	11	8	5	13	-6	4
Drew Doughty, LA	20	4	12	16	+11	14	Adam Henrique, NJ	24	5	8	13	+12	11
Zach Parise, NJ	24	8	7	15	-8	4	Dan Girardi, NYR	20	3	9	12	+6	2
Brad Richards, NYR	20	6	9	15	-2	8	David Clarkson, NJ	24	3	9	12	+8	32
Mike Richards, LA	20	4	11	15	+1	17	Marian Gaborik, NYR	20	5	6	11	+0	2
Justin Williams, LA	20	4	11	15	+8	12	Dustin Penner, LA	20	3	8	11	+4	32

Seven tied at 10 points.

GOALS

Player and Team	GP	G
Anze Kopitar, LA	20	8
Dustin Brown, LA	20	8
Ilya Kovalchuk, NJ	23	8
Claude Giroux, Phi	10	8
Zach Parise, NJ	24	8
Jeff Carter, LA	20	8
Danny Briere, Phi	11	8
Travis Zajac, NJ	24	7
Brad Richards, NYR	20	6
Ryan Callahan, NYR	20	6
Jordan Staal, Pit	6	6

SHORT-HANDED GOALS

Player and Team	GP	SH
Anze Kopitar, LA	20	2
Dustin Brown, LA	20	2
Claude Giroux, Phi	10	2
Maxime Talbot	11	2

POWER PLAY GOALS

Player and Team	GP	PPG
Ilya Kovalchuk, NJ	23	5
Jeff Carter, LA	20	4
Claude Giroux, Phi	10	3
Zach Parise, NJ	24	3
Antoine Vermette, Phx	16	3
Scott Hartnell, Phi	11	3
Stephen Weiss, Fla	7	3

ASSISTS

Player and Team	GP	A
Anze Kopitar, LA	20	12
Dustin Brown, LA	20	12
Drew Doughty, LA	20	12
Ilya Kovalchuk, NJ	23	11
Mike Richards, LA	20	11
Justin Williams, LA	20	11

PLUS/MINUS

Player and Team	GP	+/-
Anze Kopitar, LA	20	+16
Dustin Brown, LA	20	+16
Adam Henrique, NJ	24	+12
Drew Doughty, LA	20	+11

Three players tied at +9.

Goaltending*

GOALS AGAINST AVERAGE

Player and Team	GP	W-L	Avg
Jonathan Quick, LA	20	16-4	1.41
Henrik Lundqvist, NYR	20	10-10	1.82
Braden Holtby, Wash	14	7-7	1.95
Mike Smith, Phx	16	9-7	1.99
Craig Anderson, Ott	7	3-4	2.00
Pekka Rinne, Nash	10	5-5	2.07
Martin Brodeur, NJ	24	14-9	2.12

*minimum of 400 minutes

SAVE PERCENTAGE

Player and Team	GP	W-L	SA	GA	SV	SV%
Jonathan Quick, LA	20	16-4	538	29	509	.946
Mike Smith, Phx	16	9-7	602	34	568	.944
Braden Holtby, Wash	14	7-7	459	30	429	.935
Craig Anderson, Ott	7	3-4	208	14	194	.933
Henrik Lundqvist, NYR	20	10-10	554	38	516	.931
Pekka Rinne, Nash	10	5-5	296	21	275	.929
Tim Thomas, Bos	7	3-4	207	16	191	.923

NHL Awards

Award	Player and Team	Award	Player and Team
Hart Trophy (MVP)	Evgeni Malkin, Pit	Adams Award (top coach)	Ken Hitchcock, StL
Lindsay Award (NHLPA MOP)	Evgeni Malkin, Pit	Selke Trophy (top def. forward)	Patrice Bergeron, Bos
Calder Trophy (top rookie)	Gabriel Landeskog, Col	Jennings Trophy (goaltender/s on	Brian Elliott/
Vezina Trophy (top goaltender)	Henrik Lundqvist, NYR	club allowing fewest goals)	Jaroslav Halak, StL
Norris Trophy (top defenseman)	Erik Karlsson, Ott	Art Ross Trophy (most points)	Evgeni Malkin, Pit
Lady Byng Trophy		Conn Smythe Trophy	
(for gentlemanly play)	Brian Campbell, Fla	(playoff MVP)	Jonathan Quick, LA

Individual 2011–12 Regular Season Leaders

Scoring

POINTS

Player and Team	GP	G	Ast	Pts	+/-	PIM	Player and Team	GP	G	Ast	Pts	+/-	PIM
Evgeni Malkin, Pit	75	50	59	109	+18	70	Erik Karlsson, Ott	81	19	59	78	+16	42
Steven Stamkos, TB	82	60	37	97	+7	66	Marian Hossa, Chi	81	29	48	77	+18	20
Claude Giroux, Phi	77	28	65	93	+6	29	Ray Whitney, Phx	82	24	53	77	+26	28
Jason Spezza, Ott	80	34	50	84	+11	36	Joe Thornton, SJ	82	18	59	77	+17	31
Ilya Kovalchuk, NJ	77	37	46	83	-9	33	Marian Gaborik, NYR	82	41	35	76	+15	34
Phil Kessel, Tor	82	37	45	82	-10	20	Jordan Eberle, Edm	78	34	42	76	+4	10
James Neal, Pit	80	40	41	81	+6	87	Anze Kopitar, LA	82	25	51	76	+12	20
John Tavares, NYI	82	31	50	81	-6	26	Martin St Louis, TB	77	25	49	74	-3	16
Henrik Sedin, Van	82	14	67	81	+23	52	Jason Pominville, Buf	82	30	43	73	-7	12
Patrik Elias, NJ	81	26	52	78	-8	16	Loui Eriksson, Dal	82	26	45	71	+18	12

Scoring *(Cont.)*

GOALS

Player and Team	GP	G
Steven Stamkos, TB	82	60
Evgeni Malkin, Pit	75	50
Marian Gaborik, NYR	82	41
James Neal, Pit	80	40
Alex Ovechkin, Wash	78	38
Ilya Kovalchuk, NJ	77	37
Phil Kessel, Tor	82	37
Scott Hartnell, Phi	82	37
Corey Perry, Ana	80	37
Matt Moulson, NYI	82	36

ASSISTS

Player and Team	GP	Ast
Henrik Sedin, Van	82	67
Claude Giroux, Phi	77	65
Evgeni Malkin, Pit	75	59
Erik Karlsson, Ott	81	59
Joe Thornton, SJ	82	59
Ray Whitney, Phx	82	53
Patrik Elias, NJ	81	52

ASSISTS *(CONT.)*

Player and Team	GP	Ast
Anze Kopitar, LA	82	51
Jason Spezza, Ott	80	50
John Tavares, NYI	82	50

PLUS/MINUS

Player and Team	GP	+/–
Patrice Bergeron, Bos	81	+36
Tyler Seguin, Bos	81	+34
Zdeno Chara, Bos	79	+33
Chris Kelly, Bos	82	+33
Brad Marchand, Bos	76	+31
Dan Hamhuis, Van	82	+29
Patrick Sharp, Chi	74	+28
Johnny Boychuk, Bos	77	+27
Ray Whitney, Phx	82	+26
Filip Kuba, Ott	73	+26

POWER PLAY GOALS

Player and Team	GP	PPG
James Neal, Pit	80	18
Scott Hartnell, Phi	82	16
Matt Moulson, NYI	82	14
Corey Perry, Ana	80	14
Three tied with 13 goals.		

SHORT-HANDED GOALS

Player and Team	GP	SHG
Adam Henrique, NJ	74	4
Mike Richards, LA	74	4
Cal Clutterbuck, Min	74	4
Twelve tied with three goals.		

GAME-WINNING GOALS

Player and Team	GP	GW
Steven Stamkos, TB	82	12
Radim Vrbata, Phx	77	12
Johan Franzen, Det	77	10
Evgeni Malkin, Pit	75	9
Brad Richards, NYR	82	9
Ryan Callahan, NYR	76	9

Goaltending
(Minimum 25 games)

GOALS AGAINST AVERAGE

Player and Team	GP	W–L	GA	GAA
Brian Elliott, StL	38	23-10	58	1.568
Jonathan Quick, LA	69	35-21	133	1.95
Cory Schneider, Van	33	20-8	60	1.96
Henrik Lundqvist, NYR	62	39-18	123	1.97
Jaroslav Halak, StL	46	26-12	90	1.97
Jimmy Howard, Det	57	35-17	119	2.13
Mike Smith, Phx	67	38-18	144	2.21
Johan Hedberg, NJ	27	17-7	59	2.23
J.-S. Giguere, Col	32	15-11	69	2.27
Kari Lehtonen, Dal	59	32-22	136	2.33

SAVE PERCENTAGE

Player and Team	GP	W–L	GA	SV	SV%
Brian Elliott, StL	38	23-10	58	914	.940
Cory Schneider, Van	33	20-8	60	885	.937
Henrik Lundqvist, NYR	62	39-18	123	1630	.930
Mike Smith, Phx	67	38-18	144	1922	.930
Jonathan Quick, LA	69	35-21	133	1730	.929

WINS

Player and Team	GP	GAA	W	L
Pekka Rinne, Nash	73	2.39	43	18
Marc-Andre Fleury, Pit	67	2.36	42	17
Henrik Lundqvist, NYR	62	1.97	39	18
Mike Smith, Phx	67	2.21	38	18
Jonathan Quick, LA	69	1.95	35	21
Jimmy Howard, Det	57	2.13	35	17
Miikka Kiprusoff, Cal	70	2.35	35	22
Tim Thomas, Bos	59	2.36	35	19
Antti Niemi, SJ	68	2.42	34	22
Ilya Bryzgalov, Phi	59	2.48	33	16
Craig Anderson, Ott	63	2.84	33	22

SHUTOUTS

Player and Team	GP	W	L	SO
Jonathan Quick, LA	69	35	21	10
Brian Elliott, StL	38	23	10	9
Henrik Lundqvist, NYR	62	39	18	8
Mike Smith, Phx	67	38	18	8
Five tied with six shutouts.				

NHL Team-by-Team Statistical Leaders

Anaheim Ducks

SCORING

Player	GP	G	Ast	Pts	+/–	PM
Teemu Selanne, RW	82	26	40	66	-1	24
Corey Perry, RW	80	37	23	60	-7	127
Bobby Ryan, RW	82	31	26	57	+1	53
Ryan Getzlaf, C	82	11	46	57	-11	75
Saku Koivu, C	74	11	27	38	+7	50
Cam Fowler, D	82	5	24	29	-28	18
Lubomir Visnovsky, D	68	6	21	27	+7	47
Andrew Cogliano, C	82	13	13	26	-4	15
Luca Sbisa, D	80	5	19	24	-5	66
Niklas Hagman, LW	71	9	14	23	-7	14
Francois Beauchemin, D	82	8	14	22	-14	48
Nick Bonino, C	50	5	13	18	+1	8
Matt Beleskey, LW	70	4	11	15	-2	72
Sheldon Brookbank, D	80	3	11	14	+11	72
Devante Smith-Pelly, RW	49	7	6	13	-7	16
Toni Lydman, D	74	0	13	13	+0	46
Jason Blake, LW	45	7	5	12	-4	6

SCORING *(CONT.)*

Player	GP	G	Ast	Pts	+/–	PM
Kyle Palmieri, RW	18	4	3	7	+3	6
Andrew Gordon, RW	37	2	3	5	-10	6
Maxime Macenauer, C	29	1	3	4	-4	18
George Parros, RW	46	1	3	4	+1	85
Brandon McMillan, C	25	0	4	4	-10	20
Rod Pelley, C	52	2	1	3	-3	16
Nate Guenin, D	15	2	0	2	+6	6
Peter Holland, C	4	1	0	1	+0	2
Ryan O'Marra, C	9	0	1	1	-1	4

GOALTENDING

Player	GP	W	L	OT	TGA	GAA	SO
Jonas Hiller	73	29	30	12	182	2.57	4
Jeff Deslauriers	4	3	1	0	11	2.74	0
Dan Ellis	10	1	5	0	19	2.72	0
Iiro Tarkki	1	1	0	0	3	4.39	0

Boston Bruins

SCORING

Player	GP	G	Ast	Pts	+/-	PM
Tyler Seguin, C	81	29	38	67	+34	30
Patrice Bergeron, C	81	22	42	64	+36	20
David Krejci, C	79	23	39	62	-5	36
Milan Lucic, LW	81	26	35	61	+7	135
Brad Marchand, LW	76	28	27	55	+31	87
Zdeno Chara, D	79	12	40	52	+33	86
Rich Peverley, C	57	11	31	42	+20	22
Chris Kelly, C	82	20	19	39	+33	41
Nathan Horton, RW	46	17	15	32	+0	54
Benoit Pouliot, LW	74	16	16	32	+18	38
Joe Corvo, D	75	4	21	25	+10	13
Brian Rolston, RW	70	7	17	24	-5	14
Andrew Ference, D	72	6	18	24	+9	46
Dennis Seidenberg, D	80	5	18	23	+15	39
Gregory Campbell, C	78	8	8	16	-3	80
Daniel Paille, LW	69	9	6	15	-5	15
Jordan Caron, RW	48	7	8	15	+0	14
Johnny Boychuk, D	77	5	10	15	+27	53
Shawn Thornton, LW	81	5	8	13	-7	154
Adam McQuaid, D	72	2	8	10	+16	99
Greg Zanon, D	56	3	5	8	+3	18
Mike Mottau, D	35	0	2	2	-11	15
Zach Hamill, C	16	0	2	2	+3	4
Carter Camper, C	3	1	0	1	+1	0
Torey Krug, D	2	0	1	1	+0	0

GOALTENDING

Player	GP	W	L	OT	TGA	GAA	SO
Tim Thomas	59	35	19	1	132	2.36	5
Tuukka Rask	23	11	8	3	44	2.05	3
Marty Turco	5	2	2	0	16	3.68	0
Anton Khudobin	1	1	0	0	1	1.00	0

Buffalo Sabres

SCORING

Player	GP	G	Ast	Pts	+/-	PM
Jason Pominville, RW	82	30	43	73	-7	12
Thomas Vanek, LW	78	26	35	61	-6	52
Drew Stafford, RW	80	20	30	50	+5	46
Derek Roy, C	80	17	27	44	-7	54
Cody Hodgson, C	83	19	22	41	+1	10
Tyler Ennis, LW	48	15	19	34	+11	14
Christian Ehrhoff, D	66	5	27	32	-2	47
Ville Leino, C	71	8	17	25	-2	16
Nathan Gerbe, LW	62	6	19	25	+2	32
Jordan Leopold, D	79	10	14	24	+4	28
Tyler Myers, D	55	8	15	23	+5	33
Brad Boyes, RW	65	8	15	23	+2	6
Luke Adam, C	52	10	10	20	-6	14
Marcus Foligno, LW	14	6	7	13	+6	9
Andrej Sekera, D	69	3	10	13	+3	18
Patrick Kaleta, RW	63	5	5	10	-5	116
Alexander Sulzer, D	27	3	6	9	+8	8
Jochen Hecht, C	22	4	4	8	+1	6
Matt Ellis, LW	60	3	5	8	-3	25
Corey Tropp, RW	34	3	5	8	+0	20
Brayden McNabb, D	25	1	7	8	-1	15
Robyn Regehr, D	76	1	4	5	-12	56
Mike Weber, D	51	1	4	5	-19	64
Cody McCormick, C	50	1	3	4	-7	56
Paul Szczechura, C	9	1	3	4	+0	4
TJ Brennan, D	11	1	0	1	+0	6
Travis Turnbull, C	3	1	0	1	+0	5

GOALTENDING

Player	GP	W	L	OT	TGA	GAA	SO
Ryan Miller	61	31	21	7	150	2.55	6
Jhonas Enroth	26	8	11	4	63	2.70	1
Drew MacIntyre	2	0	0	0	1	1.40	0

Calgary Flames

SCORING

Player	GP	G	Ast	Pts	+/-	PM
Jarome Iginla, RW	82	32	35	67	-10	43
Olli Jokinen, C	82	23	38	61	-12	54
Alex Tanguay, LW	64	13	36	49	+7	28
Curtis Glencross, LW	67	26	22	48	-13	62
Mike Cammalleri, C	66	20	21	41	-10	26
Jay Bouwmeester, D	82	5	24	29	-21	26
Lee Stempniak, RW	61	14	14	28	-2	16
Mark Giordano, D	61	9	18	27	+0	75
Matt Stajan, C	61	8	10	18	-3	29
Blake Comeau, LW	74	5	10	15	-11	30
Chris Butler, D	68	2	13	15	-9	34
TJ Brodie, D	54	2	12	14	+3	14
Tom Kostopoulos, RW	81	4	8	12	-15	57
Scott Hannan, D	78	2	10	12	-10	38
Mikael Backlund, C	41	4	7	11	-13	16
Roman Horak, C	61	3	8	11	+3	14
Derek Smith, D	47	2	9	11	-1	12
Anton Babchuk, D	32	2	8	10	+2	6

SCORING *(CONT.)*

Player	GP	G	Ast	Pts	+/-	PM
David Moss, RW	32	2	7	9	-3	12
Blair Jones, C	43	3	5	8	-1	18
Cory Sarich, D	62	1	6	7	+1	66
Tim Jackman, RW	75	1	6	7	-21	94
Paul Byron, C	22	3	2	5	+3	2
Sven Baertschi, LW	5	3	0	3	+2	4
Akim Aliu, RW	2	2	1	3	+3	12
Lance Bouma, C	27	1	2	3	-5	11
Krys Kolanos, C	13	0	1	1	-1	2

GOALTENDING

Player	GP	W	L	OT	TGA	GAA	SO
Miikka Kiprusoff	70	35	22	11	162	2.35	4
Henrik Karlsson	9	1	4	2	24	3.17	0
Leland Irving	7	1	3	3	21	3.20	0

Carolina Hurricanes

SCORING

Player	GP	G	Ast	Pts	+/–	PM
Eric Staal, C	82	24	46	70	-20	48
Jussi Jokinen, LW	79	12	34	46	-2	54
Jeff Skinner, C	64	20	24	44	-8	56
Jiri Tlusty, C	79	17	19	36	+1	26
Tuomo Ruutu, C	72	18	16	34	-3	50
Chad LaRose, RW	67	19	13	32	-15	48
Brandon Sutter, C	82	17	15	32	-3	21
Jamie McBain, D	76	8	19	27	-7	4
Tim Brent, C	79	12	12	24	-8	27
Jay Harrison, D	72	9	14	23	-10	60
Justin Faulk, D	66	8	14	22	-16	29
Anthony Stewart, RW	77	9	11	20	-2	30
Tim Gleason, D	82	1	17	18	+12	71
Joni Pitkanen, D	30	5	12	17	-15	16
Jaroslav Spacek, D	46	5	10	15	+6	8
Bryan Allen, D	82	1	13	14	-1	76
Drayson Bowman, LW	37	6	7	13	+2	4
Patrick Dwyer, RW	73	5	7	12	+0	23
Andreas Nodl, RW	60	3	5	8	-5	8
Jerome Samson, RW	16	2	3	5	-3	8
Derek Joslin, D	44	2	2	4	-15	35
Zac Dalpe, C	16	1	2	3	-3	4
Brett Sutter, LW	15	0	3	3	-1	11
Zach Boychuk, LW	16	0	2	2	-3	0
Riley Nash, C	5	0	1	1	+1	2

GOALTENDING

Player	GP	W	L	OT	TGA	GAA	SO
Cam Ward	68	30	23	13	182	2.74	5
Justin Peters	7	2	3	2	16	2.48	1
Brian Boucher	10	1	6	1	31	3.41	0
Mike Murphy	2	0	1	0	0	0.00	0

Chicago Blackhawks

SCORING

Player	GP	G	Ast	Pts	+/–	PM
Marian Hossa, RW	81	29	48	77	+18	20
Patrick Sharp, LW	74	33	36	69	+28	38
Patrick Kane, C	82	23	43	66	+7	40
Jonathan Toews, C	59	29	28	57	+17	28
Viktor Stalberg, RW	79	22	21	43	+6	34
Duncan Keith, D	74	4	36	40	+15	42
Dave Bolland, C	76	19	18	37	+0	47
Nick Leddy, D	82	3	34	37	-12	10
Brent Seabrook, D	78	9	25	34	+21	22
Andrew Brunette, LW	78	12	15	27	-13	4
Marcus Kruger, C	71	9	17	26	+11	22
Bryan Bickell, LW	71	9	15	24	-3	48
Andrew Shaw, C	37	12	11	23	-1	50
Johnny Oduya, D	81	3	15	18	-6	33
Jamal Mayers, RW	81	6	9	15	-4	91
Michael Frolik, RW	63	5	10	15	-10	22
Niklas Hjalmarsson, D	69	1	14	15	+9	14
Steve Montador, D	52	5	9	14	+4	45
Brendan Morrison, C	39	4	7	11	-5	12
Daniel Carcillo, LW	28	2	9	11	+10	82
Jimmy Hayes, RW	31	5	4	9	-3	16
Sean O'Donnell, D	51	0	7	7	-6	23
Sami Lepisto, D	26	1	2	3	+3	4
Ben Smith, RW	13	2	0	2	-5	0
Brandon Pirri, C	5	0	2	2	+2	0
Dylan Olsen, D	28	0	1	1	-5	6

GOALTENDING

Player	GP	W	L	OT	TGA	GAA	SO
Corey Crawford	57	30	17	7	146	2.72	4
Ray Emery	34	15	9	4	83	2.81	0

Colorado Avalanche

SCORING

Player	GP	G	Ast	Pts	+/–	PM
Ryan O'Reilly, C	81	18	37	55	-1	12
Paul Stastny, C	79	21	32	53	-8	34
Gabriel Landeskog, LW	82	22	30	52	+20	51
Steve Downie, RW	75	14	27	41	-6	137
David Jones, RW	72	20	17	37	-8	32
Jamie McGinn, LW	78	20	17	37	-3	37
Milan Hejduk, RW	81	14	23	37	-12	14
Matt Duchene, C	58	14	14	28	-11	8
Erik Johnson, D	73	4	22	26	-7	26
Ryan Wilson, D	59	1	20	21	+11	33
Shane O'Brien, D	76	3	17	20	+2	105
Jan Hejda, D	81	5	14	19	-17	24
Jay McClement, C	80	10	7	17	-8	31
Peter Mueller, C	32	7	9	16	-3	8
Chuck Kobasew, RW	58	7	7	14	-10	51
Stefan Elliott, D	39	4	9	13	+2	8
Cody McLeod, LW	75	6	5	11	+0	164

SCORING *(CONT.)*

Player	GP	G	Ast	Pts	+/–	PM
Kevin Porter, C	35	4	3	7	-2	17
Mark Olver, C	24	4	3	7	+0	15
Ryan O'Byrne, D	74	1	6	7	-5	57
Matt Hunwick, D	33	3	3	6	-3	8
David Van Der Gulik, LW	25	1	5	6	+3	2
Joakim Lindstrom, C	16	2	3	5	-9	0
Brad Malone, C	9	0	2	2	+1	0
Tyson Barrie, D	10	0	0	0	-2	0
Mike Connolly, LW	2	0	0	0	+0	2
Evan Brophey, C	3	0	0	0	+0	0

GOALTENDING

Player	GP	W	L	OT	TGA	GAA	SO
Semyon Varlamov	53	26	24	3	136	2.59	4
J.-S. Giguere	32	15	11	3	69	2.27	2

Columbus Blue Jackets

SCORING

Player	GP	G	Ast	Pts	+/-	PM
Rick Nash, RW	82	30	29	59	-19	40
Vinny Prospal, LW	82	16	39	55	-11	36
Derick Brassard, C	74	14	27	41	-20	42
RJ Umberger, LW	77	20	20	40	-10	27
Jack Johnson, D	82	12	26	38	-7	39
Nikita Nikitin, D	61	7	25	32	-10	18
James Wisniewski, D	48	6	21	27	-13	37
Fedor Tyutin, D	66	5	21	26	-21	49
Mark Letestu, C	62	11	14	25	-9	8
Ryan Johansen, C	67	9	12	21	-2	24
Derek Dorsett, RW	77	12	8	20	-11	235
Aaron Johnson, D	56	3	13	16	-12	26
Derek MacKenzie, C	66	7	7	14	+4	46
Cam Atkinson, RW	27	7	7	14	+1	14
David Savard, D	31	2	8	10	+0	16
Colton Gillies, C	75	2	6	8	-9	35
John Moore, D	67	2	5	7	-23	8
Marc Methot, D	46	1	6	7	-11	24
Darryl Boyce, C	37	1	4	5	-8	35
Brett Lebda, D	30	1	3	4	-1	14
Jared Boll, RW	54	2	1	3	-8	126
Matt Calvert, LW	13	0	3	3	-5	16
Ryan Russell, LW	41	1	2	3	-7	2
Maksim Mayorov, LW	10	1	1	2	-3	2
Tomas Kubalik, RW	8	1	1	2	-3	6

GOALTENDING

Player	GP	W	L	OT	TGA	GAA	SO
Steve Mason	46	16	26	3	143	3.39	1
Curtis Sanford	36	10	18	4	86	2.60	1
Allen York	11	3	2	0	16	2.30	0

Detroit Red Wings

SCORING

Player	GP	G	Ast	Pts	+/-	PM
Henrik Zetterberg, LW	82	22	47	69	+14	47
Pavel Datsyuk, C	70	19	48	67	+21	14
Valtteri Filppula, C	81	23	43	66	+18	14
Johan Franzen, RW	77	29	27	56	+23	40
Jiri Hudler, C	81	25	25	50	+10	42
Todd Bertuzzi, RW	71	14	24	38	+23	64
Niklas Kronwall, D	82	15	21	36	-2	38
Nicklas Lidstrom, D	70	11	23	34	+21	28
Danny Cleary, RW	75	12	21	33	+2	30
Ian White, D	77	7	25	32	+23	22
Darren Helm, C	68	9	17	26	+5	12
Kyle Quincey, D	72	7	19	26	-1	89
Drew Miller, LW	80	14	11	25	+6	20
Tomas Holmstrom, LW	74	11	13	24	-9	40
Justin Abdelkader, LW	81	8	14	22	+4	62
Brad Stuart, D	81	6	15	21	+16	29
Jakub Kindl, D	55	1	12	13	+7	25
Jonathan Ericsson, D	69	1	10	11	+16	47
Cory Emmerton, C	71	6	4	10	+1	14
Brendan Smith, D	14	1	6	7	+3	13
Gustav Nyquist, C	18	1	6	7	+2	2
Jan Mursak, LW	25	1	2	3	+2	0
Chris Conner, RW	8	1	2	3	+2	0

GOALTENDING

Player	GP	W	L	OT	TGA	GAA	SO
Jimmy Howard	57	35	17	4	119	2.13	6
Joey MacDonald	14	8	5	1	29	2.16	0
Ty Conklin	15	5	6	1	44	3.28	1

Dallas Stars

SCORING

Player	GP	G	Ast	Pts	+/-	PM
Loui Eriksson, LW	82	26	45	71	+18	12
Jamie Benn, LW	71	26	37	63	+15	55
Mike Ribeiro, C	74	18	45	63	+5	66
Michael Ryder, RW	82	35	27	62	+17	46
Steve Ott, LW	74	11	28	39	+5	156
Alex Goligoski, D	71	9	21	30	+0	16
Brenden Morrow, LW	57	11	15	26	+1	97
Trevor Daley, D	79	4	21	25	+3	42
Stephane Robidas, D	75	5	17	22	-5	48
Eric Nystrom, LW	74	16	5	21	-10	24
Vernon Fiddler, C	82	8	13	21	-13	60
Sheldon Souray, D	64	6	15	21	+11	73
Radek Dvorak, RW	73	4	17	21	-16	12
Adam Burish, RW	65	6	13	19	+6	76
Tom Wandell, C	72	6	9	15	-5	16
Philip Larsen, D	55	3	8	11	+11	16
Tomas Vincour, C	47	4	6	10	-2	2
Jake Dowell, C	52	2	5	7	-3	53
Toby Petersen, C	39	2	3	5	-7	6
Ryan Garbutt, C	20	2	1	3	-1	22
Adam Pardy, D	36	0	3	3	-5	16
Mark Fistric, D	60	0	2	2	-3	41
Jordie Benn, D	3	0	2	2	+1	0

GOALTENDING

Player	GP	W	L	OT	TGA	GAA	SO
Kari Lehtonen	59	32	22	4	136	2.33	4
Richard Bachman	18	8	5	1	43	2.77	1
Andrew Raycroft	10	2	8	0	31	3.52	0

Edmonton Oilers

SCORING

Player	GP	G	Ast	Pts	+/-	PM
Jordan Eberle, RW	78	34	42	76	+4	10
Taylor Hall, LW	61	27	26	53	-3	36
R. Nugent-Hopkins, C	62	18	34	52	-2	16
Sam Gagner, C	75	18	29	47	+5	36
Ryan Smyth, LW	82	19	27	46	-5	82
Ales Hemsky, RW	69	10	26	36	-13	43
Shawn Horcoff, C	81	13	21	34	-23	24
Ryan Jones, LW	79	17	16	33	-7	42
Jeff Petry, D	73	2	23	25	-7	26
Corey Potter, D	62	4	17	21	-16	24
Ryan Whitney, D	51	3	17	20	-16	16
Eric Belanger, C	78	4	12	16	-13	32
Ladislav Smid, D	78	5	10	15	+4	44
Ben Eager, LW	63	8	5	13	-1	107
Andy Sutton, D	52	3	7	10	+5	80
Lennart Petrell, LW	60	4	5	9	-10	45
Magnus Paajarvi, LW	41	2	6	8	-7	4
Nick Schultz, D	82	1	6	7	-12	40
Anton Lander, C	56	2	4	6	-8	12
Teemu Hartikainen, LW	17	2	3	5	+1	6
Linus Omark, LW	14	2	3	5	-3	8
Theo Peckham, D	54	1	2	3	+0	80
Darcy Hordichuk, LW	43	1	2	3	-3	64
Cam Barker, D	25	2	0	2	+0	23
Josh Green, C	7	1	1	2	-6	7

GOALTENDING

Player	GP	W	L	OT	TGA	GAA	SO
Devan Dubnyk	47	20	20	3	118	2.67	2
Nikolai Khabibulin	40	12	20	7	100	2.65	2
Yann Danis	1	0	0	0	2	3.75	0

Florida Panthers

SCORING

Player	GP	G	Ast	Pts	+/−	PM
Tomas Fleischmann, LW	82	27	34	61	-7	26
Stephen Weiss, C	80	20	37	57	+5	60
Kris Versteeg, RW	71	23	31	54	+4	49
Brian Campbell, D	82	4	49	53	-9	6
Jason Garrison, D	77	16	17	33	+6	32
Tomas Kopecky, RW	80	10	22	32	-8	32
Mikael Samuelsson, RW	54	14	17	31	+1	20
Dmitry Kulikov, D	58	4	24	28	-5	36
Marcel Goc, C	57	11	16	27	+5	10
Shawn Matthias, C	79	10	14	24	-2	49
Sean Bergenheim, LW	62	17	6	23	-5	48
Mike Weaver, D	82	0	16	16	-2	14
Ed Jovanovski, D	66	3	10	13	-11	31
Wojtek Wolski, LW	31	4	8	12	-5	2
Mike Santorelli, C	60	9	2	11	-10	18
Jack Skille, RW	46	4	6	10	-9	28
Matt Bradley, RW	45	3	5	8	-3	31
Erik Gudbranson, D	72	2	6	8	-19	78
Jerred Smithson, RW	69	1	5	6	-5	34
Marco Sturm, LW	48	3	2	5	-13	25
Krystofer Barch, RW	51	2	3	5	+0	114
Scottie Upshall, LW	26	2	3	5	-3	29
Michal Repik, RW	17	2	3	5	-3	6
Keaton Ellerby, C	40	0	5	5	-3	10
John Madden, C	31	3	0	3	-4	4
Evgenii Dadonov, RW	15	2	1	3	-4	2
Tyson Strachan, D	15	1	2	3	+1	5
Tim Kennedy, LW	27	1	1	2	-11	4

GOALTENDING

Player	GP	W	L	OT	TGA	GAA	SO
Jose Theodore	53	22	16	11	125	2.46	3
Scott Clemmensen	30	14	6	6	67	2.57	1
Jacob Markstrom	7	2	4	1	17	2.66	0

Los Angeles Kings

SCORING

Player	GP	G	Ast	Pts	+/−	PM
Anze Kopitar, C	82	25	51	76	+12	20
Justin Williams, RW	82	22	37	59	+10	44
Dustin Brown, RW	82	22	32	54	+18	53
Mike Richards, C	74	18	26	44	+3	71
Drew Doughty, D	77	10	26	36	-2	69
Jeff Carter, C	55	21	13	34	-12	16
Willie Mitchell, D	76	5	19	24	+20	44
Jarret Stoll, C	78	6	15	21	+2	60
Slava Voynov, D	54	8	12	20	+12	12
Dustin Penner, LW	65	7	10	17	-7	43
Simon Gagne, LW	34	7	10	17	-1	18
Matt Greene, D	82	4	11	15	+4	58
Dwight King, LW	27	5	9	14	+3	10
Alec Martinez, D	51	6	6	12	-1	8
Kyle Clifford, LW	81	5	7	12	-5	123
Rob Scuderi, D	82	1	8	9	-7	16
Brad Richardson, C	59	5	3	8	-6	30
Colin Fraser, C	67	2	6	8	-2	67
Trevor Lewis, C	72	3	4	7	-3	26
Andrei Loktionov, C	39	3	4	7	-4	2
Trent Hunter, RW	38	2	5	7	-4	8
Jordan Nolan, C	26	2	2	4	+2	28
Ethan Moreau, LW	28	1	3	4	-3	20
Davis Drewiske, D	9	2	0	2	+0	2
Scott Parse, LW	9	2	0	2	+1	14
Kevin Westgarth, RW	25	1	1	2	-3	39

GOALTENDING

Player	GP	W	L	OT	TGA	GAA	SO
Jonathan Quick	69	35	21	13	133	1.95	10
Jonathan Bernier	16	5	6	2	35	2.36	1

Minnesota Wild

SCORING

Player	GP	G	Ast	Pts	+/−	PM
Dany Heatley, LW	82	24	29	53	+2	28
Kyle Brodziak, C	82	22	22	44	-15	66
Mikko Koivu, C	55	12	32	44	+10	28
Devin Setoguchi, RW	69	19	17	36	-17	28
Matt Cullen, C	73	14	21	35	-10	24
Cal Clutterbuck, RW	74	15	12	27	-4	103
Nick Johnson, RW	77	8	18	26	-6	45
Jared Spurgeon, D	70	3	20	23	-4	6
P.-M. Bouchard, C	37	9	13	22	-1	18
Tom Gilbert, D	67	3	19	22	-8	20
Kurtis Foster, D	51	4	10	14	-13	35
Darroll Powe, C	82	6	7	13	-20	57
Erik Christensen, C	49	7	5	12	-13	8
Marco Scandella, D	63	3	9	12	-22	19
Nate Prosser, D	51	1	11	12	-17	57
G. Latendresse, LW	16	5	4	9	+6	29
Justin Falk, D	47	1	8	9	-13	54
Nick Palmieri, RW	38	4	3	7	-10	14

SCORING *(CONT.)*

Player	GP	G	Ast	Pts	+/−	PM
Casey Wellman, C	14	2	5	7	-4	0
Steven Kampfer, D	23	2	3	5	-1	6
Clayton Stoner, D	51	1	4	5	+3	62
Warren Peters, C	58	1	4	5	-15	54
Carson McMillan, RW	11	1	2	3	+1	11
Brett Bulmer, RW	9	0	3	3	+1	6
Matt Kassian, LW	24	2	0	2	-2	55
Chad Rau, C	9	2	0	2	-1	0
Jed Ortmeyer, RW	35	1	1	2	-8	14
David McIntyre, C	7	1	1	2	-1	2
Mike Lundin, D	17	0	2	2	-1	4
Stephane Veilleux, LW	22	0	2	2	-2	15

GOALTENDING

Player	GP	W	L	OT	TGA	GAA	SO
Niklas Backstrom	46	19	18	7	105	2.43	4
Josh Harding	34	13	12	4	81	2.62	2
Matt Hackett	12	3	6	0	22	2.37	0

Montreal Canadiens

SCORING

Player	GP	G	Ast	Pts	+/-	PM
Max Pacioretty, LW	79	33	32	65	+2	56
Erik Cole, LW	82	35	26	61	+11	48
David Desharnais, C	81	16	44	60	+10	24
Tomas Plekanec, C	81	17	35	52	-15	56
P.K. Subban, D	81	7	29	36	+9	119
Tomas Kaberle, D	72	3	28	31	-18	12
Lars Eller, C	79	16	12	28	-5	66
Rene Bourque, RW	76	18	6	24	-19	68
Yannick Weber, D	60	4	14	18	-7	30
Travis Moen, LW	48	9	7	16	-3	41
Raphael Diaz, D	59	3	13	16	-7	30
Josh Gorges, D	82	2	14	16	+14	39
Brian Gionta, RW	31	8	7	15	-7	16
Mathieu Darche, LW	61	5	7	12	-4	18
Chris Campoli, D	43	2	9	11	-3	6
Scott Gomez, C	38	2	9	11	-9	14
Louis Leblanc, C	42	5	5	10	+3	28
Alexei Emelin, D	67	3	4	7	-18	30
Petteri Nokelainen, C	56	3	4	7	-6	37
Blake Geoffrion, C	35	2	3	5	+0	27
Aaron Palushaj, RW	38	1	4	5	+1	4
Mike Blunden, RW	39	2	2	4	-1	27
Frédéric St-Denis, D	17	1	2	3	+3	10
Ryan White, C	20	0	3	3	-7	61
Andrei Markov, D	13	0	3	3	-4	4
Brad Staubitz, RW	62	1	0	1	-5	121

GOALTENDING

Player	GP	W	L	OT	TGA	GAA	SO
Carey Price	65	26	28	11	160	2.43	4
Peter Budaj	17	5	7	5	44	2.55	0

New Jersey Devils

SCORING

Player	GP	G	Ast	Pts	+/-	PM
Ilya Kovalchuk, LW	77	37	46	83	-9	33
Patrik Elias, C	81	26	52	78	-8	16
Zach Parise, LW	82	31	38	69	-5	32
Adam Henrique, C	74	16	35	51	+8	7
David Clarkson, RW	80	30	16	46	-8	138
Petr Sykora, RW	82	21	23	44	+4	40
Dainius Zubrus, RW	82	17	27	44	+7	34
Alexei Ponikarovsky, LW	82	14	19	33	-3	34
Marek Zidlicky, D	63	2	20	22	-6	34
Adam Larsson, D	65	2	16	18	-7	20
Mark Fayne, D	82	4	13	17	-4	26
Andy Greene, D	56	1	15	16	+3	16
Anton Volchenkov, D	72	2	9	11	+3	34
Jacob Josefson, C	41	2	7	9	+10	6
Bryce Salvador, D	82	0	9	9	+18	66
Ryan Carter, C	72	4	4	8	-13	90
Matt Taormina, D	30	1	6	7	+6	4
Travis Zajac, C	15	2	4	6	-3	4
Mattias Tedenby, RW	43	1	5	6	-15	16
Steve Bernier, RW	32	1	5	6	+6	16
Henrik Tallinder, D	39	0	6	6	-11	16
Peter Harrold, D	11	0	2	2	+0	0
Alexander Urbom, D	5	1	0	1	+1	9
Stephen Gionta, RW	1	1	0	1	+1	0
Cam Janssen, RW	48	0	1	1	-8	75
Brad Mills, C	27	0	1	1	-10	32

GOALTENDING

Player	GP	W	L	OT	TGA	GAA	SO
Martin Brodeur	59	31	21	4	136	2.41	3
Johan Hedberg	27	17	7	2	59	2.23	4

Nashville Predators

SCORING

Player	GP	G	Ast	Pts	+/-	PM
Martin Erat, RW	71	19	39	58	+12	30
David Legwand, C	78	19	34	53	+3	26
Mike Fisher, C	72	24	27	51	+11	33
Shea Weber, D	78	19	30	49	+21	46
Ryan Suter, D	79	7	39	46	+15	30
Patric Hornqvist, RW	76	27	16	43	+9	28
Sergei Kostitsyn, LW	75	17	26	43	+8	34
Andrei Kostitsyn, LW	72	16	20	36	-1	26
Craig Smith, C	72	14	22	36	-9	30
Colin Wilson, C	68	15	20	35	+5	21
Jordin Tootoo, RW	77	6	24	30	-5	92
Matt Halischuk, RW	73	15	13	28	+9	27
Nick Spaling, LW	77	10	12	22	-7	18
Paul Gaustad, C	70	7	14	21	-1	76
Kevin Klein, D	66	4	17	21	-8	4
Gabriel Bourque, LW	43	7	12	19	-2	6
Roman Josi, D	52	5	11	16	+1	14
Hal Gill, D	76	1	12	13	-3	37
Francis Bouillon, D	66	4	7	11	-4	33
Ryan Ellis, D	32	3	8	11	+5	4
Jonathon Blum, D	33	3	4	7	-14	6
Brandon Yip, RW	35	3	4	7	+1	28
Alexander Radulov, RW	9	3	4	7	+3	4
Jack Hillen, D	55	2	4	6	+6	20
Niclas Bergfors, RW	11	1	1	2	-2	2
Brian McGrattan, RW	30	0	2	2	-1	61

GOALTENDING

Player	GP	W	L	OT	TGA	GAA	SO
Pekka Rinne	73	43	18	8	166	2.39	5
Anders Lindback	16	5	8	0	32	2.42	0

New York Islanders

SCORING

Player	GP	G	Ast	Pts	+/-	PM
John Tavares, C	82	31	50	81	-6	26
Matt Moulson, LW	82	36	33	69	+1	6
PA Parenteau, RW	80	18	49	67	-8	89
Frans Nielsen, C	82	17	30	47	-3	6
Mark Streit, D	82	7	40	47	-27	46
Kyle Okposo, RW	79	24	21	45	-15	46
Michael Grabner, RW	78	20	12	32	-18	12
Josh Bailey, C	80	13	19	32	-10	32
Travis Hamonic, D	73	2	22	24	+6	73
Andrew MacDonald, D	75	5	14	19	-5	26
Matt Martin, LW	80	7	7	14	-17	121
Milan Jurcina, D	65	3	8	11	-34	30
David Ullstrom, LW	29	4	4	8	-2	6
Steve Staios, D	65	0	8	8	-19	53
Dylan Reese, D	28	1	6	7	+0	11
Marty Reasoner, C	61	1	5	6	-25	34
Mark Eaton, D	62	1	3	4	-17	10
Casey Cizikas, C	15	0	4	4	+1	6
Jay Pandolfo, LW	62	1	2	3	-14	8
Nino Niederreiter, RW	55	1	0	1	-29	12

GOALTENDING

Player	GP	W	L	OT	TGA	GAA	SO
Evgeni Nabokov	42	19	18	3	101	2.55	2
Al Montoya	31	9	11	5	89	3.10	0
Rick DiPietro	8	3	2	3	22	3.73	0
Kevin Poulin	6	2	4	0	15	3.04	0
Anders Nilsson	4	1	2	0	10	2.75	1

New York Rangers

SCORING

Player	GP	G	Ast	Pts	+/-	PM
Marian Gaborik, RW	82	41	35	76	+15	34
Brad Richards, C	82	25	41	66	-1	22
Ryan Callahan, RW	76	29	25	54	-8	61
Derek Stepan, C	82	17	34	51	+14	22
Michael Del Zotto, D	77	10	31	41	+20	36
Carl Hagelin, LW	64	14	24	38	+21	24
Artem Anisimov, C	79	16	20	36	+12	34
Brandon Dubinsky, C	77	10	24	34	+16	110
Ryan McDonagh, D	82	7	25	32	+25	44
Dan Girardi, D	82	5	24	29	+13	20
Brian Boyle, C	82	11	15	26	+2	59
Ruslan Fedotenko, LW	73	9	11	20	-7	16
Anton Stralman, D	53	2	16	18	+9	20
Brandon Prust, LW	82	5	12	17	-1	156
John Mitchell, C	63	5	11	16	+10	8
Stu Bickel, D	51	0	9	9	+2	108
Jeff Woywitka, D	27	1	5	6	+2	8
Mike Rupp, C	60	4	1	5	-1	97
Marc Staal, D	46	2	3	5	-7	16
Steve Eminger, D	42	2	3	5	+0	28
Sean Avery, LW	15	3	0	3	+2	21
Mats Zuccarello, LW	10	2	1	3	+0	6
Michael Sauer, D	19	1	2	3	+9	21
Tim Erixon, D	18	0	2	2	-2	8
John Scott, LW	35	0	1	1	-1	53
Andre Deveaux, C	9	0	1	1	+3	29

GOALTENDING

Player	GP	W	L	OT	TGA	GAA	SO
Henrik Lundqvist	62	39	18	5	123	1.97	8
Martin Biron	21	12	6	2	50	2.46	2

Philadelphia Flyers

SCORING

Player	GP	G	Ast	Pts	+/-	PM
Claude Giroux, RW	77	28	65	93	+6	29
Scott Hartnell, LW	82	37	30	67	+19	136
Jaromir Jagr, RW	73	19	35	54	+5	30
Wayne Simmonds, RW	82	28	21	49	-1	114
Jakub Voracek, RW	78	18	31	49	+11	32
Danny Briere, RW	70	16	33	49	+5	69
Matt Read, RW	79	24	23	47	+13	12
Kimmo Timonen, D	76	4	39	43	+8	46
Matt Carle, D	82	4	34	38	+4	36
Maxime Talbot, C	81	19	15	34	+5	59
Sean Couturier, C	77	13	14	27	+18	14
Andrej Meszaros, D	62	7	18	25	+6	38
J. van Riemsdyk, LW	43	11	13	24	-1	24
Braydon Coburn, D	81	4	20	24	+10	56
Brayden Schenn, C	54	12	6	18	-7	34
Pavel Kubina, D	69	3	12	15	-2	74
Chris Pronger, D	13	1	11	12	+1	10
Nicklas Grossmann, D	74	0	11	11	+5	36
Eric Wellwood, LW	24	5	4	9	+12	2
Zac Rinaldo, C	66	2	7	9	-1	232
Marc-Andre Bourdon, D	45	4	3	7	+4	52
Harry Zolnierczyk, LW	37	3	3	6	-11	35
Andreas Lilja, D	46	0	6	6	+9	34
Erik Gustafsson, D	30	1	4	5	+12	2
Jody Shelley, LW	30	0	1	1	-6	64
Tom Sestito, LW	14	0	1	1	-3	83

GOALTENDING

Player	GP	W	L	OT	TGA	GAA	SO
Ilya Bryzgalov	59	33	16	7	141	2.48	6
Sergei Bobrovsky	29	14	10	2	78	3.02	0

Ottawa Senators

SCORING

Player	GP	G	Ast	Pts	+/-	PM
Jason Spezza, C	80	34	50	84	+11	36
Erik Karlsson, D	81	19	59	78	+16	42
Milan Michalek, LW	77	35	25	60	+4	32
Daniel Alfredsson, RW	75	27	32	59	+16	18
Nick Foligno, LW	82	15	32	47	+2	124
Colin Greening, LW	82	17	20	37	-4	46
Sergei Gonchar, D	74	5	32	37	-4	55
Filip Kuba, D	73	6	26	32	+26	26
Kyle Turris, C	55	12	17	29	+10	31
Chris Neil, RW	72	13	15	28	-10	178
Zack Smith, C	81	14	12	26	+4	98
Erik Condra, RW	81	8	17	25	+11	30
Matt Gilroy, D	67	3	17	20	+2	18
Chris Phillips, D	80	5	14	19	+12	16
Jared Cowen, D	82	5	12	17	-4	56
Bobby Butler, RW	56	6	10	16	+8	12
Kaspars Daugavins, LW	65	5	6	11	-2	12
Jesse Winchester, C	32	2	6	8	+2	22
Jim O'Brien, C	28	3	3	6	+6	4
Zenon Konopka, C	55	3	2	5	-4	193
Stephane Da Costa, C	22	3	2	5	-9	8
Peter Regin, C	10	2	2	4	+3	2
Matt Carkner, D	29	1	2	3	+0	33
Rob Klinkhammer, LW	15	0	2	2	+0	2

GOALTENDING

Player	GP	W	L	OT	TGA	GAA	SO
Craig Anderson	63	33	22	6	165	2.84	3
Robin Lehner	5	3	2	0	10	2.01	1
Ben Bishop	10	3	3	2	22	2.48	0
Alex Auld	14	2	4	2	36	3.35	0

Phoenix Coyotes

SCORING

Player	GP	G	Ast	Pts	+/-	PM
Ray Whitney, LW	82	24	53	77	+26	28
Radim Vrbata, RW	77	35	27	62	+24	24
Shane Doan, RW	79	22	28	50	-8	48
Keith Yandle, D	82	11	32	43	+5	51
Lauri Korpikoski, LW	82	17	20	37	+3	14
Antoine Vermette, C	82	11	26	37	-13	28
Martin Hanzal, C	64	8	26	34	+12	63
O. Ekman-Larsson, D	82	13	19	32	+0	32
Daymond Langkow, C	73	11	19	30	-4	14
Raffi Torres, LW	79	15	11	26	+2	83
Mikkel Boedker, RW	82	11	13	24	-2	12
Boyd Gordon, C	75	8	15	23	+9	10
Taylor Pyatt, LW	73	9	10	19	-4	23
Kyle Chipchura, C	53	3	13	16	+2	42
Gilbert Brule, C	33	5	9	14	+7	11
Rostislav Klesla, D	65	3	10	13	+13	54
Michal Rozsival, D	54	1	12	13	+8	34
Derek Morris, D	59	2	9	11	-12	38
David Schlemko, D	46	1	10	11	+7	10
Adrian Aucoin, D	64	2	7	9	+14	42
David Rundblad, D	30	1	6	7	-12	6
Patrick O'Sullivan, C	23	2	2	4	-4	2
Marc-Antoine Pouliot, C	13	0	4	4	-2	2
Michael Stone, D	13	1	2	3	+7	2
Chris Summers, D	21	0	3	3	-4	11

GOALTENDING

Player	GP	W	L	OT	TGA	GAA	SO
Mike Smith	67	38	18	10	144	2.21	8
Jason LaBarbera	19	3	9	3	43	2.54	0
Curtis McElhinney	2	1	0	0	2	1.67	0

Pittsburgh Penguins

SCORING

Player	GP	G	Ast	Pts	+/–	PM
Evgeni Malkin, C	75	50	59	109	+18	70
James Neal, LW	80	40	41	81	+6	87
Chris Kunitz, LW	82	26	35	61	+16	49
Pascal Dupuis, RW	82	25	34	59	+18	34
Jordan Staal, C	62	25	25	50	+11	34
Steve Sullivan, LW	79	17	31	48	-3	20
Kris Letang, D	51	10	32	42	+21	34
Matt Cooke, LW	82	19	19	38	+5	44
Sidney Crosby, C	22	8	29	37	+15	14
Tyler Kennedy, C	60	11	22	33	+10	29
Paul Martin, D	73	2	25	27	+9	18
Matt Niskanen, D	75	4	17	21	+9	47
Craig Adams, RW	82	5	13	18	-6	34
Brooks Orpik, D	73	2	16	18	+19	61
Deryk Engelland, D	73	4	13	17	+10	56
Arron Asham, RW	64	5	11	16	-5	76
Richard Park, RW	54	7	7	14	-1	12
Joe Vitale, C	68	4	10	14	-5	56
Zbynek Michalek, D	62	2	11	13	+0	24
Cal O'Reilly, C	33	2	5	7	-11	4
Dustin Jeffrey, LW	26	4	2	6	-4	2
Ben Lovejoy, D	34	1	4	5	+3	13
Simon Despres, D	18	1	3	4	+5	10
Alexandre Picard, D	17	0	4	4	+4	4
Jason Williams, C	8	1	1	2	+1	4
Eric Tangradi, LW	24	0	2	2	-4	16
Brian Strait, D	9	0	1	1	-2	4
Carl Sneep, D	1	0	1	1	+1	0

GOALTENDING

Player	GP	W	L	OT	TGA	GAA	SO
Marc-Andre Fleury	67	42	17	4	153	2.36	3
Brent Johnson	16	6	7	2	42	3.11	0
Brad Thiessen	5	3	1	0	16	3.72	0

San Jose Sharks

SCORING

Player	GP	G	Ast	Pts	+/–	PM
Joe Thornton, C	82	18	59	77	+17	31
Logan Couture, C	80	31	34	65	+2	16
Patrick Marleau, LW	82	30	34	64	+10	26
Joe Pavelski, RW	82	31	30	61	+18	31
Dan Boyle, D	81	9	39	48	+10	57
Ryane Clowe, LW	76	17	28	45	-5	97
Brent Burns, D	81	11	26	37	+8	34
Martin Havlat, RW	39	7	20	27	+10	22
Dominic Moore, C	79	4	21	25	-18	54
Michal Handzus, C	67	7	17	24	-6	18
Daniel Winnik, LW	84	8	15	23	-11	52
M.-E. Vlasic, D	82	4	19	23	+11	40
Torrey Mitchell, C	76	9	10	19	-6	29
Andrew Desjardins, C	76	4	13	17	+4	47
T.J. Galiardi, LW	69	9	6	15	-8	53
Jason Demers, D	57	4	9	13	-8	22
Justin Braun, D	66	2	9	11	-2	23
Brad Winchester, LW	67	6	4	10	-5	88
Tommy Wingels, C	33	3	6	9	-1	18
Benn Ferriero, RW	35	7	1	8	+0	8
Colin White, D	54	1	3	4	-5	21
Andrew Murray, C	39	1	3	4	+3	4
Jim Vandermeer, D	25	1	3	4	+3	33
Douglas Murray, D	60	0	4	4	+3	31

GOALTENDING

Player	GP	W	L	OT	TGA	GAA	SO
Antti Niemi	68	34	22	9	159	2.42	6
Thomas Greiss	19	9	7	1	40	2.30	0

St. Louis Blues

SCORING

Player	GP	G	Ast	Pts	+/–	PM
David Backes, C	82	24	30	54	+15	101
T.J. Oshie, RW	80	19	35	54	+15	50
Alex Pietrangelo, D	81	12	39	51	+16	36
Kevin Shattenkirk, D	81	9	34	43	+20	60
David Perron, LW	57	21	21	42	+19	28
Patrik Berglund, C	82	19	19	38	+4	30
Jason Arnott, C	72	17	17	34	+13	26
Chris Stewart, RW	79	15	15	30	+1	109
Alexander Steen, LW	43	15	13	28	+24	28
J. Langenbrunner, RW	70	6	18	24	+7	32
Andy McDonald, LW	25	10	12	22	+4	2
Vladimir Sobotka, LW	73	5	15	20	+12	42
Carlo Colaiacovo, D	64	2	17	19	+7	22
Matt D'Agostini, RW	55	9	9	18	+12	27
Barret Jackman, D	81	1	12	13	+20	57
Kris Russell, D	55	6	6	12	+12	25
Roman Polak, D	77	0	11	11	+6	57

SCORING *(CONT.)*

Player	GP	G	Ast	Pts	+/–	PM
Scott Nichol, C	80	3	5	8	-5	83
Chris Porter, LW	47	4	3	7	-1	11
Kent Huskins, D	25	2	5	7	+9	10
Ian Cole, D	26	1	5	6	+7	22
Ryan Reaves, RW	60	3	1	4	+0	124
Evgeny Grachev, C	26	1	3	4	-4	2
Jaden Schwartz, LW	7	2	1	3	+1	0
B.J. Crombeen, RW	40	1	2	3	-2	71
Adam Cracknell, RW	2	1	0	1	+1	0
Cade Fairchild, D	5	0	1	1	-1	0

GOALTENDING

Player	GP	W	L	OT	TGA	GAA	SO
Jaroslav Halak	46	26	12	7	90	1.97	6
Brian Elliott	38	23	10	4	58	1.56	9

Tampa Bay Lightning

SCORING

Player	GP	G	Ast	Pts	+/-	PM
Steven Stamkos, C	82	60	37	97	+7	66
Martin St Louis, RW	77	25	49	74	-3	16
Teddy Purcell, RW	81	24	41	65	+9	16
Vincent Lecavalier, C	64	22	27	49	-2	50
Ryan Malone, LW	68	20	28	48	-11	82
M. Bergeron, D	43	4	20	24	+6	20
Victor Hedman, D	61	5	18	23	-9	65
Eric Brewer, D	82	1	20	21	-5	49
Tom Pyatt, C	74	12	7	19	-19	8
Brian Lee, D	55	1	15	16	-8	35
Nate Thompson, C	68	9	6	15	-23	21
Brett Connolly, RW	68	4	11	15	-9	30
Brett Clark, D	82	2	13	15	-26	20
Bruno Gervais, D	50	6	7	13	-4	8
Ryan Shannon, RW	45	4	8	12	-11	10
JT Wyman, RW	40	2	9	11	+1	8
Tim Wallace, RW	49	3	6	9	-3	16
Adam Hall, RW	57	2	5	7	-11	17
Trevor Smith, C	16	2	3	5	+2	4
Dana Tyrell, C	26	0	5	5	-5	6
Brendan Mikkelson, D	41	1	2	3	-4	13
Keith Aulie, D	36	0	3	3	-7	29
Mike Commodore, D	30	0	2	2	+7	38
P. Labrie, LW	14	0	2	2	-2	15
Mike Angelidis, LW	6	1	0	1	-1	5
J.T. Brown, RW	5	0	1	1	+2	0

GOALTENDING

Player	GP	W	L	OT	TGA	GAA	SO
Mathieu Garon	48	23	16	4	118	2.85	1
Dwayne Roloson	40	13	16	3	128	3.66	1
Sebastien Caron	3	1	1	0	7	3.11	0
Dustin Tokarski	5	1	3	1	14	3.44	0

Toronto Maple Leafs

SCORING

Player	GP	G	Ast	Pts	+/-	PM
Phil Kessel, RW	82	37	45	82	-10	20
Joffrey Lupul, LW	66	25	42	67	+1	48
Mikhail Grabovski, C	74	23	28	51	+0	51
Tyler Bozak, C	73	18	29	47	-7	22
Dion Phaneuf, D	82	12	32	44	-10	92
Clarke MacArthur, LW	73	20	23	43	+3	37
Tim Connolly, C	70	13	23	36	-14	40
Jake Gardiner, D	75	7	23	30	-2	18
Nikolai Kulemin, LW	70	7	21	28	+2	6
John-Michael Liles, D	66	7	20	27	-14	20
Joey Crabb, RW	67	11	15	26	+1	33
Luke Schenn, D	79	2	20	22	-6	62
Cody Franson, D	57	5	16	21	-1	22
Carl Gunnarsson, D	76	4	15	19	-9	20
Matthew Lombardi, C	62	8	10	18	-19	10
Matt Frattin, RW	56	8	7	15	-4	25
David Steckel, C	76	8	5	13	-14	10
Nazem Kadri, C	21	5	2	7	+2	8
Mike Komisarek, D	45	1	4	5	-13	41
Joe Colborne, C	10	1	4	5	+2	4
Mike Brown, RW	50	2	2	4	-8	74
Colby Armstrong, RW	29	1	2	3	-8	9
Colton Orr, RW	5	1	0	1	+1	5
Ryan Hamilton, LW	2	0	1	1	-1	2

GOALTENDING

Player	GP	W	L	OT	TGA	GAA	SO
Jonas Gustavsson	42	17	17	4	112	2.92	4
James Reimer	34	14	14	4	97	3.10	3
Ben Scrivens	12	4	5	2	35	3.13	0
Jussi Rynnas	2	0	1	0	7	4.24	0

Vancouver Canucks

SCORING

Player	GP	G	Ast	Pts	+/-	PM
Henrik Sedin, C	82	14	67	81	+23	52
Daniel Sedin, LW	72	30	37	67	+14	40
Alexandre Burrows, LW	80	28	24	52	+24	90
Ryan Kesler, C	77	22	27	49	+11	56
Alexander Edler, D	82	11	38	49	+0	34
Kevin Bieksa, D	78	8	36	44	+12	94
Chris Higgins, LW	71	18	25	43	+11	16
Jannik Hansen, RW	82	16	23	39	+18	34
Dan Hamhuis, D	82	4	33	37	+29	46
David Booth, LW	62	16	14	30	-5	34
Sami Salo, D	69	9	16	25	+7	10
Mason Raymond, LW	55	10	10	20	+4	18
Maxim Lapierre, C	82	9	10	19	-3	130
Manny Malhotra, C	78	7	11	18	-11	14
Samuel Pahlsson, C	80	4	13	17	-2	34
M. Gragnani, D	58	2	13	15	+6	26

SCORING *(CONT.)*

Player	GP	G	Ast	Pts	+/-	PM
Aaron Rome, D	43	4	6	10	-4	46
Zack Kassian, RW	44	4	6	10	-2	51
Dale Weise, RW	68	4	4	8	-1	81
Keith Ballard, D	47	1	6	7	+0	64
Andrew Ebbett, C	18	5	1	6	+2	6
Byron Bitz, RW	10	1	3	4	+2	14
Andrew Alberts, D	44	2	1	3	+4	40
Christopher Tanev, D	25	0	2	2	+10	2
Mike Duco, RW	6	0	2	2	+1	5
Aaron Volpatti, LW	23	1	0	1	-2	37

GOALTENDING

Player	GP	W	L	OT	TGA	GAA	SO
Roberto Luongo	55	31	14	8	127	2.41	5
Cory Schneider	33	20	8	1	60	1.96	3

Washington Capitals

SCORING

Player	GP	G	Ast	Pts	+/-	PM
Alex Ovechkin, LW	78	38	27	65	-8	26
Alexander Semin, LW	77	21	33	54	+9	56
Marcus Johansson, C	80	14	32	46	-5	8
Dennis Wideman, D	82	11	35	46	-8	46
Nicklas Backstrom, C	42	14	30	44	-4	24
Brooks Laich, C	82	16	25	41	-8	34
Jason Chimera, LW	82	20	19	39	+4	78
Troy Brouwer, RW	82	18	15	33	-15	61
John Carlson, D	82	9	23	32	-15	22
Mathieu Perreault, C	64	16	14	30	+9	24
Dmitry Orlov, D	60	3	16	19	+1	18
Mike Knuble, RW	72	6	12	18	-15	32
Joel Ward, RW	73	6	12	18	+12	20
Karl Alzner, D	82	1	16	17	+12	29
Jeff Halpern, C	69	4	12	16	-1	24

SCORING *(CONT.)*

Player	GP	G	Ast	Pts	+/-	PM
Roman Hamrlik, D	68	2	11	13	+11	34
Keith Aucoin, RW	27	3	8	11	+4	0
Matt Hendricks, C	78	4	5	9	-6	95
Cody Eakin, C	30	4	4	8	+2	4
Mike Green, D	32	3	4	7	+5	12
Jeff Schultz, D	54	1	5	6	-2	12
Jay Beagle, RW	41	4	1	5	-2	23
John Erskine, D	28	0	2	2	+3	51

GOALTENDING

Player	GP	W	L	OT	TGA	GAA	SO
Tomas Vokoun	48	25	17	2	108	2.51	4
Michal Neuvirth	38	13	13	5	95	2.82	3
Braden Holtby	7	4	2	1	15	2.49	1

Winnipeg Jets

SCORING

Player	GP	G	Ast	Pts	+/-	PM
Blake Wheeler, RW	80	17	47	64	+3	55
Evander Kane, LW	74	30	27	57	+11	53
Dustin Byfuglien, D	66	12	41	53	-8	72
Andrew Ladd, LW	82	28	22	50	-8	64
Kyle Wellwood, C	77	18	29	47	+3	4
Bryan Little, C	74	24	22	46	-11	26
Nik Antropov, C	69	15	20	35	+0	42
Tobias Enstrom, D	62	6	27	33	+6	38
Zach Bogosian, D	65	5	25	30	-3	71
Alexander Burmistrov, C	76	13	15	28	+4	42
Tim Stapleton, C	63	11	16	27	-2	10
Jim Slater, C	78	13	8	21	-9	42
Grant Clitsome, D	63	4	13	17	-9	32
Tanner Glass, LW	78	5	11	16	-12	73
Mark Stuart, D	80	3	11	14	-4	98
Antti Miettinen, RW	45	5	8	13	-5	0

SCORING

Player	GP	G	Ast	Pts	+/-	PM
Chris Thorburn, RW	72	4	7	11	-6	83
Ron Hainsey, D	56	0	10	10	+9	23
Spencer Machacek, RW	13	2	7	9	+8	7
Mark Flood, D	33	3	4	7	-1	10
Ben Maxwell, C	15	1	5	6	+4	2
Eric Fehr, RW	35	2	1	3	-6	12
Randy Jones, D	39	1	1	2	+4	8
Brett MacLean, LW	5	0	2	2	+1	2
Mark Scheifele, C	7	1	0	1	+0	0
Jason Jaffray, LW	13	0	1	1	-1	7

GOALTENDING

Player	GP	W	L	OT	TGA	GAA	SO
Ondrej Pavelec	68	29	28	9	191	2.91	4
Chris Mason	20	8	7	1	43	2.59	2
Peter Mannino	1	0	0	0	0	0.00	0

2012 NHL Draft

First Round

The opening round of the 2012 NHL entry draft was held on June 22 in Pittsburgh, Pennsylvania.

	Team	Selection	Position
1	Edmonton	Nail Yakupov	RW
2	Columbus	Ryan Murray	D
3	Montreal	Alex Galchenyuk	C
4	N.Y. Islanders	Griffin Reinhart	D
5	Toronto	Morgan Rielly	D
6	Anaheim	Hampus Lindholm	D
7	Minnesota	Mathew Dumba	D
8	Pittsburgh	Derrick Pouliot	D
	(from Carolina)		
9	Winnipeg	Jacob Trouba	D
10	Tampa Bay	Slater Koekkoek	D
11	Washington	Filip Forsberg	C
	(from Colorado)		
12	Buffalo	Mikhail Grigorenko	C
13	Dallas	Radek Faksa	C
14	Buffalo	Zemgus Girgensons	C
	(from Calgary)		

	Team	Selection	Position
15	Ottawa	Cody Ceci	D
16	Washington	Thomas Wilson	RW
17	San Jose	Tomas Hertl	C
18	Chicago	Teuvo Teravainen	LW
19	Tampa Bay	Andrey Vasilevskiy	G
	(from Detroit)		
20	Philadelphia	Scott Laughton	C
21	Calgary	Mark Jankowski	C
	(from Buffalo through Nashville)		
22	Pittsburgh	Olli Maatta	D
23	Florida	Michael Matheson	D
24	Boston	Malcolm Subban	G
25	St. Louis	Jordan Schmaltz	D
26	Vancouver	Brendan Gaunce	G
27	Phoenix	Henrik Samuelsson	C
28	N.Y. Rangers	Brady Skjei	D
29	New Jersey	Stefan Matteau	C
30	Los Angeles	Tanner Pearson	LW

The Stanley Cup

Awarded annually to the team that wins the NHL's best-of-seven final-round playoffs. The Stanley Cup is the oldest trophy competed for by professional athletes in North America. It was donated in 1893 by Frederick Arthur, Lord Stanley of Preston.

Results

1892–93	Montreal A.A.A.
1893–94	Montreal A.A.A.
1894–95	Montreal Victorias
1895–96	Winnipeg Victorias (Feb)
1895–96	Montreal Victorias (Dec)
1896–97	Montreal Victorias
1897–98	Montreal Victorias
1898–99	Montreal Victorias (Feb)
1898–99	Montreal Shamrocks (Mar)
1899–1900	Montreal Shamrocks
1900–01	Winnipeg Victorias
1901–02	Winnipeg Victorias (Jan)
1901–02	Montreal A.A.A. (Mar)
1902–03	Montreal A.A.A. (Feb)
1902–03	Ottawa Silver Seven (Mar)
1903–04	Ottawa Silver Seven
1904–05	Ottawa Silver Seven
1905–06	Ottawa Silver Seven (Feb)
1905–06	Montreal Wanderers (Mar)
1906–07	Kenora Thistles (Jan)
1906–07	Montreal Wanderers (Mar)
1907–08	Montreal Wanderers
1908–09	Ottawa Senators
1909–10	Montreal Wanderers
1910–11	Ottawa Senators
1911–12	Quebec Bulldogs
1912–13	Quebec Bulldogs
1913–14	Toronto Blueshirts
1914–15	Vancouver Millionaires
1915–16	Montreal Canadiens
1916–17	Seattle Metropolitans

NHL WINNERS AND FINALISTS

Season	Champion	Finalist	GP in Final
1917–18	Toronto Arenas	Vancouver Millionaires	5
1918–19	No decision*	No decision*	5
1919–20	Ottawa Senators	Seattle Metropolitans	5
1920–21	Ottawa Senators	Vancouver Millionaires	5
1921–22	Toronto St. Pats	Vancouver Millionaires	5
1922–23	Ottawa Senators	Vancouver Maroons, Edmonton Eskimos	2, 4
1923–24	Montreal Canadiens	Vancouver Maroons, Calgary Tigers	2, 2
1924–25	Victoria Cougars	Montreal Canadiens	4
1925–26	Montreal Maroons	Victoria Cougars	4
1926–27	Ottawa Senators	Boston Bruins	4
1927–28	New York Rangers	Montreal Maroons	5
1928–29	Boston Bruins	New York Rangers	2
1929–30	Montreal Canadiens	Boston Bruins	2
1930–31	Montreal Canadiens	Chicago Black Hawks	5
1931–32	Toronto Maple Leafs	New York Rangers	3
1932–33	New York Rangers	Toronto Maple Leafs	4
1933–34	Chicago Black Hawks	Detroit Red Wings	4
1934–35	Montreal Maroons	Toronto Maple Leafs	3
1935–36	Detroit Red Wings	Toronto Maple Leafs	4
1936–37	Detroit Red Wings	New York Rangers	5
1937–38	Chicago Black Hawks	Toronto Maple Leafs	4
1938–39	Boston Bruins	Toronto Maple Leafs	5
1939–40	New York Rangers	Toronto Maple Leafs	6
1940–41	Boston Bruins	Detroit Red Wings	4
1941–42	Toronto Maple Leafs	Detroit Red Wings	7
1942–43	Detroit Red Wings	Boston Bruins	4
1943–44	Montreal Canadiens	Chicago Black Hawks	4
1944–45	Toronto Maple Leafs	Detroit Red Wings	7
1945–46	Montreal Canadiens	Boston Bruins	5
1946–47	Toronto Maple Leafs	Montreal Canadiens	6
1947–48	Toronto Maple Leafs	Detroit Red Wings	4
1948–49	Toronto Maple Leafs	Detroit Red Wings	4
1949–50	Detroit Red Wings	New York Rangers	7
1950–51	Toronto Maple Leafs	Montreal Canadiens	5
1951–52	Detroit Red Wings	Montreal Canadiens	4
1952–53	Montreal Canadiens	Boston Bruins	5
1953–54	Detroit Red Wings	Montreal Canadiens	7
1954–55	Detroit Red Wings	Montreal Canadiens	7

NHL WINNERS AND FINALISTS *(CONT.)*

Season	Champion	Finalist	GP in Final
1955–56	Montreal Canadiens	Detroit Red Wings	5
1956–57	Montreal Canadiens	Boston Bruins	5
1957–58	Montreal Canadiens	Boston Bruins	6
1958–59	Montreal Canadiens	Toronto Maple Leafs	5
1959–60	Montreal Canadiens	Toronto Maple Leafs	4
1960–61	Chicago Blackhawks	Detroit Red Wings	6
1961–62	Toronto Maple Leafs	Chicago Blackhawks	6
1962–63	Toronto Maple Leafs	Detroit Red Wings	5
1963–64	Toronto Maple Leafs	Detroit Red Wings	7
1964–65	Montreal Canadiens	Chicago Blackhawks	7
1965–66	Montreal Canadiens	Detroit Red Wings	6
1966–67	Toronto Maple Leafs	Montreal Canadiens	6
1967–68	Montreal Canadiens	St. Louis Blues	4
1968–69	Montreal Canadiens	St. Louis Blues	4
1969–70	Boston Bruins	St. Louis Blues	4
1970–71	Montreal Canadiens	Chicago Blackhawks	7
1971–72	Boston Bruins	New York Rangers	6
1972–73	Montreal Canadiens	Chicago Blackhawks	6
1973–74	Philadelphia Flyers	Boston Bruins	6
1974–75	Philadelphia Flyers	Buffalo Sabres	6
1975–76	Montreal Canadiens	Philadelphia Flyers	4
1976–77	Montreal Canadiens	Boston Bruins	4
1977–78	Montreal Canadiens	Boston Bruins	6
1978–79	Montreal Canadiens	New York Rangers	5
1979–80	New York Islanders	Philadelphia Flyers	6
1980–81	New York Islanders	Minnesota North Stars	5
1981–82	New York Islanders	Vancouver Canucks	4
1982–83	New York Islanders	Edmonton Oilers	4
1983–84	Edmonton Oilers	New York Islanders	5
1984–85	Edmonton Oilers	Philadelphia Flyers	5
1985–86	Montreal Canadiens	Calgary Flames	5
1986–87	Edmonton Oilers	Philadelphia Flyers	7
1987–88	Edmonton Oilers	Boston Bruins	4
1988–89	Calgary Flames	Montreal Canadiens	6
1989–90	Edmonton Oilers	Boston Bruins	5
1990–91	Pittsburgh Penguins	Minnesota North Stars	6
1991–92	Pittsburgh Penguins	Chicago Blackhawks	4
1992–93	Montreal Canadiens	Los Angeles Kings	5
1993–94	New York Rangers	Vancouver Canucks	7
1994–95	New Jersey Devils	Detroit Red Wings	4
1995–96	Colorado Avalanche	Florida Panthers	4
1996–97	Detroit Red Wings	Philadelphia Flyers	4
1997–98	Detroit Red Wings	Washington Capitals	4
1998–99	Dallas Stars	Buffalo Sabres	6
1999–2000	New Jersey Devils	Dallas Stars	6
2000–01	Colorado Avalanche	New Jersey Devils	7
2001–02	Detroit Red Wings	Carolina Hurricanes	5
2002–03	New Jersey Devils	Anaheim Mighty Ducks	7
2003–04	Tampa Bay Lightning	Calgary Flames	7
2004–05	No Stanley Cup due to season lockout		
2005–06	Carolina Hurricanes	Edmonton Oilers	7
2006–07	Anaheim Ducks	Ottawa Senators	5
2007–08	Detroit Red Wings	Pittsburgh Penguins	6
2008–09	Pittsburgh Penguins	Detroit Red Wings	7
2009–10	Chicago Blackhawks	Philadelphia Flyers	6
2010–11	Boston Bruins	Vancouver Canucks	7
2011–12	Los Angeles Kings	New Jersey Devils	6

*In 1919 the Montreal Canadiens traveled to meet Seattle, the PCHL champions. After five games had been played—the teams were tied at two wins and one tie—the series was called off by the local Department of Health because of the influenza epidemic and the death of Canadiens defenseman Joe Hall from influenza.

Conn Smythe Trophy

Awarded to the Most Valuable Player of the Stanley Cup playoffs, as selected by the Professional Hockey Writers Association. The trophy is named after the former coach, general manager, president and owner of the Toronto Maple Leafs.

1965	Jean Beliveau, Mtl
1966	Roger Crozier, Det
1967	Dave Keon, Tor
1968	Glenn Hall, StL
1969	Serge Savard, Mtl
1970	Bobby Orr, Bos
1971	Ken Dryden, Mtl
1972	Bobby Orr, Bos
1973	Yvan Cournoyer, Mtl
1974	Bernie Parent, Phi
1975	Bernie Parent, Phi
1976	Reggie Leach, Phi
1977	Guy Lafleur, Mtl
1978	Larry Robinson, Mtl
1979	Bob Gainey, Mtl
1980	Bryan Trottier, NYI
1981	Butch Goring, NYI
1982	Mike Bossy, NYI
1983	Bill Smith, NYI
1984	Mark Messier, Edm
1985	Wayne Gretzky, Edm
1986	Patrick Roy, Mtl
1987	Ron Hextall, Phi
1988	Wayne Gretzky, Edm
1989	Al MacInnis, Cgy
1990	Bill Ranford, Edm
1991	Mario Lemieux, Pit
1992	Mario Lemieux, Pit
1993	Patrick Roy, Mtl
1994	Brian Leetch, NYR
1995	Claude Lemieux, NJ
1996	Joe Sakic, Col
1997	Mike Vernon, Det
1998	Steve Yzerman, Det
1999	Joe Nieuwendyk, Dal
2000	Scott Stevens, NJ
2001	Patrick Roy, Col
2002	Nicklas Lidstrom, Det
2003	J.-S. Giguere, Ana
2004	Brad Richards, TB
2005	No Award–No Season
2006	Cam Ward, Car
2007	Scott Niedermayer, Ana
2008	Henrik Zetterberg, Det
2009	Evgeni Malkin, Pit
2010	Jonathan Toews, Chi
2011	Tim Thomas, Bos
2012	Jonathan Quick, LA

Alltime Stanley Cup Playoff Leaders
Points

	Playoff Seasons	GP	G	Ast	Pts
Wayne Gretzky, four teams	16	208	122	260	382
Mark Messier, Edm, Van, NYR	18	236	109	186	295
Jari Kurri, four teams	15	200	106	127	233
Glenn Anderson, four teams	15	225	93	121	214
Paul Coffey, six teams	16	194	59	137	196
Brett Hull, four teams	19	202	103	87	190
*Jaromir Jagr, four teams	16	180	78	111	189
Doug Gilmour, seven teams	18	182	60	128	188
Joe Sakic, Que, Col	13	172	84	104	188
Steve Yzerman, Det	20	196	70	115	185
Bryan Trottier, NYI, Pit	17	221	71	113	184
*Nicklas Lidstrom, Det	19	258	54	129	183
Ray Bourque, Bos, Col	21	214	41	139	180
Jean Beliveau, Mtl	17	162	79	97	176
Sergei Fedorov, Det, Wsh	15	183	52	124	176
Denis Savard, Chi, Mtl	16	169	66	109	175
Mario Lemieux, Pit	8	107	76	96	172
Peter Forsberg, Que, Col, Phi	13	151	64	107	171
Denis Potvin, NYI	14	185	56	108	164
Mike Bossy, NYI	10	129	85	75	160
Gordie Howe, Det, Hfd	20	157	68	92	160
Bobby Smith, Min, Mtl	13	184	64	96	160
Al MacInnis, Cgy, StL	19	177	39	121	160
Claude Lemieux, six teams	18	234	80	77	157
Adam Oates, six teams	15	163	42	114	156

Goals

	Playoff Seasons	GP	G
Wayne Gretzky, four teams	16	208	122
Mark Messier, Edm, NYR	18	236	109
Jari Kurri, five teams	15	200	106
Brett Hull, Cgy, StL, Dal, Det	19	202	103
Glenn Anderson, four teams	15	225	93
Mike Bossy, NYI	10	129	85
Joe Sakic, Que, Col	13	172	84
Maurice Richard, Mtl	15	133	82
Claude Lemieux, six teams	18	234	80
Jean Beliveau, Mtl	17	162	79
*Jaromir Jagr, Pit, Wsh, NYR, Phi	16	180	78
Mario Lemieux, Pitt	8	107	76
Dino Ciccarelli, Min, Wsh, Det	14	141	73
Esa Tikkanen, five teams	13	186	72
Bryan Trottier, NYI, Pit	17	221	71
Steve Yzerman, Det	20	196	70
Gordie Howe, Det, Hfd	20	157	68
Denis Savard, Chi Mtl	16	169	66
Joe Nieuwendyk, Cgy, Dal, NJ, Tor	16	158	66

Four tied with 64.

*Active in 2011–12.

Assists

	Playoff Seasons	GP	Ast
Wayne Gretzky, four teams	16	208	260
Mark Messier, Edm, NYR	18	236	186
Ray Bourque, Bos, Col	21	214	139
Paul Coffey, six teams	16	194	137
*Nicklas Lidstrom, Det	19	258	129
Doug Gilmour, seven teams	18	182	128
Jari Kurri, five teams	15	200	127
Sergei Fedorov, Det, Wsh	15	183	124
Glenn Anderson, four teams	15	225	121
Al MacInnis, Cgy, StL	19	177	121
Larry Robinson, Mtl, LA	20	227	116
Steve Yzerman, Det	20	196	115
Lawrence Murphy, six teams	20	215	115
Adam Oates, six teams	15	163	114
Bryan Trottier, NYI, Pit	17	221	113
Chris Chelios, Mtl, Chi, Det	24	266	113
*Jaromir Jagr, Pit, Wsh, NYR, Phi	16	180	111
Denis Savard, Chi, Mtl	16	169	109
Denis Potvin, NYI	14	185	108
Peter Forsberg, Que, Col, Phi	13	151	107
Joe Sakic, Que, Col	13	172	104

Alltime Stanley Cup Playoff Goaltending Leaders

WINS	W	L	Pct
Patrick Roy, Mtl, Col	151	94	.616
*Martin Brodeur, NJ	113	91	.554
Grant Fuhr, five teams	92	50	.648
Billy Smith, LA, NYI	88	36	.710
Ed Belfour, four teams	88	68	.564
Ken Dryden, Mtl	80	32	.714
Mike Vernon, four teams	77	56	.579
Chris Osgood, NYI, StL, Det	74	49	.602
Jacques Plante, five teams	71	36	.663
Andy Moog, four teams	68	57	.544
Dominik Hasek, Chi, Buf, Det	65	49	.570
Curtis Joseph, four teams	63	66	.488
Tom Barrasso, Buf, Pit, Ott	61	54	.530
Turk Broda, Tor	60	39	.606

*Active in 2011–12.

SHUTOUTS	GP	W	SO
*Martin Brodeur, NJ	205	113	24
Patrick Roy, Mtl, Col	247	151	23
Curtis Joseph, four teams	133	63	16
Chris Osgood, NYI, StL, Det	129	74	15

GOALS AGAINST AVG	Avg
George Hainsworth, Mtl, Tor	1.93
Turk Broda, Tor	1.98
*Martin Brodeur, NJ	2.02
Dominik Hasek, Chi, Buf, Det	2.02
Tim Thomas, Bos	2.07
*Jean-Sebastien Giguere, Ana	2.08
Chris Osgood, NYI, StL, Det	2.09
Jacques Plante, Mtl, StL, Tor, Bos	2.14

Note: At least 50 games played.
*Active in 2011–12.

Alltime Stanley Cup Team Playoff Record, by Wins

TEAM	W	L	Pct	TEAM	W	L	Pct
Montreal	410	291	.585	Vancouver	99	120	.452
Detroit	313	277	.531	Calgary*	94	114	.452
Boston	276	294	.484	Washington	93	112	.454
Toronto	251	269	.483	San Jose	77	86	.472
Pittsburgh	223	199	.528	Los Angeles	85	117	.421
Chicago	218	240	.476	Carolina§	59	68	.465
Philadelphia	214	199	.518	Anaheim	55	43	.561
NY Rangers	208	226	.479	Ottawa	54	62	.466
Edmonton	152	99	.606	Tampa Bay	37	32	.536
Dallas#	148	149	.498	Phoenix††	41	78	.345
St. Louis	142	174	.449	Florida	16	22	.421
Colorado**	132	117	.530	Nashville	18	27	.400
NY Islanders	131	102	.562	Minnesota	10	14	.417
Buffalo	124	132	.484	Columbus	0	4	.000
New Jersey†	136	118	.535				

*Atlanta Flames 1972–80. †Colorado Rockies 1976–82, Kansas City Scouts 1974–76. #Minnesota North Stars 1967–93. **Quebec Nordiques 1979–95. ††Winnipeg Jets 1979–96. §Hartford Whalers 1979–97.

Stanley Cup Playoff Coaching Records

Coach	Team	Plf Seas.	Series	Series W	Series L	Games	Games W	Games L	T	Cups	Pct
Glen Sather	Edm	10	27	21	6	†126	89	37	0	4	.706
Toe Blake	Mtl	13	23	18	5	119	82	37	0	8	.689
Scott Bowman	Five teams	28	68	49	19	353	223	130	0	9	.632
Hap Day	Tor	9	14	10	4	80	49	31	0	5	.613
*Mike Babcock	Ana, Det	8	22	14	8	117	71	46	0	1	.607
Al Arbour	StL, NYI	16	42	30	12	209	123	86	0	4	.589
Bob Hartley	Col, Atl	5	14	10	4	84	49	35	0	1	.583
Fred Shero	Phi, NYR	8	21	15	6	110	63	47	0	2	.573
*Lindy Ruff	Buf	8	18	10	8	101	57	44	0	0	.564
Jacques Demers	StL, Det, Mtl	8	18	11	7	98	55	43	0	1	.561
Mike Keenan	Five teams	13	30	18	12	173	96	77	0	1	.555

†Does not include suspended game, May 24, 1988. *Active in 2010–11.
Note: Coaches ranked by winning percentage. Minimum: 65 games.

The 10 Longest Overtime Games

Date	Result	OT	Scorer	Series	Series Winner
3-24-36	Det 1 vs Mtl M 0	116:30	Mud Bruneteau	SF	Det
4-3-33	Tor 1 vs Bos 0	104:46	Ken Doraty	SF	Tor
5-4-00	Phi 2 vs Pit 1	92:01	Keith Primeau	CSF	Phi
4-24-03	Ana 4 vs Dal 3	80:48	Petr Sykora	CSF	Ana
4-24-96	Pit 3 vs Wsh 2	79:15	Petr Nedved	CQF	Pit
4-11-07	Van 5 vs Dal 4	78:06	Henrik Sedin	CQF	Van
3-23-43	Tor 3 vs Det 2	70:18	Jack McLean	SF	Det
5-4-08	Dal 2 vs SJ 1	69:03	Brenden Morrow	CSF	Dal
3-28-30	Mtl 2 vs NYR 1	68:52	Gus Rivers	SF	Mtl
4-18-87	NYI 3 vs Wsh 2	68:47	Pat LaFontaine	DSF	NYI

Hart Memorial Trophy

Awarded annually "to the player adjudged to be the most valuable to his team." The original trophy was donated by Dr. David A. Hart, father of Cecil Hart, former manager-coach of the Montreal Canadiens. In the 1980s Wayne Gretzky won the award nine times.

Year	Winner	Key Statistics	Runner-Up
1924	Frank Nighbor, Ott	10 goals, 3 assists in 20 games	Sprague Cleghorn, Mtl
1925	Billy Burch, Ham	20 goals, 4 assists in 27 games	Howie Morenz, Mtl
1926	Nels Stewart, Mtl M	42 points in 36 games	Sprague Cleghorn, Mtl
1927	Herb Gardiner, Mtl	12 points in 44 games as defenseman	Bill Cook, NYR
1928	Howie Morenz, Mtl	33 goals, 18 assists	Roy Worters, Pitt
1929	Roy Worters, NYA	1.21 goals against, 13 shutouts	Ace Bailey, Tor
1930	Nels Stewart, Mtl M	39 goals, 16 assists	Lionel Hitchman, Bos
1931	Howie Morenz, Mtl	28 goals, 23 assists	Eddie Shore, Bos
1932	Howie Morenz, Mtl	24 goals, 25 assists	Ching Johnson, NYR
1933	Eddie Shore, Bos	27 assists in 48 games as defenseman	Bill Cook, NYR
1934	Aurel Joliat, Mtl	27 points	Lionel Conacher, Chi
1935	Eddie Shore, Bos	26 assists in 48 games as defenseman	Charlie Conacher, Tor
1936	Eddie Shore, Bos	16 assists in 46 games as defenseman	Hooley Smith, Mtl M
1937	Babe Siebert, Mtl	28 points	Lionel Conacher, Mtl M
1938	Eddie Shore, Bos	17 points in 47 games as defenseman	Paul Thompson, Chi
1939	Toe Blake, Mtl	led NHL in points (47)	Syl Apps, Tor
1940	Ebbie Goodfellow, Det	28 points	Syl Apps, Tor
1941	Bill Cowley, Bos	led NHL in assists (45) and points (62)	Dit Clapper, Bos
1942	Tom Anderson, Bos	41 points	Syl Apps, Tor
1943	Bill Cowley, Bos	led NHL in assists (45)	Doug Bentley, Chi
1944	Babe Pratt, Tor	57 points in 50 games	Bill Cowley, Bos
1945	Elmer Lach, Mtl	led NHL in assists (54) and points (80)	Maurice Richard, Mtl
1946	Max Bentley, Chi	61 points in 47 games	Gaye Stewart, Tor
1947	Maurice Richard, Mtl	led NHL in goals (45); 26 assists	Milt Schmidt, Bos
1948	Buddy O'Connor, NYR	60 points in 60 games	Frank Brimsek, Bos
1949	Sid Abel, Det	28 goals, 26 assists	Bill Durnan, Mtl
1950	Charlie Rayner, NYR	6 shutouts	Ted Kennedy, Tor
1951	Milt Schmidt, Bos	61 points in 62 games	Maurice Richard, Mtl
1952	Gordie Howe, Det	led NHL in goals (47) and points (86)	Elmer Lach, Mtl
1953	Gordie Howe, Det	led NHL in goals (49) and points (95)	Al Rollins, Chi
1954	Al Rollins, Chi	5 shutouts	Red Kelly, Det
1955	Ted Kennedy, Tor	52 points	Harry Lumley, Tor
1956	Jean Beliveau, Mtl	led NHL in goals (47) and points (88)	Tod Sloan, Tor
1957	Gordie Howe, Det	led NHL in goals (44) and points (89)	Jean Beliveau, Mtl
1958	Gordie Howe, Det	33 goals, 77 points in 64 games	Andy Bathgate, NYR
1959	Andy Bathgate, NYR	74 points in 70 games	Gordie Howe, Det
1960	Gordie Howe, Det	45 assists, 73 points	Bobby Hull, Chi
1961	Bernie Geoffrion, Mtl	50 goals, 95 points	Johnny Bower, Tor
1962	Jacques Plante, Mtl	42 wins, 2.37 goals against avg.	Doug Harvey, NYR
1963	Gordie Howe, Det	47 assists, 73 points	Stan Mikita, Chi
1964	Jean Beliveau, Mtl	50 assists, 78 points	Bobby Hull, Chi
1965	Bobby Hull, Chi	39 goals, 32 assists	Norm Ullman, Det
1966	Bobby Hull, Chi	led NHL in goals (54) and points (97)	Jean Beliveau, Mtl
1967	Stan Mikita, Chi	led NHL in assists (62) and points (97)	Ed Giacomin, NYR
1968	Stan Mikita, Chi	40 goals, 47 assists	Jean Beliveau, Mtl
1969	Phil Esposito, Bos	led NHL in assists (77) and points (126)	Jean Beliveau, Mtl
1970	Bobby Orr, Bos	led NHL in assists (87) and points (120)	Tony Esposito, Chi
1971	Bobby Orr, Bos	102 assists, 139 points	Phil Esposito, Bos
1972	Bobby Orr, Bos	80 assists, 117 points	Ken Dryden, Mtl
1973	Bobby Clarke, Phi	67 assists, 104 points	Phil Esposito, Bos
1974	Phil Esposito, Bos	led NHL in goals (68) and points (145)	Bernie Parent, Phi
1975	Bobby Clarke, Phi	89 assists, 116 points	Rogatien Vachon, LA
1976	Bobby Clarke, Phi	89 assists, 119 points	Denis Potvin, NYI
1977	Guy Lafleur, Mtl	led NHL in assists (80) and points (136)	Bobby Clarke, Phi
1978	Guy Lafleur, Mtl	led NHL in goals (60) and points (132)	Bryan Trottier, NYI
1979	Bryan Trottier, NYI	led NHL in assists (87) and points (134)	Guy Lafleur, Mtl
1980	Wayne Gretzky, Edm	51 goals, 86 assists	Marcel Dionne, LA
1981	Wayne Gretzky, Edm	led NHL in assists (109) and points (164)	Mike Liut, StL
1982	Wayne Gretzky, Edm	NHL-record 92 goals and 212 points	Bryan Trottier, NYI
1983	Wayne Gretzky, Edm	led NHL in goals (71) and points (196)	Pete Peeters, Bos
1984	Wayne Gretzky, Edm	led NHL in goals (87) and points (205)	Rod Langway, Wsh
1985	Wayne Gretzky, Edm	led NHL in goals (73) and points (208)	Dale Hawerchuk, Win
1986	Wayne Gretzky, Edm	NHL-record 163 assists and 215 points	Mario Lemieux, Pit
1987	Wayne Gretzky, Edm	led NHL in assists (121) and points (183)	Ray Bourque, Bos
1988	Mario Lemieux, Pit	led NHL in goals (70) and points (168)	Grant Fuhr, Edm

Hart Memorial Trophy *(Cont.)*

Year	Winner	Key Statistics	Runner-Up
1989	Wayne Gretzky, LA	114 assists, 168 points	Mario Lemieux, Pit
1990	Mark Messier, Edm	84 assists, 129 points	Ray Bourque, Bos
1991	Brett Hull, StL	led NHL in goals (86); 131 points	Wayne Gretzky, LA
1992	Mark Messier, NYR	72 assists, 107 points	Patrick Roy, Mtl
1993	Mario Lemieux, Pit	69 goals, 91 assists in 60 games	Doug Gilmour, Tor
1994	Sergei Fedorov, Det	56 goals, 64 assists	Dominik Hasek, Buf
1995	Eric Lindros, Phi	29 goals, 41 assists in 46 games	Jaromir Jagr, Pit
1996	Mario Lemieux, Pit	led NHL in goals (69) and points (161)	Mark Messier, NYR
1997	Dominik Hasek, Buf	5 shutouts, 2.27 goals against avg.	Paul Kariya, Ana
1998	Dominik Hasek, Buf	13 shutouts, 2.09 goals against avg.	Jaromir Jagr, Pit
1999	Jaromir Jagr, Pit	44 goals, 127 points	Alexei Yashin, Ott
2000	Chris Pronger, StL	62 points, +52 plus/minus rating	Jaromir Jagr, Pit
2001	Joe Sakic, Col	118 points, +45 plus/minus rating	Mario Lemieux, Pit
2002	Jose Theodore, Mtl	2.11 goals against avg./7 shutouts	Jarome Iginla, Cal
2003	Peter Forsberg, Col	77 assists, +52 plus/minus rating	Markus Naslund, Van
2004	Martin St. Louis, TB	94 points, +35 plus/minus rating	Jarome Iginla, Cal
2005	No Award–No Season.		
2006	Joe Thornton, Bos/SJ	29 goals, 96 assists; 125 points	Jaromir Jagr, NYR
2007	Sidney Crosby, Pit	36 goals, 84 assists; 120 points	Roberto Luongo, Van
2008	Alexander Ovechkin, Wsh	65 goals, 47 assists; 112 points	Evgeni Malkin, Pit
2009	Alexander Ovechkin, Wsh	56 goals, 54 assists; 110 points	Evgeni Malkin, Pit
2010	Henrik Sedin, Van	29 goals, 83 assists; 112 points	Sidney Crosby, Pit
2011	Corey Perry, Ana	50 goals, 48 assists; 98 points	Daniel Sedin, Van
2012	Evgeni Malkin, Pitt	50 goals, 59 assists, 109 points	Steven Stamkos, TB

Art Ross Trophy

Awarded annually "to the player who leads the league in scoring points at the end of the regular season." The trophy was presented to the NHL in 1947 by Arthur Howie Ross, former manager-coach of the Boston Bruins. The tie-breakers, in order, are: (1) most goals, (2) fewer games played, (3) first goal of the season. Bobby Orr is the only defenseman in NHL history to win this trophy, and he won it twice (1970 and 1975).

Year	Winner	Pts	Year	Winner	Pts
1919	Newsy Lalonde, Mtl	44	1956	Jean Beliveau, Mtl	88
1920	Joe Malone, Que	30	1957	Gordie Howe, Det	89
1921	Newsy Lalonde, Mtl	48	1958	Dickie Moore, Mtl	84
1922	Punch Broadbent, Ott	41	1959	Dickie Moore, Mtl	96
1923	Babe Dye, Tor	46	1960	Bobby Hull, Chi	81
1924	Cy Denneny, Ott	37	1961	Bernie Geoffrion, Mtl	95
1925	Babe Dye, Tor	23	1962	Bobby Hull, Chi	84
1926	Nels Stewart, Mtl M	44	1963	Gordie Howe, Det	86
1927	Bill Cook, NYR	42	1964	Stan Mikita, Chi	89
1928	Howie Morenz, Mtl	37	1965	Stan Mikita, Chi	87
1929	Ace Bailey, Tor	51	1966	Bobby Hull, Chi	97
1930	Cooney Weiland, Bos	32	1967	Stan Mikita, Chi	97
1931	Howie Morenz, Mtl	73	1968	Stan Mikita, Chi	87
1932	Harvey Jackson, Tor	51	1969	Phil Esposito, Bos	126
1933	Bill Cook, NYR	53	1970	Bobby Orr, Bos	120
1934	Charlie Conacher, Tor	50	1971	Phil Esposito, Bos	152
1935	Charlie Conacher, Tor	57	1972	Phil Esposito, Bos	133
1936	Sweeney Schriner, NYA	45	1973	Phil Esposito, Bos	130
1937	Sweeney Schriner, NYA	46	1974	Phil Esposito, Bos	145
1938	Gordie Drillon, Tor	52	1975	Bobby Orr, Bos	135
1939	Toe Blake, Mtl	47	1976	Guy Lafleur, Mtl	125
1940	Milt Schmidt, Bos	52	1977	Guy Lafleur, Mtl	136
1941	Bill Cowley, Bos	62	1978	Guy Lafleur, Mtl	132
1942	Bryan Hextall, NYR	56	1979	Bryan Trottier, NYI	134
1943	Doug Bentley, Chi	73	1980	Marcel Dionne, LA	137
1944	Herb Cain, Bos	82	1981	Wayne Gretzky, Edm	164
1945	Elmer Lach, Mtl	80	1982	Wayne Gretzky, Edm	212
1946	Max Bentley, Chi	61	1983	Wayne Gretzky, Edm	196
1947	*Max Bentley, Chi	72	1984	Wayne Gretzky, Edm	205
1948	Elmer Lach, Mtl	61	1985	Wayne Gretzky, Edm	208
1949	Roy Conacher, Chi	68	1986	Wayne Gretzky, Edm	215
1950	Ted Lindsay, Det	78	1987	Wayne Gretzky, Edm	183
1951	Gordie Howe, Det	86	1988	Mario Lemieux, Pit	168
1952	Gordie Howe, Det	86	1989	Mario Lemieux, Pit	199
1953	Gordie Howe, Det	95	1990	Wayne Gretzky, LA	142
1954	Gordie Howe, Det	81	1991	Wayne Gretzky, LA	163
1955	Bernie Geoffrion, Mtl	75	1992	Mario Lemieux, Pit	131

Art Ross Trophy *(Cont.)*

Year	Winner	Pts	Year	Winner	Pts
1993	Mario Lemieux, Pit	160	2003	Peter Forsberg, Col	106
1994	Wayne Gretzky, LA	130	2004	Martin St. Louis, TB	94
1995	Jaromir Jagr, Pit	70	2005	No award/no season	
1996	Mario Lemieux, Pit	161	2006	Joe Thornton, Bos/SJ	125
1997	Mario Lemieux, Pit	122	2007	Sidney Crosby, Pit	120
1998	Jaromir Jagr, Pit	102	2008	Alexander Ovechkin, Wsh	112
1999	Jaromir Jagr, Pit	127	2009	Evgeni Malkin, Pit	113
2000	Jaromir Jagr, Pit	96	2010	Henrik Sedin, Van	112
2001	Jaromir Jagr, Pit	121	2011	Daniel Sedin, Van	104
2002	Jarome Iginla, Cgy	96	2012	Evgeni Malkin, Pit	109

Note: Listing includes scoring leaders prior to inception of Art Ross Trophy in 1947–48.

Lady Byng Memorial Trophy

Awarded annually "to the player adjudged to have exhibited the best type of sportsmanship and gentlemanly conduct combined with a high standard of playing ability."

Year	Winner	Year	Winner	Year	Winner
1925	Frank Nighbor, Ott	1955	Sid Smith, Tor	1985	Jari Kurri, Edm
1926	Frank Nighbor, Ott	1956	Earl Reibel, Det	1986	Mike Bossy, NYI
1927	Billy Burch, NYA	1957	Andy Hebenton, NYR	1987	Joe Mullen, Cgy
1928	Frank Boucher, NYR	1958	Camille Henry, NYR	1988	Mats Naslund, Mtl
1929	Frank Boucher, NYR	1959	Alex Delvecchio, Det	1989	Joe Mullen, Cgy
1930	Frank Boucher, NYR	1960	Don McKenney, Bos	1990	Brett Hull, StL
1931	Frank Boucher, NYR	1961	Red Kelly, Tor	1991	Wayne Gretzky, LA
1932	Joe Primeau, Tor	1962	Dave Keon, Tor	1992	Wayne Gretzky, LA
1933	Frank Boucher, NYR	1963	Dave Keon, Tor	1993	Pierre Turgeon, NYI
1934	Frank Boucher, NYR	1964	Ken Wharram, Chi	1994	Wayne Gretzky, LA
1935	Frank Boucher, NYR	1965	Bobby Hull, Chi	1995	Ron Francis, Pit
1936	Doc Romnes, Chi	1966	Alex Delvecchio, Det	1996	Paul Kariya, Ana
1937	Marty Barry, Det	1967	Stan Mikita, Chi	1997	Paul Kariya, Ana
1938	Gordie Drillon, Tor	1968	Stan Mikita, Chi	1998	Ron Francis, Pit
1939	Clint Smith, NYR	1969	Alex Delvecchio, Det	1999	Wayne Gretzky, NYR
1940	Bobby Bauer, Bos	1970	Phil Goyette, StL	2000	Pavol Demitra, StL
1941	Bobby Bauer, Bos	1971	John Bucyk, Bos	2001	Joe Sakic, Col
1942	Syl Apps, Tor	1972	Jean Ratelle, NYR	2002	Ron Francis, Car
1943	Max Bentley, Chi	1973	Gilbert Perreault, Buf	2003	Alexander Mogilny, Det
1944	Clint Smith, Chi	1974	John Bucyk, Bos		
1945	Billy Mosienko, Chi	1975	Marcel Dionne, Det	2004	Brad Richards, TB
1946	Toe Blake, Mtl	1976	Jean Ratelle, NYR-Bos	2005	No Award
1947	Bobby Bauer, Bos	1977	Marcel Dionne, LA	2006	Pavel Datsyuk, Det
1948	Buddy O'Connor, NYR	1978	Butch Goring, LA	2007	Pavel Datsyuk, Det
1949	Bill Quackenbush, Det	1979	Bob MacMillan, Atl	2008	Pavel Datsyuk, Det
1950	Edgar Laprade, NYR	1980	Wayne Gretzky, Edm	2009	Pavel Datsyuk, Det
1951	Red Kelly, Det	1981	Rick Kehoe, Pit	2010	Martin St. Louis, TB
1952	Sid Smith, Tor	1982	Rick Middleton, Bos	2011	Martin St. Louis, TB
1953	Red Kelly, Det	1983	Mike Bossy, NYI	2012	Brian Campbell, Fla
1954	Red Kelly, Det	1984	Mike Bossy, NYI		

James Norris Memorial Trophy

Awarded annually "to the defense player who demonstrates throughout the season the greatest all-around ability in the position." James Norris was the former owner-president of the Detroit Red Wings. Bobby Orr holds the record for most consecutive times winning the award (eight, 1968–1975).

Year	Winner	Year	Winner	Year	Winner
1954	Red Kelly, Det	1969	Bobby Orr, Bos	1984	Rod Langway, Wsh
1955	Doug Harvey, Mtl	1970	Bobby Orr, Bos	1985	Paul Coffey, Edm
1956	Doug Harvey, Mtl	1971	Bobby Orr, Bos	1986	Paul Coffey, Edm
1957	Doug Harvey, Mtl	1972	Bobby Orr, Bos	1987	Ray Bourque, Bos
1958	Doug Harvey, Mtl	1973	Bobby Orr, Bos	1988	Ray Bourque, Bos
1959	Tom Johnson, Mtl	1974	Bobby Orr, Bos	1989	Chris Chelios, Mtl
1960	Doug Harvey, Mtl	1975	Bobby Orr, Bos	1990	Ray Bourque, Bos
1961	Doug Harvey, Mtl	1976	Denis Potvin, NYI	1991	Ray Bourque, Bos
1962	Doug Harvey, NYR	1977	Larry Robinson, Mtl	1992	Brian Leetch, NYR
1963	Pierre Pilote, Chi	1978	Denis Potvin, NYI	1993	Chris Chelios, Chi
1964	Pierre Pilote, Chi	1979	Denis Potvin, NYI	1994	Ray Bourque, Bos
1965	Pierre Pilote, Chi	1980	Larry Robinson, Mtl	1995	Paul Coffey, Det
1966	Jacques Laperriere, Mtl	1981	Randy Carlyle, Pit	1996	Chris Chelios, Chi
1967	Harry Howell, NYR	1982	Doug Wilson, Chi	1997	Brian Leetch, NYR
1968	Bobby Orr, Bos	1983	Rod Langway, Wsh	1998	Rob Blake, LA

James Norris Memorial Trophy *(Cont.)*

1999 ....Al MacInnis, StL	2004 ....Scott Niedermayer, NJ	2009 ....Zdeno Chara, Bos
2000 ....Chris Pronger, StL	2005 ....No Award	2010 ....Duncan Keith, Chi
2001 ....Nicklas Lidstrom, Det	2006 ....Nicklas Lidstrom, Det	2011 ....Nicklas Lidstrom, Det
2002 ....Nicklas Lidstrom, Det	2007 ....Nicklas Lidstrom, Det	2012 ....Erik Karlsson, Ott
2003 ....Nicklas Lidstrom, Det	2008 ....Nicklas Lidstrom, Det	

Calder Memorial Trophy

Awarded annually "to the player selected as the most proficient in his first year of competition in the National Hockey League." Frank Calder was a former NHL president. Sergei Makarov, who won the award in 1989–90, was the oldest recipient of the trophy, at 31. Players are no longer eligible for the award if they are 26 or older as of September 15th of the season in question.

1933 ....Carl Voss, Det	1960 ....Bill Hay, Chi	1987 ....Luc Robitaille, LA
1934 ....Russ Blinko, Mtl M	1961 ....Dave Keon, Tor	1988 ....Joe Nieuwendyk, Cgy
1935 ....Dave Schriner, NYA	1962 ....:.Bobby Rousseau, Mtl	1989 ....Brian Leetch, NYR
1936 ....Mike Karakas, Chi	1963 ....Kent Douglas, Tor	1990 ....Sergei Makarov, Cgy
1937 ....Syl Apps, Tor	1964 ....Jacques Laperriere, Mtl	1991 ....Ed Belfour, Chi
1938 ....Cully Dahlstrom, Chi	1965 ....Roger Crozier, Det	1992 ....Pavel Bure, Van
1939 ....Frank Brimsek, Bos	1966 ....Brit Selby, Tor	1993 ....Teemu Selanne, Win
1940 ....Kilby MacDonald, NYR	1967 ....Bobby Orr, Bos	1994 ....Martin Brodeur, NJ.
1941 ....Johnny Quilty, Mtl	1968 ....Derek Sanderson, Bos	1995 ....Peter Forsberg, Que
1942 ....Grant Warwick, NYR	1969 ....Danny Grant, Min	1996 ....Daniel Alfredsson, Ott
1943 ....Gaye Stewart, Tor	1970 ....Tony Esposito, Chi	1997 ....Bryan Berard, NYI
1944 ....Gus Bodnar, Tor	1971 ....Gilbert Perreault, Buf	1998 ....Sergei Samsonov, Bos
1945 ....Frank McCool, Tor	1972 ....Ken Dryden, Mtl	1999 ....Chris Drury, Col
1946 ....Edgar Laprade, NYR	1973 ....Steve Vickers, NYR	2000 ....Scott Gomez, NJ
1947 ....Howie Meeker, Tor	1974 ....Denis Potvin, NYI	2001 ....Evgeni Nabokov, SJ
1948 ....Jim McFadden, Det	1975 ....Eric Vail, Atl	2002 ....Dany Heatley, Atl
1949 ....Pentti Lund, NYR	1976 ....Bryan Trottier, NYI	2003 ....Barret Jackman, StL
1950 ....Jack Gelineau, Bos	1977 ....Willi Plett, Atl	2004 ....Andrew Raycroft, Bos
1951 ....Terry Sawchuk, Det	1978 ....Mike Bossy, NYI	2005 ....No Award
1952 ....Bernie Geoffrion, Mtl	1979 ....Bobby Smith, Min	2006.......Alexander Ovechkin, Wsh
1953 ....Gump Worsley, NYR	1980 ....Ray Bourque, Bos	2007.......Evgeni Malkin, Pit
1954 ....Camille Henry, NYR	1981 ....Peter Stastny, Que	2008.........Patrick Kane, Chi
1955 ....Ed Litzenberger, Chi	1982 ....Dale Hawerchuk, Win	2009.........Steve Mason, CBJ
1956 ....Glenn Hall, Det	1983 ....Steve Larmer, Chi	2010.........Tyler Myers, Buf
1957 ....Larry Regan, Bos	1984 ....Tom Barrasso, Buf	2011.........Jeff Skinner, Car
1958 ....Frank Mahovlich, Tor	1985 ....Mario Lemieux, Pit	2012.........Gabriel Landeskog, Col
1959 ....Ralph Backstrom, Mtl	1986 ....Gary Suter, Cgy	

Vezina Trophy

Awarded annually "to the goalkeeper adjudged to be the best at his position." The trophy is named after Georges Vezina, an outstanding goalie for the Montreal Canadiens who collapsed during a game on November 28, 1925, and died four months later of tuberculosis. The general managers of the NHL teams vote on the award.

1927 ....George Hainsworth, Mtl	1953 ....Terry Sawchuk, Det	1973 ....Ken Dryden, Mtl
1928 ....George Hainsworth, Mtl	1954 ....Harry Lumley, Tor	1974 ....Bernie Parent, Phi
1929 ....George Hainsworth, Mtl	1955 ....Terry Sawchuk, Det	Tony Esposito, Chi
1930 ....Tiny Thompson, Bos	1956 ....Jacques Plante, Mtl	1975 ....Bernie Parent, Phi
1931 ....Roy Worters, NYA	1957 ....Jacques Plante, Mtl	1976 ....Ken Dryden, Mtl
1932 ....Charlie Gardiner, Chi	1958 ....Jacques Plante, Mtl	1977 ....Ken Dryden, Mtl
1933 ....Tiny Thompson, Bos	1959 ....Jacques Plante, Mtl	Michel Larocque, Mtl
1934 ....Charlie Gardiner, Chi	1960 ....Jacques Plante, Mtl	1978 ....Ken Dryden, Mtl
1935 ....Lorne Chabot, Chi	1961 ....Johnny Bower, Tor	Michel Larocque, Mtl
1936 ....Tiny Thompson, Bos	1962 ....Jacques Plante, Mtl	1979 ....Ken Dryden, Mtl
1937 ....Normie Smith, Det	1963 ....Glenn Hall, Chi	Michel Larocque, Mtl
1938 ....Tiny Thompson, Bos	1964 ....Charlie Hodge, Mtl	1980 ....Bob Sauve, Buf
1939 ....Frank Brimsek, Bos	1965 ....Terry Sawchuk, Tor	Don Edwards, Buf
1940 ....Dave Kerr, NYR	Johnny Bower, Tor	1981 ....Richard Sevigny, Mtl
1941 ....Turk Broda, Tor	1966 ....Gump Worsley, Mtl	Michel Larocque, Mtl
1942 ....Frank Brimsek, Bos	Charlie Hodge, Mtl	1982 ....Billy Smith, NYI
1943 ....Johnny Mowers, Det	1967 ....Glenn Hall, Chi	Denis Herron, Mtl
1944 ....Bill Dur[an, Mtl	Denis DeJordy, Chi	1983 ....Pete Peeters, Bos
1945 ....Bill Durnan, Mtl	1968 ....Lorne Worsley, Mtl	1984 ....Tom Barrasso, Buf
1946 ....Bill Durnan, Mtl	1969 ....Jacques Plante, StL	1985 ....Pelle Lindbergh, Phi
1947 ....Bill Durnan, Mtl	Glenn Hall, StL	1986 ....John Vanbiesbrouck, NYR
1948 ....Turk Broda, Tor	1970 ....Tony Esposito, Chi	
1949 ....Bill Durnan, Mtl	1971 ....Ed Giacomin, NYR	1987 ....Ron Hextall, Phi
1950 ....Bill Durnan, Mtl	Gilles Villemure, NYR	1988 ....Grant Fuhr, Edm
1951 ....Al Rollins, Tor	1972 ....Tony Esposito, Chi	1989 ....Patrick Roy, Mtl
1952 ....Terry Sawchuk, Det	Gary Smith, Chi	1990 ....Patrick Roy, Mtl

Vezina Trophy (Cont.)

1991 ....Ed Belfour, Chi	1998 ....Dominik Hasek, Buf	2005 ....No Award
1992 ....Patrick Roy, Mtl	1999 ......Dominik Hasek, Buf	2006 ....Miikka Kiprusoff, Cgy
1993 ....Ed Belfour, Chi	2000 ....Olaf Kolzig, Wash	2007 ....Martin Brodeur, NJ
1994 ....Dominik Hasek, Buf	2001 ....Dominik Hasek, Buf	2008 ....Martin Brodeur, NJ
1995 ....Dominik Hasek, Buf	2002 ....Jose Theodore, Mtl	2009 ....Tim Thomas, Bos
1996 ....Jim Carey, Wsh	2003 ....Martin Brodeur, NJ	2010 ....Ryan Miller, Buf
1997 ....Dominik Hasek, Buf	2004 ....Martin Brodeur, NJ	2011 ....Tim Thomas, Bos
		2012 ....Henrik Lundqvist, NYR

Selke Trophy

Awarded annually "to the forward who best excels in the defensive aspects of the game." The trophy is named after Frank J. Selke, the architect of the Montreal Canadians dynasty that won five consecutive Stanley Cups in the late '50s. The winner is selected by a vote of the Professional Hockey Writers Association.

1978........Bob Gainey, Mtl	1990........Rick Meagher, StL	2002........Michael Peca, NYI
1979........Bob Gainey, Mtl	1991........Dirk Graham, Chi	2003........Jere Lehtinen, Dal
1980........Bob Gainey, Mtl	1992........Guy Carbonneau, Mtl	2004........Kris Draper, Det
1981........Bob Gainey, Mtl	1993........Doug Gilmour, Tor	2005........No Award
1982........Steve Kasper, Bos	1994........Sergei Fedorov, Det	2006........Rod Brind'Amour, Car
1983........Bobby Clarke, Phi	1995........Ron Francis, Pit	2007........Rod Brind'Amour, Car
1984........Doug Jarvis, Wsh	1996........Sergei Fedorov, Det	2008........Pavel Datsyuk, Det
1985........Craig Ramsay, Buf	1997........Michael Peca, Buf	2009........Pavel Datsyuk, Det
1986........Troy Murray, Chi	1998........Jere Lehtinen, Dal	2010........Pavel Datsyuk, Det
1987........Dave Poulin, Phi	1999........Jere Lehtinen, Dal	2011........Ryan Kesler, Van
1988........Guy Carbonneau, Mtl	2000........Steve Yzerman, Det	2012........Patrice Bergeron, Bos
1989........Guy Carbonneau, Mtl	2001........John Madden, NJ	

Adams Award

Awarded annually "to the NHL coach adjudged to have contributed the most to his team's success." The trophy is named in honor of Jack Adams, longtime coach and general manager of the Detroit Red Wings. The winner is selected by a vote of the National Hockey League Broadcasters' Association.

1974 .....Fred Shero, Phi	1987 ....Jacques Demers, Det	2000 .....Joel Quenneville, StL
1975 .....Bob Pulford, LA	1988 ....Jacques Demers, Det	2001 .....Bill Barber, Phi
1976 .....Don Cherry, Bos	1989 ....Pat Burns, Mtl	2002 ....Bob Francis, Phx
1977 .....Scott Bowman, Mtl	1990 ....Bob Murdoch, Win	2003 ....Jacques Lemaire, Min
1978 .....Bobby Kromm, Det	1991 ....Brian Sutter, StL	2004 ....John Tortorella, TB
1979 .....Al Arbour, NYI	1992 ....Pat Quinn, Van	2005 .....No Award
1980 .....Pat Quinn, Phi	1993 ....Pat Burns, Tor	2006 .....Lindy Ruff, Buf
1981 .....Red Berenson, StL	1994 ....Jacques Lemaire, NJ	2007 .....Alain Vigneault, Van
1982 .....Tom Watt, Win	1995 ....Marc Crawford, Que	2008 .....Bruce Boudreau, Wsh
1983 .....Orval Tessier, Chi	1996 ....Scotty Bowman, Det	2009 .....Claude Julien, Bos
1984 .....Bryan Murray, Wsh	1997 ....Ted Nolan, Buf	2010 .....Dave Tippett, Phx
1985 .....Mike Keenan, Phi	1998 ....Pat Burns, Bos	2011 .....Dan Bylsma, Pit
1986 .....Glen Sather, Edm	1999 ....Jacques Martin, Ott	2012 ....Ken Hitchcock, StL

Career Records

Alltime Point Leaders

Player	Yrs	GP	G	A	Pts	Pts/game
Wayne Gretzky, Edm, LA, StL, NYR 20		1487	894	1963	2857	1.921
Mark Messier, Edm, NYR, Van 25		1756	694	1193	1887	1.074
Gordie Howe, Det, Hfd 26		1767	801	1049	1850	1.047
Ron Francis, Hfd, Pit, Car, Tor.....................23		1731	549	1249	1798	1.039
Marcel Dionne, Det, LA, NYR 18		1348	731	1040	1771	1.314
Steve Yzerman, Det 22		1514	692	1063	1755	1.159
Mario Lemieux, Pit 17		915	690	1033	1723	1.883
*Jaromir Jagr, Pit, Wsh, NYR, Phi................18		1346	665	988	1653	1.228
Joe Sakic, Que, Col 20		1378	625	1016	1641	1.191
Phil Esposito, Chi, Bos, NYR 18		1282	717	873	1590	1.240
Ray Bourque, Bos, Col 22		1612	410	1169	1579	.980
Mark Recchi, seven teams 23		1652	577	956	1533	.928
Paul Coffey, eight teams.............................21		1409	396	1135	1531	1.087
Stan Mikita, Chi 22		1394	541	926	1467	1.052
Bryan Trottier, NYI, Pit................................18		1279	524	901	1425	1.114

*Active in 2011–12.

Alltime Goal-Scoring Leaders

Player	Yrs	GP	G	G/game
Wayne Gretzky, Edm, LA, StL, NYR	20	1487	894	.601
Gordie Howe, Det, Hfd	26	1767	801	.453
Brett Hull, Cgy, StL, Dal, Det	19	1269	741	.584
Marcel Dionne, Det, LA, NYR	18	1348	731	.542
Phil Esposito, Chi, Bos, NYR	18	1282	717	.559
Mike Gartner, Wsh, Min, NYR, Tor, Phx	19	1432	708	.494
Mark Messier, Edm, NYR, Van	25	1756	694	.395
Steve Yzerman, Det.	22	1514	692	.457
Mario Lemieux, Pit.	17	915	690	.754
Luc Robitaille, LA, Pit, NYR, Det	19	1431	668	.467
*Jaromir Jagr, Pit, Wsh, NYR, Phi	18	1346	665	.494
*Temmu Selanne, Win, Ana, SJ, Col, Ana	19	1341	663	.494
Brendan Shanahan, NJ, StL, Hfd, Det, NYR	21	1524	656	.430
Dave Andreychuk, Buf, Tor, NJ, Bos, Col, Buf, TB	23	1,639	640	.390
Joe Sakic, Que, Col	20	1,378	625	.454

Alltime Assist Leaders

Player	Yrs	GP	A	A/game
Wayne Gretzky, Edm, LA, StL, NYR	20	1487	1963	1.320
Ron Francis, Hfd, Pit, Car	23	1731	1249	.722
Mark Messier, Edm, NYR, Van	25	1756	1193	.679
Ray Bourque, Bos, Col	22	1612	1169	.725
Paul Coffey, eight teams	21	1409	1135	.806
Adam Oates, seven teams	22	1337	1079	.807
Steve Yzerman, Det.	22	1514	1063	.702
Gordie Howe, Det, Hfd	26	1767	1049	.594
Marcel Dionne, Det, LA, NYR	18	1348	1040	.772
Mario Lemieux, Pit.	17	915	1033	1.129

Alltime Penalty Minutes Leaders

Player	Yrs	GP	PIM	Min/game
Dave Williams, Tor, Van, Det, LA, Hfd	14	962	3966	4.12
Dale Hunter, Que, Wsh, Col	19	1407	3565	2.53
Tie Domi, Tor, NYR, Win	16	1020	3515	3.45
Marty McSorley, Pit, Edm, LA, NYR, SJ, Bos	17	961	3381	3.52
Bob Probert, Det, Chi	16	935	3300	3.53

Goaltending Records

ALLTIME GOALTENDING LEADERS, BY WINS

Goaltender	W	L	T	OT
*Martin Brodeur, NJ	656	371	105	58
Patrick Roy, Mtl, Col	551	315	131	29
Ed Belfour, five teams	484	320	111	44
Curtis Joseph, five teams	454	352	90	39
Terry Sawchuk, five teams	447	330	172	0
Jacques Plante, five teams	437	246	145	0
Tony Esposito, Mtl, Chi	423	306	151	0
Glenn Hall, Det, Chi, StL	407	326	163	0
Grant Fuhr, six teams	403	295	114	9
Chris Osgood, Det, NYI, StL, Det	401	216	66	42
Dominik Hasek, Chi, Buf, Ott, Det	389	223	82	32

*Active in 2011–12.

ACTIVE GOALTENDING LEADERS, BY WINS

Goaltender	W	L	T	OT
Martin Brodeur, NJ	656	371	105	58
Roberto Luongo, Van	339	283	33	68
Nikolai Khabibulin, Edm	328	328	58	58
Evgeni Nabokov, NYI	312	196	29	54
Miikka Kiprusoff, Cgy	311	199	7	67
Tomas Vokoun, Wash	287	284	35	57
Jose Theodore, Fla	282	248	30	55
Marty Turco, Bos	275	167	26	43
Ryan Miller, Buf	252	147	1	50
Henrik Lundqvist, NYR	252	155	0	54
Jean-Sebastien Giguere, Col	246	206	25	59

ALLTIME SHUTOUT LEADERS

Goaltender	Team	Yrs	GP	SO
*Martin Brodeur	NJ	19	1191	119
Terry Sawchuk	Det, Bos, Tor, LA, NYR	21	971	103
George Hainsworth	Mtl, Tor	11	465	94
Glenn Hall	Det, Chi, StL	18	906	84
Jacques Plante	Mtl, NYR, StL, Tor, Bos	18	837	82
Tiny Thompson	Bos, Det	12	553	81
Alex Connell	Ott, Det, NYA, Mtl M	12	417	81
Dominik Hasek	Chi, Buf, Ott, Det	16	735	81
Tony Esposito	Mtl, Chi	16	886	76
Ed Belfour	Chi, SJ, Dal, Tor	17	963	76

ALLTIME GOALS AGAINST AVERAGE LEADERS (PRE-1950)

Goaltender	Team	Yrs	GP	GA	GAA
Alec Connell	Ott, Det, NYA, Mtl M	12	417	830	1.91
George Hainsworth	Mtl, Tor	11	465	937	1.93
Chuck Gardiner	Chi	7	316	664	2.02
Lorne Chabot	NYR, Tor, Mtl, Chi, Mtl M, NYA	11	411	860	2.04
Tiny Thompson	Bos, Det	12	553	1183	2.08

ALLTIME GOALS AGAINST AVERAGE LEADERS (POST-1950)

Goaltender	Team	Yrs	GP	GA	GAA
Dominik Hasek	Chi, Buf, Det, Ott	16	735	1572	2.20
*Martin Brodeur	NJ	19	1191	2603	2.23
Ken Dryden	Mtl	8	397	870	2.24
*Henrik Lundqvist	NYR	7	468	1046	2.27
*Jonathan Quick	LA	5	249	559	2.30
Roman Turek	Dal, StL, Cgy	8	328	734	2.31

*Active in 2011–12. Note: Minimum 200 games played. GAA equals goals against per 60 minutes played.

Alltime Coaching Leaders, by Regular Season Wins

Coach	Team	Seasons	W	L	T	OT
Scotty Bowman	StL, Mtl, Buf, Pit, Det	30	1244	573	314	10
Al Arbour	StL, NYI	23	782	577	248	0
Dick Irvin	Chi, Tor, Mtl, Chi	27	692	527	230	0
Pat Quinn	Phi, LA, Van, Tor, Ed	20	684	528	154	34
Mike Keenan	Phi, Chi, NYR, StL, Van, Bos, Fla, Cgy	20	672	531	147	36
*Ron Wilson	Ana, Wash, SJ, Tor	18	648	561	101	91
*Joel Quenneville	StL, Col, Chi	15	624	382	77	80
Bryan Murray	Wash, Det, Fla, Ana, Ott	17	620	465	131	23
Jacques Lemaire	Mtl, NJ, Minn, NJ	17	617	458	124	63
*Jacques Martin	StL, Ott, Fla, Mtl	17	613	481	119	81
*Ken Hitchcock	Dal, Phi, CBJ, StL	15	576	365	88	81
*Lindy Ruff	Buf	14	565	422	78	83
Marc Crawford	Que, Col, Van, LA, Dal	15	549	421	103	78
Billy Reay	Tor, Chi	16	542	385	175	0
*Barry Trotz	Nash	13	503	424	60	79

*Active in 2011–12.

Single-Season Records

Goals

Player	Season	GP	G	Player	Season	GP	G
Wayne Gretzky, Edm	1981–82	80	92	Wayne Gretzky, Edm	1982–83	80	71
Wayne Gretzky, Edm	1983–84	74	87	Brett Hull, StL	1991–92	73	70
Brett Hull, StL	1990–91	78	86	Mario Lemieux, Pit	1987–88	77	70
Mario Lemieux, Pit	1988–89	76	85	Bernie Nicholls, LA	1988–89	79	70
Alexander Mogilny, Buf	1992–93	77	76	Mario Lemieux, Pit	1992–93	60	69
Phil Esposito, Bos	1970–71	78	76	Mario Lemieux, Pit	1995–96	70	69
Teemu Selanne, Win	1992–93	84	76	Mike Bossy, NYI	1978–79	80	69
Wayne Gretzky, Edm	1984–85	80	73	Phil Esposito, Bos	1973–74	78	68
Brett Hull, StL	1989–90	80	72	Jari Kurri, Edm	1985–86	78	68
Jari Kurri, Edm	1984–85	73	71	Mike Bossy, NYI	1980–81	79	68

Assists

Player	Season	GP	Asst	Player	Season	GP	Asst
Wayne Gretzky, Edm	1985–86	80	163	Bobby Orr, Bos	1970–71	78	102
Wayne Gretzky, Edm	1984–85	80	135	Mario Lemieux, Pit	1987–88	77	98
Wayne Gretzky, Edm	1982–83	80	125	Adam Oates, Bos	1992–93	84	97
Wayne Gretzky, LA	1990–91	78	122	Joe Thornton, SJ	2005–06	81	96
Wayne Gretzky, Edm	1986–87	79	121	Doug Gilmour, Tor	1992–93	83	95
Wayne Gretzky, Edm	1981–82	80	120	Pat LaFontaine, Buf	1992–93	84	95
Wayne Gretzky, Edm	1983–84	74	118	Mario Lemieux, Pit	1985–86	79	93
Mario Lemieux, Pit	1988–89	76	114	Peter Stastny, Que	1981–82	80	93
Wayne Gretzky, LA	1988–89	78	114	Wayne Gretzky, LA	1993–94	81	92
Wayne Gretzky, Edm	1987–88	64	109	Mario Lemieux, Pit	1995–96	70	92
Wayne Gretzky, Edm	1980–81	80	109	Ron Francis, Pit	1995–96	77	92
Wayne Gretzky, LA	1989–90	73	102	Joe Thornton, SJ	2006–07	82	92

Points

Player	Season	G	Asst	Pts	Player	Season	G	Asst	Pts
Wayne Gretzky, Edm	1985–86	52	163	215	Wayne Gretzky, LA	1990–91	41	122	163
Wayne Gretzky, Edm	1981–82	92	120	212	Mario Lemieux, Pit	1995–96	69	92	161
Wayne Gretzky, Edm	1984–85	73	135	208	Mario Lemieux, Pit	1992–93	69	91	160
Wayne Gretzky, Edm	1983–84	87	118	205	Steve Yzerman, Det	1988–89	65	90	155
Mario Lemieux, Pit	1988–89	85	114	199	Phil Esposito, Bos	1970–71	76	76	152
Mario Lemieux, Pit	1982–83	71	125	196	Bernie Nicholls, LA	1988–89	70	80	150
Wayne Gretzky, Edm	1986–87	62	121	183	Wayne Gretzky, Edm	1987–88	40	109	149
Mario Lemieux, Pit	1987–88	70	98	168	Jaromir Jagr, Pit	1995–96	82	62	149
Wayne Gretzky, LA	1988–89	54	114	168	Pat LaFontaine, Buf	1992–93	53	95	148
Wayne Gretzky, Edm	1980–81	55	109	164	Mike Bossy, NYI	1981–82	64	83	147

Points per Game

Player	Season	GP	Pts	Avg	Player	Season	GP	Pts	Avg
Wayne Gretzky, Edm	1983–84	74	205	2.77	Mario Lemieux, Pit	1987–88	77	168	2.18
Wayne Gretzky, Edm	1985–86	80	215	2.69	Wayne Gretzky, LA	1988–89	78	168	2.15
Mario Lemieux, Pit	1992–93	60	160	2.67	Wayne Gretzky, LA	1990–91	78	163	2.09
Wayne Gretzky, Edm	1981–82	80	212	2.65	Mario Lemieux, Pit	1989–90	59	123	2.08
Mario Lemieux, Pit	1988–89	76	199	2.62	Wayne Gretzky, Edm	1980–81	80	164	2.05
Wayne Gretzky, Edm	1984–85	80	208	2.60	Mario Lemieux, Pit	1991–92	64	131	2.05
Wayne Gretzky, Edm	1982–83	80	196	2.45	Bill Cowley, Bos	1943–44	36	71	1.97
Wayne Gretzky, Edm	1987–88	64	149	2.33	Phil Esposito, Bos	1970–71	78	152	1.95
Wayne Gretzky, Edm	1986–87	79	183	2.32	Wayne Gretzky, LA	1989–90	73	142	1.95
Mario Lemieux, Pitt	1995–96	70	161	2.30	Steve Yzerman, Det	1988–89	80	155	1.94

Note: Minimum 50 points in one season.

Goals per Game

Player	Season	GP	G	Avg	Player	Season	GP	Asst	Avg
Joe Malone, Mtl	1917–18	20	44	2.20	Wayne Gretzky, Edm	1985–86	80	163	2.04
Cy Denneny, Ott	1917–18	20	36	1.80	Wayne Gretzky, Edm	1987–88	64	109	1.70
Newsy Lalonde, Mtl	1917–18	14	23	1.64	Wayne Gretzky, Edm	1984–85	80	135	1.69
Joe Malone, Que	1919–20	24	39	1.63	Wayne Gretzky, Edm	1983–84	74	118	1.59
Newsy Lalonde, Mtl	1919–20	23	36	1.57	Wayne Gretzky, Edm	1982–83	80	125	1.56
Reg Noble, Tor	1917–18	20	30	1.50	Wayne Gretzky, LA	1990–91	78	122	1.56
Babe Dye, Ham-Tor	1920–21	24	35	1.46	Wayne Gretzky, Edm	1986–87	79	121	1.53
Cy Denneny, Ott	1920–21	24	34	1.42	Mario Lemieux, Pit	1992–93	60	91	1.52
Joe Malone, Ham	1920–21	20	28	1.40	Wayne Gretzky, Edm	1981–82	80	120	1.50
Newsy Lalonde, Mtl	1920–21	24	33	1.38	Mario Lemieux, Pit	1988–89	76	114	1.50

Note: Minimum 20 goals in one season.

Note: Minimum 35 assists in one season.

Shutout Leaders

Player	Season	SO	Length of Schedule	Player	Season	SO	Length of Schedule
George Hainsworth, Mtl	1928–29	22	44	Chuck Gardiner, Chi	1930–31	12	44
Alec Connell, Ott	1925–26	15	36	Terry Sawchuk, Det	1951–52	12	70
Alec Connell, Ott	1927–28	15	44	Terry Sawchuk, Det	1953–54	12	70
Hal Winkler, Bos	1927–28	15	44	Terry Sawchuk, Det	1954–55	12	70
Tony Esposito, Chi	1969–70	15	76	Glenn Hall, Det	1955–56	12	70
George Hainsworth, Mtl	1926–27	14	44	Bernie Parent, Phi	1973–74	12	78
Clint Benedict, Mtl M	1926–27	13	44	Bernie Parent, Phi	1974–75	12	80
Alec Connell, Ott	1926–27	13	44	Martin Brodeur, NJ	2006–07	12	82
George Hainsworth, Mtl	1927–28	13	44	Lorne Chabot, NYR	1927–28	11	44
John Roach, NYR	1928–29	13	44	Harry Holmes, Det	1927–28	11	44
Roy Worters, NYA	1928–29	13	44	Roy Worters, Pit Pirates	1927–28	11	44
Harry Lumley, Tor	1953–54	13	70	Clint Benedict, Mtl M	1928–29	11	44
Dominik Hasek, Buf	1997–98	13	82	Lorne Chabot, Tor	1928–29	11	44
Tiny Thompson, Bos	1928–29	12	44	Joe Miller, Pit Pirates	1928–29	11	44

Shutout Leaders (Cont.)

	Season	SO	Length of Schedule		Season	SO	Length of Schedule
Tiny Thompson, Bos	1932–33	11	48	Gerry McNeil, Mtl	1952–53	10	70
Terry Sawchuck, Det	1950–51	11	70	Tony Esposito, Chi	1973–74	10	78
Dominik Hasek, Buf	2000–01	11	82	Ken Dryden, Mtl	1976–77	10	80
Martin Brodeur, NJ	2003–04	11	82	Martin Brodeur, NJ	1996–97	10	82
Henrik Lundqvist, NYR	2010–11	11	82	Martin Brodeur, NJ	1997–98	10	82
Lorne Chabot, NYR	1926–27	10	44	Byron Dafoe, Bos	1998–99	10	82
Clarence Dolson, Det	1928–29	10	44	Roman Cechmanek, Phi	2000–01	10	82
John Roach, Det	1932–33	10	48	Ed Belfour, Tor	2003–04	10	82
Chuck Gardiner, Chi	1933–34	10	48	Miikka Kiprusoff, Cgy	2005–06	10	82
Tiny Thompson, Bos	1935–36	10	48	Henrik Lundqvist, NYR	2007–08	10	82
Frank Brimsek, Bos	1938–39	10	48	Steve Mason, CBJ	2008–09	10	82
Bill Durnan, Mtl	1948–49	10	60	Jonathan Quick, LA	2011–12	10	82
Harry Lumley, Tor	1952–53	10	70				

Wins

	Season	Record*		Season	Record*
Martin Brodeur, NJ	2006–07	48–23	Martin Brodeur, NJ	1997–98	43–17–8
Roberto Luongo, Van	2006–07	47–22	Martin Brodeur, NJ	1999–00	43–20–8
Bernie Parent, Phi	1973–74	47–13–12	Martin Brodeur, NJ	2005–06	43–23
Evgeni Nabokov, SJ	2007–08	46–21	Pekka Rinne, Nash	2011–12	43–26
Miikka Kiprusoff, Cgy	2008–09	45–24	Ken Dryden, Mtl	1975–76	42–10–8
Martin Brodeur, NJ	2009–10	45–25	Mike Richter, NYR	1993–94	42–12–6
Terry Sawchuk, Det	1950–51	44–13–13	Jacques Plante, Mtl	1955–56	42–12–10
Bernie Parent, Phi	1974–75	44–14–9	Jacques Plante, Mtl	1961–62	42–14–14
Terry Sawchuk, Det	1951–52	44–14–12	Roman Turek, StL	1999–00	42–15–9
Evgeni Nabokov, SJ	2009–10	44–16	Martin Brodeur, NJ	2000–01	42–17–11
Martin Brodeur, NJ	2007–08	44–27	Miikka Kiprusoff, Cgy	2005–06	42–20
Tom Barrasso, Pit	1992–93	43–14–5	Ilya Bryzgalov, Phx	2009–10	42–20
Ed Belfour, Chi	1990–91	43–19–7	Marc-Andre Fleury, Pit	2011–12	42–21

*Starting with the 2005–06 season, ties were eliminated.

Goals Against Average

(PRE-1950)					(POST-1950)			
	Season	GP	GAA			Season	GP	GAA
George Hainsworth, Mtl	1928–29	44	0.92		Brian Elliott, StL	2011–12	38	1.56
George Hainsworth, Mtl	1927–28	44	1.05		Miika Kiprusoff, Cal	2003–04	38	1.69
Alec Connell, Ott	1925–26	36	1.12		Marty Turco, Dal	2002–03	55	1.73
Tiny Thompson, Bos	1928–29	44	1.15		Tony Esposito, Chi	1971–72	48	1.770
Roy Worters, NYA	1928–29	38	1.15		Al Rollins, Tor	1950–51	40	1.774

Single-Game Records

Goals

	Date	G
Joe Malone, Que vs Tor	1-31-20	7
Newsy Lalonde, Mtl vs Tor	1-10-20	6
Joe Malone, Que vs Ott	3-10-20	6
Corb Denneny, Tor vs Ham	1-26-21	6
Cy Denneny, Ott vs Ham	3-7-21	6
Syd Howe, Det vs NYR	2-3-44	6
Red Berenson, StL vs Phi	11-7-68	6
Darryl Sittler, Tor vs Bos	2-7-76	6

Assists

	Date	A
Billy Taylor, Det vs Chi	3-16-47	7
Wayne Gretzky, Edm vs Wsh	2-15-80	7
Wayne Gretzky, Edm vs Chi	12-11-85	7
Wayne Gretzky, Edm vs Que	2-14-86	7

Note: 24 tied with 6.

Points

	Date	G	A	Pts
Darryl Sittler, Tor vs Bos	2-7-76	6	4	10
Maurice Richard, Mtl vs Det	12-28-44	5	3	8
Bert Olmstead, Mtl vs Chi	1-9-54	4	4	8
Tom Bladon, Phi vs Clev	12-11-77	4	4	8
Bryan Trottier, NYI vs NYR	12-23-78	5	3	8
Peter Stastny, Que vs Wsh	2-22-81	4	4	8
Anton Stastny, Que vs Wsh	2-22-81	3	5	8
Wayne Gretzky, Edm vs NJ	11-19-83	3	5	8
Wayne Gretzky, Edm vs Min	1-4-84	4	4	8
Paul Coffey, Edm vs Det	3-14-86	2	6	8
Mario Lemieux, Pit vs StL	10-15-88	2	6	8
Bernie Nicholls, LA vs Tor	12-1-88	2	6	8
Mario Lemieux, Pit vs NJ	12-31-88	5	3	8
Sam Gagner, Edm vs. Chi	2-2-12	4	4	8

NHL Season Leaders

Points

Season	Player and Club	Pts	Season	Player and Club	Pts
1917–18	Joe Malone, Mtl	44	1965–66	Bobby Hull, Chi	97
1918–19	Newsy Lalonde, Mtl	30	1966–67	Stan Mikita, Chi	97
1919–20	Joe Malone, Que	48	1967–68	Stan Mikita, Chi	87
1920–21	Newsy Lalonde, Mtl	41	1968–69	Phil Esposito, Bos	126
1921–22	Punch Broadbent, Ott	46	1969–70	Bobby Orr, Bos	120
1922–23	Babe Dye, Tor	37	1970–71	Phil Esposito, Bos	152
1923–24	Cy Denneny, Ott	23	1971–72	Phil Esposito, Bos	133
1924–25	Babe Dye, Tor	44	1972–73	Phil Esposito, Bos	130
1925–26	Nels Stewart, Mtl M	42	1973–74	Phil Esposito, Bos	145
1926–27	Bill Cook, NY	37	1974–75	Bobby Orr, Bos	135
1927–28	Howie Morenz, Mtl	51	1975–76	Guy Lafleur, Mtl	125
1928–29	Ace Bailey, Tor	32	1976–77	Guy Lafleur, Mtl	136
1929–30	Cooney Weiland, Bos	73	1977–78	Guy Lafleur, Mtl	132
1930–31	Howie Morenz, Mtl	51	1978–79	Bryan Trottier, NYI	134
1931–32	Harvey Jackson, Tor	53	1979–80	Marcel Dionne, LA	137
1932–33	Bill Cook, NY	50		Wayne Gretzky, Edm	137
1933–34	Charlie Conacher, Tor	52	1980–81	Wayne Gretzky, Edm	164
1934–35	Charlie Conacher, Tor	57	1981–82	Wayne Gretzky, Edm	212
1935–36	Sweeney Schriner, NYA	45	1982–83	Wayne Gretzky, Edm	196
1936–37	Sweeney Schriner, NYA	46	1983–84	Wayne Gretzky, Edm	205
1937–38	Gord Drillon, Tor	52	1984–85	Wayne Gretzky, Edm	208
1938–39	Hector Blake, Mtl	47	1985–86	Wayne Gretzky, Edm	215
1939–40	Milt Schmidt, Bos	52	1986–87	Wayne Gretzky, Edm	183
1940–41	Bill Cowley, Bos	62	1987–88	Mario Lemieux, Pit	168
1941–42	Bryan Hextall, NY	54	1988–89	Mario Lemieux, Pit	199
1942–43	Doug Bentley, Chi	73	1989–90	Wayne Gretzky, LA	142
1943–44	Herb Cain, Bos	82	1990–91	Wayne Gretzky, LA	163
1944–45	Elmer Lach, Mtl	80	1991–92	Mario Lemieux, Pit	131
1945–46	Max Bentley, Chi	61	1992–93	Mario Lemieux, Pit	160
1946–47	Max Bentley, Chi	72	1993–94	Wayne Gretzky, LA	130
1947–48	Elmer Lach, Mtl	61	1994–95	Jaromir Jagr, Pit	70
1948–49	Roy Conacher, Chi	68	1995–96	Mario Lemieux, Pit	161
1949–50	Ted Lindsay, Det	78	1996–97	Mario Lemieux, Pit	122
1950–51	Gordie Howe, Det	86	1997–98	Jaromir Jagr, Pit	102
1951–52	Gordie Howe, Det	86	1998–99	Jaromir Jagr, Pit	127
1952–53	Gordie Howe, Det	95	1999–00	Jaromir Jagr, Pit	96
1953–54	Gordie Howe, Det	81	2000–01	Jaromir Jagr, Pit	121
1954–55	Bernie Geoffrion, Mtl	75	2001–02	Jarome Iginla, Cgy	96
1955–56	Jean Beliveau, Mtl	88	2002–03	Peter Forsberg, Col	106
1956–57	Gordie Howe, Det	89	2003–04	Martin St. Louis, TB	94
1957–58	Dickie Moore, Mtl	84	2004–05	No season	
1958–59	Dickie Moore, Mtl	96	2005–06	Joe Thornton, Bos/SJ	125
1959–60	Bobby Hull, Chi	81	2006–07	Sidney Crosby, Pit	120
1960–61	Bernie Geoffrion, Mtl	95	2007–08	Alexander Ovechkin, Wsh	112
1961–62	Andy Bathgate, NY	84	2008–09	Evgeni Malkin, Pit	113
	Bobby Hull, Chi	84	2009–10	Henrik Sedin, Van	112
1962–63	Gordie Howe, Det	86	2010–11	Daniel Sedin, Van	104
1963–64	Stan Mikita, Chi	89	2011–12	Evgeni Malkin, Pit	109
1964–65	Stan Mikita, Chi	87			

Goals

Season	Player and Club	G	Season	Player and Club	G
1917–18	Joe Malone, Mtl	44	1930–31	Charlie Lonacher, Tor	31
1918–19	Odie Cleghorn, Mtl	23	1931–32	Charlie Conacher, Tor	34
1919–20	Joe Malone, Que	39		Bill Cook, NY	34
1920–21	Babe Dye, Ham-Tor	35	1932–33	Bill Cook, NY	28
1921–22	Punch Broadbent, Ott	32	1933–34	Charlie Conacher, Tor	32
1922–23	Babe Dye, Tor	26	1934–35	Charlie Conacher, Tor	36
1923–24	Cy Denneny, Ott	22	1935–36	Charlie Conacher, Tor	23
1924–25	Babe Dye, Tor	38		Bill Thoms, Tor	23
1925–26	Nels Stewart, Mtl	34	1936–37	Larry Aurie, Det	23
1926–27	Bill Cook, NY	33		Nels Stewart, Bos-NYA	23
1927–28	Howie Morenz, Mtl	33	1937–38	Gord Drillon, Tor	26
1928–29	Ace Bailey, Tor	22	1938–39	Roy Conacher, Bos	26
1929–30	Cooney Weiland, Bos	43	1939–40	Bryan Hextall, NY	24

Goals (Cont.)

Season	Player and Club	G	Season	Player and Club	G
1940–41	Bryan Hextall, NY	26	1978–79	Mike Bossy, NYI	69
1941–42	Lynn Patrick, NY	32	1979–80	Charlie Simmer, LA	56
1942–43	Doug Bentley, Chi	33		Blaine Stoughton, Hart	56
1943–44	Doug Bentley, Chi	38	1980–81	Mike Bossy, NYI	68
1944–45	Maurice Richard, Mtl	50	1981–82	Wayne Gretzky, Edm	92
1945–46	Gaye Stewart, Tor	37	1982–83	Wayne Gretzky, Edm	71
1946–47	Maurice Richard, Mtl	45	1983–84	Wayne Gretzky, Edm	87
1947–48	Ted Lindsay, Det	33	1984–85	Wayne Gretzky, Edm	73
1948–49	Sid Abel, Det	28	1985–86	Jari Kurri, Edm	68
1949–50	Maurice Richard, Mtl	43	1986–87	Wayne Gretzky, Edm	62
1950–51	Gordie Howe, Det	43	1987–88	Mario Lemieux, Pit	70
1951–52	Gordie Howe, Det	47	1988–89	Mario Lemieux, Pit	85
1952–53	Gordie Howe, Det	49	1989–90	Brett Hull, StL	72
1953–54	Maurice Richard, Mtl	37	1990–91	Brett Hull, StL	86
1954–55	Bernie Geoffrion, Mtl	38	1991–92	Brett Hull, StL	70
	Maurice Richard, Mtl	38	1992–93	Alexander Mogilny, Buf	76
1955–56	Jean Beliveau, Mtl	47		Teemu Selanne, Win	76
1956–57	Gordie Howe, Det	44	1993–94	Pavel Bure, Van	60
1957–58	Dickie Moore, Mtl	36	1994–95	Peter Bondra, Wsh	34
1958–59	Jean Beliveau, Mtl	45	1995–96	Mario Lemieux, Pit	69
1959–60	Bronco Horvath, Bos	39	1996–97	Keith Tkachuk, Phx	52
	Bobby Hull, Chi	39	1997–98	Peter Bondra, Wsh	52
1960–61	Bernie Geoffrion, Mtl	50		Teemu Selanne, Ana	52
1961–62	Bobby Hull, Chi	50	1998–99	Teemu Selanne, Ana	47
1962–63	Gordie Howe, Det	38	1999–00	Pavel Bure, Fla	58
1963–64	Bobby Hull, Chi	43	2000–01	Pavel Bure, Fla	59
1964–65	Norm Ullman, Det	42	2001–02	Jarome Iginla, Cgy	52
1965–66	Bobby Hull, Chi	54	2002–03	Milan Hejduk, Col	50
1966–67	Bobby Hull, Chi	52	2003–04	Jarome Iginla, Cgy	41
1967–68	Bobby Hull, Chi	44		Ilya Kovalchuk, Atl	41
1968–69	Bobby Hull, Chi	58		Rick Nash, CBJ	41
1969–70	Phil Esposito, Bos	43	2004–05	No season	
1970–71	Phil Esposito, Bos	76	2005–06	Jonathan Cheechoo, SJ	56
1971–72	Phil Esposito, Bos	66	2006–07	Vincent Lecavalier, TB	52
1972–73	Phil Esposito, Bos	55	2007–08	Alexander Ovechkin, Wsh	65
1973–74	Phil Esposito, Bos	68	2008–09	Alexander Ovechkin, Wsh	56
1974–75	Phil Esposito, Bos	61	2009–10	Sidney Crosby, Pit	51
1975–76	Guy Lafleur, Mtl	56		Steven Stamkos, TB	51
1976–77	Steve Shutt, Mtl	60	2010–11	Corey Perry, Ana	50
1977–78	Guy Lafleur, Mtl	60	2011–12	Steven Stamkos, TB	60

Assists

Season	Player and Club	Asst	Season	Player and Club	Asst
1917–18	statistic not kept		1940–41	Bill Cowley, Bos	45
1918–19	Newsy Lalonde, Mtl	9	1941–42	Phil Watson, NY	37
1919–20	Corbett Denneny, Tor	12	1942–43	Bill Cowley, Bos	45
1920–21	Louis Berlinquette, Mtl	9	1943–44	Clint Smith, Chi	49
1921–22	Punch Broadbench, Ott	14	1944–45	Elmer Lach, Mtl	54
1922–23	Babe Dye, Tor	11	1945–46	Elmer Lach, Mtl	34
1923–24	Billy Boucher, Mtl	6	1946–47	Billy Taylor, Det	46
1924–25	Cy Denneny, Ott	15	1947–48	Doug Bentley, Chi	37
1925–26	Frank Nighbor, Ott	13	1948–49	Doug Bentley, Chi	43
1926–27	Dick Irvin, Chi	18	1949–50	Ted Lindsay, Det	55
1927–28	Howie Morenz, Mtl	18	1950–51	Gordie Howe, Det	43
1928–29	Frank Boucher, NY	16		Ted Kennedy, Tor	43
1929–30	Frank Boucher, NY	36	1951–52	Elmer Lach, Mtl	50
1930–31	Joe Primeau, Tor	32	1952–53	Gordie Howe, Det	46
1931–32	Joe Primeau, Tor	37	1953–54	Gordie Howe, Det	48
1932–33	Frank Boucher, NY	28	1954–55	Bert Olmstead, Mtl	48
1933–34	Joe Primeau, Tor	32	1955–56	Bert Olmstead, Mtl	56
1934–35	Art Chapman, NYA	34	1956–57	Ted Lindsay, Det	55
1935–36	Art Chapman, NYA	28	1957–58	Henri Richard, Mtl	52
1936–37	Syl Apps, Tor	29	1958–59	Dickie Moore, Mtl	55
1937–38	Syl Apps, Tor	29	1959–60	Bobby Hull, Chi	42
1938–39	Bill Cowley, Bos	34	1960–61	Jean Beliveau, Mtl	58
1939–40	Milt Schmidt, Bos	30	1961–62	Andy Bathgate, NY	56

Assists *(Cont.)*

Season	Player and Club	Asst	Season	Player and Club	Asst
1962–63	Henri Richard, Mtl	50	1988–89	Wayne Gretzky, LA	114
1963–64	Andy Bathgate, NY-Tor	58		Mario Lemieux, Pit	114
1964–65	Stan Mikita, Chi	59	1989–90	Wayne Gretzky, LA	102
1965–66	Jean Beliveau, Mtl	48	1990–91	Wayne Gretzky, LA	122
	Stan Mikita, Chi	48	1991–92	Wayne Gretzky, LA	90
	Bobby Rousseau, Mtl	48	1992–93	Adam Oates, Bos	97
1966–67	Stan Mikita, Chi	62	1993–94	Wayne Gretzky, LA	92
1967–68	Phil Esposito, Bos	49	1994–95	Ron Francis, Pit	48
1968–69	Phil Esposito, Bos	77	1995–96	Ron Francis, Pit	92
1969–70	Bobby Orr, Bos	87		Mario Lemieux, Pit	92
1970–71	Bobby Orr, Bos	102	1996–97	Mario Lemieux, Pit	72
1971–72	Bobby Orr, Bos	80	1997–98	Wayne Gretzky, NYR	67
1972–73	Phil Esposito, Bos	75		Jaromir Jagr, Pit	67
1973–74	Bobby Orr, Bos	90	1998–99	Jaromir Jagr, Pit	83
1974–75	Bobby Clarke, Phi	89	1999–00	Mark Recchi, Phi	63
	Bobby Orr, Bos	89	2000–01	Jaromir Jagr, Pit	69
1975–76	Bobby Clarke, Phi	89		Adam Oates, Wsh	69
1976–77	Guy Lafleur, Mtl	80	2001–02	Adam Oates, Wsh	64
1977–78	Bryan Trottier, NYI	77	2002–03	Peter Forsberg, Col	77
1978–79	Bryan Trottier, NYI	87	2003–04	Scott Gomez, NJ	56
1979–80	Wayne Gretzky, Edm	86		Martin St. Louis, TB	56
1980–81	Wayne Gretzky, Edm	109	2004–05	No season	
1981–82	Wayne Gretzky, Edm	120	2005–06	Joe Thornton, Bos/SJ	96
1982–83	Wayne Gretzky, Edm	125	2006–07	Joe Thornton, SJ	92
1983–84	Wayne Gretzky, Edm	118	2007–08	Joe Thornton, SJ	67
1984–85	Wayne Gretzky, Edm	135	2008–09	Evgeni Malkin, Pit	78
1985–86	Wayne Gretzky, Edm	163	2009–10	Henrik Sedin, Van	83
1986–87	Wayne Gretzky, Edm	121	2010–11	Henrik Sedin, Van	75
1987–88	Wayne Gretzky, Edm	109	2011–12	Henrik Sedin, Van	67

Goals Against Average

Season	Goaltender and Club	GP	Min	GA	SO	Avg
1917–18	Georges Vezina, Mtl	21	1282	84	1	3.93
1918–19	Clint Benedict, Ott	18	1113	53	2	2.86
1919–20	Clint Benedict, Ott	24	1444	64	5	2.66
1920–21	Clint Benedict, Ott	24	1457	75	2	3.09
1921–22	Clint Benedict, Ott	24	1508	84	2	3.34
1922–23	Clint Benedict, Ott	24	1478	54	4	2.18
1923–24	Georges Vezina, Mtl	24	1459	48	3	1.97
1924–25	Georges Vezina, Mtl	30	1860	56	5	1.81
1925–26	Alec Connell, Ott	36	2251	42	15	1.12
1926–27	Clint Benedict, Mtl M	43	2748	65	13	1.42
1927–28	George Hainsworth, Mtl	44	2730	48	13	1.05
1928–29	George Hainsworth, Mtl	44	2800	43	22	0.92
1929–30	Tiny Thompson, Bos	44	2680	98	3	2.19
1930–31	Roy Worters, NYA	44	2760	74	8	1.61
1931–32	Chuck Gardiner, Chi	48	2989	92	4	1.85
1932–33	Tiny Thompson, Bos	48	3000	88	11	1.76
1933–34	Wilf Cude, Det-Mtl	30	1920	47	5	1.47
1934–35	Lorne Chabot, Chi	48	2940	88	8	1.80
1935–36	Tiny Thompson, Bos	48	2930	82	10	1.68
1936–37	Normie Smith, Det	48	2980	102	6	2.05
1937–38	Tiny Thompson, Bos	48	2970	89	7	1.80
1938–39	Frank Brimsek, Bos	43	2610	68	10	1.56
1939–40	Dave Kerr, NYR	48	3000	77	8	1.54
1940–41	Turk Broda, Tor	48	2970	99	5	2.00
1941–42	Frank Brimsek, Bos	47	2930	115	3	2.35
1942–43	Johnny Mowers, Det	50	3010	124	6	2.47
1943–44	Bill Durnan, Mtl	50	3000	109	2	2.18
1944–45	Bill Durnan, Mtl	50	3000	121	1	2.42
1945–46	Bill Durnan, Mtl	40	2400	104	4	2.60
1946–47	Bill Durnan, Mtl	60	3600	138	4	2.30
1947–48	Turk Broda, Tor	60	3600	143	5	2.38
1948–49	Bill Durnan, Mtl	60	3600	126	10	2.10

Goals Against Average *(Cont.)*

Season	Goaltender and Club	GP	Min	GA	SO	Avg
1949–50	Bill Durnan, Mtl	64	3840	141	8	2.20
1950–51	Al Rollins, Tor	40	2367	70	5	1.77
1951–52	Terry Sawchuk, Det	70	4200	133	12	1.90
1952–53	Terry Sawchuk, Det	63	3780	120	9	1.90
1953–54	Harry Lumley, Tor	69	4140	128	13	1.86
1954–55	Harry Lumley, Tor	69	4140	134	8	1.94
1955–56	Jacques Plante, Mtl	64	3840	119	7	1.86
1956–57	Jacques Plante, Mtl	61	3660	122	9	2.00
1957–58	Jacques Plante, Mtl	57	3386	119	9	2.11
1958–59	Jacques Plante, Mtl	67	4000	144	9	2.16
1959–60	Jacques Plante, Mtl	69	4140	175	3	2.54
1960–61	Charlie Hodge, Mtl	30	1800	74	4	2.47
1961–62	Jacques Plante, Mtl	70	4200	166	4	2.37
1962–63	Don Simmons, Tor	28	1680	69	1	2.46
1963–64	Johnny Bower, Tor	51	3009	106	5	2.11
1964–65	Johnny Bower, Tor	34	2040	81	3	2.38
1965–66	Johnny Bower, Tor	35	1998	75	3	2.25
1966–67	Glenn Hall, Chi	32	1664	66	2	2.38
1967–68	Gump Worsley, Mtl	40	2213	73	6	1.98
1968–69	Jacques Plante, StL	37	2139	70	5	1.96
1969–70	Ernie Wakely, StL	30	1651	58	4	2.11
1970–71	Jacques Plante, Tor	40	2329	73	4	1.88
1971–72	Tony Esposito, Chi	48	2780	82	9	1.77
1972–73	Ken Dryden, Mtl	54	3165	119	6	2.26
1973–74	Bernie Parent, Phi	73	4314	136	12	1.89
1974–75	Bernie Parent, Phi	68	4041	137	12	2.03
1975–76	Ken Dryden, Mtl	62	3580	121	8	2.03
1976–77	Michel Larocque, Mtl	26	1525	53	4	2.09
1977–78	Ken Dryden, Mtl	52	3071	105	5	2.05
1978–79	Ken Dryden, Mtl	47	2814	108	5	2.30
1979–80	Bob Sauve, Buff	32	1880	74	4	2.36
1980–81	Richard Sevigny, Mtl	33	1777	71	2	2.40
1981–82	Denis Herron, Mtl	27	1547	68	3	2.64
1982–83	Pete Peeters, Bos	62	3611	142	8	2.36
1983–84	Pat Riggin, Wsh	41	2299	102	4	2.66
1984–85	Tom Barrasso, Buf	54	3248	144	5	2.66
1985–86	Bob Froese, Phi	51	2728	116	5	2.55
1986–87	Brian Hayward, Mtl	37	2178	102	1	2.81
1987–88	Pete Peeters, Wsh	35	1896	88	2	2.78
1988–89	Patrick Roy, Mtl	48	2744	113	4	2.47
1989–90	Mike Liut, Hfd-Wsh	37	2161	91	4	2.53
	Patrick Roy, Mtl	54	3173	134	3	2.53
1990–91	Ed Belfour, Chi	74	4127	170	4	2.47
1991–92	Patrick Roy, Mtl	67	3935	155	5	2.36
1992–93	Felix Potvin, Tor	48	2781	116	2	2.50
1993–94	Dominik Hasek, Buf	58	3358	109	7	1.95
1994–95	Dominik Hasek, Buf	41	2416	85	5	2.11
1995–96	Ron Hextall, Phi	53	3102	112	4	2.17
	Chris Osgood, Det	50	2932	106	5	2.17
1996–97	Martin Brodeur, NJ	67	3838	120	10	1.88
1997–98	Ed Belfour, Dal	61	3581	112	9	1.88
1998–99	Ron Tugnutt, Ott	43	2508	75	3	1.79
1999–00	Brian Boucher, Phi	35	2038	65	4	1.91
2000–01	Marty Turco, Dal	26	1266	40	3	1.90
2001–02	Patrick Roy, Col	63	3773	122	9	1.94
2002–03	Marty Turco, Dal	55	3202	92	7	1.72
2003–04	Miikka Kiprusoff, Cgy	38	2301	65	4	1.69
2004–05	No season					
2005–06	Miikka Kiprusoff, Cgy	74	4379	151	10	2.07
2006–07	Niklas Backstrom, Min	41	2226	73	5	1.97
2007–08	Chris Osgood, Det	43	2409	84	4	2.09
2008–09	Tim Thomas, Bos	54	3259	114	5	2.10
2009–10	Tuukka Rask, Bos	45	2562	84	5	1.97
2010–11	Tim Thomas, Bos	57	3364	112	9	2.00
2011–12	Brian Elliott, StL	38	2235	58	9	1.56

Penalty Minutes

Season	Player and Club	GP	PIM	Season	Player and Club	GP	PIM
1918–19	Joe Hall, Mtl	17	135	1965–66	Reggie Fleming, Bos-NYR	69	166
1919–20	Cully Wilson, Tor	23	79	1966–67	John Ferguson, Mtl	67	177
1920–21	Bert Corbeau, Mtl	24	86	1967–68	Barclay Plager, StL	49	153
1921–22	Sprague Cleghorn, Mtl	24	63	1968–69	Forbes Kennedy, Phi-Tor	77	219
1922–23	Billy Boucher, Mtl	24	55	1969–70	Keith Magnuson, Chi	76	213
1923–24	Bert Corbeau, Tor	24	55	1970–71	Keith Magnuson, Chi	76	291
1924–25	Billy Boucher, Mtl	30	92	1971–72	Brian Watson, Pit	75	212
1925–26	Bert Corbeau, Tor	36	121	1972–73	Dave Schultz, Phi	76	259
1926–27	Nels Stewart, Mtl M	44	133	1973–74	Dave Schultz, Phi	73	348
1927–28	Eddie Shore, Bos	44	165	1974–75	Dave Schultz, Phi	76	472
1928–29	Red Dutton, Mtl M	44	139	1975–76	Steve Durbano, Pit-KC	69	370
1929–30	Joe Lamb, Ott	44	119	1976–77	Dave Williams, Tor	77	338
1930–31	Harvey Rockburn, Det	42	118	1977–78	Dave Schultz, LA-Pit	74	405
1931–32	Red Dutton, NYA	47	107	1978–79	Dave Williams, Tor	77	298
1932–33	Red Horner, Tor	48	144	1979–80	Jimmy Mann, Win	72	287
1933–34	Red Horner, Tor	42	126	1980–81	Dave Williams, Van	77	343
1934–35	Red Horner, Tor	46	125	1981–82	Paul Baxter, Pit	76	409
1935–36	Red Horner, Tor	43	167	1982–83	Randy Holt, Wsh	70	275
1936–37	Red Horner, Tor	48	124	1983–84	Chris Nilan, Mtl	76	338
1937–38	Red Horner, Tor	47	82	1984–85	Chris Nilan, Mtl	77	358
1938–39	Red Horner, Tor	48	85	1985–86	Joey Kocur, Det	59	377
1939–40	Red Horner, Tor	30	87	1986–87	Tim Hunter, Cgy	73	361
1940–41	Jimmy Orlando, Det	48	99	1987–88	Bob Probert, Det	74	398
1941–42	Pat Egan, Bklyn	48	124	1988–89	Tim Hunter, Cgy	75	375
1942–43	Jimmy Orlando, Det	40	89	1989–90	Basil McRae, Min	66	351
1943–44	Mike McMahon, Mtl	42	98	1990–91	Rob Ray, Buf	66	350
1944–45	Pat Egan, Bos	48	86	1991–92	Mike Peluso, Chi	63	408
1945–46	Jack Stewart, Det	47	73	1992–93	Marty McSorley, LA	81	399
1946–47	Gus Mortson, Tor	60	133	1993–94	Tie Domi, Win	81	347
1947–48	Bill Barilko, Tor	57	147	1994–95	Enrico Ciccone, TB	41	225
1948–49	Bill Ezinicki, Tor	52	145	1995–96	Matthew Barnaby, Buf	73	335
1949–50	Bill Ezinicki, Tor	67	144	1996–97	Gino Odjick, Van	70	371
1950–51	Gus Mortson, Tor	60	142	1997–98	Donald Brashear, Van	77	372
1951–52	Gus Kyle, Bos	69	127	1998–99	Rob Ray, Buf	76	261
1952–53	Maurice Richard, Mtl	70	112	1999–00	Denny Lambert, Atl	73	219
1953–54	Gus Mortson, Chi	68	132	2000–01	Matthew Barnaby, TB	76	265
1954–55	Fern Flaman, Bos	70	150	2001–02	Peter Worrell, Fla	79	354
1955–56	Lou Fontinato, NYR	70	202	2002–03	Jody Shelley, CBJ	68	249
1956–57	Gus Mortson, Chi	70	147	2003–04	Sean Avery, LA	76	261
1957–58	Lou Fontinato, NYR	70	152	2004–05	No season		
1958–59	Ted Lindsay, Chi	70	184	2005–06	Sean Avery, LA	75	257
1959–60	Carl Brewer, Tor	67	150	2006–07	Ben Eager, Phi	63	233
1960–61	Pierre Pilote, Chi	70	165	2007–08	Daniel Carcillo, Phx	57	324
1961–62	Lou Fontinato, Mtl	54	167	2008–09	Daniel Carcillo, Phi	74	254
1962–63	Howie Young, Det	64	273	2009–10	Zenon Konopka, TB	74	265
1963–64	Vic Hadfield, NYR	69	151	2010–11	Zenon Konopka, NYI	82	307
1964–65	Carl Brewer, Tor	70	177	2011–12	Derek Dorsett, CBJ	77	235

First played in 1947, this game started before the regular season and was used to match the defending Stanley Cup champions against the league All-Stars from other teams. In 1966 the game was moved to midseason, although there was no game that year. The format changed to a inter-conference showdown in 1969. The Challenge Cup, a series between the NHL All-Stars and the Soviet Union, was played instead of the All-Star Game in 1979. Eight years later, Rendez-Vous '87, a two-game series matching the Soviet Union and the NHL All-Stars, replaced the All-Star Game. The 1995 NHL All-Star game was cancelled due to a labor dispute. The 1998 NHL All-Star game, billed as a preview to the 1998 Winter Olympics in Nagano, Japan, matched North Amercian–born All-Stars and All-Stars born elsewhere.

Results

Year	Site	Score	MVP	Attendance
1947	Toronto	All-Stars 4, Toronto 3	None named	14,169
1948	Chicago	All-Stars 3, Toronto 1	None named	12,794
1949	Toronto	All-Stars 3, Toronto 1	None named	13,541
1950	Detroit	Detroit 7, All-Stars 1	None named	9,166
1951	Toronto	1st team 2, 2nd team 2	None named	11,469
1952	Detroit	1st team 1, 2nd team 1	None named	10,680
1953	Montreal	All-Stars 3, Montreal 1	None named	14,153
1954	Detroit	All-Stars 2, Detroit 2	None named	10,689
1955	Detroit	Detroit 3, All-Stars 1	None named	10,111
1956	Montreal	All-Stars 1, Montreal 1	None named	13,095
1957	Montreal	All-Stars 5, Montreal 3	None named	13,003
1958	Montreal	Montreal 6, All-Stars 3	None named	13,989
1959	Montreal	Montreal 6, All-Stars 1	None named	13,818
1960	Montreal	All-Stars 2, Montreal 1	None named	13,949
1961	Chicago	All-Stars 3, Chicago 1	None named	14,534
1962	Toronto	Toronto 4, All-Stars 1	Eddie Shack, Tor	14,236
1963	Toronto	All-Stars 3, Toronto 3	Frank Mahovlich, Tor	14,034
1964	Toronto	All-Stars 3, Toronto 2	Jean Beliveau, Mtl	14,232
1965	Montreal	All-Stars 5, Montreal 2	Gordie Howe, Det	13,529
1967	Montreal	Montreal 3, All-Stars 0	Henri Richard, Mtl	14,284
1968	Toronto	Toronto 4, All-Stars 3	Bruce Gamble, Tor	15,753
1969	Montreal	East 3, West 3	Frank Mahovlich, Det	16,260
1970	St. Louis	East 4, West 1	Bobby Hull, Chi	16,587
1971	Boston	West 2, East 1	Bobby Hull, Chi	14,790
1972	Minnesota	East 3, West 2	Bobby Orr, Bos	15,423
1973	NY Rangers	East 5, West 4	Greg Polis, Pit	16,986
1974	Chicago	West 6, East 4	Garry Unger, StL	16,426
1975	Montreal	Wales 7, Campbell 1	Syl Apps Jr, Pit	16,080
1976	Philadelphia	Wales 7, Campbell 5	Pete Mahovlich, Mtl	16,436
1977	Vancouver	Wales 4, Campbell 3	Rick Martin, Buf	15,607
1978	Buffalo	Wales 3, Campbell 2 (OT)	Billy Smith, NYI	16,433
1980	Detroit	Wales 6, Campbell 3	Reg Leach, Phi	21,002
1981	Los Angeles	Campbell 4, Wales 1	Mike Liut, StL	15,761
1982	Washington	Wales 4, Campbell 2	Mike Bossy, NYI	18,130
1983	NY Islanders	Campbell 9, Wales 3	Wayne Gretzky, Edm	15,230
1984	New Jersey	Wales 7, Campbell 6	Don Maloney, NYR	18,939
1985	Calgary	Wales 6, Campbell 4	Mario Lemieux, Pit	16,825
1986	Hartford	Wales 4, Campbell 3 (OT)	Grant Fuhr, Edm	15,100
1988	St. Louis	Wales 6, Campbell 5 (OT)	Mario Lemieux, Pit	17,878
1989	Edmonton	Campbell 9, Wales 5	Wayne Gretzky, LA	17,503
1990	Pittsburgh	Wales 12, Campbell 7	Mario Lemieux, Pit	16,236
1991	Chicago	Campbell 11, Wales 5	Vince Damphousse, Tor	18,472
1992	Philadelphia	Campbell 10, Wales 6	Brett Hull, StL	17,380
1993	Montreal	Wales 16, Campbell 6	Mike Gartner, NYR	17,137
1994	NY Rangers	East 9, West 8	Mike Richter, NYR	18,200
1996	Boston	East 5, West 4	Ray Bourque, Bos	17,565
1997	San Jose	East 11, West 7	Mark Recchi, Mtl	17,422
1998	Vancouver	North America 8, World 7	Teemu Selanne, Ana (World)	18,422
1999	Tampa Bay	North America 8, World 6	Wayne Gretzky, NYR (N. America)	19,758
2000	Toronto	World 9, North America 4	Pavel Bure, Fla (World)	19,300
2001	Denver	North America 14, World 12	Bill Guerin, Bos (North America)	18,646
2002	Los Angeles	World 8, North America 5	Eric Daze, Chi (North America)	18,118
2003	Sunrise, Fla.	West 6, East 5 (shootout)	Dany Heatley, Atl (East)	19,250
2004	St. Paul, Minn.	East 6, West 4	Joe Sakic, Col (West)	19,434
2005	No game played (season lockout)			
2006	No game played (2006 Winter Olympics)			
2007	Dallas	West 12, East 9	Daniel Briere, Buf (East)	18,532
2008	Atlanta	East 8, West 7	Eric Staal, Car (East)	18,644

Results (Cont.)

Year	Site	Score	MVP	Attendance
2009	Montreal	East 12, West 11	Alexei Kovalev, Mtl (East)	21,273
2010	No game played (2010 Winter Olympics)			
2011	Raleigh	Team Lidstrom 11, Team Staal 10	Patrick Sharp, Chi (Team Staal)	18,680
2012	Ottawa	Team Chara 12, Team Alfredsson 9	Marian Gaborik, NYR (Team Chara)	20,510

Hockey Hall of Fame

Located in Toronto, the Hockey Hall of Fame was officially opened on August 26, 1961. The current chairman is William C. Hay. There are, at present, 306 members of the Hockey Hall of Fame—209 players, 84 "builders," and 14 on-ice officials. (One member, Alan Eagleson, resigned from the Hall March 25, 1998.) To be eligible, player and referee/linesman candidates should have been out of the game for three years, but the Hall's Board of Directors can make exceptions.

Players

Sid Abel (1969)
Jack Adams (1959)
Glenn Anderson (2008)
Charles (Syl) Apps (1961)
George Armstrong (1975)
Irvine (Ace) Bailey (1975)
Donald H. (Dan) Bain (1945)
Hobey Baker (1945)
Bill Barber (1990)
Marty Barry (1965)
Andy Bathgate (1978)
Bobby Bauer (1996)
Ed Belfour (2011)
Jean Beliveau (1972)
Clint Benedict (1965)
Douglas Bentley (1964)
Max Bentley (1966)
Hector (Toe) Blake (1966)
Leo Boivin (1986)
Dickie Boon (1952)
Mike Bossy (1991)
Emile (Butch) Bouchard (1966)
Frank Boucher (1958)
George (Buck) Boucher (1960)
Ray Bourque (2004)
Johnny Bower (1976)
Russell Bowie (1945)
Frank Brimsek (1966)
Harry L. (Punch) Broadbent (1962)
Walter (Turk) Broda (1967)
John Bucyk (1981)
Billy Burch (1974)
Pavel Bure (2012)
Harry Cameron (1962)
Gerry Cheevers (1985)
Dino Ciccarelli (2010)
Francis (King) Clancy (1958)
Aubrey (Dit) Clapper (1947)
Bobby Clarke (1987)
Sprague Cleghorn (1958)
Paul Coffey (2004)
Neil Colville (1967)
Charlie Conacher (1961)
Lionel Conacher (1994)
Roy Conacher (1998)

Alex Connell (1958)
Bill Cook (1952)
Fred (Bun) Cook (1995)
Arthur Coulter (1974)
Yvan Cournoyer (1982)
Bill Cowley (1968)
Samuel (Rusty) Crawford (1962)
Jack Darragh (1962)
Allan M. (Scotty) Davidson (1950)
Clarence (Hap) Day (1961)
Alex Delvecchio (1977)
Cy Denneny (1959)
Marcel Dionne (1992)
Gordie Drillon (1975)
Charles Drinkwater (1950)
Ken Dryden (1983)
Terrance (Dick) Duff (2006)
Woody Dumart (1992)
Thomas Dunderdale (1974)
Bill Durnan (1964)
Mervyn A. (Red) Dutton (1958)
Cecil (Babe) Dye (1970)
Phil Esposito (1984)
Tony Esposito (1988)
Arthur F. Farrell (1965)
Bernie Federko (2002)
Viacheslav Fetisov (2001)
Ferdinand (Fern) Flaman (1990)
Frank Foyston (1958)
Ron Francis (2007)
Frank Frederickson (1958)
Grant Fuhr (2003)
Bill Gadsby (1970)
Bob Gainey (1992)
Chuck Gardiner (1945)
Herb Gardiner (1958)
Jimmy Gardner (1962)
Mike Gartner (2001)
Bernie (Boom Boom) Geoffrion (1972)
Eddie Gerard (1945)
Ed Giacomin (1987)
Rod Gilbert (1982)
Clark Gillies (2002)
Doug Gilmour (2011)
Hamilton (Billy) Gilmour (1962)

Note: Year of election to the Hall of Fame is in parentheses after the member's name.

Players *(Cont.)*

Frank (Moose) Goheen (1952)
Ebenezer R. (Ebbie)
    Goodfellow (1963)
Michel Goulet (1998)
Cammi Granato (2010)
Mike Grant (1950)
Wilfred (Shorty) Green (1962)
Jim Gregory (2007)
Wayne Gretzky (1999)
Si Griffis (1950)
George Hainsworth (1961)
Glenn Hall (1975)
Joe Hall (1961)
Doug Harvey (1973)
Dale Hawerchuk (2001)
George Hay (1958)
William (Riley) Hern (1962)
Bryan Hextall (1969)
Harry (Hap) Holmes (1972)
Tom Hooper (1962)
George (Red) Horner (1965)
Miles (Tim) Horton (1977)
Gordie Howe (1972)
Mark Howe (2011)
Syd Howe (1965)
Harry Howell (1979)
Bobby Hull (1983)
Brett Hull (2009)
John (Bouse) Hutton (1962)
Harry M. Hyland (1962)
James (Dick) Irvin (1958)
Angela James (2010)
Harvey (Busher) Jackson (1971)
Ernest (Moose) Johnson (1952)
Ivan (Ching) Johnson (1958)
Tom Johnson (1970)
Aurel Joliat (1947)
Gordon (Duke) Keats (1958)
Leonard (Red) Kelly (1969)
Ted (Teeder) Kennedy (1966)
Dave Keon (1986)
Valeri Kharlamov (2005)
Jari Kurri (2001)
Elmer Lach (1966)
Guy Lafleur (1988)
Pat LaFontaine (2003)
Edouard (Newsy) Lalonde (1950)
Rod Langway (2002)
Jacques Laperriere (1987)
Guy Lapointe (1993)
Edgar Laprade (1993)
Igor Larionov (2008)
Jean (Jack) Laviolette (1962)
Brian Leetch (2009)
Hugh Lehman (1958)
Jacques Lemaire (1984)
Mario Lemieux (1997)
Percy LeSueur (1961)
Herbert A. Lewis (1989)
Ted Lindsay (1966)
Harry Lumley (1980)
Lanny McDonald (1992)
Frank McGee (1945)

Billy McGimsie (1962)
George McNamara (1958)
Al MacInnis (2007)
Duncan (Mickey) MacKay (1952)
Frank Mahovlich (1981)
Joe Malone (1950)
Sylvio Mantha (1960)
Jack Marshall (1965)
Fred G. (Steamer) Maxwell (1962)
Mark Messier (2007)
Stan Mikita (1983)
Dicky Moore (1974)
Patrick (Paddy) Moran (1958)
Howie Morenz (1945)
Billy Mosienko (1965)
Joe Mullen (2000)
Larry Murphy (2004)
Cam Neely (2005)
Joe Nieuwendyk (2011)
Frank Nighbor (1947)
Reg Noble (1962)
Adam Oates (2012)
Herbert (Buddy) O'Connor (1988)
Harry Oliver (1967)
Bert Olmstead (1985)
Bobby Orr (1979)
Bernie Parent (1984)
Brad Park (1988)
Lester Patrick (1947)
Lynn Patrick (1980)
Gilbert Perreault (1990)
Tommy Phillips (1945)
Pierre Pilote (1975)
Didier (Pit) Pitre (1962)
Jacques Plante (1978)
Denis Potvin (1991)
Walter (Babe) Pratt (1966)
Joe Primeau (1963)
Marcel Pronovost (1978)
Bob Pulford (1991)
Harvey Pulford (1945)
Hubert (Bill) Quackenbush (1976)
Frank Rankin (1961)
Jean Ratelle (1985)
Claude (Chuck) Rayner (1973)
Kenneth Reardon (1966)
Henri Richard (1979)
Maurice (Rocket) Richard (1961)
George Richardson (1950)
Gordon Roberts (1971)
Larry Robinson (1995)
Luc Robitaille (2009)
Art Ross (1945)
Patrick Roy (2006)
Blair Russel (1965)
Ernest Russell (1965)
Jack Ruttan (1962)
Joe Sakic (2012)
Borje Salming (1996)
Denis Savard (2000)
Serge Savard (1986)
Terry Sawchuk (1971)

Note: Year of election to the Hall of Fame is in parentheses after the member's name.

Players *(Cont.)*

Fred Scanlan (1965)
Milt Schmidt (1961)
Dave (Sweeney) Schriner (1962)
Earl Seibert (1963)
Oliver Seibert (1961)
Eddie Shore (1947)
Steve Shutt (1993)
Albert C. (Babe) Siebert (1964)
Harold (Bullet Joe) Simpson (1962)
Daryl Sittler (1989)
Alfred E. Smith (1962)
Billy Smith (1993)
Clint Smith (1991)
Reginald (Hooley) Smith (1972)
Thomas Smith (1973)
Allan Stanley (1981)
Russell (Barney) Stanley (1962)
Peter Stastny (1998)
Scott Stevens (2007)
John (Black Jack) Stewart (1964)
Nels Stewart (1962)
Bruce Stuart (1961)

Hod Stuart (1945)
Mats Sundin (2012)
Frederic (Cyclone) Taylor (O.B.E.) (1947)
Cecil R. (Tiny) Thompson (1959)
Vladislav Tretiak (1989)
Harry J. Trihey (1950)
Bryan Trottier (1997)
Norm Ullman (1982)
Georges Vezina (1945)
Jack Walker (1960)
Marty Walsh (1962)
Harry Watson (1994)
Harry E. Watson (1962)
Ralph (Cooney) Weiland (1971)
Harry Westwick (1962)
Fred Whitcroft (1962)
Gordon (Phat) Wilson (1962)
Lorne (Gump) Worsley (1980)
Roy Worters (1969)
Steve Yzerman (2009)

Builders

Charles Adams (1960)
Weston W. Adams (1972)
Thomas (Frank) Ahearn (1962)
John (Bunny) Ahearne (1977)
Montagu Allan (C.V.O.) (1945)
Keith Allen (1992)
Al Arbour (1996)
Harold Ballard (1977)
David Bauer (1989)
John Bickell (1978)
Scott Bowman (1991)
Herb Brooks (2006)
George V. Brown (1961)
Walter A. Brown (1962)
Frank Buckland (1975)
Walter L. Bush (2000)
Jack Butterfield (1980)
Frank Calder (1947)
Angus D. Campbell (1964)
Clarence Campbell (1966)
Joe Cattarinich (1977)
Ed Chynoweth (2008)
Bob Cole (1996, Media)
Murray Costello (2005)
Joseph (Leo) Dandurand (1963)
Jimmy Devellano (2010)
Francis Dilio (1964)
George S. Dudley (1958)
James A. Dunn (1968)
*Robert Alan Eagleson (1989–98)
Cliff Fletcher (2004)
Emile Francis (1982)
Jack Gibson (1976)
Tommy Gorman (1963)
Frank Griffiths (1993)

William Hanley (1986)
Charles Hay (1974)
James C. Hendy (1968)
Foster Hewitt (1965)
William Hewitt (1947)
Harley Hotchkiss (2006)
Fred J. Hume (1962)
Mike Ilitch (2003)
George (Punch) Imlach (1984)
Tommy Ivan (1974)
William M. Jennings (1975)
Bob Johnson (1992)
Gordon W. Juckes (1979)
John Kilpatrick (1960)
Brian Kilrea (2003)
Seymour Knox III (1993)
Lou Lamoriello (2009)
George Leader (1969)
Robert LeBel (1970)
Thomas F. Lockhart (1965)
Paul Loicq (1961)
Frederic McLaughlin (1963)
John Mariucci (1985)
Frank Mathers (1992)
John (Jake) Milford (1984)
Hartland Molson (1973)
Scotty Morrison (1999)
Msgr. Athol (Pere) Murray (1998)
Roger Neilson (2002)
Francis Nelson (1947)
Bruce A. Norris (1969)
James Norris, Sr. (1958)
James D. Norris (1962)
William M. Northey (1947)
John O'Brien (1962)

*Eagleson resigned from Hall March 25, 1998.
Note: Year of election to the Hall of Fame is in parentheses after the member's name.

Builders *(Cont.)*

Brian O'Neill (1994)
Fred Page (1993)
Craig Patrick (1996)
Frank Patrick (1958)
Allan W. Pickard (1958)
Rudy Pilous (1985)
Norman (Bud) Poile (1990)
Samuel Pollock (1978)
Donat Raymond (1958)
John Robertson (1947)
Claude C. Robinson (1947)
Philip D. Ross (1976)
Gunther Sabetzki (1995)
Glen Sather (1997)
Daryl "Doc" Seaman (2010)
Frank J. Selke (1960)

Harry Sinden (1983)
Frank D. Smith (1962)
Conn Smythe (1958)
Edward M. Snider (1988)
Lord Stanley of Preston (1945)
James T. Sutherland (1947)
Anatoli V. Tarasov (1974)
Bill Torrey (1995)
Lloyd Turner (1958)
William Tutt (1978)
Carl Potter Voss (1974)
Fred C. Waghorn (1961)
Arthur Wirtz (1971)
Bill Wirtz (1976)
John A. Ziegler, Jr. (1987)

Referees/Linesmen

Neil Armstrong (1991)
John Ashley (1981)
William L. Chadwick (1964)
John D'Amico (1993)
Chaucer Elliott (1961)
George Hayes (1988)
Robert W. Hewitson (1963)
Fred J. (Mickey) Ion (1961)

Matt Pavelich (1987)
Mike Rodden (1962)
Ray Scapinello (2008)
J. Cooper Smeaton (1961)
Roy (Red) Storey (1967)
Frank Udvari (1973)
Andy Van Hellemond (1999)

Note: Year of election to the Hall of Fame is in parentheses after the member's name.

Olympics

Michael Phelps' Olympic swan song produced four more gold medals and two silvers, making him the most successful Oympian in history

London Calling

Becoming the first city to host the Games for a third time, London proved up to the task as the Olympics were smooth, safe, and filled with thrills

BY MERRELL NODEN

"AS I WRITE THESE WORDS THERE are semi-naked women playing beach volleyball in the middle of the Horse Guards Parade."

It wasn't hard to understand London Mayor Boris Johnson's astonishment at his city's transformation as host of this summer's Olympic Games. Oh, brave new world, indeed!

Londoners can be a cynical lot, and in the weeks leading up to the Games there had been no shortage of moaning about the Games' $14.5 billion cost, as well as the security fiasco that was revealed when, just days before the Opening Ceremonies, it became known that the company G4S had come up 3,500 security personnel short.

But in the end all went smoothly and safely, and London, the first city to stage the Olympics three times, proved to be a superb host. The organizers' most inspired idea was to use iconic London landmarks as backdrops to competitive venues. There was cycling at Hampton Court Palace, rowing at Windsor Castle, archery at Lords Cricket Ground, and a marathon course that finished almost on the steps of Buckingham Palace. London looked sensational.

The Games kicked off with an opening ceremony directed by filmmaker Danny Boyle. "Isles of Wonder" was an eccentric walk through British history and culture, from cricket on village greens to the belching smokestacks of the Industrial Revolution. The only thing more unexpected than its paean to Britain's National Health Service was a filmed gag that began with Daniel Craig as James Bond collecting the Queen from the palace and ended with her parachuting from a helicopter into the Olympic Stadium. We didn't see that in Beijing!

But as always, the staged activities paled next to the surprises the Games themselves conjured up. A nearly blind archer from South Korea, Im Dong-hyun, set a world record in the 72-arrow event. Manteo Mitchell of the U.S. ran the second half of his 1600-meter relay prelim on a broken leg, while Oscar Pistorius of South Africa ran without legs at all. Pistorius, a double amputee who competes on carbon blades called Cheetahs, reached the semifinals. Then, in one of those gestures that make the Olympics so special, Kirani James of Grenada, the eventual gold medalist, approached him and asked to trade numbers.

Still, the two biggest stars at these Games were familiar faces. There was some question about the fitness of Usain Bolt, the tall, impossibly loose Jamaican sprinter who'd won both sprints in Beijing. In the 100, Bolt used a mid-race surge to blow away a great field—Tyson Gay ran 9.80 and finished fourth!—clocking 9.63, ahead of his training partner, Yohan Blake. Bolt ran a great turn to put the 200 field away early, and then anchored a Jamaican team to a world

AL TIELEMANS

record 36.84 in the 400-meter relay. "I came here to be a legend and I did," said Bolt, and it was hard to argue with him.

If Bolt had a rival for top performer at these Games it was Michael Phelps, who, like Bolt, was something of a question mark coming in, with many expecting him to concede his crown to teammate Ryan Lochte. When Lochte won their opening race, the 400IM, and Phelps finished fourth, it looked as if Phelps might have a disappointing Games. But he came back to win six more medals, four of them gold, pushing him well past Russian gymnast Larysa Latynina's alltime record of 18 total medals, with 22. The "next" Phelps may well be a woman. Missy Franklin, a 17-year-old high school senior to be, won both backstrokes, and added two more gold medals in relays.

The big shock for the U.S. women's gymnastics team came during qualifying for the all around, when Jordyn Wieber, the reigning world champion, finished fourth, failing to advance. She recovered to help her Fab

When teammate Wieber failed to qualify for the all around final, Douglas wowed the world by taking the gold medal, becoming the first African American all around champion in Olympic history.

Five teammates win the team gold but was on the sidelines cheering her 16-year-old teammate Gabby Douglas, who won the all around title, becoming the first African American gymnast to do so.

Familiar juggernauts prevailed. The U.S. men and women won gold in basketball. Misty May-Treanor and Kerri Walsh won their third straight gold in beach volleyball. The U.S. women's soccer team slipped past Canada 4–3 in the semifinal game when Alex Morgan's header just cleared the goalie's fingertips with seconds remaining in overtime, then beat Japan for the gold. And Chinese divers took six of eight golds. David Boudia of the U.S. won the men's 10-meter platform, the first U.S. diver to win in the event since Greg Louganis in 1988.

BILL FRAKES

It always boosts the Games when the home team does well. It took Team GB a while to get going, but when it did, medals came in a veritable flood—six on one day alone, including three at the track within 45 minutes, with the Duke and Duchess of Cambridge among the enraptured spectators. First to win was heptathlete Jessica Ennis, "our Jess" to faithful fans all over Britain. Then came long jumper Greg Rutherford, and finally Mo Farah, a slip of a man, a Somali by birth, Londoner by upbringing, and Oregonian by training base. Farah won an incredibly exciting 10,000, with training partner Galen Rupp second to claim the first U.S. medal in the event since 1964.

The crowd at Olympic Stadium could not have been more delirious, and it seemed to pump up British athletes elsewhere. Britain won seven of ten medals in track cycling. Bradley Wiggins, fresh off becoming the

After a dominant 200, Bolt (in signature celebratory pose) declared himself a legend, and with wins in the 100 and 200 in consecutive Games, who could argue?

first Englishman to win the Tour de France, added to his golden summer by winning the cycling time trial. And Andy Murray avenged his Wimbledon defeat to Roger Federer. On the final night of competition, Farah again sprinted clear of a crowded field to win the 5,000, running his last mile in 3:58.

The U.S. topped the medals table, with 46 gold and 104 overall. China came second with 38 and 88. The host team won 29 and 65, its best showing since the 1908 London Games.

Still, the best measure of the host country's inarguable success was the joy and pride it showed in hosting these Games. Everyone seemed to agree: It was a jolly good show.

FOR THE RECORD • 2012 Games

2012 Summer Games

TRACK AND FIELD
Men

100 METERS
1. ...Usain Bolt, Jamaica — 9.63 OR
2. ...Yohan Blake, Jamaica — 9.75
3. ...Justin Gatlin, United States — 9.79

200 METERS
1. ...Usain Bolt, Jamaica — 19.32
2. ...Yohan Blake, Jamaica — 19.44
3. ...Warren Weir, Jamaica — 19.84

400 METERS
1. ...Kirani James, Grenada — 43.94
2. ...Luguelin Santos, Dominican Rep. — 44.46
3. ...Lalonde Gordon, Trinidad and Tobago — 44.52

800 METERS
1. ...David Lekuta Rudisha, Kenya — 1:40.91 WR
2. ...Nijel Amos, Botswana — 1:41.73
3. ...Timothy Kitum, Kenya — 1:42.53

1,500 METERS
1. ...Taoufik Makhloufi, Algeria — 3:34.08
2. ...Leonel Manzano, United States — 3:34.79
3. ...Abdalaati Iguider, Morocco — 3:35.13

5,000 METERS
1. ...Mohamed Farah, Great Britain — 13:41.66
2. ...Dejen Gebremeskel, Ethiopia — 13:41.98
3. ...Thomas Pkemei Longosiwa, Kenya — 13:42.36

10,000 METERS
1. ...Mohamed Farah, Great Britain — 27:30.42
2. ...Galen Rupp, United States — 27:30.90
3. ...Tariku Bekele, Ethiopia — 27:31.43

MARATHON
1. ...Stephen Kiprotich, Uganda — 2:08:01
2. ...Abel Kirui, Kenya — 2:08:27
3. ...Wilson Kipsang Kiprotich, Kenya — 2:09:37

110-METER HURDLES
1. ...Aries Merritt, United States — 12.92
2. ...Jason Richardson, United States — 13.04
3. ...Hansle Parchment, Jamaica — 13.12

400-METER HURDLES
1. ...Felix Sanchez, Dominican Republic — 47.63
2. ...Michael Tinsley, United States — 47.91
3. ...Javier Culson, Puerto Rico — 48.10

3,000-METER STEEPLECHASE
1. ...Ezekiel Kemboi, Kenya — 8:18.56
2. ...Mahiedine Mekhissi-Benabbad, France — 8:19.08
3. ...Abel Kiprop Mutai, Kenya — 8:19.73

4 X 100-METER RELAY
1. ...Jamaica: (Y. Blake, U, Bolt, N. Carter, M. Frater) — 36.84 WR
2. ...United States — 37.04
3. ...Trinidad and Tobago — 38.12

4 X 400-METER RELAY
1. ...Bahamas: (C. Brown, D. Pinder, M. Mathieu, R. Miller) — 2:56.72
2. ...United States — 2:57.05
3. ...Trinidad and Tobago — 2:59.40

20-KILOMETER WALK
1. ...Ding Chen, China — 1:18:46 OR
2. ...Erick Barrondo, Guatemala — 1:18:57
3. ...Zhen Wang, China — 1:19:25

50-KILOMETER WALK
1. ...Sergey Kirdyapkin, Russia — 3:35:59 OR
2. ...Jared Tallent, Australia — 3:36:53
3. ...Tianfeng Si, China — 3:37:16

HIGH JUMP
1. ...Ivan Ukhov, Russia — 7 ft 9¾ in
2. ...Erik Kynard, United States — 7 ft 7¾ in
3. ...Derek Drouin, Canada — 7 ft 6¼ in

POLE VAULT
1. ...Renaud Lavillenie, France — 19 ft 7 in OR
2. ...Bjorn Otto, Germany — 19 ft 4¾ in
3. ...Raphael Holzdeppe, Germany — 19 ft 4¾ in

LONG JUMP
1. ...Greg Rutherford, Great Britain — 27 ft 3¼ in
2. ...Mitchell Watt, Australia — 26 ft 9¼ in
3. ...Will Claye, United States — 26 ft 7¾ in

TRIPLE JUMP
1. ...Christian Taylor, United States — 58 ft 5¼ in
2. ...Will Claye, United States — 57 ft 9¼ in
3. ...Fabrizio Donato, Italy — 57 ft 4¼ in

SHOT PUT
1. ...Tomasz Majewski, Poland — 71 ft 9¾ in
2. ...David Storl, Germany — 71 ft 8% in
3. ...Reese Hoffa, United States — 69 ft 7¾ in

DISCUS THROW
1. ...Robert Harting, Germany — 223 ft 11¾ in
2. ...Ehsan Hadadi, Iran — 223 ft 8¼ in
3. ...Gerd Kanter, Estonia — 223 ft 2¼ in

HAMMER THROW
1. ...Krisztian Pars, Hungary — 264 ft 4¾ in
2. ...Primoz Kozmus, Slovakia — 260 ft 4% in
3. ...Koji Murofushi, Japan — 258 ft 2¾ in

JAVELIN
1. ...Keshorn Walcott, Trinidad and Tobago — 277 ft 5¾ in
2. ...Oleksandr Pyatnytsya, Ukraine — 277 ft 3¼ in
3. ...Antti Ruuskanen, Finland — 275 ft 11¾ in

DECATHLON — Pts
1. ...Ashton Eaton, United States — 8869
2. ...Trey Hardee, United States — 8671
3. ...Leonel Suarez, Cuba — 8523

TRACK AND FIELD
Women

100 METERS
1. ...Shelly-Ann Fraser-Pryce, Jamaica — 10.75
2. ...Carmelita Jeter, United States — 10.78
3. ...Veronica Campbell-Brown, Jamaica — 10.81

200 METERS
1. ...Allyson Felix, United States — 21.88
2. ...Shelly-Ann Fraser-Pryce, Jamaica — 22.09
3. ...Carmelita Jeter, United States — 22.14

Note: OR=Olympic Record. WR=World Record. EOR=Equals Olympic Record. EWR=Equals World Record.

TRACK AND FIELD *(CONT.)*
Women *(Cont.)*

400 METERS
1. ...Sanya Richards-Ross, United States 49.55
2. ....Christine Ohuruogu, Great Britain 49.70
3. ....DeeDee Trotter, United States 49.72

800 METERS
1. ...Mariya Savinova, Russia 1:56.19
2. ...Caster Semenya, South Africa 1:57.23
3. ...Ekaterina Poistogova, Russia 1:57.53

1,500 METERS
1. ...Asli Cakir Alptekin, Turkey 4:10.23
2. ...Gamze Bulut, Turkey 4:10.40
3. ...Maryam Yusuf Jamal, Bahrain 4:10.74

5,000 METERS
1. ...Meseret Defar, Ethiopia 15:04.25
2. ...Vivian Jepkemoi Cheruiyot, Kenya 15:04.73
3. ...Tirunesh Dibaba, Ethiopia 15:05.15

10,000 METERS
1. ...Tirunesh Dibaba, Ethiopia 30:20.75
2. ...Sally Jepkosgei Kipyego, Kenya 30:26.37
3. ...Vivian Jepkemoi Cheruiyot, Kenya 30:30.44

MARATHON
1. ...Tiki Gelana, Ethiopia 2:23:07 OR
2. ....Priscah Jeptoo, Kenya 2:23:12
3. ....Tatyana Petrova Arkhipova, Russia 2:23:29

100-METER HURDLES
1. ...Sally Pearson, Australia 12.35 OR
2. ...Dawn Harper, United States 12.37
3. ...Kellie Wells, United States 12.48

400-METER HURDLES
1. ...Natalya Antyukh, Russia 52.70
2. ...Lashinda Demus, United States 52.77
3. ...Zuzana Hejnova, Czech Republic 53.38

3,000-METER STEEPLECHASE
1. ...Yuliya Zaripova, Russia 9:06.72
2. ...Habiba Ghribi, Tunisia 9:08.37
3. ...Sofia Assefa, Ethiopia 9:09.84

4 X 100-METER RELAY
1. ...United States: (C. Jeter, T. Madison, 40.82 WR
   A. Felix, B. Knight)
2. ....Jamaica 41.41
3. .....Ukraine 42.04

4 X 400-METER RELAY
1. ...United States: (A. Felix, F. McCorory 3:16.87
   S. Richards-Ross, D. Trotter)
2. ....Russia 3:20.23
3. .....Jamaica 3:20.95

20-KILOMETER WALK
1. ...Elena Lashmanova Russia 1:25:02 WR
2. ...Olga Kaniskina, Russia 1:25:09
3. ...Shenjie Qieyang, China 1:25:16

HIGH JUMP
1. ...Anna Chicherova, Russia 6 ft 8¾ in
2. ...Brigetta Barrett, United States 6 ft 7⅞ in
3. ...Svetlana Shkolina, Russia 6 ft 7⅞ in

POLE VAULT
1. ...Jennifer Suhr, United States 15 ft 7 in
2. ...Yarisley Silva, Cuba 15 ft 7 in
3. ...Elena Isinbaeva, Russia 15 ft 5 in

LONG JUMP
1. ...Brittney Reese, United States 23 ft 4¼ in
2. ...Elena Sokolova, Russia 23 ft 2¼ in
3. ...Janay Deloach, United States 22 ft 7¼ in

TRIPLE JUMP
1. ...Olga Rypakova, Kazakhstan 49 ft 1¾ in
2. ....Caterine Ibarguen, Colombia 48 ft 6¾ in
3. ...Olha Saladuha, Ukraine 48 ft 6¼ in

SHOT PUT
1. ....Nadzeya Ostapchuk, Belarus 70 ft ⅞ in
2. ...Valerie Adams, New Zealand 67 ft 11 in
3. ...Evgeniia Kolodko, Russia 67 ft 2¼ in

DISCUS THROW
1. ...Sandra Perkovic, Croatia 226 ft 8⅜ in
2. ......Darya Pishchalnikova, Russia 221 ft 7¾ in
3. ......Yanfeng Li, China 220 ft 6½ in

JAVELIN
1. ...Barbora Spotakova, Czech Republic 228 ft 2¼ in
2. ....Christina Obergfoll, Germany 213 ft 9¾ in
3. .....Linda Stahl, Germany 212 ft 11½ in

HEPTATHLON Pts
1. ...Jessica Ennis, Great Britain 6955
2. ....Lilli Schwarzkopf, Germany 6649
3. ...Tatyana Chernova, Russia 6628

HAMMER THROW
1. ...Tatyana Lysenko, Russia 256 ft 6 in OR
2. ...Anita Wlodarczyk, Poland 254 ft 7⅛ in
3. ...Betty Heidler, Germany 253 ft ¼ in

INDIVIDUAL ARCHERY

Men
1. ...Jin Hyek Oh, South Korea
2. ....Takaharu Furukawa, Japan
3. ...Xiaoxiang Dai, China

Women
1. ...Bo Bae Ki, South Korea
2. ...Aida Roman, Mexico
3. ...Mariana Avitia, Mexico

TEAM ARCHERY

Men
1. .....Italy
2. .....United States
3. .....South Korea

Women
1. .....South Korea
2. .....China
3. .... Japan

Note: OR=Olympic Record. WR=World Record. EOR=Equals Olympic Record. EWR=Equals World Record.

BADMINTON

Men
SINGLES
1. ....Dan Lin, China
2. ....Chong Wei Lee, Malaysia
3. ....Long Chen, China

DOUBLES
1. ....Yun Cai/Haifeng Fu, China
2. ....Mathias Boe/Carsten Mogensen, Denmark
3. ....Yong Dae Lee/Jae Sung Chung, South Korea

Women
SINGLES
1. ....Xuerui Li, China
2. ....Yihan Wang, China
3. ....Saina Nehwal, India

DOUBLES
1. ....Qing Tian/Yunlei Zhao, China
2. ....Reika Kakiiwa/Mizuki Fujii, Japan
3. ....Nina Vislova/Valeria Sorokina, Russia

MIXED DOUBLES
1. ....Nan Zhang/Yunlei Zhao, China
2. ....Chen Xu/Jin Ma, China
3. ....Christinna Pedersen/Joachim Fischer, Denmark

BASKETBALL

Men
Final: United States 107, Spain 100
Russia (3rd)
United States: Kevin Durant, Chris Paul, Lebron James, Kobe Bryant, Carmelo Anthony, Kevin Love, Deron Williams, Russell Westbrook, Tyson Chandler, Andre Iguodala, Anthony Davis, James Harden

Women
Final: United States 86, France 50
Russia (3rd)
United States: Diana Taurasi, Maya Moore, Sue Bird, Candace Parker, Tina Charles, Lindsay Whalen, Tamika Catchings, Seimone Augustus, Sylvia Fowles, Angel McCoughtry, Asjha Jones, Swin Cash

BOXING – Men

LIGHT FLYWEIGHT (106 LB)
1. ....Shiming Zou, China
2. ....Kaeo Pongprayoon, Thailand
3. ....Paddy Barnes, Ireland
3. ....David Ayrapetyan, Russia

FLYWEIGHT (112 LB)
1. ....Robeisy Ramirez Carrazana, Cuba
2. ....Tugstsogt Nyambayar, Mongolia
3. ....Misha Aloian, Russia
3. ....Michael Conlan, Ireland

BANTAMWEIGHT (119 LB)
1. ....Luke Campbell, Great Britain
2. ....John Joe Nevin, Ireland
3. ....Satoshi Shimizu, Japan
3. ....Lazaro Alvarez Estrada, Cuba

LIGHTWEIGHT (132 LB)
1. ....Vasyl Lomachenko, Ukraine
2. ....Soonchul Han, South Korea
3. ....Evaldas Petrauskas, Lithuania
3. ....Yasnier Toledo Lopez, Cuba

LIGHT WELTERWEIGHT (139 LB)
1. ....Roniel Iglesias Sotolongo, Cuba
2. ....Denys Berinchyk, Ukraine
3. ....Munkh-Erdene Uranchimeg, Mongolia
3. ....Vincenzo Mangiacapre, Italy

WELTERWEIGHT (147 LB)
1. ....Serik Sapiyev, Kazakhstan
2. ....Freddie Evans, Great Britain
3. ....Taras Shelestyuk, Ukraine
3. ....Andrey Zamkovoy, Russia

MIDDLEWEIGHT (165 LB)
1. ....Serik Sapiyev, Kazakhstan
2. ....Esquiva Falcao Florentino, Brazil
3. ....Anthony Ogogo, Great Britain
3. ....Abbos Atoev, Uzbekistan

LIGHT HEAVYWEIGHT (178 LB)
1. ....Egor Mekhontcev, Russia
2. ....Adilbek Niyazymbetov, Kazakhstan
3. ....Yamaguchi Falcao Florentino, Brazil
3. ....Oleksandr Gvozdyk, Ukraine

HEAVYWEIGHT (201 LB)
1. ....Oleksandr Usyk, Ukraine
2. ....Clemente Russo, Italy
3. ....Tervel Pulev, Bulgaria
3. ....Teymur Mammadov, Azerbaijan

SUPERHEAVYWEIGHT (201+ LB)
1. ....Anthony Joshua, Great Britain
2. ....Roberto Cammarelle, Italy
3. ....Ivan Dychko, Kazakhstan
3. ....Magomedrasul Medzhidov, Azerbaijan

Women

FLYWEIGHT (112 LB)
1. ....Nicola Adams, Great Britain
2. ....Cancan Ren, China
3. ....Chungneijang Mery Kom Hmangte, India
3. ....Marlen Esparza, United States

LIGHTWEIGHT (132 LB)
1. ....Katie Taylor, Ireland
2. ....Sofya Ochigava, Russia
3. ....Mavzuna Chorieva, Tajikistan
3. ....Adriana Araujo, Brazil

MIDDLEWEIGHT (165 LB)
1. ....Claressa Shields, United States
2. ....Nadezda Torlopova, Russia
3. ....Marina Volnova, Kazakhstan
3. ....Jinzi Li, China

CANOE/KAYAK
Men

CANOE SINGLES 200 METERS
1. ....Iurii Cheban, Ukraine — 42.291
2. ....Jevgenij Shuklin, Lithuania — 42.792
3. ....Ivan Shtyl, Russia — 42.853

CANOE SINGLES 1,000 METERS
1. ....Sebastian Brendel, Germany — 3:47.176
2. ....David Cal Figueroa, Spain — 3:48.053
3. ....Mark Oldershaw, Canada — 3:48.502

CANOE DOUBLES 1,000 METERS
1. ....K. Kuschela/P. Kretschmer, Germany — 3:33.804
2. ....A. Bahdanovich/A. Bahdanovich, Belarus — 3:35.206
3. ....I. Pervukhin/A. Korovashkov, Russia — 3:36.414

CANOE SINGLE WHITEWATER SLALOM
	Pts
1. ....Tony Estanguet, France	97.06
2. ....Sideris Tasiadis, Germany	98.09
3. ....Michal Martikan, Slovakia	98.31

CANOE DOUBLE WHITEWATER SLALOM
	Pts
1. ....E. Stott/T. Baillie, Great Britain	106.41
2. ....R. Hounslow/D. Florence, Great Britain	106.77
3. ....P. Hochschorner/P. Hochschorner, Slovakia	108.28

KAYAK SINGLES 200 METERS
1. ....Ed Mckeever, Great Britain	36.246
2. ....Saul Craviotto Rivero, Spain	36.540
3. ....Mark de Jonge, Canada	36.657

CANOE/KAYAK *(CONT.)*

Men *(Cont.)*

KAYAK SINGLES 1,000 METERS
1....Eirik Veras Larsen, Norway   3:26.462
2....Adam van Koeverden, Canada   3:27.170
3....Max Hoff, Germany   3:27.759

KAYAK DOUBLES 1,000 METERS
1....R. Kokeny/R. Dombi, Hungary   3:09.646
2....E. Silva/F. Pimenta, Portugal   3:09.699
3....A. Ihle/M. Hollstein, Germany   3:10.117

KAYAK DOUBLES 200 METERS
1....A. Dyachenko/Y. Postrigay, Russia   33.507
2....V. Makhneu/R. Piatrushenka, Belarus   34.266
3....J. Schofield/L. Heath, Great Britain   34.421

KAYAK FOURS 1,000 METERS
1....Australia   2:55.085
2....Hungary   2:55.699
3....Czech Republic   2:55.850

KAYAK SINGLE WHITEWATER   Pts
1....Daniele Molmenti, Italy   93.43
2....Vavrinec Hradilek, Czech Republic   94.78
3....Hannes Aigner, Germany   94.92

Women

KAYAK SINGLES 200 METERS
1....Lisa Carrington, New Zealand   44.638
2....Inna Osypenko-Radomska, Ukraine   45.053
3....Natasa Douchev-Janic, Hungary   45.128

KAYAK SINGLES 500 METERS
1....Danuta Kozak, Hungary   1:51.456
2....Inna Osypenko-Radomska, Ukraine   1:52.685
3....Bridgitte Hartley, South Africa   1:52.923

KAYAK DOUBLES 500 METERS
1....T. Dietze/F. Weber, Germany   1:42.213
2....N. Douchev-Janic/K. Kovacs, Hungary   1:43.278
3....B. Mikolajczyk/K. Naja, Poland   1:44.000

KAYAK FOURS 500 METERS
1....Hungary   1:30.827
2....Germany   1:31.298
3....Belarus   1:31.400

KAYAK SINGLE WHITEWATER   Pts
1....Emilie Fer, France   105.90
2....Jessica Fox, Australia   106.51
3....Maialen Chourraut, Spain   106.87

CYCLING–Men

ROAD RACE
1....Alexandr Vinokurov, Kazakhstan   5:45:57
2....Rigoberto Uran Uran, Colombia   5:45:57
3....Alexander Kristoff, Norway   5:46:05

INDIVIDUAL TIME TRIAL
1....Bradley Wiggins, Great Britain   50:39.54
2....Tony Martin, Germany   51:21.54
3....Christopher Froome, Great Britain   51:47.87

TEAM PURSUIT
1....Great Britain: (E. Clancy, P. Kennaugh,   3:51.659
......S. Burke, G. Thomas)
2....Australia   3:54.581
3....New Zealand   3:55.952

SPRINT
1....Jason Kenny, Great Britain
2....Gregory Bauge, France
3....Shane Perkins, Australia

OMNIUM
1....Lasse Norman Hansen, Denmark   27 pts
2....Bryan Coquard, France   29 pts
3....Edward Clancy, Great Britain   30 pts

KEIRIN
1....Chris Hoy, Great Britain
2....Maximilian Levy, Germany
3....Teun Mulder, Netherlands
3....Simon van Velthooven, New Zealand

TEAM SPRINT
1....Great Britain: (Hoy, Kenny, Hindes)   42.600 WR
2....France   43.013
3....Germany   43.209

CROSS COUNTRY
1....Jaroslav Kulhavy, Czech Republic   1:29:07
2....Nino Schurter, Switzerland   1:29:08
3....Marco Aurelio Fontana, Italy   1:29:32

BMX
1....Maris Strombergs, Latvia   37.58 pts
2....Sam Willoughby, Australia   37.93 pts
3....C. Mario Oquendo Zabala, Colombia   38.25 pts

Women

INDIVIDUAL TIME TRIAL
1....Kristin Armstrong, United States   37:34.82
2.....Judith Arndt, Germany   37:50.29.
3.....Olga Zabelinskaya, Russia   37:57.35

OMNIUM
1....Laura Trott, Great Britain   18 pts
2....Sarah Hammer, United States   19 pts
3....Annette Edmondson, Australia   24 pts

TEAM PURSUIT
1....Great Britain: (Rowsell, Trott, King)   3:14.051
2....United States   3:19.727
3....Australia   3:18.096

SPRINT
1....Anna Meares, Australia
2....Victoria Pendleton, Great Britain
3....Shuang Guo, China

TEAM SPRINT
1....Germany: (K. Vogel, M. Welte)
2....China
3....Australia

ROAD RACE
1....Marianne Vos, Netherlands   3:35:29
2....Elizabeth Armitstead, Great Britain   3:35:29
3....Olga Zabelinskaya, Russia   3:35:31

CROSS COUNTRY
1....Julie Bresset, France   1:30:52
2....Sabine Spitz, Germany   1:31:54
3....Georgia Gould, United States   1:32:00

KEIRIN
1....Victoria Pendleton, Great Britain
2....Shuang Guo, China
3....Wai Sze Lee, Hong Kong

BMX
1....Mariana Pajon, Colombia   37.71 pts
2....Sarah Walker, New Zealand   38.13 pts
3....Laura Smulders, Netherlands   38.23 pts

Note: WR=World Record.

DIVING
Men

3-METER SPRINGBOARD	Pts	10-METER PLATFORM	Pts
1. Ilya Zakharov, Russia	555.90	1. David Boudia, United States	568.65
2. Kai Qin, China	541.75	2. Bo Qiu, China	566.85
3. Chong He, China	524.15	3. Thomas Daley, Great Britain	556.95

Women

3-METER SPRINGBOARD	Pts	10-METER PLATFORM	Pts
1. Minxia Wu, China	414.0	1. Ruolin Chen, China	422.3
2. Zi He, China	379.2	2. Brittany Broben, Australia	366.5
3. Laura Sanchez Soto, Mexico	362.4	3. Pandelela Rinong Pamg, Malaysia	359.2

EQUESTRIAN

TEAM EVENTING	Pen. Pts	INDIVIDUAL DRESSAGE	Pts
1. Germany: (I. Klimke, D. Schrade, P. Thomsen)	133.7	1. Charlotte Dujardin, Great Britain	90.089
		2. Adelinde Cornelissen, Netherlands	88.196
2. Great Britain	138.2	3. Laura Bechtolsheimer, Great Britain	84.339
3. New Zealand	144.4	**TEAM JUMPING**	**Pen. Pts**

INDIVIDUAL EVENTING	Pen. Pts		
1. Michael Jung, Germany	40.6	1. Great Britain: (P. Charles, B. Maher, S. Brash, N. Skelton)	8
2. Sara Algotsson Ostholt, Sweden	43.3	2. Netherlands	8
3. Sandra Auffarth, Germany	44.8	3. Saudi Arabia	14

TEAM DRESSAGE	Pts	INDIVIDUAL JUMPING	Pen. Pts
1. Great Britain: (C. Hester, L. Bechtolsheimer, C. Dujardin)	79.979	1. Steve Guerdat, Switzerland	0
2. Germany	78.216	2. Gerco Schroder, Netherlands	1
3. Netherlands	77.124	3. Cian O'Connor, Ireland	1

FENCING
Men

FOIL	ÉPÉE	TEAM FOIL
1. Sheng Lei, China	1. Ruben Limardo Gascon, Venezuela	1. Italy: (A. Cassara, A. Baldini, V. Aspromonte)
2. A. Abouelkassem, Egypt	2. Bartosz Piasecki, Norway	2. Japan
3. Byungchul Choi, South Korea	3. Jinsun Jung, South Korea	3. Germany
SABRE	**TEAM SABRE**	
1. Aron Szilagyi, Hungary	1. South Korea: (J. Kim, W. Young Won, B. Gu)	
2. Diego Occhiuzzi, Italy	2. Romania	
3. Nikolay Kovalev, Russia		

Women

FOIL	ÉPÉE	
1. Elisa di Francisca, Italy	1. Yana Shemyakina, Ukraine	3. Italy
2. Arianna Errigo, Italy	2. Britta Heidemann, Germany	**TEAM FOIL**
3. Valentina Vezzali, Italy	3. Yujie Sun, China	1. Italy: (V. Vezzali, A. Errigo, E. di Francisca
SABRE	**TEAM ÉPÉE**	2. Russia
1. Jiyeon Kim, South Korea	1. China: (Y. Sun, N. Li, X. Luo)	3. South Korea
2. Sofya Velikaya, Russia	2. South Korea	
3. Olga Kharlan, Ukraine	3. United States	

FIELD HOCKEY

Men	Women
1. Germany	1. Netherlands
2. Netherlands	2. Argentina
3. Australia	3. Great Britain

GYMNASTICS
Men

ALL-AROUND	Pts	PARALLEL BARS	Pts
1. Kohei Uchimura, Japan	92.690	1. Zhe Feng, China	15.966
2. Marcel Nguyen, Germany	91.031	2. Marcel Nguyen, Germany	15.800
3. Danell Leyva, United States	90.698	3. Hamilton Sabot, France	15.566

HORIZONTAL BAR	Pts	VAULT	Pts
1. Epke Zonderland, Netherlands	16.533	1. Hak Seon Yang, South Korea	16.533
2. Fabian Hambuchen, Germany	16.400	2. Denis Ablyazin, Russia	16.399
3. Kai Zou, China	16.366	3. Igor Radivilov, Ukraine	16.316

GYMNASTICS *(Cont.)*
Men *(Cont.)*

POMMEL HORSE	Pts
1. Krisztian Berki, Hungary	16.066
2. Louis Smith, Great Britain	16.066
3. Max Whitlock, Great Britain	15.600

RINGS	Pts
1. Arthur Nabarrete Zanetti, Brazil	15.900
2. Yibing Chen, China	15.800
3. Matteo Morandi, Italy	15.733

FLOOR EXERCISE	Pts
1. Kai Zou, China	15.933
2. Kohei Uchimura, Japan	15.800
3. Denis Ablyazin, Russia	15.800

TEAM COMBINED EXERCISES	Pts
1. China: (C. Zhang, K. Zou, Y. Chen, Z. Feng)	275.997
2. Japan	271.952
3. Great Britain	271.711

Women

ALL-AROUND	Pts
1. Gabrielle Douglas, United States	62.232
2. Victoria Komova, Russia	61.973
3. Aliya Mustafina, Russia	59.566

VAULT	Pts
1. Sandra Raluca Izbasa, Romania	15.191
2. McKayla Maroney, United States	15.083
3. Maria Paseka, Russia	15.050

UNEVEN BARS	Pts
1. Aliya Mustafina, Russia	16.133
2. Kexin He, China	15.933
3. Elizabeth Tweddle, Great Britain	15.916

BALANCE BEAM	Pts
1. Linlin Deng, China	15.600
2. Lu Sui, China	15.500
3. Alexandra Raisman, United States	15.066

FLOOR EXERCISE	Pts
1. Alexandra Raisman, United States	15.600
2. Catalina Ponor, Romania	15.200
3. Aliya Mustafina, Russia	14.900

TEAM COMBINED EXERCISES	Pts
1. United States: (J. Wieber, G. Douglas, K. Ross, A. Raisman, M. Maroney)	183.596
2. Russia	178.530
3. Romania	176.414

RHYTHMIC TEAM	
1. Russia	57.000
2. Belarus	55.500
3. Italy	55.450

RHYTHMIC INDIVIDUAL ALL-AROUND	
1. Evgeniya Kanaeva, Russia	116.900
2. Daria Dmitrieva, Russia	114.500
3. Liubou Charkashyna, Belarus	111.700

JUDO

Men

EXTRA-LIGHTWEIGHT
1. Arsen Galstyan, Russia
2. Hiroaki Hiraoka, Japan
3. Rishod Sobirov, Uzbekistan
3. Felipe Kitadai, Brazil

HALF-LIGHTWEIGHT
1. Lasha Shavdatuashvili, Georgia
2. Miklos Ungvari, Hungary
3. Jun-Ho Cho, South Korea
3. Masashi Ebinuma, Japan

LIGHTWEIGHT
1. Mansur Isaev, Russia
2. Riki Nakaya, Japan
3. Nyam-Ochir Sainjargal, Mongolia
3. Ugo Legrand, France

HALF-MIDDLEWEIGHT
1. Jae-Bum Kim, South Korea
2. Ole Bischof, Germany
3. Antoine Valois-Fortier, Canada
3. Ivan Nifontov, Russia

MIDDLEWEIGHT
1. Dae-Nam Song, South Korea
2. Asley Gonzalez, Cuba
3. Ilias Iliadis, Greece
3. Masashi Nishiyama, Japan

HALF-HEAVYWEIGHT
1. Tagir Khaibulaev, Russia
2. Tuvshinbayar Naidan, Mongolia
3. Dimitri Peters, Germany
3. Henk Grol, Netherlands

HEAVYWEIGHT
1. Teddy Riner, France
2. Alexander Mikhaylin, Russia
3. Rafael Silva, Brazil
3. Andreas Toelzer, Germany

Women

EXTRA-LIGHTWEIGHT
1. Sarah Menezes, Brazil
2. Alina Dumitru, Romania
3. Eva Csernoviczki, Hungary
3. Charline van Snick, Belgium

HALF-LIGHTWEIGHT
1. Kum Ae An, North Korea
2. Yanet Bermoy Acosta, Cuba
3. Priscilla Gneto, France
3. Rosalba Forciniti, Italy

LIGHTWEIGHT
1. Kaori Matsumoto, Japan
2. Corina Caprioriu, Romania
3. Marti Malloy, United States
3. Automne Pavia, France

HALF-MIDDLEWEIGHT
1. Urska Zolnir, Slovenia
2. Lili Xu, China
3. Gevrise Emane, France
3. Yoshie Ueno, Japan

MIDDLEWEIGHT
1. Lucie Decosse, France
2. Kerstin Thiele, Germany
3. Yuri Alvear, Colombia
3. Edith Bosch, Netherlands

HALF-HEAVYWEIGHT
1. Kayla Harrison, United States
2. Gemma Gibbons, Great Britain
3. Mayra Aguiar, Brazil
3. Audrey Tcheumeo, France

HEAVYWEIGHT
1. Idalys Ortiz, Cuba
2. Mika Sugimoto, Japan
3. Wen Tong, China
3. Karina Bryant, Great Britain

MODERN PENTATHLON

Men

1. ......David Svoboda, Czech Republic — 5928
2. ......Zhongrong Cao, China — 5904
3. ......Adam Marosi, Hungary — 5836

Women

1. ......Laura Asadauskaite, Lithuania — 5408
2. ......Samantha Murray, Great Britain — 5356
3. ......Yane Marques, Brazil — 5340

ROWING

Men

SINGLE SCULLS
1. ...Mahe Drysdale, New Zealand — 6:57.82
2. ...Ondrej Synek, Czech Republic — 6:59.37
3. ...Alan Campbell, Great Britain — 7:03.28

DOUBLE SCULLS
1. ...N. Cohen/J. Sullivan, New Zealand — 6:31.67
2. ...R. Battisti/A. Sartori, Italy — 6:32.80
3. ...I. Cop/L. Spik, Slovenia — 6:34.35

LIGHTWEIGHT DOUBLE SCULLS
1. ...R. Quist/M. Rasmussen, Denmark — 6:37.17
2. ...M. Hunter/Z. Purchase, Great Britain — 6:37.78
3. ...P. Taylor/S. Uru, New Zealand — 6:40.86

QUADRUPLE SCULLS
1. ...Germany — 5:42.48
2. ...Croatia — 5:44.78
3. ...Australia — 5:45.22

COXLESS PAIR
1. ...H. Bond/E. Murray, New Zealand — 6:16.65
2. ...D. Mortelette/G. Chardin, France — 6:21.11
3. ...W. Satch/G. Nash, Great Britain — 6:21.77

COXLESS FOUR
1. ...Great Britain — 6:03.97
2. ...Australia — 6:05.19
3. ...United States — 6:07.20

LIGHTWEIGHT COXLESS FOUR
1. ...South Africa — 6:02.84
2. ...Great Britain — 6:03.09
3. ...Denmark — 6:03.16

EIGHT-OARS
1. ...Germany — 5:48.75
2. ...Canada — 5:49.98
3. ...Great Britain — 5:51.18

Women

SINGLE SCULLS
1. ...Miroslava Knapkova, Czech Republic — 7:54.37
2. ...Fie Udby Erichsen, Denmark — 7:57.72
3. ...Kim Crow, Australia — 7:58.04

DOUBLE SCULLS
1. ...K. Grainger/A. Watkins, Great Britain — 6:55.82
2. ...B. Pratley/K. Crow, Australia — 6:58.55
3. ...J. Michalska/M. Fularczyk, Poland — 7:07.92

LIGHTWEIGHT DOUBLE SCULLS
1. ...S. Hosking/K. Copeland, Great Britain — 7:09.30
2. ...W. Huang/D. Xu, China — 7:11.93
3. ...A. Tsiavou/C. Giazitzidou, Greece — 7:12.09

QUADRUPLE SCULLS
1. ...Ukraine — 6:35.93
2. ...Germany — 6:38.09
3. ...United States — 6:40.63

COXLESS PAIR
1. ...H. Stanning/H. Glover, Great Britain — 7:27.13
2. ...S. Tait/K. Hornsey, Australia — 7:29.86
3. ...J. Haigh/R. Scown, New Zealand — 7:30.19

EIGHT-OARS
1. ...United States — 6:10.59
2. ...Canada — 6:12.06
3. ...Netherlands — 6:13.12

SHOOTING

Men

25M RAPID-FIRE PISTOL — Pts
1. ....Leuris Pupo, Cuba — 34
2. ....Vijay Kumar, India — 30
3. ....Feng Ding, China — 27

50M FREE PISTOL — Pts
1. ....Jongoh Jin, South Korea — 662.0
2. ....Young Rae Choi, South Korea — 661.5
3. ....Zhiwei Wang, China — 658.6

10M AIR PISTOL — Pts
1. ....Jongoh Jin, South Korea — 688.2
2. ....Luca Tesconi, Italy — 685.8
3. ....Andrija Zlatic, Serbia — 685.2

50M FREE RIFLE, THREE-POSITION — Pts
1. ....Niccolo Campriani, Italy — 1278.5
2. ....Jonghyun Kim, South Korea — 1272.5
3. ....Matthew Emmons, United States — 1271.3

50M FREE RIFLE, PRONE — Pts
1. ....Sergei Martynov, Belarus — 705.5
2. ....Lionel Cox, Belgium — 701.2
3. ....Rajmond Debevec, Slovenia — 701.0

10M AIR RIFLE — Pts
1. ....Alin George Moldoveanu, Romania — 702.1
2. ....Niccolo Campriani, Italy — 701.5
3. ....Gagan Narang, India — 701.1

SHOOTING (CONT.)

Men (Cont.)

TRAP	Pts
1. ....Giovanni Cernogoraz, Croatia	146
2. ....Massimo Fabbrizi, Italy	146
3. ....Fehaid Aldeehani, Kuwait	145

DOUBLE TRAP	Pts
1. ....Peter Robert Russell Wilson, Great Britain	188
2. ....Hakan Dahlby, Sweden	186
3. ....Vasily Mosin, Russia	185

SKEET	Pts
1. ....Vincent Hancock, United States	148
2. ....Anders Golding, Denmark	146
3. ....Nasser Al-Attiya, Qatar	144

Women

25M SPORT PISTOL	Pts
1......Jangmi Kim, South Korea	792.4
2......Ying Chen, China	791.4
3......Olena Kostevych, Ukraine	788.6

10M AIR PISTOL	Pts
1......Wenjun Guo, China	488.1
2......Celine Goberville, France	486.6
3......Olena Kostevych, Ukraine	486.6

50M STANDARD RIFLE, THREE-POSITION	Pts
1......Jamie Lynn Gray, United States	691.9
2......Ivana Maksimovic, Serbia	687.5
3......Adela Sykorova, Czech Republic	683.0

10M AIR RIFLE	Pts
1......Siling Yi, China	502.9
2......Sylwia Bogacka, Poland	502.2
3......Dan Yu, China	501.5

TRAP	Pts
1......Jessica Rossi, Italy	99
2......Zuzana Stefecekova, Slovakia	93
3......Delphine Reau, France	93

SKEET	Pts
1......Kimberly Rhode, United States	99
2......Ning Wei, China	91
3......Danka Bartekova, Slovakia	90

SOCCER

Men

1. ....Mexico
2. ....Brazil
3. ....South Korea

Women

1. ....United States
2. ....Japan
3. ....Canada

SWIMMING - Men

50-METER FREESTYLE	
1. ...Florent Manaudou, France	21.34
2. ...Cullen Jones, United States	21.54
3. ...Cesar Cielo, Brazil	21.59

100-METER FREESTYLE	
1. ...Nathan Adrian, United States	47.52
2. ...James Magnussen, Australia	47.53
3. ...Brent Hayden, Canada	47.80

200-METER FREESTYLE	
1. ...Yannick Agnel, France	1:43.14
2. ...Yang Sun, China	1:44.93
3. ...Taehwan Park, South Korea	1:44.93

400-METER FREESTYLE	
1. ...Yang Sun, China	3:40.14 OR
2. ...Taehwan Park, South Korea	3:42.06
3. ...Peter Vanderkaay, United States	3:44.69

1,500-METER FREESTYLE	
1. ...Yang Sun, China	14:31.02 WR
2. ...Ryan Cochrane, Canada	14:39.63
3. ...Oussama Mellouli, Tunisia	14:40.31

100-METER BACKSTROKE	
1. ...Matthew Grevers, United States	52.16 OR
2. ...Nick Thoman, United States	52.92
3. ...Ryosuke Irie, Japan	52.97

200-METER BACKSTROKE	
1. ...Tyler Clary, United States	1:53.41 OR
2. ...Ryosuke Irie, Japan	1:53.78
3. ...Ryan Lochte, United States	1:53.94

100-METER BREASTSTROKE	
1. ...Cameron van der Burgh, South Africa	58.46 WR
2. ...Christian Sprenger, Australia	58.93
3. ...Brendan Hansen, United States	59.49

200-METER BREASTSTROKE	
1. ...Daniel Gyurta, Hungary	2:07.28 WR
2. ...Michael Jamieson, Great Britain	2:07.43
3. ...Ryo Tateishi, Japan	2:08.29

100-METER BUTTERFLY	
1. ...Michael Phelps, United States	51.21
2. ...Chad le Clos, South Africa	51.44
3. ...Evgeny Korotyshkin, Russia	51.44

200-METER BUTTERFLY	
1. ...Chad le Clos, South Africa	1:52.96
2. ...Michael Phelps, United States	1:53.01
3. ...Takeshi Matsuda, Japan	1:53.21

200-METER INDIVIDUAL MEDLEY	
1. ...Michael Phelps, United States	1:54.27
2. ...Ryan Lochte, United States	1:54.90
3. ...Laszlo Cseh, Hungary	1:56.22

400-METER INDIVIDUAL MEDLEY	
1. ...Ryan Lochte, United States	4:05.18
2. ...Thiago Pereira, Brazil	4:08.86
3. ...Kosuke Hagino, Japan	4:08.94

4 X 100-METER MEDLEY RELAY	
1. ...United States: (M. Grevers, B. Hansen, M. Phelps, N. Adrian)	3:29.35
2. ...Japan	3:31.26
3. ...Australia	3:31.58

4 X 100-METER FREESTYLE RELAY	
1. ...France: (A. Leveaux, F. Gilot, C. Lefert, Y. Agnel)	3:09.93
2. ...United States	3:10.38
3. ...Russia	3:11.41

Note: OR=Olympic record. WR=world record. EOR=equals Olympic record. EWR=equals world record.

SWIMMING - Men (Cont.)

4 X 200-METER FREESTYLE RELAY

1. ...United States: (R. Lochte, C. Dwyer 6:59.70
   R. Berens, M. Phelps)
2. .....France   7:02.77
3. .....China   7:06.30

10 KM MARATHON

1. ...Oussama Mellouli, Tunisia   1:49:55.1
2. ...Thomas Lurz, Germany   1:49:58.5
3. ...Richard Weinberger, Canada   1:50:00.3

Women

50-METER FREESTYLE

1. ...Ranomi Kromowidjojo, Netherlands 24.05 OR
2. ...Aliaksandra Herasimenia, Belarus 24.28
3. ...Marleen Veldhuis, Netherlands   24.39

100-METER FREESTYLE

1. ...Ranomi Kromowidjojo, Netherlands 53.00 OR
2. ...Aliaksandra Herasimenia, Belarus 53.38
3. ...Yi Tang, China   53.44

200-METER FREESTYLE

1. ...Allison Schmitt, United States   1:53.61 OR
2. ...Camille Muffat, France   1:55.58
3. ...Bronte Barratt, Australia   1:55.81

400-METER FREESTYLE

1. ...Camille Muffat, France   4:01.45 OR
2. ...Allison Schmitt, United States   4:01.77
3. ...Rebecca Adlington, Great Britain 4:03.01

800-METER FREESTYLE

1. ...Katie Ledecky, United States   8:14.63
2. ...Mireia Belmonte Garcia, Spain   8:18.76
3. ...Rebecca Adlington, Great Britain 8:20.32

100-METER BACKSTROKE

1. ...Missy Franklin, United States   58.33
2. ...Emily Seebohm, Australia   58.68
3. ...Aya Terakawa, Japan   58.83

200-METER BACKSTROKE

1. ...Missy Franklin, United States   2:04.06 WR
2. ...Anastasia Zueva, Russia   2:05.92
3. ...Elizabeth Beisel, United States   2:06.55

100-METER BREASTSTROKE

1. ...Ruta Meilutyte, Lithuania   1:05.47
2. ...Rebecca Soni, United States   1:05.55
3. ...Satomi Suzuki, Japan   1:06.46

200-METER BREASTSTROKE

1. ...Rebecca Soni, United States   2:19.59 WR
2. ...Satomi Suzuki, Japan   2:20.72
3. ...Iuliia Efimova, Russia   2:20.92

100-METER BUTTERFLY

1. ...Dana Vollmer, United States   55.98 WR
2. ...Ying Lu, China   56.87
3. ...Alicia Coutts, Australia   56.94

200-METER BUTTERFLY

1. ...Liuyang Jiao, China   2:04.06 OR
2. ...Mireia Belmonte Garcia, Spain   2:05.25
3. ...Natsumi Hoshi, Japa   2:05.48

200-METER INDIVIDUAL MEDLEY

1. ...Shiwen Ye, China   2:07.57 OR
2. ...Alicia Coutts, Australia   2:08.15
3. ...Caitlin Leverenz, United States   2:08.95

400-METER INDIVIDUAL MEDLEY

1. ...Shiwen Ye, China   4:28.43 WR
2. ...Elizabeth Beisel, United States   4:31.27
3. ...Xuanxu Li, China   4:32.91

4 X 100-METER MEDLEY RELAY

1. ...United States: (M. Franklin, R. Soni, 3:52.05 WR
   D. Vollmer, A. Schmitt)
2. ...Australia   3:54.02
3. ...Japan   3:55.73

4 X 100-METER FREESTYLE RELAY

1. ...Australia: (A. Coutts, C. Campbell, 3:33.15 OR
   B. Elmslie, M. Schlanger)
2. ...Netherlands   3:33.79
3. ...United States   3:34.24

4 X 200-METER FREESTYLE RELAY

1. ...United States: (M. Franklin, D. Vollmer, 7:42.92 OR
   S. Vreeland, A. Schmitt)
2. ...Australia   7:44.41
3. ...France   7:47.49

10-KM MARATHON

1. ...Eva Risztov, Hungary   1:57:38.2
2. ...Haley Anderson, United States   1:57:38.6
3. ...Martina Grimaldi, Italy   1:57:41.8

SYNCHRONIZED DIVING

Men

3M SPRINGBOARD

		Pts
1.	...K. Qin/Y. Luo, China	477.00
2.	...I. Zakharov/E. Kuznetsov, Russia	459.63
3.	...T. Dumais/K. Ipsen, United States	446.7

10M PLATFORM

		Pts
1.	...Y. Cao/Y. Zhang, China	486.78
2.	...G. Sanchez Sanchez/ I. Garcia Navarro, Mexico	468.90
3.	...D. Boudia/N. Mccrory, United States	463.47

Women

3M SPRINGBOARD

		Pts
1.	...Z. He/M. Wu, China	346.2
2.	...A. Johnston/K. Bryant, United States	321.9
3.	...E. Heymans/J. Abel, Canada	316.8

10M PLATFORM

		Pts
1.	...H. Wang/R. Chen, China	368.40
2.	...P. Espinosa Sanchez/ A. Orozco Loza, Mexico	343.32
3.	...R. Filion/M. Benfeito, Canada	337.62

Note: OR=Olympic record. WR=world record. EOR=equals Olympic record. EWR=equals world record.

SYNCHRONIZED SWIMMING

DUET
1.........S. Romashina/N. Ishchenko, Russia
2.........O. Carbonell Ballestero/A. Fuentes Fache, Spain
3.........X. Huang/O. Liu, China

TEAM
1............................Russia
2............................China
3............................Spain

TABLE TENNIS

Men

SINGLES
1. ....Jike Zhang, China
2. ....Hao Wang, China
3. ....Dimitrij Ovtcharov, Germany

TEAM
1. ....China: (H. Wang, L. Ma, J. Zhang)
2. ....South Korea
3. ....Germany

Women

SINGLES
1. ....Xiaoxia Li, China
2. ....Ning Ding, China
3. ....Tianwei Feng, Singapore

TEAM
1. ....China: (X. Li, Y. Guo, N. Ding)
2. ....Japan
3. ....Singapore

TAEKWONDO

Men

FLYWEIGHT
1. ....Joel Gonzalez Bonilla, Spain
2. ....Daehoon Lee, South Korea
3. ....Alexey Denisenko, Russia
3. ....Oscar Munoz Oviedo, Colombia

FEATHERWEIGHT
1. ....Servet Tazegul, Turkey
2. ....Mohammad Bagheri Motamed, Iran
3. ....Rohullah Nikpah, Afghanistan
3. ....Terrence Jennings, United States

WELTERWEIGHT
1. ....S. Eduardo Crismanich, Argentina
2. ....Nicolas Garcia Hemme, Spain
3. ....Lutalo Muhammad, Great Britain
3. ....Mauro Sarmiento, Italy

HEAVYWEIGHT
1. ....Carlo Molfetta, Italy
2. ....Anthony Obame, Gabon
3. ....Xiaobo Liu, China
3. ....Robelis Despaigne, Cuba

Women

FLYWEIGHT
1. ....Jingyu Wu, China
2. ....Brigitte Yague Enrique, Spain
3. ....Chanatip Sonkham, Thailand
3. ....Lucija Zaninovic, Croatia

FEATHERWEIGHT
1. ....Jade Jones, Great Britain
2. ....Yuzhuo Hou, China
3. ....Marlene Harnois, France
3. ....Li-Cheng Tseng, Taiwan

WELTERWEIGHT
1. ....Kyung Seon Hwang, South Korea
2. ....Nur Tatar, Turkey
3. ....Paige McPherson, United States
3. ....Helena Fromm, Germany

HEAVYWEIGHT
1. ....Milica Mandic, Serbia
2. ....Anne-Caroline Graffe, France
3. ....Maria del Rosario Espinoza, Mexico
3. ....Anastasiia Baryshnikova, Russia

TEAM HANDBALL

Men
1. ....France
2. ....Sweden
3. ....Croatia

Women
1. ....Montenegro
2. ....Norway
3. ....Spain

TENNIS

Men

SINGLES
1..........Andy Murray, Great Britain
2..........Roger Federer, Switzerland
3..........Juan Martin del Potro, Argentina

DOUBLES
1..........Mike Bryan/Bob Bryan, United States
2..........Michael Llodra/Jo-Wilfried Tsonga, France
3..........Julien Benneteau/Richard Gasquet, France

Women

SINGLES
1..........Serena Williams, United States
2..........Maria Sharapova, Russia
3..........Victoria Azarenka, Belarus

DOUBLES
1..........Serena Willams/Venus Williams, United States
2..........Andrea Hlavackova/Lucie Hradecka, Czech Rep.
3..........Maria Kirilenko/Nadia Petrova, Russia

MIXED DOUBLES
1..........Max Mirnyi/Victoria Azarenka, Belarus
2..........Andy Murray/Laura Robson, Great Britain
3..........Mike Bryan/Lisa Raymond, United States

TRAMPOLINE

Men
1. ....Dong Dong, China   62.990
2. ....Dmitry Ushakov, Russia   61.769
3. ....Chunlong Lu, China   61.319

Women
1. ....Rosannagh Maclennan, Canada   57.305
2. ....Shanshan Huang, China   56.730
3. ....Wenna He, China   55.950

TRIATHLON

Men
1..........Alistair Brownlee, Great Britain — 1:46:25
2..........Javier Gomez, Spain — 1:46:36
3..........Jonathan Brownlee, Great Britain — 1:46:56

Women
1..........Nicola Spirig, Switzerland — 1:59:48.00
2..........Lisa Norden, Sweden — 1:59:48.00
3..........Erin Densham, Australia — 1:59:50.00

VOLLEYBALL

Men
1..........Russia
2..........Brazil
3..........Italy

Women
1..........Brazil
2..........United States
3..........Japan

BEACH VOLLEYBALL

Men
1....Jonas Reckermann/Julius Brink, Germany
2....Emanuel Rego/Alison Cerutti, Brazil
3....Janis Smedins/Martins Plavins, Latvia

Women
1....Misty May-Treanor/Kerri Walsh Jennings, United States
2....Jennifer Kessy/April Ross, United States
3....Larissa Franca/Juliana Silva, Brazil

WATER POLO

Men
1..........Croatia
2..........Italy
3..........Serbia

Women
1..........United States
2..........Spain
3..........Australia

WEIGHTLIFTING - Men

123 POUNDS
1..........Yun Chol Om, North Korea — 644.60 lbs
2..........Jingbiao Wu, China — 635.80 lbs
3..........Valentin Hristov, Azerbaijan — 629.20 lbs

187 POUNDS
1..........Adrian E. Zielinski, Poland — 847.00 lbs
2..........Apti Aukhadov, Russia — 847.00 lbs
3..........Kianoush Rostami, Iran — 836.00 lbs

137 POUNDS
1..........Un Guk Kim, North Korea — 719.40 lbs WR
2..........Oscar Mosquera, Colombia — 697.40 lbs
2..........Irawan Eko Yuli, Indonesia — 697.40 lbs

207 POUNDS
1..........Ilya Ilyin, Kazakhstan — 919.60 lbs WR
2..........Alexandr Ivanov, Russia — 899.80 lbs
3..........Anatoli Ciricu, Moldova — 895.40 lbs

152 POUNDS
1..........Qingfeng Lin, China — 756.80 lbs
2..........Triyatno, Indonesia — 732.60 lbs
3..........R. Constantin Martin, Romania — 730.40 lbs

231 POUNDS
1..........Oleksiy Torokhtiy, Ukraine — 906.40 lbs
2..........Navab Nasirshelal, Iran — 904.20 lbs
3..........B. Wojciech Bonk, Poland — 902.00 lbs

170 POUNDS
1..........Xiaojun Lu, China — 833.80 lbs WR
2..........Haojie Lu, China — 792.00 lbs
3..........Ivan Cambar Rodriguez, Cuba — 767.80 lbs

231+ POUNDS
1..........Behdad Salimikordasiabi, Iran — 1,001.00 lbs
2..........S. Anoushiravani Hamlabad, Iran — 987.80 lbs
3..........Ruslan Albegov, Russia — 985.60 lbs

Women

106 POUNDS
1..........Mingjuan Wang, China — 451.00 lbs
2..........Hiromi Miyake, Japan — 433.40 lbs
3..........Chun Hwa Ryang, North Korea — 422.40 lbs

152 POUNDS
1..........Jong Sim Rim, North Korea — 574.20 lbs
2..........Roxana Daniela Cocos, Romania — 563.20 lbs
3..........Maryna Shkermankova, Belarus — 563.20 lbs

117 POUNDS
1..........Zulfiya Chinshanlo, Kazakhstan — 497.20 lbs OR
2..........Shu-Ching Hsu, Taiwan — 481.80 lbs
3..........Cristina Iovu, Moldova — 481.80 lbs

165 POUNDS
1..........S. Podobedova, Kazakhstan — 640.20 lbs
2..........Natalya Zabolotnaya, Russia — 640.20 lbs OR
3..........Iryna Kulesha, Belarus — 591.80 lbs

128 POUNDS
1..........Xueying Li, China — 541.2 lbs OR
2..........Pimsiri Sirikaew, Thailand — 519.20 lbs
3..........Yuliya Kalina, Ukraine — 517.00 lbs

165+ POUNDS
1..........Lulu Zhou, China — 732.60 lbs WR
2..........Tatiana Kashirina, Russia — 730.40 lbs
3..........Hripsime Khurshudyan, Armenia — 646.80 lbs

139 POUNDS
1..........Maiya Maneza, Kazakhstan — 539 lbs OR
2..........Svetlana Tsarukaeva, Russia — 521.40 lbs
3..........Christine Girard, Canada — 519.20 lbs

Note: OR=Olympic Record. WR=World Record. EOR=Equals Olympic Record. EWR=Equals World Record.

FREESTYLE WRESTLING

MEN	MEN (CONT.)	WOMEN

121 POUNDS
1. ....Dzhamal Otarsultanov, Russia
2. ....Vladimer Khinchegashvili, Georgia
3. ....Shinichi Yumoto, Japan
3. ....Kyong Il Yang, North Korea

132 POUNDS
1. ....Toghrul Asgarov. Azerbaijan
2. ....Besik Kudukhov, Russia
3. ....Coleman Scott, United States
3. ....Yogeshwar Dutt, India

145.5 POUNDS
1. ....Tatsuhiro Yonemitsu, Japan
2. ....Sushil Kumar, India
3. ....Livan Lopez Azcuy, Cuba
3. ....Akzhurek Tanatarov, Kazakhstan

163 POUNDS
1. .....Jordan Ernest Burroughs, United States
2. ....Sadegh Saeed Goudarzi, Iran
3. ....Soslan Tigiev, Uzbekistan
3. ....Denis Tsargush, Russia

185 POUNDS
1. ....Sharif Sharifov, Azerbaijan
2. .....Jaime Yusept Espinal, Puerto Rico
3. ....Ehsan Naser Lashgari, Iran
3. ....Dato Marsagishvili, Georgia

211.5 POUNDS
1. .....Jacob Stephen Varner, United States
2. ....Valerii Andriitsev, Ukraine
3. ....George Gogshelidze, Georgia
3. ....Khetag Gazyumov, Azerbaijan

264.5 POUNDS
1. ....Artur Taymazov, Uzbekistan
2. ....Davit Modzmanashvili, Georgia
3. ....Bilyal Makhov, Russia
3. ....Komeil Ghasemi, Iran

106 POUNDS
1. ...Hitomi Obara, Japan
2. ...Mariya Stadnyk, Azerbaijan
3. ...Clarissa Chun, United States
3. ...Carol Huynh, Canada

121 POUNDS
1. ...Saori Yoshida, Japan
2. ...Tonya Lynn Verbeek, Canada
3. ...J. Renteria Castillo, Colombia
3. ...Yuliya Ratkevich, Azerbaijan

139 POUNDS
1. ...Kaori Icho, Japan
2. ...Ruixue Jing, China
3. ...B. Soronzonbold, Mongolia
3. ...Lubov Volosova, Russia

159 POUNDS
1. ...Natalia Vorobeva, Russia
2.....Stanka Zlateva Hristova, Bulgaria
3. ...Guzel Manyurova, Kazakhstan
3.   M. Unda Gonzalez de
     Audicana, Spain

GRECO-ROMAN WRESTLING

121 POUNDS
1. ....H. Mohammad Soryan Reihanpour, Iran
2. ....Rovshan Bayramov, Azerbaijan
3. ....Peter Modos, Hungary
3. ....Mingiyan Semenov, Russia

132 POUNDS
1. ....Omid Haji Noroozi, Iran
2. ....Revaz Lashkhi, Georgia
3. ....Ryutaro Matsumoto, Japan
3. ....Z. Kuramagomedov, Russia

145.5 POUNDS
1. ....Hyeonwoo Kim, South Korea
2. ....Tamas Lorincz, Hungary
3. ....Manuchar Tskhadaia, Georgia
3. ....Steeve Guenot, France

163 POUNDS
1. ....Roman Vlasov, Russia
2 ....Arsen Julfalakyan, Armenia
3. ....Emin Ahmadov, Azerbaijan
3. ....Aleksandr Kazakevic, Lithuania

185 POUNDS
1. ....Alan Khugaev, Russia
2. .....K. Mohamed Gaber Ebrahim, Egypt
3. ....Danyal Gajiyev, Kazakhstan
3. ....Damian Janikowski, Poland

211.5 POUNDS
1. ....Ghasem Gholamreza Rezaei, Iran
2. ....Rustam Totrov, Russia
3. ....Artur Aleksanyan, Armenia
3. ....Jimmy Lidberg, Sweden

264.5 POUNDS
1. ....Mijain Lopez Nunez, Cuba
2. ....Heiki Nabi, Estonia
3. ....Johan Euren, Sweden
3. ....Riza Kayaalp, Turkey

YACHTING

Men

470 - TWO-PERSON DINGHY
1. ....M. Page/M. Belcher, Australia
2. ....L. Patience/S. Bithell, Great Britain
3. ....L. Calabrese/J. de la Fuente,
     Argentina

FINN
1. ....Ben Ainslie, Great Britain
2. ....Jonas Hogh-Christensen, Denmark
3. ....Jonathan Lobert, France

ONE-PERSON DINGHY
1. ....Tom Slingsby, Australia
2. ....Pavlos Kontides, Cyprus
3. ....Rasmus Myrgren, Sweden

49ER SKIFF
1. ....I. Jensen/N. Outteridge, Australia
2. ....P. Burling/B. Tuke, New Zealand
3. ....P. Lang/A. Norregaard, Denmark

STAR
1. ....F. Loof/M. Salminen, Sweden
2. ....I. Percy/A. Simpson, Great Britain
3. ....B. Prada/R. Scheidt, Brazil

Men (Cont.)

RS:X - WINDSURFER
1. ....Dorian van Rijsselberge, Netherlands
2. ....Nick Dempsey, Great Britain
3. ....Przemyslaw Miarczynski, Poland

Women

ONE-PERSON DINGHY
1. ....Lijia Xu, China
2. ....Marit Bouwmeester, Netherlands
3. ....Evi Van Acker, Belgium

470 - TWO-PERSON DINGHY
1. ....O. Powrie/J. Aleh, New Zealand
2. ....S. Clark/H. Mills, Great Britain
3. ....L. Berkhout/L. Westerhof, Netherlands

KEEL
1. ....Spain
2. ....Australia
3. ....Finland

RS: X - WINDSURFER
1. ....Marina Alabau Neira, Spain
2. ....Tuuli Petaja, Finland
3. ....Zofia Noceti-Klepacka, Poland

FOR THE RECORD • Year by Year

Summer Olympic Games Locations and Dates

	Year	Site	Dates	COMPETITORS Men	Women	Nations	Most Medals	US Medals
I	1896	Athens, Greece	Apr 6–15	311	0	13	Greece (10-19-18—47)	11-6-2—19 (2nd)
II	1900	Paris, France	May 20– Oct 28	1319	11	22	France (29-41-32—102)	20-14-19—53 (2nd)
III	1904	St Louis, United States	July 1– Nov 23	681	6	12	United States (80-86-72—238)	
—	1906	Athens, Greece	Apr 22– May 28	77	7	20	France (15-9-16—40)	12-6-5—23 (4th)
IV	1908	London, Great Britain	Apr 27– Oct 31	1999	36	23	Britain (56-50-39—145)	23-12-12—47 (2nd)
V	1912	Stockholm, Sweden	May 5– July 22	2490	57	28	Sweden (24-24-17—65)	23-19-19—61 (2nd)
VI	1916	Berlin, Germany	CANCELED BECAUSE OF WAR					
VII	1920	Antwerp, Belgium	Apr 20– Sep 12	2543	64	29	United States (41-27-28—96)	
VIII	1924	Paris, France	May 4– July 27	2956	136	44	United States (45-27-27—99)	
IX	1928	Amsterdam, Netherlands	May 17– Aug 12	2724	290	46	United States (22-18-16—56)	
X	1932	Los Angeles, United States	July 30– Aug 14	1281	127	37	United States (41-32-31—104)	
XI	1936	Berlin, Germany	Aug 1–16	3738	328	49	Germany (33-26-30—89)	24-20-12—56 (2nd)
XII	1940	Tokyo, Japan	CANCELED BECAUSE OF WAR					
XIII	1944	London, Great Britain	CANCELED BECAUSE OF WAR					
XIV	1948	London, Great Britain	July 29– Aug 14	3714	385	59	United States (38-27-19—84)	
XV	1952	Helsinki, Finland	July 19– Aug 3	4407	518	69	United States (40-19-17—76)	
XVI	1956	Melbourne, Australia*	Nov 22– Dec 8	2958	384	67	USSR (37-29-32—98)	32-25-17—74 (2nd)
XVII	1960	Rome, Italy	Aug 25– Sep 11	4738	610	83	USSR (43-29-31—103)	34-21-16—71 (2nd)
XVIII	1964	Tokyo, Japan	Oct 10–24	4457	683	93	United States (36-26-28—90)	
XIX	1968	Mexico City, Mexico	Oct 12–27	4750	781	112	United States (45-28-34—107)	
XX	1972	Munich, W Germany	Aug 26– Sep 10	5848	1299	122	USSR (50-27-22—99)	33-31-30—94 (2nd)
XXI	1976	Montreal, Canada	July 17– Aug 1	4834	1251	92†	USSR (49-41-35—125)	34-35-25—94 (3rd)
XXII	1980	Moscow, USSR	July 19– Aug 3	4265	1088	81‡	USSR (80-69-46—195)	Did not compete
XXIII	1984	Los Angeles, United States	July 28– Aug 12	5458	1620	141#	United States (83-61-30—174)	
XXIV	1988	Seoul, S Korea	Sep 17– Oct 2	7105	2476	160	USSR (55-31-46—132)	36-31-27—94 (3rd)
XXV	1992	Barcelona, Spain	July 25– Aug. 9	7555	3008	172	Unified Team (45-38-29—112)	37-34-37—108 (2nd)
XXVI	1996	Atlanta, United States	July 19– Aug 4	6984	3766	197	United States (44-32-25—101)	
XXVII	2000	Sydney, Australia	Sept 15– Oct 1	6862	4254	199	United States (39-25-33—97)	
XXVIII	2004	Athens, Greece	Aug 11– Aug 29	11,099 total		202	United States (35-39-29—103)	

	Year	Site	Dates	COMPETITORS			Most Medals	US Medals
				Men	Women	Nations		
XXIX	2008	Beijing, China	Aug 8–Aug 24	11,028 total		204	United States (36-38-36—110)	
XXX	2012	London, England	July 27–August 12	10,903 total		205	United States (46-29-29—104)	

*The equestrian events were held in Stockholm, Sweden, June 10–17, 1956. †This figure includes Cameroon, Egypt, Morocco, and Tunisia, countries that boycotted the 1976 Olympics after some of their athletes had already competed.
‡The U.S. was among 65 countries that did not participate in the 1980 Summer Games in Moscow.
#The USSR, East Germany, and 14 other countries did not participate in the 1984 Summer Games in Los Angeles.

Alltime Olympic Medal Winners

Summer

NATIONS

Nation	Gold	Silver	Bronze	Total	Nation	Gold	Silver	Bronze	Total
United States	990	765.5	679.5	2,435	East Germany (1956–88)	153	129	127	409
USSR (1952–1988)	440	357	325	1,122	Russia	119	140	135	394
Great Britain	238.5	276.5	280.5	796.5	Romania	87	104	123	314
Germany (1896–1936, 1992–)	208.5	253	256	717.5	Finland	101	83	115	299
France	217	225	258	700	Canada	58	103	121	282
Italy	204	168	187	559	Poland	69	84	122	275
China	219	153	129	501	South Korea	93	82	91	266
Australia	137	170	180.5	487.5	Netherlands	76	83	107	266
Sweden	141.5	164	172	477.5	Bulgaria	51	84	77	212
Hungary	162	145	170	477	Cuba	71	72	62	205
Japan	129	136	160	425	West Germany (1952–88)	56	67	81	204
					Denmark	42.5	66	72	180.5

INDIVIDUALS — OVERALL

Men

Athlete, Nation	Sport	G	S	B	Tot	Athlete, Nation	Sport	G	S	B	Tot
Michael Phelps, United States	Swim	18	2	2	22	Matt Biondi, United States	Swim	8	2	1	11
Nikolai Andrianov, USSR	Gym	7	5	3	15	Viktor Chukarin, USSR	Gym	7	3	1	11
Boris Shakhlin, USSR	Gym	7	4	2	13	Carl Osburn, United States	Shoot	5	4	2	11
Edoardo Mangiarotti, Italy	Fen	6	5	2	13	Ryan Lochte, United States	Swim	5	3	3	11
Takashi Ono, Japan	Gym	5	4	4	13	Ray Ewry, United States	Track	10	0	0	10
Paavo Nurmi, Finland	Track	9	3	0	12	Carl Lewis, United States	Track	9	1	0	10
Sawao Kato, Japan	Gym	8	3	1	12	Aladár Gerevich, Hungary	Fen	7	1	2	10
Alexei Nemov, Russia	Gym	4	2	6	12	Akinori Nakayama, Japan	Gym	6	2	2	10
Mark Spitz, United States	Swim	9	1	1	11	Vitaly Scherbo, UT/Belarus	Gym	6	0	4	10
						Aleksandr Dityatin, USSR	Gym	3	6	1	10

Women

Athlete, Nation	Sport	G	S	B	Tot	Athlete, Nation	Sport	G	S	B	Tot
Larissa Latynina, USSR	Gym	9	5	4	18	Dara Torres, United States	Swim	4	1	4	9
Jenny Thompson, United States	Swim	8	3	1	12	Nadia Comaneci, Romania	Gym	5	3	1	9
Natalie Coughlin, United States	Swim	3	4	5	12	Lyudmila Tourischeva, USSR	Gym	4	3	2	9
Vera Cáslavská, Czech	Gym	7	4	0	11	Valentina Vezzali, Italy	Fenc	6	1	2	9
Agnes Keleti, Hungary	Gym	5	3	2	10	Anky van Grunsven, Neth.	Eque	3	5	1	9
Polina Astaknova, USSR	Gym	5	2	3	10	Six tied with 8.					

INDIVIDUALS — GOLD

Men

Micheal Phelps, United States	18	Mark Spitz, United States	9	Boris Shakhlin, USSR	7

Micheal Phelps, United States ...18
Ray Ewry, United States 10
Paavo Nurmi, Finland 9
Carl Lewis, United States 9

Mark Spitz, United States 9
Sawao Kato, Japan 8
Matt Biondi, United States 8
Nikolai Andrianov, USSR 7

Boris Shakhlin, USSR 7
Viktor Chukarin, USSR 7
Aladár Gerevich, Hungary 7

Women

Larissa Latynina, USSR 9
Jenny Thompson, U.S. 8
Vera Cáslavská, Czech 7
Kristin Otto, E Germany 6
Valentina Vezzali, Italy 6
Agnes Keleti, Hungary 5
Nadia Comaneci, Romania 5
Polina Astaknova, USSR 5

Krisztina Egerszegi, Hungary 5
Kornelia Ender, E Germany 4
Dawn Fraser, Australia 4
Lyudmila Tourischeva, USSR ...4
Evelyn Ashford, United States ...4
Janet Evans, United States 4
Fanny Blankers-Koen, Neth. 4
Betty Cuthbert, Australia 4

Pat McCormick, United States ..4
Bärbel Eckert Wöckel, E Ger....4
Amy Van Dyken, United States...4
Inge de Bruijn, Netherlands 4
Yana Klochkova, Ukraine 4
Dara Torres, United States 4

TRACK AND FIELD — Men

100 METERS

1896	Thomas Burke, United States	12.0
1900	Frank Jarvis, United States	11.0
1904	Archie Hahn, United States	11.0
1906	Archie Hahn, United States	11.2
1908	Reginald Walker, S Africa	10.8 OR
1912	Ralph Craig, United States	10.8
1920	Charles Paddock, United States	10.8
1924	Harold Abrahams, Great Britain	10.6 OR
1928	Percy Williams, Canada	10.8
1932	Eddie Tolan, United States	10.3 OR
1936	Jesse Owens, United States	10.3
1948	Harrison Dillard, United States	10.3
1952	Lindy Remigino, United States	10.4
1956	Bobby Morrow, United States	10.5
1960	Armin Hary, W Germany	10.2 OR
1964	Bob Hayes, United States	10.0 EWR
1968	Jim Hines, United States	9.95 WR
1972	Valery Borzov, USSR	10.14
1976	Hasely Crawford, Trinidad	10.06
1980	Allan Wells, Great Britain	10.25
1984	Carl Lewis, United States	9.99
1988	Carl Lewis, United States*	9.92 WR
1992	Linford Christie, Great Britain	9.96
1996	Donovan Bailey, Canada	9.84 WR
2000	Maurice Greene, United States	9.87
2004	Justin Gatlin, United States	9.85
2008	Usain Bolt, Jamaica	9.69 WR
2012	Usain Bolt, Jamaica	9.63 OR

*Ben Johnson, Canada, disqualified.

200 METERS

1900	John Walter Tewksbury, United States	22.2
1904	Archie Hahn, United States	21.6 OR
1906	Not held	
1908	Robert Kerr, Canada	22.6
1912	Ralph Craig, United States	21.7
1920	Allen Woodring, United States	22.0
1924	Jackson Scholz, United States	21.6
1928	Percy Williams, Canada	21.8
1932	Eddie Tolan, United States	21.2 OR
1936	Jesse Owens, United States	20.7 OR
1948	Mel Patton, United States	21.1
1952	Andrew Stanfield, United States	20.7
1956	Bobby Morrow, United States	20.6 OR
1960	Livio Berruti, Italy	20.5 EWR
1964	Henry Carr, United States	20.3 OR
1968	Tommie Smith, United States	19.83 WR
1972	Valery Borzov, USSR	20.00
1976	Donald Quarrie, Jamaica	20.23
1980	Pietro Mennea, Italy	20.19
1984	Carl Lewis, United States	19.80 OR
1988	Joe DeLoach, United States	19.75 OR
1992	Mike Marsh, United States	20.01
1996	Michael Johnson, United States	19.32 WR
2000	Konstadinos Kederis, Greece	20.09
2004	Shawn Crawford, United States	19.79
2008	Usain Bolt, Jamaica	19.30 WR
2012	Usain Bolt, Jamaica	19.32

400 METERS

1896	Thomas Burke, United States	54.2
1900	Maxey Long, United States	49.4 OR
1904	Harry Hillman, United States	49.2 OR
1906	Paul Pilgrim, United States	53.2
1908	Wyndham Halswelle, Great Britain	50.0
1912	Charles Reidpath, United States	48.2 OR
1920	Bevil Rudd, South Africa	49.6
1924	Eric Liddell, Great Britain	47.6 OR
1928	Ray Barbuti, United States	47.8
1932	William Carr, United States	46.2 WR

400 METERS (Cont.)

1936	Archie Williams, United States	46.5
1948	Arthur Wint, Jamaica	46.2
1952	George Rhoden, Jamaica	45.9
1956	Charles Jenkins, United States	46.7
1960	Otis Davis, United States	44.9 WR
1964	Michael Larrabee, United States	45.1
1968	Lee Evans, United States	43.86 WR
1972	Vincent Matthews, United States	44.66
1976	Alberto Juantorena, Cuba	44.26
1980	Viktor Markin, USSR	44.60
1984	Alonzo Babers, United States	44.27
1988	Steve Lewis, United States	43.87
1992	Quincy Watts, United States	43.50 OR
1996	Michael Johnson, United States	43.49 OR
2000	Michael Johnson, United States	43.84
2004	Jeremy Wariner, United States	44.00
2008	Lashawn Merritt, United States	43.75
2012	Kirani James, Grenada	43.94

800 METERS

1896	Edwin Flack, Australia	2:11
1900	Alfred Tysoe, Great Britain	2:01.2
1904	James Lightbody, United States	1:56 OR
1906	Paul Pilgrim, United States	2:01.5
1908	Mel Sheppard, United States	1:52.8 WR
1912	James Meredith, United States	1:51.9 WR
1920	Albert Hill, Great Britain	1:53.4
1924	Douglas Lowe, Great Britain	1:52.4
1928	Douglas Lowe, Great Britain	1:51.8 OR
1932	Thomas Hampson, Great Britain	1:49.8 WR
1936	John Woodruff, United States	1:52.9
1948	Mal Whitfield, United States	1:49.2 OR
1952	Mal Whitfield, United States	1:49.2 EOR
1956	Thomas Courtney, United States	1:47.7 OR
1960	Peter Snell, New Zealand	1:46.3 OR
1964	Peter Snell, New Zealand	1:45.1 OR
1968	Ralph Doubell, Australia	1:44.3 EWR
1972	Dave Wottle, United States	1:45.9
1976	Alberto Juantorena, Cuba	1:43.50 WR
1980	Steve Ovett, Great Britain	1:45.40
1984	Joaquim Cruz, Brazil	1:43.00 OR
1988	Paul Ereng, Kenya	1:43.45
1992	William Tanui, Kenya	1:43.66
1996	Vebjoern Rodal, Norway	1:42.58 OR
2000	Nils Schumann, Germany	1:45.08
2004	Yuriy Borzakovskiy, Russia	1:44.45
2008	Wilfred Kipkemboi Bungei, Kenya	1:44.65
2012	David Lekuta Rudisha, Kenya	1:40.91 WR

1,500 METERS

1896	Edwin Flack, Australia	4:33.2
1900	Charles Bennett, Great Britain	4:06.2 WR
1904	James Lightbody, United States	4:05.4 WR
1906	James Lightbody, United States	4:12.0
1908	Mel Sheppard, United States	4:03.4 OR
1912	Arnold Jackson, Great Britain	3:56.8 OR
1920	Albert Hill, Great Britain	4:01.8
1924	Paavo Nurmi, Finland	3:53.6 OR
1928	Harry Larva, Finland	3:53.2 OR
1932	Luigi Beccali, Italy	3:51.2 OR
1936	Jack Lovelock, New Zealand	3:47.8 WR
1948	Henri Eriksson, Sweden	3:49.8
1952	Josef Barthel, Luxemburg	3:45.1 OR
1956	Ron Delany, Ireland	3:41.2 OR
1960	Herb Elliott, Australia	3:35.6 WR
1964	Peter Snell, New Zealand	3:38.1
1968	Kipchoge Keino, Kenya	3:34.9 OR
1972	Pekkha Vasala, Finland	3:36.3
1976	John Walker, New Zealand	3:39.17
1980	Sebastian Coe, Great Britain	3:38.4
1984	Sebastian Coe, Great Britain	3:32.53 OR

Note: OR=Olympic Record. WR=World Record. EOR=Equals Olympic Record. EWR=Equals World Record. WB=World Best.

TRACK AND FIELD — Men *(Cont.)*

1,500 METERS *(Cont.)*

1988	Peter Rono, Kenya	3:35.96
1992	Fermin Cacho, Spain	3:40.12
1996	Noureddine Morceli, Algeria	3:35.78
2000	Noah Ngeni, Kenya	3:32.07 OR
2004	Hicham El Guerrouj, Morocco	3:34.18
2008	Rasheed Ramzi, Bahrain	3:32.94
2012	Taoufik Makhloufi, Algeria	3:34.08

5,000 METERS

1912	Hannes Kolehmainen, Finland	14:36.6 WR
1920	Joseph Guillemot, France	14:55.6
1924	Paavo Nurmi, Finland	14:31.2 OR
1928	Villie Ritola, Finland	14:38.0
1932	Lauri Lehtinen, Finland	14:30 OR
1936	Gunnar Höckert, Finland	14:22.2 OR
1948	Gaston Reiff, Belgium	14:17.6 OR
1952	Emil Zatopek, Czechoslovakia	14:06.6 OR
1956	Vladimir Kuts, USSR	13:39.6 OR
1960	Murray Halberg, New Zealand	13:43.4
1964	Bob Schul, United States	13:48.8
1968	Mohamed Gammoudi, Tunisia	14:05.0
1972	Lasse Viren, Finland	13:26.4 OR
1976	Lasse Viren, Finland	13:24.76
1980	Miruts Yifter, Ethiopia	13:21.0
1984	Said Aouita, Morocco	13:05.59 OR
1988	John Ngugi, Kenya	13:11.70
1992	Dieter Baumann, Germany	13:12.52
1996	Venuste Niyongabo, Burundi	13:07.96
2000	Millon Wolde, Ethiopia	13:35.49
2004	Hicham El Guerrouj, Morocco	13:14.39
2008	Kenenisa Bekele, Ethiopia	12:57.82 OR
2012	Mohamed Farah, Great Britain	13:41.66

10,000 METERS

1912	Hannes Kolehmainen, Finland	31:20.8
1920	Paavo Nurmi, Finland	31:45.8
1924	Vilho (Ville) Ritola, Finland	30:23.2 WR
1928	Paavo Nurmi, Finland	30:18.8 OR
1932	Janusz Kusocinski, Poland	30:11.4 OR
1936	Ilmari Salminen, Finland	30:15.4
1948	Emil Zatopek, Czechoslovakia	29:59.6 OR
1952	Emil Zatopek, Czechoslovakia	29:17.0 OR
1956	Vladimir Kuts, USSR	28:45.6 OR
1960	Pyotr Bolotnikov, USSR	28:32.2 OR
1964	Billy Mills, United States	28:24.4 OR
1968	Naftali Temu, Kenya	29:27.4
1972	Lasse Viren, Finland	27:38.4 WR
1976	Lasse Viren, Finland	27:40.38
1980	Miruts Yifter, Ethiopia	27:42.7
1984	Alberto Cova, Italy	27:47.54
1988	Brahim Boutaib, Morocco	27:21.46 OR
1992	Khalid Skah, Morocco	27:46.70
1996	Haile Gebrselassie, Ethiopia	27:07.34 OR
2000	Haile Gebrselassie, Ethiopia	27:18.20
2004	Kenenisa Bekele, Ethiopia	27:05.10 OR
2008	Kenenisa Bekele, Ethiopia	27:01.17 OR
2012	Mohamed Farah, Great Britain	27:30.42

MARATHON

1896	Spiridon Louis, Greece	2:58:50
1900	Michel Theato, France	2:59:45
1904	Thomas Hicks, United States	3:28:53
1906	William Sherring, Canada	2:51:23.6
1908	John Hayes, United States	2:55:18.4 OR
1912	Kenneth McArthur, S Africa	2:36:54.8
1920	Hannes Kolehmainen, Finland	2:32:35.8 WB
1924	Albin Stenroos, Finland	2:41:22.6
1928	Boughera El Ouafi, France	2:32:57
1932	Juan Zabala, Argentina	2:31:36 OR
1936	Kijung Son, Japan (Korea)	2:29:19.2 OR
1948	Delfo Cabrera, Argentina	2:34:51.6
1952	Emil Zatopek, Czechoslovakia	2:23:03.2 OR
1956	Alain Mimoun O'Kacha, France	2:25:00.0
1960	Abebe Bikila, Ethiopia	2:15:16.2 WB

MARATHON *(Cont.)*

1964	Abebe Bikila, Ethiopia	2:12:11.2 WB
1968	Mamo Wolde, Ethiopia	2:20:26.4
1972	Frank Shorter, United States	2:12:19.8
1976	Waldemar Cierpinski, E Germ.	2:09:55.0
1980	Waldemar Cierpinski, E Germ.	2:11:03.0
1984	Carlos Lopes, Portugal	2:09:21.0 OR
1988	Gelindo Bordin, Italy	2:10:32
1992	Hwang Young-Cho, S Korea	2:13:23
1996	Josia Thugwane, S Africa	2:12:36
2000	Gezahgne Abera, Ethiopia	2:10:11
2004	Stefano Baldini, Italy	2:10:55
2008	Samuel Kamau, Kenya	2:06:32 OR
2012	Stephen Kiprotich, Uganda	2:08.01

110-METER HURDLES

1896	Thomas Curtis, United States	17.6
1900	Alvin Kraenzlein, United States	15.4 OR
1904	Frederick Schule, United States	16.0
1906	Robert Leavitt, United States	16.2
1908	Forrest Smithson, United States	15.0 WR
1912	Frederick Kelly, United States	15.1
1920	Earl Thomson, Canada	14.8 WR
1924	Daniel Kinsey, United States	15.0
1928	Sydney Atkinson, S Africa	14.8
1932	George Saling, United States	14.6
1936	Forrest Towns, United States	14.2
1948	William Porter, United States	13.9 OR
1952	Harrison Dillard, United States	13.7 OR
1956	Lee Calhoun, United States	13.5 OR
1960	Lee Calhoun, United States	13.8
1964	Hayes Jones, United States	13.6
1968	Willie Davenport, United States	13.3 OR
1972	Rod Milburn, United States	13.24 EWR
1976	Guy Drut, France	13.30
1980	Thomas Munkelt, E Germany	13.39
1984	Roger Kingdom, United States	13.20 OR
1988	Roger Kingdom, United States	12.98 OR
1992	Mark McKoy, Canada	13.12
1996	Allen Johnson, United States	12.95 OR
2000	Anier Garcia, Cuba	13.00
2004	Xiang Liu, China	12.91 EWR
2008	Dayron Robles, Cuba	12.93
2012	Aries Merritt, United States	12.92

400-METER HURDLES

1900	John Walter Tewksbury, U.S.	57.6
1904	Harry Hillman, United States	53.0
1906	Not held	
1908	Charles Bacon, United States	55.0 WR
1912	Not held	
1920	Frank Loomis, United States	54.0 WR
1924	F. Morgan Taylor, United States	52.6
1928	David Burghley, Great Britain	53.4 OR
1932	Robert Tisdall, Ireland	51.7
1936	Glenn Hardin, United States	52.4
1948	Roy Cochran, United States	51.1 OR
1952	Charles Moore, United States	50.8 OR
1956	Glenn Davis, United States	50.1 EOR
1960	Glenn Davis, United States	49.3 EOR
1964	Rex Cawley, United States	49.6
1968	Dave Hemery, Great Britain	48.12 WR
1972	John Akii-Bua, Uganda	47.82 WR
1976	Edwin Moses, United States	47.64 WR
1980	Volker Beck, E Germany	48.70
1984	Edwin Moses, United States	47.75
1988	Andre Phillips, United States	47.19 OR
1992	Kevin Young, United States	46.78 WR
1996	Derrick Adkins, United States	47.54
2000	Angelo Taylor, United States	47.50
2004	Felix Sanchez, Dominican Rep	47.63
2008	Angelo Taylor, United States	47.25
2012	Felix Sanchez, Dominican Rep	47.63

TRACK AND FIELD — Men *(Cont.)*

3,000-METER STEEPLECHASE

1920	Percy Hodge, Great Britain	10:00.4 OR
1924	Vilho (Ville) Ritola, Finland	9:33.6 OR
1928	Toivo Loukola, Finland	9:21.8 WR
1932	Volmari Iso-Hollo, Finland	10:33.4*
1936	Volmari Iso-Hollo, Finland	9:03.8 WR
1948	Thore Sjöstrand, Sweden	9:04.6
1952	Horace Ashenfelter, U.S.	8:45.4 WR
1956	Chris Brasher, Great Britain	8:41.2 OR
1960	Zdzislaw Krzyszkowiak, Poland	8:34.2 OR
1964	Gaston Roelants, Belgium	8:30.8 OR
1968	Amos Biwott, Kenya	8:51
1972	Kipchoge Keino, Kenya	8:23.6 OR
1976	Anders Gärderud, Sweden	8:08.2 WR
1980	Bronislaw Malinowski, Poland	8:09.7
1984	Julius Korir, Kenya	8:11.8
1988	Julius Kariuki, Kenya	8:05.51 OR
1992	Matthew Birir, Kenya	8:08.84
1996	Joseph Keter, Kenya	8:07.12
2000	Reuben Kosgei, Kenya	8:21.43
2004	Ezekiel Kemboi, Kenya	8:05.81
2008	Brimin Kipruto, Kenya	8:10.34
2012	Ezekiel Kemboi, Kenya	8:18.56

*About 3,450 meters; extra lap by error.

4 X 100-METER RELAY

1912	Great Britain	42.4 OR
1920	United States	42.2 WR
1924	United States	41.0 EWR
1928	United States	41.0 EWR
1932	United States	40.0 EWR
1936	United States	39.8 WR
1948	United States	40.6
1952	United States	40.1
1956	United States	39.5 WR
1960	W Germany	39.5 EWR
1964	United States	39.0 WR
1968	United States	38.2 WR
1972	United States	38.19 EWR
1976	United States	38.33
1980	USSR	38.26
1984	United States	37.83 WR
1988	USSR	38.19
1992	United States	37.40 WR
1996	Canada	37.69
2000	United States	37.61
2004	Great Britain	38.07
2008	Jamaica	37.10 WR
2012	Jamaica	36.84 WR

4 X 400-METER RELAY

1908	United States	3:29.4
1912	United States	3:16.6 WR
1920	Great Britain	3:22.2
1924	United States	3:16.0 WR
1928	United States	3:14.2 WR
1932	United States	3:08.2 WR
1936	Great Britain	3:09.0
1948	United States	3:10.4 WR
1952	Jamaica	3:03.9 WR
1956	United States	3:04.8
1960	United States	3:02.2 WR
1964	United States	3:00.7 WR
1968	United States	2:56.16 WR
1972	Kenya	2:59.8
1976	United States	2:58.65
1980	USSR	3:01.1
1984	United States	2:57.91
1988	United States	2:56.16 EWR
1992	United States	2:55.74 WR
1996	United States	2:55.99
2000	United States	2:56.35

4 X 400-METER RELAY *(Cont.)*

2004	United States	2:55.91
2008	United States	2:55.39 OR
2012	Bahamas	2:56.72

20-KILOMETER WALK

1956	Leonid Spirin, USSR	1:31:27.4
1960	Vladimir Golubnichiy, USSR	1:34:07.2
1964	Kenneth Mathews, Great Britain	1:29:34.0 OR
1968	Vladimir Golubnichiy, USSR	1:33:58.4
1972	Peter Frenkel, E Germany	1:26:42.4 OR
1976	Daniel Bautista, Mexico	1:24:40.6 OR
1980	Maurizio Damilano, Italy	1:23:35.5 OR
1984	Ernesto Canto, Mexico	1:23:13.0 OR
1988	Jozef Pribilinec, Czechoslovakia	1:19:57.0 OR
1992	Daniel Plaza, Spain	1:21:45.0
1996	Jefferson Pérez, Ecuador	1:20:07
2000	Robert Korzeniowski, Poland	1:18:59 OR
2004	Ivano Brugnetti, Italy	1:19:40
2008	Valeriy Borchin, Russia	1:19:01
2012	Ding Chen, China	1:18.46 OR

50-KILOMETER WALK

1932	Thomas Green, Great Britain	4:50:10
1936	Harold Whitlock, Great Britain	4:30:41.4 OR
1948	John Ljunggren, Sweden	4:41:52
1952	Giuseppe Dordoni, Italy	4:28:07.8 OR
1956	Norman Read, New Zealand	4:30:42.8
1960	Donald Thompson, Great Britain	4:25:30 OR
1964	Abdon Parnich, Italy	4:11:12.4 OR
1968	Christoph Höhne, E Germany	4:20:13.6
1972	Bernd Kannenberg, W Germany	3:56:11.6 OR
1980	Hartwig Gauder, E Germany	3:49:24.0 OR
1984	Raul Gonzalez, Mexico	3:47:26.0 OR
1988	Viacheslav Ivanenko, USSR	3:38:29.0 OR
1992	Andrey Perlov, Unified Team	3:50:13
1996	Robert Korzeniowski, Poland	3:43:30
2000	Robert Korzeniowski, Poland	3:42:22 OR
2004	Robert Korzeniowski, Poland	3:38:46
2008	Alex Schwazer, Italy	3:37:09 OR
2012	Sergey Kirdyapkin, Russia	3:35.59 OR

HIGH JUMP

1896	Ellery Clark, United States	5 ft 11¼ in
1900	Irving Baxter, United States	6 ft 2¾ in OR
1904	Samuel Jones, United States	5 ft 11 in
1906	Cornelius Leahy, Great Britain/Ireland	5 ft 10 in
1908	Harry Porter, United States	6 ft 3 in OR
1912	Alma Richards, United States	6 ft 4 in OR
1920	Richmond Landon, United States	6 ft 4 in OR
1924	Harold Osborn, United States	6 ft 6 in OR
1928	Robert W. King, United States	6 ft 4½ in
1932	Duncan McNaughton, Canada	6 ft 5½ in
1936	Cornelius Johnson, United States	6 ft 8 in OR
1948	John L. Winter, Australia	6 ft 6 in
1952	Walter Davis, United States	6 ft 8½ in OR
1956	Charles Dumas, United States	6 ft 11½ in OR
1960	Robert Shavlakadze, USSR	7 ft 1 in OR
1964	Valery Brumel, USSR	7 ft 1¾ in OR
1968	Dick Fosbury, United States	7 ft 4¼ in OR
1972	Yuri Tarmak, USSR	7 ft 3¾ in
1976	Jacek Wszola, Poland	7 ft 4½ in OR
1980	Gerd Wessig, E Germany	7 ft 8¾ in WR
1984	Dietmar Mögenburg, W Ger	7 ft 8½ in
1988	Gennadiy Avdeyenko, USSR	7 ft 9¾ in
1992	Javier Sotomayor, Cuba	7 ft 8 in.
1996	Charles Austin, United States	7 ft 10 in OR
2000	Sergey Kliugin, Russia	7 ft 8¼ in

Note: OR=Olympic Record. WR=World Record. EOR=Equals Olympic Record. EWR=Equals World Record. WB=World Best.

TRACK AND FIELD — Men (Cont.)

HIGH JUMP (Cont.)

2004	Stefan Holm, Sweden	7 ft 8¾ in
2008	Andrey Silnov, Russia	7 ft 9 in
2012	Ivan Ukhov, Russia	7 ft 9¾ in

POLE VAULT

1896	William Hoyt, United States	10 ft 10 in
1900	Irving Baxter, United States	10 ft 10 in
1904	Charles Dvorak, United States	11 ft 5¾ in
1906	Fernand Gonder, France	11 ft 5¾ in
1908	Alfred Gilbert, United States	12 ft 2 in OR
	Edward Cooke Jr., United States	
1912	Harry Babcock, United States	12 ft 11½ in OR
1920	Frank Foss, United States	13 ft 5 in WR
1924	Lee Barnes, United States	12 ft 11½ in
1928	Sabin Carr, United States	13 ft 9¼ in OR
1932	William Miller, United States	14 ft 1¾ in OR
1936	Earle Meadows, United States	14 ft 3¼ in OR
1948	Guinn Smith, United States	14 ft 1¼ in
1952	Robert Richards, United States	14 ft 11 in OR
1956	Robert Richards, United States	14 ft 11½ in OR
1960	Don Bragg, United States	15 ft 5 in OR
1964	Fred Hansen, United States	16 ft 8¾ in OR
1968	Bob Seagren, United States	17 ft 8½ in OR
1972	Wolfgang Nordwig, E Germany	18 ft ½ in OR
1976	Tadeusz Slusarski, Poland	18 ft ½ in EOR
1980	Wladyslaw Kozakiewicz, Pol	18 ft 11½ in WR
1984	Pierre Quinon, France	18 ft 10¼ in
1988	Sergei Bubka, USSR	19 ft 4¼ in OR
1992	Maksim Tarasov, Unified Team	19 ft ¼ in
1996	Jean Galfione, France	19 ft 5¼ in OR
2000	Nick Hysong, United States	19 ft 4¼ in
2004	Timothy Mack, United States	19 ft 6¼ in
2008	Steve Hooker, Australia	19 ft 6½ in OR
2012	Renaud Lavillenie, France	19 ft 7 in OR

LONG JUMP

1896	Ellery Clark, United States	20 ft 10 in
1900	Alvin Kraenzlein, United States	23 ft 6¾ in OR
1904	Meyer Prinstein, United States	24 ft 1 in OR
1906	Meyer Prinstein, United States	23 ft 7½ in
1908	Frank Irons, United States	24 ft 6½ in OR
1912	Albert Gutterson, United States	24 ft 11¼ in OR
1920	William Petersson, Sweden	23 ft 5½ in
1924	DeHart Hubbard, United States	24 ft 5 in
1928	Edward B. Hamm, United States	25 ft 4½ in OR
1932	Edward Gordon, United States	25 ft ¾ in
1936	Jesse Owens, United States	26 ft 5½ in OR
1948	William Steele, United States	25 ft 8 in
1952	Jerome Biffle, United States	24 ft 10 in
1956	Gregory Bell, United States	25 ft 8¼ in
1960	Ralph Boston, United States	26 ft 7¾ in OR
1964	Lynn Davies, Great Britain	26 ft 5¾ in
1968	Bob Beamon, United States	29 ft 2½ in WR
1972	Randy Williams, United States	27 ft ½ in
1976	Arnie Robinson, United States	27 ft 4¾ in
1980	Lutz Dombrowski, E Germany	28 ft ¼ in
1984	Carl Lewis, United States	28 ft ¼ in
1988	Carl Lewis, United States	28 ft 7½ in
1992	Carl Lewis, United States	28 ft 5½ in
1996	Carl Lewis, United States	27 ft 10¾ in
2000	Ivan Pedrosa, Cuba	28 ft ¾ in
2004	Dwight Phillips, United States	28 ft 2¼ in
2008	Irving Jahir Saladino, Panama	27 ft 4¼ in
2012	Greg Rutherford, Great Britain	27 ft 3¼ in

TRIPLE JUMP

1896	James Connolly, United States	44 ft 11¾ in
1900	Meyer Prinstein, United States	47 ft 5¾ in
1904	Meyer Prinstein, United States	47 ft 1 in
1906	Peter O'Connor, GB/ Ire	46 ft 2¼ in

TRIPLE JUMP (Cont.)

1908	Timothy Ahearne, GB/ Ire	48 ft 11¼ in OR
1912	Gustaf Lindblom, Sweden	48 ft 5¼ in
1920	Vilho Tuulos, Finland	47 ft 7 in
1924	Anthony Winter, Australia	50 ft 11¼ in WR
1928	Mikio Oda, Japan	49 ft 11 in
1932	Chuhei Nambu, Japan	51 ft 7 in WR
1936	Naoto Tajima, Japan	52 ft 6 in WR
1948	Arne Ahman, Sweden	50 ft 6¼ in
1952	Adhemar da Silva, Brazil	53 ft 2¾ in WR
1956	Adhemar da Silva, Brazil	53 ft 7¾ in OR
1960	Jozef Schmidt, Poland	55 ft 2 in
1964	Jozef Schmidt, Poland	55 ft 3½ in OR
1968	Viktor Saneyev, USSR	57 ft ¾ in WR
1972	Viktor Saneyev, USSR	56 ft 11¾ in
1976	Viktor Saneyev, USSR	56 ft 8¾ in
1980	Jaak Uudmae, USSR	56 ft 11¼ in
1984	Al Joyner, United States	56 ft 7½ in
1988	Khristo Markov, Bulgaria	57 ft 9½ in OR
1992	Mike Conley, United States	59 ft 7½ in (w)
1996	Kenny Harrison, United States	59 ft 4¼ in OR
2000	Jonathon Edwards, G. Britain	58 ft 1¼ in
2004	Christian Olsson, Sweden	58 ft 4½ in
2008	Nelson Evora, Portugal	57 ft 11½ in
2012	Christian Taylor, United States	58 ft 5¼ in

SHOT PUT

1896	Robert Garrett, United States	36 ft 9¾ in
1900	Richard Sheldon, United States	46 ft 3¼ in OR
1904	Ralph Rose, United States	48 ft 7 in WR
1906	Martin Sheridan, United States	40 ft 5¼ in
1908	Ralph Rose, United States	46 ft 7½ in
1912	Pat McDonald, United States	50 ft 4 in OR
1920	Ville Porhola, Finland	48 ft 7¼ in
1924	Clarence Houser, United States	49 ft 2¼ in
1928	John Kuck, United States	52 ft 3⁄4 in WR
1932	Leo Sexton, United States	52 ft 6 in OR
1936	Hans Woellke, Germany	53 ft 1¾ in OR
1948	Wilbur Thompson, United States	56 ft 2 in OR
1952	Parry O'Brien, United States	57 ft ½ in OR
1956	Parry O'Brien, United States	60 ft 11¼ in OR
1960	William Nieder, United States	64 ft 6¾ in OR
1964	Dallas Long, United States	66 ft 8½ in OR
1968	Randy Matson, United States	67 ft 4¾ in
1972	Wladyslaw Komar, Poland	69 ft 6 in OR
1976	Udo Beyer, E Germany	69 ft ¾ in
1980	Vladimir Kiselyov, USSR	70 ft ½ in OR
1984	Alessandro Andrei, Italy	69 ft 9 in
1988	Ulf Timmermann, E Germany	73 ft 8¾ in OR
1992	Mike Stulce, United States	71 ft 2½ in
1996	Randy Barnes, United States	70 ft 11 in
2000	Arsi Harju, Finland	69 ft 10¼ in
2004	Yuriy Bilonog, Ukraine	69 ft 5¼ in
2008	Tomasz Majewski, Poland	70 ft 6¾ in
2012	Tomasz Majewski, Poland	71 ft 9¾ in

DISCUS THROW

1896	Robert Garrett, United States	95 ft 7½ in
1900	Rudolf Bauer, Hungary	118 ft 3 in OR
1904	Martin Sheridan, United States	128 ft 10½ in OR
1906	Martin Sheridan, United States	136 ft
1908	Martin Sheridan, United States	134 ft 2 in OR
1912	Armas Taipele, Finland	148 ft 3 in OR
1920	Elmer Niklander, Finland	146 ft 7 in
1924	Clarence Houser, United States	151 ft 4 in OR
1928	Clarence Houser, United States	155 ft 3 in OR
1932	John Anderson, United States	162 ft 4 in OR
1936	Ken Carpenter, United States	165 ft 7 in OR
1948	Adolfo Consolini, Italy	173 ft 2 in OR
1952	Sim Iness, United States	180 ft 6 in OR
1956	Al Oerter, United States	184 ft 11 in OR

(w)-wind aided

Summer Games Champions *(Cont.)*

TRACK AND FIELD — Men *(Cont.)*

DISCUS *(Cont.)*

1960	Al Oerter, United States	194 ft 2 in OR
1964	Al Oerter, United States	200 ft 1 in OR
1968	Al Oerter, United States	212 ft 6 in OR
1972	Ludvik Danek, Czechoslovakia	211 ft 3 in
1976	Mac Wilkins, United States	221 ft 5 in OR
1980	Viktor Rashchupkin, USSR	218 ft 8 in
1984	Rolf Dannenberg, W Ger	218 ft 6 in
1988	Jürgen Schult, E Germany	225 ft 9 in OR
1992	Romas Ubartas, Lithuania	213 ft 8 in
1996	Lars Riedel, Germany	227 ft 8 in OR
2000	Virgilijus Alekna, Lithuania	227 ft 4 in
2004	Virgilijus Alekna, Lithuania	229 ft 3 in
2008	Gerd Kanter, Estonia	225 ft 9½ in
2012	Robert Harting, Germany	223 ft 11¾ in

HAMMER THROW

1900	John Flanagan, United States	163 ft 1 in
1904	John Flanagan, United States	168 ft 1 in OR
1906	Not held	
1908	John Flanagan, United States	170 ft 4 in OR
1912	Matt McGrath, United States	179 ft 7 in OR
1920	Pat Ryan, United States	173 ft 5 in
1924	Fred Tootell, United States	174 ft 10 in
1928	Patrick O'Callaghan, Ireland	168 ft 7 in
1932	Patrick O'Callaghan, Ireland	176 ft 11 in
1936	Karl Hein, Germany	185 ft 4 in OR
1948	Imre Nemeth, Hungary	183 ft 11 in
1952	Jozsef Csermak, Hungary	197 ft 11 in WR
1956	Harold Connolly, United States	207 ft 3 in OR
1960	Vasily Rudenkov, USSR	220 ft 2 in OR
1964	Romuald Klim, USSR	228 ft 10 in OR
1968	Gyula Zsivotsky, Hungary	240 ft 8 in OR
1972	Anatoli Bondarchuk, USSR	247 ft 8 in OR
1976	Yuri Sedykh, USSR	254 ft 4 in OR
1980	Yuri Sedykh, USSR	268 ft 4 in WR
1984	Juha Tiainen, Finland	256 ft 2 in
1988	Sergei Litvinov, USSR	278 ft 2 in OR
1992	Andrey Abduvaliyev, Unified Team	270 ft 9 in
1996	Balazs Kiss, Hungary	266 ft 6 in
2000	Szymon Ziolkowski, Poland	262 ft 6 in
2004	Adrian Zsolt, Hungary	272 fr 11 in
2008	Primoz Kozmus, Slovenia	269 ft 1 in
2012	Krisztian Pars, Hungary	264 ft 4¾ in

JAVELIN

1908	Erik Lemming, Sweden	179 ft 10 in
1912	Erik Lemming, Sweden	198 ft 11 in WR
1920	Jonni Myyrä, Finland	215 ft 10 in OR
1924	Jonni Myyrä, Finland	206 ft 6 in
1928	Eric Lundkvist, Sweden	218 ft 6 in OR
1932	Matti Jarvinen, Finland	238 ft 6 in OR
1936	Gerhard Stöck, Germany	235 ft 8 in
1948	Kai Rautavaara, Finland	228 ft 10½ in
1952	Cy Young, United States	242 ft 1 in OR
1956	Egil Danielson, Norway	281 ft 2¼ in WR
1960	Viktor Tsibulenko, USSR	277 ft 8 in
1964	Pauli Nevala, Finland	271 ft 2 in
1968	Janis Lusis, USSR	295 ft 7 in OR
1972	Klaus Wolfermann, W Germany	296 ft 10 in OR
1976	Miklos Nemeth, Hungary	310 ft 4 in WR
1980	Dainis Kuta, USSR	299 ft 2⅜ in
1984	Arto Härkönen, Finland	284 ft 8 in
1988	Tapio Korjus, Finland	276 ft 6 in
1992	Jan Zelezny, Czechoslovakia	294 ft 2 in OR
1996	Jan Zelezny, Czech Republic	289 ft 3 in
2000	Jan Zelezny, Czech Republic	295 ft 9½ in OR
2004	Andreas Thorkildsen, Norway	283 ft 9 in
2008	Andreas Thorkildsen, Norway	297 ft 1¾ in OR
2012	Keshorn Walcott, Trinidad & Tobago	277 ft 5⅞ in

DECATHLON

		Pts
1904	Thomas Kiely, Ireland	6036
1912	Jim Thorpe, United States*	8412 WR
1920	Helge Lövland, Norway	6803
1924	Harold Osborn, United States	7711 WR
1928	Paavo Yrjölä, Finland	8053.29 WR
1932	James Bausch, United States	8462 WR
1936	Glenn Morris, United States	7900 WR
1948	Robert Mathias, United States	7139
1952	Robert Mathias, United States	7887 WR
1956	Milton Campbell, United States	7937 OR
1960	Rafer Johnson, United States	8392 OR
1964	Willi Holdorf, W Germany	7887
1968	Bill Toomey, United States	8193 OR
1972	Nikolai Avilov, USSR	8454 WR
1976	Bruce Jenner, United States	8617 WR
1980	Daley Thompson, Great Britain	8495
1984	Daley Thompson, Great Britain	8798 EWR
1988	Christian Schenk, E Germany	8488
1992	Robert Zmelik, Czechoslovakia	8611
1996	Dan O'Brien, United States	8824 OR
2000	Erki Nool, Estonia	8641
2004	Roman Seberle, Czech Rep	8893 OR
2008	Bryan Clay, United States	8791
2012	Ashton Eaton, United States	8869

*In 1913, Thorpe was disqualified for having played professional baseball in 1910. His record was restored in 1982.

TRACK AND FIELD — Women

100 METERS

1928	Elizabeth Robinson, United States	12.2 EWR
1932	Stella Walsh, Poland	11.9 EWR
1936	Helen Stephens, United States	11.5
1948	Francina Blankers-Koen, Neth	11.9
1952	Marjorie Jackson, Australia	11.5 EWR
1956	Betty Cuthbert, Australia	11.5 EWR
1960	Wilma Rudolph, United States	11.0
1964	Wyomia Tyus, United States	11.4
1968	Wyomia Tyus, United States	11.0 WR
1972	Renate Stecher, E Germany	11.07
1976	Annegret Richter, W Germany	11.08
1980	Lyudmila Kondratyeva, USSR	11.06
1984	Evelyn Ashford, United States	10.97 OR
1988	Florence Griffith Joyner, United States	10.54 WR
1992	Gail Devers, United States	10.82
1996	Gail Devers, United States	10.94
2000	Vacant*	
2004	Yuliya Nesterenko, Belarus	10.93
2008	Shelly-Ann Fraser, Jamaica	10.78
2012	Shelly-Ann Fraser-Pryce, Jamaica	10.75

200 METERS

1948	Francina Blankers-Koen, Neth	24.4
1952	Marjorie Jackson, Australia	23.7
1956	Betty Cuthbert, Australia	23.4 EOR
1960	Wilma Rudolph, United States	24.0

Note: OR=Olympic Record. WR=World Record. EOR=Equals Olympic Record. EWR=Equals World Record. WB=World Best.

*Marion Jones was stripped of her medals from the 2000 Olympics, no decision on replacing her victories has been made.

TRACK AND FIELD — Women (Cont.)

200 METERS (Cont.)

1964	Edith McGuire, United States	23.0 OR
1968	Irena Szewinska, Poland	22.5 WR
1972	Renate Stecher, E Germany	22.40 EWR
1976	Bärbel Eckert, E Germany	22.37 OR
1980	Bärbel Wöckel (Eckert), E Germ.	22.03 OR
1984	Valerie Brisco-Hooks, U.S.	21.81 OR
1988	Florence Griffith Joyner, U.S.	21.34 WR
1992	Gwen Torrence, United States	21.81
1996	Marie-José Pérec, France	22.12
2000	Vacant*	
2004	Veronica Campbell, Jamaica	22.05
2008	Veronica Campbell-Brown, Jamaica	21.74
2012	Allyson Felix, United States	21.88

400 METERS

1964	Betty Cuthbert, Australia	52.0 OR
1968	Colette Besson, France	52.0 EOR
1972	Monika Zehrt, E Germany	51.08 OR
1976	Irena Szewinska, Poland	49.29 WR
1980	Marita Koch, E Germany	48.88 OR
1984	Valerie Brisco-Hooks, U.S.	48.83 OR
1988	Olga Bryzgina, USSR	48.65 OR
1992	Marie-José Pérec, France	48.83
1996	Marie-José Pérec, France	48.25 OR
2000	Cathy Freeman, Australia	49.11
2004	T. Williams-Darling, Bahamas	49.41
2008	Christine Ohuruogu, Great Britain	49.62
2012	Sanya Richards-Ross, U. S.	49.55

800 METERS

1928	Lina Radke, Germany	2:16.8 WR
1932-56	Not held	
1960	Lyudmila Shevtsova, USSR	2:04.3 EWR
1964	Ann Packer, Great Britain	2:01.1 OR
1968	Madeline Manning, United States	2:00.9 OR
1972	Hildegard Falck, W Germany	1:58.55 OR
1976	Tatyana Kazankina, USSR	1:54.94 WR
1980	Nadezhda Olizarenko, USSR	1:53.42 WR
1984	Doina Melinte, Romania	1:57.6
1988	Sigrun Wodars, E Germany	1:56.10
1992	Ellen Van Langen, Netherlands	1:55.54
1996	Svetlana Masterkova, Russia	1:57.73
2000	Maria Mutola, Mozambique	1:56.15
2004	Kelly Holmes, Great Britain	1:56.38
2008	Pamela Jelimo, Kenya	1:54.87
2012	Mariya Savinova, Russia	1:56.19

1,500 METERS

1972	Lyudmila Bragina, USSR	4:01.4 WR
1976	Tatyana Kazankina, USSR	4:05.48
1980	Tatyana Kazankina, USSR	3:56.6 OR
1984	Gabriella Dorio, Italy	4:03.25
1988	Paula Ivan, Romania	3:53.96 OR
1992	Hassiba Boulmerka, Algeria	3:55.30
1996	Svetlana Masterkova, Russia	4:00.83
2000	Nouria Merah-Benida, Algeria	4:05.10
2004	Kelly Holmes, Great Britain	3:57.90
2008	Nancy Jebet Lagat, Kenya	4:00.23
2012	Asli Cakir Alptekin, Turkey	4:10.23

3,000 METERS

1984	Maricica Puica, Romania	8:35.96 OR
1988	Tatyana Samolenko, USSR	8:26.53 OR
1992	Elena Romanova, Unified Team	8:46.04

5,000 METERS

1996	Wang Junxia, China	14:57.88

5,000 METERS (Cont.)

2000	Gabriela Szabo, Romania	14:40.79 OR
2004	Meseret Defar, Ethiopia	14:45.65
2008	Tirunesh Dibaba Kenene, Ethiopia	15:41.40
2012	Meseret Defar, Ethiopia	15:04.25

10,000 METERS

1988	Olga Bondarenko, USSR	31:05.21 OR
1992	Derartu Tulu, Ethiopia	31:06.02
1996	Fernanda Ribeiro, Portugal	31:01.63 OR
2000	Derartu Tulu, Ethiopia	30:17.49 OR
2004	Huina Xing, China	30:24.36
2008	Tirunesh Dibaba Kenene, Ethiopia	29:54.66 OR
2012	Tirunesh Dibaba, Ethiopia	30:20.75

MARATHON

1984	Joan Benoit, United States	2:24:52 OR
1988	Rosa Mota, Portugal	2:25:40
1992	Valentin Yegorova, Unified Team	2:32:41
1996	Fatuma Roba, Ethiopia	2:26:05
2000	Naoko Takahashi, Japan	2:23:14 OR
2004	Noguchi Mizuki, Japan	2:26:20
2008	Constantina Tomescu Dita, Romania	2:26:44
2012	Tiki Gelana, Ethiopia	2:23:07 OR

80-METER HURDLES

1932	Babe Didrikson, United States	11.7 WR
1936	Trebisonda Valla, Italy	11.7
1948	Francina Blankers-Koen, Neth	11.2 OR
1952	Shirley Strickland, Australia	10.9 WR
1956	Shirley Strickland, Australia	10.7 OR
1960	Irina Press, USSR	10.8
1964	Karin Balzer, E Germany	10.5
1968	Maureen Caird, Australia	10.3 OR

100-METER HURDLES

1972	Annelie Ehrhardt, E Germany	12.59 WR
1976	Johanna Schaller, E Germany	12.77
1980	Vera Komisova, USSR	12.56 OR
1984	Benita Fitzgerald-Brown, U.S.	12.84
1988	Yordanka Donkova, Bulgaria	12.38 OR
1992	Paraskevi Patoulidou, Greece	12.64
1996	Lyudmila Engqvist, Sweden	12.58
2000	Olga Shishigina, Kazakhstan	12.65
2004	Joanna Hayes, United States	12.37 OR
2008	Dawn Harper, United States	12.54
2012	Sally Pearson, Australia	12.35 OR

400-METER HURDLES

1984	Nawal el Moutawakel, Morocco	54.61 OR
1988	Debra Flintoff-King, Australia	53.17 OR
1992	Sally Gunnell, Great Britain	53.23
1996	Deon Hemmings, Jamaica	52.82 OR
2000	Irina Privalova, Russia	53.02
2004	Faní Halkiá, Greece	52.82
2008	Melaine Walker, Jamaica	52.64
2012	Natalya Antyukh, Russia	52.70

4 X 100-METER RELAY

1928	Canada	48.4 WR
1932	United States	46.9 WR
1936	United States	46.9
1948	Netherlands	47.5
1952	United States	45.9 WR
1956	Australia	44.5 WR
1960	United States	44.5
1964	Poland	43.6
1968	United States	42.8 WR
1972	W Germany	42.81 EWR
1976	E Germany	42.55 OR

Note: OR=Olympic Record; WR=World Record; EOR=Equals Olympic Record; EWR=Equals World Record; WB=World Best.
†Marion Jones was stripped of her medals from the 2000 Olympics, no decision on replacing her victories has been made.

TRACK AND FIELD — Women (Cont.)

4 X 100-METER RELAY (Cont.)

1980	E Germany	41.60 WR
1984	United States	41.65
1988	United States	41.98
1992	United States	42.11
1996	United States	41.95
2000	Bahamas	41.95
2004	Jamaica	41.73
2008	Russia	42.31
2012	United States	40.82 WR

4 X 400-METER RELAY

1972	E Germany	3:23 WR
1976	E Germany	3:19.23 WR
1980	USSR	3:20.02
1984	United States	3:18.29 OR
1988	USSR	3:15.18 WR
1992	Unified Team	3:20.20
1996	United States	3:20.91
2000	Vacant†	
2004	United States	3:19.01
2008	United States	3:18.54
2012	United States	3:16.87

10-KILOMETER WALK

1992	Chen Yueling, China	44:32
1996	Elena Nikolayeva, Russia	41:49 OR

20-KILOMETER WALK

2000	Liping Wang, China	1:29:05
2004	Athanasía Tsoumeléka, Greece	1:29:12
2008	Olga Kaniskina, Russia	1:26:31 OR
2012	Elena Lashmanova Russia	1:25:02 WR

HIGH JUMP

1928	Ethel Catherwood, Canada	5 ft 2½ in
1932	Jean Shiley, United States	5 ft 5¼ in WR
1936	Ibolya Csak, Hungary	5 ft 3 in
1948	Alice Coachman, United States	5 ft 6 in OR
1952	Esther Brand, South Africa	5 ft 5¾ in
1956	Mildred L. McDaniel, U.S.	5 ft 9¼ in WR
1960	Iolanda Balas, Romania	6 ft ¾ in OR
1964	Iolanda Balas, Romania	6 ft 2¾ in OR
1968	Miloslava Reskova, Czech.	5 ft 11½ in
1972	Ulrike Meyfarth, W. Germany	6 ft 3½ in EWR
1976	Rosemarie Ackermann, E Germ	6 ft 4 in OR
1980	Sara Simeoni, Italy	6 ft 5½ in OR
1984	Ulrike Meyfarth, W Germany	6 ft 7½ in OR
1988	Louise Ritter, United States	6 ft 8 in OR
1992	Heike Henkel, Germany	6 ft 7½ in
1996	Stefka Kostadinova, Bulgaria	6 ft 8¾ in OR
2000	Yelena Yelesina, Russia	6 ft 7 in
2004	Yelena Slesarenko, Russia	6 ft 9 in
2008	Tia Hellebaut, Belgium	6 ft 8¾ in
2012	Anna Chicherova, Russia	6 ft 8¾ in

POLE VAULT

2000	Stacy Dragila, United States	15 ft 1 in OR
2004	Yelena Isinbayeva, Russia	16 ft 1¼ in WR
2008	Yelena Isinbayeva, Russia	16 ft 6¾ in WR
2012	Jennifer Suhr, United States	15 ft 7 in

LONG JUMP

1948	Olga Gyarmati, Hungary	18 ft 8¼ in
1952	Yvette Williams, New Zealand	20 ft 5¾ in OR
1956	Elzbieta Krzeskinska, Poland	20 ft 10 in EWR
1960	Vyera Krepkina, USSR	20 ft 10¾ in OR
1964	Mary Rand, Great Britain	22 ft 2¼ in WR
1968	Viorica Viscopoleanu, Rom	22 ft 4½ in WR
1972	Heidemarie Rosendahl, W Ger	22 ft 3 in
1976	Angela Voigt, E Germany	22 ft ¾ in
1980	Tatyana Kolpakova, USSR	23 ft 2 in OR
1984	Anisoara Stanciu, Romania	22 ft 10 in

LONG JUMP (Cont.)

1988	Jackie Joyner-Kersee, U.S.	24 ft 3½ in OR
1992	Heike Drechsler, Germany	23 ft 5¼ in
1996	Chioma Ajunwa, Nigeria	23 ft 4½ in
2000	Heike Drechsler, Germany	22 ft 11¼ in
2004	Tatyana Lebedeva, Russia	23 ft 2½ in
2008	Maurren Higa Maggi, Brazil	23 ft 1 in
2012	Brittney Reese, United States	23 ft 4¼ in

TRIPLE JUMP

1996	Inessa Kravets, Ukraine	50 ft 3½ in
2000	Tereza Marinova, Bulgaria	49 ft 10½ in
2004	Francoise M. Etone, Cameroon	50 ft 2½ in
2008	Francoise M. Etone, Cameroon	50 ft 5 in OR
2012	Olga Rypakova, Kazakhstan	49 ft 1¾ in

SHOT PUT

1948	Micheline Ostermeyer, France	45 ft 1½ in
1952	Galina Zybina, USSR	50 ft 1¾ in WR
1956	Tamara Tyshkevich, USSR	54 ft 5 in OR
1960	Tamara Press, USSR	56 ft 10 in OR
1964	Tamara Press, USSR	59 ft 6¼ in OR
1968	Margitta Gummel, E Germany	64 ft 4 in WR
1972	Nadezhda Chizhova, USSR	69 ft WR
1976	Ivanka Hristova, Bulgaria	69 ft 5¼ in OR
1980	Ilona Slupianek, E Germany	73 ft 6¼ in OR
1984	Claudia Losch, W Germany	67 ft 2¼ in
1988	Natalya Lisovskaya, USSR	72 ft 11¾ in
1992	Svetlana Kriveleva, Unified Team	69 ft 1¼ in
1996	Astrid Kumbernuss, Germany	67 ft 5½ in
2000	Yanina Korolchik, Belarus	67 ft 5½ in
2004	Yumileidi Cumba Jay, Cuba	64 ft 3¼ in
2008	Valerie Vili, New Zealand	67 ft 5½ in
2012	Nadzeya Ostapchuk, Belarus	70 ft ⅞ in

DISCUS THROW

1928	Helena Konopacka, Poland	129 ft 11¾ in WR
1932	Lillian Copeland, United States	133 ft 2 in OR
1936	Gisela Mauermayer, Germany	156 ft 3 in OR
1948	Micheline Ostermeyer, France	137 ft 6 in
1952	Nina Romaschkova, USSR	168 ft 8 in OR
1956	Olga Fikotova, Czechoslovakia	176 ft 1 in OR
1960	Nina Ponomaryeva, USSR	180 ft 9 in OR
1964	Tamara Press, USSR	187 ft 10 in OR
1968	Lia Manoliu, Romania	191 ft 2 in OR
1972	Faina Melnik, USSR	218 ft 7 in OR
1976	Evelin Schlaak, E Germany	226 ft 4 in OR
1980	Evelin Jahl (Schlaak), E Germ.	229 ft 6 in OR
1984	Ria Stalman, Netherlands	214 ft 5 in
1988	Martina Hellmann, E Germany	237 ft 2 in OR
1992	Maritza Martén, Cuba	229 ft 10 in
1996	Ilke Wyludda, Germany	228 ft 6 in
2000	Ellina Zvereva, Belarus	224 ft 5 in
2004	Natalya Sadova, Russia	219 ft 10 in
2008	S. Brown-Trafton, United States	212 ft 4¾ in
2012	Sandra Perkovic, Croatia	226 ft 8⅞ in

HAMMER THROW

2000	Kamila Skolimowska, Russia	233 ft 5 in OR
2004	Olga Kuzenkova, Russia	246 ft 1½ in OR
2008	Aksana Miankova, Belarus	250 ft 5½ in OR
2012	Tatyana Lysenko, Russia	256 ft 6 in OR

JAVELIN THROW

1932	Babe Didrikson, United States	143 ft 4 in OR
1936	Tilly Fleischer, Germany	148 ft 3 in OR
1948	Herma Bauma, Austria	149 ft 6 in
1952	Dana Zatopkova, Czechoslovakia	165 ft 7 in
1956	Inese Jaunzeme, USSR	176 ft 8 in
1960	Elvira Ozolina, USSR	183 ft 8 in OR
1964	Mihaela Penes, Romania	198 ft 7 in

TRACK AND FIELD — Women (Cont.)

JAVELIN (Cont.)

1968	Angela Nemeth, Hungary	198 ft
1972	Ruth Fuchs, E Germany	209 ft 7 in OR
1976	Ruth Fuchs, E Germany	216 ft 4 in OR
1980	Maria Colon, Cuba	224 ft 5 in OR
1984	Tessa Sanderson, Great Britain	228 ft 2 in OR
1988	Petra Felke, E Germany	245 ft OR
1992	Silke Renk, Germany	224 ft 2 in
1996	Heli Rantanen, Finland	222 ft 11 in
2000	Trine Hattestad, Norway	226 ft ½ in OR
2004	Osleidys Menendez, Cuba	234 ft 8 in OR
2008	B. Spotakova, Czech Republic	234 ft 3¾ in
2012	Barbora Spotakova, Czech Rep	228 ft 2¼ in

PENTATHLON

		Pts
1964	Irina Press, USSR	5246 WR
1968	Ingrid Becker, W Germany	5098
1972	Mary Peters, Great Britain	4801 WR
1976	Siegrun Siegl, E Germany	4745
1980	Nadezhda Tkachenko, USSR	5083 WR

HEPTATHLON

		Pts
1984	Glynis Nunn, Australia	6390 OR
1988	Jackie Joyner-Kersee, U.S.	7291 WR
1992	Jackie Joyner-Kersee, U.S.	7044
1996	Ghada Shouaa, Syria	6780
2000	Denise Lewis, Great Britain	6584
2004	Carolina Kluft, Sweden	6952
2008	Natalia Dobrynska, Ukraine	6733
2012	Jessica Ennis, Great Britain	6955

BASKETBALL — Men

1936

Final: United States 19, Canada 8
United States: R. Bishop, J. Fortenberry, C. Knowles, J. Ragland, C. Shy, W. Wheatley, F. Johnson, S. Balter, J. Gibbons, F. Lubin, A. Mollner, D. Piper, D. Swanson, W. Schmidt

1948

Final: United States 65, France 21
United States: C. Barker, D. Barksdale, R. Beard, L. Beck, V. Boryla, G. Carpenter, A. Groza, W. Jones, B. Kurland, R. Lumpp, R. Pitts, J. Renick, B. Robinson, K. Rollins

1952

Final: United States 36, USSR 25
United States: C. Hoag, B. Hougland, M. Kelley, B. Kenney, C. Lovellette, M. Freiberger, V. Glasgow, F. McCabe, D. Pippen, H. Williams, R. Bontemps, B. Kurland, W. Lienhard, J. Keller

1956

Final: United States 89, USSR 55
United States: C. Cain, B. Hougland, K.C. Jones, B. Russell, J. Walsh, W. Evans, B. Haldorson, R. Tomsic, D. Boushka, G. Ford, B. Jeangerard, C. Darling

1960

Final: United States 90, Brazil 63
United States: J. Arnette, W. Bellamy, B. Boozer, T. Dischinger, J. Lucas, O. Robertson, A. Smith, B. Haldorson, D. Imhoff, A. Kelley, L. Lane, J. West

1964

Final: United States 73, USSR 59
United States: J. Barnes, B. Bradley, L. Brown, J. Caldwell, M. Counts, R. Davies, W. Hazzard, L. Jackson, J. McCaffrey, J. Mullins, J. Shipp, G. Wilson

1968

Final: United States 65, Yugoslavia 50
United States: J. Clawson, K. Spain, J. White, M. Barrett, S. Haywood, C. Scott, W. Hosket, C. Fowler, M. Silliman, G. Saulters, J. King, D. Dee

1972

Final: USSR 51, United States 50
United States: K. Davis, D. Collins, T. Henderson, M. Bantom, B. Jones, D. Jones, J. Forbes, J. Brewer, T. Burleson, T. McMillen, K. Joyce, E. Ratleff

1976

Final: United States 95, Yugoslavia 74
United States: P. Ford, S. Sheppard, A. Dantley, W. Davis, Q. Buckner, E. Grunfeld, K. Carr, S. May, M. Armstrong, T. La Garde, P. Hubbard, M. Kupchak

1980

Final: Yugoslavia 86, Italy 77
U.S. participated in boycott.

1984

Final: United States 96, Spain 65
United States: S. Alford, L. Wood, P. Ewing, V. Fleming, A. Robertson, M. Jordan, J. Kleine, J. Koncak, W. Tisdale, C. Mullin, S. Perkins, J. Turner

1988

Final: USSR 76, Yugoslavia 63
U.S. (3rd): M. Richmond, C.E. Smith, V. Coles, H. Hawkins, J. Grayer, C.D. Smith, W. Anderson, S. Augmon, D. Majerle, D. Manning, J.R. Reid, D. Robinson

1992

Final: United States 117, Croatia 85
United States: D. Robinson, C. Laettner, P. Ewing, L. Bird, S. Pippen, M. Jordan, C. Drexler, K. Malone, J. Stockton, C. Mullin, C. Barkley, E. Johnson

1996

Final: United States 95, Yugoslavia 69
United States: C. Barkley, A. Hardaway, G. Hill, K. Malone, R. Miller, H. Olajuwon, S. O'Neal, S. Pippen, M. Richmond, J. Stockton, D. Robinson, G. Payton

2000

Final: United States 85, France 75
United States: S. Abdur-Rahim, R. Allen, V. Baker, V. Carter, K. Garnett, T. Hardaway, A. Houston, J. Kidd, A. McDyess, A. Mourning, G. Payton, S. Smith

2004

Final: Argentina 84, Italy 69
U.S. (3rd): A. Iverson, L. James, T. Duncan, C. Anthony, D. Wade, R. Jefferson, L. Odom, S. Marbury, C. Boozer, E. Okafor, A. Stoudemire, S. Marion

2008

Final: United States 118, Spain 107
U.S.: C. Anthony, C. Boozer, C. Bosh, K. Bryant, D. Howard, L. James, J. Kidd, C. Paul, T. Prince, M. Redd, D. Wade, D. Williams

2012

Final: United States 107, Spain 100
U.S.: K. Durant, C. Paul, L. James, K. Bryant, C. Anthony, K. Love, D. Williams, R. Westbrook, T. Chandler, A. Iguodala, A. Davis, J. Harden

BASKETBALL — Women

1976
Gold, USSR; Silver, United States*
United States: C. Brogdon, S. Rojcewicz, A. Meyers, L. Harris, N. Dunkle, C. Lewis, N. Lieberman, G. Marquis, P. Roberts, M. O'Connor, P. Head, J. Simpson

*In 1976 the women played a round-robin tournament, with the gold medal going to the team with the best record. The USSR won with a 5–0 record, and the USA, with a 3–2 record, was given the silver by virtue of a 95–79 victory over Bulgaria, which was also 3–2.

1980
Final: USSR 104, Bulgaria 73
U.S. participated in boycott.

1984
Final: United States 85, Korea 55
United States: T. Edwards, L. Henry, L. Woodard, A. Donovan, C. Boswell, C. Miller, J. Lawrence, C. Noble, K. Mulkey, D. Curry, P. McGee, C. Menken-Schaudt

1988
Final: United States 77, Yugoslavia 70
United States: T. Edwards, M. Ethridge, C. Brown, A. Donovan, T. Weatherspoon, B. Gordon, V. Bullett, A. Lloyd, K. McClain, J. Gillom, C. Cooper, S. McConnell

1992
Final: Unified Team 76, China 66
United States (3rd): T. Edwards, T. Weatherspoon, V. Bullett, K. McClain, C. Cooper, S. McConnell, D. Charles, C. Davis, T. Jackson, V. Orr, C. Jones, M. Dixon

1996
Final: United States 111, Brazil 87
United States: J. Azzi, R. Bolton, T. Edwards, L. Leslie, R. Lobo, K. McClain, N. McCray, C. McGhee, D. Staley, K. Steding, S. Swoopes, V. Lacey

2000
Final: United States 76, Australia 54
United States: R. Bolton-Holifield, T. Edwards, Y. Griffith, C. Holdsclaw, L. Leslie, N. McCray, D. Milton, K. Smith, D. Staley, S. Swoopes, N. Williams, K. Wolters

2004
Final: United States 74, Australia 63
United States: D. Staley, D. Taurasi, L. Leslie, S. Swoopes, T. Catchings, S. Bird, R. Riley, S. Johnson, K. Smith, Y. Griffith, S. Cash, T. Thompson

2008
Final: United States 92, Australia 65
United States: S. Augustus, S. Bird, S. Fowles, L. Leslie, D. Milton-Jones, C. Parker, C. Pondexter, T. Catchings, T. Thompson, D. Taurasi, K. Smith

2012
Final: United States 86, France 50
United States: D. Taurasi, M. Moore, S. Bird, C. Parker, T. Charles, L. Whalen, T. Catchings, S. Augustus, S. Fowles, A. McCoughtry, A. Jones, S. Cash

BOXING

LIGHT FLYWEIGHT (106 LB)
1968	Francisco Rodriguez, Venezuela
1972	Gyorgy Gedo, Hungary
1976	Jorge Hernandez, Cuba
1980	Shamil Sabyrov, USSR
1984	Paul Gonzalez, United States
1988	Ivailo Hristov, Bulgaria
1992	Rogelio Marcelo, Cuba
1996	Daniel Petrov, Bulgaria
2000	Brahim Asloum, France
2004	Yan Bhartelemy Varela, Cuba
2008	Shiming Zou, China
2012	Shiming Zou, China

FLYWEIGHT (112 LB)
1904	George Finnegan, United States
1920	Frank Di Gennara, United States
1924	Fidel LaBarba, United States
1928	Antal Kocsis, Hungary
1932	Istvan Enekes, Hungary
1936	Willi Kaiser, Germany
1948	Pascual Perez, Argentina
1952	Nathan Brooks, United States
1956	Terence Spinks, Great Britain
1960	Gyula Torok, Hungary
1964	Fernando Atzori, Italy
1968	Ricardo Delgado, Mexico
1972	Georgi Kostadinov, Bulgaria
1976	Leo Randolph, United States
1980	Peter Lessov, Bulgaria
1984	Steve McCrory, United States
1988	Kim Kwang Sun, S Korea
1992	Su Choi Chol, N Korea
1996	Maikro Romero, Cuba
2000	Wijan Ponlid, Thailand
2004	Yuriokis Toledano, Cuba

FLYWEIGHT (112 LB) (Cont.)
2008	Somit Jongjohor, Thailand
2012	Robeisy Ramirez Carrazana, Cuba

BANTAMWEIGHT (119 LB)
1904	Oliver Kirk, United States
1908	A. Henry Thomas, Great Britain
1920	Clarence Walker, S Africa
1924	William Smith, S Africa
1928	Vittorio Tamagnini, Italy
1932	Horace Gwynne, Canada
1936	Ulderico Sergo, Italy
1948	Tibor Csik, Hungary
1952	Pentti Hamalainen, Finland
1956	Wolfgang Behrendt, E Germany
1960	Oleg Grigoryev, USSR
1964	Takao Sakurai, Japan
1968	Valery Sokolov, USSR
1972	Orlando Martinez, Cuba
1976	Yong Jo Gu, N Korea
1980	Juan Hernandez, Cuba
1984	Maurizio Stecca, Italy
1988	Kennedy McKinney, United States
1992	Joel Casamayor, Cuba
1996	István Kovács, Hungary
2000	Guillermo Ortiz, Cuba
2004	Guillermo Ortiz, Cuba
2008	Badar-Uugan Enkhbat, Mongolia
2012	Luke Campbell, Great Britain

FEATHERWEIGHT (125 LB)
1904	Oliver Kirk, United States
1908	Richard Gunn, Great Britain
1920	Paul Fritsch, France
1924	John Fields, United States
1928	Lambertus van Klaveren, Netherlands
1932	Carmelo Robledo, Argentina

BOXING (*Cont.*)

FEATHERWEIGHT (125 LB) (*Cont.*)

1936	Oscar Casanovas, Argentina
1948	Ernesto Formenti, Italy
1952	Jan Zachara, Czechoslovakia
1956	Vladimir Safronov, USSR
1960	Francesco Musso, Italy
1964	Stanislav Stephashkin, USSR
1968	Antonio Roldan, Mexico
1972	Boris Kousnetsov, USSR
1976	Angel Herrera, Cuba
1980	Rudi Fink, E Germany
1984	Meldrick Taylor, United States
1988	Giovanni Parisi, Italy
1992	Andreas Tews, Germany
1996	Somluck Kamsing, Thailand
2000	Bekzat Sattarkhanox, Kazakhstan
2004	Alexei Tichtchenko, Russia
2008	Vasyl Lomachenko, Ukraine

LIGHTWEIGHT (132 LB)

1904	Harry Spanger, United States
1908	Frederick Grace, Great Britain
1920	Samuel Mosberg, United States
1924	Hans Nielsen, Denmark
1928	Carlo Orlandi, Italy
1932	Lawrence Stevens, S Africa
1936	Imre Harangi, Hungary
1948	Gerald Dreyer, S Africa
1952	Aureliano Bolognesi, Italy
1956	Richard McTaggart, Great Britain
1960	Kazimierz Pazdzior, Poland
1964	Jozef Grudzien, Poland
1968	Ronald Harris, United States
1972	Jan Szczepanski, Poland
1976	Howard Davis, United States
1980	Angel Herrera, Cuba
1984	Pernell Whitaker, United States
1988	Andreas Zuelow, E Germany
1992	Oscar De La Hoya, United States
1996	Hocine Soltani, Algeria
2000	Mario Mesa, Cuba
2004	Mario Mesa, Cuba
2008	Alexey Tishchenko, Russia
2012	Vasyl Lomachenko, Ukraine

LIGHT WELTERWEIGHT (139 LB)

1952	Charles Adkins, United States
1956	Vladimir Yengibaryan, USSR
1960	Bohumil Nemecek, Czechoslovakia
1964	Jerzy Kulej, Poland
1968	Jerzy Kulej, Poland
1972	Ray Seales, United States
1976	Ray Leonard, United States
1980	Patrizio Oliva, Italy
1984	Jerry Page, United States
1988	Viatcheslav Janovski, USSR
1992	Hector Vinent, Cuba
1996	Hector Vinent, Cuba
2000	Mahamadkadyz Abdullaev, Uzbekistan
2004	Manus Boonjumnong, Thailand
2008	Felix Diaz, Dominican Rebublic
2012	Roniel Iglesias Sotolongo, Cuba

WELTERWEIGHT (147 LB)

1904	Albert Young, United States
1920	Albert Schneider, Canada
1924	Jean Delarge, Belgium
1928	Edward Morgan, New Zealand
1932	Edward Flynn, United States
1936	Sten Suvio, Finland
1948	Julius Torma, Czechoslovakia
1952	Zygmunt Chychla, Poland
1956	Nicolae Linca, Romania

WELTERWEIGHT (147 LB) (*Cont.*)

1960	Giovanni Benvenuti, Italy
1964	Marian Kasprzyk, Poland
1968	Manfred Wolke, E Germany
1972	Emilio Correa, Cuba
1976	Jochen Bachfeld, E Germany
1980	Andres Aldama, Cuba
1984	Mark Breland, United States
1988	Robert Wangila, Kenya
1992	Michael Carruth, Ireland
1996	Oleg Saitov, Russia
2000	Oleg Saitov, Russia
2004	Bakhtiyar Artayev, Kazakhstan
2008	Bakhyt Sarsekbayev, Kazakhstan
2012	Serik Sapiyev, Kazakhstan

LIGHT MIDDLEWEIGHT (156 LB)

1952	Laszlo Papp, Hungary
1956	Laszlo Papp, Hungary
1960	Wilbert McClure, United States
1964	Boris Lagutin, USSR
1968	Boris Lagutin, USSR
1972	Dieter Kottysch, W Germany
1976	Jerzy Rybicki, Poland
1980	Armando Martinez, Cuba
1984	Frank Tate, United States
1988	Park Si-Hun, S Korea
1992	Juan Lemus, Cuba
1996	David Reid, United States
2000	Yermakhan Ibraimov, Kazakhstan

MIDDLEWEIGHT (165 LB)

1904	Charles Mayer, United States
1908	John Douglas, Great Britain
1920	Harry Mallin, Great Britain
1924	Harry Mallin, Great Britain
1928	Piero Toscani, Italy
1932	Carmen Barth, United States
1936	Jean Despeaux, France
1948	Laszlo Papp, Hungary
1952	Floyd Patterson, United States
1956	Gennady Schatkov, USSR
1960	Edward Crook, United States
1964	Valery Popenchenko, USSR
1968	Christopher Finnegan, Great Britain
1972	Vyacheslav Lemechev, USSR
1976	Michael Spinks, United States
1980	Jose Gomez, Cuba
1984	Shin Joon Sup, S Korea
1988	Henry Maske, E Germany
1992	Ariel Hernandez, Cuba
1996	Ariel Hernandez, Cuba
2000	Jorge Gutierrez, Cuba
2004	Gaydarbek Gaydarbekov, Russia
2008	James Degale, Great Britain
2012	Serik Sapiyev, Kazakhstan

LIGHT HEAVYWEIGHT (178 LB)

1920	Edward Eagan, United States
1924	Harry Mitchell, Great Britain
1928	Victor Avendano, Argentina
1932	David Carstens, S Africa
1936	Roger Michelot, France
1948	George Hunter, S Africa
1952	Norvel Lee, United States
1956	James Boyd, United States
1960	Cassius Clay, United States
1964	Cosimo Pinto, Italy
1968	Dan Poznyak, USSR
1972	Mate Parlov, Yugoslavia
1976	Leon Spinks, United States
1980	Slobodan Kacer, Yugoslavia

BOXING *(Cont.)*

LIGHT HEAVYWEIGHT (178 LB) *(Cont.)*

1984	Anton Josipovic, Yugoslavia
1988	Andrew Maynard, United States
1992	Torsten May, Germany
1996	Vassili Jirov, Kazakhstan
2000	Alexander Lebziak, Russia
2004	Andre Ward, United States
2008	Zhang Xiaoping, China
2012	Egor Mekhontcev, Russia

HEAVYWEIGHT*

1904	Samuel Berger, United States
1908	Albert Oldham, Great Britain
1920	Ronald Rawson, Great Britain
1924	Otto von Porat, Norway
1928	Arturo Rodriguez Jurado, Argentina
1932	Santiago Lovell, Argentina
1936	Herbert Runge, Germany
1948	Rafael Inglesias, Argentina
1952	H. Edward Sanders, United States
1956	T. Peter Rademacher, United States
1960	Franco De Piccoli, Italy
1964	Joe Frazier, United States
1968	George Foreman, United States
1972	Teofilo Stevenson, Cuba

HEAVYWEIGHT *(Cont.)*

1976	Teofilo Stevenson, Cuba
1980	Teofilo Stevenson, Cuba
1984	Henry Tjllman, United States
1988	Ray Mercer, United States
1992	Félix Sávon, Cuba
1996	Félix Sávon, Cuba
2000	Félix Sávon, Cuba
2004	Odlanier Fonte, Cuba
2008	Rakhim Chakhiev, Russia
2012	Oleksandr Usyk, Ukraine

SUPERHEAVYWEIGHT (UNLIMITED)

1984	Tyrell Biggs, United States
1988	Lennox Lewis, Canada
1992	Roberto Balado, Cuba
1996	Vladimir Klitchko, Ukraine
2000	Audley Harrison, Great Britain
2004	Alexander Povetkin, Russia
2008	Roberto Cammarelle, Italy
2012	Anthony Joshua, Great Britain

*Until 1984 the heavyweight division was unlimited. With the addition of the super heavyweight division, a limit of 201 pounds was imposed.

SWIMMING — Men

50-METER FREESTYLE

1904	Zoltan Halmay, Hungary (50 yds)	28.0
1988	Matt Biondi, United States	22.14 WR
1992	Aleksandr Popov, Unified Team	22.30
1996	Aleksandr Popov, Russia	22.13
2000	Anthony Ervin, United States	21.98
	Gary Hall Jr, United States	21.98
2004	Gary Hall Jr, United States	21.93
2008	Cesar Cielo Filho, Brazil	21.30 OR
2012	Florent Manaudou, France	21.34

100-METER FREESTYLE

1896	Alfred Hajos, Hungary	1:22.2 OR
1904	Zoltan Halmay, Hungary (100 yds)	1:02.8
1906	Charles Daniels, United States	1:13.4
1908	Charles Daniels, United States	1:05.6 WR
1912	Duke Kahanamoku, United States	1:03.4
1920	Duke Kahanamoku, United States	1:00.4 WR
1924	John Weissmuller, United States	59.0 OR
1928	John Weissmuller, United States	58.6 OR
1932	Yasuji Miyazaki, Japan	58.2
1936	Ferenc Csik, Hungary	57.6
1948	Wally Ris, United States	57.3 OR
1952	Clarke Scholes, United States	57.4
1956	Jon Henricks, Australia	55.4 WR
1960	John Devitt, Australia	55.2 OR
1964	Don Schollander, United States	53.4 OR
1968	Mike Wenden, Australia	52.2 WR
1972	Mark Spitz, United States	51.22 WR
1976	Jim Montgomery, United States	49.99 WR
1980	Jörg Woithe, E Germany	50.40
1984	Rowdy Gaines, United States	49.80 OR
1988	Matt Biondi, United States	48.63 OR
1992	Aleksandr Popov, Unified Team	49.02
1996	Aleksandr Popov, Russia	48.74
2000	P. van den Hoogenband, Neth	48.30
2004	P. van den Hoogenband, Neth	48.17
2008	Alain Bernard, France	47.21 OR
2012	Nathan Adrian, United States	47.52

200-METER FREESTYLE

1900	Frederick Lane, Australia	2:25.2 OR
1904	Charles Daniels, United States	2:44.2
1968	Michael Wenden, Australia	1:55.2 OR

200-METER FREESTYLE *(CONT.)*

1972	Mark Spitz, United States	1:52.78 WR
1976	Bruce Furniss, United States	1:50.29 WR
1980	Sergei Kopliakov, USSR	1:49.81 OR
1984	Michael Gross, W Germany	1:47.44 WR
1988	Duncan Armstrong, Australia	1:47.25 WR
1992	Evgueni Sadovyi, Unified Team	1:46.70 OR
1996	Danyon Loader, New Zealand	1:47.63
2000	Pieter van den Hoogenband, Neth	1:45.35 EWR
2004	Ian Thorpe, Australia	1:44.71 OR
2008	Michael Phelps, United States	1:42.96 WR
2012	Yannick Agnel, France	1:43.14

400-METER FREESTYLE

1896	Paul Neumann, Austria (500 yds)	8:12.6
1904	Charles Daniels, U.S. (440 yds)	6:16.2
1906	Otto Scheff, Austria (440 yds)	6:23.8
1908	Henry Taylor, Great Britain	5:36.8
1912	George Hodgson, Canada	5:24.4
1920	Norman Ross, United States	5:26.8
1924	John Weissmuller, United States	5:04.2 OR
1928	Albert Zorilla, Argentina	5:01.6 OR
1932	Buster Crabbe, United States	4:48.4 OR
1936	Jack Medica, United States	4:44.5 OR
1948	William Smith, United States	4:41.0 OR
1952	Jean Boiteux, France	4:30.7 OR
1956	Murray Rose, Australia	4:27.3 OR
1960	Murray Rose, Australia	4:18.3 OR
1964	Don Schollander, United States	4:12.2 WR
1968	Mike Burton, United States	4:09.0 OR
1972	Brad Cooper, Australia	4:00.27 OR
1976	Brian Goodell, United States	3:51.93 WR
1980	Vladimir Salnikov, USSR	3:51.31 OR
1984	George DiCarlo, United States	3:51.23 OR
1988	Uwe Dassler, E Germany	3:46.95 WR
1992	Evgueni Sadovyi, Unified Team	3:45.00 WR
1996	Danyon Loader, New Zealand	3:47.97
2000	Ian Thorpe, Australia	3:40.59 WR
2004	Ian Thorpe, Australia	3:43.10
2008	Park Taehwan, South Korea	3:41.86
2012	Yang Sun, China	3:40.14 OR

SWIMMING— Men *(Cont.)*

1,500-METER FREESTLYE

1908	Henry Taylor, Great Britain	22:48.4 WR
1912	George Hodgson, Canada	22:00.0 WR
1920	Norman Ross, United States	22:23.2
1924	Andrew Charlton, Australia	20:06.6 WR
1928	Arne Borg, Sweden	19:51.8 OR
1932	Kusuo Kitamura, Japan	19:12.4 OR
1936	Noboru Terada, Japan	19:13.7
1948	James McLane, United States	19:18.5
1952	Ford Konno, United States	18:30.3 OR
1956	Murray Rose, Australia	17:58.9
1960	John Konrads, Australia	17:19.6 OR
1964	Robert Windle, Australia	17:01.7 OR
1968	Mike Burton, United States	16:38.9 OR
1972	Mike Burton, United States	15:52.58 OR
1976	Brian Goodell, United States	15:02.40 WR
1980	Vladimir Salnikov, USSR	14:58.27 WR
1984	Michael O'Brien, United States	15:05.20
1988	Vladimir Salnikov, USSR	15:00.40
1992	Kieren Perkins, Australia	14:43.48 WR
1996	Kieren Perkins, Australia	14:56.40
2000	Grant Hackett, Australia	14:48.33
2004	Grant Hackett, Australia	14:43.40 OR
2008	Ousama Mellouli, Tunisia	14:40.84 OR
2012	Yang Sun, China	14:31.02 WR

100-METER BACKSTROKE

1904	Walter Brack, Germany (100 yds)	1:16.8
1908	Arno Bieberstein, Germany	1:24.6 WR
1912	Harry Hebner, United States	1:21.2
1920	Warren Kealoha, United States	1:15.2
1924	Warren Kealoha, United States	1:13.2 OR
1928	George Kojac, United States	1:08.2 WR
1932	Masaji Kiyokawa, Japan	1:08.6
1936	Adolph Kiefer, United States	1:05.9 OR
1948	Allen Stack, United States	1:06.4
1952	Yoshi Oyakawa, United States	1:05.4 OR
1956	David Thiele, Australia	1:02.2 OR
1960	David Thiele, Australia	1:01.9 OR
1968	Roland Matthes, E Germany	58.7 OR
1972	Roland Matthes, E Germany	56.58 OR
1976	John Naber, United States	55.49 WR
1980	Bengt Baron, Sweden	56.33
1984	Rick Carey, United States	55.79
1988	Daichi Suzuki, Japan	55.05
1992	Mark Tewksbury, Canada	53.98 WR
1996	Jeff Rouse, United States	54.10
2000	Lenny Krayzelburg, United States	53.72 OR
2004	Aaron Peirsol, United States	54.06
2008	Aaron Peirsol, United States	52.54 WR
2012	Matthew Grevers, United States	52.16 OR

200-METER BACKSTROKE

1900	Ernst Hoppenberg, Germany	2:47.0
1964	Jed Graef, United States	2:10.3 WR
1968	Roland Matthes, E Germany	2:09.6 OR
1972	Roland Matthes, E Germany	2:02.82 EWR
1976	John Naber, United States	1:59.19 WR
1980	Sandor Wladar, Hungary	2:01.93
1984	Rick Carey, United States	2:00.23
1988	Igor Polianski, USSR	1:59.37
1992	Martin Lopez-Zubero, Spain	1:58.47 OR
1996	Brad Bridgewater, United States	1:58.54
2000	Lenny Krayzelburg, United States	1:56.76 OR
2004	Aaron Peirsol, United States	1:54.95 OR
2008	Ryan Lochte, United States	1:53.94 WR
2012	Tyler Clary, United States	1:53.41 OR

100-METER BREASTROKE

1968	Don McKenzie, United States	1:07.7 OR

100-METER BREASTROKE *(CONT.)*

1972	Nobutaka Taguchi, Japan	1:04.94 WR
1976	John Hencken, United States	1:03.11 WR
1980	Duncan Goodhew, Great Britain	1:03.44
1984	Steve Lundquist, United States	1:01.65 WR
1988	Adrian Moorhouse, Great Britain	1:02.04
1992	Nelson Diebel, United States	1:01.50 OR
1996	Fred DeBurghgraeve, Belgium	1:00.65
2000	Domenico Fioravanti, Italy	1:00.46 OR
2004	Kosuke Kitajima, Japan	1:00.08
2008	Kosuke Kitajima, Japan	58.91 WR
2012	Cameron van der Burgh, S. Africa	58.46 WR

200-METER BREASTSTROKE

1908	Frederick Holman, Great Britain	3:09.2 WR
1912	Walter Bathe, Germany	3:01.8 OR
1920	Haken Malmroth, Sweden	3:04.4
1924	Robert Skelton, United States	2:56.6
1928	Yoshiyuki Tsuruta, Japan	2:48.8 OR
1932	Yoshiyuki Tsuruta, Japan	2:45.4
1936	Tetsuo Hamuro, Japan	2:41.5 OR
1948	Joseph Verdeur, United States	2:39.3 OR
1952	John Davies, Australia	2:34.4 OR
1956	Masura Furukawa, Japan	2:34.7 OR
1960	William Mulliken, United States	2:37.4
1964	Ian O'Brien, Australia	2:27.8 WR
1968	Felipe Munoz, Mexico	2:28.7
1972	John Hencken, United States	2:21.55 WR
1976	David Wilkie, Great Britain	2:15.11 WR
1980	Robertas Zhulpa, USSR	2:15.85
1984	Victor Davis, Canada	2:13.34 WR
1988	Jozsef Szabo, Hungary	2:13.52
1992	Mike Barrowman, United States	2:10.16 WR
1996	Norbert Rózsa, Hungary	2:12.57
2000	Domenico Fioravanti, Italy	2:10.87
2004	Kosuke Kitajima, Japan	2:09.44 OR
2008	Kosuke Kitajima, Japan	2:07.64 OR
2012	Daniel Gyurta, Hungary	2:07.28 WR

100-METER BUTTERFLY

1968	Doug Russell, United States	55.9 OR
1972	Mark Spitz, United States	54.27 WR
1976	Matt Vogel, United States	54.35
1980	Pär Arvidsson, Sweden	54.92
1984	Michael Gross, W Germany	53.08 WR
1988	Anthony Nesty, Suriname	53.00 OR
1992	Pablo Morales, United States	53.32
1996	Denis Pankratov, Russia	52.27 WR
2000	Lars Froelander, Sweden	52.00
2004	Michael Phelps, United States	51.25 OR
2008	Michael Phelps, United States	50.58 OR
2012	Michael Phelps, United States	51.21

200-METER BUTTERFLY

1956	William Yorzyk, United States	2:19.3 OR
1960	Michael Troy, United States	2:12.8 WR
1964	Kevin Berry, Australia	2:06.6 WR
1968	Carl Robie, United States	2:08.7
1972	Mark Spitz, United States	2:00.70 WR
1976	Mike Bruner, United States	1:59.23 WR
1980	Sergei Fesenko, USSR	1:59.76
1984	Jon Sieben, Australia	1:57.04 WR
1988	Michael Gross, W Germany	1:56.94 OR
1992	Melvin Stewart, United States	1:56.26 OR
1996	Denis Pankratov, Russia	1:56.51
2000	Tom Malchow, United States	1:55.35 OR
2004	Michael Phelps, United States	1:54.04 OR
2008	Michael Phelps, United States	1:52.03 WR
2012	Chad le Clos, South Africa	1:52.96

Note: OR=Olympic Record. WR=World Record. EOR=Equals Olympic Record. EWR=Equals World Record. WB=World Best.

SWIMMING — Men *(Cont.)*

200-METER INDIVIDUAL MEDLEY

1968	Charles Hickcox, United States	2:12.0 OR
1972	Gunnar Larsson, Sweden	2:07.17 WR
1984	Alex Baumann, Canada	2:01.42 WR
1988	Tamas Darnyi, Hungary	2:00.17 WR
1992	Tamas Darnyi, Hungary	2:00.76
1996	Attila Czene, Hungary	1:59.91 OR
2000	Massimiliano Rosolino, Italy	1:58.98 OR
2004	Michael Phelps, United States	1:57.14 OR
2008	Michael Phelps, United States	1:54.23 WR
2012	Michael Phelps, United States	1:54.27

400-METER INDIVIDUAL MEDLEY

1964	Richard Roth, United States	4:45.4 WR
1968	Charles Hickcox, United States	4:48.4
1972	Gunnar Larsson, Sweden	4:31.98 OR
1976	Rod Strachan, United States	4:23.68 WR
1980	Aleksandr Sidorenko, USSR	4:22.89 OR
1984	Alex Baumann, Canada	4:17.41 WR
1988	Tamas Darnyi, Hungary	4:14.75 WR
1992	Tamas Darnyi, Hungary	4:14.23 OR
1996	Tom Dolan United States	4:14.90
2000	Tom Dolan, United States	4:11.76 WR
2004	Michael Phelps, United States	4:08.26 WR
2008	Michael Phelps, United States	4:03.84 WR
2012	Ryan Lochte, United States	4:05.18

4 X 100-METER MEDLEY RELAY

1960	United States	4:05.4 WR
1964	United States	3:58.4 WR
1968	United States	3:54.9 WR
1972	United States	3:48.16 WR
1976	United States	3:42.22 WR
1980	Australia	3:45.70
1984	United States	3:39.30 WR
1988	United States	3:36.93 WR
1992	United States	3:36.93 EWR
1996	United States	3:34.84 WR
2000	United States	3:33.73 WR
2004	United States	3:30.68 WR
2008	United States	3:29.34 WR
2012	United States	3:29.35

4 X 100-METER FREESTYLE RELAY

1964	United States	3:32.2 WR
1968	United States	3:31.7 WR
1972	United States	3:26.42 WR
1984	United States	3:19.03 WR
1988	United States	3:16.53 WR
1992	United States	3:16.74
1996	United States	3:15.41 OR
2000	Australia	3:13.67 WR
2004	S Africa	3:13.17 WR
2008	United States	3:08.24 WR
2012	France	3:09.93

4 X 200-METER FREESTYLE RELAY

1906	Hungary (1,000 m)	16:52.4
1908	Great Britain	10:55.6
1912	Australia/New Zealand	10:11.6 WR
1920	United States	10:04.4 WR
1924	United States	9:53.4 WR
1928	United States	9:36.2 WR
1932	Japan	8:58.4 WR
1936	Japan	8:51.5 WR
1948	United States	8:46.0 WR
1952	United States	8:31.1 OR
1956	Australia	8:23.6 WR
1960	United States	8:10.2 WR
1964	United States	7:52.1 WR
1968	United States	7:52.33
1972	United States	7:35.78 WR
1976	United States	7:23.22 WR
1980	USSR	7:23.50
1984	United States	7:15.69 WR
1988	United States	7:12.51 WR
1992	Unified Team	7:11.95 WR
1996	United States	7:14.84
2000	Australia	7:07.05 WR
2004	United States	7:07.33
2008	United States	6:58.56 WR
2012	United States	6:59.70

10 KM MARATHON

2008	M. van der Weijden, Neth.	1:51:51.60
2012	Oussama Mellouli, Tunisia	1:49:55.1

SWIMMING — Women

50-METER FREESTYLE

1988	Kristin Otto, E Germany	25.49 OR
1992	Yang Wenyi, China	24.79 WR
1996	Amy Van Dyken, United States	24.87
2000	Inge de Bruijn, Netherlands	24.32 WR
2004	Inge de Bruijn, Netherlands	24.58
2008	Britta Steffen, Germany	24.06 OR
2012	Ranomi Kromowidjojo, Netherlands	24.05 OR

100-METER FREESTYLE

1912	Fanny Durack, Australia	1:22.2
1920	Ethelda Bleibtrey, United States	1:13.6 WR
1924	Ethel Lackie, United States	1:12.4
1928	Albina Osipowich, United States	1:11.0 OR
1932	Helene Madison, United States	1:06.8 OR
1936	Hendrika Mastenbroek, Neth	1:05.9 OR
1948	Greta Andersen, Denmark	1:06.3
1952	Katalin Szöke, Hungary	1:06.8
1956	Dawn Fraser, Australia	1:02.0 WR
1960	Dawn Fraser, Australia	1:01.2 OR
1964	Dawn Fraser, Australia	59.5 OR
1968	Jan Henne, United States	1:00.0
1972	Sandra Neilson, United States	58.59 OR
1976	Kornelia Ender, E Germany	55.65 WR
1980	Barbara Krause, E Germany	54.79 WR

100-METER FREESTYLE *(CONT.)*

1984	Carrie Steinseifer, United States	55.92
	Nancy Hogshead, United States	55.92
1988	Kristin Otto, E Germany	54.93
1992	Zhuang Yong, China	54.64 OR
1996	Le Jingyi, China	54.50 OR
2000	Inge de Bruijn, Netherlands	53.83 OR
2004	Jodie Henry, Australia	53.84
2008	Britta Steffen, Germany	53.12 OR
2012	Ranomi Kromowidjojo, Netherlands	53.00 OR

200-METER FREESTYLE

1968	Debbie Meyer, United States	2:10.5 OR
1972	Shane Gould, Australia	2:03.56 WR
1976	Kornelia Ender, E Germany	1:59.26 WR
1980	Barbara Krause, E Germany	1:58.33 OR
1984	Mary Wayte, United States	1:59.23
1988	Heike Friedrich, E Germany	1:57.65 OR
1992	Nicole Haislett, United States	1:57.90
1996	Claudia Poll, Costa Rica	1:58.16
2000	Susie O'Neill, Australia	1:58.24
2004	Camelia Potec, Romania	1:58.03
2008	Frederica Pellegrini, Italy	1:54.82 WR
2012	Allison Schmitt, United States	1:53.61 OR

Note: OR=Olympic Record. WR=World Record. EOR=Equals Olympic Record. EWR=Equals World Record. WB=World Best.

SWIMMING — Women *(Cont.)*

400-METER FREESTYLE

1924	Martha Norelius, United States	6:02.2 OR
1928	Martha Norelius, United States	5:42.8 WR
1932	Helene Madison, United States	5:28.5 WR
1936	Hendrika Mastenbroek, Neth	5:26.4 OR
1948	Ann Curtis, United States	5:17.8 OR
1952	Valeria Gyenge, Hungary	5:12.1 OR
1956	Lorraine Crapp, Australia	4:54.6 OR
1960	Chris von Saltza, United States	4:50.6 OR
1964	Virginia Duenkel, United States	4:43.3 OR
1968	Debbie Meyer, United States	4:31.8 OR
1972	Shane Gould, Australia	4:19.44 WR
1976	Petra Thümer, E Germany	4:09.89 WR
1980	Ines Diers, E Germany	4:08.76 WR
1984	Tiffany Cohen, United States	4:07.10 OR
1988	Janet Evans, United States	4:03.85 WR
1992	Dagmar Hase, Germany	4:07.18
1996	Michelle Smith, Ireland	4:07.25
2000	Brooke Bennett, United States	4:05.80
2004	Laure Manaudou, France	4:05.34
2008	Rebecca Adlington, Great Britain	4:03.22
2012	Camille Muffat, France	4:01.45 OR

800-METER FREESTYLE

1968	Debbie Meyer, United States	9:24.0 OR
1972	Keena Rothhammer, United States	8:53.68 WR
1976	Petra Thümer, E Germany	8:37.14 WR
1980	Michelle Ford, Australia	8:28.90 OR
1984	Tiffany Cohen, United States	8:24.95 OR
1988	Janet Evans, United States	8:20.20 OR
1992	Janet Evans, United States	8:25.52
1996	Brooke Bennett, United States	8:27.89
2000	Brooke Bennett, United States	8:19.67 OR
2004	Ai Shibata, Japan	8:24.54
2008	Rebecca Adlington, Great Britain	8:14.10 WR
2012	Katie Ledecky, United States	8:14.63

100-METER BACKSTROKE

1924	Sybil Bauer, United States	1:23.2 OR
1928	Marie Braun, Netherlands	1:22.0
1932	Eleanor Holm, United States	1:19.4
1936	Dina Senff, Netherlands	1:18.9
1948	Karen Harup, Denmark	1:14.4 OR
1952	Joan Harrison, South Africa	1:14.3
1956	Judy Grinham, Great Britain	1:12.9 OR
1960	Lynn Burke, United States	1:09.3 OR
1964	Cathy Ferguson, United States	1:07.7 WR
1968	Kaye Hall, United States	1:06.2 WR
1972	Melissa Belote, United States	1:05.78 OR
1976	Ulrike Richter, E Germany	1:01.83 OR
1980	Rica Reinisch, E Germany	1:00.86 WR
1984	Theresa Andrews, United States	1:02.55
1988	Kristin Otto, E Germany	1:00.89
1992	Krisztina Egerszegi, Hungary	1:00.68 OR
1996	Beth Botsford, United States	1:01.19
2000	Diana Iuliana Mocanu, Romania	1:00.21 OR
2004	Natalie Coughlin, United States	1:00.37
2008	Natalie Coughlin, United States	58.96
2012	Missy Franklin, United States	58.33

200-METER BACKSTROKE

1968	Pokey Watson, United States	2:24.8 OR
1972	Melissa Belote, United States	2:19.19 WR
1976	Ulrike Richter, E Germany	2:13.43 OR
1980	Rica Reinisch, E Germany	2:11.77 WR
1984	Jolanda De Rover, Netherlands	2:12.38
1988	Krisztina Egerszegi, Hungary	2:09.29 OR
1992	Krisztina Egerszegi, Hungary	2:07.06 OR
1996	Krisztina Egerszegi, Hungary	2:07.83
2000	Diana Iuliana Mocanu, Romania	2:08.16
2004	Kirsty Coventry, Zimbabwe	2:09.19

200-METER BACKSTROKE *(CONT.)*

2008	Kirsty Coventry, Zimbabwe	2:05.24 WR
2012	Missy Franklin, United States	1:58.33

100-METER BREASTSTROKE

1968	Djurdjica Bjedov, Yugoslavia	1:15.8 OR
1972	Catherine Carr, United States	1:13.58 WR
1976	Hannelore Anke, E Germany	1:11.16
1980	Ute Geweniger, E Germany	1:10.22
1984	Petra Van Staveren, Netherlands	1:09.88 OR
1988	Tania Dangalakova, Bulgaria	1:07.95 OR
1992	Elena Roudkovskaia, Unified Team	1:08.00
1996	Penelope Heyns, S Africa	1:07.73
2000	Megan Quann, United States	1:07.05
2004	Xue Juan Luo, China	1:06.64
2008	Liesel Jones, Australia	1:05.17 WR
2012	Ruta Meilutyte, Lithuania	1:05.47

200-METER BREASTSTROKE

1924	Lucy Morton, Great Britain	3:33.2 OR
1928	Hilde Schrader, Germany	3:12.6
1932	Clare Dennis, Australia	3:06.3 OR
1936	Hideko Maehata, Japan	3:03.6
1948	Petronella Van Vliet, Netherlands	2:57.2
1952	Eva Szekely, Hungary	2:51.7 OR
1956	Ursula Happe, W Germany	2:53.1 OR
1960	Anita Lonsbrough, Great Britain	2:49.5 WR
1964	Galina Prozumenshikova, USSR	2:46.4 OR
1968	Sharon Wichman, United States	2:44.4 OR
1972	Beverly Whitfield, Australia	2:41.71 OR
1976	Marina Koshevaia, USSR	2:33.35 WR
1980	Lina Kaciusyte, USSR	2:29.54 OR
1984	Anne Ottenbrite, Canada	2:30.38
1988	Silke Hoerner, E Germany	2:26.71 WR
1992	Kyoko Iwasaki, Japan	2:26.65 OR
1996	Penelope Heyns, S Africa	2:25.41 OR
2000	Agnes Kovacs, Hungary	2:24.35 OR
2004	Amanda Beard, United States	2:23.37 OR
2008	Rebecca Soni, United States	2:20.22 WR
2012	Rebecca Soni, United States	2:19.59 WR

100-METER BUTTERFLY

1956	Shelley Mann, United States	1:11.0 OR
1960	Carolyn Schuler, United States	1:09.5 OR
1964	Sharon Stouder, United States	1:04.7 WR
1968	Lynn McClements, Australia	1:05.5
1972	Mayumi Aoki, Japan	1:03.34 WR
1976	Kornelia Ender, E Germany	1:00.13 EWR
1980	Caren Metschuck, E Germany	1:00.42
1984	Mary T. Meagher, United States	59.26
1988	Kristin Otto, E Germany	59.00 OR
1992	Qian Hong, China	58.62 OR
1996	Amy Van Dyken, United States	59.13
2000	Inge de Bruijn, Netherlands	56.61 WR
2004	Petria Thomas, Australia	57.72
2008	Lisbeth Trickett, Australia	56.73
2012	Dana Vollmer, United States	55.98 WR

200-METER BUTTERFLY

1968	Ada Kok, Netherlands	2:24.7 OR
1972	Karen Moe, United States	2:15.57 WR
1976	Andrea Pollack, E Germany	2:11.41 OR
1980	Ines Geissler, E Germany	2:10.44 OR
1984	Mary T. Meagher, United States	2:06.90 OR
1988	Kathleen Nord, E Germany	2:09.51
1992	Summer Sanders, United States	2:08.67
1996	Susan O'Neill, Australia	2:07.76
2000	Misty Hyman, United States	2:05.88 OR
2004	Otylia Jedrzejczak, Poland	2:06.05
2008	Liu Zige, China	2:04.18 WR
2012	Liuyang Jiao, China	2:04.06 WR

Note: OR=Olympic Record. WR=World Record. EOR=Equals Olympic Record. EWR=Equals World Record. WB=World Best.

SWIMMING — Women (Cont.)

200-METER INDIVIDUAL MEDLEY

1968	Claudia Kolb, United States	2:24.7 OR
1972	Shane Gould, Australia	2:23.07 WR
1984	Tracy Caulkins, United States	2:12.64 OR
1988	Daniela Hunger, E Germany	2:12.59 OR
1992	Lin Li, China	2:11.65 WR
1996	Michelle Smith, Ireland	2:13.93
2000	Yana Klochkova, Ukraine	2:10.68 OR
2004	Yana Klochkova, Ukraine	2:11.14
2008	Stephanie Rice, Australia	2:08.45 WR
2012	Shiwen Ye, China	2:07.57 OR

400-METER INDIVIDUAL MEDLEY

1964	Donna de Varona, United States	5:18.7 OR
1968	Claudia Kolb, United States	5:08.5 OR
1972	Gail Neall, Australia	5:02.97 WR
1976	Ulrike Tauber, E Germany	4:42.77 WR
1980	Petra Schneider, E Germany	4:36.29 WR
1984	Tracy Caulkins, United States	4:39.24
1988	Janet Evans, United States	4:37.76
1992	Krisztina Egerszegi, Hungary	4:36.54
1996	Michelle Smith, Ireland	4:39.18
2000	Yana Klochkova, Ukraine	4:33.59 WR
2004	Yana Klochkova, Ukraine	4:34.83
2008	Stephanie Rice, Australia	4:29.45 WR
2012	Shiwen Ye, China	4:28.43 WR

4 X 100-METER MEDLEY RELAY

1960	United States	4:41.1 WR
1964	United States	4:33.9 WR
1968	United States	4:28.3 OR
1972	United States	4:20.75 WR
1976	E Germany	4:07.95 WR
1980	E Germany	4:06.67 WR
1984	United States	4:08.34
1988	E Germany	4:03.74 OR
1992	United States	4:02.54 WR
1996	United States	4:02.88
2000	United States	3:58:30 WR

4 X 100-METER MEDLEY RELAY (CONT.)

2004	Australia	3:57.32 WR
2008	Australia	3:52.69 WR
2012	United States	3:52.05 WR

4 X 100-METER FREESTYLE RELAY

1912	Great Britain	5:52.8 WR
1920	United States	5:11.6 WR
1924	United States	4:58.8 WR
1928	United States	4:47.6 WR
1932	United States	4:38.0 WR
1936	Netherlands	4:36.0 OR
1948	United States	4:29.2 OR
1952	Hungary	4:24.4 WR
1956	Australia	4:17.1 WR
1960	United States	4:08.9 WR
1964	United States	4:03.8 WR
1968	United States	4:02.5 OR
1972	United States	3:55.19 WR
1976	United States	3:44.82 WR
1980	E Germany	3:42.71 WR
1984	United States	3:43.43
1988	E Germany	3:40.63 OR
1992	United States	3:39.46 WR
1996	United States	3:39.29 OR
2000	United States	3:36.61 WR
2004	Australia	3:35.94 WR
2008	Netherlands	3:33.76 OR
2012	Australia	

4 X 200-METER FREESTYLE RELAY

1996	United States	7:59.87
2000	United States	7:57.80 OR
2004	United States	7:53.42 WR
2008	Australia	7:44.31 WR
2012	United States	3:33.15 OR

10 KM MARATHON

2008	Larisa Ilchenko, Russia	1:59:27.70
2012	Eva Risztov, Hungary	1:57:38.2

DIVING — Men

SPRINGBOARD		Pts
1908	Albert Zürner, Germany	85.5
1912	Paul Günther, Germany	79.23
1920	Louis Kuehn, United States	675.40
1924	Albert White, United States	97.46
1928	Pete DesJardins, United States	185.04
1932	Michael Galitzen, United States	161.38
1936	Richard Degener, United States	163.57
1948	Bruce Harlan, United States	163.64
1952	David Browning, United States	205.29
1956	Robert Clotworthy, United States	159.56
1960	Gary Tobian, United States	170.00
1964	Kenneth Sitzberger, United States	159.90
1968	Bernie Wrightson, United States	170.15
1972	Vladimir Vasin, USSR	594.09
1976	Phil Boggs, United States	619.05
1980	Aleksandr Portnov, USSR	905.02
1984	Greg Louganis, United States	754.41
1988	Greg Louganis, United States	730.80
1992	Mark Lenzi, United States	676.53
1996	Xiong Ni, China	701.46
2000	Xiong Ni, China	708.72
2004	Bo Peng, China	787.38
2008	He Chong, China	572.90
2012	Ilya Zakharov, Russia	555.90

PLATFORM		Pts
1904	George Sheldon, United States	12.66
1906	Gottlob Walz, Germany	156.0
1908	Hjalmar Johansson, Sweden	83.75
1912	Erik Adlerz, Sweden	73.94
1920	Clarence Pinkston, United States	100.67
1924	Albert White, United States	97.46
1928	Pete DesJardins, United States	98.74
1932	Harold Smith, United States	124.80
1936	Marshall Wayne, United States	113.58
1948	Sammy Lee, United States	130.05
1952	Sammy Lee, United States	156.28
1956	Joaquin Capilla, Mexico	152.44
1960	Robert Webster, United States	165.56
1964	Robert Webster, United States	148.58
1968	Klaus Dibiasi, Italy	164.18
1972	Klaus Dibiasi, Italy	504.12
1976	Klaus Dibiasi, Italy	600.51
1980	Falk Hoffmann, E Germany	835.65
1984	Greg Louganis, United States	710.91
1988	Greg Louganis, United States	638.61
1992	Sun Shuwei, China	677.31
1996	Dmitri Sautin, Russia	692.34
2000	Tian Liang, China	724.53
2004	Jia Hu, China	748.08
2008	Matthew Mitcham, Australia	537.95
2012	David Boudia, United States	568.65

DIVING — Women

SPRINGBOARD	Pts		PLATFORM	Pts
1920.....Aileen Riggin, United States	539.90	1912.....Greta Johansson, Sweden	39.90
1924.....Elizabeth Becker, United States	474.50	1920.....Stefani Fryland-Clausen, Denmark	34.60
1928.....Helen Meany, United States	78.62	1924.....Caroline Smith, United States	33.20
1932.....Georgia Coleman, United States	87.52	1928.....Elizabeth B. Pinkston, United States	31.60
1936.....Marjorie Gestring, United States	89.27	1932.....Dorothy Poynton, United States	40.26
1948.....Victoria Draves, United States	108.74	1936.....Dorothy Poynton Hill, United States	33.93
1952.....Patricia McCormick, United States	147.30	1948.....Victoria Draves, United States	68.87
1956.....Patricia McCormick, United States	142.36	1952.....Patricia McCormick, United States	79.37
1960.....Ingrid Krämer, E Germany	155.81	1956.....Patricia McCormick, United States	84.85
1964.....Ingrid Engel Krämer, E Germany	145.00	1960.....Ingrid Krämer, E Germany	91.28
1968.....Sue Gossick, United States	150.77	1964.....Lesley Bush, United States	99.80
1972.....Micki King, United States	450.03	1968.....Milena Duchkova, Czechoslovakia	109.59
1976.....Jennifer Chandler, United States	506.19	1972.....Ulrika Knape, Sweden	390.00
1980.....Irina Kalinina, USSR	725.91	1976.....Elena Vaytsekhovskaya, USSR	406.59
1984.....Sylvie Bernier, Canada	530.70	1980.....Martina Jäschke, E Germany	596.25
1988.....Gao Min, China	580.23	1984.....Zhou Jihong, China	435.51
1992.....Gao Min, China	572.40	1988.....Xu Yanmei, China	445.20
1996.....Mingxia Fu, China	547.68	1992.....Mingxia Fu, China	461.43
2000.....Mingxia Fu, China	609.42	1996.....Mingxia Fu, China	521.58
2004.....Guo Jingjing, China	633.15	2000.....Laura Wilkinson, United States	543.75
2008.....Guo Jingjing, China	415.35	2004.....Chantelle Newbery, Australia	590.31
2012.....Minxia Wu, China	414.00	2008.....Chen Ruoulin, China	447.70
		2012.....Chen Ruolin, China	422.3

GYMNASTICS — Men

ALL-AROUND	Pts		HORIZONTAL BAR *(CONT.)*	Pts
1900.....Gustave Sandras, France	302	1980.....Stoyan Deltchev, Bulgaria	19.825
1904.....Julius Lenhart, Austria	69.80	1984.....Shinji Morisue, Japan	20.00
1906.....Pierre Paysse, France	97	1988.....Vladimir Artemov, USSR	19.90
1908.....Alberto Braglia, Italy	317.0	1992.....Trent Dimas, United States	9.875
1912.....Alberto Braglia, Italy	135.0	1996.....Andreas Wecker, Germany	9.850
1920.....Giorgio Zampori, Italy	88.35	2000.....Alexei Nemov, Russia	9.787
1924.....Leon Stukelj, Yugoslavia	110.340	2004.....Igor Cassina, Italy	9.812
1928.....Georges Miez, Switzerland	247.500	2008.....Zou Kai, China	16.200
1932.....Romeo Neri, Italy	140.625	2012.....Epke Zonderland, Netherlands	16.533
1936.....Alfred Schwarzmann, Germany	113.100		
1948.....Veikko Huhtanen, Finland	229.70	PARALLEL BARS	Pts
1952.....Viktor Chukarin, USSR	115.70	1896.....Alfred Flatow, Germany	—
1956.....Viktor Chukarin, USSR	114.25	1904.....George Eyser, United States	44
1960.....Boris Shakhlin, USSR	115.95	1924.....August Güttinger, Switzerland	21.63
1964.....Yukio Endo, Japan	115.95	1928.....Ladislav Vacha, Czechoslovakia	18.83
1968.....Sawao Kato, Japan	115.90	1932.....Romeo Neri, Italy	18.97
1972.....Sawao Kato, Japan	114.65	1936.....Konrad Frey, Germany	19.067
1976.....Nikolai Andrianov, USSR	116.65	1948.....Michael Reusch, Switzerland	19.75
1980.....Aleksandr Dityatin, USSR	118.65	1952.....Hans Eugster, Switzerland	19.65
1984.....Koji Gushiken, Japan	118.70	1956.....Viktor Chukarin, USSR	19.20
1988.....Vladimir Artemov, USSR	119.125	1960.....Boris Shakhlin, USSR	19.40
1992.....Vitaly Scherbo, Unified Team	59.025	1964.....Yukio Endo, Japan	19.675
1996.....Li Xiaoshuang, China	58.423	1968.....Akinori Nakayama, Japan	19.475
2000.....Alexei Nemov, Russia	58.474	1972.....Sawao Kato, Japan	19.475
2004.....Paul Hamm, United States	57.823	1976.....Sawao Kato, Japan	19.675
2008.....Yang Wei, China	94.575	1980.....Aleksandr Tkachyov, USSR	19.775
2012.....Kohei Uchimura, Japan	92.690	1984.....Bart Conner, United States	19.95
		1988.....Vladimir Artemov, USSR	19.925
HORIZONTAL BAR	Pts	1992.....Vitaly Scherbo, Unified Team	9.900
1896.....Hermann Weingärtner, Germany	—	1996.....Rustan Sharipov, Ukraine	9.837
1904.....Anton Heida, United States	40	2000.....Li Xiaopeng, China	9.825
1924.....Leon Stukelj, Yugoslavia	19.73	2004.....Valeri Goncharov, Ukraine	9.787
1928.....Georges Miez, Switzerland	19.17	2008.....Li Xiaopeng, China	16.450
1932.....Dallas Bixler, United States	18.33	2012.....Zhe Feng, China	15.966
1936.....Aleksanteri Saarvala, Finland	19.367		
1948.....Josef Stalder, Switzerland	19.85	VAULT	Pts
1952.....Jack Günthard, Switzerland	19.55	1896.....Karl Schumann, Germany	Pts
1956.....Takashi Ono, Japan	19.60	1904.....George Eyser, United States	36
1960.....Takashi Ono, Japan	19.60	1924.....Frank Kriz, United States	9.98
1964.....Boris Shakhlin, USSR	19.625	1928.....Eugen Mack, Switzerland	9.58
1968.....Akinori Nakayama, Japan	19.55	1932.....Savino Guglielmetti, Italy	• 18.03
1972.....Mitsuo Tsukahara, Japan	19.725	1936.....Alfred Schwarzmann, Germany	19.20
1976.....Mitsuo Tsukahara, Japan	19.675	1948.....Paavo Aaltonen, Finland	19.55
		1952.....Viktor Chukarin, USSR	19.20

GYMNASTICS — Men *(Cont.)*

VAULT *(CONT.)*	Pts
1956.....Helmut Bantz, Germany	18.85
1960.....Takashi Ono, Japan	19.35
1964.....Haruhiro Yamashita, Japan	19.60
1968.....Mikhail Voronin, USSR	19.00
1972.....Klaus Köste, E Germany	18.85
1976.....Nikolai Andrianov, USSR	19.45
1980.....Nikolai Andrianov, USSR	19.825
1984.....Lou Yun, China	19.95
1988.....Lou Yun, China	19.875
1992.....Vitaly Scherbo, Unified Team	9.856
1996.....Alexei Nemov, Russia	9.787
2000.....Gervasio Deferr, Spain	9.712
2004.....Gervasio Deferr, Spain	9.737
2008.....Leszek Blanik, Poland	16.537
2012.....Hak Seon Yang, South Korea	16.533

POMMEL HORSE	Pts
1896.....Louis Zutter, Switzerland	—
1904.....Anton Heida, United States	42
1924.....Josef Wilhelm, Switzerland	21.23
1928.....Hermann Hänggi, Switzerland	19.75
1932.....Istvan Pelle, Hungary	19.07
1936.....Konrad Frey, Germany	19.333
1948.....Paavo Aaltonen, Finland	19.35
1952.....Viktor Chukarin, USSR	19.50
1956.....Boris Shakhlin, USSR	19.25
1960.....Eugen Ekman, Finland	19.375
1964.....Miroslav Cerar, Yugoslavia	19.525
1968.....Miroslav Cerar, Yugoslavia	19.325
1972.....Viktor Klimenko, USSR	19.125
1976.....Zoltan Magyar, Hungary	19.70
1980.....Zoltan Magyar, Hungary	19.925
1984.....Li Ning, China	19.95
1988.....Dmitri Bilozerchev, USSR	19.95
1992.....Vitaly Scherbo, Unified Team	9.925
1996.....Donghua Li, Switzerland	9.875
2000.....Marius Urzica, Romania	9.862
2004.....Haibin Teng, China	9.837
2008.....Xiao Oin, China	15.875
2012.....Krisztian Berki, Hungary	16.066

RINGS	Pts
1896.....Ioannis Mitropoulos, Greece	—
1904.....Hermann Glass, United States	45
1924.....Francesco Martino, Italy	21.553
1928.....Leon Stukelj, Yugoslavia	19.25
1932.....George Gulack, United States	18.97
1936.....Alois Hudec, Czechoslovakia	19.433
1948.....Karl Frei, Switzerland	19.80
1952.....Grant Shaginyan, USSR	19.75
1956.....Albert Azaryan, USSR	19.35
1960.....Albert Azaryan, USSR	19.725
1964.....Takuji Haytta, Japan	19.475
1968.....Akinori Nakayama, Japan	19.45
1972.....Akinori Nakayama, Japan	19.35
1976.....Nikolai Andrianov, USSR	19.65
1980.....Aleksandr Dityatin, USSR	19.875

RINGS *(CONT.)*	Pts
1984.....Koji Gushiken, Japan	19.85
1988.....Holger Behrendt, E Germany	19.925
1992.....Vitaly Scherbo, Unified Team	9.937
1996.....Yuri Chechi, Italy	9.887
2000.....Szilveszter Csollany, Hungary	9.862
2004.....Dimosthenis Tampakos, Greece	9.862
2008.....Chen Yibing, China	16.600
2012.....Arthur Nabarrete Zanetti, Brazil	15.900

FLOOR EXERCISE	Pts
1932.....Istvan Pelle, Hungary	9.60
1936.....Georges Miez, Switzerland	18.666
1948.....Ferenc Pataki, Hungary	19.35
1952.....K. William Thoresson, Sweden	19.25
1956.....Valentin Muratov, USSR	19.20
1960.....Nobuyuki Aihara, Japan	19.45
1964.....Franco Menichelli, Italy	19.45
1968.....Sawao Kato, Japan	19.475
1972.....Nikolai Andrianov, USSR	19.175
1976.....Nikolai Andrianov, USSR	19.45
1980.....Roland Brückner, E Germany	19.75
1984.....Li Ning, China	19.925
1988.....Sergei Kharkov, USSR	19.925
1992.....Li Xiaoshuang, China	9.925
1996.....Ioannis Melissanidis, Greece	9.850
2000.....Igors Vihrovs, Latvia	9.812
2004.....Kyle Shewfelt, Canada	9.787
2008.....Kai Zou, China	16.050
2012.....Kai Zou, China	15.933

TEAM COMBINED EXERCISES	Pts
1904.....Turngemeinde Philadelphia	374.43
1906.....Norway	19.00
1908.....Sweden	438
1912.....Italy	265.75
1920.....Italy	359.855
1924.....Italy	839.058
1928.....Switzerland	1718.625
1932.....Italy	541.850
1936.....Germany	657.430
1948.....Finland	1358.30
1952.....USSR	574.40
1956.....USSR	568.25
1960.....Japan	575.20
1964.....Japan	577.95
1968.....Japan	575.90
1972.....Japan	571.25
1976.....Japan	576.85
1980.....USSR	598.60
1984.....United States	591.40
1988.....USSR	593.35
1992.....Unified Team	585.45
1996.....Russia	576.778
2000.....China	231.919
2004.....Japan	173.821
2008.....China	286.125
2012.....China	275.997

GYMNASTICS — Women

ALL-AROUND	Pts
1952 .....Maria Gorokhovskaya, USSR	76.78
1956 .....Larissa Latynina, USSR	74.933
1960 .....Larissa Latynina, USSR	77.031
1964 .....Vera Caslavska, Czechoslovakia	77.564
1968 .....Vera Caslavska, Czechoslovakia	78.25
1972 .....Lyudmila Tousischeva, USSR	77.025
1976 .....Nadia Comaneci, Romania	79.275
1980 .....Yelena Davydova, USSR	79.15
1984 .....Mary Lou Retton, United States	79.175
1988 .....Yelena Shushunova, USSR	79.662

ALL AROUND *(CONT.)*	Pts
1992 .....Tatiana Gutsu, Unified Team	39.737
1996 .....Lilia Podkopayeva, Ukraine	39.255
2000 .....Simona Amanar, Romania	38.642
2004 .....Carly Patterson, United States	38.387
2008 .....Nastia Liukin, United States	63.325
2012 .....Gabrielle Douglas, United States	62.232

VAULT	Pts
1952 .....Yekaterina Kalinchuk, USSR	19.20
1956 .....Larissa Latynina, USSR	18.833
1960 .....Margarita Nikolayeva, USSR	19.316

GYMNASTICS - Women *(Cont.)*

VAULT *(CONT.)*	Pts
1964 .....Vera Caslavska, Czechoslovakia	19.483
1968 .....Vera Caslavska, Czechoslovakia	19.775
1972 .....Karin Janz, E Germany	19.525
1976 .....Nelli Kim, USSR	19.80
1980 .....Natalya Shaposhnikova, USSR	19.725
1984 .....Ecaterina Szabo, Romania	19.875
1988 .....Svetlana Boginskaya, USSR	19.905
1992 .....Henrietta Onodi, Hungary	9.925
Lavinia Milosovici, Romania	9.925
1996 .....Simona Amanar, Romania	9.825
2000 .....Yelena Zamolodtchikova, Russia	9.731
2004 .....Monica Rosu, Romania	9.656
2008 ....Un Jong Hong, North Korea	15.650
2012 .....Sandra Raluca Izbasa, Romania	15.191

UNEVEN BARS	Pts
1952 .....Margit Korondi, Hungary	19.40
1956 .....Agnes Keleti, Hungary	18.966
1960 .....Polina Astakhova, USSR	19.616
1964 .....Polina Astakhova, USSR	19.332
1968 .....Vera Caslavska, Czechoslovakia	19.65
1972 .....Karin Janz, E Germany	19.675
1976 .....Nadia Comaneci, Romania	20.00
1980 .....Maxi Gnauck, E Germany	19.875
1984 .....Ma Yanhong, China	19.95
1988 .....Daniela Silivas, Romania	20.00
1992 .....Lu Li, China	10.00
1996 .....Svetlana Khorkina, Russia	9.850
2000 .....Svetlana Khorkina, Russia	9.862
2004 .....Emilie Lepennec, France	9.687
2008 .....He Kexin, China	16.725
2012 .....Aliya Mustafina, Russia	16.133

BALANCE BEAM	Pts
1952 .....Nina Bocharova, USSR	19.22
1956 .....Agnes Keleti, Hungary	18.80
1960 .....Eva Bosakova, Czechoslovakia	19.283
1964 .....Vera Caslavska, Czechoslovakia	19.449
1968 .....Natalya Kuchinskaya, USSR	19.65
1972 .....Olga Korbut, USSR	19.40
1976 .....Nadia Comaneci, Romania	19.95
1980 .....Nadia Comaneci, Romania	19.80
1984 .....Simona Pauca, Romania	19.80
1988 .....Daniela Silivas, Romania	19.924
1992 .....Tatiana Lisenko, Unified Team	9.975
1996 .....Shannon Miller, United States	9.862
2000 .....Xuan Li, China	9.825
2004 .....Catalina Ponor, Romania	9.787
2008 .....Shawn Johnson, United States	16.225
2012 .....Linlin Deng, China	15.600

FLOOR EXERCISE	Pts
1952 .....Agnes Keleti, Hungary	19.36
1956 .....Agnes Keleti, Hungary	18.733

FLOOR EXERCISES *(CONT.)*	Pts
1960 .....Larissa Latynina, USSR	19.583
1964 .....Larissa Latynina, USSR	19.599
1968 .....Vera Caslavska, Czechoslovakia	19.675
1972 .....Olga Korbut, USSR	19.575
1976 .....Nelli Kim, USSR	19.85
1980 .....Nadia Comaneci, Romania	19.875
1984 .....Ecaterina Szabo, Romania	19.975
1988 .....Daniela Silivas, Romania	19.937
1992 .....Lavinia Milosovici, Romania	10.00
1996 .....Lilia Podkopayeva, Ukraine	9.887
2000 .....Yelena Zamolodtchikova, Russia	9.850
2004 .....Catalina Ponor, Romania	9.750
2008 .....Sandra Izbasa, Romania	15.650
2012 .....Alexandra Raisman, United States	15.600

TEAM COMBINED EXERCISES	Pts
1928 .....The Netherlands	316.75
1932 .....Not held	
1936 .....Germany	506.50
1948 .....Czechoslovakia	445.45
1952 .....USSR	527.03
1956 .....USSR	444.800
1960 .....USSR	382.320
1964 .....USSR	280.890
1968 .....USSR	382.85
1972 .....USSR	380.50
1976 .....USSR	466.00
1980 .....USSR	394.90
1984 .....Romania	392.02
1988 .....USSR	395.475
1992 .....Unified Team	395.666
1996 .....United States	389.225
2000 .....Romania	154.608
2004 .....Romania	114.283
2008 .....China	188.900
2012 .....United States	183.596

RHYTHMIC ALL-AROUND	Pts
1984 .....Lori Fung, Canada	57.95
1988 .....Marina Lobach, USSR	60.00
1992 .....A. Timoshenko, Unified Team	59.037
1996 .....E. Serebrianskaya, Ukraine	39.683
2000 .....Yulia Barsukova, Russia	39.632
2004 .....Alina Kabaeva, Russia	108.400
2008 .....Evgeniya Kanaeva, Russia	75.500
2012 .....Evgeniya Kanaeva, Russia	116.900

RHYTHMIC TEAM COMBINED EXERCISES	Pts
1996 .....Spain	38.933
2000 .....Russia	39.500
2004 .....China	249.750
2008 .....Russia	35.550
2012 .....Russia	57.000

SOCCER

Men

1900 .....Great Britain	1936 .....Italy	1972 .....Poland	2000 .....Cameroon
1904 .....Canada	1948 .....Sweden	1976 ....E Germany	2004 .....Argentina
1908 .....Great Britain	1952 .....Hungary	1980 ....Czechoslovakia	2008 .....Argentina
1912 .....Great Britain	1956 .....USSR	1984 .....France	2012 .....Mexico
1920 .....Belgium	1960 .....Yugoslavia	1988 .....USSR	
1924 .....Uruguay	1964 .....Hungary	1992 .....Spain	
1928 .....Uruguay	1968 .....Hungary	1996 .....Nigeria	

Women

1996 ....United States	2008 ....United States
2000 ....Norway	2012 ....United States
2004 ....United States	

Tennis

Serena Williams charges back to the top of women's tennis with wins at Wimbledon (right), the Olympics, and the U.S. Open

2012 Grand Slam Champions

Australian Open
Men's Singles

	Winner	Runner-up	Score
Quarterfinals	Novak Djokovic	David Ferrer	6–1, 6–3, 4–6, 6–3
	Andy Murray	Kei Nishikori	6–3, 6–3, 6–1
	Rafael Nadal	Tomas Berdych	6–7 (5–7), 7–6 (8–6), 6–4, 6–3
	Roger Federer	Juan Martin del Potro	6–4, 6–3, 6–2
Semifinals	Novak Djokovic	Andy Murray	6–3, 3–6, 6–7 (4–7), 6–1, 7–5
	Rafael Nadal	Roger Federer	6–7 (5–7), 6–2, 7–6 (7–5), 6–4
Final	Novak Djokovic	Rafael Nadal	5–7, 6–4, 6–2, 6–7 (5–7), 7–5

Women's Singles

	Winner	Runner-up	Score
Quarterfinals	Kim Clijsters	Caroline Wozniacki	6–3, 7–6 (7–4)
	Victoria Azarenka	Agnieszka Radwanska	6–7 (0–7), 6–0, 6–2
	Maria Sharapova	Ekaterina Makarova	6–2, 6–3
	Petra Kvitova	Sara Errani	6–4, 6–2
Semifinals	Victoria Azarenka	Kim Clijsters	6–4, 1–6, 6–3
	Maria Sharapova	Petra Kvitova	6–2, 3–6, 6–4
Final	Victoria Azarenka	Maria Sharapova	6–3, 6–0

Doubles

	Winner	Runner-up	Score
Men's Final	Leander Paes/ Radek Stepanek	Bob Bryan/ Mike Bryan	7–6 (7–1), 6–2
Women's Final	Svetlana Kuznetsova/ Vera Zvonareva	Sara Errani/ Roberta Vinci	5–7, 6–4, 6–3
Mixed Final	Bethanie Mattek-Sands/ Horia Tecau	Elena Vesnina/ Leander Paes	6–3, 5–7, 10–8

French Open
Men's Singles

	Winner	Runner-up	Score
Quarterfinals	Novak Djokovic	Jo-Wilfried Tsonga	6–1, 5–7, 5–7, 7–6 (8–6), 6–1
	Roger Federer	Juan Martin Del Potro	3–6, 6–7 (4–7), 6–2, 6–0, 6–3
	David Ferrer	Andy Murray	6–4, 6–7 (3–7), 6–3, 6–2
	Rafael Nadal	Nicolas Almagro	7–6 (7–4), 6–2, 6–3
Semifinals	Novak Djokovic	Roger Federer	6–4, 7–5, 6–3
	Rafael Nadal	David Ferrer	6–2, 6–2, 6–1
Final	Rafael Nadal	Novak Djokovic	6–4, 6–3, 2–6, 7–5

Women's Singles

	Winner	Runner-up	Score
Quarterfinals	Samantha Stosur	Dominika Cibulkova	6–4, 6–1
	Sara Errani	Angelique Kerber	6–3, 7–6 (7–2)
	Petra Kvitova	Yaroslava Shvedova	3–6, 6–2, 6–4
	Maria Sharapova	Kaia Kanepi	6–2, 6–3
Semifinals	Sara Errani	Samantha Stosur	7–5, 1–6, 6–3
	Maria Sharapova	Petra Kvitova	6–3, 6–3
Final	Maria Sharapova	Sara Errani	6–3, 6–2

Doubles

	Winner	Runner-Up	Score
Men's Final	Max Mirnyi/ Daniel Nestor	Bob Bryan/ Mike Bryan	6–4, 6–4
Women's Final	Sara Errani/ Roberta Vinci	Maria Kirilenko/ Nadia Petrova	4–6, 6–4, 6–2
Mixed Final	Sania Mirza/ Mahesh Bhupathi	Klaudia Jans-Ignacik/ Santiago Gonzalez	7–6 (7–3), 6–1

Wimbledon

Men's Singles

	Winner	Runner-Up	Score
Quarterfinals	Novak Djokovic	Florian Mayer	6–4, 6–1, 6–4
	Roger Federer	Mikhail Youzhny	6–1, 6–2, 6–2
	Andy Murray	David Ferrer	6–7 (5–7), 7–6 (8–6), 6–4, 7–6 (7–4)
	Jo-Wilfried Tsonga	Philipp Kohlschreiber	7–6 (7–5), 4–6, 7–6 (7–3), 6–2
Semifinals	Roger Federer	Novak Djokovic	6–3, 3–6, 6–4, 6–3
	Andy Murray	Jo-Wilfried Tsonga	6–3, 6–4, 3–6, 7–5
Final	Roger Federer	Andy Murray	4–6, 7–5, 6–3, 6–4

Women's Singles

	Winner	Runner-Up	Score
Quarterfinals	Angelique Kerber	Sabine Lisicki	6–3, 6–7 (7–9), 7–5
	Agnieszka Radwanska	Maria Kirilenko	7–5, 4–6, 7–5
	Serena Williams	Petra Kvitova	6–3, 7–5
	Victoria Azarenka	Tamira Paszek	6–3, 7–6 (7–4)
Semifinals	Agnieszka Radwanska	Angelique Kerber	6–3, 6–4
	Serena Williams	Victoria Azarenka	6–3, 7–6 (8–6)
Final	Serena Williams	Agnieszka Radwanska	6–1, 5–7, 6–2

Doubles

	Winner	Runner-Up	Score
Men's Final	Jonathan Marray/ Frederik Nielsen	Robert Lindstedt/ Horia Tecau	4–6, 6–4, 7–6 (7–5), 6–7 (5–7), 6–3
Women's Final	Serena Williams/ Venus Williams	Andrea Hlavackova/ Lucie Hradecka	7–5, 6–4
Mixed Final	Mike Bryan/ Lisa Raymond	Leander Paes/ Elena Vesnina	6–3, 5–7, 6–4

U.S. Open

Men's Singles

	Winner	Runner-Up	Score
Quarterfinals	Tomas Berdych	Roger Federer	7–6 (7–1), 6–4, 3–6, 6–3
	Andy Murray	Marin Cilic	3–6, 7–6 (7–4), 6–2, 6–0
	David Ferrer	Janko Tipsarevic	3–6, 7–6 (7–5), 6–2, 3–6, 7–6 (7–4)
	Novak Djokovic	Juan Martin Del Potro	6–2, 7–6 (7–3), 6–4
Semifinals	Andy Murray	Tomas Berdych	5–7, 6–2, 6–1, 7–6 (9–7)
	Novak Djokovic	David Ferrer	2–6, 6–1, 6–4, 6–2
Final	Andy Murray	Novak Djokovic	7–6 (12–10), 7–5, 2–6, 3–6, 6–2

Women's Singles

	Winner	Runner-Up	Score
Quarterfinals	Victoria Azarenka	Samantha Stosur	6–1, 4–6, 7–6 (7–5)
	Maria Sharapova	Marion Bartoli	3–6, 6–3, 6–4
	Serena Williams	Ana Ivanovic	6–1, 6–3
	Sara Errani	Roberta Vinci	6–2, 6–4
Semifinals	Victoria Azarenka	Maria Sharapova	3–6, 6–2, 6–4
	Serena Williams	Sara Errani	6–1, 6–2
Final	Serena Williams	Victoria Azarenka	2–6, 6–2, 7–5

Doubles

	Winner	Runner-Up	Score
Men's Final	Bob Bryan/ Mike Bryan	Leander Paes/ Radek Stepanek	6–3, 6–4
Women's Final	Sara Errani/ Roberta Vinci	Andrea Hlavackova/ Lucie Hradecka	6–4, 6–2
Mixed Final	Ekaterina Makarova/ Bruno Soares	Kveta Peschke/ Marcin Matkowski	7–6 (10–8), 1–6, 12–10

Major Tournament Results

Late 2011 ATP Tour Events

Date	Tournament	Site	Singles Winner	Surface	Prize Money
Oct 3	Japan Open	Tokyo, Japan	Andy Murray	Outdoor Hard	$1,214,500
Oct 3	China Open	Beijing, China	Tomas Berdych	Outdoor Hard	$2,100,000
Oct 9	Shanghai Masters	Shanghai, China	Andy Murray	Outdoor Hard	$3,240,000
Oct 17	Stockholm Open	Stockholm, Sweden	Gael Monfils	Indoor Hard	€531,000
Oct 17	Kremlin Cup	Moscow, Russia	Janko Tipsarevic	Indoor Hard	$725,000
Oct 24	Austria Trophy	Vienna, Austria	Jo Wilfried Tsonga	Indoor Hard	€575,250
Oct 24	St. Petersburg Open	St. Petersburg, Russia	Marin Cilic	Indoor Hard	$663,750
Oct 31	Valencia Open	Valencia, Spain	Marcel Granoliers	Indoor Hard	€1,357,000
Oct 31	Swiss Indoor	Basel, Switzerland	Roger Federer	Indoor Hard	€1,308,100
Nov 7	Paris Masters	Paris, France	Roger Federer	Indoor Hard	€2,227,500
Nov 20	ATP World Tour Finals	London, England	Roger Federer	Indoor Hard	$5,070,000

2012 ATP Tour Events

Date	Tournament	Site	Singles Winner	Surface	Prize Money
Jan 1	Brisbane International	Brisbane, Australia	Andy Murray	Outdoor Hard	$434,250
Jan 2	Qatar Open	Doha, Qatar	Jo Wilfried Tsonga	Outdoor Hard	$1,024,000
Jan 2	Chennai Open	Chennai, India	Milos Raonic	Outdoor Hard	$398,250
Jan 9	Heineken Open	Auckland, New Zealand	David Ferrer	Outdoor Hard	$398,250
Jan 9	Sydney International	Sydney, Australia	Jarkko Nieminen	Outdoor Hard	$434,250
Jan 15	Australian Open	Melbourne, Australia	Novak Djokovic	Outdoor Hard	A$11,806,550
Jan 30	Sud de France Open	Montpellier, France	Tomas Berdych	Indoor Hard	€398,250
Jan 30	Zagreb Indoors	Zagreb, Croatia	Mikhail Youzhny	Indoor Hard	€398,250
Jan 30	VTR Open	Vina Del Mar, Chile	Juan Monaco	Outdoor Clay	$398,250
Feb 13	Brasil Open	Sao Paulo, Brazil	Nicolas Almagro	Indoor Clay	$475,300
Feb 13	SAP Open	San Jose, California	Milos Raonic	Indoor Hard	$531,000
Feb 13	ABN/AMRO	Rotterdam, Neth.	Roger Federer	Indoor Hard	€1,207,500
Feb 20	Regions Championships	Memphis, Tennessee	Jurgen Melzer	Indoor Hard	$1,155,000
Feb 20	Copa Claro	Buenos Aires, Argentina	David Ferrer	Outdoor Clay	$484,100
Feb 20	Open 13	Marseille, France	Juan Martin Del Potro	Indoor Hard	€512,750
Feb 27	Dubai Championships	Dubai, U.A.E.	Roger Federer	Outdoor Hard	$1,700,475
Feb 27	Mexican Open	Acapulco, Mexico	David Ferrer	Outdoor Clay	$1,155,000
Feb 27	Delray Beach Int'l	Delray Beach, Fla.	Kevin Anderson	Outdoor Hard	$442,500
Mar 8	BNP Paribas Open	Indian Wells, Calif.	Roger Federer	Outdoor Hard	$4,694,969
Mar 21	Sony Open	Miami, Fla.	Novak Djokovic	Outdoor Hard	$3,973,050
Apr 9	Grand Prix Hassan II	Casablanca, Morocco	Pablo Andujar	Outdoor Clay	€398,250
Apr 9	U.S. Clay Champ'ship	Houston, Texas	Juan Monaco	Outdoor Clay	$442,500
Apr 15	Monte Carlo Masters	Monte Carlo, Monaco	Rafael Nadal	Outdoor Clay	€2,427,975
Apr 23	BRD Nastase Tiriac Tr.	Bucharest, Romania	Gilles Simon	Outdoor Clay	€398,250
Apr 23	Barcelona Open	Barcelona, Spain	Rafael Nadal	Outdoor Clay	€1,627,500
Apr 30	BMW Open	Munich, Germany	Philipp Kohlschreiber	Outdoor Clay	€398,250
Apr 30	Serbia Open	Belgrade, Serbia	Andreas Seppi	Outdoor Clay	€366,950
Apr 30	Estoril Open	Estoril, Portugal	Juan Martin del Potro	Outdoor Clay	€398,250
May 6	Madrid Open	Madrid, Spain	Roger Federer	Outdoor Clay	€3,090,150
May 13	Italia International	Rome, Italy	Rafael Nadal	Outdoor Clay	€2,427,975
May 20	Nice Open	Nice, France	Nicolas Almagro	Outdoor Clay	€398,250
May 27	French Open	Paris, France	Rafael Nadal	Outdoor Clay	€6,555,000
June 11	Gerry Weber Open	Halle, Germany	Tommy Haas	Outdoor Grass	€663,750
June 11	AEGON Championships	London, England	Marin Cilic	Outdoor Grass	€625,300
June 17	UNICEF Open	's-Hertogenbosch, Netherlands	David Ferrer	Outdoor Grass	€398,250
June 18	AEGON International	Eastbourne, England	Andy Roddick	Outdoor Grass	£403,950
June 25	Wimbledon	Wimbledon, England	Roger Federer	Outdoor Grass	£1,150,000
July 9	Hall of Fame Champ's	Newport, R.I.	John Isner	Outdoor Grass	$398,250
July 9	Swedish Open	Bastad, Sweden	David Ferrer	Outdoor Clay	€358,425
July 9	Mercedes Cup	Stuttgart, Germany	Janko Tipsarevic	Outdoor Clay	€358,425
July 9	Croatia Open	Umag, Croatia	Marin Cilic	Outdoor Clay	€358,425
July 16	German Open	Hamburg, Germany	Juan Monaco	Outdoor Clay	€900,000

2012 ATP Tour Events (Cont.)*

Date	Tournament	Site	Singles Winner	Surface	Prize Money
July 16	Atlanta Open	Atlanta, Georgia	Andy Roddick	Outdoor Hard	$477,900
July 16	Swiss Open	Gstaad, Switzerland	Thomaz Bellucci	Outdoor Clay	€358,425
July 22	Kitzbuhel Cup	Kitzbuhel, Austria	Robin Haase	Outdoor Clay	€358,425
July 23	Farmer's Classic	Los Angeles	Sam Querrey	Outdoor Hard	$557,500
July 28	Olympics	London	Andy Murray	Outdoor Grass	—
July 30	Citi Open	Washington, D.C.	Alexandr Dolgopolov	Oudoor Hard	$1,049,760
Aug 6	Rogers Cup	Toronto, Canada	Novak Djokovic	Outdoor Hard	$2,648,700
Aug 12	Western & Southern	Cincinnati, Ohio	Roger Federer	Outdoor Hard	$2,825,280
Aug 19	Winston-Salem Open	Winston-Salem, N.C.	John Isner	Outdoor Hard	$553,125
Aug 27	U.S. Open	New York City	Andy Murray	Outdoor Hard	$9,406,000
Sept 17	Moselle Open	Metz, France	Jo-Wilfried Tsonga	Indoor Hard	€398,250
Sept 17	St. Petersburg Open	St. Petersburg, Russia	Martin Klizan	Indoor Hard	$410,850
Sept 24	Thailand Open	Bangkok, Thailand	Richard Gasquet	Outdoor Hard	$551,000
Sept 24	Malaysian Open	Kuala Lumpur, Malaysia	Juan Monaco	Indoor Hard	$850,000
Oct 1	China Open	Beijing, China	Novak Djokovic	Outdoor Hard	$2,205,000
Oct 1	Japan Open	Tokyo, Japan	Kei Nishikori	Outdoor Hard	$1,280,565

*Through Oct. 1, 2012

Late 2011 WTA Tour Events

Date	Tournament	Site	Singles Winner	Surface	Total Purse
Oct 1	China Open	Bejing, China	Agnieszka Radwanska	Outdoor Hard	$4,500,000
Oct 10	HP Japan Open	Osaka, Japan	Marion Bartoli	Indoor Hard	$220,000
Oct 10	Generali Ladies Open	Linz, Austria	Petra Kvitova	Indoor Hard	$220,000
Oct 17	BNP Luxembourg Open	Luxembourg, Lux.	Victoria Azarenka	Indoor Hard	$220,000
Oct 17	WTA Kremlin Cup	Moscow, Russia	Dominika Cibulkova	Indoor Hard	$721,000
Oct 25	WTA Championships	Itanbul, Turkey	Petra Kvitova	Indoor Hard	$4,900,000
Nov 3	Tourn. of Champions	Bali, Indonesia	Ana Ivanovic	Indoor Hard	$750,000

2012 WTA Tour Events

Date	Tournament	Site	Singles Winner	Surface	Total Purse
Jan 1	Brisbane International	Brisbane, Australia	Kaia Kanepi	Outdoor Hard	$655,000
Jan 2	ASB Classic	Auckland, New Zealand	Jie Zheng	Outdoor Hard	$220,000
Jan 8	Apia International	Sydney, Australia	Victoria Azarenka	Outdoor Hard	$637,000
Jan 8	Hobart International	Hobart, Australia	Mona Barthel	Outdoor Hard	$220,000
Jan 15	Australian Open	Melbourne, Australia	Victoria Azarenka	Outdoor Hard	$12,122,762
Feb 6	GDF Suez Open	Paris, France	Angelique Kerber	Indoor Hard	$637,000
Feb 6	Pattaya Open	Patttaya City, Thailand	Daniela Hantuchova	Outdoor Hard	$220,000
Feb 13	Qatar Open	Doha, Qatar	Victoria Azarenka	Outdoor Hard	$2,168,400
Feb 13	Copa Colsanitas	Bogota, Colombia	L. Arruabarrena-Vecino	Outdor Clay	$220,000
Feb 19	Memphis International	Memphis, Tenn.	Sofia Arvidsson	Indoor Hard	$220,000
Feb 20	Dubai Championships	Dubai, U.A.E.	Agnieszka Radwanska	Outdoor Hard	$2,000,000
Feb 20	Monterrey Open	Monterrey, Mexico	Timea Babos	Outdoor Hard	$220,000
Feb 27	Mexicano Open	Acapulco, Mexico	Sara Errani	Outdoor Clay	$220,000
Feb 27	Malaysian Open	Kuala Lumpur, Mal.	Su-Wei Hsieh	Outdoor Hard	$220,000
Mar 7	BNP Paribas Open	Indian Wells, Calif.	Victoria Azarenka	Outdoor Hardi	$5,536,664
Mar 20	Sony Open	Miami, Florida	Agnieszka Radwanska	Outdoor Hard	$4,828,050
Apr 2	Family Circle Cup	Charleston, S.C.	Serena Williams	Outdoor Clay	$721,000
Apr 9	Barcelona Open	Barcelona, Spain	Sara Errani	Outdoor Clay	$220,000
Apr 9	Copenhagen Open	Copenhagen, Den.	Angelique Kerber	Indoor Hard	$220,000
Apr 23	Porsche Grand Prix	Stuttgart, Germany	Maria Sharapova	Indoor Clay	$740,000
Apr 23	Morocco Grand Prix	Fez, Morocco	Kiki Bertens	Outdoor Clay	$220,000
Apr 30	Estoril Open	Estoril, Portugal	Kaia Kanepi	Outdoor Clay	$220,000
Apr 30	Budapest Grand Prix	Budapest, Hungary	Sara Errani	Outdoor Clay	$220,000
May 5	Madrid Open	Madrid, Spain	Serena Williams	Outdoor Clay	$5,189,603
May 14	d'Italia International	Rome, Italy	Maria Sharapova	Outdoor Clay	$2,168,400
May 21	Brussels Open	Brussels, Belguim	Agnieszka Radwanska	Outdoor Clay	$637,000
May 21	Strasbourg International	Strasbourg, France	Francesca Schiavone	Outdoor Clay	$220,000
May 27	French Open	Paris, France	Maria Sharapova	Outdoor Clay	$11,315,740
June 6	AEGON Classic	Birmingham, England	Melanie Oudin	Outdoor Grass	$220,000
June 11	Gastein International	Bad Gastein, Austria	Alize Cornet	Outdoor Clay	$220,000
June 17	UNICEF Open	's-Hertogenbosch, Neth.	Nadia Petrova	Outdoor Grass	$220,000
June 18	AEGON Int'l	Eastbourne, England	Tamira Paszek	Outdoor Grass	$637,000
June 25	Wimbledon	Wimbledon, England	Serena Williams	Outdoor Grass	$11,174,883

2012 WTA Tour Events (Cont.)*

Date	Tournament	Site	Singles Winner	Surface	Total Purse
July 9	Bank of the West Classic	Stanford, Calif.	Serena Williams	Outdoor Hard	$740,000
July 9	Palermo International	Palermo, Italy	Sara Errani	Outdoor Clay	$220,000
July 16	Swedish Open	Bastad, Sweden	Polona Hercog	Outdoor Clay	$220,000
July 16	Mercury Insurance Open	Carlsbad, Calif.	Dominika Cibulkova	Outdoor Hard	$740,000
July 23	Baku Cup	Baku, Azerbaijan	Bojana Jovanovski	Outdoors Hard	$220,000
July 28	Olympics	London, England	Serena Williams	Outdoor Grass	—
July 29	Citi Open	Washington, D.C.	Magdalena Rybarikova	Outdoor Hard	220,000
Aug 7	Rogers Cup	Montreal, Canada	Petra Kvitova	Outdoor Hard	$2,168,400
Aug 13	Western & Southern Open	Cincinnati, Ohio	Li Na	Outdoor Hard	$2,168,400
Aug 19	New Haven Open	New Haven, Conn.	Petra Kvitova	Outdoor Hard	$637,000
Aug 19	Texas Open	Dallas, Texas	Roberta Vinci	Outdoor Hard	$220,000
Aug 27	U.S. Open	New York City	Serena Williams	Outdoor Hard	$9,406,000
Sept 10	Tashkent Open	Tashkent, Uzbekistan	Irina-Camelia Begu	Outdoor Hard	$220,000
Sept 10	Bell Challenge	Quebec City, Canada	Kirsten Flipkens	Indoor Hard	$220,000
Sept 17	Korea Open	Seoul, South Korea	Caroline Wozniacki	Outdoor Hard	$500,000
Sept 17	Guangzhou Open	Guangzhou, China	Su-Wei Hsieh	Outdoor Hard	$220,000
Sept 23	Pan Pacific Open	Tokyo, Japan	Nadia Petrova	Outdoor Hard	$2,168,400
Sept 29	China Open	Beijing, China	Victoria Azarenka	Outdoor Hard	$4,828,050

*Through Oct. 1, 2012

2011 Final Season Singles Points Leaders

Men

Rank	Player	Country	Points	Events
1.	Novak Djokovic	SRB	13,630	19
2.	Rafael Nadal	ESP	9,595	20
3.	Roger Federer	SUI	8,170	19
4.	Andy Murray	GBR	7,380	19
5.	David Ferrer	ESP	4,925	23
6.	Jo-Wilfried Tsonga	FRA	4,335	25
7.	Tomas Berdych	CZE	3,700	24
8.	Mardy Fish	USA	2,965	24
9.	Janko Tipsarevic	SRB	2,595	28
10.	Nicolas Almagro	ESP	2,380	27

Note: Compiled by the ATP Tour, through the end of the 2011 season.

Women

Rank	Player	Country	Points
1.	Victoria Azarenka	BLR	8585
2.	Maria Sharapova	RUS	7680
3.	Petra Kvitova	CZE	7320
4.	Caroline Wozniacki	DEN	7085
5.	Samantha Stosur	AUS	5430
6.	Agnieszka Radwanska	POL	5330
7.	Marion Bartoli	FRA	4890
8.	Vera Zvonareva	RUS	4690
9.	Li Na	CHN	4450
10.	Andrea Petkovic	GER	3950

Note: Compiled by the WTA, through the end of the 2011 season.

Grand Slam Tournaments

MEN

Australian Open Championships

Year	Winner	Finalist	Score
1905	Rodney Heath	A. H. Curtis	4–6, 6–3, 6–4, 6–4
1906	Tony Wilding	H. A. Parker	6–0, 6–4, 6–4
1907	Horace M. Rice	H. A. Parker	6–3, 6–4, 6–4
1908	Fred Alexander	A. W. Dunlop	3–6, 3–6, 6–0, 6–2, 6–3
1909	Tony Wilding	E. F. Parker	6–1, 7–5, 6–2
1910	Rodney Heath	Horace M. Rice	6–4, 6–3, 6–2
1911	Norman Brookes	Horace M. Rice	6–1, 6–2, 6–3
1912	J. Cecil Parke	A. E. Beamish	3–6, 6–3, 1–6, 6–1, 7–5
1913	E. F. Parker	H. A. Parker	2–6, 6–1, 6–2, 6–3
1914	Pat O'Hara Wood	G. L. Patterson	6–4, 6–3, 5–7, 6–1
1915	Francis G. Lowe	Horace M. Rice	4–6, 6–1, 6–1, 6–4
1916–18	No tournament		
1919	A. R. F. Kingscote	E. O. Pockley	6–4, 6–0, 6–3
1920	Pat O'Hara Wood	Ron Thomas	6–3, 4–6, 6–8, 6–1, 6–3
1921	Rhys H. Gemmell	A. Hedeman	7–5, 6–1, 6–4
1922	Pat O'Hara Wood	Gerald Patterson	6–0, 3–6, 3–6, 6–3, 6–2
1923	Pat O'Hara Wood	C. B. St John	6–1, 6–1, 6–3
1924	James Anderson	R. E. Schlesinger	6–3, 6–4, 3–6, 5–7, 6–3
1925	James Anderson	Gerald Patterson	11–9, 2–6, 6–2, 6–3
1926	John Hawkes	J. Willard	6–1, 6–3, 6–1
1927	Gerald Patterson	John Hawkes	3–6, 6–4, 3–6, 18–16, 6–3
1928	Jean Borotra	R. O. Cummings	6–4, 6–1, 4–6, 5–7, 6–3
1929	John C. Gregory	R. E. Schlesinger	6–2, 6–2, 5–7, 7–5
1930	Gar Moon	Harry C. Hopman	6–3, 6–1, 6–3
1931	Jack Crawford	Harry C. Hopman	6–4, 6–2, 2–6, 6–1
1932	Jack Crawford	Harry C. Hopman	4–6, 6–3, 3–6, 6–3, 6–1
1933	Jack Crawford	Keith Gledhill	2–6, 7–5, 6–3, 6–2
1934	Fred Perry	Jack Crawford	6–3, 7–5, 6–1
1935	Jack Crawford	Fred Perry	2–6, 6–4, 6–4, 6–4
1936	Adrian Quist	Jack Crawford	6–2, 6–3, 4–6, 3–6, 9–7
1937	Vivian B. McGrath	John Bromwich	6–3, 1–6, 6–0, 2–6, 6–1
1938	Don Budge	John Bromwich	6–4, 6–2, 6–1
1939	John Bromwich	Adrian Quist	6–4, 6–1, 6–3
1940	Adrian Quist	Jack Crawford	6–3, 6–1, 6–2
1941–45	No tournament		
1946	John Bromwich	Dinny Pails	5–7, 6–3, 7–5, 3–6, 6–2
1947	Dinny Pails	John Bromwich	4–6, 6–4, 3–6, 7–5, 8–6
1948	Adrian Quist	John Bromwich	6–4, 3–6, 6–3, 2–6, 6–3
1949	Frank Sedgman	Ken McGregor	6–3, 6–3, 6–2
1950	Frank Sedgman	Ken McGregor	6–3, 6–4, 4–6, 6–1
1951	Richard Savitt	Ken McGregor	6–3, 2–6, 6–3, 6–1
1952	Ken McGregor	Frank Sedgman	7–5, 12–10, 2–6, 6–2
1953	Ken Rosewall	Mervyn Rose	6–0, 6–3, 6–4
1954	Mervyn Rose	Rex Hartwig	6–2, 0–6, 6–4, 6–2
1955	Ken Rosewall	Lew Hoad	9–7, 6–4, 6–4
1956	Lew Hoad	Ken Rosewall	6–4, 3–6, 6–4, 7–5
1957	Ashley Cooper	Neale Fraser	6–3, 9–11, 6–4, 6–2
1958	Ashley Cooper	Mal Anderson	7–5, 6–3, 6–4
1959	Alex Olmedo	Neale Fraser	6–1, 6–2, 3–6, 6–3
1960	Rod Laver	Neale Fraser	5–7, 3–6, 6–3, 8–6, 8–6
1961	Roy Emerson	Rod Laver	1–6, 6–3, 7–5, 6–4
1962	Rod Laver	Roy Emerson	8–6, 0–6, 6–4, 6–4
1963	Roy Emerson	Ken Fletcher	6–3, 6–3, 6–1
1964	Roy Emerson	Fred Stolle	6–3, 6–4, 6–2
1965	Roy Emerson	Fred Stolle	7–9, 2–6, 6–4, 7–5, 6–1
1966	Roy Emerson	Arthur Ashe	6–4, 6–8, 6–2, 6–3
1967	Roy Emerson	Arthur Ashe	6–4, 6–1, 6–1
1968	Bill Bowrey	Juan Gisbert	7–5, 2–6, 9–7, 6–4
1969*	Rod Laver	Andres Gimeno	6–3, 6–4, 7–5

MEN *(Cont.)*
Australian Open Championships *(Cont.)*

Year	Winner	Finalist	Score
1970	Arthur Ashe	Dick Crealy	6–4, 9–7, 6–2
1971	Ken Rosewall	Arthur Ashe	6–1, 7–5, 6–3
1972	Ken Rosewall	Mal Anderson	7–6, 6–3, 7–5
1973	John Newcombe	Onny Parun	6–3, 6–7, 7–5, 6–1
1974	Jimmy Connors	Phil Dent	7–6, 6–4, 4–6, 6–3
1975	John Newcombe	Jimmy Connors	7–5, 3–6, 6–4, 7–5
1976	Mark Edmondson	John Newcombe	6–7, 6–3, 7–6, 6–1
1977 (Jan)	Roscoe Tanner	Guillermo Vilas	6–3, 6–3, 6–3
1977 (Dec)	Vitas Gerulaitis	John Lloyd	6–3, 7–6, 5–7, 3–6, 6–2
1978	Guillermo Vilas	John Marks	6–4, 6–4, 3–6, 6–3
1979	Guillermo Vilas	John Sadri	7–6, 6–3, 6–2
1980	Brian Teacher	Kim Warwick	7–5, 7–6, 6–3
1981	Johan Kriek	Steve Denton	6–2, 7–6, 6–7, 6–4
1982	Johan Kriek	Steve Denton	6–3, 6–3, 6–2
1983	Mats Wilander	Ivan Lendl	6–1, 6–4, 6–4
1984	Mats Wilander	Kevin Curren	6–7, 6–4, 7–6, 6–2
1985 (Dec)	Stefan Edberg	Mats Wilander	6–4, 6–3, 6–3
1987 (Jan)	Stefan Edberg	Pat Cash	6–3, 6–4, 3–6, 5–7, 6–3
1988	Mats Wilander	Pat Cash	6–3, 6–7, 3–6, 6–1, 8–6
1989	Ivan Lendl	Miloslav Mecir	6–2, 6–2, 6–2
1990	Ivan Lendl	Stefan Edberg	4–6, 7–6, 5–2, ret.
1991	Boris Becker	Ivan Lendl	1–6, 6–4, 6–4, 6–4
1992	Jim Courier	Stefan Edberg	6–3, 3–6, 6–4, 6–2
1993	Jim Courier	Stefan Edberg	6–2, 6–1, 2–6, 7–5
1994	Pete Sampras	Todd Martin	7–6, 6–4, 6–4
1995	Andre Agassi	Pete Sampras	4–6, 6–1, 7–6, 6–4
1996	Boris Becker	Michael Chang	6–2, 6–4, 2–6, 6–2
1997	Pete Sampras	Carlos Moya	6–2, 6–3, 6–3
1998	Petr Korda	Marcelo Ríos	6–2, 6–2, 6–2
1999	Yevgeny Kafelnikov	Thomas Enqvist	4–6, 6–0, 6–3, 7–6
2000	Andre Agassi	Yevgeny Kafelnikov	3–6, 6–3, 6–2, 6–4
2001	Andre Agassi	Arnaud Clement	6–4, 6–2, 6–2
2002	Thomas Johansson	Marat Safin	3–6, 6–4, 6–4, 7–6 (7-4)
2003	Andre Agassi	Rainer Schuettler	6–2, 6–2, 6–1
2004	Roger Federer	Marat Safin	7–6 (7–3), 6–4, 6–2
2005	Marat Safin	Lleyton Hewitt	1–6, 6–3, 6–4, 6–4
2006	Roger Federer	Marcos Baghdatis	5–7, 7–5, 6–0, 6–2
2007	Roger Federer	Fernando Gonzalez	7–6 (7–2), 6–4, 6–4
2008	Novak Djokovic	Jo-Wilfried Tsonga	4–6, 6–4, 6–3, 7–6 (7–2)
2009	Rafael Nadal	Roger Federer	7–5, 3–6, 7–6 (7–3), 3–6, 6–2
2010	Roger Federer	Andy Murray	6–3, 6–4, 7–6 (13–11)
2011	Novak Djokovic	Andy Murray	6–4, 6–2, 6–3
2012	Novak Djokovic	Rafael Nadal	5–7, 6–4, 6–2, 6–7 (5–7), 7–5

*Became Open (amateur and professional) in 1969.

MEN *(Cont.)*

French Championships

Year	Winner	Finalist	Score
1925†	Rene Lacoste	Jean Borotra	7–5, 6–1, 6–4
1926	Henri Cochet	Rene Lacoste	6–2, 6–4, 6–3
1927	Rene Lacoste	Bill Tilden	6–4, 4–6, 5–7, 6–3, 11–9
1928	Henri Cochet	Rene Lacoste	5–7, 6–3, 6–1, 6–3
1929	Rene Lacoste	Jean Borotra	6–3, 2–6, 6–0, 2–6, 8–6
1930	Henri Cochet	Bill Tilden	3–6, 8–6, 6–3, 6–1
1931	Jean Borotra	Claude Boussus	2–6, 6–4, 7–5, 6–4
1932	Henri Cochet	Giorgio de Stefani	6–0, 6–4, 4–6, 6–3
1933	Jack Crawford	Henri Cochet	8–6, 6–1, 6–3
1934	Gottfried von Cramm	Jack Crawford	6–4, 7–9, 3–6, 7–5, 6–3
1935	Fred Perry	Gottfried von Cramm	6–3, 3–6, 6–1, 6–3
1936	Gottfried von Cramm	Fred Perry	6–0, 2–6, 6–2, 2–6, 6–0
1937	Henner Henkel	Henry Austin	6–1, 6–4, 6–3
1938	Don Budge	Roderick Menzel	6–3, 6–2, 6–4
1939	Don McNeill	Bobby Riggs	7–5, 6–0, 6–3
1940	No tournament		
1941‡	Bernard Destremau	n/a	n/a
1942‡	Bernard Destremau	n/a	n/a
1943‡	Yvon Petra	n/a	n/a
1944‡	Yvon Petra	n/a	n/a
1945‡	Yvon Petra	Bernard Destremau	7–5, 6–4, 6–2
1946	Marcel Bernard	Jaroslav Drobny	3–6, 2–6, 6–1, 6–4, 6–3
1947	Joseph Asboth	Eric Sturgess	8–6, 7–5, 6–4
1948	Frank Parker	Jaroslav Drobny	6–4, 7–5, 5–7, 8–6
1949	Frank Parker	Budge Patty	6–3, 1–6, 6–1, 6–4
1950	Budge Patty	Jaroslav Drobny	6–1, 6–2, 3–6, 5–7, 7–5
1951	Jaroslav Drobny	Eric Sturgess	6–3, 6–3, 6–3
1952	Jaroslav Drobny	Frank Sedgman	6–2, 6–0, 3–6, 6–4
1953	Ken Rosewall	Vic Seixas	6–3, 6–4, 1–6, 6–2
1954	Tony Trabert	Arthur Larsen	6–4, 7–5, 6–1
1955	Tony Trabert	Sven Davidson	2–6, 6–1, 6–4, 6–2
1956	Lew Hoad	Sven Davidson	6–4, 8–6, 6–3
1957	Sven Davidson	Herbie Flam	6–3, 6–4, 6–4
1958	Mervyn Rose	Luis Ayala	6–3, 6–4, 6–4
1959	Nicola Pietrangeli	Ian Vermaak	3–6, 6–3, 6–4, 6–1
1960	Nicola Pietrangeli	Luis Ayala	3–6, 6–3, 6–4, 4–6, 6–3
1961	Manuel Santana	Nicola Pietrangeli	4–6, 6–1, 3–6, 6–0, 6–2
1962	Rod Laver	Roy Emerson	3–6, 2–6, 6–3, 9–7, 6–2
1963	Roy Emerson	Pierre Darmon	3–6, 6–1, 6–4, 6–4
1964	Manuel Santana	Nicola Pietrangeli	6–3, 6–1, 4–6, 7–5
1965	Fred Stolle	Tony Roche	3–6, 6–0, 6–2, 6–3
1966	Tony Roche	Istvan Gulyas	6–1, 6–4, 7–5
1967	Roy Emerson	Tony Roche	6–1, 6–4, 2–6, 6–2
1968*	Ken Rosewall	Rod Laver	6–3, 6–1, 2–6, 6–2
1969	Rod Laver	Ken Rosewall	6–4, 6–3, 6–4
1970	Jan Kodes	Zeljko Franulovic	6–2, 6–4, 6–0
1971	Jan Kodes	Ilie Nastase	8–6, 6–2, 2–6, 7–5
1972	Andres Gimeno	Patrick Proisy	4–6, 6–3, 6–1, 6–1
1973	Ilie Nastase	Nikki Pilic	6–3, 6–3, 6–0
1974	Bjorn Borg	Manuel Orantes	6–7, 6–0, 6–1, 6–1
1975	Bjorn Borg	Guillermo Vilas	6–2, 6–3, 6–4
1976	Adriano Panatta	Harold Solomon	6–1, 6–4, 4–6, 7–6
1977	Guillermo Vilas	Brian Gottfried	6–0, 6–3, 6–0
1978	Bjorn Borg	Guillermo Vilas	6–1, 6–1, 6–3
1979	Bjorn Borg	Victor Pecci	6–3, 6–1, 6–7, 6–4
1980	Bjorn Borg	Vitas Gerulaitis	6–4, 6–1, 6–2
1981	Bjorn Borg	Ivan Lendl	6–1, 4–6, 6–2, 3–6, 6–1
1982	Mats Wilander	Guillermo Vilas	1–6, 7–6, 6–0, 6–4
1983	Yannick Noah	Mats Wilander	6–2, 7–5, 7–6
1984	Ivan Lendl	John McEnroe	3–6, 2–6, 6–4, 7–5, .7–5
1985	Mats Wilander	Ivan Lendl	3–6, 6–4, 6–2, 6–2
1986	Ivan Lendl	Mikael Pernfors	6–3, 6–2, 6–4
1987	Ivan Lendl	Mats Wilander	7–5, 6–2, 3–6, 7–6

†1925 was the first year that entries were accepted from all countries.
‡From 1941 to 1945 the event was called Tournoi de France and was closed to all foreigners.

MEN *(Cont.)*

French Championships *(Cont.)*

Year	Winner	Finalist	Score
1988	Mats Wilander	Henri Leconte	7–5, 6–2, 6–1
1989	Michael Chang	Stefan Edberg	6–1, 3–6, 4–6, 6–4, 6–2
1990	Andres Gomez	Andre Agassi	6–3, 2–6, 6–4, 6–4
1991	Jim Courier	Andre Agassi	3–6, 6–4, 2–6, 6–1, 6–4
1992	Jim Courier	Petr Korda	7–5, 6–2, 6–1
1993	Sergi Bruguera	Jim Courier	6–4, 2–6, 6–2, 3–6, 6–3
1994	Sergi Bruguera	Alberto Berasategui	6–3, 7–5, 2–6, 6–1
1995	Thomas Muster	Michael Chang	7–5, 6–2, 6–4
1996	Yevgeny Kafelnikov	Michael Stich	7–6, 7–5, 7–6
1997	Gustavo Kuerten	Sergi Bruguera	6–3, 6–4, 6–2
1998	Carlos Moya	Alex Corretja	6–3, 7–5, 6–3
1999	Andre Agassi	Andrei Medvedev	1–6, 2–6, 6–4, 6–3, 6–4
2000	Gustavo Kuerten	Magnus Norman	6–2, 6–3, 2–6, 7–6
2001	Gustavo Kuerten	Alex Corretja	6–7, 7–5, 6–2, 6–0
2002	Albert Costa	Juan Carlos Ferrero	6–1, 6–0, 4–6, 6–3
2003	Juan Carlos Ferrero	Martin Verkerk	6–1, 6–3, 6–2
2004	Gaston Gaudio	Guillermo Coria	0–6, 3–6, 6–4, 6–1, 8–6
2005	Rafael Nadal	Mariano Puerta	6–7, 6–3, 6–1, 7–5
2006	Rafael Nadal	Roger Federer	1–6, 6–1, 6–4, 7–6
2007	Rafael Nadal	Roger Federer	6–3, 4–6, 6–3, 6–4
2008	Rafael Nadal	Roger Federer	6–1, 6–3, 6–0
2009	Roger Federer	Robin Soderling	6–1, 7–6 (7–1), 6–4
2010	Rafael Nadal	Robin Soderling	6–4, 6–2, 6–4
2011	Rafael Nadal	Roger Federer	7–5, 7–6 (7–3), 5–7, 6–1
2012	Rafael Nadal	Novak Djokovic	6–4, 6–3, 2–6, 7–5

*Became Open (amateur and professional) in 1968, but restricted to only contract professionals in 1972.

Wimbledon Championships

Year	Winner	Finalist	Score
1877	Spencer W. Gore	William C. Marshall	6–1, 6–2, 6–4
1878	P. Frank Hadow	Spencer W. Gore	7–5, 6–1, 9–7
1879	John T. Hartley	V. St Leger Gould	6–2, 6–4, 6–2
1880	John T. Hartley	Herbert F. Lawford	6–0, 6–2, 2–6, 6–3
1881	William Renshaw	John T. Hartley	6–0, 6–2, 6–1
1882	William Renshaw	Ernest Renshaw	6–1, 2–6, 4–6, 6–2, 6–2
1883	William Renshaw	Ernest Renshaw	2–6, 6–3, 6–3, 4–6, 6–3
1884	William Renshaw	Herbert F. Lawford	6–0, 6–4, 9–7
1885	William Renshaw	Herbert F. Lawford	7–5, 6–2, 4–6, 7–5
1886	William Renshaw	Herbert F. Lawford	6–0, 5–7, 6–3, 6–4
1887	Herbert F. Lawford	Ernest Renshaw	1–6, 6–3, 3–6, 6–4, 6–4
1888	Ernest Renshaw	Herbert F. Lawford	6–3, 7–5, 6–0
1889	William Renshaw	Ernest Renshaw	6–4, 6–1, 3–6, 6–0
1890	William J. Hamilton	William Renshaw	6–8, 6–2, 3–6, 6–1, 6–1
1891	Wilfred Baddeley	Joshua Pim	6–4, 1–6, 7–5, 6–0
1892	Wilfred Baddeley	Joshua Pim	4–6, 6–3, 6–3, 6–2
1893	Joshua Pim	Wilfred Baddeley	3–6, 6–1, 6–3, 6–2
1894	Joshua Pim	Wilfred Baddeley	10–8, 6–2, 8–6
1895	Wilfred Baddeley	Wilberforce V. Eaves	4–6, 2–6, 8–6, 6–2, 6–3
1896	Harold S. Mahoney	Wilfred Baddeley	6–2, 6–8, 5–7, 8–6, 6–3
1897	Reggie F. Doherty	Harold S. Mahoney	6–4, 6–4, 6–3
1898	Reggie F. Doherty	H. Laurie Doherty	6–3, 6–3, 2–6, 5–7, 6–1
1899	Reggie F. Doherty	Arthur W. Gore	1–6, 4–6, 6–2, 6–3, 6–3
1900	Reggie F. Doherty	Sidney H. Smith	6–8, 6–3, 6–1, 6–2
1901	Arthur W. Gore	Reggie F. Doherty	4–6, 7–5, 6–4, 6–4
1902	H. Laurie Doherty	Arthur W. Gore	6–4, 6–3, 3–6, 6–0
1903	H. Laurie Doherty	Frank L. Riseley	7–5, 6–3, 6–0
1904	H. Laurie Doherty	Frank L. Riseley	6–1, 7–5, 8–6
1905	H. Laurie Doherty	Norman E. Brookes	8–6, 6–2, 6–4
1906	H. Laurie Doherty	Frank L. Riseley	6–4, 4–6, 6–2, 6–3
1907	Norman E. Brookes	Arthur W. Gore	6–4, 6–2, 6–2
1908	Arthur W. Gore	H. Roper Barrett	6–3, 6–2, 4–6, 3–6, 6–4
1909	Arthur W. Gore	M. J. G. Ritchie	6–8, 1–6, 6–2, 6–2, 6–2
1910	Anthony F. Wilding	Arthur W. Gore	6–4, 7–5, 4–6, 6–2
1911	Anthony F. Wilding	H. Roper Barrett	6–4, 4–6, 2–6, 6–2, ret.

Note: Prior to 1922 the tournament was run on a challenge-round system. The previous year's winner "stood out" of an All Comers event, which produced a challenger to play him for the title.

MEN *(Cont.)*

Wimbledon Championships *(Cont.)*

Year	Winner	Finalist	Score
1912	Anthony F. Wilding	Arthur W. Gore	6–4, 6–4, 4–6, 6–4
1913	Anthony F. Wilding	Maurice E. McLoughlin	8–6, 6–3, 10–8
1914	Norman E. Brookes	Anthony F. Wilding	6–4, 6–4, 7–5
1915–18	No tournament		
1919	Gerald L. Patterson	Norman E. Brookes	6–3, 7–5, 6–2
1920	Bill Tilden	Gerald L. Patterson	2–6, 6–3, 6–2, 6–4
1921	Bill Tilden	Brian I. C. Norton	4–6, 2–6, 6–1, 6–0, 7–5
1922	Gerald L. Patterson	Randolph Lycett	6–3, 6–4, 6–2
1923	Bill Johnston	Francis T. Hunter	6–0, 6–3, 6–1
1924	Jean Borotra	Rene Lacoste	6–1, 3–6, 6–1, 3–6, 6–4
1925	Rene Lacoste	Jean Borotra	6–3, 6–3, 4–6, 8–6
1926	Jean Borotra	Howard Kinsey	8–6, 6–1, 6–3
1927	Henri Cochet	Jean Borotra	4–6, 4–6, 6–3, 6–4, 7–5
1928	Rene Lacoste	Henri Cochet	6–1, 4–6, 6–4, 6–2
1929	Henri Cochet	Jean Borotra	6–4, 6–3, 6–4
1930	Bill Tilden	Wilmer Allison	6–3, 9–7, 6–4
1931	Sidney B. Wood Jr	Francis X. Shields	walkover
1932	Ellsworth Vines	Henry Austin	6–4, 6–2, 6–0
1933	Jack Crawford	Ellsworth Vines	4–6, 11–9, 6–2, 2–6, 6–4
1934	Fred Perry	Jack Crawford	6–3, 6–0, 7–5
1935	Fred Perry	Gottfried von Cramm	6–2, 6–4, 6–4
1936	Fred Perry	Gottfried von Cramm	6–1, 6–1, 6–0
1937	Don Budge	Gottfried von Cramm	6–3, 6–4, 6–2
1938	Don Budge	Henry Austin	6–1, 6–0, 6–3
1939	Bobby Riggs	Elwood Cooke	2–6, 8–6, 3–6, 6–3, 6–2
1940–45	No tournament		
1946	Yvon Petra	Geoff E. Brown	6–2, 6–4, 6–7 (7–9), 5–7, 6–4
1947	Jack Kramer	Tom P. Brown	6–1, 6–3, 6–2
1948	Bob Falkenburg	John Bromwich	7–5, 0–6, 6–2, 3–6, 7–5
1949	Ted Schroeder	Jaroslav Drobny	3–6, 6–0, 6–3, 4–6, 6–4
1950	Budge Patty	Frank Sedgman	6–1, 6–7 (8–10), 6–2, 6–3
1951	Dick Savitt	Ken McGregor	6–4, 6–4, 6–4
1952	Frank Sedgman	Jaroslav Drobny	4–6, 6–3, 6–2, 6–3
1953	Vic Seixas	Kurt Nielsen	9–7, 6–3, 6–4
1954	Jaroslav Drobny	Ken Rosewall	13–11, 4–6, 6–2, 9–7
1955	Tony Trabert	Kurt Nielsen	6–3, 7–5, 6–1
1956	Lew Hoad	Ken Rosewall	6–2, 4–6, 7–5, 6–4
1957	Lew Hoad	Ashley Cooper	6–2, 6–1, 6–2
1958	Ashley Cooper	Neale Fraser	3–6, 6–3, 6–4, 13–11
1959	Alex Olmedo	Rod Laver	6–4, 6–3, 6–4
1960	Neale Fraser	Rod Laver	6–4, 3–6, 9–7, 7–5
1961	Rod Laver	Chuck McKinley	6–3, 6–1, 6–4
1962	Rod Laver	Martin Mulligan	6–2, 6–2, 6–1
1963	Chuck McKinley	Fred Stolle	9–7, 6–1, 6–4
1964	Roy Emerson	Fred Stolle	6–4, 12–10, 4–6, 6–3
1965	Roy Emerson	Fred Stolle	6–2, 6–4, 6–4
1966	Manuel Santana	Dennis Ralston	6–4, 11–9, 6–4
1967	John Newcombe	Wilhelm Bungert	6–3, 6–1, 6–1
1968*	Rod Laver	Tony Roche	6–3, 6–4, 6–2
1969	Rod Laver	John Newcombe	6–4, 5–7, 6–4, 6–4
1970	John Newcombe	Ken Rosewall	5–7, 6–3, 6–2, 3–6, 6–1
1971	John Newcombe	Stan Smith	6–3, 5–7, 2–6, 6–4, 6–4
1972	Stan Smith	Ilie Nastase	4–6, 6–3, 6–3, 4–6, 7–5
1973	Jan Kodes	Alex Metreveli	6–1, 9–8, 6–3
1974	Jimmy Connors	Ken Rosewall	6–1, 6–1, 6–4
1975	Arthur Ashe	Jimmy Connors	6–1, 6–1, 5–7, 6–4
1976	Bjorn Borg	Ilie Nastase	6–4, 6–2, 9–7
1977	Bjorn Borg	Jimmy Connors	3–6, 6–2, 6–1, 5–7, 6–4
1978	Bjorn Borg	Jimmy Connors	6–2, 6–2, 6–3
1979	Bjorn Borg	Roscoe Tanner	6–7, 6–1, 3–6, 6–3, 6–4
1980	Bjorn Borg	John McEnroe	1–6, 7–5, 6–3, 6–7, 8–6
1981	John McEnroe	Bjorn Borg	4–6, 7–6, 7–6, 6–4
1982	Jimmy Connors	John McEnroe	3–6, 6–3, 6–7, 7–6, 6–4
1983	John McEnroe	Chris Lewis	6–2, 6–2, 6–2

Note: Prior to 1922 the tournament was run on a challenge-round system. The previous year's winner "stood out" of an All Comers event, which produced a challenger to play him for the title.

*Became Open (amateur and professional) in 1968, but restricted to only contract professionals in 1972.

MEN *(Cont.)*
Wimbledon Championships *(Cont.)*

Year	Winner	Finalist	Score
1984	John McEnroe	Jimmy Connors	6–1, 6–1, 6–2
1985	Boris Becker	Kevin Curren	6–3, 6–7, 7–6, 6–4
1986	Boris Becker	Ivan Lendl	6–4, 6–3, 7–5
1987	Pat Cash	Ivan Lendl	7–6, 6–2, 7–5
1988	Stefan Edberg	Boris Becker	4–6, 7–6, 6–4, 6–2
1989	Boris Becker	Stefan Edberg	6–0, 7–6, 6–4
1990	Stefan Edberg	Boris Becker	6–2, 6–2, 3–6, 3–6, 6–4
1991	Michael Stich	Boris Becker	6–4, 7–6, 6–4
1992	Andre Agassi	Goran Ivanisevic	6–7, 6–4, 6–4, 1–6, 6–4
1993	Pete Sampras	Jim Courier	7–6, 7–6, 3–6, 6–3
1994	Pete Sampras	Goran Ivanisevic	7–6, 7–6, 6–0
1995	Pete Sampras	Boris Becker	6–7, 6–2, 6–4, 6–2
1996	Richard Krajicek	MaliVai Washington	6–3, 6–4, 6–3
1997	Pete Sampras	Cedric Pioline	6–4, 6–2, 6–4
1998	Pete Sampras	Goran Ivanisevic	6–7, 7–6, 6–4, 3–6, 6–2
1999	Pete Sampras	Andre Agassi	6–3, 6–4, 7–5
2000	Pete Sampras	Patrick Rafter	6–7, 7–6, 6–4, 6–2
2001	Goran Ivanisevic	Patrick Rafter	6–3, 3–6, 6–3, 2–6, 9–7
2002	Lleyton Hewitt	David Nalbandian	6–1, 6–3, 6–2
2003	Roger Federer	Mark Philippoussis	7–6 (7-5), 6–2, 7–6 (7-3)
2004	Roger Federer	Andy Roddick	4–6, 7–5, 7–6 (7-3), 6–4
2005	Roger Federer	Andy Roddick	6–2, 7–6 (7-2), 6–4
2006	Roger Federer	Rafael Nadal	6–0, 7–6, (7–5), 6–7 (2–7), 6–3
2007	Roger Federer	Rafael Nadal	7–6 (9-7), 4–6, 7–6 (7-3), 2–6, 6–2
2008	Rafael Nadal	Roger Federer	6–4, 6–4, 6–7 (5–7), 6–7 (8–10) 9–7
2009	Roger Federer	Andy Roddick	5–7, 7–6 (8–6), 7–6 (7–5), 3–6, 16–14
2010	Rafael Nadal	Tomas Berdych	6–3, 7–5, 6–4
2011	Novak Djokovic	Rafael Nadal	6–4, 6–1, 1–6, 6–3
2012	Roger Federer	Andy Murray	4–6, 7–5, 6–3, 6–4

United States Championships

Year	Winner	Finalist	Score
1881	Richard D. Sears	W.E. Glyn	6–0, 6–3, 6–2
1882	Richard D. Sears	C.M. Clark	6–1, 6–4, 6–0
1883	Richard D. Sears	James Dwight	6–2, 6–0, 9–7
1884	Richard D. Sears	H.A. Taylor	6–0, 1–6, 6–0, 6–2
1885	Richard D. Sears	G.M. Brinley	6–3, 4–6, 6–0, 6–3
1886	Richard D. Sears	R.L. Beeckman	4–6, 6–1, 6–3, 6–4
1887	Richard D. Sears	H.W. Slocum Jr	6–1, 6–3, 6–2
1888†	H. W. Slocum Jr	H.A. Taylor	6–4, 6–1, 6–0
1889	H. W. Slocum Jr	Q.A. Shaw	6–3, 6–1, 4–6, 6–2
1890	Oliver S. Campbell	H.W. Slocum Jr	6–2, 4–6, 6–3, 6–1
1891	Oliver S. Campbell	Clarence Hobart	2–6, 7–5, 7–9, 6–1, 6–2
1892	Oliver S. Campbell	Frederick H. Hovey	7–5, 3–6, 6–3, 7–5
1893†	Robert D. Wrenn	Frederick H. Hovey	6–4, 3–6, 6–4, 6–4
1894	Robert D. Wrenn	M.F. Goodbody	6–8, 6–1, 6–4, 6–4
1895	Frederick H. Hovey	Robert D. Wrenn	6–3, 6–2, 6–4
1896	Robert D. Wrenn	Frederick H. Hovey	7–5, 3–6, 6–0, 1–6, 6–1
1897†	Robert D. Wrenn	Wilberforce V. Eaves	4–6, 8–6, 6–3, 2–6, 6–2
1898†	Malcolm D. Whitman	Dwight F. Davis	3–6, 6–2, 6–2, 6–1
1899	Malcolm D. Whitman	J. Parmly Paret	6–1, 6–2, 3–6, 7–5
1900	Malcolm D. Whitman	William A. Larned	6–4, 1–6, 6–2, 6–2
1901†	William A. Larned	Beals C. Wright	6–2, 6–8, 6–4, 6–4
1902	William A. Larned	Reggie F. Doherty	4–6, 6–2, 6–4, 8–6
1903	H. Laurie Doherty	William A. Larned	6–0, 6–3, 10–8
1904†	Holcombe Ward	William J. Clothier	10–8, 6–4, 9–7
1905	Beals C. Wright	Holcombe Ward	6–2, 6–1, 11–9
1906	William J. Clothier	Beals C. Wright	6–3, 6–0, 6–4
1907†	William A. Larned	Robert LeRoy	6–2, 6–2, 6–4
1908	William A. Larned	Beals C. Wright	6–1, 6–2, 8–6
1909	William A. Larned	William J. Clothier	6–1, 6–2, 5–7, 1–6, 6–1

† No challenge round played.

MEN *(Cont.)*
United States Championships *(Cont.)*

Year	Winner	Finalist	Score
1910	William A. Larned	Thomas C. Bundy	6–1, 5–7, 6–0, 6–8, 6–1
1911	William A. Larned	Maurice E. McLoughlin	6–4, 6–4, 6–2
1912‡	Maurice E. McLoughlin	Bill Johnson	3–6, 2–6, 6–2, 6–4, 6–2
1913	Maurice E. McLoughlin	Richard N. Williams	6–4, 5–7, 6–3, 6–1
1914	Richard N. Williams	Maurice E. McLoughlin	6–3, 8–6, 10–8
1915	Bill Johnston	Maurice E. McLoughlin	1–6, 6–0, 7–5, 10–8
1916	Richard N. Williams	Bill Johnston	4–6, 6–4, 0–6, 6–2, 6–4
1917#	R.L. Murray	N. W. Niles	5–7, 8–6, 6–3, 6–3
1918	R.L. Murray	Bill Tilden	6–3, 6–1, 7–5
1919	Bill Johnston	Bill Tilden	6–4, 6–4, 6–3
1920	Bill Tilden	Bill Johnston	6–1, 1–6, 7–5, 5–7, 6–3
1921	Bill Tilden	Wallace F. Johnson	6–1, 6–3, 6–1
1922	Bill Tilden	Bill Johnston	4–6, 3–6, 6–2, 6–3, 6–4
1923	Bill Tilden	Bill Johnston	6–4, 6–1, 6–4
1924	Bill Tilden	Bill Johnston	6–1, 9–7, 6–2
1925	Bill Tilden	Bill Johnston	4–6, 11–9, 6–3, 4–6, 6–3
1926	Rene Lacoste	Jean Borotra	6–4, 6–0, 6–4
1927	Rene Lacoste	Bill Tilden	11–9, 6–3, 11–9
1928	Henri Cochet	Francis T. Hunter	4–6, 6–4, 3–6, 7–5, 6–3
1929	Bill Tilden	Francis T. Hunter	3–6, 6–3, 4–6, 6–2, 6–4
1930	John H. Doeg	Francis X. Shields	10–8, 1–6, 6–4, 16–14
1931	Ellsworth Vines	George M. Lott Jr	7–9, 6–3, 9–7, 7–5
1932	Ellsworth Vines	Henri Cochet	6–4, 6–4, 6–4
1933	Fred Perry	Jack Crawford	6–3, 11–13, 4–6, 6–0, 6–1
1934	Fred Perry	Wilmer L. Allison	6–4, 6–3, 1–6, 8–6
1935	Wilmer L. Allison	Sidney B. Wood Jr	6–2, 6–2, 6–3
1936	Fred Perry	Don Budge	2–6, 6–2, 8–6, 1–6, 10–8
1937	Don Budge	Gottfried von Cramm	6–1, 7–9, 6–1, 3–6, 6–1
1938	Don Budge	Gene Mako	6–3, 6–8, 6–2, 6–1
1939	Bobby Riggs	Welby Van Horn	6–4, 6–2, 6–4
1940	Don McNeill	Bobby Riggs	4–6, 6–8, 6–3, 6–3, 7–5
1941	Bobby Riggs	Francis Kovacs II	5–7, 6–1, 6–3, 6–3
1942	Ted Schroeder	Frank Parker	8–6, 7–5, 3–6, 4–6, 6–2
1943	Joseph R. Hunt	Jack Kramer	6–3, 6–8, 10–8, 6–0
1944	Frank Parker	William F. Talbert	6–4, 3–6, 6–3, 6–3
1945	Frank Parker	William F. Talbert	14–12, 6–1, 6–2
1946	Jack Kramer	Tom P. Brown	9–7, 6–3, 6–0
1947	Jack Kramer	Frank Parker	4–6, 2–6, 6–1, 6–0, 6–3
1948	Pancho Gonzales	Eric W. Sturgess	6–2, 6–3, 14–12
1949	Pancho Gonzales	Ted Schroeder	16–18, 2–6, 6–1, 6–2, 6–4
1950	Arthur Larsen	Herbie Flam	6–3, 4–6, 5–7, 6–4, 6–3
1951	Frank Sedgman	Vic Seixas	6–4, 6–1, 6–1
1952	Frank Sedgman	Gardnar Mulloy	6–1, 6–2, 6–3
1953	Tony Trabert	Vic Seixas	6–3, 6–2, 6–3
1954	Vic Seixas	Rex Hartwig	3–6, 6–2, 6–4, 6–4
1955	Tony Trabert	Ken Rosewall	9–7, 6–3, 6–3
1956	Ken Rosewall	Lew Hoad	4–6, 6–2, 6–3, 6–3
1957	Mal Anderson	Ashley J. Cooper	10–8, 7–5, 6–4
1958	Ashley J. Cooper	Mal Anderson	6–2, 3–6, 4–6, 10–8, 8–6
1959	Neale Fraser	Alex Olmedo	6–3, 5–7, 6–2, 6–4
1960	Neale Fraser	Rod Laver	6–4, 6–4, 9–7
1961	Roy Emerson	Rod Laver	7–5, 6–3, 6–2
1962	Rod Laver	Roy Emerson	6–2, 6–4, 5–7, 6–4
1963	Rafael Osuna	Frank Froehling III	7–5, 6–4, 6–2
1964	Roy Emerson	Fred Stolle	6–4, 6–2, 6–4
1965	Manuel Santana	Cliff Drysdale	6–2, 7–9, 7–5, 6–1
1966	Fred Stolle	John Newcombe	4–6, 12–10, 6–3, 6–4
1967	John Newcombe	Clark Graebner	6–4, 6–4, 8–6
1968*	Arthur Ashe	Tom Okker	14–12, 5–7, 6–3, 3–6, 6–3
1968**	Arthur Ashe	Bob Lutz	4–6, 6–3, 8–10, 6–0, 6–4
1969	Rod Laver	Tony Roche	7–9, 6–1, 6–3, 6–2
1969**	Stan Smith	Bob Lutz	9–7, 6–3, 6–1
1970	Ken Rosewall	Tony Roche	2–6, 6–4, 7–6, 6–3
1971	Stan Smith	Jan Kodes	3–6, 6–3, 6–2, 7–6

#National Patriotic Tournament. *Became Open (amateur and professional) in 1968. **Amateur event held.
‡ Challenge round abolished.

MEN *(Cont.)*
United States Championships *(Cont.)*

Year	Winner	Finalist	Score
1972	Ilie Nastase	Arthur Ashe	3–6, 6–3, 6–7, 6–4, 6–3
1973	John Newcombe	Jan Kodes	6–4, 1–6, 4–6, 6–2, 6–3
1974	Jimmy Connors	Ken Rosewall	6–1, 6–0, 6–1
1975	Manuel Orantes	Jimmy Connors	6–4, 6–3, 6–3
1976	Jimmy Connors	Bjorn Borg	6–4, 3–6, 7–6, 6–4
1977	Guillermo Vilas	Jimmy Connors	2–6, 6–3, 7–6, 6–0
1978	Jimmy Connors	Bjorn Borg	6–4, 6–2, 6–2
1979	John McEnroe	Vitas Gerulaitis	7–5, 6–3, 6–3
1980	John McEnroe	Bjorn Borg	7–6, 6–1, 6–7, 5–7, 6–4
1981	John McEnroe	Bjorn Borg	4–6, 6–2, 6–4, 6–3
1982	Jimmy Connors	Ivan Lendl	6–3, 6–2, 4–6, 6–4
1983	Jimmy Connors	Ivan Lendl	6–3, 6–7, 7–5, 6–0
1984	John McEnroe	Ivan Lendl	6–3, 6–4, 6–1
1985	Ivan Lendl	John McEnroe	7–6, 6–3, 6–4
1986	Ivan Lendl	Miloslav Mecir	6–4, 6–2, 6–0
1987	Ivan Lendl	Mats Wilander	6–7, 6–0, 7–6, 6–4
1988	Mats Wilander	Ivan Lendl	6–4, 4–6, 6–3, 5–7, 6–4
1989	Boris Becker	Ivan Lendl	7–6, 1–6, 6–3, 7–6
1990	Pete Sampras	Andre Agassi	6–4, 6–3, 6–2
1991	Stefan Edberg	Jim Courier	6–2, 6–4, 6–0
1992	Stefan Edberg	Pete Sampras	3–6, 6–4, 7–6, 6–2
1993	Pete Sampras	Cedric Pioline	6–4, 6–4, 6–3
1994	Andre Agassi	Michael Stich	6–1, 7–6, 7–5
1995	Pete Sampras	Andre Agassi	6–4, 6–3, 4–6, 7–5
1996	Pete Sampras	Michael Chang	6–1, 6–4, 7–6
1997	Patrick Rafter	Greg Rusedski	6–3, 6–2, 4–6, 7–5
1998	Patrick Rafter	Mark Philippoussis	6–3, 3–6, 6–2, 6–0
1999	Andre Agassi	Todd Martin	6–4, 6–7, 6–7, 6–3, 6–2
2000	Marat Safin	Pete Sampras	6–4, 6–3, 6–3
2001	Lleyton Hewitt	Pete Sampras	7–6, 6–1, 6–1
2002	Pete Sampras	Andre Agassi	6–3, 6–4, 5–7, 6–4
2003	Andy Roddick	Juan Carlos Ferrero	6–3, 7–6 (7-2), 6–3
2004	Roger Federer	Lleyton Hewitt	6–0, 7–6 (7-3), 6–0
2005	Roger Federer	Andre Agassi	6–3, 2–6, 7–6 (7–1), 6–1
2006	Roger Federer	Andy Roddick	6–2, 4–6, 7–5, 6–1
2007	Roger Federer	Novak Djokovic	7–6 (7–4), 7–6 (7–2), 6–4
2008	Roger Federer	Andy Murray	6–2, 7–5, 6–2
2009	Juan Martin del Potro	Roger Federer	3–6, 7–6 (7–5), 4–6, 7–6 (7–4), 6–2
2010	Rafael Nadal	Novak Djokovic	6–4, 5–7, 6–4, 6–2
2011	Novak Djokovic	Rafael Nadal	6–2, 6–4, 6–7 (3–7), 6–1
2012	Andy Murray	Novak Djokovic	7–6 (12–10), 7–5, 2–6, 3–6, 6–2

WOMEN
Australian Open Championships

Year	Winner	Finalist	Score
1922	Margaret Molesworth	Esna Boyd	6–3, 10–8
1923	Margaret Molesworth	Esna Boyd	6–1, 7–5
1924	Sylvia Lance	Esna Boyd	6–3, 3–6, 6–4
1925	Daphne Akhurst	Esna Boyd	1–6, 8–6, 6–4
1926	Daphne Akhurst	Esna Boyd	6–1, 6–3
1927	Esna Boyd	Sylvia Harper	5–7, 6–1, 6–2
1928	Daphne Akhurst	Esna Boyd	7–5, 6–2
1929	Daphne Akhurst	Louise Bickerton	6–1, 5–7, 6–2
1930	Daphne Akhurst	Sylvia Harper	10–8, 2–6, 7–5
1931	Coral Buttsworth	Margorie Crawford	1–6, 6–3, 6–4
1932	Coral Buttsworth	Kathrine Le Messurier	9–7, 6–4
1933	Joan Hartigan	Coral Buttsworth	6–4, 6–3
1934	Joan Hartigan	Margaret Molesworth	6–1, 6–4
1935	Dorothy Round	Nancye Wynne Bolton	1–6, 6–1, 6–3
1936	Joan Hartigan	Nancye Wynne Bolton	6–4, 6–4
1937	Nancye Wynne Bolton	Emily Westacott	6–3, 5–7, 6–4
1938	Dorothy Bundy	D. Stevenson	6–3, 6–2
1939	Emily Westacott	Nell Hopman	6–1, 6–2
1940	Nancye Wynne Bolton	Thelma Coyne	5–7, 6–4, 6–0
1941–45	No tournament		
1946	Nancye Wynne Bolton	Joyce Fitch	6–4, 6–4
1947	Nancye Wynne Bolton	Nell Hopman	6–3, 6–2
1948	Nancye Wynne Bolton	Marie Toomey	6–3, 6–1
1949	Doris Hart	Nancye Wynne Bolton	6–3, 6–4
1950	Louise Brough	Doris Hart	6–4, 3–6, 6–4
1951	Nancye Wynne Bolton	Thelma Long	6–1, 7–5
1952	Thelma Long	H. Angwin	6–2, 6–3
1953	Maureen Connolly	Julia Sampson	6–3, 6–2
1954	Thelma Long	J. Staley	6–3, 6–4
1955	Beryl Penrose	Thelma Long	6–4, 6–3
1956	Mary Carter	Thelma Long	3–6, 6–2, 9–7
1957	Shirley Fry	Althea Gibson	6–3, 6–4
1958	Angela Mortimer	Lorraine Coghlan	6–3, 6–4
1959	Mary Carter-Reitano	Renee Schuurman	6–2, 6–3
1960	Margaret Smith	Jan Lehane	7–5, 6–2
1961	Margaret Smith	Jan Lehane	6–1, 6–4
1962	Margaret Smith	Jan Lehane	6–0, 6–2
1963	Margaret Smith	Jan Lehane	6–2, 6–2
1964	Margaret Smith	Lesley Turner	6–3, 6–2
1965	Margaret Smith	Maria Bueno	5–7, 6–4, 5–2, ret.
1966	Margaret Smith	Nancy Richey	Default
1967	Nancy Richey	Lesley Turner	6–1, 6–4
1968	Billie Jean King	Margaret Smith	6–1, 6–2
1969*	Margaret Smith Court	Billie Jean King	6–4, 6–1
1970	Margaret Smith Court	Kerry Melville Reid	6–3, 6–1
1971	Margaret Smith Court	Evonne Goolagong	2–6, 7–6, 7–5
1972	Virginia Wade	Evonne Goolagong	6–4, 6–4
1973	Margaret Smith Court	Evonne Goolagong	6–4, 7–5
1974	Evonne Goolagong	Chris Evert	7–6, 4–6, 6–0
1975	Evonne Goolagong	Martina Navratilova	6–3, 6–2
1976	Evonne Goolagong Cawley	Renata Tomanova	6–2, 6–2
1977 (Jan)	Kerry Melville Reid	Dianne Balestrat	7–5, 6–2
1977 (Dec)	Evonne Goolagong Cawley	Helen Gourlay	6–3, 6–0
1978	Chris O'Neil	Betsy Nagelsen	6–3, 7–6
1979	Barbara Jordan	Sharon Walsh	6–3, 6–3
1980	Hana Mandlikova	Wendy Turnbull	6–0, 7–5
1981	Martina Navratilova	Chris Evert Lloyd	6–7, 6–4, 7–5
1982	Chris Evert Lloyd	Martina Navratilova	6–3, 2–6, 6–3
1983	Martina Navratilova	Kathy Jordan	6–2, 7–6
1984	Chris Evert Lloyd	Helena Sukova	6–7, 6–1, 6–3
1985 (Dec)	Martina Navratilova	Chris Evert Lloyd	6–2, 4–6, 6–2
1987 (Jan)	Hana Mandlikova	Martina Navratilova	7–5, 7–6
1988	Steffi Graf	Chris Evert	6–1, 7–6
1989	Steffi Graf	Helena Sukova	6–4, 6–4
1990	Steffi Graf	Mary Joe Fernandez	6–3, 6–4
1991	Monica Seles	Jana Novotna	5–7, 6–3, 6–1

*Became Open (amateur and professional) in 1969.

WOMEN *(Cont.)*
Australian Championships *(Cont.)*

Year	Winner	Finalist	Score
1992	Monica Seles	Mary Joe Fernandez	6–2, 6–3
1993	Monica Seles	Steffi Graf	4–6, 6–3, 6–2
1994	Steffi Graf	Arantxa Sánchez Vicario	6–0, 6–2
1995	Mary Pierce	Arantxa Sánchez Vicario	6–3, 6–2
1996	Monica Seles	Anke Huber	6–4, 6–1
1997	Martina Hingis	Mary Pierce	6–2, 6–2
1998	Martina Hingis	Conchita Martinez	6–3, 6–3
1999	Martina Hingis	Amelie Mauresmo	6–2, 6–3
2000	Lindsay Davenport	Martina Hingis	6–1, 7–5
2001	Jennifer Capriati	Martina Hingis	6–4, 6–3
2002	Jennifer Capriati	Martina Hingis	4–6, 7–6 (9–7), 6–2
2003	Serena Williams	Venus Williams	7–6 (7-4), 3–6, 6–4
2004	Justine Henin-Hardenne	Kim Clijsters	6–3, 4–6, 6–3
2005	Serena Williams	Lindsay Davenport	2–6, 6–3, 6–0
2006	Amelie Mauresmo	Justine Henin-Hardenne	6–1, 2–0, ret.
2007	Serena Williams	Maria Sharapova	6–1, 6–2
2008	Maria Sharapova	Ana Ivanovic	7–5, 6–3
2009	Serena Williams	Dinara Safina	6–0, 6–3
2010	Serena Williams	Justine Henin	6–4, 3–6, 6–2
2011	Kim Clijsters	Li Na	3–6, 6–3, 6–3
2012	Victoria Azarenka	Maria Sharapova	6–3, 6–0

French Championships

Year	Winner	Finalist	Score
1925†	Suzanne Lenglen	Kathleen McKane	6–1, 6–2
1926	Suzanne Lenglen	Mary K. Browne	6–1, 6–0
1927	Kea Bouman	Irene Peacock	6–2, 6–4
1928	Helen Wills	Eileen Bennett	6–1, 6–2
1929	Helen Wills	Simone Mathieu	6–3, 6–4
1930	Helen Wills Moody	Helen Jacobs	6–2, 6–1
1931	Cilly Aussem	Betty Nuthall	8–6, 6–1
1932	Helen Wills Moody	Simone Mathieu	7–5, 6–1
1933	Margaret Scriven	Simone Mathieu	6–2, 4–6, 6–4
1934	Margaret Scriven	Helen Jacobs	7–5, 4–6, 6–1
1935	Hilde Sperling	Simone Mathieu	6–2, 6–1
1936	Hilde Sperling	Simone Mathieu	6–3, 6–4
1937	Hilde Sperling	Simone Mathieu	6–2, 6–4
1938	Simone Mathieu	Nelly Landry	6–0, 6–3
1939	Simone Mathieu	Jadwiga Jedrzejowska	6–3, 8–6
1940–45	No tournament		
1946	Margaret Osborne	Pauline Betz	1–6, 8–6, 7–5
1947	Patricia Todd	Doris Hart	6–3, 3–6, 6–4
1948	Nelly Landry	Shirley Fry	6–2, 0–6, 6–0
1949	Margaret Osborne duPont	Nelly Adamson	7–5, 6–2
1950	Doris Hart	Patricia Todd	6–4, 4–6, 6–2
1951	Shirley Fry	Doris Hart	6–3, 3–6, 6–3
1952	Doris Hart	Shirley Fry	6–4, 6–4
1953	Maureen Connolly	Doris Hart	6–2, 6–4
1954	Maureen Connolly	Ginette Bucaille	6–4, 6–1
1955	Angela Mortimer	Dorothy Knode	2–6, 7–5, 10–8
1956	Althea Gibson	Angela Mortimer	6–0, 12–10
1957	Shirley Bloomer	Dorothy Knode	6–1, 6–3
1958	Zsuzsi Kormoczi	Shirley Bloomer	6–4, 1–6, 6–2
1959	Christine Truman	Zsuzsi Kormoczi	6–4, 7–5
1960	Darlene Hard	Yola Ramirez	6–3, 6–4
1961	Ann Haydon	Yola Ramirez	6–2, 6–1
1962	Margaret Smith	Lesley Turner	6–3, 3–6, 7–5
1963	Lesley Turner	Ann Haydon Jones	2–6, 6–3, 7–5
1964	Margaret Smith	Maria Bueno	5–7, 6–1, 6–2
1965	Lesley Turner	Margaret Smith	6–3, 6–4
1966	Ann Jones	Nancy Richey	6–3, 6–1
1967	Francoise Durr	Lesley Turner	4–6, 6–3, 6–4
1968*	Nancy Richey	Ann Jones	5–7, 6–4, 6–1

†1925 was the first year that entries were accepted from all countries. *Became Open (amateur and professional) in 1968, but restricted to only contract professionals in 1972.

WOMEN *(Cont.)*
French Championships *(Cont.)*

Year	Winner	Finalist	Score
1969	Margaret Smith Court	Ann Jones	6–1, 4–6, 6–3
1970	Margaret Smith Court	Helga Niessen	6–2, 6–4
1971	Evonne Goolagong	Helen Gourlay	6–3, 7–5
1972	Billie Jean King	Evonne Goolagong	6–3, 6–3
1973	Margaret Smith Court	Chris Evert	6–7, 7–6, 6–4
1974	Chris Evert	Olga Morozova	6–1, 6–2
1975	Chris Evert	Martina Navratilova	2–6, 6–2, 6–1
1976	Sue Barker	Renata Tomanova	6–2, 0–6, 6–2
1977	Mima Jausovec	Florenza Mihai	6–2, 6–7, 6–1
1978	Virginia Ruzici	Mima Jausovec	6–2, 6–2
1979	Chris Evert Lloyd	Wendy Turnbull	6–2, 6–0
1980	Chris Evert Lloyd	Virginia Ruzici	6–0, 6–3
1981	Hana Mandlikova	Sylvia Hanika	6–2, 6–4
1982	Martina Navratilova	Andrea Jaeger	7–6, 6–1
1983	Chris Evert Lloyd	Mima Jausovec	6–1, 6–2
1984	Martina Navratilova	Chris Evert Lloyd	6–3, 6–1
1985	Chris Evert Lloyd	Martina Navratilova	6–3, 6–7, 7–5
1986	Chris Evert Lloyd	Martina Navratilova	2–6, 6–3, 6–3
1987	Steffi Graf	Martina Navratilova	6–4, 4–6, 8–6
1988	Steffi Graf	Natalia Zvereva	6–0, 6–0
1989	Arantxa Sánchez Vicario	Steffi Graf	7–6, 3–6, 7–5
1990	Monica Seles	Steffi Graf	7–6, 6–4
1991	Monica Seles	Arantxa Sánchez Vicario	6–3, 6–4
1992	Monica Seles	Steffi Graf	6–2, 3–6, 10–8
1993	Steffi Graf	Mary Joe Fernandez	4–6, 6–2, 6–4
1994	Arantxa Sánchez Vicario	Mary Pierce	6–4, 6–4
1995	Steffi Graf	Arantxa Sánchez Vicario	7–5, 4–6, 6–0
1996	Steffi Graf	Arantxa Sánchez Vicario	6–3, 6–7 (4–7), 10–8
1997	Iva Majoli	Martina Hingis	6–4, 6–2
1998	Arantxa Sánchez Vicario	Monica Seles	7–6 (7–5), 0–6, 6–2
1999	Steffi Graf	Martina Hingis	4–6, 7–5, 6–2
2000	Mary Pierce	Conchita Martinez	6–2, 7–5
2001	Jennifer Capriati	Kim Clijsters	1–6, 6–4, 12–10
2002	Serena Williams	Venus Williams	7–5, 6–3
2003	Justine Henin-Hardenne	Kim Clijsters	6–0, 6–4
2004	Anastasia Myskina	Elena Dementieva	6–1, 6–2
2005	Justine Henin-Hardenne	Mary Pierce	6–1, 6–1
2006	Justine Henin-Hardenne	Svetlana Kuznetsova	6–4, 6–4
2007	Justine Henin	Ana Ivanovic	6–1, 6–2
2008	Ana Ivanovic	Dinara Safina	6–4, 6–3
2009	Svetlana Kuznetsova	Dinara Safina	6–4, 6–2
2010	Francesca Schiavone	Samantha Stosur	6–4, 7–6 (7–2)
2011	Li Na	Francesca Schiavone	6–4, 7–6 (7–0)
2012	Maria Sharapova	Sara Errani	6–3, 6–2

Wimbledon Championships

Year	Winner	Finalist	Score
1884	Maud Watson	Lilian Watson	6–8, 6–3, 6–3
1885	Maud Watson	Blanche Bingley	6–1, 7–5
1886	Blanche Bingley	Maud Watson	6–3, 6–3
1887	Charlotte Dod	Blanche Bingley	6–2, 6–0
1888	Charlotte Dod	Blanche Bingley Hillyard	6–3, 6–3
1889	Blanche Bingley Hillyard	n/a	n/a
1890	Lena Rice	n/a	n/a
1891	Charlotte Dod	n/a	n/a
1892	Charlotte Dod	Blanche Bingley Hillyard	6–1, 6–1
1893	Charlotte Dod	Blanche Bingley Hillyard	6–8, 6–1, 6–4
1894	Blanche Bingley Hillyard	n/a	n/a
1895	Charlotte Cooper	n/a	n/a
1896	Charlotte Cooper	Mrs. W. H. Pickering	6–2, 6–3
1897	Blanche Bingley Hillyard	Charlotte Cooper	5–7, 7–5, 6–2
1898	Charlotte Cooper	n/a	n/a
1899	Blanche Bingley Hillyard	Charlotte Cooper	6–2, 6–3
1900	Blanche Bingley Hillyard	Charlotte Cooper	4–6, 6–4, 6–4
1901	Charlotte Cooper Sterry	Blanche Bingley Hillyard	6–2, 6–2
1902	Muriel Robb	Charlotte Cooper Sterry	7–5, 6–1

WOMEN *(Cont.)*

Wimbledon Championships *(Cont.)*

Year	Winner	Finalist	Score
1903	Dorothea Douglass	n/a	n/a
1904	Dorothea Douglass	Charlotte Cooper Sterry	6–0, 6–3
1905	May Sutton	Dorothea Douglass	6–3, 6–4
1906	Dorothea Douglass	May Sutton	6–3, 9–7
1907	May Sutton	Dorothea Douglass Lambert Chambers	6–1, 6–4
1908	Charlotte Cooper Sterry	n/a	n/a
1909	Dora Boothby	n/a	n/a
1910	Dorothea Douglass Lambert Chambers	Dora Boothby	6–2, 6–2
1911	Dorothea Douglass Lambert Chambers	Dora Boothby	6–0, 6–0
1912	Ethel Larcombe	n/a	n/a
1913	Dorothea Douglass Lambert Chambers	n/a	n/a
1914	Dorothea Douglass Lambert Chambers	Ethel Larcombe	7–5, 6–4
1915–18	No tournament		
1919	Suzanne Lenglen	Dorothea Douglass Lambert Chambers	10–8, 4–6, 9–7
1920	Suzanne Lenglen	Dorothea Douglass Lambert Chambers	6–3, 6–0
1921	Suzanne Lenglen	Elizabeth Ryan	6–2, 6–0
1922	Suzanne Lenglen	Molla Mallory	6–2, 6–0
1923	Suzanne Lenglen	Kathleen McKane	6–2, 6–2
1924	Kathleen McKane	Helen Wills	4–6, 6–4, 6–2
1925	Suzanne Lenglen	Joan Fry	6–2, 6–0
1926	Kathleen McKane Godfree	Lili de Alvarez	6–2, 4–6, 6–3
1927	Helen Wills	Lili de Alvarez	6–2, 6–4
1928	Helen Wills	Lili de Alvarez	6–2, 6–3
1929	Helen Wills	Helen Jacobs	6–1, 6–2
1930	Helen Wills Moody	Elizabeth Ryan	6–2, 6–2
1931	Cilly Aussem	Hilde Kranwinkel	7–5, 7–5
1932	Helen Wills Moody	Helen Jacobs	6–3, 6–1
1933	Helen Wills Moody	Dorothy Round	6–4, 6–8, 6–3
1934	Dorothy Round	Helen Jacobs	6–2, 5–7, 6–3
1935	Helen Wills Moody	Helen Jacobs	6–3, 3–6, 7–5
1936	Helen Jacobs	Hilde Kranwinkel Sperling	6–2, 4–6, 7–5
1937	Dorothy Round	Jadwiga Jedrzejowska	6–2, 2–6, 7–5
1938	Helen Wills Moody	Helen Jacobs	6–4, 6–0
1939	Alice Marble	Kay Stammers	6–2, 6–0
1940–45	No tournament		
1946	Pauline Betz	Louise Brough	6–2, 6–4
1947	Margaret Osborne	Doris Hart	6–2, 6–4
1948	Louise Brough	Doris Hart	6–3, 8–6
1949	Louise Brough	Margaret Osborne duPont	10–8, 1–6, 10–8
1950	Louise Brough	Margaret Osborne duPont	6–1, 3–6, 6–1
1951	Doris Hart	Shirley Fry	6–1, 6–0
1952	Maureen Connolly	Louise Brough	6–4, 6–3
1953	Maureen Connolly	Doris Hart	8–6, 7–5
1954	Maureen Connolly	Louise Brough	6–2, 7–5
1955	Louise Brough	Beverly Fleitz	7–5, 8–6
1956	Shirley Fry	Angela Buxton	6–3, 6–1
1957	Althea Gibson	Darlene Hard	6–3, 6–2
1958	Althea Gibson	Angela Mortimer	8–6, 6–2
1959	Maria Bueno	Darlene Hard	6–4, 6–3
1960	Maria Bueno	Sandra Reynolds	8–6, 6–0
1961	Angela Mortimer	Christine Truman	4–6, 6–4, 7–5
1962	Karen Hantze Susman	Vera Sukova	6–4, 6–4
1963	Margaret Smith	Billie Jean Moffitt	6–3, 6–4
1964	Maria Bueno	Margaret Smith	6–4, 7–9, 6–3
1965	Margaret Smith	Maria Bueno	6–4, 7–5
1966	Billie Jean King	Maria Bueno	6–3, 3–6, 6–1
1967	Billie Jean King	Ann Haydon Jones	6–3, 6–4

Note: Prior to 1922 the tournament was run on a challenge-round system. The previous year's winner "stood out" of an All-Comers event, which produced a challenger to play her for the title.

WOMEN (Cont.)
Wimbledon Championships (Cont.)

Year	Winner	Finalist	Score
1968*	Billie Jean King	Judy Tegart	9–7, 7–5
1969	Ann Haydon Jones	Billie Jean King	3–6, 6–3, 6–2
1970	Margaret Smith Court	Billie Jean King	14–12, 11–9
1971	Evonne Goolagong	Margaret Smith Court	6–4, 6–1
1972	Billie Jean King	Evonne Goolagong	6–3, 6–3
1973	Billie Jean King	Chris Evert	6–0, 7–5
1974	Chris Evert	Olga Morozova	6–0, 6–4
1975	Billie Jean King	Evonne Goolagong Cawley	6–0, 6–1
1976	Chris Evert	Evonne Goolagong Cawley	6–3, 4–6, 8–6
1977	Virginia Wade	Betty Stove	4–6, 6–3, 6–1
1978	Martina Navratilova	Chris Evert	2–6, 6–4, 7–5
1979	Martina Navratilova	Chris Evert Lloyd	6–4, 6–4
1980	Evonne Goolagong Cawley	Chris Evert Lloyd	6–1, 7–6
1981	Chris Evert Lloyd	Hana Mandlikova	6–2, 6–2
1982	Martina Navratilova	Chris Evert Lloyd	6–1, 3–6, 6–2
1983	Martina Navratilova	Andrea Jaeger	6–0, 6–3
1984	Martina Navratilova	Chris Evert Lloyd	7–6, 6–2
1985	Martina Navratilova	Chris Evert Lloyd	4–6, 6–3, 6–2
1986	Martina Navratilova	Hana Mandlikova	7–6, 6–3
1987	Martina Navratilova	Steffi Graf	7–5, 6–3
1988	Steffi Graf	Martina Navratilova	5–7, 6–2, 6–1
1989	Steffi Graf	Martina Navratilova	6–2, 6–7, 6–1
1990	Martina Navratilova	Zina Garrison	6–4, 6–1
1991	Steffi Graf	Gabriela Sabatini	6–4, 3–6, 8–6
1992	Steffi Graf	Monica Seles	6–2, 6–1
1993	Steffi Graf	Jana Novotna	7–6, 1–6, 6–4
1994	Conchita Martinez	Martina Navratilova	6–4, 3–6, 6–3
1995	Steffi Graf	Arantxa Sánchez Vicario	4–6, 6–1, 7–5
1996	Steffi Graf	Arantxa Sánchez Vicario	6–3, 7–5
1997	Martina Hingis	Jana Novotna	2–6, 6–3, 6–3
1998	Jana Novotna	Nathalie Tauziat	6–4, 7–6
1999	Lindsay Davenport	Steffi Graf	6–4, 7–5
2000	Venus Williams	Lindsay Davenport	6–3, 7–6
2001	Venus Williams	Justine Henin	6–1, 3–6, 6–0
2002	Serena Williams	Venus Williams	7–6 (7–4), 6–3
2003	Serena Williams	Venus Williams	4–6, 6–4, 6–2
2004	Maria Sharapova	Serena Williams	6–1, 6–4
2005	Venus Williams	Lindsay Davenport	4–6, 7–6 (7–4), 9–7
2006	Amelie Mauresmo	Justine Henin-Hardenne	2–6, 6–3, 6–4
2007	Venus Williams	Marion Bartoli	6–4, 6–1
2008	Venus Williams	Serena Williams	7–5, 6–4
2009	Serena Williams	Venus Williams	7–6 (7–3), 6–2
2010	Serena Williams	Vera Zvonareva	6–3, 6–2
2011	Petra Kvitova	Maria Sharapova	6–3, 6–4
2012	Serena Williams	Agnieszka Radwanska	6–1, 5–7, 6–2

*Became Open (amateur and professional) in 1968, but restricted to only contract professionals in 1972.

United States Championships

Year	Winner	Finalist	Score
1887	Ellen Hansell	Laura Knight	6–1, 6–0
1888	Bertha L. Townsend	Ellen Hansell	6–3, 6–5
1889	Bertha L. Townsend	Louise Voorhes	7–5, 6–2
1890	Ellen C. Roosevelt	Bertha L. Townsend	6–2, 6–2
1891	Mabel Cahill	Ellen C. Roosevelt	6–4, 6–1, 4–6, 6–3
1892	Mabel Cahill	Elisabeth Moore	5–7, 6–3, 6–4, 4–6, 6–2
1893	Aline Terry	Alice Schultze	6–1, 6–3
1894	Helen Hellwig	Aline Terry	7–5, 3–6, 6–0, 3–6, 6–3
1895	Juliette Atkinson	Helen Hellwig	6–4, 6–2, 6–1
1896	Elisabeth Moore	Juliette Atkinson	6–4, 4–6, 6–2, 6–2
1897	Juliette Atkinson	Elisabeth Moore	6–3, 6–3, 4–6, 3–6, 6–3
1898	Juliette Atkinson	Marion Jones	6–3, 5–7, 6–4, 2–6, 7–5
1899	Marion Jones	Maud Banks	6–1, 6–1, 7–5
1900	Myrtle McAteer	Edith Parker	6–2, 6–2, 6–0
1901	Elisabeth Moore	Myrtle McAteer	6–4, 3–6, 7–5, 2–6, 6–2
1902*	Marion Jones	Elisabeth Moore	6–1, 1–0, ret.

*Five-set final abolished.

WOMEN *(Cont.)*

United States Championships *(Cont.)*

Year	Winner	Finalist	Score
1903	Elisabeth Moore	Marion Jones	7–5, 8–6
1904	May Sutton	Elisabeth Moore	6–1, 6–2
1905	Elisabeth Moore	Helen Homans	6–4, 5–7, 6–1
1906	Helen Homans	Maud Barger-Wallach	6–4, 6–3
1907	Evelyn Sears	Carrie Neely	6–3, 6–2
1908	Maud Barger–Wallach	Evelyn Sears	6–3, 1–6, 6–3
1909	Hazel Hotchkiss	Maud Barger–Wallach	6–0, 6–1
1910	Hazel Hotchkiss	Louise Hammond	6–4, 6–2
1911	Hazel Hotchkiss	Florence Sutton	8–10, 6–1, 9–7
1912†	Mary K. Browne	Eleanora Sears	6–4, 6–2
1913	Mary K. Browne	Dorothy Green	6–2, 7–5
1914	Mary K. Browne	Marie Wagner	6–2, 1–6, 6–1
1915	Molla Bjurstedt	Hazel Hotchkiss Wightman	4–6, 6–2, 6–0
1916	Molla Bjurstedt	Louise Hammond Raymond	6–0, 6–1
1917‡	Molla Bjurstedt	Marion Vanderhoef	4–6, 6–0, 6–2
1918	Molla Bjurstedt	Eleanor Goss	6–4, 6–3
1919	Hazel Hotchkiss Wightman	Marion Zinderstein	6–1, 6–2
1920	Molla Bjurstedt Mallory	Marion Zinderstein	6–3, 6–1
1921	Molla Bjurstedt Mallory	Mary K. Browne	4–6, 6–4, 6–2
1922	Molla Bjurstedt Mallory	Helen Wills	6–3, 6–1
1923	Helen Wills	Molla Bjurstedt Mallory	6–2, 6–1
1924	Helen Wills	Molla Bjurstedt Mallory	6–1, 6–3
1925	Helen Wills	Kathleen McKane	3–6, 6–0, 6–2
1926	Molla Bjurstedt Mallory	Elizabeth Ryan	4–6, 6–4, 9–7
1927	Helen Wills	Betty Nuthall	6–1, 6–4
1928	Helen Wills	Helen Jacobs	6–2, 6–1
1929	Helen Wills	Phoebe Holcroft Watson	6–4, 6–2
1930	Betty Nuthall	Anna McCune Harper	6–1, 6–4
1931	Helen Wills Moody	Eileen Whitingstall	6–4, 6–1
1932	Helen Jacobs	Carolin Babcock	6–2, 6–2
1933	Helen Jacobs	Helen Wills Moody	8–6, 3–6, 3–0, ret.
1934	Helen Jacobs	Sarah Palfrey	6–1, 6–4
1935	Helen Jacobs	Sarah Palfrey Fabyan	6–2, 6–4
1936	Alice Marble	Helen Jacobs	4–6, 6–3, 6–2
1937	Anita Lizane	Jadwiga Jedrzejowska	6–4, 6–2
1938	Alice Marble	Nancye Wynne	6–0, 6–3
1939	Alice Marble	Helen Jacobs	6–0, 8–10, 6–4
1940	Alice Marble	Helen Jacobs	6–2, 6–3
1941	Sarah Palfrey Cooke	Pauline Betz	7–5, 6–2
1942	Pauline Betz	Louise Brough	4–6, 6–1, 6–4
1943	Pauline Betz	Louise Brough	6–3, 5–7, 6–3
1944	Pauline Betz	Margaret Osborne	6–3, 8–6
1945	Sarah Palfrey Cooke	Pauline Betz	3–6, 8–6, 6–4
1946	Pauline Betz	Patricia Canning	11–9, 6–3
1947	Louise Brough	Margaret Osborne	8–6, 4–6, 6–1
1948	Margaret Osborne duPont	Louise Brough	4–6, 6–4, 15–13
1949	Margaret Osborne duPont	Doris Hart	6–4, 6–1
1950	Margaret Osborne duPont	Doris Hart	6–4, 6–3
1951	Maureen Connolly	Shirley Fry	6–3, 1–6, 6–4
1952	Maureen Connolly	Doris Hart	6–3, 7–5
1953	Maureen Connolly	Doris Hart	6–2, 6–4
1954	Doris Hart	Louise Brough	6–8, 6–1, 8–6
1955	Doris Hart	Patricia Ward	6–4, 6–2
1956	Shirley Fry	Althea Gibson	6–3, 6–4
1957	Althea Gibson	Louise Brough	6–3, 6–2
1958	Althea Gibson	Darlene Hard	3–6, 6–1, 6–2
1959	Maria Bueno	Christine Truman	6–1, 6–4
1960	Darlene Hard	Maria Bueno	6–4, 10–12, 6–4
1961	Darlene Hard	Ann Haydon	6–3, 6–4
1962	Margaret Smith	Darlene Hard	9–7, 6–4
1963	Maria Bueno	Margaret Smith	7–5, 6–4
1964	Maria Bueno	Carole Graebner	6–1, 6–0
1965	Margaret Smith	Billie Jean Moffitt	8–6, 7–5
1966	Maria Bueno	Nancy Richey	6–3, 6–1
1967	Billie Jean King	Ann Haydon Jones	11–9, 6–4

†Challenge round abolished. ‡National Patriotic Tournament.

WOMEN *(Cont.)*

United States Championships *(Cont.)*

Year	Winner	Finalist	Score
1968**	Virginia Wade	Billie Jean King	6–4, 6–4
1968#	Margaret Smith Court	Maria Bueno	6–2, 6–2
1969	Margaret Smith Court	Nancy Richey	6–2, 6–2
1969#	Margaret Smith Court	Virginia Wade	4–6, 6–3, 6–0
1970	Margaret Smith Court	Rosie Casals	6–2, 2–6, 6–1
1971	Billie Jean King	Rosie Casals	6–4, 7–6
1972	Billie Jean King	Kerry Melville	6–3, 7–5
1973	Margaret Smith Court	Evonne Goolagong	7–6, 5–7, 6–2
1974	Billie Jean King	Evonne Goolagong	3–6, 6–3, 7–5
1975	Chris Evert	Evonne Goolagong Cawley	5–7, 6–4, 6–2
1976	Chris Evert	Evonne Goolagong Cawley	6–3, 6–0
1977	Chris Evert	Wendy Turnbull	7–6, 6–2
1978	Chris Evert	Pam Shriver	7–6, 6–4
1979	Tracy Austin	Chris Evert Lloyd	6–4, 6–3
1980	Chris Evert Lloyd	Hana Mandlikova	5–7, 6–1, 6–1
1981	Tracy Austin	Martina Navratilova	1–6, 7–6, 7–6
1982	Chris Evert Lloyd	Hana Mandlikova	6–3, 6–1
1983	Martina Navratilova	Chris Evert Lloyd	6–1, 6–3
1984	Martina Navratilova	Chris Evert Lloyd	4–6, 6–4, 6–4
1985	Hana Mandlikova	Martina Navratilova	7–6, 1–6, 7–6
1986	Martina Navratilova	Helena Sukova	6–3, 6–2
1987	Martina Navratilova	Steffi Graf	7–6, 6–1
1988	Steffi Graf	Gabriela Sabatini	6–3, 3–6, 6–1
1989	Steffi Graf	Martina Navratilova	3–6, 6–4, 6–2
1990	Gabriela Sabatini	Steffi Graf	6–2, 7–6
1991	Monica Seles	Martina Navratilova	7–6, 6–1
1992	Monica Seles	Arantxa Sánchez Vicario	6–3, 6–2
1993	Steffi Graf	Helena Sukova	6–3, 6–3
1994	Arantxa Sánchez Vicario	Steffi Graf	1–6, 7–6, 6–4
1995	Steffi Graf	Monica Seles	7–6, 0–6, 6–3
1996	Steffi Graf	Monica Seles	7–5, 7–4
1997	Martina Hingis	Venus Williams	6–0, 6–4
1998	Lindsay Davenport	Martina Hingis	6–3, 7–5
1999	Serena Williams	Martina Hingis	6–3, 7–6
2000	Venus Williams	Lindsay Davenport	6–4, 7–5
2001	Venus Williams	Serena Williams	6–2, 6–4
2002	Serena Williams	Venus Williams	6–4, 6–3
2003	Justine Henin-Hardenne	Kim Clijsters	7–5, 6–1
2004	Svetlana Kuznetsova	Elena Dementieva	6–3, 7–5
2005	Kim Clijsters	Mary Pierce	6–3, 6–1
2006	Maria Sharapova	Justine Henin-Hardenne	6–4, 6–4
2007	Justine Henin	Svetlana Kuznetsova	6–1, 6–3
2008	Serena Williams	Jelena Jankovic	6–4, 7–5
2009	Kim Clijsters	Caroline Wozniacki	7–5, 6–3
2010	Kim Clijsters	Vera Zvonareva	6–2, 6–1
2011	Samantha Stosur	Serena Williams	6–2, 6–3
2012	Serena Williams	Victoria Azarenka	2–6, 6–2, 7–5

**Became Open (amateur and professional) in 1968. #Amateur event held.

Single-Year Grand Slam Winners

Singles

Don Budge, 1938
Maureen Connolly, 1953
Rod Laver, 1962, 1969
Margaret Smith Court, 1970
Steffi Graf, 1988

Doubles

Frank Sedgman and Ken McGregor, 1951
Martina Navratilova and Pam Shriver, 1984
Maria Bueno and two partners, 1960
Christine Truman (Australian),
Darlene Hard (French, Wimbledon and U.S.)
Martina Hingis and two partners, 1998
Mirjana Lucic (Australian),
Jana Novotna (French, Wimbledon and U.S.)

Mixed Doubles

Margaret Smith and Ken Fletcher, 1963
Owen Davidson and two partners, 1967
Lesley Turner (Australian),
Billie Jean King (French, Wimbledon and U.S.)

Alltime Grand Slam Champions

Alltime Grand Slam Champions (Singles, Doubles, and Mixed Doubles)

MEN

Player	Aus. S-D-M	French S-D-M	Wim. S-D-M	U.S. S-D-M	Total
Roy Emerson	6-3-0	2-6-0	2-3-0	2-4-0	28
John Newcombe	2-5-0	0-3-0	3-6-0	2-3-1	25
Frank Sedgman	2-2-2	0-3-2	1-2-2	2-2-2	22
Todd Woodbridge	0-3-1	0-1-1	0-9-1	0-3-3	22
Bill Tilden	†	0-0-1	3-1-0	7-5-4	21
Rod Laver	3-4-0	2-1-1	4-1-2	2-0-0	20
John Bromwich	2-8-1	0-0-0	0-2-2	0-3-1	19
Jean Borotra	1-1-1	1-5-2	2-3-1	0-0-1	18
Fred Stolle	0-3-1	1-2-0	0-2-3	1-3-2	18
Ken Rosewall	4-3-0	2-2-0	0-2-0	2-2-1	18
Neale Fraser	0-3-1	0-3-0	1-2-0	2-3-3	18
Adrian Quist	3-10-0	0-1-0	0-2-0	0-1-0	17
John McEnroe	0-0-0	0-0-1	3-4-0	4-5-0	17
Jack Crawford	4-4-3	1-1-1	1-1-1	0-0-0	17
Mark Woodforde	0-2-2	0-1-1	0-6-1	0-3-1	17
*Roger Federer	4-0-0	1-0-0	7-0-0	5-0-0	17

†Did not compete.

WOMEN

Player	Aus. S-D-M	French S-D-M	Wim. S-D-M	U.S. S-D-M	Total
Margaret Smith Court	11-8-2	5-4-4	3-2-5	5-5-8	62
Martina Navratilova	3-8-1	2-7-2	9-7-4	4-9-3	59
Billie Jean King	1-0-1	1-1-2	6-10-4	4-5-4	39
Doris Hart	1-1-2	2-5-3	1-4-5	2-4-5	35
Helen Wills Moody	†	4-2-0	8-3-1	7-4-2	31
Louise Brough	1-1-0	0-3-0	4-5-4	1-8-3	30**
*Serena Williams	5-4-0	1-2-0	5-5-1	4-2-1	30
Margaret Osborne duPont	†	2-3-0	1-5-1	3-8-6	29**
Elizabeth Ryan	†	0-4-0	0-12-7	0-1-2	26
Steffi Graf	4-0-0	6-0-0	7-1-0	5-0-0	23
Pam Shriver	0-7-0	0-4-1	0-5-0	0-5-0	22
*Venus Williams	0-4-1	0-2-1	5-5-0	2-2-0	22
Chris Evert	2-0-0	7-2-0	3-1-0	6-0-0	21
Darlene Hard	†	1-3-2	0-4-3	2-6-0	21
Suzanne Lenglen	†	2-2-2#	6-6-3	0-0-0	21
Nancye Wynne Bolton	6-10-4	0-0-0	0-0-0	0-0-0	20

*Active player in 2012. †Did not compete. **From 1940–45, with competition in the U.S. Championships thinned due to war, Louise Brough Clapp won four doubles titles (1942–45) and one mixed doubles title (1942); and Margaret Osborne duPont won five doubles titles (1941–45) and three mixed doubles titles (1943–45).

Alltime Grand Slam Singles Champions

MEN Player	Aus.	French	Wim.	U.S.	Total	WOMEN Player	Aus.	French	Wim.	U.S.	Total
*Roger Federer	4	1	7	5	17	Margaret Smith Court	11	5	3	5	24
Pete Sampras	2	0	7	5	14	Steffi Graf	4	6	7	5	22
Roy Emerson	6	2	2	2	12	Helen Wills Moody	†	4	8	7	19
Bjorn Borg	0	6	5	0	11	Chris Evert	2	7	3	6	18
Rod Laver	3	2	4	2	11	Martina Navratilova	3	2	9	4	18
*Rafael Nadal	1	7	2	1	11	*Serena Williams	5	1	5	4	15
Bill Tilden	†	0	3	7	10	Billie Jean King	1	1	6	4	12
Jimmy Connors	1	0	2	5	8	Maureen Connolly	1	2	3	3	9
Ivan Lendl	2	3	0	3	8	Monica Seles	4	3	0	2	9
Fred Perry	1	1	3	3	8	Suzanne Lenglen	†	2#	6	0	8
Ken Rosewall	4	2	0	2	8	Molla Bjurstedt Mallory	†	†	0	8	8
Andre Agassi	4	1	1	2	8	Maria Bueno	0	0	3	4	7
Henri Cochet	†	4	2	1	7	Evonne Goolagong	4	1	2	0	7
Rene Lacoste	†	3	2	2	7	Dorothea D.L. Chambers	†	†	7	0	7
Bill Larned	†	†	0	7	7	Justine Henin	1	4	0	2	7
John McEnroe	0	0	3	4	7	*Venus Williams	0	0	5	2	7
John Newcombe	2	0	3	2	7	*Maria Sharapova	3	1	2	1	7
Willie Renshaw	†	†	7	†	7						
Dick Sears	†	†	0	7	7						

*Active player in 2012. †Did not compete. #Suzanne Lenglen won four singles titles at the French Championships before competition was opened to entries from all nations in 1925.

Golf

Rory McIlroy cemented his No. 1 status with three late-season wins, including a dominant victory at the PGA Championship.

Men's Majors

The Masters
Augusta National GC (par 72; 7,435 yds);
Augusta, Ga., April 5–8, 2012

Player	Score	Earnings ($)
*Bubba Watson	69-71-70-68--278	1,440,000
Louis Oosthuizen	68-72-69-69--278	864,000
Peter Hanson	68-74-65-73--280	384,000
Matt Kuchar	71-70-70-69--280	384,000
Phil Mickelson	74-68-66-72--280	384,000
Lee Westwood	67-73-72-68--280	384,000
Ian Poulter	72-72-70-69--283	268,000
Padraig Harrington	71-73-68-72--284	232,000
Justin Rose	72-72-72-68--284	232,000
Adam Scott	75-70-73-66--284	232,000
Jim Furyk	70-73-72-70--285	200,000
Fred Couples	72-67-75-72--286	156,800
Sergio Garcia	72-68-75-71--286	156,800
Hunter Mahan	72-72-68-74--286	156,800
Graeme McDowell	75-72-71-68--286	156,800
Kevin Na	71-75-72-68--286	156,800
Ben Crane	69-73-72-73--287	124,000
Bo Van Pelt	73-75-75-64--287	124,000
Charles Howell III	72-70-74-72--288	96,960
Fredrik Jacobson	76-68-70-74--288	96,960
Francesco Molinari	69-75-70-74--288	96,960
Geoff Ogilvy	74-72-71-71--288	96,960
Brandt Snedeker	72-75-68-73--288	96,960
Jason Dufner	69-70-75-75--289	70,400
Anders Hansen	76-72-73-68--289	70,400
Paul Lawrie	69-72-72-76--289	70,400

*Won in playoff.

U.S. Open
Olympic Club (par 70; 6,822 yds);
San Francisco, Calif., June 14–17, 2012

Player	Score	Earnings ($)
Webb Simpson	72-73-68-68--281	1,440,000
Michael Thompson	66-75-74-67--282	695,916
Graeme McDowell	69-72-68-73--282	695,916
Padraig Harrington	74-70-71-68--283	276,841
Jason Dufner	72-71-70-70--283	276,841
Jim Furyk	70-69-70-74--283	276,841
David Toms	69-70-76-68--283	276,841
John Peterson	71-70-72-70--283	276,841
Ernie Els	75-69-68-72--284	200,280
Retief Goosen	75-70-69-71--285	163,594
Lee Westwood	73-72-67-73--285	163,594
John Senden	72-73-68-72--285	163,594
Casey Wittenberg	71-77-67-70--285	163,594
Kevin Chappell	74-71-68-72--285	163,594
Martin Kaymer	74-71-69-72--286	118,969
Aaron Watkins	72-71-72-71--286	118,969
Adam Scott	76-70-70-70--286	118,969
Steve Stricker	76-68-73-69--286	118,969
Fredrik Jacobson	72-71-68-75--286	118,969
K.J. Choi	73-70-74-69--286	118,969
Raphael Jacquelin	72-71-73-71--287	86,348
Justin Rose	69-75-71-72--287	86,348
Tiger Woods	69-70-75-73--287	86,348
Nick Watney	69-75-73-70--287	86,348
Blake Adams	72-70-70-75--287	86,348
a–Jordan Spieth	74-74-69-70--287	—

a–Amateur.

British Open
Royal Lytham & St. Annes GC (par 70; 7,128 yds);
Lancashire, England, July 19–22, 2012

Player	Score	Earnings ($)
Ernie Els	67-70-68-68--273	1,405,890
Adam Scott	64-67-68-75--274	812,292
Tiger Woods	67-67-70-73--277	464,725
Brandt Snedeker	66-64-73-74--277	464,725
Luke Donald	70-68-71-69--278	304,610
Graeme McDowell	67-69-67-75--278	304,610
Thomas Aiken	68-68-71-72--279	222,599
Nicolas Colsaerts	65-77-72-65--279	222,599
Ian Poulter	71-69-73-67--280	124,343
Zach Johnson	65-74-66-75--280	124,343
Miguel Jimenez	71-69-73-67--280	124,343
Mark Calcavecchia	71-68-69-72--280	124,343
Matt Kuchar	69-67-72-72--280	124,343
Geoff Ogilvy	72-68-73-67--280	124,343
Vijay Singh	70-72-68-70--280	124,343
Dustin Johnson	73-68-68-71--280	124,343
Alexander Noren	71-71-69-69--280	124,343
Thorbjorn Olesen	69-66-71-74--280	124,343
Steven Alker	69-69-72-71--281	79,277
Hunter Mahan	70-71-70-70--281	79,277
Louis Oosthuizen	72-68-68-73--281	79,277
Bill Haas	71-68-68-74--281	79,277

PGA Championship
Kiawah Island Resort (par 72; 7,676 yds);
Kiawah Island, S.C., August 9–12, 2012

Player	Score	Earnings ($)
Rory McIlroy	67-75-67-66--275	1,445,000
David Lynn	73-74-68-68--283	865,000
Justin Rose	69-79-70-66--284	384,500
Keegan Bradley	68-77-71-68--284	384,500
Ian Poulter	70-71-74-69--284	384,500
Carl Pettersson	66-74-72-72--284	384,500
Blake Adams	71-72-75-67--285	226,000
Jamie Donaldson	69-73-73-70--285	226,000
Peter Hanson	69-75-70-71--285	226,000
Steve Stricker	74-73-67-71--285	226,000
Ben Curtis	69-77-73-67--286	143,286
Bubba Watson	73-75-70-68--286	143,286
Tim Clark	71-73-73-69--286	143,286
Geoff Ogilvy	68-78-70-70--286	143,286
Graeme McDowell	68-76-71-71--286	143,286
Tiger Woods	69-71-74-72--286	143,286
Adam Scott	68-75-70-73--286	143,286
John Daly	68-77-73-69--287	99,667
Padraig Harrington	70-76-69-72--287	99,667
Bo Van Pelt	73-73-67-74--287	99,667

PGA Tour Results

Late 2011 PGA Tour Events

Tournament	Final Round	Winner	Score/ Under Par	Earnings ($)
Shriners Hosptials for Children Open	Oct 2	Kevin Na	261/-23	792,000
Frys.com Open	Oct 9	Bryce Molder*	267/-17	900,000
McGladrey Classic	Oct 16	Ben Crane*	265/-15	720,000
Children's Miracle Network Classic	Oct 23	Luke Donald	271/-17	846,000
Asia Pacific Classic Malaysia	Oct 30	Bo Van Pelt	261/-23	1,300,000
WGC HSBC Champions	Nov 6	Martin Kaymer	268/-20	1,200,000
**Chevron World Challenge	Dec 4	Tiger Woods	278/-10	1,200,000

2012 PGA Tour Events

Tournament	Final Round	Winner	Score/ Under Par	Earnings ($)
Hyundai Tournament of Champions	Jan 9	Steve Stricker	269/-23	1,120,000
Sony Open in Hawaii	Jan 15	Johnson Wagner	267/-13	990,000
Humana Challenge	Jan 22	Mark Wilson	264/-24	1,008,000
Farmers Insurance Open	Jan 29	Brandt Snedeker*	272/-16	1,080,000
Phoenix Open	Feb 5	Kyle Stanley	269/-15	1,098,000
AT&T Pebble Beach National Pro-Am	Feb 12	Phil Mickelson	269/-17	1,152,000
Northern Trust Open	Feb 19	Bill Haas*	277/-7	1,188,000
Mayakoba Classic at Riviera Maya	Feb 26	John Huh*	271/-13	666,000
WGC Match Play Championship	Feb 26	Hunter Mahan	2 & 1	1,400,000
Honda Classic	Mar 4	Rory McIlroy	268/-12	1,026,000
Puerto Rico Open	Mar 11	George McNeill	272/-16	630,000
WGC-Cadillac Championship	Mar 11	Justin Rose	272/-16	1,400,000
Transitions Championship	Mar 18	Luke Donald*	271/-13	990,000
Arnold Palmer Invitational	Mar 25	Tiger Woods	275/-13	1,080,000
Shell Houston Open	Apr 1	Hunter Mahan	272/-16	1,080,000
The Masters	Apr 8	Bubba Watson*	278/-10	1,440,000
The Heritage	Apr 15	Carl Pettersson	270/-14	1,026,000
Valero Texas Open	Apr 22	Ben Curtis	279/-9	1,116,000
Zurich Classic	Apr 29	Jason Dufner*	269/-19	1,152,000
Wells Fargo Championship	May 6	Rickie Fowler	274/-14	1,170,000
The Players Championship	May 13	Matt Kuchar	275/-13	1,710,000
Byron Nelson Championship	May 20	Jason Dufner	269/-11	1,170,000
Crowne Plaza Invitational at Colonial	May 27	Zach Johnson	268/-12	1,152,000
Memorial Tournament	June 3	Tiger Woods	279/-9	1,116,000
St. Jude Classic	June 10	Dustin Johnson	271/-9	1,008,000
U.S. Open Championship	June 17	Webb Simpson	281/+1	1,440,000
Travelers Championship	June 24	Marc Leishman	266/-14	1,080,000
AT&T National	July 1	Tiger Woods	276/-8	1,170,000
The Greenbrier Classic	July 8	Ted Potter, Jr.*	264/-16	1,098,000
John Deere Classic	July 15	Zach Johnson*	264/-20	828,000
True South Classic	July 22	Scott Stallings	264/-24	540,000
The Open Championship (British Open)	July 22	Ernie Els	273/-7	1,405,890
Canadian Open	July 29	Scott Piercy	263/-17	936,000
WGC-Bridgestone Invitational	Aug 5	Keegan Bradley	267/-13	1,400,000
#Reno-Tahoe Open	Aug 5	J.J. Henry	+43	540,000
*PGA Championship	Aug 12	Rory McIlroy	275/-13	1,445,000
Wyndham Championship	Aug 19	Sergio Garcia	262/-18	936,000
‡The Barclays	Aug 26	Nick Watney	274/-10	1,440,000
‡Deutsche Bank Championship	Sept 3	Rory McIlroy	264/-20	1,440,000
‡BMW Championship	Sept 9	Rory McIlroy	268/-20	1,440,000
‡TOUR Championship	Sept 23	Brandt Snedeker	270/-10	1,440,000

† Five-round tournament. * Won in playoff. **Recognized as unofficial money event by the PGA Tour. ‡Part of four-tournament FedEx Cup playoffs, with size of field lowered with each successive event. #Modified Stableford scoring sytem.

2012 FedEx Cup Playoff Results

Player	Points	Earnings ($)
1. Brandt Snedeker	4,100	10,000,000
2. Rory McIlroy	2,827	3,000,000
3. Tiger Woods	2,663	2,000,000
4. Nick Watney	2,215	1,500,000
5. Phil Mickelson	2,073	1,000,000
6. Justin Rose	1,770	800,000
7. Louis Oosthuizen	1,635	700,000
8. Dustin Johnson	1,527	600,000
9. Luke Donald	1,275	550,000
10. Lee Westwood	1,205	500,000

Kraft Nabisco Championship

Mission Hills CC (par 72; 6,738 yds); Rancho Mirage, Calif., March 29–April 1, 2012

Player	Score	Earnings ($)
Sun Young Yoo*	69-69-72-69--279	300,000
I.K. Kim	70-70-70-69--279	182,538
Yani Tseng	68-68-71-73--280	132,418
Karin Sjodin	72-67-68-74--281	77,202
Amy Yang	66-74-72-69--281	77,202
Stacy Lewis	74-71-70-66--281	77,202
Hee Kyung Seo	69-72-69-71--281	77,202
Natalie Gulbis	76-71-70-65--282	44,806
Se Ri Pak	70-69-72-71--282	44,806
Na Yeon Choi	69-72-69-72--282	44,806
Ha-Neul Kim	71-71-70-71--283	34,003
Angela Stanford	72-71-70-70--283	34,003
Eun-Hee Ji	71-69-70-73--283	34,003
Vicky Hurst	70-70-71-72--283	34,003
Karrie Webb	71-72-71-70--284	26,184
Catriona Matthew	74-70-70-70--284	26,184
Suzann Pettersen	72-74-66-72--284	26,184
Haeji Kang	69-68-72-75--284	26,184
Azahara Munoz	73-72-67-72--284	26,184
Katherine Hull	69-73-69-74--285	22,586
Paula Creamer	69-73-71-72--285	22,586
Cristie Kerr	71-70-72-73--286	20,587
Shanshan Feng	72-70-73-71--286	20,587
a-Ariya Jutanugarn	71-73-71-71--286	—
Lexi Thompson	72-72-68-74--286	20,587

a-Amateur. *Won in playoff

LPGA Championship

Locust Hill CC (par 72; 6,534 yds); Pittsford, N.Y., June 7–10, 2012

Player	Score	Earnings ($)
Shanshan Feng	72-73-70-67--282	375,000
Eun-Hee Ji	75-68-69-72--284	158,443
Suzann Pettersen	71-72-71-70--284	158,443
Stacy Lewis	72-72-70-70--284	158,443
Mika Miyazato	70-72-73-69--284	158,443
Karrie Webb	74-71-68-72--285	73,285
Ai Miyazato	70-74-73-68--285	73,285
Gerina Piller	74-71-72-68--285	73,285
Paula Creamer	70-72-73-71--286	51,742
Giulia Sergas	69-76-69-72--286	51,742
Inbee Park	72-70-72-72--286	51,742
Cristie Kerr	70-76-70-71--287	42,956
Sandra Gal	71-71-75-70--287	42,956
Hee Young Park	77-70-73-68--288	39,028
Jeong Jang	70-74-71-74--289	33,960
Karin Sjodin	75-69-73-72--289	33,960
Sun Young Yoo	72-72-71-74--289	33,960
Mina Harigae	74-72-74-69--289	33,960
Nicole Castrale	76-74-70-70--290	28,638
Se Ri Pak	70-71-76-73--290	28,638
Jenny Shin	71-75-71-73--290	28,638
Jennifer Johnson	73-71-71-75--290	28,638

U.S. Women's Open

Blackwolf Run (par 72; 6,984 yds); Kohler, Wisc., July 5–8, 2012

Player	Score	Earnings ($)
Na Yeon Choi	71-72-65-73--281	585,000
Amy Yang	73-72-69-71--285	350,000
Sandra Gal	71-70-74-74--289	218,840
Giulia Sergas	74-71-73-72--290	128,487
Ilhee Lee	72-71-77-70--290	128,487
Shanshan Feng	74-74-71-71--290	128,487
Paula Creamer	73-73-71-74--291	94,736
Mika Miyazato	71-71-73-76--291	94,736
Cristie Kerr	69-71-77-75--292	72,596
Nicole Castrale	73-70-74-75--292	72,596
Inbee Park	71-70-76-75--292	72,596
Se Ri Pak	72-73-76-71--292	72,596
Suzann Pettersen	71-68-78-75--292	72,596
Cindy LaCrosse	73-74-74-72--293	55,161
Danielle Kang	78-70-71-74--293	55,161
So Yeon Ryu	74-71-74-74--293	55,161
Lexi Thompson	70-73-72-78--293	55,161
Brittany Lincicome	69-80-74-71--294	45,263
Vicky Hurst	71-70-75-78--294	45,263
Hee Kyung Seo	72-73-80-69--294	45,263

Women's British Open

Royal Liverpool GC (par 72; 6,660 yds); Hoylake, England, Sept 13–16, 2012

Player	Score	Earnings ($)
Jiyai Shin	71-64-71-73--279	428,650
Inbee Park	72-68-72-76--288	249,668
Paula Creamer	73-72-72-72--289	174,768
Mika Miyazato	71-70-72-77--290	136,724
Karrie Webb	71-70-68-82--291	104,623
So Yeon Ryu	70-74-71-76--291	104,623
Julieta Granada	74-71-74-74--293	87,979
Katie Futcher	71-71-73-79--294	76,090
Stacy Lewis	74-70-76-74--294	76,090
Catriona Matthew	76-73-71-75--295	59,841
I.K. Kim	75-72-73-75--295	59,841
Chella Choi	72-73-72-78--295	59,841
Cristie Kerr	72-73-74-77--296	44,138
Na Yeon Choi	73-73-75-75--296	44,138
Michelle Wie	75-70-72-79--296	44,138
Cindy LaCrosse	73-75-72-76--296	44,138
Lindsey Wright	76-72-75-74--297	34,002
Vicky Hurst	71-72-79-75--297	34,002
Jenny Shin	75-68-71-83--297	34,002
a-Lydia Ko	72-71-76-78--297	-
Lexi Thompson	74-75-76-72--297	34,002
Carlota Ciganda	76-71-77-73--297	34,002

a–Amateur

LPGA Tour Results

Late 2011 LPGA Tour Events

Tournament	Final Round	Winner	Score/ Under Par	Earnings ($)
Hana Bank Championship	Oct 9	Yani Tseng	202/-14	270,000
Sime Darby Malaysia	Oct 16	Na Yeon Choi	269/-15	285,000
LPGA Taiwan Championship	Oct 23	Yani Tseng	272/-16	300,000
Mizuno Classic	Nov 6	Momoka Ueda*	200/-16	180,000
Lorena Ochoa Invitational	Nov 13	Catriona Matthew	276/-12	200,000
CME Group Titleholders	Nov 20	Hee Young Park	279/-9	500,000

2012 LPGA Tour Events*

Tournament	Final Round	Winner	Score/ Under Par	Earnings ($)
Australian Open	Feb 12	Jessica Korda*	289/-3	165,000
Honda Thailand	Feb 19	Yani Tseng	269/-19	225,000
HSBC Champions	Feb 26	Angela Stafford	278/-10	210,000
LPGA Founders Cup	Mar 18	Yani Tseng	270/-18	225,000
KIA Classic	Mar 25	Yani Tseng	274/-14	255,000
Kraft Nabisco Championship	Apr 1	Sun Young Yoo	279/-9	300,000
LPGA Lotte Championship	Apr 21	Ai Miyazato	276/-12	255,000
Mobil Bay LPGA Classic	Apr 29	Stacy Lewis	271/-17	187,500
Brazil Cup	May 6	Pornanong Phatlum	133/-13	108,000
Sybase Match Play Championship	May 20	Azahara Munoz	2&1	375,000
ShopRite Classic	June 3	Stacy Lewis	201/-12	225,000
LPGA Championship	June 10	Shanshan Feng	282/-6	375,000
Manulife Financial LPGA Classic	June 24	Brittany Lang*	268/-16	195,000
NW Arkansas Championship	July 1	Ai Miyazato	201/-12	300,000
U.S. Women's Open	July 8	Na Yeon Choi	281/-3	585,000
Evian Masters	July 29	Inbee Park	271/-17	487,500
Jamie Farr Toledo Classic	Aug 12	So Yeon Ryu	264/-20	195,000
Safeway Classic	Aug 19	Mika Miyazato	203/-13	225,000
Canadian Women's Open	Aug 26	Lydia Ko†	275/-13	—
Kingsmill Championship	Sept 10	Jiyai Shin*	268/-16	195,000
Women's British Open	Sept 16	Jiyai Shin	279/-9	428,650
Navistar Classic	Sept 23	Stacy Lewis	270/-18	195,000

*Through Oct. 1, 2012

* Won in playoff.
†Amateur

Late 2011 Champions Tour Events

Tournament	Final Round	Winner	Score/ Under Par	Earnings ($)
Insperity Championship	Oct 9	Brad Faxon	134/-10	255,000
AT&T Championship	Oct 16	Fred Couples	193/-23	270,000
Charles Schwab Cup Championship	Nov 6	Jay Don Blake	276/-8	440,000

2012 Champions Tour Events

Tournament	Final Round	Winner	Score/ Under Par	Earnings ($)
Mitsubishi Electric Championship	Jan 22	Dan Forsman	201/-15	307,000
Allianz Championship	Feb 12	Corey Pavin*	205/-11	270,000
ACE Group Classic	Feb 19	Kenny Perry	196/-20	240,000
Toshiba Senior Classic	Mar 18	Loren Roberts	205/-8	262,500
Mississippi Gulf Resort Classic	Mar 25	Fred Couples	202/-14	240,000
Encompass Insurance Pro-Am	Apr 15	Michael Allen	201/-12	240,000
Legends of Golf	Apr 22	Michael Allen/David Frost	187/-29	230,000 each
Insperity Championship	May 6	Fred Funk	202/-14	255,000
Senior PGA Championship	May 27	Roger Chapman	271/-13	378,000
Principal Charity Classic	June 3	Jay Haas	197/-16	262,500
Regions Tradition	June 10	Tom Lehman	274/-14	335,000
Montreal Championship	June 24	Mark Calcavecchia	200/-16	270,000
Senior Players Championship	July 1	Joe Daley	266/-14	405,000
First Tee Open at Pebble Beach	July 8	Kirk Triplett	206/-10	255,000
U.S. Senior Open Championship	July 15	Roger Chapman	270/-10	500,000
Senior British Open	July 29	Fred Couples	271/-9	315,600
3M Championship	Aug 5	Bernhard Langer	198/-18	262,500
Dick's Sporting Goods Open	Aug 19	Willie Wood	203/-13	270,000
Boeing Classic	Aug 26	Jay Don Blake*	206/-10	300,000
Pacific Links Hawaii Championship	Sept 16	Willie Wood	202/-14	270,000

* Won in playoff.

2012 U.S. Amateur Championships Results

Tournament	Final Round	Winner	Score	Runner-Up
Women's Amateur Public Links	June 23	Kyung Kim	4 & 2	Ashlan Ramsey
Men's Amateur Public Links	July 14	T.J. Vogel	12 & 10	Kevin Aylwin
Girls' Junior Amateur	July 21	Minjee Lee	1-up	Alison Lee
Boys' Junior Amateur	July 21	Andy Hyeon Bo Shim	4 & 3	Jim Liu
Women's Amateur	Aug 12	Lydia Ko	3 & 1	Jaye Marie Green
Men's Amateur	Aug 19	Steven Fox	37 holes	Michael Weaver
Senior Women's Amateur	Sept 13	Ellen Port	4 & 3	Jane Fitzgerald
Men's Mid-Amateur	Sept 13	Nathan Smith	1-up	Garrett Rank
Senior Amateur	Oct 4	Paul Simsom	4 & 3	Curtis Skinner
Women's Mid-Amateur	Oct 11	Liz Waynick	6 & 5	Meghan Stasi

2012 International Results

Tournament	Final Round	Winner	Score	Runner-Up
Curtis Cup	June 10	Great Britain & Ireland	10½–9½	United States
Ryder Cup	Sept 30	Europe	14½–13½	United States

PGA Tour Final 2011 Money Leaders

Name	Events	Best Finish	Scoring Average*	Money ($)
Luke Donald	19	1 (2)	68.86	6,683,214
Webb Simpson	26	1 (2)	69.25	6,347,353
Nick Watney	22	1 (2)	69.52	5,290,673
K.J. Choi	22	1 (1)	69.99	4,434,691
Dustin Johnson	21	1 (1)	70.46	4,309,961
Matt Kuchar	24	2 (2)	69.51	4,233,920
Bill Haas	26	1 (1)	70.13	4,088,637
Steve Stricker	19	1 (2)	69.36	3,992,785
Jason Day	21	2 (2)	69.71	3,962,647
David Toms	23	1 (1)	69.71	3,858,090

*Adjusted for average score of field in tournaments entered

LPGA Tour Final 2011 Money Leaders

Name	Events	Best Finish	Scoring Average	Money ($)
Yani Tseng	22	1 (7)	69.66	2,921,713
Cristie Kerr	22	2 (3)	70.71	1,470,979
Na Yeon Choi	21	1 (1)	70.53	1,357,382
Stacy Lewis	23	1 (1)	70.98	1,356,211
Suzann Pettersen	20	1 (2)	70.97	1,322,770
Brittany Lincicome	21	1 (2)	71.03	1,154,234
Angela Stanford	21	3 (3)	71.42	1,017,196
Ai Miyazato	19	1 (1)	71.63	1,007,633
Paula Creamer	21	2 (2)	70.84	926,338
Amy Yang	22	1 (1)	71.12	912,160

Champions Tour Final 2011 Money Leaders

Name	Events	Best Finish	Scoring Average	Money ($)
Tom Lehman	21	1 (3)	69.22	2,081,526
Mark Calcavecchia	22	1 (1)	69.04	1,867,991
John Cook	23	1 (3)	69.75	1,747,075
Jay Don Blake	20	1 (2)	70.05	1,531,877
Russ Cochran	18	1 (1)	69.22	1,503,090
Jeff Sluman	24	1 (1)	69.62	1,493,672
Peter Senior	22	2 (3)	69.62	1,434,119
Nick Price	21	1 (1)	69.56	1,300,443
Olin Browne	23	1 (1)	70.13	1,251,473
Mark O'Meara	20	2 (2)	69.61	1,237,797

Men's Golf

THE MAJOR TOURNAMENTS
The Masters

Year	Winner	Score	Runner-Up
1934	Horton Smith	284	Craig Wood
1935	Gene Sarazen* (144)	282	Craig Wood (149)
	(only 36-hole playoff)		
1936	Horton Smith	285	Harry Cooper
1937	Byron Nelson	283	Ralph Guldahl
1938	Henry Picard	285	Ralph Guldahl
			Harry Cooper
1939	Ralph Guldahl	279	Sam Snead
1940	Jimmy Demaret	280	Lloyd Mangrum
1941	Craig Wood	280	Byron Nelson
1942	Byron Nelson* (69)	280	Ben Hogan (70)
1943–45	No tournament		
1946	Herman Keiser	282	Ben Hogan
1947	Jimmy Demaret	281	Byron Nelson
			Frank Stranahan
1948	Claude Harmon	279	Cary Middlecoff
1949	Sam Snead	282	Johnny Bulla
			Lloyd Mangrum
1950	Jimmy Demaret	283	Jim Ferrier
1951	Ben Hogan	280	Skee Riegel
1952	Sam Snead	286	Jack Burke Jr.
1953	Ben Hogan	274	Ed Oliver Jr.
1954	Sam Snead* (70)	289	Ben Hogan (71)
1955	Cary Middlecoff	279	Ben Hogan
1956	Jack Burke Jr.	289	Ken Venturi
1957	Doug Ford	282	Sam Snead
1958	Arnold Palmer	284	Doug Ford
			Fred Hawkins
1959	Art Wall Jr.	284	Cary Middlecoff
1960	Arnold Palmer	282	Ken Venturi
1961	Gary Player	280	Charles R. Coe
			Arnold Palmer
1962	Arnold Palmer* (68)	280	Gary Player (71)
			D. Finsterwald (77)
1963	Jack Nicklaus	286	Tony Lema
1964	Arnold Palmer	276	Dave Marr
			Jack Nicklaus
1965	Jack Nicklaus	271	Arnold Palmer
			Gary Player
1966	Jack Nicklaus* (70) (72)	288	Tommy Jacobs
			Gay Brewer Jr. (78)
1967	Gay Brewer Jr.	280	Bobby Nichols
1968	Bob Goalby	277	Roberto DeVicenzo
1969	George Archer	281	Billy Casper
			George Knudson
			Tom Weiskopf
1970	Billy Casper* (69)	279	Gene Littler (74)
1971	Charles Coody	279	Johnny Miller
			Jack Nicklaus
1972	Jack Nicklaus	286	Bruce Crampton
			Bobby Mitchell
			Tom Weiskopf
1973	Tommy Aaron	283	J.C. Snead
1974	Gary Player	278	Tom Weiskopf
			Dave Stockton
1975	Jack Nicklaus	276	Johnny Miller
			Tom Weiskopf
1976	Ray Floyd	271	Ben Crenshaw
1977	Tom Watson	276	Jack Nicklaus
1978	Gary Player	277	Hubert Green
			Rod Funseth
			Tom Watson
1979	Fuzzy Zoeller* (4–3)†	280	Ed Sneed (4–4)
			Tom Watson (4–4)
1980	Seve Ballesteros	275	Gibby Gilbert
			Jack Newton
1981	Tom Watson	280	Johnny Miller
			Jack Nicklaus
1982	Craig Stadler* (4)	284	Dan Pohl (5)
1983	Seve Ballesteros	280	Ben Crenshaw
			Tom Kite
1984	Ben Crenshaw	277	Tom Watson
1985	Bernhard Langer	282	Curtis Strange
			Seve Ballesteros
			Ray Floyd
1986	Jack Nicklaus	279	Greg Norman
			Tom Kite
1987	Larry Mize* (4–3)	285	Seve Ballesteros (5)
			Greg Norman (4–4)
1988	Sandy Lyle	281	Mark Calcavecchia
1989	Nick Faldo* (5–3)	283	Scott Hoch (5–4)
1990	Nick Faldo* (4–4)	278	Ray Floyd (4–x)
1991	Ian Woosnam	277	José María Olazábal
1992	Fred Couples	275	Ray Floyd
1993	Bernhard Langer	277	Chip Beck
1994	José María Olazábal	279	Tom Lehman
1995	Ben Crenshaw	274	Davis Love III
1996	Nick Faldo	276	Greg Norman
1997	Tiger Woods	270	Tom Kite
1998	Mark O'Meara	279	David Duval
			Fred Couples
1999	José María Olazábal	280	Davis Love III
2000	Vijay Singh	278	Ernie Els
2001	Tiger Woods	272	David Duval
2002	Tiger Woods	276	Retief Goosen
2003	Mike Weir	281	Len Mattiace
2004	Phil Mickelson	279	Ernie Els
2005	Tiger Woods	276	Chris DiMarco
2006	Phil Mickelson	281	Tim Clark
2007	Zach Johnson	289	Tiger Woods
			Retief Goosen
			Rory Sabbatini
2008	Trevor Immelman	280	Tiger Woods
2009	Angel Cabrera	276	Chad Campbell
			Kenny Perry
2010	Phil Mickelson	272	Lee Westwood
2011	Charl Schwartzel	274	Jason Day
			Adam Scott
2012	Bubba Watson	278	Louis Oosthuizen

*Winner in playoff. Playoff scores are in parentheses. †Playoff cut from 18 holes to sudden death.
Note: Played at Augusta National Golf Club, Augusta, GA.

United States Open Championship

Year	Winner	Score	Runner-Up	Site
1895	Horace Rawlins	†173	Willie Dunn	Newport GC, Newport, RI
1896	James Foulis	†152	Horace Rawlins	Shinnecock Hills GC, Southampton, NY
1897	Joe Lloyd	†162	Willie Anderson	Chicago GC, Wheaton, IL
1898	Fred Herd	328	Alex Smith	Myopia Hunt Club, Hamilton, MA
1899	Willie Smith	315	George Low Val Fitzjohn W.H. Way	Baltimore CC, Baltimore, MD
1900	Harry Vardon	313	John H. Taylor	Chicago GC, Wheaton, IL
1901	Willie Anderson* (85)	331	Alex Smith (86)	Myopia Hunt Club, Hamilton, MA
1902	Laurie Auchterlonie	307	Stewart Gardner	Garden City GC, Garden City, NY
1903	Willie Anderson* (82)	307	David Brown (84)	Baltusrol GC, Springfield, NJ
1904	Willie Anderson	303	Gil Nicholls	Glen View Club, Golf, IL
1905	Willie Anderson	314	Alex Smith	Myopia Hunt Club, Hamilton, MA
1906	Alex Smith	295	Willie Smith	Onwentsia Club, Lake Forest, IL
1907	Alex Ross	302	Gil Nicholls	Philadelphia Cricket Club, Chestnut Hill, PA
1908	Fred McLeod* (77)	322	Willie Smith (83)	Myopia Hunt Club, Hamilton, MA
1909	George Sargent	290	Tom McNamara	Englewood GC, Englewood, NJ
1910	Alex Smith* (71)	298	John McDermott (75) Macdonald Smith (77)	Philadelphia Cricket Club, Chestnut Hill, PA
1911	John McDermott* (80)	307	Mike Brady (82) George Simpson (85)	Chicago GC, Wheaton, IL
1912	John McDermott	294	Tom McNamara	CC of Buffalo, Buffalo, NY
1913	Francis Ouimet* (72)	304	Harry Vardon (77) Edward Ray (78)	The Country Club, Brookline, MA
1914	Walter Hagen	290	Chick Evans	Midlothian CC, Blue Island, IL
1915	Jerry Travers	297	Tom McNamara	Baltusrol GC, Springfield, NJ
1916	Chick Evans	286	Jock Hutchison	Minikahda Club, Minneapolis. MN
1917–18	No tournament			
1919	Walter Hagen* (77)	301	Mike Brady (78)	Brae Burn CC, West Newton, MA
1920	Edward Ray	295	Harry Vardon Jack Burke Leo Diegel Jock Hutchison	Inverness CC, Toledo, OH
1921	Jim Barnes	289	Walter Hagen Fred McLeod	Columbia CC, Chevy Chase, MD
1922	Gene Sarazen	288	John L. Black Bobby Jones	Skokie CC, Glencoe, IL
1923	Bobby Jones* (76)	296	Bobby Cruickshank (78)	Inwood CC, Inwood, NY
1924	Cyril Walker	297	Bobby Jones	Oakland Hills CC, Birmingham, MI
1925	W. MacFarlane* (75–72)	291	Bobby Jones (75–73)	Worcester CC, Worcester, MA
1926	Bobby Jones	293	Joe Turnesa	Scioto CC, Columbus, OH
1927	Tommy Armour* (76)	301	Harry Cooper (79)	Oakmont CC, Oakmont, PA
1928	Johnny Farrell* (143)	294	Bobby Jones (144)	Olympia Fields CC, Matteson, IL
1929	Bobby Jones* (141)	294	Al Espinosa (164)	Winged Foot GC, Mamaroneck, NY
1930	Bobby Jones	287	Macdonald Smith	Interlachen CC, Hopkins, MN
1931	Billy Burke* (149–148)	292	George Von Elm (149–149)	Inverness Club, Toledo, OH
1932	Gene Sarazen	286	Phil Perkins Bobby Cruickshank	Fresh Meadows CC, Flushing, NY
1933	Johnny Goodman	287	Ralph Guldahl	North Shore CC, Glenview, IL
1934	Olin Dutra	293	Gene Sarazen	Merion Cricket Club, Ardmore, PA
1935	Sam Parks Jr.	299	Jimmy Thompson	Oakmont CC, Oakmont, PA
1936	Tony Manero	282	Harry Cooper	Baltusrol GC (Upper Course), Springfield, NJ
1937	Ralph Guldahl	281	Sam Snead	Oakland Hills CC, Birmingham, MI
1938	Ralph Guldahl	284	Dick Metz	Cherry Hills CC, Denver, CO
1939	Byron Nelson* (68–70)	284	Craig Wood (68–73) Denny Shute (76)	Philadelphia CC, Philadelphia, PA
1940	Lawson Little* (70)	287	Gene Sarazen (73)	Canterbury GC, Cleveland, OH
1941	Craig Wood	284	Denny Shute	Colonial Club, Fort Worth, TX
1942–45	No tournament			
1946	Lloyd Mangrum* (72–72)	284	Vic Ghezzi (72–73) Byron Nelson (72–73)	Canterbury GC, Cleveland, OH
1947	Lew Worsham* (69)	282	Sam Snead (70)	St. Louis CC, Clayton, MO
1948	Ben Hogan	276	Jimmy Demaret	Riviera CC, Los Angeles, CA
1949	Cary Middlecoff	286	Sam Snead Clayton Heafner	Medinah CC, Medinah, IL
1950	Ben Hogan* (69)	287	Lloyd Mangrum (73) George Fazio (75)	Merion GC, Ardmore, PA

United States Open Championship *(Cont.)*

Year	Winner	Score	Runner-Up	Site
1951	Ben Hogan	287	Clayton Heafner	Oakland Hills CC, Birmingham, MI
1952	Julius Boros	281	Ed Oliver	Northwood CC, Dallas, TX
1953	Ben Hogan	283	Sam Snead	Oakmont CC, Oakmont, PA
1954	Ed Furgol	284	Gene Littler	Baltusrol GC (Lower Course), Springfield, NJ
1955	Jack Fleck* (69)	287	Ben Hogan (72)	Olympic Club (Lake Course), San Fran., CA
1956	Cary Middlecoff	281	Ben Hogan Julius Boros	Oak Hill CC, Rochester, NY
1957	Dick Mayer* (72)	282	Cary Middlecoff (79)	Inverness Club, Toledo, OH
1958	Tommy Bolt	283	Gary Player	Southern Hills CC, Tulsa, OK
1959	Billy Casper	282	Bob Rosburg	Winged Foot GC, Mamaroneck, NY
1960	Arnold Palmer	280	Jack Nicklaus	Cherry Hills CC, Denver, CO
1961	Gene Littler	281	Bob Goalby Doug Sanders	Oakland Hills CC, Birmingham, MI
1962	Jack Nicklaus* (71)	283	Arnold Palmer (74)	Oakmont CC, Oakmont, PA
1963	Julius Boros* (70)	293	Jacky Cupit (73) Arnold Palmer (76)	The Country Club, Brookline, MA
1964	Ken Venturi	278	Tommy Jacobs	Congressional CC, Bethesda, MD
1965	Gary Player* (71)	282	Kel Nagle (74)	Bellerive CC, St. Louis, MO
1966	Billy Casper* (69)	278	Arnold Palmer (73)	Olympic Club (Lake Course), San Fran., CA
1967	Jack Nicklaus	275	Arnold Palmer	Baltusrol GC (Lower Course), Springfield, NJ
1968	Lee Trevino	275	Jack Nicklaus	Oak Hill CC, Rochester, NY
1969	Orville Moody	281	Deane Beman Al Geiberger Bob Rosburg	Champions GC (Cypress Creek Course), Houston, TX
1970	Tony Jacklin	281	Dave Hill	Hazeltine GC, Chaska, MN
1971	Lee Trevino* (68)	280	Jack Nicklaus (71)	Merion GC (East Course), Ardmore, PA
1972	Jack Nicklaus	290	Bruce Crampton	Pebble Beach GL, Pebble Beach, CA
1973	Johnny Miller	279	John Schlee	Oakmont CC, Oakmont, PA
1974	Hale Irwin	287	Forrest Fezler	Winged Foot GC, Mamaroneck, NY
1975	Lou Graham* (71)	287	John Mahaffey (73)	Medinah CC, Medinah, IL
1976	Jerry Pate	277	Tom Weiskopf Al Geiberger	Atlanta Athletic Club, Duluth, GA
1977	Hubert Green	278	Lou Graham	Southern Hills CC, Tulsa, OK
1978	Andy North	285	Dave Stockton J.C. Snead	Cherry Hills CC, Denver, CO
1979	Hale Irwin	284	Gary Player Jerry Pate	Inverness Club, Toledo, OH
1980	Jack Nicklaus	272	Isao Aoki	Baltusrol GC (Lower Course), Springfield, NJ
1981	David Graham	273	George Burns Bill Rogers	Merion GC, Ardmore, PA
1982	Tom Watson	282	Jack Nicklaus	Pebble Beach GL, Pebble Beach, CA
1983	Larry Nelson	280	Tom Watson	Oakmont CC, Oakmont, PA
1984	Fuzzy Zoeller* (67)	276	Greg Norman (75)	Winged Foot GC, Mamaroneck, NY
1985	Andy North	279	Dave Barr T.C. Chen Denis Watson	Oakland Hills CC, Birmingham, MI
1986	Ray Floyd	279	Lanny Wadkins Chip Beck	Shinnecock Hills GC, Southampton, NY
1987	Scott Simpson	277	Tom Watson	Olympic Club (Lake Course), San Fran., CA
1988	Curtis Strange* (71)	278	Nick Faldo (75)	The Country Club, Brookline, MA
1989	Curtis Strange	278	Chip Beck Mark McCumber Ian Woosnam	Oak Hill CC, Rochester, NY
1990	Hale Irwin* (74) (3)	280	Mike Donald (74) (4)	Medinah CC, Medinah, IL
1991	Payne Stewart* (75)	282	Scott Simpson (77)	Hazeltine GC, Chaska, MN
1992	Tom Kite	285	Jeff Sluman	Pebble Beach GL, Pebble Beach, CA
1993	Lee Janzen	272	Payne Stewart	Baltusrol GC, Springfield, NJ
1994	Ernie Els*	279	Loren Roberts Colin Montgomerie	Oakmont CC, Oakmont, PA
1995	Corey Pavin	280	Greg Norman	Shinnecock Hills GC, Southampton, NY
1996	Steve Jones	278	Davis Love III Tom Lehman	Oakland Hills CC, Birmingham, MI
1997	Ernie Els	276	Colin Montgomerie	Congressional CC, Bethesda, MD
1998	Lee Janzen	280	Payne Stewart	Olympic Club (Lake Course), San Fran., CA
1999	Payne Stewart	279	Phil Mickelson	Pinehurst Resort and CC, Pinehurst, NC
2000	Tiger Woods	272	Miguel Angel Jiménez	Pebble Beach GL, Pebble Beach, CA

United States Open Championship *(Cont.)*

Year	Winner	Score	Runner-Up	Site
			Ernie Els	
2001	Retief Goosen* (70)	276	Mark Brooks (72)	Southern Hills CC, Tulsa, OK
2002	Tiger Woods	277	Phil Mickelson	Bethpage State Park (Black), Farmingdale, NY
2003	Jim Furyk	272	Stephen Leaney	Olympia Fields CC, Olympia Fields, IL
2004	Retief Goosen	276	Phil Mickelson	Shinnecock Hills GC, Southampton, NY
2005	Michael Campbell	280	Tiger Woods	Pinehurst Resort and CC, Pinehurst, NC
2006	Geoff Ogilvy	285	Jim Furyk	Winged Foot GC, Mamaroneck, NY
			Colin Montgomerie	
			Phil Mickelson	
2007	Angel Cabrera	285	Jim Furyk	Oakmont CC, Oakmont, PA
			Tiger Woods	
2008	Tiger Woods* (71) (4)	283	Rocco Mediate (71) (5)	Torrey Pines GC (South), San Diego, CA
2009	Lucas Glover	276	Phil Mickelson	Bethpage State Park (Black), Farmingdale, NY
			David Duval	
			Ricky Barnes	
2010	Graeme McDowell	284	Gregory Havret	Pebble Beach GL, Pebble Beach, CA
2011	Rory McIlroy	268	Jason Day	Congressional CC, Bethesda, MD
2012	Webb Simpson	281	Michael Thompson	Olympic Club, San Francisco, CA

*Winner in playoff. Playoff scores are in parentheses. The 1990 and 2008 playoffs went to one hole of sudden death after an 18-hole playoff. In the 1994 playoff, Montgomerie was eliminated after 18 playoff holes, and Els beat Roberts on the 20th.
†Before 1898, 36 holes. From 1898 on, 72 holes.

The Open Championship (British Open)

Year	Winner	Score	Runner-Up	Site
1860†	Willie Park	174	Tom Morris Sr.	Prestwick, Scotland
1861‡	Tom Morris Sr.	163	Willie Park	Prestwick, Scotland
1862	Tom Morris Sr.	163	Willie Park	Prestwick, Scotland
1863	Willie Park	168	Tom Morris Sr.	Prestwick, Scotland
1864	Tom Morris, Sr.	160	Andrew Strath	Prestwick, Scotland
1865	Andrew Strath	162	Willie Park	Prestwick, Scotland
1866	Willie Park	169	David Park	Prestwick, Scotland
1867	Tom Morris Sr.	170	Willie Park	Prestwick, Scotland
1868	Tom Morris Jr.	154	Tom Morris Sr.	Prestwick, Scotland
1869	Tom Morris Jr.	157	Tom Morris Sr.	Prestwick, Scotland
1870	Tom Morris Jr.	149	David Strath	Prestwick, Scotland
			Bob Kirk	
1871	No tournament			
1872	Tom Morris Jr.	166	David Strath	Prestwick, Scotland
1873	Tom Kidd	179	Jamie Anderson	St. Andrews, Scotland
1874	Mungo Park	159	No record	Musselburgh, Scotland
1875	Willie Park	166	Bob Martin	Prestwick, Scotland
1876	Bob Martin	176	David Strath#	St. Andrews, Scotland
1877	Jamie Anderson	160	Bob Pringle	Musselburgh, Scotland
1878	Jamie Anderson	157	Robert Kirk	Prestwick, Scotland
1879	Jamie Anderson	169	Andrew Kirkaldy	St. Andrews, Scotland
			James Allan	
1880	Robert Ferguson	162	No record	Musselburgh, Scotland
1881	Robert Ferguson	170	Jamie Anderson	Prestwick, Scotland
1882	Robert Ferguson	171	Willie Fernie	St. Andrews, Scotland
1883	Willie Fernie*	159	Robert Ferguson	Musselburgh, Scotland
1884	Jack Simpson	160	Douglas Rolland	Prestwick, Scotland
			Willie Fernie	
1885	Bob Martin	171	Archie Simpson	St. Andrews, Scotland
1886	David Brown	157	Willie Campbell	Musselburgh, Scotland
1887	Willie Park Jr.	161	Bob Martin	Prestwick, Scotland
1888	Jack Burns	171	Bernard Sayers	St. Andrews, Scotland
			David Anderson	
1889	Willie Park Jr.* (158)	155	Andrew Kirkaldy (163)	Musselburgh, Scotland
1890	John Ball	164	Willie Fernie	Prestwick, Scotland
1891	Hugh Kirkaldy	166	Andrew Kirkaldy	St. Andrews, Scotland
			Willie Fernie	
1892	Harold Hilton	**305	John Ball	Muirfield, Scotland
			Hugh Kirkaldy	
1893	William Auchterlonie	322	John E. Laidlay	Prestwick, Scotland

The Open Championship (British Open) (Cont.)

Year	Winner	Score	Runner-Up	Site
1894	John H. Taylor	326	Douglas Rolland	Royal St. George's, England
1895	John H. Taylor	322	Alexander Herd	St. Andrews, Scotland
1896	Harry Vardon* (157)	316	John H. Taylor (161)	Muirfield, Scotland
1897	Harold Hilton	314	James Braid	Royal Liverpool (Hoylake), England
1898	Harry Vardon	307	Willie Park Jr.	Prestwick, Scotland
1899	Harry Vardon	310	Jack White	Royal St. George's, England
1900	John H. Taylor	309	Harry Vardon	St. Andrews, Scotland
1901	James Braid	309	Harry Vardon	Muirfield, Scotland
1902	Alexander Herd	307	Harry Vardon	Royal Liverpool (Hoylake), England
1903	Harry Vardon	300	Tom Vardon	Prestwick, Scotland
1904	Jack White	296	John H. Taylor	Royal St. George's, England
1905	James Braid	318	John H. Taylor	St. Andrews, Scotland
			Rolland Jones	
1906	James Braid	300	John H. Taylor	Muirfield, Scotland
1907	Arnaud Massy	312	John H. Taylor	Royal Liverpool (Hoylake), England
1908	James Braid	291	Tom Ball	Prestwick, Scotland
1909	John H. Taylor	295	James Braid	Deal, England
			Tom Ball	
1910	James Braid	299	Alexander Herd	St. Andrews, Scotland
1911	Harry Vardon	303	Arnaud Massy	Royal St. George's, England
1912	Ted Ray	295	Harry Vardon	Muirfield, Scotland
1913	John H. Taylor	304	Ted Ray	Royal Liverpool (Hoylake), England
1914	Harry Vardon	306	John H. Taylor	Prestwick, Scotland
1915–19	No tournament			
1920	George Duncan	303	Alexander Herd	Deal, England
1921	Jock Hutchison* (150)	296	Roger Wethered (159)	St. Andrews, Scotland
1922	Walter Hagen	300	George Duncan	Royal St. George's, England
			Jim Barnes	
1923	Arthur G. Havers	295	Walter Hagen	Troon, Scotland
1924	Walter Hagen	301	Ernest Whitcombe	Royal Liverpool (Hoylake), England
1925	Jim Barnes	300	Archie Compston	Prestwick, Scotland
			Ted Ray	
1926	Bobby Jones	291	Al Watrous	Royal Lytham & St. Annes, England
1927	Bobby Jones	285	Aubrey Boomer	St. Andrews, Scotland
1928	Walter Hagen	292	Gene Sarazen	Royal St. George's, England
1929	Walter Hagen	292	Johnny Farrell	Muirfield, Scotland
1930	Bobby Jones	291	Macdonald Smith	Royal Liverpool (Hoylake), England
			Leo Diegel	
1931	Tommy Armour	296	Jose Jurado	Carnoustie, Scotland
1932	Gene Sarazen	283	Macdonald Smith	Prince's, England
1933	Denny Shute* (149)	292	Craig Wood (154)	St. Andrews, Scotland
1934	Henry Cotton	283	Sidney F. Brews	Royal St. George's, England
1935	Alfred Perry	283	Alfred Padgham	Muirfield, Scotland
1936	Alfred Padgham	287	James Adams	Royal Liverpool (Hoylake), England
1937	Henry Cotton	290	Reginald A. Whitcombe	Carnoustie, Scotland
1938	Reginald A. Whitcombe	295	James Adams	Royal St. George's, England
1939	Richard Burton	290	Johnny Bulla	St. Andrews, Scotland
1940–45	No tournament			
1946	Sam Snead	290	Bobby Locke	St. Andrews, Scotland
			Johnny Bulla	
1947	Fred Daly	293	Reginald W. Horne	Royal Liverpool (Hoylake), England
			Frank Stranahan	
1948	Henry Cotton	294	Fred Daly	Muirfield, Scotland
1949	Bobby Locke* (135)	283	Harry Bradshaw (147)	Royal St. George's, England
1950	Bobby Locke	279	Roberto DeVicenzo	Troon, Scotland
1951	Max Faulkner	285	Tony Cerda	Portrush, Ireland
1952	Bobby Locke	287	Peter Thomson	Royal Lytham & St. Annes, England
1953	Ben Hogan	282	Frank Stranahan	Carnoustie, Scotland
			Dai Rees	
			Peter Thomson	
			Tony Cerda	
1954	Peter Thomson	283	Sidney S. Scott	Royal Birkdale, Southport, England
			Dai Rees	
			Bobby Locke	
1955	Peter Thomson	281	John Fallon	St. Andrews, Scotland
1956	Peter Thomson	286	Flory Van Donck	Royal Liverpool (Hoylake), England
1957	Bobby Locke	279	Peter Thomson	St. Andrews, Scotland

The Open Championship (British Open) *(Cont.)*

Year	Winner	Score	Runner-Up	Site
1958	Peter Thomson* (139)	278	Dave Thomas (143)	Royal Lytham & St. Annes, England
1959	Gary Player	284	Fred Bullock	Muirfield, Scotland
			Flory Van Donck	
1960	Kel Nagle	278	Arnold Palmer	St. Andrews, Scotland
1961	Arnold Palmer	284	Dai Rees	Royal Birkdale, Southport, England
1962	Arnold Palmer	276	Kel Nagle	Troon, Scotland
1963	Bob Charles* (140)	277	Phil Rodgers (148)	Royal Lytham & St. Annes, England
1964	Tony Lema	279	Jack Nicklaus	St. Andrews, Scotland
1965	Peter Thomson	285	Brian Huggett	Royal Birkdale, Southport, England
			Christy O'Connor	
1966	Jack Nicklaus	282	Doug Sanders	Muirfield, Scotland
			Dave Thomas	
1967	Robert DeVicenzo	278	Jack Nicklaus	Royal Liverpool (Hoylake), England
1968	Gary Player	289	Jack Nicklaus	Carnoustie, Scotland
			Bob Charles	
1969	Tony Jacklin	280	Bob Charles	Royal Lytham & St. Annes, England
1970	Jack Nicklaus* (72)	283	Doug Sanders (73)	St. Andrews, Scotland
1971	Lee Trevino	278	Lu Liang Huan	Royal Birkdale, Southport, England
1972	Lee Trevino	278	Jack Nicklaus	Muirfield, Scotland
1973	Tom Weiskopf	276	Johnny Miller	Troon, Scotland
1974	Gary Player	282	Peter Oosterhuis	Royal Lytham & St. Annes, England
1975	Tom Watson* (71)	279	Jack Newton (72)	Carnoustie, Scotland
1976	Johnny Miller	279	Jack Nicklaus	Royal Birkdale, Southport, England
			Seve Ballesteros	
1977	Tom Watson	268	Jack Nicklaus	Turnberry, Scotland
1978	Jack Nicklaus	281	Ben Crenshaw	St. Andrews, Scotland
			Tom Kite	
			Ray Floyd	
			Simon Owen	
1979	Seve Ballesteros	283	Ben Crenshaw	Royal Lytham & St. Annes, England
			Jack Nicklaus	
1980	Tom Watson	271	Lee Trevino	Muirfield, Scotland
1981	Bill Rogers	276	Bernhard Langer	Royal St. George's, England
1982	Tom Watson	284	Nick Price	Troon, Scotland
			Peter Oosterhuis	
1983	Tom Watson	275	Andy Bean	Royal Birkdale, Southport, England
1984	Seve Ballesteros	276	Tom Watson	St. Andrews, Scotland
			Bernhard Langer	
1985	Sandy Lyle	282	Payne Stewart	Royal St. George's, England
1986	Greg Norman	280	Gordon Brand	Turnberry, Scotland
1987	Nick Faldo	279	Paul Azinger	Muirfield, Scotland
			Rodger Davis	
1988	Seve Ballesteros	273	Nick Price	Royal Lytham & St. Annes, England
1989††	Mark Calcavecchia* (4-3-3-3)	275	Wayne Grady (4-4-4-4)	Troon, Scotland
			Greg Norman (3-3-4-x)	
1990	Nick Faldo	270	Payne Stewart	St. Andrews, Scotland
			Mark McNulty	
1991	Ian Baker-Finch	272	Mike Harwood	Royal Birkdale, Southport, England
1992	Nick Faldo	272	John Cook	Muirfield, Scotland
1993	Greg Norman	267	Nick Faldo	Royal St. George's, England
1994	Nick Price	268	Jesper Parnevik	Turnberry, Scotland
1995	John Daly* (4-3-4-4)	282	C. Rocca (5-4-7-3)	St. Andrews, Scotland
1996	Tom Lehman	271	Mark McCumber	Royal Lytham & St. Annes, England
			Ernie Els	
1997	Justin Leonard	272	Jesper Parnevik	Troon, Scotland
			Darren Clarke	
1998	Mark O'Meara* (4-4-5-4)	280	Brian Watts (5-4-5-5)	Royal Birkdale, Southport, England
1999	Paul Lawrie* (5-4-3-3)	290	Jean Van de Velde (6-4-3-5)	Carnoustie, Scotland
			Justin Leonard (5-4-4-5)	
2000	Tiger Woods	269	Thomas Bjorn	St. Andrews, Scotland
			Ernie Els	
2001	David Duval	274	Niclas Fasth	Royal Lytham & St. Annes, England
2002	Ernie Els* (4-3-5-4-4)	278	Thommas Levet (4-2-5-5-5)	Muirfield, Scotland
2003	Ben Curtis	283	Vijay Singh	Royal St. George's, England
2004	Todd Hamilton* (4-4-3-4)	274	Ernie Els (4-4-4-4)	Troon, Scotland

The Open Championship (British Open) *(Cont.)*

Year	Winner	Score	Runner-Up	Site
2005	Tiger Woods	274	Colin Montgomerie	St. Andrews, Scotland
2006	Tiger Woods	270	Chris DiMarco	Royal Liverpool (Hoylake), England
2007	Pad. Harrington* (3-3-4-5)	277	Sergio Garcia (5-3-4-4)	Carnoustie, Scotland
2008	Padraig Harrington	283	Ian Poulter	Royal Birkdale, Southport, England
2009	Stewart Cink* (4-3-4-3)	278	Tom Watson (5-3-7-5)	Turnberry, Scotland
2010	Louis Oosthuizen	272	Lee Westwood	St. Andrews, Scotland
2011	Darren Clarke	275	Phil Mickelson	Royal St. George's, England
			Dustin Johnson	
2012	Ernie Els	273	Adam Scott	Royal Lytham & St. Annes, England

*Winner in playoff. †The first event was open only to professional golfers.
‡The second annual open was open to amateurs and pros. #Tied, but refused playoff.
**Championship extended from 36 to 72 holes. ††Playoff cut from 18 holes to 4 holes.

PGA Championship

Year	Winner	Score	Runner-Up	Site
1916	Jim Barnes	1 up	Jock Hutchison	Siwanoy CC, Bronxville, NY
1917–18	No tournament			
1919	Jim Barnes	6 & 5	Fred McLeod	Engineers CC, Roslyn, NY
1920	Jock Hutchison	1 up	J. Douglas Edgar	Flossmoor CC, Flossmoor, IL
1921	Walter Hagen	3 & 2	Jim Barnes	Inwood CC, Far Rockaway, NY
1922	Gene Sarazen	4 & 3	Emmet French	Oakmont CC, Oakmont, PA
1923	Gene Sarazen	1 up 38 holes	Walter Hagen	Pelham CC, Pelham, NY
1924	Walter Hagen	2 up	Jim Barnes	French Lick CC, French Lick, IN
1925	Walter Hagen	6 & 5	William Mehlhorn	Olympia Fields CC, Olympia Fields, IL
1926	Walter Hagen	5 & 3	Leo Diegel	Salisbury GC, Westbury, NY
1927	Walter Hagen	1 up	Joe Turnesa	Cedar Crest CC, Dallas, TX
1928	Leo Diegel	6 & 5	Al Espinosa	Five Farms CC, Baltimore, MD
1929	Leo Diegel	6 & 4	Johnny Farrell	Hillcrest CC, Los Angeles, CA
1930	Tommy Armour	1 up	Gene Sarazen	Fresh Meadow CC, Flushing, NY
1931	Tom Creavy	2 & 1	Denny Shute	Wannamoisett CC, Rumford, RI
1932	Olin Dutra	4 & 3	Frank Walsh	Keller GC, St. Paul, MN
1933	Gene Sarazen	5 & 4	Willie Goggin	Blue Mound CC, Milwaukee, WI
1934	Paul Runyan	1 up	Craig Wood	Park CC, Williamsville, NY
1935	Johnny Revolta	5 & 4	Tommy Armour	Twin Hills CC, Oklahoma City, OK
1936	Denny Shute	3 & 2	Jimmy Thomson	Pinehurst CC, Pinehurst, NC
1937	Denny Shute	1 up 37 holes	Harold McSpaden	Pittsburgh FC, Aspinwall, PA
1938	Paul Runyan	8 & 7	Sam Snead	Shawnee CC, Shawnee-on-Delaware, PA
1939	Henry Picard	1 up 37 holes	Byron Nelson	Pomonok CC, Flushing, NY
1940	Byron Nelson	1 up	Sam Snead	Hershey CC, Hershey, PA
1941	Vic Ghezzi	1 up 38 holes	Byron Nelson	Cherry Hills CC, Denver, CO
1942	Sam Snead	2 & 1	Jim Turnesa	Seaview CC, Atlantic City, NJ
1943	No tournament			
1944	Bob Hamilton	1 up	Byron Nelson	Manito G & CC, Spokane, WA
1945	Byron Nelson	4 & 3	Sam Byrd	Morraine CC, Dayton, OH
1946	Ben Hogan	6 & 4	Ed Oliver	Portland GC, Portland, OR
1947	Jim Ferrier	2 & 1	Chick Harbert	Plum Hollow CC, Detroit, MI
1948	Ben Hogan	7 & 6	Mike Turnesa	Norwood Hills CC, St. Louis, MO
1949	Sam Snead	3 & 2	Johnny Palmer	Hermitage CC, Richmond, VA
1950	Chandler Harper	4 & 3	Henry Williams Jr.	Scioto CC, Columbus, OH
1951	Sam Snead	7 & 6	Walter Burkemo	Oakmont CC, Oakmont, PA
1952	Jim Turnesa	1 up	Chick Harbert	Big Spring CC, Louisville, KY
1953	Walter Burkemo	2 & 1	Felice Torza	Birmingham CC, Birmingham, MI
1954	Chick Harbert	4 & 3	Walter Burkemo	Keller GC, St. Paul, MN
1955	Doug Ford	4 & 3	Cary Middlecoff	Meadowbrook CC, Detroit, MI
1956	Jack Burke	3 & 2	Ted Kroll	Blue Hill CC, Boston, MA
1957	Lionel Hebert	2 & 1	Dow Finsterwald	Miami Valley CC, Dayton, OH
1958#	Dow Finsterwald	276	Billy Casper	Llanerch CC, Havertown, PA
1959	Bob Rosburg	277	Jerry Barber	Minneapolis GC, St. Louis Park, MN
			Doug Sanders	

PGA Championship (Cont.)

Year	Winner	Score	Runner-Up	Site
1960	Jay Hebert	281	Jim Ferrier	Firestone CC, Akron, OH
1961	Jerry Barber* (67)	277	Don January (68)	Olympia Fields CC, Olympia Fields, IL
1962	Gary Player	278	Bob Goalby	Aronimink GC, Newton Square, PA
1963	Jack Nicklaus	279	Dave Ragan Jr.	Dallas Athletic Club, Dallas, TX
1964	Bobby Nichols	271	Jack Nicklaus Arnold Palmer	Columbus CC, Columbus, OH
1965	Dave Marr	280	Billy Casper Jack Nicklaus	Laurel Valley CC, Ligonier, PA
1966	Al Geiberger	280	Dudley Wysong	Firestone CC, Akron, OH
1967	Don January* (69)	281	Don Massengale (71)	Columbine CC, Littleton, CO
1968	Julius Boros	281	Bob Charles Arnold Palmer	Pecan Valley CC, San Antonio, TX
1969	Ray Floyd	276	Gary Player	NCR CC, Dayton, OH
1970	Dave Stockton	279	Arnold Palmer Bob Murphy	Southern Hills CC, Tulsa, OK
1971	Jack Nicklaus	281	Billy Casper	PGA Nat'l GC, Palm Beach Gardens, FL
1972	Gary Player	281	Tommy Aaron Jim Jamieson	Oakland Hills CC, Birmingham, MI
1973	Jack Nicklaus	277	Bruce Crampton	Canterbury GC, Cleveland, OH
1974	Lee Trevino	276	Jack Nicklaus	Tanglewood GC, Winston-Salem, NC
1975	Jack Nicklaus	276	Bruce Crampton	Firestone CC, Akron, OH
1976	Dave Stockton	281	Ray Floyd Don January	Congressional CC, Bethesda, MD
1977†	Lanny Wadkins* (4-4-4)	282	Gene Littler (4-4-5)	Pebble Beach GL, Pebble Beach, CA
1978	John Mahaffey* (4–3)	276	Jerry Pate (4–4) Tom Watson (4–5)	Oakmont CC, Oakmont, PA
1979	David Graham* (4-4-2)	272	Ben Crenshaw (4-4-4)	Oakland Hills CC, Birmingham, MI
1980	Jack Nicklaus	274	Andy Bean	Oak Hill CC, Rochester, NY
1981	Larry Nelson	273	Fuzzy Zoeller	Atlanta Athletic Club, Duluth, GA
1982	Raymond Floyd	272	Lanny Wadkins	Southern Hills CC, Tulsa, OK
1983	Hal Sutton	274	Jack Nicklaus	Riviera CC, Pacific Palisades, CA
1984	Lee Trevino	273	Gary Player Lanny Wadkins	Shoal Creek, Birmingham, AL
1985	Hubert Green	278	Lee Trevino	Cherry Hills CC, Denver, CO
1986	Bob Tway	276	Greg Norman	Inverness CC, Toledo, OH
1987	Larry Nelson* (4)	287	Lanny Wadkins (5)	PGA Natl GC, Palm Beach Gardens, FL
1988	Jeff Sluman	272	Paul Azinger	Oak Tree GC, Edmond, OK
1989	Payne Stewart	276	Mike Reid	Kemper Lakes GC, Hawthorn Woods, IL
1990	Wayne Grady	282	Fred Couples	Shoal Creek, Birmingham, AL
1991	John Daly	276	Bruce Lietzke	Crooked Stick GC, Carmel, IN
1992	Nick Price	278	Jim Gallagher Jr.	Bellerive CC, St. Louis, MO
1993	Paul Azinger* (4–4)	272	Greg Norman (4–5)	Inverness CC, Toledo, OH
1994	Nick Price	269	Corey Pavin	Southern Hills CC, Tulsa, OK
1995	Steve Elkington* (3)	267	Colin Montgomerie (4)	Riviera CC, Pacific Palisades, CA
1996	Mark Brooks* (3)	277	Kenny Perry (x)	Valhalla GC, Louisville, KY
1997	Davis Love III	269	Justin Leonard	Winged Foot GC, Mamaroneck, NY
1998	Vijay Singh	271	Steve Stricker	Sahalee CC, Redmond, WA
1999	Tiger Woods	277	Sergio Garcia	Medinah CC, Medinah, IL
2000‡	Tiger Woods* (3-4-5)	270	Bob May (4-4-x)	Valhalla GC, Louisville, KY
2001	David Toms	265	Phil Mickelson	Atlanta AC, Duluth, GA
2002	Rich Beem	278	Tiger Woods	Hazeltine National GC, Chaska, MN
2003	Shaun Micheel	276	Chad Campbell	Oak Hill CC, Rochester, NY
2004	Vijay Singh*	280	Chris DiMarco	Whistling Straits GC, Kohler, WI
2005	Phil Mickelson	276	Steve Elkington	Baltusrol GC, Springfield, NJ
2006	Tiger Woods	270	Shaun Micheel	Medinah CC, Medinah, IL
2007	Tiger Woods	272	Woody Austin	Southern Hills CC, Tulsa, OK
2008	Padraig Harrington	277	Sergio Garcia	Oakland Hills CC, Birmingham, MI
2009	Y.E. Yang	280	Tiger Woods	Hazeltine National GC, Chaska, MN
2010	Martin Kaymer* (4-2-5)	277	Bubba Watson (3-6)	Whistling Straits GC, Kohler, WI
2011	Keegan Bradley* (3-3-4)	272	Jason Dufner (4-4-3)	Atlanta Athletic Club, Johns Creek, GA
2012	Rory McIlroy	275	David Lynn	Kiawah Island Resort, Kiawah Island, SC

*Winner in playoff. †Playoff changed from 18 holes to sudden death. ‡ Playoff changed from sudden death to three-hole playoff. #Switched from match play to stroke-play format in 1958.

THE PGA TOUR
Most Career Wins†

	Wins		Wins		Wins
Sam Snead	82	Billy Casper	51	Lloyd Mangrum	36
*Tiger Woods	74	Walter Hagen	44	*Vijay Singh	34
Jack Nicklaus	73	*Phil Mickelson	40	Horton Smith	32
Ben Hogan	64	Cary Middlecoff	40	Harry Cooper	31
Arnold Palmer	62	Gene Sarazen	39	Jimmy Demaret	31
Byron Nelson	52	Tom Watson	39	Leo Diegel	30

† Through 10/1/12. * Active player.

Alltime Major Championship Winners

	Masters	U.S. Open	British Open	PGA Champ.	U.S. Amateur	British Amateur	Total
Jack Nicklaus	6	4	3	5	2	0	20
*Tiger Woods	4	3	3	4	3	0	17
Bobby Jones	0	4	3	0	5	1	13
Walter Hagen	0	2	4	5	0	0	11
Ben Hogan	2	4	1	2	0	0	9
Gary Player	3	1	3	2	0	0	9
John Ball	0	0	1	0	0	8	9
Arnold Palmer	4	1	2	0	1	0	8
Tom Watson	2	1	5	0	0	0	8
Harold Hilton	0	0	2	0	1	4	7
Gene Sarazen	1	2	1	3	0	0	7
Sam Snead	3	0	1	3	0	0	7
Harry Vardon	0	1	6	0	0	0	7

*Active player.

Alltime Multiple Professional Major Winners

MASTERS		U.S. OPEN		BRITISH OPEN		PGA CHAMPIONSHIP	
Jack Nicklaus	6	Willie Anderson	4	Harry Vardon	6	Walter Hagen	5
Arnold Palmer	4	Ben Hogan	4	James Braid	5	Jack Nicklaus	5
*Tiger Woods	4	Bobby Jones	4	J.H. Taylor	5	*Tiger Woods	4
Jimmy Demaret	3	Jack Nicklaus	4	Peter Thomson	5	Gene Sarazen	3
Nick Faldo	3	Hale Irwin	3	Tom Watson	5	Sam Snead	3
*Phil Mickelson	3	*Tiger Woods	3	Walter Hagen	4	Jim Barnes	2
Gary Player	3	Julius Boros	2	Bobby Locke	4	Leo Diegel	2
Sam Snead	3	Billy Casper	2	Tom Morris Sr.	4	Raymond Floyd	2
Seve Ballesteros	2	*Ernie Els	2	Tom Morris Jr.	4	Ben Hogan	2
Ben Crenshaw	2	*Retief Goosen	2	Willie Park	4	Byron Nelson	2
Ben Hogan	2	Ralph Guldahl	2	Jamie Anderson	3	Larry Nelson	2
*Bernhard Langer	2	Walter Hagen	2	Seve Ballesteros	3	Gary Player	2
Byron Nelson	2	*Lee Janzen	2	Henry Cotton	3	Paul Runyan	2
*José María Olazábal	2	John McDermott	2	Nick Faldo	3	Denny Shute	2
Horton Smith	2	Cary Middlecoff	2	Robert Ferguson	3	Dave Stockton	2
Tom Watson	2	Andy North	2	Bobby Jones	3	Lee Trevino	2
		Gene Sarazen	2	Jack Nicklaus	3	*Vijay Singh	2
		Alex Smith	2	Gary Player	3		
		Payne Stewart	2	*Tiger Woods	3		
		Curtis Strange	2	*Padraig Harrington	2		
		Lee Trevino	2	Harold Hilton	2		
				Bob Martin	2		
				Greg Norman	2		
				Arnold Palmer	2		
				Willie Park Jr.	2		
				Lee Trevino	2		
				Ernie Els	2		

*Active player.

Season Money Leaders

	Earnings ($)		Earnings ($)		Earnings ($)
1934 ...Paul Runyan	6,767.00	1960 ...Arnold Palmer	75,262.85	1986 ...Greg Norman	653,296.00
1935 ...Johnny Revolta	9,543.00	1961 ...Gary Player	64,540.45	1987 ...Curtis Strange	925,941.00
1936 ...Horton Smith	7,682.00	1962 ...Arnold Palmer	81,448.33	1988 ...Curtis Strange	1,147,644.00
1937 ...Harry Cooper	14,138.69	1963 ...Arnold Palmer	128,230.00	1989 ...Tom Kite	1,395,278.00
1938 ...Sam Snead	19,534.49	1964 ...Jack Nicklaus	113,284.50	1990 ...Greg Norman	1,165,477.00
1939 ...Henry Picard	10,303.00	1965 ...Jack Nicklaus	140,752.14	1991 ...Corey Pavin	979,430.00
1940 ...Ben Hogan	10,655.00	1966 ...Billy Casper	121,944.92	1992 ...Fred Couples	1,344,188.00
1941 ...Ben Hogan	18,358.00	1967 ...Jack Nicklaus	188,998.08	1993 ...Nick Price	1,478,557.00
1942 ...Ben Hogan	13,143.00	1968 ...Billy Casper	205,168.67	1994 ...Nick Price	1,499,927.00
1943 ...No statistics compiled		1969 ...Frank Beard	164,707.11	1995 ...Greg Norman	1,654,959.00
1944 ...Byron Nelson*	37,967.69	1970 ...Lee Trevino	157,037.63	1996 ...Tom Lehman	1,780,159.00
1945 ...Byron Nelson*	63,335.66	1971 ...Jack Nicklaus	244,490.50	1997 ...Tiger Woods	2,066,833.00
1946 ...Ben Hogan	42,556.16	1972 ...Jack Nicklaus	320,542.26	1998 ...David Duval	2,591,031.00
1947 ...Jimmy Demaret	27,936.83	1973 ...Jack Nicklaus	308,362.10	1999 ...Tiger Woods	6,616,585.00
1948 ...Ben Hogan	32,112.00	1974 ...Johnny Miller	353,021.59	2000 ...Tiger Woods	9,188,321.00
1949 ...Sam Snead	31,593.83	1975 ...Jack Nicklaus	298,149.17	2001 ...Tiger Woods	5,687,777.00
1950 ...Sam Snead	35,758.83	1976 ...Jack Nicklaus	266,438.57	2002 ...Tiger Woods	6,912,625.00
1951 ...Lloyd Mangrum	26,088.83	1977 ...Tom Watson	310,653.16	2003 ...Vijay Singh	7,573,907.00
1952 ...Julius Boros	37,032.97	1978 ...Tom Watson	362,428.93	2004 ...Vijay Singh	10,905,166.00
1953 ...Lew Worsham	34,002.00	1979 ...Tom Watson	462,636.00	2005 ...Tiger Woods	10,628,024.00
1954 ...Bob Toski	65,819.81	1980 ...Tom Watson	530,808.33	2006 ...Tiger Woods	9,941,563.00
1955 ...Julius Boros	63,121.55	1981 ...Tom Kite	375,698.84	2007 ...Tiger Woods	10,867,052.00
1956 ...Ted Kroll	72,835.83	1982 ...Craig Stadler	446,462.00	2008 ...Vijay Singh	6,601,094.00
1957 ...Dick Mayer	65,835.00	1983 ...Hal Sutton	426,668.00	2009 ...Tiger Woods	10,508,163.00
1958 ...Arnold Palmer	42,607.50	1984 ...Tom Watson	476,260.00	2010 ...Matt Kuchar	4,910,477.00
1959 ...Art Wall	53,167.60	1985 ...Curtis Strange	542,321.00	2011 ...Luke Donald	6,683,214.00

* War bonds. Note: Total money listed from 1968 through 1974. Official money listed from 1975 on.

Year-by-Year Statistical Leaders

SCORING AVERAGE			DRIVING DISTANCE		Yds	DRIVING ACCURACY		Pct./Fwy
1980	Lee Trevino	69.73	1980	Dan Pohl	274.3	1980	Mike Reid	79.5
1981	Tom Kite	69.80	1981	Dan Pohl	280.1	1981	Calvin Peete	81.9
1982	Tom Kite	70.21	1982	Bill Calfee	275.3	1982	Calvin Peete	84.6
1983	Raymond Floyd	70.61	1983	John McComish	277.4	1983	Calvin Peete	81.3
1984	Calvin Peete	70.56	1984	Bill Glasson	276.5	1984	Calvin Peete	77.5
1985	Don Pooley	70.36	1985	Andy Bean	278.2	1985	Calvin Peete	80.6
1986	Scott Hoch	70.08	1986	Davis Love III	285.7	1986	Calvin Peete	81.7
1987	David Frost	70.09	1987	John McComish	283.9	1987	Calvin Peete	83.0
1988	Greg Norman	69.38	1988	Steve Thomas	284.6	1988	Calvin Peete	82.5
1989	Payne Stewart	69.485†	1989	Ed Humenik	280.9	1989	Calvin Peete	82.6
1990	Greg Norman	69.10	1990	Tom Purtzer	279.6	1990	Calvin Peete	83.7
1991	Fred Couples	69.59	1991	John Daly	288.9	1991	Hale Irwin	78.3
1992	Fred Couples	69.38	1992	John Daly	283.4	1992	Doug Tewell	82.3
1993	Greg Norman	68.90	1993	John Daly	288.9	1993	Doug Tewell	82.5
1994	Greg Norman	68.81	1994	Davis Love III	283.8	1994	David Edwards	81.6
1995	Greg Norman	69.06	1995	John Daly	289.0	1995	Fred Funk	81.3
1996	Tom Lehman	69.32	1996	John Daly	288.8	1996	Fred Funk	78.7
1997	Nick Price	68.98	1997	John Daly	302.0	1997	Allen Doyle	80.8
1998	David Duval	69.13	1998	John Daly	299.4	1998	Bruce Fleisher	81.4
1999	Tiger Woods	68.43	1999	John Daly	305.6	1999	Fred Funk	80.2
2000	Tiger Woods	67.79	2000	John Daly	301.4	2000	Fred Funk	79.7
2001	Tiger Woods	68.81	2001	John Daly	306.7	2001	Joe Durant	81.1
2002	Tiger Woods	68.13	2002	John Daly	306.8	2002	Fred Funk	81.2
2003	Tiger Woods	68.41	2003	Hank Kuehne	321.4	2003	Fred Funk	77.9
2004	Vijay Singh	69.19	2004	Hank Kuehne	314.4	2004	Fred Funk	77.2
2005	Tiger Woods	68.66	2005	Scott Hend	318.9	2005	Jeff Hart	76.0
2006	Tiger Woods	68.11	2006	Bubba Watson	319.6	2006	Joe Durant	78.4
2007	Tiger Woods	67.79	2007	Bubba Watson	315.2	2007	Jose Coceres	75.5
2008	Sergio Garcia	69.12	2008	Bubba Watson	315.1	2008	Olin Browne	80.4
2009	Tiger Woods	68.05	2009	Robert Garrigus	312.3	2009	Joe Durant	74.8
2010	Matt Kuchar	69.61	2010	Robert Garrigus	315.5	2010	Omar Uresti	76.1
2011	Luke Donald	68.86	2011	J.B. Holmes	318.4	2011	Joe Durant	75.7

Note: Scoring average per round, with adjustments made at each round for the field's course scoring average.

Note: Average uses distance of two tee shots on a predetermined par-four or par-five hole (front & back).

Note: Percentage of fairways hit on number of par-four and par-five holes played; par-three holes excluded.

THE PGA TOUR (Cont.)

Year by Year Statistical Leaders (Cont.)

GREENS IN REGULATION

1980	Jack Nicklaus	72.1
1981	Calvin Peete	73.1
1982	Calvin Peete	72.4
1983	Calvin Peete	71.4
1984	Andy Bean	72.1
1985	John Mahaffey	71.9
1986	John Mahaffey	72.0
1987	Gil Morgan	73.3
1988	John Adams	73.9
1989	Bruce Lietzke	72.6
1990	Doug Tewell	70.9
1991	Bruce Lietzke	73.3
1992	Tim Simpson	74.0
1993	Fuzzy Zoeller	73.6
1994	Bill Glasson	73.0
1995	Lenny Clements	72.3
1996	Fred Couples	71.8
	Mark O'Meara	71.8
1997	Tom Lehman	72.7
1998	Hal Sutton	71.3
1999	Tiger Woods	71.4
2000	Tiger Woods	75.2
2001	Tom Lehman	74.5
2002	Tiger Woods	74.0
2003	Joe Durant	72.9
2004	Joe Durant	73.3
2005	Sergio Garcia	71.8
2006	Tiger Woods	74.2
2007	Tiger Woods	71.0
2008	Joe Durant	71.1
2009	John Senden	70.9
2010	John Senden	72.5
2011	Bo Weekley	71.7

Note: Average of greens reached in regulation out of total holes played; hole is considered hit in regulation if any part of the ball rests on the putting surface in two shots less than the hole's par—a par-5 hit in two shots is one green in regulation.

PUTTING

1980	Jerry Pate	28.81
1981	Alan Tapie	28.70
1982	Ben Crenshaw	28.65
1983	Morris Hatalsky	27.96
1984	Gary McCord	28.57
1985	Craig Stadler	28.627†
1986	Greg Norman	1.736
1987	Ben Crenshaw	1.743
1988	Don Pooley	1.729
1989	Steve Jones	1.734
1990	Larry Rinker	1.7467†
1991	Jay Don Blake	1.7326†
1992	Mark O'Meara	1.731
1993	David Frost	1.739
1994	Loren Roberts	1.737
1995	Jim Furyk	1.708
1996	Brad Faxon	1.709
1997	Don Pooley	1.718
1998	Rick Fehr	1.722
1999	Brad Faxon	1.723
2000	Brad Faxon	1.704
2001	David Frost	1.708

PUTTING (Cont.)

2002	Bob Heintz	1.682
2003	John Huston	1.713
2004	Stewart Cink	1.723
2005	Arjun Atwal	1.710
2006	Daniel Chopra	1.712
2007	Tim Clark	1.727
2008	Bob Tway	1.718
2009	Patrick Sheehan	1.358
2010	Jerod Turner	1.372
2011	Andres Gonzales	1.411

Note: Average number of putts taken for all holes played; prior to 1986, based on average number of putts per 18 holes.

SAND SAVES

1980	Bob Eastwood	65.4
1981	Tom Watson	60.1
1982	Isao Aoki	60.2
1983	Isao Aoki	62.3
1984	Peter Oosterhuis	64.7
1985	Tom Purtzer	60.8
1986	Paul Azinger	63.8
1987	Paul Azinger	63.2
1988	Greg Powers	63.5
1989	Mike Sullivan	66.0
1990	Paul Azinger	67.2
1991	Ben Crenshaw	64.9
1992	Mitch Adcock	66.9
1993	Ken Green	64.4
1994	Corey Pavin	65.4
1995	Billy Mayfair	68.6
1996	Gary Rusnak	64.0
1997	Bob Estes	70.3
1998	Keith Fergus	71.0
1999	Jeff Sluman	67.3
2000	Fred Couples	67.0
2001	Franklin Langham	68.9
2002	J.M. Olazabal	64.9
2003	Stuart Appleby	62.1
2004	Dan Forsman	62.3
2005	Pat Perez	63.0
2006	Luke Donald	63.6
2007	Tim Clark	68.1
2008	Dudley Hart	63.7
2009	Luke Donald	64.4
2010	Luke Donald	66.4
2011	Brian Gay	63.4

Note: Percentage of up-and-down efforts from greenside bunkers only—fairway bunkers excluded.

EAGLES

1980	Dave Eichelberger	16
1981	Bruce Lietzke	12
1982	Tom Weiskopf	10
	J.C. Snead	10
	Andy Bean	10
1983	Chip Beck	15
1984	Gary Hallberg	15
1985	Larry Rinker	14
1986	Joey Sindelar	16
1987	Phil Blackmar	20
1988	Ken Green	21

EAGLES (Cont.)

1990	Lon Hinkle	14
	Duffy Waldorf	14
1990	Paul Azinger	14
1991	Andy Bean	15
1992	Dan Forsman	18
1993	Davis Love III	15
1994	Davis Love III	18
1995	Kelly Gibson	16
1996	Tom Watson	97.2
1997	Tiger Woods	104.1
1998	Davis Love III	83.3
1999	Vijay Singh	104.8
2000	Tiger Woods	72.0
2001	Phil Mickelson	73.8
2002	John Daly	78.4
2003	Tiger Woods	76.5
2004	Nick Price	90.0
2005	Brenden Pappas	70.6
2006	J.B. Holmes	72.9
2007	Chris Tidland	88.5
2008	Chad Campbell	105.8
2009	Bubba Watson	75.2
2010	Dustin Johnson	92.3
2011	Sunghoon Kang	75.6

Note: Total of eagles scored 1980–1995. Since 1996 winner determined by number of holes played per eagle.

BIRDIES

1980	Andy Bean	388
1981	Vance Heafner	388
1982	Andy Bean	392
1983	Hal Sutton	399
1984	Mark O'Meara	419
1985	Joey Sindelar	411
1986	Joey Sindelar	415
1987	Dan Forsman	409
1988	Dan Forsman	465
1989	Ted Schulz	415
1990	Mike Donald	401
1991	Scott Hoch	446
1992	Jeff Sluman	417
1993	John Huston	426
1994	Brad Bryant	397
1995	Steve Lowery	410
1996	Fred Couples	4.20
1997	Tiger Woods	4.25
1998	David Duval	4.29
1999	Tiger Woods	4.46
2000	Tiger Woods	4.92
2001	Phil Mickelson	4.49
2002	Tiger Woods	4.47
2003	Vijay Singh	4.41
2004	Vijay Singh	4.40
2005	Tiger Woods	4.57
2006	Tiger Woods	4.65
2007	Tiger Woods	4.03
2008	Ryan Palmer	4.16
2009	Tiger Woods	4.15
2010	Tom Gillis	4.06
2011	Steve Stricker	4.28

Note: 1980–95: Total birdies. Since 1996, average number of birdies per round.

† Number carried to extra decimal place to determine winner.

THE PGA TOUR *(Cont.)*
Year-by-Year Statistical Leaders *(Cont.)*

ALL-AROUND			ALL-AROUND *(Cont.)*			ALL-AROUND *(Cont.)*		
1987	Dan Pohl	170	1997	Bill Glasson	282	2007	Tiger Woods	240
1988	Payne Stewart	170	1998	John Huston	151	2008	Pat Perez	323
1989	Paul Azinger	250	1999	Tiger Woods	120	2009	Tiger Woods	151
1990	Paul Azinger	162	2000	Tiger Woods	113	2010	Matt Kuchar	270
1991	Scott Hoch	283	2001	Phil Mickelson	174	2011	Webb Simpson	239
1992	Fred Couples	256	2002	Phil Mickelson	259			
1993	Gil Morgan	252	2003	Tiger Woods	206			
1994	Bob Estes	227	2004	Jeff Ogilvy	268			
1995	Justin Leonard	323	2005	Tiger Woods	265			
1996	Fred Couples	214	2006	Tiger Woods	216			

Note: Sum of the places of standing from the other statistical categories; the player with the number closest to zero leads.

PGA Player of the Year Award

1948	Ben Hogan	1970	Billy Casper	1991	Fred Couples
1949	Sam Snead	1971	Lee Trevino	1992	Fred Couples
1950	Ben Hogan	1972	Jack Nicklaus	1993	Nick Price
1951	Ben Hogan	1973	Jack Nicklaus	1994	Nick Price
1952	Julius Boros	1974	Johnny Miller	1995	Greg Norman
1953	Ben Hogan	1975	Jack Nicklaus	1996	Tom Lehman
1954	Ed Furgol	1976	Jack Nicklaus	1997	Tiger Woods
1955	Doug Ford	1977	Tom Watson	1998	David Duval
1956	Jack Burke	1978	Tom Watson	1999	Tiger Woods
1957	Dick Mayer	1979	Tom Watson	2000	Tiger Woods
1958	Dow Finsterwald	1980	Tom Watson	2001	Tiger Woods
1959	Art Wall	1981	Bill Rogers	2002	Tiger Woods
1960	Arnold Palmer	1982	Tom Watson	2003	Tiger Woods
1961	Jerry Barber	1983	Hal Sutton	2004	Vijay Singh
1962	Arnold Palmer	1984	Tom Watson	2005	Tiger Woods
1963	Julius Boros	1985	Lanny Wadkins	2006	Tiger Woods
1964	Ken Venturi	1986	Bob Tway	2007	Tiger Woods
1965	Dave Marr	1987	Paul Azinger	2008	Padraig Harrington
1966	Billy Casper	1988	Curtis Strange	2009	Tiger Woods
1967	Jack Nicklaus	1989	Tom Kite	2010	Jim Furyk
1968	Not awarded	1990	Wayne Levi	2011	Luke Donald
1969	Orville Moody				

Vardon Trophy: Scoring Average

Year	Winner	Avg	Year	Winner	Avg	Year	Winner	Avg
1937	Harry Cooper	*500	1965	Billy Casper	70.85	1989	Greg Norman	69.49
1938	Sam Snead	520	1966	Billy Casper	70.27	1990	Greg Norman	69.10
1939	Byron Nelson	473	1967	Arnold Palmer	70.18	1991	Fred Couples	69.59
1940	Ben Hogan	423	1968	Billy Casper	69.82	1992	Fred Couples	69.38
1941	Ben Hogan	494	1969	Dave Hill	70.34	1993	Nick Price	69.11
1942–46	No award		1970	Lee Trevino	70.64	1994	Greg Norman	68.81
1947	Jimmy Demaret	69.90	1971	Lee Trevino	70.27	1995	Steve Elkington	69.62
1948	Ben Hogan	69.30	1972	Lee Trevino	70.89	1996	Tom Lehman	69.32
1949	Sam Snead	69.37	1973	Bruce Crampton	70.57	1997	Nick Price	68.98
1950	Sam Snead	69.23	1974	Lee Trevino	70.53	1998	David Duval	69.13
1951	Lloyd Mangrum	70.05	1975	Bruce Crampton	70.51	1999	Tiger Woods	68.43
1952	Jack Burke	70.54	1976	Don January	70.56	2000	Tiger Woods	67.79
1953	Lloyd Mangrum	70.22	1977	Tom Watson	70.32	2001	Tiger Woods	68.81
1954	E.J. Harrison	70.41	1978	Tom Watson	70.16	2002	Tiger Woods	68.13
1955	Sam Snead	69.86	1979	Tom Watson	70.27	2003	Tiger Woods	68.41
1956	Cary Middlecoff	70.35	1980	Lee Trevino	69.73	2004	Vijay Singh	68.84
1957	Dow Finsterwald	70.30	1981	Tom Kite	69.80	2005	Tiger Woods	68.66
1958	Bob Rosburg	70.11	1982	Tom Kite	70.21	2006	Jim Furyk	68.86
1959	Art Wall	70.35	1983	Raymond Floyd	70.61	2007	Tiger Woods	67.79
1960	Billy Casper	69.95	1984	Calvin Peete	70.56	2008	Sergio Garcia	69.12
1961	Arnold Palmer	69.85	1985	Don Pooley	70.36	2009	Tiger Woods	68.05
1962	Arnold Palmer	70.27	1986	Scott Hoch	70.08	2010	Matt Kuchar	69.61
1963	Billy Casper	70.58	1987	Don Pohl	70.25	2011	Luke Donald	68.86
1964	Arnold Palmer	70.01	1988	Chip Beck	69.46			

*Point system used, 1937–41. NOTE: As of 1988, based on minimum of 60 rounds per year. Adjusted for average score of field in tournaments entered.

THE MAJOR TOURNAMENTS
LPGA Championship

Year	Winner	Score	Runner-Up	Site
1955	Beverly Hanson† (4 & 3)	220	Louise Suggs	Orchard Ridge CC, Ft Wayne, IN
1956	Marlene Hagge*	291	Patty Berg	Forest Lake CC, Detroit, MI
1957	Louise Suggs	285	Wiffi Smith	Churchill Valley CC, Pittsburgh, PA
1958	Mickey Wright	288	Fay Crocker	Churchill Valley CC, Pittsburgh, PA
1959	Betsy Rawls	288	Patty Berg	Sheraton Hotel CC, French Lick, IN
1960	Mickey Wright	292	Louise Suggs	Sheraton Hotel CC, French Lick, IN
1961	Mickey Wright	287	Louise Suggs	Stardust CC, Las Vegas, NV
1962	Judy Kimball	282	Shirley Spork	Stardust CC, Las Vegas, NV
1963	Mickey Wright	294	Mary Lena Faulk	Stardust CC, Las Vegas, NV
			Mary Mills	
			Louise Suggs	
1964	Mary Mills	278	Mickey Wright	Stardust CC, Las Vegas, NV
1965	Sandra Haynie	279	Clifford A. Creed	Stardust CC, Las Vegas, NV
1966	Gloria Ehret	282	Mickey Wright	Stardust CC, Las Vegas, NV
1967	Kathy Whitworth	284	Shirley Englehorn	Pleasant Valley CC, Sutton, MA
1968	Sandra Post*	294	Kathy Whitworth (75)	Pleasant Valley CC, Sutton, MA
1969	Betsy Rawls	293	Susie Berning	Concord GC, Kiameshia Lake, NY
			Carol Mann	
1970	Shirley Englehorn*	285	Kathy Whitworth (78)	Pleasant Valley CC, Sutton, MA
1971	Kathy Whitworth	288	Kathy Ahern	Pleasant Valley CC, Sutton, MA
1972	Kathy Ahern	293	Jane Blalock	Pleasant Valley CC, Sutton, MA
1973	Mary Mills	288	Betty Burfeindt	Pleasant Valley CC, Sutton, MA
1974	Sandra Haynie	288	JoAnne Carner	Pleasant Valley CC, Sutton, MA
1975	Kathy Whitworth	288	Sandra Haynie	Pine Ridge GC, Baltimore, MD
1976	Betty Burfeindt	287	Judy Rankin	Pine Ridge GC, Baltimore, MD
1977	Chako Higuchi	279	Pat Bradley	Bay Tree Golf Plantation, N Myrtle Beach, SC
			Sandra Post	
			Judy Rankin	
1978	Nancy Lopez	275	Amy Alcott	Jack Nicklaus GC, Kings Island, OH
1979	Donna Caponi	279	Jerilyn Britz	Jack Nicklaus GC, Kings Island, OH
1980	Sally Little	285	Jane Blalock	Jack Nicklaus GC, Kings Island, OH
1981	Donna Caponi	280	Jerilyn Britz	Jack Nicklaus GC, Kings Island, OH
			Pat Meyers	
1982	Jan Stephenson	279	JoAnne Carner	Jack Nicklaus GC, Kings Island, OH
1983	Patty Sheehan	279	Sandra Haynie	Jack Nicklaus GC, Kings Island, OH
1984	Patty Sheehan	272	Beth Daniel	Jack Nicklaus GC, Kings Island, OH
			Pat Bradley	
1985	Nancy Lopez	273	Alice Miller	Jack Nicklaus GC, Kings Island, OH
1986	Pat Bradley	277	Patty Sheehan	Jack Nicklaus GC, Kings Island, OH
1987	Jane Geddes	275	Betsy King	Jack Nicklaus GC, Kings Island, OH
1988	Sherri Turner	281	Amy Alcott	Jack Nicklaus GC, Kings Island, OH
1989	Nancy Lopez	274	Ayako Okamoto	Jack Nicklaus GC, Kings Island, OH
1990	Beth Daniel	280	Rosie Jones	Bethesda CC, Bethesda, MD
1991	Meg Mallon	274	Pat Bradley	Bethesda CC, Bethesda, MD
			Ayako Okamoto	
1992	Betsy King	267	Karen Noble	Bethesda CC, Bethesda, MD
1993	Patty Sheehan	275	Lauri Merten	Bethesda CC, Bethesda, MD
1994	Laura Davies	279	Alice Ritzman	DuPont CC, Wilmington, DE
1995	Kelly Robbins	274	Laura Davies	DuPont CC, Wilmington, DE
1996	Laura Davies	213#	Julie Piers	DuPont CC, Wilmington, DE
1997	Chris Johnson*	281	Leta Lindley	DuPont CC, Wilmington, DE
1998	Se Ri Pak	273	Donna Andrews	DuPont CC, Wilmington, DE
1999	Juli Inkster	268	Liselotte Neumann	DuPont CC, Wilmington, DE
2000	Juli Inkster*	281	Stefania Croce	DuPont CC, Wilmington, DE
2001	Karrie Webb	270	Laura Diaz	DuPont CC, Wilmington, DE
2002	Se Ri Pak	279	Beth Daniel	DuPont CC, Wilmington, DE
2003	Annika Sorenstam*	278	Grace Park	DuPont CC, Wilmington, DE
2004	Annika Sorenstam	271	Shi Hyun Ahn	DuPont CC, Wilmington, DE
2005	Annika Sorenstam	277	Michelle Wie	Bulle Rock GC, Havre de Grace, MD
2006	Se Ri Pak*	280	Karrie Webb	Bulle Rock GC, Havre de Grace, MD
2007	Suzann Pettersen	274	Karrie Webb	Bulle Rock GC, Havre de Grace, MD
2008	Yani Tseng*	276	Maria Hjorth	Bulle Rock GC, Havre de Grace, MD
2009	Anna Nordqvist	273	Lindsey Wright	Bulle Rock GC, Havre de Grace, MD
2010	Cristie Kerr	269	Song-Hee Kim	Bulle Rock GC, Havre de Grace, MD
2011	Yani Tseng	269	Morgan Pressel	Locust Hill CC, Pittsford, NY

*Won playoff. †Won match-play final. #Shortened due to rain.

LPGA Championship *(Cont.)*

Year	Winner	Score	Runner-Up	Site
2012	Shanshan Feng	282	Eun-Hee Ji	Locust Hill CC, Pittsford, NY
			Suzann Pettersen	
			Stacy Lewis	
			Mika Miyazato	

U.S. Women's Open

Year	Winner	Score	Runner-Up	Site
1946	Patty Berg	5 & 4	Betty Jameson	Spokane CC, Spokane, WA
1947	Betty Jameson	295	Sally Sessions	Starmount Forest CC, Greensboro, NC
			Polly Riley	
1948	Babe Zaharias	300	Betty Hicks	Atlantic City CC, Northfield, NJ
1949	Louise Suggs	291	Babe Zaharias	Prince George's G & CC, Landover, MD
1950	Babe Zaharias	291	Betsy Rawls	Rolling Hills CC, Wichita, KS
1951	Betsy Rawls	293	Louise Suggs	Druid Hills GC, Atlanta, GA
1952	Louise Suggs	284	Marlene Bauer	Bala GC, Philadelphia, PA
			Betty Jameson	
1953	Betsy Rawls* (71)	302	Jackie Pung (77)	CC of Rochester, Rochester, NY
1954	Babe Zaharias	291	Betty Hicks	Salem CC, Peabody, MA
1955	Fay Crocker	299	Mary Lena Faulk	Wichita CC, Wichita, KS
			Louise Suggs	
1956	Kathy Cornelius* (75)	302	Barbara McIntire (82)	Northland CC, Duluth, MN
1957	Betsy Rawls	299	Patty Berg	Winged Foot GC, Mamaroneck, NY
1958	Mickey Wright	290	Louise Suggs	Forest Lake CC, Detroit, MI
1959	Mickey Wright	287	Louise Suggs	Churchill Valley CC, Pittsburgh
1960	Betsy Rawls	292	Joyce Ziske	Worcester CC, Worcester, MA
1961	Mickey Wright	293	Betsy Rawls	Baltusrol GC (Lower Course), Springfield, NJ
1962	Murle Breer	301	Jo Ann Prentice	Dunes GC, Myrtle Beach, SC
			Ruth Jessen	
1963	Mary Mills	289	Sandra Haynie	Kenwood CC, Cincinnati,OH
			Louise Suggs	
1964	Mickey Wright* (70)	290	Ruth Jessen (72)	San Diego CC, Chula Vista, CA
1965	Carol Mann	290	Kathy Cornelius	Atlantic City CC, Northfield, NJ
1966	Sandra Spuzich	297	Carol Mann	Hazeltine Natl GC, Chaska, MN
1967	Catherine LaCoste	294	Susie Berning	Hot Springs GC (Cascades Course),
			Beth Stone	Hot Springs, VA
1968	Susie Berning	289	Mickey Wright	Moslem Springs GC, Fleetwood, PA
1969	Donna Caponi	294	Peggy Wilson	Scenic Hills CC, Pensacola, FL
1970	Donna Caponi	287	Sandra Haynie	Muskogee CC, Muskogee, OK
			Sandra Spuzich	
1971	JoAnne Carner	288	Kathy Whitworth	Kahkwa CC, Erie, PA
1972	Susie Berning	299	Kathy Ahern	Winged Foot GC, Mamaroneck, NY
			Pam Barnett	
			Judy Rankin	
1973	Susie Berning	290	Gloria Ehret	CC of Rochester, Rochester, NY
			Shelley Hamlin	
1974	Sandra Haynie	295	Carol Mann	La Grange CC, La Grange, IL
			Beth Stone	
1975	Sandra Palmer	295	JoAnne Carner	Atlantic City CC, Northfield, NJ
			Sandra Post	
			Nancy Lopez	
1976	JoAnne Carner* (76)	292	Sandra Palmer (78)	Rolling Green CC, Springfield, PA
1977	Hollis Stacy	292	Nancy Lopez	Hazeltine Natl GC, Chaska, MN
1978	Hollis Stacy	289	JoAnne Carner	CC of Indianapolis, Indianapolis, IN
			Sally Little	
1979	Jerilyn Britz	284	Debbie Massey	Brooklawn CC, Fairfield, CT
			Sandra Palmer	
1980	Amy Alcott	280	Hollis Stacy	Richland CC, Nashville, TN
1981	Pat Bradley	279	Beth Daniel	La Grange CC, La Grange, IL
1982	Janet Anderson	283	Beth Daniel	Del Paso CC, Sacramento,CA
			Sandra Haynie	
			Donna White	
			JoAnne Carner	
1983	Jan Stephenson	290	JoAnne Carner	Cedar Ridge CC, Tulsa, OK
			Patty Sheehan	
1984	Hollis Stacy	290	Rosie Jones	Salem CC, Peabody, MA
1985	Kathy Baker	280	Judy Dickinson	Baltusrol GC (Upper Course), Springfield, NJ

U.S. Women's Open *(Cont.)*

Year	Winner	Score	Runner-Up	Site
1986	Jane Geddes* (71)	287	Sally Little (73)	NCR GC, Dayton, OH
1987	Laura Davies* (71)	285	Ayako Okamoto (73)	Plainfield CC, Plainfield, NJ
			JoAnne Carner (74)	
1988	Liselotte Neumann	277	Patty Sheehan	Baltimore CC, Baltimore, MD
1989	Betsy King	278	Nancy Lopez	Indianwood G & CC, Lake Orion, MI
1990	Betsy King	284	Patty Sheehan	Atlanta Athletic Club, Duluth, GA
1991	Meg Mallon	283	Pat Bradley	Colonial Club, Fort Worth, TX
1992	Patty Sheehan* (72)	280	Juli Inkster	Oakmont CC, Oakmont, PA
1993	Lauri Merten	280	Donna Andrew	Crooked Stick, Carmel, IN
			Helen Alfredsson	
1994	Patty Sheehan	277	Tammie Green	Indianwood G & CC, Lake Orion, MI
1995	Annika Sorenstam	278	Meg Mallon	The Broadmoor GC, Colorado Springs,CO
1996	Annika Sorenstam	272	Kris Tschetter	Pine Needles GC, Southern Pines, NC
1997	Alison Nicholas	274	Nancy Lopez	Pumpkin Ridge CC, North Plains, OR
1998	Se Ri Pak†	290	Jenny Chuasiriporn	Blackwolf Run Golf Resort, Kohler, WI
1999	Juli Inkster	272	Sherri Turner	Old Waverly GC, West Point, MS
2000	Karrie Webb	282	Cristie Kerr/ Meg Mallon	Merit GC, Libertyville, IL
2001	Karrie Webb	273	Se Ri Pak	Pine Needles GC, Southern Pines, NC
2002	Juli Inkster	276	Annika Sorenstam	Prairie Dunes CC, Hutchinson, KS
2003	Hilary Lunke*	283	Kelly Robbins	Pumpkin Ridge CC, North Plains, OR
2004	Meg Mallon	274	Annika Sorenstam	The Orchards GC, South Hadley, MA
2005	Birdie Kim	287	Brittany Lang	Cherry Hills CC, Cherry Hills Village, CO
			Morgan Pressel	
2006	Annika Sorenstam*	284	Pat Hurst	Newport CC, Newport, RI
2007	Cristie Kerr	279	Angela Park	Pine Needles GC, Southern Pines, NC
			Lorena Ochoa	
2008	Inbee Park	283	Helen Alfredsson	Interlachen CC, Edina, MN
2009	Eun-Hee Ji	284	Candie Kung	Saucon Valley CC-Old Course, Bethlehem, PA
2010	Paula Creamer	281	Na Yeon Choi	Oakmont CC, Oakmont, PA
2011	So Yeon Ryu*	281	Hee Kyung Seo	The Broadmoor GC, Colorado Springs, CO
2012	Na Yeon Choi	281	Amy Yang	Blackwolf Run Golf Resort, Kohler, WI

* Winner in playoff. † Winner on second hole of sudden death after 18-hole playoff ended in a tie.

Kraft Nabisco Championship

Year	Winner	Score	Runner-Up	Year	Winner	Score	Runner-Up
1972	Jane Blalock	213	Carol Mann	1993	Helen Alfredsson	284	Amy Benz
			Judy Rankin				Tina Barrett
1973	Mickey Wright	284	Joyce Kazmierski				Betsy King
1974	Jo Ann Prentice*	289	Jane Blalock	1994	Donna Andrews	276	Laura Davies
			Sandra Haynie	1995	Nanci Bowen	285	Susie Redman
1975	Sandra Palmer	283	Kathy McMullen	1996	Patti Sheehan	281	Kelly Robbins
1976	Judy Rankin	285	Betty Burfeindt				Meg Mallon
1977	Kathy Whitworth	289	JoAnne Carner				Annika Sorenstam
			Sally Little	1997	Betsy King	276	Kris Tschetter
1978	Sandra Post*	283	Penny Pulz	1998	Pat Hurst	281	Helen Dobson
1979	Sandra Post	276	Nancy Lopez	1999	Dottie Pepper	269	Meg Mallon
1980	Donna Caponi	275	Amy Alcott	2000	Karrie Webb	274	Dottie Pepper
1981	Nancy Lopez	277	Carolyn Hill	2001	Annika Sorenstam	281	five players
1982	Sally Little	278	Hollis Stacy	2002	Annika Sorenstam	280	Liselotte Neumann
			Sandra Haynie	2003	P. Meunier-Lebouc	281	Annika Sorenstam
1983	Amy Alcott	282	Beth Daniel	2004	Grace Park	277	Aree Song
			Kathy Whitworth	2005	Annika Sorenstam*	273	Rosie Jones
1984	Juli Inkster*	280	Pat Bradley	2006	Karrie Webb*	279	Lorena Ochoa
1985	Alice Miller	275	Jan Stephenson	2007	Morgan Pressel	285	Catriona Matthew
1986	Pat Bradley	280	Val Skinner				Brittany Lincicome
1987	Betsy King*	283	Patty Sheehan				Suzann Pettersen
1988	Amy Alcott	274	Colleen Walker	2008	Lorena Ochoa	277	Annika Sorenstam
1989	Juli Inkster	279	Tammie Green	2009	Brittany Lincicome	279	Kristy McPherson
			JoAnne Carner				Cristie Kerr
1990	Betsy King	283	Kathy Postlewait	2010	Yani Tseng	275	Suzann Pettersen
			Shirley Furlong	2011	Stacy Lewis	275	Yani Tseng
1991	Amy Alcott	273	Dottie Mochrie	2012	Sun Young Koo*	279	I.K. Kim
1992	Dottie Mochrie*	279	Juli Inkster				

*Winner in sudden-death playoff. Note: Designated fourth major in 1983; played at Mission Hills CC, Rancho Mirage, CA.

du Maurier Classic

Year	Winner	Score	Runner-Up	Site
1973	Jocelyne Bourassa*	214	Sandra Haynie	Montreal GC, Montreal
			Judy Rankin	
1974	Carole Jo Callison	208	JoAnne Carner	Candiac GC, Montreal
1975	JoAnne Carner*	214	Carol Mann	St. George's CC, Toronto
1976	Donna Caponi*	212	Judy Rankin	Cedar Brae G & CC, Toronto
1977	Judy Rankin	214	Pat Meyers	Lachute G & CC, Montreal
			Sandra Palmer	
1978	JoAnne Carner	278	Hollis Stacy	St. George's CC, Toronto
1979	Amy Alcott	285	Nancy Lopez	Richelieu Valley CC, Montreal
1980	Pat Bradley	277	JoAnne Carner	St. George's CC, Toronto
1981	Jan Stephenson	278	Nancy Lopez	Summerlea CC, Dorion, Quebec
			Pat Bradley	
1982	Sandra Haynie	280	Beth Daniel	St. George's CC, Toronto
1983	Hollis Stacy	277	JoAnne Carner	Beaconsfield GC, Montreal
			Alice Miller	
1984	Juli Inkster	279	Ayako Okamoto	St. George's G & CC, Toronto
1985	Pat Bradley	278	Jane Geddes	Beaconsfield CC, Montreal
1986	Pat Bradley*	276	Ayako Okamoto	Board of Trade CC, Toronto
1987	Jody Rosenthal	272	Ayako Okamoto	Islesmere GC, Laval, Quebec
1988	Sally Little	279	Laura Davies	Vancouver GC, Coquitlam, British Columbia
1989	Tammie Green	279	Pat Bradley	Beaconsfield GC, Montreal
			Betsy King	
1990	Cathy Johnston	276	Patty Sheehan	Westmount G & CC, Kitchener, Ontario
1991	Nancy Scranton	279	Debbie Massey	Vancouver GC, Coquitlam, British Columbia
1992	Sherri Steinhauer	277	Judy Dickinson	St. Charles CC, Winnipeg, Manitoba
1993	Brandie Burton	277	Betsy King	London Hunt and CC, London, Ontario
1994	Martha Nause	279	Michelle McGann	Ottawa Hunt and GC, Ottawa, Ont.
1995	Jenny Lidback	280	Liselotte Neumann	Beaconsfield GC, Pointe-Claire, Quebec
1996	Laura Davies	277	Nancy Lopez	Edmonton CC, Edmonton, Alberta
			Karrie Webb	
1997	Colleen Walker	278	Liselotte Neumann	Glen Abbey GC, Oakville, Ontario
1998	Brandie Burton	270	Annika Sorenstam	Essex G & CC, Windsor, Ontario
1999	Karrie Webb	277	Laura Davies	Priddis Greens G & CC, Calgary, Alberta
2000	Meg Mallon	282	Rosie Jones	Royal Ottawa GC, Aylmer, Quebec

*Winner in sudden-death playoff. Note: Designated third major in 1979. Tournament discontinued in 2001.

Women's British Open

Year	Winner	Score	Runner-Up	Site
2001	Se Ri Pak	277	Mi Hyun Kim	Sunningdale GC, Berkshire, England
2002	Karrie Webb	273	Michelle Ellis	Turnberry GC, Ailsa, Scotland
			Paula Marti	
2003	Annika Sorenstam	278	Se Ri Pak	Royal Lytham & St. Annes, England
2004	Karen Stupples	269	Rachel Teske	Sunningdale GC, Berklshire, England
2005	Jeong Jang	272	Sophie Gustafson	Royal Birkdale CC, Merseyside, England
2006	Sherri Steinhauer	281	Cristie Kerr	Royal Lytham & St. Anne's, England
2007	Lorena Ochoa	287	Jee Young Lee	Old Course, St. Andrew's, Scotland
			Maria Hjorth	
2008	Jiyai Shin	270	Yani Tseng	Sunningdale GC, Berkshire, England
2009	Catriona Matthew	285	Karrie Webb	Royal Lytham & St. Annes, England
2010	Yani Tseng	277	Katherine Hull	Royal Birkdale CC, Merseyside, England
2011	Yani Tseng	272	Brittany Lang	Carnousie GL, Carnoustie, Scotland
2012	Jiyai Shin	279	Inbee Park	Royal Liverpool GC, Hoylake, England

Note: Designated fourth major in 2001.

THE LPGA TOUR

Most Career Wins†

	Wins		Wins		Wins
Kathy Whitworth	88	Sandra Haynie	42	*Juli Inkster	31
Mickey Wright	82	Babe Zaharias	41	Amy Alcott	29
Annika Sorenstam	72	Carol Mann	38	Jane Blalock	27
Patty Berg	60	*Karrie Webb	37	Lorena Ochoa	27
Louise Suggs	58	Patty Sheehan	35	Marlene Hagge	26
Betsy Rawls	55	Betsy King	34	Judy Rankin	26
Nancy Lopez	48	Beth Daniel	33	*Se Ri Pak	25
JoAnne Carner	43	Pat Bradley	31	Donna Caponi	24

†Through 10/1/12. *Active player.

Alltime Major Championship Winners

	LPGA	U.S. Open	Nabisco	Brit. Open	‡du Maurier	#Titleholders	†Western	U.S. Am	Brit. Am	Total
Patty Berg	0	1	0	0	0	7	7	1	0	16
Mickey Wright	4	4	0	0	0	2	3	0	0	13
Louise Suggs	1	2	0	0	0	4	4	1	1	13
Babe Zaharias	0	3	0	0	0	3	4	1	1	12
*Juli Inkster	2	2	2	0	1	0	0	3	0	10
Annika Sorenstam	3	3	3	1	0	0	0	0	0	10
Betsy Rawls	2	4	0	0	0	0	2	0	0	8
JoAnne Carner	0	2	0	0	0	0	0	5	0	7
*Karrie Webb	1	2	2	1	1	0	0	0	0	7
Kathy Whitworth	3	0	0	0	0	2	1	0	0	6
Pat Bradley	1	1	1	0	3	0	0	0	0	6
Patty Sheehan	3	2	1	0	0	0	0	0	0	6
Glenna Vare	0	0	0	0	0	0	0	6	0	6
Betsy King	1	2	3	0	0	0	0	0	0	6

*Active LPGA player.
#Major from 1937–1972. †Major from 1937–1967. ‡Major from 1979–2000.

Alltime Multiple Professional Major Winners

LPGA

Mickey Wright	4
Nancy Lopez	3
Se Ri Pak	3
Patty Sheehan	3
Annika Sorenstam	3
Kathy Whitworth	3
Donna Caponi	2
Sandra Haynie	2
Mary Mills	2
Betsy Rawls	2
Laura Davies	2
*Juli Inkster	2
*Yani Tseng	2

BRITISH OPEN

*Yani Tseng	2
*Jiyai Shin	2

U.S. OPEN

Betsy Rawls	4
Mickey Wright	4
Susie Maxwell Berning	3
Hollis Stacy	3
Babe Zaharias	3
Annika Sorenstam	3
JoAnne Carner	2
Donna Caponi	2
Betsy King	2
Meg Mallon	2
Patty Sheehan	2
Louise Suggs	2
*Karrie Webb	2
*Juli Inkster	2

NABISCO/DINAH SHORE

Amy Alcott	3
Betsy King	3
Annika Sorenstam	3
*Juli Inkster	2
*Karrie Webb	2

TITLEHOLDERS

Patty Berg	7
Louise Suggs	4
Babe Zaharias	3
Dorothy Kirby	2
Marilynn Smith	2
Kathy Whitworth	2
Mickey Wright	2

WESTERN OPEN

Patty Berg	7
Louise Suggs	4
Babe Zaharias	4
Mickey Wright	3
June Beebe	2
Opal Hill	2
Betty Jameson	2
Betsy Rawls	2

DU MAURIER

Pat Bradley	3
Brandie Burton	2
JoAnne Carner	2

*Active player.

THE LPGA TOUR *(Cont.)*

Season Money Leaders

	Earnings ($)		Earnings ($)		Earnings ($)
1950...Babe Zaharias	14,800	1971...Kathy Whitworth	41,181	1992...Dottie Mochrie	693,335
1951...Babe Zaharias	15,087	1972...Kathy Whitworth	65,063	1993...Betsy King	595,992
1952...Betsy Rawls	14,505	1973...Kathy Whitworth	82,864	1994...Laura Davies	687,201
1953...Louise Suggs	19,816	1974...JoAnne Carner	87,094	1995...Annika Sorenstam	666,533
1954...Patty Berg	16,011	1975...Sandra Palmer	76,374	1996...Karrie Webb	1,002,000
1955...Patty Berg	16,492	1976...Judy Rankin	150,734	1997...Annika Sorenstam	1,236,789
1956...Marlene Hagge	20,235	1977...Judy Rankin	122,890	1998...Annika Sorenstam	1,092,748
1957...Patty Berg	16,272	1978...Nancy Lopez	189,814	1999...Karrie Webb	1,591,959
1958...Beverly Hanson	12,639	1979...Nancy Lopez	197,489	2000...Karrie Webb	1,876,853
1959...Betsy Rawls	26,774	1980...Beth Daniel	231,000	2001...Annika Sorenstam	2,105,868
1960...Louise Suggs	16,892	1981...Beth Daniel	206,998	2002...Annika Sorenstam	2,863,904
1961...Mickey Wright	22,236	1982...JoAnne Carner	310,400	2003...Annika Sorenstam	2,029,506
1962...Mickey Wright	21,641	1983...JoAnne Carner	291,404	2004...Annika Sorenstam	2,544,707
1963...Mickey Wright	31,269	1984...Betsy King	266,771	2005...Annika Sorenstam	2,588,240
1964...Mickey Wright	29,800	1985...Nancy Lopez	416,472	2006...Lorena Ochoa	2,592,872
1965...Kathy Whitworth	28,658	1986...Pat Bradley	492,021	2007...Lorena Ochoa	4,364,994
1966...Kathy Whitworth	33,517	1987...Ayako Okamoto	466,034	2008...Lorena Ochoa	2,763,193
1967...Kathy Whitworth	32,937	1988...Sherri Turner	350,851	2009...Jiyai Shin	1,807,334
1968...Kathy Whitworth	48,379	1989...Betsy King	654,132	2010...Na Yeon Choi	1,871,166
1969...Carol Mann	49,152	1990...Beth Daniel	863,578	2011...Yani Tseng	2,921,713
1970...Kathy Whitworth	30,235	1991...Pat Bradley	763,118		

LPGA Player of the Year

1966	Kathy Whitworth	1982	JoAnne Carner	1998	Annika Sorenstam
1967	Kathy Whitworth	1983	Patty Sheehan	1999	Karrie Webb
1968	Kathy Whitworth	1984	Betsy King	2000	Karrie Webb
1969	Kathy Whitworth	1985	Nancy Lopez	2001	Annika Sorenstam
1970	Sandra Haynie	1986	Pat Bradley	2002	Annika Sorenstam
1971	Kathy Whitworth	1987	Ayako Okamoto	2003	Annika Sorenstam
1972	Kathy Whitworth	1988	Nancy Lopez	2004	Annika Sorenstam
1973	Kathy Whitworth	1989	Betsy King	2005	Annika Sorenstam
1974	JoAnne Carner	1990	Beth Daniel	2006	Lorena Ochoa
1975	Sandra Palmer	1991	Pat Bradley	2007	Lorena Ochoa
1976	Judy Rankin	1992	Dottie Mochrie	2008	Lorena Ochoa
1977	Judy Rankin	1993	Betsy King	2009	Lorena Ochoa
1978	Nancy Lopez	1994	Beth Daniel	2010	Yani Tseng
1979	Nancy Lopez	1995	Annika Sorenstam	2011	Yani Tseng
1980	Beth Daniel	1996	Laura Davies		
1981	JoAnne Carner	1997	Annika Sorenstam		

Vare Trophy: Best Scoring Average*

		Avg			Avg			Avg
1953	Patty Berg	75.00	1973	Judy Rankin	73.08	1993	Nancy Lopez	70.83
1954	Babe Zaharias	75.48	1974	JoAnne Carner	72.87	1994	Beth Daniel	70.90
1955	Patty Berg	74.47	1975	JoAnne Carner	72.40	1995	Annika Sorenstam	71.00
1956	Patty Berg	74.57	1976	Judy Rankin	72.25	1996	Annika Sorenstam	70.47
1957	Louise Suggs	74.64	1977	Judy Rankin	72.16	1997	Karrie Webb	70.00
1958	Beverly Hanson	74.92	1978	Nancy Lopez	71.76	1998	Annika Sorenstam	69.99
1959	Betsy Rawls	74.03	1979	Nancy Lopez	71.20	1999	Karrie Webb	69.43
1960	Mickey Wright	73.25	1980	Amy Alcott	71.51	2000	Karrie Webb	70.05
1961	Mickey Wright	73.55	1981	JoAnne Carner	71.75	2001	Annika Sorenstam	69.42
1962	Mickey Wright	73.67	1982	JoAnne Carner	71.49	2002	Annika Sorenstam	68.70
1963	Mickey Wright	72.81	1983	JoAnne Carner	71.41	2003	Se Ri Pak	70.03
1964	Mickey Wright	72.46	1984	Patty Sheehan	71.40	2004	Grace Park	69.99
1965	Kathy Whitworth	72.61	1985	Nancy Lopez	70.73	2005	Annika Sorenstam	69.33
1966	Kathy Whitworth	72.60	1986	Pat Bradley	71.10	2006	Lorena Ochoa	69.23
1967	Kathy Whitworth	72.74	1987	Betsy King	71.14	2007	Lorena Ochoa	69.69
1968	Carol Mann	72.04	1988	Colleen Walker	71.26	2008	Lorena Ochoa	69.70
1969	Kathy Whitworth	72.38	1989	Beth Daniel	70.38	2009	Lorena Ochoa	70.16
1970	Kathy Whitworth	72.26	1990	Beth Daniel	70.54	2010	Na Yeon Choi	69.87
1971	Kathy Whitworth	72.88	1991	Pat Bradley	70.76	2011	Yani Tseng	69.66
1972	Kathy Whitworth	72.38	1992	Dottie Mochrie	70.80			

*Must play 70 rounds or more to qualify; Annika Sorenstam compiled an average of 69.02 in 60 rounds in 2003.

U.S. Senior Open

Year	Winner	Score	Runner-Up	Site
1980	Roberto DeVicenzo	285	William C. Campbell	Winged Foot GC, Mamaroneck, NY
1981	Arnold Palmer* (70)	289	Bob Stone (74)	Oakland Hills CC, Birmingham, MI
			Billy Casper (77)	
1982	Miller Barber	282	Gene Littler, Dan Sikes, Jr.	Portland GC, Portland, OR
1983	Billy Casper* (75) (3)	288	Rod Funseth (75) (4)	Hazeltine GC, Chaska, MN
1984	Miller Barber	286	Arnold Palmer	Oak Hill CC, Rochester, NY
1985	Miller Barber	285	Roberto DeVicenzo	Edgewood Tahoe GC, Stateline, NV
1986	Dale Douglass	279	Gary Player	Scioto CC, Columbus, OH
1987	Gary Player	270	Doug Sanders	Brooklawn CC, Fairfield, CT
1988	Gary Player* (68)	288	Bob Charles (70)	Medinah CC, Medinah, IL
1989	Orville Moody	279	Frank Beard	Laurel Valley GC, Ligonier, PA
1990	Lee Trevino	275	Jack Nicklaus	Ridgewood CC, Paramus, NJ
1991	Jack Nicklaus* (65)	282	Chi Chi Rodriguez (69)	Oakland Hills CC, Birmingham, MI
1992	Larry Laoretti	275	Jim Colbert	Saucon Valley CC, Bethlehem, PA
1993	Jack Nicklaus	278	Tom Weiskopf	Cherry Hills CC, Englewood, CO
1994	Simon Hobday	274	Jim Albus	Pinehurst Resort & CC, Pinehurst, NC
1995	Tom Weiskopf	275	Jack Nicklaus	Congressional CC, Bethesda, MD
1996	Dave Stockton	277	Hale Irwin	Canterbury GC, Beachwood, OH
1997	Graham Marsh	280	Hale Irwin	Olympia Fields CC, Olympia Fields, IL
1998	Hale Irwin	285	Vicente Fernandez	Riviera CC, Pacific Palisades, CA
1999	Dave Eichelberger	281	Ed Dougherty	Des Moines G & CC, Des Moines, IA
2000	Hale Irwin	267	Bruce Fleisher	Saucon Valley CC, Bethlehem, PA
2001	Bruce Fleisher	280	Isao Aoki, Gil Morgan	Salem CC, Peabody, MA
2002	Don Pooley* (18)	274	Tom Watson (19)	Caves Valley GC, Owings Mill, MD
2003	Bruce Lietzke	277	Tom Watson	Inverness GC, Toledo, OH
2004	Peter Jacobsen	272	Hale Irwin	Bellerive CC, St. Louis, MO
2005	Allen Doyle	274	D.A. Weibring	NCR GC, Kettering, OH
			Loren Roberts	
2006	Allen Doyle	272	Tom Watson	Prairie Dunes CC, Hutchinson, KS
2007	Brad Bryant	282	Ben Crenshaw	Whistling Straits GC, Kohler, WI
2008	Eduardo Romero	274	Fred Funk	Broadmoor GC, Colorado Springs, CO
2009	Fred Funk	268	Joey Sindelar	Crooked Stick GC, Carmel, IN
2010	Bernhard Langer	272	Fred Couples	Sahalee GC, Sammamish, WA
2011	Olin Browne	269	Mark O'Meara	Inverness GC, Toledo, OH
2012	Roger Chapman	270	Fred Funk, Tom Lehman,	Indianwood G & CC, Lake Orion, MI
			Corey Pavin, Bernhard Langer	

*Winner in playoff. Playoff scores are in parentheses. The 1983 playoff went to one hole of sudden death after an 18-hole playoff.

CHAMPIONS TOUR
Season Money Leaders

	Earnings ($)		Earnings ($)		Earnings ($)
1980...Don January	44,100	1991...Mike Hill	1,065,657	2002...Hale Irwin	3,028,304
1981...Miller Barber	83,136	1992...Lee Trevino	1,027,002	2003...Tom Watson	1,853,108
1982...Miller Barber	106,890	1993...Dave Stockton	1,175,944	2004...Craig Stadler	2,306,066
1983...Don January	237,571	1994...Dave Stockton	1,402,519	2005...Dana Quigley	2,170,258
1984...Don January	328,597	1995...Jim Colbert	1,444,386	2006...Jay Haas	2,420,227
1985...Peter Thomson	386,724	1996...Jim Colbert	1,627,890	2007...Jay Haas	2,581,001
1986...Bruce Crampton	454,299	1997...Hale Irwin	2,449,420	2008...Bernhard Langer	2,035,073
1987...Chi Chi Rodriguez	509,145	1998...Hale Irwin	2,861,945	2009...Bernhard Langer	2,164,451
1988...Bob Charles	533,929	1999...Bruce Fleisher	2,515,705	2010...Bernhard Langer	2,648,939
1989...Bob Charles	725,887	2000...Larry Nelson	2,708,005	2011...Tom Lehman	2,081,526
1990...Lee Trevino	1,190,518	2000...Larry Nelson	2,708,005		
1990...Lee Trevino	1,190,518	2001...Allen Doyle	2,553,582		

Most Career Wins†

	Wins		Wins
*Hale Irwin	45	Gary Player	19
Lee Trevino	29	Larry Nelson	19
Gil Morgan	25	George Archer	19
Miller Barber	24	Bruce Fleisher	18
Bob Charles	23	Mike Hill	18
Don January	22	*Jay Haas	16
Chi Chi Rodriguez	22	*Bernhard Langer	15
Jim Colbert	20	Raymond Floyd	14
Bruce Crampton	20	*Dave Stockton	14
		*Tom Watson	14

*Active player. †Through 10/1/12.

Ryder Cup Matches

Year	Results	Site
1927	United States 9½, Great Britain 2½	Worcester CC, Worcester, MA
1929	Great Britain 7, United States 5	Moortown GC, Leeds, England
1931	United States 9, Great Britain 3	Scioto CC, Columbus, OH
1933	Great Britain 6½, United States 5½	Southport and Ainsdale Courses, Southport, England
1935	United States 9, Great Britain 3	Ridgewood CC, Ridgewood, NJ
1937	United States 8, Great Britain 4	Southport and Ainsdale Courses, Southport, England
1939–1945	No tournament	
1947	United States 11, Great Britain 1	Portland GC, Portland, OR
1949	United States 7, Great Britain 5	Ganton GC, Scarborough, England
1951	United States 9½, Great Britain 2½	Pinehurst CC, Pinehurst, NC
1953	United States 6½, Great Britain 5½	Wentworth Club, Surrey, England
1955	United States 8, Great Britain 4	Thunderbird Ranch & CC, Palm Springs, CA
1957	Great Britain 7½, United States 4½	Lindrick GC, Yorkshire, England
1959	United States 8½, Great Britain 3½	Eldorado CC, Palm Desert, CA
1961	United States 14½, Great Britain 9½	Royal Lytham & St. Annes GC, St Anne's-on-the-Sea, England
1963	United States 23, Great Britain 9	East Lake CC, Atlanta
1965	United States 19½, Great Britain 12½	Royal Birkdale GC, Southport, England
1967	United States 23½, Great Britain 8½	Champions GC, Houston
1969	United States 16, Great Britain 16	Royal Birkdale GC, Southport, England
1971	United States 18½, Great Britain 13½	Old Warson CC, St. Louis
1973	United States 19, Great Britain 13	Hon Co of Edinburgh Golfers, Muirfield, Scotland
1975	United States 21, Great Britain 11	Laurel Valley GC, Ligonier, PA
1977	United States 12½, Great Britain 7½	Royal Lytham & St. Annes GC, St. Annes-on-the-Sea, Eng.
1979	United States 17, Europe 11	Greenbrier, White Sulphur Springs, WV
1981	United States 18½, Europe 9½	Walton Heath GC, Surrey, England
1983	United States 14½, Europe 13½	PGA National GC, Palm Beach Gardens, FL
1985	Europe 16½, United States 11½	Belfry GC, Sutton Coldfield, England
1987	Europe 15, United States 13	Muirfield GC, Dublin, OH
1989	Europe 14, United States 14	Belfry GC, Sutton Coldfield, England
1991	United States 14½, Europe 13½	Ocean Course, Kiawah Island, SC
1993	United States 15, Europe 13	Belfry GC, Sutton Coldfield, England
1995	Europe 14½, United States 13½	Oak Hill CC, Rochester, NY
1997	Europe 14½, United States 13½	Valderrama GC, Sotogrande, Spain
1999	United States 14½, Europe 13½	The Country Club, Brookline, MA
2002	Europe 15½, Unites States 12½	Belfry GC, Sutton Coldfield, England
2004	Europe 18½, United States 9½	Oakland Hills CC, Bloomfield Hills, MI
2006	Europe 18½, United States 9½	The K Club, County Kildare, Ireland
2008	United States 16½, Europe 11½	Valhalla GC, Louisville, KY
2010	Europe 14½, United States 13½	Celtic Manor GC, Newport, Wales
2012	Europe 14½, United States 13½	Medinah CC, Medinah, IL

Team matches held every other year between U.S. professionals and those of Great Britain/Europe. Team members selected on basis of finishes in PGA and European tour events. Match in 2001 canceled due to 9/11 terrorist attacks.

Presidents Cup Matches

Year	Results	Site
1994	United States 20, International 12	Robert Trent Jones GC, Lake Manassas, VA
1996	United States 16½, International 15½	Robert Trent Jones GC, Lake Manassas, VA
1998	International 20½ United States 11½	Royal Melbourne GC, Melbourne, Australia
2000	United States 21½, International 10½	Robert Trent Jones GC, Lake Manassas, VA
2003	International 17, United States 17	Fan Court Hotel CC, George, South Africa
2005	United States 18½, International 15½	Robert Trent Jones GC, Lake Manassas, VA
2007	United States 19½, International 14½	Royal Montreal GC, Bizard, Quebec
2009	United States 19½, International 14½	Harding Park GC, San Francisco, CA
2011	United States 19, International 15	Royal Melbourne GC, Melbourne, Australia

A biennial event played in non-Ryder Cup years designed to provide non-European players with international team and match play.

Curtis Cup Matches

Year	Results	Site
1932	United States 5½, British Isles 3½	Wentworth GC, Wentworth, England
1934	United States 6½, British Isles 2½	Chevy Chase Club, Chevy Chase, MD
1936	United States 4½ British Isles 4½	King's Course, Gleneagles, Scotland
1938	United States 5½, British Isles 3½	Essex CC, Manchester, MA
1940–46	No tournament	
1948	United States 6½, British Isles 2½	Birkdale GC, Southport, England
1950	United States 7½, British Isles 1½	CC of Buffalo, Williamsville, NY
1952	British Isles 5, United States 4	Muirfield, Scotland
1954	United States 6, British Isles 3	Merion GC, Ardmore, PA
1956	British Isles 5, United States 4	Prince's GC, Sandwich Bay, England
1958	British Isles 4½, United States 4½	Brae Burn CC, West Newton, Mass.
1960	United States 6½, British Isles 2½	Lindrick GC, Worksop, England
1962	United States 8, British Isles 1	Broadmoor CG, Colorado Springs,CO
1964	United States 10½, British Isles 7½	Royal Porthcawl GC, Porthcawl, South Wales
1966	United States 13, British Isles 5	Va. Hot Springs G & TC, Hot Springs, VA
1968	United States 10½, British Isles 7½	Royal County Down GC, Newcastle, N. Ire.
1970	United States 11½, British Isles 6½	Brae Burn CC, West Newton, MA
1972	United States 10, British Isles 8	Western Gailes, Ayrshire, Scotland
1974	United States 13, British Isles 5	San Francisco GC, San Francisco, Calif.
1976	United States 11½, British Isles 6½	Royal Lytham & St. Annes GC, England
1978	United States 12, British Isles 6	Apawamis Club, Rye, NY
1980	United States 13, British Isles 5	St. Pierre G & CC, Chepstow, Wales
1982	United States 14½, British Isles 3½	Denver CC, Denver
1984	United States 9½ British Isles 8½	Muirfield, Scotland
1986	British Isles 13, United States 5	Prairie Dunes CC, Hutchinson, KS
1988	British Isles 11, United States 7	Royal St. George's GC, Sandwich, England
1990	United States 14, British Isles 4	Somerset Hills CC, Bernardsville, NJ
1992	Great Britain/Ireland 10, United States 8	Royal Liverpool GC, Hoylake, England
1994	Great Britain/Ireland 9, United States 9	The Honors Course, Ooltewah, TN
1996	Great Britain/Ireland 11½, United States 6½	Killarney Golf & Fishing Club, Killarney, Ireland
1998	United States 10, Great Britain/Ireland 8	The Minikahda Club, Minneapolis, Minn.
2000	United States 10, Great Britain/Ireland 8	Ganton GC, North Yorkshire, England
2002	United States 11, Great Britain/Ireland 7	Fox Chapel GC, Pittsburgh, PA
2004	United States 10, Great Britain/Ireland 8	Formby GC, Merseyside, England
2006	United States 11½, Great Britain/Ireland 6½	Bandon Dunes GC, Bandon, OR
2008	United States 13, Great Britain/Ireland 7	Old Course, St. Andrews, Scotland
2010	United States 12½, Great Britain/Ireland 7½	Essex County Club, Manchester, Mass.
2012	Great Britain/Ireland 10½, United States 9½	Nairn GC, Nairn, Scotland

Women's amateur team competition every other year between the United States and Great Britain/Ireland. U.S. team members selected by USGA.

Solheim Cup Matches

Year	Results	Site
1990	United States 11½, Europe 4½	Lake Nona GC, Orlando, FL
1992	Europe 11½, United States 6½	Dalmahoy Hotel GC, Edinburgh, Scotland
1994	United States 13, Europe 7	The Greenbrier, White Sulphur Springs, WV
1996	United States 17, Europe 11	Marriott St Pierre Hotel & CC, Chepstow, Wales
1998	United States 16, Europe 12	Muirfield Village GC, Dublin, OH
2000	Europe 14½, United States, 11 ½	Loch Lomond GC, Luss, Scotland
2002	United States 15½, Europe 12 ½	Interlachen CC, Minneapolis, MN
2003	Europe 17½, United States 10 ½	Barseback G&CC, Malmo, Sweden
2005	United States 15½, Europe 12 ½	Crooked Stick GC, Carmel, IN
2007	United States 16, Europe 12	Halmstad GC, Halmstad, Sweden
2009	United States 16, Europe 12	Rich Harvest Farms GC, Sugar Grove, IL
2011	Europe 15, United States 13	Killeen Castle GC, Ireland

Women's team matches held every other year between U.S. professionals and those of Europe. Team members selected on the basis of finishes in LPGA and European tour events.

Soccer

DAVID BERNAL

Landon Donovan celebrated with his team after scoring the only goal in L.A.'s 1–0 victory over Houston in the MLS Cup Final.

FOR THE RECORD • 2011–2012

2011 Major League Soccer

2011 Final Standings

WESTERN CONFERENCE

Team	GP	W	L	T	Pts	GF	GA
†Los Angeles	34	19	5	10	67	48	28
*Seattle	34	18	7	9	63	56	37
*Real Salt Lake	34	15	11	8	53	44	36
**FC Dallas	34	15	12	7	52	42	39
**Colorado	34	12	9	13	49	46	42
Portland	34	11	14	9	42	40	48
San Jose	34	8	12	14	38	40	45
Chivas USA	34	8	14	12	36	41	43
Vancouver	34	6	18	10	28	35	55

EASTERN CONFERENCE

Team	GP	W	L	T	Pts	GF	GA
†Kansas City	34	13	9	12	51	50	40
*Houston	34	12	9	13	49	45	41
*Philadelphia	34	11	8	15	48	44	36
**Columbus	34	13	13	8	47	43	44
**New York	34	10	8	16	46	50	44
Chicago	34	9	9	16	43	46	45
D.C. United	34	9	13	12	39	49	52
Toronto FC	34	6	13	15	33	36	59
New England	34	5	16	13	28	38	58

Note: Three points for win; one point for tie. †Conference champion. *Qualified for playoffs. **Qualified for wild card play-in.

GOALS LEADERS

Player, Team	GP	G
Dwayne De Rosario, DC	33	16
Chris Wondolowski, SJ	30	16
Thierry Henry, NY	26	14
Andres Mendoza, CLB	29	13
Fredy Montero, SEA	30	12
Landon Donovan, LA	23	12
Camilo, VAN	32	12
Dominic Oduro, CHI	34	12

Four tied with 11

ASSISTS LEADERS

Player, Team	GP	A
Landon Donovan, LA	24	16
Brad Davis, HOU	34	16
David Beckham, LA	26	15
Mauro Rosales, SEA	26	13
Dwayne De Rosario, DC	33	12
Davide Chiumiento, VAN	26	9
Fredy Montero, SEA	30	9
Kyle Beckerman, RSL	29	9
Patrick Nyarko, CHI	30	9
Sebastien Le Toux, PHI	34	9
Jack Jewsbury, POR	31	8

SAVES LEADERS

Player, Team	Saves	GAA
Kasey Keller, SEA	119	1.11
Tally Hall, HOU	119	1.13
Jon Busch, SJ	113	1.33
Matt Reis, NE	111	1.59
Stefan Frei, TOR	106	1.83
Nick Rimando, RSL	102	1.14
Dan Kennedy, CHV	100	1.22
William Hesmer, CLB	98	1.36
Kevin Hartman, DAL	89	1.09

MLS Regular Season MVP: Dwayne De Rosario, DC United.

2011 MLS Playoffs

CONF. SEMIS (TWO LEGS)

Salt Lake	3	0—3
Seattle	0	2—2

Los Angeles	1	2—3
New York	0	1—1

CONF. FINALS

Salt Lake City	1
Los Angeles	3

CONF. SEMIS (TWO LEGS)

Houston	2	1—3
Philadelphia	1	0—1

Kansas City	2	2—4
Colorado	0	0—0

CONF. FINALS

Houston	2
Kansas City	0

2011 MLS CUP (November 20, 2011 in Carson, California)

Houston	0	0—0
Los Angeles	0	1—1

FIRST HALF: Scoring: None.

SECOND HALF: Scoring: 1, LA, Donovan (Keane, Beckham), 72nd minute.

Houston: Hall, Hainault, Boswell, Cameron, Taylor, Cruz (Clark 78), Camargo, Moffat, Ashe (Watson 84), Ching, Carr (Costly 66).

Los Angeles: Saunders, Franklin, Gonzalez, DeLaGarza, Dunivant, Donovan, Beckham, Juninho, Magee, Cristman (Birchall 57), Keane.

Attendance: 30,281. Referee: R. Salazar. Asst. Referees: C. Lowry, P. Manikowski.

MLS Cup MVP: Landon Donovan, Los Angeles.

Group Stage

GROUP A

Country	MP	W	L	D	Pts
*Germany	3	3	0	0	9
*France	3	2	1	0	6
Nigeria	3	1	2	0	3
Canada	3	0	3	0	0

GROUP B

Country	MP	W	L	D	Pts
*England	3	2	0	1	7
*Japan	3	2	1	0	6
Mexico	3	0	1	2	2
New Zealand	3	0	2	1	1

GROUP C

Country	MP	W	L	D	Pts
*Sweden	3	3	0	0	9
*United States	3	2	1	0	6
North Korea	3	0	2	1	1
Colómbia	3	0	2	1	1

GROUP D

Country	MP	W	L	D	Pts
*Brazil	3	3	0	0	9
*Australia	3	2	1	0	6
Norway	3	1	2	0	3
Equa. Guinea	3	0	3	0	0

*Moved on to quarterfinals.
Note: in group play, three points are awarded for a win, one for a tie.

Quarterfinals

Germany	0 0 0—0	Sweden	2	1—3
Japan	0 0 1—1	Australia	1	0—1
a.e.t.				

			England	0 1 0–1 (3)
			France	0 1 0–1 (4)
				a.e.t. (PSO)

			Brazil	0 1 1—2 (3)
			U.S.	1 0 1—2 (5)
				a.e.t. (PSO)

Semifinals

Japan	1	2—3	France	0 1—1
Sweden	1	0—1	U.S.	1 2—3

Third-Place Consolation Match

Sweden	1	1—2
France	0	1—1

2011 Women's World Cup Final

(July 17, 2011 in Frankfurt, Germany)

Japan	0	1	1 — — 2 (3)
United States	0	1	1 — — 2 (1)

FIRST HALF: Scoring: None.

SECOND HALF: Scoring: 1, United States, Morgan (Rapinoe), 69th minute; 1, Japan, Miyama, 81st minute.

EXTRA TIME: Scoring: 1, United States, Wambach (Morgan), 104th minute; 1, Japan, Sawa (Miyama), 117th minute.

PENALTY SHOOT-OUT: Scoring: 1, United States, Boxx (saved), Lloyd (missed), Heath (saved), Wambach (goal); 3, Japan: Miyama (goal), Nagasato (saved), Sakaguchi (goal), Kumagai (goal).

Japan: Kaihori, Kinga, Iwashimizu, Kumagai, Sakaguchi, Ando (Nagasato 66), Miyama, Kawasumi, Sawa, Ohno (Maruyama 66, Iwabuchi 119), Sameshima.

United States: Solo, Rampone, Le Peilbet, Boxx, O'Reilly, Lloyd, Krieger, Cheney (Morgan 46), Rapinoe (Heath 114), Buehler, Wambach.

Referee: Bibiana Steinhaus. Asst. Referees: Marina Wozniak, Katrin Rafalksi.

Final match attendance: 48,817.

2011 World Cup Golden Boot & Golden Ball Winner: Homare Sawa, Japan

The World Cup

Results—Men

Year	Champion	Score	Runner-Up	Winning Coach
1930	Uruguay	4–2	Argentina	Alberto Supicci
1934	Italy	2–1	Czechoslovakia	Vittorio Pozzo
1938	Italy	4–2	Hungary	Vittorio Pozzo
1950	Uruguay	2–1	Brazil	Juan Lopez
1954	West Germany	3–2	Hungary	Sepp Herberger
1958	Brazil	5–2	Sweden	Vicente Feola
1962	Brazil	3–1	Czechoslovakia	Aymore Moreira
1966	England	4–2	West Germany	Alf Ramsey
1970	Brazil	4–1	Italy	Mario Zagalo
1974	West Germany	2–1	Netherlands	Helmut Schoen
1978	Argentina	3–1	Netherlands	César Menotti
1982	Italy	3–1	West Germany	Enzo Bearzot
1986	Argentina	3–2	West Germany	Carlos Bilardo
1990	West Germany	1–0	Argentina	Franz Beckenbauer
1994	Brazil	0–0 (3–2)	Italy	Carlos Alberto Parreira
1998	France	3–0	Brazil	Aime Jacquet
2002	Brazil	2–0	Germany	Luis Felipe Scolari
2006	Italy	1–1 (5–3)	France	Marcello Lippi
2010	Spain	1–0 (2 OT)	Netherlands	Vicente Del Bosque

Alltime World Cup Wins

Nation	Matches	W	T	L	Goals For	Goals Against
Brazil	97	67	15	15	210	89
*Germany	99	60	19	20	206	119
Italy	80	44	21	15	126	78
Argentina	70	37	13	20	123	79
Spain	56	28	12	16	88	57
England	59	26	19	14	77	52
France	54	25	11	18	96	70
Netherlands	43	22	10	11	71	42
Uruguay	47	18	12	17	76	64
†Russia	37	17	6	14	64	44
Yugoslavia	37	17	6	14	60	46
Sweden	46	16	13	17	74	71
Poland	31	15	5	11	44	40
Hungary	32	15	3	14	87	58
Portugal	23	12	3	8	39	23
Austria	29	12	4	13	43	49
Czech Republic	33	12	5	16	47	48
Mexico	49	12	13	24	52	87
Belgium	36	10	9	17	46	64
Switzerland	29	9	6	14	38	51
Chile	29	9	6	14	34	45
Denmark	16	8	2	6	27	24
Romania	21	8	5	8	30	32
Paraguay	27	7	10	10	30	38
United States	29	7	5	17	32	57
Croatia	13	6	2	5	15	11
Turkey	10	5	1	4	20	17
South Korea	28	5	8	15	28	60
Ghana	9	4	2	3	9	10
Japan	14	4	3	7	12	16
Nigeria	14	4	2	8	17	21
Peru	15	4	3	8	19	31
Cameroon	20	4	7	9	17	34
Scotland	23	4	7	12	25	41
Ecuador	7	3	0	4	7	8
Northern Ireland	13	3	5	5	13	23
Costa Rica	10	3	1	6	12	21
Colombia	13	3	2	8	14	22
Bulgaria	26	3	8	15	22	52
Senegal	5	2	2	1	7	6
Ukraine	5	2	1	2	5	7
East Germany	6	2	2	2	5	6
Norway	8	2	3	3	7	9
Cote d'Ivoire	6	2	1	3	9	9
South Africa	9	2	4	3	11	15
Republic of Ireland	13	2	8	3	10	10
Algeria	9	2	2	5	6	12
Morocco	13	2	4	7	12	17
Saudi Arabia	13	2	2	9	9	32
Australia	10	2	3	5	8	16
Wales	5	1	3	1	4	4
Cuba	3	1	1	1	5	12
Slovakia	3	1	1	1	4	5
Jamaica	3	1	0	2	3	9
Slovenia	6	1	1	4	5	10
North Korea	7	1	1	5	6	21
Serbia	6	1	0	5	4	13
Greece	6	1	0	5	2	15
Iran	9	1	2	6	6	17
Tunisia	12	1	4	7	8	17
Angola	3	0	2	1	1	2
Israel	3	0	2	1	1	3
Indonesia	1	0	0	1	0	6
Egypt	4	0	2	2	3	6
Kuwait	3	0	1	2	2	6
Trinidad and Tobago	3	0	1	2	0	4
New Zealand	6	0	3	3	4	14
Honduras	6	0	3	3	2	6
United Arab Emirates	3	0	0	3	2	11
Haiti	3	0	0	3	2	14
Iraq	3	0	0	3	1	4
Togo	3	0	0	3	1	6
Canada	3	0	0	3	0	5
China	3	0	0	3	0	9
Dem. Rep. of Congo	3	0	0	3	0	14
Bolivia	6	0	1	5	1	20
El Salvador	6	0	0	6	1	22

*Includes West Germany 1950–90. †Includes USSR 1930–1990.
Note: Matches decided by penalty kicks are shown as drawn games.

World Cup Final Box Scores

URUGUAY 1930

Uruguay	1	3	--4
Argentina	2	0	--2

FIRST HALF: Scoring: 1, Uruguay, Dorado (12); 2, Argentina, Peucelle (20); 3, Argentina, Stabile (37).

SECOND HALF: Scoring: 4, Uruguay, Cea (57); 5, Uruguay, Iriarte (68); 6, Uruguay, Castro (89).

Argentina: Botosso, Della Toree, Paternoster, J. Evaristo, Monti, Suarez, Peucelle, Varallo, Stabile, Ferreira, M. Evaristo.

Uruguay: Ballesteros, Nasazzi, Mascheroni, Andrade, Fernandez, Gestido, Dorado, Scarone, Castro, Cea, Iriarte.

Referee: Langenus (Belgium).

ITALY 1934

Italy	0	1	1 --2
Czechoslovakia	0	1	0 --1

SECOND HALF: Scoring: 1, Czech., Puc (70); 2, Italy, Orsi (80).

OVERTIME: Scoring: 3, Italy, Schiavio (95).

Italy: Combi, Monzeglio, Allemandi, Ferraris Monti, Monti, Bertolini, Guaita, Meazza, Schiavio, Ferrari, Orsi.

Czechoslovakia: Planicka, Zenisek, Ctyroky, Kostalek, Cambal, Cambal, Krcil, Junek, Svoboda, Sobotka, Nejedly, Puc.

Referee: Eklind (Sweden).

FRANCE 1938

Italy	3	1	--4
Hungary	1	1	--2

FIRST HALF: Scoring: 1, Italy, Colaussi (5); 2, Hungary, Titkos (7); 3, Italy, Piola (16); 4, Italy, Piola (35).

SECOND HALF: Scoring: 5, Hungary, Sarosi (70); 6, Italy, Colaussi (82).

Italy: Olivieri, Foni, Rava, Serantoni, Andreolo, Locatelli, Biavati, Meazza, Piola, Ferrari, Colaussi.

Hungary: Szabo, Polger, Biro, Szalay, Szucs, Lazar, Sas, Vincze, Sarosi, Zsengeller, Titkos.

Referee: Capdeville (France).

BRAZIL 1950

Uruguay	0	2	--2
Brazil	0	1	--1

SECOND HALF: Scoring: 1, Brazil, Friaca (47); 2, Uruguay, Schiaffino (66); 3, Uruguay, Ghiggia (79).

Uruguay: Maspoli, Gonzales, Tejera, Gambretta, Varela, Andrade, Ghiggia, Perez, Miguez, Schiffiano, Moran.

Brazil: Barbosa, Augusto, Juvenal, Bauer, Banilo, Bigode, Friaca, Zizinho, Ademir, Jair, Chico.

Referee: Reader (England).

SWITZERLAND 1954

West Germany	2	1	--3
Hungary	2	0	--2

FIRST HALF: Scoring: 1, Hungary, Puskas (6); 2, Hungary, Czibor (8); 3, W Germ., Morlock (10); 4, W Germ., Rahn (18).

SECOND HALF: Scoring: 5, W Germany, Rahn (84).

West Germany: Turek, Posipal, Kohlmeyer, Eckel, Liebrich, Mai, Rahn, Morlock, O.Walter, F. Walter, Schaefer.

Hungary: Grosics, Buzansky, Lantos, Bozsik, Lorant, Zakarias, Czibor, Kocsis, Hidegkuti, Puskas, Toth.

Referee: Ling (England).

SWEDEN 1958

Brazil	2	3	--5
Sweden	1	1	--2

FIRST HALF: Scoring:1, Sweden, Liedholm (3); 2, Brazil, Vava (9); 3, Brazil, Vava (32).

SECOND HALF: Scoring: 4, Brazil, Pelé (55); 5, Brazil, Zagalo (68); 6, Sweden Simonsson (80); 7, Brazil, Pelé (90).

Brazil: Glymar, D. Santos, N. Santos, Zito, Bellini, Orlando, Garrincha, Didi, Vava, Pelé, Zagalo.

Sweden: Svensson, Bergmark, Axbom, Boerjesson, Gustavsson, Parling, Hamrin, Gren, Simonsson, Liedholm, Skoglund.

Referee: Guigue (France).

CHILE 1962

Brazil	1	2 --3
Czechoslovakia	1	0 --1

FIRST HALF: Scoring: 1, Czech., Masopust (15); 2, Brazil, Amarildo (17).

SECOND HALF: Scoring: 3, Brazil, Zito (68); 4, Brazil, Vava (77).

Brazil: Glymar, D. Santos, N. Santos, Zito, Mauro, Zozimo, Garrincha, Didi, Vava, Amarildo, Zagalo.

Czechoslovakia: Schroiff, Tichy, Novak, Pluskal, Popluhar, Masopust, Pospichal, Scherer, Kvasnak, Kadraba, Jelinek.

Referee: Latychev (USSR).

ENGLAND 1966

England	1	1	2 --3
West Germany	1	1	0 --1

FIRST HALF: Scoring: 1, W Germany, Haller (12); 2, England, Hurst (18).

SECOND HALF: Scoring: 3, England, Peters (78); 4, W. Germany, Weber (90).

EXTRA TIME: Scoring: 5, England, Hurst (101); 6, England, Hurst (120).

England: Banks, Cohen, Wilson, Stiles, J. Charlton, Moore, Ball, Hurst, Hunt, R. Charlton, Peters.

West Germany: Tilkowski, Hottges, Schmellinger, Beckenbauer, Schulz, Weber, Held, Haller, Seeler, Overath, Emmerich.

Referee: Dienst (Switzerland).

World Cup Final Box Scores *(Cont.)*

MEXICO 1970

Brazil	....	1	3 —— 4
Italy	....	1	0 —— 1

FIRST HALF: Scoring: 1, Brazil, Pelé (18); 2, Italy, Boninsegna (32).

SECOND HALF: Scoring: 3, Brazil, Gerson (65); 4, Brazil, Jairzinho (70); 5, Brazil, Alberto (86).

Brazil: Feliz, Alberto, Brito, Wilson, Piazza, Everaldo, Clodoaldo, Gerson, Jairzinho, Tostao, Pelé, Rivelino.

Italy: Albertosi, Burgnich, Cera, Rosato, Facchetti, Bertini (Juliano), Mazzola, De Sisti, Domenghini, Boninsegna (Rivera), Riva.

Referee: Glockner (E Germany).

WEST GERMANY 1974

West Germany	2	0 —— 2
Netherlands	1	0 —— 1

FIRST HALF: Scoring: 1, Netherlands, Neeskens, PK (1); 2, W Germany, Breitner, PK (26); 3, W Germany, Müller (44).

West Germany: Maier, Vogts, Beckenbauer, Schwarzenbeck, Breitner, Hoeness, Bonhof, Overath, Grabowski, Müller, Holzenbein.

Netherlands: Jongbloed, Suurbier, Rijsbergen (de Jong), Haan, Krol, Jansen, Neeskens, van Hanagem, Cruyff, Rensenbrink (van der Kerkhof).

Referee: Taylor (England).

ARGENTINA 1978

Argentina	1	0	2 —— 3
Netherlands	0	1	0 —— 1

FIRST HALF: Scoring: 1, Argentina, Kempes (38).

SECOND HALF: Scoring: 2, Netherlands, Nanninga (81).

EXTRA TIME: Scoring: 3, Arg., Kempes (104); 4, Arg., Bertoni (114).

Argentina: Fillol, Olguin, Galvan, Passarella, Tarantini, Ardiles (Larrosa), Gallego, Kempes, Bertoni, Luque, Ortiz (Houseman).

Netherlands: Jongbloed, Jansen (Suurbier), Krol, Brandts, Poortvliet, Neeskens, Haan, W. van der Kerkhoff, R. van der Kerkhoff, Rep (Nanninga), Rensenbrink.

Referee: Gonella (Italy).

SPAIN 1982

Italy	....	0	3 —— 3
West Germany	0	1 —— 1

SECOND HALF: Scoring: 1, Italy, Rossi (57); 2, Italy, Tardelli (68); 3, Italy, Altobelli (81); 4, W Germany, Breitner (83).

Italy: Zoff, Bergomi, Scirea, Collovati, Cabrini, Oriali, Gentile, Tardelli, Conti, Rossi, Graziani (Altobelli, Causio).

West Germany: Schumacher, Kaltz, Stielike, K. Foerster, B. Foerster, Dremmler (Hrubesch), Breitner, Briegel, Rummenigge (Müller), Fischner (Littbarski).

Referee: Coelho (Brazil).

MEXICO 1986

Argentina	1	2 —— 3
West Germany	0	2 —— 2

FIRST HALF: Scoring: 1, Argentina, Brown (22).

SECOND HALF: Scoring: 2, Arg., Valdano (55); 3, W Germ., Rummenigge (73); 4, W Germ., Voller (81); 5, Arg., Burruchaga (83).

Argentina: Pumpido, Brown, Cuciuffo, Ruggeri, Olarticoecha, Bastista, Giusti, Burruchaga (Trobbiani 90), Enrique, Maradona, Valdona.

West Germany: Schumacher, Jakobs, Forster, Eder, Brehme, Matthaus, Berthold, Magath (Hoeness 62), Briegel, Rummenigge, Allofs (Voller 46).

Referee: Filho (Brazil).

ITALY 1990

West Germany	0	1 —— 1
Argentina	0	0 —— 0

SECOND HALF: Scoring: 1, W Germany, Brehme, PK (84).

West Germany: Illgner, Brehme, Kohler, Augenthaler, Buchwald, Berthold (Reuter), Littbarski, Haessler, Mattaeus, Voeller, Klinsmann.

Argentina: Goychoechea, Lorenzo, Serrizuela, Sensini, Ruggeri (Monzon), Simon, Basualdo, Burruchag (Calderon), Maradona, Troglio, Dezottir.

Referee: Coelho (Brazil).

UNITED STATES 1994

Italy	....	0	0	0 —— 0
Brazil	....	0	0	0 —— 0

Brazil won on penalty kicks, 2–2.

Scoring: None. Shootout goals: Italy—2: Albertini, Evani; Brazil—3: Romario, Branco, Dunga.

Italy: Pagliuca, Benarrivo, Maldini, Baresi, Mussi (Apolloni 35), Albertini, D. Baggio (Evani 95), Berti, Donadoni, Baggio, Massaro.

Brazil: Taffarel, Jorginho (Cafu 21), Branco, Aldair, Santos, Silva, Dunga, Zinho (Viola 106), Mazinho, Bebeto, Romario.

Referee: Puhl (Hungary).

FRANCE 1998

Brazil	....	0	0 —— 0
France	....	2	1 —— 3

FIRST HALF: Scoring: 1, France, Zidane (27); 2, France, Zidane (45).

SECOND HALF: Scoring: 3, France, Petit (90).

Brazil: Taffarel, Cafu, Aldair, Baiano, Carlos, Sampaio (Edmundo 74), Dunga, Rivaldo, Leonardo, (Denilson 46), Bebeto, Ronaldo.

France: Barthez, Lizarazu, Desailly, Thuram, Leboeuf, Djorkaeff (Vieira 75) Deschamps, Zidane, Petit, Karembeu (Boghossian 57), Guivarc'h (Dugarry 66).

Referee: Belqola (Morocco).

World Cup Final Box Scores *(Cont.)*

KOREA/JAPAN 2002

Brazil.................0		**2——2**
Germany...............0		**0——0**

SECOND HALF: Scoring: 1, Brazil, Ronaldo (67); 2, Brazil, Ronaldo (79).

Brazil: Marcos, Cafu, Lucio, Roque Junior, Edmilson, Carlos, Silva, Ronaldo (Denilson, 90), Rivaldo, Ronaldinho (Juninho, 85), Kleberson.

Germany: Kahn, Linke, Ramelow, Neuville, Hamann, Klose (Bierhoff, 74), Jeremies (Asamoah, 77), Bode (Ziege, 84), Schneider, Metzelder, Frings.

Referee: Collina (Italy).

GERMANY 2006

Italy..............l	**0**	**0 ——l**
France........l	**0**	**0 ——l**

Italy won on penalty kicks, 5–3.

FIRST HALF: Scoring: 1, France, Zidane (7); 1, Italy, Materazzi (19).

SHOOTOUT GOALS: Italy—Pirlo, Materazzi, De Rossi, Del Piero, Grosso; France—Wiltord, Abidal, Sagnol.

Italy: Buffon, Zambrotta, Cannavaro, Materazzi, Grosso, Camoranesi (Del Piero 86), Pirlo, Gattuso, Perrotta (Iaquinta 61), Totti (De Rossi 61), Toni.

France: Barthez, Sagnol, Thuram, Gallas, Abidal, Ribery (Trezeguet 100), Vieira (Diarra 56), Makelele, Zidane, Malouda, Henry (Wiltord 107).

Referee: Elizondo (Argentina).

SOUTH AFRICA 2010

Spain..................0	**0**	**0**	**l——l**
Netherlands........0	**0**	**0**	**0——0**

2ND EXTRA TIME: Scoring: 1, Spain, Iniesta (Fabregas), 116.

Spain: Casillas, Pique, Puyol, Iniesta, Pedro (Navas 60), Xavi, Capdevila, Fabregas (Alonso 87), Ramos, Busquets, Villa (Torres 105).

Netherlands: Stekelenburg, Van der Wiel, Heitinga, Mathijsen, Van Brommel, Robben, Sneijder, Kuyt (Elia 71), De Jong (Van der Vaart 99), Van Bronckhorst (Braafheid 105), Van Persie.

Referee: Webb (England).

Alltime Leaders

GOALS

Player, Nation	Tournaments	Goals	Player, Nation	Tournaments	Goals
Ronaldo, Brazil	1994, '98, 2002, '06	15	Teofilo Cubillas, Peru	1970, '78, '82	10
Gerd Müller, West Germany	1970, '74	14	Grzegorz Lato, Poland	1974, '78, '82	10
Miroslav Klose, Germany	2002, '06, '10	14	Ademir, Brazil	1950	9
Just Fontaine, France	1958	13	Eusebio, Portugal	1966	9
Pelé, Brazil	1958, '62, '66, '70	12	Jairzinho, Brazil	1970, '74	9
Sandor Kocsis, Hungary	1954	11	Paolo Rossi, Italy	1982, '86	9
Jurgen Klinsmann, Germany	1990, '94, '98	11	K.H. Rummenigge, W. Germany	1978, '82, '86	9
Helmut Rahn, West Germany	1954, '58	10	Uwe Seeler, West Germany	1958, '62, '66, '70	9
Gary Lineker, England	1986, '90	10	Vava, Brazil	1958, '62	9
Gabriel Batistuta, Argentina	1998, 2002	10	Christian Vieri, Italy	1998, 2002	9

LEADING SCORER, CUP BY CUP

Year	Player, Nation	Goals	Year	Player, Nation	Goals
1930	Guillermo Stabile, Argentina	8	1978	Mario Kempes, Argentina	6
1934	Oldrich Nejedly, Czechoslovakia	5	1982	Paolo Rossi, Italy	6
1938	Leonidas da Silva, Brazil	8	1986	Gary Lineker, England	6
1950	Ademir de Menezes, Brazil	9	1990	Salvatore Schillaci, Italy	6
1954	Sandor Kocsis, Hungary	11	1994	Hristo Stoichkov, Bulgaria	6
1958	Just Fontaine, France	13		Oleg Salenko, Russia	
1962	Florian Albert, Hungary	4	1998	Davor Suker, Croatia	6
	Valentin Ivanov, USSR, Garrincha, Brazil,		2002	Ronaldo, Brazil	8
	Vava, Brazil, Drazan Jerkovic, Yugoslavia		2006	Miroslav Klose, Germany	5
	Leonel Sanchez, Chile		2010	Thomas Mueller, Germany	5
1966	Eusebio Ferreira, Portugal	9		Diego Forlan, Uruguay	
1970	Gerd Müller, W Germany	10		Wesley Sneijder, Netherlands	
1974	Gregorz Lato, Poland	7		David Villa, Spain	

Most Goals, Individual, One Game

Goals	Player, Nation	Score	Date
5	Oleg Salenko, Russia	Russia–Cameroon, 6–1	6-28-94
4	Léonidas, Brazil	Brazil–Poland, 6–5	6-5-38
4	Ernest Willimowski, Poland	Brazil–Poland, 6–5	6-5-38
4	Gustav Wetterström, Sweden	Sweden–Cuba, 8–0	6-12-38
4	Juan Alberto Schiaffino, Uruguay	Uruguay–Bolivia, 8–0	7-2-50
4	Ademir, Brazil	Brazil–Sweden, 7–1	7-9-50
4	Sandor Kocsis, Hungary	Hungary–W Germany, 8–3	6-20-54
4	Just Fontaine, France	France–W Germany, 6–3	6-28-58
4	Eusebio, Portugal	Portugal–N Korea, 5–3	7-23-66
4	Emilio Butragueño, Spain	Spain–Denmark, 5–1	6-18-86

Note: 31 players have scored 32 World Cup hat tricks. Gerd Müller of West Germany is the only man to have two World Cup hat tricks, both in 1970. The last hat tricks were 6-1-02, Miroslav Klose (Ger) vs. Saudi Arabia; 6-21-98, Gabriel Batistuta (Arg) vs. Jamaica; 6-23-90, Tomas Skuhravy (Czech) vs. Costa Rica; and 6-17-90, Michel (Spain) vs. S Korea.

Attendance and Goal Scoring, Year by Year

Year	Site	No. of Games	Goals	Goals/Game	Attendance	Avg Att
1930	Uruguay	18	70	3.89	434,500	24,139
1934	Italy	17	70	4.12	395,000	23,235
1938	France	18	84	4.67	483,000	26,833
1950	Brazil	22	88	4.00	1,337,000	60,773
1954	Switzerland	26	140	5.38	943,000	36,269
1958	Sweden	35	126	3.60	868,000	24,800
1962	Chile	32	89	2.78	776,000	24,250
1966	England	32	89	2.78	1,614,677	50,459
1970	Mexico	32	95	2.97	1,673,975	52,312
1974	W Germany	38	97	2.55	1,774,022	46,685
1978	Argentina	38	102	2.68	1,610,215	42,374
1982	Spain	52	146	2.80	1,856,277	35,698
1986	Mexico	52	132	2.54	2,441,731	46,956
1990	Italy	52	115	2.21	2,514,443	48,354
1994	United States	52	140	2.69	3,567,415	68,604
1998	France	64	171	2.67	2,775,400	43,366
2002	Korea/Japan	64	161	2.52	2,705,216	42,269
2006	Germany	64	147	2.23	3,353,655	52,400
2010	South Africa	64	145	2.27	3,178,856	49,670
Totals		708	2,046	2.89	31,597,166	44,629

Results—Women's World Cup

Year	Champion	Score	Runner-Up	Third Place	Fourth Place
1991	United States	2–1	Norway	Sweden	Germany
1995	Norway	2–0	Germany	United States	China
1999	United States	0–0 (5–4 PK)	China	Brazil	Norway
2003	Germany	2–1	Sweden	United States	Canada
2007	Germany	2–0	Brazil	United States	Norway
2011	Japan	2–2 (3–1 PK)	United States	Sweden	France

Major League Soccer Finals

MLS Cup Results

Year	Champion	Score	Runner-up	Regular Season MVP
1996	D.C. United	3–2 (OT)	Los Angeles	Carlos Valderrama, TB
1997	D.C. United	2–1	Colorado	Preki, Kansas City
1998	Chicago	2–0	D.C. United	Marco Etcheverry, D.C.
1999	D.C. United	2–0	Los Angeles	Jason Kreis, Dallas
2000	Kansas City	1–0	Chicago	Tony Meola, Kansas City
2001	San Jose	2–1 (OT)	Los Angeles	Alex Pineda Chacon, Miami
2002	Los Angeles	1–0 (OT)	New England	Carlos Ruiz, Los Angeles
2003	San Jose	4–2	Chicago	Preki, Kansas City
2004	D.C. United	3–2	Kansas City	Amado Guevara, MetroStars
2005	Los Angeles	1–0 (OT)	New England	Taylor Twellman, NE
2006	Houston	1–1 (OT, 4-3 PKs)	New England	Christian Gomez, D.C.
2007	Houston	2–1	New England	Luciano Emilio, D.C.
2008	Columbus	3–1	New York	Guillermo Schelotto, Clb
2009	Real Salt Lake	1–1 (OT, 5–4 PKs)	Los Angeles	Landon Donovan, LA
2010	Colorado	2–1 (OT)	FC Dallas	David Ferreira, DAL
2011	Los Angeles	1–0	Houston	Dwayne De Rosario, D.C.

United Soccer League Finals

Year	Champion	Score	Runner-Up	Regular Season MVP
1991	San Francisco	1–3, 2–0 (1–0 PKs)	Albany	Jean Harbor, Maryland
1992	Colorado	1–0	Tampa Bay	Taifour Diane, Colorado
1993	Colorado	3–1 (OT)	Los Angeles	Taifour Diane, Colorado
1994	Montreal	1–0	Colorado	Paulinho, Los Angeles
1995	Seattle	1–2 (SO), 3–0, 2–1 (SO)	Atlanta	Peter Hattrup, Seattle
1996	Seattle	2–0	Rochester	Wolde Harris, Colorado
1997	Milwaukee	2–1 (SO)	Carolina	Doug Miller, Rochester
1998	Rochester	3–1	Minnesota	Mark Baena, Seattle
1999	Minnesota	2–1	Rochester	John Swallen, Minnesota
2000	Rochester	3–1	Minnesota	Vitalis Takawira, Mil
2001	Rochester	2–0	Vancouver	Paul Conway, Charleston
2002	Milwaukee	2–1 (2 OT)	Richmond	Leighton O'Brien, Seattle
2003	Charleston	3–0	Minnesota	Thiago Martins, Pittsburgh
2004	Montreal	2–0	Seattle	Greg Sutton, Montreal
2005	Seattle	1–1 (4–3 on PKs)	Richmond	Jason Jordan, Vancouver
2006	Vancouver	3–0	Rochester	Joey Gjertsen, Vancouver
2007	Seattle	4–0	Atlanta	Sebastien Le Toux, Seattle
2008	Vancouver	2–1	Puerto Rico	Jonathan Steele, Puerto Rico
2009	Montreal	6–3 (two legs)	Vancouver	Cristian Arietta, Puerto Rico
2010	Puerto Rico	3–1 (two legs)	Carolina	Ryan Pore, Portland
2011	Orlando City	2–2 (3–2 PKs)	Harrisburg City	Yordany Alvarez, Orlando City
2012	Charleston	1–0	Wilmington	Kevin Molino, Orlando City

Motor Sports

Scotland's Dario Franchitti (50)
led the pack en route to his
record-setting third victory in
the Indianapolis 500

Indy Racing League

Indianapolis 500

Results of the 96th running of the Indianapolis 500 and fifth race of the 2012 Indy Racing League season. Held Sunday, May 27, 2012, at the 2.5-mile Indianapolis Motor Speedway in Indianapolis, Indiana. Distance, 500 miles; starters, 33; winning time of race, 2 hours, 58 minutes, 51.2532 seconds; average speed, 167.734 mph; margin of victory (under caution); caution flags, 8 for 39 laps; lead changes, 34 among 10 drivers.

TOP 10 FINISHERS

Pos.	Driver (start pos.)	Engine	Qual. Speed	Laps	Status
1	Dario Franchitti (16)	Honda	223.582	200	running
2	Scott Dixon (15)	Honda	223.684	200	running
3	Tony Kanaan (8)	Chevrolet	224.751	200	running
4	Oriol Servia (27)	Chevrolet	222.393	200	running
5	Ryan Briscoe (1)	Chevrolet	226.484	200	running
6	James Hinchcliffe (2)	Chevrolet	226.481	200	running
7	Justin Wilson (21)	Honda	222.929	200	running
8	Charlie Kimball (14)	Honda	223.868	200	running
9	Townsend Bell (20)	Honda	223.134	200	running
10	Helio Castroneves (6)	Chevrolet	225.172	200	running

2012 Indy Racing League Results

Date	Race	Winner (start pos.)	Engine	Avg. Speed
Mar 25	Grand Prix of St. Petersburg	Helio Castroneves (5)	Chevrolet	90.113 mph
Apr 1	Indy Grand Prix of Alabama	Will Power (9)	Chevrolet	102.081 mph
Apr 15	Grand Prix of Long Beach	Will Power (12)	Chevrolet	88.021 mph
Apr 29	Sao Paulo Indy 300	Will Power (1)	Chevrolet	88.945 mph
May 27	Indianapolis 500	Dario Franchitti (16)	Honda	167.734 mph
Jun 3	Indycar Series at Belle Isle	Scott Dixon	Honda	85.012 mph
Jun 9	Firestone 550	Justin Wilson	Honda	167.217 mph
Jun 16	IndyCar Series at Milwaukee	Ryan Hunter-Reay	Chevrolet	122.020 mph
Jun 23	Iowa Corn Indy 250	Ryan Hunter-Reay	Chevrolet	129.371 mph
Jul 8	IndyCar Series at Toronto	Ryan Hunter-Reay	Chevrolet	95.787 mph
Jul 22	Edmonton Indy	Helio Castroneves	Chevrolet	101.246 mph
Aug 5	IndyCar Series at Mid-Ohio	Scott Dixon	Honda	115.379 mph
Aug 26	Indy Grand Prix of Sonoma	Ryan Briscoe	Chevrolet	95.740 mph
Sep 2	Grand Prix of Baltimore	Ryan Hunter-Reay	Chevrolet	71.136 mph
Sep 15	MAVTV 500	Ed Carpenter	Chevrolet	168.939 mph

Note: Distances are in miles unless followed by * (laps).

2012 Final IRL Standings

Driver	Pts	Wins
Ryan Hunter-Reay	468	4
Will Power	465	3
Scott Dixon	435	2
Helio Castroneves	431	2
Simon Pagenaud	387	0
Ryan Briscoe	370	1
Dario Franchitti	363	1
James Hinchcliffe	358	0
Tony Kanaan	351	0
Graham Rahal	333	0

Daytona 500

Results of the 54th Daytona 500, the opening round of the 2012 Sprint Cup series. Held Sunday, February 27, 2012, at the 2.5-mile high-banked Daytona International Speedway. Distance, 500 miles; starters, 43; winning time of race, 3 hours, 36 minutes, 2 seconds; average speed, 140.256 mph; margin of victory, 0.21 seconds; caution flags, 10 for 42 laps; lead changes, 25 among 13 drivers.

TOP 10 FINISHERS

Pos.	Driver (start pos.)	Car	Laps	Winnings ($)
1	Matt Kenseth (4)	Ford	202	1,589,390
2	Dale Earnhardt Jr. (5)	Chevrolet	202	1,102,170
3	Greg Biffle (2)	Ford	202	804,163
4	Denny Hamlin (31)	Toyota	202	702,091
5	Jeff Burton (9)	Chevrolet	202	559,550
6	Paul Menard (37)	Chevrolet	202	427,900
7	Kevin Harvick (13)	Chevrolet	202	415,261
8	Carl Edwards (1)	Ford	202	403,466
9	Joey Logano (12)	Toyota	202	346,063
10	Mark Martin (22)	Toyota	202	323,313

2011 Sprint Chase for the Cup* Final Season Standings

Driver	Pts	Starts	Wins	Top 5	Top 10
Tony Stewart	2403	36	5	9	19
Carl Edwards	2403	36	1	19	26
Kevin Harvick	2345	36	4	9	19
Matt Kenseth	2330	36	3	12	20
Brad Keselowski	2319	36	3	10	14
Jimmie Johnson	2304	36	2	14	21
Dale Earnhardt Jr.	2290	36	0	4	12
Jeff Gordon	2287	36	3	13	18
Denny Hamlin	2284	36	1	5	14
Ryan Newman	2284	36	1	9	17
Kurt Busch	2262	36	2	8	16
Kyle Busch	2246	35	4	14	18

2011 Sprint Cup* Final Season Driver Winnings

Driver	Winnings ($)
Carl Edwards	8,485,990
Tony Stewart	6,529,870
Jimmie Johnson	6,296,360
Kevin Harvick	6,197,140
Matt Kenseth	6,183,580
Kyle Busch	6,161,020
Kurt Busch	5,936,470
Jeff Gordon	5,912,830
Clint Bowyer	5,663,950
Denny Hamlin	5,401,190
Ryan Newman	5,303,020
Brad Keselowski	5,087,740

2012 Sprint Chase for the Cup Late-Season Standings†

Driver	Pts	Starts	Wins	Top 5	Top 10
Brad Keselowski	2142	29	5	12	18
Jimmie Johnson	2137	29	3	15	20
Denny Hamlin	2126	29	5	12	15
Clint Bowyer	2117	29	2	7	18
Tony Stewart	2110	29	3	10	14
Kasey Kahne	2110	29	2	9	15
Dale Earnhardt Jr.	2103	29	1	10	18
Martin Truex Jr.	2100	29	0	6	16
Kevin Harvick	2096	29	0	4	11
Jeff Gordon	2094	29	1	9	14
Greg Biffle	2091	29	2	10	15
Matt Kenseth	2070	29	1	10	16

*Series name changed from Winston Cup to Nextel Cup after 2003 season, then to Sprint Cup beginning in 2008.
†2012 Sprint Chase for the Cup standings through October 1, 2012 (29 of 36 races).

2011-12 NASCAR Sprint Cup Results

Late 2011 Sprint Cup Series Results

Date	Track/Distance	Winner (start pos.)	Car	Laps	Winnings ($)
*Oct 9	Kansas 400	Jimmie Johnson (19)	Chevrolet	272	331,336
*Oct 15	Charlotte 500	Matt Kenseth (2)	Ford	334	284,436
*Oct 23	Talladega 500	Clint Bowyer (3)	Chevrolet	188	260,558
*Oct 30	Martinsville 500	Tony Stewart (4)	Chevrolet	500	198,983
*Nov 6	Texas 500	Tony Stewart (5)	Chevrolet	334	484,783
*Nov 13	Phoenix 500	Kasey Kahne (10)	Toyota	312	202,233
*Nov 20	Homestead/Miami 400	Tony Stewart (15)	Chevrolet	267	341,258

2012 Sprint Cup Series Results†

Date	Track/Distance	Winner (start pos.)	Car	Laps	Winnings ($)
Feb 27	Daytona 500	Matt Kenseth (4)	Ford	202	1,589,390
Mar 4	Phoenix 500	Denny Hamlin (13)	Toyota	312	238,016
Mar 11	Las Vegas 400	Tony Stewart (7)	Chevrolet	267	428,175
Mar 18	Bristol 500	Brad Keselowski (5)	Dodge	500	186,770
Mar 25	Fontana 500	Tony Stewart (9)	Chevrolet	129	323,450
Apr 1	Martinsville 500	Ryan Newman (5)	Chevrolet	515	198,808
Apr 14	Texas 500	Greg Biffle (3)	Ford	334	540,850
Apr 22	Kansas 400	Denny Hamlin (4)	Toyota	267	248,691
Apr 28	Richmond 400	Kyle Busch (5)	Toyota	400	247,783
May 6	Talladega 499	Brad Keselowski (13)	Dodge	194	305,745
May 12	Darlington 500	Jimmie Johnson (2)	Chevrolet	368	319,786
May 19	Showdown	Dale Earnhardt Jr. (3)	Chevrolet	40	N/A
May 19	All-Star Race	Jimmie Johnson (6)	Chevrolet	90	N/A
May 27	Charlotte 600	Kasey Kahne (7)	Chevrolet	400	355,675
June 3	Dover 400	Jimmie Johnson (2)	Chevrolet	400	319,411
June 10	Pocono 400	Joey Logano (1)	Toyota	160	226,725
June 17	Michigan 400	Dale Earnhardt Jr. (17)	Chevrolet	200	168,775
June 24	Sonoma 350	Clint Bowyer (6)	Toyota	112	314,089
June 30	Kentucky 400	Brad Keselowski (8)	Dodge	267	176,470
July 7	Daytona 400	Tony Stewart (42)	Chevrolet	160	340,950
July 15	Loudon 301	Kasey Kahne (2)	Chevrolet	301	220,275
July 29	Brickyard 400	Jimmie Johnson (6)	Chevrolet	160	430,461
Aug 5	Pocono 400	Jeff Gordon (27)	Chevrolet	98	233,011
Aug 12	Watkins Glen 355	Marcos Ambrose (5)	Ford	90	259,558
Aug 19	Michigan 400	Greg Biffle (13)	Ford	201	225,275
Aug 25	Bristol 500	Denny Hamlin (8)	Toyota	500	329,166
Sept 2	Atlanta 500	Denny Hamlin (7)	Toyota	327	355,716
Sept 8	Richmond 400	Clint Bowyer (4)	Toyota	400	226,114
*Sept 16	Chicago 400	Brad Keselowski (13)	Dodge	267	303,195
*Sept 23	Loudon 300	Denny Hamlin (32)	Toyota	300	273,166
*Sept 30	Dover 400	Brad Keselowski (10)	Dodge	400	221,070

† Through October 1, 2012.
* Part of 10-race Chase for the Cup.

Formula One Grand Prix Racing

Late 2011 Formula One Results

Grand Prix	Date	Winner	Car	Laps	Time
Korea	Oct 16	Sebastian Vettel	RBR-Renault	55	1:38:01.994
India	Oct 30	Sebastian Vettel	RBR-Renault	60	1:30:35.002
Abu Dhabi	Nov 13	Lewis Hamilton	McLaren-Mercedes	55	1:37:11.886
Brazil	Nov 27	Mark Webber	RBR-Renault	71	1:32:17.464

2012 Formula One Results†

Grand Prix	Date	Winner	Car	Laps	Time
Australia	Mar 18	Sebastian Vettel	RBR-Renault	58	1:29:30.259
Australia	Mar 18	Jenson Button	McLaren-Mercedes	58	1:34:09.565
Malaysia	Mar 25	Fernando Alonso	Ferrari	56	2:44:51.812
China	Apr 15	Nico Rosberg	Mercedes	56	1:36:26.929
Bahrain	Apr 22	Sebastian Vettel	RBR-Renault	57	1:35:10.990
Spain	May 13	Pastor Maldonado	Williams-Renault	66	1:39:09.145

† Through October 1, 2012.

2012 Formula One Results (Cont.)†

Monaco	May 27	Mark Webber	RBR-Renault	78	1:46:06.557
Canada	June 10	Lewis Hamilton	McLaren-Mercedes	70	1:32:29.586
Europe	June 24	Fernando Alonso	Ferrari	57	1:44:16.649
Great Britain	July 8	Mark Webber	RBR-Renault	52	1:25:11.288
Germany	July 22	Fernando Alonso	Ferrari	67	1:31:05.862
Hungary	July 29	Lewis Hamilton	McLaren-Mercedes	69	1:41:05.503
Belgium	Sept 2	Jenson Button	McLaren-Mercedes	44	1:29:08.530
Italy	Sept 9	Lewis Hamilton	McLaren-Mercedes	53	1:19:41.221
Singapore	Sept 23	Sebastian Vettel	RBR-Renault	59	2:00:26.144

† Through October 1, 2012.

2011 World Championship Final Standings

Drivers compete in Grand Prix races for the title of World Driving Champion. Points are awarded for places 1–10 as follows: 25-18-15-12-10-8-6-4-2-1.

Driver	Country	Team	Pts
Sebastian Vettel	Germany	RBR-Renault	392
Jenson Button	Great Britain	McLaren-Mercedes	270
Mark Webber	Australia	RBR-Renault	258
Fernando Alonso	Spain	Ferrari	257
Lewis Hamilton	Great Britain	McLaren-Mercedes	227
Felipe Massa	Brazil	Ferrari	118
Nico Rosberg	Germany	Mercedes	89
Michael Schumacher	Germany	Mercedes	76
Adrian Sutil	Germany	Force India-Mercedes	42
Vitaly Petrov	Russia	Renault	37

Professional Sports Car Racing

The 24 Hours of Daytona

Held at the Daytona International Speedway on Jan 28–29, 2012, the 24 Hours of Daytona serves as the opening round of the Grand American Road Racing Association's season.

Place	Drivers	Car (Class)	Distance
1	J. Pew, O. Negri Jr, AJ Allmendinger, J. Wilson	Ford Riley	761 laps
2	E. Potolicchio, R. Dalziel, A. Popow, L. Luhr, A. McNish	Ford Riley	761 laps
3	M. McDowell, F. Nasr, J. Goncalvez, G. Yacaman	Ford Riley	761 laps
4	S. Dixon, J. Pablo Montoya, D. Franchitti, J. McMurray	BMW Riley	760 laps
5	D. Law, D. Donohue, C. Fittipaldi	Corvette DP	758 laps

2012 American Le Mans Series—P1 Class

Date	Race	Winners	Car
Mar 17	12 Hours of Sebring	A. McNish, T. Kristensen, R. Capello	Audi R18
April 14	Grand Prix of Long Beach	L. Luhr, K. Graf	HPD ARX-03a
May 12	Monterey Grand Prix	L. Luhr, K. Graf	HPD ARX-03a
July 7	Northeast Grand Prix	L. Luhr, K. Graf	HPD ARX-03a
July 22	Grand Prix of Mosport	L. Luhr, K. Graf	HPD ARX-03a
Aug 4	Mid-Ohio Challenge	L. Luhr, K. Graf	HPD ARX-03a
Aug 18	Road America 500	C. Dyson, G. Smith	Lola B12/60
Sept 1	Baltimore Grand Prix	M. Marsal, E Lux	Lola B11/66
Sept 15	Laguna Seca	L. Luhr, K. Graf	HPD ARX-03a

2012 American Le Mans Series—P2 Class

Date	Race	Winners	Car
Mar 17	12 Hours of Sebring	V. Potolicchio, R. Dalziel, S. Sarrazin	HPD ARX-03b
April 14	Grand Prix of Long Beach	S. Tucker, C. Bouchut	HPD ARX-03b
May 12	Monterey Grand Prix	S. Tucker, L. Diaz, F. Montagny	HPD ARX-03b
July 7	Northeast Grand Prix	S. Tucker, C. Bouchut	HPD ARX-03b
July 22	Grand Prix of Mosport	M. Plowman, D. Heinemeier Hansson	Morgan
Aug 4	Mid-Ohio Challenge	C. Bouchut, S. Tucker	HPD ARX-03b
Aug 18	Road America 500	M. Plowman, D. Heinemeier Hansson	Morgan
Sept 1	Baltimore Grand Prix	S. Tucker, C. Bouchut	HPD ARX-03b
Sept 15	Laguna Seca	S. Tucker, C. Bouchut	HPD ARX-03b

2012 American Le Mans Series—Prototype Challenge

Date	Race	Winners	Car
Mar 17	12 Hours of Sebring	A. Popow, E.J. Viso, B. Frisselle	Oreca FLM09
April 14	Grand Prix of Long Beach	A. Popow, R. Dalziel	Oreca FLM09
May 12	Monterey Grand Prix	C. Braun, J. Bennett	Oreca FLM09
July 7	Northeast Grand Prix	C. Braun, J. Bennett	Oreca FLM09
July 22	Grand Prix of Mosport	B. Junqueira, T. Drissi	Oreca FLM09
Aug 4	Mid-Ohio Challenge	M. Franchitti, R. Junco	Oreca FLM09
Aug 18	Road America 500	A. Popow, T. Kimber-Smith, J. Bennett	Oreca FLM09
Sept 1	Baltimore Grand Prix	A. Popow, R. Dalziel	Oreca FLM09
Sept 15	Laguna Seca	J. Bennett, C. Braun	Oreca FLM09

2012 American Le Mans Series—GT Class

Date	Race	Winners	Car
Mar 19	12 Hours of Sebring	J. Hand, D. Müller, J. Summerton	BMW E92 M3
April 16	Grand Prix of Long Beach	O. Gavin, T. Milner	Chevrolet Corvette C6 ZR1
May 12	Monterey Grand Prix	O. Gavin, T. Milner	Chevrolet Corvette C6 ZR1
July 7	Northeast Grand Prix	J. Bergmeister, P Long	Porsche 911 GT3 RSR
July 22	Grand Prix of Mosport	S. Sharp, J. Van Overbeek	Ferrari F458 Italia
Aug 4	Mid-Ohio Challenge	O. Gavin, T. Milner	Chevrolet Corvette C6 ZR1
Aug 18	Road America 500	J. Müller, B. Auberlen	BMW E92 M3
Sept 1	Baltimore Grand Prix	W. Henzler, B. Sellers	Porsche 911 GT3 RSR
Sept 15	Laguna Seca	O. Gavin, T. Milner	Chevrolet Corvette C6 ZR1

2012 American Le Mans Series—GT Challenge

Date	Race	Winners	Car
Mar 17	12 Hours of Sebring	B. Sweedler, T. Bell, D. von Moltke	Porsche 911 GT3
April 14	Grand Prix of Long Beach	D. Faulkner, P. LeSaffre	Porsche 911 GT3
May 12	Monterey Grand Prix	J. Bleekemolen, T.Pappas	Porsche 911 GT3
July 7	Northeast Grand Prix	C. MacNeil, L. Keen	Porsche 911 GT3
July 22	Grand Prix of Mosport	E. Di Guida, S. Pumpelly	Porsche 911 GT3
Aug 4	Mid-Ohio Challenge	T. Pappas, J. Bleekemolen	Porsche 911 GT3
Aug 18	Road America 500	C. MacNeil, J. Bleekemolen	Porsche 911 GT3
Sept 1	Baltimore Grand Prix	A. Carter, P. Pilet	Porsche 911 GT3
Sept 15	Laguna Seca	C. MacNeil, L. Keen	Porsche 911 GT3

Late 2012 American Le Mans Series Championship Standings†

P1 CLASS	Pts	P2 CLASS	Pts	PROTOTYPE CLASS	Pts
Klaus Graf	175	Christophe Bouchut	172	Alex Popow	161
Lucas Luhr	175	Scott Tucker	172	Jonathan Bennett	136
Chris Dyson	162	David Heinemeier Hansson	156	Colin Braun	136
Guy Smith	162	Martin Plowman	156	Bruno Junqueira	98
Eric Lux	87	Patrick Dempsey	53	Duncan Ende	70
Michael Marsal	74	Luis Diaz	51	Henri Richard	70

GT CLASS	Pts	GTC CLASS	Pts
Oliver Gavin	146	Cooper MacNeil	161
Tommy Milner	146	Leh Keen	127
Antonio Garcia	101	Damien Faulkner	116
Jan Magnussen	101	Peter LeSaffre	116
Four tied with 99		Spencer Pumpelly	96
		Chris Cumming	91

† Through October 1, 2012. Includes all races except season-ending Petit Le Mans.

24 Hours of Le Mans

Held at Le Mans, France, on June 16–17, 2012, the 24 Hours of Le Mans is the most prestigious international event in endurance racing.

Place	Drivers	Car	Laps
1	M. Fassler, A. Lotterer, B Treluyer	Audi R18 e-tron quattro	378 (133.28 mph)
2	D. Capello, T. Kristensen, A. McNish	Audi R18 e-tron quattro	377
3	M. Bonanomi, O. Jarvis, M. Rockenfeller	Audi R18 Ultra	375
4	N. Prost, N. Jani, N. Heidfeld	Lola B12/60 Coupe - Toyota	367
5	R. Dumas, L. Duval, M. Gené	Audi R18 Ultra	366

FOR THE RECORD • Year by Year

Indianapolis 500

First held in 1911, the Indianapolis 500—200 laps of the 2.5-mile Indianapolis Motor Speedway Track (called the Brickyard in honor of its original pavement)—grew to become the most famous auto race in the world. Though the Memorial Day weekend event lost participants and prestige in the mid-1990s due to feuding in the world of U.S. open-wheel racing, it annually attracts crowds of over 100,000.

Year	Winner (start pos.)	Chassis-Engine	Avg Speed	Pole Winner	Speed
1911	Ray Harroun (28)	Marmon-Marmon	74.590	Lewis Strang	First entered
1912	Joe Dawson (7)	National-National	78.720	Gil Anderson	First entered
1913	Jules Goux (7)	Peugeot-Peugeot	75.930	Caleb Bragg	Drew pole
1914	Rene Thomas (15)	Delage-Delage	82.470	Jean Chassagne	Drew pole
1915	Ralph DePalma (2)	Mercedes-Mercedes	89.840	Howard Wilcox	98.90
1916	Dario Resta (4)	Peugeot-Peugeot	84.000	John Aitken	96.69
1917–18	No race				
1919	Howard Wilcox (2)	Peugeot-Peugeot	88.050	Rene Thomas	104.78
1920	Gaston Chevrolet (6)	Frontenac-Frontenac	88.620	Ralph DePalma	99.15
1921	Tommy Milton (20)	Frontenac-Frontenac	89.620	Ralph DePalma	100.75
1922	Jimmy Murphy (1)	Duesenberg-Miller	94.480	Jimmy Murphy	100.50
1923	Tommy Milton (1)	Miller-Miller	90.950	Tommy Milton	108.17
1924	L.L. Corum	Duesenberg-Duesenberg	98.230	Jimmy Murphy	108.037
	Joe Boyer (21)				
1925	Peter DePaolo (2)	Duesenberg-Duesenberg	101.130	Leon Duray	113.196
1926	Frank Lockhart (20)	Miller-Miller	95.904	Earl Cooper	111.735
1927	George Souders (22)	Duesenberg-Duesenberg	97.545	Frank Lockhart	120.100
1928	Louis Meyer (13)	Miller-Miller	99.482	Leon Duray	122.391
1929	Ray Keech (6)	Miller-Miller	97.585	Cliff Woodbury	120.599
1930	Billy Arnold (1)	Summers-Miller	100.448	Billy Arnold	113.268
1931	Louis Schneider (13)	Stevens-Miller	96.629	Russ Snowberger	112.796
1932	Fred Frame (27)	Wetteroth-Miller	104.144	Lou Moore	117.363
1933	Louis Meyer (6)	Miller-Miller	104.162	Bill Cummings	118.524
1934	Bill Cummings (10)	Miller-Miller	104.863	Kelly Petillo	119.329
1935	Kelly Petillo (22)	Wetteroth-Offy	106.240	Rex Mays	120.736
1936	Louis Meyer (28)	Stevens-Miller	109.069	Rex Mays	119.664
1937	Wilbur Shaw (2)	Shaw-Offy	113.580	Bill Cummings	123.343
1938	Floyd Roberts (1)	Wetteroth-Miller	117.200	Floyd Roberts	125.681
1939	Wilbur Shaw (3)	Maserati-Maserati	115.035	Jimmy Snyder	130.138
1940	Wilbur Shaw (2)	Maserati-Maserati	114.277	Rex Mays	127.850
1941	Floyd Davis	Wetteroth-Offy	115.117	Mauri Rose	128.691
	Mauri Rose (17)				
1942–45	No race				
1946	George Robson (15)	Adams-Sparks	114.820	Cliff Bergere	126.471
1947	Mauri Rose (3)	Deidt-Offy	116.338	Ted Horn	126.564
1948	Mauri Rose (3)	Deidt-Offy	119.814	Rex Mays	130.577
1949	Bill Holland (4)	Deidt-Offy	121.327	Duke Nalon	132.939
1950	Johnnie Parsons (5)	Kurtis-Offy	124.002	Walt Faulkner	134.343
1951	Lee Wallard (2)	Kurtis-Offy	126.244	Duke Nalon	136.498
1952	Troy Ruttman (7)	Kuzma-Offy	128.922	Fred Agabashian	138.010
1953	Bill Vukovich (1)	KK500A-Offy	128.740	Bill Vukovich	138.392
1954	Bill Vukovich (19)	KK500A-Offy	130.840	Jack McGrath	141.033
1955	Bob Sweikert (14)	KK500C-Offy	128.209	Jerry Hoyt	140.045
1956	Pat Flaherty (1)	Watson-Offy	128.490	Pat Flaherty	145.596
1957	Sam Hanks (13)	Salih-Offy	135.601	Pat O'Connor	143.948
1958	Jim Bryan (7)	Salih-Offy	133.791	Dick Rathmann	145.974
1959	Rodger Ward (6)	Watson-Offy	135.857	Johnny Thomson	145.908
1960	Jim Rathmann (2)	Watson-Offy	138.767	Eddie Sachs	146.592
1961	A.J. Foyt (7)	Trevis-Offy	139.130	Eddie Sachs	147.481
1962	Rodger Ward (2)	Watson-Offy	140.293	Parnelli Jones	150.370
1963	Parnelli Jones (1)	Watson-Offy	143.137	Parnelli Jones	151.153
1964	A.J. Foyt (5)	Watson-Offy	147.350	Jim Clark	158.828
1965	Jim Clark (2)	Lotus-Ford	150.686	A.J. Foyt	161.233
1966	Graham Hill (15)	Lola-Ford	144.317	Mario Andretti	165.899
1967	A.J. Foyt (4)	Coyote-Ford	151.207	Mario Andretti	168.982
1968	Bobby Unser (3)	Eagle-Offy	152.882	Joe Leonard	171.559
1969	Mario Andretti (2)	Hawk-Ford	156.867	A.J. Foyt	170.568
1970	Al Unser (1)	PJ Colt-Ford	155.749	Al Unser	170.221
1971	Al Unser (5)	PJ Colt-Ford	157.735	Peter Revson	178.696
1972	Mark Donohue (3)	McLaren-Offy	162.962	Bobby Unser	195.940

Year	Winner (start pos.)	Chassis-Engine	Avg speed	Pole Winner	Speed
1973	Gordon Johncock (11)	Eagle-Offy	159.036	Johnny Rutherford	198.413
1974	Johnny Rutherford (25)	McLaren-Offy	158.589	A.J. Foyt	191.632
1975	Bobby Unser (3)	Racers Eagle-Offy	149.213	A.J. Foyt	193.976
1976	Johnny Rutherford (1)	McLaren-Offy	148.725	Johnny Rutherford	188.957
1977	A.J. Foyt (4)	Coyote-Ford	161.331	Tom Sneva	198.884
1978	Al Unser (5)	Lola-Cosworth	161.361	Tom Sneva	202.156
1979	Rick Mears (1)	Penske-Cosworth	158.899	Rick Mears	193.736
1980	Johnny Rutherford (1)	Chaparral-Cosworth	142.862	Johnny Rutherford	192.256
1981	Bobby Unser (1)	Penske-Cosworth	139.084	Bobby Unser	200.546
1982	Gordon Johncock (5)	Wildcat-Cosworth	162.026	Rick Mears	207.004
1983	Tom Sneva (4)	March-Cosworth	162.117	Teo Fabi	207.395
1984	Rick Mears (3)	March-Cosworth	163.612	Tom Sneva	210.029
1985	Danny Sullivan (8)	March-Cosworth	152.982	Pancho Carter	212.583
1986	Bobby Rahal (4)	March-Cosworth	170.722	Rick Mears	216.828
1987	Al Unser (20)	March-Cosworth	162.175	Mario Andretti	215.390
1988	Rick Mears (1)	Penske-Chevrolet	144.809	Rick Mears	219.198
1989	Emerson Fittipaldi (3)	Penske-Chevrolet	167.581	Rick Mears	223.885
1990	Arie Luyendyk (3)	Lola-Chevrolet	185.981*	Emerson Fittipaldi	225.301
1991	Rick Mears (1)	Penske-Chevrolet	176.457	Rick Mears	224.113
1992	Al Unser Jr. (12)	Galmer-Chevrolet	134.477	Roberto Guerrero	232.482
1993	Emerson Fittipaldi (9)	Penske-Chevrolet	157.207	Arie Luyendyk	223.967
1994	Al Unser Jr. (1)	Penske-Mercedes	160.872	Al Unser Jr.	228.011
1995	Jacques Villeneuve (5)	Reynard-Ford	153.616	Scott Brayton	231.616
1996	Buddy Lazier (5)	Reynard-Ford	147.956	Tony Stewart	233.100†
1997	Arie Luyendyk (1)	G Force-Oldsmobile	145.827	Arie Luyendyk	231.468
1998	Eddie Cheever (17)	Dallara-Oldsmobile	145.155	Billy Boat	223.503
1999	Kenny Brack (8)	Dallara-Oldsmobile	153.176	Arie Luyendyk	225.179
2000	Juan Montoya (2)	G Force-Oldsmobile	167.607	Greg Ray	223.471
2001	Helio Castroneves (11)	Dallara-Oldsmobile	153.601	Scott Sharp	226.037
2002	Helio Castroneves (13)	Dallara-Chevrolet	166.499	Bruno Junqueira	231.342
2003	Gil de Ferran (10)	Panoz-Toyota	156.291	Helio Castroneves	231.725
2004	Buddy Rice (1)	G Force-Honda	138.518	Buddy Rice	222.024
2005	Dan Wheldon (16)	Dallara-Honda	157.603	Tony Kanaan	227.566
2006	Sam Hornish Jr.(1)	Dallara-Honda	157.085	Sam Hornish Jr.	228.985
2007	Dario Franchitti (3)	Dallara-Honda	151.744	Helio Castroneves	225.817
2008	Scott Dixon (1)	Dallara-Honda	143.567	Scott Dixon	226.366
2009	Helio Castroneves (1)	Dallara-Honda	150.138	Helio Castroneves	224.864
2010	Dario Franchitti (3)	Dallara-Honda	161.623	Helio Castroneves	227.970
2011	Dan Wheldon (6)	Dallara-Honda	170.265	Alex Tagliani	227.472
2012	Dario Franchitti (16)	Dallara-Honda	167.734	Ryan Briscoe	226.484

*Track record, winning speed. †Track record, qualifying speed.

Indianapolis 500 Rookie of the Year Award

1952	Art Cross	1974	Pancho Carter	1994	Jacques Villeneuve*
1953	Jimmy Daywalt	1975	Bill Puterbaugh	1995	Gil de Ferran*
1954	Larry Crockett	1976	Vern Schuppan	1996	Tony Stewart
1955	Al Herman	1977	Jerry Sneva	1997	Jeff Ward
1956	Bob Veith	1978	Rick Mears*	1998	Steve Knapp
1957	Don Edmunds		Larry Rice	1999	Robby McGehee
1958	George Amick	1979	Howdy Holmes	2000	Juan Montoya*
1959	Bobby Grim	1980	Tim Richmond	2001	Helio Castroneves*
1960	Jim Hurtubise	1981	Josele Garza	2002	Alex Barron
1961	Parnelli Jones*	1982	Jim Hickman		Tomas Scheckter
	Bobby Marshman	1983	Teo Fabi	2003	Tora Tagaki
1962	Jimmy McElreath	1984	Michael Andretti	2004	Kosuke Matsuura
1963	Jim Clark*		Roberto Guerrero	2005	Danica Patrick
1964	Johnny White	1985	Arie Luyendyk*	2006	Marco Andretti
1965	Mario Andretti*	1986	Randy Lanier	2007	Phil Giebler
1966	Jackie Stewart	1987	Fabrizio Barbazza	2008	Ryan Hunter-Reay
1967	Denis Hulme	1988	Billy Vukovich III	2009	Alex Tagliani
1968	Billy Vukovich	1989	Bernard Jourdain	2010	Simona De Silvestro
1969	Mark Donohue*		Scott Pruett	2011	JR Hildebrand
1970	Donnie Allison	1990	Eddie Cheever*	2012	Rubens Barrichello
1971	Denny Zimmerman	1991	Jeff Andretti		
1972	Mike Hiss	1992	Lyn St. James		
1973	Graham McRae	1993	Nigel Mansell		

*Future winner of Indy 500.

Champ Car World Series Champions

From 1909 to 1955, this championship was awarded by the American Automobile Association (AAA), and from 1956 to 1979 by the United States Auto Club (USAC). During the 1979 season, Championship Auto Racing Teams (CART) split from the USAC and conducted the championship. Known as PPG CART World Series until 1998. Series name changed to Champ Car World Series for 2005 racing season. On Februray 22, 2008, the Champ Car World Series merged with the Indy Racing League.

Year	Champion	Year	Champion	Year	Champion
1909	George Robertson	1942–45	No racing	1978	Tom Sneva
1910	Ray Harroun	1946	Ted Horn	1979	A.J. Foyt (USAC)
1911	Ralph Mulford	1947	Ted Horn	1979	Rick Mears (CART)
1912	Ralph DePalma	1948	Ted Horn	1980	Johnny Rutherford
1913	Earl Cooper	1949	Johnnie Parsons	1981	Rick Mears
1914	Ralph DePalma	1950	Henry Banks	1982	Rick Mears
1915	Earl Cooper	1951	Tony Bettenhausen	1983	Al Unser
1916	Dario Resta	1952	Chuck Stevenson	1984	Mario Andretti
1917	Earl Cooper	1953	Sam Hanks	1985	Al Unser
1918	Ralph Mulford	1954	Jimmy Bryan	1986	Bobby Rahal
1919	Howard Wilcox	1955	Bob Sweikert	1987	Bobby Rahal
1920	Tommy Milton	1956	Jimmy Bryan	1988	Danny Sullivan
1921	Tommy Milton	1957	Jimmy Bryan	1989	Emerson Fittipaldi
1922	Jimmy Murphy	1958	Tony Bettenhausen	1990	Al Unser Jr.
1923	Eddie Hearne	1959	Rodger Ward	1991	Michael Andretti
1924	Jimmy Murphy	1960	A.J. Foyt	1992	Bobby Rahal
1925	Peter DePaolo	1961	A.J. Foyt	1993	Nigel Mansell
1926	Harry Hartz	1962	Rodger Ward	1994	Al Unser Jr.
1927	Peter DePaolo	1963	A.J. Foyt	1995	Jacques Villeneuve
1928	Louis Meyer	1964	A.J. Foyt	1996	Jimmy Vasser
1929	Louis Meyer	1965	Mario Andretti	1997	Alex Zanardi
1930	Billy Arnold	1966	Mario Andretti	1998	Alex Zanardi
1931	Louis Schneider	1967	A.J. Foyt	1999	Juan Montoya
1932	Bob Carey	1968	Bobby Unser	2000	Gil de Ferran
1933	Louis Meyer	1969	Mario Andretti	2001	Gil de Ferran
1934	Bill Cummings	1970	Al Unser	2002	Cristiano da Matta
1935	Kelly Petillo	1971	Joe Leonard	2003	Paul Tracy
1936	Mauri Rose	1972	Joe Leonard	2004	Sebastian Bourdais
1937	Wilbur Shaw	1973	Roger McCluskey	2005	Sebastian Bourdais
1938	Floyd Roberts	1974	Bobby Unser	2006	Sebastian Bourdais
1939	Wilbur Shaw	1975	A.J. Foyt	2007	Sebastian Bourdais
1940	Rex Mays	1976	Gordon Johncock		
1941	Rex Mays	1977	Tom Sneva		

Alltime Champ Car* Leaders

WINS		POLE POSITIONS	
A.J. Foyt	67	Mario Andretti	67
Mario Andretti	52	A.J. Foyt	53
Michael Andretti	42	Bobby Unser	49
Al Unser	39	Rick Mears	40
Bobby Unser	35	Michael Andretti	32
Al Unser Jr	31	Sebastian Bourdais	28
Paul Tracy	31	Al Unser	27
Rick Mears	29	Paul Tracy	25
Sebastian Bourdais	29	Johnny Rutherford	23
Johnny Rutherford	27	Gordon Johncock	20
Rodger Ward	26	Rex Mays	19
Gordon Johncock	25	Danny Sullivan	19
Bobby Rahal	24	Bobby Rahal	18
Ralph DePalma	24	Emerson Fittipaldi	17
Tommy Milton	23	Gil de Ferran	16
Tony Bettenhausen	22	Tony Bettenhausen	14
Emerson Fittipaldi	22	Juan Montoya	14
Earl Cooper	20	Don Branson	14
Jimmy Bryan	19	Tom Sneva	14
Jimmy Murphy	19	Parnelli Jones	12
Danny Sullivan	17		
Ralph Mulford	17		

*Series known as CART prior to 2003 season

Major Events
Daytona 500

Year	Winner	Car	Avg Speed	Pole Winner	Qual. Speed
1959	Lee Petty	Oldsmobile	135.520	Cotton Owens	143.198
1960	Junior Johnson	Chevrolet	124.740	Fireball Roberts	151.556
1961	Marvin Panch	Pontiac	149.601	Fireball Roberts	155.709
1962	Fireball Roberts	Pontiac	152.529	Fireball Roberts	156.995
1963	Tiny Lund	Ford	151.566	Johnny Rutherford	165.183
1964	Richard Petty	Plymouth	154.345	Paul Goldsmith	174.910
1965	Fred Lorenzen	Ford	141.539	Darel Dieringer	171.151
1966	Richard Petty	Plymouth	160.627	Richard Petty	175.165
1967	Mario Andretti	Ford	149.926	Curtis Turner	180.831
1968	Cale Yarborough	Mercury	143.251	Cale Yarborough	189.222
1969	Lee Roy Yarbrough	Ford	157.950	David Pearson	190.029
1970	Pete Hamilton	Plymouth	149.601	Cale Yarborough	194.015
1971	Richard Petty	Plymouth	144.462	A.J. Foyt	182.744
1972	A.J. Foyt	Mercury	161.550	Bobby Isaac	186.632
1973	Richard Petty	Dodge	157.205	Buddy Baker	185.662
1974	Richard Petty	Dodge	140.894	David Pearson	185.017
1975	Benny Parsons	Chevrolet	153.649	Donnie Allison	185.827
1976	David Pearson	Mercury	152.181	A.J. Foyt	185.943
1977	Cale Yarborough	Chevrolet	153.218	Donnie Allison	188.048
1978	Bobby Allison	Ford	159.730	Cale Yarborough	187.536
1979	Richard Petty	Oldsmobile	143.977	Buddy Baker	196.049
1980	Buddy Baker	Oldsmobile	177.602*	A.J. Foyt	195.020
1981	Richard Petty	Buick	169.651	Bobby Allison	194.624
1982	Bobby Allison	Buick	153.991	Benny Parsons	196.317
1983	Cale Yarborough	Pontiac	155.979	Ricky Rudd	198.864
1984	Cale Yarborough	Chevrolet	150.994	Cale Yarborough	201.848
1985	Bill Elliott	Ford	172.265	Bill Elliott	205.114
1986	Geoff Bodine	Chevrolet	148.124	Bill Elliott	205.039
1987	Bill Elliott	Ford	176.263	Bill Elliott	210.364†
1988	Bobby Allison	Buick	137.531	Ken Schrader	193.823
1989	Darrell Waltrip	Chevrolet	148.466	Ken Schrader	196.996
1990	Derrike Cope	Chevrolet	165.761	Ken Schrader	196.515
1991	Ernie Irvan	Chevrolet	148.148	Davey Allison	195.955
1992	Davey Allison	Ford	160.256	Sterling Marlin	192.213
1993	Dale Jarrett	Chevrolet	154.972	Kyle Petty	189.426
1994	Sterling Marlin	Chevrolet	156.931	Loy Allen Jr	190.158
1995	Sterling Marlin	Chevrolet	141.710	Dale Jarrett	193.498
1996	Dale Jarrett	Ford	154.308	Dale Earnhardt	189.510
1997	Jeff Gordon	Chevrolet	148.295	Mike Skinner	189.813
1998	Dale Earnhardt	Chevrolet	172.712	Bobby Labonte	192.415
1999	Jeff Gordon	Chevrolet	161.551	Jeff Gordon	195.067
2000	Dale Jarrett	Ford	155.669	Dale Jarrett	191.091
2001	Michael Waltrip	Chevrolet	161.783	Bill Elliott	183.570
2002	Ward Burton	Dodge	142.971	Jimmie Johnson	185.831
2003	Michael Waltrip	Chevrolet	133.870	Jeff Green	186.606
2004	Dale Earnhardt Jr.	Chevrolet	156.345	Greg Biffle	188.387
2005	Jeff Gordon	Chevrolet	135.173	Dale Jarrett	188.312
2006	Jimmie Johnson	Chevrolet	142.667	Jeff Burton	188.887
2007	Kevin Harvick	Chevrolet	149.335	David Gilliland	186.320
2008	Ryan Newman	Dodge	152.672	Jimmie Johnson	187.075
2009	Matt Kenseth	Ford	132.816	Martin Truex Jr.	188.001
2010	Jamie McMurray	Chevrolet	137.284	Mark Martin	191.188
2011	Trevor Bayne	Ford	130.326	Dale Earnhardt Jr.	186.089
2012	Matt Kenseth	Ford	140.256	Carl Edwards	194.738

Note: The Daytona 500, held annually in February, now opens the NASCAR season with 200 laps around the 2.5-mile high-banked Daytona International Speedway. Starting in 1988, cars racing at Daytona have used restrictor plates that curb power and acceleration. *Track record, winning speed. †Track record, qualifying speed.

Brickyard 400

Year	Winner	Car	Avg Speed	Pole Winner	Qual. Speed
1994	Jeff Gordon	Chevrolet	131.977	Rick Mast	172.414
1995	Dale Earnhardt	Chevrolet	155.206	Jeff Gordon	172.536
1996	Dale Jarrett	Ford	139.508	Jeff Gordon	176.419
1997	Ricky Rudd	Ford	130.814	Ernie Irvan	177.736
1998	Jeff Gordon	Chevrolet	126.772	Ernie Irvan	179.394

Brickyard 400 (Cont.)

Year	Winner	Car	Avg Speed	Pole Winner	Qual. Speed
1999	Dale Jarrett	Ford	148.194	Jeff Gordon	179.612
2000	Bobby Labonte	Pontiac	155.912*	Ricky Rudd	181.068
2001	Jeff Gordon	Chevrolet	130.790	Jimmy Spencer	179.666
2002	Bill Elliott	Dodge	125.033	Tony Stewart	182.960
2003	Kevin Harvick	Chevrolet	134.554	Kevin Harvick	184.343
2004	Jeff Gordon	Chevrolet	115.037	Casey Mears	186.293†
2005	Tony Stewart	Chevrolet	148.782	Elliott Sadler	184.117
2006	Jimmie Johnson	Chevrolet	137.182	Jeff Burton	182.778
2007	Tony Stewart	Chevrolet	117.379	Reed Sorenson	184.207
2008	Jimmie Johnson	Chevrolet	115.117	Jimmie Johnson	181.763
2009	Jimmie Johnson	Chevrolet	145.882	Mark Martin	182.054
2010	Jamie McMurray	Chevrolet	136.054	Juan Pablo Montoya	182.278
2011	Paul Menard	Chevrolet	140.762	David Ragan	182.994
2012	Jimmie Johnson	Chevrolet	137.680	Denny Hamlin	182.763

Note: Held at the 2.5-mile Indianapolis Motor Speedway.*Track record, winning speed. †Track record, qualifying speed.

Talladega 500

Year	Winner	Car	Avg Speed	Pole Winner	Qual Speed
1970	Pete Hamilton	Plymouth	152.321	Bobby Isaac	199.658
1971	Donnie Allison	Mercury	147.419	Donnie Allison	185.869
1972	David Pearson	Mercury	134.400	Bobby Isaac	192.428
1973	David Pearson	Mercury	131.956	Buddy Baker	193.435
1974	David Pearson	Mercury	130.220	David Pearson	186.086
1975	Buddy Baker	Ford	144.94	Buddy Baker	189.947
1976	Buddy Baker	Ford	169.887	Dave Marcis	189.197
1977	Darrell Waltrip	Chevrolet	164.887	A.J. Foyt	192.424
1978	Cale Yarborough	Oldsmobile	155.699	Cale Yarborough	191.904
1979	Bobby Allison	Ford	154.770	Darrell Waltrip	195.644
1980	Buddy Baker	Oldsmobile	170.481	David Pearson	197.704
1981	Bobby Allison	Buick	149.376	Bobby Allison	195.864
1982	Darrell Waltrip	Buick	156.697	Benny Parsons	200.176
1983	Richard Petty	Pontiac	135.936	Cale Yarborough	202.650
1984	Cale Yarborough	Chevrolet	172.988	Cale Yarborough	202.692
1985	Bill Elliott	Ford	186.288	Bill Elliott	209.398
1986	Bobby Allison	Buick	157.698	Bill Elliott	212.229
1987	Davey Allison	Ford	154.228	Bill Elliott	221.809†
1988	Phil Parsons	Oldsmobile	156.547	Davey Allison	198.969
1989	Davey Allison	Ford	155.869	Mark Martin	193.061
1990	Dale Earnhardt	Chevrolet	159.571	Bill Elliott	199.388
1991	Harry Gant	Oldsmobile	165.620	Ernie Irvan	195.186
1992	Davey Allison	Ford	167.609	Ernie Irvan	192.831
1993	Ernie Irvan	Chevrolet	155.412	Dale Earnhardt	192.355
1994	Dale Earnhardt	Chevrolet	157.478	Ernie Irvan	193.298
1995	Mark Martin	Ford	178.902	Terry Labonte	196.532
1996	Sterling Marlin	Chevrolet	149.999	Ernie Irvan	192.855
1997	Mark Martin	Ford	188.354*	John Andretti	193.627
1998	Dale Jarrett	Ford	159.318	Ken Schrader	196.153
1999	Dale Earnhardt	Chevrolet	166.632	Joe Nemechek	198.331
2000	Dale Earnhardt	Chevrolet	165.681	Joe Nemechek	190.279
2001	Dale Earnhardt Jr.	Chevrolet	164.185	Stacy Compton	185.240
2002	Dale Earnhardt Jr.	Chevrolet	183.665	qualifying cancelled	—
2003	Michael Waltrip	Chevrolet	156.045	Elliott Sadler	189.943
2004	Jeff Gordon	Chevrolet	129.396	Ricky Rudd	191.180
2005	Dale Jarrett	Ford	143.818	Elliott Sadler	189.260
2006	Brian Vickers	Chevrolet	157.602	David Gilliland	191.712
2007	Jeff Gordon	Chevrolet	143.438	Michael Waltrip	189.070
2008	Kyle Busch	Toyota	157.409	Joe Nemechek	187.396
2009	Brad Keselowski	Chevrolet	147.565	Juan Pablo Montoya	188.171
2010	Kevin Harvick	Chevrolet	150.590	qualifying cancelled	—
2011	Jimmie Johnson	Chevrolet	156.261	Jeff Gordon	178.248
2012	Brad Keselowski	Dodge	160.192	Jeff Gordon	191.623

*Track record, winning speed. †Track record, qualifying speed.

Charlotte 600

Year	Winner	Car	Avg Speed	Pole Winner
1960	Joe Lee Johnson	Chevrolet	107.752	Joe Lee Johnson
1961	David Pearson	Pontiac	111.634	Richard Petty
1962	Nelson Stacy	Ford	125.552	Fireball Roberts
1963	Fred Lorenzen	Ford	132.418	Junior Johnson
1964	Jim Paschal	Plymouth	125.772	Junior Johnson
1965	Fred Lorenzen	Ford	121.772	Fred Lorenzen
1966	Marvin Panch	Plymouth	135.042	Paul Goldsmith
1967	Jim Paschal	Plymouth	135.832	Cale Yarborough
1968	Buddy Baker	Dodge	104.207	Donnie Allison
1969	Lee Roy Yarbrough	Mercury	134.631	Donnie Allison
1970	Donnie Allison	Ford	129.680	Bobby Isaac
1971	Bobby Allison	Mercury	140.442	Charlie Glotzbach
1972	Buddy Baker	Dodge	142.255	Bobby Allison
1973	Buddy Baker	Dodge	134.890	Buddy Baker
1974	David Pearson	Mercury	135.720	David Pearson
1975	Richard Petty	Dodge	145.327	David Pearson
1976	David Pearson	Mercury	137.352	David Pearson
1977	Richard Petty	Dodge	137.636	David Pearson
1978	Darrell Waltrip	Chevrolet	138.355	David Pearson
1979	Darrell Waltrip	Chevrolet	136.674	Neil Bonnet
1980	Benny Parsons	Chevrolet	119.265	Cale Yarborough
1981	Bobby Allison	Buick	129.326	Neil Bonnett
1982	Neil Bonnett	Ford	130.508	David Pearson
1983	Neil Bonnett	Chevrolet	140.406	Buddy Baker
1984	Bobby Allison	Buick	129.233	Harry Gant
1985	Darrell Waltrip	Chevrolet	141.807	Bill Elliott
1986	Dale Earnhardt	Chevrolet	140.406	Geoff Bodine
1987	Kyle Petty	Ford	131.483	Bill Elliott
1988	Darrell Waltrip	Chevrolet	124.460	Davey Allison
1989	Darrell Waltrip	Chevrolet	144.077	Alan Kulwicki
1990	Rusty Wallace	Pontiac	137.650	Ken Schrader
1991	Davey Allison	Ford	138.951	Mark Martin
1992	Dale Earnhardt	Chevrolet	132.980	Bill Elliott
1993	Dale Earnhardt	Chevrolet	145.504	Ken Schrader
1994	Jeff Gordon	Chevrolet	139.445	Jeff Gordon
1995	Bobby Labonte	Chevrolet	151.952	Jeff Gordon
1996	Dale Jarrett	Ford	147.581	Jeff Gordon
1997	Jeff Gordon	Chevrolet	136.745	Jeff Gordon
1998	Jeff Gordon	Chevrolet	136.424	Jeff Gordon
1999	Jeff Burton	Ford	151.367	Bobby Labonte
2000	Matt Kenseth	Ford	142.640	Dale Earnhardt Jr
2001	Jeff Burton	Ford	138.107	Ryan Newman
2002	Mark Martin	Ford	137.729	Jimmie Johnson
2003	Jimmie Johnson	Chevrolet	126.198	Ryan Newman
2004	Jimmie Johnson	Chevrolet	142.763	Jimmie Johnson
2005	Jimmie Johnson	Chevrolet	114.698	Ryan Newman
2006	Kasey Kahne	Dodge	128.840	Scott Riggs
2007	Casey Mears	Chevrolet	130.222	Ryan Newman
2008	Kasey Kahne	Dodge	135.772	Kyle Busch
2009	David Reutimann	Toyota	120.899	Ryan Newman
2010	Kurt Busch	Dodge	144.966	Ryan Newman
2011	Kevin Harvick	Chevrolet	132.414	Brad Keselowski
2012	Kasey Kahne	Chevrolet	155.687*	Aric Almirola

Note: Held at the 1.5 mile high-banked Lowe's Motor Speedway in Charlotte on Memorial Day weekend.
*Track record, winning speed.

Darlington 500

Year	Winner	Car	Avg Speed	Pole Winner
1950	Johnny Mantz	Plymouth	76.260	Wally Campbell
1951	Herb Thomas	Hudson	76.900	Marshall Teague
1952	Fonty Flock	Oldsmobile	74.510	Dick Rathman
1953	Buck Baker	Oldsmobile	92.780	Fonty Flock
1954	Herb Thomas	Hudson	94.930	Buck Baker
1955	Herb Thomas	Chevrolet	92.281	Tim Flock
1956	Curtis Turner	Ford	95.067	Buck Baker
1957	Speedy Thompson	Chevrolet	100.100	Paul Goldsmith
1958	Fireball Roberts	Chevrolet	102.590	Fireball Roberts
1959	Jim Reed	Chevrolet	111.836	Fireball Roberts
1960	Buck Baker	Pontiac	105.901	Cotton Owens
1961	Nelson Stacy	Ford	117.880	Fireball Roberts
1962	Larry Frank	Ford	117.965	Fireball Roberts
1963	Fireball Roberts	Ford	129.784	Fireball Roberts
1964	Buck Baker	Dodge	117.757	Richard Petty
1965	Ned Jarrett	Ford	115.924	Junior Johnson
1966	Darel Dieringer	Mercury	114.830	Lee Yarborough
1967	Richard Petty	Plymouth	131.933	David Pearson
1968	Cale Yarborough	Mercury	126.132	Charlie Glotzbach
1969	Lee Roy Yarbrough	Ford	105.612	Cale Yarborough
1970	Buddy Baker	Dodge	128.817	David Pearson
1971	Bobby Allison	Mercury	131.398	Bobby Allison
1972	Bobby Allison	Chevrolet	128.124	David Pearson
1973	Cale Yarborough	Chevrolet	134.033	David Pearson
1974	Cale Yarborough	Chevrolet	111.075	Richard Petty
1975	Bobby Allison	Matador	116.825	David Pearson
1976	David Pearson	Mercury	120.534	David Pearson
1977	David Pearson	Mercury	106.797	Darrell Waltrip
1978	Cale Yarborough	Oldsmobile	116.828	David Pearson
1979	David Pearson	Chevrolet	126.259	Bobby Allison
1980	Terry Labonte	Chevrolet	115.210	Darrell Waltrip
1981	Neil Bonnett	Ford	126.410	Harry Gant
1982	Cale Yarborough	Buick	126.703	David Pearson
1983	Bobby Allison	Buick	123.343	Neil Bonnett
1984	Harry Gant	Chevrolet	128.270	Harry Gant
1985	Bill Elliott	Ford	121.254	Bill Elliott
1986	Tim Richmond	Chevrolet	121.068	Tim Richmond
1987	Dale Earnhardt	Chevrolet	115.520	Davey Allison
1988	Bill Elliott	Ford	128.297	Bill Elliott
1989	Dale Earnhardt	Chevrolet	135.462	Alan Kulwicki
1990	Dale Earnhardt	Chevrolet	123.141	Dale Earnhardt
1991	Harry Gant	Oldsmobile	133.508	Davey Allison
1992	Darrell Waltrip	Chevrolet	129.114	Sterling Marlin
1993	Mark Martin	Ford	137.932	Ken Schrader
1994	Bill Elliott	Ford	127.915	Geoff Bodine
1995	Jeff Gordon	Chevrolet	121.231	John Andretti
1996	Jeff Gordon	Chevrolet	135.757	Dale Jarrett
1997	Jeff Gordon	Chevrolet	121.149	Bobby Labonte
1998	Jeff Gordon	Chevrolet	139.031*	Dale Jarrett
1999	Jeff Burton	Ford	100.816	Kenny Irwin
2000	Bobby Labonte	Pontiac	108.275	Jeremy Mayfield
2001	Ward Burton	Dodge	122.773	Kurt Busch
2002	Jeff Gordon	Chevrolet	118.617	Sterling Marlin
2003	Terry Labonte	Chevrolet	120.744	Ryan Newman
2004	Jimmie Johnson	Chevrolet	125.044	Kurt Busch
2005	Greg Biffle	Ford	135.127	Kasey Kahne
2006	Greg Biffle	Ford	123.031	Kasey Kahne
2007	Jeff Gordon	Chevrolet	124.372	Clint Bowyer
2008	Kyle Busch	Toyota	140.350	Greg Biffle
2009	Mark Martin	Chevrolet	119.687	Matt Kenseth
2010	Denny Hamlin	Toyota	126.605	Jamie McMurray
2011	Regan Smith	Chevrolet	129.678	Kasey Kahne
2012	Jimmie Johnson	Chevrolet	133.802	Greg Biffle

Note: Through 2004, results listed were for the Southern 500, traditionally the second race of the year at the 1.366-mile Darlington (S.C.) Raceway. Starting in 2005, Darlington only hosted one race a year, in May.

*Track record, winning speed.

Sprint Cup* NASCAR Champions

Year	Driver	Car	Wins	Poles	Winnings ($)
1949	Red Byron	Oldsmobile	2	1	5,800
1950	Bill Rexford	Oldsmobile	1	0	6,175
1951	Herb Thomas	Hudson	7	4	18,200
1952	Tim Flock	Hudson	8	4	20,210
1953	Herb Thomas	Hudson	11	10	27,300
1954	Lee Petty	Dodge	7	3	26,706
1955	Tim Flock	Chrysler	18	19	33,750
1956	Buck Baker	Chrysler	14	12	29,790
1957	Buck Baker	Chevrolet	10	5	24,712
1958	Lee Petty	Oldsmobile	7	4	20,600
1959	Lee Petty	Plymouth	10	2	45,570
1960	Rex White	Chevrolet	6	3	45,260
1961	Ned Jarrett	Chevrolet	1	4	27,285
1962	Joe Weatherly	Pontiac	9	6	56,110
1963	Joe Weatherly	Mercury	3	6	58,110
1964	Richard Petty	Plymouth	9	8	98,810
1965	Ned Jarrett	Ford	13	9	77,966
1966	David Pearson	Dodge	14	7	59,205
1967	Richard Petty	Plymouth	27	18	130,275
1968	David Pearson	Ford	16	12	118,824
1969	David Pearson	Ford	11	14	183,700
1970	Bobby Isaac	Dodge	11	13	121,470
1971	Richard Petty	Plymouth	21	9	309,225
1972	Richard Petty	Plymouth	8	3	227,015
1973	Benny Parsons	Chevrolet	1	0	114,345
1974	Richard Petty	Dodge	10	7	299,175
1975	Richard Petty	Dodge	13	3	378,865
1976	Cale Yarborough	Chevrolet	9	2	387,173
1977	Cale Yarborough	Chevrolet	9	3	477,499
1978	Cale Yarborough	Oldsmobile	10	8	530,751
1979	Richard Petty	Chevrolet	5	1	531,292
1980	Dale Earnhardt	Chevrolet	5	0	588,926
1981	Darrell Waltrip	Buick	12	11	693,342
1982	Darrell Waltrip	Buick	12	7	873,118
1983	Bobby Allison	Buick	6	0	828,355
1984	Terry Labonte	Chevrolet	2	2	713,010
1985	Darrell Waltrip	Chevrolet	3	4	1,318,735
1986	Dale Earnhardt	Chevrolet	5	1	1,783,880
1987	Dale Earnhardt	Chevrolet	11	1	2,099,243
1988	Bill Elliott	Ford	6	6	1,574,639
1989	Rusty Wallace	Pontiac	6	4	2,247,950
1990	Dale Earnhardt	Chevrolet	9	4	3,083,056
1991	Dale Earnhardt	Chevrolet	4	0	2,396,685
1992	Alan Kulwicki	Ford	2	6	2,322,561
1993	Dale Earnhardt	Chevrolet	6	2	3,353,789
1994	Dale Earnhardt	Chevrolet	4	2	3,400,733
1995	Jeff Gordon	Chevrolet	7	9	4,347,343
1996	Terry Labonte	Chevrolet	2	4	4,030,648
1997	Jeff Gordon	Chevrolet	10	1	4,201,227
1998	Jeff Gordon	Chevrolet	13	7	6,175,867
1999	Dale Jarrett	Ford	4	0	3,608,829
2000	Bobby Labonte	Pontiac	4	2	4,041,750
2001	Jeff Gordon	Chevrolet	6	8	6,649,076
2002	Tony Stewart	Pontiac	3	4	4,695,150
2003	Matt Kenseth	Ford	1	2	4,038,120
2004	Kurt Busch	Ford	3	1	4,200,330
2005	Tony Stewart	Chevrolet	5	3	6,987,530
2006	Jimmie Johnson	Chevrolet	5	1	8,909,140
2007	Jimmie Johnson	Chevrolet	10	4	7,646,420
2008	Jimmie Johnson	Chevrolet	7	6	7,354,860
2009	Jimmie Johnson	Chevrolet	7	4	7,339,630
2010	Jimmie Johnson	Chevrolet	6	2	7,264,780
2011	Tony Stewart/	Chevrolet	5	1	6,529,870
	Carl Edwards	Ford	1	3	8,485,990

*Series name changed from Winston Cup after 2003 season, to Nextel Cup 2004–07, and then to Sprint Cup beginning in 2008.

Alltime NASCAR Leaders

	WINS		WINS	POLE WINNERS		POLE WINNERS	
Richard Petty	200	Rusty Wallace	55	Richard Petty	123	Bobby Isaac	49
David Pearson	105	Lee Petty	54	David Pearson	113	*Ryan Newman	49
*Jeff Gordon	86	Ned Jarrett	50	*Jeff Gordon	72	Junior Johnson	46
Bobby Allison	84	Junior Johnson	50	Cale Yarborough	69	Buck Baker	45
Darrell Waltrip	84	Herb Thomas	48	Darrell Waltrip	59	Herb Thomas	39
Cale Yarborough	83	*Tony Stewart	47	Bobby Allison	58	Buddy Baker	38
Dale Earnhardt	76	Buck Baker	46	Bill Elliott	55	Geoff Bodine	37
*Jimmie Johnson	58	David Pearson	45	*Mark Martin	55	Tim Flock	37

*Active drivers. Note: NASCAR wins leaders and pole position leaders through Oct 1, 2012.

Formula One Grand Prix Racing

World Driving Champions

Year	Winner	Car	Year	Winner	Car
1950	Guiseppe Farina, Italy	Alfa Romeo	1978	Mario Andretti, U.S.	Lotus-Ford
1951	Juan-Manuel Fangio, Argentina	Alfa Romeo	1979	Jody Scheckter, S. Africa	Ferrari
1952	Alberto Ascari, Italy	Ferrari	1980	Alan Jones, Australia	Williams-Ford
1953	Alberto Ascari, Italy	Ferrari	1981	Nelson Piquet, Brazil	Brabham-Ford
1954	Juan-Manuel Fangio, Argentina	Maserati-Mercedes	1982	Keke Rosberg, Finland	Williams-Ford
1955	Juan-Manuel Fangio, Argentina	Mercedes	1983	Nelson Piquet, Brazil	Brabham-BMW
			1984	Niki Lauda, Austria	McLaren-Porsche
1956	Juan-Manuel Fangio, Argentina	Ferrari	1985	Alain Prost, France	McLaren-Porsche
			1986	Alain Prost, France	McLaren-Porsche
1957	Juan-Manuel Fangio, Argentina	Maserati	1987	Nelson Piquet, Brazil	Williams-Honda
			1988	Ayrton Senna, Brazil	McLaren-Honda
1958	Mike Hawthorn, Grt. Britain	Ferrari	1989	Alain Prost, France	McLaren-Honda
1959	Jack Brabham, Australia	Cooper-Climax	1990	Ayrton Senna, Brazil	McLaren-Honda
1960	Jack Brabham, Australia	Cooper-Climax	1991	Ayrton Senna, Brazil	McLaren-Honda
1961	Phil Hill, U.S.	Ferrari	1992	Nigel Mansell, Great Britain	Williams-Renault
1962	Graham Hill, Great Britain	BRM	1993	Alain Prost, France	Williams-Renault
1963	Jim Clark, Scotland	Lotus-Climax	1994	Michael Schumacher, Ger.	Benetton-Ford
1964	John Surtees, Great Britain	Ferrari	1995	Michael Schumacher, Ger.	Benetton-Renault
1965	Jim Clark, Scotland	Lotus-Climax	1996	Damon Hill, Great Britain	Williams-Renault
1966	Jack Brabham, Australia	Brabham-Repco	1997	Jacques Villeneuve, Can.	Williams-Renault
1967	Denny Hulme, New Zealand	Brabham-Repco	1998	Mika Hakkinen, Finland	McLaren-Mercedes
			1999	Mika Hakkinen, Finland	McLaren-Mercedes
1968	Graham Hill, Great Britain	Lotus-Ford	2000	Michael Schumacher, Ger.	Ferrari
1969	Jackie Stewart, Scotland	Matra-Ford	2001	Michael Schumacher, Ger.	Ferrari
1970	Jochen Rindt, Austria*	Lotus-Ford	2002	Michael Schumacher, Ger.	Ferrari
1971	Jackie Stewart, Scotland	Tyrell-Ford	2003	Michael Schumacher, Ger.	Ferrari
1972	Emerson Fittipaldi, Brazil	Lotus-Ford	2004	Michael Schumacher, Ger.	Ferrari
1973	Jackie Stewart, Scotland	Tyrell-Ford	2005	Fernando Alonso, Spain	Renault
1974	Emerson Fittipaldi, Brazil	McLaren-Ford	2006	Fernando Alonso, Spain	Renault
1975	Niki Lauda, Austria	Ferrari	2007	Kimi Raikkonen, Finland	Ferrari
1976	James Hunt, Great Britain	McLaren-Ford	2008	Lewis Hamilton, Great Britain	McLaren-Mercedes
1977	Niki Lauda, Austria	Ferrari	2009	Jenson Button, Great Britain	Brawn-Mercedes
			2010	Sebastian Vettel, Germany	RBR-Renault
			2011	Sebastian Vettel, Germany	RBR-Renault

*The championship was awarded posthumously, after Rindt was killed during practice for the Italian Grand Prix.

Alltime F/I Grand Prix Winners

Driver	Wins	Driver	Wins
*Michael Schumacher, Germany	91	Jim Clark, Great Britain	25
Alain Prost, France	51	Niki Lauda, Austria	25
Ayrton Senna, Brazil	41	Juan-Manuel Fangio, Argentina	24
Nigel Mansell, Great Britain	31	Nelson Piquet, Brazil	23
*Fernando Alonso, Spain	30	*Sebastian Vettel	23
Jackie Stewart, Great Britain	27		

Alltime F/I Grand Prix Pole Winners

Driver	Poles	Driver	Poles
*Michael Schumacher, Germany	68	Nigel Mansell, Great Britain	32
Ayrton Senna, Brazil	65	Juan-Manuel Fangio, Argentina	29
Alain Prost, France	33	Mika Hakkinen, Finland	26
Jim Clark, Great Britain	33	Niki Lauda, Austria	24
*Sebastian Vettel, Germany	33	Nelson Piquet, Brazil	24
		*Lewis Hamilton, Great Britain	24

*Active driver in 2011. Note: Grand Prix winners and pole winners through Oct 1, 2012.

The 24 Hours of Daytona

Year	Winner	Car	Avg Speed	Distance
1962	Dan Gurney	Lotus 19-Class SP11	104.101 mph	3 hrs (312.42 mi)
1963	Pedro Rodriguez	Ferrari-Class 12	102.074 mph	3 hrs (308.61 mi)
1964	Pedro Rodriguez/Phil Hill	Ferrari 250 LM	98.230 mph	2,000 km
1965	Ken Miles/Lloyd Ruby	Ford	99.944 mph	2,000 km
1966	Ken Miles/Lloyd Ruby	Ford Mark II	108.020 mph	24 hrs (2,570.63 mi)
1967	Lorenzo Bandini/Chris Amon	Ferrari 330 P4	105.688 mph	24 hrs (2,537.46 mi)
1968	Vic Elford/Jochen Neerpasch	Porsche 907	106.697 mph	24 hrs (2,565.69 mi)
1969	Mark Donohue/Chuck Parsons	Chevy Lola	99.268 mph	24 hrs (2,383.75 mi)
1970	Pedro Rodriguez/Leo Kinnunen	Porsche 917	114.866 mph	24 hrs (2,758.44 mi)
1971	Pedro Rodriguez/Jackie Oliver	Porsche 917K	109.203 mph	24 hrs (2,621.28 mi)
1972*	Mario Andretti/Jacky Ickx	Ferrari 312/P	122.573 mph	6 hrs (738.24 mi)
1973	Peter Gregg/Hurley Haywood	Porsche Carrera	106.225 mph	24 hrs (2,552.7 mi)
1974	(No race)			
1975	Peter Gregg/Hurley Haywood	Porsche Carrera	108.531 mph	24 hrs (2,606.04 mi)
1976†	Peter Gregg/Brian Redman/ John Fitzpatrick	BMW CSL	104.040 mph	24 hrs (2,092.8 mi)
1977	John Graves/Hurley Haywood/ Dave Helmick	Porsche Carrera	108.801 mph	24 hrs (2,615 mi)
1978	Rolf Stommelen/ Antoine Hezemans/Peter Gregg	Porsche Turbo	108.743 mph	24 hrs (2,611.2 mi)
1979	Ted Field/Danny Ongais/ Hurley Haywood	Porsche Turbo	109.249 mph	24 hrs (2,626.56 mi)
1980	Volkert Meri/Rolf Stommelen/ Reinhold Joest	Porsche Turbo	114.303 mph	24 hrs
1981	Bob Garretson/Bobby Rahal/ Brian Redman	Porsche Turbo	113.153 mph	24 hrs
1982	John Paul Jr/John Paul Sr/ Rolf Stommelen	Porsche Turbo	114.794 mph	24 hrs
1983	Preston Henn/Bob Wollek/ Claude Ballot-Lena/A.J. Foyt	Porsche Turbo	98.781 mph	24 hrs
1984	Sarel van der Merwe/ Graham Duxbury/Tony Martin	Porsche March	103.119 mph	24 hrs (2,476.8 mi)
1985	A.J. Foyt/Bob Wollek/ Al Unser/Thierry Boutsen	Porsche 962	104.162 mph	24 hrs (2,502.68 mi)
1986	Al Holbert/Derek Bell/Al Unser Jr.	Porsche 962	105.484 mph	24 hrs (2,534.72 mi)
1987	Chip Robinson/Derek Bell/ Al Holbert/Al Unser Jr.	Porsche 962	111.599 mph	24 hrs (2,680.68 mi)
1988	Martin Brundle/John Nielsen/ Raul Boesel	Jaguar XJR-9	107.943 mph	24 hrs (2,591.68 mi)
1989	John Andretti/Derek Bell/ Bob Wollek	Porsche 962	92.009 mph	24 hrs (2,210.76 mi)
1990	Davy Jones/Jan Lammers/ Andy Wallace	Jaguar XJR-12	112.857 mph	24 hrs (2,709.16 mi)
1991	Hurley Haywood/ John Winter/ Frank Jelinski/ Henri Pescarolo/ Bob Wollek	Porsche 962C	106.633 mph	24 hrs (2,559.64 mi)
1992	Massahiro Hasemi/ Kazuoyshi Hoshino/ Toshio Suzuki/ Anders Olofsson	Nissan R91CP	112.987 mph	24 hrs (2,712.72 mi)
1993	P.J. Jones/Mark Dismore/ Rocky Moran	Toyota Eagle MK III	103.537 mph	24 hrs (2,484.88 mi)
1994	Paul Gentilozzi/ Scott Pruett/ Butch Leitzinger/ Steve Millen	Nissan 300 ZX	104.80 mph	24 hrs (2,693.67 mi)
1995	Jurgen Lassig/ Christophe Buochut/ Giovanni Lavaggi/ Marco Werner	Porsche Spyder K8	102.28 mph	690 laps (2,456.4 mi)
1996	Wayne Taylor/ Scott Sharp/ Jim Pace	Oldsmobile Mark III	103.32 mph	697 laps (2,481.32 mi)
1997	Elliot Forbes-Robinson/ John Schneider/Rob Dyson/ John Paul Jr/Butch Leitzinger/James Weaver/Andy Wallace	Ford R & S MK III	102.292 mph	690 laps (2,456.4 mi)
1998	Arie Luyendyk/Didier Theys/ Mauro Baldi	Ferrari 333 SP	105.565 mph	711 laps (2,531.16 mi)
1999	Elliott Forbes-Robinson/ Butch Leitzinger/ Andy Wallace	Ford R & S MK III	104.9 mph	708 laps (2,520.48 mi)
2000	Olivier Beretta/Karl Wendlinger/ Dominique Dupuy	Dodge Viper	107.207 mph	723 laps (2,573.88 m)

*Race shortened due to fuel crisis. †Course lengthened from 3.81 miles to 3.84 miles.

The 24 Hours of Daytona *(Cont.)*

Year	Winner	Car	Avg Speed	Distance
2001	Ron Fellows/Chris Kneifel/ Franck Freon/Johnny O'Connell	Corvette	97.293 mph	656 laps (2,335.360 mi)
2002	Didier Theys/Fredy Lienhard/ Max Papis/Mauro Baldi	Dallara-Judd (SRP)	106.143 mph	716 laps (2,548.96 mi)
2003	Kevin Buckler/Michael Schrom Timo Bernhard/Jorg Bergmeister	Porsche GT3 RS	114.068 mph (top speed)	694 laps (2,470.64 mi)
2004	Forest Barber/Terry Borcheller Andy Pilgrim/Christian Fittipaldi	Pontiac Doran	117.651 mph	526 laps (1,872.56 mi)
2005	Wayne Taylor/Max Angelelli Emmanuel Collard	Pontiac Riley	119.397 mph	710 laps (2,527.60 mi)
2006	Scott Dixon/Dan Wheldon Casey Mears	Lexus Riley	108.826 mph	734 laps (2,613.04 mi)
2007	Scott Pruett/Salvador Duran Juan Montoya	Lexus Riley	99.020 mph	668 laps (2,378.08 mi)
2008	Scott Pruett/Memo Rojas Juan Montoya/Dario Franchitti	Lexus Riley	103.057 mph	695 laps (2,474.20 mi)
2009	Darren Law/David Donohue Buddy Rice/Antonio Garcia	Porsche Riley	108.994 mph	735 laps (2,616.60 mi.)
2010	Terry Borcheller/Joao Barbosa Ryan Dalziel/Mike Rockenfeller	Porsche Riley	111.930 mph	755 laps (2,687.77 mi.)
2011	Joey Hand/Scott Pruett Graham Rahal/Memo Rojas	BMW Riley	106.877 mph	721 laps (2,566.76 mi.)
2012	John Pew, Oswaldo Negri Jr, AJ Allmendinger, Justin Wilson	Ford Riley	112.834 mph	761 laps (2,709.16 mi.)

World Sportscar Champions

Year	Winner	Car	Year	Winner	Car
1978	Peter Gregg	Porsche 935	1989	Geoff Brabham	Nissan GTP
1979	Peter Gregg	Porsche 935	1990	Geoff Brabham	Nissan GTP
1980	John Fitzpatrick	Porsche 935	1991	Geoff Brabham	Nissan NPT
1981	Brian Redman	Chevy Lola	1992	Juan Fangio II	Toyota EGL MKIII
1982	John Paul Jr	Chevy Lola	1993	Juan Fangio II	Toyota EGL MKIII
1983	Al Holbert	Chevy March	1994	Wayne Taylor	Mazda Kudzu
1984	Randy Lanier	Chevy March	1995	Fermin Velez	Ferrari 333 SP
1985	Al Holbert	Porsche 962	1996	Wayne Taylor	Mazda Kudzu
1986	Al Holbert	Porsche 962	1997	Butch Leitzinger	Ford R&S MKIII
1987	Chip Robinson	Porsche 962	1998	Butch Leitzinger	Ford R&S MKIII
1988	Geoff Brabham	Nissan GTP			

Year	Prototype	GTC	GT
1999	Elliott Forbes-Robinson	Olivier Beretta	Cort Wagner
2000	Allan McNish	Olivier Beretta	Sascha Maassen
2001	Emanuele Pirro	Terry Borcheller	Jörg Müller
2002	Tom Kristensen	Ron Fellows	Lucas Luhr
2003	Frank Biela/Marco Werner	Ron Fellows/John O'Connell	Sascha Maassen/L. Luhr
2004	Frank Biela/Emanuele Pirro	Oliver Gavin/Olivier Beretta	Patrick Long/Jorg Bergmeister
2005	Frank Biela/Emanuele Pirro	Oliver Gavin/Olivier Beretta	Patrick Long/Jorg Bergmeister
2006	R. Capello/A. McNish	Oliver Gavin/Olivier Beretta	Johannes van Overbeek
2007	R. Capello/A. McNish	Oliver Gavin/Olivier Beretta	Mika Salo/Jaime Melo
2008	Lucas Luhr/Marco Werner	Jan Magnussen/J. O'Connell	Jorg Bergmeister/Wolf Henzler
2009	David Brabham/Scott Sharp	Oliver Gavin/Olivier Beretta	Jorg Bergmeister/Patrick Long
2010	D. Brabham/Simon Pagenaud	Tim. Pappas/Jer. Bleekemolen	Jorg Bergmeister/Patrick Long
2011	Guy Smith/Chris Dyson	Timothy Pappas	Joey Hand/Dirk Mueller

Year	Winning Drivers	Car
1923	André Lagache/René Léonard	Chenard & Walker
1924	John Duff/Francis Clement	Bentley
1925	Gérard de Courcelles/André Rossignol	La Lorraine
1926	Robert Bloch/André Rossignol	La Lorraine
1927	J. Dudley Benjafield/Sammy Davis	Bentley
1928	Woolf Barnato/Bernard Rubin	Bentley
1929	Woolf Barnato/Sir Henry Birkin	Bentley Speed 6
1930	Woolf Barnato/Glen Kidston	Bentley Speed 6
1931	Earl Howe/Sir Henry Birkin	Alfa Romeo 8C-2300 sc
1932	Raymond Sommer/Luigi Chinetti	Alfa Romeo 8C-2300 sc
1933	Raymond Sommer/Tazio Nuvolari	Alfa Romeo 8C-2300 sc
1934	Luigi Chinetti/Philippe Etancelin	Alfa Romeo 8C-2300 sc
1935	John Hindmarsh/Louis Fontés	Lagonda M45R
1936	RACE CANCELLED	
1937	Jean-Pierre Wimille/Robert Benoist	Bugatti 57G sc
1938	Eugène Chaboud/Jean Tremoulet	Delahaye 135M
1939	Jean-Pierre Wimille/Pierre Veyron	Bugatti 57G sc
1940–48	RACES CANCELLED	
1949	Luigi Chinetti/Lord Selsdon	Ferrari 166MM
1950	Louis Rosier/Jean-Louis Rosier	Talbot-Lago
1951	Peter Walker/Peter Whitehead	Jaguar C
1952	Hermann Lang/Fritz Reiss	Mercedes-Benz 300 SL
1953	Tony Rolt/Duncan Hamilton	Jaguar C
1954	Froilan Gonzales/Maurice Trintignant	Ferrari 375
1955	Mike Hawthorn/Ivor Bueb	Jaguar D
1956	Ron Flockhart/Ninian Sanderson	Jaguar D
1957	Ron Flockhart/Ivor Bueb	Jaguar D
1958	Olivier Gendebien/Phil Hill	Ferrari 250 TR58
1959	Carroll Shelby/Roy Salvadori	Aston Martin DBR1
1960	Olivier Gendebien/Paul Frère	Ferrari 250 TR59/60
1961	Olivier Gendebien/Phil Hill	Ferrari 250 TR61
1962	Olivier Gendebien/Phil Hill	Ferrari 250P
1963	Lodovico Scarfiotti/Lorenzo Bandini	Ferrari 250P
1964	Jean Guichet/Nino Vaccarella	Ferrari 275P
1965	Jochen Rindt/Masten Gregory	Ferrari 250LM
1966	Chris Amon/Bruce McLaren	Ford Mk2
1967	Dan Gurney/A.J. Foyt	Ford Mk4
1968	Pedro Rodriguez/Lucien Bianchi	Ford GT40
1969	Jacky Ickx/Jackie Oliver	Ford GT40
1970	Hans Herrmann/Richard Attwood	Porsche 917
1971	Helmut Marko/Gijs van Lennep	Porsche 917
1972	Henri Pescarolo/Graham Hill	Matra-Simca MS670
1973	Henri Pescarolo/Gérard Larrousse	Matra-Simca MS670B
1974	Henri Pescarolo/Gérard Larrousse	Matra-Simca MS670B
1975	Jacky Ickx/Derek Bell	Mirage-Ford MB
1976	Jacky Ickx/Gijs van Lennep	Porsche 936
1977	Jacky Ickx/Jurgen Barth/Hurley Haywood	Porsche 936
1978	Jean-Pierre Jaussaud/Didier Pironi	Renault-Alpine A442
1979	Klaus Ludwig/Bill Whittington/Don Whittington	Porsche 935
1980	Jean-Pierre Jaussaud/Jean Rondeau	Rondeau-Ford M379B
1981	Jacky Ickx/Derek Bell	Porsche 936-81
1982	Jacky Ickx/Derek Bell	Porsche 956
1983	Vern Schuppan/Hurley Haywood/Al Holbert	Porsche 956-83
1984	Klaus Ludwig/Henri Pescarolo	Porsche 956B
1985	Klaus Ludwig/Paolo Barilla/John Winter	Porsche 956B
1986	Derek Bell/Hans-Joachim Stuck/Al Holbert	Porsche 962C
1987	Derek Bell/Hans-Joachim Stuck/Al Holbert	Porsche 962C
1988	Jan Lammers/Johnny Dumfries/Andy Wallace	Jaguar XJR9LM
1989	Jochen Mass/Manuel Reuter/Stanley Dickens	Sauber-Mercedes C9-88
1990	John Nielsen/Price Cobb/Martin Brundle	TWR Jaguar XJR-12
1991	Volker Weidler/Johnny Herbert/Bertrand Gachof	Mazda 787B
1992	Derek Warwick/Yannick Dalmas/Mark Blundell	Peugeot 905B
1993	Geoff Brabham/Christophe Bouchut/Eric Helary	Peugeot 905
1994	Yannick Dalmas/Hurley Haywood/Mauro Baldi	Porsche 962
1995	Yannick Dalmas/J.J. Lehto/Masanori Sekiya	McLaren BMW
1996	Manuel Reuter/Davy Jones/Alexander Wurz	TWR Porsche
1997	Michele Alboreto/Stefan Johansson/Tom Kristensen	TWR Porsche
1998	Allan McNish/Laurent Aiello/Stephane Ortelli	Porsche GT One
1999	Yannick Dalmas/Joachim Winkelhock/Pierluigi Martini	BMW V12 LMR
2000	Frank Biela/Tom Kristensen/Emanuele Pirro	Audi R8
2001	Frank Biela/Tom Kristensen/Emanuele Pirro	Audi R8
2002	Frank Biela/Tom Kristensen/Emanuele Pirro	Audi R8
2003	Rinaldo Capello/Tom Kristensen/Guy Smith	Bentley EXP Speed 8
2004	Rinaldo Capello/Seiji Ara/Tom Kristensen	Audi R8
2005	J.J. Lehto/Marco Werner/Tom Kristensen	Audi R8
2006	Frank Biela/Emanuele Pirro/Marco Werner	Audi R10
2007	Frank Biela/Emanuele Pirro/Marco Werner	Audi R10
2008	Rinaldo Capello/Tom Kristensen/Allan McNish	Audi R10
2009	Marc Gene/Alexander Wurz/David Brabham	Peugeot 908
2010	Timo Bernhard/Romain Dumas/Mike Rockenfeller	Audi R15
2011	Marcel Fassler/Andre Lotterer/Benoit Treluyer	Audi R18
2012	Marcel Fassler/Andre Lotterer/Benoit Treluyer	Audi R18 e-tron quattro

Horse Racing

With Mario Guttierez aboard, I'll Have Another drove through the stretch to a stirring victory in the Kentucky Derby, the first of his two Triple Crown wins in 2012.

The Triple Crown

138th Kentucky Derby

May 5, 2012. Grade I, 3-year-olds; 11th race, Churchill Downs, Louisville. All: 126 lbs. Distance: 1¼ miles. Purse: $2,000,000 guaranteed. Track: fast. Off: 6:31 p.m. Winner: I'll Have Another (By Flower Alley out of Arch's Gal Edith by Arch); Times: 22.32, 45.39, 1:09.80, 1:35.19, 2:01.83. Won: driving. Breeder: Harvey Clarke (Kentucky).

Horse	Finish-PP	Margin	Jockey/Trainer
I'll Have Another	1–19	1½	Mario Gutierrez/Doug O'Neill
Bodemeister	2–6	neck	Mike Smith/Bob Baffert
Dullahan	3–5	3¾	Kent Desormeaux/Dale Romans
Went The Day Well	4–13	½	John Velazquez/H. Graham Motion
Creative Cause	5–8	4	Joel Rosario/Mike Harrington
Liaison	6–20	6½	Martin Garcia/Bob Baffert
Union Rags	7–4	7¾	Julien Leparoux/Michael Matz
Rousing Sermon	8–7	2	Jose Lezcano/Jerry Hollendorfer
Hansen	9–14	1¼	Ramon Dominguez/Michael Maker
Daddy Nose Best	10–10	½	Garrett Gomez/Steven Asmussen
Optimizer	11–2	7¼	Jon Court/D. Wayne Lukas
Alpha	12–11	¾	Rajiv Maragh/Kiaran McLaughlin
El Padrino	13–16	3½	Rafael Bejarano/Todd Pletcher
Done Talking	14–17	1¼	Sheldon Russell/Hamilton Smith
Saber Cat	15–18	5¼	Corey Nakatani/Steven Asmussen
Gemologist	16–15	1½	Javier Castellano/Todd Pletcher
Trinniberg	17–9	3	Willie Martinez/Bisnath Parboo
Prospective	18–12	15½	Luis Contreras/Mark Casse
Take Charge Indy	19–3	—	Calvin Borel/Patrick Byrne
Daddy Long Legs	Eased–1	—	Colm O'Donoghue/Aidan O'Brien

137th Preakness Stakes

May 19, 2012. Grade I, 3-year-olds; 12th race, Pimlico Race Course, Baltimore. All 126 lbs. Distance: 1³⁄₁₆ miles; Stakes value: $1,000,000. Track: fast. Off: 6:20 p.m. Winner: I'll Have Another (By Flower Alley out of Arch's Gal Edith by Arch); Times: 23.79, 47.68, 1:11.72, 1:36.69, 1:55.94. Won: driving. Breeder: Harvey Clarke (Kentucky).

Horse	Finish-PP	Margin	Jockey/Trainer
I'll Have Another	1–9	neck	Mario Gutierrez/Doug O'Neill
Bodemeister	2–7	8¾	Mike Smith/Bob Baffert
Creative Cause	3–6	3	Joel Rosario/Mike Harrington
Zetterholm	4–8	3¼	Junior Alvarado/Richard Dutrow
Teeth Of The Dog	5–2	neck	Joe Bravo/Michael Matz
Optimizer	6–10	2¼	Corey Nakatani/D. Wayne Lukas
Cozzetti	7–11	7¹⁄₂	Jose Lezcano/Dale Romans
Tiger Walk	8–1	2¼	Ramon Dominguez/Ignacio Correas IV
Daddy Nose Best	9–8	3¼	Julien Leparoux/Steven Asmussen
Went The Day Well	10–5	3¾	John Velazquez/H. Graham Motion
Pretension	11–3	—	Javier Santiago/Christopher Grove

144th Belmont Stakes

June 9, 2012. Grade I, 3-year-olds; 11th race, Belmont Park, Elmont, NY. All: 126 lbs. Distance: 1½ miles. Stakes value: $1,000,000. Track: fast. Off: 6:41 p.m. Winner: Union Rags (By Dixie Union out of Tempo by Gone West); Times: 23.72, 49.23, 1:14.72, 1:38.85, 2:04.39, 2:30.42. Won: driving. Breeder: Phyllis Wyeth (Kentucky).

Horse	Finish-PP	Margin	Jockey/Trainer
Union Rags	1–3	neck	John Velazquez/Michael Matz
Paynter	2–9	1¾	Mike Smith/Bob Baffert
Atigun	3–4	5½	Julien Leparoux/Kenneth McPeek
Street Life	4–1	2½	Jose Lezcano/Chad Brown
Five Sixteen	5–7	1	Rosie Napravnik/Dominick Schettino
Unstoppable U	6–2	head	Junior Alvarado/Kenneth McPeek
Dullahan	7–5	7¼	Javier Castellano/Dale Romans
My Adonis	8–11	3¾	Ramon Dominguez/Kelly Breen
Ravelo's Boy	9–6	8¾	A Solis/Manuel Azpurua
Optimizer	10–1	—	Corey Nakatani/D. Wayne Lukas
Guyana Star Dweej	Eased–8	—	Kent Desormeaux/Doodnauth Shivmangal

Grade I North American Stakes Races

Late 2011–2012*

Date	Race	Track	Distance	Winner	Trainer/Jockey	Purse ($)
Oct 1	Joe Hirsch Turf Classic	Belmont	1½ miles	Cape Blanco	A. O'Brien/J. Spencer	500,000
Oct 1	Flower Bowl Stakes	Belmont	1¼ miles	Stacelita	C. Brown/R. Dominguez	500,000
Oct 1	Jockey Club Gold Cup St.	Belmont	1¼ miles	Flat Out	S. Dickey/A. Solis	750,000
Oct 1	Vosburgh Stakes	Belmont	6 furlongs	Giant Ryan	B. Parbhoo/C. Velasquez	350,000
Oct 1	Beldame Stakes	Belmont	1⅛ miles	Havre de Grace	J.L. Jones/R. Dominguez	350,000
Oct 1	Lady's Secret Stakes	Santa Anita	1¹⁄₁₆ miles	Zazu	J. Sadler/J. Rosario	250,000
Oct 1	Norfolk Stakes	Santa Anita	1¹⁄₁₆ miles	Creative Cause	M. Harrington/ J. Rosario	250,000
Oct 1	Yellow Ribbon Stakes	Santa Anita	1¼ miles	Dubawl Heights	S. Callaghan/J. Rosario	250,000
Oct 2	Oak Leaf Stakes	Santa Anita	1¹⁄₁₆ miles	Weemissfrankie	P. Eurton/ R. Bejarano	250,000
Oct 7	Alcibiades Stakes	Keeneland	1¹⁄₁₆ miles	Stephanie's Kitten	W. Catalano/J. Velasquez	400,000
Oct 8	Ancient Title Stakes	Santa Anita	6 furlongs	Amazombie	W. Spawr/M. Smith	250,000
Oct 8	Frizette Stakes	Belmont	1 mile	My Miss Aurelia	S. Asmussen/C. Nakatani	300,000
Oct 8	Champagne Stakes	Belmont	1 mile	Union Rags	M. Matz/J. Castellano	300,000
Oct 8	First Lady Stakes	Keeneland	1 mile	Never Retreat	C. Block/J. Peparoux	350,000
Oct 8	Shadwell Turf Mile	Keeneland	1 mile	Gio Ponti	C. Clement/R. Dominguez	600,000
Oct 8	Dixiana Breeders' Futurity	Keeneland	1¹⁄₁₆ miles	Dullahan	D. Romans/K. Desormeaux	400,000
Oct 8	Jamaica Handicap	Belmont	1⅛ miles	Western Aristocrat	J. Noseda/C. Nakatani	250,000
Oct 9	Spinster Stakes	Keeneland	1⅛ miles	Aruna	H. Motion/ R. Dominguez	500,000
Oct 10	Oklahoma Derby	Remington Park	1⅛ miles	Pleasant Prince	W. Ward/J. Rosario	400,000
Oct 15	Queen Elizabeth II Chall. Cup	Keeneland	1⅛ miles	Together	A. O'Brien/C. O'Donoghue	400,000
Oct 16	Nearctic Stakes	Woodbine	6 furlongs	Regally Ready	S. Asmussen/C. Nakatani	495,050
Oct 16	E.P. Taylor Stakes	Woodbine	1¼ miles	Miss Keller	R. Affeld/J. Velazquez	990,100
Oct 16	Canadian Int'l Stakes	Woodbine	1½ miles	Sarah Lynx	J. Hammond/C. Soumillon	1,485,150
Nov 4	Breeders Cup Juvenile Fillies	Churchill Downs	1¹⁄₁₆ miles	My Miss Aurelia	S. Asmussen/C. Nakatani	2,000,000
Nov 4	Breeders Cup F & M Turf	Churchill Downs	1⅜ miles	Perfect Shirl	R. Attfield/J. Velazquez	2,000,000
Nov 4	Breeders Cup Ladies' Classic	Churchill Downs	1⅛ miles	Royal Delta	W. Mott/J. Lezcano	2,000,000
Nov 4	Breeders Cup F & M Sprint	Churchill Downs	7 furlongs	Musical Romance	W. Kaplan/L. Leyva	1,000,000
Nov 5	Breeders Cup Juvenile Turf	Churchill Downs	1 mile	Wrote	A. O'Brien/R. Moore	1,000,000
Nov 5	Breeders Cup Mile	Churchill Downs	1 mile	Court Vision	D. Romans/R. Albarado	2,000,000
Nov 5	Breeders Cup Turf	Churchill Downs	1½ miles	St Nicholas Abbey	A. O'Brien/J. O'Brien	3,000,000
Nov 5	Breeders Cup Classic	Churchill Downs	1¼ miles	Drosselmeyer	W. Mott/M. Smith	5,000,000
Nov 5	Breeders Cup Juvenile	Churchill Downs	1¹⁄₁₆ miles	Hansen	M. Maker/R. Dominguez	2,000,000
Nov 5	Breeders Cup Sprint	Churchill Downs	6 furlongs	Amazombie	W. Spawr/M. Smith	1,500,000
Nov 5	Breeders Cup Dirt Mile	Churchill Downs	1 mile	Caleb's Posse	D.K. Von Hemel/R. Maragh	1,000,000
Nov 19	Hollywood Turf Cup Stakes	Hollywood	1½ miles	Sanagas	H.G. Motion/R. Maragh	250,000
Nov 25	Clark Handicap	Churchill Downs	1⅛ miles	Wise Dan	C. Lopresti/J. Velazquez	500,000
Nov 25	Matriarch Stakes	Hollywood	1 mile	Star Billing	J. Shirreffs/V. Espinoza	250,000
Nov 26	Cigar Mile Handicap	Aqueduct	1 mile	To Honor And Serve	W. Mott/J. Lezcano	250,000
Nov 27	Hollywood Derby	Hollywood	1¼ miles	Ultimate Eagle	M. Pender/M. Pedroza	250,000
Dec 10	Hollywood Starlet Stakes	Hollywood	1¹⁄₁₆ miles	Killer Graces	J. Hollendorfer/J. Talamo	400,000
Dec 17	CashCall Futurity	Hollywood	1¹⁄₁₆ miles	Liaison	B. Baffert/R. Bejarano	750,000
Dec 26	Malibu Stakes	Santa Anita	7 furlongs	The Factor	B. Baffert/M. Garcia	300,000
Dec 31	La Brea Stakes	Santa Anita	7 furlongs	Teddy's Promise	R. Ellis/V. Espinoza	300,000
Jan 28	Santa Monica Stakes	Santa Anita	7 furlongs	Home Sweet	J. Sadler/J. Rosario	300,000
Feb 11	Donn Handicap	Gulfstream	1⅛ miles	Hymn Book	C. McGaughey/J. Velazquez	500,000
Feb 11	Gulfstream Turf Handicap	Gulfstream	1⅛ miles	Get Stormy	T. Bush/R. Dominguez	300,000
Mar 3	Frank E. Kilroe Mile	Santa Anita	1 mile	Willyconker	D. O'Neill/ J. Rosario	300,000
Mar 3	Santa Anita Handicap	Santa Anita	1¼ miles	Ron The Greek	W.Mott/J. Lezcano	750,000
Mar 3	Las Virgenes Stakes	Santa Anita	1 mile	Eden's Moon	B. Baffert/M. Garcia	250,000
Mar 17	Santa Margarita Stakes	Santa Anita	1⅛ miles	Include Me Out	R. Ellis/J. Talamo	300,000
Mar 31	Florida Derby	Gulfstream	1⅛ miles	Take Charge	C. Borel/P. Byrne	1,000,000
Mar 31	Santa Anita Oaks	Santa Anita	1¹⁄₁₆ miles	Willa B Awesome	W. Solis/M. Pedroza	300,000
Apr 7	Carter Handicap	Aqueduct	7 furlongs	Jackson Bend	N. Zito/C. Nakatani	400,000
Apr 7	Wood Memorial	Aqueduct	1⅛ miles	Gemologist	T. Pletcher/ J. Castellano	1,000,000
Apr 7	Santa Anita Derby	Santa Anita	1⅛ miles	I'll Have Another	D. O'Neill/M. Gutierrez	750,000
Apr 7	Ashland Stakes	Keeneland	1¹⁄₁₆ miles	Karlovy Vary	G. Arnold/J. Graham	500,000
Apr 12	Madison Stakes	Keeneland	7 furlongs	Groupie Doll	W. Bradley/R. Maragh	300,000
Apr 13	Maker's 46 Mile Stakes	Keeneland	1 mile	Data Link	C. McGaughey/A. Solis	300,000
Apr 13	Apple Blossom Handicap	Oaklawn	1¹⁄₁₆ miles	Plum Pretty	B. Baffert/R. Bejarano	500,000

* Through Oct. 1, 2012

2012*

Date	Race	Track	Distance	Winner	Trainer/Jockey	Purse ($)
Apr 14	Blue Grass Stakes	Keeneland	1⅛ miles	Dullahan	D. Romans/K. Desormeaux	750,000
Apr 14	Arkansas Derby	Oaklawn	1⅛ miles	Bodemeister	B. Baffert/M. Smith	1,000,000
Apr 14	Jenny Wiley Stakes	Keeneland	1¹⁄₁₆ miles	Daisy Devine	A. McKeever/J. Graham	300,000
May 4	Kentucky Oaks	Churchill Downs	1⅛ miles	Believe You Can	J.L. Jones/R. Napravnik	1,000,000
May 5	Kentucky Derby	Churchill Downs	1¼ miles	I'll Have Another	D. O'Neill/M. Gutierrez	2,000,000
May 5	Woodford Reserve Turf Classic	Churchill Downs	1⅛ miles	Little Mike	D. Romans/J. Bravo	500,000
May 5	Humana Distaff	Churchill Downs	7 furlongs	Groupie Doll	W. Bradley/R. Maragh	300,000
May 19	Preakness Stakes	Pimlico	1³⁄₁₆ miles	I'll Have Another	D. O'Neill/M. Gutierrez	1,000,000
May 28	Metropolitan Handicap	Belmont	1 mile	Shackleford	D. Romans/J. Velazquez	750,000
May 28	Acorn Stakes	Belmont	1 mile	Contested	B. Baffert/J. Castellano	300,00
May 28	Ogden Phipps Handicap	Belmont	1¹⁄₁₆ miles	It's Tricky	K. McLaughlin/ E. Castro	400,000
May 28	Gamley Stakes	Hollywood	1⅛ miles	Belle Royale	S. Callaghan/J. Rosario	250,000
June 9	Belmont Stakes	Belmont	1½ miles	Union Rags	M. Matz/J. Velazquez	1,000,000
June 9	Just a Game Stakes	Belmont	1 mile	Tapitsfly	D. Romans/R. Dominguez	500,000
June 9	Manhattan Handicap Turf	Belmont	1¼ miles	Desert Blanc	C. Brown/R. Dominguez	500,000
June 9	Charles Whittingham Memorial	Hollywood	1¼ miles	Acclamation	D. Warren/P. Valenzuela	250,000
June 16	Stephen Foster Handicap	Churchill Downs	1⅛ miles	Ron The Greek	W. Mott/J. Lezcano	400,000
June 16	Vanity Handicap	Hollywood	1⅛ miles	Love The WayYou Are	M. Cho/G. Gomez	250,000
June 23	Mother Goose Stakes	Belmont	1¹⁄₁₆ miles	Zo Impressive	T. Albertrani/R. Maragh	300,000
June 30	Shoemaker Mile	Hollywood	1 mile	Jeranimo	M. Pender/G. Gomez	300,000
June 30	Triple Bend Handicap	Hollywood	7 furlongs	Camp Victory	M. Mitchell/J. Talamo	250,000
July 7	United Nations Stakes	Monmouth	1⅜ miles	Turbo Compressor	T. Pletcher/J. Bravo	500,000
July 7	Hollywood Gold Cup	Hollywood	1¼ miles	Game On Dude	B. Baffert/C. Sutherland	500,000
July 7	Princess Rooney Handicap	Calder	6 furlongs	Musical Romance	W. Kaplan/J. Leyva	400,000
July 14	Man O'War Stakes	Belmont	1⅜ miles	Point of Entry	C. McGaughey/J. Lezcano	600,000
July 14	American Oaks Stakes	Hollywood	1¼ miles	Lady Of Shamrock	J. Sadler/M. Smith	350,000
July 21	Eddie Read Stakes	Del Mar	1⅛ miles	Acclamation	D. Warren/P. Valenzuela	300,000
July 21	Coaching Club American Oaks	Saratoga	1⅛ miles	Questing	K. McLaughlin/I. Ortiz Jr.	300,000
July 28	Diana Stakes	Saratoga	1⅛ miles	Winter Memories	J. Toner/J. Castellano	600,000
July 29	Bing Crosby Stakes	Del Mar	6 furlongs	Amazombie	W. Spawr/M. Smith	300,000
July 29	Haskell Invitational	Monmouth	1⅛ miles	Paynter	B. Baffert/R. Bejarano	1,000,000
Aug 4	Whitney Invitational	Saratoga	1⅛ miles	Fort Larned	I.R. Wilkes/B. Hernandez Jr.	750,000
Aug 4	Clement L. Hirsch Stakes	Del Mar	1¹⁄₁₆ miles	Include Me Out	R. Ellis/J. Talamo	300,000
Aug 4	Prioress Stakes	Saratoga	6 furlongs	Emma's Encore	H.A. Jerkens/J. Alvarado	300,000
Aug 5	Alfred G. Vanderbilt Handicap	Saratoga	6 furlongs	Poseidon's Warrior	R.E. Reed Jr./I. Ortiz Jr.	400,000
Aug 18	Sword Dancer Invitational	Saratoga	1½ miles	Point of Entry	C. McGaughey/J. Velazquez	600,000
Aug 18	Arlington Million Stakes	Arlington	1¼ miles	Little Mike	D. Romans/R. Dominguez	1,000,000
Aug 18	Beverly D. Stakes	Arlington	1³⁄₁₆ miles	I'm A Dreamer	D. Simcock/H. Turner	750,000
Aug 18	Secretariat Stakes	Arlington	1¼ miles	Bayrir	A De Royer-Dupre/C. Lemaire	500,000
Aug 18	Alabama Stakes	Saratoga	1¼ miles	Questing	K. McLaughlin/I. Ortiz Jr.	600,000
Aug 18	Del Mar Oaks	Del Mar	1⅛ miles	Lady of Shamrock	J. Sadler/M. Smith	300,000
Aug 24	Ballerina Stakes	Saratoga	7 furlongs	Turbulent Descent	T. Pletcher/J. Velazquez	500,000
Aug 25	King's Bishop Stakes	Saratoga	7 furlongs	Willy Beamin	R. Dutrow/A. Garcia	500,000
Aug 25	Test Stakes	Saratoga	7 furlongs	Contested	B. Baffert/R. Bejarano	500,000
Aug 25	Travers Stakes	Saratoga	1¼ miles	Golden Ticket	K. McPeek/D. Cohen	1,000,000
Aug 26	Pacific Classic	Del Mar	1¼ miles	Dullahan	D. Romans/J. Rosario	1,000,000
Aug 26	Personal Ensign Stakes	Saratoga	1⅛ miles	Love And Pride	T. Pletcher/J. Velazquez	600,000
Sept 1	Del Mar Debutante	Del Mar	1⅛ miles	Executiveprivilege	B. Baffert/R. Bejarano	300,000
Sept 1	Forego Stakes	Saratoga	7 furlongs	Emcee	K. McLaughlin/A. Garcia	500,000
Sept 1	Woodward Stakes	Saratoga	1⅛ miles	To Honor And Serve	W. Mott/J. Velazquez	750,000
Sept 2	Spinaway Stakes	Saratoga	7 furlongs	So Many Ways	A. Dutrow/J. Castellano	300,000
Sept 5	Del Mar Futurity	Del Mar	7 furlongs	Rolling Fog	B. Baffert/R. Bejarano	300,000
Sept 22	Cotillion Stakes	Parx	1¹⁄₁₆ miles	Miss Aurelia	S. Asmussen/C. Nakatani	1,000,000

* Through Oct. 1, 2012

FOR THE RECORD • Year by Year

THOROUGHBRED RACING

Kentucky Derby

Run at Churchill Downs, Louisville, KY, on the first Saturday in May.

Year	Winner (Margin)	Jockey	Second	Third	Time
1875	Aristides (1)	Oliver Lewis	Volcano	Verdigris	2:37¾
1876	Vagrant (2)	Bobby Swim	Creedmoor	Harry Hill	2:38¼
1877	Baden-Baden (2)	William Walker	Leonard	King William	2:38
1878	Day Star (2)	Jimmie Carter	Himyar	Leveler	2:37¼
1879	Lord Murphy (1)	Charlie Shauer	Falsetto	Strathmore	2:37
1880	Fonso (1)	George Lewis	Kimball	Bancroft	2:37½
1881	Hindoo (4)	Jimmy McLaughin	Lelex	Alfambra	2:40
1882	Apollo (½)	Babe Hurd	Runnymede	Bengal	2:40¼
1883	Leonatus (3)	Billy Donohue	Drake Carter	Lord Raglan	2:43
1884	Buchanan (2)	Isaac Murphy	Loftin	Audrain	2:40¼
1885	Joe Cotton (Neck)	Erskine Henderson	Bersan	Ten Booker	2:37¼
1886	Ben Ali (½)	Paul Duffy	Blue Wing	Free Knight	2:36½
1887	Montrose (2)	Isaac Lewis	Jim Gore	Jacobin	2:39¼
1888	MacBeth II (1)	George Covington	Gallifet	White	2:38¼
1889	Spokane (Nose)	Thomas Kiley	Proctor Knott	Once Again	2:34½
1890	Riley (2)	Isaac Murphy	Bill Letcher	Robespierre	2:45
1891	Kingman (1)	Isaac Murphy	Balgowan	High Tariff	2:52¼
1892	Azra (Nose)	Alonzo Clayton	Huron	Phil Dwyer	2:41½
1893	Lookout (5)	Eddie Kunze	Plutus	Boundless	2:39¼
1894	Chant (2)	Frank Goodale	Pearl Song	Sigurd	2:41
1895	Halma (3)	Soup Perkins	Basso	Laureate	2:37½
1896	Ben Brush (Nose)	Willie Simms	Ben Eder	Semper Ego	2:07¼
1897	Typhoon II (Head)	Buttons Garner	Ornament	Dr. Catlett	2:12½
1898	Plaudit (Neck)	Willie Simms	Lieber Karl	Isabey	2:09
1899	Manuel (2)	Fred Taral	Corsini	Mazo	2:12
1900	Lieut. Gibson (4)	Jimmy Boland	Florizar	Thrive	2:06¼
1901	His Eminence (2)	Jimmy Winkfield	Sannazarro	Driscoll	2:07¾
1902	Alan-a-Dale (Nose)	Jimmy Winkfield	Inventor	The Rival	2:08¾
1903	Judge Himes (¾)	Hal Booker	Early	Bourbon	2:09
1904	Elwood (½)	Frankie Prior	Ed Tierney	Brancas	2:08½
1905	Agile (3)	Jack Martin	Ram's Horn	Layson	2:10¾
1906	Sir Huon (2)	Roscoe Troxler	Lady Navarre	James Reddick	2:08⅕
1907	Pink Star (2)	Andy Minder	Zal	Ovelando	2:12⅗
1908	Stone Street (1)	Arthur Pickens	Sir Cleges	Dunvegan	2:15⅕
1909	Wintergreen (4)	Vincent Powers	Miami	Dr. Barkley	2:08⅕
1910	Donau (½)	Fred Herbert	Joe Morris	Fighting Bob	2:06⅖
1911	Meridian (¾)	George Archibald	Governor Gray	Colston	2:05
1912	Worth (Neck)	Carroll H. Schilling	Duval	Flamma	2:09⅖
1913	Donerail (½)	Roscoe Goose	Ten Point	Gowell	2:04⅘
1914	Old Rosebud (8)	John McCabe	Hodge	Bronzewing	2:03⅖
1915	Regret (2)	Joe Notter	Pebbles	Sharpshooter	2:05⅖
1916	George Smith (Neck)	Johnny Loftus	Star Hawk	Franklin	2:04
1917	Omar Khayyam (2)	Charles Borel	Ticket	Midway	2:04⅗
1918	Exterminator (1)	William Knapp	Escoba	Viva America	2:10⅘
1919	Sir Barton (5)	Johnny Loftus	Billy Kelly	Under Fire	2:09⅘
1920	Paul Jones (Head)	Ted Rice	Upset	On Watch	2:09
1921	Behave Yourself (Head)	Charles Thompson	Black Servant	Prudery	2:04⅕
1922	Morvich (½)	Albert Johnson	Bet Mosie	John Finn	2:04⅗
1923	Zev (1½)	Earl Sande	Martingale	Vigil	2:05⅖
1924	Black Gold (½)	John Mooney	Chilhowee	Beau Butler	2:05⅕
1925	Flying Ebony (1½)	Earl Sande	Captain Hal	Son of John	2:07⅗
1926	Bubbling Over (5)	Albert Johnson	Bagenbaggage	Rock Man	2:03⅗
1927	Whiskery (Head)	Linus McAtee	Osmond	Jock	2:06
1928	Reigh Count (3)	Chick Lang	Misstep	Toro	2:10⅖
1929	Clyde Van Dusen (2)	Linus McAtee	Naishapur	Panchio	2:10⅘
1930	Gallant Fox (2)	Earl Sande	Gallant Knight	Ned O.	2:07⅗
1931	Twenty Grand (4)	Charles Kurtsinger	Sweep All	Mate	2:01⅘
1932	Burgoo King (5)	Eugene James	Economic	Stepenfetchit	2:05⅕

Kentucky Derby *(Cont.)*

Year	Winner (Margin)	Jockey	Second	Third	Time
1933	Brokers Tip (Nose)	Don Meade	Head Play	Charley O.	2:06⅘
1934	Cavalcade (2½)	Mack Garner	Discovery	Agrarian	2:04
1935	Omaha (1½)	Willie Saunders	Roman Soldier	Whiskolo	2:05
1936	Bold Venture (Head)	Ira Hanford	Brevity	Indian Broom	2:03⅗
1937	War Admiral (1¾)	Charles Kurtsinger	Pompoon	Reaping Reward	2:03⅕
1938	Lawrin (1)	Eddie Arcaro	Dauber	Can't Wait	2:04⅘
1939	Johnstown (8)	James Stout	Challedon	Heather Broom	2:03⅗
1940	Gallahadion (1½)	Carroll Bierman	Bimelech	Dit	2:05
1941	Whirlaway (8)	Eddie Arcaro	Staretor	Market Wise	2:01⅖
1942	Shut Out (2½)	Wayne Wright	Alsab	Valdina Orphan	2:04⅖
1943	Count Fleet (3)	John Longden	Blue Swords	Slide Rule	2:04
1944	Pensive (4½)	Conn McCreary	Broadcloth	Stir Up	2:04⅕
1945	Hoop Jr. (6)	Eddie Arcaro	Pot o' Luck	Darby Dieppe	2:07
1946	Assault (8)	Warren Mehrtens	Spy Song	Hampden	2:06⅗
1947	Jet Pilot (Head)	Eric Guerin	Phalanx	Faultless	2:06⅘
1948	Citation (3½)	Eddie Arcaro	Coaltown	My Request	2:05⅖
1949	Ponder (3)	Steve Brooks	Capot	Palestinian	2:04⅕
1950	Middleground (1¼)	William Boland	Hill Prince	Mr. Trouble	2:01⅗
1951	Count Turf (4)	Conn McCreary	Royal Mustang	Ruhe	2:02⅗
1952	Hill Gail (2)	Eddie Arcaro	Sub Fleet	Blue Man	2:01⅗
1953	Dark Star (Head)	Hank Moreno	Native Dancer	Invigorator	2:02
1954	Determine (1½)	Ray York	Hasty Road	Hasseyampa	2:03
1955	Swaps (1½)	Bill Shoemaker	Nashua	Summer Tan	2:01⅘
1956	Needles (¾)	Dave Erb	Fabius	Come On Red	2:03⅖
1957	Iron Liege (Nose)	Bill Hartack	Gallant Man	Round Table	2:02⅕
1958	Tim Tam (½)	Ismael Valenzuela	Lincoln Road	Noureddin	2:05
1959	Tomy Lee (Nose)	Bill Shoemaker	Sword Dancer	First Landing	2:02⅕
1960	Venetian Way (3½)	Bill Hartack	Bally Ache	Victoria Park	2:02⅖
1961	Carry Back (¾)	John Sellers	Crozier	Bass Clef	2:04
1962	Decidedly (2¼)	Bill Hartack	Roman Line	Ridan	2:00⅖
1963	Chateaugay (1¼)	Braulio Baeza	Never Bend	Candy Spots	2:01⅘
1964	Northern Dancer (Neck)	Bill Hartack	Hill Rise	The Scoundrel	2:00
1965	Lucky Debonair (Neck)	Bill Shoemaker	Dapper Dan	Tom Rolfe	2:01⅕
1966	Kauai King (½)	Don Brumfield	Advocator	Blue Skyer	2:02
1967	Proud Clarion (1)	Bobby Ussery	Barbs Delight	Damascus	2:00⅗
1968	Forward Pass (Disq.)	Ismael Valenzuela	Francie's Hat	T.V. Commercial	2:02⅕
1969	Majestic Prince (Neck)	Bill Hartack	Arts and Letters	Dike	2:01⅘
1970	Dust Commander (5)	Mike Manganello	My Dad George	High Echelon	2:03⅖
1971	Canonero II (3¾)	Gustavo Avila	Jim French	Bold Reason	2:03⅕
1972	Riva Ridge (3¼)	Ron Turcotte	No Le Hace	Hold Your Peace	2:01⅘
1973	Secretariat (2½)	Ron Turcotte	Sham	Our Native	1:59⅖
1974	Cannonade (2¼)	Angel Cordero Jr.	Hudson County	Agitate	2:04
1975	Foolish Pleasure (1¾)	Jacinto Vasquez	Avatar	Diabolo	2:02
1976	Bold Forbes (1)	Angel Cordero Jr.	Honest Pleasure	Elocutionist	2:01⅗
1977	Seattle Slew (1¾)	Jean Cruguet	Run Dusty Run	Sanhedrin	2:02⅕
1978	Affirmed (1½)	Steve Cauthen	Alydar	Believe It	2:01⅕
1979	Spectacular Bid (2¾)	Ronald J. Franklin	General Assembly	Golden Act	2:02⅖
1980	Genuine Risk (1)	Jacinto Vasquez	Rumbo	Jaklin Klugman	2:02
1981	Pleasant Colony (¾)	Jorge Velasquez	Woodchopper	Partez	2:02
1982	Gato Del Sol (2½)	Eddie Delahoussaye	Laser Light	Reinvested	2:02⅕
1983	Sunny's Halo (2)	Eddie Delahoussaye	Desert Wine	Caveat	2:02⅕
1984	Swale (3¼)	Laffit Pincay Jr.	Coax Me Chad	At the Threshold	2:02⅖
1985	Spend A Buck (5)	Angel Cordero Jr.	Stephan's Odyssey	Chief's Crown	2:00⅕
1986	Ferdinand (2¼)	Bill Shoemaker	Bold Arrangement	Broad Brush	2:02⅘
1987	Alysheba (¾)	Chris McCarron	Bet Twice	Avies Copy	2:03⅖
1988	Winning Colors (Neck)	Gary Stevens	Forty Niner	Risen Star	2:02⅕
1989	Sunday Silence (2½)	Pat Valenzuela	Easy Goer	Awe Inspiring	2:05
1990	Unbridled (3½)	Craig Perret	Summer Squall	Pleasant Tap	2:02
1991	Strike the Gold (1¾)	Chris Antley	Best Pal	Mane Minister	2:03
1992	Lil E. Tee (1)	Pat Day	Casual Lies	Dance Floor	2:03
1993	Sea Hero (2½)	Jerry Bailey	Prairie Bayou	Wild Gale	2:02⅖
1994	Go for Gin (2½)	Chris McCarron	Strodes Creek	Blumin Affair	2:03⅗
1995	Thunder Gulch (2¼)	Gary Stevens	Tejano Run	Timber Country	2:01⅕

Kentucky Derby *(Cont.)*

Year	Winner (Margin)	Jockey	Second	Third	Time
1996	Grindstone (Nose)	Jerry Bailey	Cavonnier	Prince of Thieves	2:01
1997	Silver Charm (Head)	Gary Stevens	Captain Bodgit	Free House	2:02⅖
1998	Real Quiet (½)	Kent Desormeaux	Victory Gallop	Indian Charlie	2:02⅒
1999	Charismatic (Neck)	Chris Antley	Menifee	Cat Thief	2:03⅕
2000	Fusaichi Pegasus (1½)	Kent Desormeaux	Aptitude	Impeachment	2:01.12
2001	Monarchos (4¾)	Jorge Chavez	Invisible Ink	Congaree	1:59.97
2002	War Emblem (4)	Victor Espinoza	Proud Citizen	Perfect Drift	2:01.13
2003	Funny Cide (1¾)	Jose Santos	Empire Maker	Peace Rules	2:01.19
2004	Smarty Jones (2¾)	Stewart Elliott	Lion Heart	Imperialism	2:04.06
2005	Giacomo (½)	Mike Smith	Closing Argument	Afleet Alex	2:02.75
2006	Barbaro (1½)	Edgar Prado	Bluegrass Cat	Steppenwolfer	2:01.36
2007	Street Sense (2¼)	Calvin Borel	Hard Spun	Curlin	2:02.17
2008	Big Brown (4¾)	Kent Desormeaux	Eight Belles	Denis of Cork	2:01.82
2009	Mine That Bird (6¾)	Calvin Borel	Pioneer of the Nile	Musket Man	2:02.66
2010	Super Saver (2½)	Calvin Borel	Ice Box	Paddy O'Prado	2:04.45
2011	Animal Kingdom (2¾)	John Velazquez	Nehro	Mucho Macho Man	2:02.04
2012	I'll Have Another (1½)	Mario Gutierrez	Bodemeister	Dullahan	2:01.83

Note: Distance: 1½ miles (1875–95), 1¼ miles (1896–present).

Preakness

Run at Pimlico Race Course, Baltimore, Md., two weeks after the Kentucky Derby.

Year	Winner (Margin)	Jockey	Second	Third	Time
1873	Survivor (10)	G. Barbee	John Boulger	Artist	2:43
1874	Culpepper (¾)	W. Donohue	King Amadeus	Scratch	2:56½
1875	Tom Ochiltree (2)	L. Hughes	Viator	Bay Final	2:43½
1876	Shirley (4)	G. Barbee	Rappahannock	Algerine	2:44¾
1877	Cloverbrook (4)	C. Holloway	Bombast	Lucifer	2:45½
1878	Duke of Magenta (6)	C. Holloway	Bayard	Albert	2:41¾
1879	Harold (3)	L. Hughes	Jericho	Rochester	2:40½
1880	Grenada (¾)	L. Hughes	Oden	Emily F.	2:40½
1881	Saunterer (½)	T. Costello	Compensation	Baltic	2:40½
1882	Vanguard (Neck)	T. Costello	Heck	Col Watson	2:44½
1883*	Jacobus (4)	G. Barbee	Parnell		2:42½
1884*	Knight of Ellerslie (2)	S. Fisher	Welcher		2:39½
1885	Tecumseh (2)	Jim McLaughlin	Wickham	John C.	2:49
1886	The Bard (3)	S. Fisher	Eurus	Elkwood	2:45
1887	Dunboyne (1)	W. Donohue	Mahoney	Raymond	2:39½
1888	Refund (3)	F. Littlefield	Judge Murray	Glendale	2:49
1889*	Buddhist (8)	W. Anderson	Japhet		2:17½
1890	Montague (3)	W. Martin	Philosophy	Barrister	2:36¾
1894	Assignee (3)	Fred Taral	Potentate	Ed Kearney	1:49¼
1895	Belmar (1)	Fred Taral	April Fool	Sue Kittie	1:50½
1896	Margrave (1)	H. Griffin	Hamilton II	Intermission	1:51
1897	Paul Kauvar (1½)	C. Thorpe	Elkins	On Deck	1:51¼
1898	Sly Fox (2)	C. W. Simms	The Huguenot	Nuto	1:49⅗
1899	Half Time (1)	R. Clawson	Filigrane	Lackland	1:47
1900	Hindus (Head)	H. Spencer	Sarmation	Ten Candles	1:48⅖
1901	The Parader (2)	F. Landry	Sadie S.	Dr. Barlow	1:47⅕
1902	Old England (Nose)	L. Jackson	Major Daingerfield	Namtor	1:45⅘
1903	Flocarline (½)	W. Gannon	Mackey Dwyer	Rightful	1:44⅘
1904	Bryn Mawr (1)	E. Hildebrand	Wotan	Dolly Spanker	1:44⅕
1905	Cairngorm (Head)	W. Davis	Kiamesha	Coy Maid	1:45⅘
1906	Whimsical (4)	Walter Miller	Content	Larabie	1:45
1907	Don Enrique (1)	G. Mountain	Ethon	Zambesi	1:45⅖
1908	Royal Tourist (4)	E. Dugan	Live Wire	Robert Cooper	1:46⅖
1909	Effendi (1)	Willie Doyle	Fashion Plate	Hilltop	1:39⅘
1910	Layminster (½)	R. Estep	Dalhousie	Sager	1:40⅗
1911	Watervale (1)	E. Dugan	Zeus	The Nigger	1:51

Preakness *(Cont.)*

Year	Winner (Margin)	Jockey	Second	Third	Time
1912	Colonel Holloway (5)	C. Turner	Bwana Tumbo	Tipsand	1:56⅗
1913	Buskin (Neck)	J. Butwell	Kleburne	Barnegat	1:53⅖
1914	Holiday (¾)	A. Schuttinger	Brave Cunarder	Defendum	1:53⅘
1915	Rhine Maiden (1½)	Douglas Hoffman	Half Rock	Runes	1:58
1916	Damrosch (1½)	Linus McAtee	Greenwood	Achievement	1:54⅘
1917	Kalitan (2)	E. Haynes	Al M. Dick	Kentucky Boy	1:54⅖
1918*	War Cloud (¾)	Johnny Loftus	Sunny Slope	Lanius	1:53⅗
1918*	Jack Hare, Jr (2)	C. Peak	The Porter	Kate Bright	1:53⅖
1919	Sir Barton (4)	Johnny Loftus	Eternal	Sweep On	1:53
1920	Man o' War (1½)	Clarence Kummer	Upset	Wildair	1:51⅗
1921	Broomspun (¾)	F. Coltiletti	Polly Ann	Jeg	1:54⅕
1922	Pillory (Head)	L. Morris	Hea	June Grass	1:51⅗
1923	Vigil (1¼)	B. Marinelli	General Thatcher	Rialto	1:53⅗
1924	Nellie Morse (1½)	J. Merimee	Transmute	Mad Play	1:57⅕
1925	Coventry (4)	Clarence Kummer	Backbone	Almadel	1:59
1926	Display (Head)	J. Maiben	Blondin	Mars	1:59⅘
1927	Bostonian (½)	A. Abel	Sir Harry	Whiskery	2:01⅗
1928	Victorian (Nose)	Sonny Workman	Toro	Solace	2:00⅕
1929	Dr. Freeland (1)	Louis Schaefer	Minotaur	African	2:01⅗
1930	Gallant Fox (¾)	Earl Sande	Crack Brigade	Snowflake	2:00⅗
1931	Mate (1½)	G. Ellis	Twenty Grand	Ladder	1:59
1932	Burgoo King (Head)	E. James	Tick On	Boatswain	1:59⅘
1933	Head Play (4)	Charles Kurtsinger	Ladysman	Utopian	2:02
1934	High Quest (Nose)	R. Jones	Cavalcade	Discovery	1:58⅕
1935	Omaha (6)	Willie Saunders	Firethorn	Psychic Bid	1:58⅖
1936	Bold Venture (Nose)	George Woolf	Granville	Jean Bart	1:59
1937	War Admiral (Head)	Charles Kurtsinger	Pompoon	Flying Scot	1:58⅖
1938	Dauber (7)	M. Peters	Cravat	Menow	1:59⅘
1939	Challedon (1¼)	George Seabo	Gilded Knight	Volitant	1:59⅘
1940	Bimelech (3)	F. A. Smith	Mioland	Gallahadion	1:58⅗
1941	Whirlaway (5½)	Eddie Arcaro	King Cole	Our Boots	1:58⅘
1942	Alsab (1)	B. James	Requested Sun Again	(dead heat for second)	1:57
1943	Count Fleet (8)	Johnny Longden	Blue Swords	Vincentive	1:57⅖
1944	Pensive (¾)	Conn McCreary	Platter	Stir Up	1:59⅕
1945	Polynesian (2½)	W. D. Wright	Hoop Jr.	Darby Dieppe	1:58⅘
1946	Assault (Neck)	Warren Mehrtens	Lord Boswell	Hampden	2:01⅖
1947	Faultless (1¼)	Doug Dodson	On Trust	Phalanx	1:59
1948	Citation (5½)	Eddie Arcaro	Vulcan's Forge	Boyard	2:02⅖
1949	Capot (Head)	Ted Atkinson	Palestinian	Noble Impulse	1:56
1950	Hill Prince (5)	Eddie Arcaro	Middleground	Dooley	1:59⅕
1951	Bold (7)	Eddie Arcaro	Counterpoint	Alerted	1:56⅖
1952	Blue Man (3½)	Conn McCreary	Jampol	One Count	1:57⅖
1953	Native Dancer (Neck)	Eric Guerin	Jamie K.	Royal Bay Gem	1:57⅘
1954	Hasty Road (Neck)	Johnny Adams	Correlation	Hasseyampa	1:57⅖
1955	Nashua (1)	Eddie Arcaro	Saratoga	Traffic Judge	1:54⅗
1956	Fabius (¾)	Bill Hartack	Needles	No Regrets	1:58⅖
1957	Bold Ruler (2)	Eddie Arcaro	Iron Liege	Inside Tract	1:56⅕
1958	Tim Tam (1½)	I. Valenzuela	Lincoln Road	Gone Fishin'	1:57⅕
1959	Royal Orbit (4)	William Harmatz	Sword Dancer	Dunce	1:57
1960	Bally Ache (4)	Bobby Ussery	Victoria Park	Celtic Ash	1:57⅗
1961	Carry Back (¾)	Johnny Sellers	Globemaster	Crozier	1:57⅗
1962	Greek Money (Nose)	John Rotz	Ridan	Roman Line	1:56⅕
1963	Candy Spots (3½)	Bill Shoemaker	Chateaugay	Never Bend	1:56⅕
1964	Northern Dancer (2¼)	Bill Hartack	The Scoundrel	Hill Rise	1:56⅘
1965	Tom Rolfe (Neck)	Ron Turcotte	Dapper Dan	Hail to All	1:56⅕
1966	Kauai King (1¾)	Don Brumfield	Stupendous	Amberoid	1:55⅖
1967	Damascus (2¼)	Bill Shoemaker	In Reality	Proud Clarion	1:55⅕
1968	Forward Pass (6)	I. Valenzuela	Out of the Way	Nodouble	1:56⅘
1969	Majestic Prince (Head)	Bill Hartack	Arts and Letters	Jay Ray	1:55⅗
1970	Personality (Neck)	Eddie Belmonte	My Dad George	Silent Screen	1:56⅕
1971	Canonero II (1½)	Gustavo Avila	Eastern Fleet	Jim French	1:54
1972	Bee Bee Bee (1¼)	Eldon Nelson	No Le Hace	Key to the Mint	1:55⅗
1973	Secretariat (2½)	Ron Turcotte	Sham	Our Native	1:54⅖

Preakness (Cont.)

Year	Winner (Margin)	Jockey	Second	Third	Time
1974	Little Current (7)	Miguel Rivera	Neapolitan Way	Cannonade	1:54⅗
1975	Master Derby (1)	Darrel McHargue	Foolish Pleasure	Diabolo	1:56⅖
1976	Elocutionist (3)	John Lively	Play the Red	Bold Forbes	1:55
1977	Seattle Slew (1½)	Jean Cruguet	Iron Constitution	Run Dusty Run	1:54⅖
1978	Affirmed (Neck)	Steve Cauthen	Alydar	Believe It	1:54⅖
1979	Spectacular Bid (5½)	Ron Franklin	Golden Act	Screen King	1:54⅕
1980	Codex (4¾)	Angel Cordero Jr.	Genuine Risk	Colonel Moran	1:54⅕
1981	Pleasant Colony (1)	Jorge Velasquez	Bold Ego	Paristo	1:54⅗
1982	Aloma's Ruler (½)	Jack Kaenel	Linkage	Cut Away	1:55⅖
1983	Deputed Testamony (2¾)	Donald Miller Jr.	Desert Wine	High Honors	1:55⅖
1984	Gate Dancer (1½)	Angel Cordero Jr.	Play On	Fight Over	1:53⅗
1985	Tank's Prospect (Head)	Pat Day	Chief's Crown	Eternal Prince	1:53⅖
1986	Snow Chief (4)	Alex Solis	Ferdinand	Broad Brush	1:54⅘
1987	Alysheba (½)	Chris McCarron	Bet Twice	Cryptoclearance	1:55⅘
1988	Risen Star (1¼)	E. Delahoussaye	Brian's Time	Winning Colors	1:56⅕
1989	Sunday Silence (Nose)	Pat Valenzuela	Easy Goer	Rock Point	1:53⅘
1990	Summer Squall (2¼)	Pat Day	Unbridled	Mister Frisky	1:53⅗
1991	Hansel (Head)	Jerry Bailey	Corporate Report	Mane Minister	1:54
1992	Pine Bluff (¾)	Chris McCarron	Alydeed	Casual Lies	1:55⅗
1993	Prairie Bayou (½)	Mike Smith	Cherokee Run	El Bakan	1:56⅗
1994	Tabasco Cat (¾)	Pat Day	Go For Gin	Concern	1:56⅖
1995	Timber Country (½)	Pat Day	Oliver's Twist	Thunder Gulch	1:54⅖
1996	Louis Quatorze (3¼)	Pat Day	Skip Away	Editor's Note	1:53⅖
1997	Silver Charm (Head)	Gary Stevens	Free House	Captain Bodgit	1:54⅖
1998	Real Quiet (2¼)	Kent Desormeaux	Victory Gallop	Classic Cat	1:54⅗
1999	Charismatic (1½)	Chris Antley	Menifee	Badge	1:55⅕
2000	Red Bullet (3¾)	Jerry Bailey	Fusaichi Pegasus	Impeachment	1:56.04
2001	Point Given (2¼)	Gary Stevens	A P Valentine	Congaree	1:55.51
2002	War Emblem (¾)	Victor Espinoza	Magic Weisner	Proud Citizen	1:56.36
2003	Funny Cide (9¾)	Jose Santos	Midway Road	Scrimshaw	1:55.61
2004	Smarty Jones (11½)	Stewart Elliott	Rock Hard Ten	Eddington	1:55.59
2005	Afleet Alex (7)	Jeremy Rose	Scrappy T	Giacomo	1:55.04
2006	Bernardini (5¼)	Javier Castellano	Sweetnorthernsaint	Hemingway's Key	1:54.65
2007	Curlin (Head)	Robby Albarado	Street Sense	Hard Spun	1:53.46
2008	Big Brown (5¼)	Kent Desormeaux	Macho Again	Icabad Crane	1:54.80
2009	Rachel Alexandra (1)	Calvin Borel	Mine That Bird	Musket Man	1:55.08
2010	Lookin at Lucky (1¾)	Martin Garcia	First Dude	Jackson Bend	1:55.47
2011	Shackleford (½)	Jesus Castanon	Animal Kingdom	Astrology	1:56.47
2012	I'll Have Another (Neck)	Mario Gutierrez	Bodemeister	Creative Cause	1:55.94

*Preakness was a two-horse race in 1883, '84 and '89. It was not run 1891–1893; and in 1918, it was run in two divisions.
Note: Distance: 1½ miles (1873–88), 1¼ miles (1889), 1½ miles (1890), 1 1/16 miles (1894–1900), 1 mile and 70 yards (1901–1907), 1 1/16 miles (1908), 1 mile (1909–10), 1⅛ miles (1911–24), 1 3/16 miles (1925–present).

Belmont

Run at Belmont Park, Elmont, NY, three weeks after the Preakness Stakes. Held previously at two locations in the Bronx (NY): Jerome Park (1867–1889) and Morris Park (1890–1904).

Year	Winner (Margin)	Jockey	Second	Third	Time
1867	Ruthless (Head)	J. Gilpatrick	De Courcy	Rivoli	3:05
1868	General Duke (2)	R. Swim	Northumberland	Fannie Ludlow	3:02
1869	Fenian (Unknown)	C. Miller	Glenelg	Invercauld	3:04¼
1870	Kingfisher (½)	E. Brown	Foster	Midday	2:59½
1871	Harry Bassett (3)	W. Miller	Stockwood	By-the-Sea	2:56
1872	Joe Daniels (¾)	James Rowe	Meteor	Shylock	2:58¼
1873	Springbok (4)	James Rowe	Count d'Orsay	Strachino	3:01¾
1874	Saxon (Neck)	G. Barbee	Grinstead	Aaron Pennington	2:39½
1875	Calvin (2)	R. Swim	Aristides	Milner	2:40¼
1876	Algerine (Head)	W. Donahue	Fiddlestick	Barricade	2:40½

Belmont (Cont.)

Year	Winner (Margin)	Jockey	Second	Third	Time
1877	Cloverbrook (1)	C. Holloway	Loiterer	Baden-Baden	2:46
1878	Duke of Magenta (2)	L. Hughes	Bramble	Sparta	2:43½
1879	Spendthrift (5)	S. Evans	Monitor	Jericho	2:42¾
1880	Grenada (½)	L. Hughes	Ferncliffe	Turenne	2:47
1881	Saunterer (Neck)	T. Costello	Eole	Baltic	2:47
1882	Forester (5)	James McLaughlin	Babcock	Wyoming	2:43
1883	George Kinney (2)	James McLaughlin	Trombone	Renegade	2:42½
1884	Panique (½)	James McLaughlin	Knight of Ellerslie	Himalaya	2:42
1885	Tyrant (3½)	Paul Duffy	St. Augustine	Tecumseh	2:43
1886	Inspector B (1)	James McLaughlin	The Bard	Linden	2:41
1887*	Hanover (28-32)	James McLaughlin	Oneko		2:43½
1888*	Sir Dixon (12)	James McLaughlin	Prince Royal		2:40¼
1889	Eric (Head)	W. Hayward	Diable	Zephyrus	2:47
1890	Burlington (1)	S. Barnes	Devotee	Padishah	2:07¾
1891	Foxford (Neck)	E. Garrison	Montana	Laurestan	2:08¾
1892*	Patron (Unknown)	W. Hayward	Shellbark		2:17
1893	Comanche (Head)	Willie Simms	Dr. Rice	Rainbow	1:53¼
1894	Henry of Navarre (2-4)	Willie Simms	Prig	Assignee	1:56½
1895	Belmar (Head)	Fred Taral	Counter Tenor	Nanki Pooh	2:11½
1896	Hastings (Neck)	H. Griffin	Handspring	Hamilton II	2:24½
1897	Scottish Chieftain (1)	J. Scherrer	On Deck	Octagon	2:23¼
1898	Bowling Brook (8)	P. Littlefield	Previous	Hamburg	2:32
1899	Jean Bereaud (Head)	R. R. Clawson	Half Time	Glengar	2:23
1900	Ildrim (Head)	N. Turner	Petrucio	Missionary	2:21½
1901	Commando (½)	H. Spencer	The Parader	All Green	2:21
1902	Masterman (2)	John Bullmann	Ranald	King Hanover	2:22½
1903	Africander (2)	John Bullmann	Whorler	Red Knight	2:23⅕
1904	Delhi (3½)	George Odom	Graziallo	Rapid Water	2:06⅗
1905	Tanya (1/2)	E. Hildebrand	Blandy	Hot Shot	2:08
1906	Burgomaster (4)	L. Lyne	The Quail	Accountant	2:20
1907	Peter Pan (1)	G. Mountain	Superman	Frank Gill	Unknown
1908	Colin (Head)	Joe Notter	Fair Play	King James	Unknown
1909	Joe Madden (8)	E. Dugan	Wise Mason	Donald MacDonald	2:21⅗
1910*	Sweep (6)	J. Butwell	Duke of Ormonde		2:22
1913	Prince Eugene (½)	Roscoe Troxler	Rock View	Flying Fairy	2:18
1914	Luke McLuke (8)	M. Buxton	Gainer	Charlestonian	2:20
1915	The Finn (4)	G. Byrne	Half Rock	Pebbles	2:18⅖
1916	Friar Rock (3)	E. Haynes	Spur	Churchill	2:22
1917	Hourless (10)	J. Butwell	Skeptic	Wonderful	2:17⅘
1918	Johren (2)	Frank Robinson	War Cloud	Cum Sah	2:20⅖
1919	Sir Barton (5)	Johnny Loftus	Sweep On	Natural Bridge	2:17⅖
1920*	Man o' War (20)	Clarence Kummer	Donnacona		2:14⅕
1921	Grey Lag (3)	Earl Sande	Sporting Blood	Leonardo II	2:16⅘
1922	Pillory (2)	C. H. Miller	Snob II	Hea	2:18⅘
1923	Zev (1½)	Earl Sande	Chickvale	Rialto	2:19
1924	Mad Play (2)	Earl Sande	Mr. Mutt	Modest	2:18⅘
1925	American Flag (8)	Albert Johnson	Dangerous	Swope	2:16⅘
1926	Crusader (1)	Albert Johnson	Espino	Haste	2:32⅕
1927	Chance Shot (1½)	Earl Sande	Bois de Rose	Flambino	2:32⅖
1928	Vito (3)	Clarence Kummer	Genie	Diavolo	2:33⅕
1929	Blue Larkspur (¾)	Mack Garner	African	Jack High	2:32⅘
1930	Gallant Fox (3)	Earl Sande	Whichone	Questionnaire	2:31⅗
1931	Twenty Grand (10)	Charles Kurtsinger	Sun Meadow	Jamestown	2:29⅗
1932	Faireno (1½)	T. Malley	Osculator	Flag Pole	2:32⅘
1933	Hurryoff (1½)	Mack Garner	Nimbus	Union	2:32⅗
1934	Peace Chance (6)	W. D. Wright	High Quest	Good Goods	2:29⅕
1935	Omaha (1½)	Willie Saunders	Firethorn	Rosemont	2:30⅗
1936	Granville (Nose)	James Stout	Mr. Bones	Hollyrood	2:30
1937	War Admiral (3)	Charles Kurtsinger	Sceneshifter	Vamoose	2:28⅗
1938	Pasteurized (Neck)	James Stout	Dauber	Cravat	2:29⅖
1939	Johnstown (5)	James Stout	Belay	Gilded Knight	2:29⅗
1940	Bimelech (¾)	F. A. Smith	Your Chance	Andy K	2:29⅗
1941	Whirlaway (2½)	Eddie Arcaro	Robert Morris	Yankee Chance	2:31
1942	Shut Out (2)	Eddie Arcaro	Alsab	Lochinvar	2:29⅕
1943	Count Fleet (25)	Johnny Longden	Fairy Manhurst	Deseronto	2:28⅕

Belmont *(Cont.)*

Year	Winner (Margin)	Jockey	Second	Third	Time
1944	Bounding Home (½)	G. L. Smith	Pensive	Bull Dandy	2:32⅕
1945	Pavot (5)	Eddie Arcaro	Wildlife	Jeep	2:30⅕
1946	Assault (3)	Warren Mehrtens	Natchez	Cable	2:30⅘
1947	Phalanx (5)	R. Donoso	Tide Rips	Tailspin	2:29⅗
1948	Citation (8)	Eddie Arcaro	Better Self	Escadru	2:28⅕
1949	Capot (½)	Ted Atkinson	Ponder	Palestinian	2:30⅕
1950	Middleground (1)	William Boland	Lights Up	Mr. Trouble	2:28⅗
1951	Counterpoint (4)	D. Gorman	Battlefield	Battle Morn	2:29
1952	One Count (2½)	Eddie Arcaro	Blue Man	Armageddon	2:30⅕
1953	Native Dancer (Neck)	Eric Guerin	Jamie K.	Royal Bay Gem	2:38⅗
1954	High Gun (Neck)	Eric Guerin	Fisherman	Limelight	2:30⅘
1955	Nashua (9)	Eddie Arcaro	Blazing Count	Portersville	2:29
1956	Needles (Neck)	David Erb	Career Boy	Fabius	2:29⅘
1957	Gallant Man (8)	Bill Shoemaker	Inside Tract	Bold Ruler	2:26⅗
1958	Cavan (6)	Pete Anderson	Tim Tam	Flamingo	2:30⅕
1959	Sword Dancer (¾)	Bill Shoemaker	Bagdad	Royal Orbit	2:28⅖
1960	Celtic Ash (5½)	Bill Hartack	Venetian Way	Disperse	2:29⅗
1961	Sherluck (2¼)	Braulio Baeza	Globemaster	Guadalcanal	2:29⅕
1962	Jaipur (Nose)	Bill Shoemaker	Admiral's Voyage	Crimson Satan	2:28⅘
1963	Chateaugay (2½)	Braulio Baeza	Candy Spots	Choker	2:30⅕
1964	Quadrangle (2)	Manuel Ycaza	Roman Brother	Northern Dancer	2:28⅖
1965	Hail to All (Neck)	John Sellers	Tom Rolfe	First Family	2:28⅖
1966	Amberold (2½)	William Boland	Buffle	Advocator	2:29⅗
1967	Damascus (2½)	Bill Shoemaker	Cool Reception	Gentleman James	2:28⅘
1968	Stage Door Johnny (1¼)	Hellodoro Gustines	Forward Pass	Call Me Prince	2:27⅕
1969	Arts and Letters (5½)	Braulio Baeza	Majestic Prince	Dike	2:28⅘
1970	High Echelon (¾)	John L. Rotz	Needles N Pins	Naskra	2:34
1971	Pass Catcher (¾)	Walter Blum	Jim French	Bold Reason	2:30⅖
1972	Riva Ridge (7)	Ron Turcotte	Ruritania	Cloudy Dawn	2:28
1973	Secretariat (31)	Ron Turcotte	Twice a Prince	My Gallant	2:24
1974	Little Current (7)	Miguel A. Rivera	Jolly Johu	Cannonade	2:29⅕
1975	Avatar (Neck)	Bill Shoemaker	Foolish Pleasure	Master Derby	2:28⅕
1976	Bold Forbes (Neck)	Angel Cordero Jr.	McKenzie Bridge	Great Contractor	2:29
1977	Seattle Slew (4)	Jean Cruguet	Run Dusty Run	Sanhedrin	2:29⅗
1978	Affirmed (Head)	Steve Cauthen	Alydar	Darby Creek Road	2:26⅘
1979	Coastal (3¼)	Ruben Hernandez	Golden Act	Spectacular Bid	2:28⅗
1980	Temperence Hill (2)	Eddie Maple	Genuine Risk	Rockhill Native	2:29⅘
1981	Summing (Neck)	George Martens	Highland Blade	Pleasant Colony	2:29
1982	Conquistador Cielo (14½)	Laffit Pincay, Jr.	Gato Del Sol	Illuminate	2:28⅕
1983	Caveat (3½)	Laffit Pincay Jr.	Slew o'Gold	Barberstown	2:27⅘
1984	Swale (4)	Laffit Pincay Jr.	Pine Circle	Morning Bob	2:27⅕
1985	Creme Fraiche (½)	Eddie Maple	Stephan's Odyssey	Chief's Crown	2:27
1986	Danzig Connection (1¼)	Chris McCarron	Johns Treasure	Ferdinand	2:29⅘
1987	Bet Twice (14)	Craig Perret	Cryptoclearance	Gulch	2:28⅕
1988	Risen Star (14¾)	Eddie Delahoussaye	Kingpost	Brian's Time	2:26⅖
1989	Easy Goer (8)	Pat Day	Sunday Silence	Le Voyageur	2:26
1990	Go and Go (8¼)	Michael Kinane	Thirty Six Red	Baron de Vaux	2:27⅕
1991	Hansel (Head)	Jerry Bailey	Strike the Gold	Mane Minister	2:28
1992	A.P. Indy (¾)	Eddie Delahoussaye	My Memoirs	Pine Bluff	2:26
1993	Colonial Affair (2¼)	Julie Krone	Kissin Kris	Wild Gale	2:29⅘
1994	Tabasco Cat (2)	Pat Day	Go For Gin	Strodes Creek	2:26⅘
1995	Thunder Gulch (2)	Gary Stevens	Star Standard	Citadeed	2:32
1996	Editor's Note (1)	Rene Douglas	Skip Away	My Flag	2:28⅘
1997	Touch Gold (¾)	Chris McCarron	Silver Charm	Free House	2:28⅘
1998	Victory Gallop (Nose)	Gary Stevens	Real Quiet	Thomas Jo	2:28⅘
1999	Lemon Drop Kid (Head)	Jose Santos	Vision and Verse	Charismatic	2:27⅘
2000	Commendable (1½)	Pat Day	Aptitude	Unshaded	2:31.19
2001	Point Given (12¼)	Gary Stevens	A P Valentine	Monarchos	2:26.56
2002	Sarava (½)	Edgar Prado	Medaglia d'Oro	Sunday Break	2:29.71
2003	Empire Maker (¾)	Jerry Bailey	Ten Most Wanted	Funny Cide	2:28.26
2004	Birdstone (1)	Edgar Prado	Smarty Jones	Royal Assault	2:27.59
2005	Afleet Alex (4¾)	Jeremy Rose	Andromeda's Hero	Nolan's Cat	2:28.75

Belmont *(Cont.)*

Year	Winner (Margin)	Jockey	Second	Third	Time
2006	Jazil (1¼)	Fernando Jara	Bluegrass Cat	Sunriver	2:27.86
2007	Rags to Riches (Head)	John Velazquez	Curlin	Tiago	2:28.74
2008	Da' Tara (5¼)	Alan Garcia	Denis of Cork	Ready's Echo	2:29.65
2009	Summer Bird (2⅝)	Kent Desormeaux	Dunkirk	Mine That Bird	2:27.54
2010	Drosselmeyer (1¾)	Mike Smith	Fly Down	First Dude	2:31.57
2011	Ruler On Ice (¾)	Jose Valdivia Jr.	Stay Thirsty	Brilliant Speed	2:30.88
2012	Union Rags (Neck)	John Velazquez	Paynter	Atigun	2:30.42

*Belmont was a two-horse race in 1887, '88, '92, 1910 and '20; and was not held in 1911–1912.
Note: Distance: 1 mile 5 furlongs (1867–89), 1¼ miles (1890–1905), 1⅜ miles (1906–25), 1½ miles (1926–present).

Triple Crown Winners

Year	Horse	Jockey	Owner	Trainer
1919	Sir Barton	John Loftus	J. K. L. Ross	H. G. Bedwell
1930	Gallant Fox	Earle Sande	Belair Stud	James Fitzsimmons
1935	Omaha	William Saunders	Belair Stud	James Fitzsimmons
1937	War Admiral	Charles Kurtsinger	Samuel D. Riddle	George Conway
1941	Whirlaway	Eddie Arcaro	Calumet Farm	Ben Jones
1943	Count Fleet	John Longden	Mrs J. D. Hertz	Don Cameron
1946	Assault	Warren Mehrtens	King Ranch	Max Hirsch
1948	Citation	Eddie Arcaro	Calumet Farm	Jimmy Jones
1973	Secretariat	Ron Turcotte	Meadow Stable	Lucien Laurin
1977	Seattle Slew	Jean Cruguet	Karen L. Taylor	William H. Turner Jr.
1978	Affirmed	Steve Cauthen	Harbor View Farm	Laz Barrera

Boxing

Heavyweight champion
Wladimir Klitschko easily
disposed of Jean Mark
Mormeck to retain his WBA
and IBF titles

FOR THE RECORD • 2011—2012

Current World Champions†

Division	Weight Limit	WBA Champion	WBC Champion	IBF Champion
Heavyweight	None	Wladimir Klitschko	Vitali Klitschko	Wladimir Klitschko
Cruiserweight	200	Guillermo Jones	Krzysztof Wlodarczyk	Yoan Pablo Hernandez
Light Heavyweight	175	Beibut Shumenov	Chad Dawson	Tavoris Cloud
Super Middleweight	168	Andre Ward	Andre Ward	Carl Froch
Middleweight	160	Felix Sturm	Sergio Gabriel Martinez	Daniel Geale
Super Welterweight	154	Floyd Mayweather Jr.	Saul Alvarez	Cornelius Bundrage
Welterweight	147	Paulie Malignaggi	Floyd Mayweather Jr.	Randall Bailey
Super Lightweight	140	Danny Garcia	Danny Garcia	Lamont Peterson
Lightweight	135	Vacant	Antonio DeMarco	Miguel Vazquez
Super Featherweight	130	Takashi Uchiyama	Takahiro Aoh	Juan Carlos Salgado
Featherweight	126	Chris John	Daniel Ponce De Leon	Billy Dib
Super Bantamweight	122	Guillermo Rigondeaux	Abner Mares	Nonito Donaire
Bantamweight	118	Anselmo Moreno	Shinsuke Yamanaka	Leo Santa Cruz
Super Flyweight	115	Tepparith Kokietgym	Yota Sato	Juan Carlos Sanchez Jr.
Flyweight	112	Hernan Marquez	Toshiyuki Igarashi	Moruti Mthalane
Light Flyweight	108	Roman Gonzalez	Kompayak Porpramook	John Riel Casimero
Strawweight	105	Kazuto Ioka	Vacant	Mario Rodriguez

Note: WBA=World Boxing Association; WBC=World Boxing Council; IBF=International Boxing Federation. Champions as of October 1, 2012. †In divisions in which WBA has designated "super" champion and "regular" champion, list shows "super" champion only. Does not include "interim" title holders.

Title and Major Boxing Matches of Late 2011 and 2012**

Abbreviations: WBC=World Boxing Council; WBA= World Boxing Association; IBF=International Boxing Federation; KO=knockout; TKO=technical knockout; UD=unanimous decision; SD=split decision; MD=majority decision; TD=technical decision; DQ=disqualification; NC=no contest. Bouts from Oct. 1, 2011 to Oct. 1, 2012.

	Date	Winner	Loser	Result	Title/Org.	Site
HEAVYWEIGHT	Dec 3	Alexander Povetkin	Cedric Boswell	KO 8	WBA	Helsinki, Finland
	Feb 18	Vitali Klitschko	Dereck Chisora	UD	WBC	Munich, Germany
	Feb 25	Alexander Povetkin	Marco Huck	MD	WBA	Baden-Wurttemberg, Germany
	Mar 3	Wladimir Klitschko	Jean Marc Mormeck	KO 4	IBF	Dusseldorf, Germany
	July 7	Wladimir Klitschko	Tony Thompson	TKO 6	WBA/IBF	Bern, Switzerland
	Sept 8	Vitali Klitschko	Manuel Charr	TKO 4	WBC	Moscow, Russia
	Sept 29	Alexander Povetkin	Hasim Rahman	TKO 2	WBA	Hamburg, Germany
CRUISERWEIGHT	Nov 5	Guillermo Jones	Michael Marrone	TKO 6	WBA	Hollywood, Florida
	Nov 30	Krzysztof Wlodarczyk	Danny Green	TKO 11	WBC	Mt. Claremont, Australia
	Feb 4	Yoan Pablo Hernandez	Steve Cunningham	UD	IBF	Frankfurt, Germany
	Sep 15	Yoan Pablo Hernandez	Troy Ross	UD	IBF	Bamberg, Germany
LIGHT HEAVYWEIGHT	Oct 15	Chad Dawson	Bernard Hopkins	TKO 2	WBC	Los Angeles, California
	Feb 18	Tavoris Cloud	Gabriel Campillo	SD	IBF	Corpus Christi, Texas
	Apr 28	Chad Dawson	Bernard Hopkins	MD	WBC	Atlantic City, NJ
	June 2	Beibut Shumenov	Enrique Ornelas	UD	WBA	Las Vegas, Nevada
SUPER MIDDLEWEIGHT	Nov 5	Lucian Bute	Glencoffe Johnson	UD	IBF	Quebec City, Canada
	Dec 17	Andre Ward	Carl Froch	UD	WBA/WBC	Atlantic City, New Jersey
	Feb 18	Brian Magee	Rudy Markussen	KO 5	WBA	Brondby, Denmark
	May 26	Carl Froch	Lucian Bute	TKO 5	IBF	Nottingham, England
	Sep 8	Andre Ward	Chad Dawson	TKO 10	WBA/WBC	Oakland, California

**Does not include fights for "interim" titles or WBO title fights.

MIDDLEWEIGHT

Date	Winner	Loser	Result	Title/Org.	Site
Nov 19	Julio Cesar Chavez Jr.	Peter Manfredo Jr.	TKO 5	WBC	Houston, Texas
Dec 2	Felix Sturm	Martin Murray	SD	WBA	Baden-Württemberg, Ger.
Dec 9	Gennady Golovkin	Lajuan Simon	KO 1	WBA	Dusseldorf, Germany
Feb 4	Julio Cesar Chavez Jr.	Marco Antonio Rubio	UD	WBC	San Antonio, Texas
Mar 7	Daniel Geale	Osumanu Adama	UD	IBF	Hobart, Australia
Apr 13	Felix Sturm	Sebastian Zbik	RTD	WBA	Nordrhein-Westfalen, Ger.
May 12	Gennady Golovkin	Makoto Fuchigami	TKO 3	WBA	Brovari, Ukraine
June 16	Julio Cesar Chavez Jr.	Andy Lee	TKO 7	WBC	El Paso, Texas
Sep 1	Daniel Geale	Felix Sturm	SD	IBF	Oberhausen, Germany
Sep 1	Gennady Golovkin	Grzegorz Proska	TKO 5	WBA	Verona, New York
Sep 15	Sergio Gabriel Martinez	Julio Cesar Chavez Jr.	UD	WBC	Las Vegas, Nevada

JR. MIDDLEWT.
(SUPER WELTERT.)

Date	Winner	Loser	Result	Title/Org.	Site
Nov 11	Austin Trout	Frank LoPorto	TKO 6	WBA	El Paso, Texas
Nov 26	Saul Alvarez	Kermit Cintron	TKO 5	WBC	Mexico City, Mexico
Dec 3	Miguel Angel Cotto	Antonio Margarito	TKO 10	WBA	New York, New York
May 5	Floyd Mayweather Jr.	Miguel Angel Cotto	UD	WBA	Las Vegas, Nevada
May 5	Saul Alvarez	Shane Mosley	UD	WBC	Las Vegas, Nevada
June 2	Austin Trout	Delvin Rodriguez	UD	WBA	Carson, California
June 30	Cornelius Bundrage	Cory Spinks	TKO 7	IBF	Indio, California
Sep 15	Saul Alvarez	Josesito Lopez	TKO 5	WBC	Las Vegas, Nevada

WELTERWEIGHT

Date	Winner	Loser	Result	Title/Org.	Site
April 29	Paul Malignaggi	V. Senchenko	TKO 9	WBA	Donetsk, Ukraine
June 9	Randall Bailey	Mike Jones	KO 11	IBF	Las Vegas, Nevada

SUPER LIGHTWEIGHT (JUNIOR WELTERWEIGHT)

Date	Winner	Loser	Result	Title/Org.	Site
Dec 10	Lamont Peterson	Amir Khan	SD	WBA/IBF	Washington, D.C.
Mar 24	Danny Garcia	Erik Morales	UD	WBC	Houston, Texas
Jul 14	Danny Garcia	Amir Khan	TKO 4	WBC	Las Vegas, Nevada

LIGHTWEIGHT

Date	Winner	Loser	Result	Title/Org.	Site
Oct 15	Antonio DeMarco	Jorge Linares	TKO 11	WBC	Los Angeles
Dec 3	Brandon Rios	John Murray	TKO 11	WBA	New York
Jan 21	Miguel Vazquez	Ammeth Diaz	UD	IBF	Guadalajara, Mexico
Feb 14	Brandon Rios	Richard Abril	SD	WBA	Las Vegas, Nevada
Mar 17	Antonio DeMarco	Miguel Roman	KO 5	WBC	Los Mochis, Mexico
Sep 8	Antonio DeMarco	John Molina	TKO 1	WBC	Oakland, California

SUPER FEATHERWEIGHT (JUNIOR LIGHTWEIGHT)

Date	Winner	Loser	Result	Title/Org.	Site
Nov 6	Takahiro Ao	Devis Boschiero	SD	WBC	Tokyo, Japan
Dec 10	Juan Carlos Salgado	Miguel Beltran Jr.	NC	IBF	Los Mochis, Mexico
Dec 31	Takashi Uchiyama	Jorge Solis	TKO 11	WBA	Yokohama, Japan
Apr 6	Takahiro Ao	Terdsak Kokietgym	UD	WBC	Tokyo, Japan
Apr 28	Juan Carlos Salgado	Martin Honorio	MD	IBF	Cancun, Mexico
Jul 16	Takashi Uchiyama	Michael Farenas	TD	WBA	Kasukabe, Japan
Aug 18	Juan Carlos Salgado	Jonathan Barros	UD	IBF	Puebla, Mexico

FEATHERWEIGHT

Date	Winner	Loser	Result	Title/Org.	Site
Oct 14	Celestino Caballero	Jonathan Barros	UD	WBA	Buenos Aires, Argentina
Nov 19	Billy Dib	Alberto Servidei	KO 1	IBF	Sydney, Australia
Nov 30	Chris John	Stanyslav Merdov	UD	WBA	Mt. Claremont, Australia
Dec 3	Jhonny Gonzalez	Roinet Caballero	KO 2	WBC	Mexico City, Mexico
Dec 31	Celestino Caballero	Satoshi Hsono	UD	WBA	Yokohama, Japan
Mar 7	Billy Dib	Eduardo Escobedo	TKO 6	IBF	Hobart, Australia
Apr 28	Jhonny Gonzalez	Elio Rojas	UD	WBC	Cancun, Mexico
May 5	Chris John	Shoji Kimura	UD	WBA	Singapore
Sep 15	Daniel Ponce De Leon	Jhonny Gonzalez	TD	WBC	Las Vegas, Nevada

**Does not include fights for "interim" titles or WBO title fights.

	Date	Winner	Loser	Result	Title/Org.	Site
SUPER BANTAMWEIGHT (JUNIOR FEATHERWEIGHT)	Oct 29	Takalani Ndlovu	Giovanni Caro	SD	IBF	Colima, Mexico
	Jan 20	Guillermo Rigondeaux	Rico Ramos	KO 6	WBA	Las Vegas Nevada
	Apr 21	Abner Mares	Eric Morel	UD	WBC	El Paso, Texas
	Apr 24	Jeffrey Mathebula	Takalani Ndlovu	UD	IBF	Carson, California
	June 9	Guillermo Rigondeaux	Teon Kennedy	TKO 5	WBA	Las Vegas, Nevada
	July 7	Nonito Donaire	Jeffrey Mathebula	UD	IBF	Carson, California
BANTAMWEIGHT	Oct 22	Nonito Donaire	Omar Andres Narvaez	UD	WBC	New York, New York
	Nov 6	Shinsuke Yamanaka	Christian Esquivel	TJO 11	WBC	Tokyo, Japan
	Dec 3	Anselmo Moreno	Vic Darchinyan	UD	WBA	Anaheim, California
	Dec 3	Abner Mares	Joesph Agbeko	UD	IBF	Anaheim, California
	Dec 7	Koki Kameda	Mario Macias	KO 4	WBA	Osaka, Japan
	Apr 4	Koki Kameda	Nouldy Manakane	UD	WBA	Kanagawa, Japan
	Apr 6	Shinsuke Yamanaka	Vic Darchinyan	UD	WBC	Tokyo, Japan
	Apr 21	Anselmo Moreno	David De La Hoya	TKO 9	WBA	El Paso, Texas
	June 2	Leo Santa Cruz	Vusi Malinga	UD	IBF	Carson, California
	Sept 15	Leo Santa Cruz	Eric Morel	TKO 5	IBF	Las Vegas, Nevada
SUPER FLYWEIGHT (JUNIOR BANTAMWEIGHT)	Oct 8	Roberto Guerrero	Raul Martinez	TD	IBF	Tijuana, Mexico
	Nov 4	Suriyan Sor Rungvisai	Nobuo Nashiro	UD	WBC	Bangkok, Thailand
	Feb 11	Juan Carlos Sanchez Jr	Roberto Guerrero	UD	IBF	Los Mochis, Mexico
	Mar 27	Yota Sato	S. Sor Rungvisai	UD	WBC	Tokyo, Japan
	Apr 4	Tepparith Kokietgym	Tomonobu Shimizu	TKO 9	WBA	Yokohama, Japan
	May 19	Juan Carlos Sanchez Jr	Juan Alberto Rosas	UD	IBF	Puerto Vallarta, Mexico
	Jul 8	Yota Sato	Sylvester Lopez	UD	WBC	Yokohama, Japan
	Sep 1	Tepparith Kokietgym	Nobuo Nashiro	MD	WBA	Osaka, Japan
FLYWEIGHT	Oct 21	Pong. Wonjongkam	Edgar Sosa	UD	WBC	Bangkok, Thailand
	Oct 28	Moruti Mthalane	Andrea Sarritzu	TKO 7	IBF	Cagliari, Italy
	Oct 29	Hernan Marquez	Luis Concepcion	TKO 1	WBA	Hermosillo, Mexico
	Dec 23	Pong. Wonjongkam	Hirofumi Mukai	D	WBC	Bangkok, Thailand
	Mar 2	Sonny Boy Jaro	Pong. Wonjongkam	KO 6	WBC	Chonburi, Thailand
	Jul 16	Toshiyuki Igarashi	Sonny Boy Jaro	SD	WBC	Kasukabe, Japan
	Sep 1	Moruti Mthalane	Ricardo Nunez	TKO 8	IBF	Panama City, Panama
LIGHT FLYWEIGHT (JUNIOR FLYWEIGHT)	Dec 23	K. Porpramook	Adrian Hernandez	KO 10	WBC	Bangkok, Thailand
	Feb 10	John Riel Casimero	Luis Alberto Lazarte	TKO 10	IBF	Buenos Aires, Argentina
	Apr 28	Roman Gonzalez	Ramon G. Hirales	TKO 4	WBA	Pomona, California
	May 3	K. Porpramook	Jonathan Taconing	TD	WBC	Buriram, Thailand
	Aug 4	John Riel Casimero	Pedro Guevara	SD	IBF	Mazatlan, Mexico
STRAWWEIGHT (MINI FLYWT.) (MINIMUM WT.)	Oct 24	Akira Yaegashi	P. Porpramook	TKO 10	WBA	Tokyo, Japan
	Dec 31	Kazuto Ioka	Y.T. Chalermchai	TKO 1	WBC	Osaka, Japan
	Mar 30	Nkosinathi Joyi	Katsunari Takayama	UD	IBF	East London, South Africa
	Jun 20	Kazuto Ioka	Akira Yaegashi	UD	WBA	Osaka, Japan
	Sep 1	Mario Rodriguez	Nkosinathi Joyi	KO 7	IBF	Guasave, Mexico

**Does not include fights for "interim" titles or WBO title fights.

World Champions**

Sanctioning bodies: the National Boxing Association (NBA), the New York State Athletic Commission (NY), the World Boxing Association (WBA), the World Boxing Council (WBC), and the International Boxing Federation (IBF).

Heavyweights (Weight: Unlimited)

Champion	Reign	Champion	Reign	Champion	Reign	Champion	Reign
John L. Sullivan*	1885–92	Muhammad Ali*	1964–70†	Trevor Berbick WBC	1986	Hasim Rahman* WBC,	
James J. Corbett*	1892–97	Ernie Terrell WBA	1965–67	Mike Tyson WBC	1986–87	IBF	2001–05
Bob Fitzsimmons*	1897–99	Joe Frazier* NY	1968–70	James Smith WBA	1986–87	Chris Byrd IBF	2002–06
James J. Jeffries*	1899–05†	Jimmy Ellis WBA	1968–70	Tony Tucker IBF	1987	Roy Jones Jr. WBA	2003–05
Marvin Hart*	1905–06	Joe Frazier*	1970–73	Mike Tyson*	1987–90	Lennox Lewis* WBC	2001–04
Tommy Burns*	1906–08	George Foreman*	1973–74	Buster Douglas*	1990	John Ruiz, WBA	2003–05
Jack Johnson*	1908–15	Muhammad Ali*	1974–78	Evander Holyfield*	1990–92	Vitali Klitschko WBC	2004–05
Jess Willard*	1915–19	Leon Spinks*	1978	Lennox Lewis WBC	1993–95	Hasim Rahman WBC	2005–06
Jack Dempsey*	1919–26	Ken Norton WBC	1978	Riddick Bowe*	1992–93	Nikolay Valuev WBA	2005–07
Gene Tunney*	1926–28†	Larry Holmes WBC	1978–80	Evander Holyfield*	1993–94	Oleg Maskaev WBC	2006–08
Max Schmeling*	1930–32	Muhammad Ali*	1978–79†	Michael Moorer*	1994	Wladimir Klitschko.	
Jack Sharkey*	1932–33	John Tate WBA	1979–80	George Foreman*	1994–95	IBF/WBA	2006–
Primo Carnera*	1933–34	Mike Weaver WBA	1980–82	Oliver McCall WBC	1995	Ruslan Chagaev WBA	2007–08
Max Baer*	1934–35	Larry Holmes*	1980–85	Frank Bruno WBC	1995–96	Samuel Peter WBC	2008
James J. Braddock*	1935–37	Michael Dokes WBA	1982–83	Bruce Seldon WBA	1995–96	Nikolai Valuev WBA	2008–09
Joe Louis*	1937–49†	Gerrie Coetzee WBA	1983–84	Mike Tyson WBA	1996	Vitali Klitschko WBC	2008–
Ezzard Charles*	1949–51	Tim Witherspoon		Michael Moorer IBF	1996–97	David Haye WBA	2009–11
Jersey Joe Walcott*	1951–52	WBC	1984	Shannon Briggs*	1997–98	Alexander Povetkin	
Rocky Marciano*	1952–56†	Pinklon Thomas WBC	1984–86	Lennox Lewis* WBC	1997–01	WBA	2011–
Floyd Patterson*	1956–59	Greg Page WBA	1984–85	E. Holyfield WBA, IBF	1996–99		
Ingemar Johansson*	1959–60	Michael Spinks*	1985–87	Lennox Lewis	1999–01		
Floyd Patterson*	1960–62	Tim Witherspoon		E. Holyfield WBA	2000–01		
Sonny Liston*	1962–64	WBA	1986	John Ruiz WBA	2001–03		

Cruiserweights (Weight Limit: 200 pounds)

Champion	Reign	Champion	Reign	Champion	Reign	Champion	Reign
Marvin Camel* WBC	1980	Evander Holyfield*	1988†	Imamu Mayfield IBF	1997–98	David Haye WBC	2007–08
Carlos De Leon* WBC	1980–82	Toufik Belbouli WBA	1989	Fabrice Tiozzo WBA	1997–00	David Haye WBA	2007–08†
Ossie Ocasio WBA	1982–84	Robert Daniels WBA	1989–91	J.C. Gomez* WBC	1998–02†	Giacobbe Fragomeni	
S.T. Gordon* WBC	1982–83	Carlos De Leon* WBC	1989–90	Arthur Williams IBF	1998–99	WBC	2008–09
Carlos De Leon* WBC	1983–85	Glenn McCrory IBF	1989–90	Vassiliy Girov* IBF	1999–03	Tomasz Adamek IBF	2008–09†
Marvin Camel IBF	1983–84	Jeff Lampkin IBF	1990	Virgil Hill WBA	2000–02	Zsolt Erdei WBC	2009–10
Lee Roy Murphy IBF	1984–86	M. Duran* WBC	1990–91	Wayne Braithwaite		Guillermo Jones	
Piet Crous WBA	1984–85	Bobby Czyz WBA	1991–92†	WBC	2002–05	WBA	2009–
Alfonso Ratliff*		Anaclet Wamba* WBC	1991–95†	J.M. Mormeck WBA	2002–06	Kryzysztof Wlodarczyk	
WBC	1985	James Pritchard IBF	1991	James Toney* IBF	2003	WBC	2010–
Dwight Braxton WBA	1985–86	James Warring IBF	1991–92	Melvin Davis IBF	2004–05	Steve Cunningham,	
Bernard Benton* WBC	1985–86	Alfred Cole IBF	1992–96	J.M. Mormeck WBC	2005–06	IBF	2010–11
Carlos De Leon* WBC	1986–88	Orlin Norris WBA	1993–95	O'Neil Bell IBF	2005–06	Yoan Pablo Hernandez,	
Evander Holyfield*		Nate Miller WBA	1995–97	O'Neil Bell WBC/WBA	2006–07	IBF	2011–
WBA	1986–88	M. Dominguez*		Steve Cunningham			
Ricky Parkey IBF	1986–87	WBC	1996–98	IBF	2006–08		
Evander Holyfield*		A. Washington IBF	1996–97	J.M. Mormeck			
WBA, IBF	1987–88	Uriah Grant IBF	1997	WBC/WBA	2007		

*Lineal champion. †Champion relinquished title to retire or switch weight classes, or had title stripped by boxing organization.
**In case of WBA, includes both "super" and "regular" champions. Does not include interim or WBO title holders.

Light Heavyweights (Weight Limit: 175 pounds)

Champion	Reign	Champion	Reign	Champion	Reign	Champion	Reign
Jack Root*	1903	Jose Torres*	1965–66	Bobby Czyz IBF	1986–87	Silvio Branco WBA	2003–04
George Gardner*	1903	Dick Tiger*	1966–68	Leslie Stewart WBA	1987	Antonio Tarver	
Bob Fitzsimmons*	1903–05	Bob Foster*	1968–74†	Virgil Hill* WBA	1987–91	WBC, IBF	2003
Jack O'Brien*	1905–12†	Vicente Rondon WBA	1971–72	Pr Charles Williams		Roy Jones Jr. WBC	2003
Jack Dillon*	1914–16	John Conteh WBC	1974–77	IBF	1987–93	Glencoffe Johnson	
Battling Levinsky*	1916–20	Victor Galindez* WBA	1974–78	Thomas Hearns WBC	1987†	IBF	2004–05
Georges Carpentier*	1920–22	Miguel A. Cuello WBC	1977–78	Donny Lalonde WBC	1987–88	Fabrice Tiozzo WBA	2004–05
Battling Siki*	1922–23	Mate Parlov WBC	1978	Sugar Ray Leonard		Antonio Tarver* WBC	2004–05
Mike McTigue*	1923–25	Mike Rossman*		WBC	1988	Silvio Branco WBA	2005–07
Paul Berlenbach*	1925–26	WBA	1978–79	Dennis Andries WBC	1989	Clinton Woods IBF	2005–08
Jack Delaney*	1926–27†	Marvin Johnson*		Jeff Harding WBC	1989–90	Tomasz Adamek WBC	2005–07
Jimmy Slattery NBA	1927	WBC	1978–79	Dennis Andries WBC	1990–91	Stipe Drews WBA	2007
Tommy Loughran*	1927–29†	Victor Galindez*		Thomas Hearns* WBA	1991–92	Chad Dawson WBC	2007–08
Maxie Rosenbloom*	1930–34	WBA	1979	Jeff Harding WBC	1991–94		2008–09†
George Nichols NBA	1932	M.S. Muhammad*		Iran Barkley* WBA	1992	Danny Green WBA	2007–08
Bob Godwin NBA	1933	WBC	1979–81	Virgil Hill* WBA	1992–97	Hugo Garay WBA	2008–09
Bob Olin*	1934–35	Marvin Johnson		Henry Maske IBF	1993–96	Antonio Tarver IBF	2008
John Henry Lewis*	1935–38†	WBA	1979–80	Mike McCallum WBC	1994–95	Adrian Diaconu WBC	2008–09
Melio Bettina	1939	E.M. Muhammad*		Fabrice Tiozzo WBC	1995–96	Gabriel Campillo WBA	2009–10
Billy Conn*	1939–40†	WBA	1980–81	D. Michalczewski*		Jean Pascal WBC	2009–11
Anton Christoforidis	1941	Michael Spinks* WBA	1981–83	IBF	1997†	Tavoris Cloud IBF	2009–
Gus Lesnevich*	1941–48	Dwight Qawi WBC	1981–83	Roy Jones Jr.		Beibut Shumenov,	
Freddie Mills*	1948–50	Michael Spinks*	1983–85†	WBC, WBA	1997–03	WBA	2010–
Joey Maxim*	1950–52	J. B. Williamson WBC	1985–86	William Guthrie IBF	1997–98	Bernard Hopkins,	
Archie Moore*	1952–62†	Slobodan Kacar IBF	1985–86	Reggie Johnson IBF	1998–99	WBC	2011
Harold Johnson NBA	1961	Marvin Johnson*		Roy Jones Jr.*	1999–03	Chad Dawson WBC	2011–
Harold Johnson*	1962–63	WBA	1986–87	Bruno Girard WBA	2001–03		
Willie Pastrano*	1963–65	Dennis Andries WBC	1986–87	Mehdi Sahnoune			
				WBA	2003		

Super Middleweights (Weight Limit: 168 pounds)

Champion	Reign	Champion	Reign	Champion	Reign	Champion	Reign
Murray Sutherland*		Nigel Benn WBC	1992–96	Markus Beyer WBC	1999–00	Mikkel Kessler WBC	2006–07
IBF	1984	James Toney IBF	1992–94	Bruno Girard* WBA	2000–01†	Robert Stieglitz IBF	2007
Chong-Pal Park* IBF	1984–87	Michael Nunn* WBA	1992–94	Glenn Catley WBC	2000–01	Alejandro Berrio IBF	2007
Chong-Pal Park* WBA	1987–88	Steve Little* WBA	1994	Eric Lucas WBC	2000–03	Joe Calzaghe, WBC	2007–08
G. Rocchigiani IBF	1988–89	Frank Liles* WBA	1994–99	Byron Mitchell WBA	2000–03	Lucian Bute IBF	2007–12
F. Obelmejias* WBA	1988–89	Roy Jones Jr. IBF	1994–96	Sven Ottke WBA	2003†	Joe Calzaghe WBA	2007–08
Sugar Ray Leonard		Thulane Malinga WBC	1996	Anthony Mundine WBA	2003	Carl Froch WBC	2008–10
WBC	1988–90†	V. Nardiello WBC	1996	Markus Beyer WBC	2003–04	Mikkel Kessler WBA	2008–09
In-Chul Baek* WBA	1989–90	Robin Reid WBC	1996–97	Sven Ottke, IBF	2003–05	Andre Ward‡ WBA	2009–
Lindell Holmes IBF	1990–91	Charles Brewer IBF	1997–98	Cristian Sanavia WBC	2004	Mikkel Kessler WBA	2010†
Chris Tiozzo* WBA	1990–91	Thulane Malinga		Manny Siaca, WBA	2004	Carl Froch WBC	2011
Mauro Galvano WBC	1990–92	WBC	1997–98	Mikel Kessler WBA	2004–07	Andre Ward WBC	2011–
Victor Cordova* WBA	1991	Richie Woodhall WBC	1998–99	Markus Beyer WBC	2004–06	Carl Froch IBF	2012–
Darrin Van Horn IBF	1991–92	Sven Ottke IBF	1998–03	Jeff Lacy IBF	2005		
Iran Barkley IBF	1992	Byron Mitchell* WBA	1999–00	Joe Calzaghe IBF	2006–07		

---

*Lineal champion. ‡ Super champion. †Champion relinquished title to retire or switch weight classes, or had title stripped by boxing organization.
**In case of WBA, includes both "super" and "regular" champions. Does not include interim or WBO title holders.

Middleweights (Weight Limit: 160 pounds)

Champion	Reign	Champion	Reign	Champion	Reign	Champion	Reign
Jack Dempsey*	1884–91	Marcel Cerdan*	1948–49	Alan Minter*	1980	Hassine Cherifi WBC	1998–99
Bob Fitzsimmons*	1891–97†	Jake La Motta*	1949–51	Marvin Hagler*	1980–87	Keith Holmes WBC	1999–00
Kid McCoy*	1897–98	Sugar Ray Robinson*	1951	Sugar Ray Leonard*	1987†	Felix Trinidad WBA	2001
Tommy Ryan*	1898–07†	Randy Turpin*	1951	Frank Tate IBF	1987–88	William Joppy WBA	2001–03
Stanley Ketchel*	1908	Sugar Ray Robinson*	1951–52†	Sumbu Kalambay		Bernard Hopkins*	
Billy Papke*	1908	Bobo Olson*	1953–55	WBA	1987–89	WBC/IBF	2001–05
Stanley Ketchel*	1908–10†	Sugar Ray Robinson*	1955–57	Thomas Hearns*		Bernard Hopkins WBA	2003–05
Frank Klaus*	1913	Gene Fullmer*	1957	WBC	1987–88	Jermain Taylor IBF	2005
George Chip*	1913–14	Sugar Ray Robinson*	1957	Iran Barkley* WBC	1988–89	Jermain Taylor WBA	2005–06
Al McCoy*	1914–17	Carmen Basilio*	1957–58	Michael Nunn IBF	1988–91	Jermain Taylor WBC	2005–07
Mike O'Dowd*	1917–20	Sugar Ray Robinson*	1958–60	Roberto Duran* WBC	1989–90†	Arthur Abraham IBF	2005–09†
Johnny Wilson*	1920–23	Gene Fullmer NBA	1959–62	Mike McCallum WBA	1989–91	Felix Sturm WBA	2006
Harry Greb*	1923–26	Paul Pender*	1960–61	Julian Jackson WBA	1990–93	Javier Castillejo WBA	2006–07
Tiger Flowers*	1926	Terry Downes*	1961–62	Michael Nunn* IBF	1991	Felix Sturm WBA	2007–
Mickey Walker*	1926–31†	Paul Pender*	1962–63†	James Toney* IBF	1991–93†	Kelly Pavlik WBC	2007–10
Gorilla Jones*	1931–32	Dick Tiger WBA	1962–63	Reggie Johnson WBA	1992–94	Sebastian Sylvester	
Marcel Thil*	1932–37	Dick Tiger*	1963	Roy Jones Jr.* IBF	1993–95†	IBF	2009–11
Fred Apostoli*	1937–39	Joey Giardello*	1963–65	G. McClellan WBC	1993–95†	Sergio Gabriel Martinez,	
Al Hostak NBA	1938	Dick Tiger*	1965–66	Jorge Castro WBA	1994–95	WBC	2010–11†
Solly Krieger NBA	1938–39	Emile Griffith*	1966–67	Bernard Hopkins*		Sebastian Zbik WBC	2011
Al Hostak NBA	1939–40	Nino Benvenuti*	1967	IBF	1994–	Julio Cesar Chavez Jr.,	
Ceferino Garcia*	1939–40	Emile Griffith*	1967–68	Shinji Takehara WBA	1995–96	WBC	2011–12
Ken Overlin*	1940–41	Nino Benvenuti*	1968–70	Jullian Jackson WBC	1995	Gennady Golovkin,	
Tony Zale NBA	1940–41	Carlos Monzon*	1970–77†	Quincy Taylor WBC	1995–96	WBA	2011–
Billy Soose*	1941	Rodrigo Valdez WBC	1974–76	Keith Holmes WBC	1996–98	Daniel Geale IBF	2011–
Tony Zale*	1941–47	Rodrigo Valdez*	1977–78	William Joppy WBA	1996–97	Sergio Gabriel Martinez,	
Rocky Graziano*	1947–48	Hugo Corro*	1978–79	J.C. Green WBA	1997	WBC	2012–
Tony Zale*	1948	Vito Antuofermo*	1979–80	William Joppy WBA	1998–01		

Junior Middleweights (Weight Limit: 154 pounds)

Champion	Reign	Champion	Reign	Champion	Reign	Champion	Reign
Emile Griffith (EBU)	1962–63	Roberto Duran WBA	1983–84	Terry Norris* WBC	1995–97	Oscar De La Hoya	
Dennis Moyer*	1962–63	Mark Medal IBF	1984	Terry Norris* IBF	1995–96†	WBC	2006–07
Ralph Dupas*	1963	Thomas Hearns*	1984–86†	L. Boudouani WBA	1996–99	Cory Spinks IBF	2006–08
Sandro Mazzinghi*	1963–65	Mike McCallum*		Raul Marquez IBF	1997	Travis Simms WBA	2007
Nino Benvenuti*	1965–66	WBA	1984–87†	Keith Mullings* WBC	1997–99	Floyd Mayweather Jr.	
Ki-Soo Kim*	1966–68	Carlos Santos IBF	1984–86	Yori Boy Campas IBF	1997–98	WBC	2007
Sandro Mazzinghi*	1968	Buster Drayton IBF	1986–87	Fernando Vargas IBF	1998–00	Joachim Alcine WBA	2007–08
Freddie Little*	1969–70	Duane Thomas		F. Javier Castillejo*		Vernon Forrest WBC	2007–08
Carmelo Bossi*	1970–71	WBC	1986–87	WBC	1999–01	Sergio Mora WBC	2008
Koichi Wajima*	1971–74	Matthew Hilton IBF	1987–88	David Reid WBA	1999–01	Verno Phillips IBF	2008†
Oscar Albarado*	1974–75	Lupe Aquino WBC	1987	Felix Trinidad WBA	2000–01	Daniel Santos WBA	2008–09
Koichi Wajima*	1975	Gianfranco Rosi		Felix Trinidad		Vernon Forrest	
Miguel de Oliveira WBC	1975–76	WBC	1987–88	WBA, IBF	2001†	WBC	2008–09
Jae-Do Yuh*	1975–76	Julian Jackson WBA	1987–90	Oscar De La Hoya*		Cory Spinks IBF	2009–10
Elisha Obed WBC	1975–76	Donald Curry WBC	1988–89	WBC	2001–03	Sergio Gabriel Martinez	
Koichi Wajima*	1976	Robert Hines IBF	1988–89	Fernando Vargas		WBC	2009–10†
Jose Duran*	1976	Darrin Van Horn IBF	1989	WBA	2001–02	Yuri Foreman WBA	2009–10
Eckhard Dagge WBC	1976–77	Rene Jacquot WBC	1989	Ronald Wright IBF†	2001–04	Miguel Cotto WBA‡	2010–
Miguel Angel		John Mugabi* WBC	1989–90	Oscar De La Hoya*		Manny Pacquiao WBC	2010–11†
Castellini*	1976–77	Gianfranco Rosi IBF	1989–94	WBC/WBA	2002–03	Saul Alvarez WBC	2011–
Eddie Gazo*	1977–78	Terry Norris* WBC	1990–93	Shane Mosley* WBC	2003–04	Austin Trout WBA	2011–
Rocky Mattioli WBC	1977–79	Gilbert Dele WBA	1991	Alejandro Garcia WBA	2003–05	Cornelius Bundrage	
Masashi Kudo*	1978–79	Vinny Pazienza		Ronald Wright		IBF	2011–
Maurice Hope WBC	1979–81	WBA	1991–92	WBA/WBC	2004–05	Miguel Angel Cotto	
Ayub Kalule*	1979–81	Julio C. Vasquez WBA	1992–94	Verno Phillips IBF	2004–05	WBA	2011
Wilfred Benitez WBC	1981–82	Simon Brown* WBC	1993–94	Ricardo Mayora		Floyd Mayweather Jr.	
Sugar Ray Leonard*	1981–82†	Terry Norris* WBC	1994	WBC	2005–06	WBA	2012–
Tadashi Mihara WBA	1981–82	Vincent Pettway IBF	1994–95	Alex T. Garcia WBA	2005–06		
Davey Moore WBA	1982–83	Luis Santana* WBC	1995–95	Roman Karmazin			
Thomas Hearns*		Paul Vaden IBF	1995	IBF	2005–06		
WBC	1982–84	Carl Daniels WBA	1995	Jose A. Rivera WBA	2006–07		

*Lineal champion. ‡Super champion. †Champion relinquished title to retire or switch weight classes, or had title stripped by boxing organization.
**In case of WBA, includes both "super" and "regular" champions. Does not include interim or WBO title holders.

Welterweights (Weight Limit: 147 pounds)

Champion	Reign	Champion	Reign	Champion	Reign	Champion	Reign
Paddy Duffy*	1888–90†	Jimmy McLarnin*	1934–35	Sugar Ray Leonard*	1980–82†	Andrew Lewis WBA	2001–02
Mysterious Billy Smith*		Barney Ross*	1935–38	Donald Curry* WBA	1983–85	Vernon Forrest IBF	2001
	1892–94	Henry Armstrong*	1938–40	Milton McCrory		Vernon Forrest* WBC	2001–03
Tommy Ryan*	1894–98†	Fritzie Zivic*	1940–41	WBC	1983–85	Ricardo Mayorga	
Mysterious Billy Smith*		Red Cochrane*	1941–46	Donald Curry*	1985–86	WBA	2002
	1898–1900	Marty Servo*	1946	Lloyd Honeyghan*	1986–87	Michele Piccirillo IBF	2002–03
Rube Ferns*	1900	Sugar Ray		Jorge Vaca* WBC	1987–88	Ricardo Mayorga*	
Matty Matthews*	1900–01	Robinson*	1946–51†	Mark Breland WBA	1987	WBC	2003–05
Rube Ferns*	1901	Johnny Bratton*	1951	Marlon Starling		Jose Rivera WBA	2003
Joe Walcott*	1901–04	Kid Gavilan*	1951–54	WBA	1987–88	Cory Spinks	
The Dixie Kid*	1904–05†	Johnny Saxton*	1954–55	Lloyd Honeyghan*		IBF, WBC, WBA	2003–05
Honey Mellody*	1906–07	Tony DeMarco*	1955	WBC	1988–89	Zab Judah	
Mike Sullivan*	1907–08†	Carmen Basilio*	1955–56	Tomas Molinares		WBA/WBC/IBF	2005–06
Jimmy Gardner*	1908†	Johnny Saxton*	1956	WBA	1988–89	Luis Collazo WBA	2006
Jimmy Clabby*	1910–11†	Carmen Basilio*	1956–57†	Simon Brown IBF	1988–91	Ricky Hatton WBA	2006
Waldemar Holberg*	1914	Virgil Akins*	1958	Mark Breland WBA	1989–90	Carlos Baldomir WBC	2006
Tom McCormick*	1914	Don Jordan*	1958–60	Marlon Starling*		F. Mayweather, Jr. IBF	2006
Matt Wells*	1914–15	Kid Paret*	1960–61	WBC	1989–90	Miguel Cotto WBA	2006–08
Mike Glover*	1915	Emile Griffith*	1961	Aaron Davis WBA	1990–91	F. Mayweather Jr.	
Jack Britton*	1915	Kid Paret*	1961–62	Maurice Blocker*		WBC	2006–08
Ted "Kid" Lewis*	1915–16	Emile Griffith*	1962–63	WBC	1990–91	Kermit Cintron IBF	2006–08
Jack Britton*	1916–17	Luis Rodriguez*	1963	Meldrick Taylor WBA	1991–92	A. Margarito IBF	2008
Ted "Kid" Lewis*	1917–19	Emile Griffith*	1963–66†	Simon Brown* WBC	1991	Joshua Clottey IBF	2008–09†
Jack Britton*	1919–22	Curtis Cokes*	1966–69	Buddy McGirt* WBC	1991–93	Ant. Margarito WBA	2008–09
Mickey Walker*	1922–26	Jose Napoles*	1969–70	Crisanto Espana		Andre Berto WBC	2008–11
Pete Latzo*	1926–27	Billy Backus*	1970–71	WBA	1992–94	Shane Mosley WBA	2009
Joe Dundee*	1927–29	Jose Napoles*	1971–75	Felix Trinidad IBF	1993–00	Isaac Hlatshwayo IBF	2009
Jackie Fields*	1929–30	Hedgemon Lewis NY	1972–73	Pernell Whitaker*		Vyacheslav Senchenko	
Young		Angel Espada WBA	1975–76	WBC	1993–97		2009–12
Jack Thompson*	1930	John H. Stracey*	1975–76	Ike Quartey WBA	1994–97†	Dejan Zavec IBF	2009–11
Tommy Freeman*	1930–31	Carlos Palomino*	1976–79	Oscar De La Hoya*		Victor Ortz WBC	2011
Young		Pipino Cuevas WBA	1976–80	WBC	1997–99	F. Mayweather Jr.,	
Jack Thompson*	1931	Wilfredo Benitez*	1979	James Page WBA	1998–01	WBC	2011–
Lou Brouillard*	1931–32	Sugar Ray Leonard*	1979–80	Felix Trinidad*		Andre Berto IBF	2011†
Jackie Fields*	1932–33	Roberto Duran*	1980	IBF, WBC	1999–00†	Randall Bailey IBF	2012–
Young Corbett III*	1933	Thomas Hearns		Shane Mosley*		Paul Malignaggi WBA	2012–
Jimmy McLarnin*	1933–34	WBA	1980–81	WBA	2000–02		
Barney Ross*	1934						

Super Lightweights (Weight Limit: 140 pounds)

Champion	Reign	Champion	Reign	Champion	Reign	Champion	Reign
Pinkey Mitchell*	1922–25	Perico Fernandez		Joe Louis Manley		Julio César Chávez*	
Red Herring*	1925	WBC	1974–75	IBF	1986–87	WBC	1994–96
Mushy Callahan*	1926–30	S. Muangsurin WBC	1975–76	Terry Marsh IBF	1987	Kostya Tszyu IBF	1995–97
Jack (Kid) Berg*	1930–31	Wilfred Benitez*	1976–79†	Juan Coggi WBA	1987–90	Frankie Randall WBA	1996–97
Tony Canzoneri*	1931–32	M. Velasquez WBC	1976	Rene Arredondo WBC	1987	Oscar De La Hoya*	
Johnny Jadick*	1932–33	S. Muangsurin WBC	1976–78	R. Mayweather* WBC	1987–89	WBC	1996–97†
Sammy Fuller*	1932–33	A. Cervantes WBA	1977–80	James McGirt IBF	1988	Khalid Rahilou WBA	1997–98
Battling Shaw*	1933	Sang-Hyun Kim WBC	1978–80	Meldrick Taylor IBF	1988–90	Vincent Phillips* IBF	1997–99
Tony Canzoneri*	1933	Saoul Mamby WBC	1980–82	Julio César Chávez*		Sharmba Mitchell	
Barney Ross*	1933–35†	Aaron Pryor* WBA	1980–83	WBC	1989–94	WBA	1998–01
Tippy Larkin*	1946	Leroy Haley WBC	1982–83	Julio César Chávez*		Kostya Tszyu WBC	1998–04
Carlos Ortiz*	1959–60	Aaron Pryor* IBF	1983–85†	IBF	1990–91	Terronn Millett* IBF	1999–00
Duilio Loi*	1960–62	Bruce Curry WBC	1983–84	Loreto Garza WBA	1990–91	Zab Judah* IBF	2000–01
Eddie Perkins*	1962	Johnny Bumphus		Juan Coggi WBA	1991	KostyaTszyu*†	
Duilio Loi*	1962–63†	WBA	1984	Edwin Rosario WBA	1991–92	WBA	2001–03
Roberto Cruz WBA	1963	Bill Costello WBC	1984–85	Rafael Pineda IBF	1991–92	Kostya Tszyu* IBF	2003–05
Eddie Perkins*	1963–65	Gene Hatcher WBA	1984–85	Akinobu Hiranaka		Vivian Harris WBA	2003–05
Carlos Hernandez*	1965–66	Ubaldo Sacco WBA	1985–86	WBA	1992	Arturo Gatti WBC	2004–05
Sandro Lopopolo*	1966–67	Lonnie Smith* WBC	1985–86	Pernell Whitaker IBF	1992–93†	F. Mayweather Jr.	
Paul Fujii*	1967–68	Patrizio Oliva WBA	1986–87	Charles Murray IBF	1993–94	WBC	2005–06
Nicolino Loche*	1968–72	Gary Hinton IBF	1986	Juan Coggi WBA	1993–94	Carlos Maussa	
Pedro Adigue WBC	1968–70	Rene Arredondo*		Jake Rodriguez IBF	1994–95	WBA	2005–06
Bruno Arcari WBC	1970–74	WBC	1986	Frankie Randall* WBC	1994	Ricky Hatton IBF	2005–06
Alfonso Frazer*	1972	Tsuyoshi Hamada		Frankie Randall WBA	1994–96	Souleymane M'baye	
Antonio Cervantes*	1972–76	WBC	1986–87	Juan Coggi WBA	1996	WBA	2006–07

*Lineal champion. †Champion relinquished title to retire or switch weight classes, or had title stripped by boxing organization.
**In case of WBA, includes both "super" and "regular" champions. Does not include interim or WBO title holders.

Super Lightweights (Cont.)

Champion	Reign	Champion	Reign	Champion	Reign	Champion	Reign
Juan Urango IBF	2006–07	Timothy Bradley		Devon Alexander,		Lamont Peterson /IBF	2011–
Junior Witter WBC	2006–08	WBC	2008–09	IBF	2010†	Danny Garcia	
Gavin Rees WBA	2007–08	Andreas Kotelnik		Marcos Maidana WBA	2010	WBA/WBC	2012–
Ricky Hatton IBF	2007	WBA	2008–09	Zab Judah IBF	2011		
Lovemore N'Dou		Devon Alexander		Timothy Bradley			
IBF	2007	WBC	2009–11	WBC	2011†		
Paul Malignaggi		Amir Khan WBA‡	2009–	Erik Morales WBC	2011–12		
IBF	2007–09†	Juan Urango IBF	2009–10	Amir Khan WBA/IBF	2011		

Lightweights (Weight Limit: 135 pounds)

Champion	Reign	Champion	Reign	Champion	Reign	Champion	Reign
Jack McAuliffe*	1886–94†	Joe Brown*	1956–62	Julio César Chávez*		Steve Johnston*	
Kid Lavigne*	1896–99	Carlos Ortiz*	1962–65	WBA	1987–88	WBC	1999–00
Frank Erne*	1899–1902	Ismael Laguna*	1965	Jose Luis Ramirez		Julien Lorcy WBA	1999
Joe Gans*	1902–04	Carlos Ortiz*	1965–68	WBC	1987–88	Stefano Zoff WBA	1999
Jimmy Britt*	1904–05	Carlos Teo Cruz*	1968–69	Vinny Pazienza IBF	1987–88	Paul Spadafora IBF	1999–03
Battling Nelson*	1905–06	Mando Ramos*	1969–70	Julio César Chávez*	1988–89†	Gilbert Serrano WBA	1999–00
Joe Gans*	1906–08	Ismael Laguna*	1970	Greg Haugen IBF	1988–89	T. Hatakeyama WBA	2000–01
Battling Nelson*	1908–10	Ken Buchanan*	1970–72	P. Whitaker*		Jose Luis Castillo*	
Ad Wolgast*	1910–12	Roberto Duran*	1972–79†	WBC, IBF	1989–90	WBC	2000–02
Willie Ritchie*	1912–14	Chango Carmona		Edwin Rosario WBA	1989–90	Julien Lorcy WBA	2001
Freddie Welsh*	1915–17	WBC	1972	Juan Nazario WBA	1990	Raul Balbi WBA	2001
Benny Leonard*	1917–25†	Rodolfo Gonzalez		P. Whitaker*		F. Mayweather* WBC	2002–03
Jimmy Goodrich*	1925	WBC	1972–74	WBA, WBC	1990–92†	Leonard Dorin WBA	2002–03
Rocky Kansas*	1925–26	Ishimatsu Suzuki		Julio César Chávez		Javier Jauregui IBF	2003–04
Sammy Mandell*	1926–30	WBC	1974–76	IBF	1990–91	Julio Diaz IBF	2004–05
Al Singer*	1930	Estaban DeJesus		Julio César Chávez		Lakva Sim WBA	2004
Tony Canzoneri*	1930–33	WBC	1976–78	WBC	1990–92	Juan Diaz WBA	2004–08
Barney Ross*	1933–35†	Jim Watt WBC*	1979–81	Pernell Whitaker*		Jose Luis Castillo	
Tony Canzoneri*	1935–36	Ernesto Espana		IBF	1991–92†	WBC	2004–05
Lou Ambers*	1936–38	WBA	1979–80	Edwin Rosario WBA	1991–92	Diego Corrales WBC	2005–06
Henry Armstrong*	1938–39	Hilmer Kenty WBA	1980–81	Miguel Gonzalez		Jesus Chavez IBF	2005–07
Lou Ambers*	1939–40	Sean O'Grady WBA	1981	WBC	1992–95	Joel Casamayor	
Sammy Angott NBA	1940–41	Claude Noel WBA	1981	Joey Gamache		WBC	2006–08
Lew Jenkins*	1940–41	Alexis Arguello*		WBA	1992–93	Julio Diaz IBF	2007
Sammy Angott*	1941–42†	WBC	1981–82†	Dingaan Thobela		Juan Diaz	2007–08
Beau Jack* NY	1942–43	Arturo Frias WBA	1981–82	WBA	1993	David Diaz WBC	2008
Bob Montgomery*		Ray Mancini* WBA	1982–84	Fred Pendleton* IBF	1993–94	Yusuke Kobori WBA	2008–09
NY	1943	Alexis Arguello	1982–83	Orzubek Nazarov		Nate Campbell IBF	2008–09†
Sammy Angott NBA	1943–44	Edwin Rosario WBC	1983–84	WBA	1993–98	Manny Pacquiao	
Beau Jack* NY	1943–44	Choo Choo Brown		Rafael Ruelas* IBF	1994–95	WBC	2008–09†
Bob Montgomery*		IBF	1984	Oscar De La Hoya*		Juan Manual Marquez	
NY	1944–47	L. Bramble* WBA	1984–86	IBF	1995†	WBA	2009–12†
Juan Zurita NBA	1944–45	Jose Luis Ramirez		Phillip Holiday IBF	1995–97	Edwin Valero WBC	2009–10†
Ike Williams*	1947–51	WBC	1984–85	Jean B. Mendy*		Miguel Vazquez IBF	2010–
James Carter*	1951–52	Harry Arroyo IBF	1984–85	WBC	1996–97	Humberto Soto WBC	2010–11
Lauro Salas*	1952	Jimmy Paul IBF	1985–86	Steve Johnston*		Miguel Acosta WBA	2010–11
James Carter*	1952–54	Hector Camacho		WBC	1997–98	Brandon Rios WBA	2011†
Paddy DeMarco*	1954	WBC	1985–86	Shane Mosley IBF	1997–99†	Antonio DeMarco WBC	2011–
James Carter*	1954–55	Greg Haugen IBF	1986–87	Jean B. Mendy WBA	1998–99	Vacant WBA	2012–
Wallace Smith*	1955–56	Edwin Rosario* WBA	1986–87	Cesar Bazan* WBC	1998–99		

*Lineal champion. †Champion relinquished title to retire or switch weight classes, or had title stripped by boxing organization.
**In case of WBA, includes both "super" and "regular" champions. Does not include interim or WBO title holders.

Super Featherweights (Weight Limit: 130 pounds)

Champion	Reign
Johnny Dundee*	1921–23
Jack Bernstein*	1923
Johnny Dundee*	1923–24
Steve (Kid) Sullivan*	1924–25
Mike Ballerino*	1925
Tod Morgan*	1925–29
Benny Bass*	1929–31
Kid Chocolate*	1931–33
Frankie Klick*	1933–34†
Sandy Saddler*	1949–50†
Harold Gomes*	1959–60
Gabriel (Flash) Elorde*	1960–67
Yoshiaki Numata*	1967
Hiroshi Kobayashi*	1967–71
Rene Barrientos WBC	1969–70
Yoshiaki Numata WBC	1970–71
Alfredo Marcano*	1971–72
R. Arredondo WBC	1971–74
Ben Villaflor*	1972–73
Kuniaki Shibata*	1973
Ben Villaflor*	1973–76
Kuniaki Shibata WBC	1974–75
Alfredo Escalera WBC	1975–78
Samuel Serrano*	1976–80
Alexis Arguello WBC	1978–80
Yasutsune Uehara*	1980–81
Rafael Limon WBC	1980–81
C. Boza-Edwards WBC	1981
Samuel Serrano*	1981–83
R. Navarrete WBC	1981–82
Rafael Limon WBC	1982
Bobby Chacon WBC	1982–83
Roger Mayweather*	1983–84
Hector Camacho WBC	1983–84
Rocky Lockridge*	1984–85
Hwan-Kil Yuh IBF	1984–85
Julio César Chávez WBC	1984–87
Lester Ellis IBF	1985
Wilfredo Gomez*	1985–86
Barry Michael IBF	1985–87
Alfredo Layne* WBA	1986
Brian Mitchell* WBA	1986–91†
Rocky Lockridge IBF	1987–88
Azumah Nelson* WBC	1988–94
Tony Lopez IBF	1988–89
Juan Molina IBF	1989–90
Tony Lopez IBF	1990–91
Joey Gamache WBA	1991
Brian Mitchell IBF	1991
Genaro Hernandez WBA	1991–95
Juan Molina IBF	1991–95
James Leija* WBC	1994
Gabriel Ruelas* WBC	1994–95
Eddie Hopson IBF	1995
Tracy Patterson IBF	1995
Azumah Nelson* WBC	1995–97
Choi Yong-Soo WBA	1995–98
Arturo Gatti IBF	1995–98†
Genaro Hernandez* WBC	1997–98
Roberto Garcia IBF	1998–99
Floyd Mayweather Jr.* WBC	1998–01†
T. Hatakeyama WBA	1998–99
Lakva Sim WBA	1999
Diego Corrales IBF	1999–01
Jong Kwon Baek WBA	1999–00
Joel Casamayor WBA	2000–02
Steve Forbes IBF	2000–02†
Acelino Freitas* WBA	2002–04
Y. Nantchachai WBA	2002–05
S. Singmanassak WBC	2002–03
Jesus Chavez WBC	2003–04
Carlos Hernandez IBF	2003–04
Erik Morales WBC/IBF	2004–05
Erik Morales IBF	2004–05
Marco A. Barrera WBC	2005–07
Vicente Mosquera WBA	2005–06
Robbie Peden IBF	2005
Marco A. Barrera, IBF	2005–06
Cassius Baloyi IBF	2006
Edwin Valero WBA	2006–08
Gairy St. Clair IBF	2006
Malcolm Klassen IBF	2006–07
Mzonke Fana IBF	2007–08
Juan Manuel Marquez WBC	2007–08
Manny Pacquiao WBC	2008
Jorge Linares WBA	2008–09
Cassius Baloyi IBF	2008–09
Humberto Soto WBC	2008–10†
Malcom Klassen IBF	2009
Juan Carlos Salgado IBF	2009
Juan Carlos Salgado WBA	2009–10
Robert Guerrero IBF	2009–10†
Takashi Uchiyama WBA	2010–
Vitaly Tajbert WBC	2010
Takahiro Aoh WBC	2010–
Mzonke Fana IBF	2010–11†
Juan Carlos Salgado IBF	2011–

Featherweights (Weight Limit: 126 pounds)

Champion	Reign
Torpedo Billy Murphy*	1890
Young Griffo*	1890–92†
George Dixon*	1892–97
Solly Smith*	1897–98
Dave Sullivan*	1898
George Dixon*	1898–1900
Terry McGovern*	1900–01
Young Corbett II*	1901–03†
Abe Attell*	1903–04
Tommy Sullivan*	1904–05†
Abe Attell*	1906–12
Johnny Kilbane*	1912–23
Eugene Criqui*	1923
Johnny Dundee*	1923–24†
"Kid" Kaplan*	1925–26†
Tony Canzoneri*	1927–28
Andre Routis*	1928–29
Battling Battalino*	1929–32†
Tommy Paul NBA	1932–33
Kid Chocolate NY	1932–33†
Freddie Miller NBA	1933–36
Mike Beloise NY	1936–37
Petey Sarron NBA	1936–37
Maurice Holtzer*	1937–38
Henry Armstrong*	1937–38†
Joey Archibald* NY	1938–39
Leo Rodak NBA	1938–39
Joey Archibald	1939–40
Petey Scalzo NBA	1940–41
Harry Jeffra*	1940–41
Joey Archibald*	1941
Richie Lamos NBA	1941
Chalky Wright*	1941–42
Jackie Wilson NBA	1941–43
Willie Pep*	1942–48
Jackie Callura NBA	1943
Phil Terranova NBA	1943–44
Sal Bartolo NBA	1944–46
Sandy Saddler*	1948–49
Willie Pep*	1949–50
Sandy Saddler*	1950–57†
Kid Bassey*	1957–59
Davey Moore*	1959–63
Sugar Ramos*	1963–64
Vicente Saldivar*	1964–67†
Paul Rojas NBA	1968
Jose Legra WBC	1968–69
Shozo Saijyo WBA	1968–71
J. Famechon* WBC	1969–70
Vicente Saldivar* WBC	1970
Kuniaki Shibata* WBC	1970–72
Antonio Gomez WBA	1971–72
C. Sanchez* WBC	1972
Ernesto Marcel WBA	1972–74
Jose Legra* WBC	1972–73
Eder Jofre* WBC	1973–74†
Ruben Olivares WBA	1974
Bobby Chacon WBC	1974–75
Alexis Arguello* WBA	1974–76†
Ruben Olivares WBC	1975
Poison Kotey WBC	1975–76
Danny Lopez* WBC	1976–80
Rafael Ortega WBA	1977
Cecilio Lastra WBA	1977–78
Eusebio Pedroza* WBA	1978–85
S. Sanchez* WBC	1980–82†
Juan LaPorte WBC	1982–84
Wilfredo Gomez WBC	1984
Min-Keun Oh IBF	1984–85
Azumah Nelson WBC	1984–88
Barry McGuigan* WBA	1985–86
Ki Young Chung IBF	1985–86
Steve Cruz* WBA	1986–87
Antonio Rivera IBF	1986–88
A. Esparragoza* WBA	1987–91
Calvin Grove IBF	1988
Jorge Paez IBF	1988–91
Jeff Fenech WBC	1988–90†
Marcos Villasana WBC	1990–91
Paul Hodkinson WBC	1991–93
Troy Dorsey IBF	1991
Manuel Medina IBF	1991–93
Yung Kyun Park* WBA	1991–93
Gregorio Vargas WBC	1993
Tom Johnson IBF	1993–97†
Eloy Rojas* WBA	1993–96
Kevin Kelley WBC	1993–95
A. Gonzalez WBC	1995
Manuel Medina WBC	1995–95
Luisito Espinosa WBC	1995–99

*Lineal champion. †Champion relinquished title to retire or switch weight classes, or had title stripped by boxing organization.
**In case of WBA, includes both "super" and "regular" champions. Does not include interim or WBO title holders.

Featherweights *(Cont.)*

Champion	Reign	Champion	Reign	Champion	Reign
Wilfredo Vazquez* WBA	1996–98	Manuel Medina IBF	2001–02	Jorge Linares WBC	2007–08
Hector Lizarraga IBF	1997–98	Marco A. Barrera*WBA/WBC	2001–03	Oscar Larios WBC	2008–09
Naseem Hamed* WBA	1998†	Johnny Tapia IBF	2002	Cristobal Cruz IBF	2008–10
Naseem Hamed*	1998–01	Marco A. Barrera* WBC	2002†	Takahiro Aoh WBC	2009
Freddy Norwood WBA	1998	Erik Morales WBC	2002–03	Elio Rojas WBC	2009–10†
Manuel Medina IBF	1998–99	Juan Marquez IBF	2003–06	Yuriorkis Gamboa WBA	2009–11†
Antonio Cermeno WBA	1998–99	Chris John WBA‡	2003	Hozumi Hasegawa WBC	2010–11
Cesar Soto WBC	1999	In Jin Chi WBC	2004–06	Orlando Salido IBF	2010†
Freddy Norwood WBA	1999–00	Valdemir Pereira, IBF	2006	Yuriorkis Gamboa IBF	2010–11
Naseem Hamed* WBC	1999†	Eric Aiken IBF	2006	Jhonny Gonzalez WBC	2011–12
Paul Ingle IBF	1999–00	T. Koshimoto, WBC	2006	Jonathan Barros WBA	2011
Guty Espadas WBC	2000–01	Rudolfo Lopez WBC	2006	Billy Dib WBA	2011–
Erik Morales WBC	2000–02	Robert Guerrero IBF	2006	Celestino Caballero WBA	2011–
Derrick Gainer WBA	2000–03	Orlando Salido IBF	2006	Chris John WBA	2012–
Mbulelo Botile IBF	2001	In Jin Chi WBC	2006–07	Daniel Ponce De Leon, WBC	2012–
Frankie Toledo IBF	2001	Robert Guerrero IBF	2007–08†		

Super Bantamweights (Weight Limit: 122 pounds)

Champion	Reign	Champion	Reign	Champion	Reign
Jack (Kid) Wolfe*	1922–23	J.J. Estrada WBA	1988–89	Osamu Sato WBA	2002
Carl Duane*	1923–24	Fabrice Benichou IBF	1989–90	Salim Medjkoune WBA	2002–03
Rigoberto Riasco* WBC	1976	Jesus Salud WBA	1989–90	Oscar Larios WBC	2002–05
R. Kobayashi* WBC	1976	Welcome Ncita IBF	1990–92	Mahyar Monshipour WBA	2003–06
Dong-Kyun Yum* WBC	1976–77	Paul Banke* WBC	1990	Israel Vazquez IBF	2004–05
Wilfredo Gomez* WBC	1977–83†	Luis Mendoza WBA	1990–91	Israel Vazquez WBC	2005–07
Soo-Hwan Hong WBA	1977–78	Pedro Decima* WBC	1990–91	S. Sithchatchawal WBA	2006
Ricardo Cardona WBA	1978–80	K. Hatanaka* WBC	1991	C. Caballero WBA	2006–10†
Leo Randolph WBA	1980	Daniel Zaragoza* WBC	1991–92	IBF	2008–09†
Sergio Palma WBA	1980–82	Raul Perez WBA	1992	Michael Hunter IBF	2006
Leonardo Cruz WBA	1982–84	Thiery Jacob* WBC	1992	Steve Molitor IBF	2006–08
Jaime Garza*	1983	Tracy Patterson* WBC	1992–94	Rafael Marquez WBC	2007
Bobby Berna IBF	1983–84	Wilfredo Vasquez WBA	1992–95	Israel Vazquez WBC	2007–08†
Loris Stecca WBA	1984	Kennedy McKinney IBF	1993–94	Ricardo Cordoba WBA	2008–09
Seung-Il Suh IBF	1984–85	Vuyani Bungu IBF	1994–99†	Toshiaki Nishioka WBC	2008–12
Victor Callejas WBA	1984–86	H. Acero* Sanchez WBC	1994–95	Bernard Dunne WBA	2009
Juan Meza* WBC	1984–85	Antonio Cermeno WBA	1995–98†	Poon. Kratingdaenggym WBA	2009–10
Ji-Won Kim IBF	1985–86	Daniel Zaragoza* WBA	1995–97	Steve Molitor IBF	2010–11
Lupe Pintor*	1985–86	Erik Morales* WBC	1997–00†	Ryol Li Lee WBA	2010–11
S. Payakaroon* WBC	1986–87	Enrique Sanchez WBA	1998	Akifumi Shimoda WBA	2011
Seung-Hoon Lee IBF	1987–88	Nestor Garza WBA	1998–00	Rico Ramos WBA	2011–12
Louie Espinoza WBA	1987	Benedict Ledwaba IBF	1999–01	Takalani Ndlovu IBF	2011–12
Jeff Fenech* WBC	1987†	Clarence Adams WBA	2000–01†	Guillermo Rigondeaux WBA	2012–
Julio Gervacio WBA	1987–88	Willie Jorrin WBC	2000–02	Nonito Donaire IBF	2012–
Daniel Zaragoza* WBC	1988–90	Manny Pacquiao IBF	2001–04	Abner Mares WBC	2012–
Jose Sanabria IBF	1988–89	Yober Ortega WBA	2001–02		
B. Pinango WBA	1988	Y. Sithyodthong WBA	2002		

Bantamweights (Weight Limit: 118 pounds)

Champion	Reign	Champion	Reign	Champion	Reign	Champion	Reign
Spider Kelly	1887	Kewpie Ertle	1915	Sixto Escobar*	1936–37	Lionel Rose*	1968–69
Hughey Boyle	1887–88	Pete Herman*	1917–20	Harry Jeffra*	1937–38	Ruben Olivares*	1969–70
Spider Kelly	1889	Joe Lynch*	1920–21	Sixto Escobar*	1938–39†	Chucho Castillo*	1970–71
Chappie Moran	1889–90	Pete Herman*	1921	Georgie Pace NBA	1939–40	Ruben Olivares*	1971–72
George Dixon	1890–91	Johnny Buff*	1921–22	Lou Salica*	1940–42	Rafael Herrera*	1972
Pedlar Palmer	1895–99	Joe Lynch*	1922–24	Manuel Ortiz*	1942–47	Enrique Pinder*	1972–73
Terry McGovern*	1899–00†	Abe Goldstein*	1924	Harold Dade*	1947	Romeo Anaya*	1973
Harry Harris	1901	Cannonball Martin*	1924–25	Manuel Ortiz*	1947–50	Arnold Taylor*	1973–74
Harry Forbes*	1901–03	Phil Rosenberg*	1925–27†	Vic Toweel*	1950–52	Rafael Herrera WBC	1973–74
Frankie Neil*	1903–04	Bud Taylor NBA	1927–28	Jimmy Carruthers*	1952–54†	Soo-Hwan Hong*	1974–75
Joe Bowker*	1904–05†	Bushy Graham NY	1928–29	Robert Cohen*	1954–56	Rodolfo Martinez	
Jimmy Walsh*	1905–06†	Panama Al Brown*	1929–35	Paul Macias NBA	1955–57	WBC	1974–76
Owen Moran	1907–08	Sixto Escobar NBA	1934–35	Mario D'Agata	1956–57	Alfonso Zamora*	1975–77
Monte Attell	1909–10	Baltazar Sangchilli*	1935–36	Alphonse Halimi*	1957–59	Carlos Zarate* WBC	1976–79
Frankie Conley	1910–11	Lou Salica NBA	1935	Joe Becerra*	1959–60†	Jorge Lujan	1977–80
Johnny Coulon*	1910–14	Sixto Escobar NBA	1935–36	Eder Jofre*	1961–65	Lupe Pintor* WBC	1979–83†
Kid Williams*	1914–17	Tony Marino*	1936	Fighting Harada*	1965–68	Julian Solis	1980

*Lineal champion. †Champion relinquished title to retire or switch weight classes, or had title stripped by boxing organization.
**In case of WBA, includes both "super" and "regular" champions. Does not include interim or WBO title holders.

Bantamweights (Cont.)

Champion	Reign	Champion	Reign	Champion	Reign	Champion	Reign
Jeff Chandler*	1980–84	Luisito Espinosa WBA	1989–91	W. McCullough WBC	1995–96	H. Hasegawa WBC	2005–10
Albert Davila WBC	1983–85	Israel Contreras WBA	1991–92	Harold Mestre IBF	1995	Luis Perez IBF	2007
Richard Sandoval*	1984–86	Greg Richardson		Mbulelo Botile IBF	1995–97	Joseph Agbeko IBF	2007–09
Satoshi Shingaki IBF	1984–85	WBC	1991	Nana Konadu* WBA	1996–98	Anselmo Moreno	
Jeff Fenech IBF	1985	J. Tatsuyoshi, WBC	1991–92	S. Singmanassak		WBA	2008–
Daniel Zaragoza WBC	1985	Eddie Cook WBA	1992–93	WBC	1996–97	Yohnny Perez IBF	2009–10
Miguel Lora WBC	1985–88	Victor Rabanales		Tim Austin IBF	1997–03	Fernando Montiel	
Gaby Canizales*	1986	WBC	1992–93	J.Tatsuyoshi WBC	1997–98	WBC	2010–11
Bernardo Pinango*	1986–87†	Jung-Il Byun WBC	1993	Johnny Tapia* WBA	1998–99	Joseph Agbeko IBF	2010–11
W. Vasquez WBA	1987–88	Jorge Julio WBA	1993	V. Sahaprom* WBC	1998–05	Koki Kameda WBA	2010–
Kevin Seabrooks* IBF:	1987–88	Yasuei Yakushiji WBC	1993–95	Paulie Ayala* WBA	1999–01†	Nonito Donaire WBC	2011–12
Kaokor Galaxy WBA	1988	Junior Jones WBA	1994	Eidy Moya WBA	2001–02	Abner Mares IBF	2011–12
Moon Sung-Kil WBA	1988–89	John M. Johnson		Johnny Bredahl WBA	2002–05	Leo Santa Cruz IBF	2012–
Kaokor Galaxy WBA	1989	WBA	1994	Rafael Marquez IBF	2003–07	Shinsuke Yamanaka	
Raul Perez WBC	1988–91	D. Chuvatana WBA	1994–95	W. Sidorenko WBA	2005–08	WBC	2012–
O. Canizales* IBF	1988–95†	V. Sahaprom* WBA	1995–96				

Super Flyweights (Weight Limit: 115 pounds)

Champion	Reign	Champion	Reign	Champion	Reign	Champion	Reign
Rafael Orono* WBC	1980–81	Juan Polo Perez IBF	1989–90	Johnny Tapia IBF	1997–99†	Vic Darchinyan	
Chul-Ho Kim* WBC	1981–82	Nana Konadu* WBC	1989–90	Satoshi Iida WBA	1997–98	WBC, WBA	2008–10†
Gustavo Ballas WBA	1981	Sung-Kil Moon*		In-Joo Cho* WBC	1998–00	IBF	2006–09†
Rafael Pedroza WBA	1981–82	WBC	1990–93	Jesus Rojas WBA	1998–99	Simphiwe Nongqayi	
Jiro Watanabe WBA	1982–84	Robert Quiroga IBF	1990–93	Mark Johnson IBF	1999–00	IBF	2009–10
Rafael Orono* WBC	1982–83	Julio Borboa IBF	1993–94	Hideki Todaka IBF	1999–00	Juan Alberto Rosas,	
Payao Poontarat*		Katsuya Onizuka		Felix Machado IBF	2000–03	IBF	2010
WBC	1983–85	WBA	1993–94	M. Tokuyama* WBC	2000–04	Cristian Mijares IBF	2010–11†
Joo-Do Chun IBF	1983–85	Jose Luis Bueno*		Leo Gamez WBA	2000–01	Hugo Cazares WBA	2010–11
Jiro Watanabe*	1984–86	WBC	1993–94	Celes Kobayashi		Tomas Rojas WBC	2010–11
Kaosai Galaxy WBA	1984	Lee Hyung-Chul		WBA	2001–02	Suriyan Sor Rungvisai,	
Ellyas Pica IBF	1985–86	WBA	1994–95	Alexander Munoz		WBC	2011–12
Cesar Polanco IBF	1986	H. Kawashima* WBC	1994–97	WBA	2002–05	Tomonobu Shimizu,	
Gilberto Roman*		Harold Grey IBF	1994–95	Luis Alberto Perez IBF	2003–06	WBA	2011–12
WBC	1986–87	Alimi Goitia WBA	1995–96	Katsushige Kawashima		Roberto Guerrero IBF	2011–12
Ellyas Pical IBF	1986	Carlos Salazar IBF	1995–96	WBC	2004–05	Juan Carlos Sanchez Jr.	
Santos Laciar* WBC	1987	Yokthai Sith-Oar		M. Tokuyama WBC	2005–06	IBF	2012–
Tae-Il Chang IBF	1987	WBA	1996–97	Jose M. Castillo IBF	2005–06	Tepparith Kokietgym	
Sugar Rojas* WBC	1987–88	Harold Grey IBF	1996	Nobuo Nashiro WBA	2006–08	WBA	2012–
Ellyas Pical IBF	1987–89	Danny Romero IBF	1996–97	Cristian Mijares WBC	2006–08	Yota Sato WBC	2012–
Giberto Roman*		Gerry Penalosa*		Dmitri Kirilov IBF	2007–08		
WBC	1988–89	WBC	1997–98				

Flyweights (Weight Limit: 112 pounds)

Champion	Reign	Champion	Reign	Champion	Reign	Champion	Reign
Sid Smith*	1913	Jackie Paterson*	1943–48	Erbito Salavarria*	1970–73†	Luis Ibarra WBA	1981
Bill Ladbury*	1913–14	Rinty Monaghan*	1948–50†	B. Gonzalez WBA	1972	Juan Herrera WBA	1981–82
Percy Jones*	1914†	Terry Allen*	1950	V. Borkorsor WBC	1972–73†	P. Cardona* WBC	1982
Joe Symonds*	1914–16	Dado Marino*	1950–52	Venice Borkorsor*	1973†	Santos Laciar WBA	1982–85
Jimmy Wilde*	1916–23	Yoshio Shirai*	1952–54	Chartchai Chionoi WBA	1973–74	Freddie Castillo* WBC	1982
Pancho Villa*	1923–25†	Pascual Perez*	1954–60	B. Gonzalez* WBA	1973–74	E. Mercedes* WBA	1982–83
Fidel La Barba*	1925–27†	Pone Kingpetch*	1960–62	Shoji Oguma* WBC	1974–75	Charlie Magri* WBC	1983
Frenchy Belanger*		Masahiko Harada*	1962–63	S. Hanagata WBA	1974–75	Frank Cedeno* WBC	1983–84
NBA	1927–28	Pone Kingpetch*	1963	Miguel Canto* WBC	1975–79	Soon-Chun Kwon	
Izzy Schwartz NY	1927–29	Hiroyuki Ebihara*	1963–64	Erbito Salavarria		IBF	1983–85
Frankie Genaro*		Pone Kingpetch*	1964–65	WBA	1975–76	Koji Kobayashi*	
NBA	1928–29	Salvatore Burrini*	1965–66	Alfonso Lopez WBA	1976	WBC	1984
Spider Pladner* NBA	1929	H. Accavallo WBA	1966–68	G. Espadas WBA	1976–78	Gabriel Bernal*	
Frankie Genaro*		Walter McGowan*	1966	B. Gonzalez WBA	1978–79	WBC	1984
NBA	1929–31	Chartchai Chionoi*	1966–69	Chan-Hee Park*		Sot Chitalada* WBC	1984–88
Midget Wolgast NY	1930–35	Efren Torres*	1969–70	WBC	1979–80	Hilario Zapate WBA	1985–87
Young Perez* NBA	1931–32	Hiroyuki Ebihara WBA	1969	Luis Ibarra WBA	1979–80	Chong-Kwan Chung	
Jackie Brown* NBA	1932–35	B. Villacampo WBA	1969–70	Tae-Shik Kim WBA	1980	IBF	1985–86
Benny Lynch*	1935–38†	Chartchai Chionoi*	1970	Shoji Oguma* WBC	1980–81	Bi-Won Chung IBF	1986
Small Montana NY	1935–37	B. Chartvanchai		Peter Mathebula WBA	1980–81	Hi-Sup Shin IBF	1986–87
Peter Kane*	1938–43	WBA	1970	Santos Laciar WBA	1981	Dodie Penalosa IBF	1987
Little Dado NY	1938–40	Masao Ohba WBA	1970–73	Antonio Avelar* WBC	1981–82	Fidel Bassa WBA	1987–89

*Lineal champion. †Champion relinquished title to retire or switch weight classes, or had title stripped by boxing organization.
**In case of WBA, includes both "super" and "regular" champions. Does not include interim or WBO title holders.

Flyweights *(Cont.)*

Champion	Reign	Champion	Reign	Champion	Reign	Champion	Reign
Choi-Chang Ho IBF	1987–88	Yuri Arbachakov*		Manny Pacquiao* WBC	1998–99	Daisuke Naito WBC	2007–09
Rolando Bohol IBF	1988	WBC	1992–97	Leo Gamez WBA	1999	Nonito Donaire IBF	2007–09†
Yong-Kang Kim*		Rodolfo Blanco IBF	1992–93	Irene Pacheco IBF	1999–05	Denkaosan Kaovichit	
WBC	1988–89	David Griman WBA	1992–94	S. Pisnurachan WBA	1999–00	WBA	2008–10
Duke McKenzie IBF	1988–89	P. Sithbangprachan IBF	1993–95	M. Sinsurat* WBC	1999–00	Koki Kameda WBC	2009–10
Sot Chitalada* WBC	1989–91	S.S. Ploenchit WBA	1994–96	Malcolm Tunacao* WBC	2000–01	Moruti Mthalane IBF	2009–
Dave McAuley IBF	1989–92	Francisco Tejedor IBF	1995	Eric Morel WBA	2000–03	Daiki Kameda WBA	2010–11†
Jesus Rojas WBA	1989–90	Danny Romero IBF	1995–96	P. Wonjongkam*		Pongsaklek Wonjongkam	
Yul-Woo Lee WBA	1990	Mark Johnson IBF	1996–99†	WBC	2001–07	WBC	2010–12
L. Tamakuma WBA	1990–91	Jose Bonilla WBA	1996–98	Lorenzo Parra WBA	2003–07	Luis Concepcion WBA	2011
M. Kittikasem* WBC	1991–92	Chatchai Sasakul*		Vic Darchinyan IBF	2005–07	Hernan Marquez WBA	2011–
Yong Kang Kim		WBC	1997–98	Takefumi Sakata		Sonny Boy Jaro WBC	2012
WBA	1991–92	Hugo Soto WBA	1998–99	WBA	2007–08	T. Igarashi WBC	2012–

Light Flyweights (Weight Limit: 108 pounds)

Champion	Reign	Champion	Reign	Champion	Reign
Franco Udella WBC	1975	Yul-Woo Lee WBC	1989	Jorge Arce* WBC	2002–05
Jaime Rios WBA	1975–76	M. Kittikasem IBF	1989–90	Jose Burgos IBF	2003–05
Luis Estaba* WBC	1975–78	H. Gonzalez WBC	1989–90	Brian Viloria WBC	2005–06
Juan Guzman WBA	1976	Michael Carbajal IBF	1990–94	R. Vasquez WBA	2005–06
Yoko Gushiken WBA	1976–81	R. Pascua WBC	1990	Will Grigsby IBF	2005–06
Freddy Castillo* WBC	1978	M. C. Castro WBC	1991	Koki Kameda WBA	2006–07
Sor Vorasingh* WBC	1978	H. Gonzalez WBC	1991–93	Omar Nino Rivero WBC	2006–07
Sung-Jun Kim* WBC	1978–80	Hirokia Ioka* WBA	1991–92	Ulises Solis IBF	2006–09
Shigeo Nakajima* WBC	1980	Myung-Woo Yuh* WBA	1993†	Juan Carlos Reveco WBA	2007
Hilario Zapata* WBC	1980–82	Michael Carbajal* WBC	1993–94	Edgar Sosa WBC	2007–09
Pedro Flores WBA	1981	Leo Gamez WBA	1993–95	Brahim Asloum WBA	2007–09†
Hwan-Jin Kim WBA	1981	H. Gonzalez* WBC, IBF	1994–95	Giovanni Segura WBA‡	2009–10†
Katsuo Tokashiki WBA	1981–83	Choi Hi-Yong WBA	1995–96	Brian Viloria IBF	2009–10
Amado Urzua* WBC	1982	S. Sor Jaturong WBC, IBF	1995–96	Rodel Mayol WBC	2009–10
Tadashi Tomori* WBC	1982	Saman Jaturong* WBC	1995–99	Omar Nino Romero WBC	2010
Hilario Zapata* WBC	1982–83	Carlos Murillo WBA	1996	Carlos Tamara IBF	2010
Jung-Koo Chang* WBC	1983–88†	Keiji Yamaguchi WBA	1996	Juan Carlos Reveco WBA	2010–11
Lupe Madera WBA	1983–84	Michael Carbajal IBF	1996–97	Luis Alberto Lazarte IBF	2010–11
Dodie Penalosa IBF	1983–86	Phichitchor Siriwat WBA	1996–00	Gilberto Keb Bass WBC	2010–11
Francisco Quiroz WBA	1984–85	Mauricio Pastrana IBF	1997–98†	Ulises Solis IBF	2011–12†
Joey Olivo WBA	1985	Will Grigsby IBF	1998–99	Adrian Hernandez WBC	2011
Myung-Woo Yuh* WBA	1985–91	Ricardo Lopez IBF	1999–02	Roman Gonzalez WBA	2011–
Jum-Hwan Choi IBF	1986–88	Yo-Sam Choi* WBC	1999–02	K. Porpramook WBC	2011–
Tacy Macalos IBF	1988–89	Beibis Mendoza WBA	2000–01	John Riel Casimero IBF	2012–
German Torres WBC	1988–89	Rosendo Alvarez WBA	2001–05		

Strawweights (Weight Limit: 105 pounds)

Champion	Reign	Champion	Reign	Champion	Reign
Kyung-Yun Lee* IBF	1987	R. Sor Vorapin IBF	1996–97	Yukata Niida WBA	2004–08
Hiroki Ioka* WBC	1987–88	Zolani Petelo* IBF	1997–00†	K. Takayama WBC	2005
Leo Gamez WBA	1988–89	W. Chor Charoen WBC	1998–00	Eagle Junlaphan WBC	2005–07
S. Sithnaruepol IBF	1988–89	R. Lopez* WBA, WBC	1998–99†	M. Rachman IBF	2005–07
N. Kiatwanchai* WBC	1988–89	Songkram Popaoin WBA	1999	Florante Condes IBF	2007–08
Bong-Jun Kim WBA	1989–91	Noel Arambulet WBA	1999–00	O. Sithsamerchai WBC	2007–11
Nico Thomas IBF	1989	Jose Aguirre* WBC	2000–04	Roman Gonzalez WBA	2008–10†
Eric Chavez IBF	1989–90	Joma Gamboa WBA	2000	Raul Garcia IBF	2008–10
Jum-Hwan Choi* WBC	1989–90	Keitaro Hoshino WBA	2000–01	Kwanthai Sithmorseng WBA	2010–11
Hideyuki Ohashi* WBC	1990	Chana Porpaoin WBA	2001	Nkosinathi Joyi IBF	2010–12
F. Lookmingkwan IBF	1990–92	Roberto Leyva IBF	2001–02	Muhammad Rachman WBA	2011
Ricardo Lopez* WBC	1990–98†	Yutaka Niida WBA	2001†	Kazuto Ioka WBC	2011–12†
Hi-Yong Choi WBA	1991–92	Miguel Barrera IBF	2002–03	Pornsawan Porpramook WBA	2011
Manny Melchor IBF	1992	Noel Arambulet WBA	2002–04	Akira Yaegashi WBA	2011–12
Hideyuki Ohashi WBA	1992–93	Edgar Cardenas IBF	2003	Kazuto Ioka WBC	2012–
R.S. Voraphin IBF	1992–96	Daniel Reyes IBF	2003–05	Vacant WBC	2012–
Chana Porpaoin WBA	1993–95	Eagle Junlaphan WBC	2004	Mario Rodriguez IBF	2012–
Rosendo Alvarez WBA	1995–98	Isaac Bustos WBC	2004–05		

*Lineal champion.   †Champion relinquished title to retire or switch weight classes, or had title stripped by boxing organization.
**In case of WBA, includes both "super" and "regular" champions. Does not include interim or WBO title holders.

Lineal Heavyweight Champions

Champion	Reign	Age*	Career	W-L-D (KO)	SD
John L. Sullivan	1885–92	26	1878–92	38-1-3 (33)	0
James J. Corbett	1892–97	26	1884–03	11-4-2 (7)	1
Bob Fitzsimmons	1897–99	33	1880–16	74-8-3 (67)	0
James J. Jeffries†	1899–05	24	1896–10	18-1-2 (15)	7
Marvin Hart	1905–06	28	1899–10	28–7–4 (19)	0
Tommy Burns	1906–08	24	1900–20	46-5-8 (37)	11
Jack Johnson	1908–15	30	1894–28	77-13-14 (48)	9
Jess Willard	1915–19	33	1911–23	23-6-1 (20)	1
Jack Dempsey	1919–26	24	1914–27	60-6-8 (50)	5
Gene Tunney†	1926–28	29	1915–28	61-1-1 (45)	2
Max Schmeling	1930–32	24	1924–48	56-10-4 (39)	1
Jack Sharkey	1932–33	29	1924–36	38-13-3 (14)	0
Primo Carnera	1933–34	26	1928–37	88-14-0 (69)	2
Max Baer	1934–35	25	1929–41	72-12-0 (53)	0
James J. Braddock	1935–37	29	1926–38	51-26-7 (26)	0
Joe Louis†	1937–49	23	1934–51	68-3-0 (54)	25
Ezzard Charles	1949–51	27	1940–59	96-25-1 (59)	8
Jersey Joe Walcott	1951–52	37	1930–53	53-18-1 (33)	1
Rocky Marciano†	1952–56	29	1947–56	49-0-0 (43)	6
Floyd Patterson	1956–59	21	1952–72	55-8-1 (40)	4
Ingemar Johansson	1959–60	26	1952–63	26-2-0 (17)	0
Floyd Patterson	1960–62	25	1952–72	55-8-1 (40)	2
Sonny Liston	1962–64	30	1953–70	50-4-0 (39)	1
Muhammad Ali	1964–71	22	1960–81	56-5-0 (37)	9
Joe Frazier	1971–73	27	1965–81	32-4-1 (27)	2
George Foreman	1973–74	24	1969–97	76-5-0 (68)	2
Muhammad Ali	1974–78	32	1960–81	56-5-0 (37)	10
Leon Spinks	1978	24	1977–95	26-17-3 (14)	0
Muhammad Ali†	1978–79	36	1960–81	56-5-0 (37)	0
Larry Holmes	1980–85	29	1973–2002	69-6-0 (44)	20
Michael Spinks	1985–88	29	1977–88	32-1-0 (21)	3
Mike Tyson	1988–90	21	1985–2005	49-4-0 (43)	2
Buster Douglas	1990	29	1981–99	38-6-1 (25)	0
Evander Holyfield	1990–92	28	1984–	38-5-2 (26)	3
Riddick Bowe	1992–93	25	1989–96	40-1-0 (32)	2
Evander Holyfield	1993–94	31	1984–94; 1995–	44-10-2 (29)	0
Michael Moorer	1994	26	1988–97	52-4-1 (40)	0
George Foreman	1994–97	45	1969–97	76-5-0 (68)	3
Shannon Briggs	1997–98	25	1992–00	32-3-1 (25)	0
Lennox Lewis	1998–01	32	1989–2004	41-2-1 (32)	5
Hasim Rahman	2001	28	1994–	50-7-2 (41)	0
Lennox Lewis†	2001–04	36	1989–2004	41-2-1 (32)	2
John Ruiz	2001–03	31	1992–2010	44-9-1 (30)	2
Chris Byrd	2002–06	35	1993–2009	41-5-1 (20)	3
Roy Jones, Jr.	2003	34	1989–	54-8-0 (40)	0
John Ruiz	2003–05	33	1992–2010	41-6-1 (28)	2
Vitali Klitschko†	2004–05	34	1996–2005; 2007–	44-2-0 (40)	1
Hasim Rahman	2005-06	33	1994–	50-7-2 (40)	1
ikolay Valuev	2005–07 2008–09	32	1993–2009	50-2-0 (34)	1
Oleg Maskaev	2006–08	37	1993–2009	36-7-0 (27)	0
Wladimir Klitschko‡	2006–	33	1996–	58-3-0 (51)	0
NRuslan Chagaev	2007–08	28	2001–	29-2-1 (18)	1
Samuel Peter	2008	28	2004–11	34-5-0 (27)	0
Vitali Klitschko^	2008–	38	1996–2005; 2007–	44-2-0 (40)	1
Nikolay Valuev	2008–09	36	1993–2009	50-2-0 (34)	0
David Haye	2009–11	30	2002–	26-2-0 (24)	0
Alexander Povetkin	2011–	31	2005–	24-0-0 (16)	0

*Age when boxer won world championship.
† Boxer retired or relinquished world title.
‡ Maintains WBA Super Champion status
^ Boxer returned from retirement.

Matt Hedges (6) of North Carolina went head-to-head with UNC Charlotte's Robby Thomas (29) during North Carolina's 1–0 win in the NCAA title game

TONY QUINN/ICON SMI

NCAA
Sports

NCAA Team Champions

Fall 2011

			Champion	Runner-Up
Cross-Country	MEN	Division I:	Wisconsin	Oklahoma St
		Division II:	Western St	Adams St
		Division III:	North Central (Ill.)	Haverford
	WOMEN	Division I:	Georgetown	Washington
		Division II:	Augustana (S.D.)	Western St
		Division III:	Washington-St. Louis	Middlebury
Field Hockey	WOMEN	Division I:	Maryland	North Carolina
		Division II	West Chester	UMass-Lowell
		Division III:	The College of NJ	Middlebury
Football	MEN	FCS (I-AA):	North Dakota St	Sam Houston St
		Division II:	Pittsburg St	Wayne St
		Division III:	UW-Whitewater	Mount Union
Soccer	MEN	Division I:	North Carolina	Charlotte
		Division II:	Fort Lewis	Lynn
		Division III:	Ohio Wesleyan	Calvin
	WOMEN	Division I:	Stanford	Duke
		Division II:	Saint Rose	Grand Valley St
		Division III:	Messiah	Wheaton (Ill.)
Volleyball	WOMEN	Division I:	UCLA	Illinois
		Division II:	Concordia-St. Paul	Cal St-San Bernardino
		Division III:	Wittenberg	Christopher Newport
Water Polo	MEN		USC	UCLA

Winter 2011-12

			Champion	Runner-Up
Bowling	WOMEN		Md.-Eastern Shore	Fairleigh Dickinson
Basketball	MEN	Division I:	Kentucky	Kansas
		Division II:	Western Washington	Montevallo
		Division III:	UW-Whitewater	Cabrini
	WOMEN	Division I:	Baylor	Notre Dame
		Division II:	Shaw	Ashland
		Division III:	Illinois Wesleyan	George Fox
Fencing			Ohio State	Princeton
Gymnastics	MEN		Illinois	Oklahoma
	WOMEN		Alabama	Florida
Ice Hockey	MEN	Division I:	Boston College	Ferris St
		Division III:	St. Norbert	SUNY-Oswego
	WOMEN	Division I:	Minnesota	Wisconsin
		Division III:	RIT	Norwich
Rifle			TCU	Kentucky
Skiing			Vermont	Utah
Swimming and Diving	MEN	Division I:	California	Texas
		Division II:	Drury	UC-San Diego
		Division III:	Denison	Kenyon
	WOMEN	Division I:	California	Georgia
		Division II:	Wayne St (Mich.)	Drury
		Division III:	Emory	Williams

Winter 2011-2012 *(Cont.)*

			Champion	Runner-Up
Wrestling	MEN	Division I:	Penn St	Minnesota
		Division II:	Neb.-Kearney	St. Cloud St
		Division III:	Wartburg	Augsburg (Minn.)
Indoor Track and Field	MEN	Division I:	Florida	Arkansas
		Division II:	Grand Canyon	Adams St
		Division III:	North Central (Ill.)	WI-Eau Claire
	WOMEN	Division I:	Oregon	Kansas
		Division II:	Grand Valley St	Adams St
		Division III:	Wartburg	UW-Oshkosh

Spring 2012

			Champion	Runner-Up
Baseball		Division I:	Arizona	South Carolina
		Division II:	West Chester	Delta State
		Division III:	Marietta	Wheaton
Golf	MEN	Division I:	Texas	Alabama
		Division II:	Nova Southeastern	Chico St
		Division III:	Oglethorpe	Transylvania
	WOMEN	Division I:	Alabama	Southern Cal
		Division II:	Nova Southeastern	Florida Southern
		Division III	Methodist	DePauw
Lacrosse	MEN	Division I:	Loyola Maryland	Maryland
		Division II:	Dowlin	Limestone
		Division III:	Salisbury	SUNY-Cortland
	WOMEN	Division I:	Northwestern	Syracuse
		Division II	CW Post	West Chester
		Division III:	Trinity (CT)	Salisbury
Rowing	WOMEN	Division I:	Virginia	Michigan
		Division II	Humboldt St	Western
	Washington			
		Division III:	Williams	Bates
Softball		Division I:	Alabama	Oklahoma
		Division II:	Valdosta St	UC-San Diego
		Division III:	Pacific Lutheran	Linfield
Tennis	MEN	Division I:	Southern Cal	Virginia
		Division II:	Armstrong Atlantic St	West Florida
		Division III:	Emory	Kenyon
	WOMEN	Division I:	Florida	UCLA
		Division II:	Armstrong Atlantic St	BYU-Hawaii
		Division III:	Williams	Chicago
Outdoor Track and Field	MEN	Division I:	Florida	LSU
		Division II:	Adams St	Lincoln (Mo.)
		Division III:	McMurry	UW-LaCrosse
	WOMEN	Division I:	LSU	Oregon
		Division II:	Grand Valley St	Lincoln (Mo.)
		Division III:	Wartburg	UW-Oshkosh
Volleyball	MEN		UC-Irvine	Southern Cal
	WOMEN	Division I:	UCLA	Illinois
		Division II:	Concordia-St. Paul	Cal St-San Bern.
		Division III:	Wittenberg	Chris. Newport
Water Polo	MEN		Southern Cal	UCLA
	WOMEN		Stanford	Southern Cal

NCAA Division I Individual Champions

Fall 2011 – Cross Country (Div. I)

MEN

Champion	Runner-Up
Lawi Lalang, Arizona	Chris Derrick, Stanford

WOMEN

Champion	Runner-Up
Sheila Reid, Villanova	Jordan Hasay, Oregon

Winter 2011–12
Gymnastics

MEN

	Champion	Runner-Up
All-around	Jake Dalton, Oklahoma	Sam Mikulak, Mich./C.J. Maestes, Ill.
Vault	Paul Ruggeri, Illinois / Eddie Penev, Stanford – tied, co-champions	
Parallel bars	Jake Dalton, Oklahoma	Paul Ruggeri, Illinois
Horizontal bar	Sam Mikulak, Michigan	Glen Ishino, California
Floor exercise	Eddie Penev, Stanford	Jake Dalton, Oklahoma
Pommel horse	Glen Ishino, California	Craig Hernandez, Penn St
Rings	C.J. Maestes, Illinois	Scott Rosenthal, Penn St

WOMEN

	Champion	Runner-Up
All-around	Kytra Hunter, Florida	Kat Ding, Georgia
Balance beam	Geralen Stack-Eaton, Alabama	Megan Ferguson, Oklahoma
Uneven bars	Kat Ding, Georgia	Sami Shapiro, Stanford
Floor exercise	Kat Ding, Georgia	Geralen Stack-Eaton, Alabama
		Elyse Hopfner-Hibbs, UCLA
Vault	Kytra Hunter, Florida	Diandra Milliner, Alabama

Skiing

MEN

	Champion	Runner-Up
Slalom	Epsen Lysdahl, Denver	Tim Kelley, Vermont
Giant slalom	Adam Zika, Colorado	Ryan Wilson, Utah
10-kilometer free	Erik Soderman, N Michigan	Miles Havlick, Utah
20-kilometer classic	Miles Havlick, Utah	David Norris, Montana State

WOMEN

	Champion	Runner-Up
Slalom	Kate Ryley, Vermont	Kristina Riis-Johannessen, Vermont
Giant slalom	Rebecca Nadler, Harvard	Kate Ryley, Vermont
5-kilometer free	Maria Graefnings, Utah	Caitlin Patterson, Vermont
15-kilometer classic	Amy Glen, Vermont	Sophie Caldwell, Dartmouth

Wrestling

	Champion	Runner-Up
125 lb	Matt McDonough, Iowa	Nicholas Megaludis, Penn St
133 lb	Logan Stieber, Ohio St	Jordan Oliver, Oklahoma St
141 lb	Kellen Russell, Michigan	Montell Marion, Iowa
149 lb	Frank Molinaro, Penn St	Dylan Ness, Minnesota
157 lb	Kyle Drake, Cornell	Derek St. John, Iowa
165 lb	David Taylor, Penn St	Brandon Hatchett, Lehigh
174 lb	Edward Ruth, Penn St	Nick Amuchastegui, Stanford
184 lb	Steve Bosak, Cornell	Quentin Wright, Penn St
197 lb	Cam Simaz, Cornell	Christopher Honeycutt, Edinboro
285 lb	Anthony Nelson, Minnesota	Zachary Rey, Lehigh

Swimming and Diving — Men

	Champion	Time	Runner-Up	Time
50-yd freestyle	James Feigen, Texas	19.01	Vladimir Morozov	19.08
100-yd freestyle	James Feigen, Texas	41.95	Marcelo Chierighini, Auburn	42.34
200-yd freestyle	Daxon Hill, Texas	1:32.51	Dmitri Colupaev, Southern Cal	1:32.91
500-yd freestyle	Martin Grodzki, Georgia	4:12.95	Cristian Quintero, Southern Cal	4:13.07
1650-yd freestyle	Martin Grodzki, Georgia	14:24.08*	Chad LaTourette, Stanford	14:24.35
100-yd backstroke	Thomas Shields, California	44.86	David Nolan, Stanford	45.53
200-yd backstroke	Cory Chitwood, Arizona	1:39.66	David Nolan, Stanford	1:39.74
100-yd breaststroke	Kevin Cordes, Arizona	51.71	Carlos Almeida, Louisville	51.78
200-yd breaststroke	Carlos Almeida, Louisville	1:51.88	Trevor Hoyt, California	1:51.90
100-yd butterfly	Thomas Shields, California	44.76	Giles Smith, Arizona	45.77
200-yd butterfly	Will Hamilton, California	1:40.94	Thomas Shields, California	1:41.07
200-yd IM	Marcin Tarczynski, California	1:41.97	Marcin Cieslak, Florida	1:42.26
400-yd IM	Austen Thompson, Arizona	3:39.15	Kyle Whitaker, Michigan	3:41.37
200-yd free relay	California	1:16.58	Auburn	1:16.67
400-yd free relay	Texas	2:49.83	California/Auburn	2:50.34
800-yd free relay	Texas	6:15.55	California	6:15.70
200-yd medley relay	Arizona	1:23.53a	California	1:23.91
400-yd medley relay	California	3:03.24	Arizona	3:04.83
1-meter diving	Drew Livingston, Texas	448.10	Kristian Ipsen, Stanford	410.15
3-meter diving	Kristian Ipsen, Stanford	469.20	Drew Livingston, Texas	454.25
Platform	Ben Grado, Arizona	487.25	David Bonuchi, Missouri	456.00

*NCAA record. a-American record.

Winter 2011-12 (*Cont.*)
Swimming and Diving — Women

	Champion	Time/Pts	Runner-Up	Time/Pts
50-yd freestyle	Liv Jensen, California	21.48	Margo Geer, Arizona	21.64
100-yd freestyle	A. Vanderpool-Wallace, Auburn	46.88	Megan Romano, Georgia	47.01
200-yd freestyle	Megan Romano, Georgia	1:41.21	Karlee Bispo, Texas	1:42.78
500-yd freestyle	Haley Anderson, Southern Cal	4:34.48	Amber McDermott, Georgia	4:35.09
1650-yd freestyle	Stephanie Peacock, N Carolina	15:38.79*	Wendy Trott, Georgia	15:38.94
100-yd backstroke	Cindy Tran, California	50.31	Megan Romano, Georgia	51.37
200-yd backstroke	Elizabeth Beisel, Florida	1:50.58	Madeline Dirado, Stanford	1:51.42
100-yd breaststroke	Breeja Larson, Texas A&M	57.71	Ashley Danner, George Mason	59.02
200-yd breaststroke	Caitlin Leverenz, California	2:04.76	Haley Spencer, Minnesota	2:07.24
100-yd butterfly	Sara Isakovic, California	51.49	Olivia Scott, Auburn	51.61
200-yd butterfly	Katinka Hosszu, Southern Cal	1:51.32	Cammile Adams, Texas A&M	1:52.40
200-yd IM	Caitlin Leverenz, California	1:51.77	Katinka Hosszu, Southern Cal	1:54.45
400-yd IM	Katinka Hosszu, Southern Cal	3:56.54*	Caitlin Leverenz, California	3:57.89a
200-yd free relay	Stanford	1:26.85	California	1:27.22
400-yd free relay	Stanford	3:10.77a	Auburn	3:11.49
800-yd free relay	Georgia	6:55.96	California	6:57.50
200-yd medley relay	California	1:34.24	Arizona	1:35.71
400-yd medley relay	California	3:28.10*	Arizona	3:29.13
1-meter diving	Tory Ishimatsu, Southern Cal	354.10	Jaele Patrick, Texas A&M	348.90
3-meter diving	Jaele Patrick, Texas A&M	410.15	Bianca Alvarez, Ohio St	386.30
Platform	Chen Ni, IUPUI	343.05	Victoria Lamp, Tennessee	333.45

*NCAA record.   a-American record.

Indoor Track and Field — Men

	Champion	Time/Mark	Runner-Up	Time/Mark
60-meter dash	Jeff Demps, Florida	6.56	Andrew Riley, Illinois	6.57
60-meter hurdles	Jarret Eaton, Syracuse	7.54	Devon Hill, Miami	7.55
200-meter dash	Akheem Gauntlett, Arkansas	20.62	Maurice Mitchell, Florida St	20.66
400-meter dash	Mike Berry, Oregon	45.93	Marek Niit, Arkansas	46.04
800-meter run	Mason McHenry, Arizona St	1:47.96	Michael Preble, Texas A&M	1:48.11
4x400-meter relay	Baylor	3:07.86	Indiana	3:10.75
Mile run	Chris O'Hare, Tulsa	4:01.66	Rich Peters, Boston U	4:01.78
3,000-meter run	Lawi Lalang, Arizona	7:46.64	Chris Derrick, Stanford	7:46.81
5,000-meter run	Lawi Lalang, Arizona	13:25.11	Chris Derrick, Stanford	13:26.88
Distance medley	Notre Dame	9:35.48	Indiana	9:35.67
High jump	Nick Ross, Arizona	§2.23m	Darius King, Indiana	2.23m
Pole Vault	Andrew Irwin, Arkansas	5.55m	Marvin Reitze, South Carolina	5.50m
Long jump	Damar Forbes, LSU	7.99m	Marquise Goodwin, Texas	7.98m
Triple jump	Omar Craddock, Florida	16.75m	Chris Benard, Arizona St	16.50m
Shot put	Jordan Clarke, Arizona St	20.86m	Jacob Thormaehlen, Texas	20.50m
Weight throw	Marcel Lomnicky, Virginia Tech	22.05m	Jeremy Postin, Florida	21.51m
Heptathlon	Curtis Beach, Duke	6,138 pts	Japheth Cato, Wisconsin	6,082 pts

Indoor Track and Field — Women

	Champion	Time/Mark	Runner-Up	Time/Mark
60-meter dash	English Gardner, Oregon	7.12	Octavious Freeman, Central Florida	7.15
60-meter hurdles	Christina Manning, Ohio St	7.91	Brianna Rollins, Clemson	7.93
200-meter dash	Kimberlyn Duncan, LSU	22.74	Kamaria Brown, Texas A&M	23.05
400-meter dash	Regina George, Arkansas	52.54	Lanie Whittaker, Florida	52.80
800-meter run	Nachelle Mackie, BYU	2:03.30	Natalja Piliusina, Oklahoma St	2:04.48
4x400-meter relay	Tennessee	3:34.13	Texas Tech	3:34.66
Mile run	Lucy Van Dalen, Stony Brook	4:39.76	Aisha Praught, Illinois St	4:39.85
3,000-meter run	Aisha Praught, Georgetown	9:15.44	Deborah Maier, California	9:15.74
5,000-meter run	Betsy Saina, Iowa St	15:38.83	Deborah Maier, California	15:40.74
Distance medley	Washington	11:05.20	Oregon	11:05.85
High jump	Brigetta Barrett, Arizona	1.96m	Krystle Schade, Alabama	1.84m
Pole vault	Tina Sutej, Arkansas	4.45m	Krystle Schade, Alabama	4.40m
Long jump	Whitney Gipson, TCU	6.91m*	Leah Eber, Purdue	6.43m
Triple jump	Andrea Geubelle, Kansas	13.67m	Tori Franklin, Michigan St	13.34m
Shot Put	Julie Labonte, Arizona	17.68m	Skylar White, Baylor	17.42m
Weight throw	Ida Storm, UCLA	21.48m	Brittany Smith, Illinois St	20.89m
Pentathlon	Brianne Theisen, Oregon	4,536 pts	Dorcas Akinniyi, Wisconsin	4,299 pts

Rifle

	Champion	Pts	Runner-Up	Pts
Smallbore	Sarah Scherer, TCU	688.6	Michael Matthews, USMA	687.6
Air rifle	Petra Zublasing, West Virginia	696.2	Abigail Stanec, Mississippi	693.5

§-Final place determined by which athlete cleared height first. *Collegiate record.

Spring 2012

Golf

	Champion	Score	Runner-Up	Score
MEN	Thomas Pieters, Illinois	208	Julien Brun, TCU	211
WOMEN	Chirapat Jao-Javanil, Oklahoma	282	Brooke Pancake, Alabama	286

Outdoor Track and Field

MEN

	Champion	Time/Mark	Runner-Up	Time/Mark
100-meter dash	Andrew Riley, Illinois	10.28	Harry Adams, Auburn	10.28
200-meter dash	Maurice Mitchell, Florida St	20.40	Ameer Webb, Texas A&M	20.65
400-meter dash	Tony McQuay, Florida	44.58	Mike Berry, Oregon	44.75
4x100-meter relay	LSU	38.38	Florida St	38.57
800-meter run	Charles Jock, UC-Irvine	1:45.59	Erik Sowinski, Iowa	1:45.90
1,500-meter run	Andrew Bayer, Indiana	3:43.82	Miles Batty, BYU	3:43.83
4x400-meter relay	Florida	3:00.02	Southern Cal	3:00.64
5,000-meter run	Cameron Levins, S Utah	13:40.05	Paul Chelimo, UNC-Greensboro	13:41.04
10,000-meter run	Cameron Levins, S Utah	28:07.14	Stephen Sambu, Arizona	28:09.52
110-meter hurdles	Andrew Riley, Illinois	13.53	Wayne Davis II, Texas A&M	13.60
400-meter hurdles	Amaechi Morton, Stanford	48.79	Jamele Mason, Texas Tech	48.89
3,000-meter steeple	Donn Cabral, Princeton	8:35.44	Craig Forys, Michigan	8:40.66
High jump	Erik Kynard, Kansas St	2.34m	Derek Drouin, Indiana	2.31m
Pole vault	Jack Whitt, Oral Roberts	5.65m	Michael Woepse, UCLA	5.55m
Long jump	Clive Chafausipo, Oral Roberts	7.82m	Stephan Scott-Ellis, Washington St	7.80m
Triple jump	Omar Craddock, Florida	16.92m	Hasheem Halim, Virginia Tech	16.49m
Shot put	Jordan Clarke, Arizona St	20.40m	Stephen Saenz, Auburn	19.78m
Discus throw	Chad Wright, Nebraska	62.79m	Mason Finley, Kansas	61.02m
Hammer throw	Alexander Ziegler, Virginia Tech	75.78m	Jeremy Postin, Florida	69.47m
Javelin throw	Tim Glover, Illinois St	81.69m	Matthias Treff, Virginia Tech	75.83m
Decathlon	Kurt Felix, Boise St	8,062 pts	Romain Martin, UT-Arlington	7,956 pts

WOMEN

	Champion	Time/Mark	Runner-Up	Time/Mark
100-meter dash	English Gardner, Oregon	11.10	Kimberlyn Duncan, LSU	11.11
200-meter dash	Kimberlyn Duncan, LSU	22.86	Kai Selvon, Auburn	23.19
400-meter dash	Ashley Spencer, Illinois	50.95	Rebecca Alexander, LSU	51.20
4x100-meter relay	LSU	42.75	Texas A&M	42.82
800-meter run	Nachelle Mackie, BYU	2:01.06	Charlene Lipsey, LSU	2:01.40
1,500-meter run	Katie Flood, Washington	4:12.65	Emily Infeld, Georgetown	4:14.02
4x400-meter relay	Oregon	3:24.54†	LSU	3:24.59
5,000-meter run	Abbey D'Agostino, Dartmouth	16:11.34	Megan Goethals, Washington	16:11.37
10,000-meter run	Natosha Rogers, Texas A&M	32:41.63	Aliphine Tuliamuk, Wichita State	32:45.43
100-meter hurdles	Christina Manning, Ohio State	12.89	Brianna Rollins, Clemson	12.91
400-meter hurdles	Cassandra Tate, LSU	55.22	Turquoise Thompson, UCLA	55.28
3,000-meter steeple	Shalaya Kipp, Colorado	9:49.02	Genevieve LaCaze, Florida	9:50.25
High jump	Brigetta Barrett, Arizona	1.93m	Shanay Briscoe, Texas	1.90m
Pole vault	Katerina Stefanidi, Stanford	4.45m†	Morgann Leleux, Georgia	4.40m
Long jump	Whitney Gipson, TCU	6.82m	Tori Bowie, So. Mississippi	6.66m
Triple jump	Shanieka Thomas, San Diego St	13.96m	Andrea Geubelle, Kansas	13.84m
Shot put	Tia Brooks, Oklahoma	18.44m	Kearsten Peoples, Missouri	17.31m
Discus throw	Whitney Ashley, San Diego St	59.99m	Beth Rohl, Michigan St	56.85m
Hammer throw	Brittany Smith, Illinois State	68.45m	Jenny Ozorai, Southern Cal	65.91m
Javelin throw	Brianna Bain, Stanford	54.93m	Emily Tyrrell, Montana St	50.50m
Heptathlon	Brianne Theisen, Oregon	6,440 pts†	Barbara Nwaba, UC-S. Barbara	5,927 pts

†NCAA meet record.

Tennis

		Champion	Score	Runner-Up
MEN	Singles	Steve Johnson, Southern Cal	6–4, 6–4	Eric Quigley, Kentucky
	Doubles	C. Buchanan/B. Rola, Ohio St	7–6 (4), 6–3	R. Carvalho/G. Escobar, Texas Tech
WOMEN	Singles	Nicole Gibbs, Stanford	2–6, 7–6 (5), 6–3	Mallory Burdette, Stanford
	Doubles	N. Gibbs/M. Burdette, Stanford	6–2, 6–4	N. Gilchrist/C. Gullickson, Georgia

DIVISION I

Year	Champion	Coach	Score	Runner-Up	Most Outstanding Player
1947	California*	Clint Evans	8–7	Yale	No award
1948	USC	Sam Barry	9–2	Yale	No award
1949	Texas*	Bibb Falk	10–3	Wake Forest	Charles Teague, Wake Forest, 2B
1950	Texas	Bibb Falk	3–0	Washington St	Ray VanCleef, Rutgers, CF
1951	Oklahoma*	Jack Baer	3–2	Tennessee	Sidney Hatfield, Tennessee, P-1B
1952	Holy Cross	Jack Barry	8–4	Missouri	James O'Neill, Holy Cross, P
1953	Michigan	Ray Fisher	7–5	Texas	J.L. Smith, Texas, P
1954	Missouri	John (Hi) Simmons	4–1	Rollins	Tom Yewcic, Michigan St, C
1955	Wake Forest	Taylor Sanford	7–6	Western Michigan	Tom Borland, Oklahoma St, P
1956	Minnesota	Dick Siebert	12–1	Arizona	Jerry Thomas, Minnesota, P
1957	California*	George Wolfman	1–0	Penn St	Cal Emery, Penn St, P-1B
1958	USC	Rod Dedeaux	8–7†	Missouri	Bill Thom, USC, P
1959	Oklahoma St	Toby Greene	5–3	Arizona	Jim Dobson, Oklahoma St, 3B
1960	Minnesota	Dick Siebert	2–1‡	USC	John Erickson, Minnesota, 2B
1961	USC*	Rod Dedeaux	1–0	Oklahoma St	Littleton Fowler, Oklahoma St, P
1962	Michigan	Don Lund	5–4	Santa Clara	Bob Garibaldi, Santa Clara, P
1963	USC	Rod Dedeaux	5–2	Arizona	Bud Hollowell, USC, C
1964	Minnesota	Dick Siebert	5–1	Missouri	Joe Ferris, Maine, P
1965	Arizona St	Bobby Winkles	2–1#	Ohio St	Sal Bando, Arizona St, 3B
1966	Ohio St	Marty Karow	8–2	Oklahoma St	Steve Arlin, Ohio St, P
1967	Arizona St	Bobby Winkles	11–2	Houston	Ron Davini, Arizona St, C
1968	USC*	Rod Dedeaux	4–3	Southern Illinois	Bill Seinsoth, USC, 1B
1969	Arizona St	Bobby Winkles	10–1	Tulsa	John Dolinsek, Arizona St, LF
1970	USC	Rod Dedeaux	2–1	Florida St	Gene Ammann, Florida St, P
1971	USC	Rod Dedeaux	7–2	Southern Illinois	Jerry Tabb, Tulsa, 1B
1972	USC	Rod Dedeaux	1–0	Arizona St	Russ McQueen, USC, P
1973	USC*	Rod Dedeaux	4–3	Arizona St	Dave Winfield, Minnesota, P-OF
1974	USC	Rod Dedeaux	7–3	Miami (Fla.)	George Milke, USC, P
1975	Texas	Cliff Gustafson	5–1	S Carolina	Mickey Reichenbach, Texas, 1B
1976	Arizona	Jerry Kindall	7–1	Eastern Michigan	Steve Powers, Arizona, P-DH
1977	Arizona St	Jim Brock	2–1	S Carolina	Bob Horner, Arizona St, 3B
1978	USC*	Rod Dedeaux	10–3	Arizona St	Rod Boxberger, USC, P
1979	CSU–Fullerton	Augie Garrido	2–1	Arkansas	Tony Hudson, CSU–Fullerton, P
1980	Arizona	Jerry Kindall	5–3	Hawaii	Terry Francona, Arizona, LF
1981	Arizona St	Jim Brock	7–4	Oklahoma St	Stan Holmes, Arizona St, LF
1982	Miami (Fla.)*	Ron Fraser	9–3	Wichita St	Dan Smith, Miami (Fla.), P
1983	Texas*	Cliff Gustafson	4–3	Alabama	Calvin Schiraldi, Texas, P
1984	CSU–Fullerton	Augie Garrido	3–1	Texas	John Fishel, CSU–Fullerton, LF
1985	Miami (Fla.)	Ron Fraser	10–6	Texas	Greg Ellena, Miami (Fla.), DH
1986	Arizona	Jerry Kindall	10–2	Florida St	Mike Senne, Arizona, LF
1987	Stanford	Mark Marquess	9–5	Oklahoma St	Paul Carey, Stanford, RF
1988	Stanford	Mark Marquess	9–4	Arizona St	Lee Plemel, Stanford, P
1989	Wichita St	Gene Stephenson	5–3	Texas	Greg Brummett, Wichita St, P
1990	Georgia	Steve Webber	2–1	Oklahoma St	Mike Rebhan, Georgia, P
1991	LSU	Skip Bertman	6–3	Wichita St	Gary Hymel, LSU, C
1992	Pepperdine	Andy Lopez	3–2	CSU–Fullerton	Phil Nevin, CSU–Fullerton, 3B
1993	LSU	Skip Bertman	8–0	Wichita St	Todd Walker, LSU, 2B
1994	Oklahoma	Larry Cochell	13–5	Georgia Tech	Chip Glass, Oklahoma, CF
1995	CSU–Fullerton*	Augie Garrido	11–5	USC	Mark Kotsay, CSU–Fullerton, CF-P
1996	LSU*	Skip Bertman	9–8	Miami (Fla.)	Pat Burrell, Miami (Fla.), 3B
1997	LSU*	Skip Bertman	13–6	Alabama	Brandon Larson, LSU, SS
1998	USC	Mike Gillespie	21–14	Arizona St	Wes Rachels, USC, 2B
1999	Miami (Fla.)	Jim Morris	6–5	Florida St	Marshall McDougall, FSU 3B/2B
2000	LSU*	Skip Bertman	6–5	Stanford	Trey Hodges, LSU, P
2001	Miami (Fla.)*	Jim Morris	12–1	Stanford	Charlton Jimerson, Miami (Fla.), OF
2002	Texas	Augie Garrido	12–6	South Carolina	Huston Street, Texas, P
2003	Rice	Wayne Graham	14–2^	Stanford	John Hudgins, Stanford, P
2004	CSU–Fullerton	George Horton	3–2^	Texas	Jason Windsor, CSU–Fullerton
2005	Texas	Augie Garrido	6–2^	Florida	David Maroul, Texas

*Undefeated teams in College World Series play.
†12 innings.   ‡10 innings.   #15 innings.   ^Score of decisive game of best-of-three series.

Baseball (Cont.)

DIVISION I (CONT.)

Year	Champion	Coach	Score	Runner-Up	Most Outstanding Player
2006	Oregon St	Pat Casey	3–2^	North Carolina	Jonah Nickerson, Oregon St, P
2007	Oregon St	Pat Casey	9–3^	North Carolina	Jorge Reyes, Oregon St, P
2008	Fresno St	Mike Batesole	6–1^	Georgia	Tommy Mendonca. Fresno St, 3B
2009	LSU	Paul Mainieri	11–4^	Texas	Jared Mitchell, LSU, OF
2010	South Carolina	Ray Tanner	2–1^†	UCLA	Jackie Bradley Jr., South Carolina, OF
2011	South Carolina	Ray Tanner	5–2^	Florida	Scott Wingo, South Carolina, 2B
2012	Arizona	Andy Lopez	4–1^	South Carolina	Robert Refsnyder, Arizona, OF

*Undefeated teams in College World Series play. †11 innings. ^Score of decisive game of best-of-three series.

DIVISION II

Year	Champion	Year	Champion	Year	Champion
1968	Chapman	1984	CSU–Northridge	2000	SE Oklahoma St
1969	Illinois St	1985	Florida Southern	2001	St. Mary's (Tex.)
1970	CSU-Northridge	1986	Troy St	2002	Columbus St
1971	Florida Southern	1987	Troy St	2003	Central Missouri St
1972	Florida Southern	1988	Florida Southern	2004	Kennesaw St
1973	UC–Irvine	1989	Cal Poly–SLO	2005	Florida Southern
1974	UC–Irvine	1990	Jacksonville St	2006	Tampa
1975	Florida Southern	1991	Jacksonville St	2007	Tampa
1976	Cal Poly–Pomona	1992	Tampa	2008	Mount Olive
1977	UC–Riverside	1993	Tampa	2009	Lynn
1978	Florida Southern	1994	Central Missouri St	2010	Southern Indiana
1979	Valdosta St	1995	Florida Southern	2011	West Florida
1980	Cal Poly–Pomona	1996	Kennesaw St	2012	West Chester
1981	Florida Southern	1997	CSU–Chico		
1982	UC–Riverside	1998	Tampa		
1983	Cal Poly–Pomona	1999	CSU–Chico		

DIVISION III

Year	Champion	Year	Champion	Year	Champion
1976	CSU-Stanislaus	1989	N. Carolina Wesleyan	2002	Eastern Connecticut St
1977	CSU-Stanislaus	1990	Eastern Connecticut St	2003	Chapman
1978	Glassboro St	1991	Southern Maine	2004	UW-Stevens Pt
1979	Glassboro St	1992	William Paterson	2005	Wisconsin
1980	Ithaca	1993	Montclair St	2006	Marietta
1981	Marietta	1994	UW-Oshkosh	2007	Kean
1982	Eastern Connecticut St	1995	La Verne	2008	Trinity (Conn.)
1983	Marietta	1996	William Paterson	2009	St. Thomas (Minn.)
1984	Ramapo	1997	Southern Maine	2010	Illinois Wesleyan
1985	UW-Oshkosh	1998	Eastern Connecticut St	2011	Marietta
1986	Marietta	1999	N.Carolina Wesleyan	2012	Marietta
1987	Montclair St	2000	Montclair St		
1988	Ithaca	2001	St. Thomas (Minn.)		

Ice Hockey

Men

DIVISION I

Year	Champion	Coach	Score	Runner-Up	Most Outstanding Player
1948	Michigan	Vic Heyliger	8–4	Dartmouth	Joe Riley, Dartmouth, F
1949	Boston College	John Kelley	4–3	Dartmouth	Dick Desmond, Dartmouth, G
1950	Colorado College	Cheddy Thompson	13–4	Boston University	Ralph Bevins, Boston University, G
1951	Michigan	Vic Heyliger	7–1	Brown	Ed Whiston, Brown, G
1952	Michigan	Vic Heyliger	4–1	Colorado College	Kenneth Kinsley, Colorado Coll, G
1953	Michigan	Vic Heyliger	7–3	Minnesota	John Matchefts, Michigan, F
1954	Rensselaer	Ned Harkness	5–4 (OT)	Minnesota	Abbie Moore, Rensselaer, F
1955	Michigan	Vic Heyliger	5–3	Colorado College	Philip Hilton, Colorado College, D
1956	Michigan	Vic Heyliger	7–5	Michigan Tech	Lorne Howes, Michigan, G
1957	Colorado College	Thomas Bedecki	13–6	Michigan	Bob McCusker, Colorado Coll, F
1958	Denver	Murray Armstrong	6–2	North Dakota	Murray Massier, Denver, F
1959	North Dakota	Bob May	4–3 (OT)	Michigan St	Reg Morelli, North Dakota, F
1960	Denver	Murray Armstrong	5–3	Michigan Tech	Lou Angotti, Michigan Tech, F
					Bob Marquis, Boston U, F
					Barry Urbanski, Boston U, G
1961	Denver	Murray Armstrong	12–2	St. Lawrence	Bill Masterton, Denver, F

Men (Cont.)
DIVISION I (CONT.)

Year	Champion	Coach	Score	Runner-Up	Most Outstanding Player
1962	Michigan Tech	John MacInnes	7–1	Clarkson	Lou Angotti, Michigan Tech, F
1963	North Dakota	Barney Thorndycraft	6–5	Denver	Al McLean, North Dakota, F
1964	Michigan	Allen Renfrew	6–3	Denver	Bob Gray, Michigan, G
1965	Michigan Tech	John MacInnes	8–2	Boston College	Gary Milroy, Michigan Tech, F
1966	Michigan St	Amo Bessone	6–1	Clarkson	Gaye Cooley, Michigan St, G
1967	Cornell	Ned Harkness	4–1	Boston University	Walt Stanowski, Cornell, D
1968	Denver	Murray Armstrong	4–0	North Dakota	Gerry Powers, Denver, G
1969	Denver	Murray Armstrong	4–3	Cornell	Keith Magnuson, Denver, D
1970	Cornell	Ned Harkness	6–4	Clarkson	Daniel Lodboa, Cornell, D
1971	Boston University	Jack Kelley	4–2	Minnesota	Dan Brady, Boston University, G
1972	Boston University	Jack Kelley	4–0	Cornell	Tim Regan, Boston University, G
1973	Wisconsin	Bob Johnson	4–2	Vacated	Dean Talafous, Wisconsin, F
1974	Minnesota	Herb Brooks	4–2	Michigan Tech	Brad Shelstad, Minnesota, G
1975	Michigan Tech	John MacInnes	6–1	Minnesota	Jim Warden, Michigan Tech, G
1976	Minnesota	Herb Brooks	6–4	Michigan Tech	Tom Vanelli, Minnesota, F
1977	Wisconsin	Bob Johnson	6–5 (OT)	Michigan	Julian Baretta, Wisconsin, G
1978	Boston University	Jack Parker	5–3	Boston College	Jack O'Callahan, Boston Univ, D
1979	Minnesota	Herb Brooks	4–3	North Dakota	Steve Janaszak, Minnesota, G
1980	North Dakota	John Gasparini	5–2	Northern Michigan	Doug Smail, North Dakota, F
1981	Wisconsin	Bob Johnson	6–3	Minnesota	Marc Behrend, Wisconsin, G
1982	North Dakota	John Gasparini	5–2	Wisconsin	Phil Sykes, North Dakota, F
1983	Wisconsin	Jeff Sauer	6–2	Harvard	Marc Behrend, Wisconsin, G
1984	Bowling Green	Jerry York	5–4 (OT)	Minn.–Duluth	Gary Kruzich, Bowling Green, G
1985	Rensselaer	Mike Addesa	2–1	Providence	Chris Terreri, Providence, G
1986	Michigan St	Ron Mason	6–5	Harvard	Mike Donnelly, Michigan St, F
1987	North Dakota	John Gasparini	5–3	Michigan St	Tony Hrkac, North Dakota, F
1988	Lake Superior St	Frank Anzalone	4–3 (OT)	St. Lawrence	Bruce Hoffort, Lake Superior St, G
1989	Harvard	Bill Cleary	4–3 (OT)	Minnesota	Ted Donato, Harvard, F
1990	Wisconsin	Jeff Sauer	7–3	Colgate	Chris Tancill, Wisconsin, F
1991	Northern Michigan	Rick Comley	8–7 (3OT)	Boston University	Scott Beattie, Northern Michigan, F
1992	Lake Superior St	Jeff Jackson	4–2	Wisconsin	Paul Constantin, Lake Superior St, F
1993	Maine	Shawn Walsh	5–4	Lake Superior St	Jim Montgomery, Maine, F
1994	Lake Superior St	Jeff Jackson	9–1	Boston University	Sean Tallaire, Lake Superior St, F
1995	Boston University	Jack Parker	6–2	Maine	Chris O'Sullivan, Boston Univ, F
1996	Michigan	Red Berenson	3–2 (OT)	Colorado College	Brendan Morrison, Michigan, F
1997	North Dakota	Dean Blais	6–4	Boston University	Matt Henderson, North Dakota, F
1998	Michigan	Red Berenson	3–2 (OT)	Boston College	Marty Turco, Michigan, G
1999	Maine	Shawn Walsh	3–2 (OT)	New Hampshire	Alfie Michaud, Maine, G
2000	North Dakota	Dean Blais	4–2	Boston College	Lee Goren, North Dakota, F
2001	Boston College	Jerry York	3–2 (OT)	North Dakota	Chuck Kobasew, Boston Coll, F
2002	Minnesota	Don Lucia	4–3 (OT)	Maine	Grant Potulny, Minnesota, F
2003	Minnesota	Don Lucia	5–1	New Hampshire	Thomas Vanek, Minnesota, F
2004	Denver	George Gwozdecky	1–0	Maine	Adam Berkhoel, Denver, G
2005	Denver	George Gwozdecky	4–1	North Dakota	Peter Mannino, Denver
2006	Wisconsin	Mike Eaves	2–1	Boston College	Robbie Earl, Wisconsin, F
2007	Michigan St	Rick Comley	3–1	Boston College	Justin Abdelkader, Michigan St, F
2008	Boston College	Jerry York	4–1	Notre Dame	Nathan Gerbe, Boston Coll, F
2009	Boston University	Jack Parker	4–3 (OT)	Miami (Ohio)	Colby Cohen, Boston University, D
2010	Boston College	Jerry York	5–0	Wisconsin	Ben Smith, Boston College, F
2011	Minn.–Duluth	Scott Sandelin	3–2 (OT)	Michigan	J.T. Brown, Minn.-Dultuh, F
2012	Boston College	Jerry York	4–1	Ferris St	Parker Milner, Boston College, G

DIVISION II (Discontinued)

Year	Champion	Coach	Score	Runner-Up
1978	Merrimack	Thom Lawler	12–2	Lake Forest
1979	Lowell	Bill Riley Jr	6–4	Mankato St
1980	Mankato St	Don Brose	5–2	Elmira
1981	Lowell	Bill Riley Jr	5–4	Plattsburgh St
1982	Lowell	Bill Riley Jr	6–1	Plattsburgh St
1983	RIT	Brian Mason	4–2	Bemidji St
1984	Bemidji St	R.H. (Bob) Peters	14–4*	Merrimack
1993	Bemidji St	R.H. (Bob) Peters	15–6*	Mercyhurst
1994	Bemidji St	R.H. (Bob) Peters	7–6*	Ala.–Huntsville
1995	Bemidji St	R.H. (Bob) Peters	11–6*	Mercyhurst
1996	Ala.–Huntsville	Doug Ross	10–1*	Bemidji St
1997	Bemidji St	R.H. (Bob) Peters	7–4*	Ala.–Huntsville
1998	Ala.–Huntsville	Doug Ross	11–4*	Bemidji St
1999	St. Michael's (Vt.)	Lou DiMasi	12–9*	New Hamp. Coll

*Two-game, total-goal series.

Men *(Cont.)*
DIVISION III

Year	Champion	Coach	Score	Runner-Up
1984	Babson	Bob Riley	8–0	Union (N.Y.)
1985	RIT	Bruce Delventhal	5–1	Bemidji St
1986	Bemidji St	R.H. (Bob) Peters	8–5	Vacated
1987	Vacated			Oswego St
1988	UW-River Falls	Rick Kozuback	7–1, 3–5, 3–0	Elmira
1989	UW-Stevens Point	Mark Mazzoleni	3–3, 3–2	RIT
1990	UW-Stevens Point	Mark Mazzoleni	10–1, 3–6, 1–0	Plattsburgh St
1991	UW-Stevens Point	Mark Mazzoleni	6–2	Mankato St
1992	Plattsburgh St	Bob Emery	7–3	UW-Stevens Point
1993	UW-Stevens Point	Joe Baldarotta	4–3	UW-River Falls
1994	UW-River Falls	Dean Talafous	6–4	UW-Superior
1995	Middlebury	Bill Beaney	1–0	Fredonia St
1996	Middlebury	Bill Beaney	3–2	RIT
1997	Middlebury	Bill Beaney	3–2	UW-Superior
1998	Middlebury	Bill Beaney	2–1	UW-Stevens Point
1999	Middlebury	Bill Beaney	5–0	UW-Superior
2000	Norwich	Michael McShane	2–1	St. Thomas (Minn.)
2001	Plattsburgh St	Bob Emery	6–2	RIT
2002	UW-Superior	Dan Stauber	3–2	Norwich
2003	Norwich	Michael McShane	2–1	Oswego St
2004	Middlebury	Bill Beaney	1–0	St. Norbert
2005	Middlebury	Bill Beaney	5–0	St. Thomas (Minn.)
2006	Middlebury	Bill Beaney	3–0	St. Norbert
2007	Oswego St	Ed Gosek	4–3	Middlebury
2008	St. Norbert	Tim Coghlin	2–0	Plattsburgh St
2009	Neumann	Dominick Dawes	4–1	Gustavus Adolphus
2010	Norwich	Michael McShane	2–1	St. Norbert
2011	St. Norbert	Tim Coghlin	4–3	Adrian
2012	St. Norbert	Tim Coghlin	4–1	Oswego St

Women - DIVISION I

Year	Champion	Coach	Score	Runner-Up
2001	Minn.-Duluth	Shannon Miller	4–2	St. Lawrence
2002	Minn.-Duluth	Shannon Miller	3–2	Brown
2003	Minn.-Duluth	Shannon Miller	4–3 (2 OT)	Harvard
2004	Minnesota	Laura Holldorson	6–2	Harvard
2005	Minnesota	Laura Holldorson	4–3	Harvard
2006	Wisconsin	Mark Johnson	3–0	Minnesota
2007	Wisconsin	Mark Johnson	4–1	Minnesota
2008	Minn.-Duluth	Shannon Miller	4–0	Wisconsin
2009	Wisconsin	Mark Johnson	5–0	Mercyhurst
2010	Minn.-Duluth	Shannon Miller	3–2 (3 OT)	Cornell
2011	Wisconsin	Mark Johnson	4–1	Boston Univ.
2012	Minnesota	Brad Frost	4–2	Wisconsin

Soccer
Men - DIVISION I

Year	Champion	Coach	Score	Runner-Up
1959	St. Louis	Bob Guelker	5–2	Bridgeport
1960	St. Louis	Bob Guelker	3–2	Maryland
1961	West Chester	Mel Lorback	2–0	St. Louis
1962	St. Louis	Bob Guelker	4–3	Maryland
1963	St. Louis	Bob Guelker	3–0	Navy
1964	Navy	F.H. Warner	1–0	Michigan St
1965	St. Louis	Bob Guelker	1–0	Michigan St
1966	San Francisco	Steve Negoesco	5–2	LIU–Brooklyn
1967	Michigan St	Gene Kenney	0–0	Game called due to
	St. Louis	Harry Keough		inclement weather
1968	Maryland	Doyle Royal	2–2 (2 OT)	
	Michigan St	Gene Kenney		
1969	St. Louis	Harry Keough	4–0	San Francisco
1970	St. Louis	Harry Keough	1–0	UCLA
1971	Vacated		3–2	St. Louis
1972	St. Louis	Harry Keough	4–2	UCLA
1973	St. Louis	Harry Keough	2–1 (OT)	UCLA
1974	Howard	Lincoln Phillips	2–1 (4 OT)	St. Louis

Men - DIVISION I *(CONT.)*

Year	Champion	Coach	Score	Runner-Up
1975	San Francisco	Steve Negoesco	4–0	SIU–Edwardsville
1976	San Francisco	Steve Negoesco	1–0	Indiana
1977	Hartwick	Jim Lennox	2–1	San Francisco
1978	Vacated		2–0	Indiana
1979	SIU–Edwardsville	Bob Guelker	3–2	Clemson
1980	San Francisco	Steve Negoesco	4–3 (OT)	Indiana
1981	Connecticut	Joe Morrone	2–1 (OT)	Alabama A&M
1982	Indiana	Jerry Yeagley	2–1 (8 OT)	Duke
1983	Indiana	Jerry Yeagley	1–0 (2 OT)	Columbia
1984	Clemson	I.M. Ibrahim	2–1	Indiana
1985	UCLA	Sigi Schmid	1–0 (8 OT)	American
1986	Duke	John Rennie	1–0	Akron
1987	Clemson	I.M. Ibrahim	2–0	San Diego St
1988	Indiana	Jerry Yeagley	1–0	Howard
1989	Santa Clara	Steve Sampson	1–1 (2 OT)	
	Virginia	Bruce Arena		
1990	UCLA	Sigi Schmid	1–0 (OT)	Rutgers
1991	Virginia	Bruce Arena	0–0* (3-1 PKs)	Santa Clara
1992	Virginia	Bruce Arena	2–0	San Diego
1993	Virginia	Bruce Arena	2–0	South Carolina
1994	Virginia	Bruce Arena	1–0	Indiana
1995	Wisconsin	Jim Launder	2–0	Duke
1996	St. John's (N.Y.)	Dave Masur	4–1	Florida International
1997	UCLA	Sigi Schmid	2–1	Virginia
1998	Indiana	Jerry Yeagley	3–1	Stanford
1999	Indiana	Jerry Yeagley	1–0	Santa Clara
2000	Connecticut	Ray Reid	2–0	Creighton
2001	North Carolina	Elmar Bolowich	2–0	Indiana
2002	UCLA	Tom Fitzgerald	1–0	Stanford
2003	Indiana	Jerry Yeagley	2–1	St. John's (N.Y.)
2004	Indiana	Jerry Yeagley	1–1 (3-2 PKs)	UC–Santa Barbara
2005	Maryland	Sasho Cirovski	1–0	New Mexico
2006	UC–Santa Barbara	Tim Vom Steeg	2–1	UCLA
2007	Wake Forest	Tony da Luz	2–0	Ohio St
2008	Maryland	Sasha Cirovski	1–0	North Carolina
2009	Virginia	George Gelnovatch	0–0 (3–2 PKs)	Akron
2010	Akron	Caleb Porter	1–0	Louisville
2011	North Carolina	Carlos Somoano	1–0	Charlotte

*Under a rule passed in 1991, the NCAA determined that when a score is tied after regulation and overtime, and the championship is determined by penalty kicks, the official score will be 0–0.

Men - DIVISION II

Year	Champion	Year	Champion	Year	Champion
1972	SIU–Edwardsville	1986	Seattle Pacific	2000	CSU–Dominguez Hills
1973	Missouri–St. Louis	1987	Southern Conn St	2001	Tampa
1974	Adelphi	1988	Florida Tech	2002	Sonoma St
1975	Baltimore	1989	New Hampshire College	2003	Lynn
1976	Loyola (Md.)	1990	Southern Conn St	2004	Seattle
1977	Alabama A&M	1991	Florida Tech	2005	Fort Lewis
1978	Seattle Pacific	1992	Southern Conn St	2006	Dowling (N.Y.)
1979	Alabama A&M	1993	Seattle Pacific	2007	Franklin Pierce
1980	Lock Haven	1994	Tampa	2008	Cal St.–Dominguez Hills
1981	Tampa	1995	Southern Conn St	2009	Fort Lewis
1982	Florida International	1996	Grand Canyon	2010	Northern Kentucky
1983	Seattle Pacific	1997	CSU–Bakersfield	2011	Fort Lewis
1984	Florida International	1998	Southern Conn St		
1985	Seattle Pacific	1999	Southern Conn St		

Men - DIVISION III

Year	Champion	Year	Champion	Year	Champion
1974	Brockport St	1982	N.C.–Greensboro	1990	Glassboro St
1975	Babson	1983	N.C.–Greensboro	1991	UC–San Diego
1976	Brandeis	1984	Wheaton (Ill.)	1992	Kean
1977	Lock Haven	1985	N.C.–Greensboro	1993	UC–San Diego
1978	Lock Haven	1986	N.C.–Greensboro	1994	Bethany (W.V.)
1979	Babson	1987	N.C.–Greensboro	1995	Williams
1980	Babson	1988	UC–San Diego	1996	The College of New Jersey
1981	Glassboro St	1989	Elizabethtown	1997	Wheaton (Ill.)

Men - DIVISION III *(CONT.)*

Year	Champion	Year	Champion	Year	Champion
1998	Ohio Wesleyan	2003	Trinity (Tex.)	2008	Messiah
1999	St. Lawrence	2004	Messiah	2009	Messiah
2000	Messiah	2005	Messiah	2010	Messiah
2001	Richard Stockton	2006	Messiah	2011	Ohio Wesleyan
2002	Messiah	2007	Middlebury		

Women - DIVISION I

Year	Champion	Coach	Score	Runner-Up
1982	North Carolina	Anson Dorrance	2–0	Central Florida
1983	North Carolina	Anson Dorrance	4–0	George Mason
1984	North Carolina	Anson Dorrance	2–0	Connecticut
1985	George Mason	Hank Leung	2–0	North Carolina
1986	North Carolina	Anson Dorrance	2–0	Colorado College
1987	North Carolina	Anson Dorrance	1–0	Massachusetts
1988	North Carolina	Anson Dorrance	4–1	North Carolina St
1989	North Carolina	Anson Dorrance	2–0	Colorado College
1990	North Carolina	Anson Dorrance	6–0	Connecticut
1991	North Carolina	Anson Dorrance	3–1	Wisconsin
1992	North Carolina	Anson Dorrance	9–1	Duke
1993	North Carolina	Anson Dorrance	6–0	George Mason
1994	North Carolina	Anson Dorrance	5–0	Notre Dame
1995	Notre Dame	Chris Petrucelli	1–0	Portland
1996	North Carolina	Anson Dorrance	1–0	Notre Dame
1997	North Carolina	Anson Dorrance	2–0	Connecticut
1998	Florida	Becky Burleigh	1–0	North Carolina
1999	North Carolina	Anson Dorrance	2–0	Notre Dame
2000	North Carolina	Anson Dorrance	2–1	UCLA
2001	Santa Clara	Jerry Smith	1–0	North Carolina
2002	Portland	Clive Charles	2–1	Santa Clara
2003	North Carolina	Anson Dorrance	6–0	Connecticut
2004	Notre Dame	Randy Waldrum	1–1 (OT 4–3)	UCLA
2005	Portland	Garrett Smith	4–0	UCLA
2006	North Carolina	Anson Dorrance	2–1	Notre Dame
2007	USC	Ali Khosroshahin	2–0	Florida St
2008	North Carolina	Anson Dorrance	2–1	Notre Dame
2009	North Carolina	Anson Dorrance	1–0	Stanford
2010	Notre Dame	Randy Waldrum	1–0	Stanford
2011	Stanford	Paul Ratcliffe	1–0	Duke

Women - DIVISION II

Year	Champion	Year	Champion	Year	Champion
1988	CSU–Hayward	1996	Franklin Pierce	2004	Metro St
1989	Barry	1997	Franklin Pierce	2005	Nebraska-Omaha
1990	Sonoma St	1998	Lynn	2006	Metro St
1991	CSU–Dominguez Hills	1999	Franklin Pierce	2007	Tampa
1992	Barry	2000	UC-San Diego	2008	Seattle Pacific
1993	Barry	2001	UC-San Diego	2009	Grand Valley St
1994	Franklin Pierce	2002	Christian Brothers	2010	Grand Valley St
1995	Franklin Pierce	2003	Kennesaw St	2011	St. Rose

Women - DIVISION III

Year	Champion	Year	Champion	Year	Champion
1986	Rochester	1995	UC–San Diego	2004	Wheaton (Ill.)
1987	Rochester	1996	UC–San Diego	2005	Messiah
1988	William Smith	1997	UC–San Diego	2006	Wheaton (Ill.)
1989	UC–San Diego	1998	Macalester	2007	Wheaton (Ill.)
1990	Ithaca	1999	UC–San Diego	2008	Messiah
1991	Ithaca	2000	The College of New Jersey*	2009	Messiah
1992	Cortland St	2001	Ohio Wesleyan	2010	Hardin-Simmons
1993	Trenton St	2002	Ohio Wesleyan	2011	Messiah
1994	Trenton St	2003	Oneonta St		

*formerly Trenton St

Track & Field

There was no way Usain Bolt could keep his fans quiet after his scintillating victory in the 200 meter final at the Olympics in London

BILL FRAKES

2012 Olympics

London, England July 27–August 12, 2012

Men

100 METERS
1. ..Usain Bolt, Jamaica 9.63 OR
2. ..Yohan Blake, Jamaica 9.75
3. ..Justin Gatlin, U.S. 9.79

200 METERS
1. ..Usain Bolt, Jamaica 19.32
2. ..Yohan Blake, Jamaica 19.44
3. ..Warren Weir, Jamaica 19.84

400 METERS
1. ..Kirani James, Grenada 43.94
2. ..Luguelin Santos, Dominican Rep. 44.46
3. ..Lalonde Gordon, Trinidad & Tobago 44.52

800 METERS
1. ....David Lekuta Rudisha, Kenya 1:40.91 WR
2. ..Nijel Amos, Botswana 1:41.73
3. ..Timothy Kitum, Kenya 1:42.53

1,500 METERS
1. ..Taoufik Makhloufi, Algeria 3:34.08
2. ..Leonel Manzano, U.S. 3:34.79
3. ..Abdalaati Iguider, Morocco 3:35.13

5,000 METERS
1. ..Mohamed Farah, G.B. 13:41.66
2. ..Dejen Gebremeskel, Eth. 13:41.98
3. ..Thomas P. Longosiwa, Kenya 13:42.36

10,000 METERS
1. ..Mohamed Farah, G.B. 27:30.42
2. ..Galen Rupp, United States 27:30.90
3. ..Tariku Bekele, Ethiopia 27:31.43

MARATHON
1. ...Stephen Kiprotich, Uganda 2:08:01
2. ..Abel Kirui, Kenya 2:08:27
3. ....Wilson Kipsang Kiprotich, Kenya 2:09:37

110-METER HURDLES
1. ..Aries Merritt, United States 12.92
2. ..Jason Richardson, United States 13.04
3. ..Hansle Parchment, Jamaica 13.12

400-METER HURDLES
1. .. Felix Sanchez, Dominican Republic 47.63
2. ..Michael Tinsley, United States 47.91
3. ..Javier Culson, Puerto Rico 48.10

3,000-METER STEEPLECHASE
1. ..Ezekiel Kemboi, Kenya 8:18.56
2. ..M. Mekhissi-Benabbad, France 8:19.08
3. ..Abel Kiprop Mutai, Kenya 8:19.73

4 X 100-METER RELAY
1. ...Jamaica: (Y. Blake, U, Bolt, 36.84 WR
.....N. Carter, M. Frater)
2. ..United States 37.04
3. ..Trinidad and Tobago 38.12

4 X 400-METER RELAY
1. ..Bahamas: (C. Brown, D. Pinder 2:56.72
.....M. Mathieu, R. Miller)
2. ..United States 2:57.05
3. ..Trinidad and Tobago 2:59.40

20-KILOMETER WALK
1. ..Ding Chen, China 1:18:46 OR
2. ..Erick Barrondo, Guatemala 1:18:57
3. ..Zhen Wang, China 1:19:25

50-KILOMETER WALK
1. ..Sergey Kirdyapkin, Russia 3:35:59 OR
2. ..Jared Tallent, Australia 3:36:53
3. ..Tianfeng Si, China 3:37:16

HIGH JUMP
1. ..Ivan Ukhov, Russia 7 ft 9¾ in
2. ..Erik Kynard, United States 7 ft 7¾ in
3. ..Derek Drouin, Canada 7 ft 6¼ in

POLE VAULT
1. ..Renaud Lavillenie, France 19 ft 7 in OR
2. ..Bjorn Otto, Germany 19 ft 4¾ in
3. ..Raphael Holzdeppe, Germany 19 ft 4¾ in

LONG JUMP
1. ..Greg Rutherford, G Britain 27 ft 3¼ in
2. ..Mitchell Watt, Australia 26 ft 9¼ in
3. ..Will Claye, United States 26 ft 7¾ in

TRIPLE JUMP
1. ..Christian Taylor, United States 58 ft 5¼ in
2. ..Will Claye, U.S. 57 ft 9¾ in
3. ..Fabrizio Donato, Italy 57 ft 4¼ in

SHOT PUT
1. ..Tomasz Majewski, Poland 71 ft 9¾ in
2. ..David Storl, Germany 71 ft 8⅝ in
3. ..Reese Hoffa, United States 69 ft 7¾ in

DISCUS THROW
1. ..Robert Harting, Germany 223 ft 11¾ in
2. ..Ehsan Hadadi, Iran 223 ft 8¼ in
3. ..Gerd Kanter, Estonia 223 ft 2¼ in

HAMMER THROW
1. ..Krisztian Pars, Hungary 264 ft 4¾ in
2. ..Primoz Kozmus, Slovakia 260 ft 4⅜ in
3. ..Koji Murofushi, Japan 258 ft 2¾ in

JAVELIN
1. ..Keshorn Walcott, Trin. and Tob. 277 ft 5⅞ in
2. ....Oleksandr Pyatnytsya, Ukraine 277 ft 3¾ in
3. ..Antti Ruuskanen, Finland 275 ft 11¾ in

DECATHLON
Pts
1. ..Ashton Eaton, United States 8869
2. ..Trey Hardee, United States 8671
3. ..Leonel Suarez, Cuba 8523

Women

100 METERS
1. ..Shelly-Ann Fraser-Pryce, Jamaica 10.75
2. ..Carmelita Jeter, United States 10.78
3. ..Veronica Campbell-Brown, Jamaica 10.81

200 METERS
1. ..Allyson Felix, United States 21.88
2. ....Shelly-Ann Fraser-Pryce, Jamaica 22.09
3. ....Carmelita Jeter, United States 22.14

400 METERS
1. ..Sanya Richards-Ross, United States 49.55
2. ....Christine Ohuruogu, Great Britain 49.70
3. ....DeeDee Trotter, United States 49.72

800 METERS
1. ..Mariya Savinova, Russia 1:56.19
2. ..Caster Semenya, South Africa 1:57.23
3. ..Ekaterina Poistogova, Russia 1:57.53

1,500 METERS
1. ..Asli Cakir Alptekin, Turkey 4:10.23
2. ..Gamze Bulut, Turkey 4:10.40
3. ..Maryam Yusuf Jamal, Bahrain 4:10.74

5,000 METERS
1. ..Meseret Defar, Ethiopia 15:04.25
2. ....Vivian Jepkemoi Cheruiyot, Kenya 15:04.73
3. ..Tirunesh Dibaba, Ethiopia 15:05.15

10,000 METERS
1. ..Tirunesh Dibaba, Ethiopia 30:20.75
2. ....Sally Jepkosgei Kipyego, Kenya 30:26.37
3. ....Vivian Jepkemoi Cheruiyot, Kenya 30:30.44

MARATHON
1. ..Tiki Gelana, Ethiopia 2:23:07 OR
2. ..Priscah Jeptoo, Kenya 2:23:12
3. ...Tatyana Petrova Arkhipova, Russia 2:23:29

100-METER HURDLES
1. ..Sally Pearson, Australia 12.35 OR
2. ..Dawn Harper, United States 12.37
3. ..Kellie Wells, United States 12.48

400-METER HURDLES
1. ..Natalya Antyukh, Russia 52.70
2. ..Lashinda Demus, United States 52.77
3. ..Zuzana Hejnova, Czech Republic 53.38

3,000-METER STEEPLECHASE
1. ..Yuliya Zaripova, Russia 9:06.72
2. ..Habiba Ghribi, Tunisia 9:08.37
3. ..Sofia Assefa, Ethiopia 9:09.84

4 X 100-METER RELAY
1. ...United States: (C. Jeter, T. Madison 40.82 WR
A. Felix, B. Knight)
2. ..Jamaica 41.41
3. ..Ukraine 42.04

Note: OR=Olympic Record. WR=World Record. EOR=Equals Olympic Record. EWR=Equals World Record.

London, England July 27–August 12, 2012
Women (*Cont.*)

4 X 400-METER RELAY
1....United States: (A. Felix,F. McCorory 3:16.87
S. Richards-Ross, D. Trotter)
2. ..Russia   3:20.23
3. ..Jamaica   3:20.95

20-KILOMETER WALK
1. ..Elena Lashmanova Russia   1:25:02 WR
2. ..Olga Kaniskina, Russia   1:25:09
3. ..Shenjie Qieyang, China   1:25:16

HIGH JUMP
1. ..Anna Chicherova, Russia   6 ft 8¾ in
2. ..Brigetta Barrett, United States 6 ft 7⅞ in
3. ..Svetlana Shkolina, Russia   6 ft 7⅞ in

POLE VAULT
1. ..Jennifer Suhr, United States   15 ft 7 in
2. ..Yarisley Silva, Cuba   15 ft 7 in
3. ..Elena Isinbaeva, Russia   15 ft 5 in

LONG JUMP
1. ..Brittney Reese, United States 23 ft 4¼ in
2. ..Elena Sokolova, Russia   23 ft 2¼ in
3. ..Janay Deloach, United States 22 ft 7¼ in

TRIPLE JUMP
1. ..Olga Rypakova, Kazakhstan   49 ft 1¾ in
2. ..Caterine Ibarguen, Colombia   48 ft 6¾ in
3. ..Olha Saladuha, Ukraine   48 ft 6¼ in

SHOT PUT
1. ..Nadzeya Ostapchuk, Belarus   70 ft ⅞ in
2. ..Valerie Adams, New Zealand   67 ft 11 in
3. ..Evgeniia Kolodko, Russia   67 ft 2¼ in

DISCUS THROW
1. ..Sandra Perkovic, Croatia   226 ft 8¾ in
2. ..Darya Pishchalnikova, Russia 221 ft 7¾ in
3. ..Yanfeng Li, China   220 ft 6½ in

HAMMER THROW
1. ..Tatyana Lysenko, Russia   256 ft 6 in OR
2. ..Anita Wlodarczyk, Poland 254 ft 7¼ in
3. ..Betty Heidler, Germany   253 ft ¼ in

JAVELIN
1. ..Barbora Spotakova, Czech Rep. 228 ft 2¼ in
2....Christina Obergfoll, Germany 213 ft 9¾ in
3. ..Linda Stahl, Germany   212 ft 11½ in

HEPTATHLON   Pts
1. ..Jessica Ennis, Great Britain   6955
2. ..Lilli Schwarzkopf, Germany   6649
3. ..Tatyana Chernova, Russia   6628

Note: OR=Olympic Record. WR=World Record. EOR=Equals Olympic Record. EWR=Equals World Record.

World and American Outdoor Records

As of October 1, 2012. World outdoor records are recognized by the International Amateur Athletics Federation (IAAF). American records recognized by U.S.A. Track & Field. (A) represents an American record, (W) represents a World record.

Men

Event	Mark	Record Holder	Date	Site
100 meters	9.58	Usain Bolt, Jamaica (W)	8-16-09	Berlin
	9.69	Tyson Gay (A)	9-20-09	Shanghai
200 meters	19.19	Usain Bolt, Jamaica (W)	8-20-09	Berlin
	19.32	Michael Johnson (A)	8-01-96	Atlanta
400 meters	43.18	Michael Johnson, U.S. (W,A)	8-26-99	Seville, Spain
800 meters	1:41.01	David Lekuta Rudisha, Kenya (W)	8-29-10	Rieti, Italy
	1:42.60	Johnny Gray (A)	8-28-85	Koblenz, Germany
1,000 meters	2:11.96	Noah Ngeny, Kenya (W)	9-05-99	Rieti, Italy
	2:13.90	Rick Wohlhuter (A)	8-31-03	Oslo
1,500 meters	3:26.00	Hicham El Guerrouj, Morocco (W)	7-14-98	Rome
	3:29.30	Bernard Lagat (A)	8-28-05	Rieti, Italy
Mile	3:43.13	Hicham El Guerrouj, Morocco (W)	7-07-99	Rome
	3:46.91	Alan Webb (A)	7-21-07	Brasschaat, Belguim
2,000 meters	4:44.79	Hicham El Guerrouj, Morocco (W)	9-07-99	Berlin
	4:52.44	Jim Spivey (A)	9-15-87	Lausanne, Switzerland
3,000 meters	7:20.67	Daniel Komen, Kenya (W)	9-01-96	Rieti, Italy
	7:29.00	Bernard Lagat (A)	8-29-10	Rieti, Italy
3,000-m Steeplechase	7:53.63	Saif Saaeed Shaheen, Qatar (W)	9-03-04	Brussels
	8:06.81	Evan Jaeger (A)	7-20-12	Monaco
5,000 meters	12:52.79	Kenenisa Bekele, Ethiopia (W)	5-31-04	Hengelo, Netherlands
	12:53.60	Bernard Lagat (A)	7-22-11	Fontvielle, Monaco
10,000 meters	26:17.53	Kenenisa Bekele, Ehtiopia (W)	8-26-05	Brussels
	26:48.00	Galen Rupp (A)	9-16-11	Brussels
Marathon	2:03:38	Patrick Makau Musyoki, Kenya (W)	9-25-11	Berlin
	2:05.38	Khalid Khannouchi (A)	4-14-02	London
110-meter hurdles	12.80	Aries Merritt, United States (W, A)	9-7-12	Brussels
400-meter hurdles	46.78	Kevin Young, United States (W, A)	8-6-92	Barcelona
20-kilometer walk	1:17.16	Vladimir Kanaykin, Russia (W)	9-29-07	Saransk, Russia
	1:23:40	Tim Seaman (A)	3-07-99	Chula Vista, Calif.
50-kilometer walk	3:34:14	Denis Nizhegorodov, Russia (W)	5-11-08	Cheboksary, Russia
4 x 100-meter relay	36.84	Jamaica (Nesta Carter, Michael Prater, Yohan Blake, Usain Bolt)	8-11-12	London
4 x 100-meter relay	37.04	Trell Kimmons, Justin Gatlin (A) Tyson Gay, Ryan Bailey	8-11-12	London

Men (*Cont.*)

4 x 200-meter relay	1:18.68	U.S. (Mike Marsh, Leroy Burrell, (W,A)	4-17-94	Walnut, Calif.
		Floyd Heard, Carl Lewis)		
4 x 400-meter relay	2:54.29	United States (Andrew Valmon, (W,A)	7-22-93	Stuttgart, Germany
		Quincy Watts, Harry Reynolds,		
		Michael Johnson)		
4 x 800-meter relay	7:02.43	Kenya (Wilfred Bungei, (W)	8-25-06	Brussels
		William Yiampoy, Joseph Mutua,		
		Ismael Kombich)		
	7:02.82	Jebreh Harris, Khadevis Robinson, (A)	8-25-06	Brussels
		Sam Burley, David Krummenacker		
4 x 1,500-meter relay	14:36.28	Kenya (W)	9-04-09	Brussels
		(William Biwoot Tanui, Gideon Gathimba,		
		Geoffrey Kipkoech Rono, Augustine Kiprono Choge)		
	14:46.30	Dan Aldridge, Andy Clifford, (A)	6-24-79	Bourges, France
		Todd Harbour, Tom Dults		
High jump	2.45m	Javier Sotomayor, Cuba (W)	7-27-93	Salamanca, Spain
	2.40m	Charles Austin (A)	8-07-91	Zurich
Pole vault	6.14m	Sergei Bubka, Ukraine (W)	7-31-94	Sestriere, Italy
	6.04m	Brad Walker (A)	6-08-08	Eugene, Oregon
Long jump	8.95m	Mike Powell, United States (W, A)	8-30-91	Tokyo
Triple jump	18.29m	Jonathan Edwards, U.K. (W)	8-07-95	Göteborg, Sweden
	18.09m	Kenny Harrison (A)	7-27-96	Atlanta
Shot put	23.12m	Randy Barnes, United States (W, A)	5-20-90	Westwood, Calif.
Discus throw	74.08m	Jürgen Schult, East Germany (W)	6-06-86	Neubrandenburg, Germ.
	72.34m	Ben Plucknett (A)	7-07-81	Stockholm
Hammer throw	86.74m	Yuriy Sedykh, USSR (W)	8-30-86	Stuttgart, Germany
	82.52m	Lance Deal (A)	9-17-96	Milan
Javelin throw	98.48m	Jan Zelezny, Czech Republic (W)	5-25-96	Jena, Germany
	91.29m	Breaux Greer (A)	6-21-07	Indianapolis
Decathlon	9039 pts	Ashton Eaton, United States (W, A)	6-23-12	Eugene, Oregon

Note: The decathlon consists of 10 events: the 100 meters, long jump, shot put, high jump and 400 meters on the first day; the 110-meter hurdles, discus, pole vault, javelin and 1,500 meters on the second.

Women

Event	Mark	Record Holder	Date	Site
100 meters	10.49	Florence Griffith Joyner, U.S. (W, A)	7-16-88	Indianapolis
200 meters	21.34	Florence Griffith Joyner, U.S. (W, A)	9-29-88	Seoul
400 meters	47.60	Marita Koch, E Germany (W)	10-6-85	Canberra, Australia
	48.70	Sanya Richards (A)	9-17-06	Athens
800 meters	1:53.28	Jarmila Kratochvílová, Czech. (W)	7-26-83	Munich
	1:56.40	Jearl Miles-Clark (A)	8-11-99	Zurich
1,000 meters	2:28.98	Svetlana Masterkova, Russia (W)	8-23-96	Brussels
	2:31.80	Regina Jacobs (A)	7-02-99	Brunswick, Maine
1,500 meters	3:50.46	Yunxia Qu, China (W)	9-11-93	Beijing
	3:57.12	Mary Slaney (A)	7-26-83	Stockholm
Mile	4:12.56	Svetlana Masterkova, Russia (W)	8-14-96	Zurich
	4:16.71	Mary Slaney (A)	8-21-85	Zurich
2,000 meters	5:25.36	Sonia O'Sullivan, Ireland (W)	7-08-94	Edinburgh
	5:32.70	Mary Slaney (A)	8-03-84	Eugene, Oregon
3,000 meters	8:06.11	Junxia Wang, China (W)	9-13-93	Beijing
	8:25.83	Mary Slaney (A)	9-07-85	Rome
3,000-m Steeplechase	8:58.81	Gulnara Samitova-Galkina, Russia (W)	8-17-08	Beijing
	9:12.50	Jenny Barringer (A)	8-17-09	Berlin
5,000 meters	14:11.15	Tirunesh Dibaba, Ethiopia (W)	6-06-08	Oslo
	14:44.76	Molly Huddle (A)	8-27-10	Brussels
10,000 meters	29:31.78	Junxia Wang, China (W)	9-08-93	Beijing
	30:22.22	Shalane Flanagan (A)	8-15-08	Beijing
Marathon	2:15:25	Paula Radcliffe, Great Britain (W)	4-13-03	London
	2:19:36	Deena Kastor (A)	4-23-06	London
100-meter hurdles	12.21	Yordanka Donkova, Bulgaria (W)	8-20-88	Stara Zagora, Bulgaria
	12.33	Gail Devers (A)	7-23-00	Sacramento, Calif.
400-meter hurdles	52.34	Yuliya Pechenkina, Russia (W)	8-08-03	Tula, Russia
	52.61	Kim Batten (A)	8-11-95	Gothenburg, Sweden
20-kilometer walk	1:25:08	Vera Sokolova, Russia (W)	2-26-11	Sochi, Russia
	1:33:28.15	Teresa Vaill (A)	6-25-05	Carson, Calif.

Women (Cont.)

4 x 100-meter relay	40.82	United States (Tianna Madison, (W, A) 8-10-12 Allyson Felix, Bianca Knight, Carmelita Jeter)		London
4 x 200-meter relay	1:27.46	United States (LaTasha Jenkins, (W, A) 4-29-00 LaTasha Colander-Richardson, Nanceen Perry, Marion Jones)		Philadelphia
4 x 400-meter relay	3:15.17	USSR (Tatyana Ledovskaya, (W) 10-01-88 Olga Nazarova, Maria Pinigina, Olga Bryzgina)		Seoul
	3:15.51	Denean Howard, Diane Dixon (A) 10-01-88 Valerie Brisco, Florence Griffith-Joyner		Seoul
4 x 800-meter relay	7:50.17	USSR (Nadezhda Olizarenko, (W) 8-05-84 Lyubov Gurina, Lyudmila Borisova, Irina Podyalovskaya)		Moscow
	8:17.91	Chanelle Price, Phoebe Wright (A) 4-24-09 Rolanda Bell, Sarah Bowman		Philadelphia
High jump	2.09m	Stefka Kostadinova, Bulgaria (W)	8-30-87	Rome
	2.05m	Chaunte Howard-Lowe (A)	8-26-10	Des Moines, Iowa
Pole vault	5.06m	Yelena Isinbayeva, Russia (W)	8-28-09	Zurich
	4.92m	Jenn Stuczynski (A)	7-06-08	Eugene, Ore.
Long jump	7.52m	Galina Chistyakova, USSR (W)	6-11-88	Leningrad
	7.49m	Jackie Joyner-Kersee (A)	7-31-94	Sestriere, Italy
Triple jump	15.50m	Inessa Kravets, Ukraine (W)	8-10-95	Gothenburg, Sweden
	14.45m	Tiombe Hurd (A)	7-11-04	Sacramento, Calif.
Shot put	22.63m	Natalya Lisovskaya, USSR (W)	6-07-87	Moscow
	20.18m	Ramona Pagel (A)	6-25-88	San Diego, Calif.
Discus throw	76.80m	Gabriele Reinsch, East Germany (W)	7-09-88	Neubrandenburg, Germ.
	67.74m	Stephanie Brown-Trafton (A)	5-7-12	Wailuku, Haw.
Hammer throw	79.42m	Betty Heidler, Germany (W)	5-21-11	Halle, Germany
	74.19m	Jessica Colby (A)	6-1-12	Eugene, Ore.
Javelin throw	72.28m	Barbora Spotakova, Czech Rep. (W)	9-13-08	Stuttgart
	66.679m	Kara Patterson (A)	6-25-10	Des Moines, Iowa
Heptathlon	7291 pts	Jackie Joyner-Kersee, U.S. (W,A)	9-24-88	Seoul

Note: The heptathlon consists of 7 events: the 100-meter hurdles, high jump, shot put and 200 meters on the first day; the long jump, javelin and 800 meters on the second.

World and American Indoor Records

As of October 1, 2012. World Indoor records are recognized by the International Amateur Athletics Federation (IAAF). American indoor records are recognized by USA Track and Field. (A) represents an American record, (W) represents a World record.

Men

Event	Mark	Record Holder	Date	Site
50 meters	5.56	Donovan Bailey, Canada (W)	2-09-96	Reno, Nev.
	5.56	Maurice Greene (A)	2-12-99	Los Angeles
55 meters*	6.00	Lee McRae (A)	3-14-86	Oklahoma City
60 meters	6.39	Maurice Greene (W, A)	2-03-98	Madrid
	6.39	Maurice Greene (W, A)	3-03-01	Atlanta
200 meters	19.92	Frankie Fredericks, Namibia (W)	2-18-96	Liévin, France
	20.10	Wallace Spearmon (A)	3-11-05	Fayetteville, Ark.
400 meters	44.57	Kerron Clement (W, A)	3-12-05	Fayetteville, Ark.
800 meters	1:40.91	David Lekuta Rudisha, Kenya (W)	8-09-12	London
	1:45.00	Johnny Gray (A)	3-08-92	Sindelfingen, Germany
1,000 meters	2:14.96	Wilson Kipketer, Denmark (W)	2-20-00	Birmingham, England
	2:17.86	David Krummenacker (A)	1-27-02	Boston
1,500 meters	3:31.18	Hicham El Guerrouj, Morocco (W)	2-02-97	Stuttgart, Germany
	3:33.34	Bernard Lagat (A)	2-11-05	Fayetteville, Ark.
Mile	3:48.45	Hicham El Guerrouj, Morocco (W)	2-12-97	Ghent, Belgium
	3:49.89	Bernard Lagat (A)	2-11-05	Fayetteville, Ark.
3,000 meters	7:24.90	Daniel Komen, Kenya (W)	2-06-98	Budapest, Hungary
	7:32.43	Bernard Lagat (A)	2-17-07	Birmingham, England

*No recognized world record.

Men (Cont.)

Event	Mark	Record Holder	Date	Site
5,000 meters	12:49.60	Kenenisa Bekele, Ethiopia (W)	2-20-04	Birmingham, England
	13:07.15	Bernard Lagat (A)	2-9-12	New York City
50-meter hurdles	6.25	Mark McKoy, Canada (W)	3-05-86	Kobe, Japan
	6.35	Greg Foster (A)	1-31-87	Ottawa
	6.35	Greg Foster (A)	1-27-85	Rosemont, Illinois
55-meter hurdles*	6.89	Renaldo Nehemiah (A)	1-20-79	New York City
60-meter hurdles	7.30	Colin Jackson, Great Britain (W)	3-6-94	Sindelfingen, Germany
	7.36	Greg Foster (A)	1-16-87	Los Angeles
	7.36	Allen Johnson (A)	3-06-04	Budapest, Hungary
5,000-meter walk	18:07.08	Mikhail Shchennikov, Russia (W)	2-14-95	Moscow
	19:15.88	Tim Seaman (A)	3-07-87	Indianapolis
4 x 200-meter relay	1:22.11	United Kingdom (Linford Christie, (W) Darren Braithwaite, Ade Mafe, John Regis)	3-03-91	Glasgow
	1:22.71	National Team (A) (Thomas Jefferson, Raymond Pierre, Antonio McKay, Kevin Little)	3-03-91	Glasgow
4 x 400-meter relay	3:02.83	United States (W, A) (Milton Campbell, Deon Minor Dameon Johnson, Andre Morris)	3-07-99	Maebashi, Japan.
4 x 800-meter relay	7:13.94	United States (W, A) (Joey Woody, Karl Paranya, Rich Kenah, David Krummenacker)	2-06-00	Boston
High jump	2.43m	Javier Sotomayor, Cuba (W)	3-4-89	Budapest, Hungary
	2.40m	Hollis Conway (A)	3-10-91	Seville
Pole vault	6.15m	Sergei Bubka, Ukraine (W)	2-21-93	Donetsk, Ukraine
	6.02m	Jeff Hartwig (A)	3-10-02	Sindelfingen, Germany
Long jump	8.79m	Carl Lewis (W, A)	1-27-84	New York City
Triple jump	17.92m	Teddy Tamgho, France (W)	3-6-11	Paris
	17.76m	Mike Conley (A)	2-27-87	New York City
Shot put	22.66m	Randy Barnes (W, A)	1-20-89	Los Angeles
Weight throw*	25.86m	Lance Deal (A)	3-04-95	Atlanta
Pentathlon*	4478 pts	Steve Fritz, (A)	1-14-95	Lawrence, Kan.
Heptathlon	6645 pts	Ashton Eaton (W, A)	3-10-12	Istanbul

*No recognized world record.

Women

Event	Mark	Record Holder	Date	Site
50 meters	5.96	Irina Privolova, Russia (W)	2-09-95	Madrid
	6.02	Gail Devers (A)	2-22-99	Liévin, France
55 meters*	6.56	Gwen Torrence (A)	3-14-87	Oklahoma City, Okla.
60 meters	6.92	Irina Privalova, Russia (W)	2-11-93	Madrid
	6.92	Irina Privalova, Russia (W)	2-09-95	Madrid
	6.95	Gail Devers (A)	3-12-93	Toronto
	6.95	Marion Jones (A)	3-07-98	Maebashi, Japan
200 meters	21.87	Merlene Ottey, Jamaica (W)	2-13-93	Liévin, France
	22.33	Gwen Torrence (A)	3-02-66	Atlanta
400 meters	49.59	Jarmila Kratochvílová, Czecho. (W)	3-07-82	Milan
	50.54	Francena McCorory (A)	3-13-10	Fayetteville, Ark.
800 meters	1:55.82	Jolanda Batagelj, Slovenia (W)	3-03-02	Vienna
	1:58.71	Nicole Teter (A)	3-02-02	New York City
1,000 meters	2:30.94	Maria Mutola, Mozambique (W)	2-25-99	Stockholm
	2:34.19	Jennifer Toomey (A)	2-20-04	Birmingham, England
1,500 meters	3:58.28	Yelena Soboleva, Russia (W)	2-18-06	Moscow
	3:59.98	Regina Jacobs, United States (A)	2-01-03	Boston
Mile	4:17.14	Doina Melinte, Romania (W)	2-09-90	East Rutherford, N.J.
	4:20.50	Mary Slaney (A)	2-19-82	San Diego
3,000 meters	8:23.72	Meseret Defar, Ethiopia (W)	2-03-07	Stuttgart
	8:33.25	Shalane Flanagan (A)	1-27-07	Boston
5,000 meters	14:24.37	Meseret Defar, Ethiopia (W)	2-18-09	Stockholm
	14:47.62	Shalane Flanagan (A)	2-07-09	Boston
50-meter hurdles	6.58	Cornelia Oschkenat, E Germany (W)	2-20-88	Berlin
	6.67	Jackie Joyner-Kersee (A)	2-10-95	Reno, Nev.
55-meter hurdles*	7.37	Jackie Joyner-Kersee (A)	2-03-89	New York City
60-meter hurdles	7.68	Susanna Kallur, Sweden (W)	2-20-08	Berlin
	7.72	Lolo Jones (A)	3-13-10	Doha, Qatar

Women *(Cont.)*

Event	Mark	Record Holder	Date	Site
3,000-meter walk	11:40.33	Claudia Stef, Romania	1-30-99	Bucharest, Romania
	12:20.79	Debbi Lawrence (A)	3-12-93	Toronto
4 x 200-meter relay	1:32.41	Russia (Y. Kondratyeva, (W)	1-29-05	Glasgow
		I. Khabarova, Y. Pechonkina, Y. Gushchina)		
	1:33.24	Flirtisha Harris, Chryste Gaines, (A)	2-12-94	Glasgow
		Terri Dendy, Michele Collins		
4 x 400-meter relay	3:23.37	Russia (Y. Gushchina, (W)	1-28-06	Glasgow
		O. Kotlyarova, O. Zaytseva, O. Krasnomovets)		
	3:27.34	Debbie Dunn, DeeDee Trotter (A)	3-14-10	Doha, Qatar
		Natasha Hastings, Allyson Felix		
4 x 800-meter relay	8:06.24	Russia, (A. Bulanova, E. Martynova (W)	2-18-11	Moscow
		E. Kofanova, A. Balakshina)		
	8:28.41	Wisconsin (Sarah Renk, (A)	3-14-92	Indianapolis
		Kim Sherman, Sue Gentes, Amy Wickus)		
High jump	2.08m	Kajsa Bergqvist, Sweden (W)	2-4-06	Arnstadt, Germany
	2.02m	Chaunte Lowe (A)	2-26-98	Albuquerque, N.M.
Pole vault	5.01m	Yelena Isinbaeva, Russia (W)	2-23-12	Stockholm
	4.88m	Jennifer Suhr (A)	2-4-12	Boston
Long jump	7.37m	Heike Drechsler, East Germany (W)	2-13-88	Vienna
	7.23m	Brittney Reese (A)	3-11-12	Istanbul
Triple jump	15.36m	Tatyana Lebedeva, Russia (W)	3-6-04	Budapest, Hungary
	14.23m	Sheila Hudson-Strudwick (A)	3-4-95	Atlanta
Shot put	22.50m	Helena Fibingerová, Czecho. (W)	2-19-77	Jablonec, Czecho.
	19.89m	Jillian Camarena-Williams (A)	2-11-12	Fayetteville, Ark.
Weight throw*	25.56m	Brittany Riley (A)	3-10-07	Fayetteville, Ark.
Pentathlon	5013 pts	Natallia Dobrynska, Ukraine (W)	3-9-12	Istanbul
	4753 pts	DeDee Nathan (A)	3-4/5-99	Maebashi, Japan
	4753 pts	Hyleas Fountain (A)	3-12/13-10	Doha, Qatar

*No recognized world record.

World Track and Field Championships

Men

100 METERS

1983	Carl Lewis, United States	10.07
1987*	Carl Lewis, United States	9.93 WR
1991	Carl Lewis, United States	9.86 WR
1993	Linford Christie, Great Britain	9.87
1995	Donovan Bailey, Canada	9.97
1997	Maurice Greene, United States	9.86
1999	Maurice Greene, United States	9.80
2001	Maurice Greene, United States	9.82
2003	Kim Collins, St. Kitts & Nevis	10.07
2005	Justin Gatlin, United States	9.88
2007	Tyson Gay, United States	9.85
2009	Usain Bolt, Jamaica	9.58WR
2011	Yohan Blake, Jamaica	9.92

200 METERS

1983	Calvin Smith, United States	20.14
1987	Calvin Smith, United States	20.16
1991	Michael Johnson, United States	20.01
1993	Frank Fredericks, Namibia	19.85
1995	Michael Johnson, United States	19.79
1997	Ato Boldon, Trinidad and Tobago	20.04
1999	Maurice Greene, United States	19.90
2001	Konstadínos Kedéris, Greece	20.04
2003	John Capel, United States	20.30
2005	Justin Gatlin, United States	20.04
2007	Tyson Gay, United States	19.76
2009	Usain Bolt, Jamaica	19.19WR
2011	Usain Bolt, Jamaica	19.40

400 METERS

1983	Bert Cameron, Jamaica	45.05
1987	Thomas Schoenlebe, E Germany	44.33
1991	Antonio Pettigrew, United States	44.57
1993	Michael Johnson, United States	43.65
1995	Michael Johnson, United States	43.39
1997	Michael Johnson, United States	44.12
1999	Michael Johnson, United States	43.18 WR
2001	Avard Moncur, Bahamas	44.64
2003	Jerome Young, United States	44.50
2005	Jeremy Wariner, United States	43.93
2007	Jeremy Wariner, United States	43.45
2009	LaShawn Merritt, United States	44.06
2011	Kirani James, Grenada	44.60

800 METERS

1983	Willi Wulbeck, W Germany	1:43.65
1987	Billy Konchellah, Kenya	1:43.06
1991	Billy Konchellah, Kenya	1:43.99
1993	Paul Ruto, Kenya	1:44.71
1995	Wilson Kipketer, Denmark	1:45.08
1997	Wilson Kipketer, Denmark	1:43.38
1999	Wilson Kipketer, Denmark	1:43.30
2001	André Bucher, Switzerland	1:43.70
2003	Djabir Saïd-Guerni, Algeria	1:44.81
2005	Rashid Ramzi, Brunei	1:44.24
2007	Alfred Kirwa Yego	1:47.09
2009	Mbulaeni Mulaudzi, South Africa	1:45.29
2011	David Lekuta Rudisha, Kenya	1:43.91

WR=World record.   *Ben Johnson, Canada, disqualified.

Men (Cont.)

1,500 METERS

1983	Steve Cram, Great Britain	3:41.59
1987	Abdi Bile, Somalia	3:36.80
1991	Noureddine Morceli, Algeria	3:32.84
1993	Noureddine Morceli, Algeria	3:34.24
1995	Noureddine Morceli, Algeria	3:33.73
1997	Hicham El Guerrouj, Morocco	3:35.83
1999	Hicham El Guerrouj, Morocco	3:27.65
2001	Hicham El Guerrouj, Morocco	3:30.68
2003	Hicham El Guerrouj, Morocco	3:31.77
2005	Rashid Ramzi, Brunei	3:37.88
2007	Bernard Lagat, United States	3:34.77
2009	Yusuf Kamel, Bahrain	3:35.93
2011	Asbel Kiprop, Kenya	3:35.69

3,000-METER STEEPLECHASE

1983	Patriz Ilg, West Germany	8:15.06
1987	Francesco Panetta, Italy	8:08.57
1991	Moses Kiptanui, Kenya	8:12.59
1993	Moses Kiptanui, Kenya	8:06.36
1995	Moses Kiptanui, Kenya	8:04.16
1997	Wilson Boit Kipketer, Kenya	8:05.84
1999	Christopher Koskei, Kenya	8:11.76
2001	Reuben Kosgei, Kenya	8:15.16
2003	Saif Saaeed Shaheen, Qatar	8:04.39
2005	Saif Saaeed Shaheen, Qatar	8:13.31
2007	Brimin Kipruto, Kenya	8:13.82
2009	Ezekiel Kemboi, Kenya	8:00.43
2011	Ezekiel Kemboi, Kenya	8:14.85

5,000 METERS

1983	Eamonn Coghlan, Ireland	13:28.53
1987	Said Aouita, Morocco	13:26.44
1991	Yobes Ondieki, Kenya	13:14.45
1993	Ismael Kirui, Kenya	13:02.75
1995	Ismael Kirui, Kenya	13:16.77
1997	Daniel Komen, Kenya	13:07.38
1999	Salah Hissou, Morocco	12:58.13
2001	Richard Limo, Kenya	13:00.77
2003	Eliud Kipchoge, Kenya	12:52.79
2005	Benjamin Limo, Kenya	13:32.55
2007	Bernard Lagat, United States	13:45.87
2009	Kenenisa Bekele, Ethiopia	13:17.09
2011	Mohamed Farah, U.K.	13:23.36

10,000 METERS

1983	Alberto Cova, Italy	28:01.04
1987	Paul Kipkoech, Kenya	27:38.63
1991	Moses Tanui, Kenya	27:38.74
1993	Haile Gebrselassie, Ethiopia	27:46.02
1995	Haile Gebrselassie, Ethiopia	27:12.95
1997	Haile Gebrselassie, Ethiopia	27:24.58
1999	Haile Gebrselassie, Ethiopia	27:57.27
2001	Charles Kamathi, Kenya	27:53.25
2003	Kenenisa Bekele, Ethiopia	26:49.57
2005	Kenenisa Bekele, Ethiopia	27:08.33
2007	Kenenisa Bekele, Ethiopia	27:05.90
2009	Kenenisa Bekele, Ethiopia	26:46.31
2011	Ibrahim Jeilan, Ethiopia	27:13.81

MARATHON

1983	Rob de Castella, Australia	2:10:03
1987	Douglas Wakiihuri, Kenya	2:11:48
1991	Hiromi Taniguchi, Japan	2:14:57
1993	Mark Plaatjes, United States	2:13:57
1995	Martín Fiz, Spain	2:11:41
1997	Abel Anton, Spain	2:13:16
1999	Abel Anton, Spain	2:13:36

MARATHON (Cont.)

2001	Gezahegne Abera, Ethiopia	2:12:42
2003	Jaouad Gharib, Morocco	2:08.31
2005	Jaouad Gharib, Morocco	2:10:10
2007	Luke Kibet, Kenya	2:15:59
2009	Abel Kirui, Kenya	2:06.54
2011	Abel Kirui, Kenya	2:07:38

110-METER HURDLES

1983	Greg Foster, United States	13.42
1987	Greg Foster, United States	13.21
1991	Greg Foster, United States	13.06
1993	Colin Jackson, Great Britain	12.91 WR
1995	Allen Johnson, United States	13.00
1997	Allen Johnson, United States	12.93
1999	Colin Jackson, Great Britain	13.04
2001	Allen Johnson, United States	13.04
2003	Allen Johnson, United States	13.12
2005	Ladji Doucoure, France	13:07
2007	Liu Xiang, China	12.95
2009	Ryan Brathwaite, Barbados	13.14
2011	Jason Richardson, United States	13.16

400-METER HURDLES

1983	Edwin Moses, United States	47.50
1987	Edwin Moses, United States	47.46
1991	Samuel Matete, Zambia	47.64
1993	Kevin Young, United States	47.18
1995	Derrick Adkins, United States	47.98
1997	Stéphane Diagana, France	47.70
1999	Fabrizio Mori, Italy	47.72
2001	Felix Sánchez, Dominican Rep.	47.49
2003	Felix Sánchez, Dominican Rep.	47.25
2005	Bershawn Jackson, United States	47.30
2007	Kerron Clement, United States	47.61
2009	Kerron Clement, United States	47.91
2011	David Greene, United Kingdom	48.26

20-KILOMETER WALK

1983	Ernesto Canto, Mexico	1:20:49
1987	Maurizio Damilano, Italy	1:20:45
1991	Maurizio Damilano, Italy	1:19:37
1993	Valentin Massana, Spain	1:22:31
1995	Michele Didoni, Italy	1:19:59
1997	Daniel Garcia, Mexico	1:21:43
1999	Ilya Markov, Russia	1:23:34
2001	Roman Rasskazov, Russia	1:20:31
2003	Jefferson Pérez, Ecuador	1:17.21 WR
2005	Jefferson Pérez, Ecuador	1:18:35
2007	Jefferson Pérez, Ecuador	1:22:20
2009	Valeriy Borchin, Russia	1:18.41
2011	Valeriy Borchin, Russia	1:19.56

50-KILOMETER WALK

1983	Ronald Weigel, East Germany	3:43:08
1987	Hartwig Gauder, East Germany	3:40:53
1991	Aleksandr Potashov, USSR	3:53:09
1993	Jesus Angel Garcia, Spain	3:41:41
1995	Valentin Kononen, Finland	3:43:42
1997	Robert Korzeniowski, Poland	3:44:46
1999	German Skurygin, Russia	3:44:23
2001	Robert Korzeniowski, Poland	3:42:08
2003	R. Korzeniowski, Poland	3:36:03 WR
2005	S. Kirdyapkin, Russia	3:38:08
2007	Nathan Deakes, Australia	3:43:53
2009	Sergey Kirdyapkin, Russia	3:38.35
2011	Sergey Bakulin, Russia	3:41.24

WR=World record.

Men (Cont.)

4 X 100-METER RELAY

1983	United States (Emmit King, Willie Gault, Calvin Smith, Carl Lewis)	37.86
1987	United States (Lee McRae, Lee McNeil, Harvey Glance, Carl Lewis)	37.90
1991	United States (A. Cason L. Burrell, D. Mitchell, C. Lewis)	37.50 WR
1993	United States (J. Drummond, A. Cason, D. Mitchell, L. Burrell)	37.48
1995	Canada (Robert Esmie, Glenroy Gilbert, Bruny Surin, Donovan Bailey)	38.31
1997	Canada (Robert Esmie, Glenroy Gilbert, Bruny Surin, Donovan Bailey)	37.86
1999	United States (Jon Drummond, Tim Montgomery, Brian Lewis, Maurice Greene)	37.59
2001	United States (Mickey Grimes, Bernard Williams, Dennis Mitchell, Tim Montgomery)	37.96
2003	United States (J. Capel, B. Williams D.Patton, J. Johnson)	38.06
2005	Trinidad and Tobago (L. Doucoure, R. Pognon, E. De Lepine, Dovy Lueyi)	38.08
2007	United States (D. Patton, W. Spearmon, T. Gay, L. Dixon)	37.78
2009	Jamaica (Steve Mullings, Michael Frater, Usain Bolt, Asafa Powell)	37.31
2011	Jamaica (Nesta Carter, Michael Frater, Yohan Blake, Usain Bolt)	37.04WR

4 X 400-METER RELAY

1983	USSR (S. Lovachev,A. Troschilo, N. Chernyetski, V. Markin)	3:00.79
1987	United States (Danny Everett Rod Haley, Antonio McKay, Butch Reynolds)	2:57.29
1991	Great Britain (Roger Black Derek Redmond, John Regis, Kriss Akabusi)	2:57.53
1993	United States (Andrew Valmon, Quincy Watts, Butch Reynolds, Michael Johnson)	2:54.29 WR
1995	United States (Marlon Ramsey, Derek Mills, Butch Reynolds, Michael Johnson)	2:57.32
1997	United States (J. Young, A. Pettigrew, C. Jones, T. Washington)	2:56.47
1999	United States (Jerome Davis, Antonio Pettigrew, Angelo Taylor, Michael Johnson)	2:56.45
2001	United States (L. Byrd, A. Pettigrew, D. Brew, A. Taylor)	2:57.54
2003	United States (C. Harrison, T. Washington, D. Brew, J. Young)	2:58.88
2005	United States (D. Brew, R. Andrew, D. Williamson, B. Wariner)	2:56.91
2007	United States (LaShawn Merritt, Angelo Taylor, Darold Williamson, Jeremy Wariner)	2:55.56
2009	United States (Angelo Taylor, Jeremy Wariner, Kerron Clement, LaShawn Merritt)	2:57.86
2011	United States (Greg Nixon, Bershawn Jackson, Angelo Taylor, LaShawn Merritt)	2:59.31

HIGH JUMP

1983	Gennadi Avdeyenko, USSR	2.32m
1987	Patrik Sjoberg, Sweden	2.38m
1991	Charles Austin, United States	2.38m
1993	Javier Sotomayor, Cuba	2.40mWR
1995	Troy Kemp, Bahamas	2.37m
1997	Javier Sotomayor, Cuba	2.37m
1999	Vyacheslav Voronin, Russia	2.37m
2001	Martin Buss, Germany	2.36m
2003	Jacques Freitag, South Africa	2.35m
2005	Yuriy Krymarenko,Ukraine	2.32m
2007	Donald Thoma, Bahamas	2.35m
2009	Yaroslav Rybakov, Russia	2.32m
2011	Jesse Williams, United States	2.35m

POLE VAULT

1983	Sergei Bubka, USSR	5.70m
1987	Sergei Bubka, USSR	5.85m
1991	Sergei Bubka, USSR	5.95m
1993	Sergei Bubka, Ukraine	6.00m
1995	Sergei Bubka, Ukraine	5.92m
1997	Sergei Bubka, Ukraine	6.01m
1999	Maksim Tarasov, Russia	6.02m
2001	Dmitri Markov, Australia	6.05mWR
2003	Guiseppe Gibilisco, Italy	5.90m
2005	Rens Blom, Netherlands	5.80m
2007	Brad Walker, United States	5.86m
2009	Steven Hooker, Australia	5.90m
2011	Pawel Wojciechowski, Poland	5.90m

LONG JUMP

1983	Carl Lewis, United States	8.55m
1987	Carl Lewis, United States	8.67m
1991	Mike Powell, United States	8.95mWR
1993	Mike Powell, United States	8.59m
1995	Iván Pedroso, Cuba	8.71m
1997	Iván Pedroso, Cuba	8.51m
1999	Iván Pedroso, Cuba	8.62m
2001	Iván Pedroso, Cuba	8.43m
2003	Dwight Phillips, United States	8.29m
2005	Dwight Phillips, United States	8.60m
2007	Irving Saladino, Panama	8.57m
2009	Dwight Phillips, United States	8.54m
2011	Dwight Phillips, United States	8.45m

TRIPLE JUMP

1983	Zdislaw Hoffmann, Poland	17.42m
1987	Hristo Markov, Bulgaria	17.92m
1991	Kenny Harrison, United States	17.78m
1993	Mike Conley, United States	17.86m
1995	Jonathan Edwards, G.B.	18.29m WR
1997	Yoelvis Quesada, Cuba	17.85m
1999	Charles Friedek, Germany	17.59m
2001	Jonathan Edwards, G. Britain	17.92m
2003	Christian Olsson, Sweden	17.72m
2005	Walter Davis, United States	17.57m
2007	Nelson Evora, Portugal	17.74m
2009	Phillips Idowu, United Kingdom	17.73m
2011	Christian Taylor, United States	17.96m

SHOT PUT

1983	Edward Sarul, Poland	21.39m
1987	Werner Günthör, Switz.	22.23mWR
1991	Werner Günthör, Switz.	21.67m
1993	Werner Günthör, Switz.	21.97m
1995	John Godina, United States	21.47m
1997	John Godina, United States	21.44m
1999	C.J. Hunter, United States	21.79m
2001	John Godina, United States	21.87m

Men *(Cont.)*

SHOT PUT *(Cont.)*

2003	Andrei Mikahnevic, Bulgaria	21.69m
2005	Adam Nelson, United States	21.73m
2007	Reese Hoffa, United States	22.04m
2009	Christian Cantwell, United States	22.03m
2011	David Storl, Germany	21.78m

DISCUS THROW

1983	Imrich Bugar, Czechoslovakia	67.72m
1987	Juergen Schult, E Germany	68.74m
1991	Lars Riedel, Germany	66.20m
1993	Lars Riedel, Germany	67.72m
1995	Lars Riedel, Germany	68.76m
1997	Lars Riedel, Germany	68.54m
1999	Anthony Washington, U.S.	69.08m
2001	Lars Riedel, Germany	69.72m
2003	Virgilijus Alekna, Lithuania	69.69m
2005	Virgilijus Alekna, Lithuania	70.17mWR
2007	Gerd Kanter, Estonia	68.94m
2009	Robert Harting, Germany	69.43m
2011	Robert Harting, Germany	68.97m

HAMMER THROW

1983	Sergei Litvinov, USSR	82.68m
1987	Sergei Litvinov, USSR	83.06m
1991	Yuriy Sedykh, USSR	81.70m
1993	Andrey Abduvaliyev, Tajikistan	81.64m
1995	Andrey Abduvaliyev, Tajikistan	81.56m
1997	Heinz Weis, Germany	81.78m
1999	Karsten Kobs, Germany	80.24m
2001	Szymon Ziolkowski, Poland	83.38m
2003	Ivan Tikhon, Belarus	83.05m
2005	Ivan Tikhon, Belarus	83.89mWR
2007	Ivan Tsikhan, Belarus	83.63m

HAMMER THROW *(Cont.)*

2009	Primoz Kozmus, Slovenia	80.84m
2011	Koji Murofushi, Japan	81.24m

JAVELIN

1983	Detlef Michel, East Germany	89.48m
1987	Seppo Räty, Finland	83.54m
1991	Kimmo Kinnunen, Finland	90.82m
1993	Jan Zelezny, Czech Rep.	85.98m
1995	Jan Zelezny, Czech Rep.	89.58m
1997	Marius Corbett, South Africa	88.40m
1999	Aki Parviainen, Finland	89.52m
2001	Jan Zelezny, Czech Rep.	92.80mWR
2003	Sergey Makarov, Russia	85.44m
2005	Andrus Varnik, Estonia	87.17m
2007	Tero Pitkämäki, Finland	90.33m
2009	Andreas Thorkildsen, Norway	89.59m
2011	Matthias de Zordo, Germany	86.27m

DECATHLON

1983	Daley Thompson, Great Britain	8666 pts
1987	Torsten Voss, East Germany	8680 pts
1991	Dan O'Brien, United States	8812 pts
1993	Dan O'Brien, United States	8817 pts
1995	Dan O'Brien, United States	8695 pts
1997	Tomás Dvorák, Czech Rep.	8837 pts
1999	Tomás Dvorák, Czech Rep.	8744 pts
2001	Tomás Dvorák, Czech Rep.	8902 ptsWR
2003	Tom Pappas, United States	8750 pts
2005	Bryan Clay, United States	8732 pts
2007	Roman Sebrle, Czech Rep.	8676 pts
2009	Trey Hardee, United States	8790 pts
2011	Trey Hardee, United States	8607 pts

Women

100 METERS

1983	Marlies Gohr, East Germany	10.97
1987	Silke Gladisch, East Germany	10.90
1991	Katrin Krabbe, Germany	10.99
1993	Gail Devers, United States	10.82
1995	Gwen Torrence, United States	10.85
1997	Marion Jones, United States	10.83
1999	Marion Jones, United States	10.70
2001	Zhanna Pintusevich-Block, Ukraine	10.82
2003	Kelli White, United States	10.85
2005	Lauryn Williams, United States	10.93
2007	Veronica Campbell, Jamaica	11.01
2009	Shelly-Ann Fraser, Jamaica	10.73
2011	Carmelita Jeter, United States	10.90

200 METERS

1983	Marita Koch, East Germany	22.13
1987	Silke Gladisch, East Germany	21.74
1991	Katrin Krabbe, Germany	22.09
1993	Merlene Ottey, Jamaica	21.98
1995	Merlene Ottey, Jamaica	22.12
1997	Zhanna Pintusevich, Ukraine	22.32
1999	Inger Miller, United States	21.77
2001	Marion Jones, United States	22.39
2003	Kelli White, United States	22.05
2005	Allyson Felix, United States	22.16
2007	Allyson Felix, United States	21.81
2009	Allyson Felix, United States	22.02
2011	Veronica Campell-Brown, Jamaica	22.22

400 METERS

1983	Jarmila Kratochvilova, Czech.	47.99
1987	Olga Bryzgina, USSR	49.38
1991	Marie-José Pérec, France	49.13

400 METERS *(Cont.)*

1993	Jearl Miles, United States	49.82
1995	Marie-José Pérec, France	49.28
1997	Cathy Freeman, Australia	49.77
1999	Cathy Freeman, Australia	49.67
2001	Amy Mbacke Thiam, Senegal	49.86
2003	Ana Guevara, Mexico	48.89
2005	Darling Williams, Bahamas	49.55
2007	Christine Ohuruogu, Great Britain	49.61
2009	Sanya Richards, United States	49.00
2011	Amantie Montsho, Botswana	49.56

800 METERS

1983	Jarmila Kratochvilova, Czech.	1:54.68
1987	Sigrun Wodars, East Germany	1:55.26
1991	Lilia Nurutdinova, USSR	1:57.50
1993	Maria Mutola, Mozambique	1:55.43
1995	Ana Quirot, Cuba	1:56.11
1997	Ana Quirot, Cuba	1:57.14
1999	Ludmila Formanová, Czech Rep.	1:56.68
2001	Maria Mutola, Mozambique	1:57.17
2003	Maria Mutola, Mozambique	1:59.89
2005	Zulia Calatayud, Cuba	1:58.82
2007	Janeth Jepkosgei, Kenya	1:56.04
2009	Caster Semenya, South Africa	1:55.45
2011	Mariya Savinova, Russia	1:55.87

1,500 METERS

1983	Mary Slaney, United States	4:00.90
1987	Tatyana Samolenko, USSR	3:58.56
1991	Hassiba Boulmerka, Algeria	4:02.21
1993	Dong Liu, China	4:00.50
1995	Hassiba Boulmerka, Algeria	4:02.42
1997	Carla Sacramento, Portugal	4:04.24

WR=World record.

1,500 METERS *(Cont.)*

1999	Svetlana Masterkova, Russia	3:59.53
2001	Gabriela Szabo, Romania	4:00.57
2003	Tatyana Tomashova, Russia	3:58.52
2005	Tatyana Tomashova, Russia	4:00.35
2007	Maryam Yusuf Jamal, Bahrain	3:58.75
2009	Maryam Yusuf Jamal, Bahrain	4:03.74
2011	Jennifer Simpson, United States	4:05.40

3,000 METERS

1983	Mary Slaney, United States	8:34.62
1987	Tatyana Samolenko, USSR	8:38.73
1991	Tatyana Dorovskikh, USSR	8:35.82
1993	Qu Yunxia, China	8:28.71

3,000 METER STEEPLECHASE

2005	Docus Inzikuru, Uganda	9:18.24
2007	Yekaterina Volkova, Russia	9:06.57
2009	Marta Dominguez, Spain	9:07.32
2011	Yuliya Zaripova, Russia	9:07.03

5,000 METERS

1995	Sonia O'Sullivan, Ireland	14:46.47
1997	Gabriela Szabo, Romania	14:57.68
1999	Gabriela Szabo, Romania	14:41.82
2001	Olga Yegorova, Russia	15:03.39
2003	Tirunesh Dibaba, Ethiopia	14:51.72
2005	Tirunesh Dibaba, Ethiopia	14:38.59
2007	Meseret Defar, Ethiopia	14:57.91
2009	Vivian Cheruiyot, Kenya	14:57.97
2011	Vivian Cheruiyot, Kenya	14:55.36

10,000 METERS

1987	Ingrid Kristiansen, Norway	31:05.85
1991	Liz McColgan, Great Britain	31:14.31
1993	Wang Junxia, China	30:49:30
1995	Fernanda Ribeiro, Portugal	31:04.99
1997	Sally Barsosio, Kenya	31:32.92
1999	Gete Wami, Ethiopia	30:24.56
2001	Derartu Tulu, Ethiopia	31:48.81
2003	Berhane Adere, Ethiopia	30:04.18
2005	Tirunesh Dibaba, Ethiopia	30:24.02
2007	Tirunesh Dibaba, Ethiopia	31:55.41
2009	Linet Masai, Kenya	30:51.24
2011	Vivian Cheruiyot, Kenya	30:48.98

MARATHON

1983	Grete Waitz, Norway	2:28:09
1987	Rosa Mota, Portugal	2:25:17
1991	Wanda Panfil, Poland	2:29:53
1993	Junko Asari, Japan	2:30:03
1995	Manuela Machado, Portugal	2:25:39*
1997	Hiromi Suzuki, Japan	2:29:48
1999	Jong Song-Ok, North Korea	2:26:59
2001	Lidia Simon, Romania	2:26.01
2003	Catherine Ndereba, Kenya	2:23:55
2005	Paula Radcliffe, Great Britain	2:20:57
2007	Catherine Ndereba, Kenya	2:30:37
2009	Xue Bai, China	2:25.15
2011	Edna Kiplagat, Kenya	2:28.43

100-METER HURDLES

1983	Bettine Jahn, East Germany	12.35
1987	Ginka Zagorcheva, Bulgaria	12.34
1991	Lyudmila Narozhilenko, USSR	12.59
1993	Gail Devers, United States	12.46
1995	Gail Devers, United States	12.68
1997	Ludmila Engquist, Sweden	12.50
1999	Gail Devers, United States	12.37
2001	Anjanette Kirkland, United States	12.42
2003	Perdita Felicien, Canada	12.53

*400 meters short. WR=World Record.

100-METER HURDLES *(Cont.)*

2005	Michelle Perry, United States	12:66
2007	Michelle Perry, United States	12:46
2009	Brigitte Foster-Hylton, Jamaica	12.51
2011	Sally Pearson, Australia	12.28

400-METER HURDLES

1983	Yekaterina Fesenko, USSR	54.14
1987	Sabine Busch, East Germany	53.62
1991	Tatyana Ledovskaya, USSR	53.11
1993	Sally Gunnell, Great Britain	52.74WR
1995	Kim Batten, United States	52.61
1997	Nezha Bidouane, Morocco	52.97
1999	Daimi Pernia, Cuba	52.89
2001	Nezha Bidouane, Morocco	53.34
2003	Jana Pittman, Australia	53.22
2005	Yuliya Pechonkina, Russia	52.90
2007	Jana Rawlinson, Australia	53.31
2009	Melaine Walker, Jamaica	52.42
2011	Lashinda Demus, United States	52.47

20-KILOMETER WALK

1999	Hongyu Liu, China	1:30:50
2001	Olimpiada Ivanova, Russia	1:27:48
2003	Yelena Nikolayeva, Russia	1:26:52
2005	Olimpjada Ivanova, Russia	1:25:41
2007	Olga Kaniskina, Russia	1:30:09
2009	Olga Kaniskina, Russia	1:28.09
2011	Olga Kaniskina, Russia	1:29.42

4 X 100-METER RELAY

1983	East Germany (S. Gladisch, M. Koch, I. Auerswald, M. Gohr)	41.76
1987	United States (A. Brown, D. Williams, F. Griffith, P. Marshall)	41.58
1991	Jamaica (Dalia Duhaney, Juliet Cuthbert, Beverley McDonald, Merlene Ottey)	41.94
1993	Russia (Olga Bogoslovskaya, Galina Malchugina, Natalya Voronova, Irina Privalova)	41.49
1995	United States (Celena Mondie-Milner, Carlette Guidry, Chryste Gaines, Gwen Torrence)	42.12
1997	United States (C. Gaines, M. Jones, I. Miller, G. Devers)	41.47
1999	Bahamas (S. Fynes, C. Sturrup, P. Davis-Thompson, D. Ferguson)	41.92
2001	United States (Kelli White, Chryste Gaines, Inger Miller, Marion Jones)	41.71
2003	France (P. Girard, M. Hurtis S. Félix, C. Arron)	41.78
2005	Jamaica, (A. Daigie, M. Lee, M. Billiams	41.78
2007	United States (Lauryn Williams, Allyson Felix, Mikele Barber, Torri Edwards)	41.98
2009	Jamaica (Simone Facey, S. Fraser, Aleen Bailey, Kerron Stewart)	42.06
2011	United States (Bianca Knight, Allyson Felix, Marshevet Myers, Carmelita Jeter)	41.56

4 X 400-METER RELAY

1983	East Germany (Kerstin Walther, Sabine Busch, Marita Koch, Dagmar Rubsam)	3:19.73
1987	East Germany (Dagmar Neubauer, Kirsten Emmelmann, Petra Müller, Sabine Busch)	3:18.63
1991	USSR (Tatyana Ledovskaya, Lyudmila Dzhigalova, Olga Nazarova, Olga Bryzgina)	3:18.43

4 X 400-METER RELAY *(Cont.)*

1993	United States (Gwen Torrence, Maicel Malone, Natasha Kaiser-Brown, Jearl Miles)	3:16.71
1995	United States (Kim Graham, Rochelle Stevens, Camara Jones, Jearl Miles)	3:22.39
1997	Germany (A. Feller, U. Rohlander, A. Rucker, G. Breuer)	3:20.92
1999	Russia (Tatyana Chebykina, Svetlana Goncharenko, Olga Kotylarova, Natalya Nazarova)	3:21.98
2001	Jamaica (Sandie Richards, Catherine Scott, Debbie Ann Parris, Lorraine Fenton)	3:20.65
2003	United States (M. Barber, D. Washington, J. Miles-Clark, S. Richards)	3:22.63
2005	Russia (Y. Pechonkina, O. Krasnomovets, N. Antyukh, S. Pospelova)	3:20.95
2007	United States (D. Trotter, A. Felix, M. Wineberg, S.Richards)	3:18.55
2009	United States (Debbie Dunn, A. Felix, Lashinda Demus, Sanya Demus)	3:17.83
2011	United States (Sanya Richards-Ross, A. Felix, Jessica Beard, Francena McCrory)	3:18.09

HIGH JUMP

1983	Tamara Bykova, USSR	2.01m
1987	Stefka Kostadinova, Bulgaria	2.09mWR
1991	Heike Henkel, Germany	2.05m
1993	Ioamnet Quintero, Cuba	1.99m
1995	Stefka Kostadinova, Bulgaria	2.01m
1997	Hanne Haugland, Norway	1.99m
1999	Inga Babakova, Ukraine	1.99m
2001	Hestrie Cloete, South Africa	2.00m
2003	Hestrie Cloete, South Africa	2.06m
2005	Kajsa Bergvist, Sweden	2.02m
2007	Blanka Vlasic, Croatia	2.05m
2009	Blanka Vlasic, Croatia	2.04m
2011	Anna Chicerova, Russia	2.03m

POLE VAULT

1999	Stacy Dragila, United States	4.06mEWR
2001	Stacy Dragila, United States	4.75m
2003	Svetlana Feofanova, Russia	4.75m
2005	Yelena Isinbayeva, Russia	5.01mWR
2007	Yelena Isinbayeva, Russia	4.80m
2009	Anna Rogowska, Poland	4.75m
2011	Fabiana Murer, Brazil	4.85m

LONG JUMP

1983	Heike Daute, E Germany	7.27m
1987	Jackie Joyner-Kersee, U.S.	7.36mWR
1991	Jackie Joyner-Kersee, U.S.	7.32m
1993	Heike Drechsler, Germany	7.11m
1995	Fiona May, Italy	6.98m
1997	Lyudmila Galkina, Russia	7.05m
1999	Niurka Montalvo, Spain	7.06m
2001	Fiona May, Italy	6.87m
2003	Eunice Barber, France	6.99m
2005	Tianna Madison, United States	6.89m
2007	Tatyana Lebedeva, Russia	7.03m
2009	Brittney Reese, United States	7.10m
2011	Brittney Reese, United States	6.82m

TRIPLE JUMP

1993	Ana Biryukova, Russia	15.09m
1995	Inessa Kravets, Ukraine	15.50mWR
1997	S. Kasparkova, Czech Rep.	15.20m
1999	Paraskevi Tsiamita, Greece	14.88m
2001	Tatyana Lebedeva, Russia	15.25m
2003	Tatyana Lebedeva, Russia	15.18m

TRIPLE JUMP *(Cont.)*

2005	Trecia Smith, Jamaica	15.11m
2007	Yargeris Savigne, Cuba	15.28m
2009	Yargeris Savigne, Cuba	14.95m
2011	Olha Saladuha, Ukraine	14.94m

SHOT PUT

1983	Helena Fibingerova, Czech.	21.05m
1987	Natalya Lisovskaya, USSR	21.24mWR
1991	Zhihong Huang, China	20.83m
1993	Zhihong Huang, China	20.57m
1995	Astrid Kumbernuss, Germany	21.22m
1997	Astrid Kumbernuss, Germany	20.71m
1999	Astrid Kumbernuss, Germany	19.85m
2001	Yanina Korolchik, Belarus	20.61m
2003	Svetlana Krivelyova, Russia	20.63m
2005	Nadezhda Ostapchuk, Russia	20.51m
2007	Valerie Vili, New Zealand	20.54m
2009	Valerie Vili, New Zealand	20.44m
2011	Valerie Adams, New Zealand	21.24m

HAMMER THROW

1999	Mihaela Melinte, Romania	75.20mWR
2001	Yipsi Moreno, Cuba	70.65m
2003	Yipsi Moreno, Cuba	70.30m
2005	Olga Kuzenkova, Russia	75.10m
2007	Betty Heidler, Germany	74.76m
2009	Anita Wlodarczyk, Poland	77.96mWR
2011	Tatyana Lysenko, Russia	77.13

JAVELIN

1983	Tiina Lillak, Finland	70.82m
1987	Fatima Whitbread, United Kingdom	76.64m
1991	Xu Demei, China	68.78m
1993	Trine Solberg-Hattestad, Norway	69.18m
1995	Natalya Shikolenko, Belarus	67.56m
1997	Trine Hattestad, Norway	68.78m
1999	Mirela Manjani-Tzelili, Greece	67.09m
2001	Osleidys Menendez, Cuba	69.53m
2003	Mirela Manjani, Greece	66.52m
2005	Osleidys Menendez, Cuba	71.70m
2007	Barbora Spotakova, Czech Rep.	67.07m
2009	Steffi Nerius, Germany	67.30m
2011	Maria Abakumova, Russia	71.99m

DISCUS THROW

1983	Martina Opitz, East Germany	68.94m
1987	Martina Hellmann, East Germany	71.62mWR
1991	Tsvetanka Khristova, Bulgaria	71.02m
1993	Olga Burova, Russia	67.40m
1995	Ellina Zvereva, Belarus	68.64m
1997	Beatrice Faumuina, New Zealand	66.82m
1999	Franka Dietzsch, Germany	68.14m
2001	Ellina Zvereva, Belarus	67.10m
2003	Irina Yatchenko, Belarus	67.32m
2005	Franka Dietzsch, Germany	66.56m
2007	Franka Dietzsch, Germany	66.61m
2009	Dani Samuels, Australia	65.44m
2011	Yanfeng Li, China	66.52m

HEPTATHLON

1983	Ramona Neubert, E. Germany	6714 pts
1987	Jackie Joyner-Kersee, U.S.	7128 pts
1991	Sabine Braun, Germany	6672 pts
1993	Jackie Joyner-Kersee, U.S.	6831 pts
1995	Ghada Shouaa, Syria	6651 pts
1997	Sabine Braun, Germany	6739 pts
1999	Eunice Barber, France	6861 pts
2001	Yelena Prokhorova, Russia	6694 pts
2003	Carolina Kluft, Sweden	7001 pts
2005	Carolina Kluft, Sweden	6887 pts
2007	Carolina Kluft, Sweden	7032 pts
2009	Jessica Ennis, United Kingdom	6731 pts
2011	Tatyana Chernova, Russia	6880 pts

WR=World Record. EWR=Equals world record.

Miscellaneous Sports

Lindsay Vonn continued to dominate women's skiing, winning her fourth overall World Cup title in the last five years

Miscellaneous Sport Champions

Archery

		Winner (Recurve)	Winner (Compound)
	2012 U.S. National Field Championships		
	MEN	Jake Kaminski	Dave Cousins
	WOMEN	Heather Koehl	Jamie Van Natta

Bowling

		Money Winner ($)	Highest Average (pts.)
	2011–12 PBA Tour		
	TOUR LEADERS	Sean Rash	Sean Rash
		($140,250)	(228.13)
	2011–12 PBA Senior Tour	Money Winner ($)	Highest Average (pts.)
	TOUR LEADERS	Walter Ray Williams Jr.	Walter Ray Williams Jr.
		($35,900)	(233.41)

Curling

		Winner	Runner-up
	2012 World Championships		
	MEN	Canada (8–7)	Scotland
	WOMEN	Switzerland (7–6)	Sweden
	2012 U.S. Club National Championships	Winner	Runner-up
	MEN	Minnesota	Washington
	WOMEN	Washington	Minnesota

Cycling

		Winner	Time
	2012 ROAD RACE WORLD CHAMPIONSHIP	Philippe Gilbert, Belgium	6:10:41
	2012 TOUR DE FRANCE	Bradley Wiggins, G.B.	87:34:47

Sled Dog Racing

		Winner	Time
	2012 IDITAROD	Dallas Seavey	9 days, 4:29:26

Figure Skating

		Winner	Country
	2012 ISU World Championships		
	MEN	Patrick Chan	Canada
	WOMEN	Carolina Kostner	Italy
	PAIRS	Aliona Savchenko/	Germany
		Robin Szolkowy	
	ICE DANCING	Tessa Virtue/	Canada
		Scott Moir	
	2012 U.S. Figure Skating Nat'l Championships	Winner	Club
	MEN	Jeremy Abbott	Detroit SC
	WOMEN	Ashley Wagner	SC of Wilmington
	PAIRS	Caydee Denney/	Broadmoor SC/
		John Coughlin	Kansas City FSC
	ICE DANCING	Meryl Davis/	Arctic FSC/
		Charlie White	Detroit SC

Handball

		Winner	Runner-up
	2012 U.S. One-Wall Nat'l Championships		
	MEN	John Wright	Joe Kaplan
	WOMEN	Tracy David	Sandy Ng
	2012 U.S. Three-Wall Nat'l Championships	Winner	Runner-up
	MEN	Sean Lenning	Tyree Bastidas
	WOMEN	Megan Mehilos	Tracy Davis

Lacrosse

		Winner (Score)	Runner-up
	League		
	AMERICAN LACROSSE LEAGUE	Magerks (11–10)	GMH Philadelphia
	NATIONAL LACROSSE LEAGUE	Rochester Knighthawks (9–6)	Edmonton Rush
	MAJOR LEAGUE LACROSSE	Chesapeake Bayhawks (16-6)	Denver Outlaws

Little League Baseball

		Winner	Runner-up	Score
	WORLD SERIES CHAMPION	Tokyo, Japan	Goodlettsville, Tenn.	12–2

Motor Boat Racing

		Winning Boat	Winning Driver
	American Power Boat Association		
	GOLD CUP CHAMPION (UNLIMITED)	U-96 Spirit of Qatar	Dave Villwock

Polo

		Winner	Runner-up
	2012 U.S. Open		
	U.S. POLO ASSOCIATION	Zacara (10–8)	Lechuza Caracas

Rodeo

2011 PRCA World Champions	Winner(s)
ALL-AROUND	Trevor Brazile
SADDLE BRONC RIDING	Taos Muncy
BAREBACK RIDING	Kaycee Feild
BULL RIDING	Shane Proctor
STEER WRESTLING	Luke Branquinho
STEER ROPING	Trevor Brazile
CALF TIE-DOWN ROPING	Tuf Cooper
TEAM ROPING (Header, Heeler)	Turtle Powell, Jhett Johnson

Rowing

2012 Intercollegiate Rowing Association	Winner	Runner-Up
MEN (VARSITY EIGHTS)	Washington	Brown

Rugby

2012 Rugby Union	Winner	Runner-Up
COLLEGE PREMIER DIVISION	BYU	Arkansas State

2012 USA Rugby League	Winner	Runner-Up
U.S. CHAMPION	Jacksonville Axemen	Boston 13s

Skiing

FIS World Cup Season Points Champion	Men's Winner (Season)	Women's Winner (Season)
OVERALL	Marcel Hirscher, Aus.	Lindsay Vonn, U.S.
DOWNHILL	Klaus Kroell, Austria	Lindsey Vonn, U.S.
SLALOM	Andre Myhrer, Sweden	Marlies Schild, Austria
GIANT SLALOM	Marcel Hirscher, Aus.	Viktoria Rebensburg, Ger.
SUPER G	Aksel Lund Svindal, Nor.	Lindsey Vonn, U.S.
COMBINED	Ivica Kostelic, Croatia	Lindsey Vonn, U.S.

Softball

2012 U.S. ASA Championship	Major Fast Pitch Winner
MEN	New York Gremlins
WOMEN	Tournament cancelled

Speed Skating

2012 ISU All-Around World Champion	Winner
MEN	Sven Kramer, Netherlands
WOMEN	Ireen Wust, Netherlands

Squash

2012 U.S. Open Championship	Winner
MEN	Ramy Ashour
WOMEN	Nicol David

Triathlon

2012 Ironman World Championship	Winner	Time
MEN	Pete Jacobs	8:18:37
WOMEN	Leanda Cave	9:15.53

2012 U.S. Elite Triathlon Championship	Winner	Time
MEN	Jarrod Shoemaker	1:52:44
WOMEN	Sarah Haskins	2:03:05

Volleyball

2012 U.S. Adult Championship (Open Div.)	Winner	Runner-Up
MEN	Team Lights Out	Team Paul Mitchell

Wrestling

2012 U.S. Olympic Team Trials	Freestyle	Greco-Roman
121 LBS.	Nick Simmons	Spenser Mango
132 LBS.	Coleman Scott	Ellis Coleman
145.5 LBS.	Jared Frayer	Justin Lester
163 LBS.	Jordan Burroughs	Ben Provisor
185 LBS.	Travis Paulson	Chas Betts
211.5 LBS.	Jake Varner	RC Johnson
264.5 LBS.	Tervel Dlagnev	Dremiel Byers
TEAM	Sunkist	U.S. Army

Bowling

2011-12 PBA TOUR RESULTS

Date	Event	Winner/s	Earnings ($)	Runner-Up
Nov 5–18	Viper Open	Stuart Williams	15,000	Ildemaro Ruiz
Nov 5–18	WSOB Chameleon Open	Jason Belmonte	16,100	Sean Rash
Nov 7–18	WSOB Scorpion Open	Dom Barrett	16,000	Sean Rash
Nov 8–18	Shark Open	Jason Belmonte	15,000	Chris Barnes
Nov 9–19	PBA World Championship	Osku Palermaa	50,000	Ryan Shafer
Nov 11–20	Carmen Salvino Classic	Andres Gomez	16,100	Wes Malott
Nov 15–20	PBA Elite Players Championship	Jason Belmonte	35,000	Mike DeVaney
Jan 20–22	Cheetah Open	Eugene McCune	10,000	Pete Weber
Jan 23–29	USBC Masters	Mike Fagan	50,000	Chris Barnes
Feb 17–20	Ricart Ford Open	Scott Newell	10,100	Ryan Ciminelli
Feb 20–26	69th U.S. Open	Pete Weber	60,000	Mike Fagan
Mar 9–11	Detroit Open	Norm Duke	10,000	Mika Koivuniemi
Mar 30–Apr 1	Dick Weber Playoffs	Norm Duke	20,000	Parker Bohn III
Apr 8–15	PBA Tournament of Champions	Sean Rash	80,000	Ryan Ciminelli

2012 SENIOR PBA TOUR RESULTS

Date	Event	Winner	Earnings ($)	Runner-Up
Apr 21–24	Senior Sun Bowl	Lennie Boresch Jr.	7,600	Ricky Beck
Apr 28–May 2	Don Carter Open	Walter Ray Williams Jr.	7,500	Bo Goergen
May 6–9	Mooresville Classic	Bob Learn Jr.	8,000	Ron Profitt
May 14–17	Dayton Classic	John Petraglia	8,000	Ron Mohr
June 3–8	Senior U.S. Open	Amleto Monacelli	15,000	Walter Ray Williams Jr.
June 10–15	USBC Senior Masters	Mike Edwards	16,000	Hugh Miller
June 17–20	Northern California Classic	Walter Ray Williams Jr.	8,100	Hugh Miller
Aug 6	South Shore Open	Hugh Miller	7,600	Rick Minier
Aug 11	Decatur Open	Ron Mohr	7,500	Harry Sullins

TOUR LEADERS - PBA: 2011-12

MONEY LEADERS	Events	Earnings ($)	AVERAGE	Events	Average
Sean Rash	13	140,250.00	Sean Rash	13	228.13
Jason Belmonte	13	137,375.00	Mike Fagan	13	227.53
Mike Fagan	13	116,950.00	Jason Belmonte	13	226.42
Pete Weber	14	97,820.00	Ryan Ciminelli	14	225.93
Osku Palermaa	11	79,110.00	Bill O'Neill	13	225.85

TOUR LEADERS - SENIOR PBA: 2012

MONEY LEADERS	Events	Earnings ($)	AVERAGE	Events	Average
Walter Ray Williams Jr	9	35,900.00	Walter Ray Williams Jr	9	233.41
Hugh Miller	6	26,850.00	Wayne Webb	7	229.85
Amleto Monacelli	6	26,150.00	Mike Edwards	4	228.71
Mike Edwards	4	25,500.00	Lennie Boresch Jr	8	228.66
Ron Mohr	9	19,900.00	Bob Learn Jr	8	228.33

PBA CAREER STATISTICS

CAREER EARNINGS		CAREER TITLES	
*Walter Ray Williams Jr.	$4,362,605.50	*Walter Ray Williams Jr.	47
*Pete Weber	$3,544,239.00	Earl Anthony	43
*Norm Duke	$3,050,518.88	*Norm Duke	37
*Parker Bohn III	$2,815,192.17	*Pete Weber	36
Brian Voss	$2,477,062.88	Mark Roth	34
*Amleto Monacelli	$2,165,374.30	*Parker Bohn III	32
Mike Aulby	$2,097,520.33	Dick Weber	30
*Chris Barnes	$2,014,857.17	Mike Aulby	29
Tom Baker	$1,944,474.00	Don Johnson	26
*Jason Couch	$1,763,711.83	Brian Voss	25

Note: Career leaders through Oct. 1, 2012. *Active in 2011–12 season.

Cycling

Tour de France Winners

Year	Winner	Time	Year	Winner	Time
1903	Maurice Garin, France	94 hrs, 33 min	1962	Jacques Anquetil, France	114 hrs, 31 min, 54 sec
1904	Henry Cornet, France	96 hrs, 5 min, 56 sec	1963	Jacques Anquetil, France	113 hrs, 30 min, 5 sec
1905	Louis Trousselier, France	110 hrs, 26 min, 58 sec	1964	Jacques Anquetil, France	127 hrs, 9 min, 44 sec
1906	Rene Pottier, France	Not available	1965	Felice Gimondi, Italy	116 hrs, 42 min, 6 sec
1907	Lucien Petit-Breton, France	158 hrs, 54 min, 5 sec	1966	Lucien Aimar, France	117 hrs, 34 min, 21 sec
1908	Lucien Petit-Breton, France	Not available	1967	Roger Pingeon, France	136 hrs, 53 min, 50 sec
1909	Francois Faber, Luxembourg	157 hrs, 1 min, 22 sec	1968	Jan Janssen, Netherlands	133 hrs, 49 min, 32 sec
1910	Octave Lapize, France	162 hrs, 41 min, 30 sec	1969	Eddy Merckx, Belgium	116 hrs, 16 min, 2 sec
1911	Gustave Garrigou, France	195 hrs, 37 min	1970	Eddy Merckx, Belgium	119 hrs, 31 min, 49 sec
1912	Odile Defraye, Belgium	190 hrs, 30 min, 28 sec	1971	Eddy Merckx, Belgium	96 hrs, 45 min, 14 sec
1913	Philippe Thys, Belgium	197 hrs, 54 min	1972	Eddy Merckx, Belgium	108 hrs, 17 min, 18 sec
1914	Philippe Thys, Belgium	200 hrs, 28 min, 48 sec	1973	Luis Ocana, Spain	122 hrs, 25 min, 34 sec
1915–18 NO RACE			1974	Eddy Merckx, Belgium	116 hrs, 16 min, 58 sec
1919	Firmin Lambot, Belgium	231 hrs, 7 min, 15 sec	1975	Bernard Thevenet, France	114 hrs, 35 min, 31 sec
1920	Philippe Thys, Belgium	228 hrs, 36 min, 13 sec	1976	Lucien Van Impe, Belgium	116 hrs, 22 min, 23 sec
1921	Leon Scieur, Belgium	221 hrs, 50 min, 26 sec	1977	Bernard Thevenet, France	115 hrs, 38 min, 30 sec
1922	Firmin Lambot, Belgium	222 hrs, 8 min, 16 sec	1978	Bernard Hinault, France	108 hrs, 18 min
1923	Henri Pelissier, France	222 hrs, 15 min, 30 sec	1979	Bernard Hinault, France	103 hrs, 6 min, 50 sec
1924	Ottavio Bottechia, Italy	226 hrs, 18 min, 21 sec	1980	Joop Zoetemelk, Netherlands	109 hrs, 19 min, 14 sec
1925	Ottavio Bottechia, Italy	219 hrs, 10 min, 18 sec	1981	Bernard Hinault, France	96 hrs, 19 min, 38 sec
1926	Lucien Buysse, Belgium	238 hrs, 44 min, 25 sec	1982	Bernard Hinault, France	92 hrs, 8 min, 46 sec
1927	Nicolas Frantz, Luxembourg	198 hrs, 16 min, 42 sec	1983	Laurent Fignon, France	105 hrs, 7 min, 52 sec
1928	Nicolas Frantz, Luxembourg	192 hrs, 48 min, 58 sec	1984	Laurent Fignon, France	112 hrs, 3 min, 40 sec
1929	Maurice Dewaele, Belgium	186 hrs, 39 min, 16 sec	1985	Bernard Hinault, France	113 hrs, 24 min, 23 sec
1930	Andre Leducq, France	172 hrs, 12 min, 16 sec	1986	Greg LeMond, United States	110 hrs, 35 min, 19 sec
1931	Antonin Magne, France	177 hrs, 10 min, 3 sec	1987	Stephen Roche, Ireland	115 hrs, 27 min, 42 sec
1932	Andre Leducq, France	154 hrs, 12 min, 49 sec	1988	Pedro Delgado, Spain	84 hrs, 27 min, 53 sec
1933	Georges Speicher, France	147 hrs, 51 min, 37 sec	1989	Greg LeMond, United States	87 hrs, 38 min, 35 sec
1934	Antonin Magne, France	147 hrs, 13 min, 58 sec	1990	Greg LeMond, United States	90 hrs, 43 min, 20 sec
1935	Romain Maes, Belgium	141 hrs, 32 min	1991	Miguel Induráin, Spain	101 hrs, 1 min, 20 sec
1936	Sylvere Maes, Belgium	142 hrs, 47 min, 32 sec	1992	Miguel Induráin, Spain	100 hrs, 49 min, 30 sec
1937	Roger Lapebie, France	138 hrs, 58 min, 31 sec	1993	Miguel Induráin, Spain	95 hrs, 57 min, 9 sec
1938	Gino Bartali, Italy	148 hrs, 29 min, 12 sec	1994	Miguel Induráin, Spain	103 hrs, 38 min, 38 sec
1939	Sylvere Maes, Belgium	132 hrs, 3 min, 17 sec	1995	Miguel Induráin, Spain	92 hrs, 44 min, 59 sec
1940–46 NO RACE			1996	Bjarne Riis, Denmark	95 hrs, 57 min, 16 sec
1947	Jean Robic, France	148 hrs, 11 min, 25 sec	1997	Jan Ullrich, Germany	100 hrs, 30 min, 35 sec
1948	Gino Bartali, Italy	147 hrs, 10 min, 36 sec	1998	Marco Pantani, Italy	92 hrs, 49 min, 46 sec
1949	Fausto Coppi, Italy	149 hrs, 40 min, 49 sec	#1999	Lance Armstrong, United States	91 hrs, 32 min, 16 sec
1950	Ferdi Kubler, Switzerland	145 hrs, 36 min, 56 sec	#2000	Lance Armstrong, United States	92 hrs, 33 min, 8 sec
1951	Hugo Koblet, Switzerland	142 hrs, 20 min, 14 sec	#2001	Lance Armstrong, United States	86 hrs, 17 min, 28 sec
1952	Fausto Coppi, Italy	151 hrs, 57 min, 20 sec	#2002	Lance Armstrong, United States	82 hrs, 5 min, 12 sec
1953	Louison Bobet, France	129 hrs, 23 min, 25 sec	#2003	Lance Armstrong, United States	83 hrs, 41 min, 12 sec
1954	Louison Bobet, France	140 hrs, 6 min, 5 sec	#2004	Lance Armstrong, United States	83 hrs, 36 min, 2 sec
1955	Louison Bobet, France	130 hrs, 29 min, 26 sec	#2005	Lance Armstrong, United States	82 hrs, 34 min, 5 sec
1956	Roger Walkowiak, France	124 hrs, 1 min, 16 sec	†2006	Oscar Pereiro, Spain	82 hrs, 48 min, 30 sec
1957	Jacques Anquetil, France	129 hrs, 46 min, 11 sec	2007	Alberto Contador, Spain	91 hrs, 26 sec
1958	Charly Gaul, Luxembourg	116 hrs, 59 min, 5 sec	2008	Carlos Sastre, Spain	87 hrs, 52 min, 52 sec
1959	Federico Bahamontes, Spain	123 hrs, 46 min, 45 sec	2009	Alberto Contador, Spain	85 hrs, 48 min, 35 sec
1960	Gastone Nencini, Italy	112 hrs, 8 min, 42 sec	*2010	Alberto Contador, Spain	91 hrs, 58 min, 48 sec
1961	Jacques Anquetil, France	122 hrs, 1 min, 33 sec	2011	Cadel Evans, Australia	86 hrs, 12 min, 22 sec
			2012	Bradley Wiggins, Great Britain	87 hrs, 34 min, 47 sec

†Floyd Landis, the initial winner, was officially stripped of his title on Sept. 20, 2007 by the ICU after a hearing affirmed that he had tested positive for using banned substances during Stage 17 of the 2006 Tour.

*Alberto Contador was stripped of his 2010 Tour de France title and suspended for two years after a test sample showed trace amounts of a performance-enhancing stimulant in one of that race's final stages.

#Lance Armstrong was stripped of all seven of his titles in 2012 and banned for life by the U.S. Anti-Doping Agency.

WORLD CHAMPIONS
Women

1906 .....Madge Sayers-Cave, Great Britain	1951 .....Jeannette Altwegg, Great Britain	1984 .....Katarina Witt, E. Germany
1907 .....Madge Sayers-Cave, Great Britain	1952 .....Jacqueline duBief, France	1985 .....Katarina Witt, E. Germany
1908 .....Lily Kronberger, Hungary	1953 .....Tenley Albright, United States	1986 .....Debi Thomas, United States
1909 .....Lily Kronberger, Hungary	1954 .....Gundi Busch, W. Germany	1987 .....Katarina Witt, E. Germany
1910 .....Lily Kronberger, Hungary	1955 .....Tenley Albright, United States	1988 .....Katarina Witt, E. Germany
1911 .....Lily Kronberger, Hungary	1956 .....Carol Heiss, United States	1989 .....Midori Ito, Japan
1912 .....Opika von Meray Horvath, Hungary	1957 .....Carol Heiss, United States	1990 .....Jill Trenary, United States
1913 .....Opika von Meray Horvath, Hungary	1958 .....Carol Heiss, United States	1991 .....Kristi Yamaguchi, United States
1914 .....Opika von Meray Horvath, Hungary	1959 .....Carol Heiss, United States	1992 .....Kristi Yamaguchi, United States
1915–21 NO COMPETITION	1960 .....Carol Heiss, United States	1993 .....Oksana Baiul, Ukraine
1922 .....Herma Plank-Szabo, Austria	1961 .....NO COMPETITION	1994 .....Yuka Sato, Japan
1923 .....Herma Plank-Szabo, Austria	1962 .....Sjoukje Dijkstra, Netherlands	1995 .....Chen Lu, China
1924 .....Herma Plank-Szabo, Austria	1963 .....Sjoukje Dijkstra, Netherlands	1996 .....Michelle Kwan, United States
1925 .....Herma Jaross-Szabo, Austria	1964 .....Sjoukje Dijkstra, Netherlands	1997 .....Tara Lipinski, United States
1926 .....Herma Jaross-Szabo, Austria	1965 .....Petra Burka, Canada	1998 .....Michelle Kwan, United States
1927 .....Sonja Henie, Norway	1966 .....Peggy Fleming, United States	1999 .....Maria Butyrskaya, Russia
1928 .....Sonja Henie, Norway	1967 .....Peggy Fleming, United States	2000 .....Michelle Kwan, United States
1929 .....Sonja Henie, Norway	1968 .....Peggy Fleming, United States	2001 .....Michelle Kwan, United States
1930 .....Sonja Henie, Norway	1969 .....Gabriele Seyfert, E. Germany	2002 .....Irina Slutskaya, Russia
1931 .....Sonja Henie, Norway	1970 .....Gabriele Seyfert, E. Germany	2003 .....Michelle Kwan, United States
1932 .....Sonja Henie, Norway	1971 .....Beatrix Schuba, Austria	2004 .....Shizuka Arakawa, Japan
1933 .....Sonja Henie, Norway	1972 .....Beatrix Schuba, Austria	2005 .....Irina Slutskaya, Russia
1934 .....Sonja Henie, Norway	1973 .....Karen Magnussen, Canada	2006 .....Kimmie Meissner, United States
1935 .....Sonja Henie, Norway	1974 .....Christine Errath, E. Germany	2007 .....Miki Ando, Japan
1936 .....Sonja Henie, Norway	1975 .....Dianne DeLeeuw, Netherlands	2008 .....Mao Asada, Japan
1937 .....Cecilia Colledge, Great Britain	1976 .....Dorothy Hamill, United States	2009 .....Yu-Na Kim, South Korea
1938 .....Megan Taylor, Great Britain	1977 .....Linda Fratianne, United States	2010 .....Mao Asada, Japan
1939 .....Megan Taylor, Great Britain	1978 .....Annett Poetzsch, E. Germany	2011 .....Miki Ando, Japan
1940–46 .NO COMPETITION	1979 .....Linda Fratianne, United States	2012 .....Carolina Kostner, Italy
1947 .....Barbara Ann Scott, Canada	1980 .....Annett Poetzsch, E. Germany	
1948 .....Barbara Ann Scott, Canada	1981 .....Denise Biellmann, Switzerland	
1949 .....Alena Vrzanova, Czechoslovakia	1982 .....Elaine Zayak, United States	
1950 .....Alena Vrzanova, Czechoslovakia	1983 .....Rosalynn Sumners, United States	

Men

1896 .....Gilbert Fuchs, Germany	1928 .....Willy Bockl, Austria	1960 .....Alan Giletti, France
1897 .....Gustav Hugel, Austria	1929 .....Gillis Grafstrom, Sweden	1961 .....NO COMPETITION
1898 .....Henning Grenander, Sweden	1930 .....Karl Schafer, Austria	1962 .....Donald Jackson, Canada
1899 .....Gustav Hugel, Austria	1931 .....Karl Schafer, Austria	1963 .....Donald McPherson, Canada
1900 .....Gustav Hugel, Austria	1932 .....Karl Schafer, Austria	1964 .....Manfred Schneldorfer, W. Germany
1901 .....Ulrich Salchow, Sweden	1933 .....Karl Schafer, Austria	1965 .....Alain Calmat, France
1902 .....Ulrich Salchow, Sweden	1934 .....Karl Schafer, Austria	1966 .....Emmerich Danzer, Austria
1903 .....Ulrich Salchow, Sweden	1935 .....Karl Schafer, Austria	1967 .....Emmerich Danzer, Austria
1904 .....Ulrich Salchow, Sweden	1936 .....Karl Schafer, Austria	1968 .....Emmerich Danzer, Austria
1905 .....Ulrich Salchow, Sweden	1937 .....Felix Kaspar, Austria	1969 .....Tim Wood, United States
1906 .....Gilbert Fuchs, Germany	1938 .....Felix Kaspar, Austria	1970 .....Tim Wood, United States
1907 .....Ulrich Salchow, Sweden	1939 .....Graham Sharp, Great Britain	1971 .....Andrej Nepela, Czechoslovakia
1908 .....Ulrich Salchow, Sweden	1940–46 .NO COMPETITION	1972 .....Andrej Nepela, Czechoslovakia
1909 .....Ulrich Salchow, Sweden	1947 .....Hans Gerschwiler, Switzerland	1973 .....Andrej Nepela, Czechoslovakia
1910 .....Ulrich Salchow, Sweden	1948 .....Dick Button, United States	1974 .....Jan Hoffmann, E. Germany
1911 .....Ulrich Salchow, Sweden	1949 .....Dick Button, United States	1975 .....Sergei Volkov, USSR
1912 .....Fritz Kachler, Austria	1950 .....Dick Button, United States	1976 .....John Curry, Great Britain
1913 .....Fritz Kachler, Austria	1951 .....Dick Button, United States	1977 .....Vladimir Kovalev, USSR
1914 .....Gosta Sandhal, Sweden	1952 .....Dick Button, United States	1978 .....Charles Tickner, United States
1915–21 .NO COMPETITION	1953 .....Hayes Alan Jenkins, United States	1979 .....Vladimir Kovalev, USSR
1922 .....Gillis Grafstrom, Sweden	1954 .....Hayes Alan Jenkins, United States	1980 .....Jan Hoffmann, E. Germany
1923 .....Fritz Kachler, Austria	1955 .....Hayes Alan Jenkins, United States	1981 .....Scott Hamilton, United States
1924 .....Gillis Grafstrom, Sweden	1956 .....Hayes Alan Jenkins, United States	1982 .....Scott Hamilton, United States
1925 .....Willy Bockl, Austria	1957 .....David W. Jenkins, United States	1983 .....Scott Hamilton, United States
1926 .....Willy Bockl, Austria	1958 .....David W. Jenkins, United States	1984 .....Scott Hamilton, United States
1927 .....Willy Bockl, Austria	1959 .....David W. Jenkins, United States	1985 .....Aleksandr Fadeev, USSR

WORLD CHAMPIONS *(Cont.)*
Men *(Cont.)*

1986	Brian Boitano, United States	1995	Elvis Stojko, Canada	2004	Evgeni Plushenko, Russia
1987	Brian Orser, Canada	1996	Todd Eldredge, United States	2005	Stephane Lambiel, Switzerland
1988	Brian Boitano, United States	1997	Elvis Stojko, Canada	2006	Stephane Lambiel, Switzerland
1989	Kurt Browning, Canada	1998	Alexei Yagudin, Russia	2007	Brian Joubert, France
1990	Kurt Browning, Canada	1999	Alexei Yagudin, Russia	2008	Jeffrey Buttle, Canada
1991	Kurt Browning, Canada	2000	Alexei Yagudin, Russia	2009	Evan Lysacek, United States
1992	Viktor Petrenko, CIS	2001	Evgeni Plushenko, Russia	2010	Daisuke Takahaski, Japan
1993	Kurt Browning, Canada	2002	Alexei Yagudin, Russia	2011	Patrick Chan, Canada
1994	Elvis Stojko, Canada	2003	Evgeni Plushenko, Russia	2012	Patrick Chan, Canada

Pairs

1908	Anna Hubler, Heinrich Burger, Germany	1966	Ljudmila Protopopov, Oleg Protopopov, USSR
1909	Phyllis Johnson, James H. Johnson, Great Britain	1967	Ljudmila Protopopov, Oleg Protopopov, USSR
1910	Anna Hubler, Heinrich Burger, Germany	1968	Ljudmila Protopopov, Oleg Protopopov, USSR
1911	Ludowika Eilers, Walter Jakobsson, Germany/Finland	1969	Irina Rodnina, Aleksey Ulanov, USSR
1912	Phyllis Johnson, James H. Johnson, Great Britain	1970	Irina Rodnina, Aleksey Ulanov, USSR
1913	Helene Engelmann, Karl Majstrik, Germany	1971	Irina Rodnina, Aleksey Ulanov, USSR
1914	Ludowika Jakobsson-Eilers, Walter Jakobsson-Eilers, Finland	1972	Irina Rodnina, Aleksey Ulanov, USSR
1915–21	NO COMPETITION	1973	Irina Rodnina, Aleksandr Zaytsev, USSR
1922	Helene Engelmann, Alfred Berger, Germany	1974	Irina Rodnina, Aleksandr Zaytsev, USSR
1923	Ludowika Jakobsson-Eilers, Walter Jakobsson-Eilers, Finland	1975	Irina Rodnina, Aleksandr Zaytsev, USSR
1924	Helene Engelmann, Alfred Berger, Germany	1976	Irina Rodnina, Aleksandr Zaytsev, USSR
1925	Herma Jaross-Szabo, Ludwig Wrede, Austria	1977	Irina Rodnina, Aleksandr Zaytsev, USSR
1926	Andree Joly, Pierre Brunet, France	1978	Irina Rodnina, Aleksandr Zaytsev, USSR
1927	Herma Jaross-Szabo, Ludwig Wrede, Austria	1979	Tai Babilonia, Randy Gardner, United States
1928	Andree Joly, Pierre Brunet, France	1980	Maria Cherkasova, Sergei Shakhrai, USSR
1929	Lilly Scholz, Otto Kaiser, Austria	1981	Irina Vorobieva, Igor Lisovsky, USSR
1930	Andree Brunet-Joly, Pierre Brunet-Joly, France	1982	Sabine Baess, Tassilio Thierbach, E. Germany
1931	Emilie Rotter, Laszlo Szollas, Hungary	1983	Elena Valova, Oleg Vasiliev, USSR
1932	Andree Brunet-Joly, Pierre Brunet-Joly, France	1984	Barbara Underhill, Paul Martini, Canada
1933	Emilie Rotter, Laszlo Szollas, Hungary	1985	Elena Valova, Oleg Vasiliev, USSR
1934	Emilie Rotter, Laszlo Szollas, Hungary	1986	Ekaterina Gordeeva, Sergei Grinkov, USSR
1935	Emilie Rotter, Laszlo Szollas, Hungary	1987	Ekaterina Gordeeva, Sergei Grinkov, USSR
1936	Maxi Herber, Ernst Bajer, Germany	1988	Elena Valova, Oleg Vasiliev, USSR
1937	Maxi Herber, Ernst Bajer, Germany	1989	Ekaterina Gordeeva, Sergei Grinkov, USSR
1938	Maxi Herber, Ernst Bajer, Germany	1990	Ekaterina Gordeeva, Sergei Grinkov, USSR
1939	Maxi Herber, Ernst Bajer, Germany	1991	Natalia Mishkutienok, Artur Dmitriev, USSR
1940–46	NO COMPETITION	1992	Natalia Mishkutienok, Artur Dmitriev, CIS
1947	Micheline Lannoy, Pierre Baugniet, Belgium	1993	Isabelle Brasseur, Lloyd Eisler, Canada
1948	Micheline Lannoy, Pierre Baugniet, Belgium	1994	Evgenia Shishkova, Vadim Naumov, Russia
1949	Andrea Kekessy, Ede Kiraly, Hungary	1995	Radka Kovarikova, Rene Novotny, Czech Republic
1950	Karol Kennedy, Peter Kennedy, United States	1996	Marina Eltsova, Andrey Buskhov, Russia
1951	Ria Baran, Paul Falk, W. Germany	1997	Mandy Wötzel, Ingo Steuer, Germany
1952	Ria Baran Falk, Paul Falk, W. Germany	1998	Jenni Meno, Todd Sand, United States
1953	Jennifer Nicks, John Nicks, Great Britain	1999	Elena Berezhnaya, Anton Sikharulidze, Russia
1954	Frances Dafoe, Norris Bowden, Canada	2000	Maria Petrova, Aleksei Tikhonov, Russia
1955	Frances Dafoe, Norris Bowden, Canada	2001	Jamie Salé, David Pelletier, Canada
1956	Sissy Schwarz, Kurt Oppelt, Austria	2002	Xue Shen, Hongbo Zhao, China
1957	Barbara Wagner, Robert Paul, Canada	2003	Xue Shen, Hongbo Zhao, China
1958	Barbara Wagner, Robert Paul, Canada	2004	Tatiana Totmianina, Maxim Marinin, Russia
1959	Barbara Wagner, Robert Paul, Canada	2005	Tatiana Totmianina, Maxim Marinin, Russia
1960	Barbara Wagner, Robert Paul, Canada	2006	Qing Pang, Jian Tong, China
1961	NO COMPETITION	2007	Shen Xue, Zhao Hongbo, China
1962	Maria Jelinek, Otto Jelinek, Canada	2008	Aliona Savchenko, Robin Szolkowy, Germany
1963	Marika Kilius, Hans-Jurgen Baumler, W Germany	2009	Aliona Savchenko, Robin Szolkowy, Germany
1964	Marika Kilius, Hans-Jurgen Baumler, W Germany	2010	Qin Pang, Jian Tong, China
1965	Ljudmila Protopopov, Oleg Protopopov, USSR	2011	Aliona Savchenko, Robin Szolkowy, Germany
		2012	Aliona Savchenko, Robin Szolkowy, Germany

WORLD CHAMPIONS *(Cont.)*

Dance

1950 ....Lois Waring, Michael McGean, United States	1982 ....Jayne Torvill, Christopher Dean, Great Britain
1951 ....Jean Westwood, Lawrence Demmy, Great Britain	1983 ....Jayne Torvill, Christopher Dean, Great Britain
1952 ....Jean Westwood, Lawrence Demmy, Great Britain	1984 ....Jayne Torvill, Christopher Dean, Great Britain
1953 ....Jean Westwood, Lawrence Demmy, Great Britain	1985 ....Natalia Bestemianova, Andrei Bukin, USSR
1954 ....Jean Westwood, Lawrence Demmy, Great Britain	1986 ....Natalia Bestemianova, Andrei Bukin, USSR
1955 ....Jean Westwood, Lawrence Demmy, Great Britain	1987 ....Natalia Bestemianova, Andrei Bukin, USSR
1956 ....Pamela Wieght, Paul Thomas, Great Britain	1988 ....Natalia Bestemianova, Andrei Bukin, USSR
1957 ....June Markham, Courtney Jones, Great Britain	1989 ....Marina Klimova, Sergei Ponomarenko, USSR
1958 ....June Markham, Courtney Jones, Doreen D. Denny, Courtney Jones, Great Britain	1990 ....Marina Klimova, Sergei Ponomarenko, USSR
1960 ....Doreen D. Denny, Courtney Jones, Great Britain	1991 ....Isabelle Duchesnay, Paul Duchesnay, France
1961 ....NO COMPETITION	1992 ....Marina Klimova, Sergei Ponomarenko, CIS
1962 ....Eva Romanova, Pavel Roman, Czechoslovakia	1993 ....Renee Roca, Gorsha Sur, United States
1963 ....Eva Romanova, Pavel Roman, Czechoslovakia	1994 ....Oksana Grishuk, Evgeny Platov, Russia
1964 ....Eva Romanova, Pavel Roman, Czechoslovakia	1995 ....Oksana Grishuk, Evgeny Platov, Russia
1965 ....Eva Romanova, Pavel Roman, Czechoslovakia	1996 ....Oksana Grishuk, Evgeny Platov, Russia
1966 ....Diane Towler, Bernard Ford, Great Britain	1997 ....Oksana Grishuk, Evgeny Platov, Russia
1967 ....Diane Towler, Bernard Ford, Great Britain	1998 ....Anjelika Krylova, Oleg Ovsyannikov, Russia
1968 ....Diane Towler, Bernard Ford, Great Britain	1999 ....Anjelika Krylova, Oleg Ovsyannikov, Russia
1969 ....Diane Towler, Bernard Ford, Great Britain	2000 ....Marina Anissina, Gwendal Peizerat, France
1970 ....Ljudmila Pakhomova, Aleksandr Gorshkov, USSR	2001 ....Barbara Fusar Poli, Maurizio Margaglio, Italy
1971 ....Ljudmila Pakhomova, Aleksandr Gorshkov USSR	2002 ....Irina Lobacheva, Ilia Averbukh, Russia
1972 ....Ljudmila Pakhomova, Aleksandr Gorshkov USSR	2003 ....Shae-Lynn Bourne, Victor Kraatz, Canada
1973 ....Ljudmila Pakhomova, Aleksandr Gorshkov USSR	2004 ....Tatiana Navka, Roman Kostomarov, Russia
1974 ....Ljudmila Pakhomova, Aleksandr Gorshkov USSR	2005 ....Tatiana Navka, Roman Kostomarov, Russia
1975 ....Irina Moiseeva, Andreij Minenkov, USSR	2006 ....Albena Denkova, Maxim Staviski, Bulgaria
1976 ....Ljudmila Pakhomova, Aleksandr Gorshkov, USSR	2007 ....Albena Denkova ,Maxim Staviski, Bulgaria
1977 ....Irina Moiseeva, Andreij Minenkov, USSR	2008 ....Isabelle Delobel, Olivier Schoenfelder, France
1978 ....Natalia Linichuk, Gennadi Karponosov, USSR	2009 ....Oksana Domnina, Maxim Shabalin, Russia
1979 ....Natalia Linichuk, Gennadi Karponosov, USSR	2010 ....Tessa Virtue, Scott Moir, Canada
1980 ....Krisztina Regoeczy, Andras Sallai, Hungary	2011 ....Meryl Davis, Charlie White, United States
1981 ....Jayne Torvill, Christopher Dean, Great Britain	2012 ....Tessa Virtue, Scott Moir, Canada

CHAMPIONS OF THE UNITED STATES

Women

The championships held in 1914, 1918, 1920 and 1921 under the auspices of the International Skating Union of America were open to Canadians, although the competitions were considered to be United States championships. Beginning in 1922, the championships have been held under the auspices of the United States Figure Skating Association.

1914 ....Theresa Weld, SC of Boston	1932 ....Maribel Y. Vinson, SC of Boston	1947 ....Gretchen Van Zandt Merrill, SC of Boston
1915–17.NO COMPETITION	1933 ....Maribel Y. Vinson, SC of Boston	1948 ....Gretchen Van Zandt Merrill, SC of Boston
1918 ....Rosemary S. Beresford, New York SC	1934 ....Suzanne Davis, SC of Boston	1949 ....Yvonne Claire Sherman, SC of New York
1919 ...NO COMPETITION	1935 ....Maribel Y. Vinson, SC of Boston	1950 ....Yvonne Claire Sherman, SC of New York
1920 ....Theresa Weld, SC of Boston	1936 ....Maribel Y. Vinson, SC of Boston	1951 ....Sonya Klopfer, Junior SC of New York
1921 ....Theresa Weld Blanchard, SC of Boston	1937 ....Maribel Y. Vinson, SC of Boston	1952 ....Tenley E. Albright, SC of Boston
1922 ....Theresa Weld Blanchard, SC of Boston	1938 ....Joan Tozzer, SC of Boston	1953 ....Tenley E. Albright, SC of Boston
1923 ....Theresa Weld Blanchard, SC of Boston	1939 ....Joan Tozzer, SC of Boston	1954 ....Tenley E. Albright, SC of Boston
1924 ....Theresa Weld Blanchard, SC of Boston	1940 ....Joan Tozzer, SC of Boston	1955 ....Tenley E. Albright, SC of Boston
1925 ....Beatrix Loughran, New York SC	1941 ....Jane Vaughn, Philadelphia SC & HS	1956 ....Tenley E. Albright, SC of Boston
1926 ....Beatrix Loughran, New York SC	1942 ....Jane Vaughn Sullivan, Philadelphia SC & HS	1957 ....Carol E. Heiss, SC of New York
1927 ....Beatrix Loughran, New York SC	1943 ....Gretchen Van Zandt Merrill, SC of Boston	1958 ....Carol E. Heiss, SC of New York
1928 ....Maribel Y. Vinson, SC of Boston	1944 ....Gretchen Van Zandt Merrill, SC of Boston	1959 ....Carol E. Heiss, SC of New York
1929 ....Maribel Y. Vinson, SC of Boston	1945 ....Gretchen Van Zandt Merrill, SC of Boston	1960 ....Carol E. Heiss, SC of New York
1930 ....Maribel Y. Vinson, SC of Boston	1946 ....Gretchen Van Zandt Merrill, SC of Boston	1961 ....Laurence R. Owen, SC of Boston
1931 ....Maribel Y. Vinson, SC of Boston		

CHAMPIONS OF THE UNITED STATES (Cont.)
Women (Cont.)

1962....Barbara Roles Pursley,
    Arctic Blades FSC
1963....Lorraine G. Hanlon,
    SC of Boston
1964....Peggy Fleming,
    Arctic Blades FSC
1965....Peggy Fleming,
    Arctic Blades FSC
1966....Peggy Fleming,
    City of Colorado Springs
1967....Peggy Fleming, Broadmoor SC
1968....Peggy Fleming, Broadmoor SC
1969....Janet Lynn, Wagon Wheel FSC
1970....Janet Lynn, Wagon Wheel FSC
1971....Janet Lynn, Wagon Wheel FSC
1972....Janet Lynn, Wagon Wheel FSC
1973....Janet Lynn, Wagon Wheel FSC
1974....Dorothy Hamill, SC of New York
1975....Dorothy Hamill, SC of New York

1976....Dorothy Hamill, SC of New York
1977....Linda Fratianne, Los Angeles FSC
1978....Linda Fratianne, Los Angeles FSC
1979....Linda Fratianne, Los Angeles FSC
1980....Linda Fratianne, Los Angeles FSC
1981....Elaine Zayak, SC of New York
1982....Rosalynn Sumners, Seattle SC
1983....Rosalynn Sumners, Seattle SC
1984....Rosalynn Sumners, Seattle SC
1985....Tiffany Chin, San Diego FSC
1986....Debi Thomas, Los Angeles FSC
1987....Jill Trenary, Broadmoor SC
1988....Debi Thomas, Los Angeles FSC
1989....Jill Trenary, Broadmoor SC
1990....Jill Trenary, Broadmoor SC
1991....Tonya Harding, Carousel FSC
1992....Kristi Yamaguchi, St Moritz ISC
1993....Nancy Kerrigan, Colonial FSC
1994....Tonya Harding, Portland FSC

1995....Nicole Bobek, Los Angeles FSC
1996....Michelle Kwan, Los Angeles FSC
1997....Tara Lipinski, Detroit SC
1998....Michelle Kwan, Los Angeles FSC
1999....Michelle Kwan, Los Angeles FSC
2000....Michelle Kwan, Los Angeles FSC
2001....Michelle Kwan, Los Angeles FSC
2002....Michelle Kwan, Los Angeles FSC
2003....Michelle Kwan, Los Angeles FSC
2004....Michelle Kwan, Los Angeles FSC
2005....Michelle Kwan, Los Angeles FSC
2006....Sasha Cohen, Orange County FSC
2007....Kimmie Meissner,
    Univ. of Delaware FSC
2008....Mirai Nagasu, Pasadena FSC
2009....Alissa Czisny, Detroit SC
2010....Rachael Flatt, Broadmoor SC
2011....Alissa Czisny, Detroit SC
2012....Ashley Wagner, SC of Wilmington

Men

1914....Norman M. Scott,
    WC of Montreal
1915–17 NO COMPETITION
1918....Nathaniel W. Niles, SC of Boston
1919....NO COMPETITION
1920....Sherwin C. Badger, SC of Boston
1921....Sherwin C. Badger, SC of Boston
1922....Sherwin C. Badger, SC of Boston
1923....Sherwin C. Badger, SC of Boston
1924....Sherwin C. Badger, SC of Boston
1925....Nathaniel W. Niles, SC of Boston
1926....Chris I. Christenson,
    Twin City FSC
1927....Nathaniel W. Niles, SC of Boston
1928....Roger F. Turner, SC of Boston
1929....Roger F. Turner, SC of Boston
1930....Roger F. Turner, SC of Boston
1931....Roger F. Turner, SC of Boston
1932....Roger F. Turner, SC of Boston
1933....Roger F. Turner, SC of Boston
1934....Roger F. Turner, SC of Boston
1935....Robin H. Lee, SC of New York
1936....Robin H. Lee, SC of New York
1937....Robin H. Lee, SC of New York
1938....Robin H. Lee, Chicago FSC
1939....Robin H. Lee, St Paul FSC
1940....Eugene Turner, Los Angeles FSC
1941....Eugene Turner, Los Angeles FSC
1942....Robert Specht, Chicago FSC
1943....Arthur R. Vaughn Jr.,
    Phila. SC & HS
1944–45.NO COMPETITION
1946....Dick Button,
    Philadelphia SC & HS
1947....Dick Button,
    Philadelphia SC & HS
1948....Dick Button,
    Philadelphia SC & HS
1949....Dick Button,
    Philadelphia SC & HS

1950....Dick Button, SC of Boston
1951....Dick Button, SC of Boston
1952....Dick Button, SC of Boston
1953....Hayes Alan Jenkins,
    Cleveland SC
1954....Hayes Alan Jenkins,
    Broadmoor SC
1955....Hayes Alan Jenkins,
    Broadmoor SC
1956....Hayes Alan Jenkins,
    Broadmoor SC
1957....David Jenkins, Broadmoor SC
1958....David Jenkins, Broadmoor SC
1959....David Jenkins, Broadmoor SC
1960....David Jenkins, Broadmoor SC
1961....Bradley R. Lord, SC of Boston
1962....Monty Hoyt, Broadmoor SC
1963....Thomas Litz, Hershey FSC
1964....Scott Ethan Allen,
    SC of New York
1965....Gary C. Visconti, Detroit SC
1966....Scott Ethan Allen,
    SC of New York
1967....Gary C. Visconti, Detroit SC
1968....Tim Wood, Detroit SC
1969....Tim Wood, Detroit SC
1970....Tim Wood, City of
    Colorado Springs
1971....John Misha Petkevich,
    Great Falls FSC
1972....Kenneth Shelley,
    Arctic Blades FSC
1973....Gordon McKellen Jr.,
    SC of Lake Placid
1974....Gordon McKellen Jr.,
    SC of Lake Placid
1975....Gordon McKellen Jr.,
    SC of Lake Placid
1976....Terry Kubicka, Arctic Blades FSC
1977....Charles Tickner, Denver FSC
1978....Charles Tickner, Denver FSC

1979....Charles Tickner, Denver FSC
1980....Charles Tickner, Denver FSC
1981....Scott Hamilton,
    Philadelphia SC & HS
1982....Scott Hamilton,
    Philadelphia SC & HS
1983....Scott Hamilton,
    Philadelphia SC & HS
1984....Scott Hamilton,
    Philadelphia SC & HS
1985....Brian Boitano, Peninsula FSC
1986....Brian Boitano, Peninsula FSC
1987....Brian Boitano, Peninsula FSC
1988....Brian Boitano, Peninsula FSC
1989....Christopher Bowman,
    Los Angeles FSC
1990....Todd Eldredge, Los Angeles FSC
1991....Todd Eldredge, Los Angeles FSC
1992....Christopher Bowman,
    Los Angeles FSC
1993....Scott Davis, Broadmoor SC
1994....Scott Davis, Broadmoor SC
1995....Todd Eldredge, Detroit SC
1996....Rudy Galindo, St Moritz ISC
1997....Todd Eldredge, Detroit SC
1998....Todd Eldredge, Detroit SC
1999....Michael Weiss, Washington FSC
2000....Michael Weiss, Washington FSC
2001....Timothy Goebel, Winterhurst FSC
2002....Todd Eldredge, Los Angeles FSC
2003....Michael Weiss, Washington FSC
2004....Johnny Weir, SC of New York
2005....Johnny Weir, SC of New York
2006....Johnny Weir, SC of New York
2007....Evan Lysacek, DuPage FSC
2008....Evan Lysacek, DuPage FSC
2009....Jeremy Abbott, Broadmoor SC
2010....Jeremy Abbott, Detroit SC
2011....Ryan Bradley, Broadmoor SC
2012....Jeremy Abbott, Detroit SC

CHAMPIONS OF THE UNITED STATES *(Cont.)*
Pairs

1914   Jeanne Chevalier, Norman M. Scott, WC of Montreal

1915–17 .NO COMPETITION

1918   Theresa Weld, Nathaniel W. Niles, SC of Boston

1919   No competition

1920   Theresa Weld, Nathaniel W. Niles, SC of Boston

1921   Theresa Weld Blanchard, Nathaniel W. Niles, SC of Boston

1922   Theresa Weld Blanchard, Nathaniel W. Niles, SC of Boston

1923   Theresa Weld Blanchard, Nathaniel W. Niles, SC of Boston

1924   Theresa Weld Blanchard, Nathaniel W. Niles, SC of Boston

1925   Theresa Weld Blanchard, Nathaniel W. Niles, SC of Boston

1926   Theresa Weld Blanchard, Nathaniel W. Niles, SC of Boston

1927   Theresa Weld Blanchard, Nathaniel W. Niles, SC of Boston

1928   Maribel Y. Vinson, Thornton L. Coolidge, SC of Boston

1929   Maribel Y. Vinson, Thornton L. Coolidge, SC of Boston

1930   Beatrix Loughran, Sherwin C. Badger, SC of New York

1931   Beatrix Loughran, Sherwin C. Badger, SC of New York

1932   Beatrix Loughran, Sherwin C. Badger, SC of New York

1933   Maribel Y. Vinson, George E. B. Hill, SC of SC of Boston

1936   Maribel Y. Vinson, George E. B. Hill, SC of Boston

1937   Maribel Y. Vinson, George E. B. Hill, SC of Boston

1938   Joan Tozzer, M. Bernard Fox, SC of Boston

1939   Joan Tozzer, M. Bernard Fox, SC of Boston

1940   Joan Tozzer, M. Bernard Fox, SC of Boston

1941   Donna Atwood, Eugene Turner, Mercury FSC/Los Angeles FSC

1942   Doris Schubach, Walter Noffke, Springfield Ice Birds

1943   Doris Schubach, Walter Noffke, Springfield Ice Birds

1944   Doris Schubach, Walter Noffke, Springfield Ice Birds

1945   Donna Jeanne Pospisil, Jean-Pierre Brunet, SC of New York

1946   Donna Jeanne Pospisil, Jean-Pierre Brunet, SC of New York

1947   Yvonne Claire Sherman, Robert J. Swenning, SC of New York

1948   Karol Kennedy, Peter Kennedy, Seattle SC

1949   Karol Kennedy, Peter Kennedy, Seattle SC

1950   Karol Kennedy, Peter Kennedy, Broadmoor SC

1951   Karol Kennedy, Peter Kennedy, Broadmoor SC

1952   Karol Kennedy, Peter Kennedy, Broadmoor SC

1953   Carole Ann Ormaca, Robin Greiner, SC of Fresno

1954   Carole Ann Ormaca, Robin Greiner, SC of Fresno

1955   Carole Ann Ormaca, Robin Greiner, St Moritz ISC

1956   Carole Ann Ormaca, Robin Greiner, St Moritz ISC

1957   Nancy Rouillard Ludington, Ronald Ludington, Commonwealth FSC/SC of Boston

1958   Nancy Rouillard Ludington, Ronald Ludington, Commonwealth FSC/SC of Boston

1959   Nancy Rouillard Ludington, Ronald Ludington, Commonwealth FSC

1960   Nancy Rouillard Ludington, Ronald Ludington, Commonwealth FSC

1961   Maribel Y. Owen, Dudley S. Richards, SC of Boston

1962   Dorothyann Nelson, Pieter Kollen, Village of Lake Placid

1963   Judianne Fotheringill, Jerry J. Fotheringill, Broadmoor SC

1964   Judianne Fotheringill, Jerry J. Fotheringill, Broadmoor SC

1965   Vivian Joseph, Ronald Joseph, Chicago FSC

1966   Cynthia Kauffman, Ronald Kauffman, Seattle SC

1967   Cynthia Kauffman, Ronald Kauffman, Seattle SC

1968   Cynthia Kauffman, Ronald Kauffman, Seattle SC

1969   Cynthia Kauffman, Ronald Kauffman, Seattle SC

1970   Jo Jo Starbuck, Kenneth Shelley, Arctic Blades FSC

1971   Jo Jo Starbuck, Kenneth Shelley, Arctic Blades FSC

1972   Jo Jo Starbuck, Kenneth Shelley, Arctic Blades FSC

1973   Melissa Militano, Mark Militano, SC of New York

1974   Melissa Militano, Johnny Johns, SC of New York/Detroit SC

1975   Melissa Militano, Johnny Johns, SC of New York/Detroit SC

1976   Tai Babilonia, Randy Gardner, LA FSC

1977   Tai Babilonia, Randy Gardner, LA FSC

1978   Tai Babilonia, Randy Gardner, Los Angeles FSC/Santa Monica FSC

1979   Tai Babilonia, Randy Gardner, Los Angeles FSC/Santa Monica FSC

1980   Tai Babilonia, Randy Gardner, Los Angeles FSC/Santa Monica FSC

1981   Caitlin/Peter Carruthers, SC of Wilmington

1982   Caitlin/Peter Carruthers, SC of Wilmington

1983   Caitlin/Peter Carruthers, SC of Wilmington

1984   Caitlin/Peter Carruthers, SC of Wilmington

1985   Jill Watson, Peter Oppegard, LA FSC

1986   Gillian Wachsman, Todd Waggoner, SC of Wilmington

1987   Jill Watson, Peter Oppegard, LA FSC

1988   Jill Watson, Peter Oppegard, LA FSC

1989   Kristi Yamaguchi, Rudy Galindo, St Moritz ISC

1990   Kristi Yamaguchi, Rudy Galindo, St Moritz ISC

1991   Natasha Kuchiki, Todd Sand, LA FSC

1992   Calla Urbanski, Rocky Marval, U of Delaware FSC/SC of New York

1993   Calla Urbanski, Rocky Marval, U of Delaware FSC/SC of New York

1994   Jenni Meno, Todd Sand, Winterhurst FSC/Los Angeles FSC

1995   Jenni Meno, Todd Sand, Winterhurst FSC/Los Angeles FSC

1996   Jenni Meno, Todd Sand, Winterhurst FSC/Los Angeles FSC

1997   Kyoko Ina, Jason Dungjen, SC of New York

1998   Kyoko Ina, Jason Dungjen, SC of New York

1999   Danielle Hartsell, Steve Hartsell, Detroit SC

2000   Kyoko Ina, John Zimmerman, SC of New York/Birmingham FSC

2001   Kyoko Ina, John Zimmerman, SC of New York/Birmingham FSC

2002   Kyoko Ina, John Zimmerman, SC of New York/Birmingham FSC

2003   Tiffany Scott, Philip Dulebohn, Colonial FSC/Univ of Delaware FSC

2004   Rena Inoue, John Baldwin, All Year FSC

2005   Kathryn Orscher, Garrett Lucash, Charter Oak FSC

2006   Rena Inoue, John Baldwin, All Year FSC

2007   Brooke Castile, Benjamin Okolski, Arctic FSC

2008   Keauna McLaughlin, Los Angeles FSC/Rockne Brubaker, Broadmoor SC

2009   Keauna McLaughlin, Los Angeles FSC/Rockne Brubaker, Broadmoor SC

2010   Caydee Denney, SW Florida FSC/Jeremy Barrett, SW Florida FSC

2011   Caitlin Yankowskas, Broadmoor SC/John Coughlin, Kansas City FSC

2012   Caydee Denney, Broadmoor SC/John Coughlin, Kansas City FSC

CHAMPIONS OF THE UNITED STATES *(Cont.)*
Dance

1914	Waltz: Theresa Weld, Nathaniel W. Niles, SC of Boston	
1915–19	NO COMPETITION	
1920	Waltz: Theresa Weld, Nathaniel W. Niles, SC of Boston Fourteenstep: Gertrude Cheever Porter, Irving Brokaw, New York SC	
1921	Waltz and Fourteenstep: Theresa Weld Blanchard, Nathaniel W. Niles, SC of Boston	
1922	Waltz: Beatrix Loughran, Edward M. Howland, New York SC/ SC of Boston Fourteenstep: Theresa Weld Blanchard, Nathaniel W. Niles, SC of Boston	
1923	Waltz: Mr. & Mrs. Henry W. Howe, New York SC Fourteenstep: Sydney Goode, James B. Greene, New York SC	
1924	Waltz: Rosaline Dunn, Frederick Gabel, New York SC Fourteenstep: Sydney Goode, James B. Greene, New York SC	
1925	Waltz and Fourteenstep: Virginia Slattery, Ferrier T. Martin, New York SC	
1926	Waltz: Rosaline Dunn, Joseph K. Savage, New York SC Fourteenstep: Sydney Goode, James B. Greene, New York SC	
1927	Waltz and Fourteenstep: Rosaline Dunn, Joseph K. Savage, New York SC	
1928	Waltz: Rosaline Dunn, Joseph K. Savage, New York SC Fourteenstep: Ada Bauman Kelly, George T. Braakman, New York SC	
1929	Waltz and Original Dance combined: Edith C. Secord, Joseph K. Savage, SC of New York	
1930	Waltz: Edith C. Secord, Joseph K. Savage, SC of New York Original: Clara Rotch Frothingham, George E. B. Hill, SC of Boston	
1931	Waltz: Edith C. Secord, Ferrier T. Martin, SC of New York Original: Theresa Weld Blanchard, Nathaniel W. Niles, SC of Boston	
1932	Waltz: Edith C. Secord, Joseph K. Savage, SC of New York Original: Clara Rotch Frothingham, George E. B. Hill, SC of Boston	
1933	Waltz: Ilse Twaroschk, Frederick F. Fleishmann, Brooklyn FSC Original: Suzanne Davis, Frederick Goodridge, SC of Boston	
1934	Waltz: Nettie C. Prantel, Roy Hunt, SC of New York Original: Suzanne Davis, Frederick Goodridge, SC of Boston	
1935	Waltz: Nettie C. Prantel, Roy Hunt, SC of New York	
1936	Marjorie Parker, Joseph K. Savage, SC of New York	
1937	Nettie C. Prantel, Harold Hartshorne, SC of New York	
1938	Nettie C. Prantel, Harold Hartshorne, SC of New York	
1939	Sandy Macdonald, Harold Hartshorne, SC of New York	
1940	Sandy Macdonald, Harold Hartshorne, SC of New York	
1941	Sandy Macdonald, Harold Hartshorne, SCNY	
1942	Edith B. Whetstone, Alfred N. Richards, Jr, Philadelphia SC & HS	
1943	Marcella May, James Lochead Jr., Skate & Ski Club	
1944	Marcella May, James Lochead Jr., Skate & Ski Club	
1945	Kathe Mehl Williams, Robert J. Swenning, SC of New York	
1946	Anne Davies, Carleton C. Hoffner Jr., Washington FSC	
1947	Lois Waring, Walter H. Bainbridge Jr., Baltimore FSC/Washigton FSC	
1948	Lois Waring, Walter H. Bainbridge Jr., Baltimore FSC/Washington FSC	
1949	Lois Waring, Walter H. Bainbridge Jr., Baltimore FSC/Washington FSC	
1950	Lois Waring, Michael McGean, Baltimore FSC	
1951	Carmel Bodel, Edward L. Bodel, St. Moritz ISC	
1952	Lois Waring, Michael McGean, Baltimore FSC	
1953	Carol Ann Peters, Daniel C. Ryan, Washington FSC	
1954	Carmel Bodel, Edward L. Bodel, St Moritz ISC	
1955	Carmel Bodel, Edward L. Bodel, St Moritz ISC	
1956	Joan Zamboni, Roland Junso, Arctic Blades FSC	
1957	Sharon McKenzie, Bert Wright, Los Angeles FSC	
1958	Andree Anderson, Donald Jacoby, Buffalo SC	
1959	Andree Anderson Jacoby, Donald Jacoby, Buffalo SC	
1960	Margie Ackles, Charles W. Phillips Jr., Los Angeles FSC/Arctic Blades FSC	
1961	Diane C. Sherbloom, Larry Pierce, Los Angeles FSC/ WC of Indianapolis	
1962	Yvonne N. Littlefield, Peter F. Betts, Arctic Blades FSC/ Paramount, CA	
1963	Sally Schantz, Stanley Urban, SC of Boston/Buffalo SC	
1964	Darlene Streich, Charles D. Fetter Jr., WC of Indianapolis	
1965	Kristin Fortune, Dennis Sveum, Los Angeles FSC	
1966	Kristin Fortune, Dennis Sveum, Los Angeles FSC	
1967	Lorna Dyer, John Carrell, Broadmoor SC	
1968	Judy Schwomeyer, James Sladky, WC of Indianapolis/Genesee FSC	
1969	Judy Schwomeyer, James Sladky, WC of Indianapolis/Genesee FSC	
1970	Judy Schwomeyer, James Sladky, WC of Indianapolis/Genesee FSC	
1971	Judy Schwomeyer, James Sladky, WC of Indianapolis/Genesee FSC	
1972	Judy Schwomeyer, James Sladky, WC of Indianapolis/Genesee FSC	
1973	Mary Karen Campbell, Johnny Johns, Lansing SC/Detroit SC	
1974	Colleen O'Connor, Jim Millns, Broadmoor SC/ City of Colorado Springs	
1975	Colleen O'Connor, Jim Millns, Broadmoor SC	
1976	Colleen O'Connor, Jim Millns, Broadmoor SC	
1977	Judy Genovesi, Kent Weigle, SC of Hartford/Charter Oak FSC	
1978	Stacey Smith, John Summers, SC of Wilmington	
1979	Stacey Smith, John Summers, SC of Wilmington	
1980	Stacey Smith, John Summers, SC of Wilmington	
1981	Judy Blumberg, Michael Seibert, Broadmoor SC/ISC of Indianapolis	
1982	Judy Blumberg, Michael Seibert, Broadmoor SC/ISC of Indianapolis	
1983	Judy Blumberg, Michael Seibert, Pittsburgh FSC	
1984	Judy Blumberg, Michael Seibert, Pittsburgh FSC	
1985	Judy Blumberg, Michael Seibert, Pittsburgh FSC	
1986	Renee Roca, Donald Adair, Genesee FSC/Academy FSC	
1987	Suzanne Semanick, Scott Gregory, U of Delaware SC	
1988	Suzanne Semanick, Scott Gregory, U of Delaware SC	
1989	Susan Wynne, Joseph Druar, Broadmoor SC/Seattle SC	
1990	Susan Wynne, Joseph Druar, Broadmoor SC/Seattle SC	
1991	Elizabeth Punsalan, Jerod Swallow, Broadmoor SC	
1992	April Sargent, Russ Witherby, Ogdensburg FSC/ U of Delaware FSC	
1993	Renee Roca, Gorsha Sur, Broadmoor SC	
1994	Elizabeth Punsalan, Jerod Swallow, Broadmoor SC/Detroit SC	
1995	Renee Roca, Gorsha Sur, Broadmoor SC	
1996	Elizabeth Punsalan, Jerod Swallow, Detroit SC	
1997	Elizabeth Punsalan, Jerod Swallow, Detroit SC	

CHAMPIONS OF THE UNITED STATES *(CONT.)*
Dance *(Cont.)*

1998	Elizabeth Punsalan, Jerod Swallow, Detroit SC	2003	Naomi Lang, Peter Tchernyshev, American Academy FSC	2008	Tanith Belbin, Ben Agosto, Arctic FSC
1999	Naomi Lang, Peter Tchernyshev, Detroit SC	2004	Tanith Belbin, Ben Agosto, Detroit SC	2009	Meryl Davis, Arctic FSC/ Charlie White, Detroit SC
2000	Naomi Lang, Peter Tchernyshev, Detroit SC	2005	Tanith Belbin, Ben Agosto, Detroit SC	2010	Meryl Davis, Arctic FSC/ Charlie White, Detroit SC
2001	Naomi Lang, Peter Tchernyshev, Detroit SC	2006	Tanith Belbin, Ben Agosto, Arctic FSC	2011	Meryl Davis, Arctic FSC/ Charlie White, Detroit SC
2002	Naomi Lang, Peter Tchernyshev, American Academy FSC	2007	Tanith Belbin, Ben Agosto, Arctic FSC	2012	Meryl Davis, Arctic FSC/ Charlie White, Detroit SC

Gymnastics

WORLD CHAMPIONS — Men

All-Around

Year	Champion, Nation
1903	Joseph Martinez, France
1905	Marcel Lalue, France
1907	Joseph Czada, Czechoslovakia
1909	Marcos Torres, France
1911	Ferdinand Steiner, Czechoslovakia
1913	Marcos Torres, France
1922	Peter Sumi, Yugoslavia
	F. Pechacek, Czechoslovakia
1926	Peter Sumi, Yugoslavia
1930	Josip Primozic, Yugoslavia
1934	Eugene Mack, Switzerland
1938	Jan Gajdos, Czechoslovakia
1950	Walter Lehmann, Switzerland
1954	Valentin Mouratov, USSR
	Victor Chukarin, USSR
1958	Boris Shaklin, USSR
1962	Yuri Titov, USSR
1966	Mikhail Voronin, USSR
1970	Eizo Kenmotsu, Japan
1974	Shigeru Kasamatsu, Japan
1978	Nikolai Andrianov, USSR
1979	Alexander Ditiatin, USSR
1981	Yuri Korolev, USSR
1983	Dimitri Bilozertchev, USSR
1985	Yuri Korolev, USSR
1987	Dimitri Bilozertchev, USSR
1989	Igor Korobchinsky, USSR
1991	Grigori Misutin, CIS
1993	Vitaly Scherbo, Belarus
1994	Ivan Ivankov, Belarus
1995	Li Xiaoshuang, China
1997	Ivan Ivankov, Belarus
1999	Nicolae Krukov, Russia
2001	Feng Jing, China
2003	Paul Hamm, United States
2005	Hiroyuki Tomita, Japan
2007	Yang Wei, China
2009	Kohei Uchimura, Japan
2011	Kohei Uchimura, Japan

Pommel Horse

Year	Champion, Nation
1930	Josip Primozic, Yugoslavia
1934	Eugene Mack, Switzerland
1938	Michael Reusch, Switzerland
1950	Josef Stalder, Switzerland
1954	Grant Chaguinjan, USSR
1958	Boris Shaklin, USSR
1962	Miroslav Cerar, Yugoslavia
1966	Miroslav Cerar, Yugoslavia
1970	Miroslav Cerar, Yugoslavia
1974	Zoltan Magyar, Hungary
1978	Zoltan Magyar, Hungary
1979	Zoltan Magyar, Hungary
1981	Michael Mikolai, East Germany
1983	Dmitri Bilozertchev, USSR
1985	Valentin Moguilny, USSR
1987	Zsolt Borkai, Hungary
	Dmitri Bilozertchev, USSR
1989	Valentin Moguilny, USSR
1991	Valeri Belenki, USSR
1992	Pae Gil Su, North Korea
	Vitaly Scherbo, CIS
	Li Jing, China
1993	Pae Gil Su, North Korea
1994	Marius Urzica, Romania
1995	Li Donghua, Switzerland
1996	Pae Gil Su, North Korea
1997	Valeri Belenki, Germany
1999	Alexei Nemov, Russia
2001	Marius Urzica, Romania
2003	Teng Haibin, China
	Takehiro Kashima, Japan
2005	Qin Xiao, China
2007	Qin Xiao, China
2009	Hongtao Zhang, China
2011	Krisztian Berki, Hungary

Floor Exercise

Year	Champion, Nation
1930	Josip Primozic, Yugoslavia
1934	Georges Miesz, Switzerland
1938	Jan Gajdos, Czechoslovakia
1950	Josef Stalder, Switzerland
1954	Valentin Mouratov, USSR
	Masao Takemoto, Japan
1958	Masao Takemoto, Japan
1962	Nobuyuki Aihara, Japan
	Yukio Endo, Japan
1966	Akinori Nakayama, Japan
1970	Akinori Nakayama, Japan
1974	Shigeru Kasamatsu, Japan
1978	Kurt Thomas, United States
1979	Kurt Thomas, United States
	Roland Brucker, East Germ.
1981	Yuri Korolev, USSR
	Li Yuejui, China
1983	Tong Fei, China
1985	Tong Fei, China
1987	Lou Yun, China
1989	Igor Korobchinsky, USSR
1991	Igor Korobchinsky, USSR
1993	Grigori Misutin, Ukraine
1994	Vitaly Scherbo, Belarus
1995	Vitaly Scherbo, Belarus
1996	Vitaly Scherbo, Belarus
1997	Alexei Nemov, Russia
1999	Alexei Nemov, Russia
2001	Marian Dragulescu, Romania
2003	Paul Hamm, United States
	Jordan Jovtchev, Bulgaria
2005	Diego Hypolito, Brazil
2007	Zou Kai, China
2009	Marian Dragulescu, Romania
2011	Kohei Uchimura, Japan

WORLD CHAMPIONS — Men *(Cont.)*

Rings

Year	Champion, Nation
1930	Emanuel Loffler, Czechoslovakia
1934	Alois Hudec, Czechoslovakia
1938	Alois Hudec, Czechoslovakia
1950	Walter Lehmann, Switzerland
1954	Albert Azarian, USSR
1958	Albert Azarian, USSR
1962	Yuri Titov, USSR
1966	Mikhail Voronin, USSR
1970	Akinori Nakayama, Japan
1974	N. Andrianov, USSR D. Grecu, Rom.
1978	Nikolai Andrianov, USSR
1979	Alexander Ditiatin, USSR
1981	Alexander Ditiatin, USSR
1983	Dimitri Bilozertchev, USSR
1985	Li Ning, China, Yuri Korolev, USSR
1987	Yuri Korolev, USSR
1989	Andreas Aguilar, West Germ.
1991	Grigory Misutin, USSR
1992	Vitaly Scherbo, CIS
1993	Yuri Chechi, Italy
1994	Yuri Chechi, Italy
1995	Yuri Chechi, Italy
1996	Yuri Chechi, Italy
1997	Yuri Chechi, Italy
1999	Zhen Dong, China
2001	Jordan Jovtchev, Bulgaria
2003	Jordan Jovtchev, Bulgaria Dimosthenis Tampakos, Greece
2005	Yuri Van Gelder, Netherlands
2007	Diego Hypolito, Brazil
2009	Mingyong Yan, China
2011	Yibing Chen, China

Parallel Bars

Year	Champion, Nation
1930	Josip Primozic, Yugoslavia
1934	Eugene Mack, Switzerland
1938	Michael Reusch, Switzerland
1950	Hans Eugster, Switzerland
1954	Victor Chukarin, USSR
1958	Boris Shaklin, USSR
1962	Miroslav Cerar, Yugoslavia
1966	Sergei Diamidov, USSR
1970	Akinori Nakayama, Japan
1974	Eizo Kenmotsu, Japan
1978	Eizo Kenmotsu, Japan
1979	Bart Conner, United States
1981	Koji Gushiken, Japan Alexandr Ditiatin, USSR
1983	Vladimir Artemov, USSR Lou Yun, China
1985	Sylvio Kroll, East Germany Valentin Moguilny, USSR
1987	Vladimir Artemov, USSR
1989	Li Jing, China Vladimir Artemov, USSR
1991	Li Jing, China
1992	Li Jin, China, Alexei Voropaev, CIS
1993	Vitaly Scherbo, Belarus
1994	Huang Liping, China
1995	Vitaly Scherbo, Belarus
1996	Rustam Sharipov, Ukraine
1997	Zhang Jinjing, China

Parallel Bar *(Cont.)*

Year	Champion, Nation
1999	Joo-Hyung Lee, South Korea
2001	Sean Townsend, U.S.
2003	Li Xiao-Peng, China
2005	Mitja Petkovsek, Slovenia
2007	Mitja Petkovsek, Slovenia
2009	Guanyin Yang, China
2011	Danell Leyva, United States

Horizontal Bar

Year	Champion, Nation
1930	Istvan Pelle, Hungary
1934	Ernst Winter, Germany
1938	Michael Reusch, Switzerland
1950	Paavo Aaltonen, Finland
1954	Valentin Mouratov, USSR
1958	Boris Shaklin, USSR
1962	Takashi Ono, Japan
1966	Akinori Nakayama, Japan
1970	Eizo Kenmotsu, Japan
1974	Eberhard Gienger, W Germany
1978	Shigeru Kasamatsu, Japan
1979	Kurt Thomas, United States
1981	Alexander Takchev, USSR
1983	Dimitri Bilozertchev, USSR
1985	Tong Fei, China
1987	Dimitri Bilozertchev, USSR
1989	Li Chunyang, China
1991	Li Chunyang, China R. Buechner, Germ
1992	Grigori Misutin, CIS
1993	Sergei Kharkov, Russia
1994	Vitaly Scherbo, Belarus
1995	Andreas Wecker, Germany
1996	Jesús Carballo, Spain
1997	Jani Tanskanen, Finland
1999	Jesus Carballo, Spain
2001	Vlasios Maras, Greece
2003	Takehiro Kashima, Japan
2005	Vlasios Maras, Greece
2007	Fabian Hambuechen, Germ.
2009	Kai Zou, China
2011	Kai Zou, China

Vault

Year	Champion, Nation
1934	Eugene Mack, Switzerland
1938	Eugene Mack, Switzerland
1950	Ernst Gebendinger, Switzerland
1954	Leo Sotornik, Czechoslovakia
1958	Yuri Titov, USSR
1962	Premysel Krbec, Czechoslovakia
1966	Haruhiro Yamashita, Japan
1970	Mitsuo Tsukahara, Japan
1974	Shigeru Kasamatsu, Japan
1978	Junichi Shimizu, Japan
1979	Alexander Ditiatin, USSR
1981	Ralf-Peter Hemmann, East Germany
1983	Arthur Akopian, USSR
1985	Yuri Korolev, USSR
1987	Lou Yun, China Sylvio Kroll, East Germany

Vault *(Cont.)*

Year	Champion, Nation
1989	Joreg Behrend, East Germany
1991	Yoo Ok Youl, South Korea
1992	Yoo Ok Youl, South Korea
1993	Vitaly Scherbo, Belarus
1994	Vitaly Scherbo, Belarus
1995	G. Misutin, Ukraine A. Nemov, Russia
1996	Alexei Nemov, Russia
1997	Sergei Fedorchenko, Kazakhstan
1999	Li Xiao-Peng, China
2001	Marian Dragulescu, Romania
2003	Li Xiao-Peng, China
2005	Eichi Sekiguchi, Japan
2007	Leszek Blanik, Poland
2009	Marian Dragulescu, Romania
2011	Hak-seon Yang, South Korea

WORLD CHAMPIONS — Women

All-Around

Year	Champion, Nation
1934	Vlasta Dekanova, Czechoslovakia
1938	Vlasta Dekanova, Czechoslovakia
1950	Helena Rakoczy, Poland
1954	Galina Roudiko, USSR
1958	Larissa Latynina, USSR
1962	Larissa Latynina, USSR
1966	Vera Caslavska, Czechoslovakia
1970	Ludmilla Tourischeva, USSR
1974	Ludmilla Tourischeva, USSR
1978	Elena Mukhina, USSR
1979	Nelli Kim, USSR
1981	Olga Bicherova, USSR
1983	Natalia Yurchenko, USSR
1985	Elena Shoushounova, USSR
	Oksana Omeliantchik, USSR
1987	Aurelia Dobre, Romania
1989	Svetlana Bouguinskaia, USSR
1991	Kim Zmeskal, United States
1993	Shannon Miller, United States
1994	Shannon Miller, United States
1995	Lilia Podkopayeva, Ukraine
1997	Svetlana Khorkina, Russia
1999	Maria Olaru, Romania
2001	Svetlana Khorkina, Russia
2003	Svetlana Khorkina, Russia
2005	Chellsie Memmel, United States
2007	Shawn Johnson, United States
2009	Bridget Sloan, United States
2011	Jordyn Wieber, United States

Floor Exercise

Year	Champion, Nation
1950	Helena Rakoczy, Poland
1954	Tamara Manina, USSR
1958	Eva Bosakava, Czechoslovakia
1962	Larissa Latynina, USSR
1966	Natalia Kuchinskaya, USSR
1970	Ludmilla Tourischeva, USSR
1974	Ludmilla Tourischeva, USSR
1978	Nelli Kim, USSR
	Elena Mukhina, USSR
1979	Emilia Eberle, Romania
1981	Natalia Ilenko, USSR
1983	Ecaterina Szabo, Romania
1985	Oksana Omeliantchik, USSR
1987	Elena Shoushounova, USSR
	Daniela Silivas, Romania
1989	Svetlana Bouguinskaia, USSR
	Daniela Silivas, Romania
1991	Cristina Bontas, Romania
	Oksana Tchusovitina, USSR
1992	Kim Zmeskal, United States
1993	Shannon Miller, United States
1994	Dina Kochetkova, Russia
1995	Gina Gogean, Romania
1996	Gina Gogean, Romania
1997	Gina Gogean, Romania
1999	Andreea Raducan, Romania
2001	Andreea Raducan, Romania
2003	Daiane Dos Santos, Brazil
2005	Nastia Liukin, United States
2007	Shawn Johnson, United States
2009	Elizabeth Tweddle, United Kingdom
2011	Kseniia Afanaseva, Russia

Uneven Bars

Year	Champion, Nation
1950	Gertchen Kolar, Austria
	Anna Pettersson, Sweden
1954	Agnes Keleti, Hungary
1958	Larissa Latynina, USSR
1962	Irina Pervuschina, USSR
1966	Natalia Kuchinskaya, USSR
1970	Karin Janz, East Germany
1974	Annelore Zinke, East Germany
1978	Marcia Frederick, United States
1979	Ma Yanhong, China
	Maxi Gnauck, East Germany
1981	Maxi Gnauck, East Germany
1983	Maxi Gnauck, East Germany
1985	Gabriele Fahnrich, East Germany
1987	Daniela Silivas, Romania
	Doerte Thuemmler, East Germany
1989	Fan Di, China
	Daniela Silivas, Romania
1991	Gwang Suk Kim, North Korea
1992	Lavinia Milosivici, Romania
1993	Shannon Miller, United States
1994	Luo Li, China
1995	Svetlana Khorkina, Russia
1996	Svetlana Khorkina, Russia
1997	Svetlana Khorkina, Russia
1999	Svetlana Khorkina, Russia
2001	Svetlana Khorkina, Russia
2003	Chellsie Memmel, U.S.
	Hollie Vise, United States
2005	Nastia Liukin, United States
2007	Ksenia Semenov, Russia
2009	Kexin He, China
2011	Viktoria Komova, Russia

Balance Beam

Year	Champion, Nation
1950	Helena Rakoczy, Poland
1954	Keiko Tanaka, Japan
1958	Larissa Latynina, USSR
1962	Eva Bosakova, Czech.
1966	Natalia Kuchinskaya, USSR
1970	Erika Zuchold, East Germany
1974	Ludmilla Tourischeva, USSR
1978	Nadia Comaneci, Romania
1979	Vera Cerna, Czechoslovakia
1981	Maxi Gnauck, East Germany
1983	Olga Mostepanova, USSR
1985	Daniela Silivas, Romania
1987	Aurelia Dobre, Romania
1989	Daniela Silivas, Romania
1991	Svetlana Boguinskaia, USSR
1992	Kim Zmeskal, United States
1993	Lavinia Milosivici, Romania
1994	Shannon Miller, United States
1995	Mo Huilan, China
1996	Dina Kochetkova, Russia
1997	Gina Gogean, Romania
1999	E. Zamolodchikova, Russia
2001	Andreea Raducan, Romania
2003	Fan Ye, China
2005	Nan Zhang, China
2007	Nastia Liukin, United States
2009	Linlin Deng, China
2011	Lu Sui, China

Vault

Year	Champion, Nation
1950	Helena Rakoczy, Poland
1954	T. Manina, USSR
	Anna Pettersson, Sweden
1958	Larissa Latynina, USSR
1962	Vera Caslavska, Czech.
1966	Vera Caslavska, Czech.
1970	Erika Zuchold, East Germany
1974	Olga Korbut, USSR
1978	Nelli Kim, USSR
1979	Dumitrita Turner, Romania
1981	Maxi Gnauck, East Germany
1983	Boriana Stoyanova, Bulgaria
1985	Elena Shoushounova, USSR
1987	Elena Shoushounova, USSR
1989	Olesia Durnik, USSR
1991	Lavinia Milosovici, Romania
1992	Henrietta Onodi, Hungary
1993	Elena Piskun, Belarus
1994	Gina Gogean, Romania
1995	L. Podkopayeva, Ukraine
	Simona Amanar, Romania
1996	Gina Gogean, Romania
1997	Simona Amanar, Romania
1999	Jie Ling, China
2001	Svetlana Khorkina, Russia
2003	Oksana Chusovitina, Uzbekistan
2005	Fei Cheng, China
2007	Fei Cheng, China
2009	Kayla Williams, United States
2011	McKayla Maroney, United States

CHAMPIONS OF THE UNITED STATES — Men

All-Around

Year	Champion
1963	Art Shurlock
1964	Rusty Mitchell
1965	Rusty Mitchell
1966	Rusty Mitchell
1967	Katsuzoki Kanzaki
1968	Yoshi Hayasaki
1969	Steve Hug
1970	Makoto Sakamoto, Mas Watanabe
1971	Yoshi Takei
1972	Yoshi Takei
1973	Marshall Avener
1974	John Crosby
1975	Tom Beach, Bart Conner
1976	Kurt Thomas
1977	Kurt Thomas
1978	Kurt Thomas
1979	Bart Conner
1980	Peter Vidmar
1981	Jim Hartung
1982	Peter Vidmar
1983	Mitch Gaylord
1984	Mitch Gaylord
1985	Brian Babcock
1986	Tim Daggett
1987	Scott Johnson
1988	Dan Hayden
1989	Tim Ryan
1990	John Roethlisberger
1991	Chris Waller
1992	John Roethlisberger
1993	John Roethlisberger
1994	Scott Keswick
1995	John Roethlisberger
1996	Blaine Wilson
1997	Blaine Wilson
1998	Blaine Wilson
1999	Blaine Wilson
2000	Blaine Wilson
2001	Sean Townsend
2002	Paul Hamm
2003	Paul Hamm
2004	Paul Hamm
2005	Todd Thornton
2006	Alexander Artemev
2007	David Durante
2008	David Sender
2009	Jonathan Horton
2010	Jonathan Horton
2011	Danell Leyva
2012	John Orozco

Floor Exercise

Year	Champion
1963	Tom Seward
1964	Rusty Mitchell
1965	Rusty Mitchell
1966	Dan Millman
1967	Katsuzoki Kanzaki, Ron Aure
1968	Katsuzoki Kanzaki
1969	Steve Hug, Dave Thor
1970	Makoto Sakamoto
1971	John Crosby
1972	Yoshi Takei
1973	John Crosby

Floor Exercise (Cont.)

Year	Champion
1974	John Crosby
1975	Peter Korman
1977	Ron Galimore
1978	Kurt Thomas
1979	Ron Galimore
1980	Ron Galimore
1981	Jim Hartung
1982	Jim Hartung
1983	Mitch Gaylord
1984	Peter Vidmar
1985	Mark Oates
1986	Robert Sundstrom
1987	John Sweeney
1988	Mark Oates, Charles Lakes
1989	Mike Racanelli
1990	Bob Stelter
1991	Mike Racanelli
1992	Gregg Curtis
1993	Kerry Huston
1994	Jeremy Killen
1995	Daniel Stover
1996	Jay Thornton
1997	Jason Gatson
1998	Jason Gatson
1999	Jason Gatson
2000	Blaine Wilson
2001	Sean Townsend
2002	Morgan Hamm
2003	Morgan Hamm
2004	Paul Hamm
2005	Guillermo Alvarez
2006	Jonathan Horton
2007	Paul Hamm
2008	Morgan Hamm
2009	Steven Legendre
2010	Joshua Dixon
2011	Jacob Dalton
2012	Jacob Dalton

Pommel Horse

Year	Champion
1963	Larry Spiegel
1964	Sam Bailie
1965	Jack Ryan
1966	Jack Ryan
1967	Paul Mayer, Dave Doty
1968	Katsuoki Kanzaki
1969	Dave Thor
1970	Mas Watanabe
1971	Leonard Caling
1972	Sadao Hamada
1973	Marshall Avener
1974	Marshall Avener
1975	Bart Conner
1977	Gene Whelan
1978	Jim Hartung
1979	Bart Conner
1980	Jim Hartung
1981	Jim Hartung
1982	Jim Hartung
1983	Bart Conner
1984	Tim Daggett
1985	Phil Cahoy
1986	Phil Cahoy
1987	Tim Daggett

Pommel Horse (Cont.)

Year	Champion
1988	Kevin Davis
1989	Kevin Davis
1990	Patrick Kirksey
1991	Chris Waller
1992	Chris Waller
1993	Chris Waller
1994	Mihai Begiu
1995	Mark Sohn
1996	Josh Stein
1997	John Roethlisberger
1998	John Roethlisberger
1999	John Roethlisberger
2000	John Roethlisberger
2001	Brett McClure
2002	Paul Hamm
2003	Paul Hamm
2004	Brett McClure
2005	Yewki Tomita
2006	Alexander Artemev
2007	Alexander Artemev
2008	Yewki Tomita
2009	Luke Stannard
2010	Daniel Ribiero
2011	Alexander Naddour
2012	Alexander Naddour

Rings

Year	Champion
1963	Art Shurlock
1964	Glen Gailis
1965	Glen Gailis
1966	Glen Gailis
1967	Fred Dennis, Don Hatch
1968	Yoshi Hayasaki
1969	Fred Dennis, Bob Emery
1970	Makoto Sakamoto
1971	Yoshi Takei
1972	Yoshi Takei
1973	Jim Ivicek
1974	Tom Weeder
1975	Tom Beach
1977	Kurt Thomas
1978	Mike Silverstein
1979	Bart Conner
1980	Jim Hartung
1981	Jim Hartung
1982	Jim Hartung, Peter Vidmar
1983	Mitch Gaylord
1984	Jim Hartung
1985	Dan Hayden
1986	Dan Hayden
1987	Scott Johnson
1988	Dan Hayden
1989	Scott Keswick
1990	Scott Keswick
1991	Scott Keswick
1992	Tim Ryan
1993	John Roethlisberger
1994	Scott Keswick
1995	Paul O'Neill
1996	Kip Simons
1997	Blaine Wilson
1998	Jeff Johnson
1999	Blaine Wilson
2000	Blaine Wilson

Rings (Cont.)

Year	Champion
2001	Sean Townsend
2002	Blaine Wilson
2003	Blaine Wilson
2004	Raj Bhavsar
2005	Sean Golden
2006	Kevin Tan
2007	Kevin Tan
2008	Kevin Tan
2009	Jonathan Horton
2010	Brandon Wynn
2011	Brandon Wynn
2012	Jonathan Horton

Vault

Year	Champion
1963	Art Shurlock
1964	Gary Hery
1965	Brent Williams
1966	Dan Millman
1967	Jack Kenan, Sid Jensen
1968	Rich Scorza
1969	Dave Butzman
1970	Makoto Sakamoto
1971	Gary Morava
1972	Mike Kelley
1973	Gary Morava
1974	John Crosby
1975	Tom Beach
1977	Ron Galimore
1978	Jim Hartung
1979	Ron Galimore
1980	Ron Galimore
1981	Ron Galimore
1982	Jim Hartung, Jim Mikus
1983	Chris Reigel
1984	Chris Reigel
1985	Scott Johnson, Mark Oates
1986	Scott Wilbanks
1987	John Sweeney
1988	John Sweeney, Bill Paul
1989	Bill Roth
1990	Lance Ringnald
1991	Scott Keswick
1992	Trent Dimas
1993	Bill Roth
1994	Keith Wiley
1995	David St. Pierre
1996	Blaine Wilson
1997	Blaine Wilson
1998	Brent Klaus
1999	Guard Young
2000	Blaine Wilson
2001	Jason Furr
2002	Paul Hamm
2003	Raj Bhavsar
2004	David Sender
2005	Sean Golden
2006	David Sender
2007	Sean Golden
2008	David Sender
2009	Jake Dalton
2010	Steven Legendre
2011	Jacob Dalton
2012	Sean Senters, Jacob Dalton

CHAMPIONS OF THE UNITED STATES - Men *(Cont.)*

Parallel Bars		Parallel Bars *(Cont.)*		Horizontal Bar		Horiz. Bar *(Cont.)*	
Year	Champion	Year	Champion	Year	Champion	Year	Champion
1963	Tom Seward	1991	Scott Keswick	1963	Art Shurlock	1988	Dan Hayden
1964	Rusty Mitchell	1992	Jair Lynch	1964	Glen Gailis	1989	Tim Ryan
1965	Glen Gailis	1993	Chainey Umphrey	1965	Rusty Mitchell	1990	Trent Dimas,
1966	Ray Hadley	1994	Steve McCain	1966	Katsuzoki Kanzaki		Lance Ringnald
1967	Katsuzoki Kanzaki,	1995	John Roethlisberger	1967	Katsuzoki Kanzaki,	1991	Lance Ringnald
	Tom Goldsborough	1996	Jair Lynch		Jerry Fontana	1992	Jair Lynch
1968	Yoshi Hayasaki	1997	Blaine Wilson	1968	Yoshi Hayasaki	1993	Steve McCain
1969	Steve Hug	1998	Blaine Wilson	1969	Rich Grisby	1994	Scott Keswick
1970	Makoto Sakamoto	1999	Jason Gatson	1970	Makoto Sakamoto	1995	John Roethlisberger
1971	Brent Simmons	2000	Trent Wells	1971	Yoshi Takei	1996	Bill Roth
1972	Yoshi Takei	2001	Sean Townsend	1972	Tom Lindner	1997	Douglas Stibel
1973	Marshall Avener	2002	Sean Townsend	1973	John Crosby	1998	Jason Gatson
1974	Jim Ivicek	2003	Jason Gatson	1974	Brent Simmons	1999	Jamie Natalie
1975	Bart Conner	2004	Alexander Artemev	1975	Tom Beach	2000	Trent Wells,
1977	Kurt Thomas	2005	D.J. Bucher	1977	Kurt Thomas		Jamie Natalie
1978	Bart Conner	2006	Alexander Artemev	1978	Kurt Thomas	2001	Daniel Diaz-Luong
1979	Bart Conner	2007	David Durante	1979	Yoichi Tomita	2002	Blaine Wilson
1980	Phil Cahoy, Larry Gerard	2008	Justin Spring	1980	Jim Hartung	2003	Paul Hamm
1981	Bart Conner	2009	Tim McNeill	1981	Bart Conner	2004	Paul Hamm
1982	Peter Vidmar	2010	Danell Leyva	1982	Mitch Gaylord	2005	D.J. Bucher
1983	Mitch Gaylord	2011	Danell Leyva	1983	Mario McCutcheon	2006	Chris Brooks
1984	Peter Vidmar, Mitch	2012	Danell Leyva	1983	Mario McCutcheon	2007	Justin Spring
	Gaylord, Tim Daggett			1984	Peter Vidmar,	2008	Joseph Hagerty
1985	Tim Daggett				Tim Daggett,	2009	Jonathan Horton
1986	Tim Daggett				Mitch Gaylord	2010	Chris Brooks
1987	Scott Johnson			1985	Dan Hayden	2011	Danell Leyva
1988	D. Hayden, K. Davis			1986	D. Hayden, D. Moriel	2012	Danell Leyva
1989	Conrad Voorsanger			1987	David Moriel		
1990	Trent Dimas						

CHAMPIONS OF THE UNITED STATES — Women

All-Around		All-Around *(Cont.)*		Vault *(Cont.)*	
Year	Champion	Year	Champion	Year	Champion
1963	Donna Schanezer	1992	Kim Zmeskal	1970	Cathy Rigby
1965	Gail Daley	1993	Shannon Miller	1971	Joan Moore Gnat/Adele Gleaves
1966	Donna Schanezer	1994	Dominique Dawes	1972	Cindy Eastwood
1968	Linda Scott	1995	Dominique Moceanu	1973	Roxanne Pierce Mancha
1969	Joyce Tanac	1996	Shannon Miller	1974	Dianne Dunbar
	Schroeder	1997	V. Adler/ K. Powell	1975	Kolleen Casey
1970	Cathy Rigby	1998	Kristen Maloney	1976	Debbie Wilcox
1971	Joan Moore Gnat	1999	Kristen Maloney	1977	Lisa Cawthron
	Linda Metheny Mulvihill	2000	Elise Ray	1978	Rhonda Schwandt/Sharon Shapiro
1972	Joan Moore Gnat	2001	Tasha Schwikert	1979	Christa Canary
	Cathy Rigby	2002	Tasha Schwikert	1980	J. McNamara/B. Kline
1973	Joan Moore Gnat	2003	Courtney Kupets	1981	Kim Neal
1974	Joan Moore Gnat	2004	Courtney Kupets/Carly Patterson	1982	Yumi Mordre
1975	Tammy Manville	2005	Nastia Liukin	1983	Dianne Durham
1976	Denise Cheshire	2006	Nastia Liukin	1984	Mary Lou Retton
1977	Donna Turnbow	2007	Shawn Johnson	1985	Yolanda Mavity
1978	Kathy Johnson	2008	Shawn Johnson	1986	Joyce Wilborn
1979	Leslie Pyfer	2009	Bridget Sloan	1987	Rhonda Faehn
1980	Julianne McNamara	2010	Rebecca Bross	1988	Rhonda Faehn
1981	Tracee Talavera	2011	Jordyn Wieber	1989	Brandy Johnson
1982	Tracee Talavera	2012	Jordyn Wieber	1990	Brandy Johnson
1983	Dianne Durham			1991	Kerri Strug
1984	Mary Lou Retton	**Vault**		1992	Kerri Strug
1985	Sabrina Mar			1993	Dominique Dawes
1986	Jennifer Sey	Year	Champion	1994	Dominique Dawes
1987	Kristie Phillips	1963	Donna Schanezer	1995	Shannon Miller
1988	Phoebe Mills	1965	Gail Daley	1996	Dominique Dawes
1989	Brandy Johnson	1966	Donna Schanezer	1997	Vanessa Atler
1990	Kim Zmeskal	1968	Terry Spencer	1998	Dominique Moceanu
1991	Kim Zmeskal	1969	Joyce Tanac Schroeder	1999	Vanessa Atler
			Cleo Carver	2000	Kristen Maloney

CHAMPIONS OF THE UNITED STATES— Women *(Cont.)*

Vault *(Cont.)*

Year	Champion
2001	Mohini Bhardwaj
2002	Elizabeth Tricase
2003	Annia Hatch
2004	Liz Tricase
2005	Alicia Sacramone
2006	Alicia Sacramone
2007	Alicia Sacramone
2008	Alicia Sacramone
2009	Kayla Williams
2010	Alicia Sacramone
2011	McKayla Maroney
2012	Alicia Sacramone

Uneven Bars

Year	Champion
1963	Donna Schanezer
1965	Irene Haworth
1966	Donna Schanezer
1968	Linda Scott
1969	Joyce Tanac Schroeder, Lisa Nelson
1970	Roxanne Pierce Mancha
1971	Joan Moore Gnat
1972	Cathy Rigby
1973	Roxanne Pierce Mancha
1974	Diane Dunbar
1975	Leslie Wolfsberger
1976	Leslie Wolfsberger
1977	Donna Turnbow
1978	Marcia Frederick
1979	Marcia Frederick
1980	Marcia Frederick
1981	Julianne McNamara
1982	Marie Roethlisberger
1983	Julianne McNamara
1984	Julianne McNamara
1985	Sabrina Mar
1986	Marie Roethlisberger
1987	Melissa Marlowe
1988	Chelle Stack
1989	Chelle Stack
1990	Sandy Woolsey
1991	Elisabeth Crandall
1992	Dominique Dawes
1993	Shannon Miller
1994	Dominique Dawes
1995	Dominique Dawes
1996	Dominique Dawes
1997	Kristy Powell
1998	Elise Ray
1999	Jamie Dantzscher, Jennie Thompson
2000	Elise Ray
2001	Katie Heenan
2002	Tasha Schwikert
2003	Katie Heenan
2004	Courtney Kupets
2005	Nastia Liukin
2006	Nastia Liukin
2007	Nastia Liukin
2008	Nastia Liukin
2009	Bridget Sloan
2010	Rebecca Bross
2011	Jordyn Wieber
2012	Gabrielle Douglas

Balance Beam

Year	Champion
1963	Leissa Krol
1965	Gail Daley
1966	Irene Haworth, Linda Scott
1968	Linda Scott
1969	Lonna Woodward
1970	Joyce Tanac Schroeder
1971	Linda Metheny Mulvihill
1972	Kim Chace
1973	Nancy Thies Marshall
1974	Joan Moore Gnat
1975	Kyle Gayner
1976	Carrie Englert
1977	Donna Turnbow
1978	Christa Canary
1979	Heidi Anderson
1980	Kelly Garrison-Steves
1981	Tracee Talavera
1982	Julianne McNamara
1983	Dianne Durham
1984	Pam Bileck, Tracee Talavera
1986	Angie Denkins
1987	Kristie Phillips
1985	Kelly Garrison-Steves
1988	Kelly Garrison-Steves
1989	Brandy Johnson
1990	Betty Okino
1991	Shannon Miller
1992	Kerri Strug, Kim Zmeskal
1993	Dominique Dawes
1994	Dominique Dawes
1995	Doni Thompson, Monica Flammer
1996	Dominique Dawes
1997	Kendall Beck
1998	Dominique Moceanu
1999	Vanessa Atler
2000	Alyssa Beckerman, Amy Chow
2001	Tasha Schwikert
2002	Tasha Schwikert
2003	Hollie Vise
2004	Courtney Kupets
2005	Nastia Liukin
2006	Nastia Liukin
2007	Shawn Johnson
2008	Nastia Liukin
2009	Ivana Hong
2010	Rebecca Bross
2011	Alicia Sacramone
2012	Aly Raisman

Floor Exercise

Year	Champion
1963	Donna Schanezer
1965	Gail Daley
1966	Donna Schanezer
1968	Linda Scott
1970	Cathy Rigby
1971	Joan Moore Gnat, Linda Metheny Mulvihill
1972	Joan Moore Gnat
1973	Joan Moore Gnat
1974	Joan Moore Gnat
1975	Kathy Howard
1976	Carrie Englert
1977	Kathy Johnson
1978	Kathy Johnson
1979	Heidi Anderson
1980	Beth Kline
1981	Michelle Goodwin
1982	Amy Koopman
1983	Dianne Durham
1984	Mary Lou Retton
1985	Sabrina Mar
1986	Yolanda Mavity
1987	Kristie Phillips
1988	Phoebe Mills
1989	Brandy Johnson
1990	Brandy Johnson
1991	Kim Zmeskal, Dominique Dawes
1992	Kim Zmeskal
1993	Shannon Miller
1994	Dominique Dawes
1995	Dominique Dawes
1996	Dominique Dawes
1997	Lindsay Wing
1998	Vanessa Atler
1999	Elise Ray
2000	Kristen Maloney
2001	Tabitha Yim
2002	Tasha Schwikert
2003	Ashley Postell
2004	Carly Patterson
2005	Alicia Sacramone
2006	Alicia Sacramone, Randi Stageberg
2007	Shawn Johnson
2008	Shawn Johnson
2009	Bridget Sloan
2010	Mattie Larson
2011	Jordyn Wieber
2012	Aly Raisman

Skiing World Cup Season Title Holders

Men – OVERALL

1967 ....Jean-Claude Killy, France	1990 ....Pirmin Zurbriggen, Switzerland
1968 ....Jean-Claude Killy, France	1991 ....Marc Girardelli, Luxembourg
1969 ....Karl Schranz, Austria	1992 ....Paul Accola, Switzerland
1970 ....Karl Schranz, Austria	1993 ....Marc Girardelli, Luxembourg
1971 ....Gustavo Thoeni, Italy	1994 ....Kjetil André Aamodt, Norway
1972 ....Gustavo Thoeni, Italy	1995 ....Alberto Tomba, Italy
1973 ....Gustavo Thoeni, Italy	1996 ....Lasse Kjus, Norway
1974 ....Piero Gros, Italy	1997 ....Luc Alphand, France
1975 ....Gustavo Thoeni, Italy	1998 ....Hermann Maier, Austria
1976 ....Ingemar Stenmark, Sweden	1999 ....Lasse Kjus, Norway
1977 ....Ingemar Stenmark, Sweden	2000 ....Hermann Maier, Austria
1978 ....Ingemar Stenmark, Sweden	2001 ....Hermann Maier, Austria
1979 ....Peter Lüscher, Switzerland	2002 ....Stephan Eberharter, Austria
1980 ....Andreas Wenzel, Liechtenstein	2003 ....Stephan Eberharter, Austria
1981 ....Phil Mahre, United States	2004 ....Hermann Maier, Austria
1982 ....Phil Mahre, United States	2005 ....Bode Miller, United States
1983 ....Phil Mahre, United States	2006 ....Benjamin Raich, Austria
1984 ....Pirmin Zurbriggen, Switzerland	2007 ....Aksel Lund Svindal, Norway
1985 ....Marc Girardelli, Luxembourg	2008 ....Bode Miller, United States
1986 ....Marc Girardelli, Luxembourg	2009 ....Aksel Lund Svindal, Norway
1987 ....Pirmin Zurbriggen, Switzerland	2010 ....Carlo Janka, Switzerland
1988 ....Pirmin Zurbriggen, Switzerland	2011 ....Ivica Kostelic, Croatia
1989 ....Marc Girardelli, Luxembourg	2012 ....Marcel Hirscher, Austria

Women – OVERALL

1967 ....Nancy Greene, Canada	1990 ....Petra Kronberger, Austria
1968 ....Nancy Greene, Canada	1991 ....Petra Kronberger, Austria
1969 ....Gertrud Gabl, Austria	1992 ....Petra Kronberger, Austria
1970 ....Michèle Jacot, France	1993 ....Anita Wachter, Austria
1971 ....Annemarie Pröll, Austria	1994 ....Vreni Schneider, Switzerland
1972 ....Annemarie Pröll, Austria	1995 ....Vreni Schneider, Switzerland
1973 ....Annemarie Pröll, Austria	1996 ....Katja Seizinger, Germany
1974 ....Annemarie Moser-Proell, Austria	1997 ....Pernilla Wiberg, Sweden
1975 ....Annemarie Moser-Proell, Austria	1998 ....Katja Seizinger, Germany
1976 ....Rosi Mitermaier, W Germany	1999 ....Alexandra Meissnitzer, Austria
1977 ....Lise-Marie Morerod, Switzerland	2000 ....Renate Goetschl, Austria
1978 ....Hanni Wenzel, Liechtenstein	2001 ....Janica Kostelic, Croatia
1979 ....Annemarie Moser-Proell, Austria	2002 ....Michaela Dorfmeister, Austria
1980 ....Hanni Wenzel, Liechtenstein	2003 ....Janica Kostelic, Austria
1981 ....Marie-Thérèse Nadig, Switzerland	2004 ....Anja Paerson, Sweden
1982 ....Erika Hess, Switzerland	2005 ....Anja Paerson, Sweden
1983 ....Tamara McKinney, United States	2006 ....Janica Kostelic, Croatia
1984 ....Erika Hess, Switzerland	2007 ....Nicole Hosp, Austria
1985 ....Michela Figini, Switzerland	2008 ....Lindsey Vonn, United States
1986 ....Maria Walliser, Switzerland	2009 ....Lindsey Vonn, United States
1987 ....Maria Walliser, Switzerland	2010 ....Lindsey Vonn, United States
1988 ....Michela Figini, Switzerland	2011 ....Maria Hoefl-Riesch, Germany
1989 ....Vreni Schneider, Switzerland	2012 ....Lindsay Vonn, United States

Wrestling

United States National Champions

1983
FREESTYLE
105.5 ......Rich Salamone
114.5 ......Joe Gonzales
125.5 ......Joe Corso
136.5 ......Rich Dellagatta*
149.5 ......Bill Hugent
163 ......Lee Kemp
180.5 ......Chris Campbell
198 ....Pete Bush
220 ....Greg Gibson
Hvy........Bruce Baumgartner
Team ......Sunkist Kids
GRECO-ROMAN
105.5 ......T.J. Jones
114.5 ......Mark Fuller
125.5 ......Rob Hermann
136.5 ......Dan Mello
149.5 ......Jim Martinez
163 ....James Andre
180.5 ......Steve Goss
198 ....Steve Fraser*
220 ....Dennis Koslowski
Hvy........No champion
Team ......Minn. Wrestling Club

1984
FREESTYLE
105.5 ......Rich Salamone
114.5 ......Charlie Heard
125.5 ......Joe Corso
136.5 ......Rich Dellagatta*
149.5 ......Andre Metzger
163 ....Dave Schultz*
180.5 ......Mark Schultz
198 ....Steve Fraser
220 ....Harold Smith
Hvy........Bruce Baumgartner
Team ......Sunkist Kids
GRECO-ROMAN
105.5 ......T.J. Jones
114.5 ......Mark Fuller
136.5 ......Dan Mello
149.5 ......Jim Martinez*
163 ....John Matthews
180.5 ......Tom Press
198 ....Mike Houck
220 ....No champion
Hvy........No champion
Team ......Adirondack 3-Style, Wash.

1985
FREESTYLE
105.5 ......Tim Vanni
114.5 ......Jim Martin
125.5 ......Charlie Heard
136.5 ......Darryl Burley
149.5 ......Bill Nugent*
163 ....Kenny Monday
180.5 ......Mike Sheets
198 ....Mark Schultz
220 ....Greg Gibson
286 ....Bruce Baumgartner
Team ......Sunkist Kids

1985(Cont.)
GRECO-ROMAN
105.5 ......T.J. Jones
114.5 ......Mark Fuller
125.5 ......Eric Seward*
136.5 ......Buddy Lee
149.5 ......Jim Martinez
163 ....David Butler
180.5 ......Chris Catallo
198 ....Mike Houck
220 ....Greg Gibson
286 ....Dennis Koslowski
Team ......U.S. Marine Corps

1986
FREESTYLE
105.5 ......Rich Salamone
114.5 ......Joe Gonzales
125.5 ......Kevin Darkus
136.5 ......John Smith
149.5 ......Andre Metzger*
163 ....Dave Schultz
180.5 ......Mark Schultz
198 ....Jim Scherr
220 ....Dan Severn
286 ....Bruce Baumgartner
Team ......Sunkist Kids (Div. I)
           Hawkeye Wrestling Club (Div. II)
GRECO-ROMAN
105.5 ......Eric Wetzel
114.5 ......Shawn Sheldon
125.5 ......Anthony Amado
136.5 ......Frank Famiano
149.5 ......Jim Martinez
163 ....David Butler*
180.5 ......Darryl Gholar
198 ....Derrick Waldroup
220 ....Dennis Koslowski
286 ....Duane Koslowski
Team........U.S. Marine Corps (Div. I)
           U.S. Navy (Div. II)

1987
FREESTYLE
105.5 ......Takashi Irie
114.5 ......Mitsuru Sato
125.5 ......Barry Davis
136.5 ......Takumi Adachi
149.5 ......Andre Metzger
163 ....Dave Schultz*
180.5 ......Mark Schultz
198 ....Jim Scherr
220 ....Bill Scherr
286 ....Bruce Baumgartner
Team ......Sunkist Kids (Div. I)
           Team Foxcatcher (Div. II)
GRECO-ROMAN
105.5 ......Eric Wetzel
114.5 ......Shawn Sheldon
125.5 ......Eric Seward
136.5 ......Frank Famiano
149.5 ......Jim Martinez
163 ....David Butler
180.5 ......Chris Catallo
198 ....Derrick Waldroup*

1987(Cont.)
GRECO-ROMAN (CONT.)
220 ....Dennis Koslowski
286 ....Duane Koslowski
Team........U.S. Marine Corp (Div. I)
           U.S. Army (Div. II)

1988
FREESTYLE
105.5 ......Tim Vanni
114.5 ......Joe Gonzales
125.5 ......Kevin Darkus
136.5 ......John Smith*
149.5 ......Nate Carr
163 ....Kenny Monday
180.5 ......Dave Schultz
198 ....Melvin Douglas III
220 ....Bill Scherr
286 ....Bruce Baumgartner
Team ......Sunkist Kids (Div. I)
           Team Foxcatcher (Div. II)
GRECO-ROMAN
105.5 ......T.J. Jones
114.5 ......Shawn Sheldon
125.5 ......Gogi Parseghian*
136.5 ......Dalen Wasmund
149.5 ......Craig Pollard
163 ....Tony Thomas
180.5 ......Darryl Gholar
198 ....Mike Carolan
220 ....Dennis Koslowski
286 ....Duane Koslowski
Team........U.S. Marine Corps (Div. I)
           Sunkist Kids (Div. II)

1989
FREESTYLE
105.5 ......Tim Vanni
114.5 ......Zeke Jones
125.5 ......Brad Penrith
136.5 ......John Smith
149.5 ......Nate Carr
163 ....Rob Koll
180.5 ......Rico Chiapparelli
198 ....Jim Scherr*
220 ....Bill Scherr
286 ....Bruce Baumgartner
Team ......Sunkist Kids (Div. I)
           Team Foxcatcher (Div. II)
GRECO-ROMAN
105.5 ......Lew Dorrance
114.5 ......Mark Fuller
125.5 ......Gogi Parseghian
136.5 ......Isaac Anderson
149.5 ......Andy Seras*
163 ....David Butler
180.5 ......John Morgan
198 ....Michial Foy
220 ....Steve Lawson
286 ....Craig Pittman
Team ......USMC (Div. I)
           Jets USA (Div. II)

*Outstanding wrestler.

United States National Champions *(Cont.)*

1990
FREESTYLE
105.5 ....Rob Eiter
114.5 ....Zeke Jones
125.5 ......Joe Melchiore
136.5 ....John Smith
149.5 ......Nate Carr
163 ....Rob Koll
180.5 ....Royce Alger
198 ....Chris Campbell*
220 ....Bill Scherr
286 ....Bruce Baumgartner
Team ....Sunkist Kids (Div. I)
      Team Foxcatcher (Div. II)

GRECO-ROMAN
105.5 ....Lew Dorrance
114.5 ....Sam Henson
125.5 ......Mark Pustelnik
136.5 ....Isaac Anderson
149.5 ......Andy Seras
163 ....David Butler
180.5 ....Derrick Waldroup
198 ....Randy Couture*
220 ....Chris Tironi
286 ....Matt Ghaffari
Team ....Jets USA (Div. I)
      California Jets (Div. II)

1991
FREESTYLE
105.5 ....Tim Vanni
114.5 ....Zeke Jones
125.5 ......Brad Penrith
136.5 ....John Smith*
149.5 ......Townsend Saunders
163 ....Kenny Monday
180.5 ....Kevin Jackson
198 ....Chris Campbell
220 ....Mark Coleman
286 ....Bruce Baumgartner
Team ....Sunkist Kids (Div. I)
      Jets USA (Div. II)

GRECO-ROMAN
105.5 ....Eric Wetzel
114.5 ....Shawn Sheldon
125.5 ......Frank Famiano
136.5 ....Buddy Lee
149.5 ......Andy Seras
163 ....Gordy Morgan
180.5 ....John Morgan*
198 ....Michial Foy
220 ....Dennis Koslowski
286 ....Craig Pittman
Team ....Jets USA (Div. I)
      Sunkist Kids (Div. II)

1992
FREESTYLE
105.5 ....Rob Eiter
114.5 ......Jack Griffin
125.5 ......Kendall Cross*
136.5 ....John Fisher
149.5 ......Matt Demaray
163 ....Greg Elinsky
180.5 ....Royce Alger
198 ....Dan Chaid
220 ....Bill Scherr
286 ....Bruce Baumgartner
Team ....Sunkist Kids (Div. I)
      Team Foxcatcher (Div. II)

GRECO-ROMAN
105.5 ....Eric Wetzel
114.5 ....Mark Fuller
125.5 ......Dennis Hall
136.5 ....Buddy Lee*
149.5 ......Rodney Smith
163 ....Travis West
180.5 ....John Morgan
198 ....Michial Foy
220 ....Dennis Koslowski
286 ....Matt Ghaffari
Team .......N.Y. Athletic Club (Div. I)
      Sunkist Kids (Div. II)

1993
FREESTYLE
105.5 ....Rob Eiter
114.5 ....Zeke Jones
125.5 ......Brad Penrith
136.5 ....Tom Brands
149.5 ......Matt Demaray
163 ....Dave Schultz*
180.5 ....Kevin Jackson
198 ....Melvin Douglas
220 ....Kirk Trost
286 ....Bruce Baumgartner
Team ....Sunkist Kids (Div. I)
      Team Foxcatcher (Div. II)

GRECO-ROMAN
105.5 ....Eric Wetzel
114.5 ....Shawn Sheldon
125.5 ......Dennis Hall*
136.5 ....Shon Lewis
149.5 ......Andy Seras
163 ....Gordy Morgan
180.5 ....Dan Henderson
198 ....Randy Couture
220 ....James Johnson
286 ....Matt Ghaffari
Team .......N.Y. Athletic Club (Div. I)
      Sunkist Kids (Div. II)

1994
FREESTYLE
105.5 ....Tim Vanni
114.5 ....Zeke Jones
125.5 ......Terry Brands
136.5 ....Tom Brands
149.5 ......Matt Demaray
163 ....Dave Schultz
180.5 ....Royce Alger
198 ....Melvin Douglas
220 ....Mark Kerr
286 ....Bruce Baumgartner*
Team ....Sunkist Kids (Div. I)
      Team Foxcatcher (Div. II)

GRECO-ROMAN
105.5 ....Isaac Ramaswamy
114.5 ....Shawn Sheldon
125.5 ......Dennis Hall
136.5 ....Shon Lewis
149.5 ......Andy Seras*
163 ....Gordy Morgan
180.5 ....Dan Henderson
198 ....Derrick Waldroup
220 ....James Johnson
286 ....Matt Ghaffari
Team ....Armed Forces (Div. I)
      N.Y. Athletic Club (Div. II)

1995
FREESTYLE
105.5 ....Tim Vanni
114.5 ....Zeke Jones
125.5 ......Terry Brands
136.5 ....Tom Brands
149.5 ......Matt Demaray
163 ....Dave Schultz
180.5 ....Royce Alger
198 ....Melvin Douglas
220 ....Mark Kerr
286 ....Bruce Baumgartner*
Team ....Sunkist Kids (Div. I)
      Team Foxcatcher (Div. II)

GRECO-ROMAN
105.5 ....Isaac Ramaswamy
114.5 ....Shawn Sheldon
125.5 ......Dennis Hall
136.5 ....Shon Lewis
149.5 ......Andy Seras*
163 ....Gordy Morgan
180.5 ....Dan Henderson
198 ....Derrick Waldroup
220 ....James Johnson
286 ....Matt Ghaffari
Team ....Armed Forces (Div. I)
      N.Y. Athletic Club (Div. II)

*Outstanding wrestler.